Sylvia Porter's
NEW MONEY BOOK
for the 80's

Books by Sylvia Porter

HOW TO MAKE MONEY IN GOVERNMENT BONDS
IF WAR COMES TO THE AMERICAN HOME
HOW TO LIVE WITHIN YOUR INCOME (with J. K. Lasser)
MANAGING YOUR MONEY (with J. K. Lasser)
HOW TO GET MORE FOR YOUR MONEY
SYLVIA PORTER'S INCOME TAX GUIDE (Annual)
SYLVIA PORTER'S MONEY BOOK
SYLVIA PORTER'S NEW MONEY BOOK FOR THE 80'S

SYLVIA PORTER'S
New Money Book
FOR THE 80'S

DOUBLEDAY & COMPANY, INC.
GARDEN CITY, NEW YORK
1979

ISBN: 0-385-12612-3
Library of Congress Catalog Card Number 76–20275
Copyright © 1975, 1979 by Sylvia Porter

IN MEMORY OF
G. SUMNER COLLINS

CONTENTS

ACKNOWLEDGMENTS

A book as comprehensive as this never could be the product of just one person's experience, energy, and expertise. I have tapped the resources of literally thousands of individual experts, public and private organizations, businesses, consumer and public interest groups, unions, as well as a cross section of federal, state, and local government agencies. To the extent that I have succeeded in putting together an informative, readable, and interesting book, I owe them profound gratitude. To the extent that I have failed, the shortcomings are mine alone.

Above all others, I owe appreciation and gratitude to Brooke Shearer, my associate. She not only helps in writing my daily newspaper column, but also has been my close collaborator on this new edition of the *Money Book for the 80's*.

Also my deep thanks go to: Janice Lowen Agee; Cheryl Belli; Carol Brandt; Paul Carlin; Evan Cooper; Charlotte Crenson; Dr. Robin Elliott; Alan Ettman; Christine Evers; Robert B. Feduniak; Karen Ferguson; James F. Fox; Dr. Eli Ginzberg; Leon Gold; Sally Gold; Harvey H. Harris; Gloria B. Hill; Karl Hoyle; William L. Jiler; Carolyn M. Johnston; April Klimley; Fabian Linden; Ken McCormick; Ferris Mack; Harold I. Meyerson; Ernest Morgan; Franz Pick; Milton A. Schiff; Edwin S. Shapiro; Leigh Smith; Miraed Peake Smith; Irving L. Straus; Michael Sumichrast; Harry Turton; Ben Weberman; Frank Wylie.

Air Conditioning and Refrigeration Institute; American Automobile Association; American Bankers Association; American Dental Association; American Hospital Association; American Institute of Architects; American Legion; American Medical Association; American Movers Conference; American National Red Cross; American Psychiatric Association; American Society of Appraisers; American Society of Travel Agents; American Stamp Dealers Association; American Telephone & Telegraph Co.; American Youth Hostels, Inc.; Amtrak; Associated American Artists; Association of Home Appliance Manufacturers; Avis Rent a Car System, Inc.

Better Business Bureau of Metropolitan New York, Inc.; Bicycle Institute of America; Blue Cross; Blue Shield; *Bride's Magazine;* Bureau of Building Marketing Research; Car Tours in Europe, Inc.; Celanese Corp.; Chase Manhattan Bank; Chris-Craft Industries, Inc.; College Entrance Examination Board; College Scholarship Service; Commodity Research Bureau; Consumer Education Extension Service; Consumer Federation of America; Consumers Union; Credit Union National Association, Inc.; Edmund Publications Corp.; Electronics Industries Association; Fasig-Tipton Co., Inc.

Greyhound Lines, Inc.; Group Health Association of America; Health Insurance Institute; Health Research Group; Household Finance Corporation; H. R. Harmer, Inc.; Institute of Life Insurance; Insurance Institute for Highway Safety; Insurance Information Institute; International Association of Chiefs of Police, Inc.; Jewelry Industry Council.

Ladies' Home Journal; Lightning Protection Institute; Mazda; Merrill Lynch, Pierce, Fenner & Smith; Mobile Homes Manufacturers Association; *Modern Maturity* magazine; National Alliance of Television & Electronic Service Associations; National Association of Home Builders; National Association of Realtors; National Consumer Law Center; National Family Opinion Research; National Fire Protection Association; National League of Insured Savings Associations; National Live Stock & Meat Board; National Parking Association; National Safety Council; National Society of Interior Designers; New York State College of Agriculture and Life Sciences; New York Stock Exchange; No-Loan Mutual Fund Association; Northeastern University; Outdoor Power Institute; Perera, Fifth Avenue, Inc.; Planned Parenthood; Recreational Vehicle Institute; Research Institute of America; Rhode Island Consumers Council; The Singer Company; Small Claims Study Group; Sotheby Parke Bernet, Inc.; Stratford Furniture Co.; Swann Galleries; The Conference Board; The National Association of Food Chains; Union Dime Savings Bank; Village Music Studio; Vintage Cars of Rockland; Yale University.

The United States Departments of: Agriculture, Health, Education, and Welfare, Housing and Urban Development, Transportation, and Treasury; the Internal Revenue Service; the Federal Housing Administration, General Services Administration, National Highway Traffic Safety Administration, Occupational Safety and Health Administration, Social Security Administration, and Veterans Administration; the Federal Bureaus of the Census, Customs, Labor Statistics, and the Women's Bureau; the Civil Aeronautics Board, Consumer Product Safety Commission, Federal Trade Commission, Food and Drug Administration, and the Interstate Commerce Commission; the Federal Deposit Insurance Corporation, the Federal Reserve Board, the Federal Savings and Loan Insurance Corporation, and the National Credit Union Administration; the Office of Education and the Office of Consumer Affairs.

FOREWORD

How much money are you earning? How much are you spending each month? Are you managing to save enough? Should you borrow? Are you investing your dollars wisely?

These questions are of the most vital concern to you. Yet many of you seldom discuss them, even among your dearest friends and family members.

The private money matters of individuals the nation over remain a mystery. In an age that places great emphasis on full disclosure, frankness, and public revelation of private lives, personal finances are still taboo.

Why? Why are private financial affairs one of the few types of affairs still locked in the closet?

One overriding explanation for the silence is . . . your own lack of information.

Who can talk about what they don't know? And most of you know little about the economics of your own everyday life. You have only a vague notion of how much money you spend each month and even less of an idea of precisely where it goes.

Your reluctance to look hard at your own financial habits feeds on itself; you end up frightened, guilty, confused. Since you feel neither trained nor qualified to deal with money, you procrastinate, sometimes crashing head over heels into debt, other times falling prey to a fast-talking con artist or "expert" who sounds as though he knows all the answers. And often you just muddle through, hoping that you can make it through life before your ignorance catches up with you, and you discover too late the answers to so many of the questions you never took the time or worked up the courage to ask.

This substantially expanded, revised, and reorganized book is designed to help you avoid such futile fumbling. It is written on the assumption that you know next to nothing about buying a house, creating a family budget, planning for your independence in your older years, financing your child's education after high school. My aim is simplicity in every sphere of personal and family finance. My prayer is that the hints crammed into these pages will not only show you how to survive in the U.S. economic jungle but also how to triumph in the marketplace.

Despite my attempts to make this an easy-to-read (in fact, enjoyable) guide to money matters, many of you who buy it will put it on the shelf—unopened. Okay. This is a first step: an investment. But this book's purpose is to be used, in many different ways and at many different times, depending on what kind of assistance you are seeking.

Scan it from cover to cover and you will have completed a quick course in consumer economics.

Pick it up from time to time to study the guides in a single chapter or two, *before* you borrow money, invest in the securities markets, speculate in commodities or "far-out" mediums, sign up for a corporation's dividend investment plan.

Look at the glossary of terms, the bafflegab sections at the end of each chapter whenever you come across financial language that you do not fully understand (wage garnishment, vesting requirements, price-earning ratios, for instance). And when you have questions or complaints and don't know where to turn, consult the chapter telling you how and where to get help.

Do-it-on-your-own! And help yourself make your own life in the United States financially rewarding in the two decades left of the twentieth century.

December 1978

1

INFLATION AND THE WORLD IN WHICH YOU LIVE

INFLATION QUIZ

After having been in so relentless a price squeeze for so many years, most consumers feel they are experts on inflation. But how much do you *really* know about inflation and its effects on the goods and services that you buy? To find out, take this little inflation quiz.

The answers are enclosed by parentheses and follow each question.

1. How many times during the last ten years has inflation reached the double-digit range?

A. three times.   **B.** once.   **C.** twice.

Answer: **(C).** In 1973–74 and in 1978–79.

2. How have U.S. auto prices risen compared to all other U.S. goods and services during the last five years?

A. more slowly.   **B.** about the same.   **C.** more quickly.   **D.** much more quickly.

Answer: **(D).** About 100 per cent faster.

3. Let's say you went to a market in the late 1960s and spent $20 on food, how much would the same items have cost you in the late 1970s?

A. $55.   **B.** $33.   **C.** $42.   **D.** $60.

Answer: **(C).** $42.

4. Between the start and the end of the 1970s, which of the following basic necessities rose in price the fastest: food, housing, medical care, transportation, energy?

A. food.   **B.** housing.   **C.** energy.   **D.** transportation.   **E.** medical care.

Answer: **(C).** Energy rose at an average rate of 10 per cent a year during this period.

5. In the late 1970s, which of the following factors contributed most significantly to the higher cost of housing: interest rates, labor costs, land prices, building materials, or real estate taxes?

A. land prices. **B.** real estate taxes. **C.** labor costs and interest rates. **D.** interest rates and building materials.

Answer: **(D).** Interest rates and building materials.

6. How much do government-mandated safety and pollution-control devices add to the average price of an American-made car?

A. $185–$500. **B.** $501–$1,000. **C.** $1,000 or more.

Answer: **(A).** Official opinion is widely divided on whether the price tag is at the bottom or the top of the (A) range.

WHAT FORM OF INFLATION ARE WE FIGHTING?

OVERALL DEFINITION

Inflation, in the simplest of words, is an unhealthily rapid rise in prices over a relatively short span of time.

Its results, expressed in one way: a sharp erosion in the buying power of the currency you use to conduct all your transactions at home and in your business or profession; plus a dwindling in the future buying power of the funds you put away in cash savings or the equivalent (life insurance, U.S. savings bonds, the like); an undermining in the value of most other investments.

Its results, expressed in another way: an upsurge in your living costs, which few can offset successfully and which, therefore, puts you in a budget squeeze, reduces your standard of living despite pay hikes you may win, all but destroys your confidence and peace of mind.

TWO TYPES OF INFLATION

But that's not the whole tale, for there are two types of inflation—drastically different from each other.

The first type is called "demand-pull," which means that demands for goods and services during a specified period are exceeding the available supplies of those goods and services and this excess of demand (fueled by more than adequate cash or credit in the hands of buyers) is "pulling up" prices.

A classic illustration of demand-pull inflation occurred in food prices—especially meat prices—during the early post-World War II period. Millions of newly prosperous U.S. workers and their families sharply hiked their demands for meat, more millions steadily increased their purchases of higher quality meats, shoppers the nation over loaded their supermarket carts with roasts, steaks, lamb, veal.

The continued buying of a limited supply of meats rapidly pulled up meat prices, until the spiral culminated in the blowoff in meat prices in the wild inflation of 1974—and (at least temporarily) interrupted the long-term upsurge in our consumption of meats.

The second type is called "cost-push," which means that mounting costs of producing goods and services during a specified period are "pushing up" prices. For many, many years—possibly the longest span in modern times—we have been in the clutch of cost-push inflation in the United States. And no end to this form of inflation is yet in sight. The leapfrogging of prices over wages, then wages over prices, then prices over wages, and on and on continues.

Meanwhile, intolerable though it is, an annual inflation rate of 8–9 per cent feels "better" than the double-digit rates of the late Nixon-early Ford years. But below is what would happen to your dollar's buying power if it were to continue to lose value at "only" an 8 per cent rate.

There are two assumptions in the following figures. The first is that the U.S. dollar was worth 100 cents in the fall of 1978. The second assumption is that a share of the typical marketbasket of a city family cost $1 at that time: Source—U. S. Bureau of Labor Statistics: annual inflation rate—8 per cent.

INFLATION'S IMPACT AT AN ANNUAL RATE OF 8 PER CENT

YEAR	$1 WORTH	GOODS, SERVICES COST
1978 (fall)	100 cents	$ 1.00
1979	93	$ 1.08
1989	43	$ 2.33
1999	20	$ 5.03
2009	9	$10.87

This is *not* tolerable. You couldn't make plans for anything worthwhile on the basis of an inflation rate of this magnitude—not for independence in your older years, not for the education of your children or future education of yourselves, not for care of your loved ones. *Nothing!*

EXPECTATIONS OF INFLATION: A SELF-FULFILLING PROPHECY

Perhaps the most insidious evil in the overall evil of pernicious inflation is the spreading expectation that inflation will become permanent—a "psychology of inflation" that is dangerously self-fulfilling.

As millions of Americans become resigned to the prospect that the price spiral is a fact of life to be accepted for the indefinite future, these unhealthy developments follow:

• More and more workers demand wage hikes to keep up with past price increases and to get a jump ahead of future price increases—thereby adding to the current inflation rate.

• More and more union leaders insist on cost of living adjustment clauses in their union contracts to give them automatic pay raises as the Consumer Price Index climbs. As the 1980s approached, an estimated half of our total population —Social Security and welfare recipients as well as workers—already were covered by "COLAs."

• More and more businesses boost prices in anticipation of the wage demands and of the eventual imposition of mandatory wage-price controls.

• More and more consumers try to buy big- and small-ticket items "ahead" to beat the price increases they are sure will come.

• The whole sick pyramid collapses into a business slump, which leads to "reflation" policies and a new round of inflation.

As the decade of the 1970s closed, there were signs everywhere that this psychology of inflation was becoming ever more powerful and entrenched in the marketplace. To illustrate:

(1) Only a few years ago, inflation-sensitive, "alternative" mortgages were being sharply denounced by consumer, labor, and other groups—and bills to permit federally chartered savings and loan associations to offer new types of mortgages were heavily defeated in Congress. Now new types of home loans are being offered—and widely accepted by homeowners—in dozens of states. Some of the mortgages have interest rates that vary with major money market rates.

Opposition to the alternative mortgages has dwindled, if not disappeared entirely. It well may be that the fixed-rate, level-payment mortgage is on the way to becoming the "alternative" and the new types—the rollover, graduated-payment, variable, reverse mortgages—are to become the "norm."

(2) When computer-assisted check-out systems began to appear in supermarkets and department stores several years ago, shoppers protested, fearing that prices on products and shelves would disappear. In some areas, laws were passed to outlaw the removal of prices from individual items and/or shelves, and some merchants voluntarily agreed to continue marking goods with price tags.

Resistance to this labor-saving and inflation-inspired change has declined, too. Shoppers continue to patronize stores which don't price-mark each product—even though none of the predicted savings from the change has been passed on to consumers.

(3) The automatic fuel adjustment clause is an example of a now commonplace inflation-adjustment mechanism. It enables many utilities to pass along increased fuel costs to consumers in the form of higher rates—boosts which need no review by state regulators.

(4) And a tiny but most revealing sign of how even the government had adapted to inflation came from the U. S. Postal Service. In the late 1970s it issued a series of postage stamps that carried no value marking—only an eagle carrying the letter "A". The reason—the Postal Service needed an unmarked stamp that could be used until its requested rate hikes were approved. The Postal Service says it has no more unmarked stamps in storage. But that's not so reassuring in view of the fact that this in no way stops it from requesting another printing—just in case.

These are just a few of the many accommodations the marketplace has already made to inflation. Undoubtedly more will come as the 1980s progress.

"A COUNTRY WHERE NOBODY SPEAKS THE TRUTH"

"Inflation is like a country where nobody speaks the truth."

This perceptive observation comes from Dr. Henry Wallich, an astute governor of the Federal Reserve Board, whose upbringing in pre-World War II Germany has made him particularly sensitive to the more subtle—but corrosive—side effects of persistent inflation.

The key danger is that paper money—a medium of exchange, a measure of value—becomes so debased that nothing stated in dollars and cents any longer means what it says.

The never-ending inflation of the last two decades is leading us to a situation where, Wallich says, "Everybody makes contracts knowing perfectly well that they will not be kept in terms of constant values. We do not know whether the most valuable part of the contract may not turn out to be the paper it is written on."

It becomes all but impossible for anyone to make a long-term commitment, whether the commitment is between a buyer and seller, an employer and employee, or a lender and borrower.

In the face of inflation-induced uncertainty, it is only human for you to try to protect yourself—no matter what the transaction—by constantly demanding a bit more than you expect or offering a little less than you otherwise would.

Honesty disappears.

Deception becomes a way of life.

Inflation eats away at our moral values, and deceit begins to dominate the way we conduct our economic affairs—as individuals, as businessmen, and as political leaders.

As the 1980s opened, our proud nation was in the grip of this cycle. The documentation is widespread and horrifying:

• An estimated 9 million Americans hold part-time jobs or otherwise earn money which they don't report on their income tax forms.

• Taxes and dividends are being paid from profits that don't exist, or if they could be shown to exist by appropriate accounting adjustments, they are not backed by cash flows. And adds Wallich, "In addition to misleading the stockholder and the public, these conditions push business into becoming more speculative."

• The phenomenon of "downsizing" or "packaging to price" is a form of deception that consumers encounter every day. The price of the item remains unchanged or rises only slightly, but you, the buyer, get less for your money than you did before. Candy bars, for example, are smaller, paper towels contain fewer sheets of paper, seats on some jumbo jets are narrower and packed closer together, and warranties on cars and TV sets cover much less than a mere ten years ago.

• Inflation has also brought about hidden quality changes. Solid walnut or oak furniture, for instance, has been replaced by plywood or particle board covered with a hardwood veneer. The pages of books are seldom stitched together with thread but are bound with glue, and newspapers as well as magazines have cut printing, paper, and postage costs by reducing the size of their pages.

• At the same time, our politicians follow policies that, if not openly dishonest, are not honest either. They make promises, knowing full well that they cannot be kept in real terms, because as the government at all levels overspends, the value of the benefits it is supposed to deliver automatically shrinks.

Deception, deceit, dishonesty—these are inflation's hidden side-effects. And even the most imaginative, boldest anti-inflation government policies will be slow to correct them.

THE CHARACTERISTICS OF CLASS

Where does your income rank?

ARE YOU RICH?

You are if you have a household income of $50,000 and over. This is the class of the rich and there are only about 800,000 homes in it. But while you make up 1 per cent of our nation's population, you get 6 per cent of our entire personal income.

ARE YOU AFFLUENT?

You are if your household income is $25,000 to $50,000, and if so, you are also in a skinny minority of 10 per cent of our households. But if you are in this class you have at your disposal some 26 per cent of our nation's total earnings and your per capita income is more than twice the nationwide average.

ARE YOU UPPER-MIDDLE?

Your household income is $15,000 to $25,000 and some 18 million—or about one out of every four of the nation's families—are in this class. Your per capita income exceeds $5,000, which is a third again as much as the national average.

ARE YOU AVERAGE?

Then your household income is $10,000 to $15,000 and you join nearly one fifth of all America's homes. What's more, in contrast to the affluent and the rich, many of you are thirty-four years of age or younger and less than 25 per cent of you are over fifty-five.

ARE YOU BELOW PAR?

That's you, if your household income is $5,000 to $10,000, and you represent one of every five homes. Your per capita income is only $2,600 a year and, despite the size of your group, only 10 per cent of all spending power flows to you.

In the United States in the late 1970s, you qualify for this bottom class if your household income is under $5,000. In this bracket, including one of every five households, lie many of our social problems. Here are the retired, the widowed, the lone female, often over sixty-five years old, the less educated. But happily the importance of your "class" continues to shrink.

Where do you belong? In the past quarter century the distribution of incomes has undergone a dramatic upheaval and realignment. Each year more than a million of our households are moving from the middle into the upper income brackets, a process which has been fundamentally altering our social and economic life-styles.

There are two characteristics of class inherent in this realignment which shout a direct personal message to you:

The first is that the higher the income class the higher the education. Among the below-average, only about 20 per cent of all household heads have had any exposure to college. In the $15,000 to $25,000 bracket, some 40 per cent of all household heads have had at least some college training. In the $25,000 to $50,000 bracket, this is up to 45 per cent with college degrees and an additional 15 per cent with some college training. In the class of the rich, an exceptionally high 54 per cent of all household heads have college degrees and 90 per cent are white-collar workers. You can't miss it! The tie is undeniable. The message is clear.

The second is the high incidence of the working wife in the upper-middle bracket—and in fact in well over half of all the $15,000 to $25,000 homes the wife is employed. There are relatively few working wives among the below-average; they rise to 45 per cent among average households and then up again.

The U.S. economy was an income "pyramid" a mere few generations ago, with most in the below-middle classes, a tiny few at the top. It has become "diamond-shaped," with most people in the middle, fewer at the bottom, still fewer at the top—and if incomes continue rising merely at the annual rate of the past twenty years, the average family income in the United States will top $15,500 in the early 1980s. It remains, though, a far cry from the ideal "reverse pyramid," with most of us at the top and middle, virtually none at the bottom.

Why You Feel "Broke" at Highest Pay Ever

Let's say that in the early-mid 1970s, you, the breadwinner in a family of four, earned a partially after-tax income of $15,000—meaning after deduction for federal income and Social Security taxes, but not including the huge bite from state and local taxes. Let's say also that by the start of the 1980s your annual pay hikes had raised your partially after-tax income to more than $22,500.

That's a hefty pay increase of over 50 per cent in less than five years. But it has been merely enough to keep your purchasing power even so that your family can buy about the same marketbasket of goods and services at the beginning of the 1980s as it could with your much smaller after-tax income years ago.

But wait. The cost of living, as measured by the official price indices, had increased "only" around 45 per cent in that time span. How come, then, that an income rise of more than 50 per cent is essential just to stay even in buying power?

The first answer is that as you move up the pay scale, you move, too, into ever-higher income tax brackets and your pay is subjected to ever-higher income tax rates. Federal income tax rates alone squeeze more and more out of your gross, leave you with less and less for your net-after-taxes. Call it the tax-bracket "creep," or call it the progressive tax "squeeze," or whatever—the result is the same. As your salary or other income rises, under our progressive tax system, you pay a greater percentage of it to the federal government. The gap yawns wider and wider between your gross and your net.

This is just one reason you feel so "broke" at a time when you're earning the highest pay of your entire life.

A second answer is that on $22,500, you are paying far more in Social Security taxes than you paid on the earlier salary of $15,000. The amount of your wages on which you pay Social Security taxes has been steadily raised and is slated to continue climbing. At the same time, the Social Security tax rate on incomes has been in a steady uptrend too.

This is a regressive tax—hitting lower income people harder than those at the top. But the result is the same here, too. As your salary or other income rises, you pay a higher Social Security tax to the Social Security system. The gap yawns still wider between your gross and your net.

A third answer is that you are using far more services than ever before and all services which depend heavily on individual labor cost more than ever before. Living in a "service" society commands a price and since you have chosen that life, you must pay the price demanded.

You send your laundry to the local cleaner instead of doing it at home—or you buy a washer-dryer and pay for that big-ticket item. You use public transportation, which has climbed in price at a pace far faster than the cost of cars. You go out to the movies and pay prices that would have stunned you only a few years ago. All these service costs have zoomed, at a rate far outpacing the rates of increases in other areas. And your demand for more and more services seems without end.

And finally, although much more subtle, is the factor of your ever-expanding aspirations, your continual upgrading in your demands. The luxuries of yesterday are the necessities of today. You have become accustomed to yearly increases in your spending budget to new peaks, resent any interruption in the trend. Whatever form the upgrading takes, the general rise in aspirations is undeniable. And any sudden retreats are no more than temporary.

These then are four reasons you feel so "broke" at a time when you're earning the highest pay of your entire life.

"Era of Aspirations"

You're a young family in the $15,000 to $20,000 income range—striving for the "surplus income" family status but still well below it. You have a couple of elementary-school-age kids, you live in the suburbs, and the family breadwinner commutes to work in his car or car pool in which he must share use of his automobile. Are two cars a luxury or a necessity?

Your children are in high school and you, their mother, want to go back to a full-time job to help finance their future education. Is a household employee, at least part-time, a luxury or a necessity?

Is home air conditioning, for you who live in the very hot states, a luxury in this era? Is automatic transmission in a car still just an option or has it become "basic equipment"? Does anyone today consider a TV set an unqualified luxury?

We have long been in an "era of aspirations" in our economy. In this era, most of us will spend a shrinking share of our income on the traditional necessities of food, clothing, shelter, and transportation while we spend a steadily increasing share of our income for goods and services which reflect our hopes and wants.

The implications for our economy and for you are profound.

Even now, the proportion of our total buying power available for spending on the "aspirations" rather than the necessities of life is estimated at a record high. Our total "discretionary spending"—defined as "purchases resulting from decisions relatively free of pressure of necessity or force of habit"—is enormous.

As Dr. George Katona, author of *The Mass Consumption Society*, put it: " . . . not just a thin upper class, but the majority of households have acquired discretionary purchasing power. In the new wants-or-aspirations economies, in contrast to needs-economies, many consumer expenditures may be postponed or may be bunched at a given time. Therefore, in addition to consumers' ability to buy, consumers' willingness to buy also exerts a great influence on economic trends."

But . . . does our huge capacity to buy most of the things we want, over and beyond the things we actually need, make us happier? Not by any means. Again, in Katona's words:

"If what you have today appears insufficient tomorrow, disappointment and frustration may become frequent occurrences. Stress, tension and anxiety may even grow far beyond what has prevailed in less affluent societies. Moreover, because of the persistent gap between the well-being of the affluent to very-affluent 85–90 per cent of our society and the other 10–15 per cent who remain outside the mass consumption society, deprivations are felt more strongly than ever before."

And the ironic clincher: "The higher the aspirations, the more chance that people will be disappointed."

You Work Until Early May Just to Pay Taxes!

If you are merely an average worker-taxpayer, every dollar you earn until one day early in May each year will go to pay your taxes—federal, state, and local.

No matter what you may think, for more than a full four months—through April—you have not been working to earn money for yourself and your family. You have been working to earn enough to fulfill your tax obligations to the various levels of government, according to Tax Foundation calculations.

Of your eight-hour work day, taxes alone take a stunning two hours—plus. In terms of the amount of work you put in to cover your expenses, none absorbs as much as taxes.

Taxes are the biggest single item in your family budget, far outweighing what you put into paying for your house and household operations, food and drink, transportation, etc.

May Day is an ancient spring festival. It also is celebrated as a Marxist holiday (with May Day parades a familiar spectacle in many United States cities as well as other lands that are openly socialistic-communistic). In the international language of air navigation, "Mayday" is an urgent, frightening cry for help.

And it is "Tax Freedom Day" too, says the Tax Foundation, "the day when we have all finished paying our taxes." (That would be so for the "average taxpayer"; for others, above average, the date might come even later.)

"Our research does not go into taxpayers' reactions to their responsibilities to pay taxes," says a Tax Foundation spokesman, "but it would be my guess they are happy and relieved to have completed this obligation. Whether May Day is perceived as a joyous spring festival or a cry for help remains to be seen. In my view, four full months a year to work for the government is just about enough."

This view is much too conservative, I think. In fact, I'll go on the line with the observation that the information in this report is infuriating you.

Worse, if what you are wondering is how to get out of this squeeze, the answer is that you won't—until you are willing to forfeit some of the government services for which your taxes are paying. And judging from your responses so far, this you simply are not willing to do—whether the services are for the police-fire protection of your family at the local level or for the military defense of your nation's freedoms at the federal level.

The solution surely is not in printing more greenbacks to pay for the services. That way lies utter destruction of our currency's value. And we already have done fearful damage to our dollar's buying power by inflating our money supply during previous splurges of spending on projects deemed deeply desirable if not essential.

When it comes down to the bottom line, the alternatives are: control spending at the three levels of government or maintain (even increase) current tax burdens.

Following is the Tax Bite in the Eight-Hour Day, late 1970s, as estimated by the Tax Foundation, headquartered in New York City. (It doesn't change much from year to year.)

ITEM	HOURS AND MINUTES
Taxes, total	2 hrs., 39 min.
Federal taxes	1 hr., 41 min.
State and local taxes	50 min.
Food and beverages	1 hr., 5 min.
Housing, house operation	1 hr., 32 min.
Clothing	29 min.
Transportation	39 min.
Medical care	25 min.
Recreation	19 min.
All other	52 min.

"All other" includes consumer spending for items such as personal care, personal business, private education, savings.

WHAT YOUR TAX DOLLAR BUYS

Although, as part of my work, I *must* study the big, fat U. S. Government budget books loaded with multibillion-dollar figures and supposedly simplified by well-drawn charts designed to show where the federal budget dollar comes from and where it goes, I admit that the annual budget reports bore and befuddle me into a state of stupefaction. If this is true of me, what must it suggest about your reaction?

How, then, can I translate these significant totals into terms both of us can understand? I can try to do it by breaking down an annual budget total of the late 1970s into terms of your own paycheck and taxes—and, thus, really show what share of your tax dollar is going where.

Say you are an office worker, with a wife and two dependent children, earning $16,500–$17,500 a year. That's the Tax Foundation's "Charlie Green," a mythical but typical American worker. Now, here's what the Tax Foundation estimated Charlie Green paid in federal taxes in one year at the end of the 1970s, and "you" are Charlie Green in real life.

A total of $1,688 in income taxes, $998 in Social Security taxes, and $1,849 in other federal taxes. ("Other taxes" includes your share of corporate income taxes, your employer's Social Security taxes, excises, customs, etc.) The total you are paying comes to $4,535.

A total of $4,535 in taxes is comprehensible. And below is where that money went in that year. (The dollar totals change from year to year, of course. But the meaning remains unchanged!)

U.S. SPENDING FOR	CHARLIE'S (YOUR) SHARE OF TOTAL
Income security	30.8%—$1,396
National defense	22.6%—$1,204
Health	9.2%—$ 418
Interest	9.2%—$ 417
Education, employment services	5.7%—$ 259
Commerce, transportation	4.1%—$ 188
Veterans' affairs	4.0%—$ 183
Environment, energy	4.0%—$ 182
Community development	2.2%—$ 101
Revenue sharing, general assistance	2.0%—$ 90
Agriculture	1.6%—$ 73
Internal affairs	1.4%—$ 62
Science, space	1.0%—$ 46
Law enforcement	0.8%—$ 37
General government	0.8%—$ 36
Contingencies, pay raises	0.5%—$ 23

(Slight differences in totals due to offsetting receipts not classified by function.)

No matter how much bigger (or moderately smaller) your own income and tax payments are, your relationship to the budget will be roughly the same as Charlie Green's.

The prime point is the share of your dollars going to income security—meaning Social Security benefits of all kinds and welfare. While taking moderately less than in previous years, our social welfare load is becoming ever and ever heavier.

And then there's the equally revealing fact that all the uproar over the cost of general government is about spending that accounts for a fraction of a penny per tax dollar.

And all the millions (or billions) of words of debate about a national energy policy, not to mention natural resources and environment, have resulted in a puny four cents of every tax dollar going to energy. This is the same share that went to energy-environment spending in fiscal 1977.

2

BUDGETS ARE BACK IN STYLE

If you don't have a budget, now is the right time to start one. If you do keep a budget, now is the right time to re-examine your priorities, perhaps thoroughly overhaul them, surely tighten your controls.

Personal budget-keeping is back in style—and for good reasons. Our total cost of living rose at an oppressively rapid rate throughout the 1970s; prices of many necessities and semi-luxuries skyrocketed. Against this background, it is increasingly essential for you to get the maximum benefit from your income and to protect your savings.

Fewer and fewer of you can rely strictly on your instinctive sense of money management. Fewer and fewer of you should even try to get by with only a loose outline of your living expenses and anticipated earnings.

THE SHAPE OF *YOUR* BUDGET

How to finance not only your day-to-day needs but also your aspirations—that's the objective of people everywhere, in every income group, in every circumstance. And many of you are seeking help because you have an uncomfortable feeling that you ought to be able to manage better than you do.

If, therefore, you feel you want or need a budget, you should start one. And if this is you, get this fundamental point straight now: your family's budget will be radically different from that of families living near you. And it will without question differ in many key respects from any "average" spending-saving pattern of any "average" American family. The average family exists only on paper and its average budget is a fiction, invented by statisticians for the convenience of statisticians.

The shape of your own budget will depend directly on your own or your family's individual goals and priorities. Would you prefer to spend $6,500 on a new car or on a year of education? Would $500 worth of color television mean more, or less, to you than $500 worth of, say, guitar lessons? There is no sense in attempting to fit into a ready-to-wear financial pattern which ignores your own personal wants and desires.

The budget you draw also will depend heavily on the composition of your family. A young working couple without children may have relatively low housing costs, relatively high entertainment and clothes costs, and a good opportunity to save substantial amounts toward future family goals. Drastically different will be the spending-savings blueprint of the young couple with growing children and a heavily mortgaged house.

In essence, there is no such thing as an average budget and you should not even look for a standardized format. Search instead for a simple, flexible financial outline to help you achieve the goals you truly want.

WHICH SYSTEM OF MONEY MANAGEMENT FOR YOU?

You can get your first basic guidance from the experience and methods of others. The shopkeeper on your corner has part of the answer in the way he handles his store's income and outgo and fits the two together with a margin left for "reserve." Your parents had part of the answer in the way they measured their earnings and their prospects for earnings, then divided their spending into so much for essentials, so much for savings, so much for luxuries. The giant corporation has much of the answer in the ways it keeps its books, prepares for bad as well as good times, and provides a cushion for the unexpected and unpredictable.

You may now be handling all your income and outgo on a basis of "Here's what's in my pocket, here's what has been spent." Income, in short, is what you actually have in your hands; outgo is what you are paying to other people. What's coming to you later isn't important this minute. What you owe later isn't important either. The big thing is what you have and what you spend now. Accountants call that operating on a "cash basis"—but, as millions discover, it doesn't go far enough.

It is obvious that what most people need is a system of money management which will:

(1) tell you what money is coming in during the next several weeks or months;

(2) tell you what has to be put aside today for future security and independence and for those big unavoidable bills due in the next several weeks or months;

(3) tell you what is left over for the day-to-day expenses, ranging from food to a new household gadget;

(4) tell you, too, how much is left, if any, for luxuries and semi-luxuries;

(5) relate your income and expenses to a reasonably long period of time so that you can avoid fumbling along from minute to minute and day to day;

(6) show you how to run your personal affairs the way most successful businessmen run their affairs;

(7) achieve your financial priorities.

This system, incidentally, is what accountants call operating on an "accrual" basis, but dismiss that fancy-sounding word right here. The important point is that no business can get anywhere unless it knows what money is coming in tomorrow as well as today and unless it knows also what is to be done with tomorrow's as well as today's cash.

A family or person cannot get far without this type of planning either.

Money is earned to be spent. When you spend, you buy more than material things such as bread or shoes; you make decisions which determine your whole way of life. Your decisions bring you closer to—or perhaps send you further away from—your ambitions, your aspirations, the things and non-things which are really most worthwhile to you.

Money never remains just coins and pieces of paper. It is constantly changing into the comforts of daily life. Money can be translated into the beauty of living, a support in misfortune, an education, or future security. It also can be translated into a source of bitterness.

It may seem that so many of your decisions are forced by circumstances that you have very little chance to control your own money. Perhaps, however, your income appears too small to go around only because you did not take into account the "nibblers"—the little items that nibble away at your income until there is nothing left. Perhaps you have debts left at the end of the year only because you ignored the "bouncers"—the big expenses that turn up a couple of times a year and make giant dents in your income. Or perhaps you're in trouble only because you haven't considered the "sluggers"—the unexpected expenses, such as sickness and major household repairs, that can throw even a good spending plan way off balance.

Start from the premise that no income you will earn will ever be large enough to cover *all* your wants. Accept the theory that the more income you have the greater will be your desires. Make up your mind that if you want something badly enough you will sacrifice other things for it.

Take the trouble to think out your own philosophy of living and your ambitions for the future. Develop a plan of control over your spending. Then you will make progress toward the kind of living which means most to you.

THREE PRELIMINARY NOTES ON BUDGETING

Although no system in itself can completely eliminate your money problems the following preliminary notes will certainly help:

(1) You must work together if you are married. Your plan must be a joint project and you must talk about a wide variety of things before trying to put down a single figure about income or outgo.

(2) You must provide for personal allowances in your plan—and let each person decide what to do with his or her own allotment. None of you should have to account for every cent of your allowance; that is a personal matter. Similarly, if you're a wife at home, you should not be asked to submit an item-by-item explanation of what happened to the food money. Never permit a budget to become a straitjacket—or it will surely fail. And most important, I repeat, do not try to fit yourself into other people's budgets or try to make the spending averages of other families solve your own problems.

(3) You must keep your records simple. Then they will be fun to maintain as well as helpful. All that is required from your records is a blueprint for each month's spending, a history of where money goes each month, and an overall pic-

ture to help you whenever a financial emergency arises. You can get vital information from simple records, and the simpler the records, the more they will reveal.

FOUR SIMPLE FORMS TO CREATE A PERSONAL MONEY MANAGER

You are about to create a personal money manager that, no matter what your income, will do four things:

(1) tell you where your money is coming from—and when it is coming;

(2) provide for the necessities first, then the comforts and self-improvements, then the luxuries—when you have the money to spend for them;

(3) give you a means for saving—a plan to pay off debts or to keep out of debt;

(4) build good habits for spending—for today and tomorrow.

You can do this job very successfully if you, as a family, will learn to complete four simple forms.

Form I. Here is how I get my income.

Form II. Here is what I must put aside to cover my unavoidable expenses and my savings.

Form III. Here is where I find how much I have available for my day-to-day expenses.

Form IV. Here is how I will spend the money available for my day-to-day expenses during this period.

FORM I—FAMILY INCOME

The mistake most people make in beginning a money management plan is that they don't start at the beginning. The *beginning* surely is to find out how much money you have coming in to spend for all purposes during the year.

To reach this vital figure, take a sheet of paper and write down every item of income you expect during the year. Convert each total to a monthly basis. If you are a husband-and-wife working couple or are just living together under one roof, include the earnings of both.

(1) List not only the amounts of your regular take-home pay, translated into equal monthly totals, but also any income you anticipate from stock dividends, commissions, interest on bonds or savings accounts, yearly cash gifts from relatives, rent, bonuses, tax refunds due you, amounts owed to you by others. Also include profits from any sales of securities, your car, real estate, your home, assuming, of course, you sell any of these at a profit. Anything else? List it.

(2) Estimate each item of income as accurately and realistically as you can. When in doubt, put down the *minimum*.

(3) List only the net amounts of your regular paychecks—after subtracting withheld income taxes, your Social Security contributions, union dues, company pension plan payments you make, any group insurance or other payments which your company automatically deducts from your paycheck, etc.

(4) If your income is irregular—as it well may be if you are an artist, writer,

teacher, small businessman, work part-time or on a commission basis—divide the total you expect for the year by 12. Always keep your estimates low.

(5) If you are not certain how much your income will be for the entire year, list only the amounts you can accurately predict for a shorter period—again, converted to a monthly basis.

Form I   Family Income

WHAT WILL WE GET FROM	JAN.	FEB.	MAR.	APR.	MAY	JUNE	JULY	AUG.	SEPT.	OCT.	NOV.	DEC.	YEARLY TOTAL	NOTES
Husband's job														
Wife's job														
Business interests														
Interest														
Dividends														
Rent														
Gifts														
Company bonus or bonuses														
Tax refunds														
Moonlighting job														
Profits from sales														
Alimony														
Other														
Other														
Totals for the month														

(6) If your income increases, don't get carried away; a pay raise always looks bigger than it really is. Before you start even to touch your raise, revise your budget income sheet to place the addition in accurate perspective. Add only the extra *net* (take-home) total—not the amount before taxes and other deductions.

(7) Using the same yardstick, if your income takes an unexpected dive, revise all your monthly totals downward as soon as the drop occurs. Remember, the amounts of money you'll have to spend will be based on the amounts actually coming in at any given time.

Your inventory of income must reflect *facts*. On this sheet, there is little room for flexibility and *none* for fuzziness.

Form II   Fixed Expenses – Including Savings

WHAT WE MUST SPEND AND SAVE	JAN.	FEB.	MAR.	APR.	MAY	JUNE	JULY	AUG.	SEPT.	OCT.	NOV.	DEC.	YEARLY TOTAL	NOTES
Rent or mortgage														
Fuel bills														
Telephone														
Electricity, gas														
Water														
Installment payment A														
Installment payment B														
Education (or other) payment														
Real estate taxes														
Income taxes														
Home and life insurance														
Auto insurance														
Medical, dental														
What we must set aside for savings alone														
Other														
Total for each month														

You have now broken down your income into 12 spending periods. You have taken the first step away from the "feast or famine" cash basis.

Knowing what you have available to spend each month, you will know how your expenses must be divided to match that real monthly income. When you have set up this kind of money manager, you'll be amazed how different your overall income-expense picture will appear!

FORM II—FIXED EXPENSES

Now let's consider expenses.

There are three classes of outgo: (1) the unavoidable expenses—the big items such as insurance premiums, repayment of personal debts, real estate taxes—which must be paid no matter what the inconvenience; (2) savings and rainy-day reserves; and (3) day-to-day living expenses.

The key to a good system of money management lies in spreading your big expenses and your savings so that each month bears a share of them. When you put aside $20 every month to meet a $240 yearly insurance premium, for instance, you will not risk spending that insurance money on an unnecessary luxury.

Take a second sheet of paper. On it list all of your fixed expenses during the coming year and convert each of these to a monthly basis.

Among the more obvious fixed expenses to include on your monthly list are:

(1) Rent or mortgage payments.

(2) Predictable, regular household bills for such items as electricity, gas, fuel, telephone, water, garbage collection, cable TV, lawn mowing.

(3) Installment payments you make regularly for your car, washing machine, Christmas or Hanukkah Club, charge or credit card accounts, personal or education loan, etc.

(4) Big once- or twice-a-year obligations such as real estate taxes, payments for tuition and fees, auto, life, and homeowner's insurance premiums, dues to your professional society, pledged contributions.

(5) Medical and dental expenses which can be accurately pinpointed for the year (e.g., costs of annual checkups, eye exams, orthodontia); health insurance premiums; predictable drug and vitamin bills.

(6) Federal and state income taxes which have not been withheld.

(7) Automobile and commuting expenses which you can accurately estimate, such as commuter train tickets and car pool costs, monthly parking bills, car registration and inspection, average gas and oil bills for your car or cars.

(8) Membership dues—e.g., union, club, or professional association.

Among the less obvious fixed expenses to include are your monthly personal allowances for each family member. The amount of allowances you allot to each will depend partly on what expenses each person is expected to meet out of the allowance. Is the allowance supposed to pay for gifts? Lunches? Clothes? Music lessons? Charitable contributions?

Without a money management plan, if you have to pay a life insurance premium of $240, a property tax bill of $96, and a personal loan of $600—all in January—you would have to dig up $936 somewhere. And that might be tough indeed. But you probably know beforehand that in January you must meet those payments. When your money management plan is in full effect, you would set aside $78 out of each month's income and then you would be able to take the January financial blows in stride.

Of course, when you start your plan, you might find it impossible to provide for those big expenses. For example, let's assume that the $936 is due in January and it is now November. You might have to get a loan or make the November, December, and January income bear the full brunt. But once that hurdle has been passed, you would divide the expenses by 12 to find out how much of the burden each month's income should bear.

Some of your large debts, such as loans from a member of the family, may be past due. Try to pay these as soon as possible and clear your slate.

INCLUDE YOUR SAVINGS!

At this point, let me back up and assure you that item (2) under the above "classes of outgo" was not a misprint. Rather, a savings reserve is the least obvious—but still vital—expense you must include in your monthly list.

Put down a total you can reasonably expect to save each month. *Treat savings as an expense and budget for savings as you budget for rent or mortgage payments, and you will discipline yourself into building a nest egg.* "Pay yourself" first—as soon as you get your paycheck—and your small monthly totals will become big totals over a period of time.

Include in your savings total an emergency fund equal to at least two months' income, to cover you should you be hit by big unforeseen expenses such as illness, unexpected home repairs, moving expenses. Note: the emergency part of your savings fund should be kept in a readily accessible ("liquid") form—for instance, a savings account.

As a starter, earmark 5 per cent of your total monthly income for savings, and boost the percentage from there if you can swing it.

If you have already saved the recommended equivalent of two months' income, freeze this amount as your emergency reserve. While you may want more or less than two months' income in reserve, be guided on this basically by the size of your other financial cushions: the amount of unemployment compensation for which you are eligible in the event that you are laid off or fired from your job and cannot find another one; the amount of your disability benefits which would be paid under Social Security or by your employer or through your health insurance policies; other health insurance benefits due you in the event of a medical crisis; your non-working wife's ability to take a job if an emergency arises or, if she has a job, to carry the family for a period; your credit-worthiness.

If you haven't the fund on hand now, figure how much more you will have to save before you reach the total. Then decide how long a time you'll need to save the amount necessary to lift your fund to the proper level. Don't try to save the extra amount too fast. Decide what you can put aside each month until the fund is assured and enter that amount on Form II as a fixed expense until your emergency fund is equal to the suggested level. Once it is there, keep it at that comfortable level.

As for *how* you will save, you have many alternatives today.

(1) An automatic deduction plan from your checking account is offered by many banks. Under this plan, you authorize the bank to transfer to a simple savings account your specified sum at fixed intervals. You will receive the bank's stated interest rate on the amounts you accumulate in your savings account.

(2) Payroll savings plans are offered by many corporations under which a portion of your paycheck is automatically deducted (by your authorization) and also is deposited in a savings account.

(3) Under other corporate employee savings plans now available to millions, a corporation may add its own contribution to the amount you authorize to be deducted regularly from your paycheck. Your savings then may be invested in U.S. savings bonds, mutual funds, or company stock.

You'll find many other intriguing and important guides on pages 33–34 and pages 798–811.

Whatever method you choose, these fundamentals will remain unaltered:

The "secret" to saving is to put aside little amounts regularly and let the little amounts mount up to big totals.

The great value of your emergency reserve is protection for you against the unexpected and thus preservation of your peace of mind when the unexpected comes.

FORM III—WHAT YOU HAVE LEFT FOR DAY-TO-DAY EXPENSES

Now that you have taken care of your inflexible expenses—which you must regard as already spent from each paycheck—you are ready to begin work on budgeting for day-to-day expenses.

Take a third sheet of paper for Form III. As illustrated, put down your total income divided into 12 equal parts. Put down your unavoidable expenses and your savings, divided into 12 equal parts. The difference is what you have available for day-to-day living expenses.

This much is easy.

Form III   Day-to-Day Expenses

	JAN.	FEB.	MAR.	APR.	MAY	JUNE	JULY	AUG.	SEPT.	OCT.	NOV.	DEC.
From Form I, your monthly income												
From Form II, the total of your unavoidable expenses and savings for the year, divided by 12.												
What you have available for your day-to-day living expenses												

FORM IV—BUDGETING YOUR DAY-TO-DAY EXPENSES

Form IV will show you whether you will have to do some major juggling to make ends meet. You can't argue with the fixed figures on Form II, but you can juggle the items you will list on Form IV.

This is important: on Form IV, don't try to figure ahead for a full year. That's too difficult. Simply plan your regular day-to-day living expenses for a month or two ahead.

These will vary considerably but they are a substantial and crucial part of your budget. They also are expenses over which you have the most control.

Because you probably won't even be able to remember many of the little items

Form IV   Budgeting Day-to-Day Expenses

WHAT WE WILL SPEND FOR DAY-TO-DAY LIVING THIS MONTH	JAN.	FEB.	MAR.	APR.	MAY	JUNE	JULY	AUG.	SEPT.	OCT.	NOV.	DEC.	NOTES
For food and related items	$	$	$	$	$	$	$	$	$	$	$	$	
For household services and expenses													
For furnishings and equipment													
For clothes													
For transportation													
For medical care													
For personal care													
For education and recreation													
For gifts and contributions													
For other things and non-things													
TOTAL	$	$	$	$	$	$	$	$	$	$	$	$	
Total available for the month (from last line of Form III)	$			$	$	$	$	$	$	$	$	$	

when you begin your list, keep a detailed record of *all* your living expenses just for a couple of weeks. From this, you'll get an accurate idea of how much you're spending and for what. After you've obtained this guide, stop keeping records in such stultifying detail.

Here are the main categories of day-to-day expenses:

(1) *Food and related items:* the amounts of your regular grocery bills; what you spend to eat out in restaurants (including tips); candy and snacks from vending machines; soft drinks, beer, wine, and liquor; cigarettes; pet foods and supplies; personal and household items such as toothpaste and cosmetics which you buy at the supermarket.

(2) *Household services and expenses:* home repairs and improvements; any maintenance costs not counted in your fixed expenses; cleaning supplies; household help.

(3) *Furnishings and equipment:* what you buy outright for cash and down payments for large and small appliances, glass, china, silverware, curtains, rugs, upholstering, accessories, other items.

(4) *Clothes:* everything, ranging from repairs and alterations, through laundry and dry cleaning, to the seemingly insignificant accessories which can mount up to alarming totals.

(5) *Transportation:* car repairs, tune-ups, oil changes, new tires; bus, train, taxi, and air fares; parking charges; bridge tolls.

(6) *Medical care:* doctor and dentist bills not listed under your fixed expenses; drugs; eyeglasses; hospital and nursing expenses not covered by medical insurance; veterinarian bills for your pets.

(7) *Personal care:* the barber and hairdresser; toilet articles; cosmetics and other items not paid for by each family member's personal allowance and *not* in your supermarket bills.

(8) *Education and recreation:* books; theater, movie, and concert tickets; entertaining friends; newspaper and magazine subscriptions; musical instruments and music lessons; hobby equipment; vacation and holiday expenses; the upkeep of your pleasure boat, swimming pool, or riding horse; tuition and fees not included on Form II.

(9) *Gifts and contributions:* what is not paid out of personal allowances.

(10) *Other things and non-things:* only you can fill out this item.

DON'TS TO GUIDE YOU

Just a glance at the list on Form IV shows why it is futile to attempt a precise budget at the start. Unless you are the exceptional person who always has kept exact records of your spending, you will have to estimate the totals. Later it will be possible to be more accurate.

Don't set spending limits which are impossible to meet. It may be hard to fix a range until you've tried this money management system for a few months. That's expected. You'll learn by experience what the limits are and what they should be.

Don't start out by slashing one classification arbitrarily, "on paper." A major expense category cannot be cut just because the figure appears so big when listed.

"Food" is the category that most of you will try to slash first. But if you cut this too low, you'll discover you've set an impossible target.

Don't forget that the big expenses are on Form II. The classifications on Form IV cover only the usual day-to-day expenses. Major costs, such as orthodontia for your child, may be spread over a whole year of income periods. If "spreading" is easier for you, transfer other big items from Form IV to Form II.

Don't ignore your wants and don't try to kid yourself. When you're setting your allocations, be realistic. If your menu says steak, don't put down a figure for stew.

Don't fail to leave room for unexpected expenses. These are certain to arise and you never know in advance what they will be. They may range from a destroyed flat tire to an office contribution for a wedding gift.

Don't underestimate the importance of detailed records during the first month of your money management plan. When the next period rolls around and it turns out that your guesses weren't right, cross out the inaccurate estimates and put down what was really spent for each item.

With these hints to help, you can fill out Form IV, marking down your estimates, adding them up for each month, and comparing them with the total amount available. The result easily could be a big minus, indicating that you're spending or planning to spend more than your projected income. If your expense total, including savings, comes out way above your income total and the tally indicates you're heading into a flood of red ink, some items here must be cut.

But you can't cut unless you vow to make the cuts good. This money management plan is more than a pencil-pushing game.

What Role Do Your Children Play?

In any successful family spending plan, your children must play some part—especially when the things *they* want are to be considered. Although the responsibilities to be given children will undoubtedly vary from family to family, here are ten widely accepted rules:

(1) Begin giving your child an allowance just as soon as he or she understands the use of money for getting the things he or she wants.

(2) Have an understanding on what the allowance is to cover. At first it can relate only to such things as toys and special treats, but adjustments should be made from time to time in the size of the allowance and hence in its use. Many teenage boys and girls can handle allowances that cover their clothing. By the time they are mature, they will have had some experience in looking ahead and in saving for special things.

(3) In addition to having a clear understanding with your child on just what an allowance is or is not supposed to cover, renegotiate the contract at least once a year to take new obligations into account.

(4) Make your child's allowance a fair share in terms of your family's consumption in general.

(5) Take into account what your child's friends and schoolmates have. The allowance certainly should not be so much lower that the child feels constantly

deprived. But it also should not be greatly in excess of what others get; that's just as bad.

(6) As your child gets older, give him a voice in deciding what his allowance should be. Let him share in a family round table on the spending plan. He will thus gain a greater appreciation of fair sharing.

(7) Give your child full responsibility for spending his allowance, although your advice may be required for some things and should be available at all times. If he makes mistakes, he should come to recognize his responsibility for them and put up with the results. In unusual situations you might, perhaps, help him out in advance from the following week's allowance.

(8) While your child is learning to plan ahead, give him the allowance only for short periods. Perhaps give first for the day, then for the week, and only later for somewhat longer periods. Very early in their lives, your children should learn where the family's money comes from and the effort that goes into earning it. A child's spending should, therefore, be made in part dependent on his own efforts. Children often can be taught the simple lessons of earning and spending by being paid extra for special household tasks. But *do not* carry this too far; your child may acquire the habit of putting all helpfulness on a "pay me" basis. Pay only for exceptional—and not routine—household chores. Do not confuse this sort of payment with the allowance.

(9) As for saving, teenagers are notorious non-savers. They tend to spend income as fast as possible and often on apparently frivolous things. But at the same time they are deeply attracted by such big-ticket items as motorcycles, autos, stereos. Once a teenager sets an expensive item as a goal, the message usually seeps through that the purchase requires saving over a long period. Encourage your youngster to keep a savings goal within reasonable limits and not to make it a prolonged drudgery. Encourage your youngster also to learn how to manage a checking and/or savings account.

Here are some rough guides, developed by Household Finance Corporation, on what children in various age brackets might be expected to buy and pay for out of their allowances:

Under 6: candy, gum, ice cream, small toys, gifts for others, books, playthings, paints, crayons, blocks, and dolls.

Ages 6–9: movies, amusements, toys, books, magazines, hobbies, club dues, special savings for sports equipment, carfare and lunches at school, school activities and school expenses, gifts for birthdays and holidays and contributions.

Ages 9–12: fees for skating rinks, pools, etc., club dues, hobby materials, sports equipment and repairs, games and special events, carfare and lunches at school, gifts for birthdays and holidays, contributions, trips, school supplies, clothing, and upkeep.

Ages 12–18: the above, plus money for dates, grooming, cosmetics, jewelry, clothing, school activities, savings for special purposes such as travel and a future education.

Finally, on charge accounts, expert opinion divides violently—with one side warning that it is extremely reckless to give a teenager a charge account and the other arguing that, since charge accounts are so much a part of American life, a youngster should learn early how to buy on credit.

My compromise rule would be to teach your teenager to use credit modestly and wisely and to pay bills promptly. As an allowance is "learning money," so installment buying is vital financial education. The crucial point is that the earlier a youngster learns to live within a fixed income the better prepared he or she will be to manage money soundly as an adult.

These guides may seem no more than simple common sense—but isn't that fundamentally what proper money management always is?

BUDGETING IF YOU'RE IN COLLEGE

Now let's assume you're a college student living—or trying to live—on an allowance. How can the money management plan help you?

Some of you are at home during school years and are on weekly allowances; many others of you live away and receive your checks every month. But for all of you the problem is identical: college years are a constant—and usually losing—battle to make financial ends meet.

Halfway through the week or month, most of you are either broke or on the brink. Some of you live high the first few days you get your money, then scramble for help toward the end. Some of you have only far-apart intervals when you are out of debt. The vast majority of you are either flush or frantic.

But your allowance is a paycheck. It deserves the respect and care you will give a paycheck after graduation. Just as your parents get the most for their dollars by living by certain financial rules, so you in college can get the greatest satisfaction out of your allowance if you live by certain financial rules.

Whether you live at home or away from home, whether you're at the fanciest of schools or on a scholarship or working your way through, the fundamental principles of money management apply equally.

Here are your "Allowance ABCs." Try them for size.

(1) Plan the spending of your allowance with your parents before you leave for college, and then keep planning on your own from the day you arrive at school.

It's nonsense to say that $40 a week will be fine when $40 a week won't do at all for what you have to cover. Plan realistically and with a clear understanding of what your allowance is to take care of. Then, when you arrive at school, work out your day-to-day budget to cover your necessities and luxuries. Be honest with yourself. (If Cokes and coffee are going to cost X cents a day, plan for X cents a day.) If your allowance is supposed to cover such items as new panty hose, dry cleaning, shoe repair, oil, gas, auto maintenance, and so forth, budget these costs —don't ignore them. This is *your* budget; it should fit *you*.

(2) Deposit your money in a bank account and draw on it only as you need the money. If you carry a wad of cash with you, you'll risk being mugged and the temptation to spend it recklessly may become irresistible. Discipline yourself via your bank account; the lessons you learn now will be valuable throughout your life.

If your school has banking facilities, use them. If not, a nearby bank will accept your deposit even if it's just a few dollars. While you may be slapped with service charges, the bank's advantages could far outweigh the disadvantages; check it out. And while you are learning how to make deposits, to draw checks, to balance a checkbook, etc., you are getting excellent training in personal financial management.

(3) If you and your parents can manage it, also start an account in a nearby savings bank, or try to build one through the term.

There always will be large extra expenses—a special event or a crisis—for which you'll need or want to spend money. Your savings account should be earmarked for your tuition, rent, and extraordinary expenses only. If you can't start with this savings nest egg, try to juggle your seven-days-a-week spending plan so you can save a bit and build one yourself.

(4) Don't figure down to pennies. No money plan ever should be that precise. For your protection and pleasure, give yourself a margin of safety.

(5) Keep some simple records to show you where your allowance is going and why. A record for one week alone would be enough to reveal your errors of omission and commission. For one week, list on a sheet of paper what you spend and where and when you spend it. See how this week's total fits into the monthly total allotted to you. If need be, push your spending around to make it fit. When you've found the right pattern, stick with it. Keep your list in a convenient spot where you will see it from day to day.

(6) Stretch your dollars by learning how to buy items you must have (toiletries, for instance) during special sales or in economy sizes, etc. If you're buying your own wardrobe, stretch your dollars further by buying simple basic styles which will last longer and cost least in upkeep. Also investigate how easy it will be for you to save by pooling purchases with your friends so you can buy in bulk at bargain prices.

(7) If your evidence is clear after a trial that your funds are too limited, renegotiate your allowance. Your records will be your evidence.

Where Should You Keep Your Money?

You have established a budget to make sure your income covers your expenses each month. You are now ready for your next step in money management: a system to control your money in real life as well as on paper.

For your careful plans can easily blow up into chaotic confusion unless you do have a system to help you put your money where it is supposed to be. There are six basic systems from which you can choose:

(1) the joint checking account;
(2) separate checking accounts;
(3) the savings account;
(4) the combination of savings and checking accounts;
(5) the allowance method;
(6) the broken sugar bowl method.

Whichever control system you choose, it must be:

Efficient. Your "control" should direct your cash where you want it to go.

Easy to operate. This is a "must." The major objection to most financial advice is that it is too complex. If a method is complicated or burdensome, you will abandon it in less than a month.

Suited to your income. How much money you have to manage should guide you on how to control the management.

Your problem is not merely managing your income and outgo "on paper"; it is also a matter of controlling your cash income and cash outgo so that the money goes where it is scheduled to go.

The four budget forms can be of immeasurable help in showing you how to match your income to your outgo but they cannot give you the complete control over your actual spending which will come from intelligent use of one or more of the following six systems.

THE JOINT CHECKING ACCOUNT

If you're a young husband-and-wife team and you decide on the joint checking account method, you'll establish a checking account at a neighborhood bank in both your names. Into that account will go all your earnings. Each of you may write checks on that account to meet your expenses. When this system is adopted, the husband usually writes the checks for the big fixed expenses and for the savings (Form II). The wife writes the checks for the day-to-day and week-to-week expenses (the items on Form IV).

Advantages

Since each of you has a definite responsibility to meet specific expenses you develop a cooperative spirit. Similarly, since each of you has a sense of "owning money," you develop a keener understanding of the value of money.

With a *joint* checking account your average monthly balance will be higher than the balances in two *separate* checking accounts and thus you will have a better chance of avoiding or minimizing bank service charges.

With only one checkbook, you'll find it easier to keep records and file your income tax returns. (If you do have two checkbooks, be sure you tally your stubs every month to prevent overdrawing.)

In an emergency, either of you can sign checks and get money.

Disadvantages

This method can be a success only if both of you are careful about drawing on this joint account. And even then you may get into trouble unless you constantly watch the balance in your account and keep each other thoroughly informed about the checks each is drawing. Monthly tallies of stubs are important.

SEPARATE CHECKING ACCOUNTS

The separate checking account method is fairly satisfactory if there is only one breadwinner and you have a moderate to high income and many expenditures. When you use this control system, all the salary or income of the family will generally be deposited in one account in the husband's name. He then will deposit an agreed-upon sum in the second account, which will be in the wife's name.

The husband's account will be used to meet the major, fixed-expense items and to cover savings (Form II). The wife's account will be used to pay for the day-to-day or week-to-week expenses (the items on Form IV).

The main control in this system is the husband's account—for from it will come not only the amounts for fixed expenses and for the wife's account but also the totals for savings.

Usually the wife will cash a check on her account each week or at another regular interval to pay for food and household operation expenses. Expenditures for food and for operation of the house will thus be controlled automatically by the amount of money deposited in her account.

Advantages

The portion of your income determined as necessary for food and clothing expenditures is automatically separated from other funds. Also, by cashing weekly, semimonthly, or monthly checks for food expenditures, you, the wife, automatically control the family's food costs for the period.

Since the clothing allowance will be regularly deposited in the wife's account, you'll allow funds to accumulate as desired and this will permit you to take advantage of special sales and bargains. You might leave the clothing allowance mostly untouched for two or three months, then use the funds at a pre- or post-season sale to achieve important savings. The money will be available; that is the key point.

Your checkbooks will contain all the information necessary for a complete summary of your purchases and expenditures, assuming you fill out the stubs conscientiously.

Control of your income is divided between the two of you. Each of you has responsibility for your portion of your income and expenditures. Your separate accounts can give you better control of your income and outgo than a joint banking account.

Disadvantages

The separate account control system isn't practical unless your family income is fairly large. You must have sufficient money at your disposal to permit the establishment of separate bank accounts and justify what service fees may be involved.

Unexpected expenditures may cause considerable mixups in your accounting. In fact, a key difficulty with this system—and indeed, with the joint account method, too—is in the handling of miscellaneous expenditures.

A reasonable solution to this problem is a petty cash fund to meet the "extras" that arise in every household. This fund should be operated on the same principle as the petty cash fund in a business office. A specified amount—say $200—might be deposited in the fund. Each time you have to draw on this fund—as when you have to buy extra food for guests—you'll put a slip of paper with a notation describing the expense into the cash box in place of the money taken out. If you, the wife, take out $25, you'll put in a chit: "Entertainment—$25." Thus the total of cash in the fund plus the total of notations on the slips always ought to equal the amount of the original fund.

The chits furnish a record to show where the money went, so that if the petty cash fund is being used to stretch the other funds, the situation can be remedied —either through stricter control of your expenditures or by revision of your spending plan to raise the inadequate fund to the necessary level. Each month or pay period, refill the emergency fund and bring it back to its original mark.

THE SAVINGS ACCOUNT

If you don't have a fairly substantial income and you don't write many checks each month, the savings account method may be the best spending control for you. Savings accounts can serve you best if:

(1) You deduct from your monthly income or your regular weekly paycheck the totals needed for your fixed major costs and for savings—Form II of your record—and place them in a savings account for safekeeping.

(2) You deduct for your monthly allowances out of your remaining cash and keep those funds at home or in another account. Savings accounts pay interest, and since these accounts can be set up to permit joint withdrawals, either of you can use them freely. Many institutions will help you pay large bills by giving you bank checks made out exactly the way you want them for the now-and-then expenses.

Some savings institutions also will help you control your spending and savings by encouraging "special purpose" accounts—for vacation funds, travel funds, insurance funds, tax funds, etc. The purpose of each fund will be marked on the deposit books, and these books will give you a complete picture of your savings for each objective. A combination of these "special funds" with a rainy-day savings account for unexpected expenses thus can provide both a system of control and a detailed record of your savings.

This idea of using separate accounts for special purposes is becoming increasingly popular, though it is really nothing more than an extension of the long-used Christmas Club plan. The value of these special funds lies simply in the fact that they encourage setting aside a stipulated sum each week (no matter how small) so that the regular saving of little amounts builds toward the stated goal.

Advantages

Like any form of "forced savings," the scheme has the great advantage of earmarking your funds before you receive them—and before you are tempted to spend them elsewhere. It can be an excellent control over the money that must be set aside to meet the items on Form II.

Your money is placed in a thrift account on which interest is paid and compounded. As the account grows, there is a real psychological spur to save more.

Disadvantages

The savings account method is not suitable if you must write many checks every month.

You must have sufficient savings funds to justify the opening of several "special purpose" accounts.

You may earn next to nothing in interest if you keep depleting your account or accounts. Also some of the special savings accounts pay little or no interest.

Although you may deposit funds by mail to your savings account, you must visit the bank personally each time you make a withdrawal. Another inconvenience is that you must pay many bills with cash if you make a savings account the sole "home" for your income.

THE COMBINATION OF SAVINGS AND CHECKING ACCOUNTS

Or your best method of spending control may be a combination of several methods. One such combination is:

(1) the establishment of a checking account from which you draw funds each week or month to pay for all regular and recurring expenditures (some of the items on Form II and all on Form IV); and

(2) the establishment of a savings account in which you accumulate cash for the major expenses that come up only occasionally during the year and for savings (the rest of the items on Form II). You'll maintain your "emergency fund" in this separate savings account.

Advantages

Your income is divided and your day-to-day expenses are separated from your other expenses. Through your checkbook stubs you can keep an accurate and up-to-date record of your spending.

Through your savings account, you can accumulate cash to take advantage of sales and other bargains when they are available. Also the savings account part of this system will help you develop the savings habit which is so essential to achieving financial security. You will take pride in watching your nest egg grow and, possibly, will make a real effort to meet more of your expenses from your regular checking account.

Disadvantages

Fees may well be charged for maintenance of a no-minimum account or for a regular checking account if the balance falls below the bank's established minimum.

Separation of your savings from your checking account may push your average balance in your regular account way down.

THE ALLOWANCE METHOD

The allowance method of money management is used by millions of couples in America, many of them having adopted it automatically when they married.

Admittedly, it is a simple system. The husband of the non-jobholding wife usually controls the distribution of the money. Every payday he gives an allowance to his wife for the day-to-day living expenses—the items that are primarily on Form IV. After deducting this allowance, the husband uses the balance to meet all the major items—those on Form II.

The wife may deposit the allowance in a separate account or draw checks on a joint account up to the limit of the allowance—or just keep the money in a strongbox at home.

Advantages

The allowance method is simple, involving merely the distribution of a set allowance to the wife every payday or week or month.

Disadvantages

The allowance made to the wife is often too small, and she takes only a minimum of responsibility for management of the family income. She is often forced to ask for more money to cover essential or luxury expenditures. Such an arrangement discourages cooperative management.

If the allowance is not carefully calculated to cover all the items on Form IV, the control will be too loose.

THE BROKEN SUGAR BOWL METHOD

Many young couples—particularly those still in school or just out of school—use envelopes, marking one "for rent," another "for clothing," a third "for food," and so forth. Or they may have a cashbox at home which is divided into compartments labeled "rent," "clothing," "food," and the like. Or it may be that they label small glass jars.

This is nicknamed the "broken sugar bowl method" because many older people remember that when they were children there were always several old sugar bowls hidden behind the other dishes in the kitchen closet or pantry in which there were always a few dollars for specified expenses.

But the name applied to this money management arrangement doesn't matter. The point is that under this system you'll divide your cash income into fixed amounts to meet the regular and now-and-then expenses. Into each labeled bowl, jar, envelope, or compartment you'll put the dollars agreed upon as necessary to meet that particular living expense.

Both husband and wife will have equal access to the bowls or jars or envelopes. Generally, as in other systems, each will take on the responsibility for meeting certain expenses. This method is designed for very small incomes.

Advantages

When you use the sugar bowl method, presumably the money is always where it is supposed to be—and in cash to cover any specific expense. The system may be used just as separate bank accounts are used to apportion responsibility. And how simple can you get?

Disadvantages

It is always risky to keep money in the house—even comparatively small amounts. Also, while the cash is conveniently available for easy spending, it may be too available. When the money is there, the temptation to use it carelessly is there too. And when a sudden shortage develops, the obvious shortcut is to shift money from one bowl or envelope to another. While the utter simplicity of the broken sugar bowl method of spending control may be commendable, it is hardly a "control."

HIS-AND-HER BUDGETS

America is a land of working couples. Tens of millions of you who are and will be brides will continue working long after the wedding. Millions of you will quit working for pay only during the years your children are babies. Most of you will return to work when your children go off to school.

Money management takes on a special aspect in today's two-paycheck American homes. For with both of you earning salaries, specific questions are bound to come up:

How do you divide the money you bring in? Who pays for what around the house? If you had an ideal partnership, who would pay for what—how and why?

Here are ten basic rules I've worked out over years of discussion with experts on family finance, interviews with husbands and wives in every income bracket across the country, my personal experience as a working wife through my entire adult life. Many of you might (and many have) called them "sexist," "old-fashioned," even worse. These are *my* rules, no one else's, but I'm sure all of you can benefit from some of them, some of you can benefit from all of them, and any one of them can be revised to fit your individual circumstances.

(1) Make your marriage or your non-marriage relationship a *financial partnership;* discuss your income and plan your spending as a husband-and-wife team.

The wife who insists she should pay for only the part-time housekeeper and put the rest of her paycheck in her savings account is selfish and wrong. If you're a team in other ways, be a team financially as well. If your mutual decision is that the wife's paycheck should be saved, excellent—but make the decision as a couple. Otherwise, deceit and suspicion are virtually inevitable. This is a fundamental rule.

(2) Pool part of your individual paychecks in a family fund which is to be used to cover essential household expenses.

In many households, the pooling will be automatic, for both paychecks are being used to buy things and non-things the family wants. *It should be automatic.* How much of the wife's paychecks will go into the pool may vary from home to home, depending on the wife's income and the family's circumstances, but the key point is that there should be a pool.

(3) Decide which of you will be responsible for paying specific bills out of the pool. As a husband you might take over payment of "outside bills"—rent, mortgage, insurance, taxes, the like. As a wife, you might take over management of the "household bills"—food, entertainment at home, ordinary household overhead. To me, this is a logical division of responsibility. It's entirely okay if you have other ideas, but talk them out to your mutual satisfaction. For instance, some experts say a woman who has been accustomed to her independence for a long period may be actively unhappy unless, as a working wife, she continues to

have "my" telephone, "my" bank account, etc. So be it—as long as she and her husband agree on the division and there is no secret resentment of the situation.

(4) Use the combination savings account and checking account method as your money control.

If you don't carefully separate your savings from your regular checking account, your savings easily can dribble away without your knowing just how or why. For most couples, the two-account "control" works best.

(5) If the wife's job necessitates the added expense of household help, the wife's paycheck should cover it. This is a rule I came to instinctively, for in most homes, if the wife did not hold an outside job, she could, if she had to, get along without any extra help. Thus, this is "her" expense which she should handle. If the expense is to be paid out of the family pool, the wife should directly make the payment. Or the wife may withhold a specified part of her earnings for this expense. Whatever the details, it should be understood that this expense is in the wife's department.

(6) Extra expenses for entertainment at home should be handled by the wife, but when you go out, it's the husband's deal. Again, this is my viewpoint only.

(7) If you're a young couple planning to have children, the husband's paycheck should cover all basic household expenses, and part of the wife's earnings should be earmarked for the initial expenses of a baby. You must be prepared for the time when, for a while at least, you'll scale down to one paycheck. You may decide to share this planning by earmarking funds out of each paycheck—but at least *plan*. A couple without the financial responsibilities of children obviously has more leeway to shift spending and saving.

(8) Follow faithfully the budget rules for Form II. With both of you earning money, you'll really benefit from spreading payment of your big bills so that each month bears a share.

In addition, plan your installment buying as a team and with caution so that even if you're hit by an emergency your total monthly bills will be well within your capacity to repay. Under no circumstances take on *any* installment debt without a joint agreement.

(9) The rules on personal allowances are particularly vital for you. If you want to do something absurd with your personal allowance, that's your business. Your allowance is yours alone.

(10) Make a pledge to each other today that when you get into a squeeze in the future—which you will, for nearly everyone does—you'll choose a quiet evening alone to argue it out and decide how to escape from it. And when you talk about it, call it "our" squeeze, not "yours."

A superficial point? Oh no. The wife who in the heat of a money fight says, "We wouldn't have any savings at all unless I worked," is begging for resentment and the retort that she wouldn't have any home unless her husband paid for the rent or mortgage. It's imperative to avoid discussing your money mess when you're both frantic. If you can't figure a way out yourselves, seek help from a consumer credit counselor.

One good source is the Consumer Credit Counseling Service, a non-profit, community-sponsored group with well over 200 offices around the country. They give free and confidential help to people who want to establish a budget, as well as to those who want to get out of debt. Their clients come from all age, income, and education categories.

To start you off now, here is a chart to use to build your own his-and-her budget. Add to it as you wish; switch it around as you see fit; make it yours.

WHO PAYS FOR WHAT?

WHO PAYS FOR:	HE	SHE	BOTH
Rent or mortgage, home repairs, utilities			
Food at home			
Clothing			
Household help			
Auto loan, repairs, maintenance			
Recreation (outside)			
Entertainment (at home)			
Entertainment (outside home)			
Life and health insurance			
New baby			
Education (adult, college)			
Gifts and contributions			
Vacations, recreation			
Income and property taxes			
Savings			
Other expenses			

"MINGLING SINGLES"

Shocker No. 1: The number of unmarried couples living together in the United States skyrocketed by more than 800 per cent in the 1970s as against a 10 per cent rise in the number of married couples. While the overall total of "mingles"— a word to describe those living with non-relatives in a single household—is still relatively small, the implications of the mingles movement could be far-reaching.

Shocker No. 2: The "singles" phenomenon has now reached enormous proportions. The young singles segment of our population is expanding more than five times as fast as the nation as a whole. During the past decade alone, the number of young men living alone nearly tripled, while the number of women in the same age group—under twenty-five—living alone doubled.

Shocker No. 3: In some areas of the United States, sales of homes to singles exceeded 25 per cent of all home sales as the 1970s ended. The consensus among authorities is that the trend will accelerate during the decade of the 1980s.

Whether you like it or not, the traditional household unit in this country is undergoing far-reaching changes. Proof of the impact of singles-mingles on the marketplace is on every side: the establishment of dwelling complexes for singles only, such social organizations as "Parents Without Partners," special singles-only tours, cruises, social events, eating and drinking places, country clubs, etc.

"There are serious questions among the young, particularly the better-educated, about the validity of family-orientation," social researcher Daniel Yankelovich observed in the late 1970s. In contrast, family-orientation "is a key value for the rest of the population."

"Singlehood has emerged as an intensely ritualized and newly respectable style of American life," added *Newsweek* magazine. "The discovery that America's unmarried population wields an annual spending power of $40 billion has spawned an explosive growth industry aimed at satisfying the unwed's every whim."

The singles mingles tend to be:

"More affluent . . . Highly mobile . . . Very self-concerned . . . Oriented to immediate enjoyment vs. long-term concerns . . . Fashion and appearance conscious . . . Active both in lifestyle and leisure pursuits."

A BUDGET IF YOU'RE JUST LIVING TOGETHER

What, then, if you're among the millions of young Americans who today are just living together under one roof—with no legal ties, no established rules for behavior except those you and your peers agree are okay, and certainly no guidelines for management of your individual incomes and expenses?

You could easily and successfully follow the rules in the preceding pages for a working man and wife. But you may be far more fascinated by the following real-life system of budgeting created over the past two years by a young technical consultant and his schoolteacher living companion. The two insist that, once their system was perfected, it ended two years of destructive fighting about money (an even more brutal cause of split-ups among the non-married than among the married).

"Basically," says Dick, "the system consists of four (yes four) checking accounts which we call 'yours,' 'mine,' 'ours,' and 'car.'

"In addition, we have savings accounts. We keep a required minimum balance in each checking account to avoid service charges, which would run between 12 and 18 per cent for us, but higher for frequent check writers. To reduce the temptation to dip into the minimums, we delete the balances from our records and pretend they don't exist."

Here are details which are provocatively similar in many ways to the his-and-her budgets:

• All income from both individuals goes into the "ours" account. Each has a checkbook and the money deposited is arbitrarily split in half between each checkbook as a hedge against overdrawing. If either book runs dangerously low, temporary transfers are made. Then, at the end of each month, the books are balanced and the joint bank statement reconciled.

• Out of this "ours" account come virtually all living expenses—food, rent, utilities, etc.—which these two have agreed to share on a regular basis.

• Once a month a modest total is transferred from the "ours" account to each individual account ("yours and "mine") as each person's personal allowance. "This figure was chosen arbitrarily and is still experimental," says Dick. "We expect to adjust it after we have had more experience with it." The personal allowance covers clothes and other items "which have a large potential for conflict over what is or is not extravagant" and for "simply spending as we please." Neither accounts to the other for what happens to each month's personal allowance.

The special account for the car is an ingenious twist. "This is the largest single expense we have, costing more than rent and food combined," says Dick. "And we feel that it's important for us both to be conscious of what cars really cost." They are making a vital point. Also, watching the real costs of their car tends to discourage excessive driving.

A simple record is kept of the number of miles driven and deposits of 30¢ per mile are regularly transferred from the "our" account. The 30¢ covers all operating expenses, plus a margin of 10¢ a mile for depreciation. (This figure is subject to revision upward as costs dictate.) The "car" fund includes forced savings for a new car in the future.

Another ingenious system for food shopping involves the initialing of all store register tapes or chits and periodic checking and reconciling of the records.

There are many gaps in this couple's system—but if you add their hints to all you've read in "Your Personal Money Manager," you will be way, way ahead of the vast majority of budget-keepers.

Without any difficulty, you can shift the details to fit your own situation. You, for instance, may prefer to contribute equal amounts—rather than all—of your income to your joint checking and savings accounts. Whether you're a married couple or merely living together, you may feel it's unfair for both of you to bear an equal share of the food costs if the man regularly eats far more food and far more expensive food than the woman. Or you may argue that it's unfair for both of you to bear an equal share of the phone bills if the woman does most of the long-distance talking.

Whatever your own decisions, I guarantee that personal budget-keeping will help you curb your living costs—and help bring peace of mind.

(Like the working husband and wife, use the chart "Who Pays for What?" as a basic guide and switch it around to fit your own needs and desires.)

How Much Are You Worth?

You easily may feel flat broke or, at a minimum, painfully squeezed when you are creating a budget and a system to manage your money. But I'll wager that if you figure your "net worth" even at this sticky stage you'll be happily surprised by the outcome. Try it right now—and see if you don't discover you're richer than you think in many ways!

Here's a simple method to put a specific figure on your worth. Take a pencil and three sheets of paper. Mark the first sheet "Assets" and list:

(1) The amount of money you have in checking and savings accounts, in savings and loan associations, in credit unions, in time deposits, in cash on hand, in a strongbox at home or elsewhere.

(2) The cash value of your life insurance. This is the amount you actually could borrow back on request.

(3) The cash value of your United States Savings Bonds. This is not the maturity value but the amount you would get if you turned in your bonds now.

(4) The amount of cash or its equivalent you could withdraw tomorrow from profit sharing, employee savings, retirement programs, etc. A rough calculation will do.

(5) The current market value of stocks and mutual fund shares you may own. Not the purchase price, but what you'd get if you sold the stocks tomorrow.

(6) The current market value of other securities you may own—marketable federal government, municipal, or corporate bonds—and the market value of other investments you may have, such as mortgages you have extended to others.

(7) The price you would get if you put your house and land, summer house, or other real estate on the market this week. Get a conservative estimate from a reliable real estate agent.

(8) The price you would get if you offered your car (or cars) to a used-car dealer or sold it privately for cash right now. Be cold-blooded about it. Also, your boat, motorcycle, airplane, trailer, snowmobile, the like.

(9) The market value of your household goods—furniture, rugs, appliances, TV, stereo, linen, silverware. Make your own *conservative* estimate, then *slash* it by 75 per cent and you'll be on safe ground.

(10) The market value of your other personal assets, such as jewelry, paintings, furs, rare books, art objects, coins, stamps, antiques, clothes, etc. Cut your own conservative estimate here too, by 75 per cent.

(11) The price you'd get if you sold out your investment in any unincorporated business, farm, or other ventures.

(12) Amounts of money other *responsible* people owe you.

(13) A conservative estimate of the value of any other asset you can think of.
Add the totals.

Take a second sheet, mark it "Liabilities," and list:

(1) The total amount you owe on your mortgage or mortgages and on your car, boat, motorcycle, etc.

(2) The amount you owe on other installment debts, charge accounts, credit cards, other personal debts and bills.

(3) The amount you owe for taxes which have not been withheld.

(4) Sums you've committed for college or other types of education.

(5) Any other liability you can think of.
Add these totals.

Take a third sheet, mark it "Net Worth," and:

Simply subtract the total on your second sheet from the total on your first. *The difference between what you own and what you owe is your net worth.*

You should be unexpectedly pleased by the outcome, for you are only average if your net worth runs into many thousands of dollars. You are part of the vast majority of Americans if you have some cash in the bank and in savings accounts and own a car. And while you have debts, you also have substantial assets to offset the debts. This is the norm in no other nation in the world.

IN CASE YOU'RE CURIOUS . . . HOW DO YOU COMPARE?

HERE'S WHAT OTHER PEOPLE SPEND

An "average" family living on an "average" budget does not exist, I repeat. Even if you and your neighbor lead very similar lives on very similar incomes, your budgets may be radically different. Your own ages, your children's ages—not to mention your hobbies or jobs or dozens of other aspects—would make this so.

But, if you're merely normal, you're still curious about the spending patterns of others.

So to start with, here's what average Americans were spending in the early 1970s of each pretax dollar in each major category (before the wild inflation that hit our country starting in the mid-1970s):

FOR	AMERICANS WERE SPENDING OF EACH DOLLAR
Food	20.1¢
Housing, excluding mortgage principal payments	31.4¢
Transportation	21.4¢
Clothing and upkeep	7.8¢
Medical care	6.4¢
Recreation, personal care, and education	11.4¢
Miscellaneous	1.5¢

AND HOW DOES YOUR SPENDING COMPARE WITH OTHERS IN YOUR BRACKET?

In briefest summary, if you're an average family at the top of the income scale, the share of your before-tax income ($25,000 or more) going to food and shelter is much less than the proportion spent on these basic expenses of life by families in the lowest before-tax income brackets ($3,000 or less). That's logical.

In dollar totals, of course, the higher-income family spends more (it has more dollars to spend). Specifically, the share going for food if you're in the $25,000 or more bracket is roughly 19 per cent as against 23 per cent if you're in the below $3,000 income level. (The gap yawns even wider when the focus is solely on spending for food at home: 9 per cent by the higher family earners as against 20 per cent by the lowest family earners.)

Housing reveals a similar pattern, with proportions for shelter (including utilities, furnishings, and maintenance) tapering down from 38 per cent if you're at the bottom of the income ladder to 28 per cent at the upper end. The dollar totals are diametrically opposed: climbing from the bottom of the income ladder to the top.

The more money you have, though, the more you tend to spend in percentages as well as dollar totals on such discretionary items as clothing and recreation. Again, it's no more than logical.

If you're in the $25,000-and-over class, 9.4 per cent of your before-tax earnings goes for clothing, 10.9 per cent for recreation.

Also provocative: medical expenses account for an above-average share of the living expenses of families in each income class below $10,000—primarily because in these families there often is a heavier concentration of elderly and illness-prone members.

WHAT ABOUT THE SIZE OF YOUR FAMILY?

How does the size of your family compare?

On average, at the top of the income scale, average families are larger (3.8 members), a statistical absurdity but nevertheless revealing. At the bottom, the average is 3 members, and the average rises as the income level rises. The biggest proportion of homeowners is in the highest income brackets too.

Do not permit the figures to mislead you by forgetting that spending is deeply influenced by where you live and that these are only averages. Your spending will vary according to the region in which you live, whether yours is a rural family, a suburban unit or resident of an inner city. It will be vitally affected by whether you rent or whether you are a homeowner.

3

HOW TO BUY JUST ABOUT EVERYTHING... AND SAVE 5 TO 50 PER CENT, TOO

Your Key Weapons Against Rising Costs

It could be that you are an extraordinarily perceptive shopper. Even so, I'll wager that I can show you how to become a far more effective shopper. In fact, I'll go further and wager that despite the *real* economic world in which you live and its challenges to you, you'll find ways to shave your costs from a minimum of 5 per cent to as much as 50 per cent or more in every area of your family budget.

Behind the overall increases in your living costs each year, there always will be sharp variations of which you can take advantage. There always will be moves you can make to cushion the impact of inflation on your own budget. Your fundamental safeguards are awareness of the trends and understanding of the ways to protect yourself against the trends. Now here are your four key weapons:

(1) *Substituting* for these items, wherever and whenever you can, others of a similar nature on which prices are holding the line.

(2) *Switching* to less expensive versions of increasingly costly goods and services.

(3) *Shopping* harder than ever for the best possible deal on items you must have and on which prices are soaring.

(4) *Eliminating* items which are of no real value and even are of harm to you.

For instance, contributing tremendously to the increases in food prices have been costs of meat. But within this food category, you can make many delicious substitutions. And you have great control over how often you eat out, even greater control over what you eat when you are out.

Again, to illustrate, overall transportation costs have been climbing steadily—but among the real "villains" behind this inflation have been soaring parking charges and public transportation costs. You can't do much but you can do some things to save on public transportation costs—and you do plenty to curb your parking charges.

You can switch to other forms of entertainment from activities that are going out of sight. You certainly can save on cigarettes simply by quitting smoking.

You have a wide variety of choices in clothing. I could go on and on but there is no need.

With basic guidance, you can use your own imagination and carry on superly from here.

A DOZEN WISE RULES FOR SHOPPING FOR EVERYTHING

(1) Shop around. Prices do vary even from day to day on items ranging from food to furniture, from cars to cosmetics. Comparison-shop at stores in your area. Keep an eye on the ads. Know which stores have built their reputations by offering values on certain types of merchandise.

(2) Watch for genuine sales and specials and study the "calendar for bargains." (See pages 48–51.) Not everything advertised is at a better price today than it will be tomorrow. Hunt out the real bargains. There always are some around. Stock up on things you need when prices are seasonally reduced, as at semi-annual clothing sales or inventory clearance sales. Watch and learn which stores put what things on sale and when—particularly on big-ticket major things.

(3) Watch for differences in quality. It well may be that the extra luxury or utility of the higher-priced items is really worth the extra costs. But don't spend unnecessarily for quality; but only the grade of the item you need. Grades A and B tomatoes, for instance, look best—but Grade C, the lowest in price, will be just as good in stews and casseroles.

(4) Hold periodic family councils to discuss money matters. You can cut back on costs better in an atmosphere of co-operation and understanding.

(5) Keep control of your credit purchases, make sure your monthly charge account balances are at a reasonable minimum, and shop for credit with utmost care. (See pages 822–25.)

(6) Be careful about impulse buying. Supermarket shoppers consistently buy more than they put down on their shopping lists. Don't permit impulse to trick you into buying things you don't need or even want.

(7) Buy what's right for you. In clothing, for example, classic styles may be more appropriate for you (and last longer) than the latest fashion craze. And many combinations of the same basic garment may be a far sounder purchase than any spectacular outfit. Let your own experience guide you.

(8) Buy in bulk but only when you'll use it all. All things are not necessarily "cheaper by the dozen." Spoilage and discards can eat up your apparent savings on quite a variety of bulk and "economy" purchases. Check whether the bulk price really is more attractive than what you would pay for a smaller size or amount before you stock up on things you buy regularly.

(9) Investigate the private brands in food, clothing, and appliance lines which may be priced more favorably than national brands. Test the quality, learn which private labels you can rely upon. On major purchases, be sure service facilities are available.

(10) Read the label information. Clothing labels will tell you essential facts about materials used and proper cleaning methods. Even the fanciest packages often carry important data that you will neglect to your sorrow.

(11) Give a plus to low maintenance. Many product improvements in recent years have concentrated on easy care—ranging from permanent-press fabrics and stain repellents to extra-durable furniture. They're worth the slightly higher price tags that may be attached. But don't pay more for convenience than it is worth to you—the other side of "easy care."

(12) Consider service and "returns." Deal with retailers and manufacturers who stand solidly behind what they sell and who never balk at servicing or replacing a product. If they go out of their way to serve you, they want your business, and they deserve it.

Save Money with "Cents Off"

"Save $1.36 . . . Redeem these coupons at any store selling these products," says the ad in the local newspaper. Then follows almost a full page of discount coupons . . . "Save 10 cents on any size," "Save 40 cents on every jar," "20 cents off on next purchase" . . . On and on go the coupons—10 cents, 12 cents, 15 cents, 40 cents—to totals which save a wise shopper an estimated $2 or $3 or 10 per cent on a $20–$30 weekly food bill alone.

The cents-off coupon revolution is sweeping the nation and is still gathering power. Manufacturers are now distributing billions of cents-off coupons in a single year as a reduced price incentive to lure you into buying their products.

The average cents-off value has jumped from 10 cents in 1970 to 15–20 cents and higher and the number of consumers using cents-off coupons as an integral part of their grocery shopping is greater than ever before.

There are now dozens of businesses offering coupons—primarily through newspapers, but also through magazines or direct mail.

Today's shopper is much more aware of value, and is relatively sophisticated about brands' sizes, weights, and prices. The cents-off coupon seems here to stay.

The big brand manufacturers know how the shopper has changed and are committed to cents-off coupons as one of the best ways to offer a true value without changing the size, weight, or price of their brand.

Why do manufacturers "coupon"? What are they attempting to achieve by cutting the price of their products?

There are four prime reasons:

(1) To get you to try the product, whether it be a new product or an established one.

(2) To get a jump on and beat the competition.

(3) To assure that you'll continue using the product.

(4) To add an attention-getter to regular advertising and push the supermarket into featuring the brand, as well.

And what should you do to take advantage of this ongoing cents-off revolution?

Check the retailers' weekly specials;

Shop the manufacturers' coupons every week;

Take the coupons with you to the supermarket and put them to work for your pocketbook's welfare.

While it would be unrealistic to suppose that you'll make use of every coupon offered, a sampling of housewives reveals that shoppers who use coupons most are big spenders whose transactions in a store run above average. Large families with incomes of more than $15,000 are the heaviest users of coupons. Also, housewives over thirty years of age use coupons more than younger shoppers.

Typical comments cited for the rising interest in coupons: "They save me money," "They reduce the cost of products I buy," "They tell us about products and encourage us to try new products," "I can see real cash savings on my food bill."

Tip: Be sure to look in your newspaper every day, or favorite magazines as well as "throwaway" shopper circulars for manufacturers' cents-off coupons to save money!

QUIZ YOURSELF INTO BUYING WISELY

When you're wondering whether you should or should not buy, give yourself this quiz, prepared by the Council for Family Financial Education, and find out.

1. Do you really need this item? Yes No
2. Is the price reasonable? Yes No
3. Is this the best time to buy the item? Yes No
4. If this is a bargain, is it a current model (if that matters to you)? Yes No
5. If "on sale" is the price a true sale price? Yes No
6. Are you sure no less expensive item can be substituted? Yes No
7. Are you sure there are no major disadvantages? Yes No
8. If excessive in price, will it truly satisfy an inner need? (If not excessive, just check "yes.") Yes No
9. Have you checked and researched the item? Yes No
10. Do you know the retailer's reputation? Yes No
11. Does this retailer offer any special services with the item? Yes No

Score your answers as follows:
9–11 yeses—buy the product:
6–8 yeses—think again:
Fewer than 6 yeses—forget it.

CALENDAR FOR BARGAINS

February is an excellent month in which to buy air conditioners, used cars, rugs, and lamps. Do so—and you can save 10 to 30 per cent or even more on each item's cost.

August is a fine month in which to buy furs, fans, gardening equipment, and men's coats. Do so—and you can easily save 10 to 30 per cent or more.

Buy refrigerators in January . . . Buy millinery in July . . . Buy toys during the post-Christmas clearances . . . And bathing suits during the post-July 4 markdowns . . .

These are the seasonal savings—and they are and will continue to be available throughout the years. Merely by planning your spending to take advantage of the seasonal sales the year round, you can easily slash your spending by hundreds of dollars! Just by ignoring the seasonal "bargain calendar" I submit below, you can "waste" hundreds of dollars.

There are three major periods for storewide clearance sales: after Easter, after July 4, and after Christmas. These are excellent times to pick up clothes, linens, dozens of other items, although you may run into shortages of styles, sizes, and colors if you don't shop early in the sales. There also are the well-publicized August white sales; specials for George Washington's birthday; for Columbus Day; Veterans Day; similar holidays.

And this applies just as strongly to foods. Again to illustrate: If you can manage to resist buying fresh strawberries until June or July—when prices drop sharply from their peaks at the beginning of the strawberry season in April—you will save money on this delicacy. On the other hand, if you are unable to resist buying watermelons as they begin to appear on supermarket shelves in June—instead of waiting until August when watermelon prices will have dropped sharply —your indulgence will cost you plenty.

Do not let the simplicity of the following calendars for foods and non-foods mislead you into downgrading their importance to your pocketbook! These bargain guides alone can put you well on the way to beating any foreseeable price spiral in the future. This *strategy of timing your buying* alone can more than offset any apparent annual rise in the cost of living.

IF YOU WANT TO BUY	GOOD MONTHS TO BUY ARE
Air conditioners	February, July, August
Appliances	January
Art supplies	January, February
Bathing suits	After July 4, August
Batteries and mufflers	September
Bedding	February, August
Bicycles	January, February, September, October, November
Blankets	January, May, November, December
Books	January
Building materials, lumber	June
Camping equipment	August
Carriages	January, August
Cars (new)	August, September
(used)	February, November, December
Car seat covers	February, November
Children's clothing	July, September, November, December
China	January, February, September, October
Christmas gifts	Any time but Christmas
Clothes (spring)	March

IF YOU WANT TO BUY	GOOD MONTHS TO BUY ARE
Clothes dryers	January, February, March, April
Coats (women's, children's)	April, August, November, December
(men's)	January, August
(winter)	March
Costume jewelry	January
Curtains	February
Dishes	January, February, September
Drapes and curtains	February, August
Dresses	January, April, June, November
Fans	August
Fishing equipment	October
Frozen foods	June
Fuel oil	July
Furniture	January, February, June, August, September
Furs	January, August
Gardening equipment	August, September
Glassware	January, February, September, October
Handbags	January, May, July
Hardware	August, September
Hats (children's)	July, December
(men's)	January, July
(women's)	February, April, July
Home appliances	July
Home furnishings	January, February, August
Hosiery	March, October
Housecoats	April, May, June, October, November
Housewares	January, February, August, September
Infants' wear	January, March, April, July
Lamps	February, August, September
Laundry appliances	March
Linens	January, May
Lingerie	January, May, July
Luggage	March
Men's clothing	August, January
Men's shirts	January, February, July
Paints	August, September
Party items	December
Piece goods	June, September, November
Quilts	January, November, December
Radios, phonographs	January, February, July
Ranges	April, November
Refrigerators and freezers	January, July

IF YOU WANT TO BUY	GOOD MONTHS TO BUY ARE
Rugs and carpets	January, February, July, August, May, September
School clothes	August, October
School supplies	August, October
Shoes (boys' and girls')	January, March, July
(men's and women's)	January, July, November, December
Silverware	February, October
Skates	March
Ski equipment	March
Sportswear	January, February, May, July
Stereo equipment	January, February, July
Storm windows	January, February, March
Suits (men's and boys')	April, November, January
Summer clothes and fabrics	June, July
Summer sports equipment	July
Tablecloths	January, May
Television sets	May, June
Tires	May, end of August
Toiletries	January, July
Toilet water and colognes	July
Towels	January, May, August
Toys	January, February
Water heaters	January, November

HOW TO SAVE MONEY READING THE ADS

You rarely will find bargains advertised! Do read, listen, and watch carefully. Use your informed skepticism and try to learn from the ads themselves which ones offer genuine bargains and which are trying to part you from your money by misusing words such as "Sales," "Free," "Reduced," "Close-out," or "Savings."

Here are tips on the ads with which you will be bombarded during the 1980s:

SALES

"Silver place setting, manufacturer's suggested retail list price $78.45, our sale price . . . $46.95."

"7 Day Sale . . . XYZ camera only $39.95, value $79.95."

"Post holiday savings start now! . . . Stereo components, receivers valued at $570, priced for closeout at $387."

These ads are hypothetical—but they represent what will be the most widespread deceptive advertising practices in print and airwave media in the 1980s: ads for non-existent savings claims based on fictitious comparative prices.

If you know how to read and listen to ads, learn the techniques that will help you differentiate between deceptive and honest advertising. Otherwise, you'll almost surely be stuck.

And you cannot rely on the media to police ads to the extent that would eliminate deceptions. The media have neither the money, time, knowledge nor the inclination even to attempt so vast a policing job. Essentially, it is in your own interest to bring the same money sense to looking at ads that you would bring to shopping at a department store, however large and reputable the store may be.

Consider, for instance, the silver place setting—in which the saving in the advertised "sale" was based on the manufacturer's suggested retail price. This claim is one of the most frequently misused by retailers attempting to advertise a savings claim for many categories of merchandise. The saving is often—although not always—non-existent because the advertiser and his competition rarely, if ever, sell the merchandise at the "list price."

Or consider the hypothetical camera ad, in which the company is offering a 50 per cent saving as part of a "7 Day Sale." The claim is "our price, $39.95, value $79.95." The word "value" should mean the price at which the identical merchandise is being then offered by the advertiser's competitors throughout the same trade area. If you check the competition before buying this camera, you well might find all of them offering the identical item at $39.95. What saving?

Or consider the post-holiday savings, in which the key phrase is "valued at." At which stores is it "valued at" the higher price? If you check, you might find all having "post-holiday" clearouts and offering you the same "savings."

"FREE"

Still another long-standing deception involves the word "free": "free skiing at our hotel" or "free swimming and tennis for our guests."

The word "free" should mean that the item offered is an unconditional gift. Or if a purchase is required, the details should be clearly stated, the ordinary price should not be increased, the quality or quantity should not be reduced, and the "free" offer should be temporary. If the offer is not temporary, then it is a continuous combination offer, no part of which is free.

In short, be wary of making any purchase because you are getting something "free." It probably isn't—and you probably aren't.

Here's a basic test for a savings claim: has the advertiser sold a significant quantity of the identical merchandise at the higher price recently? If so, he can say "regularly" or "usually." Be suspicious of any company which is always having a sale on the identical items. You'll almost surely not save on these.

And here's a simple way to check the validity of any advertiser's sales offer. Collect his ads for several weeks. You may find the company has a "sale" of the same goods every week. Or you may find after the sales end that there has been no increase in the prices on the advertised "bargains."

ENERGY AND FUEL SAVINGS CLAIMS

You will be lured on every side in the 1980s with ads claiming that a product will reduce fuel consumption, curb heat loss, increase insulation, improve operating efficiency, reduce electrical consumption, etc. Major areas for deceptive advertising will be: windows, fuel oil burner devices, electrical appliances, automobile gasoline savings devices, home insulation materials, and solar energy. Study these hypothetical ads:

Windows: "Replacement window specialists. Complete insulated window . . . genuine thermal insulated windows, no storm windows needed, fully guaranteed. Backed by over 30 years window experience." Or "Thermal insulated windows cut heat loss by 60 per cent . . . our company guarantees to save you 30 per cent on your fuel bills . . . or we will pay the difference in cash . . . maintenance free . . . weather stripping that seals out drafts and dirt . . . seals in heat in winter—seals out heat in summer."

Most suspicious are the superlative or absolute claims for insulation or energy efficiency in these ads. No insulation is "complete." Contrary to the ads, you may find you do need storm windows. Some consumers have reported their homes draftier than before they had installed the so-called "thermal" windows. Wind conditions at your home site are a vital factor.

Question any company that advertises its product is "fully guaranteed." This should mean you're entitled to your money back, no questions asked, at any time, for any reason. And I repeat and re-emphasize, do not expect the media in which you are reading, seeing, or hearing the ad to have done all the questioning for you. It couldn't and can't.

On a claim such as "30 years window experience," find out how long the company has been in business. Or on a claim such as "thermal insulated windows cut heat loss by 60 per cent," ask for test data to back up the claim. If you're spending several thousand dollars for windows to help reduce your fuel bill, it may even be worth the fee an engineer will charge you to check the claims. And don't overlook the information your local public utility will provide.

Any time a company guarantees "to save you 30 per cent on your fuel bills," get terms and conditions in writing. And what good is any guarantee if the company isn't in existence?

Be constantly on the alert for phony savings. The "sale" price may be the regular price. Or the regular price may be significantly higher than the competition's.

Fuel Oil Burner Devices: "Saves energy . . . cuts fuel costs up to 43 per cent, provides soot-free heating."

There is no such thing as "soot-free" combustion in a fuel oil burner. Get the documentation to substantiate the fuel reduction claim. Ask: Were the tests for this claim conducted in the laboratory? Or in actual home heating situations? Was anything else done to the furnace before or after the advertised device was installed—such as adjusting the oil nozzle or cleaning the burners?

Look out for savings claims based on undisclosed tie-in sales. To "guarantee" the advertised savings, the company may require that you buy a long-term service contract, fuel oil, or burner.

Electrical Appliances: "Save 34 per cent on operation of our air conditioner."

In bold type will appear the savings claim and name of the manufacturer. In small type buried way down may be a hedge clause that says the savings claim is based on a comparison with another model of the same manufacturer that is less efficient.

Check for the "EER" or Energy Efficiency Rating. The higher the rating, the more efficient the air conditioner. Look for the "EYCO," a dollar figure showing the estimated yearly cost of operation.

Automobile Gasoline Savings Devices: "Increase gas mileage up to 33 per cent. Save dollars per tank . . . Just drop this revolutionary new gasoline additive in your tank. One container lasts 12 months or 15,000 miles." These ads also might contain testimonials and tests on specific cars to show reductions in mpg.

These "miracles" just aren't. (See pages 357–60.) Ask the company for documentation you can believe; check with a car dealer or auto mechanic you trust. Any hesitancy to prove the validity of the claims should immediately warn you of a possible gyp.

CREDIT ADS

"A dream come true . . . This beautiful Colonial Homestead, easy to buy, down payments are low, as low as 5 per cent! . . . Seven spectacular models, from an unheard-of $38,995, only 5 per cent total down payment." Or:

"Just think, your own custom-built and maintenance-free lakeside vacation retreat . . . Just $150 a month. The full price $36,499 . . . Includes house and land."

They sound familiar—yet these hypothetical ads highlight for you violations of the disclosure rules of the Federal Truth in Lending Act and its amendments. Among other things, this law requires that if an advertiser mentions one feature of credit in an ad—such as the down payment total—the ad must disclose all other vital terms, such as the number, amount, and period of payments that follow.

In the first ad, for instance, the ad also should have revealed the number of payments (weekly, monthly, etc.), and annual percentage rate expressed as a "per cent" and labeled "annual percentage rate."

In the second ad, the same disclosures should have been made. Also, while it used the phrase "full price," this was, in fact, the cash price. "Full price" would include interest payments and would be nearly double.

In the automobile financing field in particular, and in installment buying in general, credit double-talk is a real threat to the innocent consumer.

"Instant credit," "credit guaranteed," "no credit application refused," or "no money down"—all these should be dismissed as come-ons. The merchant who lures you with "no money down" may in fact require you to obtain a separate loan for part or all of the down payment in order to qualify for this "no money down" offer.

In the automobile leasing field, ads will multiply in the 1980s. A sample: "A luxurious 1980 automobile, blank-blank dollars a month, equity lease, minimum maintenance included, additional maintenance optional."

Basically, there are two types of auto leases: "closed-end" and "open-end." The open-end lease is also known as an "equity" lease. Under this open-end or equity lease, the lessee may be required to pay an additional expense at the end of the lease period based on the price at which the vehicle may be sold at the end of the lease agreement. According to Better Business Bureau standards, when a specific rate is advertised, this obligation, if it exists, must be advertised.

But frequently it is not—even though the obligation may run into hundreds of dollars. Watch out for this pitfall.

Be wary, when leasing a car, of such phrases in ads as "full insurance," "adequate insurance," "fully protected." These phrases are nearly always meaningless. As for such pledges as "full maintenance" or "maintenance by us," these should mean that you, the customer, are not obligated to pay for any type of maintenance.

Finally, be on guard against claims that there is no cost for credit—often made by stores in low-income areas which sell furniture. The charge is there, probably hidden in the purchase price.

Under one amendment to the Truth in Lending Act, ads for extension of credit repayable in more than four installments must, unless a finance charge is imposed, state that "the cost of credit is included in the price quoted for the goods and services." By no means do all businessmen obey the law.

SELF-IMPROVEMENT BOOKS

Mail-order books promoting self-improvement, self-help, self-anything-you-want will continue to ride the greatest boom ever in the 1980s. The "ME" movement is money in the bank to mail-order promoters of do-it-yourself miracles. They reflect and capitalize on the average American's deep disillusionment with the sort of help offered from other sources.

During the 1970s, though, the phenomenon developed to an extraordinary degree—and it will explode even more in the 1980s. And many of the mail-order books, now so popular with gullible readers and TV-radio listeners, sadly confirm that in this area the "fringe" promoters are flourishing.

"Reduce while you snooze! . . . Weight loss failures have shed pounds of ugly fat this way! . . . Finally, here is a fast, simple, safe way to take it off and keep it off. You won't put it back on. If you do, you pay nothing!" Or:

"Go to the fat experts' fat expert! . . . If you don't lose 16 pounds in 16 days, you pay nothing . . . We'll make this offer to fat experts, models, corporation presidents . . . With this program, you are allowed more to eat than you can possibly want." Or:

"I beat the doctor. My doctor said, 'Stay away from liquor. Your blood pressure and cholesterol are too high. Lose 45 pounds and stay away from liquor.' I lost 45 pounds in 140 days and drank my liquor too."

These are all hypothetical ads, but I'll wager they sound completely familiar to millions of you, who see similar ads every day in every form of the media.

Typically, you are asked to send from $7.95 to $12.95 to learn how one author "beat the doctor," or how another advised "the fat experts' fat expert." The book, when you receive it, will outline the author's experiences and opinions.

But unfortunately, the ad for the book does not make it clear that the book contains only the author's experiences and opinions.

Rarely does an ad prominently state, "It is the author's opinion that . . ." "from the author's personal experiences which are limited to . . ."

What you read or see or hear, in short, may imply successes going far beyond the actual contents of the book.

• Before you write out your check, read the whole ad, not just the headline and pictures. The fine print may go a long way toward qualifying if not contradicting the prominent copy.

• Realize that the experiences of the authors and testimonials from people identified only by initials nearly always reflect the most successful results—probably not the average and certainly not the least successful.

• In medical problems, the experience of one person is frequently not relevant to what's needed for another.

• Be suspicious of any book which offers a "cure" or "permanent treatment" for a medical condition such as arthritis, which has defied medical science for decades.

• In evaluating any weight-loss book, keep in mind that the way to lose weight is by a balanced program of reduced caloric intake and exercise, under professional supervision.

• Don't be lulled by a "money back guarantee." If you scream enough, you'll probably get a refund after some delay. But these promoters know that, in most cases, you won't request a refund. You'll simply shrug and say, "Oh, well, I learned my lesson." You forget that you learned the same lesson last year—from another promoter.

EASY MONEY

An even more powerful self-help book lure than quick weight loss or a miracle cure for arthritis is easy money. Surely, you've been frequently tempted by ads such as these:

"Only $15 a week can get you $125,000, no risk, government backed . . . You don't have to have money to get money . . . Everything is legal . . . Let me tell you how to outsmart the banks at the money game . . . Just send $10 for my book." Or:

"In debt? Don't worry! You can stay in debt, and make a profit! It's all legal! . . . I was boxed in by this credit-crazy system . . . For years, I didn't know what to do. I worked hard. I was starting a family but I had a volcano of old bills threatening to erupt in my face . . . Then I discovered how to attack the bill collectors . . . My book tells you four rules for dealing with dunning notices and 'final bills.' Just send $8.95." Or:

"Money news . . . Recent study tells you how to keep working in a depressed economy . . . Just send $5.98."

These ads also are hypothetical—although in each ad, each individual statement may be factually accurate. Yet, taken together, the statements, the illustrations, the testimonials—all the contents—may be entirely misleading.

An author can write what he wishes to write—and as long as the content of the ad for the book accurately reflects the content of the book itself, there is little basis for challenging the advertising.

In fact, the First Amendment has been interpreted as protecting not only the content of the book itself but also advertisements for the book which accurately reflect its content.

But a most disturbing development is that the success of mail-order self-improvement books—in areas across the board—has become so spectacular that subsidiaries of some nationally known companies have moved into mail order and are promoting what might gently be called "questionable" books. These companies have the money and the know-how to hire writers, and to publicize books that lure you with claims which play on your fears or frustrations, pander to your dreams.

No government agency passes on the validity of opinions or experiences contained in books. This is essentially a protection of our freedoms. So, you must rely on your own common sense, enlightened skepticism. And if you buy under a "money back guarantee," you must be sure to return the book within the allotted time.

• Keep in mind, too, that basically there is no quick, easy way to make money. Certainly, anyone who has a "system" will not give it to you in a $5.98 book.

• An ad that claims a book will return you $125,000 for only $15 a week should make you suspicious at once.

• Most of the get-rich books are no different from any other get-rich-quick scheme. The promoter's goal is to take your money for himself. If he can convince you that he is doing you a favor in the process, you won't think you've been had and you'll help publicize his book to your friends.

• Don't be fooled by an author's claim that he has discovered a great secret, such as "debt is profitable." Sure, debt can be useful, it's no secret that it can be profitable too—and our economy of the 1970s was built on a vast foundation of debt, public and private. But while each statement in the debt ad may be true by itself, the whole impression you get is clearly false.

For most of these ads touting get-rich-quick books, the first paragraph should be a testimonial by the author himself, reading:

"I grossed $1,000,000 in three months. I wrote a book about how to get rich, put a $10 price tag on it, took out some fancy full-page ads, and sold it to 100,000 people!"

Advertising Bafflegab

Here is what common terms in advertising should mean, but the Better Business Bureau of Metropolitan New York cautions that these are some of the most misused words in the language.

CLEARANCE A reduction in price from the advertiser's own previous price charged in the regular course of business, used to indicate that the merchandise previously offered but not sold is being offered at a price concession and will not be offered again in the immediate future. Thus, advertising which states that new merchandise is being received for a "clearance" is misleading since the merchandise has not yet been offered by the advertiser.

CLEARANCE CENTER Usually is a misleading term, since investigation has shown that the merchandise at the "clearance center" is available for the first time.

The use of "clearance center" in a company name or trade style (name in which company is doing business) is misleading unless all the merchandise offered at the "clearance center" was previously offered but not sold at the advertiser's retail store.

CLOSEOUT   Manufacturer has discontinued production permanently and the retailer has purchased remaining supplies at price concession which he passes on to consumer.

COMPARABLE VALUE   To be used when the item advertised is similar, but not identical, to merchandise regularly selling for the value stated as a comparative. This phrase is to be used only when the customer can readily detect the similarities as well as the differences. It is misleading when used to sell merchandise which only an expert could classify as "comparable," such as appliances, photographic equipment, and electronic products, since it is impossible for the average consumer to determine whether or not the items compared are of the same grade, quality, and alike in all other technical aspects.

EMERGENCY   Merchandise offered at price concession because of some unusual, non-recurring event, such as fire, remodeling, lost lease, etc. When used, ad also should indicate reason for the "emergency," its duration, and specific merchandise offered at a price concession because of this situation.

FACTORY OUTLET   To be used only when the seller is actually the manufacturer.

FORMERLY SOLD AT   If comparison is made to the price at which identical merchandise was formerly sold in the market in which it is being advertised by principal retail outlets, the advertising shall clearly indicate that it is *not* the current selling price. Under no circumstances, where few or no sales were made, shall the advertiser use the "formerly sold at" term to imply that substantial sales actually were made at that former price.

GOING-OUT-OF-BUSINESS   Advertiser is terminating business, and has obtained the license usually required. If in doubt, ask for the license number and check it out!

INTRODUCTORY OFFER   Indicates merchandise available at a price concession which will, in the immediate or near future, be sold at a higher price.

LIQUIDATION   Advertiser, in fact, intends to terminate business, is converting assets to cash, and offers a price concession. Use of term in any other circumstances is deceptive.

MADE-TO-SELL-FOR   Raises the question, "Made for whom to sell to whom for what???" Therefore, this is an ambiguous and misleading term. Does the item sell generally at that price?

MANUFACTURER'S LIST   LIST   SUGGESTED RETAIL   Used as a comparative price, from which merchandise is reduced, allegedly for "sale." Usually deceptive, and, at best, confusing, since all these three terms refer to a price rarely charged in a highly competitive trade area, so the savings claim implied is without basis. Consumer may verify by asking retailer where merchandise is being sold at comparative price quoted.

ORIGINALLY   Refers to a previous price, on which there has been an interim price reduction. Example: "originally $100, now $80" indicates there has been a previous reduction to $90 or another intermediate figure. This "original" comparative must be limited to a one-year period. Artificial Christmas trees that appear in late November or early December preceding Christmas are deceptively advertised as "originally $_____" if the advertiser is quoting the price of the prior year's peak selling period price. Advertisers of seasonal merchandise from ice skates to air conditioners are often offenders of this principle.

PUBLISHED AT CATALOG PRICE BASICALLY These three terms are, frequently, used to advertise books or record albums and even though they may be factually correct, they can be misleading. Correctly used, they must meet this test: was the merchandise recently sold by the advertiser or is it selling elsewhere at the "published at" or "catalog" price?

REGULARLY This must pertain to the advertiser's immediately preceding price for the identical merchandise, the price charged in the regular course of business, that price at which the item actually sold, not simply the "marked" selling price.

SOLD NATIONALLY and/or ADVERTISED NATIONALLY AT . . . may be used if the advertiser can substantiate these statements. Nationally means generally appearing throughout the United States.

SALE A reduction from the advertiser's own previous price.

SPECIAL Merchandise temporarily offered at a price concession, which will end when either, (a), the supply of items is exhausted, or, (b), item is to be sold at usual price after "special" ends.

SPECIAL PURCHASE Means that the advertiser has purchased merchandise at a price concession from a manufacturer or distributor who had, in the past, sold, or would, in the future, sell, the same merchandise at a higher price.

TWO-FOR-ONE Sales and coupon offers must meet this test: items actually sold, individually, for the now offered "two-for-one" price. Further, the advertiser must have a reasonable and substantial supply of items, or indicate in the advertisement that the number of such items is "limited" to a specific number. Otherwise, such advertising practice is considered deceptive.

UP TO _____% OFF Used in advertisement which includes a number of different items, such as several men's suits, must mean that at least 10 per cent of said items have been reduced up to the given percentage. This is to prevent the advertiser from misleading the public by including, perhaps, one suit at that reduction, while the remainder of the items are negligibly reduced.

VALUE Price actually charged in the trade area for the identical merchandise by a number (not just one) of the advertiser's competitors.

WHOLESALE OR BELOW WHOLESALE Price paid by the retailer for his merchandise. Advertisements by retail stores for merchandise so described, usually misleading, since the retailer could hardly stay in business if he continually sold his goods at the same price, or less, than he paid for them.

WAREHOUSE SALE Reduced merchandise offered only in the advertiser's warehouse and not available in his retail store.

THE U. S. GOVERNMENT MAY HAVE A GOOD BUY FOR YOU

Are you in the market for a used car? An aircraft? Plumbing and heating equipment?

Or perhaps you're looking for a good buy in a typewriter or an office machine for your business? Medical items, textiles, hardware, furniture?

The U. S. Government may have a good buy for you. A wide variety of personal property located the nation over is continuously being offered for sale by the federal government. The General Services Administration and the Department of Defense are the principal government agencies engaged in selling personal property.

The condition of the property offered for sale may range from good to poor, may be new or used, may require minor or extensive repair. It may not even be salvageable and have only scrap value.

But sales of civil agency personal property are regularly conducted by the GSA, the giant purchasing arm of the federal government—including a long list of consumer-type items. Each of the ten GSA regional offices conducts sales and each office maintains a mailing list for the geographical area it serves.

Note to you: Obtain an application to have your name placed on the GSA mailing list by writing to the GSA, Federal Supply Service, Personal Property Department in the regional area serving your locality. (See your phone book under U. S. Government.)

The Defense Department handles sales of its own property and is the source of large quantities of various types of property, including commercial, industrial, and consumer merchandise.

Property designated as surplus by the military is sold through Defense Property Disposal Sales Offices. There are five offices located throughout the continental United States and Hawaii. A centralized mailing list is maintained for sales conducted by these Defense Property Disposal Sales Offices.

Note to you: Get a Department of Defense Surplus Property Bidders Application to have your name placed on the mailing list by writing: DOD Surplus Sales, P.O. Box 1370, Battle Creek, Michigan, 49016.

When the classes of property you specify in your application are placed on sale in the geographical areas designated, you will be sent an Invitation For Bid (IFB). IFBs contain descriptions of the property, specific locations, dates and time for inspection, as well as other detailed information about the sales. Notices of sales to the public also may appear in newspaper, radio, and TV announcements, trade journals, notices in public buildings such as post offices, and through announcements in the Department of Commerce publication, "Commerce Business Daily."

Note to you: You may obtain a subscription to this publication by writing to the nearest Department of Commerce field office or the Superintendent of Documents, Government Printing Office, Washington, D.C. 20402. The subscription is expensive; check the price before you subscribe.

Personal property is sold to the public on the basis of competitive bids, and in quantities suitable for individuals as well as for businesses. No priorities or preferences are given to groups or individuals.

Property is frequently sold by sealed bid with an Invitation For Bid mailed to you, a prospective buyer. You enter the prices on the bid forms contained in the

IFB and return the forms to the specified government office with a bid deposit. If you're a successful bidder, you will be notified.

Spot bids also are used, with the bidder writing the bid and submitting it during the sale. Awards are made item by item as the sale progresses. If you're on the mailing lists, you'll receive information on the property and instructions for placing bids. You may be able to make special arrangements to submit bids if you can't attend the sale in person.

Public auctions are another vehicle used by the government. These follow traditional commercial auctioning methods. Catalogs are provided. Government-approved auctioneers are in charge.

4

YOU MUST EAT—HOW TO DO IT BEST AT LEAST COST

FOOD PRICES IN PERSPECTIVE

NO END IN SIGHT TO INFLATED COSTS

The urgency for cutting down your food bills is underscored by one stark fact: since the early 1970s the cost of food has gone up faster than costs of all other commodities and services except energy and medical care. The harsh impact of inflation hits you every time you go through a supermarket check out counter. The overall increase in one recent five-year span was a staggering 52½ per cent.

Food prices have, in fact, soared more rapidly than in any other peacetime period in the nation's history—and the U. S. Department of Agriculture itself glumly predicts more of the same well into the new decade of the 1980s, with meat prices showing the sharpest increases of all.

For virtually all American families except those of you in the upper income brackets, food is the biggest item in your weekly household budget. At the end of the 1970s, food accounted for fully half of the budget for millions of low-income families with two school-age children. A similar family with an annual income of $12,000 spent at least and perhaps more than 25 per cent of its household budget for food. As always, the people punished the hardest are those who can least afford high prices.

Thus, it is even more imperative for the overwhelming majority of Americans to save on food to prevent deterioration in your quality of life. *And you can do it without drastic sacrifices*—can reduce your food costs at least 10 per cent by observing simple tips for careful, sensible shopping. You can slash your costs more than 20 per cent merely by "trading down" to products that are just as nutritious as expensive "convenience" items.

You buy food at least once or twice a week in contrast to big-ticket purchases made only occasionally—furniture, appliances, automobiles. Food is among the very few cash-and-carry items left in the typical budget.

It is the one area where you can correct costly mistakes and start saving from the day you make up your mind to concentrate on intelligent shopping.

WHY HAVE BEEF PRICES BEEN SOARING?

The short answer: a sharp cutback in beef supplies. Higher production costs combined with adverse weather in some areas and an overabundance of beef in the mid-late 1970s compelled cattlemen to cut way back on their herds or to go out of business entirely.

This steep drop in cattle inventories pushed up beef prices and will continue to do so. Add to this the inflationary pressures on the farm-to-retail spread—the difference between what a cattleman gets for a steer and what a steak costs at the grocery store. While middlemen charges as well as rapid hikes in farm prices may be absorbed in part over the short run, eventually they are passed on by the retailer to you and me, the consumer.

But still, smaller supplies and the widening farm-to-retail spread are only part of the explanation why beef prices have been jumping.

Basic, too, is your demand for meat, which, despite higher prices, remains strong. When you demand more and more meat, when you steadily increase your purchases of high-quality beef, your buying pulls up the price. This dynamic is what economists term "demand-pull" inflation.

Your taste for beef also has been fueled by changing life-styles and attitudes. Almost six out of ten women now work outside of the home. Almost half of the mothers with children under eighteen hold jobs. Families are smaller. All of these factors contribute to a strong preference for quick and easy foods.

A prime candidate is hamburger. We are indeed more and more of a hamburger society. Ground beef plus beef used in processed products accounted for a startling 45 per cent of per-capita beef consumption, as the 1970s ended.

Because ground beef is cooked quickly and can be used in such a variety of ways, many family cooks prefer it to other cuts which take longer to prepare.

The increased preference for hamburger coupled with a reduction in supply has pushed up the national average price of ground beef sharply. Chuck, which can be boned and ground for hamburger, also has risen in price.

And again, the at-home craving for hamburger is just one part of this tale. Although seafood is now the fastest-growing restaurant item, your family still eats a lot of beef when you go out.

Might your demand for beef level off or even drop? The beef industry is sensitive to this, although not overly worried.

So many of us are concerned about limiting the amount of fat in our diets and want leaner steaks and roasts as well as smaller portions. Higher beef prices may spur interest in some meat extenders or substitutes containing vegetable protein.

But the industry sees these products as helping to maintain the consumption of beef by lower-income families and keeping them from being priced out of the market completely.

In one out of every four meals prepared at home, beef is still served as the main course. Your demand for it is powerful. And as long as the U.S. economy remains relatively healthy and incomes continue to rise, your buying is likely to remain strong, even in the face of higher-higher prices.

CATTLE CYCLE—WHAT IT IS AND MEANS TO YOU

Cattle production (like business in general and other commodity businesses) has its up and down cycles. But in the cattle business, the cycles run much longer —about ten to twelve years from a low point in the cattle herd to the next.

The reason the cycle lasts so long is because it can take up to four years from the time a cow/calf producer decides to increase his basic herd—holds a female calf from market, raises her, breeds her, raises the new calf, and sends the animal to slaughter—until the extra meat arrives at your supermarket.

In the closing months of the 1970s, we reached the low point in the cattle cycle, or ended what cattlemen call a "liquidation phase." During that phase, cattle producers cut back their herds in response to financial losses caused by lower cattle prices, rising costs plus drought. Some producers were forced out of the business entirely.

But for you and me, consumers, those years meant plentiful supplies of beef at relatively low prices.

Now, at the start of the 1980s the herd reduction period is over. The basic cow herd is being built back up, but to do this cows must be kept off the market for breeding. So for a time beef supplies dwindle further.

This is a costly process for you and me.

It will be the mid 1980s, experts estimate, before supplies become excessive enough to begin to push prices back down. At that point the cycle will go into operation all over again.

HOW MUCH DOES YOUR FAMILY COST TO FEED?

The amount *your* family spends on food depends on:
• the size of your family paycheck (the lower your income bracket, the higher the proportion of your budget goes for food);
• the age of each family member (teenagers are the most expensive to feed);
• the amount of entertaining your family does;
• the types of foods you eat—and don't eat;
• the importance of food as compared to your other needs and wants;
• food price levels at a given time and in a given place;
• how much time and effort various members of your family are able and willing to spend on food preparation;
• the area of the country in which you live;
• how much you eat out in restaurants, fast-food places, etc.;
• whether or not you have a family vegetable garden or raise other foods, and whether your family preserves or freezes significant amounts of homegrown foods.

DO SMALL FAMILIES PAY MORE?

And what if yours is a smaller- or larger-sized family—how much does yours cost to feed? Here are key guides:

For each $1.00 a six-person family spends on food, a four-person household spends $1.03, a two-person household spends $1.07, and a single individual living alone spends $1.11.

On a per-person basis, the large family always pays less than the small family —a point which is becoming increasingly important as food prices continue spiraling ever upward. In fact, the one-person household in the United States pays fully 11 per cent more for the same list of foods than the family consisting of two parents and four children, according to a study by the U. S. Agriculture Department.

NON-FOODS IN FOOD STORES

How complex is the story of your rising food budget? Merely to suggest the ramifications:

• Part of your higher grocery-supermarket bills can be traced to your ever-rising preference for gourmet foods and relatively expensive condiments.

• Part can be traced to your ever-rising fondness for snacks, which have become a kind of "fourth meal" in the American home.

• Part of the bigger bills can be traced, as you all admit, to your taste for convenience foods and to the huge wave of big-eating teenagers moving through our population.

What's more, the tremendous strides we have made in food distribution have made possible nationwide availability of foods grown thousands of miles away.

The modern distribution system also is providing year-round availability of most seasonal foods. This, too, adds to costs. Clearly, anyone who buys fresh corn on the cob in Maine in February is going to pay a lot more for the corn than in Kansas in August.

A huge volume of the food we eat is imported from nations as distant as Brazil and Ghana. So weather and other factors affecting the whole food supply-demand picture in other nations also bear on the prices we pay in our supermarkets for such items as coffee, tea, cocoa, bananas, spices. And all of us, all consumers, pay for the cost to the manufacturer of developing an estimated 5,000 new food items each year—of which only 1,500 reach food-store shelves and only 500 last as long as one year. In 1928, grocery stores handled an average of 867 food and non-food items. Today, their shelves are stocked with more than 11,000 items.

But the big surge in spending has been in *non-foods*—and these now represent about one fourth of our total store bills.

Item: Among the fastest sale gainers in the nation's supermarkets and grocery stores in recent years have been non-foods, ranging from paper towels and greeting cards to dishwasher compounds, furniture polish, and deodorant soaps. Also among the fastest gainers have been cat food, canned soft drinks, and dietetic soft drinks.

Item: More than half of all the toothpaste we buy in the United States is from supermarkets and grocery stores, not drugstores. We now buy more than half of all our aspirin in food stores, and nearly half of our shampoo and shaving products. In addition, we get one third of our first-aid equipment in supermarkets plus an astounding one in ten of our phonograph records and more than one in ten of our comic books and magazines.

One less obvious force propelling the non-food upswing in food stores is the domestic do-it-yourself trend in our land. You are spending sharply increased amounts in supermarkets for such things as home spot-cleaning fluids, self-polishing floor waxes, shoe polishes, housewares.

Another force is the steady upgrading in our health and sanitary standards. This explains the huge increases in supermarket sales of aerosol household deodorizers and disinfectants, plastic film wraps for food storage, garbage-can liners, drain cleaners, deodorant soaps, personal deodorants, all types of first-aid equipment.

Here is how you divided up a $20 bill in the supermarket-grocery in the late 1970s. The relationships have not changed in many years, and this breakdown will clinch the tale of your spending for non-foods as well as foods in the supermarket in the 1980s.

CLASSIFICATION	TOTAL
Perishables	
Baked goods, snacks	$ 1.21
Dairy products (including eggs and margarine)	1.22
Frozen foods	1.00
Meat, fish, poultry	4.42
Produce	2.12
TOTAL FOR PERISHABLES	$ 9.97
Dry Groceries	
Beer	$ .86
Wine and distilled spirits	.13
Baby foods (excluding cereals)	.07
Cereals and rice	.33
Candy and chewing gum	.21
Canned foods	1.19
Coffee and tea (including instants)	.53
Dried foods	.24
Soft drinks	.49
Sugar	.29
All other foods	1.37
TOTAL FOR DRY GROCERIES	$ 5.71
Other Groceries	
Paper goods	$ .49
Soaps, detergents, laundry	.36
Other household products	.44
Pet foods	.30
Tobacco products	.70
Miscellaneous	.13
TOTAL FOR OTHER GROCERIES	$ 2.42

CLASSIFICATION	TOTAL
General Merchandise	
Health and beauty aids	$ .72
Prescriptions	.08
Housewares	.21
All other general merchandise	.89
TOTAL FOR GENERAL MERCHANDISE	1.90
GRAND TOTAL	$20.00

THE HIGH COST OF CONVENIENCE FOODS

If you serve your family a store-bought pizza pie, it will cost you about 60 per cent more than if you put the ingredients together yourself. Or if you serve prepared hashed brown potatoes, it'll cost nearly twice the amount per serving it would cost if you had hashed them at home. And the cost of one slice of store-bought apple pie also may be double the cost of a home-baked pie.

Your willingness to pay extra for expensive maid service built into the foods you buy is a well-known force behind rising food prices, but you persist in under-estimating how much your own demands for convenience foods are adding to your own food budgets. You don't *have* to buy the ready-made pizza at almost twice the price of making the pie at home—but you do.

As you wheel your cart through today's fantastic selection of supermarket foods, you are increasingly apt to choose the package of frozen beans with butter already added, the box of breakfast cereal coated with sugar or mixed with freeze-dried fruit over the box of plain cereal, the just-add-milk pancake mix over the half-dozen separate ingredients which go into pancakes.

The Department of Agriculture calculates that your per capita consumption of fresh fruits and vegetables has been dropping steadily and your consumption of canned fruit has remained fairly stable. But your consumption of canned and frozen vegetables has been climbing steeply. Most dramatically, your purchases of frozen potato products and processed items like instant mashed potatoes have skyrocketed while consumption of fresh potatoes has declined.

A full 10 per cent of the eggs you now consume are pre-emptied and preprocessed, and during the 1980s, says the Agriculture Department, the proportion of eggs in forms ranging from cake mixes to "instant" scrambled eggs will soar to one third of your total egg consumption.

Today about half of all supermarkets have a delicatessen department. Many also have their own kitchens in which sixty to a hundred different items are prepared—most of them higher-priced convenience foods.

There's absolutely no basis for expecting any of these trends to slow, much less reverse. And now you have advanced to the convenience of the *whole take-home meal*—the carton of chicken or fish and chips or whatever, bought at the fast-food, limited-menu store—and this meal certainly costs more than the made-from-scratch version.

"PAYING MORE FOR LESS"

As readily as we pay extra for the built-in maid service that comes with convenience foods, we willingly pay additional amounts for "packaged" will power.

Anxious about our overweight, we are spending in the range of $300 million a year on special diet products, featuring fewer calories but also often providing smaller portions and less food value.

"Paying more for less" is just another signal of our spreading nutritional illiteracy and susceptibility to inviting ads and supermarket displays—or both. Whatever the explanations, the result is costly to you and me.

There's a diet counterpart these days for just about every food you can think of —fruits, vegetables, jellies, salad dressing, TV dinners, sour cream, cookies, eggs, etc.

Yet, you can easily convert many of these items into diet specials yourself at far less cost.

To illustrate, you can buy a package of low-cal, fruit-flavored gelatin dessert to make four servings of ten calories each. But you can claim a saving of more than 300 per cent merely by buying unflavored gelatin and flavoring it yourself with leftover coffee, fruit juice, diet soda, or whatever.

Then there are many foods which are both low in calories and in price, which should form the basics of your diet.

Consider low-fat milk products. While fluid skim milk usually costs a few cents per quart less than whole milk, the real saver in money and weight is non-fat dry milk. It cuts calories in half, reduces cholesterol intake, is usually priced at roughly half what you pay for fluid skim or whole milk.

Or consider the simple apple. If bought fresh by the pound, these cost half as much as the price for the equivalent in foil-wrapped dried apple slices.

Low-income consumers always have been the target of the United States Agriculture Department for most of its nutritional information. But the unspoken assumption that only these consumers are malnourished and in need of education is unrealistic! Obesity is as much a symptom of malnutrition as starvation. Middle- and upper-income families need to be educated on a balanced diet as much as anyone.

You can get sensible, if not inspiring, nutritional aids from the USDA: "Food and Your Weight," Home & Garden Bulletin No. 74 (cost, less than $1.00); "Calories & Weight," a USDA calorie guide (AIB 365) (cost $1.00 in the late 1970s). But both would help you compare calories in regular foods with those listed on the labels of their diet counterparts. Both publications are available from the Superintendent of Documents, U. S. Printing Office, Washington, D.C. 20402.

WHAT'S A "LOW CALORIE" FOOD?

Within any twenty-four-hour period, some 20 million Americans thirteen years old and over will drink a sugar-free, carbonated soft drink.

More than 7 million will chew sugar-free gum; roughly 3 million will use low-calorie salad dressing; about a million will consume a portion of diet yogurt.

These survey results, prepared for the Calorie Control Council, a diet-food trade association, merely hint at Americans' reliance on low-calorie foods—and for an obvious reason.

Approximately 40 million Americans, about twice the population of Canada, are overweight. To help these 40 million to select foods which will genuinely save them calories, the Food and Drug Administration created new labeling rules as the 1970s closed for foods that you will find useful in weight control (if you learn and heed them).

Foods labeled "low calorie" can contain no more than forty calories per ordinary serving.

Foods marked "reduced calorie" must contain at least one-third fewer calories than another food of the same type. Such "reduced calorie foods" also must carry a statement comparing them to the same food as it is normally eaten. "Reduced calorie" peaches, for instance, have to carry a label stating, "peaches packed in water contain 38 calories per one-half cup serving, 62 per cent less than 'Brand X' peaches packed in syrup."

Food products claiming to be either low or reduced in calories must carry a complete nutrition label. You must be told how many calories are in a serving, as well as the amounts of protein, carbohydrate, fat, and percentage of U. S. Recommended Daily Allowances for vitamins and minerals.

Foods which are normally low in calories, such as cucumbers, cannot be labeled "low-calorie" immediately before the name. This would suggest, says the Food and Drug Administration, that the particular cucumber was lower in calories than other cucumbers. The vegetable can, however, be labeled "cucumber, a low-calorie food."

If a food is to carry such terms as "diet," "dietetic," or "artificially sweetened," it either must be labeled as low or reduced calorie or indicate that it is useful for certain other dietary purposes (low-sodium diets, for instance).

The same applies for such terms as "sugar free," "sugarless," or "no sugar." Since you reasonably might assume foods carrying these designations to be useful in weight control, the food must meet the requirements for low- or reduced-calorie foods, be so labeled or carry a clarifying statement, such as "not a reduced calorie food," or "not for weight control," or "useful only in avoiding tooth decay."

And finally in the interests of the roughly 5 million diabetics in the United States, the Food and Drug Administration has required that a food cannot be labeled "diabetic" unless it is useful for such individuals. If it is, then it must carry the statement "Diabetics: This product may be useful in your diet on the advice of a physician."

These requirements may sound complicated when spelled out this way. But in fact, they are meant to bring uniformity to the array of terms formerly used to suggest that a food is helpful for overweight people or those on special diets.

But if you are dieting, reliance solely on the new labeling rules and a few of the low-calorie items they govern won't help you much. Reduced-calorie foods are really of value only to those of you with pounds to shed when combined with increased exercise and the consumption of smaller portions than you have been eating.

Although most of you are looking for a "quick fix" to your overweight problem, you will NOT find the answer through crash dieting, monotonous diets, or a single low-calorie product.

The fundamental answer always has been and is: a balanced but reduced diet of commonly available foods.

A last word from the Food and Drug Administration: if you must lose weight, start moving! For the longer you remain overweight, the less likely it is that you will succeed in your reducing program.

OTHER "HIDDEN" FORCES PUSHING UP FOOD PRICES

What I have described so far are only the obvious factors. There also are many other "hidden" forces which may not appear of significance when considered separately but which do add up to real pressure on your food budget when considered as a group. To illustrate with a sampling:

Pollution controls: The steps that farmers, food processors, and others take to reduce runoff of chemical fertilizers into water supplies, to curtail use of dangerous pesticides, to dispose of by-products in ways that won't pollute the air and water.

Tightened food inspection rules: Regulations which have raised the food standards in this country to the highest in the history of man and made our current food supply the safest ever—despite admitted gaps still remaining.

Rising skepticism about food additives, colorings, etc.: Our questioning the safety of these substances—including preservatives—is forcing food processors to stiffen their standards for using the substances, to increase their spending on research, to risk higher losses from spoilage.

Better labeling: This improvement for us has added to the costs of some foods.

Import quotas: These restrictions cost us literally billions of dollars each year.

Then there's the weather (droughts, killing frosts), always a factor. There are periodic, costly dock strikes. There are numerous labor practices which limit productivity and raise labor costs. And there is the organic farming boom which may swell food budgets by hundreds of millions of dollars.

YOUR CHANGING EATING HABITS

Here are key trends and changes in your eating habits:

(1) From a nutritional viewpoint, you are eating less well than in the mid 1950s. Only half of all American households are eating a good diet today, according to a massive and alarming Agriculture Department study. Nearly one family in ten in the $10,000-and-up income bracket has a diet rated as poor, and overall, one in five families has a diet rated as poor. Our per capita national consumption of such nutritional cornerstones as milk, fresh fruits, and vegetables has been declining steadily—replaced to a considerable extent by sweet snacks, sweet soft drinks, etc.

In the past two generations the proportion of calories we as a nation eat in the form of starches had dropped from 68 to 48 per cent, while the proportion in the form of sugar and other sweeteners has soared from 32 to 52 per cent. The old-fashioned fresh potato, one of the richest sources of key vitamins and minerals if you eat it in its skin, is being shunned, although potatoes actually contain fewer calories on an ounce-for-ounce basis than lima beans, prunes, rice, bran flakes, and most fruits canned in heavy syrup.

(2) "Isolated eating" is in a strong uptrend. Breakfast, for millions of Americans, has become nothing more than a foraging expedition through the refrigerator and food cupboards, with each family member gulping down whatever foods are at hand and then hurrying off to work or school. Or it's "instant" breakfast made up of what is hoped to be nutritious imitations.

Lunch also, for millions of children and jobholders, has become an institutional meal, served in school cafeterias or company restaurants. Only the homebound mother and her preschool children may eat lunch together. In fact, for a startling number of families, even sitting down to dinner is now strictly a weekend affair. The kids eat when they come home from school; if the father hasn't eaten downtown, he eats when he comes home hours later; the mother eats whenever.

The haphazard eating is blurring the old demarcation lines between meals. An increasing part of what is eaten is in the form of snacks.

(3) You are often skipping meals altogether, in most cases in your efforts to lose weight. According to a recent study, about one in five Americans in the nineteen-to-twenty-four age bracket regularly skips lunch; 16 per cent skip breakfast; one in ten forgoes the evening meal.

(4) Eating out is on the increase—in restaurants, snack bars, fast-food stores and stands. The proportion of our food dollar going for eating out (as contrasted with eating at home) is now crossing 30 per cent.

(5) There has been a steady expansion of the office and factory coffee break. With orange juice or some similar beverage, pastries or rolls, and coffee now included, the coffee break has become a substitute for breakfast at home for workers at every level across the land.

This is not nearly as farfetched as it may appear, for as today's housewife finds she is little more than a short-order cook for her family, she will channel her culinary efforts into special meals for special occasions. She will do her short-order cooking as efficiently and quickly as possible, simultaneously investing ever larger amounts of her time and money in cooking schools, gourmet food guides, chafing dishes, barbecue pits, hibachis, etc. And, incidentally, the evidence is that she is teaching her daughter to cook this way too—to prepare foods on a piecemeal basis rather than systematically as a full meal.

BASIC RULES FOR SAVING ON FOOD

If you make an error in buying furniture, you're almost surely stuck. It may take you years to correct your mistake and you'll probably come out with a painful loss. But *if* you make an error in buying fruit, you can quickly learn from your mistake and only days later come out ahead when you again go shopping for food.

To be specific, here are twenty-five keys to saving:

(1) To begin with, plan before you go shopping. Always have a pad handy so you can note food items you need as your supplies run low. Group together the same kinds of foods and supplies to simplify your shopping in any store. Inspect your refrigerator, freezer, and cabinet or pantry shelves to see what you have on hand and what you need. Consult the store ads as you make up your shopping list and group the items on your list into the following categories:

> Groceries and canned foods
> Bakery products and cereals
> Dairy products
> Fresh fruits and vegetables
> Frozen foods
> Meat, fish, and poultry
> Non-foods (cleaning products, paper, etc.)
> Other

When your shopping list is ready, go over it to be sure you have chosen foods on the basis of their nutritional value—the amounts and proportions of protein, vitamins, minerals they contain—rather than strictly on the basis of their "taste appeal." Spend your money first for those items, then go on to other foods that you merely want.

Use your list as you shop, and also take along whatever throwaway shopper ads might lead you to the bargains. Glance too at the price specials advertised in store windows—for clues to items you might want to add.

Don't buy any items not on your list. Instead, wait a week, then see whether you really want or need the items you didn't buy.

(2) Avoid snacks—among the most expensive food extras you can buy. They easily can add 10 per cent to your weekly food bill but will be among the least valuable nutritionally. Or, as an alternative, stick to snacks and beverages which have some nutritionally redeeming value—i.e., orange juice versus orange pop, fresh fruit versus candy, and whole-grain crackers, oatmeal-raisin-peanut butter cookies versus chocolate or cream-filled ones.

(3) Buy a set of 3-by-5-inch index cards and a file box. As you put the groceries away, record the cost of each purchase on a separate card. The index cards will quickly become a key reference file.

By checking the recorded prices against advertised specials and newspaper discount coupons, you easily can determine if the "special" is a saving.

(4) Look on the bottom shelves of your supermarket. The people who stock the supermarket shelves are just like the rest of us. They would rather not bend to reprice items more than necessary. As a result, you may find some wonderful bargains priced below current levels.

(5) Keep a sharp eye on the check-out cash register, for that's where many unintentional mistakes are made.

(6) Buy, learn how to use, and carry with you on all food shopping trips a

small, inexpensive, hand-held calculator. The pocket calculator will allow you to keep track of your expenditures as you go through the store, and if yours is an area without unit pricing, the calculator will help you compute cost-per-measure quickly.

(7) Keep in mind—as you make out your food lists and as you actually shop for food—what you'll do with inevitable leftovers. If you plan to make split pea soup using a hambone, for example, buy the split peas when you buy the ham. Also use the little leftovers in your refrigerator—bits of cheese, a dab of tuna fish or chicken, a slice or two of salami or ham—to make a smörgåsbord that can serve as a complete lunch or supper. Or use the leftovers in a soup. Or make them the basis for a delicious platter of hors d'oeuvres. That's how hors d'oeuvres came into being, you know—out of bits of leftovers.

(8) Store your leftovers in glass containers which you have emptied and washed. Glass retains the flavor of food longer than other containers and keeps leftovers looking more appetizing. It also keeps food fresher, an added "plus" especially when you're planning a midweek leftover meal such as a "thick soup."

(9) If you possibly can, shop in person in the store; this will *always* give you the best value for your money and there is no real or comparably inexpensive substitute for this practice. You select the food, you pay cash, you carry your purchases home. If you shop by telephone, have food delivered to your home, and charge these food purchases, you will pay for these conveniences—and the costs over a year will add up to whopping totals.

Do not—if you are a non-jobholding wife and can avoid it—let your husband come along on the weekly supermarket shopping trip (unless your husband routinely does the shopping). Husbands are notorious impulse buyers and almost inevitably overload the shopping cart with non-essentials and badly chosen brands and varieties of needed items.

Do not go shopping for food on an empty stomach. Shopping hungry is another way to boost your impulse buying. Surveys reveal those who shop after meals spend up to 17 per cent *less* than those who shop when hungry.

(10) Particularly for such big items as meat, shift your menus as prices dictate.

(11) Shop the specials and stock your freezer and pantry with foods you need or want when they are marked down.

(12) Consider quality in relation to your use of the food. If corn on the cob is the heart of your meal, of course you will buy the best quality you can afford. But if you're using corn as part of another dish, you'll do just as well with a much less expensive form of corn.

(13) Check the prices of "no-frills," other bargain-priced foods, and private brands versus nationally advertised brands of foods you use frequently. Every food chain and many independent stores sell these cheaper foods, at savings running to as much as 20–30 per cent. The reasons: no advertising expenses are built in; no salesmen or promotion campaigns are pushing up the costs; and in many cases transportation is a smaller expense on private than on nationally advertised brands. The quality of many private-label products compares favorably with that of nationally advertised brands. And many brands are of identical quality because they're packed for retailers by the processors of the nationally advertised brands.

Buy the brand you like best but try the less expensive private-label product at least once.

Talk to others in the market who are looking at the new products you're considering. They already may have tried the item, and you can benefit from their experience and advice.

(14) Check the containers with care when you buy frozen foods and never buy an item that is covered with frost. Select only food that is stored below the freezer line at 0° or below. Under *no* circumstances buy a can of food that is bulging— and if you uncover such a can in your own pantry, toss it out.

(15) Buy such foods as meat by cost per portion rather than by overall price. To find this cost, divide the price of the amount you purchase by the number of portions the amount will supply. More on this later.

(16) Buy such foods as bread or cereals by cost per ounce or pound. There is no waste involved here, so see which package offers the most weight for the identical price. More on this later, too.

Buy bulk items such as flour and sugar in bags rather than in boxes. By so doing, you're likely to save an average of nearly 20 per cent.

(17) Compare package sizes in relation to how quickly you will consume the contents. The "family economy size" is no bargain to you if you end up throwing out a lot of leftovers.

(18) Analyze the real cost of cooking from scratch versus buying "built-in maid service." It's not the usual result, but the cost of ingredients to prepare something at home may sometimes be *more* than the prepackaged convenience equivalent—especially if staples are left over.

(19) Compare different forms of food. More and more foods are sold in to-day's market in different forms—fresh, canned, frozen, chilled, and dried. Save money by comparing costs between different forms. As just one illustration of possible savings, per-serving costs of condensed soup run as little as one third the cost of water-added varieties. Before buying a particular item, check to see whether it's cheaper to *buy it fresh, canned, or frozen.* Relative costs change with seasonal patterns. Taste well may be your deciding factor; the difference in nutrition may be insignificant.

When you shop for low-calorie foods, stick to ordinary foods as much as possible—fresh celery, carrots, and radishes, plain beef consommé or chicken broth, fresh fruits and vegetables, regular canned tuna fish, low-fat milk—and avoid higher-priced items on the special diet shelf.

(20) Always remember the seasonal specials. Many of the fruits and vegetables which come to market in abundance in summer, cost 50 per cent less than in winter. But don't buy the *first* of a crop; prices will go down as the supply increases. Also time buying of canned and frozen fruits and vegetables to take advantage of the end-of-summer surpluses after new packs come in. And when these specials are advertised, stock up.

(21) Weigh the cost of gasoline—and time—in choosing a supermarket. The least expensive supermarket in your area almost surely won't be the cheapest for you if you have to drive twice the distance to reach it.

As a general rule, small convenience stores which stay open long hours seven days a week charge the highest prices. Next come small neighborhood "Mom and Pop" stores. Then supermarkets and the food discount stores.

(22) Substitute among protein foods as prices dictate. Try beef or pork liver instead of calf's liver; poultry instead of red meats; bean, cheese, and egg dishes instead of meat dishes. Among today's best protein bargains: chicken, hamburger, eggs, cottage cheese, peanut butter, dry beans, American process cheese.

(23) Use the recipes and food-buying tips offered to you by the Department of Agriculture, your local consumer organizations, and your local newspaper's food editor.

(24) Also use the Agriculture Department's publications, which are designed to help you. The department is loaded with booklets and pamphlets on how to buy, raise, store, cook, and combine food of all kinds—available from the Publications Division, Office of Communication, U. S. Department of Agriculture, Washington, D.C. 20250.

Among the key titles:

Your Money's Worth in Foods (Home and Garden Bulletin No. 183)

Family Fare: A Guide to Good Nutrition (Home and Garden Bulletin No. 1)

Beef and Veal in Family Meals (Home and Garden Bulletin No. 118)

Family Food Buying, A Guide for Calculating Amounts to Buy and Comparing Costs (Home Economics Research Report No. 37)

Toward the New, A Report on Better Foods and Nutrition from Agricultural Research (Agriculture Information Bulletin No. 341)

The Food We Eat (Miscellaneous Publication No. 870)

Nutritive Value of Foods (Home and Garden Bulletin No. 72)

Family Food Budgeting for Good Meals and Good Nutrition (Home and Garden Bulletin No. 94)

(25) Hunt for nutrition bargains and *don't* overbuy meat. Use the following guides, developed by the U. S. Department of Agriculture on the minimum amounts of each major type of food we at various ages should consume daily for proper nutrition:

Milk: children under nine years, 2 to 3 cups; nine to twelve years, 3 or more cups; teenagers, 4 or more cups; adults, 2 or more cups; pregnant women, 3 or more cups; nursing mothers, 4 or more cups. (Note: Cheese, ice cream, and milk used in cooking count as part of the day's milk.)

Meat: 2 or more servings of either beef or veal, pork, lamb, poultry, fish, shellfish, eggs—with dry beans, peas, nuts as alternates.

Vegetables and fruits: 4 or more servings with a dark green or deep yellow vegetable at least every other day; a citrus fruit or other fruit or vegetable rich in vitamin C daily; other vegetables and fruits, including potatoes.

Bread and cereal: 4 or more servings—whole grain, enriched, or restored—of breads, bakery foods, cereals, crackers, grits, macaroni, spaghetti, noodles, rice.

STILL MORE SAVINGS VIA "TRADING DOWN"

Do you realize how much you could reduce your food bill by "trading down" in the supermarket today—by choosing the least expensive version available of each item on your grocery list? You're surely generally aware that you could achieve big savings simply by doing this instead of trading up to the highest-quality, most convenient, fanciest label foods. But would you have guessed that the savings I recorded in a recent shopping experiment of my own amounted to 41 per cent?

For the experiment, I asked an eagle-eyed young housewife-friend to wheel two shopping carts through a huge supermarket in my area of the country; first she would load cart number 1 with the most expensive possible items and then load cart number 2 with the least expensive.

In the milk category, it was regular fresh milk in cart number 1 and powdered milk in cart number 2. And "potatoes" meant fancy Idahos for cart number 1 but plain old Maine spuds for cart number 2. And so on down the line . . .

When she checked the two carts for me, the bargain cart came to $32.47 less than the most expensive assortment. I won't give you the complete breakdown on the carts, because prices for specific items vary so widely from time to time and area to area. But the total is representative—and if you multiplied it by fifty-two weeks, you would have savings amounting to close to $2,000—or even more—a year!

Here is my full shopping list, with the dollar difference *and* the percentage savings between high- and low-priced items:

ITEM	$ DIFFERENCE	% SAVINGS
Beer (6-pack)	$2.50	330
Salad oil (1 qt.)	2.10	275
Liquid detergent (1 qt.)	.64	260
Steak (3 lbs.)	7.20	251
Vegetable soup (4 cans)	1.24	235
Cookies (1 box)	.60	222
Onions (3 lbs.)	1.11	212
Spaghetti (2 boxes)	.56	210
Milk (8 qts.)	1.94	98
Frankfurters (2 lbs.)	1.86	91
Frozen peas (6 pkgs.)	2.16	91
Veal (2 lbs.)	3.60	90
Flour (5 lbs.)	.64	85
White bread (2 loaves)	.52	53
Bacon (2 lbs.)	1.40	42
Cat food (3 cans)	.27	40
Potatoes (10 lbs.)	.47	37
Frozen orange juice (4 6-oz. cans)	.56	33
Hamburger (3 lbs.)	1.20	29
Tomatoes (2 large cans)	.20	24
Mayonnaise (large jar)	.14	20
Eggs (2 doz.)	.24	16
Pears (2 large cans)	.12	13
Butter (2 lbs.)	.60	11
Coffee (2 lbs.)	.60	11

The rundown speaks for itself. In some cases, splurge items cost two to three times as much as non-splurge items. In some cases, too, the shopper has obviously sacrificed quality (although probably not much nutritional value). In other cases, though, there's no significant difference between the cart number 1 item and the cart number 2 item.

Convenience, too, was ignored in cart number 2—e.g., no pre-peeled vegetables, no butter added to frozen foods, no pre-pattied hamburgers, no individual servings of this or that. But, of course, convenience is part of the sacrifice a careful shopper must pay to reap the maximum savings from trading down.

I'm not suggesting you stick strictly to the cheapest available foods or other items. Most of you don't want to nor do you need to. But even though you can afford to splurge and trade up, not down, is it not fascinating to see how much you could save if you tried to trade down? And you need not go this far. All you need really do is to buy essentially the same foods in less expensive form.

Here, for instance, are two menus which reveal that you can more than double the cost of your meal by choosing the more expensive variety of meat, fruit, or vegetable or, conversely, you can cut it fully 60 per cent by choosing the less expensive variety.

Less Expensive	More Expensive
Grapefruit half	Cantaloupe
Chuck steak	Sirloin steak
Baked potato with sour cream	Frozen creamed potato with chives
Frozen peas buttered at home	Frozen peas in butter sauce
Tossed salad	Salad with tomatoes, avocados
Rye bread	Garlic bread
Chocolate pudding	Frozen éclairs

These two menus were priced toward the close of the decade. For four persons, the cheaper menu actually was less than half the dollar total of the more expensive.

SHOPPING THE DISCOUNT STORES

Discounting has become the biggest, hottest trend in food retailing today. And you are shouting your preference for this no-frills, big-scale, money-saving method of food buying.

How much do you save by shopping in discount food stores? According to a major study by A&P, weekly savings run around 11 per cent. Other studies indicate overall savings generally at from 5 to 15 per cent.

There are two key types of discount operations: general merchandise discount stores which include a food department, and separate stores devoted solely to food.

If you shop in discount stores you'll probably have to travel some distance—and in view of fuel costs, have to space your shopping trips more widely to reap in full the bargains they offer. You'll probably forfeit many of the usual supermarket amenities—ranging from carry-out service to Muzak. You probably won't find trading stamps in these places. You may even have to pick some of your foods out of cut cases instead of neat shelf displays—and in some cases you may have to make do with a smaller variety of products.

But if none of these aspects bothers you and if you have the gas, oil, and use of a car at least once a week, try out the local discount stores. Ask friends about their experience with these stores. Read newspaper ads and compare prices. Then see how much money *you* can save.

"NO FRILLS" FOODS

In your local supermarket, you well may see whole shelves of canned foods which frequently carry simple labels and price tags up to 40 per cent lower than you usually pay! And you well may wonder: What's this all about? Are these cheap foods equal to the brand-name foods to which you are accustomed? And are they safe?

The answer is that you are seeing a new line of foods, canned and packaged, called "no name," "no frills," or simply "generic." They all carry the labels disclosing the contents and they all are priced at deep discounts, ranging from 10 to as much as 40 per cent below nationally advertised brands or goods sold in the supermarket chains under house labels. They are certainly equal in nutrition but they may be slightly less pleasing to your eye in color or size or content. As measured by the United States Department of Agriculture's guidelines, they are usually standard grades instead of fancy grades. And they are neither advertised among the weekly specials nor are they elaborately packaged. Thus, the possible savings to you.

You cannot buy these "no frills" food everywhere nor do the companies selling them stock them in all their stores as the 1980s begin. Check the stores near you to see whether any have them available. It's a great way to slash your food budget even in periods of climbing food prices.

Start Your Own Food Buying Club

If food co-operatives, food warehouses, and other wholesale outlets are operating in your area, by all means use them too. You'll buy staples such as rice, sugar, flour in 25- or 50-pound bags; you'll bag your own purchases and you'll pick the produce you want to buy straight out of packing cases.

You'll also achieve savings ranging from 20 per cent up.

Or you can join with other families to start your own food-buying club.

HOW THE CLUBS WORK

Here are tips from New York City's Department of Consumer Affairs on how these clubs work and on how to make a success out of this type of arrangement:

• A buying club may consist of as few as ten to twelve families. Clubs often sell items to members practically at cost. Their small size eliminates the need for the usual supermarket overhead—such as trucks, large distribution centers, hired helpers.

• Members must be compatible—both in personality and in food tastes. Each member must be willing to do his or her share of the work load, to avoid having to hire the outside help which raises costs and defeats the purpose of small-group buying.

• There must be several people for each job: driving, simple bookkeeping, distributing, and buying. This system permits rotation of tasks and prevents any one member from being too heavily burdened.

• Members must be willing to do as much shopping as possible through the club.

• Buying is usually done by two or more buyers going once a week to wholesale markets, which are generally listed in the Yellow Pages. Each week, one buyer who has gone the week before accompanies a novice, to lend his or her previous experience (for example; a and b, then b and c, then c and d). The general shopping list for produce is: two types of fruit, one cooking vegetable, salad vegetables, potatoes, and onions. Meat is often ordered in advance from a distributor or a reliable local butcher who will give discounts.

• After the food is purchased, it is taken to a prearranged point for distribution, often a member's house or apartment. The food is sold at a price to cover the purchase price plus gasoline, oil, other incidentals.

• Buying clubs do *not* compete with each other. In fact, small clubs find it beneficial to co-operate in exchanging names of stores, recipes, and new ideas. Several buying clubs may co-operate on large-scale purchases for which an individual club would not receive a discount.

• A key problem for the clubs may be losses resulting from spoilage of unsold goods. This leftover food might be sold to outsiders via a "leftover list" of names of people who may be called after members have shopped.

• Another problem might arise when members feel that small children prevent them from participating. Some buying clubs have successfully added a baby-sitting system to their operation on buying days.

• Members should pay for their food not later than the day before the next week's buying. Members who regularly fail to pay on time, refuse to help, or do little buying harm the club. It is often best for the club to drop such members.

There must be open discussion of disagreements in order to reach constructive answers to the club's problems, whatever they turn out to be.

• Buying clubs of this type report big savings. The clubs find, moreover, that the quality of their food improves as well. And they have more bargaining power since wholesalers try to please large purchasers.

WHOLESALE UNITS

Here are the wholesale units in which food is boxed or weighed for wholesale:

DAIRY AND PRODUCE

1. American cheese—5 lbs.
2. Eggs—30 doz.
3. Rice—25, 50, 100 lbs. (bags)
4. Lettuce—24 (box)
5. Tomatoes—20 lbs. (box)
6. Potatoes—50 lbs. (bag)

7. Onions—50 lbs. (bag)
8. Apples—36 or 40 lbs. (box)
9. Oranges—48, 56, 64, 72, 80 (box)
10. Bananas—40 lbs. (box)

MEATS (may vary from place to place)

1. Chicken—one
2. Ground chuck—10 lbs. or more
3. Bacon—12 lbs. (box)
4. Frankfurters—12 lbs. (box)
5. Flank steak—15 lbs.
6. Stew beef—10 lbs.
7. Pork chops—16–20 lbs.
8. Spare ribs—30 lbs.
9. Liver—8–11 lbs.

WHERE TO GET INFORMATION

An excellent source of further information on food-buying clubs and co-ops and on shopping for wholesale foods is: The Cooperative League of the U.S.A., Suite 1100, 1828 L Street, N.W., Washington, D.C. 20036.

FROM FARMER DIRECTLY TO YOU

The direct marketing of farm products to consumers—using farmers' markets, "tailgate" markets and "pick-your-own" farms—also has achieved a legitimacy and clout it never had before.

Farmers' markets, roadside produce stalls as well as food co-ops are hardly new ideas, and throughout the U.S. individuals and groups have been forming them in mounting numbers in recent years as alternative marketing networks.

Farmers as well as you, consumers the nation over, can benefit from this food marketing scheme and can, of course, copy it. The advantages are many and intriguing.

For instance, food shoppers may save from 25 to 50 per cent! The average saving of shoppers involved in any direct marketing plan in one northeast state was in this 25–50 per cent range as the 1980s neared on such produce as vegetables, fruit, milk, eggs, etc.—the saving representing the markup that retailers add to cover waste, spoilage, handling costs.

NEW COMPETITOR IN FOOD INDUSTRY—YOU

In sum, YOU are the new, unexpectedly tough type of competition springing up in the food industry the nation over.

You, as an individual and in groups, are forming food co-ops and food-buying clubs, also supporting roadside markets, farmers' markets, "pick-your-own" farms, community gardens, canning centers.

While buying directly from growers is an ancient idea, you have re-embraced it to an extraordinary degree. What you, the budget-conscious shopper, are saying in unmistakable terms is that the conveniences of the supermarkets—ranging from the vast array of products to the huge parking lots and background music as you buy—are no longer worth the costs added to the family food bill.

What's more, joining you in supporting direct marketing schemes are small farmers, particularly in the Eastern sections of the United States. In the past thirty years, the United States has lost at least 3 million farmers, as small farmers have been forced out of existence by the big agribusinesses and major food chains. Not able to deliver the total volume and variety demanded by big chains or wholesalers, they have been compelled to close down.

Unable to supply food chains with adequate quantities of one brand for their hundreds of stores, small food processors also have been pushed out of business.

The result: many farmers have been turning to consumers directly at the precise time that many consumers have been searching for ways to cut the costs of our present food-marketing system.

An overview of the new farmer-to-consumer schemes divides them into two categories:

(1) Individual producer-to-individual consumer or one-to-one programs. Here belongs the traditional roadside produce stall and "pick-your-own" farms, where you, the consumer, swap your labor for the freshest produce and low prices while the farmer gets a better price than he would at wholesale.

(2) Groups—middle-income families who band together to hold down food expenditures, natural food advocates, or organizations set up to provide low-cost food to the poor in inner cities.

The beginning generally is the establishment of buying clubs, with the goal of buying in wholesale lots and dividing the lot into single family orders that have been taken in advance.

An evolution may change a buying club into a structured food co-op. These, in turn, may develop into chains of retail stores, with dual pricing structures: one price for the general public, another for members of the profit-sharing venture.

CAN YOUR KITCHEN PASS THE FOOD STORAGE TEST?

Have you found that "perfect" place under the sink to store food? Do you store foods in the cabinets that are so conveniently built in over the stove? Do you automatically use the taste test to be sure foods are still good?

If your answer is yes to any of these questions, you are one of millions of Americans who are throwing away startlingly large sums of money each year in the kitchen—possibly hundreds of dollars in your own case alone—because of your improper storage of food.

"It'll never happen, but if the Food and Drug Administration were to inspect every family kitchen in the United States for proper storage of foods, most of them probably would flunk," was the candid admission of a member of the Food and Drug Administration's consumer education and information staff. To be specific:

Under the sink is not only far from the "perfect" place to store food; it's also a dangerous spot. Pipes passing through the area can leak and provide unsealable openings to draw bugs as well. Avoid this popular spot, the FDA warns.

As for storage shelves near your stove, you're inviting loss because the foods dry up in these places. Even dry mixes, which may be held at room temperature, will not keep well near the stove, food handling experts emphasize.

And the taste test is actually a way of begging for medical bills. You don't have to swallow foods that have gone bad to be poisoned. If it's old food and you have reasons to doubt its freshness, don't taste. Throw it away.

Almost always when I write about saving money on food, I have stressed food shopping hints. But it well may be that more of your food dollars are lost through improper storage of food than through poor shopping practices!

To assure the safety and quality of the food you have bought, proper storage is imperative. So: draw up a check list to inspect your kitchen; be your own inspector; make a list of the changes that you discover are needed—and then make them.

• Thoroughly check the cabinets underneath the kitchen sink, or any cabinets through which water pipes, drain pipes, or heating pipes pass. This is a favorite spot to store sacks of onions or potatoes. Perhaps you have placed liquids or canned goods here—but foods never should be stored in these cabinets. They attract insects, even rodents, through openings that you'll find almost impossible to seal adequately. Also, leakage from the pipes can damage the food products, causing cans, for instance, to become overheated or rusty.

• Never store anything you plan to eat next to potent household chemicals. Bottles of cleaning chemicals can too easily be mistaken for bottles of soft drinks or other foods. Oil and vinegar may make a delicious salad dressing—but not oil and a tasteless but dangerous chemical.

• Give special care to foods that should be refrigerated or frozen, for bacteria in these foods multiply with amazing rapidity under favorable conditions. Cold foods should be kept cold. With this guide in mind, look at the open surfaces in your kitchen. Any meat thawing at room temperature? Do you put away that carton of milk or quart of orange juice as soon as you return from the supermarket?

• Rethink your ways of keeping bread, for, say FDA experts, under normal conditions, bread keeps fresher longer at room temperatures than in the refrigerator. In hot, humid weather, bread is better protected against mold in the refrigerator.

• Go over your stock of canned goods, reaching all the way to the back of the most inaccessible shelf. Dust on the cans? It's time to clean the tops. Any foreign matter on the tops of the cans will be pressed into the food itself during the opening.

• When you pick up the can, if it sticks slightly, it could have leakage, the FDA warns. Return the can to the store.

• When checking your pantry, reread the labels on the foods stored. Perhaps some should have been refrigerated. Not all boxed or canned goods can be held at room temperature. Canned cheeses such as Brie and Camembert, for instance, should be kept under refrigeration even before opening.

• Double-check the directions on your container of grated Parmesan cheese. Some containers require refrigeration after opening; other containers don't.

• Protect your syrups from mold by keeping them in the refrigerator. If crystals form in refrigerated honey or syrup, place the containers in hot water before use.

• Keep peanut butter in the refrigerator after opening. Let it stand at room temperature for a while before use.

• Get clear in your mind that refrigeration and freezing do not kill bacteria in food; they simply stop the bacteria from spreading. When food is thawed, the bacteria become active and resume spreading. Thus, foods should be prepared as soon as possible after thawing.

• Many foods that are stored in the refrigerator deteriorate rapidly and should be prepared for the table within a day or two of home storage. For instance: broths, gravies, stuffings, chicken salad, potato salad, poultry, fish, liver, kidneys, brains and giblets.

• Wrap fresh meat for freezing loosely enough to allow air to circulate but not loose enough to let the product dry out. But leftovers should be tightly wrapped and covered.

• Always arrange food in the freezer so that the oldest package is used first.

• Don't stack foods. Refrigerator shelves should not be covered since this impedes air circulation. Produce belongs in lower compartments. This prevents crystalization.

• Immerse leftover egg yolks in cold water and cover them in the refrigerator. Don't keep them more than four days. Whites of eggs require no water. Place milk, meats, and poultry in the coldest part of the appliance—the area nearest the freezing unit.

How to Read Food Labels

Q. *What is the difference between chicken "patties" and chicken "burgers"—in terms of the amount of chicken each contains?*
A. Chicken burgers must consist of 100 per cent chicken. If cereals or other fillers are used, they must be labeled patties.

Q. *How much meat must spaghetti with meatballs contain?*
A. Twelve per cent or more meat.

Q. *What's the difference between "beef and gravy" and "gravy and beef"?*
A. In beef and gravy, the primary ingredient is beef. With gravy and beef, it's the other way around.

These and other vital details, which are at least implied by the labels of hundreds of food products you buy regularly—or which may be stated among our many federal food standards—are key clues to how much of a bargain you are getting for your food dollar. Many labels tell you, too, how much of major nutrients, especially protein, are contained in each can or package.

The true value of what you are buying lies in what amounts of basic ingredients you are getting—not simply in the net weight of the food. Thus, by knowing something about food standards and some of the rules for reading food labels, you can consistently stretch your food dollar.

Here is a valuable rundown on labels and standards to use to compare products and prices in the supermarket:

• Under federal law, every package of food, drugs, or cosmetics must contain the following information on its label in plain English: name of the product; name and address of manufacturer, packer, or distributor; net amount of contents or weight in pounds and ounces and in the total number of ounces; details of dietary characteristics, if appropriate; note of whether the product contains artificial coloring, flavoring, or chemical preservatives; a list of the ingredients, except for certain products (e.g., mayonnaise, macaroni, bread, jams, ketchup, canned fruits and vegetables) for which federal "standards of identity" defining basic ingredients have been established.

• Next, certain descriptive details are required for certain products, primarily canned fruits and vegetables; the variety (white or yellow corn, for instance); style of pack (whole, diced); material in which packaged (sugar, syrup, water).

• Ingredients must be listed in *descending* order of their volume (if a beef stew list shows beef way down and potatoes way up on the list, this is your clue that you are buying mostly potatoes).

• If the food is an imitation and not as nutritious as the product it resembles, this fact must be stated, and if there is a picture of the product within, it must be accurate.

• Baby food labels must state the nutritional elements they contain—proteins, vitamins, minerals—plus, in the case of strained baby foods, a list of the ingredients.

• Meats and other foods to which special vitamins and minerals have been added or which are claimed to have special nutritional properties ("enriched") must carry labels telling their calorie content, amounts of proteins, and amounts of key vitamins and minerals.

• On the major cuts of the carcasses, meats may carry the U. S. Department of Agriculture's inspection stamp. Federally inspected poultry—fresh or frozen—carries a stamp "inspected for wholesomeness."

• Then there are federal standards covering a host of prepared and convenience foods, especially those containing meat or poultry, that are not stated on the label.

• In addition, you may or may not find on a food package a brand name; directions for storage or suggestions for cooking; a food quality grade set by the Department of Agriculture.

"NUTRITIONAL RETURN": BEST FOOD-BUYING RULE OF ALL?

Q. *Which of these canned soups is the most nutritious: (a) turkey noodle; (b) onion; (c) lentil-tomato; (d) Manhattan-style clam chowder?*

A. Lentil-tomato is twelve times as nutritious as onion soup—and therefore twelve times the bargain if the price for each can is the same. Lentil-tomato is nearly seven times as nutritious as turkey noodle soup and five times as vitamin-mineral-protein-packed as Manhattan clam chowder.

Q. *Which of these vegetables is the best nutritionally: (a) frozen collard greens; (b) frozen green beans; (c) celery; (d) canned carrots?*

A. Frozen collard greens are twice as nutritious as canned carrots, five times as nutritious as cut green beans and eighteen times as nutritious as an equivalent amount of celery.

Q. *Which of these fruits has the most nutrition value:* (*a*) *cantaloupe;* (*b*) *strawberries;* (*c*) *plum;* (*d*) *pear?*

A. A serving of cantaloupe contains twice the nutrition that a helping of strawberries contains, five times as much nutritional value as a pear and nine times as much as a plum.

These samplings underline one of the least known but surely most important food saving rules you have today:

Specifically, that among the hundreds of "how to save" rules I and others have submitted to you, "the nutritional return" on your food dollar well may be the most valuable of all—although few of you have any concept of it.

For instance, simply by choosing lentil-tomato soup, you can get a whopping twelve times the food value that you can get from an equal amount of onion soup. Or by selecting collard greens over frozen green beans, you'll get five times the food bargain, in terms of the actual benefit of the food to you. Or by buying cantaloupe instead of plums, you'll get nine times the nutritional return for each dollar you spend on each fruit.

The scoring system involves "plus" points for the amounts of protein, key vitamins and minerals, starch and fiber, naturally occurring sugar and unsaturated fat (from vegetables, oils, nuts, fish, and margarine). Foods get "minus" points for sugar and corn syrup added by the manufacturer and for saturated fats (e.g., those found in meats and dairy products). Minus points also are given when fat becomes more than 20 per cent of the food's weight after removal of all moisture.

To illustrate, according to the Washington-headquartered Center for Science in the Public Interest, here's how a hamburger scores on the "Nutrition Scoreboard":

Protein 20; Carbohydrate 0; Vitamins 19; Minerals 8; Subtotal, 47; Fat —13; Total, Plus 34.

And here's how one popular candy bar scores:

Protein 3; Carbohydrate, natural, 3; Added sugar and corn syrup —48; Fat —4; Vitamins 7; Minerals 6; Total, Minus 33.

And which are the richest foods available today?

The "top five" vegetables with their scores are: collard greens, frozen (126); kale, with stems and midribs (118); broccoli, frozen (116); turnip greens (111); spinach, frozen (104).

The highest scoring meats are beef liver (172); chicken liver (158); liver sausage (104); chicken breast (62); tuna fish (55).

The highest scoring fruits are cantaloupe (99); watermelon (74); orange (68); strawberries (50); grapefruit (45).

The top snacks are: granola and milk; almonds; peach; peanuts, plain granola. The best dairy products are: skim milk; buttermilk; low fat yogurt; Swiss cheese; whole milk. Other big "nutrition bargains" are: orange juice, V-8 juice, tomato juice, rye, whole-wheat and pumpernickel bread, brown rice, enriched pasta, cheese and cottage cheese.

Valuable nutrition information has in recent years been added to the labels of many foods. A label now tells you how many calories are in a serving and also the amount of protein, fat, carbohydrates, and the percentage of U.S. Recommended Daily Allowances (U.S. RDA) of important vitamins and minerals. With this information you can plan better meals for your family as well as get better value for your money.

More meaningful disclosures still are essential, however, in these areas:

Drained weight: If we knew the net weight of soups, minus water, for instance, we could compare the volume of real food—meat, vegetables, etc.—in various soups. In many cases, we would find concentrated, thick meaty soup is a much greater value at 45 cents a can than a watered-down equivalent at 30 cents.

Key ingredients: Labels should tell us much more clearly what proportion of "beef stew" actually is beef, what proportion of fruit is in a fruit drink.

Recommended food storage conditions: Labels should specify how long a package of frozen beans may be kept in the freezer, for instance.

A universal simple "ABC" grading system: Such a system for foods would eliminate our confusion because of the variety of federal food-grading systems (especially important in meat).

"TRUTH IN MEAT" LABELING

Look carefully in your supermarket meat counter. Has the piece of beef you've known as "California roast" been transformed into a "Beef Chuck—Under Blade Roast"? Has the old-time "London broil" been renamed a "Beef Flank Steak"? Or the traditional "Delmonico steak" reappeared as "Beef Rib—Eye Steak"?

Starting in late 1973, a whole new system of meat labeling was introduced in supermarkets, meat markets, and grocery stores from coast to coast. The "Truth in Meat" program is voluntary but it is the meat industry's big push to let you know not only what you're getting for your money but also how to cook it.

Thus, here's what to look for in the stores where you do your meat buying:

• Each package of meat labeled with the name of the animal species (beef, veal, pork, lamb); the "primal cut"—breast or brisket, shoulder (chuck) arm, shoulder (chuck) blade; rib, loin, sirloin (hip), and leg (round); and one of its more than three hundred common, standardized retail names. (In addition, if it wants to, a store may add its own fanciful name—such as "his and her" steaks or "Paradise roast.") Hamburger, though, is "ground beef" or "ground sirloin" or "ground chuck." T-bone steak is beefloin T-bone.

• The lean meat ratio of ground meat labeled, with the maximum percentage of fat set at 25 per cent.

• A variety of booklets and meat identification charts available next to meat counter—giveaways detailing both the "what you're getting" and "how to cook it" angles.

The system has been hailed by the meat industry as "the most significant meat-counter improvement since the introduction of self-service nearly four decades ago." But it is just one more step toward real consumer information protection at the meat counter. There's a long way to go.

"OPEN DATING"

"Open dating" means the clear marking on all packages or containers of perishable or semi-perishable foods with a date "pull" after which they should be removed from sale to you. These products are guaranteed to have a normal period of use in the home after the date. As a result of this form of labeling, disappearing from store shelves are the cryptic grocery codes that tell store managers the condition of the foods on sale but make a secret of the same information to us.

To get the maximum benefit:

(1) Learn the basic fact that the date on a package or container of perishable foods is frequently the "pull" date—the last permissible day of sale for that item from its normal shelf position in the store. After that day the product must be removed from regular sale.

(2) If you see an item on sale after that date, it should be in an off-shelf special display position and be offered at a greatly reduced price. It also must still be safe for consumption, of course.

(3) If you find cryptic codes on some items, ask the store for an explanation or for a free explanatory booklet and be sure you understand.

(4) If you do discover that you have bought an out-of-date item that was not on special sale as such, take it back at once and demand a refund.

(5) Use your own head about the proper storage and refrigeration of perishables. According to a Rutgers University study, temperature is seven times as important as time in maintaining freshness—and that applies whether you have the food on hand or whether it is still in the store. Don't buy perishables and then stop on the way home to have lunch or pick up your children or whatever.

How to Compare Unit Costs per Pound of Food

WHICH IS THE BIGGER BARGAIN?

Q. *Which is the bigger bargain: $4.77 for a box of powder to make 20 quarts of a popular drink or $3.27 for a box to make 12 quarts of the same brand of the drink?*

A. The 20-quart package works out to 24¢ a quart and is therefore a bigger bargain than the 12-quart package which works out to 27¢ a quart.

Q. *Which is cheaper: a 1-lb. 2-oz. jar of a spread costing 53¢ or a 12-oz. jar of the same brand costing 35¢?*

A. Neither. In both cases, the per pound cost is 47¢.

Q. *Which is more economical: a 1-lb. 14-oz. can of a sliced fruit costing 47¢ or an 8½-oz. can costing 21¢?*

A. The larger can—by far. The cost is 25¢ a pound in the larger can, but 40¢ a pound in the small can.

These illustrations underline the extent to which you, the manager of the family pocketbook, can make errors in your purchases if you do not know the price per measure as well as the total dollar price.

At the same time, the comparisons indicate the enormous savings which you can achieve by buying large versus small packages. You don't have to be a mathematical genius to figure out, just from these few examples, that you could save hundreds of dollars per year—without necessarily sacrificing any quality in any item—just by buying the large package sizes instead of the small.

But there are infuriating exceptions. In one study of one major dry detergent, the per ounce cost of the *largest* available size (more than 16 pounds) was significantly *greater* than the cost of either of the next two smaller sizes.

The trend across the land is toward new laws requiring retailers to provide shelf labels under each item with a price per ounce, quart, pound, or other unit as well as with the total retail price for the package. Most of the major retail food chains now use some kind of unit pricing system. In almost every major city the pricing system has become available. Increasing numbers of states have laws requiring unit pricing on a statewide basis.

In this era of record and rising food prices, unit pricing could be the U.S. food shopper's biggest money-saving weapon. For it is virtually your sole means of comparing the true unit cost of what you buy in the supermarket.

HOW TO USE UNIT PRICING

Next time you go to the food store, look on the edge of the shelf under the article you are considering buying. If the store uses unit pricing, you will find a label which tells the cost per measure (pound, pint, number, etc.) of the item. That's the unit price. This breaks down the total cost of the particular package or can into a simple standard so that you can now choose between brands and sizes on the basis of price.

You'll find other numbers on most labels, but they'll be inventory numbers which you need not bother about.

For instance, say you are buying a canned juice.

A 46-ounce can of a store brand is priced two for 65¢, the unit price is 23¢ a quart; a 1-quart bottle of brand A sells for 35¢ a quart; an 18-ounce of brand B sells at two for 35¢, the unit price is 31¢ a quart; a six-pack of 5½-ounce cans of brand B sells at 51¢, the unit price is 49¢ a quart.

If you look at the unit prices, it will be easy to find the best buy. And surely it's worthwhile to discover that you can buy more than two quarts of the first for the price of one quart of the fourth. With prices given per quart, all you need to do is look and compare.

Of course, you will shop for quality and in terms of your personal preferences too—but why not use unit pricing to save money when quality is not of prime importance and when you have no special preferences? *Why not use the weapon now that you have it?*

To be blunt about it, if you don't use unit pricing, your lethargy will border on plain stupidity.

PACKAGE WEIGHT (IN OUNCES)	COST PER POUND IF THE COST PER PACKAGE IS:				
	5¢	10¢	15¢	20¢	25¢
1	$ .80	$1.60	$2.40	$3.20	$4.00
2	.40	.80	1.20	1.60	2.00
3	.27	.53	.80	1.07	1.33
4	.20	.40	.60	.80	1.00
5	.16	.32	.48	.64	.80
6	.13	.27	.40	.53	.67
7	.11	.23	.34	.46	.57
8	.10	.20	.30	.40	.50
9	.09	.18	.27	.36	.44
10	.08	.16	.24	.32	.40
11	.07	.15	.22	.29	.36
12	.07	.13	.20	.27	.33
13	.06	.12	.18	.25	.31
14	.06	.11	.17	.23	.29
15	.05	.11	.16	.21	.27
16	.05	.10	.15	.20	.25
17	.05	.09	.14	.19	.24
18	.04	.09	.13	.18	.22
19	.04	.08	.13	.17	.21
20	.04	.08	.12	.16	.20
21	.04	.08	.11	.15	.19
22	.04	.07	.11	.15	.18
23	.03	.07	.10	.14	.17
24	.03	.07	.10	.13	.17
25	.03	.06	.10	.13	.16
26	.03	.06	.09	.12	.15
27	.03	.06	.09	.12	.15
28	.03	.06	.09	.11	.14
29	.03	.06	.08	.11	.14
30	.03	.05	.08	.11	.13
31	.03	.05	.08	.11	.13
32	.03	.05	.08	.10	.13
33	.02	.05	.07	.10	.12
34	.02	.05	.07	.09	.12
35	.02	.05	.07	.09	.11
36	.02	.04	.07	.09	.11
37	.02	.04	.06	.09	.11
38	.02	.04	.06	.08	.11
39	.02	.04	.06	.08	.10
40	.02	.04	.06	.08	.10

PACKAGE WEIGHT (IN OUNCES)	COST PER POUND IF THE COST PER PACKAGE IS:				
	30¢	35¢	40¢	45¢	50¢
1	$4.80	$5.60	$6.40	$7.20	$8.00
2	2.40	2.80	3.20	3.60	4.00
3	1.60	1.87	2.13	2.40	2.67
4	1.20	1.40	1.60	1.80	2.00
5	.96	1.12	1.28	1.44	1.60
6	.80	.93	1.07	1.20	1.33
7	.69	.80	.91	1.03	1.14
8	.60	.70	.80	.90	1.00
9	.53	.62	.71	.80	.89
10	.48	.56	.64	.72	.80
11	.44	.51	.58	.65	.73
12	.40	.47	.53	.60	.67
13	.37	.43	.49	.55	.62
14	.34	.40	.46	.51	.57
15	.32	.37	.43	.48	.53
16	.30	.35	.40	.45	.50
17	.28	.33	.38	.42	.47
18	.27	.31	.36	.40	.44
19	.25	.29	.34	.38	.42
20	.24	.28	.32	.36	.40
21	.23	.27	.30	.34	.38
22	.22	.25	.29	.33	.36
23	.21	.24	.28	.31	.35
24	.20	.23	.27	.30	.33
25	.19	.22	.26	.29	.32
26	.18	.22	.25	.28	.31
27	.18	.21	.24	.27	.30
28	.17	.20	.23	.26	.29
29	.17	.19	.22	.25	.28
30	.16	.19	.21	.24	.27
31	.15	.18	.21	.23	.26
32	.15	.18	.20	.23	.25
33	.15	.17	.19	.22	.24
34	.14	.16	.19	.21	.24
35	.14	.16	.18	.21	.23
36	.13	.16	.18	.20	.22
37	.13	.15	.17	.19	.22
38	.13	.15	.17	.19	.21
39	.12	.14	.16	.18	.21
40	.12	.14	.16	.18	.20

NOTES: *Change the weight on a package to ounces if necessary:*
    1 pound = 16 ounces
    1 pint = 16 fluid ounces

UNIT COST TABLE

Unit pricing is not yet universal—not by far.

And one survey revealed, shoppers made the "wrong" choices a shocking 40 per cent of the time on which can or bottle or package was cheapest—on a per-ounce or per-pound basis—*when the packages were not unit-priced*. These errors translated into an average of 10¢ on every $1.00 spent in the grocery store. Thus, on a food bill of $100, $10 may be going down the drain simply because you are not choosing the most economical food.

So until unit pricing is in every store, see the "Cost Weight Table" which you can translate on your own into extraordinary savings. Copy it and put it into your purse to refer to when you shop from now on.

To calculate the unit cost of a product, no matter what size or shape package it comes in, first locate the net weight of the food package in the left-hand column. Then locate the total price of the package along the top of the table. These reference points will lead you directly to the price per pound in the appropriate middle column. By comparing the unit cost of one package with another size, you can discover which is the better bargain.

This will help you figure out weights which are in between a single pound or pint. For instance, 1 pound 10 ounces or 1 pint 10 ounces may be translated into 16 ounces plus 10 ounces, or 26 ounces. Thus, if a product weighs 26 ounces and is priced at 35¢, the price per pound is 22¢.

You can use this table if a package weighs more than 40 ounces or more than 50 cents. Just divide the weight and price of any package weighing more than 40 ounces by 2 and, with the resulting figures, use the table above. Or just divide the price and weight of any package priced at more than 50¢ by 2 and also use the table above.

HOW TO SAVE ON MEAT

GENERAL MONEY-SAVING HINTS

The retail price you pay for meat is not necessarily a reliable guide to its quality, nutritive value, *or* tenderness. Meat prices, instead, depend on such factors as the popularity of a given meat cut or brand or grade; the season of the year; the type of store in which the meat is sold; the type and amount of handling and processing.

As a general rule, beef prices are lower in winter and higher in late summer. Steak prices tend to be highest during the summer "cookout" months and roasts cost more in the late fall and early winter "oven-cooking" months. In contrast, veal prices tend to be lowest in the spring and summer and highest in the winter.

Now here are vitally important general hints for saving money on meat—including "old" ones which a surprising number of Americans have been pulling out of their memories and "new" ones recently put together by consumer economists:

• Shift your family to less expensive cuts of each type of meat. Since nearly four fifths of the beef we buy is *not* naturally tender enough to broil, barbecue, or roast, in this area you will find your biggest meat bargains. With a little special handling, the less expensive cuts can be made virtually as tender and tasteful as the costlier cuts.

Important note: The nutrient content of these cuts is at least as great as that of the more expensive cuts while the fat content in most cases is significantly lower. Nutritionists unanimously agree that consumption of leaner beef should be encouraged for health reasons and as a brake on rising prices. (See Protein Bargains chart, pages 97–99, for details on this point.) For example, you can buy good chuck steaks and roasts at bargain prices. Short ribs are another delicious cut of beef which you can barbecue indoors or out. So are beef shank, brisket, and short loin. Lamb chops cut from the shoulder often cost 20 to 40 cents less per pound than rib or loin chips.

Among the other less expensive cuts and types of meat are: ground beef, stew meat, pot roast, beef shank, brisket, short loin, heel of round roast, pork shoulder and rump, lamb shanks, ground lamb.

Among steaks, some of the least expensive cuts are blade and arm chuck steaks, flank steak, sirloin tip, and bottom round. The "broiling steaks"—sirloin, porterhouse, etc.—rarely are bargains except as occasional sales features.

• Experiment with the help of your gourmet cookbook, preparing such "variety" meats as liver, heart, sweetbreads, tripe, kidneys, tongue, brains. Most of these rank high in nutrition. They also are among the "great" foods in Europe and are served in the finest French restaurants everywhere.

• Save simply by learning the cooking rules in your cookbook. You will save an impressive amount on meats, for instance, if you roast them at no more than 300° to 325° F. They will shrink less; be more tender; be easier to carve. Remember, the higher the temperature of your oven, the more your meats will shrink.

• Check what "family packs" are available—such as bulk hamburger, chops, chicken. Meat in larger quantities is almost invariably offered at lower prices than in smaller packages. You can always do a bit of home butchering—e.g., cutting your own rib steaks from an extra-thick roast beef or cutting a whole pork loin three ways. (An inexpensive hack saw with a good blade will substitute for a butcher's saw when you have to cut through bone.) You can then use the center section as chops, which will cost you considerably less than if you buy the chops in a package by themselves. Or, if you buy bologna, buy it in a chunk. By slicing it at home, you may cut an impressive percentage per pound from the piece.

• Try buying 2- or 3-pound boxes of bacon "ends and pieces." It may be slightly less lean than regularly packaged bacon and it's not cut uniformly. But it comes from the same animal and may cost only one third or one half what regular bacon costs. Also, consider bacon a condiment rather than meat in view of its high cost per serving and try to serve only two pieces per person instead of three or four. Typically, a pound of bacon dwindles to 3 to 5 ounces and some brands yield as little as 10 to 18 per cent of their original volume.

• Study and compare prices of canned meats—ham, beef roast, corned beef, chopped beef, luncheon loaves, meat in barbecue sauce, turkey, and chicken, to name just a few. Every ounce of these is edible. Canned-meat meals tend to be even greater money- and time-savers for small families.

• Don't overfeed your family with meat, a definitely concentrated source of calories. Overweight is one of our country's leading health problems, and the top cause for overweight is overeating. Meat also tends to be high in cholesterol. There is no reason to feed any family member more than 6 to 8 ounces of meat in one meal. Or try experimenting with even smaller servings (e.g., 3 ounces per meal) for a week—and see who, if anybody, screams.

• When you buy ground beef, try the least expensive forms first and "work your way up" if these don't satisfy your tastes. In a major study of hamburger, Consumers Union found that the price difference from hamburger grade to grade— e.g., from ground beef to ground chuck to ground round—was as much as 40 cents a pound in the same store, although analysis showed that the differences in amounts of fat, water, and protein were "indistinguishable."

• Try buying meat at local discount stores, where you frequently can achieve significant savings over supermarkets (though they may not offer the convenience of the supermarket).

• Shop for meat in terms of meals—and consider, as you buy, what you'll do with the leftovers. Plan to use all the meat you buy. Melt down fat trimmings for drippings; simmer bones and lean cuttings for soup stock and gravy.

• If scales are available for you to use in the supermarket in which you shop, *use them* to reweigh prepriced meat packages. And if you find any discrepancy, point this out immediately to the store manager.

• Read labels with care. Also remember that 3½ pounds is not 3 pounds 5 ounces but 3 pounds 8 ounces.

• Check and compare prices of prefrozen and imported meat. For example, you'll almost surely save by buying frozen lamb which has been imported from Australia or New Zealand.

THE TRUE COST OF A SERVING OF MEAT

Buy according to the true value of any type or cut of meat—as measured in terms of the true cost of a given portion of the final cooked product.

As a rule of thumb, you get two or three cooked servings from each pound of roast beef, pork, lamb, or veal, whole ham, chicken or turkey, trimmed fish, certain types of steaks and chops. And you get only one or two servings from each pound of meat loaded with fat, bone, and gristle—such as rib chops, spareribs, short ribs, plate and breast of veal, lamb shank, chicken wings and backs, T-bone or porterhouse steaks.

Here is a rundown of servings per pound of various meats. Fill in the current cost of each item in your area. Then figure the cost per serving by dividing the per-pound price by the number of servings. This is your key guide to where the bargains are.

MEAT	APPROXIMATE SERVINGS PER POUND	RETAIL PRICE PER POUND	COST PER SERVING
Beef			
Hamburger	4	————	————
Sirloin steak	3	————	————
Round steak	3	————	————
Rump roast, boneless	3	————	————
Chuck roast	3	————	————
Rib roast, with bone	2	————	————
Pork, fresh			
Pork chops	2½	————	————
Loin roast	2½	————	————
Pork, smoked			
Canned ham, boneless	4	————	————
Cooked ham, with bone	3½	————	————
Picnic shoulder, with bone	2½	————	————
Poultry			
Turkey	2	————	————
Frying chicken	2	————	————

PROTEIN BARGAINS

Compare meat prices by finding out how much of a "protein bargain" you are getting.

To illustrate: here is a breakdown on three key price categories of beef you can buy today—showing the relative amounts of protein, fat, and calories in one lean 3½-ounce cooked serving of each cut:

	PROTEIN (GRAMS)	FAT (GRAMS)	TOTAL CALORIES
Most Tender Cuts			
Standing rib roast	25	15	242
Tenderloin	26	13	224
Porterhouse steak	25	15	247
T-bone steak	26	19	280
Club steak	25	17	262
Rib steak	26	11	208
Top sirloin steak	22	21	285
Medium Tender Cuts			
Standing rump roast or rolled rump roast	32	11	235
Sirloin tip roast	30	4	168
Sirloin tip steak	27	6	166

	PROTEIN (GRAMS)	FAT (GRAMS)	TOTAL CALORIES
Medium Tender Cuts			
Heel of round	33	5	189
Full cut round steak	38	8	229
Top round steak	39	7	229
Bottom round steak or roast	36	10	238
Eye of round steak or roast	38	6	219
Stew meat—round	33	13	260
Flank steak	34	7	209
Less Tender Cuts			
Short ribs or cross ribs	32	15	272
English cut or Boston cut	33	14	263
Blade chuck pot roast, blade chuck steak, or boneless shoulder steak	35	17	298
Arm chuck pot roast, arm chuck or bone, less shoulder steak	35	8	219
Rolled shoulder roast	33	14	263

Just divide the prevailing price by the number of calories or amount of protein in any of these cuts. The resulting figure will tell you how much of a calorie bargain or protein bargain each cut is.

An even more direct route to the best protein bargains is knowing the cost of various forms of protein—meats, fishes, and meat alternatives. To calculate the price per gram of protein, divide the current price per pound (or quart or dozen) being charged in your area for the foods listed in the table below by the number of grams listed.

FOOD	GRAMS OF PROTEIN PER POUND
Lima beans	78.9
Peanut butter	72.0
Pork and beans	27.5
Beef liver	88.9
Chicken	72.3
Eggs	71.0 (per dozen)
Cottage cheese	64.0

FOOD	GRAMS OF PROTEIN PER POUND
American cheese	107.0
Tuna fish	118.5
Hamburger	86.4
Milk	33.8 (per quart)
Ocean perch	69.9
Fish sticks	78.7
Chili con carne	39.3
Whole ham	58.2
Frankfurters	56.0
Beef chuck steak	43.0
Round steak	79.6
Pizza	41.7
Bologna	48.7
Bacon	42.8
Rib roast	47.4
Sirloin steak	63.6

Of course, protein is by no means the only key nutrient. It's vitally important to know that pork is rich in thiamin, that cheese is rich in calcium, that beans contain large amounts of vitamin B₆ and magnesium. Probably your best source of nutritional details is the U. S. Department of Agriculture's Home and Garden Bulletin No. 94, entitled "Family Food Budgeting for Good Meals and Good Nutrition."

HOW TO USE BEEF "GRADES"

• Learn the U. S. Department of Agriculture grades of meat and use them not only to compare price and quality (tenderness, juiciness, and flavor) but also as a guide to the best meat for a particular type of meal.

The five top USDA beef grades are: prime, normally available only in restaurants, fancy meat stores, and from specialty mail-order houses; choice and good, the two grades most commonly found in supermarkets and butcher shops; standard and commercial, definitely inferior as far as your palate is concerned.

The top veal grades are: prime, choice, good, standard, and utility.

The top lamb grades are: prime, choice, and good. Spring lamb should bear the U. S. Government certification "Genuine Spring Lamb."

Choose lower meat grades. For instance, with beef, good versus choice; with lamb, choice versus prime. They may be less tender, but they are also leaner and equally nourishing. Using anything above U.S. good for chopped beef or stew meat is a waste of money, because in these cuts you do not need to worry, for example, about how tender the meat is.

Lower grades should cost even less. However, the taste may be equal if you cook them right—e.g., as pot roast—or if you apply such tenderizing techniques as grinding, pounding, marinating, pot-roasting, using commercial tenderizers, and cubing.

• As another guide to quality, study meat color and texture.

For general freshness, beef should be somewhere between light and dark red. Roasts and most steaks should be at least lightly "marbled" with fat.

Veal should be very pale grayish pink in color; the flesh should be firm and smooth. It should have almost no fat—just a thin coat outside.

Pork, too, should be pale pink and should have only a thin layer of fat.

Lamb should be a dull pink. Spring lamb should be colored somewhere between pink and red—not too dark—and it should have a velvety texture. The bone should be pinkish and there should be a slight amount of marbling.

BUT NUMBER 1: SHOP THE MEAT SPECIALS!

Your number 1 way to save on meat is to shop regularly and seriously for meat specials and stock your home freezer with your purchases. *You can save as much as one third on your meat bills* simply by buying meat at special rather than regular prices. Supermarket managers are well aware that meat prices determine where you will do the bulk of your shopping and offer specials every week. As a general rule, there are sales on beef twice a month, with poultry, pork, and lamb featured during other weeks. See preceding pages for table dramatizing the point.

Thursday, Friday, and Saturday remain the big days for meat specials, but also watch for specials on such off days as Monday, Tuesday, and even Sunday. (Try to shop as early in the day as possible.)

When you shop for advertised meat specials, make sure the price marked on the package reflects the advertised special. And if you can't find any packages left at the special price, remind the supermarket manager that a Federal Trade Commission rule requires that advertised specials be adequately stocked *at* or below the advertised special prices. At the very least, you should get a rain check.

Watch closely to see whether more fat has been left on the meat that's on sale —particularly on beef and pork chops.

Important note: On any given day you'll probably find only a limited number of items on special, and you'll also find that many if not most stores in your area will offer a very similar set of specials—particularly on weekends.

SAVINGS BY BUYING BEEF IN BULK

How about saving money by buying beef in bulk? Okay. No matter how casual a shopper you are, it's increasingly likely that you will try to curb your meat costs by buying beef in bulk and storing it in your home freezer.

But it's a good way to go—only *if* you are on guard against the estimated hundreds of "bait and switch" beef swindlers in the United States today . . . *if* you instead patronize one of thousands of entirely ethical freezer meat operators situated all over the country . . . and *if* you know and scrupulously obey the rules when you buy beef or other types of meat via the wholesale route.

Below you will find eleven specific rules for this type of buying:

(1) Do not buy a side of beef in hasty response to a tempting ad. If you really want and need as much beef as this and if you can arrange to store it properly, plan your purchase ahead, then shop intelligently for the meat.

(2) Before you buy, decide whether you will want a large quantity of steaks or whether your family will be happy with less fancy cuts or whether you would prefer to have a wide variety of cuts, including lots of stew meat and hamburger.

(3) To help yourself reach these decisions, study the beef-cut charts posted in your butcher shop or available from the U. S. Department of Agriculture in Washington.

(4) Use the following guide to tell you what proportion of what cuts you are likely to find in bulk beef.

In general, if you want more steaks and roasts, you'll probably want a hindquarter. A typical, trimmed beef hindquarter originally weighing about 200 pounds consists of 58 per cent steaks and oven roasts.

Here's the breakdown:

HINDQUARTER

Round steak	20.6%
Boneless rump roast	6.0
Sirloin steak	13.0
T-bone, porterhouse, club steak	10.1
Flank steak	.9
Total lean trim	17.1
Fat, bone, and shrinkage	32.3
TOTAL	100.0%

If you want a lot of stew beef and hamburger, you'll probably be best off with a forequarter. A typical, trimmed forequarter, originally weighing 215 to 220 pounds, breaks down into 37 per cent stew and ground meat.

Here's the breakdown on this:

FOREQUARTER

Rib roast	13.5%
Short ribs	6.4
Blade chuck	20.9
Arm chuck	12.5
Boneless brisket	4.1
Total lean trim	23.9
Fat, bone, and shrinkage	18.7
TOTAL	100.0%

If you want a wide variety of cuts, a half carcass will probably be the purchase for you. The usable meat from a whole beef carcass breaks down into approximately 25 per cent steaks, 25 per cent roasts, 25 per cent ground beef or stew, 25 per cent waste.

More specifically, a typical U.S. choice beef carcass weighing 300 pounds is likely to break down this way:

Retail Cuts	Per Cent of Carcass	Pounds
Round steak	11.0%	33.0 lbs.
Rump roast (boneless)	3.3	9.9
Porterhouse, T-bone, club steak	5.1	15.3
Sirloin steak	8.3	24.9
Rib roast	6.1	18.3
Chuck blade roast	8.9	26.7
Chuck arm roast (boneless)	5.8	17.4
Ground beef	11.1	33.3
Stew meat	10.3	30.9
Brisket	2.1	6.3
Flank steak	.5	1.5
Kidney	.3	.9
Total usable retail cuts	72.8	218.4
Waste (fat, bone, shrinkage)	27.2	81.6
TOTAL	100.0%	300.0 lbs.

And here are a few more important guides on other meats:

A lamb with a carcass weight of 50 pounds trims out to about 75 per cent legs, chops, and shoulders, 15 per cent breast and stew, 10 per cent bones and waste.

The breakdown for a typical lamb is:

Retail Cuts	Per Cent of Carcass	Pounds
Loin and sirloin chops	16.5%	8.25 lbs.
Rib shops	8.2	4.10
Legs (short cut)	20.5	10.25
Shoulder roast	22.3	11.15
Foreshanks	3.1	1.55
Breast	7.9	3.95
Flank	2.9	1.45
Stew meat	1.9	.95
Kidney	.5	.25
Total usable retail cuts	83.8	41.90
Waste (fat, bone, shrinkage)	16.2	8.10
TOTAL	100.0%	50.00 lbs.

A hog carcass weighing 175 pounds or so divides up into about 50 per cent hams, shoulders, and bacon, 20 per cent loins, ribs, and sausage, and most of the rest lard.

(5) Don't overlook the importance of "yield grades" in helping you avoid waste! In addition to the basic guides given you above, do you know that typical amounts of waste vary from beef side to beef side—from a minimum of about 20 per cent to as much as 34 per cent—a fact which greatly influences the real-life price you might pay for and the value you get from this beef?

The "yield grade" is among your best yardsticks of value if you are trying to save money by buying beef in bulk—for it gives you the vital clues on the percentages of the various boneless retail cuts you'll get after fat and bone have been trimmed away.

There are five yield grades, numbered 1 through 5, with 1 the highest, 5 the lowest.

The typical difference in amount of meat yields is 4.6 per cent between grades.

Here are the percentage yields of each grade level for a 600-pound beef carcass:

GRADE	FAT TRIM	BONE	EDIBLE MEAT
1	7.5%	10.5%	82.0%
2	12.6	10.0	77.4
3	17.7	9.5	72.8
4	22.8	9.0	68.2
5	27.9	8.5	63.6

And here is a more detailed comparison of the percentages of beef carcass weight of USDA yield grades 2 and 4. It's assumed that the meat is trimmed to a half inch of fat.

CUT	YIELD GRADE 2	YIELD GRADE 4
Rump, boneless	3.5%	3.1%
Inside round	4.5	3.7
Outside round	4.6	4.2
Round tip	2.6	2.4
Sirloin	8.7	7.9
Short loin	5.2	5.0
Rib, short cut (7″)	6.2	6.0
Blade chuck	9.4	8.4
Chuck, arm, boneless	6.1	5.5
Brisket, boneless	2.3	1.9
Flank steak	.5	.5
Lean trim	11.3	9.3
Ground beef	12.2	10.0
Fat	12.7	22.9
Bone	9.9	8.9
Kidney	.3	.3
TOTAL	100.0%	100.0%

With these statistics in mind when you are shopping for a side or a quarter of beef, you can get a good idea of the amounts of meat various grades will yield you after cutting and trimming. This will permit you to make sound comparisons with prices charged on beef cuts during the supermarket specials in your area.

And this in turn will tell you how much of a bargain—or non-bargain—each side of wholesale beef really is to you.

(6) When buying in bulk, figure not only what you are paying per pound for the actual meat minus fat, bones, etc., but also what price you are paying for cutting, packaging, and quick freezing. These procedures can substantially add to the net cost of your meat if they are not included in the basic price.

(7) If the ads include such terms as "beef order," "steak package," or "steak bundle," find out precisely what these terms mean and cover.

(8) If unbelievably low-priced "bonuses" are thrown in to sweeten the deal, use your head. No butcher can afford giveaways that are "unbelievable" and stay in business. *You* are the sucker.

(9) And never forget for a minute that the bait-and-switch racketeers use this sort of lure—for instance, ads for sides or quarters of beef at fantastically low prices—in order to bait you and then switch you to a much higher-priced carcass.

(10) If the deal involves payments by you on time, check whether the terms are spelled out as required under the Truth in Lending law—the total finance charge, the yearly percentage interest rate, the number and schedule of payments. Also, which bank or finance company actually will hold the paper you sign?

(11) Learn well the key signs of fresh, good-quality beef and other meats. For example, with beef, the bone should be ivory white, the sign of a young steer, not yellowed; the fat should be white as against yellow and there shouldn't be an excessive amount of fat; the tenderest beef is well marbled, meaning it has streaks of fat throughout the meat, but marbling also means calories and saturated fat.

How to Use Your Home Freezer for Top Savings

THE RULES

To take the maximum advantage of meat and other specials, and to have the convenience of a "supermarket" in your own home, you must have a home freezer.

But your savings must be compared to the cost of owning a home freezer—including depreciation, repairs, and electricity.

And there are disadvantages—in addition to annual costs summarized in the preceding paragraph. They include: the possibility of spoilage due to a power failure; the certainty of electricity rate rises in the years ahead; the nuisance of defrosting; the need to plan meals well in advance because the frozen food must be brought to room temperature or will need longer cooking time; the need to have space in which to keep the freezer; other minor annoyances.

But to millions, the advantages seem to win—which leads to the rules for getting the utmost benefits from your freezer:

• Package the meats to be frozen in sizes your family is likely to use and make sure each is tightly wrapped before freezing.

• Set your freezer at the lowest possible temperature the day before you intend to put in any large amount of meat to be frozen and, once frozen, hold the temperature at below 0° F.

• Don't add too much "warm" meat at a time—not more than 2 pounds per cubic feet of storage space. This means that large purchases, like the 100 pounds of meat, should be prefrozen by the meat packer in his large, high-powered freezer.

• Date and label with its contents each package of food you put in the freezer and consume your frozen food on a "first in, first out" basis.

• Stock your freezer as full as feasible for you; use the food frequently and re-stock; the higher the turnover of food, the lower the per pound cost to you.

• Keep all foods covered. Clean interiors regularly, including the defrost drainage tubes. Vacuum and wipe down coils and other mechanisms; dirt accumulation makes for inefficient operating.

• Open doors as little as possible to cut down frost. Defrost as often as necessary to keep no more than a fourth to a half inch of frost from accumulating. Don't place unit in a warm area—such as near the furnace. Check the gasket frequently to make certain it seals the door tightly.

• If you live in an area where your electricity goes off for as long as a day or so, set your freezer thermostat at 10° to 20° below zero or as low as it will go. If the power stays off longer, either take your frozen food to a freezer locker or put blocks of dry ice in your freezer. A 25-pound block should be enough to keep the contents of your freezer below zero for two to three days.

• Make sure your frozen food packages are firm, clean, and well sealed.

• Buy frozen foods at the last stop on your shopping trip.

• Keep foods in your freezer only for the recommended periods of time.

• And once you buy a freezer, *use* it.

HOW MUCH WILL YOU USE ONE?

Whether a freezer will be a money saver for you will depend on how much you use it, but the odds are it will *not* save you money—unless you live on a farm, or must drive a long distance to shop.

In the late 1970s it cost $180 a year to own a 480-pound capacity manual defrost freezer (about 16 cubic feet), including depreciation, electricity, and average repairs. If you stored and used only 480 pounds of food in your freezer during the year, costs worked out to an average of 37.5 cents a pound. If you stored 540 pounds, the cost dropped to 33.3 cents a pound and if you stored and used 900 pounds of food, down to 20 cents. With a 480-pound capacity freezer, you would have to use more than 900 pounds of frozen food a year and save more than 20 cents a pound on the food you buy for the freezer before it would begin to break even. Your bargains would have to average at least a pound less than prices at the time you eat the food to come out ahead with a frost-free freezer.

Here are a few more clues to the key costs of operating a home freezer today:

Depreciation. Figure this annual cost as one fifteenth of the initial purchase price, including any finance charge.

Electricity. If your local electric rates are, say, 6 cents per kilowatt hour, costs are about $80 a year to keep a 450- to 500-pound freezer 80 per cent full.

Repairs. Freezers are among the least troublesome appliances and repair costs normally average under $10 a year.

Packaging. Typical costs of materials run 5 to 6 cents per pound of food you package and freeze yourself.

Lost Interest. On the purchase price of the freezer and also on your outlay for the food you buy to fill it.

HOW TO BUY

Now here are the basic points to ponder when you are considering the purchase of a home freezer:

• Decide in advance whether an upright or chest model is best for you. The chest type requires more floor space, and it is less convenient because much unloading and rearranging are required to get food in and out on a proper rotation plan designed to eliminate spoilage. However, this type gives you extra counter space on which to work, accumulates less frost, maintains more even temperatures for longer storage times, and uses about half as much electricity as an upright freezer. The upright takes less floor space and is easier to defrost, but may cost $25 to $55 more than a chest-type freezer.

• Decide also what size freezer is adequate and appropriate for your family. Today's freezers come with capacities ranging from 3 to 31 cubic feet, but the most popular models have 12 to 17 cubic feet of storage space. The general rule is you'll want 3 to 4 cubic feet for each member of the family and 5 or 6 per person if you have a vegetable garden and thus do a lot of home freezing or if you shop only every ten days or two weeks.

• Be sure to have adequate space for—and a sturdy floor under—your freezer. When full, this appliance can weigh as much as half a ton.

• Set a budget for your freezer: In the late 1970s, price tags ranged from about $365 for a no-frills 11-cubic-foot freezer to $375–$425 for a luxury 16- to 17-cubic-foot model, and $485–$550 for a luxury 17- to 18-cubic-foot, frost-free model.

• Decide which "extras" you really want and need. Frost-free (self-defrosting) freezers are considerably more convenient than models you must defrost yourself. But you'll pay $75 to $115 more for this feature. A self-defrosting freezer also costs substantially more to operate than a standard upright model, and nearly three times as much as a manual defrost chest. Similarly, a "flash defroster" feature may cut defrosting time to 15 minutes but you'll pay $60 or so extra for this time saving.

• Among the other extras you can get—at a price—when you buy a freezer today are:
an interior light;
a special fast-freezing compartment;
a warning signal showing a dangerous temperature rise or power cutoff;
special baskets, trays, and racks for storage;
a built-in door lock.

• Finally, find out—*before* you buy a freezer—whether there is a warranty and exactly what it covers. Does it cover just repairs for the freezer? Or your losses in food spoilage as well if and when the freezer breaks down? And who will honor the warranty?

• Take special care to investigate the reliability of the dealer before you buy—for if and when a freezer breaks down, it must be repaired within twenty-four hours if you are to avoid losing your entire investment in its contents. Your dealer is of critical importance at that time.

BEWARE: THE DISHONEST "FREEZER FOOD PLAN"

There are two major traps associated with buying and owning a home freezer: the dishonest "freezer food plan" and the "bait and switch" in bulk beef buying.

Under the freezer food plan, you buy a freezer and also sign up for regular purchases of bargain-priced foods to put in it. The savings on the food, the ads say, actually will pay for the freezer itself. In effect, you'll get the freezer "free."

But if you commit yourself to such a deal and it turns out to be a come-on, you well may discover that you are obligated to pay a grossly inflated price for the freezer as well as grossly expensive finance charge on the installment loan you use to make the purchase.

The freezer you get may be much larger (and more expensive to operate) than your family really needs.

The seller may fail to deliver the promised food on the promised timetable. Or he may substitute inferior varieties of meats and other items for which you've signed up. Or he may welch on providing the "bonuses" or "free gifts" he used to lure you into the deal.

The guarantee may turn out to be worthless.

What the freezer plan salesman has done is to dazzle you with a promise of whopping savings on future food purchases—to the point where you fail to notice that he has jacked up the price of the freezer part of the deal as much as $200 to $300 over the price of a regular freezer.

Then, after you have signed a contract for the deal, he, in turn, sells it to a finance company and simply fades out of the picture—leaving you quite possibly badly stuck.

Your obvious ways to avoid the freezer plan trap are:

• Compare prices of the freezer you'd buy through regular retailers with those charged by the freezer plan salespeople.

• Also compare costs of the food offered through these plans with the costs of food you buy on special at the local supermarket.

• Be suspicious of any deal in which the food to be provided is advertised vaguely as "enough food for a family of four."

And once you have decided that you want to buy a certain freezer food plan, check the following points in the contract before you sign:

(1) Does the contract state clearly that you have to pay for the freezer?

(2) Does it state the price of the freezer, the total price of the food you are buying, the finance or carrying charges, and any other additional charges?

(3) Does it state the model, year of manufacture, and cubic capacity of the freezer?

(4) Does it state that food prices change and thus the price offer in the present plan will not remain the same?

(5) Does it state the quantity and types of food you will receive, their exact weights, and the grades of the food?

(6) Does it state that the food, should it spoil, is covered by insurance but that you have to pay for this insurance?

(7) Does it state the minimum and maximum quantities of food you must buy?

(8) If the salesman tells you he is making an introductory offer, is this specified in the contract?

(9) Is there a guarantee on the freezer? If so, does it clearly state what is guaranteed and for how long? (Don't believe unreasonable statements like "lifetime" or "unconditional" guarantees.)

BEWARE: "BAIT AND SWITCH" IN BULK BEEF BUYING

A while ago an inspector for the Virginia Department of Agriculture and Commerce visited a bulk-meat retail plant in northern Virginia which had advertised a side of beef at less than half the price the beef, in suitable cuts, was quoted in the supermarkets. On making a test purchase, the inspector (who didn't identify himself as a VDAC agent) was told that the bargain-priced beef was old, tough, and wouldn't be satisfactory for general cooking. He was also advised that the cutting and trimming loss on the meat would be high, as much as 70 per cent of the gross weight. He was then guided to a more expensive meat—USDA choice—and told this beef would be much better and the cutting loss would be less than 20 per cent.

After indicating that he would take a quantity of the higher-priced meat, the inspector began bargaining with the meat dealer. He finally bought 188 pounds of choice beef at a "reduced price."

Back at the VDAC laboratory in Richmond, the inspector weighed the beef and found he had received a little over 120 pounds—a 36 per cent cutting loss against the guarantee of less than 20 per cent.

Thus, the 120 pounds of meat actually cost much more than the original quoted price for the hanging, uncut beef. And on top of this, more than half of the 120 pounds delivered represented hamburger!

This test purchase of bulk beef also revealed that close to $100 could have been saved on the same quantities of the same grade and cuts at a simultaneous local supermarket sale. The bulk dealer was charged and convicted of "advertising without intent to sell" and "delivering less than the quantity represented." He was fined $1,000 and costs on each count.

In meat, the dangers are very real that you'll be caught in a "bait and switch" racket. Your warning signals of deception will include:

• The ads will fail to disclose that as much as half of the weight will be lost in cutting, dressing, and trimming—in effect, doubling the price per pound. Or the operator's "estimated" trimming loss will turn out to be a "mistake"—costing you, the consumer, a painful sum.

• The low advertised prices will not be honest offers to sell beef but instead will be lures to bring you into the stores. Here, salesmen will downgrade the advertised meat in order to sell you higher-priced beef.

• The advertised "sale" or "special" prices will be the regular prices, not temporary bargains. The ads will place heavy emphasis on the scary aspects of soaring prices and potential food shortages.

• Credit disclosures required under the Truth in Lending law on installment purchases will be omitted altogether from the ad.

• Even if you agree to buy the better meat at a higher price, the seller may still deliver inferior meat—and you have no way of knowing exactly what has been delivered to you. (In one case reported by the Federal Trade Commission, a "bait and switch" operator sold a single "model" carcass of beef ten times during a single day!)

• Although there may be a money-back guarantee if you're dissatisfied, you may have a hard time actually getting either a replacement of the meat or a refund of your money—because of fine-print conditions and limitations which didn't appear in the advertised guarantee.

• You may discover, when your order of beef is delivered to you, that the stated maximum of ground beef (e.g., 12 per cent) is exceeded.

• The operator's definition of a "half of beef" may turn out to be the two forequarters, or front half of the beef—where the steaks and other choice cuts *aren't,* but where much of the waste and bone *are.*

• The advertised "heavy Western Beef" may turn out to be *cow* meat which is just laden with yellow fat.

Here are guidelines that will protect you:

• To find an honest freezer meat provisioner who may be able to lead you to a real meat-in-bulk bargain, ask about dealers who are well established in your community and whose services your friends can recommend personally. The honest dealer will *not* advertise sides of beef at prices you know are unrealistically low. He will not try to lure you into a deal in which you're persuaded to buy beef at sky-high prices.

• Do not sign up for any bulk meat deal until you have exhaustively checked the reputation of the dealer. Do not permit any meat dealer to use high-pressure sales tactics on you. Give yourself plenty of time to think and to figure out what you are getting for your money.

• Find out whether the meat has been graded and what grade it is. If it is graded utility, it is likely to be tough and stringy and the net yield after cutting also may be low. Meats sold in most supermarkets are usually USDA choice.

• Have the dealer tell you how much trimming loss there will be and what net amount of meat you will receive. Then you can calculate exactly what you will be paying per pound for the meat.

• Once you have calculated the real net costs of the meat *after* trimming and cutting, compare these costs with prices of meats sold on specials.

• Know what cuts of meat—and how much—you will get with your delivered package. It is ridiculous for you to pay for a lot of stew meat when you really want steak, or vice versa.

• If you think you have been gypped, complain and complain loudly to the dealer. If you are not satisfied, do not hesitate to complain to local or state authorities.

The "bait and switch" racket is old and tenacious. It is particularly widespread and particularly vicious in meats because most of us are so ignorant about the rules for judging what is or is not a bargain. Heed these warnings well.

How to Spot Bargains in Poultry

A KEY IS FORM IN WHICH YOU BUY

Although poultry is among the least costly and most popular of main-dish foods, the form in which you buy it often will determine how big a bargain it is.

For example, chicken sold whole generally will be a few cents cheaper per pound than chicken cut up. Whole chicken also will usually be a better buy than chicken breasts or legs.

You also can achieve dramatic savings by buying specials on 5-pound boxes of chicken legs or breasts.

A chicken should be neither too white nor too yellow but rather a creamy color. Figure about one pound per person for whole chicken.

WAYS TO SAVE ON BUYING TURKEYS

Turkeys are relatively inexpensive, too, and now come in quarters, in the form of legs only, breast slices, rolled roasts, etc. Turkey can be barbecued as easily and as quickly as chicken.

You'll get more meat for your money from whole ready-to-cook turkey than from boned, rolled turkey roast. The bigger the bird, the more meat it will have in proportion to bone. A turkey weighing less than 12 pounds is one-half waste. Thus, half of a 20-pound bird may cost less than a whole 10-pound one. Look for a plump, squarish turkey for maximum meat yield. And check the label for a note of "parts missing."

Buy prepared turkey roasts or rolls on the basis of cost per serving.

Other Guides

• If you invest in the convenience of a self-basting turkey which has had oil, water, flavors, fats, phosphates, and other materials injected into it to make it more tender and more flavorful, you are paying the same price per pound for these ingredients as you're paying for the gobbler. In addition, most basting fats are highly saturated, the American Heart Association warns.

• "Turkey loaf" may, by law, contain as little as 35 per cent turkey.

• In other products, such as turkey and gravy, the proportion of turkey also is 35 per cent if *"turkey"* is the first word mentioned on the label. However, if the label says, for example, "giblet gravy and sliced turkey," the proportion of turkey may be as small as 15 per cent.

• The turkey label may or may not tell you what grade the bird is (A, B, or C) since grading is not legally required. There probably will be an indication of the turkey's "class," though—for instance, "young hen," "mature," "broiler," etc.

How to Shop for Fish

Are you among the millions turning to fish as a low-cholesterol protein substitute? If so, do you know how to buy fish? Or do you frequently waste money in the fish market? Worse still, eat fish that is contaminated, leading directly to swollen medical bills?

The chances are you are ignorant of many of the basic rules for buying fish. Here are money-saving tips from the National Marine Fisheries Service, a division of the U. S. Department of Commerce.

• Be much more on guard in buying fish and fish products than in purchasing meat and poultry, for there is no mandatory federal inspection in this area. There is only a voluntary program, which covers a mere 30 per cent of the fish products processed in the United States.

• Those products which have been inspected will carry the seal: "U. S. Department of Commerce, Packed Under Federal Inspection." You also may see a Grade A shield which is given to top quality products. But since most fish *is not* inspected, you must depend on your sight, touch, and smell to determine freshness.

• Fresh fish usually is sold in one of these four forms, each of which will give you a different yield:

(1) Whole or round fish. This you must scale and gut before cooking, so you probably can use only about 60 per cent of the fish.

(2) Dressed. This form is cleaned and ready to cook. But since it still has the bones and skin, you can eat only 80 per cent.

(3) Fish steaks. This form consists of cross-section slices of a large, dressed fish. Once the bones are removed, 90 per cent of this form can be used.

(4) Fillets. These slices are cut away from the backbone, are ready to cook and you can consume 100 per cent of it.

THE SIGNALS

• The purchase of seafood, fresh or frozen, demands special care. If you're buying fresh seafood, be sure the lobster, crab, clams, or oysters are alive at the time of purchase; reject them otherwise. If you're buying frozen seafood, be sure the fish is solidly frozen and has a pleasant odor. Frozen fish may be glazed (dipped in water and quickly frozen to produce an icy glaze that protects the fish from dehydration). If the glaze is melted or chipped, don't buy it. The unprotected fish may appear cottony white—a condition known as "freezer burn" which indicates the beginning of cellular breakdown.

• Avoid damaged frozen packages. If the package is damaged, it could mean a loss in quality. And don't buy packages stacked above the freezing line in the store freezer, for these could be in the process of thawing or actually thawed.

• Know your labels when buying breaded fish. If the label reads "regular breading," it contains 50 per cent fish; "lightly breaded" means it contains 65 per cent fish. When you open the package, check for coating defects. If there are any cracks in the breading, return the package.

• In buying canned seafood, check the condition of the can. If it is bulging, the fish may be spoiled. If the can is dented or rusty, avoid it.

• When you open the can, make sure the flesh is firm. If the fish is over-cooked, the flesh next to the can will be darker—and you should return it to the store.

• If the fish is packed in oil, the oil should be clear, not milky. If the can is not filled properly to the top, take it back to your store.

• When buying shrimp, keep in mind that shrimp is sold by color and count size: the smaller the size of the shrimp, the less expensive per pound. The count size per pound should be listed on the package.

• Be a label watcher when buying canned tuna. Albacore is the only kind that can carry the label "white meat." Tuna that is "light meat" comes from the yellow fin, skip jack, and blue fin varieties. If the can contains bonito, a fish similar to tuna, it must carry the label "bonito."

ORGANIC FOODS

BOON OR RIPOFF?

An astonishing phenomenon in recent years has been the explosive growth in the numbers of Americans who will eat only organically grown fruits, vegetables, and meats. Millions of you, worried about the safety and quality of foods grown with chemical additives, fertilizers, and pesticides, have become devoted to "natural" or organic foods, and insist the extra cost in terms of health is well worth it. Millions of others enter counterclaims, argue the health advantages are unfounded and the whole thing is a ripoff of consumers.

Both the U. S. Department of Agriculture and the Food and Drug Administration are emphatic in dismissing the benefits attributed to organic foods.

As far back as 1976, the Department of Agriculture published a study by Cynthia Cromwell in its *Family Economic Review,* which declared in part:

"Consumers continue to buy the more expensive organic foods even though they are not necessarily more nutritious, and the special conditions required for the growth and processing of such foods are not regulated or assured."

What is an organic food? For years there was no legal definition for the term. Producers, manufacturers, retailers, and advertisers, therefore, could use it loosely in ads and labels.

At the close of the 1970s, however, government regulators proposed to permit advertisers to use "organic" only if the food were produced without pesticides, artificial fertilizers, and was free of synthetic additives, preservatives, hormones, and antibiotics.

They suggested the term "health food" be banned from ads completely because it could not be defined in any meaningful way.

And they proposed that advertisers could claim that a food was "natural" only if it had been processed slightly and contained no artificial ingredients.

COMPARATIVE PRICES

One point is certain, however. Organic foods are very expensive—in many instances costing two to three times more than the regular products. In the late 1970s, the Department of Agriculture compared the cost of regular food in a Washington, D.C., supermarket with organics sold in a large natural food store.

Of forty-seven items on the list, six organics were slightly cheaper than regular products. But seven organics—mainly meat and poultry—were more than triple and eleven were more than double the cost of corresponding regular products. For some inexplicable reason, organic green cabbage was 550 per cent more expensive. The 22 remaining items were from 20 to 90 per cent higher in the natural food store.

Vitamins

The same story involved vitamins. In the late 1970s, the prices of four vitamins in a neighborhood pharmacy and a shop specializing in organic products, for 100 tablets or capsules, showed the organic vitamins priced two to three times their counterpart in the regular pharmacy.

WHAT IS "ORGANIC" FOOD?

Exactly what constitutes "organic" food? According to the National Farmers Organization in Iowa, it is "food grown without pesticides; grown without artificial fertilizers; grown in soil whose humus content is increased by the addition of organic matter" and "food which has not been treated with preservatives, hormones, antibiotics, etc."

Organically grown beef and other meats are raised on organically managed land; are fed with foods which are free from pesticides and herbicides, antibiotics, feed additives, growth and other medicinal hormones; and tend toward grass grazing over grain feeding.

How do organic foods differ from "natural" foods and "health" foods? As noted, there are no precise legal definitions but there are some guidelines which are widely agreed upon:

• Natural foods contain no preservatives, emulsifiers, or artificial ingredients. They are sold to provide consumers with an alternative to conventional foods which may contain such additives and preservatives.

• Organic foods are more or less the same as natural foods, except that "organic" implies greater care of soils and plant environment to exclude pesticides and artificial fertilizers.

• Health foods are different from the other two categories. They include dietetic, vegetarian, and other products not necessarily free of chemical additives.

But what could possibly be the advantage of chewing on desiccated liver when you can buy—and probably eat with pleasure—regular fresh liver at far lower cost? Are such products as dulse and kelp, soybean flour, rose hips, sesame seeds, and safflower oil really necessary for *your* good health? Is it honestly worth it to pay so much more for specially grown "organic" foods—in terms of their purity and nutritional value to you, the consumer?

You well may be among the millions of us who feel caught between the crossfire of claims and counterclaims by organic food buffs, food faddists, the Food and Drug Administration in Washington, nutritionists on both sides of the organic food argument today.

On one side are the organic food supporters who are (1) issuing dire warnings that we are being poisoned en masse by additives, preservatives, emulsifiers, pesticides, chemical fertilizers, other foreign substances which are routinely added to so many foods we eat, and who (2) point out quite persuasively that many food manufacturers and processors first remove most or all key nutrients and perhaps put back only a few of them in certain "fortified" foods.

On the other side are many of the world's top nutritionists who (1) insist that most foods on today's supermarket shelves are just as safe, healthy, and nutritious as their more expensive organic counterparts and (2) argue that the only difference between "natural" and synthetic vitamins is that the natural ones cost more.

THE QUESTION OF ADDITIVES

The FDA lists some six hundred different food additives—artificial colors and flavors, monosodium glutamate, synthetic sugar and salt substitutes and preservatives, emulsifiers, and other chemicals—as GRAS (Generally Recognized as Safe). However, the FDA admits that few of these additives have been extensively tested. In the past, the FDA's overall approach has been to consider an additive safe unless and until it is proven to be otherwise. However, adamant consumer advocates have been increasingly challenging that attitude—and the rules have been steadily tightened.

Caught somewhere in between are the majority of us who are legitimately worried about the questions raised in recent years concerning pesticides and additives and about our national case of malnutrition. And there's no doubt, as one New York City expert remarked, some labels "read like a qualitative analysis of the East River."

In sum, the dilemma is that most of us just don't know whether we're being ripped off by organic food stores or whether organic foods are really better for us and are worth paying twice the price for them.

And a final touch: we simply have no way of knowing for certain whether the "organic" foods we do buy actually were produced without chemicals or were processed without either removing important nutrients or adding forbidden substances.

TEN RULES FOR BUYING ORGANIC FOODS

If *you* are sold or even partially sold on the idea of organic foods, here are ten basic guidelines on how to buy them and how to get the most for your money:

(1) Start by patronizing the biggest and best established organic food store in your area, then explore others and compare products and prices as you go. Check knowledgeable friends for hints. Stick to stores that appear neat and clean. Stay away from the ill-kept ones with open flour, grain, and seed bins into which all of

you are invited to dip your hands to get what you want. Also avoid stores which offer an obviously kooky line of products along with the organic foods: vibrators, fountain-of-youth products, hair restorers, etc.

(2) Interview the proprietor and listen with care. How much control does he keep over the product he sells? What proof (such as certification from known food growers) can he offer you that the foods he sells actually are organically grown? Does he personally know his major suppliers and the farmers? Since there are relatively few large-scale growers of organic foods, it's no great chore to be acquainted with them all. Or if he doesn't know his suppliers and growers personally, does he at least require them to provide affidavits on the authenticity of their organic foods? Can you see these affidavits?

(3) Study organic food labels for details on: ingredients; where, who, and by whom grown (you can easily get to know the names of reputable growers, processors, and distributors); conditions under which the foods were grown and processed, including types of soil, water, and fertilizers used; appropriate disclaimers on pesticides, additives, herbicides, commercial fertilizers; recipes.

(4) Check with care the contents of breakfast cereal products—consisting of rolled oats, soybean oil, brown sugar, perhaps a few other items. Many varieties on the market are neither organically grown nor particularly nutritious. Note whether the contents of other products—such as juices—are not precisely the same as the contents of their regular supermarket counterparts.

(5) On vitamins, study the source of their "natural" components, as well as the proportions of each substance. Be sure the amounts of ingredients listed are for one tablet or capsule (not five or six).

(6) Comparison-shop, especially on high-priced items. An excellent way to do this is to compare prices of staple items.

(7) Ask yourself: will your family eat the foods? You won't improve your health—and certainly not your budget—by buying foods which end up in the garbage pail (or even the compost heap). Also will you really invest the necessary time to prepare meals from organic "raw materials"?

(8) Be skeptical of exorbitantly priced "organic" toothpastes, shampoos, facial creams, raw sugar (chemically identical to refined sugar), similar products. Certainly be wary if salesclerks tout any of those wares as "wonder foods."

(9) Buy such items as whole grains, wheat germ, cereals, soy beans, lentils, and other beans in bulk.

(10) If you have any questions about various foods and how they're grown, write to their producers or suppliers. The top producers and suppliers will respond to your legitimate inquiries. Be wary of any firm which gives you a runaround or no reply at all.

BEWARE! ORGANIC FOOD TRAPS

As you might suspect, the deceivers and gypsters have been crowding into this field and making a mockery of the very definition of organic food. All kinds of packagers have been buying up ordinary foods, labeling them "organic," and passing them off on naïve retailers and an innocent public.

Says the president of one of the nation's largest organic food wholesalers: "Ninety per cent of the 'organic' apple juices now being sold in California is not made from organically grown apples. At least half of the organically grown rice now being sold on the East Coast, isn't."

How, then, can you, a food shopper who buys this type of product, protect yourself against the profiteering charlatans? By using this rundown of current traps in the field:

Deceptive labeling: Probably the biggest trap is using an "organic," "natural," "nature's own," etc., label when this is not the case. Although this sort of deception violates proposed government labeling rules, some unscrupulous retailers may still simply paste an "organic" label over the brand name of a non-organic product or its package. Or the "organically grown" food may be merely food which hasn't been sprayed with pesticides—but which fails to meet other generally accepted criteria for organic foods.

Many unscrupulous suppliers, for instance, sell "natural organic" honey (a major health food product), although they have had no control over the antibiotics which may have been used in bee feed or over what types of sprays are used around the bees' base.

Non-organic foods: Often mixed in with organic products in organic food stores, leading you to believe they're somehow special and worth paying extra for.

Small type: Frequently dried fruits which are labeled "natural organic" have preservatives listed in tiny type in an inconspicuous section of the label.

Exaggerated claims: Some protein supplements are being sold with the promise that they'll improve not only your physical fitness but even your appearance.

Sheer misinformation: This is often aimed at innocent older people who are constantly worried about their health. Some food store operators, once they've sold a customer one bottle of vitamins or minerals, will then try to sell another to "balance" the first one.

Overpricing: The 50 per cent markups on vitamin pills and protein supplements are common. Moreover, most vitamin C now being sold as "natural" consists almost entirely of ascorbic acid—the same stuff you find in "unnatural" vitamin C.

Nutrition nonsense: Almost everybody is trying to climb on the health food bandwagon and make a healthy profit in the process. Of questionable nutritional value surely are "organic" variations in toothpaste, refined oils, refined sea salt, syrup.

Low calorie fruits and vegetables: These may be labeled as "natural organic" but actually they're the same as all diet foods.

Your best—and most obvious—safeguards are to know the proprietor of the store you patronize and study carefully the labels of each product you buy. And if you feel you've been deceived or cheated, report the details to your local Better Business Bureau and your Consumer Protection Agency.

HOME AND COMMUNITY GARDENS

A REWARDING TREND GAINS IMPETUS

Perhaps the most constructive reaction to soaring food prices is the enormous increase in family and community gardens for growing vegetables and fruits. As we go into the 1980s, more than half the 75 million families in the United States are cultivating gardens in their back yards and millions more of you have "mini farms" on rooftops, windowsills, patios, and in containers scattered around apartments.

A development of more significance is the great upsurge in community gardens. Countless groups of neighbors on all social and income levels have formed co-operatives to raise produce on vacant lots and plots in the middle of big cities and appalling slums.

Why the wide appeal of gardening? (1) a preference for the taste of fresh fruits and vegetables; (2) to save money; (3) as a hobby. Reason No. 2 is rapidly rising into the prime position in the grow-your-own trend.

CAN YOU REALLY SAVE MONEY?

Reports from official sources indicated a backyard garden measuring 25×30 feet could in the late 1970s return savings of $300–$400 a year with conscientious care. Those last two words, "conscientious care," hold the secret to a green thumb.

A standard joke in suburbs and small towns concerns the misadventures and frustrations of home gardening. "I could've bought two pounds of tomatoes at the supermarket for what it cost me to grow one in my back yard." "My cucumbers were so small and shriveled they looked like gherkins." "We would've starved if we had to depend on our garden, but we had the fattest insects you ever saw."

Sure, there are failures and disappointments in home gardening, but they usually can be traced to inexperience, neglect, or disregard of simple rules for planting and nurturing the crops. "You should aim to get back at least ten times the amount of your cash investment in a garden," says the director of Gardens for All, Inc., a non-profit organization based in Burlingon, Vermont. Proof that this goal is attainable is the fact that some five million additional families have been annually starting gardens since the early-mid 1970s, when food prices began to climb sharply.

WHAT TO GROW

Before planting a garden, get specific information on the varieties of vegetables best suited to your location and type of soil, optimal planting dates, and special advice that may be necessary for your particular needs.

This information is readily available from your county agricultural agent— listed in your telephone directory—and from your state agricultural experiment station. The stations generally are attached to state universities. Don't hesitate to call them for advice; that's their function. A phone call or a letter will bring you the pertinent information you need to get started.

The most popular vegetable is the tomato, grown in virtually all home gardens. Next on the popularity list are beans (lima, green, wax); cucumbers; peppers; radishes and scallions. If you try to raise lettuce, be warned: it's extremely sensitive to heat.

Not many fruits are grown in home gardens because they are perishable and/or tricky. Strawberries are your best bet if you want to have a go at fruit. You may have some success with apple trees on your property, but it's advisable to forget melons, peaches, pears, and other berries.

MICROWAVE OVENS

COOL, QUICK COOKING, SPACE-AGE STYLE

Among the appliances that went on the market in the 1970s was the microwave oven—a device that has captured the dollars of families able to afford it. The undeniable appeal of the microwave oven is that it cooks a complete meal in a matter of minutes without generating heat in the kitchen—but doubts remain about the radiation the oven emits.

Still regarded as a novelty a few years ago, microwave ovens were selling at the rate of 2 million units a year in the late 1970s against a declining trend in conventional cooking appliances. Manufacturers confidently predict 40 million units will be in use by 1985, a total that will embrace nearly half of our nation's households.

Obviously microwave cooking is a great time-saver. Another strong, lesser known attraction—the ovens are advertised as America's first fully developed space-age appliance—is a significant saving in energy.

SAVINGS IN ENERGY

If you are an average family of four, you could have saved an estimated $28 a year in electricity bills by using a microwave oven instead of a conventional electric range as the decade ended. In the 1980s, the savings will increase in direct relation to rising electricity rates and will go a long way toward amortizing the costs of a microwave oven, ranging in the late 1970s from $170 for a portable model to $440 for a full-size range up to $625 for a device with elaborate controls.

The quantity of food you cook determines the amount of energy consumed by a microwave oven. In a series of tests conducted by Pacific Gas & Electric Company, it was found that the microwave oven saves energy when cooking or reheating small amounts of food, but loses that advantage for larger portions of several different dishes.

Independent laboratory tests show appreciable savings in energy when microwave ovens are used exclusively for cooking. Conversely, when used in conjunction with, or supplementing, the conventional range, the microwave oven uses more energy. For instance, the microwave is faster and cheaper for baking four potatoes, but the gas burner of a range is faster and cheaper for cooking a package of frozen vegetables.

ARE THE OVENS SAFE?

That's the key question, and the future of the microwave industry hinges on the answer. Manufacturers point to the record, which shows there have been no documented cases of injury since the oven was introduced in 1950. Since then, particularly in the last few years, many improvements designed for safety have been made.

The public's fear of microwave radiation has resulted in stringent requirements for the construction and use of the ovens by the Food and Drug Administration's Bureau of Radiological Health. When used in accordance with the manufacturer's instructions and serviced periodically by authorized repairmen, harmful leakages are not likely. Nor is there a hazard from stored microwave energy in food or the appliance.

There is, however, concern about the allowable level of radiation emission on the basis of long-term effect. Prolonged exposure to a high level of microwave energy has produced eye damage in test animals under laboratory conditions.

SAFEGUARDS TO BE OBSERVED

To be safe, heed these precautions:

(1) Have an expert regularly inspect your oven to make sure there is no radiation leakage. In many communities the local health department will test an oven brought to its offices. Or you may be able to arrange a test of an old or possibly damaged oven by calling the nearest FDA district office.

(2) Clean your oven scrupulously. Crumbs and grime that build up around door seals can cause radiation leakage.

(3) Never turn on the oven when it's empty. Microwaves can be reflected back into the heating element and burn it out faster than normal when there is no food or liquid for absorption. Similarly, foil should not be used.

(4) Be certain you have the correct household voltage for your oven. A portable model needs its own 110–120-volt circuit. A full-size range needs a separate 220-volt line.

WHISKEY AND WINE

HOW TO CUT YOUR LIQUOR BILLS

When did you last add up your liquor bills and face up to how much this one item contributes to your pocketbook pinch?

If you're merely moderate drinkers, spend only $10 a week on liquor, and throw only three cocktail parties a year involving liquor bills of only $50 each, your annual liquor bill amounts to $670. If you're heavier drinkers and entertain lots of friends and neighbors, your annual bill easily may be in the $1,000 to $2,000 range.

Okay. How can you save on liquor without going on the wagon?

• Sample "house brands" of liquor sold locally—especially at delicatessen-type stores (whose house brands often are made by the nation's top distillers). If the house brands taste at least as good to you as the more expensive names you have been buying, adopt them for regular use or at least for large cocktail parties.

• When you throw a cocktail party, offer some "house special," building interestingly on one of the less expensive liquors—gin, vodka, rum. Of course, if you use fruit juices and mixers extensively, it's less important to have expensive, top-quality brands than if you're serving martinis or scotch on the rocks, or Bourbon and branch water. Or try something like a May wine punch with fresh strawberries; you might find that many of your guests actually would prefer this lighter and less costly drink.

• Shop for bargains in cocktail mixers as well as in the cocktails themselves. To me, many of the large-size, lower-cost mixers taste as good as the well-known brands costing 20 to 25 per cent more. But in any event, stick to the larger-size bottles when you're shopping for a party.

• Consider the premixed bottled cocktails (martinis, manhattans, etc.)—*if* they will eliminate your need to hire a bartender. Otherwise they're no bargain since you pay a premium of 25 per cent or so for the convenience.

• Consider less expensive Virgin Island rum as an alternative to Puerto Rican rum.

• Try out imported whiskey which has been bottled in the United States rather than abroad.

• If you happen to be fans of "B&B," save 20 per cent on this liqueur by buying a bottle of Benedictine and another of inexpensive French cognac and mixing your own B&B.

• Unless higher proof (e.g., 100 proof) liquor is far more expensive than its lower proof counterpart (e.g., 86 proof), the higher proof is probably the better deal. You simply dilute it yourself.

• Look for liquor sales. Although liquor prices often tend to be controlled in any given area by state laws and other factors, sales *do* happen in some places, and bargains can be found. The best time to find liquor sales—and to stock up— is after a big holiday.

• Finally, consider the liquor cost on a *per ounce* basis. If a fifth costs $6.40, the cost per ounce is 25¢ and a quart of the identical liquor would have to cost less than $8.00 to be a bargain. There are 32 ounces in a quart and 25⅗ ounces in a fifth (four fifths of a quart.)

THE TRUTH ABOUT BOTTLED WATERS

Q. *What's the latest "nouveau," American "chic" in drinking in homes and restaurants across the land?*

A. Bottled water, that's what—a European habit which goes back to the times of Julius Caesar and Michelangelo, which is immortalized in the story of Ponce de León and his search for the fabled fountain of youth. While our nation is known the world over for having the best tap water available anywhere, sales of bottled waters as the 1980s neared were reaching the $200 million a year mark, triple the total as recently as a decade earlier. And whatever the reason—chic or dieting or fear of contamination—one of every two hundred Americans now drinks bottled water, with the perpendicular climb showing no signs of slowing.

The fad is not restricted to any one part of the United States. The five states that consume 90 per cent of the country's production—California, New York, Illinois, Texas, and Florida—represent five very different parts of the country, different climates and life-styles. The one apparent link is that they all have heavily populated city areas—suggesting a special appeal to sophisticated tastes and a popularity in trendier establishments.

But if you are part of this switch, do you know what you really are drinking? Do you know how to buy? The odds are you don't.

(1) A first key fact is that it's just about impossible for one bottled water to be described as better than another. The difference depends entirely on your individual tastes.

Don't be fooled by fancy names or bottles. Drink what tastes good to you.

(2) No matter what the conflicting claims (spurred by an authoritative survey in the late 1970s, that the average municipal drinking water contained twenty-two carcinogens that would produce cancer), all bottled waters must meet certain bacteriological, chemical, and physical standards, must be bottled under strict regulations covering cleanliness of processing, containers, shipping, and storage. And all must be labeled under Food and Drug Administration rules.

(3) Many of the terms used to describe a water's source are confusing:

• Bottled waters described as "artesian" (water pumped from a well), "natural spring," or "mineral water" (spring waters) come from natural springs or wells. They are bottled, minerals intact, directly from the source, unfiltered and unprocessed.

• Bottled waters described as "purified," "artificial," "formulated," "drinking water," or "springlike" also come to just about the same thing. The terms mean the water has been scientifically treated to remove such impurities as chlorine and sulphates. Minerals are frequently added. Although the levels may differ, the contents of purified bottled waters are generally the same as artesian, natural spring, or mineral waters.

• As for purification treatments, the different types include distillation, deionization, electrolysis, or filtration. Most purified bottled waters are filtered.

• You also easily may be befuddled by the mineral (or salt) content. It's misrally sparkling) means that carbon dioxide gases captured at the source are leading, though, to limit the term "mineral water" to natural spring waters, because all bottled waters, except distilled, have minerals. (Distilled water, while drinkable, should be consumed by your car battery or clothes iron.) Minerals give bottled water its flavor.

(4) If you're choosing between carbonated or non-carbonated (still water), it's your taste which must dictate your purchase. Naturally carbonated (or natuadded to the water during bottling.

(5) On price: roughly 75 per cent of bottled waters on the market are purified, and tend to cost a little less than the imported varieties (so chic to order a Perrier or an Evian with a slice of lemon peel, you know). But don't forget: one bottled water can't be called better than another. It's all a matter of personal taste So experiment on your own and reach an intelligent decision.

WINE DRINKING IN PERPENDICULAR RISE

Shocker: Our consumption of wine has now skyrocketed to more than 400 million gallons a year and by early in the 1980s more wine will be sold in the United States than distilled spirits, predicts a leading newsletter of the wine industry.

Shocker: As of the late 1970s, our per-person drinking of wine (man, woman, child included) is around 1.8 gallons a year. In a span of merely a few years, the estimate is it will soar to 3.1 gallons and by 1985 California table shipments alone are slated to be larger than total U.S. consumption today.

Shocker: Just since 1960, adult consumption of table wines in the Unites States has more than tripled, while dessert wine intake has been slashed almost in half. Our growing sophistication and taste could not be more clearly demonstrated than by our switch from the heavily sweet wines of previous years to dry, light wines.

Shocker: Already a retail market of nearly $3 billion, U.S. drinking of wines is projected at growing 6 per cent a year into the mid 1980s, far above the rate of the last few years.

And which suppliers are leading the upsurge? Domestically, it's still California. This state's share of the table-wine market is expected to remain close to 70 per cent through 1985.

And imports? *Not* France—as most of you would guess—for France has been bedeviled by short supplies and zooming wine prices. *Not* Spain or Portugal, two other contenders.

The leader in imports and still climbing fast is *Italy*. In the late 1970s, Italy accounted for 48.6 per cent of all imported wine shipments. To put that startling finding into perspective, as recently as 1970 Italy had only 20 per cent of the table-wine market in our country while France had 35 per cent. Portugal also had 20 per cent, Spain, 10 per cent, and Germany, 15 per cent.

An obvious reason has to be competitive pricing—the area where France has been lagging most. Also marketing techniques have been significantly improved. And with American tastes so vastly refined, high quality has to be a factor too. Italian wines are now government inspected and certified.

But why the spectacular shift to wines in the first place? Among the reasons:

(1) Many European wines were sampled by visiting Americans in the 1960s and early 1970s, when millions of Americans toured Europe with what were then high-value dollars. When these tourists came home, they continued to order labels and varieties they had enjoyed in Europe (particularly Italy).

(2) Younger Americans have been reared on soft drinks, colas, and other good-tasting beverages—and they are choosing wine on the basis of taste. Side by side with the turn to wine has been the clear trend toward lighter liquors.

(3) White goods, such as vodka, gin, and white rum, have shared in the trend away from brown whiskeys—along with wines.

(4) Changing life-styles in our land have made the sodden drunk an outcast. The old frontier tradition appears ridiculous.

(5) Economics—an undeniable force. Wines are cheaper than hard liquors. And in hard liquors, too, the trend toward economy is reflected in the preference

for larger sizes (quarts and half gallons). And as more meals are eaten away from home, an increased use of wine is noted. Wine is being offered in rising totals in outlets such as hospitals and ball parks.

(6) The white wine craze (and craze it is) has become part of the American scene, with the spritzer (white wine with club soda ice) an unmistakable party favorite.

(7) Finally, emerging is a demand for premium or high-quality wines (costing more than $5.00 per fifth). Wine is not competing primarily against distilled spirits and malt beverages, but against other forms of beverages used familiarly with meals.

THE MYSTIQUE OF WINE

A Boston business executive didn't know whether he should pay more or less for an older vintage of the same wine and was too embarrassed to ask.

A young couple in Dallas threw out the opened bottles of wine left over from their wine and cheese party rather than risk doing something wrong.

A New York housewife bought a gallon of wine for a small dinner party of moderate drinkers, not knowing how much to buy or where to find proper guidance.

Typically, we face an average of two hundred choices each time we buy wine. In all, there are ten thousand different wines available in the United States at any one time—a variety that makes us insecure, confused, often intimidated and imprudent wine shoppers.

The result of all this is that any but the most experienced wine aficionado often will (1) buy a very expensive wine, equating high price with quality; (2) buy a very cheap but unpleasant wine and then throw it all away; (3) buy the same wine all the time; (4) not buy wine at all. (After tasting a light wine I served at my home a while ago, a well-meaning guest volunteered to make up a list of modestly priced but delicious whites and reds for me to buy, so I would feel "safe" with my future purchases. My response was open delight and inner embarrassment, but I'm honest enough to confess I used his list to advantage when he finally sent it.)

Contrary to the unspoken, deep fears of the novice wine consumer, an extensive knowledge of the history, methods of viticulture and viniculture, and the soil and climate conditions of grape-growing areas is not a prerequisite for buying a wine you like at a price well within the limits of your budget.

You wouldn't think of compiling a complete dossier and history of stringbeans before buying them for dinner.

It's enough to know that you want to spend $4.50 to $5.00 a bottle for dinner, or perhaps $5.00 to $6.00 for a special occasion, and that you like a red wine with steak, a white wine with fish, and a dry sherry or similar drink before dinner.

Without doubt, you and I are more knowledgeable and sophisticated consumers of wine and have a more relaxed attitude about serving wine regularly with dinner or in place of hard liquor at the cocktail hour than in the late 1930s when Chianti in straw-wrapped bottles was the only wine Americans knew. And even then, in general we associated wine only with spaghetti and red-checkered tablecloths.

Today, women are making 65 to 70 per cent of the wine purchase decisions—an unmistakable majority—against 40 per cent just twenty years ago. And women have even greater influence in states where wine is sold in the supermarkets.

A majority of women buying wine in supermarkets are planning to serve it at dinner, and table wine now accounts for 61 per cent of the total wine market.

We accepted Chianti without the straw as the classic red wine it is, rather than as a potential candleholder, when we learned that straw was so expensive it would raise the price of the wine. Now we are as concerned about value and taste as about charm and mystique.

To the Boston executive, the expert advice is: ask your retailer for a wine vintage chart to see which year was better for which wines.

To the Dallas couple, it's: recork your wine and keep it in the refrigerator for about a week.

To the New York housewife, buy half a bottle of wine per person, three four-ounce servings, for a two-course meal.

GUIDES FOR BUYING

• Learn to read wine labels. By law, each wine-producing region provides you with valuable purchasing information on the label. Ask your retailer for printed material of explanation or write to the various wine information bureaus. If you will buy and study just one basic wine book, you'll get the fundamentals. Then follow up with newspapers and magazine wine columns to stay current on wine for sale in your area at good prices.

• Compare prices and look for specials. Wine retailers, like food stores, offer loss leaders to draw customers in to shop. And take advantage of special bottlings which producers offer at excellent value to commemorate a special event.

• Buy by the case. It is common practice for retailers to offer 10 per cent discounts per case and more on six cases.

• Store wines properly so they don't spoil. A cool, quiet dry closet or corner where bottles can be stored on their sides is all you need for wines to be consumed soon after you buy them.

• Look for a knowledgeable and reliable retailer who stocks wines in a wide price range and takes proper care of the wines on his shelves. Don't hesitate to browse or ask questions.

• Figure the cost of wine as part of the cost of all your dinner beverages. If dinner costs-out to $1.50 per person, $1.00 more per person for wine is reasonable and will add considerably more ambience than less expensive soda. Also, there's little doubt that, in most cases, serving wine as an aperitif as well as a meal accompaniment will turn out much less expensive than offering the usual before-dinner cocktails.

• Decide how much wine you need before you shop. The rule of thumb is a half bottle of wine or 12 ounces per person for dinner for a two- or three-course meal.

If you are serving two wines, figure 6 ounces of each per person. Add another half bottle per person if wine is the aperitif.

• Don't overlook smaller and larger bottles. Wine usually comes in 25-ounce fifths, 6.5-ounce splits, 12-ounce half bottles, and 51.2-ounce magnums. A split of Chianti, for instance, would be ample for dinner for one and a magnum more convenient for larger groups. American jug wines are economical as everyday wines.

• Develop your wine palate. Buying what you like is the best way to get the most for your money. Start a set of 3×5 index cards or a loose-leaf notebook, or just keep labels that you soak off bottles, to note the name and type of wine, who produced it and where, what it tastes like, what food you drank it with and how much you paid. Your palate soon will be your best guide to value.

• When you find producers, importers, or shippers whose wines you consistently like, stay with them. If one importer's Spanish wines agree with your palate, their Italian, French, and German wines are likely to as well.

Keep a wine corner in your refrigerator and a few assorted-size containers. Leftover wine must be recorked firmly or decanted into a smaller container. The less air the longer the wine will last. Properly stored, it keeps about a week in your refrigerator. Combine small amounts of leftover red or white into separate containers. Keep in the refrigerator for cooking purposes. Invest in a good corkscrew, wine rack, ice bucket, a set of stemmed all-purpose wineglasses.

Unlearn the misconception that older is better. Vintage simply signifies the year the grapes used to make that wine were picked and a vintage chart can tell you which years were good or bad in each wine region. Experience will tell you when a wine is ready to drink. Rule of thumb is: white wines should be consumed when young and red wines at varying ages.

HOW TO SAVE ON PARTIES

If you have given parties you must be aware that costs easily can run double or even triple the amount you have budgeted. Yet there are many ways to save substantial sums on your party without compromising its gaiety or quality. Here are the fundamental rules.

• Whatever type of party it is—whether it's a cocktail or a dinner party—set a per-person budget and stay with it. Liquor, hors d'oeuvres, and other trimmings in the late 1970s probably cost between $3.00 and $8.00 a head; a dinner party could cost from $8.00 up, but it's possible to put on a fairly elegant spread for around $12 a person. How much can you *really* afford to spend? How many people do you *really* want to invite?

• Consider one big party—which would undoubtedly be cheaper (and easier) —rather than a smattering of medium-sized parties throughout the year. But if your home cannot take a large number of guests, try parties on successive days— or a brunch and a cocktail party on the same day. By so doing, you can take maximum advantage of mass cooking, flowers, whatever party equipment you've rented, other extras you're paying for.

• As suggested earlier, buy the larger sizes of liquor—quarts over fifths, and half gallons over any of the smaller sizes. A case almost always is cheaper than the purchase of individual bottles, of course. A quart serves sixteen two-ounce drinks, so if everybody drinks an average of three drinks, one quart will serve about five people. Ask your liquor dealer if he will take back unopened bottles; many will.

• When mixing drinks, use a measure and follow a recipe if the drink requires this. Don't overpour.

• Don't overprepare. It's false economy to prepare a pitcher of some drink and then find you'll serve only a couple of drinks during the entire party. Plan your ingredients, have them ready, then prepare your drinks as you are asked for them.

• Buy the largest available bottles of mixers and the least expensive varieties of soda, mix, tomato juice, etc. Have ginger ale and other non-alcoholic beverages available; some people do prefer these.

• Serve wine and punches at a fraction of what cocktails would cost. You'll be delighted to discover how many of your guests will be grateful. Also try Irish coffee, café diable, such non-alcoholic drinks as espresso and cappuccino. These are far less expensive than liqueurs. And if yours is a dinner party, try the European custom of serving a predinner aperitif—such as a glass of champagne or a white wine or vermouth.

• Instead of hiring a bartender, have your spouse (or a close friend) mix the first drink for everybody and then suggest that everybody mix his (her) own after that. People tend to drink less, incidentally, if an overgracious host doesn't plunge for empty glasses the instant they are drained. Or hire a college student to tend bar with the help of a few notes and advance lessons on how to mix what. If it's a dinner party try to hire a reliable, mature teenager in your area (or your own daughter) to help with preparations and cleaning up afterward.

• Place the bar where people aren't apt to congregate, and set the food in another corner. This will help distribute your guests and, incidentally, draw them away from the bar and toward your food.

• Even if you're the type who insists on flowers for every table in the house, consider buying just a dozen or so well-chosen ones, plus a bundle of pretty greenery. One or two flowers in the right-size vase can look just as good as a profusion, if you arrange them right.

• In summer, take everything you can from your garden, and from friends and neighbors. Don't order florist flowers over the telephone. Find out if any neighborhood florists offer a special of the week. Take advantage of these.

• Save on hors d'oeuvres by serving only made-in-U.S. items. Don't feel you must offer a full-scale delicatessen. One beautifully presented wheel of good domestic cheese or a platter of well-chosen cold cuts surrounded by a variety of crackers will be economical and will avoid the inevitable waste of a big variety.

Save on more elaborate food by making your foods from scratch and substituting your time for more expensive packaged convenience foods.

• Also save by serving cold foods. Buckets of ice for cold snacks are far less costly than renting or buying the necessary equipment for hot foods.

• And give a break to the millions of us who are struggling to keep trim figures. All we want is the simplest, lowest-cal crackers and rabbit food.

You probably can dwarf my list. The point is that real savings *are* possible. All *you* need do is plan.

THE HIGH COST OF EATING OUT

TREND: UP, UP, UP

If you are among the tens of millions of us who must or want to eat out regularly, you are acutely aware that the cost of restaurant meals has been skyrocketing. Just in one recent ten-year span, the cost of eating out jumped 224 per cent nationally!

And no relief appears in sight. The long-range outlook for restaurant meal prices is up, up, up—with the estimate that even as the 1980s near, we are spending $3.00 out of every $10 of food dollars for food outside our homes.

The enormous jump in prices for food away from home has forced most of you to exercise restraint in choosing dining places. The share of the away-from-home food market of conventional restaurants, lunch rooms, and cafeterias has been falling steadily while the share of fast food places has been soaring.

FAST FOOD PLACES ENDORSED

"The dramatic rise in the sales of fast food establishments is a fascinating social and economic phenomenon," the Department of Agriculture itself acknowledges. "Rising consumer incomes made it possible. Continued increases in the number of working wives, besides increasing family income, stimulated a demand for places where the family could eat at a modest price, serving food that both kids and adults like, in a relaxed atmosphere.

"Although fast foods are much maligned as a contributor to bad diets, a Consumers Union study showed that a hamburger, french fries, salad, and milk shake provide a remarkably well-balanced meal. Thus, the fast food places have met a need of the sixties and seventies and the public has taken to them with enthusiasm. Besides, they provide an opportunity for family togetherness at mealtime without the distraction of television."

RULES FOR CURBING COSTS

But you *can* hold down your eating-out costs and not sacrifice the quality of the food you get. Here are ways to slash your restaurant bills 10 to 25 per cent.

(1) Avoid restaurants where you must give individual tips to a large staff: head-waiter, maître d'hotel, doorman, hatcheck girl, rest-room attendant—as well as your own waiter. These tips alone can add up to $15 or much, much more.

(2) Have a couple of drinks at home before you go, and restrict yourself to one (or no) drinks at the restaurant.

(3) Look for good new restaurants which do not yet have their liquor licenses but which permit you to bring your own bottle of wine—with savings depending on the amount of wine and liquor you normally drink.

(4) Keep in mind that the typical markup on wine in restaurants is around 100 per cent; so do your fancy wine drinking at home.

(5) Favor restaurants which have relatively short, simple menus. You save because food is not wasted in the kitchen and you can get a far more elegant meal for your money if the chef and his staff can concentrate on a few menu items.

(6) Pass up restaurants that serve oversized portions with prices to match. You don't need all that food; it's actually harmful. And at a time of record-high food costs, worldwide shortages and starvation, such servings are obscene. By this simple change in your habits, we can save incalculable tons of wasted food and billions of dollars.

(7) Steer clear of purely snob appeal restaurants—unless it's really worth cash to you to sit across the room from a celebrity or a tycoon.

(8) Patronize restaurants in neighborhoods where you can benefit from the fact that rents and other overhead costs may be 30 to 50 per cent lower than in midtown. If you're trying to save money, this alone can do it for you.

And a final note: don't be mesmerized by exotic, fanciful adjectives or writing on a menu. You're not eating the menu.

The trend of prices for food at restaurants will still be up, but with these guides you can maneuver nicely within that trend to eat out and even save.

5

YOUR HOME

How to Find and Finance It
Buy and Build It
Furnish and Beautify It
Insure and Protect It
Remodel and Expand It
Sell . . . and Finally
Move out of It!

What Do You Really Want?

When you start planning to buy, build, or rent a roof to go over your head, you face some of the biggest financial decisions of your life and also an all-time high number of formidable competitors for that roof.

The mere fact that during the decade of the 1980s 4 million or more Americans will be marrying each year spells serious shortages of most forms of housing throughout the nation. For this means that 2 million-plus new couples will be created each year, probably exceeding the average number of new houses being built. What's more, there are far more single people living alone, mingling singles living together but not married, and groups who want to buy homes of their own. And of course each year millions of dwelling units disappear because of old age or disasters or other developments.

You are facing historically high rents as well as record high home-buying and home-building costs.

If you are in the market to buy a house and you do not buy wisely, it could be the most expensive mistake of your life. On the other hand, if you do buy wisely, your investment is virtually certain to grow in value over the years.

Thus your first rule is: take plenty of time to hunt for a house or an apartment. Being in a hurry puts you squarely into a sellers' market and it almost inevitably will cost you money. Being at ease will make it more likely that you will find a place truly suitable to your family's needs. The typical U.S. shopper for an old house takes two months and visits five different houses before he finds the right one. For new-house shoppers, the norm is three months and ten different houses. Allot even more time if you possibly can—especially if you intend to settle in for several years.

Before you even begin to shop for a house in which to move your family, sit everybody down and throw out the question: "What do we *really* want?"

An apartment or a house?

A house in the suburbs on a paved street with a sidewalk and lawns?

A house in the country with woods or a field between you and the next house?

A house close to the center of town?

A new one-story house loaded with every convenience, a two-car garage, and an acre of land—or an older, roomier house with elbow room outside as well as in, which needs major fixing up?

A house, if you want to do a lot of entertaining, with a separate dining room? Or one, if you're the type of family which congregates mainly in the kitchen for meals, with ample eating space there?

Do you want a wood house? Or a stucco one? A brick or a precast concrete one? Clapboards or shingles or shakes? Or aluminum siding? Paint or stain or just weathered wood?

How much can you afford to pay?

What type of neighborhood do you want to live in?

What style house do you want? Colonial? Ranch? Split-level? One-story or two-story?

How much land do you want? Will you want a garden?

How many rooms do you need?

How long do you plan to live in the house?

Do you want a house you can resell quickly?

What kinds of neighbors do you want? Informal, dungarees-on-Sunday, drop-in-for-a-drink types? The mentally stimulating, intellectually inclined set? A wide variety of social-economic-ethnic backgrounds?

Do you want a big rambling lawn to sit on (and mow)?

How highly does each member of the family value privacy?

If you're now under thirty-five the vast majority of you plan to move to a new home (or a first home of your own) within the next five years. If you're typical, you'd prefer to live in your own house rather than in an apartment, to buy rather than to rent, and you're willing to pay the price of doing so.

The average house bought in the late 1970s had about 1,400 square feet of improved floor space. The average new house has more than 1,700 square feet, six rooms (three of them bedrooms), at least two bathrooms, and a garage.

But no family is average. Your own needs surely differ greatly from the needs of everybody else. So arm yourselves with the facts and get ready to shop for a roof over your head which really suits your individual needs, dreams, and budget.

The Rush to Buy

Before the mid 1970s, most people tended to associate home buying with middle-aged families with a bunch of children to accommodate. This is no longer true, even though the initial prices of homes and the costs of maintaining them have skyrocketed.

The traditional picture of what constitutes a "typical home buyer" has changed. So, too, has the notion of what type of housing best suits a single person, a newly married or unmarried couple, a family of three or four, or an older person.

In the late 1970s, for example, the typical buyer of existing homes was only twenty-five to thirty years old, earned between $15,000 and $25,000 as a professional or skilled worker, was married without children, and bought a home in the suburbs.

Why this rush to buy?

(1) One explanation is psychological. During times of strong inflation when you see that the prices of such basic goods as cars and houses are rising rapidly, you vow to hurry to buy because you expect these "necessities" only to cost more in the future. Millions of Americans hold this attitude toward shelter. In brief, faced with uncertainty over whether or not your incomes will keep pace with prices, you will cut back on spending in general but will speed up your plans to buy a home.

Faced with relentlessly rising prices, many correctly regard the purchase of a house as one of the best investments they can make. Taken together these two expectations—"housing-as-a-hedge-against-inflation" plus "buy-now-because-you-won't-be-able-to-afford-it-later"—become self-fulfilling if shared by enough people. Individuals continue to buy even as prices continue to rise.

Of course, there are other demographic reasons spurring the desire for homes and people's willingness to pay for them. Among them:

(2) The postwar baby boom, the great wave of childbearing that started in 1946 and continued until 1961, is largely responsible for the housing boom of the late 1970s to 80s, just as it was responsible first for overcrowded maternity wards, then schools, then the job market. While the total population grew by 5.3 per cent earlier in the 1970s, the twenty-five-to-thirty-four-year group—the beginning home-buying crowd—grew by more than 27 per cent.

(3) At the same time American households have become increasingly fragmented. Fewer people share the same living quarters. Many now live alone, with a friend or in a small group. As a result, new households are forming at a rate that is almost three times as rapid as the growth of the overall population. These new households want shelter and are helping to bid up the price of homes.

(4) Families want fewer children, and many couples have postponed having their first or additional children until they either advance further in their careers, travel more widely, improve their economic situation, or all of these things. Holding off on having children enables would-be home buyers to devote more of their resources to down payment.

(5) There has been a spectacular rise in the percentage of wives who work. In the late 1970s, 54 per cent of American wives held jobs, against only 24 per cent in 1950. An extra income is extremely important to a couple wanting to buy a home. As the 1980s neared, for example, 50 per cent of all home buyers relied on more than one paycheck.

(6) Women also are more likely to hold a higher-paying job than they were previously. They account, for instance, for one of every eight doctors today and one of every four first-year medical students; in 1962 they accounted for just one out of every eighteen doctors.

(7) This improvement in the educational level of women and their corresponding ability to move into higher-paying professions is true in general of those born after World War II, who are now bidding up the price of homes. About 90 per cent of those born in or after 1945 have finished high school and one quarter

are college graduates. In contrast, as recently as 1940, about three fourths of the people in the United States had not graduated from high school and less than 5 per cent were college graduates.

(8) In addition to becoming better educated, wealthier, more fragmented, and younger, the overall population has shifted over the last several decades. There have been three major migrations. First, people have moved from non-metropolitan areas, particularly from rural farm locations, to the cities. Second, the white population has moved out of the central city into the suburbs, especially in the Northeast and North Central states. And finally, there has been a general shift from North to South and from the central parts of the country to the coastal regions, particularly the Far West and Florida. These movements have caused many changes, not the least of which has occurred in the housing field. Prices have moved up drastically in some regions and increased only moderately in others.

Home prices tend to be higher today in large cities and in the West, lower in smaller towns and in the North Central part of the country—such states as Iowa, Ohio, Indiana, Kansas, Nebraska, Missouri, Michigan, Minnesota, Wisconsin, and North and South Dakota. There the median sales (half above, half below) price of a new home in the last years of the 1970s was just under $41,000. In the West, it was $53,000.

Is home ownership a forgotten dream? This question has been fiercely debated during the last few years. Studies by a wide range of experts have "proven" both sides of the issue. A traditional rule of thumb has been that a family's gross income should be at least five times its mortgage payments. On this basis, only four out of ten U.S. families could afford a home by 1978, while seven out of ten could do so in 1950.

This standard test of affordability is now ignored today by many would-be owners and by borrowers. Millions are willing to devote more of their resources to buying and maintaining a home and to cutting back on other expenses than previously. As the 1980s approached, typical home buyers devoted more than 30 per cent of their take-home pay to owning and running a new home, compared to 23 per cent in 1965.

In short, home ownership is a forgotten dream for only the lowest-income individual and family.

The rest of you want homes and are willing to go to considerable lengths to buy one. Your new house is likely to be smaller and have less land than you would prefer, but you will buy anyway and overall, be pleased with your good investment.

Should You Buy or Rent?

TAX ADVANTAGES IN BUYING

In the late 1970s, mortgage interest rates soared to record highs in many major cities. Interest payments on the typical home were about two and a half times what they were ten years ago. Home construction costs rose at a yearly rate of as much as 20 per cent in some areas, partially because of the skyrocketing costs of building materials and land. And average prices of new homes across the land had, I repeat, shot well past $50,000.

Let's say that against this background, you are trying to decide whether to put down $12,500 on a $50,000 house and pay off a 10 per cent mortgage over the next thirty years or whether it would be cheaper to rent a house or apartment of similar size in the same neighborhood. How great are the differences?

To answer this question, let's assume that you have a yearly income of about $26,000 and thus fall roughly into the 30 per cent income tax bracket.

Here is a chart which shows your income and annual tax bracket under the two conditions—both buying and renting, during the first year in your new place.

Buying vs. Renting—Tax Advantage

ITEM	BUYER	RENTER
Gross Income	$26,000	$26,000
Deductions		
Real Estate Tax	960.00	None
Mortgage Interest	3,740.62	None
Other Deductions	2,500.00	2,500.00
Personal Deductions	3,000.00	3,000.00
Total Deductions	$10,202.62	$5,500.00

To see how the tax advantages of buying work in terms of monthly payments, look at the table below. It reflects the hypotheticals already given. You will note that the buyer actually is paying $303.57 each month rather than the apparent $421.09—a savings of $117.52 or nearly 28 per cent. Compare this actual monthly cost to the rent you would be charged for living in a comparable house or apartment. In some areas you might well have to pay $400 to $700 per month to rent the same house.

ITEMS		AMOUNT—IN $
Monthly Payments		
Interest		$311.72
Principal		17.37
Property Tax		80.00
Insurance		12.00
Total Monthly Costs		$421.09
Tax Deductions		
Interest	$311.72	
Property Tax	80.00	
Total deductions	$391.72	
Tax savings: $392.60×30%		$117.52
(assuming 30% tax bracket)		

ACTUAL MONTHLY COST $303.57

You can use this example as a rough guide to figure out the tax advantages that you will gain by purchasing a home. Depending on your income and your tax bracket, the price of the house, taxes, insurance, and the terms of your mortgage, the tax savings will vary. If you can come up with a down payment, it generally pays to buy, especially if you plan to live in the house for more than a couple of years. In succeeding years, your interest payments will drop and your repayment of principal will increase, so your tax deductions will be slightly lower each year. By the thirtieth year, your mortgage interest will be just $205.84, repayment of principal, $3,734.23.

OTHER FACTORS FAVORING HOME OWNERSHIP

In addition to the tax savings connected with buying rather than renting, you can be fairly confident that your investment will be both stable and high-yielding. What's more, you will have leverage—that is, you can put down a little and own a lot. And once you buy, you can trade up to a bigger house.

There are other emotional and social advantages to home ownership. Pride in your home is one example. You also may change and improve your house or apartment and its grounds as you wish. Your long-term commitment to the neighborhood gives you a stake in the community and its development.

DISADVANTAGES, TOO

There are disadvantages to home ownership, too. Among them:
• You almost surely will have to make a hefty down payment for a house (probably as much as 25 to 30 per cent of the purchase price) and sign a mortgage which binds you to regular payments for as long as thirty years.
• You will be committed to the care of your home over this same period—much like the obligation of time, energy, and money in rearing a child. Home repairs and upkeep can be costly. You will also have to be your own landlord, superintendent, garbage man, fix-it man, etc.
• If you are forced to move there is always a chance that it might take you months to sell your house for what you consider a fair price.

IN FAVOR OF RENTING

Among the positives connected with renting:
• Renting gives you more financial flexibility than home ownership. If your income drops or your job involves frequent transfers, your commitment lasts only as long as your lease.
• Renting holds distinct advantages if you are moving into a new neighborhood, particularly in a fast-growing suburb. If possible, rent for a year or so to become thoroughly acquainted with the area before making a final decision to invest and settle.
• Renting means that taxes, insurance, major repairs, etc. are the landlord's responsibility, although paid for by you in the monthly rent.

A New or an Old House?

"New" houses are generally considered to be those that were built within the last few years. "Older" homes are the ones which were built five to ten years ago or more. New and used houses appreciate in value at about the same rate—between 10 and 15 per cent a year. Both are good investments. You probably will buy an older house simply because there are more of these from which to choose —roughly fifty times as many.

IN FAVOR OF THE OLD

So here are some of the pros of buying an older house:

• You may be able to buy an older house for about 10 to 15 per cent less than a new one—in terms of the space you get for each home-buying dollar. Also, if you're buying from the owner, he may be willing to bargain on price, for the simple reason that home selling is not his sole business. (The exception is in areas where old-fashioned houses are "in.")

• The rooms—and the house as a whole—may be more spacious. Try to assign values to such extras as porches, entrance rooms, basement space, sheds, the like —in terms of dollars and in terms of their intangible value to you.

• Try especially to measure the worth of the character and warmth you'll find in so many older houses. It's up to you to put your own money tag on the "feeling" you get in one house versus another.

• The construction, including materials and workmanship, can be of considerably higher quality. The walls may be thicker, the floor hardwood, etc.

• Frequently the house will be located in an established neighborhood. It will be located relatively close to shops, schools, churches, and transportation facilities. The land surrounding the house itself will have been landscaped too.

• Its kinks and shortcomings—such as a dilapidated porch, old bath or kitchen, peeling wallpaper, or exposed water pipes—will advertise themselves loudly to you when you inspect the house. Flaws in a new development house—a badly poured foundation or poorly spaced joists under the floor—may be hidden.

• The variety of shapes, sizes, and designs of older houses from which to choose probably will be greater than the variety in new homes offered by builders or developers. And old house styles, remember, have stood the tests of time.

• Taxes tend to rise less sharply for older houses than for newer ones—and the burden of special assessments for improvements such as utilities and town water systems may be less since many of these amenities will already have been installed and paid for.

AGAINST THE OLD

Of course, the above is merely one side of the older-home-buying tale—and it would be a disservice to you if I were to stop at this. To suggest some of the points against the older house:

• You may sometimes find it tougher to get a mortgage on an older house than on a new one, and other terms—down payment, duration of mortgage—also may be less favorable on the older house.

• The older house may need costly repairs, termite fumigation, and remodeling. The major modernization jobs can run into big-time money unless your family includes devoted and gifted do-it-yourselfers.

• Your upkeep costs may be greater than for a new house, simply because there's more space to heat and light, more surface to paint, more trees to prune, more rooms to clean.

• Older houses tend to be less tight, have poorer insulation than newer ones, meaning there's greater heat loss.

• You may be offered more space than you actually want—and you may find utterly useless certain types of space: butlers' pantries, libraries, large attics. In the same category might go the lack of scientific design in many older houses, so that traffic may flow awkwardly from room to room.

• Few older houses will have central air conditioning, new built-in appliances, and other conveniences which are often part of new homes.

• And you really don't know the full cost of your older house until you have repaired and remodeled—and these expenses may more than offset that 10 to 15 per cent lower cost.

This is a balanced and honest picture which can save you money, time, and headaches as you probe the older house market.

How to Shop for a Neighborhood

Let's say your family has agreed that a house is for you and it will be a good investment. You know in general where you would like to live, what type of house you would live to live in, how much house you can really afford.

Your next steps are to find the specific community and the precise neighborhood which will be most comfortable and convenient for you and in which living costs—over and above the costs of the house itself—will be best suited to your budget. The neighborhood you choose is crucial to whether your investment in your house ultimately turns out to be excellent, just fair, or an out-and-out disaster.

To help you shop for a community and a neighborhood, make inquiries in these key areas:

PROPERTY TAXES

Even in the late 1970s—when our collective, nationwide property tax bill was under fierce attack—the new and naïve home buyer may underestimate what a huge and growing expense property taxes are. In some rural and exurban towns, local taxes pay only for schools, roads, and miscellaneous expenses. In other, larger cities and towns, taxes cover not only these basics but also the costs of an enormous range of services: the town water supply and sewage disposal system, garbage collection and disposal, the fire and police departments, health and welfare, the towering costs of preventing and eliminating pollution.

The tax on a house, in practice, is a *going charge* just as rent is. Next to your mortgage payment, your tax bill is likely to be your second biggest home ownership cost, and property taxes for years have been among the fastest-rising items in your total living costs. Even if your home deteriorates, your property taxes almost surely will continue to rise, for cities rarely reduce the valuation of a home. They are, however, deductible from your federal tax returns, as your mortgage interest payments are.

Of course, property taxes vary widely from community to community. But the closer you get to a big city, the higher rates tend to be, and the farther out in the rural countryside you go, the lower they tend to be. Northern states tend to impose higher taxes than Southern areas. Consider these factors when you are choosing a place to live and estimating your costs of home ownership. And when you investigate tax rates in a community, find out how land and houses of the type you would like to buy are valued.

Good sources for this information will be a real estate agent, people living in the neighborhood, and officials at the town offices.

Look out, too, for special assessments. Here you will find a wide range, depending on the project involved and the community.

A new road, for example, may result in an assessment on the homeowners concerned, which can make a mockery of any carefully worked-out family housing budget. A neighborhood landscaping project, on the other hand, may not be too costly and also may greatly enhance the value of the property. Special assessments are a variable item, but woe to the family who forgets them! They will always come up sometime!

Ask a real estate agent, a courteous banker, and any other knowledgeable sources you can find, these questions on property taxes in each community and neighborhood in which you are considering buying:

• When a property changes hands, what usually happens to taxes on that property? In many communities new homeowners are routinely sledgehammered by the tax assessors and slapped with tax bills which are far higher than the amounts the former owners were paying.

• What does the community provide in return for your taxes? Low taxes may not be a bargain if they mean inferior schools, second-rate police protection, poor snow removal and garbage disposal services. On the other hand, high taxes may be well worth it—if a community is committed to high educational systems, water fluoridation, good health and recreational facilities, clean and green roadsides.

• What new bond issues are being debated or scheduled in each community—for schools, sewage treatment facilities, road-building equipment, public parks and playgrounds, hospitals, etc? What will be the likely impact of the issues on tax rates? Or, if a costly new school is being planned or built, for which a bond issue already has been voted, what tax hikes may already have been announced for the coming year?

• Is a major re-evaluation of properties in the offing—and what will be the likely hike in the valuation of houses in the community and neighborhood in which you wish to settle? In some areas, tax reassessments have doubled or even tripled tax bills for certain homeowners.

Take the time to visit the town hall or county seat or local planning commission. Ask for details on property and other local taxes in the area in which you think you would like to buy. Get the facts on how fast these taxes have been rising. Ask for estimates on likely future trends—especially if new roads, schools, sewers, and other community improvement projects are in the works.

And listen to local gossip. It can be far more accurate than you suspect.

SCHOOLS

School costs are usually a community's biggest budget item—and thus the local taxpayer's biggest financial commitment. So wherever you settle, schools are crucially important in your comparisons of one community or neighborhood against another.

If you have or may have children, check the quality of local schools by talking with parents of children already enrolled, or by visiting with schoolteachers and PTA members. Ask to sit in on a couple of actual classes and, if you have school-age children, take them along.

Judge the quality of education provided not only by the school's physical plant. Judge also by how the teachers are accepted by the children in their classes; by how creative and stimulating the classroom atmosphere is; by what amount of money is spent per pupil as compared to the national and state averages; by the school's special services and facilities such as science and language laboratories; by the library, psychiatric, and guidance counseling services; by how open-minded school officials are toward promising new teaching techniques.

Inquire at the school superintendent's office about the district's achievement test rating and compare this rating with state and national scores on pupil achievement.

Find out what kindergartens, nursery schools, and day-care centers are available—and what costs are involved.

Look into the school bus services and study the bus route.

Investigate what other cultural-educational facilities the community offers, such as libraries, music, theaters.

CONVENIENCE

Ideally, your house should be as convenient as feasible for those who must commute to work.

For instance, if the family breadwinner must commute every day, how great a distance will that be? What forms of transportation are available? What are traffic conditions like? How reliable are the trains and buses?

Try a trial run yourself on the commuters' route during rush hour before you decide on a location. Do not underestimate the fact that almost any kind of commuting implies costly wear and tear—on yourself as well as your car.

Calculate commuting costs for a year—and compare these with commuting costs from houses in other communities where you are considering buying or renting. These costs can range from $1.00 to $10 or more a day, so make the effort to track down specifics. Also, figure on these costs rising fairly steeply in the years ahead. Remember this point: if you could, through the choice of the neighborhood in which you buy a house, eliminate just $1.00 from the daily commutation, this could add up to savings of $250 or more a year.

Ideally, your house also should be near a good shopping district where the prices are within your budget.

It should be near the church you will attend, if you are a churchgoer.

It should be in a location where children can play. Preschool children should have parks, playgrounds, or other play facilities within half a mile of the house.

It should be reasonably close to service stations, medical facilities, banks, airports, and theaters.

And if you or your spouse or both of you are likely to want to go back to college in the near future, you should plan to live near a university or community college.

CHARACTER

You almost surely would prefer to live in an area in which you can find people of more or less compatible background and interests. So take the time to drive—and walk—around communities and neighborhoods which appeal to you, either because you know and like people who live there or because you like the area's general appearance.

Look for a neighborhood that is stabilized or, even better, is improving. Make sure it is not deteriorating, for as the value of your neighbors' houses decreases the value of your house will be affected too. Check for signs of deterioration by noting the general state of surrounding dwellings, whether they are well-tended or neglected; by counting the number of "for sale" signs and studying the trend of sale prices in the locality; by investigating the encroachment of commercial establishments; by counting the number of dwellings for rent. Experienced appraisers agree that when more than one quarter of the houses in a neighborhood are rented, rather than owned, the neighborhood is declining.

Ask about recent crime trends in the community or neighborhood—especially the record of burglaries and break-ins.

Inquire about how local officials and citizens' groups are going about enforcing laws against polluting the community's air and water—and whether they have a reputation for toughness.

Among the signs of an economically healthy community:

• A record of relatively full employment in periods of recession as well as in booms.

• A slow but steady growth in job opportunities and population—or at least no significant population decline. The town offices will have facts and figures from recent census reports—and these will spell out the trends for you.

• Steadily rising income levels.

• Steadily rising real estate values.

ZONING AND PLANNING

Make a point of inquiring about zoning regulations affecting the neighborhood and the entire community. You should be able to locate a serious, local planning-conservation commission dedicated to keeping community growth attractive and orderly.

If you envision building a new wing or a guest cottage or a garage in the future, find out before you buy whether zoning rules would permit such an addition.

Ask about the zoning rules not only on the property you want to buy but also on nearby tracts of undeveloped land—and other property in the neighborhood. What, for instance, about overnight parking on the street in which you might choose to live?

And ask to see the master land use plan for the community as a whole and its surroundings. (If there is no plan, that in itself is a signal for you to find out why not.)

CHECK LIST FOR SIZING UP A NEIGHBORHOOD

The following abbreviated check list should be useful to you in sizing up a neighborhood—and comparing the merits of one neighborhood with those of another:

	NEIGHBORHOOD A	NEIGHBORHOOD B
Is neighborhood attractive?		
Are good public schools available?		
Are there sound zoning ordinances?		
How much will the yearly property taxes be?		
What is the outlook for special assessments?		
Are there any objectionable noises or smells?		
How many miles (and minutes) to workplace?		
What public transportation is available?		
Is bus or train stop nearby?		
What will monthly commuting costs be?		
Will second car be needed?		
How many miles (and minutes) to shopping center?		
How many miles (and minutes) to nearest grocery store?		
Are there parks and/or playgrounds nearby?		
How far away is the church you'll attend?		
Where are theaters, movies, libraries?		
How far is school bus stop?		
Will you be able to keep pets?		
Are streets well lighted?		
Is adequate police and fire protection provided?		
Are pollution controls enforced?		

HOW TO SHOP FOR A HOUSE

You have decided, within reasonable limits, where you want to live and what kind of a house you want to own. You are now ready to begin your search for a specific house.

WHERE DO YOU BEGIN?

You can get in your car and simply start cruising around whatever neighborhoods you have already checked out and like, looking for the "for sale" signs and querying residents on available houses, prices, and possibilities.

You can, if you're looking for a house in or near the neighborhood where you have been living, simply get word around among friends, acquaintances, and tradespeople of the type of house you're looking for.

You can start merely by studying the local newspaper. You may be lucky enough to spot a good house advertised for sale by its owner, and in any event the newspaper real estate ads will give you clues to prices being asked for the category of house in which you're interested.

In fact, it is worth spending a day or two checking out these ways of locating a house, just to see what may be available among properties not listed by real estate agents.

But the chances are you'll begin your serious search by consulting a real estate broker or agent—preferably a Realtor who is a member of the National Association of Realtors and who subscribes to the association's code of ethics. (Realtor is a trademark registered by the NAR.)

He or she not only has a large bank of information on what types of property are available, where, and at what prices. He also is familiar with the housing market in general. He knows details on zoning and highway building plans. A Realtor can arrange appointments for you to see the type of house you want, inspect these houses with you, give you informed advice on likely costs of maintenance, taxes, repairs, and other matters. He can help you assess the future of neighborhoods, the value of the home as a long-range investment, tell you what is the cheapest kind of mortgage available to you.

Choose a Realtor with care!

Look for one you feel you can trust implicitly. Tell him or her how much you can afford, as exactly as you possibly can, what type of property you would like to own—and where.

Typical Realtors' fees are 6 per cent of the selling price of a house and 10 per cent of the price of raw land. These fees are paid by the person selling the house or land—not the buyer, although the seller frequently jacks up his price to cover the Realtor's fee.

Most Realtors keep in touch with other Realtors and agents in the area who might have the type of property for which you are shopping. And he or she also may be tied into a new computer system which keeps a huge amount of information on listings throughout the area or even the United States. The largest system of this type in operation today—to which hundreds of Realtors in all states subscribe—is Realtron, a Detroit-based computer service real estate data bank.

HOW CAN YOU AFFORD A HOUSE TODAY?

"Demand" is not merely wanting something, in the technical lingo of economists, bankers, and businessmen. You also must be able to pay for what you want—and despite the horrifying escalation in the prices of new homes, demand for housing remains strong and "you" are finding ways to finance the American dream of owning your own home.

How are you managing it? In the young as well as older age groups, in moderate as well as wealthier income classes?

(1) You are seeking out older and relatively less costly homes, thereby avoiding new homes as their average prices cross into formidable figures.

Documentation: Half of America's home buyers as the 1980s begin are under age thirty, and are buying houses priced under $40,000. Moderate-income families are doing the same. Of those of you earning between $15,000 and $25,000, an overwhelming 75 per cent are buying housing costing less than $50,000; one third of all of you who are first-time home buyers, no matter what your age or income, are buying houses built before 1950.

(2) More and more of you are buying homes first and then marrying or having children later in life—if at all. Because your households are smaller, more of your resources, as a couple or an individual, can be spent on your home.

Documentation: More than half of all of you buying homes between the ages of twenty-five and thirty are either single or young marrieds without children; 4 per cent of all homes are going to unmarried couples, so-called "single couples"; 17 per cent are going to single individuals; 66 per cent of first-time buyers are one- or two-member households.

(3) A second income is becoming an increasingly crucial factor in your capacity to buy a home.

Documentation: Of all home-buying families, 50 per cent of you rely on more than one earner; in nearly 30 per cent of all households, the second earner contributes 30 to 50 per cent of the total household income.

(4) Your opportunities for less expensive homes are more plentiful in smaller cities and the North Central region of our nation—so that's where you are trending.

Documentation: In large cities, 38 per cent of all homes cost more than $60,000 as the decade ended, against less than 11 per cent in this expense class in cities of under 250,000 population. In the West, homes are much more costly than in other areas.

What comes through in all these findings is the fact that in the face of a cost upsurge that has made a roof over your head less and less affordable, you will not give up the dream of home ownership and you will find your own ways to make the dream come true.

How long can this hold true?

No one, certainly not the objective experts, will state a positive answer. But "demand" should remain powerful at least until the 1990s—assuming the economy continues healthy and mortgage funds do not dry up.

"ZERO LOT-LINE HOMES"

"Zero lot-line homes" . . . Note well this inelegant-sounding string of words, for they stand for a concept in home building that rapidly swept across the country in the late 1970s and enabled home builders to provide you with the kind of detached, single-family houses you want at prices you can afford.

How did builders do it?

By reducing the size of the lot by from 25 to 43 feet and placing the house on or close to one of the side boundary lines. Hence the name: zero lot-line homes.

To maintain privacy, the wall of the house abutting the boundary sideline contains no windows or windows placed higher than usual. The rest of the house is especially designed, often with skylights and arches, to bring sunlight into what otherwise would be a dark interior. The single side yard is large enough for a garden, barbecue, or patio area.

Begun in the early 1970s in California, where land has long been costly and homes built closer together, zero lot-line homes have been springing up in such widely separated cities as St. Louis, Miami, Chicago, Denver, and Dallas.

Municipal zoning officials, who once insisted that detached houses be built a certain minimum distance from the boundary lines of their lots, have taken a second look at these restrictions. Many now see the zero lot-line concept as a way to reduce urban sprawl, while protecting new households from being priced out of the single-family home market.

Zero lot-line homes often are less expensive than traditional detached houses. Lot costs amount to around 32 per cent of the sales price of a house in the Denver-Apsen area, for instance. Zero lot-line houses reduce prices in this area by increasing the density of houses from, say, four to five per acre to ten or twelve per acre.

Side yard space is traded for higher densities. Buyers like the homes, but equally important, the mortgage lenders like them. It is much easier to get financing for single-family houses than for townhouses or condominiums.

Privacy is the big thing. The houses are not just part of a row and neighbors can't be heard pounding on the walls, the patios are not right on top of one another.

The smaller yards are viewed as a plus, particularly in the drought-prone West, for as the cost of public water goes up, home buyers want smaller lots so it will cost them less to water their lawns. In some new subdivisions around Denver, people are forbidden to plant grass on more than 40 per cent of their lot.

Although a key attraction of zero lot-line homes is their relatively low price—many sell for $43,000 to $71,000, and that's becoming a "moderate price range" in this era!—the design principle also is being used in luxury homes.

You could find truly posh ZLL houses, with the "essential" feature of the swimming pool, selling for as much as $225,000 in such cities as Dallas and resort areas as Newport Beach, California, as the 1980s neared.

The future for the zero lot-line home appears bright indeed.

WHERE DO YOU FIND THE BARGAINS?

You might try to buy from the owner directly. Realtors usually get a commission of about 6 per cent, which equals $3,000 on a $50,000 house.

You might, for instance, find a bargain on a property on which the mortgage has been foreclosed. This could be a house that a bank or other lender is eager to sell before the house starts to deteriorate from disuse. A new housing or condo project could go bankrupt and give you an opportunity for a bargain.

Or you might find housing buys at the outskirts of a suburb, in the path in which the population appears to be moving. You won't find all the conveniences of the suburbs, such as superhighways and shopping centers. But you will find lower property taxes and lower land prices. If this interests you, check out the possibility of employment in the suburb adjoining this exurb—as well as all the commuting angles if either or both of you are working in the central city.

Or you could find house bargains in a neighborhood which is now run-down but which was once attractive. Look closely at neighborhoods which seem in line for urban renewal or intensive restoration. Washington's Georgetown district and New York City's Greenwich Village are classic examples of formerly depressed neighborhoods which have become ultrafashionable and ultraexpensive. This area of bargains can be exceedingly tricky and dangerous, though. You must be able to distinguish between a run-down neighborhood in line for rebirth and a deteriorating section doomed by a new superhighway, housing project, factory, or other commerical development.

Or your source of bargains could be the house with several unfinished rooms which deter other buyers but which you would be perfectly content to finish off later as your family expands. And if your family includes a do-it-yourselfer, you have a natural money saver built in.

And finally, there's the charming "freak house" or the crazy combination of Victorian and colonial—which has been on the market for months or years and has been knocked way down in price. If you are willing and able to invest the necessary amounts to restore and modernize it, if your family finds it comfortable, and if you plan to live in it for quite a few years, the "freak" you fall in love with may be a perfect answer for you—and available at a real bargain price, too. This goes even though you, in turn, may have a tough time selling your freak at the price you think it's worth years hence.

Try to buy off season—during the hot months of July and August when most people are on vacation or during the cold months of January and February when demand usually drops. Prices tend to be higher during the peak home shopping months of March, April, May, and then September and October.

Get the real estate section of your local paper as early as possible and try to view the home as soon in the day as you can. Make an offer if you're interested even if it sounds low. The owner may be anxious to sell and might accept your bid. You don't know if you don't try.

HOUSE SHOPPING DO'S AND DON'TS

Take a notebook and pencil with you when you go on a house-hunting tour and, if possible, a Polaroid camera as well. Write down the name, address, and phone number of each owner—and the name and number of the real estate agent handling the deal. Make notes on all points of special interest to you—and note also the specific problems which you spot in each. Snap a couple of pictures of each house which tempts you—for later reference and to show other family members.

By all means, use the check lists in this section to help you rate one house against another.

If it is an older house you are inspecting, query the seller on these points:

• Why he wants to sell the house—especially if his reasons have to do with the building's problems.

• What his tax bills are—and are likely to be in the near future, and how fast they have been rising.

• How much the utility bills run each year. (Ask to see actual copies of a year's bills, particularly most recent months.)

• Which major improvements have been made—and specifics on such matters as how deep the artesian well is, the location and type of the septic tank and leaching field, the status of the war against the invading termites.

• Also, if you and your family tend to be away from home a lot—on business trips, vacations—find out whether the house can be easily turned off, closed up, and left to take care of itself.

Don't be swayed because you first saw a house when the dogwood or the lilac bushes were in bloom. You are not buying bushes and trees. You are buying a house! Look at the house both during the day and at night, when it's gray and raining as well and bright and shining, when it's cold as well as hot.

Don't stray too far from the original "dream house" your family agreed it wanted. If there are such specialized rooms as family rooms, dens, sewing rooms, tool shed, "rec" rooms which you did not include in your original requirements, you'll pay a considerable sum for this space. Do you need it? Do you even want it?

And don't let yourselves be stampeded into a deal. Many real estate brokers will exert at least some pressure on you—for example, by telling you that another buyer is hot on the track of the house you are viewing. Many a family, in fact, has jumped into a purchase of a not really suitable house just to keep it away from a competitor.

Do consider, as you hunt for a house, its future resale value. The biggest pluses include a good location, in a stable but progressive community; good-sized living spaces; adequate closet and other storage space; good kitchen and laundry facilities; and a convenient arrangement of rooms.

Do, before you buy an older house, have a contractor or housing inspector look over the house and estimate costs of any major, basic repairs in these seven key areas: foundation and basement, roof, heating plant, plumbing, electrical wiring, sewage system, paint on the outside of the house. If you cannot find a qualified contractor, professional engineer, or other consultant to advise you on the structural soundness of the house, the town engineer may be willing to do so.

Do also consult individual specialists such as plumbers, electricians, roofers, and exterminators for advice if you fear other major problems may exist. These people will probably give you their advice free—on the basis that you'll use their services if it turns out that major repairs are needed. Or you may find a consulting firm which specializes in going over a house, uncovering its faults, and estimating costs of correcting them.

APPRAISING THE HOUSE

Surely, in view of the investment you are making, you owe it to yourself to spend a small sum to discover—before you buy—whether the house is likely to fall apart, burn down, be ravaged by termites. Surely you will be willing to pay an appraiser a fee to hear whether the house's asking price is fair and reasonable.

An appraiser should assess the design and structural aspects of the house; delve into prices at which comparable properties are being sold; inform you on the quality and character of the neighborhood, zoning regulations, population trends, property tax levels and prospects; estimate the community's economic growth patterns.

Ask the Chicago-based American Institute of Real Estate Appraisers or the National Association of Realtors (155 East Superior Street, Chicago, Ill. 60611) for names of qualified appraisers in your area. Although you have no real yardstick of an appraiser's competence, one guide you can use is whether the appraiser is a member of the American Institute of Real Estate Appraisers or a member of the Society of Real Estate Appraisers which certifies appraisers who can pass an examination in this field and meet other professional standards as well. Look for the designations M.A.I. (Member of the Appraisal Institute), R.M. (Residential Member), or S.R.A. (Senior Residential Appraiser) following the appraiser's name in the Yellow Pages.

Expect to pay at least $75 to $200 for an appraisal—and make sure you get a written report on the inspector's findings.

Your best sources of names of qualified home appraisers and/or inspectors are:

> your Realtor (who may be qualified to make the appraisal himself);
>
> any bank which extends mortgages;
>
> an established builder or local builders' association;
>
> the town engineer;
>
> the Yellow Pages—under either "Appraisers—Real Estate" or "Real Estate Appraisers."

AN APPRAISAL QUESTIONNAIRE

Here are questions for you and/or your professional appraiser to use as a guide in judging design and structural aspects of a house:

• Are there termites? If termite damage already has occurred, how serious is it and what must be done to correct it? If an underground termite shield has been installed around the outside of the house, is it installed properly? Do other houses in the neighborhood have termite problems—a clue that your house also could be a target?

• What is the condition of the electrical circuits? How many and where are the outlets—and is the number adequate for your needs? How old is the wiring and is it sufficient to carry the load of appliances and lighting your family would put on it? Inadequate wiring is hazardous and shortens the life of your appliance.

• What is the state of the plumbing and water supply? Is the water pure? Soft? What does it taste like? Is there adequate water pressure—especially when several faucets or appliances are running at the same time? Enough hot water? Are the plumbing pipes of brass, copper, galvanized iron, or plastic, and in what condition are these pipes? Is any major plumbing work likely to be needed before you can move in? Do all the faucets, drains, and other plumbing fixtures work well? Is each bathroom complete with all the fixtures and accessories you need?

• What type of sewer system is there—and where are the drainage pipes, septic tank, cesspool, or whatever? If there is a cesspool or septic tank, are drains provided with a grease trap? Is it a proper system in terms of soil types in the area, state and local zoning and/or health codes? Is there any visible seepage aboveground? If the owner does not have enough information to satisfy you, see if the local government has a record of the building permit application, which describes the type of sewage system installed.

• What type of hot water heater is there? What are the monthly costs for normal use? How many baths or showers can be taken, one after another, within a given period of time such as one hour? And, once the hot water supply has been depleted, how long does it take to heat another round of baths and showers?

• What is the age and condition of the furnace? Is it capable of heating the house to at least 70° when the outside temperature reaches the lowest point for this area? Has it been well serviced or does it contain fire hazards? What are the yearly costs of heating the house?

• Of what material are the foundation walls and are these walls in good condition? On what type of footing does the foundation sit? If the house doesn't rest on solid rock, does it have, as it should, poured concrete footings below the frost line in the area?

• What type of basement is there? Is it properly ventilated? Is it dry—or have any leaking basement problems already been corrected? Is there a drain in the basement? (Check this on a rainy day.) What protection does the house have against invasion by water—from the ground or from flooding resulting from rain? Is there, for example, a heavy plastic "vapor barrier" between your foundation floor and the ground underneath? Do the outsides of the foundation walls have a moistureproof coating? Are there footing drains under the ground outside the house leading away from it at the base of the foundation? Are you likely to have a leaky, wet basement?

• What type of soil is the house built on? Is there any evidence of settlement which could cause damage to the foundation?

• Is the house solidly built? Does it meet local zoning laws?

• Of what materials is the house built—especially the "basics" such as girders, columns, sills, joists? Are they of the proper size and spacing?

• Are the floors in good condition—and hard enough for the wear and tear they are likely to suffer? Will they support a heavy load such as a piano or water bed? Are they noisy when someone walks on them? Jumping up and down on floors may reassure the jumper that the floors won't collapse under such provocation. It also will yield a clue to how rigid (good) or springy (not good) the floor is. But this test might not reveal serious decay in the sills or other supports holding up the floor, too narrow or otherwise inadequate joists beneath the floor, termite damage, and other problems. Take a flashlight, go down to the basement or crawl space, and examine the ground floor from its underside if it is not covered with plaster or paneling.

• What is the condition of the attic and is it strong enough for storage purposes or for building extra living quarters if needed? Is it well ventilated? Are the framing and sealing around the chimney tight enough to prevent leaks when it rains?

• In what condition is the garage? Will your car or cars fit in it? Is it big enough to provide the type of storage and work spaces you need? If the garage is on a second floor, are the floor and framing strong enough to support a car?

• Are the plaster or plasterboard walls and ceilings smooth? Or are there cracks which could be evidence of settling of the house? How easily can any cracks be filled? In the case of plasterboard, are the seams neatly sealed?

• Is the inside trim, such as moldings and baseboards, in good condition? What about hardware such as locks and knobs? Do doors close properly and are there good outside door locks? Are the windows weather-stripped? Are the kitchen cabinet doors properly hung?

• If there is a fireplace, does the damper open and close properly—to prevent heat escape when the fireplace is not being used? Is there a heatilator which will cut fuel bills and, if so, is it rusty or is it sound?

• Is the house insulated? What type and how thick is this insulation—especially overhead, but also in the exterior walls? If new or more insulation is needed, how expensive a project is that likely to be?

• What material has been used for exterior walls? What condition are the walls in? Is the exterior of the house attractive-looking? Will walls and/or trim need scraping and painting—and how much of a job is that likely to be? (A new paint job on the outside of an average-size house may cost into the thousands, depending on how much scraping, caulking, priming, and other preparation are needed.)

• In what condition is the roof and will any roofing repairs be needed? How many years will the present roof last?

• If the house—or roof—is shingled, what type of shingles are they? Wood? Asphalt? Some other material? If shingles are wood, are they the chemically fireproofed type? If forest fires or fires generally are a real hazard in the area, how much would it cost to substitute some other type of roofing for untreated wood shingles?

• What about the gutters and downspouts? What maintenance is necessary to keep them in workable condition?

• Are the storm windows and doors in good condition? What about screens?

• In what condition is the masonry throughout—such as foundations, basement floor, walkways, fireplace, chimneys? Is mortar tight and solid or loose and flaky? If there are serious cracks or missing bricks, or if chimneys are improperly lined, what would it entail to correct these problems? (Note: cracks in the foundation do not necessarily mean a major masonry project is needed—but check this point carefully.)

•Which major appliances are included in the deal, and which will you have to buy? Today, more than 80 per cent of new homes being built include dishwashers; 90 per cent include stoves, and 61 per cent have a central air-conditioning system.

•How easy—or difficult will the house be to keep clean? (Note: a house which is air conditioned tends to be easier to keep clean than one which is not.)

•Is there enough light?

•What is the exposure of the house: does it face east, west, north, or south? A northern exposure may mean that a garden will be relatively difficult to cultivate and also may mean higher fuel bills in winter. But it may be more comfortable in summer. As a general rule, a southern, eastern, western exposure or some combination of these is more agreeable than a house facing the north, northeast, or northwest. This is particularly true for kitchens, porches, patios, and living rooms.

For more guidance on checking out a house send for the booklet *Basic Housing Inspection* (U. S. Department of Health, Education, and Welfare, Room 1587, Parklawn Building, 5600 Fishers Lane, Rockville, Maryland 20852; free).

CHECK LISTS

CHECK LIST FOR COMPARING SPECIFIC HOUSES

The following abbreviated check list will help you compare and rate one specific house against another.

	HOUSE NO. 1	HOUSE NO. 2
Location of house		
Name of owner or builder		
His address and telephone number		
Realtor's name		
Realtor's telephone number		
Price asked		
Down payment required by lender		
Term of mortgage		
Monthly mortgage payments		
Estimated closing costs		
Yearly property taxes		
Deed restrictions, if any		
Estimated cost of immediate repairs		
Type or style of house		
Total floor space (sq. ft.)		
Number of rooms		
Bedrooms		
Bathrooms		

CHECK LISTS (continued)

	HOUSE NO. 1	HOUSE NO. 2
Dimensions of living room	————	————
(*Measure.* Empty rooms appear		
deceptively large.)		
Size of kitchen	————	————
Dining room?	————	————
Fireplace?	————	————
Type of heating system	————	————
How many closets?	————	————
How big are the closets?	————	————
Is there at least one closet for each		
bedroom?	————	————
Is there a linen closet?	————	————
Other storage space?	————	————
Is there a separate laundry room?	————	————
Utility room?	————	————
"Mud" room?	————	————
Garage?	————	————
Size of garage? How many cars?	————	————
Does it have electrical outlets?	————	————
How much garage storage space?	————	————
Is there an entrance from garage to		
kitchen?	————	————
What type of water supply?	————	————
What type of sewer system?	————	————
Sanitary?	————	————
Storm?	————	————
Basement?	————	————
—or crawl space?	————	————
How big?	————	————
Which appliances are included?		
Stove	————	————
Range hood	————	————
Refrigerator	————	————
Dishwasher	————	————
Garbage disposal	————	————
Clothes washer and dryer	————	————
Air conditioning	————	————
Freezer	————	————
Other	————	————
Is carpeting included?	————	————
Is there a separate entrance hall?	————	————
Are kitchen and living room		
protected from through traffic?	————	————

CHECK LISTS (continued)

	HOUSE NO. 1	HOUSE NO. 2
Are bedrooms near baths?		
Do the size and layout permit enough privacy?		
How soundproof is the house— especially bedrooms?		
Are there enough outside doors?		
Are they equipped with foolproof locks?		
How difficult would escape be if fire broke out? (High, small bed- room windows a minus.)		
Does house have "character"?		
Notes on other good *and* bad points		

CHECK LIST FOR THE KITCHEN

Now, starting through the house, make notes on these important aspects of the kitchen (the most costly room per square foot) in each house you are considering:

Overall dimensions
Size of sink
Amount of counter space and other work surfaces
Amount of shelf and cabinet space
Location of sink in relation to stove
Location of refrigerator in relation to stove and sink
Location of counter in relation to stove and sink
Stove vent fan
Overhead lighting
Lighting for work surfaces
Type and condition of appliances
Type of and ease of cleaning kitchen floor
View of outdoor play area
Light from outside
Distance to family room or living room
Size of eating area
Condition of pipes
Wall covering

CHECK LIST FOR THE LIVING ROOM

And note these important aspects of the living room in each house you might buy:

Are floors sturdy, attractive?
If carpeted, what is underneath?

Is there a fireplace and does it work?
Does chimney draw well?
Is there adequate wall space for furniture? Pictures?
Are views to the outside attractive?
Are there bookshelves?
Are type and color of wall coverings suitable?
If there is a sliding glass door, does it work?
Is it shatterproof?
Do windows and doors permit cross-ventilation?

CHECK LIST FOR THE BATHROOMS

Is grout in tiled areas in good condition?
How handy—and how large—is the linen closet?
Is the medicine cabinet large enough?
Are there outlets for a razor, hair dryer, etc.?
Is lighting, especially near mirror, adequate?
Is there an exhaust fan?
Can door locks be opened easily from outside in event of an emergency?

CHECK LIST FOR OUTSIDE OF THE HOUSE

Now, on the outside of each house, explore these questions:

Is siding of good construction and in good condition?
Are windows and doors weather-stripped?
Is there proper flashing over doors and windows?
What are the type and condition of the gutters?
Are storm and screen windows in good condition?
Is chimney masonry in good condition?
Is porch in sound condition?
How up to date is the paint job?
Is the roof in good shape?
Are there enough hose connections?

CHECK LIST TO JUDGE THE LOT

Here, finally, is a compact check list which will help you judge the lot which goes with a house—assuming you have already jotted down the size and shape of the lot and the location of the property lines.

Is lot big enough for your needs?
Is parking space adequate?
Does driveway permit turning around?
Is its length or grade excessive if area is snowy?
Is general topography attractive?
Is there a patio?
Or terrace?
Or back yard?
What dimensions?

How many big trees are there?

Do they appear healthy?

Is there enough privacy from neighborhood?

Can garbage cans be concealed?

Is there a garden or room for a garden?

Will the soil type permit a garden?

Are wires or gutters obtrusive?

Are views pleasant?

How much landscaping has been done?

What About Buying a Co-operative Apartment?

HOW A CO-OP WORKS

Today, Americans of all types and all income brackets—from millionaires to those existing on poverty incomes, from swinging singles to elderly retirees—are buying and living in co-operative apartments and condominiums. These types of housing, in fact, are now the most rapidly expanding of all permanent housing categories in the United States. Of every seven new apartments, one is a co-op or condominium.

Many of the rules for buying a house apply to co-ops and condominiums as well. For if you enter into an agreement for a co-operative or condominium, you are buying. But there are significant variations and difference too.

First, here's how a co-operative works:

• A co-operative is a corporation, with shareholders, elected directors, and officers. Each shareholder has a voice in how the entire co-op is managed (usually by a professional manager or management firm).

• When you buy shares in a co-operative building you are buying stock in the whole corporation which in turn owns and runs the building. The larger your apartment, the larger your "share" will be in the overall organization. Today's range of co-op prices runs all the way from thousands to many hundreds of thousands of dollars.

• In addition to the purchase price of your shares in a co-operative, you pay a monthly maintenance charge which covers the mortgage on the entire building, property taxes, and general maintenance of the building as a whole. The amount of the maintenance charge depends on the size and location of your apartment.

• That portion of the maintenance fee which is earmarked to pay for mortgage interest and property taxes is deductible from your federal income taxes—with the exception of publicly subsidized co-ops, where only the non-subsidized portion is deductible.

• As a member of a non-profit co-operative, you are your own landlord. You help set the standards for the entire building. You help choose your own neighbors and you get the "profit" a landlord would otherwise get—in the form of lower monthly maintenance charges.

• Your costs compare favorably with the costs of renting. The Federal Housing

Administration estimates that the cost of living in a co-operative is about 20 per cent less than the cost of renting. Also an advantage is that resident-shareholders tend to take better care of their surroundings than do rental housing tenants.

• Unlike the person who rents a house or apartment, the shareholder in a co-operative can benefit from an increase in the value of his share of the project. As the overall value of the co-operative unit rises—in response to housing shortages and other factors—the value of each family's share rises too.

KEY DISADVANTAGES

• If too few shareholders sign up to share ownership and costs, those who have already bought in must accept hikes in their maintenance charges.

• Or if one or more other occupants default on their payments, you must make up for these losses.

• You usually must get the approval of the board of directors before you may sell to someone else or before you may make any major alterations in your apartment.

• Buyers sometimes must have all cash.

• In some areas, prices may be ridiculously inflated.

VITAL QUESTIONS TO INVESTIGATE

Before you buy shares in a co-operative, investigate these vital points:

• What size loan or, in a few places, mortgage can you get from a lender on the shares you might buy? Normally the proportion is 50 to 80 per cent of the appraised value of your shares, but sometimes the proportion is far lower.

• What interest rate will be charged on the loan? Typically, in the late 1970s this rate was at least 1 to 2 per cent above regular mortgage interest rates—and sometimes it was more.

• What is the neighborhood like? This is an important clue to whether or not an investment in a co-operative is likely to be sound.

• What is the record on sale of the other apartments? Have they been sold to financially responsible individuals? Remember, you are, in effect, going into business with the other families in the building. You may be financially responsible; your next-door neighbor may not be.

• If it is a new building, do you have reason to believe the builder is financially responsible and is in a position to fulfill whatever deal he makes?

• What efforts has the builder made, if any, to reduce the risks involved to responsible investors when some default on their payments? It is crucially important to find out the extent of your risk.

• Is the price fair? To find out, add up all your monthly costs—including the maintenance charges, utility costs, and debt service—and compare these with the amount it would cost you to rent a similar apartment.

• Is the management professional and skilled? How will your gripes be handled?

• If you had to or wanted to get out of the deal, exactly what would be the mechanics of doing so?

What About Buying a Condominium?

HOW A CONDOMINIUM WORKS

Buying a condominium is very much like buying a house or apartment, since you, the purchaser, get legal title to your own dwelling and are responsible for paying property taxes.

The key difference between a co-operative and a condominium, as one observer put it, is this:

"A co-operative is a batch of people owning one structure. A condominium is a batch of people owning a batch of structures."

• In a condominium, you buy your apartment—or house or second house—outright, with the usual down payment, mortgage, and legal paperwork. At the same time you are buying a share of the condominium's community property and facilities, which may include elevators, laundry rooms, garage, gardens, golf clubs, swimming pool, or a marina.

• You agree to pay monthly maintenance costs (although these tend to be far lower than in a co-operative) and you may deduct that portion of the costs going for mortgage interest and property taxes from your federal tax return.

• Since you have a deed (or "condominium declaration") and are the owner of your condominium, you may resell it or give it to anyone you choose—although the other owners often reserve a right of first refusal. And you usually are permitted to do anything you choose within your own four walls.

• You finance a condominium just as you would a house. Both the Federal Housing Administration and the Veterans Administration now back mortgages on condominiums. A mortgage is usually much easier to get for a condominium than for a co-op.

• An exceedingly important difference between a condominium and a co-operative is that, if others default or the whole condominium project fails, you are not held financially responsible for the failure. This becomes the problem of the mortgage lenders involved, not you.

• As a general rule, co-operatives are strictly apartments while condominiums may be "duplexes," "fourplexes," or "sixplexes"; separate "townhouses"— usually row houses and usually built in clusters; apartments or vacation cottages; or facilities at a "condominium campground."

• You have the advantage when you own a condominium of building up equity in the house or apartment as you pay off your mortgage. You also have the use of important community facilities.

• You can, when you own a condominium, particularly in a vacation resort, rent it to others—and, if its primary purpose is to produce income, you can get the added tax advantages of being able to deduct your expenses for repairs, maintenance, depreciation, etc.—with definite limitations on your deductions, though, if you use the property personally and rent it only when you don't use it.

CONDOMINIUM PITFALLS

The condominium boom, however, is not all joys of tax-sheltered easy living, no lawn mowing or snow shoveling, community pools, health clubs, etc.

But just pointing out that there are weaknesses and that there have been serious abuses is not enough. How do you, a buyer, avoid the pitfalls? Here are several basic guides if you are considering the purchase of a condominium:

• The most fundamental rule of all is a thorough investigation of the seller/developer to be sure he is highly reputable, well financed, and experienced in the field. Don't fail to check all resources available to you—including the local real estate board, local Better Business Bureau, banks, friends. Use the same basic rules in shopping for and judging a condominium as you would if you were buying shares in a co-operative or buying a separate house outright.

• Do not permit your deposit funds to be commingled with other developer funds, and instead, request that they be deposited into an escrow account with interest in your name. Ask, too, that any bank statement related to the account be forwarded to your attention. Don't compromise on this.

• Do not accept the statement of the real estate developer on real estate taxes. Be certain the information given you is accurate, and confirm what you have been told with local assessing authorities.

• Make sure you fully understand all lease situations, for there are increasing instances of developers maintaining fee ownership to the land under the condominium (thus creating a leasehold). Some hold onto the parking garage, others to the recreational amenities. These leaseholds do not necessarily present a problem to you, but they are vital in comparing costs. For instance, if Condominium A is priced at $55,000 with the seller maintaining ownership of the land and leasing it back to you at $500 a year, a comparable Condominium B with the land included is clearly worth more.

• Check whether the common area charge budget is realistic. If a developer establishes an unrealistically low budget to minimize the carrying charges and make the units more salable, the result can be poor service and inadequate maintenance until the budget is increased and the extra costs passed on to you.

• Investigate the management to make sure it is experienced and well regarded, for management will have a direct impact on the value of your investment.

• Do not accept mere promises of a swimming pool, clubhouse, tennis courts, etc. These amenities should be available before the developers start marketing their units.

• Find out about provisions for parking—particularly if you have two or more cars. Be sure the space is adequate for you.

• Study with care the condominium association rules, so you understand the meaning of such terms as "right of first refusal," "usage provisions," "rental restrictions," "pet restrictions." Don't risk learning their meaning after you have bought. Each condominium has its own rules on pets. What about children? Many do not allow children under the age of sixteen as permanent residents although they permit children to visit or remain on the premises for temporary periods and under certain regulations.

• If an apartment building is being converted to a condominium ("condo-conversion"), check whether the developer is certifying to the condition of the structure, electrical heat, plumbing, the like. In these cases, additional considerations must be the soundproofing of the building, adequate utilities, a strong structure. Hire a lawyer who knows condominium conversions to manage the transfer of title and definition of your property boundaries. Anticipate the rise in taxes that often follows conversion of an apartment condominium.

If you are now renting, don't overestimate the tax savings in condominium ownership. Your tax bracket is your adjusted gross, not your gross-earnings tax bracket. And whatever benefits accrue will be in the government's hand until receipt of your tax refund.

Finally, under an IRS ruling in the 1970s, condominium owner associations are not exempt from federal income tax (previously, they had been). This opened up important tax questions which demand your close scrutiny.

Of course, the advantages of condominium ownership remain and the concept is valid in an era of steep and rising maintenance costs. But you must recognize and know how to avoid the pitfalls if you are to enjoy a condominium's benefits.

Excellent booklets on condos are available from: (1) the Department of Housing and Urban Development, *Questions About Condominiums,* free from either HUD regional offices or HUD headquarters, Washington, D.C. 20401; (2) the National Association of Home Builders, *Condominium Buyer's Guide,* $1.00 from NAHB, 15 and M Streets, N.W., Washington, D.C. 20005.

What About Buying in a Development?

IMPORTANT QUESTIONS

Millions of American families are now living, either temporarily or permanently, in housing developments—for the very good reason that developments, or tract houses, often offer the most economical deal in housing today. Just because they are developments, professional home builders are able to use mass-produced "modular" segments, computer-standardized designs clustered together, attached townhouses, and other means to control costs. And thus they are able to offer home buyers major financial advantages.

Many development houses sell for amounts ranging around $50,000, but prices can exceed $100,000.

Typically, the home buyer may choose from several basic plans—any of which can be modified to suit his family's individual tastes and needs.

If you are thinking of buying in a housing development, consider these important questions:

• How much open, undeveloped outdoor space has been left for the use and enjoyment of everybody?

• Has the developer built around existing trees and shrubbery—or simply razed everything and superimposed a rigid plan on top of bare ground?

• Is the development planned so that there are cul-de-sacs and dead-end streets which prohibit fast, through traffic from whizzing by your house? Is there planning for parking? Sun exposure? Views from windows?

• Are the houses well constructed from good-quality materials? A few chats with residents who have lived in similar houses in the community should reveal any major shortcomings in the design and construction of the houses. Supplement your conversations with your own close inspection plus the judgment of an outside builder-consultant.

• Are the houses situated on well-prepared building sites? If they were filled in by bulldozers, were they permitted to settle for a year or more before building was begun?

• Is there enough topsoil to plant a lawn and/or garden?

• Is the lot large enough to afford your family the amount of privacy you need and want? Or will you have to spend money to build a fence to separate yourselves from neighbors who are too close or too noisy?

IF YOU BUY ON THE BASIS OF A MODEL

If you decide to buy on the basis of a model, several months before your own house will be completed, discuss your special housing needs and wants as soon as possible with the builder. And negotiate the price you'll actually pay on this basis.

For example, you may want to forgo central air conditioning—at a possible saving of about $1,500—and use that money for more kitchen appliances. Or if you are planning a Japanese garden you may prefer to have the builder landscape your house with gravel instead of topsoil.

Before you make a decision based on a model home, get a full set of floor plans and specifications for the house you are agreeing to buy in writing—including everything from landscaping promises to wallpaper designs and paint colors.

Finally, do not sign any contract to buy a development (or any other) house, or put down the usual $50 to $100 "binder," before your lawyer has exhaustively checked the deal.

HOW TO AVOID "QUESTIONABLE" DEVELOPMENT BUILDERS

The field of development housing is riddled with promoters using high-pressure sales tactics and builders with exceedingly sleazy reputations. Nevertheless, there are ways to recognize the good, honest builder. Before you make any financial commitment on a house which has not yet been built or not yet been completed:

Ask whether he lives within the development—one sign he is willing to listen to his buyers' grievances.

Inquire whether or not he is a member of the National Association of Home Builders—no guarantee of, but definitely a clue to, his ethics.

Visit houses he has built previously to see if they are well built and well landscaped.

Check his reputation with the local Chamber of Commerce, local Better Business Bureau, the bank where he has his accounts, and his major suppliers.

See if he offers a warranty developed by the National Association of Home Builders. Called the Home Owners Warranty (HOW), it gives you protection against major structural defects for up to ten years.

Try to find a couple of families or individuals who bought their present homes five or ten years ago from the builder-developer from whom you are considering buying. Ask their opinions on how the builder rectified construction errors and in general fulfilled his obligations.

Take your time in reaching your decision until you are satisfied—thoroughly—that all is well.

NEW TOWNS

Finally, there's the entirely new town—usually a community planned for a population of tens of thousands of families. Most new towns are situated in the exurbs of big cities. They come complete with shopping centers, parks, playgrounds, cultural facilities—and, often, jobs in offices and factories. And most new towns offer a variety of types of housing—ranging from small, inexpensive apartments to big, expensive individual houses.

The key advantages of new towns are that they:

eliminate the agonies of commuting, assuming the worker holds a job in the new town or nearby;

offer adequately large parks and other open spaces and fewer driving hazards because of their good, large-scale, long-range professional planning;

have the convenience of nearby schools, shopping centers and cultural attractions, a varied population, reasonable nearness to big cities;

generally do not have such big-city problems as high crime rates, filthy air and waterways, embarrassing slums.

However, unlike cities, new towns offer no "roots," traditional "charms," or ties with past history.

AND WHAT ABOUT A MOBILE HOME?

CHEAPEST LIVING SPACE AVAILABLE

Only recently the "Model T" of the U.S. housing industry, mobile homes now account for virtually all new homes in the $20,000-and-under price bracket, more than two out of three new homes in the $25,000-and-under price bracket, and half of all new homes.

But before you join the millions of mobile home inhabitants, be sure you have a firm grasp on the basic economics involved.

• The typical mobile home in the late 1970s measured 14 by 66 feet and cost about $17,000 furnished. This is about $18 per square foot—or half the cost of a conventional home. For minimum accommodations, the cheapest mobile home runs as little as $6.00 to $7.00 per square foot or only $5,000 to $6,000 in all.

• In addition to the basic purchase price, you, a prospective mobile home buyer, must weigh the costs of renting space in a mobile home park (assuming you don't own land on which to put your unit), the cost of installing the home, insurance premiums, the cost of financing, and the resale value.

• The typical rent charged for space in a mobile home park in the late 1970s was $55 a month, with water, sewage, twice weekly trash pickup, and snow removal usually included. This fee depends on the nature and location of the development itself, as well as your view and lot size. It can be in the $100 to $135 range.

• The cost of setting up a home varies according to the mobile home park's rules. The basic setup, which includes putting the home on a concrete pad, leveling it, removing the wheels, etc., cost about $450 as the 1980s neared. Hookups for electricity and plumbing can run another $400. In addition, some parks require that all units be outfitted with metal "skirting," to cover the open space beneath the home, steps from the home's platform, and an awning. Depending on the unit's size, the mobile home owner can expect to pay about 15 per cent of the retail price for installation. Of course, such extras as central air conditioning add more.

• Insurance premiums on mobile homes are higher than those for conventional houses, thanks mostly to past high fire and wind loss. A mobile home buyer was likely to pay from $85 to $150 a year in insurance premiums on a $12,000 mobile unit in the closing years of the 1970s, while the owner of a $44,000 conventional home might have paid between $67 and $85 a year in premiums.

• Getting a loan on a mobile home is relatively easy, but it's not cheap. The units aren't considered real property by most financial institutions and state governments, although in some areas this is changing. Banks and finance companies have lumped mobile homes into the same consumer credit category as motorboats, cars, and color televisions, so they're largely ineligible for the low-interest, long-term mortgages given conventional homes.

To give you a better idea of what you'll have to pay for a moderate-price mobile home unit, associates of the industry's Manufactured Housing Institute guided me in preparing this breakdown of latest reported data:

Average 1976 mobile home price	$11,750
Down payment (about 16 per cent)	1,850
Balance to be financed	9,900
Monthly payments twelve years (including three-year insurance policy and basic setup)	172
Total financing cost with 12½ per cent interest	14,850
Total 144 monthly payments	24,750
Land rental per month	55
Installation (varies depending on owner's and park's wishes)	1,000

Government-guaranteed loans are available through the Federal Housing Administration and the Veterans Administration, but the financial community's reaction (so far) to these programs has been lukewarm. From 1970 when the FHA began insuring mobile home loans to December 1975, only thirty-two thousand loans had been made. To attract more investors the FHA has since boosted the interest rate to 12 per cent. The program provides for loans of up to $10,000 (or $15,000 for double-wide homes) with repayment periods of twelve and fifteen years respectively. The VA backs loans up to $12,500 for up to twelve years to buy a single-wide unit ($20,000 for twenty years for a double-wide), and up to $27,000 for twenty years for a double-wide with an undeveloped lot included.

• The taxes on a mobile home vary greatly from one state or one locality to another. Some states tax the homes as personal property, if you rent the land on which the home sits. Other states merely levy a licensing fee, ranging from about $5 to $50 a year. Still others, such as Virginia, tax mobile homes at the same rate as real property and in addition will collect a one-time title tax of 3 per cent of the retail price of the unit.

• A few years back, you could estimate that your mobile home would depreciate 40 to 50 per cent over the first five years. But now, as the units have risen in price, improved in quality, and increasingly been set up on developed lots, their value has sometimes even held steady.

• While a mobile home may not be as inexpensive to buy and maintain as you first thought, the average direct cost of owning a typical unit still runs roughly about half what it would cost you today to own a median-priced conventional home.

KEY DISADVANTAGES

However, among the key disadvantages of many of these homes are: They tend to depreciate quickly—an average of 12 to 50 per cent over the first five years. They offer smaller living space, inadequate amounts of storage space, and lack privacy from neighbors. They tend to be aesthetically poor. Moreover, some mobile homes have had serious safety defects. For instance, few provided exits on both ends as well as in the middle, necessary to allow escape in a fire.

To protect mobile home buyers from such defects, the Department of Housing and Urban Development began in the mid 1970s to require that all new units meet certain design and safety standards.

HIGHER STANDARDS

To suggest the scope of the standards:

• A smoke detector must be installed in all sleeping areas and fire-resistant materials must be used in furnace and water heater compartments as well as around the cooking range.

• Windows and doors must be removable from the inside, permitting emergency exits.

• To protect the homes from wind damage, manufacturers must provide tie-down straps, but not the anchors. The homeowner or park manager must connect the straps to an anchoring system. (Only a minority of states now have tie-down requirements for mobile homes.) A tie-down system that keeps your home safe from high winds can reduce your homeowner's insurance by as much as 10 per cent.

• To prevent freezing, plumbing fixtures must be insulated or otherwise protected, and exterior openings around piping must be sealed against the entrance of rodents.

• Should a home not be suitable for the installation of an air-conditioning system, the manufacturer must disclose this.

• Homes designed for cold regions of the United States must include more effective overall insulation. HUD estimates if you own an effectively insulated home, you'll save about $40 per year in heating costs—helping to offset other increased costs.

The federal requirements are tougher than the mobile home code set by the American National Standards Institute (ANSI) and the National Fire Protection Association (NFPA). Still, however, HUD standards contain about 90 per cent of the existing code—already enforced by most states and met by 98 per cent of all mobile homes built since the early 1970s.

Moreover, certification by anyone—whether HUD or ANSI or NFPA—does not mean a unit will be defect-free. The President's Office of Consumer Affairs receives hundreds of complaints a year from homeowners who object to defects —even though their unit may meet state or industry codes.

Similarly, a Federal Trade Commission staff report on mobile home sales and service pointed out that "although a manufacturer may attempt in good faith to meet a complex standard such as ANSI or the HUD standard, it is an engineering fact of life that no matter how strictly adherence to a standard is enforced, many mobile homes will . . . contain standard deviations."

More disturbing, many homeowners find it difficult to get repairs even when their home falls under a warranty. The knowledge, willingness, and experience of dealers vary widely. A homeowner may be buffeted from dealer to manufacturer in a search for help without recourse except through a costly court fight.

The battle for reforms isn't over, not by a long shot. But the progress to date has been consistent and considerable.

IS MOBILE HOME PARK LIVING FOR YOU?

You've examined the pros and cons of owning a mobile home, checked out the alternative types of housing available to you in your circumstances and income range, comparison-shopped for a mobile unit you like and can afford. Now what?

(1) Before you buy, investigate where you will place your home. If you own property you would like to use, make certain that the local zoning regulations permit you to install your home; that you'll have access to water, power, and sewage disposal; that you won't be hit by drainage or flooding problems.

(2) If you decide to rent or buy space in a mobile home development or park, be sure a lot is available to you. The average rate of park occupancy in the 1970s was 94 per cent.

Zoning regulations are a key factor in limiting the number and nature of mobile parks, although in some areas, these are slowly becoming less restrictive. Some parks themselves are restricted to only those who bought their units from a park owner or a park manager-home dealer.

(3) Find out all the limits on children and age. Some parks do not allow residents with children or with more than, say, three offspring. Others are limited to homeowners of a specified age: twenty and over or in areas popular with retirees, age sixty may be the minimum.

(4) Once you find a park you think you will like and which will admit you, get a copy of the park's rules and regulations and read with care. While many

people enjoy the security and orderliness that park rules provide, you may find the regulations an invasion of your privacy and regimentation of your living style.

(5) Consider this sampling of rules to which you must agree if you rent space in many parks:

• Small pets will be allowed, but must be approved by management. They must be walked on a short leash, and a monthly charge in the $5.00-or-over range must be paid per pet.

• In the adult section of the park, children are limited to a two-week visit. Maximum number of children under sixteen allowed in the home is three.

• No auction or moving or garage sales or commercial business may be conducted in the park.

• Between 10 P.M. and 8 A.M., no loud talking, radio, TV, or other noise capable of disturbing a neighbor will be permitted.

• Additional occupants must be approved by the manager and will be charged $5 per month or more after two weeks' occupancy.

• Drunkenness or immoral conduct will not be tolerated.

• Only decorative fences no higher than 18 inches are permitted.

(6) There may be regulations which severely limit your or the manager's responsibility for proper upkeep.

A set of rules might stipulate, for instance, that the "lessor shall not be liable for any damages occasioned by failure to keep the park premises in repair . . . for any damage due to plumbing, gas, water, or sewage . . . snow or ice." Or a park manager may be allowed to enter your rental space for inspection, repairs, alterations, etc., without liability to you for any loss.

(7) Investigate most cautiously your safeguards should there be problems over your lease, for you are known legally as a "tenant at will" in a mobile park and you have little protection. If you break your lease, the park owner or manager may re-enter the space and your home and remove your home and belongings from the park, often at your expense. Some park rules provide that you must even pay the park manager's legal fees if you take him to court to enforce any terms of your lease or to regain the lot.

(8) Talk to park residents about policies and community activites. Check into all extra charges, on top of rent, you might have to pay, such as for guests or pets.

(9) Find out how utilities are metered; if you are required to use specified servicemen or may use your own.

(10) Ask if there is a residents' association and what kind of role it has been able to play in determining park rules.

In sum, mobile homes are a bargain. But you are taking formidable risks if you buy without major preparation.

SHOPPING RULES

If you are shopping for a mobile home:

• Choose a dealer with the utmost care, since he may not only be selling you a home but also arranging the financing terms for you. Usually the dealer from whom you buy a mobile home then sells your loan contract to a bank or finance company. Also, he is the sole person responsible for honoring the home's warranty or for performing repairs which may be needed.

• Check the reputation of any dealer with whom you are considering doing business with the local banks, local business associations, and the Better Business Bureau. One indication of a dealer's reliability is whether he belongs to the Chicago-based Manufactured Housing Institute. You also can go to a local mobile home park, simply knock on a few doors of homes similar to the one which interests you, and ask the occupants about the dealer's reputation.

• Compare what is and is not included in the purchase price. Normally, new mobile homes today are sold complete with kitchen range, refrigerator, water heater, furniture, draperies, carpeting, lamps—and furnace. Normally also you pay extra for such optional equipment as air conditioning, dishwasher, garbage disposals, clothes washers and dryers, screen and storm windows, shutters, house-type doors and windows.

• Before you sign up for any financing deal offered by the dealer, investigate and compare rates and terms offered by other lenders.

• If you are not a veteran and therefore do not qualify for a mobile home loan backed by the VA, ask your local banks and/or savings and loan associations about mobile home interest rates. If you own the land on which the home will be placed and if it's properly zoned, these lenders may extend a more or less conventional mortgage loan. However, interest rates charged on non-insured mobile home loans by banks and other lenders are usually closer to those charged on automobile loans.

• Collect all the facts on the financing terms—including the annual interest rate, the total dollar finance charge over the life of the loan, the amount of the down payment, the repayment period, the amount of any miscellaneous costs related to the deal. Compare these terms—especially the total finance charge—on each mobile home you consider buying.

• Get estimates on the costs of all accessories and extras you will want or will be required to have by the rules of the mobile home park. The list of accessories ranges from front doorsteps and skirting to cover the crawl space underneath the home to shutters, and panels of aluminum around the roofline, patio cover, and carport to "connect" these accessories visually. These can add at least 10 to 15 per cent to the price you pay for a mobile home.

• Check all the usual fixtures and equipment of a house—from air conditioning to storm windows—to make sure, first, that they are there (assuming you want and need them); second, where they are; and third, that they are in good operating condition. See that the furnace has a "gun" burner rather than the obsolete and dangerous "pot" burner. Find out whether the hot water heater capacity is the minimum seventeen gallons or a more adequate thirty or forty gallons.

• Find out whether the front tow hitch is removable—a plus on the better homes.

• Compare the weights of equal-size homes. Generally, heavier ones are better.

• Ask the dealer whether he will pay the costs of setting up and leveling your mobile home at its destination (even if he doesn't agree to do this at first, it may be a good bargaining point for you), along with the installation of the skirting around the bottom of the home. Many provide free delivery and installation anywhere within seventy-five or one hundred miles, and charge only a minor fee per mile outside the free area.

• If a lot is included in the deal make sure a lot number and description of the lot appear in the mobile home sales contract.

• Look for the MHMA-TCA seals (Mobile Homes Manufacturers Association —Trailer Coach Association) near the doorways which tell you that the home meets certain basic building standards, a requirement in order to get FHA- or VA-backed financing.

• Look also for the Underwriters Laboratories (UL) safety seal of approval, which virtually guarantees safe electrical wiring.

• Ask the dealer to show you the *Official Mobile Market Report,* the Blue Book of mobile homes published and updated every four months by the Judy Berner Publishing Company of Westmont, Illinois. This will help you compare current retail prices for all major models.

• If the furniture appears cheap or shoddy, ask the dealer how much of a discount he would give you if you furnished the mobile home yourself. His response may at least be an indication to you of the quality of the furniture he's offering with the home.

• Be sure a written warranty goes with each major appliance included in the home—including furnace, water heater, dishwasher, refrigerator, clothes washer and dryer.

• Before you sign any contract, also insist on getting the manufacturer's written warranty on the home itself, usually good for one year. Insist too that the dealer correct any defects you detect in it. If you cannot get satisfaction, request a service report from Consumer Action Bureau, Mobile Homes Manufacturers Association, Box 35, Chantilly, Virginia 22021 (east of the Rockies), or Consumer Affairs Council, Trailer Coach Association, 3855 La Palma Avenue, Anaheim, California 92806 (west of the Rockies).

• Finally, before you buy a mobile home consider all the alternative types of bargain-priced housing being produced today—including prefabricated permanent homes, homes built of modular units, houses and apartments (mainly in the cities and city fringes) which are being gutted and "instantly" fitted with entire new "packaged" interiors, and publicly subsidized low-cost housing.

THE LEGAL MECHANICS OF BUYING A HOME

THE CONTRACT FOR SALE

When you have made at least a tentative decision to buy a house, you'll be asked to sign a commitment to buy, at a given price. This is a legal contract and it is called a contract for sale or "purchase agreement" or "contract," "bid," "binder," "offer to buy," "deposit receipt," "memo." You also will probably have to make a "good faith" deposit of a small percentage of the purchase price. This is also called "earnest money."

Some of the items that should be specified in a contract for sale are:

the purchase price;

when and how the purchase price is to be paid;

a brief legal description of the property (not simply a street address);

a description of any other property including furniture, carpets, and appliances included in the sale;

an agreement as to who will pay what portion of property taxes, insurance, water charges, and other costs which become (or became) due during the year;

the date on which the buyer will get possession of the property;

a guarantee that the seller will provide an abstract of title, title warranty, plus details on what type of title;

a statement that the seller will provide a specified type of deed at the time of settlement with details on any deed restrictions and that he also will provide a marketable title;

any other agreements reached between the buyer and seller—for instance, your right to cancel the deal if you can't get a mortgage;

a provision for the return of your initial deposit in the event the sale falls through for some reason other than your own failure to fulfill your part of the deal;

the signature of the seller.

Your lawyer can guide you on other legal points which may be involved in your transaction. Consult him on any questions or doubts you may have on this and all other documents involved in property buying.

Do not rely on verbal explanations from the seller or his agents on what any contract means.

THE TITLE SEARCH (OR ABSTRACT OF TITLE)

The title search is the next step in a real estate transaction. The title to a piece of property you buy represents your right, as owner, to free use of it (within the limitations of laws and zoning ordinances and perhaps also the deed itself)—and therefore also your right to sell or mortgage it later. A title search is a history of the title, showing former transactions affecting the ownership, such as existence of liens and encumbrances and any other factors which bear on the title to the property.

The chief purpose of a title search is to make sure that the title is not "clouded"—that no one other than the present owner has a claim against the property. Generally, an attorney or title insurance company searches the title to your new home. Shop around for the most reasonable title fee.

THE DEED

After the title has been examined, the seller's lawyer draws up a deed. A deed describes a property in detail and formally conveys title of the property from the seller to you. There are several types of deeds: sheriff's deed, quitclaim deed, warranty deed, etc.

The warranty deed is the most commonplace. It guarantees that the seller will defend the title against anyone who may claim an interest, although this warranty is only as good as the man who makes it. Other deeds—for instance, quitclaim deeds—give the buyer only such rights and interests as the seller may have in the property.

When you, the buyer, receive the deed, make certain that it is properly recorded in the town or county records. Deeds require federal revenue stamps, for which the seller must pay.

TITLE INSURANCE

Title insurance is generally a must for anybody who is buying real estate, unless it's located in a new development. The Federal Housing Administration will not insure a mortgage unless there is title insurance on the property for which the mortgage is intended. And banks often refuse to extend a mortgage unless there is title insurance protecting them.

After your title search has eliminated known risks—such as possible claims against your property or unpaid back taxes—title insurance then protects the bank or other mortgage lender against "hidden" risks and claims which may not have been uncovered by the search. For example: claims by missing heirs, a forged deed, some defect in the records, liens of laborers for work on the property, other obligations of the previous owners. There also may be rights of individuals on the land, called squatter's rights.

There are said to be some one thousand different possible claims which could be made against your ownership of a given property.

Title insurance, for which you pay a one-time premium at the time of the closing, also covers the costs of legally defending your title in the event it is later challenged, and of paying off any claims which turn out to be valid.

Or Should You Build?

ADVANTAGES

No house is perfect for everyone. One family will want a bathroom next to each bedroom; another will have a passion for huge hall closets; a third will want a workshop in the cellar; a fourth will want a huge living room and tiny bedrooms. The key reason for building rather than buying is that you may have a new dwelling, with all the advantages of recent inventions and scientific developments, plus a layout tailored to your family's living preferences.

It is almost always more costly to build your own house than to buy an existing one—old or new. But for millions of Americans, the advantages of building their own homes still outweigh the cost disadvantages.

To illustrate, if you build your own house, you can:

create something of your own, which expresses your own personality and also the personality of your family;

build it at whatever pace you wish and can afford—room by room or wing by wing—fanning out into new living space as each room or wing is finished;

choose exactly which materials, fixtures, colors you want, including higher-quality materials than those you might find in a ready-built house;

save at least a part of the labor costs by doing part of the building yourself and getting other family members to pitch in;

design the house to meet your own family's specific needs and wants—in terms of arrangement of living spaces, lighting, exposure, decorations;

keep control over construction as it progresses, making changes and undoing errors as needed, having your say, if you want, on every single nut, bolt, and hinge which goes into it;

include only those appliances, conveniences, and labor-saving systems that you really want and can afford;

choose any building site you want, in any neighborhood, with any exposure and any surroundings—assuming, that is, the site is for sale;

and clear the land just as you wish—saving whichever greenery and opening up whatever views you wish.

DISADVANTAGES

Of course there are disadvantages when you build your own house—over and above the cost disadvantage. If your dream is a highly unusual, individualistic house, you may risk—when the time comes to resell it—not finding a buyer whose family fits into the house. It may be difficult to retrieve the full amount you laid out for special materials and custom craftsmanship. You must (or should) assume the costs of an architect.

And, despite all the bids and estimates you get, you can never be positive just how the final costs will total up—because the near certainty is that there will be underestimates, that you will expand your ambitions for your new home any number of times during the course of construction, and that utterly unanticipated extras will come up (they always do).

HOW TO FIND THE RIGHT SITE

Before you invest a penny in your dream house you must find the right property on which to build. Here's how to go about it:

• Find out from the town clerk's office the zoning regulations in the neighborhood in which the property you like is situated.

• Ask for a survey of the lot. Exactly where are the boundaries? (Walk the lines yourself.)

• Plan to invest in a title search, no matter how little the lot costs.

• Find out from local lenders whether they will make home-building loans in your neighborhood. A good source of information is the Federal Housing Administration's nearest branch office. The FHA considers the neighborhood as well as the individual house when it insures loans.

• Inspect the lot after a heavy rain; if possible, after several days of downpour. That will show how rapidly surface water leaves the site. If a plot is filled, the fill may settle and take the house along with it.

• Be wary of land subdivisions still in the "blueprint stage." These always are a gamble.

• Avoid sites which are close to things that will reduce the value of the property or detract from pleasant living—such as city dumps, mortuaries, industrial buildings, railroads, high-tension wires, heavy traffic, garbage incinerators.

• Make sure not only that the lot is large enough for the house you intend to build on it but also that the house and lot go together as a unit and that they relate pleasantly to other properties in the vicinity. What is the view like? How much privacy is there? You will almost certainly want to sell someday. A house and lot suited to each other and suited to the surroundings will prove far more salable later than ones which stand out and just don't belong together or don't belong where they are.

• Check whether all public services will be available—or can be built—on your property: water, sewer (storm and sanitary), gas, electricity, telephone, street lighting, fire and police protection, trash removal. Don't be satisfied with vague statements such as: "The company will run the lines" or "'They' will extend the water main." If the services are not already installed, get your information on future plans from residents in the vicinity or go to the town or city hall and find out where to get the facts. And also find out how these services are to be paid for.

Note these key points if you buy in areas in which these services are not publicly provided:

If you must supply your own water and sewage-disposal facilities you will need a much larger lot than otherwise. For an individual sewage-disposal system, the lot must be large enough to permit location of the tank and leaching field at a proper distance from your house and your neighbors' houses.

You must be certain that you can get an adequate supply of safe and potable water at reasonable cost.

You also must consider the nature of the soil: it should be sufficiently porous to assure adequate drainage.

• Satisfy yourself that the price being asked is reasonable—by consulting your real estate broker, your lawyer, and local bank officials. Typically, the cost of an improved lot is slightly less than one quarter of the total value of the property after your house is built.

HOW TO CHOOSE AN ARCHITECT

Unless you can find a ready-made house plan which really suits you, you must hire an architect. Thousands of such plans are now available—many of them drawn up by architects—from shelter magazines, dealers in building materials, mail-order houses. But if your dream house is even relatively elaborate you may be better off with an architect.

You wouldn't try to treat your child's first serious illness: you'd call in your doctor. You wouldn't tell a construction crew how to build a highway: you'd hire a highway engineer. It is merely common sense to recognize your ignorance about building a house, just as you recognize it in many other fields. A trained architect will know about new developments in design, building materials, and techniques —and how they may help in building your house.

A competent architect will be prepared to:

> study your family's living needs and try to match these to your budget;

> advise on your choice of building site and also on where a structure should be located on it;

> make rough preliminary sketches of your house-to-be;

> put together rough cost estimates;

> make detailed drawings and materials lists;

> provide whatever technical information is needed to draw up a contract with the contractor;

> advise on a choice of contractors, take competitive bids for the job, and choose the most favorable one;

> observe construction to make sure it is carried out according to plan;

> decide whether and how changes and substitutions proposed by you and your contractor can be carried out;

> check and authorize payments to the contractor;

> inspect the finished building and arrange for your final payment to the contractor after your building has been satisfactorily completed.

Architects' fees tend to depend on the value of the job and on the amount of designing, supervising, and other work involved. They may be computed as a percentage of total building costs, as a fixed fee plus expenses, or as a multiple of the architect's direct expenses. The figure arrived at is usually between 6 and 15 per cent of the total building costs. Normally, you pay this fee in installments—your payments beginning with an acceptable rough sketch of your house and ending when the house is actually completed.

An architect, however, may be able to save you at least the amount of his own fees by helping you avoid expensive mistakes and leading you to efficiencies in building which neither you nor the builder may have even considered.

These savings, of course, are on top of the sheer convenience to you of having someone else deal with contractors, subcontractors, zoning boards, and health officials.

How do you find a competent, suitable architect?

• Look for an architect who is a member of the Washington-based American Institute of Architects.

• Before you make a deal with any one architect, study other houses he has designed—inside as well as out, if possible. How well does your taste agree with his?

• Ask the architect's former clients, if possible, how well he stuck to his original cost estimates—or by how much he overshot the budget they gave him. You can get an impression whether or not the customers were generally satisfied with the architect's work.

• Talk over your ideas, plans, and costs with at least two architects and ask each to make at least a rough preliminary sketch—to see how each translates your ideas onto paper. Or ask them to show you examples of their work as similar as possible in scope to your project.

• Discuss fees with any architect whose services you might want to use—and find out the minimum percentage of the costs he'll work for. Quite possibly a younger architect who is a little hungrier for business than are his older and busier colleagues will charge less. Consider, too (if the architect's fees seem too high), buying his advice on an hourly basis—at least at the outset. Perhaps he could leave a lot of the supervisory work to you (if you're qualified) or to your builder-contractor.

• Find out from each architect which measures each would take to cut building costs.

• Make sure you like and respect the architect you finally choose—and that both of you are able to communicate ideas easily to each other.

HOW TO CHOOSE A CONTRACTOR

Your architect will probably recommend one or more builders after he has worked out plans and drawings which satisfy you. He'll probably get written bids from at least two contractors on the job of building your house.

At this point the following guides in finding a good contractor will be of great value to you.

• Carefully check the reputation of each—with the local bank, the local Better Business Bureau, local building suppliers, and former customers. And inspect previous houses each contractor has built.

• Then compare not only the amount of each bid but also the manner in which each intends to do the job, what types of materials each would use, the completion date, and the guarantee of the work.

• Check each builder's addresses, business as well as home. If his home is located near any of the homes he has built, it's an encouraging sign of his reliability.

• Ask about each builder at the local office of the National Association of Home Builders. As a general rule, builders who are members of the NAHB are reliable: however, not all good, reliable builders are members of this organization.

• Ask the local FHA office to see its "DSI list," which is a nationwide list of all contractors the FHA has found unsatisfactory. Also ask to see the local list of workmanship ratings. Both must be made available to you under the Freedom of Information Act, and can serve as valuable guides, though not the last word, on the reliability of contractors you are considering. Among the reasons for the

FHA's blackballs are: overpricing, misrepresentation of products, false guarantees, falsifying credit information, fraudulent "model home" come-ons. The DSI list is also available from HUD Printing Office, 451 7th Street S.W., Washington, D.C. 20410.

• Beware of any unusually low bid on the job you want done. If you accept such a bid you are likely to be risking bad workmanship and the use of inferior materials. Good builders use top grades of lumber and other building supplies and hire highly skilled carpenters, masons, plumbers, and others. These costs must be reflected in the builder's bid.

• Make sure the contractor carries adequate insurance protection to cover the men who work for him. Get a statement to this effect in writing from his insurance company.

Beware also of any contractor or supplier who advertises that the FHA endorses his work or products. The FHA does not make such endorsements.

• In the case of individual workers who do not carry such protection, make sure the liability part of your own homeowner's insurance policy does provide this type of protection against accidents and injuries on the job.

• Study "Your Home Improvement Contractor and Your Contract" later in this chapter. Some of these guides also may help you choose a contractor to build a new house.

• Ask the builder if he offers the NAHB Home Owners Warranty, a voluntary ten-year home protection plan. During the first years, the builder provides you, the home buyer, the protection against possible defects caused by faulty workmanship and defective materials. In addition, for the first two years, the builder protects you against major defects in construction and defects caused by faulty installation of plumbing, electrical, heating, and cooling systems, exclusive of defects covered by manufacturers' warranties. From the third to the tenth year, any major construction defects are covered by a private insurance company.

HOW TO CUT THE HIGH COST OF BUILDING

In the late 1970s the cost of building most houses ranged between $28 and $32 per square foot of living space—plus the cost of the lot, not counting unimproved basement space. For the highest-quality houses, building costs may run $35 to $50 or more per square foot.

According to a survey by the National Association of Home Builders, here's where each $50,000 spent in the late 1970s to build a typical single-family house went:

ITEM	% OF COST	AMOUNT
Labor	15	$7,500
Materials	35	$17,500
Land	26	13,000
Builder's overhead and profit	14	7,000
Financing costs	10	5,000
TOTAL		$50,000

Against this background, these are your fundamental money-saving guidelines:

• Try to design economies into your house. For example, a two-story house costs less to build, per foot of floor space, than a one-story house. A rectangular floor plan costs less than a U-shaped, L-shaped, or other-shaped house. Standard gable roofs tend to be less expensive than other types of roofs. Using treated wood instead of masonry for the foundation—a technique approved by the FHA —can save several hundred dollars.

• Time your building project, if possible, to take advantage of economic cycles in the area in which you are building. Perhaps you can manage to schedule it during a slack season (such as winter). Or perhaps you are building during a phase of high unemployment in the building trades. If you can take advantage of cycles of this type, you can save thousands of dollars.

• Consider most seriously hiring the largest builder with a good reputation in your area. The savings bigger builders are likely to achieve on your behalf for materials alone can be spectacular.

• Also consider building a "manufactured" house. Through this type of construction, homeowners in many cases are achieving savings of 20 per cent or more in overall home building costs.

Prefab housing covers a broad range. It can be large sections of a wall, preassembled at a factory building supply store, an entire side of a house built in some standard size, or a "package" of prebuilt parts which a builder or homeowner can put together into a whole house. One reason for the big savings available on prefabs is that you are spared the architect's fee—plus 10 to 20 per cent in labor costs.

Modular housing units are factory-built rooms, groups of rooms, sections of a house, or even whole apartments (but not whole houses). They are delivered to the construction site on a flatbed or similar conveyance. Usually a builder puts several of these modular rooms or other units together to make a complete house.

• Or consider as an alternative to the all-prefab house the part-prefab/part-custom-built house, which may make many economies possible and also permit individuality.

• And what about making yours an expandable house, if you cannot afford to build the entire house at one time? The principle of the expandable house is simple: build what you can afford now and what will meet your present needs; postpone building for future requirements and more spacious living. Our early New England houses were built in this fashion—section by section to accommodate expanding families.

If this is an answer to your building problem, plan the complete house first. Then separate it into its logical parts and decide on the sequence of additions. The house should be complete in appearance and function at each stage. The basic unit always should provide all the facilities for the normal life of a small family: living room, bedroom, bath, dining space, kitchen, closet and storage space, lighting and heating equipment, hot water heater, and laundry facilities— even though some rooms may have to serve two or more purposes.

Here are additional guides for expandable houses:

Be sure your lot is big enough and shaped correctly not only for your basic house but also for all future extensions.

Carefully check community restrictions, included in zoning ordinances or restrictive covenants in deeds. These restrictions may control the size and price of a house built in a given locality, ruling out the first unit of an expandable house as a dwelling, even though the expanded house would meet all other requirements.

Plan all stages in the progress of your expansion so that there is no wasted space and there is convenient circulation from room to room.

Design your additions to minimize the disturbance to your family while the building is going on.

Select your materials for their ultimate use. For instance, plywood might be used for an exterior wall which you plan to turn into an interior wall later.

Frame the openings to later additions in the early stages. A window can be installed temporarily in a space framed for a future door.

Rough in from the start pipes, ducts, cables which you will need for later additions to save ripping out and rebuilding walls and floors later.

The expandable house need not be expanded. If your family's needs do not grow, you may not want any expansion. As long as yours is a complete house in function and appearance, you will not endanger its resale value.

Ordinarily the cost of building a house in separate stages would be higher than building it all at once. But by careful planning you can keep the additional costs to a minimum. In general, the greater ultimate cost will be more than offset by savings in maintenance, interest, taxes, and insurance during the period between the building of your basic unit and your later additions.

• Finally, consider building your house yourself. Given the enormous variety of prefab materials and house sections, a dazzling variety of do-it-yourself equipment in hardware and building supply stores, and house-building kits complete with instructions as well as alluring materials and drawings, record numbers are building their own homes.

You must coldly appraise whether or not you are qualified to build your own house, whether or not you can afford to absorb the cost of mistakes you might make, whether or not you can even dare try to do the tasks normally done by such experts as plumbers and electricians.

You may have trouble getting a bank to extend a mortgage to you—especially if you are not a professional. You also almost surely will have to pay a relatively higher price for the materials you use, since you may not be eligible for the discounts available to builders or for the savings available to development builders. (Refer to the preceding comparison chart on material costs.)

But you will, of course, reap big savings on the high cost of labor. Also you pay any labor you hire with your after-tax dollars while the labor you invest yourself may be "worth" 20 or 30 or 40 per cent more, depending on your tax bracket. To illustrate with a rough calculation: if you're in the 20 per cent federal income tax bracket, the $5,000 worth of your own labor you put into your house may translate into real savings of $6,000. (This is the amount you would have to earn in order to pay an outsider $5,000.)

Here are rules for investing in such major, costly components of your house as a roof, heating plant, plumbing system, etc.:

Plumbing: When you get into the plumbing aspects of your house, you're into an area which is hopelessly hamstrung by obsolete building codes, by city or town inspectors who are dead set against modern efficiencies and the newer, less expensive materials for plumbing pipes and fittings, and by deeply ingrained union traditions which dictate against many of the money-saving methods you or your architect might want to try. Still, there are ways you can economize (and not economize) on the purchase of plumbing supplies and services and in the general upkeep of your plumbing facilities.

Use plastic, if zoning codes permit, for cold water pipes and also for drainage pipes and save money by using three-inch instead of far more expensive four-inch pipes. Use copper for all hot water pipes.

If there is a great distance between the hot water heater and faucets, insulate the hot water pipes to avoid waste of hot water.

As far as possible, stick to standard, stock plumbing fixtures and to prefabricated modular bathroom units. Today, moderately priced prefab bathrooms, complete with everything from soap dishes to storage shelves, tub, and toothbrush holders, are on the market and can be installed within a few hours. The deeper you get into custom plumbing, the more expensive it is.

Heating systems: In deciding what type of heating system to install, you will have to weigh both installation and operating costs. If you are reasonably confident you will occupy the house more than just a few years, operating costs, involving expensive fuels, will be more important than installation costs. Nevertheless, here are the approximate costs of building various types of heating systems into a 2,000-square-foot house in the Baltimore-Washington area in the late 1970s.

Electric baseboard	$2,000
Gas-forced air	2,300
Electric-forced air	2,300
Oil-forced air	3,000
Solar	8,500

Operating costs include fuel and maintenance.

Fuel prices vary across the country, but in the mid 1970s piped-in natural gas, where available, usually was the cheapest fuel, followed closely by oil. In the Northeast, however, oil was the cheapest. Electricity is almost invariably the most expensive way to keep warm, in many areas more than twice as expensive as the cheapest available fuel. LP (liquefied petroleum) gas is somewhere in the middle. Sunlight, of course, is free, though most solar heating setups require some backup fuel.

Here's a formula for comparing current home fuel prices in your area:

(1) Find out the going price of oil (per gallon), of gas (per therm), and of electricity (per kilowatt hour). When you ask about gas and electricity rates, be sure you get the rates applying to home heating.

(2) Multiply the price of electricity by 33 and the price of gas (whatever kind you can buy) by 1.4.

(3) Compare these numbers with the price of a gallon of fuel oil. The smallest number is the cheapest fuel.

Caution: Consult local builders, heating system contractors, and fuel suppliers on prices and known trends in your area.

Do not be swayed by minor price differences. Although large differences probably will continue for a long time, small ones could reverse overnight.

As for which type of fuel will increase fastest in price in the long run, the answer is no one really knows. The future is hopelessly befuddled by Middle Eastern policies and politics, conservation issues, world supply-demand balances, the world's capacity to develop the necessary technology to clean up one fuel or convert another fuel into forms that are acceptable, economical, and usable.

The only certainty is that costs of all home heating fuels except sunlight will continue up, up, and up.

Here are other key points, pros and cons, to consider in choosing one type of heating system over another:

• Oil and LP (liquified petroleum) gas systems require storage tanks on your grounds (or underground). Storage tanks can be a minus because they consume space and because they can run dry. They're a plus, though, in that no one can turn off your supply as long as there's fuel in your tank. In contrast, you have no control over your natural gas or electricity supply lines.

• Oil furnaces require some electricity, and thus, if the power goes off, they may shut off altogether and stay off. That's a major disadvantage to you if you're frequently away from home and you live in a cold climate. Certain types of gas heating systems, though, are immune to blackouts and brownouts—a key advantage in an era when these are likely to become ever more widespread.

• Electric heat is relatively inexpensive to install, is very quiet, demands little space—and permits you the flexibility of individual room thermostats. However, the most common types of electric heating systems require thorough insulation of your house if they are to be at all economical, and obviously electric heat is no help to you during a power failure. Also, do not install electric heat strictly on the basis of promises that nuclear power plants will soon lower your electric rates. Serious controversy exists over the possible dangers of many proposed plants and many already under construction are facing long delays before completion. Some plants in operation have actually turned out to be among the least economical sources of electricity.

Finally, do not assume, if larger-volume users of electricity (industrial users and families with all-electric homes) are getting more favorable rates in your area, that this practice will prevail indefinitely. Do not, therefore, opt for electricity on this basis.

• Do not believe claims that one source of heat is cleaner or safer than others. All heat sources are equally clean and safe if you maintain and properly service your heating plant.

• Do insulate well, no matter what type of fuel you decide to use. Choose double-pane windows (even triple-pane windows in very cold climates) and avoid huge glass areas. If you decide on gas or oil, install large tanks and keep them full. You may even wish to design your new house so part of it can be left unheated at times, particularly if you live in a cold area.

• Do give some consideration to alternative types of backup heating, such as a heating fireplace, to tide you through temporary shortages of your primary fuel and minimize the danger of frozen pipes. But, however romantic and cozy and old-fashioned the fireplace may be, it is one of the least efficient sources of home heat. Reason: it may take all night for a fire you've enjoyed for only a few evening hours to die down, and during this time more heat goes up the chimney than the heat your fireplace provided while it was blazing.

As for maintenance, electric baseboard systems are virtually maintenance-free. Gas furnaces need occasional cleaning, and oil furnaces require somewhat more frequent attention. In any heating system, motors, fans, pumps, and thermostats fail occasionally, so systems with more of these items lose some reliability. Because few solar-heated houses have been built, their maintenance costs are unknown.

For guides on how to save heat once your system is installed, see Chapter 6, "Family's Energy-Saving Guide."

The roof: Get advice from your builder and/or architect on the life expectancy of each material you are considering using in your roof. Don't make false economies—for example, by choosing a lightweight shingle when, for only a slightly higher cost, you could get a heavier grade which would last two or three times as long.

The roof is likely to be among the most expensive aspects of any new house. And the price range is enormous between the more expensive roofing materials, such as slate and clay tile, and the less expensive ones, such as asphalt shingles and liquid asphalt topped with gravel. But probably the most important factor to consider is that one roofing material may tend to last only ten years, after which you will need a whole new roofing job, while the next material may be expected to last as long as you will.

The walls: Old-fashioned plaster is almost always more expensive than dry-wall (or plasterboard or gypsum board) construction—a key reason why the latter is the far more widely used of the two today. But plaster is likely to look better and to last a lot longer than dry wall. So again, before you decide between the two (if these indeed are your only two choices), get time and cost estimates on the entire job of installing properly and painstakingly each type of wall.

Sewage disposal: Avoid putting in a too small septic tank or an inadequate leaching field. Most houses today require a tank with a capacity of at least nine hundred to one thousand gallons, and local zoning and/or health regulations well may specify requirements for other aspects of your sewage disposal system. So be sure to consult these rules before you start digging. Or, if no rules exist, get the advice of a sanitary engineer.

The floor: Choose your flooring for each room on the basis of the wear it actually is likely to get—as well as its looks and cost. Today's three most popular types of flooring are hardwood (e.g., oak, maple, birch); carpeting (frequently directly over a plywood subfloor); and tile (such as vinyl, vinyl-asbestos, and asbestos).

A CHART FOR ESTIMATING YOUR HOME BUILDING COSTS

ITEM	ESTIMATED COST
The lot	_____
Survey fees	_____
Building permit	_____
Architect's fee (if any)	_____
Materials	_____
Labor	_____
Homeowner's insurance	_____
Landscaping	_____
Interest on loans	_____
Closing costs	_____
Other	_____
TOTAL	_____

How to Shop for a Home Mortgage

WARNING

If you are among the mounting numbers of Americans who have all but given up on the United States ever getting the inflation spiral under control and have truly accepted a psychology of inflation, you will turn every rule of thumb you read in the following pages inside out.

You will "walk through Alice's Looking Glass," and instead of putting down the largest payment on your mortgage that you can manage, you will put down the smallest you can get away with—in anticipation of repaying your mortgage with dollars of steadily depreciating value.

Instead of paying off your mortgage in the shortest time you can manage, you will try to stretch out your loan for the longest span you are permitted—in the belief that the dollars you will be using to repay your loan in later years will be worth a fraction of what they are worth today.

And thus (if you have given up) you will respond to every basic point below. I have not given up—and thus, I submit the fundamental rules of sound home ownership and home financing. But I must, in all fairness, give you the other side of the argument and give it to you *first*, so that you will be able to choose the way you want to go.

HOW MUCH HOUSE CAN YOU AFFORD?

As your home is likely to be the biggest single investment you'll make in your entire lifetime, so the mortgage you take on to finance it is likely to be the biggest single debt of your life. And the monthly payments you assume on that mortgage are likely to be the biggest single item in your budget.

To find the most favorable terms, you'll have to shop with utmost care among all types of lenders and all types of mortgages available in your area. The obvious sources to check will be: savings and loan associations; full service commercial banks; savings banks; life insurance companies; mortgage companies and credit unions. Others are pension funds and individuals. You'll want to ask each source details about rates, points, closing costs, all the other terms highlighted for you in the pages ahead.

Most of you probably consider the amount of the monthly payment the key to the cost of the mortgage. Actually, this is the least significant figure to use as your guide to true costs. In fact, a low monthly payment probably means a long life for a mortgage and, as a result, the highest possible overall interest costs to you.

In this high-interest era, it's not at all uncommon to commit yourself to pay more in interest over the lifetime of your mortgage than the total amount of the mortgage itself. As just one example, a $10,000 mortgage with an extremely low rate of only 8 per cent interest over a period of twenty-five years would be $13,154.

Before you start shopping for a mortgage you must decide how much mortgage —which really means how much house—you can afford. This goes beyond the down payment and beyond the monthly payment to your entire mortgage obligation over the next twenty to thirty years.

(Incidentally, you borrow money to build our own house in much the same way as you borrow to buy an already built one. Construction loans are made on the basis of your plans and specifications and your schedule for paying building costs and are replaced once the house is completed by a regular long-term mortgage.)

One long-standing rule of thumb for the average American family is:

You can afford to buy a house costing roughly two and one half times your gross (before tax) yearly income. For example, if your family's gross annual income is $15,000, you can afford a house costing $35,000 to $40,000; if it's $20,000, your range is $45,000 to $50,000.

If your income tends to fluctuate sharply you can use an average of your yearly income over the past few years as a yardstick. If you are in a high-income bracket, figure on spending relatively less than two and a half times your gross income on a new home.

Even if you are in the lower brackets, the sum you pay for a house should be less than two and a half times your gross income if you will be carrying a heavy debt load on other purchases; if your family is large; if you plan to buy an old house requiring a lot of repairs; if you will have heavy near-future financial obligations for the college education of your children; if property taxes and living costs in the neighborhood in which you plan to buy are high (and likely to rise further as you make improvements); if your income is irregular; if your down payment is low; and if your job may force you to move unexpectedly.

On the other hand, in any income bracket, you can afford to pay more for your house if you plan and are able to do a lot of the necessary maintenance and repairs on the house yourself; if your family is small; if your property taxes are low and likely to remain so; if you are virtually certain your income will increase at regular intervals; if the home you buy involves low upkeep costs; if the house is loaded with all the appliances you might otherwise have to buy—and if you are able to make a relatively large down payment from your savings.

Another long-standing rule is that you should count on laying out one to one and a half weeks' take-home pay for each month's total housing expenses including all the costs of owning and operating your home—ranging from your monthly payments on mortgage principal and interest, insurance and taxes, repairs and maintenance, heat and utilities, to garbage collection.

By this yardstick, if you have a take-home income of $800 a month, you could safely carry housing costs totaling at least $300 a month, and if you have a take-home income of $1,250 a month, you could safely carry costs totaling in the $500 range.

Your yearly home mortgage costs will probably amount to about two thirds of your total home ownership costs. This will give you an idea of how much to budget for property taxes, insurance, and upkeep utilities. These are only approximations and the expenses will vary widely among families and areas of the country.

Admittedly, the formulas above are no guarantee that you'll avoid financial errors in your home purchase and financing. You may, even if you are within the limits, be trying to take on too much too soon. You may be reaching for too much house. You may be way off base in other areas—emotional if not financial. And remember this fundamental point about owning a house in the suburbs: the "hidden" cost of car ownership will add substantially to your home ownership cost. In the suburbs and exurbs, home ownership often means two cars are a necessity, not a luxury. But at least the formulas give you the bench marks.

Since your home mortgage is such a big part of your financial life, it should be an area in which know-how helps you achieve big savings. And it is. In fact, there are four areas in which you can chalk up impressive savings: the amount of the down payment; the number of years the mortgage spans; the interest rate; "points," closing costs, and other "extras" that go along with most mortgages.

WHAT SHOULD YOUR DOWN PAYMENT BE?

How much of your savings nest egg should you put down as an initial payment? The key dollars-and-cents rule is to make the largest down payment that is feasible for you.

The average mortgage on a new home now covers about three fourths of the purchase price—so this is one guide for you on the amount of down payment you are expected to make. But do not fail to leave enough money on hand to cover such extraordinary initial expenses as fees for lawyers, surveyors, appraisers, architects, involved in the purchase; recording fees, title search, insurance fees, and closing charges on the loan; insurance and taxes on your new home; property taxes for the current year; moving costs and immediate repair bills. And there always will be unexpected expenses.

The more you pay down, the lower will be your interest costs over the years ahead and the lower will be the overall cost of the loan to you. The more you pay down, the greater will be your equity (ownership) in your home, and thus the greater your sense of security and protection should you be hit by an unanticipated financial emergency. The more you pay down, the smaller will be your monthly mortgage payments, permitting you additional leeway to spend on other things or non-things and to rebuild your savings nest egg. The more you pay down, the easier it will be for you to obtain a mortgage loan on interest terms most favorable to you.

If you can't put down a reasonably solid initial payment for your house, the odds are you can't afford the house. If this is the case, your best bet is to keep renting and building your nest egg until you can.

Here's a table which pounds home the generalities on down payments on home mortgages. Assume you're buying a $50,000 house and can get a mortgage for a twenty-five-year period at 9½ per cent. (The rates will change from year to year and from one part of the country to another, but the relationships between low down payment and high interest costs are what count.)

DOWN PAYMENT	AMOUNT BORROWED	MONTHLY PAYMENT	TOTAL FINANCE CHARGE
$ 2,500	$47,500	$415.01	$77,001
5,000	45,000	393.16	72,949
7,500	42,500	371.32	68,896
10,000	40,000	349.48	64,844
20,000	30,000	262.11	48,633

HOW LONG SHOULD THE TERM OF YOUR MORTGAGE BE?

The second fundamental way you can save on your mortgage is to keep its life-span just as short as you can reasonably manage.

Here's a table which pounds home the generalities on mortgage terms. It assumes a 9½ per cent, $40,000 loan over various periods of time:

REPAYMENT PERIOD	MONTHLY PAYMENT	TOTAL INTEREST
15 years	$417.69	$35,184
20 years	372.85	49,485
25 years	349.48	64,844
30 years	336.34	81,083
35 years	328.64	98,031

WHAT WILL THE INTEREST RATE BE?

Although most mortgage lenders in any given city or area of the United States are likely to charge about the same rates at any given time, you still may find a variation of ½ to 1 per cent—a difference which can be highly significant in terms of your total interest costs.

You must shop for terms. You cannot fudge this job. Here's a table which translates these generalities. The details are on a $40,000 thirty-year mortgage, at various interest rates:

INTEREST RATE	MONTHLY PAYMENT	TOTAL INTEREST
8%	$293.51	$65,662
8½	307.57	70,724
9	321.85	75,866
9½	336.34	81,083
10	351.03	86,370
10½	365.90	91,722
11	380.93	97,134
11½	396.12	102,602

POINTS, CLOSING COSTS, PREPAYMENT, LATE PAYMENT PENALTIES

And this is not all. In addition to the interest rate, the term, and the down payment on your home, there are less obvious costs which are inevitably tucked into the loan. Here are the key "extras"—and ways you can save on them:

Points: Because of state-regulated interest ceilings, many lenders add "points" to their basic mortgage charges when the general trend of interest rates is up. This holds for FHA and VA as well as conventional mortgage loans. If a lender charges you 5 points, it means he deducts 5 per cent from the face value of your mortgage at the beginning. You must, however, repay the full amount of the mortgage. To illustrate, on a $20,000 mortgage, $1,000 would be deducted, leaving only $19,000 actually available to you. This is the equivalent of adding more than ½ per cent to your basic interest rate.

If the lender charges you 10 points, this is the equivalent of adding an extra 1¼ per cent to the rate you are paying.

Points also can be added as an "up front" cost—a charge you must pay at closing—instead of a reduction in the loan amount. In these instances, you must include the points in calculating how much cash you will need (see "Closing costs" below).

Since the number of points you are charged will vary from institution to institution in any given area, be sure to find out how many points each lender in your area would charge you. Also explore the possibility that the seller of the house might share the cost of points.

Closing costs: These, too, can vary quite dramatically from lender to lender, and since they ranged in the late 1970s from 2 to 10 per cent of the loan, they represent a major area for possible savings. On a $50,000 house, closing costs alone typically total $1,000 to $2,500—and you have to pay this amount in cash. There is virtually no room for negotiation on certain closing items: property taxes, fire insurance, title insurance, credit life insurance (if required). There is little room for bargaining over the appraisal fee, credit report fee, and survey fee. But there are other closing costs which may be negotiable, such as the bank's charge for processing your mortgage application and legal fees. You also might ask your own lawyer whether it is possible that the seller of the house might share the cost of such items as local recording fees, surveys, termite inspection, or even the title search. Shopping among lenders might help you to minimize closing costs. In any event, get a copy of the seller's closing costs, to be sure you are not both paying for the same items.

Note: A large building firm selling you a new house and arranging the mortgage is likely to offer overall closing costs lower than a small builder.

Here's an example, by category, of closing costs, and related expenses paid by the purchaser of a $50,000 house bought in the late 1970s with a mortgage from a savings and loan association. (This example is located in the Chicago area; fees can vary widely from region to region.)

Legal fees (your lawyer)	$ 200
Service charge (points)	600
Title insurance	82
Mortgage interest and property tax installment due between closing (the 15th of the month in this case) and the first regular mortgage payment	160
Appraisal	60
Homeowner's insurance (first year)	150
TOTAL	$1,252

Prepayment: Some lenders will not allow any prepayment without forfeit of an interest refund on the amount you prepay. Some exact a penalty for prepaying more than a fixed amount or for prepaying any amount during the first year of the loan. Some impose no penalties at all. So try to get the privilege of prepaying your mortgage at no or minimum penalties. Prepayment could save you hundreds or even thousands of dollars if you get a cash windfall or should mortgage interest rates decline sharply.

Late payment: Also check how long a grace period is provided after each payment due date before a penalty is applied and find out how big the penalty is. Late charges are typically 4 and 6 per cent of the overdue payment, but can be even larger.

OTHER AREAS TO EXPLORE

In addition, here are other areas to explore and in which to make comparisons between one mortgage deal and the next:

• How quickly can you get the loan?

• Can the life of the mortgage be extended at a later date if you choose? Can you "reborrow" after you've made several payments by increasing your monthly payment or extending your mortgage's life? If you can, what will be the deal on interest rates on the new borrowing versus the original mortgage? An open-end mortgage can be an attractive arrangement for you if the provisions for interest rates and closing costs are in your favor and there is a minimum of red tape. Check with care.

• What type and how much home insurance must you carry to get the mortgage? Must you deposit funds (probably at no interest) with the lender to pay for this insurance? Are you permitted to arrange your insurance on your own and get the most favorable terms you can? If you do not have this freedom of action, the restriction is a minus. There is no reason why the lender of your mortgage money should also make a profit on the insurance he demands to protect this investment.

• And, if you're buying an older house or apartment, can you work out a private arrangement with the seller in which he would transfer his lower-rate FHA- or VA-backed mortgage to you?

Note: When you get your mortgage, you may want to take out a credit life insurance policy which would pay off your mortgage should disaster strike. This is a term policy which declines in coverage as your mortgage loan is reduced.

Main Types of Mortgage Loans

Here are the advantages and disadvantages of the main types of mortgage loans available to you in the late 1970s.

Loans Guaranteed by the Veterans Administration

Advantages: Up to 100 per cent of the appraisal value of a home can be borrowed and thus no down payment is required (although the bank or other lending institution through which the VA loan is made may require a down payment). You get the privilege of partial prepayment without penalty. The VA makes a special effort to help veterans keep their homes by encouraging lenders to extend forbearance and indulgence to the veteran if he has repayment difficulty.

Disadvantages: There is a certain amount of red tape involved. Only eligible veterans qualify. An appraisal is required, and thus an appraisal fee is added to the closing costs. However, the appraisal often serves to lower the buyer's asking price, so it may save more than it costs.

For details on current terms for VA-backed mortgages consult your local VA office or write the Veterans Administration, Washington, D.C. 20420.

Loans Insured by the Federal Housing Administration

Advantages: The repayment period can stretch as long as thirty years, or even thirty-five years in some special cases. The down payment is very low: in the late 1970s, 3 per cent of the property's first $25,000 appraised value (but only $200 for eligible veterans) and 5 per cent of the remainder of the assessed value.

Disadvantages: There may be a lot of red tape involved; and a long wait while the loan is being processed and while the FHA determines whether or not the house meets the FHA's standards of construction, liability, and location.

For details on current terms for FHA-backed mortgages consult the Federal Housing Administration, Department of Housing and Urban Development, 451 7th Street S.W., Washington, D.C. 20410.

Conventional (non-FHA or -VA) Mortgages

Advantages: There is no set maximum amount which can be borrowed. There is a minimum of red tape and the waiting period is usually just a few days or weeks. A conventional mortgage is usually the fastest and easiest to get and virtually anybody in good financial standing is eligible.

Disadvantages: Down payments, frequently regulated by law, are relatively larger (typically 20 per cent of the appraised value in the late 1970s), unless private mortgage insurance (PMI) is carried on the loan.

Private mortgage insurance, a rapidly growing industry, has permitted home buyers to combine the convenience of conventional mortgages with the low down payments of FHA-type insured loans.

At a savings and loan association in the late 1970s, although the typical down payment was 20 per cent, you could borrow up to $60,000 ($90,000 if the home was located in Alaska, Guam, or Hawaii) with a down payment of only 5 per cent, and up to $75,000 ($112,000 in Alaska, Guam, or Hawaii) with a down payment of only 10 per cent. A savings and loan association could exceed these ceilings on low down payment loans, but only on a specified proportion of their total lending volume. PMI normally is required when the down payment is less than 20 per cent.

RURAL AND SMALL TOWN MORTGAGES

These low-cost loans were avilable to elderly and low-income rural Americans from the Farmers Home Administration (FmHA) with a repayment period up to thirty-three years as the 1980s neared. The mortgage interest rate you pay depends on the size of your family and family income.

The only disadvantages of a FmHA mortgage are that: FmHA funds occasionally may be limited; and then not all applicants succeed in getting these loans. Under a newer program initiated in the late 1970s, FmHA guarantees mortgages made by private lenders—much in the same way as FHA acts. You may find out what your local situation is by calling your local FmHA office, Department of Agriculture, or write to the Farmers Home Administration, Department of Agriculture, Washington, D.C. 20250.

PURCHASE MONEY MORTGAGES

The purchase money mortgage is one in which the seller finances the upaid balance of the purchase price—at an interest rate and under terms negotiated directly with you, the buyer.

"AMI-ERS"

GPM, RAM, VRM—a battery of new missile systems? No. These acronyms stand for innovations in a much more prosaic and close-to-the-pocketbook sphere —home mortgage loans. And they are among the variations developing of the traditional fixed-rate, fixed-term, level-payment mortgage which has dominated the U.S. housing market for almost a half century.

The major attraction of these "alternative mortgage instruments" (abbreviated to "AMI-ers") is that they are custom-tailored to fit your needs and pocketbooks in many categories of home buyers.

GRADUATED PAYMENT MORTGAGE (GPM)

Like many other products especially designed, these new home loans can cost more than conventional mortgages over the long term. Consider, for instance, the GPM, or graduated payment mortgage. This variation is custom-made for you if you are a young person with a relatively low income at this, the beginning of your career, with expectations of a higher income as the years pass. Monthly payments on this type of loan follow the same pattern as your earnings: starting small, growing larger, then leveling off. Say you're a buyer of a home with a $40,000 thirty-year mortgage at 9½ per cent. Under one graduated payment mortgage plan, you would pay about $255 per month at first, with your payments rising 7½ per cent a year for the next five years, then holding.

The attraction: your initial monthly payments would be about $80 less per month than they would be with a conventional loan of the same size.

The drawback, once the five-year graduated payment span is over: you, the borrower, would be paying nearly $30 a month more for the remaining twenty-four years of the loan.

The net result: your total payments on this GPM loan would be $127,601 against $121,083 on a conventional mortgage, or a difference of $6,518 against you.

REVERSE ANNUITY MORTGAGE (RAM)

The RAM, or reverse annuity mortgage, serves those at the opposite end of the life cycle. It is designed to meet the needs of older men and women who don't want to move out of their houses but who find it tough to keep up with rising property taxes and home maintenance costs.

Say you are an elderly couple or individual near retirement or actually retired. Your income is relatively low, yet you live in a mortgage-free home which is valued far above its original cost to you. It's a larger house than you need or want, but you don't want to move. How can you turn this asset into cash without selling it?

One possible answer is the so-called reverse mortgage.

In effect, the plan—under study and experimentation by a few financial institutions as the 1980s approached—works like this. You retain the right to live in your home, with the lender sending you the loan principal either in one lump sum or a stream of monthly payments. Thus, the reverse mortgage enables you to get back some of the equity in your home without your having to move elsewhere.

The concept seems simple and certainly appealing to millions of Americans—but there are so many ways to design these mortgages and they are so new that they pose many legal, tax, and regulatory problems for both borrowers and lenders. The problems, however, mostly stem from the novelty and unconventionality of the idea and are by no means unsurmountable.

"I can see the potential for a lot of good but also for a lot of problems," says an economist with the American Association of Retired Persons. "There are millions of possibilities and millions of pitfalls."

Among the questions to be considered:

• Do you want to sacrifice part of your estate that otherwise would go to your heirs?

• If you suddenly came into a sum of money you could profitably invest, can you get out of the reverse mortgage plan, and what would it cost you?

• What would be the total costs of fees to cover appraisal, title insurance, points, other related expenses?

Traditional home financing is itself complicated and the variations of reverse mortgages are almost unlimited. With a type of mortgage so new, untried, unregulated, unstandardized, it's even more essential that you fully understand all details of any plan.

Depending on your age, sex, marital status, and other factors, the payments vary in size but they are generally smaller than those received from a fixed-term reverse mortgage. The reason: the reverse annuity mortgage generally lasts a lifetime and you, the borrower, are not faced with the risk of having to sell your home to pay off the loan or having to raise needed funds through other means. The loan is paid off by your estate or sale of your house when you die.

Reverse mortgages probably will not become commonplace until well into the 1980s.

VARIABLE-RATE MORTGAGE (VRM)

The variable-rate mortgage is probably the most common of the AMI-ers. It is custom-tailored to the general facts of borrowing and lending in a prolonged phase of inflation rather than the financial needs of any class of borrowers.

With a VRM, the monthly payments, length of the loan, or a combination of both move up—and maybe down—in tandem with interest rates. The changes usually occur once or twice a year and there is often a ceiling on how high the interest rate can move. This customarily is 2½ per cent over the life of the loan.

If you borrow with a VRM, you frequently can choose to extend your payoff period instead of increasing your monthly payments. Some lenders allow you, as a VRM holder, to carry your loans with you when you buy another home or permit qualified new buyers to assume the mortgage at its then prevailing rate.

But have no illusions about the VRMs: they favor the lender in any period of prolonged increases in interest rates; and even without VRMs, you, a borrower, can refinance your mortgage when rates fall to a point where it's to your advantage—provided, of course, that your mortgage has prepayment privileges.

VRMs developed largely as a result of the upsurge in interest rates during 1973–74. Then depositors pulled their funds out of savings institutions to reinvest at higher rates elsewhere in such enormous amounts that the lending institutions found themselves desperately short of mortgage money. (There are ceilings on what the institutions can pay on savings.) This dilemma is what initially spurred the introduction of VRMs.

After some initial skepticism, the public had begun to accept the VRM concept as the 1980s opened.

ROLLOVER OR RENEGOTIABLE MORTGAGE

The rollover or renegotiable mortgage is another variation of the inflation-sensitive type of mortgage.

Changes in the loan rate are made much less often than with variable-rate mortgages, generally every three or five years. You, a borrower, are sometimes offered an initial interest rate below what you might obtain on a traditional fixed-rate mortgage. This plan is widely used in Canada.

Before you go "conventional," therefore, check what else might be available that would be of benefit to you. Be thorough!

HOW YOUR EQUITY BUILDS

"Mort" means "dead." When you pay off your mortgage, you amortize it or "kill" it and it's "dead." As you put the mortgage to "death," your equity or stake in the house which the mortgage helped you buy or build increases.

But in the early years of your mortgage a giant share of your monthly payments goes just for interest and a picayune proportion goes toward killing your mortgage and thereby building your equity.

Thus your equity increases very slowly in the early years and accelerates only as the mortgage nears maturity.

For instance, after the tenth year of payments on a thirty-year mortgage at 8½ per cent, you will still owe more than 88 per cent of the loan. Even at the twenty-year mark, you will have 62 per cent of the mortgage still to pay. In the twenty-eighth year of your thirty-year mortgage, you will still owe about 17 per cent.

The Bafflegab of Real Estate

Here, for quick reference, is a guide to the bafflegab of buying and selling real estate.

ABSTRACT   Short legal history of a property tracing ownership over the years and noting such encumbrances as unpaid taxes and liens.

AMORTIZATION   Reduction of a debt through monthly mortgage payments (or some other schedule of repayment in which the loan principal is reduced), along with payments of interest and other loan costs.

APPRAISAL   Estimate, made by the Federal Housing Administration, the Veterans Administration, a private lender, or other qualified appraiser, of the current market value of a property.

ASSESSMENT   Special charge imposed by local government on homeowners to cover costs of special projects such as street paving or new sewer systems from which the homeowners presumably benefit.

BINDER   Tentative agreement, between a buyer and seller of real estate, to the terms of the transaction—usually involving a deposit of a small amount of money.

BROKER   Professional who is licensed by the state in which he works to assist buyers and sellers of property.

CERTIFICATE OF TITLE   Legal statement to the effect that property ownership is established by public records.

CLOSING   The occasion on which the buyer and seller of a property—or their representatives—meet to exchange payment for the deed to a property.

CLOSING COSTS   Costs, other than the basic purchase price of a piece of property, which are imposed at the time a real estate deal is closed. Closing costs can include lawyers' fees, title insurance, taxes, and several other items.

COMMISSION   Fee which a seller of property pays to a real estate agent for his services—usually amounting to 6 to 10 per cent of the sale price.

CONDOMINIUM   Individually owned real estate consisting of a dwelling unit and an undivided interest in joint facilities and areas which serve the multi-unit complex.

CO-OPERATIVE   A form of real estate ownership in which each individual owns stock in a corporation, giving him the right to live in one of the units owned and administered by the corporation.

DEED   Legal, written document used to transfer ownership of property from seller to buyer.

DEFAULT   In this context, failure by a buyer to meet a mortgage payment or other requirement of the sale—which may result in forfeiture of the property itself.

DEPOSIT (or "EARNEST MONEY")   Sum of money, normally a small fraction of the sale price of the property, which a prospective buyer gives to a seller to secure a sales contract. See "Binder."

DEPRECIATION   Decrease in the value of property due to wear and tear, obsolescence, or the action of the elements. Differs from deterioration, which signifies abnormal loss of quality.

EARNEST MONEY   A deposit. See above.

EASEMENT   Right granted to one property owner by another to use the grantor's land for certain purposes—for example, a right-of-way for an access road or for power lines.

ENCUMBRANCE (or DEFECT OF RECORD)   Claim against the title of a parcel of real estate by a third party, other than the buyer or seller (e.g., a lien due to unpaid taxes or a mortgage delinquency), which challenges the property's ownership and tends to reduce its value.

EQUITY   In real estate terms, value built up in a property over the years, including the down payment, repaid portion of the mortgage principal, and appreciation (or depreciation) in the property's market value. The amount of equity in a property is the total current value of the property minus debts against the property.

ESCROW   The placing of money or other items of value in the custody of a bank or other third party until the terms of a real estate transaction are fulfilled by the two parties involved. Also: amounts paid by a homeowner into an account, usually administered by the mortgage lender, to provide for recurring expenses such as real estate taxes and homeowner insurance premiums. This type of escrow usually is included in the total monthly payments to the lender.

FHA   Federal Housing Administration, which insures mortgage holders against losses from default on loans made according to the Administration's policies.

FORECLOSURE   Sale by a bank or other lender of a property on which payments are seriously in default—in order to satisfy the debt at least partially.

LIEN   Claim against a property which sometimes is kept as security for the repayment of a debt.

LISTING   Registration of a property with one or more real estate brokers or agents, entitling the broker who actually sells the property to a commission. An exclusive listing gives one individual broker the exclusive right to handle the sale of a property; a multiple listing permits a special group of brokers to handle the transaction.

MORTGAGE Legal claim on property, given as security by a borrower to the lender of the funds in case repayment of the loan is not made.

OPTION Often sold by a seller of property to prospective buyer, giving the latter the right to buy the property at a specified price within a specified period of time.

PLAT Pictorial plan or map of a land subdivision or housing development.

POINTS Part of the settlement costs of exchanging real estate. One point is 1 per cent of the amount of the mortgage. Points are paid to the mortgage lender. In some cases, the term simply means a service charge imposed by the lender to cover part of the administrative costs of processing the loan. In other cases, particularly when a FHA loan is involved, the points amount to an adjustment in the interest rate to bring an artificially administered rate up to the market rate at the time. Points, in this second sense, technically are paid by the seller of the property. However, since the price of the house normally is adjusted to allow for this, points always effectively increase the interest rate on the loan to the buyer. They tend to eliminate the interest rate advantage of government-insured or-guaranteed loans.

PURCHASE MONEY MORTGAGE Mortgage granted directly by a seller to the buyer of the seller's property, in which the seller may take back the property if the buyer does not pay off the mortgage as agreed. In brief, the seller of the house lends the buyer the money with which to buy the house.

QUITCLAIM DEED Deed which releases any interest a seller or other individual may have in a given piece of land. See "Deed."

REAL ESTATE (REAL PROPERTY) Land, and any structures situated on it.

REALTOR Real estate agent who is a member of the National Association of Realtors. A copyrighted word, always capitalized.

SETBACK A common restriction provided under zoning ordinances specifying the distance a new house must be set back from a road or from the lot boundaries.

SURVEY The determination, by means of examination of land records and also field measurements based on these records, of the exact boundaries and location of a property.

TITLE Legal document containing all necessary facts to prove ownership of property.

TITLE DEFECT Fact or circumstance which challenges such ownership.

INSURING YOUR HOME

BASIC GUIDELINES

You have found the house (or apartment) which really meets your needs and fits your budget. You have tracked down the most advantageous mortgage available in your area. Now, before you even set foot in the place, you must have it insured against fire, theft, and any other real threats which exist in your region and your neighborhood. The most widely used way to do this today is through a homeowner's insurance policy.

Here are your basic guides:

Deal with an insurance agent who is respected by your neighbors and friends who have been dealing with him over the years. Your bank and lawyer are other good sources of advice on reputable insurance agents.

Sit down with the agent and go over all of the possible types, coverages, deductibles, and other aspects of property liability insurance which might apply to you and your home.

Ask the previous owners or occupants of your house what kinds and amounts of insurance they carried. Use this as a starting point only, though, for it is more than likely they were underinsured. Also ask which major additions or improvements—such as a new attached garage or a new wing or a new bathroom—have been made since their policy was last reviewed and updated. Then report to your insurance agent the details and costs of such additions and request an appropriate upward revision of your basic coverage for the house.

Consider having the house professionally appraised—if you do not have a fairly good idea how much your house or apartment and its contents are now worth. A local real estate agent probably can recommend an appraiser who would do this job for you at reasonable cost. See page 151 for guides on how to find a qualified appraiser. As an alternative, ask the contractor who built the house to estimate the cost of rebuilding it should it be totally destroyed.

At an absolute minimum, ask your insurance agent for his appraisal of your house in terms of trends in building and home repair costs in your area. Or ask him for one of the do-it-yourself appraisal kits provided by many insurance companies today. Some of these kits give you only a rough idea of cost trends; others detail building trade wage scales, materials costs, and other items in various areas of the United States.

Keep in mind that, just in a five-year span in the 1970s, overall home construction costs soared by more than 55 per cent—meaning that a house which cost $30,000 to build in 1972 would have cost more than $46,500 to replace only six years later.

Insure your house for at least 80 per cent of its replacement value—in order to collect in full for loss or damage. If your coverage is less than this (as it is today for the majority of American homeowners), your insurance would pay only for the depreciated value of your house, rather than for the actual replacement cost. To illustrate this important difference:

If a fire in your ten-year-old home causes $10,000 worth of damage and if your house is underinsured, you'll be reimbursed for $10,000 minus the amount by which the insurance adjuster decides your house has depreciated during the decade (if any). No matter how well insured your house is, any personal property losses would be reimbursed not for their replacement value but rather for their depreciated cash value—unless you have extra coverage for this personal property.

Here are typical coverages provided by a homeowner's policy for a $50,000 house in the late 1970s: $40,000 for the house itself (80 per cent of its value); $4,000 for unattached garages and other buildings on your property; $20,000 for personal property losses: $4,000 for extra living expenses in the event fire forces you out of your house temporarily; $25,000 in personal liability for each instance in which you are held liable (except for automobile liability); $500 in medical payments for each person injured on your property; and $500 for physical damage to the property of others, for which you might not be legally held liable but for which you voluntarily decide to help compensate the person who was hit by the loss. Personal liability of $250 also covers accidents off the premises if they are caused by the homeowner, a member of his family who lives with him, or his pet. Provisions for legal expenses in the event of lawsuits against the policyholder are included too.

Make an inventory of the contents of your house—including factual descriptions of the appearance, type, and condition of each item of value; snapshots of each room taken from two or more different angles; detailed photographs, descriptions, and professional appraisals of each painting, musical instrument, rare book, or other item of significant value.

Keep a copy of this inventory in your safety-deposit box to help support any insurance claim you may make later. Keep all records, photographs, up-to-date appraisals made by qualified appraisers, and other documentation of the value of such items in your safety-deposit box.

Note that, as a general rule, the contents of your house and other personal property will be insured automatically for 50 per cent of the amount of insurance on your home. If you have especially valuable possessions such as paintings, sculptures, antiques, furs, stamp or coin collections, stereo equipment or jewelry, make sure their combined value falls within the limits of coverage of personal belongings—$20,000 in the above example—and if not, consider insuring them separately. You probably will find you have to insure them separately anyway, because such property is often classified "high risk" and assigned only nominal coverage unless extra premiums are paid.

Also, if you live in a city or suburb with a high crime rate and if your insurance company refuses to offer you coverage against burglaries, robberies, etc., consider applying through a nearby commercial insurance firm for a federal crime insurance policy issued by the Federal Insurance Administration, Department of Housing and Urban Development. A federal crime insurance policy will be valuable, comparatively inexpensive—and very important to you if you are not able to buy burglary and theft insurance through the normal commercial channels.

Note: If you rent a house or apartment you can get a special tenant's homeowner's insurance policy covering your personal belongings and providing liability protection as well.

If you own a condominium apartment, you can buy coverage for your personal property and any additions or alterations made by you and not insured under the condominium association's policy. As in a tenant's policy, you also have personal liability protection. Mobile home owners can obtain a special homeowner's policy.

HOW TO GET THE RIGHT COVERAGE AND SAVE TOO

As a general rule, a homeowner's insurance policy covers your home and belongings against a wide variety of perils, including fire, lightning, windstorms, tornadoes, explosions, and riots, on top of the other coverage it provides.

The so-called "broad form" homeowner's policy adds to this list such perils as falling objects, building collapse, exploding hot water heaters and heating systems, pipe freezing, weight of ice and snow, and electrical damage to appliances.

The more expensive "all risks" policy covers you against every possible threat to your property except earthquakes, volcanic eruption, landslides, floods, tidal waves, sewage backups, nuclear radiation, war, and a few other possibilities.

Flood insurance is available through the National Flood Insurance Program. It is offered only in communities which have passed and enforce federally approved zoning restrictions on future flood plain development. Your insurance agent can tell you the limitations and other details as well as how to buy the coverage.

Obviously, the more dangers you insure your house against, the more your coverage will cost you. So go over the whole list with your insurance agent. Decide realistically which risks are a significant threat to your home. Buy the coverage which is suitable for your house.

Don't, however, overinsure your house by basing your coverage on an inflated appraisal of its value or by including the value of your building site, foundation, or underground pipes and wiring in your valuation.

Take advantage of the deductibles now available in homeowner's insurance policies. You might save a full 20 per cent in premium cost just by raising the deductible on your basic coverage from $100 to $500.

If you belong to a professional organization, find out if it offers low-cost group homeowner's insurance to members. As just one example, the National Education Association offers such a plan to teachers the nation over—costing considerably less than ordinary individual policies. Group homeowner's insurance is an increasingly popular employee fringe benefit, offered by both organizations and employers. Check into this possibility.

Finally shop among insurance companies. If you don't have time to shop when you buy your house, do so when it is time to renew your coverage. Rates can vary widely for the same coverage.

HOW TO BOOST YOUR HOMEOWNER'S COVERAGE

To expand your home insurance protection, you can:

• Simply increase the current overall limits of the coverage on your home and/or its contents.

• Add a "floater policy" to give you extra coverage of certain personal effects such as jewelry, art works, professional tools, musical instruments.

• Increase your personal liability coverage. The typical yearly cost of hiking this coverage from $25,000 to $300,000 was only $10 to $15 in the late 1970s.

• Add a new "inflation guard endorsement" in your homeowner's policy. Every three months, your coverage automatically increases by whatever per cent you have decided—1, 2, 3 per cent, even more if you wish. This feature automatically hikes your coverage as home replacement costs rise.

Whatever you do, vow to have your policy updated every year—because this is a vitally important financial protection against the soaring costs of repairing or replacing your house, and also because the values of any fine-art works, antiques, stamp collections you may own are likely to soar over the years.

Don't risk finding out the hardest, cruelest, and costliest way how drastically underinsured your home is.

BUT IS YOUR HOME ADEQUATELY INSURED FOR THE 1980s?

Q. *"We built our house in 1965 at a total cost of $40,000 and on the advice of our insurance agent, bought a homeowner's policy way back then for $30,000. Since then, he has raised the policy twice to $50,000 and now he's telling us to increase the insurance again! Is this a rip-off?"*

A. It definitely is *not* a rip-off. For even at $50,000, the house you built for $40,000 in 1965 is woefully underinsured. To prove that to yourself, honestly answer this one simple question:

Would you sell your home for $50,000 today? If you lost your home this day, the face amount of your homeowner's policy is the *maximum* amount you could be paid, you know.

Yet, the fact is that as of the late 1970s, the house you built in 1965 for $40,000 would have cost $85,880 to replace—far more than double its original cost, or $45,880 more, to be exact.

Our galloping inflation of the past few decades has had a horrendous impact on building costs particularly. Even a house bought or built only five years ago and fully insured at that date is likely to be underinsured now. An informed estimate is that as a result of the bulge in construction costs, *more than half of all U.S. single-family homes now lack adequate homeowner's insurance*. A fully insured house purchased in the early 1960s probably is no more than 50 per cent insured in the closing years of the 1970s.

AND ARE YOU REALLY COVERED?

At a political reception over a weekend a short while back, a woman I had never met before noticed my name tag and then assaulted me with a highly emotional tale about having returned that very morning from a vacation to discover her home had been seriously vandalized during her absence. Her plea: "What should I do?"

"Call your insurance agent first thing Monday morning," I suggested, and then I decided to get the answer too.

Yes, she is covered for her loss up to the limits of her homeowner's insurance policy—unless her house had been vacant for a period of more than thirty consecutive days immediately preceding the loss. (She had been gone for only two weeks.)

"This question is among the thirty most commonly asked," volunteered a spokesman for Liberty Mutual Insurance Companies of Boston with whom I talked. So, herewith, some of the other thirty questions and their answers which easily may concern millions of you:

Q. *If your pets cause damage to your personal belongings what coverage do you have?*

A. None. There is no coverage under your homeowner's policy for loss or damage to personal belongings caused by a pet or other domestic animal.

Q. *If there is a windstorm and the trees in your yard are damaged, what coverage do you have?*

A. None. There is no coverage under your homeowner's policy for windstorm damage to trees or other shrubs.

Q. *For purposes of insurance, what is the definition of burglary? Of robbery? Of theft?*

A. Burglary is the breaking or entering into a building for the purpose of committing a felony while the building is locked and secured and leaving visible signs of forced entry.

Robbery is stealing from you with the threat (or potential threat) of physical harm or violence. Victims are present when a robbery is committed and often a weapon (such as a revolver or knife) is evident.

Theft is defined as a loss where stealing can be presumed from the accompanying circumstances, if not entirely proved. For instance, if you, a homeowner, let a stranger into your home and that evening you discover something is missing from the area where the individual was, it can be generally assumed that a theft has occurred.

Q. *If your home is damaged from a covered peril to the extent of forcing you to live elsewhere while repairs are being made, will your insurance policy cover this expense?*

A. Yes. This coverage comes under the heading of additional living expenses, a coverage which is included in all homeowner's and tenant's policies. The amount of coverage you have for additional living expenses is generally 20 per cent of the amount of coverage on your dwelling. If you have $20,000 coverage on your home, you may have coverage for up to $4,000 for additional living expenses.

Q. *If you or a member of your family is injured on your property, what coverage do you have?*

A. None. There is no coverage under your homeowner's policy for injury sustained by you or a member of your household.

Q. *If your home or personal belongings are damaged by water as the result of a pipe bursting in your plumbing or heating system, what coverage do you have?*

A. You are covered up to your policy limits for the resulting damage and for any additional damage necessarily caused in the course of repairing the faulty system. You are not covered, however, for the cost of repairing or replacing the system itself. Also, for water damage to be a covered loss, it must be sudden and accidental. If it results from a slow leak over a period of weeks or months, it would not be covered.

Q. *What is a "loss off premises"?*

A. That's a loss you incur while you are away from home. As an example, a theft from your hotel or motel room while you, the policyholder, are on a vacation or business trip.

Your homeowner's policy does provide you with protection against "loss off premises." Check your policy for details.

The Bafflegab of Home Insurance

BURGLARY AND THEFT INSURANCE   Coverage which reimburses you for property which has been stolen from you or your home.

DEDUCTIBLES   Maximum amounts you, the policyholder, are required to pay in each claim or accident before your insurance payments begin. The higher the deductible you choose, the lower your premium costs.

EXTENDED COVERAGE   Protection against loss or damage to property caused by windstorm, hail, smoke, explosion, riots, vehicles, and aircraft.

FIRE INSURANCE   Coverage against losses due to fire and lightning and also against damage caused by water in home fires. You can have extended coverage for an additional premium.

HOMEOWNER'S POLICY   Home insurance "packages" cover the perils listed below under "Property Insurance" and also include coverage of personal property and of personal liability.

LIABILITY INSURANCE   Protection against loss resulting from claims or lawsuits brought against you in the event that through accident you cause injury to another person or damage to his property.

MEDICAL PAYMENTS INSURANCE   Type of insurance, usually included in your liability insurance policy, which reimburses others, no matter who is at fault, for minor accidental injury and/or funeral expenses up to the limit of the coverage.

PERSONAL LIABILITY INSURANCE   Insurance included in homeowner's policies, which reimburses you for money you have had to pay for virtually any kind of property damage or bodily injury you have caused for other people. Damage caused by your automobile, however, is not covered. Nor are injury and damage associated with your business.

PROPERTY INSURANCE   Financial protection against loss or damage to your property as a result of theft, fire, smoke, windstorm, hail, explosion, aircraft, motor vehicles, vandalism, malicious mischief, riots and civil commotion, and various other perils. The protection against perils other than fire is called "extended coverage."

UMBRELLA LIABILITY INSURANCE   Insurance against losses above and beyond those covered by your basic liability insurance policies. This type of insurance is often written for sums in the $1 million range. It is used mainly by well-to-do doctors, other professionals, and business executives who may be vulnerable to malpractice suits and other big liability claims.

How to Buy "House Equipment"

A HOUSE IS NOT A HOME

As the illustrious—albeit infamous—house mother Polly Adler put it more than a generation ago: a house is not a home.

A house is the shell. A home means furniture, appliances large and small, entertainment equipment, rugs, curtains, and you-name-what-else (not to mention people) it will take to make the shell your home.

In all, we spend tens of billions of dollars each year on furniture, appliances, and other "household durables."

Furniture, in fact, ranks among the biggest investments you will make in your lifetime. Yet the danger is that you will go about this purchase in near-total ignorance or innocence.

QUESTIONS AND ANSWERS ON FURNITURE

The following questions and answers will illustrate your basic guides to furniture buying.

Q. *Should you buy a whole houseful (or apartmentful) of furniture all at once when you set up housekeeping?*

A. Few Americans, even older ones, are in a position to make an investment involving so much money and forethought. A more realistic approach would be to draw up a two-, three-, or five-year furniture-buying plan to meet your own particular needs.

Q. *How do you accomplish this?*

A. Lay your plan out in advance. You will then know precisely where you stand in your home furnishing from year to year. You also will know what first-year purchases can be switched to other uses as time goes on—e.g., a first-year wrought-iron table and chairs might go from the living room to the terrace or recreation room the second year, or a first-year throw rug for the dining alcove might go to the bedroom the third year, etc. And you will be able to fit the whole plan without difficulty into your personal money manager. (See pages 19–22.)

Q. *Where should you begin?*

A. Decide what type and size furniture will look the best and then focus on the basic, essential pieces you'll need right away—such as a bed, couch, table and chairs, good portable lamp, bureau, dresser, mirror. Decide in advance what job you want each piece to perform in terms of durability, beauty, practicality, economy.

Fill out the "basics" you can't afford to buy new with good-quality secondhand furniture from secondhand stores, thrift shops, junk shops, railroad salvage stores, auctions, garage sales, Salvation Army and Goodwill Industries, want ads in local newspapers, family and friends. Look hard at used bedding and upholstery. Good-quality used furniture is a better deal in both durability and attractiveness than low-quality new furniture. Seconds or slightly damaged new furniture also can be a bargain, but before you buy, find out how much necessary repairs would cost. Another good investment might be unfinished furniture which you can finish yourself to blend with your other furnishings. Clean, classical furniture at moderate prices has become popular.

Q. *How can you save in buying new, finished furniture?*

A. Choose basic designs rather than "fad" furniture which may cost just as much but soon go out of style. Select with an eye toward the future: sturdy but inexpensive canvas fold-up chairs, for example, might do now for the dining area and can be used later as porch furniture. Shop during furniture clearance sales, usually in August and after Christmas. Check your newspaper for these sales. Department store clearance centers have become big in the field selling in-line goods at lower markups. Also, consider the mass merchandisers and warehouse-type centers for value and price.

Q. *What should you look for in purchasing a convertible couch?*

A. There are four major considerations for selecting a convertible couch:

• Seating comfort. Some convertible couches offer added features which provide additional seating comfort. One manufacturer offers, for example, an exclusive free-floating seat deck that prevents the cushions from resting directly on the metal sleeper mechanism. Seating comfort is particularly important, of course, if the convertible is to be used mainly as a sofa and only occasionally as a sleeper.

• Sleeping comfort. Look for extra support bars on the mechanism and an extra-firm mattress. While in the store, don't be afraid to lie down on the mattress just as you would before purchasing a conventional mattress and box spring.

If the convertible is going to be used regularly or frequently for sleeping, invest in a queen-size or super-queen-size sofa-sleeper if space permits. Extra features such as tilt-up mechanism for TV viewing are optional. Also check for plastic caps on the mechanism legs to protect floors.

Many convertibles come standard with foam mattresses but some manufacturers offer optional innerspring mattresses, which may be desirable if the couch is to be used regularly for sleeping. However, do not expect any convertible to offer the complete comfort and support obtainable from a full-size mattress and box spring set, even those convertibles which are marketed by bedding producers.

• Easy to open. You should expect your convertible to open quickly, quietly, and effortlessly, regardless of whether it's used practically every night or only occasionally. It should be just as easy to close.

• Cleaning ease. The metal mechanism in a convertible sofa adds considerably to the weight of the unit. Casters are desirable for easy moving and cleaning. Check to see if there is a cover over the entire sleeper unit with no gap between it and the frame for protection.

You may also want to choose a more heavy-duty fabric on a convertible than you would on a stationary couch. These would include an olefin or nylon or olefin blend. Cushions should be reversible regardless of cover chosen. Most man-made fibers and blends used for upholstery fabrics now have a better "feel" and improved coloration than a few years ago.

Q. *What should you look for in buying a recliner?*

A. In buying a recliner, who's going to use it is important. A recliner often becomes a one-person chair in the household. In the past, it was generally the man of the house's chair, but now some designs may be more suitable for women, and a few manufacturers offer his and her models. The recliner purchased should be comfortable to the main person who will be using it.

The Stratford Company has come up with a simple three-point test to tell if any recliner properly fits your body. It involves checking three basic body support points while sitting in the chair:

(1) Back of the knees. In both the upright and reclining positions, the nook at the back of the knee should meet the top seam of the seat cushion. If not, leg muscles will be strained.

(2) Lower back. It should have firm support of the back cushion resting against it.

(3) Head. If the head is unnaturally pushed forward or strained too far back by the headrest when in both reclining and upright positions, the chair is not for you. (Some recliners, however, have attached adjustable headrest cushions, or small matching head pillows accompanying the chair.)

Q. *There's a tremendous price range in beds you see advertised; what's the rule for saving money here?*

A. Spend as much as you can afford for a mattress and a box spring that will remain comfortable for a long time. You'll probably spend *twenty-five years of your lifetime*—if you're average—in bed. Don't skimp, and beware of "drastic reductions" and "fantastic bargains" in beds. Stay away from soft foam or foam flake mattresses—although good foams may be very good and also easier to handle. Make sure there's enough padding in your mattress so that you can't feel the innersprings through the padding. Also be sure the stitching is neat and firm, the ticking is durable. Before buying, lie down on the mattress and test its buoyancy and firmness. Your body weight should be supported equally at every point. The bedspring (box spring, usually) should have the same features as the mattress and should be bought at the same time.

It's a good idea to have a sleeping space 38 inches wide and 6 inches longer than your height (with a ½-inch allowance, plus or minus).

The mattress should have handles so it can be turned easily. It should have a strong outer fabric so that it will last, and ventilation on both sides to minimize dampness. Read the label attached to the mattress to find out if it has been treated to resist stains and whether it meets flammability standards.

Q. *How much should you budget for furniture if you are planning to move relatively soon to another home?*

A. That depends on your individual priorities and means. But one guide is to avoid a big outlay for any item of furniture which probably wouldn't be appropriate in other quarters.

Q. *What type of furniture is appropriate for a young couple with a small child?*

A. It can be risky to own a lot of really fine furniture while you're rearing young children, unless you confine it to quarters which are out of bounds for the children. Otherwise, your best choice would probably be solid, simple furniture which can stand plenty of wear and tear and which can be replaced later.

Q. *How much should you earmark for accessories and strictly decorative items such as pictures, curtains, etc.?*

A. This will be determined by how much is left after you've collected your big items. If you find there's almost nothing left, you can use many attractive but inexpensive decorative items, such as wall posters and blown-up photographs, instead of pictures, and curtains made of burlap or unbleached muslin. But don't count curtains as "accessories" if you need them to give you privacy in your apartment or house.

Q. *What about the economics of patching up old, badly worn pieces of furniture?*

A. Don't throw good money after bad. When an item is finished, throw it out with no regrets.

Q. *What happens if you decide you don't like a big piece of furniture after it has been delivered to your home?*

A. The store from which you bought it is not legally required to take it back (it's a very costly hauling job for the retailer), so find out store policy on furniture returns, especially sale items, before you buy. Laws vary from state to state on the refund of deposits. Also ask the store to put in writing its policies on damage to furniture in transit to your home, installation, and/or servicing of items. Finally, is there a written warranty and, if so, exactly what does it cover?

Q. *What about reupholstering an old chair instead of buying a new one? Does this save money?*

A. The cost for reupholstering even a medium-size chair may shock you, for upholstering is largely a hand operation, and labor costs are high. This may be the best reason for replacing an old chair with a new piece of furniture, if the chair frame is of questionable quality. If, however, a chair or sofa is an antique or a sound, old piece of furniture, it's probably well worth the cost of getting it reupholstered.

Before calling in an upholsterer, telephone several upholsterers for a non-binding, over-the-phone indication of what labor charges would be for a particular type of chair or sofa. Fabric costs usually must be added to labor costs. Ask upholsterers who stock their own fabrics if their labor charge is the same whether their own fabrics are used or you supply them. Try to agree on a firm delivery date with the shop that gets your business. Ask if you can visit the owner's workshops—so you can get some idea of whether the work is sloppy or meticulous.

Prices tend to be somewhat lower in small owner-operated shops but it also may take a small shop longer to complete a job. Department stores near you may have upholstering departments. The work often will be done in your own home and be no more costly than that done by the small shops.

The construction of a chair often dictates the method of restoring. Expect to pay more for reupholstery of tufted or channel-back chairs or sofas.

Q. *What are the comparative costs of reupholstering and buying a new chair?*

A. It can cost as much as $200 to $300 to reupholster a wing chair. A new one of average quality runs about $300 and up. The key to your choice should be the quality of the frame and springs of your chair or couch compared with that of a new piece. Wood frames in furniture bought a generation ago usually are better quality than the softer woods in upholstered furniture now on the market. A chair bought at a secondhand shop and reupholstered may prove a better buy in the long run than a new one.

Q. *How do you figure costs of fabrics in reupholstering?*

A. Fabric costs are fairly consistent from one upholsterer to another. Fabrics usually come 54 inches wide and range from as little as $5.00 a yard to as much as $75 a yard and more, with a good selection in the $10 to $20 range. It takes about 6 yards to cover a wing chair and almost twice that for a three-cushion sofa.

Q. *Are there guides for spotting good quality in furniture?*

A. All joinings should be clean, tight-fitting, difficult to detect, and put together with screws instead of nails.

Drawers should slide smoothly. There also should be stops to prevent them from being pulled all the way out. Drawers should be finished.

Backs of the furniture should be all wood—and not, as in cheap furniture, made of heavy cardboard.

Furniture doors should be well hung and fitted, and should open and close easily.

Undersides should be sanded and stained to match more visible parts.

The hardware, such as knobs, pulls, and handles, should be firmly attached, tastefully designed, and in keeping with the quality of the piece it adorns. Brass and other metal hardware should be rust-resistant and tarnish-proof.

Federal Trade Commission rules require furniture to be tagged if synthetic materials are used, or if the material is veneer. If such furniture does not have these tags prominently displayed, or if the tags are difficult to decipher, steer clear of the store.

Q. *What about the quality of upholstered furniture?*

A. It is harder to detect quality in upholstered furniture because the upholstery hides the construction. But you can get a good idea of the quality and type of materials used in an upholstered piece from the label, which, by law, must itemize all materials used in it. Ask questions about the quality and type of construction of the piece, the material used in the padding, colorfastness of the outer covering, durability. Look at the material to see if patterns match at seams and if seams and welts are straight.

FTC rules also give you some protection with upholstered furniture, requiring clear and conspicuous labels substantiating special claims for the fabrics.

Deal only with stores which have good reputations.

Also test the pieces you want to buy. Sit in them, see if they're the right height and size for your comfort, as soft or hard as you like your furniture to be. Sit on the furniture in the store the way you like to sit at home.

Q. *Should you buy furniture on time?*

A. Cash is the cheapest way to pay for furniture, of course. Moreover, interest charges by retail stores on furniture bought on the installment plan are higher than interest charges on many other forms of credit. So, if you do buy on time, shop among the various available sources of credit for your most advantageous deal.

Q. *What are the best stores in which to buy furniture?*

A. You'll find this out by comparing prices, quality, and service among furniture stores, chain stores, department stores, discount stores. Look at different price levels for the same item. Compare quality as nearly as you can determine it. Patronize no-frills, low-cost furniture "clearance centers" operated by major furniture stores where you buy for cash and take home your purchases yourself. Warehouse stores have become important in the last few years. They offer delivery and good value.

Don't be afraid to shop. The honest merchant will want you to look around in his store. Most furniture stores are honest. But there are retailers who will try to take advantage of you and high-pressure you into buying something you cannot afford or may not even want. Before you buy, find out from friends what their experiences with the store have been. Also check on the reputation of a store by calling or writing the local Better Business Bureau.

Q. *Chairs, tables, couches—these can be very expensive items. Where is there room for savings?*

A. Use your own individual skills to finish lower-cost unfinished furniture yourself. Rely on color and arrangement, rather than expensive craftsmanship, to achieve good style.

Q. *What if you love fine old furniture but just can't pay the price for it?*

A. If you're inclined toward antiques—but can't afford the real thing—consider "honest copies" made decades after the originals by lesser craftsmen.

Q. *Are there any special guides for wood?*

A. The leading native woods are: walnut, oak, pine, spruce, redwood, cedar, cherry, pecan or hickory, maple, birch. Each has a distinctive color and grain pattern. The major foreign hardwood is mahogany. It shrinks or swells less than almost any other wood.

Q. *Do you save by buying a complete bedroom or dining-room set, instead of individual items?*

A. You may, if you actually need each item offered in the package. But you won't save any money if the roomful includes things you hadn't intended to buy in the first place.

Q. *What about the bargain specials—lamps, racks—offered free with complete sets?*

A. Don't be misled by stores that toss in lamps, ashtrays, magazine racks, and other accessories to make up a "bargain" room of furniture. Reputable stores try this on occasion too, and it's no bargain. Price the basic furniture so you'll know exactly what you're paying for what.

Q. *What about furniture ads which say "wholesale prices to you"?*

A. Don't be misled by any ads claiming "wholesale prices" or "factory to you." A retailer cannot sell to customers at wholesale prices. How would he make a profit? And if factories sold wholesale to everyone, who would want to be a retailer?

Q. *What about "introductory" discount cards to furniture showrooms?*

A. If you get a "card of introduction" to a furniture showroom, do not buy until you have compared its "discount prices" with the regular prices at other stores. Make sure that the discount cards or cards of admission or introduction really do give discounts. And also make sure that "warehouse" stores are truly warehouses and not retail stores actually charging higher prices than regular stores.

Q. *What about guarantees and warranties on furniture?*

A. A reputable merchant is your best protection, for furniture is seldom guaranteed. Mattresses, however, are usually "guaranteed" by the manufacturer for ten to twenty years. Get a copy of the guarantee, read it with care, and save it for future reference. (See pages 1204–7 for details on your rights and how to get your money's worth on any type of warranty.)

Q. *How long do you have to wait for furniture to be delivered?*

A. If the furniture you have ordered is available, you will probably get it right away. However, if the furniture is not available and has to be ordered from the manufacturer, you may have to wait from six to twelve weeks or more! Get delivery promises in writing, and put down as small a deposit as possible. Don't get rid of your old furniture until you get the new. Most dealers will tell you if there will be a delay in delivery.

If you have serious late delivery problems, contact the Furniture Industry Consumer Advisory Panel, P.O. Box 2436, High Point, North Carolina 27261, or one of the consumer rights organizations listed.

Q. *Should you hire an interior designer?*

A. Before you hire a professional designer, find out if your local stores offer, as many now do, free counseling services on home furnishing problems, either at the store or at your home. You also can get good decorating ideas just by studying the variety of furniture ensembles (or model rooms) on display at most large stores. You may soon feel confident to go ahead on your own.

But if you're planning and can afford a substantial furnishing job and if you have neither the interest nor talent to tackle the job yourself, by all means consider hiring a professional interior designer. Clever designers often can save you money: by buying furniture and materials at substantial discounts; by finding practical uses for unused spaces; by turning inexpensive "raw material" into imaginative and attractive designs; by helping you sidestep the pitfalls—economic and otherwise—of dealing through untrained, unsophisticated retail salespeople;

by making sure you avoid costly decorating errors (e.g., dashing colors, oversize pieces of furniture); by knowing where the best bargains are in the goods you need.

Q. *How do you shop for this type of service?*

A. Ask the American Society of Interior Designers (730 Fifth Avenue, New York, New York 10019) for names of reputable members in your area. Ask friends who have worked with interior designers what their experiences—and costs—have been.

Be sure you communicate well, both ways, with the person you choose and that the designer will build on your ideas, tastes, and preferences in whatever job he or she takes on for you.

Insist on sketches and drawings from the designer, showing the plan or scheme to be followed. Such sketches are a crucially important clue to what a room or rooms will look like when finished.

Ask the designer to help you plan if you are furnishing and decorating your first home and if you have to spread out your purchases over several years.

Discuss costs and fees in advance and be sure these details are in a written contract for a given job. Write in this contract' what services and which furnishings will be included, what completion date is anticipated, and on what schedule you will pay for the work done.

Q. *What charges should you be prepared for?*

A. Typically, you pay one third of the total agreed-upon price when you sign the contract, another one third when the designer orders the furnishings you want, and the balance when the job is done.

Typical designers' fees for a preliminary consultation in the late 1970s covered a startlingly wide range and procedures also varied, so be sure you check them out thoroughly in advance. Some designers, including architects who offer interior designing services, charge clients only the difference between the wholesale and retail value of whatever furniture and materials they buy for you. Others charge a flat fee.

QUESTIONS AND ANSWERS ON RUGS AND CARPETING

Q. *What about wall-to-wall carpeting?*

A. Wall-to-wall is the answer if you have unsightly floors or wish to avoid the double labor of waxing floors and cleaning rugs. However, rising installation costs for wall-to-wall are taking a bigger and bigger bite of the carpet budget. If your floors look good, consider a room-size rug or area rug. Rugs are a smart buy if you're just starting out, or if you're a family on the move from apartment to apartment or city to city. Choose colors which will give you decorating flexibility with future furniture purchases.

Q. *How do you judge fibers?*

A. Wool is preferred by some experts because of its balance of such desired qualities as resilience, ease of cleaning, and durability. However, the continuing high price of wool has greatly reduced the selection of wool carpets in the stores, so be prepared to pay a premium price for those available. You can still find a wide choice of wool area rugs in many designs and styles. Wool carpets and rugs should be mothproofed and they may present an allergy problem for some people.

Nylon is today's leading carpet fiber and you will find the widest selection of nylon styles in the stores at reasonable prices. Though general inflation has affected costs, competitive factors have kept nylon prices at stable levels. Nylon is the most wear-resistant fiber and allows most water-soluble stains to be easily removed. Look especially for second- and third-generation nylons, which offer the important benefits of soil-hiding and static control. These improved nylons require less frequent cleaning and hold their appearance longer.

Acrylics resemble wool in looks and performance. They are easily cleaned. Look at the label to see if the manufacturer has applied a soil-retardant finish. This is an important benefit. Acrylics today are modified to meet flammability regulations.

Polyester is also a major carpet fiber today. It has good wear resistance and a soft "hand" or touch similar to wool. Polyester's resilience is good in dense constructions. Some manufacturers are offering nylon-polyester blends to improve the wear and resilience factors.

Q. *Are the rug-carpet sales any good?*

A. Yes. And you can save from 20 to as much as 50 per cent on carpets and rugs if you wait for the periodic traditional sales which take place in January–February and July–August. Most department stores and long-established rug stores have legitimate sales at least annually, during which you can save up to 20 to 25 per cent. Sometimes, too, you may be able to find an item that is being discontinued by the mill at savings up to 50 per cent. But deal only with reliable stores.

Q. *What about carpet flammability?*

A. Under the Flammable Fabrics Act, all newly manufactured or imported carpets, rugs, and carpet tiles must meet federal flammability standards. If the carpet dealer cannot provide you with the appropriate assurance that a carpet or carpeting is fire-resistant, write to the manufacturer. And if you get no assurance there, shop elsewhere.

Q. *How do you judge carpet quality?*

A. The old rule of "the deeper, the denser, the better" still applies. The face yarns take the punishment, so the thicker the tufts, and the closer they are to each other, the more wear you can expect. Bend the carpet back to see how thick the pile is. Also closely examine the tufts to see they are securely anchored to the backing. Virtually all American-made carpets use a latex coating to provide sufficient "tuft bind." But many carpets also use a double backing for "extra body" and this will conceal the latex coating from the back.

Incidentally, the term "broadloom," often associated with quality of a carpet, refers merely to the width of the carpeting.

Q. *What's the best way to clean wall-to-wall carpeting—and the cost?*

A. Use a rug-cleaning establishment which specializes in cleaning carpeting in the home. As of the late 1970s, these companies usually charged about 15 to 20 cents a square foot and some offered reduced rates during slow seasons, such as the early part of the year.

For an easily understandable rundown on all aspects of carpeting write for a copy of *Carpet and Rug Care Guide,* Carpet and Rug Institute, Dalton, Georgia 30720 (10 cents).

HOW TO AVOID "CARPET SHARKS"

"Wall-to-wall nylon carpet . . . two rooms plus hall or stairway . . . Complete with padding and custom installation . . . $119."

"Three rooms of wall-to-wall carpeting . . . Free tickets to a Broadway show and a free vacuum cleaner . . . All for $115."

These and hundreds of similar ads are typical of the "carpet shark," who knows little about carpeting but every trick in the book on making a sale—often at a price many times the carpet's value. And once he has made a sale and the carpet has been installed, there is absolutely nothing a victim can do about it. One victim reported paying $2,064 for a carpet worth $650. Another paid $3,000 for a small carpet valued at a few hundred dollars.

To illustrate the pitfalls, let's say you respond to a come-on ad offering rooms of carpeting, completely installed, for $100 or so. A high-pressure salesman arrives at your door and immediately downgrades the carpet his company advertised. Sample remarks made by a fast-buck salesman to a "detective" planted by one Better Business Bureau:

"If you take it up, you will have to resand your floors. Be careful how you vacuum it—it will run like a stocking from the corners. With baseboard heating like you have, it will crumple right up and won't last six months."

The salesman has instructions to sell not the low-priced carpet to you but some other, vastly overpriced product. If you insist on buying the $100 carpeting, he simply refuses to sell.

Another type of carpet gypster advertises "industrial" or "commercial" carpeting at bargain prices—claiming that the carpet is left over from a big job in a hotel or office building and that such carpeting wears longer than regular covering. As it turns out, you may end up paying the gypster up to three times the price you would pay at your local store for the same stuff. "The fact is," says one industry expert, "that there is no established commercial standard and seldom is there enough carpeting left over from a commercial installation to cover an average-sized bathroom."

Still another trick is called yardage "jumping" or "stealing." This simply means telling you that you need 30 yards of carpeting instead of the 15 yards you actually should buy. A variation of this gyp is the phony reference to "factory units" of carpet measurement—another way to induce you to buy more carpet than you need.

How do you spot a carpet shark?

• Beware of ads that offer an "astonishingly low" price. You just can't have three rooms of carpeting installed for less than $100. Many reputable dealers figure as a rule of thumb you'll get one year of wear for each dollar per yard that you spend.

• Steer clear of the salesman who tries to switch you from his company's advertised special. "Bait and switch" techniques are outlawed in most states, but enforcement of the law is difficult.

• Insist on a sample of the carpet to be installed, to at least be sure the same carpet you ordered is actually delivered.

• Don't fall for "free" offers along with "bargain" carpeting. The offers aren't free.

• Deal only with established, reputable dealers. Be wary of any carpet ad which gives only a telephone number—but no address—of the carpet company.

YOUR APPLIANCES

AN ENORMOUS HOUSEHOLD EXPENSE

No matter how and where you live in this country—whether as a single person or married, with or without kids, in a house or apartment, or in a boat or trailer —you will use appliances and various forms of household equipment. You will spend tens of thousands of dollars to buy these big-ticket items. Then you will spend more thousands (countless thousands) to repair, to power, to modernize, or to remodel these big-ticket items.

We in this country now own more than one billion appliances—an average of sixteen appliances for each home. Our annual spending for small appliances alone—ranging from electric toothbrushes to ice crushers and pencil sharpeners —topped $2.5 billion as the 1970s closed. Our outlay for the large appliances now exceeds $8 billion a year.

RULES FOR BUYING APPLIANCES

Recognize the danger of buying expensive appliances on impulse. Ask yourself: Do I need, do I want, can I really use this appliance? Can I afford the addition it will make to my electricity or gas bill? Do I have storage or counter room for it?

Consult Consumers Union ratings, descriptions, and comparisons of the type of appliance you're buying, as well as its "frequency of repair" record—a clue to how much of a lemon (or non-lemon) each brand and model are likely to be.

Start with no-frill models. Every manufacturer has lower-priced models which are the same equipment as the high-priced models, minus extras. Look first at the least expensive model to see whether it will fit your needs, and then decide how many of the refinements in more expensive models you need, and whether they're worth the price. You well may find the deluxe models are a nuisance and all you really want is the basic, least expensive—and least expensive to operate— machine.

Look for model clearance sales where you easily can save money. When old models are being cleared out, you can get an excellent buy. But be sure the guarantee·or warranty applies to the old model and you will have no trouble getting service or parts for it.

Be sure before you buy a major appliance that it fits not only through the door but also into the space you have available for it. Many people buy appliances, then find they can't get them into the area they planned to use. Or they find that their landlords won't permit the use of a washing machine or dryer in the apartment. This problem is acute with waste disposals, which are restricted by local ordinance. So think it out before you buy. Measure the area where you intend to place the appliance. Be sure the floor is strong enough. Check the manufacturer's directions on how much space you must leave between the appliance and a wall for the safest and most efficient use (typically at least one half inch for a refrigerator or freezer, several inches for a free-standing range).

Consider whether the appliance will be large enough. Will a 10-cubic-foot refrigerator be large enough for your future needs when you have children in coming years?

Comparison-shop, for appliance prices can vary substantially from store to store—and buy only from a dealer whose reputation is good for service as well as sales. Ask the salesmen if their stores service the appliances they sell. Many dealers sell a number of brands and refer customers to factory-authorized shops for service. Be sure such service is available in your area.

Know what the price includes. Will the dealer make free delivery, directly into your home? Will he install those appliances that require it, and will he charge for installation? Are warranty and service included in the price? What is covered and what is not covered by the warranty? (See pages 1204–7 for a detailed rundown on warranties.)

If you are buying an appliance on time, compare total finance charges offered by each dealer—not just monthly payments.

As an indicator of safety, look for the Underwriters Laboratories seal on the body of all electrical appliances, the Blue Star Seal of the American Gas Association Laboratories on gas appliances, or the CSA (Canadian Standard Association) mark of approval. (If the UL seal is only on the plug or cord, that is all that is approved.)

Make sure you have adequate electrical circuits to handle the appliance before you buy. Ask your landlord about this, if you're renting. Or, if you own your home, ask the local utility for a free check on these circuits. If it won't oblige, hire a qualified electrician to do it.

Be sure the type of gas you have (e.g., natural gas, propane gas, etc.) suits the gas appliances you buy. The gas company and appliance dealer can guide you.

Check your local repair shops to find out what appliance service they offer. The appliance might be trouble-free for months, but when repairs are needed or even the smallest part has to be replaced, it will be costly if you must travel a long distance to get what you need. Find a good repair shop before an emergency arises.

If your appliance develops problems after the warranty runs out, deal only with service agencies authorized by the manufacturer or with a reputable local service firm.

In deciding whether to throw away an appliance rather than repair it, consider your time, travel, and inconvenience. Consider also whether the problem is functional or merely one of appearance. And don't waste money trying to repair a too old appliance. If the appliance is much older than the following life-expectancy guide—based on Department of Agriculture findings—put your money into a replacement instead.

LIFE EXPECTANCY OF APPLIANCES

APPLIANCE	AVERAGE LIFE-SPAN
Sewing machine	24 years
Vacuum cleaner, upright	18 years
Ranges, electric or gas	16 years
Refrigerator	16 years
Toaster, automatic	15 years
Freezer	15 years
Vacuum cleaner, tank	15 years
Clothes dryer	14 years
Washing machine, automatic and semi-automatic	11 years
Television set	11 years
Washing machine, wringer and spin dry	10 years
Toaster, non-automatic	7 years

HOW TO BUY "BARGAIN" APPLIANCES

When you see a bargain-priced appliance offered "as is," how can you tell whether or not it's likely to fall apart just after you get it home? What do retailers mean when they claim they are selling items at "wholesale" prices? What does "free home trial" of a major appliance really mean?

These are some of the questions you must consider as you venture into today's increasingly complex and trap-ridden appliance marketplace. In response, here is a short list of money- and nerve-saving rules on appliance bargains and non-bargains:

• Be alert to what you're buying. If it's a "floor model" or "demonstrator"—or a damaged, scratched, beat-up "as is" item—are you getting enough of a discount?

• Similarly, if you're tempted by a bargain appliance advertised as "reconditioned" or "rebuilt," the key question to ask is: by whom? If a gadget or machine is advertised as "factory-rebuilt," this should mean rebuilt by the original manufacturer. Again, what warranty applies?

• Recognize that claims by appliance retailers of "wholesale" prices are, as the Better Business Bureaus warn, "usually wholesale bunk."

• If a "free home trial" is offered, make sure that you have no obligation to buy. Watch out for the unscrupulous dealer who may attempt to get you to sign a purchase contract which you are led to believe is simply a receipt for the "free home trial."

• One real way to save money when you buy appliances is to buy them second-hand. This obviously can be a gamble, since you usually buy them "as is." But if the dealer is reputable, he may guarantee the used appliance he is selling you or otherwise agree to fix it if problems arise. And one advantage of a slightly used appliance is that its bugs and kinks may already have been discovered—and fixed —before you get it.

• Finally, if you discover you have bought a lemon, or if a dealer fails to live up to a warranty or service contract, gather the facts to support your complaint, and complain—loudly! You'll help not only yourself but also every reliable appliance manufacturer and dealer, and all the rest of us in the market for appliances today. (See Chapter 29, "How and Where to Get Help," for valuable information on how to complain and get action on appliance agonies as well as other categories of consumer miseries.)

HOW TO CUT REPAIR COSTS

Always somewhere on the horizon is the dreamy promise by one company or another to provide a comprehensive, economical maintenance and repair service for appliances. But so far the dream hasn't materialized. Meanwhile, when you deal with appliance servicemen, you must be on the alert for an array of deep pitfalls—ranging from having to pay for unneeded or unsatisfactory work to losing deposits on work and parts not provided.

This is one reason why U.S. consumers throw away billions of dollars of defective and worn-out household goods each year—in many cases because we do not know how to fix them, we cannot find anyone else to do the job, or the repair costs just aren't worth it.

Certainly do not fail to take all the preventive maintenance measures you are supposed to take. If the owner's manual calls, for example, for regular defrosting, or periodic cleaning, or removal of lint from appliance screens and filters, do these things on schedule. To remind yourself, compile a special calendar for maintenance measures on your household appliances and post it in a prominent place.

Study from the start the owner's manual which came with the appliance. Keep a file of all these manuals for the lifetime of the respective devices and machines. They are your number-one source of information on how to operate an appliance properly, what to check if something goes wrong, common errors to avoid, etc. Merely reading each instruction booklet could eliminate the need for half the appliance service calls you are making today.

Before you call in a serviceman, check the electric plug to make sure the appliance is plugged in firmly. Also check dials, buttons, switches, and safety valves, to make sure they haven't been accidentally pushed in the wrong direction. And check appropriate fuses both in the appliance and in the cellar to make sure they have not blown.

These steps alone could save you, the consumer, more than 25 per cent of appliance service costs—and could result in really significant savings after your warranties have run out.

CHECK LIST OF MOST COMMON APPLIANCE PROBLEMS

For quick reference, here's a chart of today's most common appliance problems—and what to do about them before you call a serviceman. The chart was prepared by a small consumer magazine, *Everybody's Money,* published by the Credit Union National Association.

APPLIANCE	PROBLEM	DON'T CALL SERVICEMAN UNTIL YOU CHECK
Automatic washer	Motor won't go	(1) Fuse—is it in washer fuse box? (2) Plug—is it in outlet?
	Won't fill	(1) Is water turned on?
Automatic dryer	Slow drying	(1) Overloaded lint screen (2) Insufficient fuse rating (3) Too heavy loads (4) Too wet clothes
	Runs noisily	(1) Dryer resting unevenly on floor (2) Loose belt
Vacuum cleaner	Cleans poorly	(1) Clogged nozzle (2) Hose obstruction (3) Very full bag (4) Bag needs replacing
Toaster	Release won't work	(1) Mechanism may be jammed with crumbs, raisins, etc. Clean every two weeks by sliding out trap or turning toaster upside down
Electric range	Oven or elements won't heat	(1) Is automatic oven control set back at manual? (2) Main cartridge in house fuse box may be blown; use 40-amp fuse for older-type range, 45- or 60-amp for new double ovens
Oil or gas furnace	Won't come on	(1) Fuse in house fuse box may be blown (2) Thermostat may be set too low (3) Fuel tank may be empty (4) Pilot light may be out

APPLIANCE	PROBLEM	DON'T CALL SERVICEMAN UNTIL YOU CHECK
Dishwasher	Motor won't go	(1) Impeller may be jammed with small pieces of food or broken glass (2) The fuse may be blown
	Cleans unsatisfactorily	(1) Improper dish stacking (2) Too much detergent (3) Wrong type of detergent
Refrigerator	Doesn't keep food cold	(1) Poor door seal (2) Door left open too long, too often (3) Shelf paper on refrigerator shelves preventing air circulation (4) Thermostat set too high
	Food freezes in refrigerator compartment	(1) Return air louvers in freezer compartment blocked by loose wrapping paper (2) Thermostat set too low
Garbage disposal	Doesn't grind	(1) Use self-service wrench or push blade-activating button (2) Jammed with food

TELEVISION

HOW TO GET THE BEST DEAL

More than nine out of ten American households now own at least one TV set, millions of families own two or three sets, and more than one half of U.S. households now possess color TV sets.

With TV ownership as broad as this in our country, you would think we were a nation of pros when it comes to buying TV sets. We aren't. Millions continue to be lured into buying sets at prices and on terms they simply can't afford. Or they get the wrong kind of antenna setup and cancel out the advantages of the extra money they have paid for the basic set. Or they just don't know what to do when the TV set conks out a few months after they've bought it.

What can you do to prevent these problems? How can you get the best possible deal for the hundreds of dollars you'll almost certainly spend for TV sets in the years directly ahead?

• To start with, arrive at a clear idea of what kind of—and how much—TV you want. In the late 1970s, a typical black and white TV set had a 12-inch screen (measured diagonally). This, by Federal Trade Commission regulation, is the area in which the picture can actually be seen. It's portable—weights having come down from a few years ago as a result of sets now being transistorized. The big market in color sets is the 19-inch table model. Most sets produce a better signal with an outside antenna than with a built-in one. Most have controls for on and off, brightness and contrast in the front of the set.

• Decide what price you can afford to pay. As the 1980s began, most black and white TV sets cost under $100. But by all means find out what that price tag does and doesn't cover. Ask about warranties. What is included? Does it carry service? Where do you get it? From whom? The dealer or a service depot? How far is the depot from where you live?

• Inquire with care into what the warranty provides. As of the late 1970s, a typical black and white TV set is guaranteed for ninety days—for parts and carry-in service only—and one year for the picture tube, again not counting labor costs. Color sets typically carry a warranty running one year for parts and labor, two to five years for the picture tube.

However, TV warranty terms vary widely. And a TV dealer is not obligated to give you a new TV set if the one you have just bought turns out to be a lemon. He's required only to get it back into operating condition.

• Study the TV picture. Key aspects which you can check in any large TV showroom are:

Sharpness, resolution (detail), focus (the sharpness of the horizontal scanning lines), the interlacing or evenness in the spacing of these lines, non-linearity (which makes TV actors get fatter as they move toward the edge of the screen), and lack of distortion.

Brightness of the set is governed by the voltage of the picture tube. Modern tubes should have about 1,000 volts for each diagonal inch on the viewing screen.

AGC—or automatic gain control—is another important factor in a TV picture: it maintains the brightness and contrast setting when you switch from a strong to a weak signal and vice versa.

• Get the answers to these other key questions:

How does a particular set perform in the location of your house—particularly if your house is in an area in which signals tend to be weak or certain stations are hard to get?

How will the set look in your living room?

Practically all TV sets now are solid state. It is important to find a fully qualified TV repair shop, which requires a better serviceman than in earlier years when the repairman just changed a tube.

How are the circuit boards arranged? In some models there are a limited number of plug-in boards fitted with certain key parts. In the event of a breakdown (which will happen to the average set about once a year), you simply remove the ailing circuit board and plug in another—with a minimum of hunting time (and repair costs) to locate the source of the trouble.

• Finally, does the apartment or area in which you live offer cable TV—providing extra-good reception, especially in areas with formerly poor reception? If cable TV is offered, how much will it cost to hook into it—and what monthly fees will you have to pay the company which owns the cable?

EXTRA GUIDELINES FOR COLOR TV

As the 1980s begin, you can purchase superior color TV with a fairly large screen and improved features for under $400. But the improved features so prominently advertised by manufacturers can confuse as well as benefit you. How, then, do you shop wisely?

• Start familiarizing yourself with three basic terms: Solid-state circuitry, now available from every domestic and foreign manufacturer, is perhaps the single most important innovation in color TV. In-line picture tubes, built into many makes of 17- and 19-inch sets, are being used by a large percentage of manufacturers who believe they are fuzzy-free and fiddle-free. Automatic or one-button tuning is offered by virtually every manufacturer. On most sets, it's a simple control that eliminates the need to fiddle with a handful of knobs to adjust color for each channel. Brightness, contrast, color, and tint are preset.

• Look for the number of stages through which the picture signal is amplified, called IF stages. Most sets push the signal through three stages, though some of the less expensive models have two. But lack of that third stage can mean less resolution in the picture, particularly in areas where the signal is weak. You can determine the number of IF stages by a glance at the set's specifications.

• Check the range of house voltage the set can take. A wider range gives you more protection against future brownouts. Most sets accept 108 to 132 volts, but some will work in as wide a range as 70 to 140 volts.

• Don't skimp on an antenna. A $50 antenna can be worth every penny in terms of improved reception and in helping you get the results you want from an expensive TV set. A color TV requires a better antenna than a black and white model.

• Don't overlook service. Deal only with a reliable store that will offer you the assurance of the services you will need.

• Do not permit yourself to be rushed into buying. Decide in advance what you want. Take time to brief yourself on what to expect.

Color TV now significantly outsells black and white in the United States—and it can add a whole new dimension to your viewing pleasure, even during summer reruns. But you may regret the day you bought your set unless you know the simple rules that will help you maneuver through the maze of claims and counterclaims.

TV REPAIRS

HOW TO SLASH THESE COSTS

TV repairs are a category unto themselves. For one thing, a TV set—particularly color TV—is by far the most complex and sophisticated device in most households, and the one most likely to need service. Some TVs are "dead on arrival" from the store. Question the store's policy on a "dead on arrival" set—will it exchange it readily for your protection? For another, the field of TV repairs always has been plagued by more than its share of incompetent and unscrupulous repairmen. In fact an estimated $150 million of the $1 billion plus Americans spend annually on TV repairs is wasted through incompetence or fraud. The TV repairman can be among the most frustrating and painfully expensive service people you must deal with.

Still, there are ways in which you can reduce the frustrations and the costs. First, to cut down on the overall number of TV service calls:

• Try using another receptacle. It's possible the problem is with the first receptacle, not the set itself. Of course, make sure the set is plugged in.

• Check the antenna and lead-in from the antenna, which might have been torn by a storm or accidentally disconnected from the back of the set by your child or your dog.

• Try the adjustment controls to make sure they are operating properly, and if they are not, consult your TV owner's manual for guidance on how to get them back in working order.

• If your problem is "ghosts"—or multiple images on a TV screen—this is seldom due to defects in the set. These images are caused by interference or other problems in the location in which you live (e.g., nestled between a couple of skyscrapers), and therefore usually cannot be remedied by a TV repairman. Thus, before you ask a serviceman to lay your TV ghosts to rest, ask your neighbors whether they have been having problems similar to yours. And find out what results they have had when they called in professionals to solve them.

Only if these steps shed no light on your problem, call a serviceman. Jot down details on just what happened when the set broke down; these are vital guides for him. Also have your bill of sale ready to show him, so he can check your warranty coverage.

• If you are choosing a TV service firm for the first time, ask your friends where they have found reliable and satisfactory service. If you are in doubt about any company's record, ask the local Better Business Bureau if it has any adverse information on the company. If you are tempted by an estimated low cost of repairs, back up; this is not the basis upon which to choose a TV repairman. In states which license TV technicians, stick with the licensed shops and report any complaints to the licensing authority.

• If it is necessary to take your set to the shop for repairs, get a written estimate of the approximate repair costs—before the repairman takes the set out of your house. Depending on the complexity of the trouble, your bill might vary from the estimate by 20 per cent or so. Whether or not you authorize its removal, you should expect to pay the service call charge for the technician to come to your home and diagnose your set's trouble and sometimes also an extra pickup and delivery charge. Note: You'll probably save money if you take your set to the service shop and have the work done there rather than in your home. Be prepared to pay a charge just for checking over your TV, whether or not any work is done, since the checking ties up costly equipment and manpower.

• Don't underestimate the fact that a good TV technician must maintain thousands of dollars' worth of diagnostic and repair equipment—plus an inventory of spare parts. He may have as much as two to four years of specialized education and training behind him. He can no more afford to make a free house call than a doctor can. The average cost to the operator of an ethical TV repair service in the late 1970s was approximately $18–$30 per hour.

• Insist on and keep itemized bills for any and all repairs—for reference if the repairs fail to hold up properly. As with other appliances, see if you can pay for any repairs within thirty days. In this time, you should find out whether or not the set was repaired correctly.

BEWARE: UNRELIABLE TV REPAIRMEN

Steer clear of the "sundowner" who moonlights in TV repairs—operating out of his home and advertising only a telephone number, often an answering service, but no address. The sundowner accepts any and all work he can get but may take weeks or months to service your TV set. It can be extremely difficult to reach this type of repairman—since you do not know his address and he may pay no attention to telephone messages. He also may simply walk off with your TV set and never show up again.

Avoid the "baiter" who advertises ridiculously low prices for TV service calls, then slaps on extra-steep charges for parts. For instance: "$1 per call, plus parts." This practice is also known as "lowballing." Or, once the baiter gets your set in the shop, he may uncover an endless, expensive array of problems, all of which will necessitate new parts and much expensive labor. The baiter may then turn into a "setnapper," demanding a "ransom" in the form of an unreasonable bill before he will release your TV.

Surely you need no further analysis to convince you that the TV service firm which made free service calls or even charged only a couple of dollars for a service call would go broke almost overnight.

Also stay away from the repair outfit that lists itself under a dozen different names in the Yellow Pages to bring in as much business as possible—without regard to whether or not the outfit can handle the repairs. If you get tangled up with one of these firms, you may get neither service nor your set back.

SOUND EQUIPMENT

WHAT'S WHAT IN HOME LISTENING

If you are over age forty, you probably continue to clutch an image of this basic home listening equipment:

One metal box fitted with several knobs, which is a radio; another box with a round turntable on top and an arm fitted with a diamond needle on which you play 12-inch records, singly or in stacks; perhaps a couple of speakers connected to one of these boxes to enrich the sound of the records you're playing. And that's it.

But if you're in your teens or twenties or thirties, you well may speak an entirely different language: of stereophonic sound; of cartridges, cassettes, and consoles; of tapes and tape decks; of vastly complex, often vastly expensive "component systems" with parts you can string through your house.

Let's, though, ignore age and just assume you're an amateur considering investing in a home listening system. Let's also say you do have some money to spend and you're ready.

Your first step is to familiarize yourself with what's what in the world of home listening:

An AM radio receives the standard list of stations, local and distant.

An FM radio gives you different stations but a higher quality of sound and, possibly, better programming.

Monaural sound, e.g., in a standard phonograph or radio, comes from a single speaker and generally is the least expensive kind of sound available today.

Stereophonic sound comes from two separate speakers spaced five feet or more apart and hooked up to a phonograph, radio, or tape player, and gives the impression of two-dimensional sound as you might hear it in a concert hall or discotheque. You can listen to the radio, a phonograph record, or a prerecorded tape on a complete stereo hookup.

Prerecorded, eight-track tape cartridges are the modern equivalent of phonograph records. They cannot be recorded upon by you, unless you have special equipment. You buy them prerecorded—with music or whatever—and they play nearly as long as a phonograph record. Eight-track tape cartridges also are somewhat more expensive than phonograph records. You play one by slipping it into a cartridge tape deck or "eight-track deck"—a much easier operation than putting on an LP record.

Tape cassettes are small, encased reels of recorded music or words, or blank reels on which you may do the recording yourself. You may play these on a cassette tape recorder or a cassette tape deck, which might be considered the modern equivalent of the turntable on a phonograph.

Important note: You cannot play an eight-track cartridge in a cassette tape deck. Nor can you play a tape cassette in an eight-track deck.

Both cartridges and cassettes last far longer and wear far better than phonograph records.

HOW TO SHOP FOR SOUND EQUIPMENT

Now that you have this short dictionary of sound equipment, how and where do you begin shopping for it?

As with all types of home equipment, you must first decide what you want the equipment to do for you and how much you can afford to spend for it.

If you have small children, possibly your best bet is an inexpensive old-fashioned portable record player or inexpensive cassette player permitting them to do their own recording as well as listening. Some players are available for less than $20, although the average price for this type of equipment is more like $40. Remarkably, prices have not changed in years.

If the finest sound reproduction is important to you, you'll certainly want some kind of stereophonic equipment. A good compact stereo system today costs between $300 and $500—but a system can be bought for as little as $140. It may be semi-portable or non-portable. Generally it consists of two speakers, plus a "chassis" containing a turntable and record changer, a receiver and an amplifier to boost the volume of sound coming from both receiver and record player. In some versions a tape deck may supplement or replace the turntable-record changer.

If you want to create something special which has the advantage of fine stereophonic sound, look into a "component system" which you (or the dealer from whom you buy the system) can put together yourself. A component system consists of a collection of whatever parts you want—ranging from turntables to tape decks, tuners, amplifiers, receivers, speakers, antennas, and headphones. Of course, the cost of such a system depends on the type and quality of the components you choose and also on how much of the effort of putting it together you contribute yourself. But typical prices of good component systems range from $350 to $1,000.

If you are gifted electronically, the system you put together yourself well may outperform any other type of home sound equipment you can buy ready-made.

As an alternative, probably the ultimate in versatility is a custom built-in system for your house. There are firms specializing in custom-designing such systems —and for fees in the $1,500 to $3,500 range, they'll design and install a sound system throughout your house, with speakers that can play different music in every room—all controlled from a master unit. Options include computer-controlled automatic tape recorders, automatic volume reduction when you pick up the phone, an automatic fifty-record player, an automatic twenty-four-cassette player/recorder, a transmitter for reception on a pocket radio so you can even listen outdoors. Needless to say, such extras can jack the basic price considerably higher.

RULES FOR BUYING

Once you have decided what type of sound equipment you want and how much you can afford to pay for it, follow these rules when you actually go out to make the purchase:

• Check carefully into discounts—ranging up to 30 per cent—which are offered widely in this type of equipment since it is a highly competitive field. Obviously a no-name brand with a near-worthless warranty sold at a drastically reduced price may be no bargain. But substantial discounts occur also in the best stores and on the best equipment. Nail down what is covered by the warranty.

• Don't be misled by claims that a machine or system is "portable." Look at it. Would it take a lumberjack to lift it?

• Don't be tempted by bargain "kits" which now come in an enormous variety and from which you are supposed to assemble your own systems or components —unless you are truly qualified to do so. If you're unskilled in electronics, keep this in mind while you're shopping! However, if you are a reasonably skilled hobbyist and can follow directions faithfully, you may be able to save a lot of money by going the kit route.

• Be sure you make room in your budget and your home for adequate facilities in which to store the tapes and records you'll buy. Such facilities will pay for themselves many times over through a longer life for the tapes.

• Don't, though, buy the many accessories available simply because they're there. Most useful among the accessories are headphones (if other family members would be annoyed by having to listen to the selection you're playing) and outdoor antennas (sometimes necessary for good FM stereo reception).

• Stick strictly to brands of equipment which have achieved a reputation for quality and reliability. And stick to dealers with solid reputations and service facilities known to be responsible.

• Don't buy any stereo or other equipment without listening to the sound it produces. Go to a store which has a quiet area for test-listening and listen to a variety of music to be sure the sound pleases you. Try to arrange to try out two or three sets for a couple of days in your own home. "Comparative" listening in your own home is probably your best way to judge quality of sound.

• If you are buying a component system, remember the system as a whole is no better than its weakest link. It would be silly to buy a set of expensive speakers and skimp on your amplifier.

• In judging quality or performance, don't let the advertised power ratings of amplifiers confuse you. All other things being equal, the higher an amplifier's power rating, the more nearly distortion-free will be the sound it produces. "Overbuying" power, though, is not a substitute for a well-engineered amplifier and is often a waste of money. Moreover, there are various ways to rate an amplifier's power—and they are not necessarily comparable. Check with a dealer you trust to avoid buying more power than you need.

How to Slash Your Household Utility Bills

Just by knowing the reasonable ways to shave the amounts you pay you can significantly reduce your overall home ownership costs. For all of these bills are climbing fast and relentlessly.

HOW TO CUT YOUR TELEPHONE BILLS

If you dial a long-distance phone call on your own, you may slash its cost more than 60 per cent below what the same call would cost if you made it person-to-person.

If you call long-distance from a pay phone booth or from a hotel room or you make the call collect, charge it to another number or to a credit card, you may pay a premium of as much as 50 per cent over the cost of the same call normally dialed from home.

If you make a long-distance call over the weekend or fairly late during any evening and you dial direct, your cost may be less than half what it would be if made during weekdays.

And if you organize your thoughts so you can say what you have to say in a minute, you could call coast-to-coast for 25 cents, nights and weekends, as the 1970s ended.

Telephone rates are being raised for many types of service and being simultaneously reduced for many other types of calls. The cuts—especially for direct dialing and off-hours calls—are clearly designed to help the heavily burdened telephone system make optimum use of its facilities and personnel, an understandable goal indeed.

At the same time, by knowing what Ma Bell is doing, you can save money on your phone bills and/or make more calls without spending more. Since phone bills are a major expense in millions of homes, here are key hints:

• Know how much money you can save by direct dialing.

• Know how much you can save by making your calls in off-hours and on weekends.

• Take advantage of the coast-to-coast after 11 P.M. special rate if you dial and talk only one minute (example: "I made it home safely, Mom!"). The time difference works in your favor if you live in the East. Also try to place as many coast-to-coast personal and business calls as feasible before 8 A.M.

• Invest in an egg timer, an old but still worthwhile trick to cut your telephone talk and expense.

• Organize your calls—particularly when the whole family is calling a distant relative—to avoid wasteful, costly, and irritating repetition of "How are . . . ? I'm fine . . ." Get each family member to make a note in advance of what he or she wants to say. Then the conversation will not drag out.

• If you reach a wrong number, ask the operator immediately to credit you for the call. And if your self-dialed call fails to go through and you are forced to get help from the operator, be sure to request that you be billed for the call at the dialed rate.

• If you need information on a long-distance number, dial the area code for that place plus 555-1212 and ask the operator for the number you want. *This service was still free in the late 1970s.* Then dial the call yourself. Do not call your own local operator and ask her to get you the person, for then you will be placing the most costly person-to-person type of call. Use your phone book; you'll find many of the area codes you seek.

• If you're calling an organization, find out whether it has a toll-free number you can use by dialing (800) 555-1212 and asking the toll-free information operator.

• Always report the length of time your phone is out of order. In some states the Public Service Commission requires your phone company to credit you with refunds for any extended interruption in service.

• Choose the number and type of your extensions with care, for each regular extension will probably cost you $1.00 or so a month. The monthly charges for a Princess or Touch-Tone may be 50 to 100 per cent more than the cost of a regular extension.

• Regulatory changes in the late 1970s allow you to purchase telephones and install them in your home. They must be connected through a telephone company-installed jack and you must report the instrument(s) to your local phone company. In most areas, the monthly extension rate is lower if you have your own phone. But if you do buy a telephone, you will be responsible for repair and maintenance, whereas the telephone company's monthly rate includes repair and maintenance.

• Examine your telephoning habits to see if they lend themselves to less expensive categories of service.

For instance, if you do not use the phone much, you may be able to switch to a party line and save money with little inconvenience.

If you make few local calls, you might find local service, which results in a low monthly bill but a surcharge of 6 to 8 cents per local call in excess of a specified maximum (generally fifty to sixty per month), to your advantage. In some areas it might pay you to choose a limited geographical area of toll-free service to get a lower monthly bill.

• If you have children away at school, arrange specific times when you'll call them from home by direct dial—instead of having them make expensive coin calls to you.

• Always double-check your phone bills for possible mistakes and for evidence that others may be charging calls to your number. Report any evidence of this to the telephone business office at once—before you pay your bill—and ask for the company's assistance. Your basic telephone service charge should run the same from month to month. If you have any doubts, ask the telephone company business office for a rundown on the latest basic charges and check your bills against this rundown.

• If you are going on a trip, direct-dial your reservations from home. This will save you from making more costly coin phone calls en route to your various destinations.

HOW TO READ A UTILITY METER

With the outlook for energy prices still upward, it becomes more and more vital for you to learn how to read your electric and gas meters so that you can check whether your efforts to conserve energy and thereby to offset climbing energy costs are effective. It also makes increasingly good sense to check with care the accuracy of your bills to find out how much energy you really are using to cool or to heat your home.

Yet, while just about all of you can follow the run-up of your bills at the supermarket check-out counter, millions of you still put reading electric and gas meters and checking these bills in the same category as learning a new form of math. Thus, here's a simple list of guidelines.

(1) On electric meters, read dials from left to right (note that numbers run clockwise on some dials, counterclockwise on others). If a pointer is between two numbers, read the lower one, unless the pointer is between nine and zero (the zero stands for ten). There are four dials on most meters that record kilowatt hours by units of 10,000, 1,000, 100, and 10. Jotting down the pointer number on each gives you the cumulative total.

To find your monthly consumption, take two readings one month apart, and compare the earlier and later totals.

The figures above each dial show how many kilowatt hours are recorded each time the pointer makes a complete revolution.

(2) On gas meters, read as you would electric meters. The difference is that your total must be multiplied by 100 because each time the pointer moves from one number to another on the right-hand dial, the use of 100 cubic feet of gas has been recorded Thus, a total reading might be 317,700 (3,177×100). Since the meter was last set at zero, it has recorded consumption of 317,700 cubic feet of natural gas.

Some gas meters have more than four dials. If yours does and you cannot decide by what number to multiply the reading, call your gas company for directions.

(3) To estimate how much gas or electricity your heating system uses, the Federal Energy Administration suggests you read the meter immediately after your family goes to bed and again before it gets up. Subtract the evening from the morning reading to find out how much energy was consumed for heating during the night, when it's likely that your lights and appliances are off. Divide that total by the number of hours between readings to find out the amount of kilowatt hours or cubic feet of natural gas used per hour.

(4) To check how much power your air-conditioning system uses, take two readings one hour apart while it is running. Subtract the earlier from the later reading to see how much electricity was consumed in that hour. Repeat the process while the conditioner is off. Subtract the amount of electricity used when the conditioner was off than the amount used when the conditioner was on.

(5) To discover the electricity used by any major appliance, figure the consumption on a day when the appliance is used at least twice. Compare it to the consumption of electricity on a day when the appliance was not used at all.

These are only rough calculations, of course—and you can't even make these if you live in a rental housing unit with a large master meter or meters to register consumption for the landlord, who then recovers the cost from you through rent. But nevertheless, with these indicators of your energy consumption, you can study your next utility bill to be sure you understand the charges, and can compare the charges with previous months to get an idea of whether your consumption is increasing or decreasing. If you're mystified call the consumer service department of your utility for help.

For more guidance on how to understand your utility costs, send a postcard to Consumer Information Center, Pueblo, Colorado 81009, and request *Understanding Your Utility Bill,* No. 589E. It's free.

SEE "FAMILY'S ENERGY-SAVING GUIDE" (CHAPTER 6)

For hundreds of money-saving tips on how to cut your expenses for energy in every room of your home (as well as outside your home), see pages 278–96.

How to Protect Your Home Against Fire

TAKE A "TRIP"

Each year, thousands of Americans die in residential fires, most perishing at night while asleep. Each year, hundreds of thousands more are painfully injured and horribly disfigured by household fires. And so many are easily preventable, so, so unnecessary.

Leading causes of building fires, according to the National Fire Protection Association in Boston, are smoking and matches, defective or inadequate electrical wiring and other equipment, defective or careless use of flues, combustibles near hot ashes, coals, and heaters, misuse of matches by children. If all of these causes could be magically eliminated, so would more than one half of the building fires in this country.

Whether you rent or own your home, you are in the majority if you are permitting many of the greatest fire dangers to remain in and around your house—and thus also risking the possibility of huge financial losses.

Take a brief "inspection trip" through your house or apartment today. Examine every square foot of it for fire hazards and see if you can answer "yes" to all of these questions:

Do your gas and your electric appliances bear the seal of the American Gas Association and that of Underwriters Laboratories?

Is your kitchen equipped with a suitable, properly charged extinguisher for grease and/or electric fires? Does everybody in your family know how to use it? And does everyone know that such fires should never be doused with water?

Are your ashtrays large enough and plentiful enough for the amount of smoking which occurs in your house?

Are your small children well informed on the subject of matches and fires? For those who have developed an insatiable curiosity about them, have you taken the necessary time and patience to teach them how to use matches properly and skillfully?

Are such items as your chafing dishes and fondue pots protected by metal trays underneath to catch any alcohol overflow?

Do you have your furnaces, hot water heaters, and chimneys serviced and/or inspected regularly for safety?

Is the gas can for your lawn mower, chain saw, etc. stored properly and in a safe place? And what about those highly flammable substances with which you start barbecue fires?

Have you cleaned up and cleared out any piles of old papers and/or oil rags which may have collected in your attic, basement, or garage?

Are your household cleaning fluids of the non-flammable type?

If you cannot answer yes to all of these questions you are taking absolutely needless risks.

FUNDAMENTAL SAFEGUARDS

• Have a specific, well-rehearsed fire escape plan, in which each member knows exactly what to do, where to go, and whom and how to call for help. If you have storm windows and screens in your windows, your children should know how to take them off in an emergency.

• Consider installing a few devices to sound a warning if a fire starts: it is all too easy to fail to awake when there is a fire. (See next section.)

• Be on guard against lightning and know the risks. If your house is situated on top of a hill or on a flat plain it is a dangerous lure for lightning, an important cause of home fires. It also is vulnerable if it is in the suburbs or near a highway. If your house (or a house you are considering buying) fits the above description, inquire about a proper, effective lightning protection system. To be effective, the system should be capable of intercepting lightning bolts from the roof, metal equipment, antennas, power lines, and nearby trees which are taller than your house. A proper system also is marked by a "Master Label" plate, issued by Underwriters Laboratories.

• Minimize the fire risks of your roof. The fire risk of a house roofed with untreated wood shingles is far greater than that of a slate-roofed house or an asphalt-shingled house. (And homeowner's insurance rates on wood-shingle-roofed houses are higher in some states than the rates on houses with less dangerous types of roofing.)

• In fact, if you are buying or building or remodeling a house, inquire about the flammability characteristics of all materials in the house—including paints, insulation material, curtains and carpets, wood and imitation wood paneling, etc.

• Check and beware of all electrical hazards: appliance wires which continually overheat; fuses which blow repeatedly; TV pictures which contract when your refrigerator or furnace goes on. If any of these signs occur, call your electrician immediately to check into the problem.

And here are the best rules to help you prevent a disastrous home fire caused by defective electrical wiring:

Don't string inexpensive extension cords all over the place—and risk overloading your wiring system.

Don't use too light dime-store cords for heavy appliances such as electric irons, space heaters, rotisseries, and power tools.

Don't try to stretch the electrical capacity by putting in heavier and heavier fuses. "Overfusing" is a fairly common practice—but potentially a very dangerous one. (For most household circuits, the safe limit is 15 amperes.)

Don't put pennies behind your fuses to get them to carry a bigger load—because, again, what you well may end up with is overloaded wiring.

Do, particularly if you have any reason to suspect that your present wiring is inadequate, ask a qualified electrician (or, in many states, one who is licensed by the state) to go over your electrical system carefully. It may take as long as a full day and cost you anywhere from $50 to $150. But it will be one of the best investments you could possibly make.

Do be prepared to let the electrician remedy any problems he uncovers. Note: He won't be able to assess the condition of wires hidden behind walls and under floors without taking your house apart and doing a complete rewiring job. But he can go over all the wires, switches, outlets, and fuse boxes which are visible and accessible. And, if you discuss with him the number and type of appliances you have added to the system since it was originally installed, he also can at least make an informed guess as to how much and what type of additional wiring may be necessary.

SMOKE ALARMS—AN ESSENTIAL

Item: In the late 1970s, the president of a Minneapolis company bought 2,600 home smoke detectors on one day to be distributed free to each of the firm's employees. His poignant explanation:

"I read a story about a fire in a home that killed most of a man's family—and he was quoted afterward as saying that he'd planned to buy a smoke detector the very next day. That did it for me. I just felt I should do something . . ."

One simple, lifesaving home smoke detector cost a mere $35 as the decade closed—not much more than a dinner for a family of four in a very modest restaurant. Authorities are in virtually unanimous accord about the value of a fire safety system in any residence. Installation is supported by fire departments, fire-prevention organizations, public safety advocates, the federal government, the insurance industry. There is no argument that getting all family members out of a house is the prime safety factor.

In the face of all this evidence, it is appalling that less than 10 per cent of the nation's 75 million households are protected by smoke alarms, according to Insurance Information Institute estimates. It is even more shocking in view of the fact that smoke reveals the presence of fire much earlier than heat, and smoke detectors can be extremely valuable as an early warning system.

For many years, smoke detectors and alarm systems have been commonplace in business establishments, but it is only in recent years that they have been produced to meet the requirements of homeowners. Spurred by extensive advertising, unit sales have been rising sharply, are now around 5 million a year. Companies in the field are up to about 130—and some models are down in price from $40 to $25.

Today, two types of smoke detector are on the market: the photoelectric smoke detector and the ionization chamber smoke detector. The photoelectric smoke detector uses a photoelectric bulb that sends forth a beam of light. The ionization chamber smoke detector contains a small radiation source that produces electrically charged air molecules called ions. When smoke enters either detector, an alarm is triggered. The radioactive material in an ionization chamber detector is not a hazard and the detectors meet basic safety requirements, assures the National Bureau of Standards.

WHICH DETECTOR?

Which detector is better?

Ionization detectors offer the earliest warning and perhaps provide better protection, according to a Consumers Union test published in *Consumer Reports*. "Both types of detectors are equally effective in the home," according to the National Bureau of Standards. "If properly installed, they can provide adequate warning."

Some differences exist between the two when they operate close to the origin of the fire. Ionization detectors will respond more quickly to flaming fires. Photoelectric detectors generally will respond faster to smoldering fires. While the differences are not critical, the detector you buy should be approved by a major testing laboratory such as Underwriters Laboratories, Inc. (UL).

Because smoke rises, the best place to install a detector is on the ceiling or high on an inside wall just below the ceiling. In a multi-level air-conditioned home, you need a detector on each level. Install your detectors particularly near bedrooms, as well as in areas where fires could develop and remain unnoticed for some time. Do not install a smoke detector within three feet of an air supply register that might blow the smoke away from the detector. If you usually sleep with your doors closed, consider installing an additional detector inside the bedroom.

For maximum protection, connect your detectors, so that if one is activated, they all sound an alarm.

Every week, test your detectors to be sure all batteries are working, that whatever system you have is in top condition, etc.

A smoke detector in working condition should give you at least three minutes to evacuate the house. Have a family escape plan! Get out—and use a neighbor's phone to call the fire department.

For additional information, write "Smoke Detectors," National Fire Prevention and Control Administration, Commerce Department, Washington, D.C. 20230.

CHRISTMAS TREE: ITS HAZARDS

The instant you put your Christmas trees and decorations up each year, tragedies will begin: thousands of fires directly related to the trees will occur, resulting in wanton destruction, even death. Instead of the hundreds of millions of dollars you spend on Christmas trees each year bringing you joy and happiness, the huge sum will bring you unforgettable misery.

"Every year we warn people about the potential fire hazard of Christmas trees, yet every year the number of fires increases to new highs. You would think that people would have gotten the message by now," says the chairman of the Continental Insurance Companies, the nation's fifth largest writer of property and casualty insurance.

It makes no sense at all because with proper handling and the wide range of safe holiday materials available today, "there is no reason why everyone can't have a fire-free and decorative holiday."

The rules for keeping your Christmas tree from becoming a fire hazard are so easy. Heed them well.

• If you buy a natural Christmas tree, be sure it is fresh and green and store it in a cool place with its base in water. A dry tree is an excellent fire conductor and never should stand near a radiator, warm air duct, fireplace, TV set, outlet, or other heat source.

• Before setting the tree in its stand, make a fresh diagonal saw cut across its base to help the tree absorb more water, last longer, and be fire-resistant. Check the water in the stand daily and refill when necessary to bring the water level above the saw cut.

• Since an artificial tree can be beautiful but just as dangerous as a natural tree, be sure any plastic variety you buy carries a "slow-burning" seal of Underwriters Laboratories.

• Never string lights on metal trees; the combination can produce a painful or even fatal electrical shock. Instead, illuminate the tree with an indirect spotlight. For trees with built-in electrical systems, check for an Underwriters Lab label.

• If you're reusing last year's light systems, look for worn insulation, loose bulb sockets, broken plugs. On outdoor lights, see that the weatherproof cords and fixtures are intact. Always turn off the decorative lighting before leaving home or going to bed.

• Be particularly careful about combustible decorations. Cotton tissue paper, some foamed plastics, and glass wool (angel hair) are highly flammable and should be kept away from lighted candles. Use decorations labeled "non-combustible" or "flame-retardant."

• Take down your Christmas decorations shortly after the holidays and store them early. You can keep a lasting memory of a beautiful holiday season while slashing the risk of fire, injury, or damage.

Also, do not ever downgrade the fact that the winter months are the peak months for home fires, and the danger is heightened by weather conditions that may slow the response of fire departments to an alarm.

So, as the holiday season nears, test your windows (and storm windows) to see that they open easily. If they don't, show everyone how to break them with a chair or nightstand and how to drape a blanket or bedspread over the window frame to protect against glass fragments.

Tell your baby-sitters and holiday visitors the details of all your fire protection equipment, rules, and fire emergency plans.

Have your home heating equipment cleaned and checked for repairs.

And particularly while your Christmas decorations are up, be sure every member of your family (including you!) knows how to react quickly and calmly should a fire occur.

To help prepare you for a possible emergency, you can get a free booklet, *How to Abandon a Burning House Without Panicking,* by writing Continental Insurance Companies, Public Relations Department, 80 Maiden Lane, New York, New York 10038.

IF YOUR HOME IS HIT BY STORM

It could be snow and ice, it could be high winds and flooding—whatever the "natural disaster," at some time your home almost surely will be endangered by one of these furies.

If you return to a storm-damaged home, what should and what should you not do? Here are extremely valuable money- and life-saving guides:

Entering damaged building: Elementary as it may seem, do not enter a damaged building until you are sure it is not about to collapse. Turn off the gas at the meter or tank, let the house air for several minutes to eliminate foul odors or escaped gas. Don't use any open flame (lighting a cigarette) until you check. Don't turn on the electrical system; it may have become short-circuited. Watch out for holes in the floor or loose boards.

If flooding has caused wood to swell and you must force your entry because of swollen doors, try to get in by a window. Knock down hanging plaster; watch for loose plaster everywhere.

Use even greater caution if damage has been caused by high winds. Be certain your house still rests firmly on its foundation. Be on guard against broken power lines.

Drying and cleaning: Don't rush to move back in; be sure the house is dry and clean. Walks and fences damaged by floodwaters also are a hazard.

Checking electrical systems: Have an electrician check the system for short circuits before you turn on any lights or appliances. Wear rubber-soled shoes or boots and rubber gloves. Water in conduits and connection boxes and dampness or exposed wires can cause fires. You could be electrocuted replacing fuses under these conditions.

Checking heating systems: Before starting a fire in a hot-air heating plant, examine the inside of the heater, wash any sediment from the flues with a hose or swab on a long stick. Make sure there is an adequate draft for your fireplace to avoid heavy smoke. If yours is an oil-burning system, have an experienced inspector examine your storage tank to make sure the seams have not opened so dirt and water can enter. Clean all parts of the burner. Promptly inspect chimneys subjected to wind or water action. Defective chimneys can cause fires and carbon monoxide gas poisoning.

Salvaging your furniture: Millions of families have lost millions of dollars because even minor basement flooding has damaged their furniture. Take your wooden furniture outdoors. Take out as many drawers, slides or other working parts as possible. Do not force stuck drawers. If necessary, remove the back and push out the drawers. And don't leave furniture in the sun as it can warp. Take it indoors to store and dry slowly after you have cleaned it.

Furniture frequently develops white spots or a whitish film or cloudiness from dampness. Where the whole surface is affected, you might try to treat it by rubbing the wood with a cloth wrung out of camphorated oil followed by an immediate wipe dry and polishing, HUD experts suggest.

To remove loose mold, brush your upholstery, mattresses, rugs, and carpets. Do it outside to prevent scattering mildew spores in your house. Run a vacuum cleaner attachment over the surface. Dry the article, if necessary, with a fan or electric heater.

Sun and air the item to prevent mold growth.

Clean all metals at once, especially iron.

This is merely a sampling of guides to help you minimize—even eliminate—the losses that will follow if your home is hit by the disasters sure to strike tens of millions. And they'll strike no matter where you live—north or south, warm weather area or cold.

For additional information, write the Consumer Information Center, Pueblo, Colorado 81009, for brochure 277D, *When You Return to a Storm Damaged Home.* It's free.

How to Baffle a Burglar

HOW SAFE IS YOUR HOUSE FROM BURGLARY?

You are a typical couple and you're now preparing for your vacation. You have just bought a new lock for your front door as extra protection while you're away. You have arranged to have deliveries of milk and newspapers stopped when you leave. You have even installed an automatic light that goes on every evening to keep would-be burglars away. Moreover, you do not own any valuable jewelry or furs that might make your house a target for burglars.

234 SYLVIA PORTER'S NEW MONEY BOOK FOR THE 80'S

Q. *How safe is your house from burglary?*

A. Not necessarily one bit safer than the house next door where none of these precautions has been taken by your vacationing neighbors.

Any professional burglar can pick his way through the locks most of us use today. No amount of homeowner's insurance can spare you the agony of having your home burgled or the losses over and above the limits of your insurance policy or the heartache which is inevitable when a thief makes off with prized personal possessions. A hep burglar also can easily spot the automatic light which goes on at sundown in the same window each night. And today's typical burglar knows that it's easier to "fence" such items as TV sets, typewriters, and cameras than it is to resell expensive jewelry or fancy fur pieces. In sum, if you have been picked as a victim, the odds are you will be hit.

Burglary is one of the most costly, pervasive, and rapidly growing crimes in the United States today. Burglaries now account for nearly one half of all serious crimes reported by the FBI and our annual losses to burglars now run into hundreds of millions. What's more, burglary is booming not only in the big cities but also in the suburbs, the exurbs, and even out in the once secure countryside. All this in the face of the fact that we spend more than $200 million a year on burglary alarm systems and protection devices.

Here, therefore, are often overlooked do's and don'ts for you, which will greatly reduce the risk of having your home burglarized while you're away:

DO'S AND DON'TS

Do, if you are installing a big plate-glass window or door, insist on reinforced glass instead of plain glass.

Do arrange to keep your lawn mowed while you're away on vacation.

Do ask the police department to check your house regularly while you're away; inform the police which friend or neighbor has your itinerary and key to your house, and give the police the exact dates of your departure and return.

Do, if possible, leave a car conspicuously parked in your driveway, or, if you don't own a second car, at least lock your garage door to disguise the fact that there are no cars around. A non-operating junk car you are using for parts would be ideal for this purpose.

Do arrange, if possible, to keep not one but several indoor low-wattage lights burning at night. For good measure, leave a radio on near the front door as well —or have it hitched to the timer which turns on lights at night.

Do use a cylinder-type lock bolt on all outside doors, including your cellar door, with the slot protected by metal. And make sure the bolt goes far enough into the slot so that it can't be pushed back with a thin instrument such as a pocketknife or even a plastic card. Spring-type locks, also, are easily forced, and a 175-pound man can barge right through the typical lock chain. Consult an established locksmith for advice on the latest pickproof door locks—and if you're installing a new lock, put it in above eye level and put in a double-cylinder lead lock. This makes the lock picker's job that much more difficult. Don't rely on any lock which can be opened by a master key.

Do make sure your door hinges are on the inside rather than the outside of the doors, or at least make sure the pins in the hinges cannot be removed.

Do keep unused doors locked at all times.

Do realize that Christmas-New Year's—the greatest holiday week of the year—also is the period when burglaries of homes and apartments reach their peak. During this time—when gifts are scattered throughout the place, when you are visiting friends and relatives freely and on impulse, when week-long trips are commonplace—it's just natural not to be cautious. But instead become supercautious. Under no circumstances leave any doors unlocked even for a few minutes.

Do have locks and keys changed if you move to a new house or apartment, or if you accidentally lose your keys.

Don't put identification of any sort on your keys.

Don't leave ladders in plain sight and don't leave all your window shades down, a sure sign you are away.

Don't have your telephone disconnected while you're on vacation.

Don't leave notes on your front door indicating you are away.

Don't advertise the fact you're away by allowing a notice of your vacation to be published in the local newspaper social column, an excellent source of information for burglars. Other favorite sources of this information are wedding and funeral notices. Make sure your house is well protected while you're attending such occasions.

Don't assume that burglars operate only at night. There are now as many daytime burglaries as there are nighttime burglaries, and the number of daytime burglaries is soaring.

Do check the reputation and references of any new person working in or around your house.

Do invest in a peephole, so you can see who's knocking before you open the door.

Do be wary of suspicious callers who actually may be casing your house for burglary possibilities, and don't fall for suspicious invitations to get you out of the house. In one classic case, a burglar sent a set of free tickets to a suburban couple, then looted their home while his "guests" were enjoying the show.

Don't, if you have an electronic device which opens your garage doors, forget that if you can open the door by crossing a beam of light so can a thief. The best garage opener is a box with a key which, when turned, automatically opens the door for you.

Do investigate today's rapidly growing array of anti-burglar devices. But don't make any sizable investment before you have shopped carefully, checked the effectiveness of a device you're considering buying with the police—and make sure the alarm has been approved by Underwriters Laboratories.

One good place to begin shopping for advice on a burglar system is the listing for "Burglar Alarm Systems" in the Yellow Pages of your telephone book. Deal with a reputable dealer and be prepared to spend at least $250 to $300 for an alarm system. But first ask yourself: "Just what am I protecting, and against what likely type of burglar?"

Among the moderately priced devices available are:

• "Panic buttons" next to your front door or bed, wired into the local police headquarters.

• "Seeing eyes"—infrared or ultrasonic devices which sense a person (including, possibly, you or a pet) entering a house and sounding an alarm.

• "Burglar pins" which can be set into big sliding glass doors to prevent entry through them.

• "Hotliners" hitched to a standard telephone jack and activated by a switch which might be mounted on a strategically located door or window, which automatically dial the police and/or fire department or neighbors and transmit a recorded announcement such as: "There is a burglary in progress at the home of John Smith at 33 Blank Drive, Middletown, New Jersey."

Pay some attention to the power source of whatever alarm system you select. Automatically recharging batteries are best, because they work even during power failures.

Do make a record of the serial numbers of cameras, guns, TV sets, typewriters, and appliances you own, to aid in recovery of these items if they are stolen. Pawnbrokers and legitimate secondhand dealers are required by law to file sales reports with the police.

Do find out whether your police department endorses an Operation Identification or a similar plan. With such a plan, the police provide forms to record the serial numbers of valuables, and rent or lend equipment to engrave an identification number (such as your driver's license number) on the items themselves. Homeowners are then given decals to warn burglars of their participation. Communities which have Operation Identification programs report burglary rates in participating homes well under the rate in non-participating homes.

If your community has no Operation Identification, you might suggest that one be launched by a local civic group or organization. For further information on how to go about this write Burgess Vibocrafters, Inc., Route 83, Grayslake, Illinois 60030 for a free "Action Kit."

Finally, if you can manage it, try to find a reliable "house sitter" to spend nights in your home while you're away and keep up its "lived-in" appearance: a responsible widow, a college student you know well, someone you can trust.

YOUR SECOND HOME

A PLEASURE AND AN INVESTMENT

Some 3 million American families own second homes, and the vacation home has become one of the most rapidly growing types of housing in our country. What's more, the trend is as strong among younger families and couples as among older ones.

The key force behind the powerful surge in vacation housing is our ever expanding amount of leisure time—added to our ever more desperate need to escape from congested, smoggy cities and suburbs. A spur too is the fact that a vacation home can help a family of four or five members save significantly on the costs of weekend holidays and long vacations with all the hotel-motel-restaurant bills involved. As just one example, a two-day ski weekend for a family of four easily can cost $350 to $400. At popular summer and winter resorts, houses often rent for from $2,000 to $6,000 per season. (For many, many more ways to save on vacations, see Chapter 13, "How to Slash the Costs of Your Vacations in the 1980's.")

A third factor is that, at a time of soaring real estate values, a second home in attractive, relaxing surroundings may be one of the best long-term investments a family can make.

Commercial bank policies on mortgages and loan terms for vacation homes vary widely. Savings and loan associations are extending loans for repairs and improvements on vacation homes in addition to regular FHA-backed home mortgages. But city banks often refuse to finance out-of-town property, so open a savings account where you plan to buy and establish a contact with a bank there. This also will give you a good source of information on reliable local real estate brokers, lawyers, accountants, insurance agents, and contractors.

Today, you can choose from among literally thousands of different prefabricated vacation home kits—ranging from A-frames to log cabins, hunting lodges, and seashore saltbox houses. Prices start at less than $8,000 and go all the way up to $50,000 or more. You can either hire a builder to put this type of house together for you or you can do it yourself—at great savings. You also can use precut sections in at least some parts of the house—as a labor saver. One reason for the big savings available on prefabs is that you are spared the 10 to 15 per cent architect's fee—but if you do invest in a prefab vacation house, it's important both aesthetically and structurally to choose one which has been designed by an architect.

Economical condominium vacation homes, too, are springing up everywhere—in many cases surrounded by golf courses, tennis courts, lakes, or seashores.

Most vacation homes, though, are still relatively small "cottage"-type structures. Most are single-story. Most are valued at more than $30,000 if within a hundred miles of their owners' primary homes. Many lack conventional plumbing and central heating.

KEY QUESTIONS

Let's say you are contemplating buying or building a second home. Ask yourself these key questions:

How much can you really afford for a second home?

How much time do you really intend to spend in the house or cabin or cottage? Two weeks in summer? Occasional weekends? Every weekend?

During which times of the year?

How much will transportation to and from your prospective vacation home cost? What about the availability of gas if you intend to travel by car?

Honestly, what is your family's idea of a pleasant vacation? Relaxing on a beach? Hiking in the woods? Fishing and hunting? Skiing? Golfing? Reading? Partying with others?

How much responsibility are you willing to take on food, upkeep, maintenance, etc.?

How important are creature comforts to you when you're on vacation?

How many of the big-city conveniences do you want and need?

How near or far do you want (need) to be from your present home?

What are the chances you might decide to convert your second home later into a place for year-round retirement or vacationing?

Only after you have answered as honestly as you can all of these questions should you choose a specific place and a specific type of house. For the basic rules, simply follow the guides for buying your primary home.

You're Going to Rent

WHAT DO YOU WANT?

Let's switch emphasis entirely for a while and say that your reasons for renting outweigh the reasons for buying. In deciding to rent you are joining two out of every five U.S. families who now rent the homes in which they live.

But even though your decision has been made, you still have quite a few alternatives. Among them:

A house; an apartment; a duplex; a townhouse, plus the many far-out versions of the townhouse; apartments aimed at one particular category of people, such as young married people, elderly couples, singles; mobile homes which you can rent as well as buy; apartments and houses in the city or the suburbs or the country.

If you rent a house, you'll get considerably more space than if you rent an apartment, often including a yard or garden. You'll also probably have to pay a large share of the costs of maintaining and repairing the house, of utilities and yard upkeep.

The trend in apartments today, though, is strongly toward making them as much as possible like "compact houses"—with all the space and conveniences of a full-fledged house, but without the responsibilities of mortgage payments, insurance, property taxes, etc. that come with owning a big, sprawling house.

Increasingly, also, apartment building and townhouse developments are being equipped with such luxuries as swimming pools, saunas, tennis courts, social centers, gyms, golf courses, clothes-washing centers, even baby-sitting services.

Before you start hunting for a house or apartment to rent, ask yourself these questions:

Just how much space, including storage space, do you really need and want?

How dependent are you on labor-saving appliances such as dishwashers and clothes washers? These are expensive to buy yourself if you feel you must have them in your apartment. On the other hand, if they're included and you don't really care whether you have them or not, you'll be taking on needless expense, since you'll be forced to pay for them via your rent bill.

Where would be the most convenient location for you—in terms of commuting time and costs to work, as well as convenience to schools, shopping facilities, and other services you'll need?

How eager are you to do your own decorating and furniture buying? If this type of thing bores you, stick to apartments which are at least partially furnished. But if decorating interests you, don't absorb the costs, again through the monthly rent, of using somebody else's old beds, sofas, etc. Figure out what new furniture you will need for a new place. A big place may seem a bargain "at the price," until you figure out what it will cost to decorate and maintain it.

How much outdoor yard space do you really want—and would you really use? Is a small balcony worth the amount it may add to your rent?

HOW MUCH RENT CAN YOU REALLY AFFORD?

How much house and apartment can you really afford to rent?

The traditional rule is that you can afford to pay one week's take-home pay in monthly rent and related expenses.

There may, for example, be repairs which must be met by the tenant. These may range from fixing a closet shelf to the purchase of a new refrigerator. And you may have to pay for gas, electricity, telephone, water, and workmen's liability insurance for men and women working on the property.

There may be the cost of a garage if you rent in a city and own a car. In some big cities, garage rent is now running $100 to $150 a month and this expense has become an item next to the house rent itself. (See pages 378–79 for ways to cut your parking bills.)

There also are miscellaneous expenses that drain off the half dollars here, the dollar bills there. Tips are an example of this.

And, if you are renting a single house (or even an apartment in some parts of the country), you'll probably have to pay the heating bills. High fuel costs may throw your shelter budget out of balance.

YOUR LEASE

This is a written or verbal agreement between you, the tenant, and your landlord, stating all of the key terms of your occupancy. It is virtually your only form of legal protection—although you'll probably quickly find out that most landlords retain most of the rights and that you have very few.

The lease you get should be a written one, signed and dated by both you and your landlord. Before you sign it, have your lawyer look it over for you. I suggest this even though most leases in use today are standard forms and you probably don't need a lawyer's services if you have the know-how to read it yourself and you are sure you are dealing with an honest landlord.

The lease usually includes:
• the date you may move in;
• the length of time the lease is in force;
• a description of the property you are renting;
• the amount of rent to be paid;
• the dates the rent is due;
• the form in which payment of rent is to be made;
• the deposit which may be required—what it covers and under what circumstances it is forfeited;

- the conditions under which you may renew the lease;
- who pays what expenses, such as utility bills;
- the conditions under which the rent may be raised;
- the signatures of the parties to the lease.

The lease also may indicate that you are permitted to make any reasonable alterations. For other alterations you may be required to get permission from the landlord. Ordinarily, temporary alterations you make must be removed at the expiration of your lease, provided that you can do this without damage to the property.

Ordinarily the lease requires you to keep the property in good condition and to leave it in as good a state as when you moved in, with the exception of ordinary wear and tear.

Once you move in, your landlord has no right of entry, except in emergencies or to make repairs. Even then, he must check with you first if at all possible. To be safe, be sure this is spelled out in the lease.

Reading the small print in leases may be a tedious job. But every bit of that print is important to you. And the longer the lease, the more important is it that you do thoroughly understand it. Be sure all blank spaces are filled or crossed out.

A few points you might overlook:

Be sure that whatever verbal arrangements you have made with your landlord are written into your lease. Take an inspection tour with the landlord and make notes on all damage you can observe to walls, fixtures, appliances, floors. Give him one copy and keep the other yourself. Get in writing what is considered "normal" wear and tear.

Check the cancellation clause. Does it require you to give notice thirty to sixty days before a move? If you fail to give notice, is the lease automatically renewed under the old terms for another year?

Check the provisions on repairs. Otherwise you might be unpleasantly shocked when you ask who is responsible for which repairs. Normally, your landlord is responsible for periodic repainting and other major repairs and maintenance services. You, the tenant, are responsible for minor repairs.

But get the specifics: who pays, for example, for rug and carpet cleaning, painting, window washing, electrical work, plumbing problems, fixing broken furnaces and air conditioners? If periodic painting is provided, does this mean proper scraping and preparation of the walls, windowsills, etc.—or just slapping on more paint? Does it mean one coat or two coats? Who pays if an exterminator's services are needed to deal with cockroaches? If garage or parking space is provided, is it free or is it extra?

Check the regulations on subletting the property. If your circumstances change suddenly, you may have to sublet. Make sure you really have the flexibility which made you want to rent in the first place.

Watch out for restrictions—and make sure you can live with those in your lease. If you have children or pets, will they be permitted? Can you conduct a business from your home? What are the rules on noisemaking? Are there any restrictions on visitors you may have in your apartment? Extra roommates? Have stricken from the lease any restrictions the landlord says won't apply to you.

Find out what are the superintendent's duties.

Double-check on any security deposit requirement. Are you required to make one (usually amounting to one month's rent, but sometimes two or more months' rent)? How large a deposit? When and under what conditions will it be returned? Will interest be paid to you on this deposit?

What about insurance? Is the landlord responsible if his own negligence causes bodily injury to you or your family or loss of your personal property?

Look at the basic equipment—such as the heating plant, the wiring, and the plumbing. If it is not in good order, will the landlord agree in writing to have repairs made before you move in?

An increasingly important point in this era: what provisions has the landlord made to protect you against burglars—in terms of really adequate, up-to-date door locks, doorman, burglary alarm systems, tie-ins with the nearest police station?

Beware also these traps which turn up in some leases:

• An open-ended agreement by you to permit the landlord to show your apartment to prospective buyers anytime he pleases, without the usual limit of only a couple of weeks or one month before you are scheduled to vacate the apartment.

• A "waiver of notice" clause which permits your landlord to evict you and literally throw your belongings out the window onto the street if you violate even some obsolete, fine-print provisions of your lease. (For instance, taking a vacation trip without notifying your landlord.)

• A "waiver of tort liability" clause which frees your landlord of any responsibility for injury or damage which may befall you on his property—even if you have repeatedly warned him about hazards such as dangerously torn stairway carpeting.

• A "confession of judgment" clause which, in effect, waives your right to defend yourself in court against summary eviction or other arbitrary actions by the landlord.

• A clause permitting the landlord to cancel your lease when he finds a buyer for the apartment.

• A requirement that you, the tenant, pay property taxes on the house or apartment.

CHECK LIST FOR APARTMENTS

                                                                    Yes   *No*

Is building sound, attractive, well built?
Is it well managed and maintained?
Are corridors and entranceways clean and well lighted?
Is protection from burglars provided?
Is there a doorman?
Is landscaping pleasant?
Is there enough outdoor space?

CHECK LIST (CONTD)   *Yes   No*

Are extras you want included (such as swimming pool, steam baths, a gym for men and women)?
Is there parking space, indoor or outdoor?
Is there a receiving room for packages?
Is laundry equipment available?
Are fire escapes adequate?
Are there fire extinguishers?
Is trash collected or disposed of?
Are there storage rooms or facilities?
Are there elevators?
Are mailboxes locked?
Is routine maintenance—window washing, decorating, painting—provided?
Are servicemen available for emergency repairs?
Is the floor plan convenient?
Is the apartment big enough?
Are rooms light enough?
Are wall spaces adequate for your furniture?
Is the apartment soundproof?
Is decorating (if any) attractive?
Are views attractive?
Are there enough windows, and are they well located?
Are there screens and storm windows?
Are major appliances you need installed?
Are appliances in good condition?
Is wiring sufficient?
Is ventilation adequate?
Will cleaning be easy?
Are there separate heat controls for each part of the apartment?
Are there enough electric outlets and are they well located?
Do windows and doors, including cabinet doors, open and close easily?
Is there air conditioning?
Is there a fireplace? Does it work?
Is there carpeting?
Is there a balcony?
Are there workable blinds or shades?

HOME IMPROVEMENTS: DO IT YOURSELF? OR DON'T?

IF YOU ARE REMODELING: BEWARE!

As the 1980s open, we are spending more than $3 billion a year just to remodel, improve, and maintain our homes. Yet home remodeling is an area in which we regularly waste billions of dollars through our own widespread ignorance. Many of us don't know how to shop for and save on materials. Many don't have even vague guidelines for dealing with contractors or tackling a major building project. We tend to be suckers when we are up against today's home improvement gypsters who continue to cash in on our conspicuous innocence.

"A man needs absolutely nothing to go into this business," said no less an authority than the president of the National Remodelers Association. "Then he finds out it's not so easy. When his back is against the wall, he starts cheating the homeowner, cutting corners, not paying his bills. Guys like that decimate this industry."

That's a shocker. And it's even more of a shocker since the unlicensed contractor is the target, too, of much of the legitimate home improvement industry. For the fact is that while many communities require that contractors be licensed and some make it a misdemeanor to do business as an unlicensed contractor, the inexperienced, unlicensed home remodeler can operate out of the law's reach for a long time.

"If a man knows a little about carpentry, for example, or has a mechanical ability, he'll try to go into the home-remodeling business," said another industry leader. "The result almost always is slipshod."

Even if your contractor is entirely legitimate, there is a great risk of controversies and complications in an undertaking as big as home renovation. And with most projects averaging well over $1,000 and some well into the $10,000 to $20,000 range, your best protection is your own education. Therefore:

(1) Shop for your contractor, restricting yourself to reputable firms with established reputations. Get at least three bids.

(2) When you ask for an estimate, ask the contractor to be explicit about materials used and any extras to be included, so you can get a better comparison on bids.

(3) Seek out previous customers of your would-be contractor. A well-established contractor will be delighted to provide names of previous customers.

(4) Make sure the contractor is insured for on-the-job accidents and, if necessary, will give you follow-up service.

(5) Study with healthy skepticism contractor advertising. An industry cliché is that contractor advertising at an unbelievable price will be unbelievable.

(6) Put all your agreements on paper. Make your contract specific. Get a written confirmation of all promises and guarantees. Accept nothing pledged orally only.

(7) Set a completion date in the written agreement.

(8) If your community regulates local home improvement companies, check your local municipal or consumer affairs agency and/or the Better Business Bureau for any blemishes on your contractor's record. Do this before you sign anything.

(9) Investigate all your local zoning ordinances so you know, for instance, how close you can build an addition to a property line and what are your responsibilities for repairs. It's your responsibility to know the local regulations before making any structural changes in your house.

(10) Prepare for months of remodeling discomfort—and be sure the firm is responsible for cleaning up after the job is done.

COSTS OF COMMON IMPROVEMENTS

While we are a nation of do-it-yourselfers, millions tackle jobs for which they are utterly unqualified and, as a result, waste huge sums of money. At the same time, millions of others don't realize that, with the help of today's "miracle" materials and gadgets for the home improvement market, there are many money-saving jobs they could do easily.

At the very top of any list of rules for slashing home improvement costs must be: do it yourself and save 50 per cent or more of the cost of many home improvements. Here is a short list of typical cost ranges in the late 1970s.

JOB	COST RANGE
Replacing water pipes in basement	$300–$600
Replacing hot air furnace (no major ductwork)	$1,800–$2,800
Replacing concrete basement floor, rubble removal	$3.00–$5.00 per sq. ft.
Reroofing over existing asphalt shingles	$90–$125 per 100 sq. ft.
Upgrading electrical service to 150 or 200 amperes, including circuit breakers	$1,500–$3,000
Re-siding house	$5,000
Sanding and refinishing wood floor	$.75–$.80 per sq. ft.
Insulating attic floor and rafters	$1.00–$1.25 per sq. ft.
Installing new bathroom	$3,500–$8,000
Remodeling existing bath	$2,000–$5,000
Installing tile shower	$500–$800
Installing complete central air-conditioning system	$2,000–$5,000
Removing a 15-foot supporting wall	$2,000–$3,000
Remodeling kitchen including cabinets, appliances, floor, counter top, plumbing, wiring, decorating	$10,000–$15,000
Adding a second story to a one-story house	$14,000–$20,000
Finishing off basement into a recreation room (no plumbing)	$3,000–$6,000
New attic room	$3,000–$4,000
New two-car garage	$4,000–$8,000
Exterior painting	$2,000–$4,000
New swimming pool	$10,000–$15,000

With these costs and with the development of so many of the miracle aides as a spur, it is not surprising that the do-it-yourself trend is so powerful.

We now do more than one third of the painting inside and outside our homes.

Of every six U.S. homeowners, one does his own home plumbing.

We do a full one fifth of the roofing work on our homes and a full two fifths of all flooring work.

We do one fourth of all outside improvements.

We do the great majority of odd jobs around our homes.

And, of course, the man in the house is no longer by any means the family's sole do-it-yourselfer. According to one recent study, more than three out of four wives are now doing a wide range of home repairs themselves, including painting, patio repairs, unclogging water pipes, repairing fences, installing TV antennas, putting in insulation and masonry. In all, nearly half of all repairs in households with family incomes between $7,500 and $15,000 are done by women.

Among the most obvious do-it-yourself jobs for which you are probably qualified or which you could learn fairly easily are: interior and/or exterior painting, wallpapering, window glazing, weather-stripping, installing insulation, taping and filling wallboard seams.

GUIDELINES FOR DO-IT-YOURSELFERS

Here are a few general, but fundamental, guidelines on home improvements for do-it-yourselfers:

• By all means, do as many home repair jobs as you are qualified to do yourself. While you're at it, also recruit any qualified—or at least willing—members of your family to help you. Today's expanding availability of convenient materials and supplies makes it ever simpler. Among the materials and supplies are: "miracle" glues, roll-on paints, prefabricated building materials, sophisticated power tools, caulking guns, prepasted wallpapers, "instant" lawns, and do-it-yourself fix-it kits with easy instructions on how to do just about anything around the home.

• Do not tackle the ambitious and difficult jobs, however, unless you are qualified: for instance, roofing, re-siding, putting in a lawn, building bookshelves or kitchen cupboards, laying a floor, sanding down and staining a floor, installing a major appliance. Also stay away from such demanding and potentially hazardous jobs as the installation of electrical wiring or fuel lines. Doing these yourself may void your fire insurance.

• Don't skimp on materials. For instance, don't buy improperly cured lumber: you may find that it buckles or contracts after it has been nailed in place.

• Pick appropriate materials. When choosing flooring and floor coverings—linoleum, carpeting, etc.—get local builders to advise you on which product grades will give you the durability you'll actually need in the area to be floored or covered. There's no sense in splurging on a super grade of hardwood or linoleum or carpeting for a room in which there will be only a minimum of traffic. At the same time, it scarcely makes economic sense to buy a light-duty grade of flooring or carpeting for a children's rumpus room—to save $50 to $100.

• Buy the most economical lengths and sizes you can of lumber, plywood, tiles, floor coverings, curtain material—to avoid costly waste. If, for example, your new garage calls for 8-foot two-by-four studs, you would do much better buying 16-foot lengths which can be cut in half than 12-foot lengths, which could translate into a waste of one third of your lumber.

• Shop for remnants and also discontinued patterns in such items as roofing, linoleum, carpeting—for potentially big savings. And buy enough extra to use for patching later if necessary.

• In your estimate of how long a job will take you, allow plenty of time for shopping around.

• Before you embark on any major do-it-yourself construction or remodeling project, check your local zoning ordinances and/or building codes to make sure your plans and specifications conform. If a reputable local contractor is involved in the work, he will surely be fully aware of the rules—but if you're serving as your own contractor, obeying the zoning laws will be your responsibility.

• Don't buy sophisticated, costly tools unless you will use them extensively in the future. Try to rent them instead.

RULES FOR HANDLING REPAIRS

Now here are a few specifics on handling repairs for any economy-minded householder.

When an item is damaged, repair it immediately. Delay will, if anything, make the repair more costly or encourage you to throw the article away and lose your entire investment.

Give your house an annual checkup so you can anticipate trouble and slash repair costs. Winter can cause subtle damage to a house. Periodically check your gutters, windowsills, drains, etc. to find damage before it becomes extensive.

Take advantage of the knowledge of any experienced owner of a hardware store: he is selling advice and service as well as products. Let him help you to train yourself to handle minor repairs and thereby save substantial sums each year.

Look into buying a "medical plan" for your house, now available in some areas. These will handle any needed repairs to plumbing, heating, electrical, or air-conditioning systems for a fixed annual fee (typically $180, depending on the condition of your house). Some offer 24-hour, 365-day emergency services, too.

Also helpful to you might be a clearinghouse and referral service for household repairs, guaranteeing speed and quality—for a fee.

HOME REPAIRS: WARRANTIES

Q. *How long does a major-brand dishwasher last?*
A. About eight years.

Q. *How long will it take before a water heater with a five-year warranty springs a leak?*
A. Five to ten years.

Q. *What's the average life of a forced-air furnace?*
A. Fifteen years.

If you're considering buying a house more than ten years old, expect something to go wrong. Maintenance records of the vital systems in older houses usually are non-existent. A huge 3.5 million or more houses will be resold in the United States each year in the 1980s, and if you're a typical buyer of one of these, you'll be virtually ignorant of how long the heating, plumbing, wiring, and built-in appliances will last.

How, then, can you, an uninformed consumer, protect yourself against the future likelihood of costly repairs?

Since the early 1970s, more than one hundred companies have emerged from coast to coast, offering warranty plans that cover the cost of home repairs—and today warranties on resale homes are available in thirty-five states. (California residents buy more warranty plans than anybody else; Ohio residents are second.) You, the home buyer, may sign a contract calling for a fixed annual fee and deductible clause. In return, the cost of your home repairs will be paid by the company.

As an illustration of how the plans work, the largest company in the United States selling comprehensive home service contracts charges an annual fee of $220 to $250 with a deductible of $25 or $50 respectively.

Under its plan, the company will service, repair, or replace the heating, air-conditioning, electrical, and plumbing systems, as well as built-in appliances (oven, dishwasher, etc.). Some of its plans also cover certain structural defects in floors, walls, ceilings, and foundations, at extra cost.

Your house is not inspected before a contract is signed and the company places no limit on the size or age of the house and cost of repairs. (Repairs on a covered house have cost as much as $6,000.)

In areas where it has a concentration of customers, the company has its own in-house repairmen. It also has a network of 2,500 licensed contractors in the thirty-five states, who are authorized to charge up to $50 for parts and labor without prior approval from the parent corporation. Beyond that, the company decides if bids from other contractors are required. And it samples repair work done to check performance and price.

You are guaranteed one-hour emergency service plus regular service within forty-eight hours—except where a house is in a remote area. In that case, another time limit is specified in the contract. Service calls cost between $20 and $50 and are applied toward the deductible amount. To minimize inconvenience and avoid unnecessary cost, you, a customer, will be given free advice (if you choose) on how to solve your problem or instruction on how to correct such simple malfunctions as a pilot light that might have gone out. You may call the company toll-free for repairs twenty-four hours a day, seven days a week.

This basic plan is for one year, but you also can get two- and three-year plans. Condominiums as well as single-family homes are covered. The plans are marketed exclusively through real estate brokers, who do not receive a fee for selling the plan.

Brokers have found that the warranty plans are an effective selling point and that they enhance the chances of a marginally financed buyer to get a mortgage because the lender feels the new homeowner is protected against destructively high repair costs.

Thus, the key question: if you are offered a repair warranty by a responsible company in the field, should you rush to buy?

No!

First, consider how handy you are around the house as well as the house's age and condition and decide whether you really need a plan of this sort.

Then, carefully investigate the company.

Read your contract with utmost caution to make sure it spells out precisely what the warranty covers, the cost of service calls for your area, whether they are deductible, if you can phone the company toll-free.

Inquire about the company's repairmen. They should be licensed contractors, not just handymen.

Ask your broker about the names of other home buyers who have bought the warranties, check to see if they are satisfied with the services. Finally, take nothing for granted, no matter how great the lure!

FINANCING YOUR HOME IMPROVEMENTS

FUNDAMENTAL RULES FOR HOME IMPROVEMENT LOANS

Let's assume you are undertaking a home improvement and must borrow money to manage it. Be guided by these fundamental rules.

• Do not agree to the loan terms which may be offered by your home improvement contractor without first comparing them with terms offered by local lending institutions. Go first to your local bank, credit union, savings association, or savings bank and ask each what would be the very least expensive way for you to raise the cash you need. See pages 829–53 for details.

• Inquire about Title I and other loans which are insured by the FHA. The maximum interest rate is significantly lower than typical lending institution charges. This type of loan is now being made for up to $10,000 repayable within twelve years for almost any project which will improve the basic livability or utility of your house and grounds. Included are many major appliances but not luxury improvements such as swimming pools. The only key qualifications you, a borrower, must have are: you must be a good credit risk and you must own (or have a substantial interest in) the property to be improved. You can get an FHA-insured loan from dealers and contractors participating in the program as well as from the usual array of lenders.

• If you're lucky, your present mortgage may contain a clause permitting you to borrow an amount up to that you have already paid off at the same interest rate you are already paying—plus a nominal fee. Consider borrowing via this route if it's open to you.

• Consider also borrowing against the cash value of your life insurance policy. The pros and cons of this also are fully explained on pages 841–42.

• Look too into one little-known source of home improvement loans: the so-called "little FHA" loans, available in limited numbers to lower-income homeowners living in very dilapidated small rural communities. Interest rates on these federally subsidized loans are as low as you can find anywhere, and the loans are repayable over a period up to twenty-five years. You can inquire about such loans at the local Farmers Home Administration office or the U. S. Department of Agriculture.

Your Home Improvement Contractor and Your Contract

HOW TO CHOOSE A CONTRACTOR

The primary duties of a home improvement contractor are to order and pay for materials involved in the job he has contracted to perform and to see that the materials are shipped to the site on schedule; to make sure that the appropriate workers and subcontractors are at the right place at the right time: and to direct and co-ordinate construction.

Typically you pay a contractor in one of these three ways:

• in one lump sum covering all costs of materials, labor, and the contractor's profits;

• on a "cost plus" arrangement—the actual cost of the project plus 10 to 15 per cent of this total as the contractor's fee;

• on a "maximum total" basis, which means that a maximum cost of the project is agreed upon by homeowner and contractor, including the contractor's profits—plus any savings he can achieve by completing the project for less than the agreed-upon maximum.

Of course, if you, the homeowner, later change your mind on design or materials or some other aspect of the project, deviating from the original plans and specifications, you should expect costs to be escalated accordingly. Typically, you make periodic payments as work progresses and a final payment when the job has been satisfactorily completed.

In a few areas of the United States, home improvement contractors must be licensed—giving homeowners some protection against shoddy work and broken home improvement contracts. But for the vast majority of us the problems of finding honest, qualified contractors to do any major home improvements, or figuring out what should and should not go into a home improvement contract, can be truly staggering.

Here then are basic rules every homeowner or would-be homeowner should follow in choosing a contractor, drawing up a home improvement contract, and making sure the contract is properly carried out.

(1) Choose a contractor for any home improvement job with the utmost care.

Your key yardsticks for judging a contractor are: his credit standing with his suppliers; his reputation for reliability, fair dealing, and getting a job done on schedule; his experience, competence, and taste; his relationship with his workers, subcontractors, and suppliers; his patience and willingness to submit a reasonably detailed estimate when dealing with you.

(2) Get bids in writing on any sizable home improvement from two or more local contractors—with all important aspects of the work spelled out in detail. But make sure each bid is for the same building specification, the same quality of materials, the same deadlines, etc. Do all you can to double-check the bases for bids and estimates.

(3) Beware of "par selling," a practice banned by the Federal Housing Administration, in which an advance salesman rather than the home improvement contractor himself sets the price of a particular job.

(4) See earlier in this chapter for advice on choosing a contractor to build a new house, for the same guides—such as on insurance, sources of information, etc.—apply to home improvements.

HOW TO WRITE A HOME IMPROVEMENT CONTRACT

Once you have chosen a contractor, you move to the problem of drawing up a contract for your job. On this contract will hang hundreds or even thousands of dollars—your potential financial losses if the contractor fails to do the job as you want and expect it to be done. On this contract also will hang your entire legal protection against shoddy workmanship, inferior materials, non-completion of the job, and many other hazards.

Under the 1969 federal Truth in Lending law, you have a "right of rescission" or "cooling-off period" lasting three business days after you sign a contract involving a home improvement loan in which you put up your home as security for the loan. A contractor must give you the appropriate "Notice of Rescission," and if you change your mind about going ahead with the work, you may cancel the contract during this period by written notice to the contractor. The contractor is not legally permitted to begin work before the end of the rescission period.

However, if the home improvement contract does not involve a loan, you are strictly on your own.

Here is what should be included in a home improvement contract:

• First, indisputably foremost, and clearly, the full costs of the job. Don't haggle over the costs if the contractor is honest and his bid seems reasonable compared with other bids. You well might sacrifice quality by so doing.

• If the contractor also has arranged the financing of your job, the full financing costs of the loan and the payment schedule you'll be expected to meet.

• The specifications of all key materials, including brand names, and a work completion schedule.

• If the work is guaranteed by the contractor—as many types of home improvements should be—all details of the guarantee, particularly the period during which the guarantee will remain in effect. Most important: what happens if the materials or workmanship don't hold up as the contractor said they would? And don't confuse a manufacturer's guarantee of his materials against defects with the guarantee you also must get from the contractor covering proper installation of the materials.

• An automatic arbitration clause—so that if cost estimates are greatly exceeded by the contractor you can submit the problem to an impartial board of arbitrators. Today such services are available in many U.S. cities.

• A clause binding the contractor to be responsible for any damage caused by his (or his workers') negligence. In some states, builders are now liable for damages from poor construction on the basis of "implied warranty." Check with your lawyer to learn what protection your state provides.

• A provision requiring the builder to do a thorough clean-up job after work is completed. Getting rid of the junk left over from any building project—interior or exterior—can be a splitting headache and a major expense.

KEY RULES AND WARNINGS

Under no circumstances sign a contract with any blank spaces left on it. Have the items which don't apply marked "Void" or crossed out.

If the contract is for repairs which are covered by insurance (e.g., fire damage), check with your insurance company on costs and terms before you sign.

Never sign any complicated deal without consulting your lawyer, and if you don't have a lawyer, get one.

Do not sign a work completion certificate before you get proof (such as duplicate bills) that the contractor has paid all subcontractors who have supplied labor or materials for your project. If you fail to do this, you could be liable for these payments and the subcontractors could legally obtain a mechanic's lien on your house—since they still "own" certain materials incorporated into it. As an alternative, you might get the contractor, subcontractors, and others involved to sign "lien waivers" before you make your final payment. This will absolve you from any further responsibility for subcontractors' bills.

Never pay a contractor in full before the work is done to your satisfaction, or as specified in your contract.

Never pay in cash.

Finally, remember that you have every right to terminate a contract if the contractor fails to carry out the terms of the contract or if he performs the job improperly. Generally, you do this by sending a written notice to the contractor. You pay for the work which has been completed—minus damages. Similarly, a contractor has the right to end a contract if you fail to pay on the schedule to which you agreed.

These may seem tedious details. But heed them, for the rules were created out of the experiences of hundreds of thousands of disappointed homeowners. They will be crucially important in protecting you in your own home improvements.

WHAT ABOUT BEING YOUR OWN CONTRACTOR?

Being your own contractor means lining up all the specialists you'll need—e.g., carpenters, electricians, masons, and plumbers—choosing and ordering materials, supervising the work as it progresses. It means timing everything so precisely that lumber is on hand when the cabinetmaker appears or there's a backlog of indoor work to do when it rains for days, etc. And it means being on the job or getting to the job often to make decisions and changes as needed.

By doing all this yourself, you'll save the typical 10 per cent (or more) the contractor may add onto your bill for his services. You also may be able to wangle from a local building materials supplier the discount (also usually 10 per cent) he usually gives contractors.

Being your own contractor may make sense if, say, 90 per cent of the job you want done involves only one skill, such as plumbing. Here, the economical thing to do would be to call in your regular plumber, let him round up the equipment and materials he'll use—then call in an electrician or mason, etc., when the job progresses to that stage.

However, if the job involves meshing the skills of many different tradesmen and craftsmen and you're a babe in the home improvement woods, leave the contracting job to a pro. He'll save you a lot more money in the long run than the fee he charges you.

HOUSE PAINTING GUIDELINES

If you are to avoid the house paint and painting traps into which millions fall each year, make sure that every detail of the work done by professionals is included in a written estimate and leave nothing to "negotiations."

If the shutters must be taken off, know in advance who will do this, how much will be charged, etc. Be warned: no detail should be too small or you will find "additional labor and time charges" on your final bill and you will be able to do absolutely nothing about it.

Don't hire any paint contractor without carefully checking his qualifications and references and be immediately suspicious of any contractor who offers any long-term "guarantees"—ten, fifteen, even twenty years. The reasonable guarantee is for five years on a two-coat exterior paint job.

DOING YOUR OWN PAINTING

If you are typical of millions, you will tackle the job of painting part or all of your house or apartment, mostly in the spring.

And if you're merely a casual, much less a dedicated do-it-yourselfer, you will try the job on your own to slash costs. The do-it-yourselfer can save about 80 per cent compared to contracting a paint job, assuming he plans the job carefully, picks the right paint for the right surface, and deals with a reputable paint dealer who handles high-quality, brand-name paints.

You'll lose on time spent, of course, but if time on the project is not your primary concern, there's no disputing the potential savings by doing the work on your own.

As one illustration, you probably could paint an average-sized room that required a minimum of preparation for as little as $15 to $20 as the 1970s ended. A professional might charge $100 for the same room.

As another illustration, say a gallon of paint costs $9.00 and takes three hours to apply. At a rate of $15 per hour, a contractor would charge $54 to apply the gallon of paint (including the paint). The paint alone is about 20 per cent of this total cost.

The most expensive error you can make is buying poor-quality paint, for you soon will have to do the job over. Take the time to read the label on most brand-name paints, for it will list the contents as well as how and where to use the paint.

The content analysis is divided into two categories: percentage of dry pigment (important) and percentage of vehicle (liquid portion). A good rule of thumb is to buy a brand-name paint with a high content of TiO_2. It may cost a bit more but it will save you money in the long run. It will cover the area more effectively and hold up longer.

Also check the label to find out on what surfaces the paint is most effective, how much of the surface can be coated, and how to prepare the surface for coating. Other do's and don'ts:

• Dust or wash dirty walls and examine plaster walls for cracks. Hairline cracks should be filled with spackling, larger cracks with special patching plaster. The plaster must be completely dried before you begin to cover it.

• Stir the paint to mix color pigments at the bottom of the can. But latex paints should not be stirred vigorously because this creates air bubbles in the paint which will ruin the job. In latex paints, the amount of TiO_2 can vary from 23 to 63 per cent of the pigment content.

• Don't dip the brush more than one third into the paint. This reduces splattering and dripping.

• Don't try to cover too much area too quickly. When painting ceilings, for instance, work across the width of the room, so you can start a second lap before the first has dried. When painting walls, start at the upper left-hand corner and work down toward the floor. (Southpaws should work from right to left.)

• Don't paint woodwork with too large a brush. Remove wax or varnish if necessary before retouching floors. Varnished floors may require the removal of all the old coating.

• Don't paint undesirable architectural features (radiators, pipes) in a color that contrasts with the wall. This emphasizes them. But don't choose neutral colors either just because they're safe.

• Have a continuing color flow through your home from room to room, using harmonious colors in adjoining areas.

• Study color swatches in both daylight and night light because colors often change under artificial lighting. The color sample always should be lighter than the final results you want

• Of course, remove hardware from doors and windows. Loosen lighting fixtures or cover them with masking tape. Cover floors and furnishings with old sheets or drop cloths for those inevitable splatters, and clean up as you go. Paint is easier to remove when wet.

• For a free brochure on painting, write the National Paint and Coating Association, 1500 Rhode Island Avenue N.W., Washington, D.C. 20005.

REMODELING YOUR KITCHEN

Your kitchen is the traditional room to remodel, one of the busiest in the house, also the most expensive to change.

And it is the location of many home accidents that can happen while moving hot utensils, operating a garbage disposal unit, even using light or appliance switches near the sink.

Since the kitchen is the control center of your house, carefully review your plans not just for attractiveness, efficiency, and permanence but, equally important, for safety. Safe kitchens should be well lighted, well ventilated, and designed for maximum efficiency by even the do-it-yourself builder As for costs, errors and hazards can be prohibitively expensive to correct or eliminate when your house has been completed and equipment already installed. But careful planning now will prevent major structural changes in the future.

• A key element in kitchen planning is the coupling of safety and efficiency with suitable space standards. You must consider the kitchen location and arrangement in relationship to the rest of the house, fixtures, and appliances.

• Since the sink, wall cabinets, and range are difficult to move, the location of the windows and doors probably will limit you to the choice of one of five basic kitchen arrangements: (1) the U-shaped kitchen, (2) the L-shaped kitchen, (3) the parallel-wall kitchen, (4) the broken-U kitchen, and (5) the straight kitchen.

The L-shaped kitchen fits well on two walls and provides a good location for dining or even laundry equipment on the opposite wall. The U-shaped kitchen is usually compact, step-saving, and out of the traffic flow. The broken-U arrangement often fits well in room combinations such as kitchen-dining or kitchen-family, and maximizes use of space.

If you pick the parallel-wall kitchen arrangement, provide for the recommended width of 4 feet, 6 inches between facing equipment—enough for two people to work and pass each other. Avoid placing the refrigerator or oven so the door opens across a frequently used doorway.

• Plan to keep traffic to back yard or adjacent dining room or meal-serving area out of the kitchen work area. The heart of the kitchen is the so-called work triangle—formed by a working line between the sink, range, and refrigerator. The sum of the sides of the work triangle should not exceed 23 feet.

• Be sure your base cabinets and counter tops with wall cabinets above do not exceed 24 inches in depth. This permits easy access to the rear of wall cabinets without standing on stools or dangerous makeshift aids. Do not place the top shelves of cabinets more than 72 inches above the floor—and wall-cabinet depth should not exceed 12 inches. For counter tops without wall cabinets above, a 30-inch depth is the maximum.

• Cabinet counters should be flush with installed appliances to provide a smooth clear work area, at a height of 36 inches from the floor.

• Install your doors to swing against the side or end of a cabinet or out of the kitchen. Where standard hinged doors may present a hazard, use sliding doors or folding doors.

On appliances, install refrigerators where the interior is accessible to the work triangle and the door-swing does not interfere with traffic flow or other doors or drawers. For double-door refrigerator/freezer combinations, the refrigerator should swing away from the work triangle.

• Be sure there is a minimum of 18 inches of counter space on each side of range or 24 inches on at least one side of separate oven units to provide adjacent space for setting hot utensils with room for their handles.

• Select a range with controls at the front or side. Eliminate storage areas above burners to reduce risk of burns.

• Set range hoods 56 to 60 inches above the floor. Exhaust systems incorporated within the hood should direct their flow outside of the house—never into any house space.

• Locate receptacles and switches for lighting and electrical systems as far as possible from water outlet fixtures.

• Place hanging and wall-mounted lighting fixtures no lower than 6 feet, 8 inches above the finished floor except where installed above a permanent structure.

• Install a ground-fault circuit-interrupter (GFCI) in kitchen circuits to provide safety from shock.

Request *A Design Guide for Home Safety* from the Superintendent of Documents, U. S. Government Printing Office, Washington, D.C. 20402. The cost of the guide is modest.

HOME IMPROVEMENT TRAPS—AND HOW TO AVOID THEM

Side by side with today's home improvement boom you will find an astonishingly wide range of gyps, misrepresentations, and come-ons—a vast swindler's net into which you can be sucked at any time unless you are aware and constantly alert.

Home improvements are, in fact, among the top fields for racketeers. You can literally lose hundreds or even thousands of dollars in one fell swoop on home non-improvements. By one estimate, as much as $1.00 out of every $15 we spend to remodel, repair, and refurbish our homes goes into the hands of gypsters and "miracle" materials which don't work.

This era of technical-chemical-mechanical wonders has created not only a wide array of phony "foolproof" basement sealers but also one-coat paints which are supposed to last forever; home siding which supposedly never fades, cracks, or chips; "instant" floor coating which anybody can just paint on; spray-on roofing, and on and on and on.

Of course, many of today's miracle materials do hold up as advertised; the epoxy glues, certain caulking compounds, and hard plastic wood finishes are three product categories which leap to mind. But as a general rule these materials must be applied properly and professionally. And manufacturers of such materials will not guarantee the final job of applying them, despite what local dealers may claim.

How, then, do you spot—and avoid—today's top home improvement gyps? Here is a short rundown and explanation to guide you.

"BAIT AND SWITCH"

In this trick, an ad holds out the bait of an unbelievably low price and the salesman then switches you, the gullible customer, to a higher-priced model.

You respond to a come-on offering, for example, floor tile at, say $.10 per square foot. When the salesman arrives at your door, he harshly downgrades the product advertised, refuses to sell it to you, and switches you to a vastly overpriced product at 40, 50, or even 80 cents per square foot—if you let him.

DRIVEWAY RESURFACING

Itinerant gypsters will tell you they "just happen to be in the area," have just enough materials left from previous jobs to do your driveway, and offer to do the job at a "bargain" price. But their materials and workmanship will be either shoddy or totally ineffective. They may merely spray black oil on your driveway.

Or they may simply make off with your advance payment—without performing any resurfacing work at all.

Among the notorious purveyors of the driveway resurfacing swindle are the "Terrible Williamsons." The Williamsons are a clan of several hundred itinerant swindlers who have been victimizing Americans from coast to coast for two full generations. In addition to driveway resurfacing rackets they also are infamous for bilking their victims through other gyps ranging from roofing and basement waterproofing jobs to lightning-rod installation and barn painting.

If the swindle involves your roof, one of them may ring your bell and show you a handful of loose shingles which he says have dropped off your roof. Unless you sign up for a roofing job, he warns, your entire roof may cave in. If you bite, you'll pay an exorbitant price for a shoddy job. If the scheme involves chimney repairs, he will show you a loose brick which, he warns, signals the imminent collapse of your present chimney.

The Williamsons' favorite targets are naïve old ladies but they prey equally viciously on younger Americans. Better Business Bureau files are loaded with reports on the Terrible Williamsons who have charged $300 for applying an ineffective roof "sealer"; coated driveways with gunk which remained sticky for weeks; painted barns with a concoction of aluminum dust and used crankcase oil which washed off with the first rain; installed lightning rods with "conductors" consisting of nothing more than painted ropes.

The Williamsons (who also go under such Scottish names as Stewart, MacMillan, and MacDonald) usually work out of trucks, and usually manage to leave town before the police catch up with them—or before their victims discover they've been bilked.

There's no hard rule for spotting a Terrible Williamson or any other gypster in this area. You simply must apply the same cautions you would to any dealer in home improvement goods and services.

On driveway resurfacing, though, your best move is to consult established local experts and demand a contract specifying the work to be done, type and depth of asphalt to be used, type and thickness of the road base, completion date—plus a guarantee that the job will hold up for a stated period of time.

CHAIN REFERRAL

The typical come-on here is an ad for a complete home re-siding job at what is touted as a startlingly low price—with the extra provision that, if you permit the company to use your home as a model to illustrate a "before and after" advertisement of the firm's workmanship in your community, you'll get a hefty commission for each new customer you find. This commission, it is promised, will be at least enough to cover the total cost of the re-siding job. You might even make hundreds of dollars on top of the price of the job.

The gypster also may tell you the siding is unconditionally guaranteed for, say, twenty years, that it will never need repainting or repairing, and that it will be impervious to such perils as hail, storms, and fire. On top of it all, you'll be assured that by signing up for this type of siding you'll cut your heating bills by one third.

If this tempts you, beware! For you are about to become a victim of a "chain

referral" sales scheme. The product being sold, almost always at an unconscionable price, may be aluminum siding, wall-to-wall carpeting, a home intercom or
fire alarm system, a water softener, electric broiler, a vacuum cleaning system,
etc. But the sales technique is usually the same for whatever product is being
sold.

The salesman explains that the "bargain" he is offering is made possible by the
fact that there are no advertising costs. You'll earn your own "savings" by participating, as an alternative to advertising, in a word-of-mouth promotion campaign.
You are urged to get started at once earning commissions for your referrals. All
you need do is make a modest down payment and sign a paper confirming the
deal.

But the form you sign may be an ironclad contract which the salesman will sell
to a financial institution. You'll be legally obligated to pay the amount stated in
the contract and the amount will almost surely be several times the value of the
product you are buying.

Over and beyond the pitfall of the contract, the giant hurdle is referring the
required number of "qualified" prospects. The reason is simple mathematics. Assume that the first person contacted in your community is supposed to refer eight
more persons. Those eight would then have to refer another eight each in order
to get their "free" siding. That makes 64 referrals so far, and if each of these is
supposed to get another eight . . . The numbers balloon to 512, then 4,096 on
the next round, then 32,768 . . . 262,144 . . . 2,097,152 . . .

"CREW SWITCHING"

A team of high-pressure salesmen divides into two crews. "A" fans out into one
part of town, selling products ranging from awnings to wall-to-wall carpeting.
Crew "B," under a different company name, but selling the same products, heads
for another part of town. Both quote fantastically inflated prices, almost never
make a sale—and now comes the catch.

The crews switch. Crew "A" approaches the same houses Crew "B" already
has visited and this time quotes much lower prices. Crew "B" goes into "A's" territory and ridicules the "other company" for its high prices.

What you don't know is that the two outfits are working together, that all the
prices quoted are inflated—the second almost as much as the first—and that you
are being softened up for the kill. If you do not double-check the offers and the
reputations of the companies, the chances are you will be gypped on whatever
you buy.

THE LEAKY BASEMENT

Not long ago an elderly Chicagoan was bilked out of $9,000 by an itinerant
"engineer" who poured water into cracks in the old man's basement floor, then
managed to persuade him that his house was sitting on a cesspool. The $9,000
went, of course, for utterly unneeded repairs and non-repairs performed by the
"engineer."

Another homeowner, a New Yorker, paid $750 for a basement waterproofing
job which failed to stem the tide of spring flooding. He was then told by the wa-

terproofing company that the job covered "only the specific area where our process is applied, not leaks which appear elsewhere."

Damp, leaky basements are a bane to millions of homeowners, and in many cases the problem is exceedingly difficult to solve. This very difficulty is an open invitation to the unscrupulous operator with his array of miracle wet-basement cures.

Against this background, it is merely common sense to have the job done by professionals who understand such matters as soil types, water tables, etc. Be prepared for the fact that a reliable contractor may take time to solve the problem and the work may require several treatments before it is licked. Beware of any "guarantee" that the waterproofing will be 100 per cent effective, for no claim of this sort is valid. And invalid too is any claim that a basement waterproofing method is "government-approved."

THE PHONY FURNACE "INSPECTOR"

If you have any degree of hidden fear that your heating plant may be somehow defective and that, as a result, you might be running the danger of a devastating home fire, you are probably more vulnerable than you realize to the persuasive patter of the furnace gypster.

Here are the basic earmarks by which you'll recognize this crook—and the rules for keeping out of his way:

A stranger appears at your door and offers to "inspect" your furnace. He may drop the name of your local gas and electric company, or some nationally known furnace manufacturer. If yours is an older heating plant, he may poke around the mortar holding the firebricks together, discover that it's powdery, and declare the furnace is "dangerous." What you may not know is that in this type of installation it's perfectly normal for the mortar to be powdery.

Or he may offer you bargain-priced furnace-cleaning services—and, after dismantling your heating plant, tell you that it's a wonder you haven't already been asphyxiated by carbon monoxide or that you are extremely fortunate your house has not burned down around you. He refuses even to put the furnace back together.

These swindlers—and there are many variations—have one key goal: to scare you into buying a new furnace or expensive parts from them—whether or not you need the equipment—at prices far above the amounts which a reliable local heating contractor would charge.

Seek the advice of established local dealers on the condition of your furnace—or see if the local fire department will send somebody to check the safety aspects of your furnace for you.

THE FRAUDULENT PLUMBING AND ELECTRICAL WIRING "REPAIRMAN"

This swindler is closely related to the crooked furnace inspector, for he also deals in scare tactics and exploits the average homeowner's near total innocence on such matters as water pressure, circuit breakers, and wiring capacity.

What should you do to avoid any furnace-repair racket or similar gyp?

Beware of anybody who comes to your door uninvited and offers to "inspect" your electrical wiring or plumbing system. Call in your regular electrician if you have any reason to suspect wiring problems or your regular plumber if your pipes aren't working properly.

TERMITE SWINDLES

Part of the home "improvement" gyp tale—and yet so pervasive and expensive that he deserves a section all his own—is the termite swindler. Here is a typical illustration of how this gypster works:

A truck pulls into your driveway and a man introducing himself as a "termite inspector" informs you that a termite problem has cropped up in your neighborhood. He may tell you that he has found termites in the trees and shrubs around your house. Or he may offer to "inspect" your home—free—to see whether termites have moved inside. He disappears into your basement, later emerges with the frightening news that your own house has become infested. As proof, he displays a jar of live termites he says he has found downstairs.

The "inspector" may tell you that you are lucky because your termite problem has been discovered "in the nick of time" and he urges you to act immediately, "before your house collapses." He then summons a couple of men from his truck and tells them to bring a tankful of insecticide. You will pay only for the number of gallons actually sprayed in your cellar and there will be a ten-year guarantee on the job. A little later the men return to inform you that the job took 85 gallons at $4.00 a gallon—or $340.

But termites don't live in trees or shrubs. There may not be a single termite in your home either. Even if there are, the chemical spray used by the termite gypsters is probably worthless because termites generally live ten to twenty feet underground. Reputable exterminators normally do not guarantee a single termite control job for as long as ten years.

The hard facts about termites and termite control are these:

Termites are a very real menace in virtually every part of the United States. They feed primarily on wood, paper, and leather. They can indeed do extensive damage to the structural members supporting your house.

Each year 20 million American homes are damaged, some severely, by colonies of voracious termites. Out of every five homes, two are under attack in every state except Alaska by these wood-chewing gluttons.

But termites work very slowly and even if they invaded your house you can afford to take weeks or months to decide on a course of action.

Also, ridding a house of termites may involve injection of poisonous chemicals, under pressure, into the ground around infested areas and perhaps under basement floors. Termite control may involve excavation around the foundation and the construction of mechanical barriers to block entry by termites around the house or under the basement. Sometimes badly infested sills must be replaced as well.

The cost to you of termite control is generally based on the number of linear feet treated and the amount of excavation and reconstruction needed. It is not unusual for a legitimate termite control job to cost hundreds of dollars.

Typically, the legitimate termite exterminator will guarantee his work, usually for three or more years. But the guarantees may not hold if you make additions to the house, such as a new wing or a new porch—unless you termite-proof these, too.

Here are your key guides to avoiding termite gypsters:

• If you think you have a termite problem, call one or more reputable exterminating firms, ask for expert opinions and estimates. Some firms will inspect your home free; others may charge $15 to $20.

• Investigate their references of work done in other homes.

But first do a little inspecting on your own:

• Take a screwdriver and push it into wooden beams or footings. If the screwdriver penetrates the wood and reveals it has been hollowed out from the inside, that's a bad sign. Look too for another sure visual sign: the presence of "mud tubes." These are hollow mud tunnels usually on the outside of home foundations or walls or support columns or even rising up unsupported from the ground to floor in crawl spaces.

• Get costs spelled out in advance—including the details and costs of posttreatment service, which might involve periodic inspections to make sure construction, planting, etc. have not cracked the long-life chemical barrier used to bar termites.

If you have any doubt about a firm's reputation or control techniques, check with your Better Business Bureau, Chamber of Commerce, county agricultural agent, or state agricultural college.

• Be sure to get a guarantee. This normally will specify that if termites are detected in annual inspections (usually limited to the first three years after treatment) follow-up treatment will be provided at no extra cost. Some agreements also include insurance policies guaranteeing payment to cover repair or replacement of any part of your home damaged by termites after completion of professional treatment. The term of these policies is usually three years, with maximum coverage normally $25,000.

SWIMMING POOL GYPS

This is still another category of home improvement which has become riddled with traps and problems for the homeowner. To illustrate with a classic "bait and switch":

You see an ad in your local newspaper for a sizable aboveground swimming pool costing only $499—with all the trimmings. But when you look over the pool the salesman tells you that the vinyl liner is not heavy enough to hold water, that the deck is not real redwood but only redwood stain, and that maintenance will cost you more each year than the sales price. He may not even have such a pool on hand. And, of course, the cost doesn't include delivery. However, perhaps you'd be interested in a larger pool, costing . . .

How do you avoid the swindlers and build a swimming pool intelligently?

First and foremost, recognize that most swimming pools are expensive, so don't expect to buy a deluxe kidney-shaped model at wading-pool prices.

Luxury "extras" can run into the thousands of dollars—and can include anything from special filtration systems and heating apparatus to telephone jacks and bathing cabanas with showers.

Other hidden costs of pools are property tax hikes if yours is a belowground pool, for this is a property improvement. Also you will pay for increases in your liability insurance in your homeowner's policy, for any pool is an invitation to accidents. In addition, if you finance your swimming pool, you'll pay high interest costs, of course. Then there will be increased water and electric bills.

But there is no disputing the money-saving angles too—such as the reduced costs of going to public or club pools, the fewer trips away from home for weekend vacations. And there's no dismissing the fact that a swimming pool enhances the value of your property.

Don't buy a swimming pool from a catalog. Take time to do some basic research, since this may be a big investment. Consult the literature of local Better Business Bureaus, the National Swimming Pool Institute (2000 K Street, Washington, D.C. 20006), or your regional swimming pool association. Find out what materials are sturdiest and most appropriate for the type of pool you want.

Check your zoning regulations. Almost all communities have rules covering fences, filters, drains, etc.

Get bids on the pool you want from two or three reputable local contractors whose credentials you have checked.

Understand what's covered by each bid and, of course, by the final contract. If there is a provision for a "normal" amount of excavation for an aboveground pool, just what does the contractor consider "normal"? Will fill be provided—or only leveling? What about the filtration and drainage systems?

Get a written timetable for the pool's construction or installation, but obey the fundamental rules on home improvements: never sign a completion form until all work has been completed, never give a pool salesman a check in his own name at the time of the sale, and don't pay in full before all work is completed.

Get a detailed guarantee in writing from the contractor and study not only what it provides but also who is responsible for fulfilling it. The guarantee should cover all labor, materials, the timetable, and optional equipment.

LANDSCAPING AND GARDENING TRAPS

In this area also the gypsters are giving homeowners an ever intensifying headache.

Tens of millions of you are now going in for home gardening and spending hundreds of millions of dollars a year on supplies alone. A single family, for instance, easily can spend hundreds (or thousands) in a year if it invests in such machinery as plows, minitractors, rototillers, elaborate lawn and garden sprinkler systems.

As a reflection of this boom—and a spur to it too—you will find a dazzling variety of landscaping specialists (qualified or unqualified), of nursery stock (both retail and mail order), of supplies of all kinds in hardware and garden supply stores. You also will, if you are not informed, be an easy target for the important fringe of deceivers and racketeers on all sides.

For instance, "Trees of Heaven" which "grow 50 feet high in just one year" may sound great in the advertisements—and grow they do. But among botanists this particular variety is nicknamed the "stink tree"—hardly one you'd like grow-ing in your back yard.

The "amazing climbing vine peach," a plant you're led to believe will grow a great crop of peaches, is alluring too. But actually this one bears only an inedible type of melon.

Then there are "miracle" multiple-fruit trees pictured as laden with several different varieties bursting forth simultaneously. The chances of matching the ads in real life at home are minuscule.

There are legions of utterly incompetent "tree surgeons" abroad in our land-scape who will come to your door and try to scare you by telling you your trees are infested with this or that insect or fungus. If you let them, they will carve up your healthy trees and spew useless pesticides on others—every move at fantastic prices.

There is the springtime humus racketeer. This swindler arrives in a truck at your door, offers an impressive-sounding topsoil to bring your garden back to life, and says that several bushels at $1.00 apiece should do the job.

You give him the go-ahead, turn back to your chores. Then he presents you with a bill from $200 to $300, claiming he has sprinkled hundreds of bushels of restorative substances on your lawn and threatening you with a lawsuit if you don't pay up. You have no way of knowing how much "humus" he actually has spread around and you're lucky if the stuff doesn't kill your lawn altogether.

And there are the gypsters who show up every year with a new miracle cure for your lawn. A typical example is one product recently marketed as a preparation to revive worn-out brown lawns. The stuff was a potion of green dye and fertil-izer which streaked and washed off with the first rain.

YOUR MAJOR WEAPONS AGAINST HOME INPROVEMENT RACKETEERS

To summarize your major weapons against the home improvement racketeers and fast-buck sharpsters:

• Beware of anybody who comes to your door and tells you he "just happens" to be in the neighborhood and "just happens" to have enough material left over to perform some job for you at bargain rates.

• Ask the salesman for his name and the name and address of his company. Demand his credentials. Then, in his presence, call the local banks and/or local Better Business Bureau to check out his reputation. Don't get talked into buying anything without checking your need, double-checking company prices, and tri-ple-checking the arrangements for future servicing.

• Ask to see other jobs the company has done.

• Don't fall for any form of high-pressure sales tactics and consider them a warning to you not to deal with their users.

• Be extra cautious about taking merchandise "on approval" from any un-known salesman.

• Watch out for any guarantee that a product such as siding or linoleum or car-peting will last twenty to thirty years. What company can guarantee you that it will even be in business thirty years from now?

But if you discover that you have been gypped by an unscrupulous contractor or by an incompetent odd-job man, howl—to your local Better Business Bureau, newspapers and radio stations, the state attorney general's office, the nearest consumer protection agency. See Chapter 28, "Know Your Rights!—and How to Use Them!" to show you how to extend the range of your indignation and get action.

If you're victimized, your yells may at least save others. And possibly you'll get help in forcing the individual who bilked you to make good on your deal.

How to Cut Costs Outside Your House

Even if you manage to sidestep all the landscape gyp artists and phony siding salesmen and gardening frauds, you still will be faced with the problem of how to shop for the goods and services you will need for the upkeep and beautification of the outside of your house.

HOW TO BUY LAWN AND GARDEN SUPPLIES

Here first are basic rules to guide you on buying garden supplies generally:

Plants and seeds: You won't get the gorgeous color results shown in catalogs unless you painstakingly follow directions in planting, fertilizing, thinning, and cultivating. You may not get any results if you live in a climate where certain plant varieties just can't be grown. Before you buy, read directions on packages of seeds and plants to see how much work and expertise are involved in growing them. Check, in seed catalogs, the number of days it takes each variety to mature. Ask your county agricultural agent for advice on what can be grown where.

Trees: These can run into big money and proper tree planting can take hours of your time and effort. On the other hand, improper planting easily can mean a total loss of your investment. Before you buy, make sure the tree will grow in your area. Follow directions precisely. Before you choose a type of tree, decide exactly what you want from it. Shade? Privacy? Spring blossoms? A color splash? Edible fruit? Then ask a qualified nursery which type will best fit your expectations. Or consult low-cost literature from the U. S. Department of Agriculture on various categories of trees and shrubs.

Fertilizer: Using inappropriate fertilizers can devastate your lawn or kill your vegetables and flowers. Ask your state agricultural experiment station to test your soil and recommend a fertilizer program for you—at little or no cost.

Sprinkler systems: Since this can be a very costly investment, deal only with a reputable firm which will not only install the system according to a plan but will also service it later. Insist on standard-sized pipes, valves, and sprinkler heads in case they need to be replaced later. Be sure the system will conform to local watering restrictions in summer months. Be wary of a company which asks for advance payment—often a sign that the firm is not soundly financed.

Lawns: Seek advice from a reputable dealer or from the U. S. Department of Agriculture on which products your lawn actually needs. A key warning, though: seed your lawn properly in the first place. Seeding can be an expensive operation, perhaps involving heavy machinery for grading and rolling, plus expert assistance —but it'll be worth it if you thereby avoid having to redo the whole job later.

HOW TO BUY A POWER LAWN MOWER

The average price of the basic walk-behind power mower is over $200. Add a thousand-plus to that figure for the monster riding job. The money-saving rules in this area are indeed important, therefore—and the number-one rule of them all is:

Buy out of season if possible, timing your purchase to preseason or postseason sales. And in season or off season, look for promotions which include free accessories with your mower.

In addition, in order to save money no matter when you buy:

Buy the size needed for your particular lawn—enough power and width of cut to do the job and no more. To illustrate: small lawn, 19-inch hand-propelled, lightweight, easily maneuvered; large lawn, 21-inch self-propelled; extra large lawn, only then consider a riding mower or a lawn and garden tractor.

Buy from a qualified retailer who, you have assured yourself, will provide proper service and replacement parts.

Choose a reputable brand-name mower to ensure quality and the service backup you'll need. Compare the quality features of various brands before you buy.

By no means buy on price alone. Comparison-shop for product and safety features too. The cheapest buy may be the most expensive because of its shorter life, more servicing, and fewer safety features—and the manufacturer and retailer guarantee must be considered a tangible part of the mower's price.

Buy only the essential features that suit your lawn's needs and yours. For instance, a self-propelled mower will be easier for older people to operate, while a mower with an electric starter will be especially appealing to women. Don't buy unnecessary attachments and thereby build up your mower's price.

Buy a mower with an Outdoor Power Equipment Institute (OPEI) safety seal on it. This seal, usually on the back of the mower, signifies that a model of that mower has been approved by an independent testing laboratory as meeting the power lawn mower safety specifications established by the American National Standards Institute.

Check your motor warranty with utmost care. It will be a vital factor in your long-range maintenance costs.

Curb—even slash—your maintenance costs by following closely the manufacturer's instructions in your owner's manual. Always operate the mower as prescribed. Do not abuse the mower. It is designed to cut grass, not brush, earth, or gravel.

To limit your power mower repairs, follow these rules for continuing maintenance: check the oil and fuel level before each mowing; keep the air cleaner clean; wash out the underside of the mower after each mowing; keep your entire mower clean and free of grass and dirt buildup. Follow these rules for periodic maintenance: check the blade for sharpness and balance; clean or repair spark plugs at least once a year; check belts and pulleys for adjustment; occasionally check all bolts for tightness; make repairs as soon as trouble appears; drain both oil and gas before storing your mower in the fall; have your mower tuned up annually by an authorized service center.

If you're among the millions who are buying new mowers each year, look for the certification label on the power mower from the Outdoor Power Equipment Institute. OPEI is the national trade association representing manufacturers producing 90 per cent of consumer walk-behind and riding lawn mowers, garden tractors, tillers, edger/trimmers, shredder/grinders, yard vacuums, leaf blowers, snow throwers, and gasoline engines for these products. The certification label attests that the product has met safety and laboratory testing standards.

How to Sell Your House

DO YOU HAVE THE KNOW-HOW?

In northern Westchester, New York, where I have a home, several of my close friends have sold their houses for the usual assortment of reasons. Some have sold through a real estate broker and paid the fees involved; others have gone the do-it-yourself route and saved the commissions. Still others are nagged by doubts over which course to follow.

If you're among the millions also planning to sell and debating the broker-or-no-broker question, ask yourself:

Do I have the expert know-how required to put my own home on the market, sell it within a reasonable period of time, and get good value for it?

Can I accurately appraise the value of a house—my own in particular—in today's market?

Can I handle the legal-financial complexities?

Do I know how to market my home and show it to its best advantage? Am I willing and able to devote the time and effort to do the job on my own?

If your own answer to these questions is yes, there are many good guides available at bookstores. Or send for a short, helpful booklet, called *For Sale by Owner,* written and published by Maine's Bureau of Consumer Protection. You can get a copy by sending $1.00 and your request to the Bureau of Consumer Protection, State House Office Building, Augusta, Maine 04333.

On the other hand, if you answered no to any of the above questions, then go the real estate broker route, for selling a home yourself can be time-consuming, frustrating, and net you less than you might have received with a broker's help. You actually may lose money because you can't judge your home's true value, don't grasp the legal and financial aspects, or don't have the sales know-how to realize a good profit within a reasonable—and reasonable is a key word—time.

But what if you decide to use a broker? How can you find one who will do a really first-rate job for you?

(1) Look at the broker's track record. And that record should include the broker's ability to advise you on financing, various mortgages, interest rates, laws and regulations affecting your sale, etc. Does the broker have a proven method of selling homes? A good reputation in your community?

(2) Does the broker belong to national, state, and local real estate boards and organizations? Which?

(3) Do the firm's sales associates have a strong foundation in real estate basics? Does the firm have a training program and ongoing education programs for its associates? Are the sales counselors dedicated career people?

(4) Can the broker evaluate a house for its good and bad points, then show it to its best advantage? And can the broker advise you on which improvements would add value to the property and which would not?

(5) Is the broker familiar with the community? Aware of social or economic problems which might affect the value of property? Able to provide information about schools, churches, shopping, transportation, cultural and sports activities, other areas?

(6) Does the broker have a method to screen clients to eliminate the uninterested or unqualified? Is the number of qualified buyers brought to the house adequate?

(7) Does the broker show a genuine concern for you, your needs in such areas as timing of your sale so you can fulfill other obligations you may have, getting proper financing arrangements that also meet your requirements, the like?

(8) If you are asking for—or really require—unusual service, is the broker able and willing to provide that extra care for which you will not pay any cash compensation?

(9) Do you have confidence that, with a broker, you will realize the maximum profit possible from what is probably the most valuable asset you now own or perhaps ever will own?

As any no answer to the first set of questions signaled a don't-do-it-yourself sale, so a positive yes to the most crucial of the second set of questions signals a use-a-broker technique. These are valuable guides for millions of you.

BASIC DO'S AND DON'TS

Selling your house, and particularly selling it at the top possible price, is not an easy job. But the efforts you, the homeowner, make—to get qualified advice on the worth of your house, to find a reputable real estate broker, to make the home repairs and improvements which will improve the terms of your sale and to avoid the ones which aren't worth it—can mean literally thousands of dollars to you when you actually sell.

Here are basic do's and don'ts on selling your house. Use them not only in selling your house but also as guidelines in repairing and remodeling it—with a view toward selling years hence.

Do consult one or more licensed real estate brokers, or Realtors, who are well informed on the values in your neighborhood and with whom you feel you can have an honest, open relationship.

There are three ways to list a home for sale: an exclusive right-to-sell listing, an open listing, and a multiple listing.

If you're in a hurry to sell, the exclusive right-to-sell listing contract is a good bet. With this kind of listing, you inform only one Realtor or broker of your home's availability and give him or her time to sell it. The broker then has the incentive to put a lot of effort into the sale.

If you are not in a hurry, you might choose an open listing, in which case you list the house with several brokers, each of whom may offer it to potential customers. The first one to find a buyer gets the commission. But with this type of listing, the incentive for each broker is lower, so the sale may take longer.

Or you may opt for the most common selling method, the multiple listing. You list the house with a single agent who in turn shares it with other co-operating brokers. He or she also shares the commission with whichever broker finds the buyer.

Do ask the Realtor to estimate the value of your house and, if you have any major disagreement on this score, check other brokers in your area for their opinions as well. (Or hire an independent appraiser whose fee may run $125 to $300 but could be well worth it if he or she can pinpoint the correct price range for your house.) Beware of the broker whose price estimate is thousands of dollars above the estimates of other brokers; he may simply be trying to get your listing and be utterly incapable of delivering a buyer at this estimated price later.

Don't make the mistake of asking a much higher price for your house than it's worth. If you do this, the salesman may lose interest in selling your house and the house may remain unsold for months or years.

According to one estimate, if the sale price you set is within 5 per cent of its actual fair market value you are ten times more likely to sell it within a reasonable period of time than if you price it 15 to 20 per cent above the fair market value. A good policy is to set your price about 5 to 10 per cent above the amount your Realtor considers fair—and bargain from there.

Do view your house with as much cold objectivity as you can muster. Try to see it—and its faults—as if you were the buyer rather than the seller. This will not only help you in arriving at a realistic price range but also give you clues on what repairs should be made.

Do invest in minor improvements both inside and outside the house, such as repairing cracks in the plaster, washing dirty walls, doing a limited amount of painting, fixing broken tiles and leaky faucets, replacing ripped screens, etc. If it's summertime and the house feels like an oven, it may be worthwhile to invest in a secondhand room air conditioner. Often $100 spent for such improvements can return $1,000 in your sale price.

Don't, though, "overinvest," in, say, new additions to the house or a complete kitchen modernization job. It may turn out that prospective buyers would have designed these improvements entirely differently and your investment might go down the drain.

Do ask your Realtor to make appointments with you for showing the house to prospective buyers, so that the customer won't have to wade through an accumulation of the week's laundry or an obstacle course of children's toys. Make sure, when a prospective buyer visits, that the house is neat and clean—particularly the kitchen, living room, and bathrooms, which are the most important rooms to most buyers. Also make sure the house is well lighted when it is being inspected and keep your lawn and garden reasonably trim in summer and walkways cleared of snow and ice in winter.

Do whatever you can to warm up the atmosphere of your house—by having a fire going in the fireplace, arranging the porch or outdoor furniture attractively, putting a few flowers around.

Do prepare a couple of pages of basic facts about your house and property which you or your agent can give to would-be buyers. Sample data sheets might, for instance, mention the favorable location to schools, shopping center, bus stops or train; the number of closets, extra storage areas; special financing possibilities; landscaping; other favorable aspects.

Don't interfere with the broker and client while they're going through the house. Get lost if you can; otherwise just "sit down and shut up." Don't have any music playing during the inspection; your choice of music easily could distract or offend the visitor. And don't permit noisy children and dogs to accost your customer.

Do, if today's interest rates are a major barrier to a sale and you have a lower-rate mortgage, consider acting as the lender yourself by arranging to transfer the existing mortgage on your house to the buyer. Consider, too, extending a second mortgage to help make up the difference in the amount owed you at the same interest rates being charged by your local bank or other lender.

Do recognize the importance of final settlement costs on any house in the $30,000 and up range.

WHEN YOU MOVE

THE AGONIES OF MOVING

Dave was notified at Christmas of his promotion and transfer across the country to a new job. He and Kay then sold their house and in effect simply wasted time until the date he had told the company he would be ready: June 25.

By this decision, Dave and Kay wasted money as well as time, and all because they followed the outmoded U.S. tradition of summertime moving.

Of all the millions of American families who move each year, more than 60 per cent move between June 1 and September 20. To cope with this rush, the moving industry must operate on a twenty-four-hour basis and in this period it charges maximum prices.

But there's no doubt that many of these millions would be better off with a non-summer move. In spring, in fall, in winter they would get more efficient and quicker service; they should be charged a minimum, not a maximum rate; their moves would be safer too.

Although the proportion of families moving every year is one out of five, the proportion in the twenty-two to twenty-four age bracket is nearly 50 per cent; for newly married Americans, the mobility rate is a fantastic 84 per cent; and for executives in their thirties the rate soars to 97 per cent!

We are moving from city to suburb to exurb. We are congregating as never before in the nation's congested population belts along the east and west coasts. We are moving from east to west.

And millions of us are moving overseas—at least temporarily—to work for the government or for the great companies and industries doing business around the world.

Many young Americans, and particularly those whose jobs involve frequent transfers, now live in a dozen or more houses and apartments over the course of their lifetime.

Moving always has been one of the biggest and costliest agonies a family goes through. Almost always, the expenses turn out to be greater than expected; goods are often delivered late; when they are delivered, they often are damaged or important items are missing altogether. There's only a fifty-fifty chance that you'll be satisfied with your next move.

How you, the individual or family being transported, handle the move can make all the difference between a nightmare and a smooth, businesslike transaction.

Thus, to guide you when you move, here are basic rules for cutting costs, choosing a reliable mover, preventing and insuring losses—plus other vital and money-saving pointers on moving.

HOW TO CUT YOUR MOVING COSTS

• Find out which costs, if any, your or your spouse's employer will pay toward the move. Some companies today offer these fringe benefits to key employees being transferred to another location—above and beyond payment of direct moving expenses:

> buying a house the employee is unable to sell;
>
> helping to track down a suitable house at the new location;
>
> providing temporary household help at both the old and the new homes during the moving period;
>
> paying points added to the basic interest rate on new mortgages;
>
> paying the family's travel expenses to the new location—and also paying the costs of family excursions, before the move, to explore the new town or city;
>
> even assuming the costs of moving such things as boats, second cars, cats and dogs, and other "difficult items" (although they have been known to balk at paying for moving woodpiles, compost heaps, and flagstones from the patio).

If you are moving abroad, most major companies will pay the full costs of housing, feeding, and transporting your whole family during the usual three-to-six-week period between the time the employee must vacate his home and the time he is able to line up a house or apartment abroad.

Many companies provide special allowances to employees being transferred abroad to pay any costs above those prevailing in the United States—plus other allowances for such special expenses as storage of household belongings, foreign language courses, and adapting appliances to electrical systems abroad.

• If at all possible avoid scheduling your move between June and the end of September. The best times to move, instead, are between mid-October and mid-

May and during the second or third week of the month. Try also to give the mover at least thirty to forty-five days' notice and some choice of moving days. Try not to schedule your move on the first or last day of the month—the most active moving days, when many leases expire.

Simply by timing your move so it doesn't fall during peak months and days, you'll save 10 to 15 per cent on some carriers and also get far more efficient service. The tradition of the summer move dates back to an era when vacations were almost always a summer affair and the United States was an agriculture-oriented economy. It has been rooted in the belief that it is bad to transfer children during a school year.

But new staggered school terms permit far more flexibility in transfers than ever before, and there is even an argument in favor of moving children during a school year. Many educators now believe that a midterm change can be mentally and socially stimulating, compared with having to spend a lonely summer in a strange neighborhood. Children can acquire new friends easily in a school environment, but during summer vacation there are few sources beyond next-door neighbors.

• Before getting estimates, get rid of stuff you won't need or want in your new home. This is especially important if yours is a long-distance move in which costs are based largely on weight. (Sample: heavy old appliances.)

If you are moving only to another part of town, send out your furniture for repairs or reupholstering and your rugs and drapes for cleaning, then have the articles delivered to your new home.

If your attic is loaded with junk accumulated over the years, consider advertising items of interest in the local newspaper—and see if anybody turns up to make an offer on them. If you're dubious about people's interest in what you may consider pure junk, just take a look at what's being sold today in "antique" shops, secondhand stores, and auctions.

Or, as an alternative, stage your own "garage sale." Such an event can earn you some change and can be amusing as well.

HOW TO CHOOSE A MOVER

There are four types of household moves; local, intrastate, interstate, and international. All major national carriers are usually in a position to have their local agent handle all four types.

• On a long-distance move, inquire about the reputations of movers at your destination as well as your present location. Ask friends, neighbors, and business associates who have moved recently to steer you to a reliable carrier. And your local County or State Consumer Protection Agency can at least tell you if there have been many complaints about a mover with whom you are consider doing business.

• Then ask at least two or three movers to come to your house and estimate costs. Show each all of your belongings to be moved. Don't forget the attic, basement, garage, or even summer cottage. Be sure to point out all the heaviest items you'll want to move. Refuse to let a mover take an inventory over the phone. A reputable mover depends on an accurate estimate to know how many shipments will fit in the van.

Find out exactly which services each mover would include in the deal—and how much each would charge.

Do not, however, award the job to any one mover strictly on the basis of the cost estimate. An unrealistically low estimate is a "low ball"—and it is used by unscrupulous movers as well as unreliable repairmen simply to get the job away from others who stick to more realistic figures. Similarly, a mover's vague claim that he is "bonded" or "certified" or "insured" may be no guarantee to you of his reliability.

• Make sure any mover who is making estimates for you gives you the very helpful Interstate Commerce Commission pamphlet entitled *Summary of Information for Shippers of Household Goods,* outlining your rights and obligations as well as the mover's. Interstate carriers must give you a very useful booklet called *Loss and Damage of Household Goods—Prevention and Recovery.*

• Normally, movers do not quote flat rates. In most cases, long-distance movers are regulated by federal and state law. The amount you pay depends on the amount of weight of your shipment and the distance to be shipped. A local mover may charge for his travel time between his base and your house and the number of hours it takes to perform the special services you require such as packing.

• Explore alternatives to the professional mover to reduce the cost of moving. If you have only a relatively small collection of not too valuable belongings and also have the time to supervise the move fairly closely, a one-man panel van variety of mover may be fine. But be on guard: this business is loaded with fly-by-nights, and if you deal with a small, unknown outfit, you do so strictly at your own risk, particularly on a long-distance move.

Every time you make a trip to inspect your new house or community, take at least a few things with you in your car—especially paintings, sculptures, lamp-shades, bric-a-bracs which otherwise would have to be specially crated.

Of course, you can always rent a haul-it-yourself truck or trailer, which you can now get in almost any size and shape—if you have the time, energy, and skill to do the whole moving job yourself. Between 10 and 15 per cent of Americans who move do so themselves on short moves—often at savings of 50 per cent or more—and the number of do-it-yourselfers is increasing steadily.

The cost of renting a large truck ranges upward from $25 a day, plus 17 cents per mile, plus the cost of gas and insurance. Some rental companies today provide, for a fee, special pads, packing boxes, etc., plus instructions on how to use them to their best advantage.

Key points to check on before you rent a trailer or van include:

What surcharge, if any, will be levied at your destination for the return of the vehicle?

What type and how much insurance is provided in case of accident or damage to your belongings?

What happens if the rental van breaks down on the road?

What are the costs of "extras" you might need: the furniture pads, packing boxes, hand trucks, the like? Or are any or all of these free?

How large a deposit will you have to make at the outset and will you have to pay cash for the remainder of what you owe at your destination?

HOW TO PREVENT AND INSURE LOSSES

Interstate movers are responsible for damages or losses only up to 60 cents per pound per article. However, the 60-cents-a-pound liability limit won't be much consolation if you find your set of Meissen china in smithereens when it arrives.

• So if your belongings are worth more than this, which they almost surely are, declare a realistic total value of the goods being shipped—and pay the extra charge of 50 cents for each $100 of value you declare for full added value protection.

If you neither accept the 60-cents-per-pound liability limit nor declare the actual value of your shipment, the mover's liability limit is automatically $1.25 per pound—for the same 50 cents per $100.

It is quite possible, though, that your homeowner's insurance policy covers your belongings while they are being moved—and if so, there may be no need to get any additional coverage for the move. Or, if your employer is absorbing the costs of your move, he may have special insurance policies to cover you. Or you may be able to have a rider added to your homeowner's policy to cover your move at lower cost than the extra expense of full coverage through the mover.

• If your belongings must be stored, ask that they be held on a "storage in transit" basis. Otherwise, the mover may not be considered responsible for damage occurring in storage.

• Your key area in which to compare charges—and achieve savings—is in what movers call "accessorial charges." These are for such services as packing, unpacking, furnishing containers, lugging pianos up and down steps, etc. The charge for these is on a "per unit" or "per service" basis and must be separately itemized. Thus, you need not pay for unpacking unless you ordered it.

• To save time and confusion, have appropriate servicemen disconnect and service appliances such as refrigerators, room air conditioners, washing machines, stereo sets—as well as your telephone and electricity—before the movers arrive. Unhooking such items needs an expert hand and this is generally your responsibility.

Also among your responsibilities: moving small items of relatively great value, such as jewelry, coin and stamp collections, furs, the contents of your safe-deposit box. Your bank may be able to advise you on special courier services specializing in transporting such valuables.

• Save money by doing at least some of the packing yourself. Movers generally will sell you containers at $2.50 or so apiece, cartons at 75 cents each, and large cardboard wardrobes for about $4.25. (Or you can get cartons free from grocery and liquor stores.) You are usually responsible if what you have packed is damaged in transit. In any event, be sure to let the movers pack such tricky items as large mirrors, appliances, and fine cabinets.

• When packing, make your own detailed inventory of your belongings. You won't have time to do it on moving day, and the one the driver makes may be incomplete. It will be a big job, but invaluable in the event of a loss.

• Make sure each carton is marked with a list of contents—or fitted with color-coded tags corresponding to each room in your new home. Try to categorize your belongings so only one or two boxes must be labeled "miscellaneous." Then, as your possessions are being unloaded, have them put as near as possible to where you ultimately will want them. Or make a sketch of the floor plan of your new home, with notations on which items should be put where—and give a copy to the mover. This will save you the energy and high cost of hiring somebody else to help you shove them around from room to room later. And mark one box "load last." This is the box containing things you'll need immediately when you arrive —e.g., sheets, towels, toiletries, light bulbs, baby food, etc.

• When your goods are picked up, the van driver or other representatives of the mover will make a written inventory of everything you are having shipped—with notes on items which are "marred and scarred." Ask for a copy of the complete form, and be sure you understand the code letters on it. Check this inventory carefully and if you have any disagreement with it, note the disagreements on the inventory. (An unscrupulous mover may mark everything as marred and scratched at the beginning—to remove the chance of any blame for damage at the end.)

• Be on hand to supervise delivery. Plan to check each item as it is unpacked against the inventory. Be sure, also, that the bill of lading indicates the agreed-upon pickup and delivery dates and times, the estimated shipping costs and other charges, and any special arrangements you have made with the mover.

OTHER MONEY-SAVING POINTERS

• Do not tip your mover. Tipping is illegal in any interstate move and in most states. Report any pressure for tipping to the Interstate Commerce Commission, Washington, D.C. 20423.

• Make sure the pickup and delivery dates, and all other agreements between you and the carrier, appear on the "order and service" as well as the bill of lading. By law, interstate movers must deliver your goods during a span of several consecutive days to which you have agreed. Legally, they may not deliver your goods early. Fines up to $500 may be imposed for any infraction of ICC rules.

• By law, each shipment must be weighed on certified scales—and if you, the customer, want to witness the weighing, you have the right to do so. The order for service must include the location of the scales. So if you have any doubts whatsoever about the weight of your shipment, request a reweigh—witnessed by you. This will cost you nothing if the mover is off target or attempting to cheat you by more than 120 pounds or 25 per cent of the estimated weight, whichever is less. At the weighing scale, be on the alert for the unethical practice of weighing the empty truck with an empty gasoline tank and loaded truck with a full tank. The Interstate Commerce Commission has estimated that the weight on one shipment out of ten is illegally bumped to increase the charges paid by the shipper. If you suspect that the weight on your shipment is not correct do not hesitate to request a reweigh *before* the shipment is unloaded.

• Give the mover a telephone number and address where you can be reached if necessary while your shipment is in transit. Also, get the driver's name, van number, shipment number, and intended route in case you need to trace the shipment through the mover's home office.

• Make every effort to beat the van to your new home. Otherwise, you'll risk an extra charge for the delay beyond the "free waiting time" permitted on interstate moves.

• Be prepared to pay by cash, money order, traveler's check, certified or cashier's check when the moving van arrives at its destination. Personal checks are generally not accepted. Don't obtain the entire amount of your estimated moving charges in check form unless you know definitely what the final charge will be. You might find yourself overpaying the mover and having to wait 60 to 120 days for your change. Instead, get a cashier's check for 75 to 80 per cent of the estimated moving charges and cash or traveler's checks for the balance. If you cannot come up quickly with the required amount of cash or an acceptable substitute, the mover will put all your goods in storage at your expense—and also charge you additional sums to transport the goods from the warehouse back to your house.

By law, movers must estimate how much money customers must have at the time of delivery if requested to do so by the customer. Movers may require their customers to pay no more than the estimated cost plus 10 per cent before unloading shipments if the customer requests delivery on this basis. And according to the ICC rules, a mover must advise you of the actual weight and charges on your shipment as soon as the shipment is weighed and billed if you request this notification at the time an estimate is prepared. If you request delivery or payment of the estimated charges plus 10 per cent, you have fifteen business days in which to come up with the money to cover the balance due.

• Get a receipt (or "freight bill") for the amount you actually pay. This also states the weight of your shipment, mileage, the rate per 100 pounds, and the charges for transportation, added value protection, other special services which have been performed.

• If any loss or damage has occurred in transit to any of your belongings, note details on the mover's inventory of your shipment or on the delivery receipt at the time of delivery. This notation is probably your best evidence to support a claim you may later make in a letter to the home office of the carrier. Also point out the damages or missing items to the mover before he leaves your house. Check the truck yourself for any items may have been left inside it.

In filing a claim, list lost and damaged articles separately, plus estimates of costs of repairs or replacement. Include expenses caused by delays or losses, such as hotel or motel bills. Also, give the other basic facts such as the date of the move, the weight and destination of the shipment, and the mover's order number.

Movers, incidentally, are required by law to acknowledge your claim within 30 days and to "pay, decline, or make firm compromise settlement offer" within 120 days of the date on which the claim was received.

Normally, you may file claims up to nine months after the delivery date.

Your best bet, if a mover welshes on any part of the deal he has made, is to call the nearest ICC office and ask for advice. Or get in touch with the ICC's Bureau of Operations (Washington, D.C. 20423).

Finally, remember these other points which are closely related to most moves:

Have a bank and insurance agent lined up at your new destination.

Get the rules and forms, if you are moving to another state, for switching over your automobile license and registration—and find out what the automobile insurance and inspection rules are.

Get a free "change of address kit" from any post office and use it to advise friends, banks, utilities, newspaper and magazine publishers, creditors, and other appropriate individuals of your new address and phone number—well in advance of your move.

Ask your physician and dentist for advice on physicians and dentists in your new location—or check with the local or county medical society there for names of qualified medical personnel (consult, also pages 431–522 on the costs of good health, for hints on how to shop for physicians, dentists, and other medical services).

Arrange for the transfer of your medical and dental records and the prescriptions for your eyeglasses.

If you are taking prescription drugs, make sure you have an ample supply when you move.

Arrange with local utilities and service people at your new home to have your telephone, electricity, appliances, etc. turned on before, or shortly after, you arrive.

FORGOTTEN: HOUSING FOR THE ELDERLY

More than thirty years ago, the original 1949 Housing Act set as a national goal "a decent home and a suitable living environment for every American family." And despite conspicuous exceptions within minority groups and a housing crash during the mid 1970s, a decent home has indeed become reality for virtually every major segment of the U.S. population.

The one glaring exception: our elderly.

• Nearly 12 per cent of our elderly lived in housing officially classified as substandard as the 1980s neared, a proportion 50 per cent higher than that in the overall population. Among aged blacks, one in four lives in substandard housing (lacking adequate plumbing), about twice the proportion for whites.

• For every elderly American living in a sunny retirement village or acceptable apartment building, at least three more live in squalor, unsafe buildings, back bedrooms in rooming houses, urban ghettos, outmoded or isolated houses in small towns or rural areas.

• Even in cities trying hard to meet the housing needs of the elderly, the waiting period for decent shelters may be five to ten years or more—forcing many simply to stop applying.

Mounting numbers are being trapped—between soaring home ownership and maintenance costs, property valuations and property taxes on one side and the unavailability of less expensive, more appropriate types of housing on the other. Aged homeowners paid an average of 8 per cent of their income for real estate taxes alone in the late 1970s, versus 3.4 per cent for the typical city family of four, and the burden is heaviest on lowest-income families.

Rents have been climbing everywhere, along with property taxes. The average older American spends more than one third of his or her income on housing, against 23 per cent budgeted by younger families, and for the poorest, the share is higher. More than two out of three older Americans with annual incomes below $3,000—almost 1.5 million households—pay 35 per cent or more of their incomes for rent alone. Many pay 60 to 80 per cent!

A first key problem is that because shelter is a fixed, untouchable expense, millions are now being compelled to cut their food consumption, to reduce or eliminate important medications, to give up trips to see friends, grandchildren, movies, certainly to forget new clothes.

A second little-recognized problem for the elderly is built-in physical barriers to freedom and mobility within their own homes. Every year, hundreds of thousands aged sixty-five or over become disabled within their own homes because of injuries and tens of thousands die from accidents under their own roofs.

Such minor obstacles as steps put a majority of the nation's offices, other workplaces, public transportation, and churches—as well as houses and apartments—off limits to countless numbers of elderly citizens. Housing which really satisfies the elderly's needs must be equipped with such features as special ramps for wheelchairs and walkers, railings, and bathroom grab bars.

A third vital but drastically underplayed problem is that of loneliness and isolation. Nearly one in four elderly Americans lives alone, and fully half of all widows and widowers live alone. Grandparents have been squeezed out of the family house by trends toward smaller houses and separation of generations. Grandparents are reluctant to be baby-sitters and their children are reluctant to be grandparent-sitters.

For literally millions, their cramped, dilapidated houses and apartments have become prisons of loneliness. This chilling account of the isolation of so many of our elderly in our era was given in a report in the 1970s by the Senate Special Committee on Aging:

"More than one social worker has told us of visits to dwellings . . . (where) an elderly person had died, unnoticed by his neighbors, forgotten by his family. And many elderly couples or single persons . . . live almost entirely within their own walls, overwhelmed by illness, despair, or fear of crime."

In Conclusion

This chapter is intended to help you make major housing decisions wisely. But your housing education shouldn't end here, for the more you learn the more you'll save. Among the best sources of additional information are government publications, and chief among these is the Department of Agriculture yearbook, *Handbook for the Home*. It is available for a modest price from the Superintendent of Documents, Washington, D.C. 20402. Another but much more expensive source is *Houses: The Illustrated Guide to Construction, Design and Systems*

(National Association of Realtors, 155 East Superior Street, Chicago, Illinois 60611); also *The Complete Book of Home Buying: A Consumer's Guide to Today's Inflationary Housing Market* by Michael Sumichrast and Ronald Shafer (Dow-Jones Books, 22 Cortlandt Street, New York, New York 10007, $11.95).

6

FAMILY'S ENERGY-SAVING GUIDE

INTRODUCTION

Did you know that if you are a careful automobile driver, you can get at least 30 per cent more mileage than the average driver, 50 per cent more than the wasteful one? Or, that more than half the energy you use in your home goes for heating and cooling—of which heating water alone takes a giant 15 per cent? Or, that if you live in an all-electric home, about 23 per cent of your total electric bill goes for water heating . . . and if you live in a non-electrically heated home, an awesome 41 per cent of your total electric bill is traceable to your electric water heater alone? Or, that a big-ticket appliance, which is more expensive initially, may cost you less over a period of years than a cheaper product just because the initially more expensive item is also more energy-efficient?

Possibly you did—but whatever your answer, I am taking for granted that you *do* know that at 55 miles per hour, most cars get about 21 per cent more miles per gallon than at 70 mph; you *do* know that you can save on gas by avoiding stop-and-go traffic and minimizing braking; you *do* know you save energy merely by turning off all lights when not needed and being sensibly restrained in your use of ornamental lights for Christmas and other occasions. Not so widely publicized or so obvious are these other energy and money-saving hints:

HEATING (AND COOLING) YOUR HOME

By now, you must be acutely aware of how much energy you can save for yourself and your nation by proper insulation of your home—including the attic and walls. You also must have been told repeatedly that on top of saving as much as 20–30 per cent by effective insulation, you can slash your energy costs another 10 per cent or more by caulking and weatherstripping your doors and windows. Common sense alone must convince you to close off unoccupied rooms and turn off the heat or air conditioning in these rooms. Of course, what applies to heating your home applies with equal importance to cooling it. I shall, therefore, add merely one warning: Insulate your home against heat and cold now! In addition:

(1) Have your furnace serviced once every year, preferably right now. A needed but not obvious adjustment could save you as much as 10 per cent in your fuel consumption.

(2) If you need a new furnace, buy one that includes an automatic flue gas damper, which reduces heat loss when your furnace is not in operation.

(3) Make sure your furnace is the right size for your needs and avoid wasting energy by buying any unit that is larger than you need.

(4) Clean or replace filters on heating or cooling equipment every thirty days. Clogged filters make your systems work harder and less efficiently.

(5) If you use electric heating, consider a "heat pump" system, which uses outside air in both heating and cooling; it can slash your use of electricity for heating by 60 per cent or more.

(6) Vacuum or dust your radiator surfaces frequently.

(7) In addition to insulating the obvious areas, insulate your hot-water storage tank and piping.

(8) Install storm windows and doors, both at moderate costs. Double glass also helps insulate your home against heat as well as cold. Combination screen and storm windows are desirable because you need not remove them during the hot-weather months. Equally effective in cold weather, and at a total cost for the average home of only $10, would be a sheet of clear plastic film tightly taped to the inside of the window and door frames. You might prefer this low-cost energy saver if you're renting the house. Either type of protection could cut your fuel costs by about 15 per cent.

(9) In winter climates, lower your thermostat to 68° during the day, 60° at night. If these settings reduce your home's temperature an average of six degrees, you will cut your heating costs about 15 per cent. An extra blanket or electric blanket will help you control your nighttime heating needs. Buy a clock thermostat that will automatically turn your heat down at a regular hour before you go to bed and turn it up at your usual wake-up time. In hot-weather climates, set your air-conditioning thermostat no lower than a reasonably comfortable, energy-efficient 78°. If this setting raises your home's temperature six degrees (from 72 to 78), your home-cooling costs should drop an estimated 47 per cent! Avoid constant fiddling with your thermostat setting. Frequent changes in winter cause excessive operating costs and require increased energy to reheat a space. In summer, though, if you plan to be away for several days, turn off your air conditioning and ask a friend to turn it back on several hours before you return.

(10) Locate your thermostat away from the windows, doors, and possible drafts so that it won't keep your furnace running when the rest of the house is sufficiently warm.

(11) Since warm air rises, make sure all openings to your attic are well sealed so that heat doesn't escape to non-living areas.

(12) Always tightly close the chimney damper when your fireplace is not in use. Otherwise, as much as 20 per cent of your heated or cooled air will be wasted up the chimney. Consider fireplace glass enclosures.

(13) Run your air conditioners only on really hot days and set the fan speed at

high. In humid weather, set the fan at low speed to remove more moisture; this makes you comfortable with less cooling.

(14) In addition to cleaning or replacing air-conditioner filters at least once a month (dirty filters require more electricity to turn the fan), carefully vacuum-clean accessible parts of your air-conditioning equipment.

(15) Avoid spending money to buy more cooling capacity than you need to do the job. Energy-efficient ratios (EERs) are available for most air-conditioning units (the higher the EER, the more efficient the conditioner).

(16) Use draperies and curtains not only for decoration, but also for saving energy. Open drapes wide during winter days to let in the sun, then close them at night to prevent heat loss that can amount up to as much as 30 per cent. In warm weather, close drapes and curtains to keep out heat from the sun (that can swell your air-conditioning needs by up to 50 per cent). The use of lined or insulated draperies can also reduce energy consumption. Lower and raise your window shades and blinds according to the same common-sense rules.

(17) Keep curtains from covering baseboard heaters and wall registers. If necessary, devise practical deflectors out of aluminum foil to move the heat away from the drapes (which don't need it) and into the rooms (which do).

(18) Remove tops from boxed radiators to release maximum heat; replace with grillwork if the bare appearance offends your aesthetic sensibilities.

(19) Guard against wasting heat by keeping your doors open any length of time in winter while you say good night to your guests. Say your goodbyes *before* you open the doors. Keep all windows and outside doors closed as much as possible to hold warm air in your house.

(20) Install a humidifier-furnace or console type. It makes the air feel warmer so you can be comfortable with less heat. A dehumidifier can be just as helpful in hot weather, maintaining comfort at higher temperature levels.

(21) When entertaining a large group during holiday and winter seasons, lower the thermostat a degree or two before the guests arrive. People generate heat.

IN THE KITCHEN

(1) Use your automatic dishwasher (if you have one) instead of washing dishes by hand. If you do hand-wash, stopper the sink or use a dishpan. A running-water wash or rinse will use about 30 gallons of water per meal, while a full dishwasher cycle consumes 11 to 16 gallons.

(2) Fill the dishwasher—but don't overload it—before you turn it on. An average dishwasher uses 14 gallons of hot water per load; if every dishwasher user in the United States eliminated just one load a week, we would save the equivalent of about 9,000 barrels of oil each day—or enough to heat 140,000 homes during the winter.

(3) Scrape dishes before loading them in the washer. When rinsing is necessary—which is seldom—use cold water.

(4) Let your dishes dry in the air. After the final rinse, turn off the dishwasher

and open the door. If you turn off the dry cycle, you can save 45 per cent of the energy consumed by your dishwasher.

(5) Clean dishwasher filters frequently.

(6) Use cold running water only in your food waste disposer. Cold water congeals fats, greases, and oils into solid particles and flushes them safely down the drain. Run the cold water for a few seconds before and about 30 seconds after operating the disposal.

(7) Before deciding on whether to buy a refrigerator/freezer that defrosts automatically or must be naturally defrosted, note that the manual appliances not only cost less but also consume less energy. If yours must be manually defrosted, though, defrost at least twice a month so that frost never is allowed to build up to more than one quarter of an inch. Defrost your freezer at least once a year.

(8) Place your refrigerator/freezer in a cool location for maximum efficiency. Avoid placing it against an uninsulated wall facing the sun, for such a location will make your appliance work harder and thereby consume more energy.

(9) Check seals around your refrigerator and freezer doors to make sure they are airtight. If they're not, adjust the latch or replace the seal. An easy way to check the condition of gaskets on refrigerator and freezer doors is to place a dollar bill against the frame and close the door on it. If the bill can be pulled out with a gentle tug—or, if the bill drops out—the gasket needs replacement or the door requires adjustment.

(10) Open your refrigerator and freezer doors as seldom as possible; store perishable foods on shelves rather than in the door to avoid contact with the warm air. Plan ahead and remove all ingredients for each meal at one time to avoid unnecessary door openings.

(11) While most freezers operate more economically when fully loaded, don't overcrowd your refrigerator so as to interfere with circulation of air and thus allow developments of "hot pockets."

(12) Remove excess store wrappings from foods before placing in refrigerator or freezer. Paper acts as insulation.

(13) At least twice a year, move both your refrigerator and freezer, disconnect the plugs and carefully vacuum the coils and compressor to remove all energy-wasting dust.

(14) If you will be away for an extended period, empty your refrigerator, disconnect it from the power outlet, clean it thoroughly and leave the door open. If you will be away only a few days, raise the refrigerator's temperature setting slightly to compensate for the reduction in times the door will be opened.

(15) To reduce cooking time, completely thaw frozen meats and remove all meats from the refrigerator at least an hour before cooking.

(16) Cook by time and temperature and restrain yourself from opening the oven door repeatedly or peeking under the lids during surface cooking. "Peeking" merely wastes energy. When you are roasting meat, a meat thermometer will help you prevent overcooking and avoid unnecessary waste of energy.

(17) Preheat your oven no longer than 10–12 minutes. Preheating any longer just wastes energy.

(18) If you're using the oven for a meal, plan an all oven-cooked meal (for instance, a meat loaf with baked potatoes), or fill the oven with other foods that can be used at a later time with a bit of heating. After the oven is off, use leftover heat to warm plates or heat rolls.

(19) When feasible, prepare meals with small appliances, such as frypans, broilers, etc. These require less energy than your range.

(20) Use heat-treated glass or ceramic pots and pans in a conventional oven, to enable you to lower the heat by up to 25 degrees without sacrificing efficiency.

(21) If cooking with water, use a minimal amount so your food can heat fast.

(22) Once boiling begins, reduce the heat of a surface unit. High heat settings only make the water evaporate faster.

(23) Use a steamer or pressure cooker to cook several foods simultaneously, when possible. If your pressure cooker has partition inserts, cook three or four different items at once; you can save heat, energy, time, and money.

(24) Select pots and pans that have absolutely flat bottoms that cover each burner. More heat then enters the pot and less is lost to the surrounding air.

(25) Match the pots and pans to the size of each of your surface units. If a pot is too small for the unit extra heat will escape. Put your pots and pans on the range before the heat is turned on to avoid wasting energy.

(26) Use tight lids on your pots and pans to keep the heat inside.

(27) Check your range to see whether it produces a pure blue flame or a yellow flame. Yellow indicates improper energy-wasting combustion. Have the range adjusted. Also, be sure the pilot light is not consuming more energy than necessary.

(28) Keep the heat reflector below the stove heaters clean, so you get the maximum reflection of heat.

(29) Turn off your electric range just before cooking is finished to make use of residual heat to finish the job and keep the food warm until serving.

(30) Check oven door seal for air tightness just as you check seals on your refrigerator and freezer doors.

(31) When activating the self-cleaning cycle on an electric oven, start the cycle right after cooking, while oven is still hot.

(32) Recycle all your non-returnable aluminum containers, for it takes one third of a cup of oil or its fuel equivalent to produce each can.

(33) Consider purchase of electronic (or microwave) ovens designed for fast preparation of meals. These ovens can slash consumption of electricity 50 to 75 per cent compared with standard electric ranges. But proper care and use of these ovens is imperative for your safety (see page 119), and only qualified technicians should be permitted to repair them.

(34) Try to concentrate use of all your kitchen appliances in off-hours—late evening, early morning—to help lighten the burden on the country's electric utilities and their need to use back-up generating equipment that is not energy efficient.

IN THE BATHROOM

(1) Install a flow restrictor (available at most plumbing supply stores) in the pipe at the showerhead to limit the flow of water to an entirely adequate four gallons per minute. This will save you large amounts of hot water and the energy used to heat it. Installation is easy.

(2) Take more showers and fewer tub baths. An average tub bath uses 10–15 gallons of hot water, against 8–12 gallons for a shower bath of under five minutes' duration. A quick shower will use less than half as much hot water as a bath in a regular-size tub.

(3) Impress upon your teenagers (who tend to stay in the shower longer, thus using more hot water) that hot water equals energy equals expense—and that shorter showers are now family policy.

(4) Tell your husband not to waste hot water by keeping the faucet running as he shaves. He can pour as much as six gallons of hot water down the drain during a five-minute shave. Make him close the sink drain while he shaves.

IN BOTH KITCHEN AND BATHROOM

(1) Use bath and kitchen ventilating fans only as needed.

(2) Repair any and all leaky faucets—particularly hot water faucets—as quickly as possible. Hot water wasted by dripping faucets costs you money, probably much more than you dream of. Following are typical examples of how much hot water and electricity you can waste through leaky faucets:

DROPS PER MINUTE	GALLONS PER MONTH	KWH PER MONTH	COST* PER MONTH
60	192	48	1.68
90	310	78	2.73
120	429	107	3.75

* Cost based on a very low, now unrealistic, 3.5 cents per kilowatt hour [KWH].

A pinhole leak can waste up to 170 gallons a day; a fast drip, 970 gallons a day; a toilet leak, up to 3,000 gallons a day!

IN THE "FAMILY" OR TV ROOM

(1) "Instant-on" television sets, especially the tube types, use energy even when the screen is dark, so eliminate this waste by plugging the set into an outlet controlled by a wall switch—and turn the set on and off with the switch. Or ask your TV serviceman to install an additional on-off switch on the set itself or in the cord to the outlet. (Of course, turn off any TV set when you have finished viewing.)

(2) Apply the same turn-off rule to any and all radios in use.

(3) When buying a new TV set, radio or stereo, remember that the solid-state appliances require less electricity than conventional tube-type sets.

HEATING YOUR WATER

(1) When buying a new water heater, select one with thick insulation on the shell. Do not purchase a tank with greater capacity than you need; ask the dealer for advice on the size appropriate to the number of people in your family.

(2) Install your water heater as close as possible to the areas of major use—to minimize heat loss through the pipes—and insulate those pipes.

(3) Save on the amount of fuel consumed by your hot water heater by lowering the thermostat to the temperature adequate for your purposes. Water at 140° is sufficient for all household chores; most people find 110° to 120° adequate. By keeping your thermostat down, you'll also be saving the life of your heater; high temperatures increase the rate of corrosion. Always turn down the temperature when you plan to be away for a prolonged period.

(4) Also prolong the life of your water-heating unit by flushing out the tank once a month to eliminate rust and lime deposits. A well-maintained water heater should last ten to fifteen years.

(5) Use cold water, rather than hot, in household cleaning, whenever you can. Many household cleaning products work better in cold water.

AVERAGE HOT WATER USED PER DAY

2 Adults+1 Child=60 Gal.
2 Adults+2 Children=70 Gal.
2 Adults+3 Children=80 Gal.

ESTIMATED HOT WATER USE

Tub bath	10–15 gal.
Shower (under 5 min.)	8–12 gal.
Automatic washer	25–35 gal.
Automatic dishwasher	11–16 gal.
Hand-wash dishes (each time)	9–14 gal.
Shampoo	5–7 gal.
Cleaning	3–8 gal.
Food Preparation	5 gal.

LIGHTING YOUR HOME

(1) Remove one electric bulb out of every three in areas where bright light is not essential and replace it with either a burned-out bulb or a bulb of the next lower wattage. Concentrate bright lighting where it is needed—for reading, working, and safety (such as stairwells). This one simple step should save you, in an average home, about 4 per cent in electricity costs and slash U.S. energy consumption about 50 million kilowatt-hours of electricity per day (enough to light about 16,000,000 homes).

(2) Use one large bulb instead of several small bulbs in areas where higher illumination is needed. The larger bulb is more efficient.

(3) Use individual switches that can be turned on and off independently. One light switch controlling several light fixtures is far more costly than the individual switches.

(4) Use long-life incandescent lamps only in hard-to-reach places where high levels of light are not required. They are less efficient than ordinary bulbs.

(5) Install solid-state dimmer switches when you replace a light switch. They allow more efficient use of light.

(6) Use fluorescent lights in such places as on desks, in the kitchen, laundry, and bath. One 40-watt fluorescent tube gives more light than three 60-watt incandescent bulbs.

(7) When your fluorescent lights are not in use, it is better to leave the fixtures on for an hour than to switch them on and off. Turning on and off shortens the life of fluorescent lamps. But turn off incandescent lighting when not in use.

(8) Decorate with white or light-colored translucent lamp shades; they reflect maximum light.

(9) Move your precious house plants to windows where they will get the benefit of natural light (you can hang them from the ceiling hooks to get maximum sun) or place them near lamps. Fluorescent tubes can give your house plants adequate lighting, even in dark corners.

(10) Use outdoor lights only where necessary. Extinguish decorative gaslights unless essential for safety. Six or seven gaslights use as much natural gas as a gas-heated home! If you must use outdoor lighting for security/safety, install a timer or photocell unit to turn off the lights automatically.

In the Laundry

(1) Wash clothes in warm or cold water, and always rinse in cold. Use hot water only if essential. If everyone washed clothes in warm or cold water, we'd save the equivalent of 100,000 barrels of oil a day, enough to heat 1,600,000 homes through the winter.

(2) Fill your clothes washer and dryer (unless there are special instructions to the contrary), but do not overload. If every household cut the use of its clothes washer-dryer by 25 per cent, the nation's savings would be equivalent to 35,000 barrels of oil a day, enough to heat more than 400 *billion* gallons of water a day.

(3) Take clothes out of the dryer the instant they are dry. Every minute of extra running time is waste, expensive to you and your country. Use automatic drying controls.

(4) Divide your drying loads into heavy and lightweight items. Your dryer doesn't have to run as long to dry the lightweight items. Also dry your clothes in consecutive loads, so that the energy you use to raise the dryer to the desired temperature doesn't go to waste.

(5) Since small loads require much less water than big ones, always use the water level control on your washer.

(6) On heavily soiled garments, use a presoak product or soak cycle. Reduce washing time and protect your fabrics by pretreating stains when they are fresh. You may have to wash these clothes only once instead of twice.

(7) When buying a new washer, buy the right size for your needs: a large washer may permit you to do your washing in a single load rather than in several loads in a smaller machine, thus requiring less energy.

(8) Provide a vent to the outside so moisture removed from the dryer doesn't remain in the room. If your laundry area is steamy, the clothes will take longer to dry.

(9) Follow detergent instructions carefully in your laundry (and dishwasher too). Oversudsing makes your equipment work harder and consume more energy than necessary.

(10) Keep the lint screen in your dryer clean by removing the lint screen collects after *each* load.

(11) Don't waste power ironing fabrics that require little or no ironing—and consider this upkeep factor as well as initial price when you buy fabrics. Iron all your clothes at the same time when possible, to avoid heating of the iron several times a week. If you must interrupt your ironing (say, to answer the phone), turn the iron off or unplug it.

(12) First iron fabrics that require lower temperatures, and work up to those requiring higher heat. An iron heats faster than it cools, so less energy is needed to go from low to high than the reverse. Turn off iron five minutes or so before clothes have been ironed, and finish ironing with heat stored in the soleplate.

(13) Schedule your washer-dryer use for later afternoon-evening, or for very early morning to ease the load on the nation's electrical systems and reduce the risks of brownouts and blackouts.

IN YARD, GARDEN, WORKSHOP

(1) Buy power tools that use the lowest power sufficient for the work you need done.

(2) Keep cutting edges on all your electrical tools as sharp as possible, so they operate at maximum speed and use less power. Properly lubricate and clean all your electrical tools so they require minimum power.

(3) Use hand tools, hand lawn mowers, hand clippers, pruners, etc., when adequate for your purposes.

(4) Never allow the machinery in your gas-powered equipment to idle for any length of time. Get into the habit of turning off the power when finished with one job, and turning it back on when ready for the next.

(5) If you are installing awnings, try to place them at heights that will not block sun's rays in winter, but which also will give you protection from high sun in summer.

(6) Instead of awnings, consider attaching sun screens to the outside of your windows. Cost is nominal and screens are effective in winter and summer.

(7) Plant deciduous trees and vines on the south, east, and west sides of your home. In warm weather, they will provide protective shade from the sun, and in

cold weather, after the leaves fall, will permit the sun to penetrate and heat those areas.

(8) Save money by not heating your garage. Instead, buy a good battery that will start your car when it's cold.

(9) If you have a private or condominium/apartment swimming pool, seriously consider *not* heating it. But if your pool is heated, a pool cover can reduce your heating costs by 30 per cent . . . and if the covers are removed during the day, additional savings can be chalked up. In many areas, a good pool cover, plus the sun, can effectively eliminate the need for pool heating. Turn off decorative lighting in and around pool areas—with the possible exception of one light for security and safety—and suggest this to your landlord or homeowners' association (if yours is an apartment or condominium pool). A pool temperature of 78° is most desirable, says the American Red Cross, and afternoon swims will avoid costly all-night heating for early morning warm-ups. Since your pool filter pump is your biggest electric user, save by reducing your filter time and by keeping grids and leaf baskets clean. Take maximum advantage of the sun as your heating device.

Annual Energy Requirements and Operating Costs of Electric Household Appliances

APPLIANCE	ANNUAL KILOWATT-HOUR CON-SUMPTION	ANNUAL OPERATING COST BASED ON RATE OF:*		
		3¢ PER KILOWATT-HOUR	5¢ PER KILOWATT-HOUR	7¢ PER KILOWATT-HOUR
Water heater	4,219	$126.57	$210.95	$295.33
Refrigerator (17.5 cu. ft.)	2,250	67.50	112.50	157.50
Freezer (16.5 cu. ft.)	1,820	54.60	91.00	127.40
Clothes dryer	993	29.79	49.65	69.51
Room air conditioner **	860	25.80	43.00	60.20
Range	700	21.00	35.00	49.00
Color TV				
— tube type	528	15.84	26.40	36.96
— solid state	320	9.60	16.00	22.40
Dehumidifier	377	11.31	18.85	26.39
Dishwasher	363	10.89	18.15	25.41
Lighting	360	10.80	18.00	25.20
Attic fan	290	8.70	14.50	20.30
Black and white TV				
— tube type	220	6.60	11.00	15.40
— solid state	100	3.00	5.00	7.00
Air cleaner	216	6.48	10.80	15.12
Microwave oven	190	5.70	9.50	13.30
Humidifier	163	4.89	8.15	11.41
Bed covering	147	4.41	7.35	10.29

APPLIANCE	ANNUAL KILOWATT-HOUR CON-SUMPTION	ANNUAL OPERATING COST BASED ON RATE OF:*		
		3¢ PER KILOWATT-HOUR	5¢ PER KILOWATT-HOUR	7¢ PER KILOWATT-HOUR
Coffee maker	140	4.20	7.00	9.80
Radio-record player	109	3.27	5.45	7.63
Washing machine	103	3.09	5.15	7.21
Frying pan	100	3.00	5.00	7.00
Roaster	60	1.80	3.00	4.20
Trash compactor	50	1.50	2.50	3.50
Vacuum cleaner	46	1.38	2.30	3.22
Toaster	39	1.17	1.95	2.73
Hair dryer	25	.75	1.25	1.75
Clock	17	.51	.85	1.19
Toothbrush	1	.03	.05	.07

*Kilowatt-hour rates vary widely. The sample rates of 3¢, 5¢ and 7¢ per kilowatt-hour are intended as guidelines. Utilities list the rate per kilowatt-hour on the monthly statements to customers.

** Based on 1,000 hours of operation per year. This figure will vary widely depending on area and specific size of unit.

SOURCE: Edison Electric Institute

TEST YOUR ENERGY QUOTIENT

Score

1. WHAT IS YOUR THERMOSTAT SETTING?

If your thermostat is set at 68°F. or less during daytime in winter, score 6 points; 5 points for 69°; 4 points for 70°. If your thermostat is set above 70°, score 0.

If you have whole-house air conditioning and you keep your temperature at 78°F. in the summer, score 5 points; 4 points for 77°; 3 points for 76°. If you have no air conditioning, score 7 points. If your thermostat is set below 76°, score 0.

In winter, if you set your thermostat back to 60°F. or less at night, score 10 points; 9 points for 61°; 8 points for 62°; 7 points for 63°; 6 points for 64°; 5 points for 65°. If your thermostat is set above 65° at night, you score 0.

2. IS YOUR HOUSE DRAFTY?

To check for drafts, hold a flame (candle or match) about 1 inch from where windows and doors meet their frames. If the flame doesn't move, there is no draft around your windows and you score 10 points. If the flame moves, score 0.

Score

If there is no draft around your doors, add 5 points. If there is a draft, score 0.

If you have a fireplace and keep the damper closed or block the air flow when it is not in use, add 4 points.

If you do not have a fireplace, add 4 points.

If you leave the damper open when the fireplace is not being used, score 0.

3. HOW WELL IS YOUR ATTIC INSULATED?

Check to determine the inches of ceiling insulation recommended for your zone. If you already have the recommended thickness of insulation, score 30 points.

If you have 2 inches less insulation than you should, score 25 points.

If you have 4 inches less insulation than you should, score 15 points.

If you have 6 inches less than you should, score 5 points.

If you have less than 2 inches of insulation in your attic, score 0.

4. IS YOUR FLOOR INSULATED?

If you have unheated space under your house and there is insulation under your floor, add 10 points; if there is no insulation, score 0.

If you have a heated or air-conditioned basement, or if there is no space under your house, score 10.

5. DO YOU HAVE STORM WINDOWS?

If you live in an area where the temperature frequently falls below 30°F. in winter and you use storm windows, score 20 points. If you do not have storm windows, score 0.

YOUR ENERGY QUOTIENT TOTAL _____

SOURCES: Federal Energy Administration; Edison Electric Institute; Alabama Power; Arkansas Power & Light; National Association of Realtors; Potomac Edison; San Diego Gas & Electric.

(test evaluation on next page)

How Well Did You Score?

If you scored 90 or above, you already are an energy saver and are using energy more efficiently on average than 80 per cent of Americans. If you scored under 90, you are spending more money on energy than you need to. Check the quiz again to see where you lost the most points, for those are the areas in which you can make the greatest savings in your annual fuel bill while improving the comfort, appearance, and resale value of your home as well.

HOW DOES YOUR HOME MEASURE UP FOR ENERGY CONSERVATION?

	YES	NO
Cracked windows	( )	( ) .
Well-fitted, weather-stripped windows	( )	( )
Double or storm windows installed	( )	( )
Properly fitted or weather-stripped outside doors	( )	( )
Storm doors installed	( )	( )
Glass doors on fireplace	( )	( )
Are unused rooms kept closed off?	( )	( )

HOW MUCH DO YOU SAVE IN HEATING COSTS BY TURNING DOWN YOUR THERMOSTAT AT NIGHT? A TALE OF 29 CITIES

CITY	LOWER 5° F.	LOWER 10°
Atlanta	11%	15%
Boston	7	11
Buffalo	6	10
Chicago	7	11
Cincinnati	8	12
Cleveland	8	12
Columbus, OH	7	11
Dallas	11	15
Denver	7	11
Des Moines	7	11
Detroit	7	11
Kansas City, MO	8	12
Los Angeles	12	16
Louisville	9	13
Madison, WI	5	9
Miami	12	18
Milwaukee	6	10
Minneapolis	5	9
New York	8	12
Omaha	7	11
Philadelphia	8	12
Pittsburgh	7	11

CITY	LOWER 5° F.	LOWER 10°
Portland, OR	9	13
Salt Lake City	7	11
San Francisco	10	14
Seattle	8	12
St. Louis	8	12
Syracuse	7	11
Washington	9	13

NOTE: It's not true that you won't save energy by turning down your thermostat at night because it takes so much energy to reheat your house in the morning. Depending on where you live, as dramatized in the above table, a 5° F. thermostat setback will save you 5 to 11 per cent and a 10° F. setback will save you 9 to 16 per cent from your preconservation use.

HOW TO JUDGE INSULATION

Many insulating materials look alike. How, then, do you buy the insulation that will best meet your standards for performance, quality, and safety.

How do you judge the product?

Contrary to most of the clichés by which we live—"don't judge a book by its cover" or "clothes do *not* make the man"—you'll find your most valuable guides on the insulation package itself.

• Look first for the label of the NAHB (National Association of Homebuilders) Research Foundation, Inc. For this label tells you that samples of the insulation have been tested by independent experts and that they meet the performance specifications stated on the package.

• Second, having checked the label, look for the "R-value" designation. R-value indicates insulation's ability to resist heat transfer—into the house in the summer, out of it in fall and winter. The higher the R-value, the greater a material's ability to cut heat gain and loss throughout your house. One brand of insulation may be thicker than another, but if they're both marked with the same R-value, they'll both resist heat flow equally well.

Therefore, when inspecting the package for insulation dimensions, always be concerned with R-values, not inches. The only inch designation you, the consumer, should note is a material's width. Insulation, in blanket or batt form, is sold in widths (of 15–16 inches or 23–24 inches) to fit between conventional framing joists and studs in all American homes.

• To select the proper R-value for the area of your home to be insulated, consult your local building materials dealer, local established insulation contractor or your utility company.

• Also vitally important, check the type of insulation you're buying—either blanket (often called batt insulation) or loose-fill. Blanket insulation is usually packaged in bags or convenient rolls, and loose-fill is packaged in bags. It's obviously hard to mistake blanket-type insulation packaged in rolls, but it's relatively easy to confuse the two types of insulation when they are both packaged in bags—unless you study the label.

• If you are a do-it-yourselfer, blanket-type insulation, prefabricated by the manufacturer to yield a uniform thickness and density, will assure you of a consistent R-value. It'll be simple for you to precalculate the amount of coverage with each package. Loose-fill-type insulation, though, must be carefully poured or blown to a certain thickness and density to achieve a desired R-value for each square foot of coverage.

With loose insulation, instructions for achieving so many square feet of coverage at a given R-value may be found on the package, but it still will be far too easy for you, an amateur, to make a mistake during insulation.

• Study with care the material makeup of the insulation and the ingredients it contains.

Ask questions particularly about the differences in materials in the areas of fire safety, moisture resistance, potential corrosive chemicals or additives (such as starch) which can permit the growth of bacteria and attract vermin.

• Make a list of the key points you should investigate on the package of insulation before visiting any insulation dealer or talking to a contractor.

• And one final guide: don't delay. From the moment your house is properly insulated, you'll start to save money on your consumption of energy. Shortages might develop; prices might be pushed up by heavy demands. You have nothing to gain by delaying.

INSULATION: BEWARE "UNPROFESSIONAL PROFESSIONAL"

If you're among America's millions of "unhappy handymen" about to hire a professional to insulate your home, beware of the "unprofessional professional."

As always when a particular business booms—and the business of energy conservation is an almost classic illustration—unscrupulous fringe operators and relatively uninformed individuals crowd in to grab a piece of the action and profit.

Insulation contracting is certainly no exception. It is only common sense to check prospective contracting firms thoroughly to be sure their motives are in your best interests. You'll find the professional firms in the Yellow Pages of your phone book under "Insulation Contractors: Cold & Heat."

• Compare one contractor against another to make sure you are hiring the right one. It's not easy, but a little homework will make the task much less difficult and protect you against the fringe operator.

• Ask each contractor for references. Check with the local Better Business Bureau, your local utility, previous customers—and don't hesitate to probe for facts about the firm's reliability and performance in other jobs.

• Find out whether the contractor uses "batt" or "loose-fill" insulation. Some firms handle both; others, only one type. Batts are the familiar insulation blankets, prefabricated by the manufacturer into uniform thickness and density. Loose-fill is insulation in a chopped-up form, which is "blown" between attic floor joists and wall studs with special pneumatic equipment.

Loose insulation is good for areas which are hard to reach, but batts offer the special advantage of assured thermal performance. While there can be variations in the installed thickness of loose insulation (which may affect its ability to keep your home warm in winter and cool in summer), the variations are reduced with batts because the material is prefabricated into dimensionally consistent blankets before it's installed.

• Discuss with each contractor the R-value of the material to be installed. R-value represents insulation's ability to resist heat transfer—into the home in summer, out of it in fall and winter. Thus, specify your insulation needs in R-values, not inches, for 10 inches of one manufacturer's product may not have the same R-value as 10 inches of another's.

• Make sure the contractor will provide you with a certificate stating the R-value of the material installed and identifying the manufacturer of the insulation. If and when you decide to sell your home, you then will have proof that it has been properly insulated.

• Do not fail to get a written warranty against faulty workmanship. Most reliable contractors will be happy to provide warranty references, and just about any other information requested. They'll even tell you whether they're fully insured—and you should ask, since accidents sometimes occur. This is the best way to protect yourself against a possible lawsuit in the future.

• Ask for competitive bids. This is fundamental in most fields of this nature, and in insulation one contractor whose work might be of just as high quality as a competitor's, might charge you considerably less.

In getting more than one quote, describe the job's requirements precisely the same way to each bidder to make certain you can realistically compare the merits of each proposal.

Prices charged by contractors vary, of course, depending on local labor costs and the complexity of the job you want done. But a reliable yardstick is that you'll pay approximately one third more to have a contractor install insulation in your attic than if you try to do the job yourself.

• Expect to pay for proper insulation—combining quality materials and good workmanship—which can cost up to $1,000 for a three-bedroom house.

• Don't commit yourself to high-priced insulation by a contractor until you have at least taken such inexpensive and effective steps on your own as caulking and weatherstripping your doors and windows.

It's wise spending, though, if you're honestly one of the nation's unhappy handymen (or women). The contractor will save you time as well as the cost and inconvenience of having to do most of the job all over again to correct your mistakes.

• For more information on home energy send for the Commerce Department booklet, "Making the Most of Your Energy Dollars in Home Heating and Cooling." It costs less than $1.00, is available from the U. S. Government Printing Office, Washington, D.C. 20402. The guide contains climate maps, sample costs, and worksheets that you can use to calculate the amount of energy—and money—that can be saved, depending on where you live, your type of home, local fuel costs, etc.

• When buying or installing insulation, also evaluate the product's flammability.

Check with local authorities to be sure the products you are considering meet the safety requirements of local building codes. Under no circumstances install insulation near heat or expose it to light fixtures.

• For short, helpful government-published insulation safety guides, get "Home Insulation Safety" fact sheet No. 91, free, from the Consumer Product Safety Commission by calling the commission's toll-free hotline and the "Insulation" fact sheet DOE-CS-0017, free, from the U. S. Department of Energy, Washington, D.C. 20585.

WARNING: SOLAR ENERGY PITFALLS

Warning: If you are considering installing a solar hot-water unit to preheat water in your home, first make sure your home is suitable for a solar energy unit. Not all homes are. It is easier to put a solar heating system on a new home, for instance, than on an existing unit. Initially, check out other, less expensive domestic hot water units.

Warning: Before you make any move at all, investigate the company with which you plan to do business. While some larger corporations have moved into this field with their subsidiaries, the boom is attracting large numbers of young, small companies with no track records at all to give you guidance. You can obtain a list of reputable manufacturers of solar equipment by writing the Solar Information Center, Rockville, Maryland.

Warning: A solar system that can heat your entire house can cost up to $10,000 to $12,000. It might take you ten years to get your cost back. Look into the potential trouble points in equipment and what the equipment can literally do. Educate yourself. For a valuable book with answers to the most frequently asked questions, send a postcard to Consumer Information Center, Pueblo, Colorado 81009 and request "Solar Energy and Your Home," 646 E. It's free.

There is no doubt that solar energy has moved out of the theoretical category and onto the Main Streets of our land. Projections of U.S. homes with solar units by 1985 range from 2,500,000 to above 11 million.

The most impressive fact is that the buying is being spurred by the most practical of all reasons—to save money over the long run. The first impetus is coming in solar hot-water units, which can be installed in an average home in three or four days at a cost ranging from a low of $1,000 to as high as $3,000.

A unit of this sort can slash your hot water costs, possibly by 50 per cent or more. But the dangers inherent in the ballooning of this industry and in eager buying by a generally ignorant public are emerging. The warnings already emphasized are merely a sampling of the pocketbook threats you might face. To continue:

• To find service suppliers and manufacturers plus prices, consult a reputable directory. "Solar Industry Index" is published by Solar Energy Industries Association in Washington, D.C. "Buying Solar" is a guideline for choosing equipment and is published by the President's Office of Consumer Affairs with the Federal Energy Administration. It's available from the U. S. Government Printing Office, Washington, D.C. 20402. "Solar Source Book" is published by Solar Energy Institute of America, also headquartered in Washington, D.C. 20005. Check prices of each directory before you buy.

• To find a contractor in your area or a builder to install a solar energy system or build a solar home, inquire at your local association of home builders. Some electric or gas utility companies have lists of experienced contractors. Try your local utility. Or the Solar Information Center may have lists of interested builders and contractors.

• Try to see some solar homes near you. If you don't know any homes you can see, the Solar Information Center and your state energy office may have lists of solar homes.

• For detailed information about building a solar energy home or installing a system in your present home, ask the advice of a professional. Help also should be available from the American Institute of Architects, Washington, D.C.; the American Society of Heating, Refrigerating and Air Conditioning Engineers, New York, New York; the National Association of Home Builders, Washington, D.C. 20005; and the Solar Energy Industries Association, 1001 Connecticut Avenue, N.W., Washington D.C. 20036.

Take your time! This is the basic warning between every line in this report on pitfalls. Find out first, protect yourself.

7

GETTING TO AND FROM—
BY WHEELS, WINGS, AND WATER

Your Love Affair with Mobility Is Undiminished

Americans of all ages have been carrying on a love affair with mobility for most of the twentieth century; and our love affair goes way beyond the obvious automobile. It also has come to embrace airplanes, buses, motorcycles, bicycles, mopeds, boats, snowmobiles, almost any machine that moves.

In the late 1970s, we in America, owned some 150 million cars and trucks, about two vehicles for every three of us—and roughly one for each adult. Almost three out of five families operate two or more cars, and fewer than one in five household units is without a car at all.

In the Soviet Union, in contrast, the ratio is about one vehicle for every fifty citizens.

Each year, Americans drive their passenger cars alone more than *1 trillion* miles—a figure which is equal to more than five thousand trips between the earth and sun. For many of us, a car has become almost a "second home"—literally as well as figuratively—with the rise in "motor homes," and other "passenger trucks," those living quarters on wheels which have surged in popularity since the 1960s.

Most revealing of all, the car is the *second* biggest item in the American family budget!

We earmark now a huge 13 to 15 cents of every spending dollar just to own and operate our family cars. The total was well over $225 billion each year as the 1980s neared, or more than $1,000 annually for every man, woman, and child in the country.

I'm taking for granted, therefore, that you know *something* about buying and running your automobile. But no matter how extensive your familiarity with cars, I'll also wager you are far from fully aware of the savings you can achieve in your car buying, financing, insuring, running, repairing, and finally selling your car.

Do You Need a Car?

The first and most obvious way to save money on a car—or anything else—is to do without it. So, the first decision you must make is: do I (we) really need to own a car!

For the great majority of you, of course, the answer is yes. Almost four fifths of the passenger car mileage driven each year—some 800 billion miles annually —is traveled for reasons *other than* personal pleasure: commuting to and from work (or at least to and from the train or bus depot); actual on-the-job business travel; essential family business such as shopping, going (or taking the children) to and from school, trips to and from doctors, church, or civic meetings.

Only about 20 per cent of our yearly mileage is for such purposes as vacations, weekend outings, visiting friends and relatives, or pure sight-seeing.

But even with your high rate of "essential" driving, there are alternatives to owning a car—and this becomes more evident if you are discussing your family's second, third, or even fourth set of wheels. Although, over the past three quarters of a century, Americans have increasingly *turned away* from other forms of travel —except for air travel—you have done so because of the convenience of the personal car, not for want of other means of locomotion.

In fact, with the costs of garaging, parking, and insurance soaring to stratospheric heights in the cities, urban residents of America are starting to rely more and more on other forms of transportation—subways, buses, trains, taxis, bicycles, mopeds, and rental cars, even jogging and walking. Car and van pools also have been multiplying in response to increases in world fuel prices.

In the suburban and rural areas, a personal passenger car is almost a "must," though even in these locations, the need for double and triple car ownership must be weighed with care. But, in urban localities, if you are concerned about cutting your budget, the question is seriously whether you need to own a car at all—or whether your purchase is more for prestige or out of habit.

To help you make your decisions about car ownership, look first at the true costs of owning—and running—a car.

The Real Costs of Car Ownership and Operation

WHAT COSTS CONSIST OF

How much does it cost to run a car? Until the fuel problems and the galloping inflation of the 1970s, few Americans paid close attention to their automobile ownership and operating costs—primarily because, until then, the expense of running cars had been dropping steadily—in relationship, that is, to personal income.

Between World War II in the mid 1940s and the end of the Vietnam conflict in the early 1970s, outlays for an individual car had dropped about 50 per cent (in terms of your incomes) and you were fulfilling your urge for mobility through the purchase of two and even three cars per family.

The 1970s changed all that. More and more, you, owners of the nation's 120 million passenger cars (and 30 million trucks), wanted to know: "How much does it cost to run a car?"

The question is, almost literally, akin to asking: "How high is up?" Car costs depend on such a wide variety of factors that an accurate answer, to fit any given circumstance, requires such precise knowledge as:

What kind of car? How much did it cost to buy? Was it financed? How? How many miles a year is it driven? Where? What is the age of the driver and his or her residence? How many years will the vehicle be kept? What will its resale value be when it is sold, or what will the scrap or "junker" price be at that time? Was the car purchased new or used?

Inquiries from motorists—even sophisticated businessmen—indicate that few of you who drive understand what your automobile costs are. Even government cost studies for years omitted automobile financing charges, though two out of three new cars sold are purchased on the installment plan.

The lack of financial knowledge about automobiles is understandable, since the computation of car costs can be extremely complex and can involve a number of unknown factors.

For instance, if you are under twenty-five years old, male, live and drive in a major metropolitan area, garage your car there, commute over toll roads to work, travel a typical 8,000 to 10,000 miles a year, have a standard-size domestic-make automobile with the usual options, are financing your car, and if you trade every year, *your costs in the late 1970s were probably at least 75 cents a mile!*

But if you are middle-aged, married, live in a small suburb or rural area, don't commute with your auto, pay no highway or bridge tolls, and if you bought your subcompact car thirdhand when it was six years old and plan to drive it that 8,000 to 10,000 miles annually for another three or four years, *your costs might be as little as 10 to 15 cents a mile.*

The average, in the late 1970s, for an intermediate-size car, bought new, driven a typical ten thousand miles a year, and kept a normal three to four years, *was nearly 35 cents a mile*—excluding parking and tolls.

CAR SIZE, YEARS OF OWNERSHIP, MAJOR FACTORS

The two most significant factors in determining your car ownership costs are its size (and thus purchase price) and the number of years you plan to keep it.

To illustrate on size, a typical recent-model, standard-size car will cost 12 to 15 per cent *more* than an intermediate-make driven under similar conditions. But a subcompact will run about 25 per cent *less* than the intermediate, 33 per cent under the standard-size model.

In practice, therefore, assuming you were a typical driver in the late 1970s, the minicar would save you $800 to $1,200 a year in typical driving, *under* the cost of a standard-size car, with your annual savings depending on how long you keep the vehicle and how far you drive it.

As for the second major factor in car costs—length of ownership—in the late 1970s, the typical intermediate, purchased new, driven 10,000 miles a year, and *traded every year,* cost 35 to 36 cents a mile.

But discounting anticipated inflation, that same car, driven the same 10,000 miles a year, *but kept ten years,* until it had traveled 100,000 miles, would cost on the average only 20 to 23 cents a mile.

So the *average* cost per mile, over the entire ten-year period, is only about 60 per cent of the first-year per-mile expenses.

When you combine the two factors of car size and duration of ownership, the key point that emerges is that you can realize a per-mile *saving* of about 60 per cent by buying a smaller, less expensive automobile and becoming a once-a-decade trader rather than an annual new-car buyer.

To put these figures in perspective: at late 1970s prices, they meant that you—as a yearly new-car buyer—were spending close to $40,000 over a ten-year, 100,000-mile driving period, ignoring inevitable inflation, and excluding tolls and parking, if you drive a standard-size domestic model.

But in a subcompact, your decade costs would be well under $20,000—a walloping $20,000 difference. These totals obviously will change as the years go by. They will be higher! However, the *percentage* savings would remain relatively constant. They have so remained over the past generation.

Furthermore, there are ways you can save even more on your automotive expenses—to slash *more than* 60 per cent from typical ownership and operating outlays, enabling you to do your driving for about one third the national average! These ways to save will become apparent as you learn more about just what your car costs are, how to calculate them and how to estimate them in advance.

WHAT ARE YOUR REAL CAR COSTS?

You, like many motorists, may believe "operating costs" consist only of gasoline, oil, tires, batteries, filters, other replacement parts, and labor, for example.

Or you might add highway and bridge tolls, parking and garaging fees—and even calculate the expenses of washing and waxing.

But these costs comprised only about half of the $225-billion-a-year outlay you were paying in the late 1970s. They covered only the so-called "variable" auto expenses, those which depend primarily on the number of miles a car is run each year.

Other charges, also amounting to about half the overall outlays, consist of the *"fixed"* or standing expenditures. Primary among these is *depreciation.* This is the difference between the vehicle's purchase price (list price less discount plus delivery, preparation, and taxes) and the unit's trade-in or resale value after it has been used.

The fixed expenses also include insurance, registration, and other licensing and inspection fees. In this fixed category, too, is interest—the cost of a loan if the vehicle is financed, and the interest you, the buyer, lose on your money if you take it from savings and pay cash.

Fixed outlays—including the prorated depreciation—are calculated on a yearly basis, as they are usually incurred, and they remain essentially the same regardless of the annual vehicle mileage.

Confusing this "fixed" and "variable" terminology, though, is the fact that for tax, expense-account, and other reasons, vehicle costs often are expressed on a *per-mile* basis rather than as an annual dollar amount.

When the cents-per-mile costs are figured, the "fixed" annual charges actually fluctuate, because substantially the same total dollar charges are spread over a changing number of miles traveled.

So-called "variable" or running costs, though, tend to remain just about the same when expressed on a per-mile basis. (These costs, which include maintenance and repairs, do tend to rise somewhat if you put on extremely high mileage during your later years of ownership, however.)

THE ELEMENTS OF VEHICLE COSTS

DEPRECIATION

The primary factor in determining vehicle costs is depreciation—the difference between the actual purchase price of the car or truck and its eventual resale value —divided by the number of years the unit is driven.

Depreciation is probably the most difficult of all factors to determine. Few of you actually know—even approximately—how much you have paid for a car. In many cases, you simply add the monthly payments and any down payment you may have made.

This produces a false result. It includes the trade-in allowance on our *previous* vehicle; and, if the new unit has been financed, it lumps the interest costs into the total.

The correct way involves checking the actual list price—including options, delivery, and preparation. That gives you the *retail price*.

Then, take the so-called "allowance" the dealer gave you for your old vehicle. Following this, obtain the *wholesale value of that old car*—which almost certainly will be less than the "allowance" you received.

Subtract the wholesale value of the car from the "allowance" you received for it. That produces the discount your dealer gave you. Subtract this, in turn, from the retail price. Add any sales tax. Now you have the *purchase price* of the car.

But you still cannot calculate the annual depreciation. To do so you must penetrate an unforeseeable future: you must guess how many years you will keep the vehicle; approximately how many miles you will drive each year; and what the value of the vehicle will be when you trade it.

Only if you foresee all that will you have the data you need to calculate the annual depreciation cost to you, the current owner.

READY-MADE DEPRECIATION ESTIMATES

Surely this detailed information about depreciation will help impress upon you that depreciation is the single most important element in calculating car costs— and usually the most difficult factor with which you must contend.

Of course, if you buy your car new and keep it until you junk it, your task is relatively simple: figure what you paid for the car, less any "junker" value it may have. That would be your depreciation. Divide that figure by the number of miles you run your car, and you have the cost-per-mile of the depreciation.

If you trade or sell your car at any time earlier, you must reduce this full depreciation.

You will be relieved to know that the *approximate* depreciation rate percentages for most typical domestic cars have been estimated by various organizations through years of experience.

Here are expert estimates on what you should figure for depreciation *each year,* subtracted from your original new car purchase price:

First Year	30–32%
Second Year	24–26
Third Year	18–20
Fourth Year	7–8
Fifth Year	3–5
Sixth Year	3–5
Seventh Year	3–5
Eighth Year	1–2
Ninth Year	1–2
Tenth Year	1–2

THE INFLATION FACTOR

You no doubt have noticed how heavily the annual depreciation is "front-loaded"—how much greater it is during the early years in contrast to the low rates in the twilight years of the car's life. Obviously, these figures are averages and your own car's depreciation may vary widely. But for typical American-made automobiles, the figures are a good guideline.

Be fully aware, too, that any long-term depreciation calculation must take into account the realities of inflation. The annual rates listed above are in so-called "constant dollar" figures. What this "constant dollar" total assumes is that if you buy a $6,000 car one year and trade it five years later, you'd be able to buy the same car then for the same price. Obviously, this is most unlikely, so your depreciation will be somewhat less.

But under the same assumptions, your outlay for the identical car also will be higher later on. A quick example: suppose that inflation in the next five years is a truly modest 20 per cent—just 3¾ per cent annually. This means the car that cost you $6,000 this year will set you back $7,200 five years from now. If the depreciation on your current set of wheels is 80 per cent in terms of constant dollars over the five-year period, as the table indicates, that would be $4,800, so your car's wholesale price might be expected to come in at $1,200.

In the five-year period, though, you've had 20 per cent inflation, so your car's wholesale value would rise to $1,440. That's almost one quarter of the $6,000 original purchase price, but only one fifth of the new, $7,200 buying cost. In effect your depreciation still has been 80 per cent.

The depreciation rates listed also assume a typical 10,000-miles-per-year of travel. If your car has gone fewer than 50,000 miles in five years, its wholesale value should be higher, providing you've cared for it properly.

If the car has traveled *more* than 50,000 miles, the trade-in price should be less.

(See guides on mileage and odometers, pages 398–99.)

To put the depreciation picture into even sharper focus, if you trade your newly purchased car every year, your depreciation costs normally will run about half of your total annual operating expenses; if you keep your car ten years, depreciation will be about one quarter of your total costs.

Note how this works out as you tabulate all the elements of your car costs.

THE COSTS OF INSURING YOUR CAR

Next in importance in calculating the costs of a typical car these days comes insurance. Insurance premiums have been zooming in recent years, faster than any other element of car cost.

In later sections you will read vital tips on savings on insurance, too. But in our society, insurance is a key part of your automobile expenses. For a typical intermediate-size car, driven three years at the national norm of about 10,000 miles annually, insurance alone has been averaging $600 to $700 per year, even though, in some less populated areas, preferred risk drivers paid hundreds less for normal cars. Young drivers in urban population centers, especially those owning high-performance cars, paid well into the thousands, each year, for their insurance coverage.

OTHER FIXED COSTS

Other of your automobile's fixed costs—those which do not depend primarily on how many miles you travel—include licensing, fees, inspection charges, property taxes, and the like.

These are not major factors in your ownership costs; they are usually under 2 per cent of total annual expenses, but they are expenses which you must include. As illustrations, you must consider yearly "property" levies in some states, or vehicle inspection charges, as well as driver's licenses and registration fees.

Taxes on the purchase price of the car itself are included in the depreciation calculation, while taxes on gasoline (federal, state, and local), oil, parts, accessories, and maintenance labor charges are put in the variable expenses.

GARAGING, PARKING, AND TOLLS

Charges for garaging, parking, and bridge and highway tolls vary so widely that often they are not even included in national driving cost averages. Estimates which place the countrywide norm at 15 per cent of typical car costs are no more than sheer guesses.

For example, in the New York metropolitan area, bridge, tunnel, and highway tolls alone for a suburban commuter from New Jersey could amount to $3.00 or more a day as the 1980s neared—$15 a week, $750 a year for the average New York City worker, 20–25 per cent of the overall operating cost in the late 1970s for a typical intermediate car of recent vintage.

Parking is another item which can vary over a wide cost range. In big-city downtown areas, this item alone was running close to $1,500 a year, roughly 45 per cent of total operating costs for the "national average" car. At the other extreme would be the rural or suburban dweller who did not commute: his or her garaging would be close to zero. (See pages 378–79 on parking costs.)

Don't ignore the expense because you park your car in your own garage. You must prorate your home-ownership expenses for garaging. True, your expenses would continue whether you had a car or not; but you might have purchased a house *without* a garage if you had not owned a car in the first place.

Allocate the cost where it properly belongs. A handy way to do this is to total your monthly mortgage payments, add in any property taxes and your home insurance, then calculate the square footage of your house and garage. Get the approximate size of the garage and figure its ratio to the overall area of the structure.

Multiply your total annual home expenditures by the garage space percentage, and you have an annual cost for your garage. If your home expenses come to $5,000 annually and your garage is 10 per cent of the square footage of your entire home, your annual garage costs would be $500—a not inconsiderable sum, for it's a nickel a mile at the 10,000-miles-per-year national norm.

If you rent your home, apply the same formula, using your yearly rent, rather than your mortgage, tax, and interest payments.

INTEREST: THE FORGOTTEN FACTOR

Many automobile expense estimates of fixed car costs end here. Even the Federal Highway Administration's car cost calculations do not include your finance charges in its totals, despite the fact that two thirds of all new cars purchased by individuals are bought on the installment plan.

And even if you purchased your car for cash, you presumably took the money out of a savings account where it was earning interest for you.

On cars which are purchased "on time," you have a double expense: the finance charges *paid* on the portion of your purchase price which you finance; and the interest *lost* on the part of the purchase price which you paid as a down payment.

But, you may say, the down payment was covered by the car I traded in. No, I reply: you could have sold that used car and put the proceeds in the bank—at interest.

If you are to calculate the cost of your car, then truly calculate the cost of your car: don't hedge, don't soft-pedal your *actual* outlays to reduce your *apparent* expenditures so you can make car ownership easier to justify.

Car ownership *can* be justified in a multitude of cases. But you can't make a really intelligent decision on whether you should be owning a car unless you are ruthlessly realistic about exactly how much the privilege (or necessity) is setting you back.

On pages 310–12 discussing financing your car, you'll find tips on how much your particular car may be costing you in finance charges, and how much "interest lost" may be costing. But the figure is substantial. And the greater the amount that you finance, and the longer the terms of the loan, the more it is costing you.

In the late 1970s, with the double impact of higher automobile purchase prices and steep loan rates, the category of "interest paid-and-lost" came to more than 12 per cent of total annual ownership and operating costs of recent-model cars.

If you bought your car and kept it ten years, the ratio was slightly lower— under 10 per cent. But if you purchased a used car, it was significantly higher. The used car buyer's total costs are less, but your interest *rate* on a financed car is higher. (More about used cars—much more—later in this section.)

Thus, the so-called "fixed," or "standing" expenses of car ownership are: depreciation, insurance, licenses, fees, etc.; garaging, parking, and tolls; and interest paid and/or lost.

VARIABLE CAR OPERATING EXPENSES

In addition to these fixed or standing expenses, you must take into account the "variable" or "running" expenses of car ownership and operation. These fall into two categories: gasoline, oil, and other service station items such as lubrication, spark plugs, and batteries; and maintenance and repair charges—dictated by your warranty or required by the car's age.

During the late 1970s, these two categories averaged 25 per cent of overall *recent-model* expenditures—and 40 per cent of the *ten-year* ownership average. Maintenance expenses rise significantly as a car ages and rolls up high mileage; at the same time the average depreciation drops in later years, producing the sharp rise in the ratio spent for old as opposed to newer cars.

GASOLINE STILL "A BARGAIN"

Gasoline alone, for a typical domestic make in the late 1970s, when new cars were averaging 17 to 18 miles per gallon and gasoline was on its way to $1.00 a gallon, came to about 15 per cent of a car's cost of operation if kept three years.

Despite the uproar about zooming gasoline prices following the Arab oil embargo and crisis in Iran, the longer view is that over the years between 1950 and the late 1970s, per-gallon gasoline prices rose 141 per cent—slightly *below* the nation's overall 152 per cent inflation rate in those years.

FIGURING YOUR OWN CAR COSTS

With this knowledge about the elements of calculating car costs, at least you can get an approximate idea of what your wheels are actually costing you (or will cost you).

Following is a check list of typical late 1970s prices and their ratio to overall annual car operating costs, and costs per mile traveled:

Annual New Car Costs

CAR COST ITEMS (AT 10,000 MILES PER YEAR) 1978 Intermediate Purchase Price $5,578*	3-YEAR USE		10-YEAR USE		YOUR CAR'S ANNUAL COSTS
	$ COST ANNUALLY	% OF TOTAL	$ COST ANNUALLY	% OF TOTAL	
FIXED "STANDING" COSTS					
Annual depreciation average (Yr. 1) = 30-32% of purch. price; (Yr. 2) = 24-26%; (3) = 18-20%; (4) = 7-8%; (5-7) = 3-5%; (8-10) = 2% annually	$ 1,422	43%	$ 547	24%	
Licenses, fees, etc.	51	2%	51	2%	
Insurance (assumes collision coverage dropped after car loan is repaid)	647	20%	550	25%	
Interest† (assumes 3-yr. loan for car kept 3 years, 4-yr. loan for car kept 10 years; 1/3 down, 2/3 financed)	413	12%	208	9%	
Subtotal of fixed or "standing" expenses	$ 2,533	77%	$ 1,356	60%	
VARIABLE "RUNNING" COSTS					
Maintenance, repairs (annual average; outlays range from $161 1st yr. to $446 10th yr.)	$ 231	7%	$ 321	15%	
Gasoline, oil, lube, etc. (service station charges)	548	16%	566	25%	
Subtotal variable or "running" expenses	$ 779	23%	$ 887	40%	
TOTAL FIXED AND VARIABLE COSTS — ANNUAL	$ 3,312	100%	$ 2,243	100%	
10-YEAR TOTALS	$33,120		$22,430		

*With normally purchased options; list price less 12% discount plus 5.1% taxes.

†Assumes finance purchase, including interest lost on down payment. Straight cash purchase, also including interest lost on payment, about $100 less. Variations from rounding.

YOUR "CASH FLOW" CAR COSTS

The actual car cost expenditures estimates above show you your true passenger car transport expenses. But this figure is not what you actually must lay out each month. The so-called actual "cash flow" outlays might be more, or less.

To figure your monthly out-of-pocket expenses, use this list:

	Car #1	Car #2	Car #3

Monthly Installment Payments
    (licenses included?)
Monthly Insurance Costs
    (if not included above)
Gasoline, oil, parts
    accessories, tires, batteries, spark plugs,
    required maintenance (average your annual
    mileage over the past several years, then
    divide by 12 to get your monthly mileage;
    use the per-mile figures listed previously
    for a typical car; for smaller cars use about
    80 per cent of the figures previously given;
    for larger cars, 120 per cent. To this, add
    whatever the inflation has been since that
    time.)*
Tolls
    (daily tolls times 22 if you commute)
Daily or Monthly Rate Parking

    TOTAL

The total should not be more than one quarter (25 per cent) of your monthly take-home pay.

---

* A good way to estimate the running costs is to use the Consumer Price Index. It was about 180 (in terms of 1967 as 100) when the figures were calculated. If it is now 210, divide this by 180, giving 1.166. Multiply the running expenses by this figure to get an estimate of your current expected outlays.

COST DIFFERENCES IN CAR SIZES

Now zero in on car size, and how much it can save (or cost) you. With car sizes and weights—and costs—in a flux, as Detroit scrambles each year to meet the government fuel economy strictures, size comparisons are difficult.

But here are the costs per mile for various sizes of cars over different periods of years at varying annual mileage rates, as compiled by the Hertz Corporation, which buys, runs, and sells more cars and trucks each year than any other private organization. (The figures are for models of the late 1970s but the relationships have remained roughly the same over the past decade since the subcompacts were first introduced; as cars are downsized, the ratios are expected to remain as they were then.)

Per-Mile Expenses at Various Annual Mileages
for Different Years of Service and Car Type

YEARS USED	MILES DRIVEN PER YEAR		
	10,000	15,000	25,000

SUBCOMPACT

	10,000	15,000	25,000
1 Year	.2723¢	.2037¢	.1491¢
2 Years	.2655	.1996	.1478
3 Years	.2580	.1953	.1470
4 Years	.2376	.1825	.1424
5 Years	.2352	.1753	—
6 Years	.2081	.1654	—
7 Years	.1957	—	—
8 Years	.1870	—	—
9 Years	.1805	—	—
10 Years	.1756	—	—

INTERMEDIATE

	10,000	15,000	25,000
1 Year	.3494¢	.2597¢	.1881¢
2 Years	.3408	.2545	.1864
3 Years	.3312	.2488	.1852
4 Years	.3051	.2324	.1790
5 Years	.2891	.2231	—
6 Years	.2659	.2097	—
7 Years	.2509	.2016	—
8 Years	.2395	—	—
9 Years	.2305	—	—
10 Years	.2243	—	—

STANDARD

	10,000	15,000	25,000
1 Year	.3856¢	.2897¢	.2129¢
2 Years	.3793	.2859	.2123
3 Years	.3691	.2798	.2107
4 Years	.3406	.2618	.2036
5 Years	.3233	.2515	—
6 Years	.2992	.2372	—
7 Years	.2817	.2278	—
8 Years	.2682	—	—
9 Years	.2596	—	—
10 Years	.2528	—	—

The figures illustrate that the smaller (and lighter) the car, the less expensive it is to operate. If you take the *standard-size* car as your norm—at 10,000 miles a year of travel—the intermediate is about 12 per cent less and the subcompact a substantial 33 per cent under the standard.

These approximate savings of 12 per cent and 33 per cent also extend over the lifetime of the car, into its tenth year of use—and they apply to higher annual mileages, too.

Your annual mileage, incidentally, sharply changes your per-mile expenses, since your fixed annual outlays are spread over a greater number of miles. Of course, your total dollar costs each year are higher as the miles you drive increase.

KEEPING CARS LONGER SAVES, TOO

The year-by-year per-mile averages in the tables also emphasize the fact that you, as an annual trader, pay far more for your car than you do if you keep your vehicle longer. Owners of ten-year-old cars pay only about three fifths what the annual trader is spending. But, of course, the annual trader is driving a "new" car every year, the ten-year trader drives a new one just once a decade.

Despite the folklore about old cars costing more than new ones, this simply is not so.

Assuming you didn't buy a lemon, that you haven't abused your car, that you've maintained it properly and not been in an accident, during the first ten years or 100,000 miles of a car's life **it is never cheaper to trade in a car rather than repair it and keep it!**

Maintenance expenses do rise in later years—often quite sharply in the sixth through tenth years of the vehicle's life. But these increases in upkeep costs are more than offset by the lower depreciation charges in later years.

If you bought your car for the average $3,493 a typical new model cost in 1973, it may *seem* uneconomic to pay $400 to $500 in 1980—10 to 15 per cent of the auto's original cost—for an engine overhaul on a seven-year-old car driven 70,000 miles. But that car should have at least 30,000 more miles in it before it needs to be junked (and recent studies indicate it could be as much as 55,000 to 60,000 or more). And a new auto at that time would cost $6,000 to $6,500.

You may want to trade in your seven-year-old car for a new one because of any number of reasons, but sound economic judgment and financial prudence are not among them. In later sections of this chapter, you will find year-by-year operating cost breakouts which illustrate this fact.

Whether you figure your expenses by the true costs, or by your monthly cash-flow outlays, for cars big or small, traded annually, or every decade, the numbers are substantial.

And these numbers are simply averages. Parking, garaging, and tolls could add as much as 66 per cent to your basic outlays; and urban-area, high-risk insurance premiums could tack on another 33 per cent, in effect doubling these costs.

But there are ways to cut these expenditures, as well. You will read in pages to come some of those ways—as well as hints on avoiding false-economy mistakes.

So read the full chapter, including the sections on alternatives to buying cars, to decide if you truly must own one. Then, armed with the statistics and percentages listed above, you can intelligently determine whether you can afford a *new* one, or whether you must settle for a *used* jalopy.

How to Buy a New Car

You are in the market for a *new* car. How do you choose a reliable car dealer? When is the best time of the year to buy? Which accessories are worth the extra cost? How can you tell whether or not you are getting a fair deal if you're trading in your old car?

TEN BASIC GUIDES

(1) In advance, set a maximum price you are willing and able to pay for the car—everything included.

If you are a family with average income and expenses, plan to hold your monthly payments on a car you are buying over a period of three and a half to four years to one half or less of your monthly housing costs (mortgage and taxes *or* rent). The average amount paid for a new car in the late 1970s was about 75 per cent of the national average income, or roughly $5,500.

Here was the general price range of most models in various car sizes:

Subcompact (or minicompacts): between $3,000 and $3,500 (and subcompact station wagons cost $150 to $250 more than sedans).

Compacts: between $3,500 and $4,500.

Intermediates: between $4,500 and $5,500.

Big four-door sedans: between $5,000 and $6,500.

But, more important: what will your carrying costs be—your monthly payments *plus* your other fixed and monthly car costs—exclusive of depreciation?

(2) Also in advance, decide in some detail what *kind* of car you want.

This includes make, size, body type, engine, transmission. Will the size you choose meet your actual family needs, including those of growing children? Are you looking for an all-purpose family first car? Or one mainly for your job? Or primarily for long trips? Or just to go back and forth from the railroad station? What kind of weather will you be driving in? In what kind of traffic conditions? How much cargo room do you regularly need—honestly? (Roof racks or rented trailers are more economical for very occasional cargo hauling than an investment in a station wagon.)

(3) Do your homework before you buy.

Among your best sources are: the "Annual Roundup for New Car Buyers" issue of *Consumer Reports,* which includes frequency-of-repair records for popular makes and models, published in April and available at newsstands; the yearly "Buying Guide" issue of *Consumer Reports,* published in December and available at newsstands or from Consumers Union of U.S., Inc., 256 Washington Street, Mount Vernon, New York 10550; Edmund's *New Car Prices* (American makes) or *Foreign Car Prices,* from Edmund Publications Corporation, 515 Hempstead Turnpike, West Hempstead, New York 11552; Car/Puter's *New Car Yearbook,* from Davis Publications, Inc., 300 Lexington Avenue, New York, New York 10017; such auto and motor journals as *Car & Driver, Road and Track, Motor Trend, Automotive News,* which compare performance, price, and other aspects of each new model. (Check current prices for each publication.) Ford Motor

Company publishes *Car Buying Made Easier,* which is full of easily under-standable information on car buying. For a free copy, write: Ford Motor Company Listens, The American Road, Dearborn, Michigan 48121. (The box number usually is the year in which you write.)

(4) Use the following abbreviated chart to rate various new cars you are con-sidering buying and to compare costs:

	CAR 1	CAR 2	CAR 3
Net cash price:			
Taxes:			
Preparation costs:			
Cost of other extras:			
Cost of options you want:			
Key warranty coverage:			
Miles			
Years			
Parts			
Labor			
Other			
Expected gas mileage:			
Safety features:			
Passing ability			
Stopping distance			
Tire reserve load			
Space:			
Ride:			
Frequency-of-repair record:			
Handling:			
Luggage space:			
Passenger space:			
Ease of getting in and out:			
Looks:			
Dealer's reputation:			
Availability of parts, service:			
Efficiency of service:			

(5) Be honest with yourself about how important status is to you, as expressed by an automobile.

If you had to make a trade-off, would you prefer a more expensive model with almost no extras? Or the best of the lower-priced models, with budget room for the extras you want?

(6) Ask yourself how long you intend to keep the car. As indicated above, the longer you keep the car, the lower its cost will be, since depreciation is greatest in the earlier years.

Thus, if you expect to drive the car into the ground, a good time to buy is in the July-August-September period—what the car manufacturers call the "build-out" time. Statistics show a good, alert car buyer can average 10 to 15 per cent off list price, but in the third-quarter time span, this may be as high as 20 to 25 per cent. In effect you are buying a "semi-used" car, eight to eleven months old. Another way to do this is to purchase a current-model used rental car. (See pages 387–88.)

However, if you plan to keep your car only a few years, buy early in the model year. A snowy Monday in January of a slow car year is probably the best time of all to buy a new auto.

(7) All other things being equal, buy a car which a dealer has in stock. Obviously, color, options, two-door, four-door styles, plus make and size are important considerations; but be prepared to bend one way or another, or be ready to shop several dealers *in your own area* for one which has in stock a vehicle acceptable to you. The dealer is paying interest on *his* purchase of that car, too, and wants to unload it. And his markup margin on options may be two to three times his profit margin on cars.

(8) Make up your mind in advance and in the quiet of your own home what options are really important to you. Typically, purchased accessories can add one third or more to the total list price of your car. Be flexible, choosing a car in stock which may be minus what you consider a key item. You always can purchase most options from discount stores and install them yourself. This was dramatized during the 1970s by the rage for citizens band radios. Obviously, larger engines, heavier suspensions for boat towing, automatic transmissions, and the like are items you can't "add on" easily. But virtually all others are negotiable, if the price is right, even air conditioning, or the color of the car itself.

(9) Consider the *gasoline mileage*—and other maintenance costs—of the car. But don't overstress such aspects. You can get a *relative* idea of what mileage you'll achieve by looking at the stickers on the car windows, but that is about all.

The mileage you really attain depends upon so many factors that it is impossible to make these comparisons properly. Keep in mind that there is no free lunch. A car that is fuel-miserly simply may be one with an axle and transmission ratio so low that it is difficult to accelerate across a street before the light changes.

(10) Beware of diesel-engine cars in that respect, too. Diesel fuel as the 1980s neared cost about the same as gasoline, but fewer stations carried it. You'll also pay thousands of dollars in premium for a diesel engine.

Unless you plan to drive 20,000 to 25,000 miles a year and keep your car twenty years, stick to a traditional gasoline power plant.

SHOPPING FOR AUTO OPTIONS

CHOOSE WITH CAUTION

Since options easily can add one third to the basic price of your car, and often can boost its price by 50 per cent, accessories are important considerations for you as a car buyer.

Because the dealer's markup on options can be extremely high, he also can "trade" better with a highly optioned car than he can with basic transportation.

In addition, some options retain more of their value at trade-in time than do others.

Finally, many options can add to your car operating costs. The expenses listed in an earlier section presumed that a car was equipped with a standard engine, but that it had air conditioning, power steering, power brakes, automatic transmission, radio, and heater.

More than 75 per cent of all cars sold are equipped this way, but the figures can mislead you. More than half of all new domestic cars sold, compacts and larger, are purchased primarily for *non*-personal driving. Thus, the "fleets" dictate a large measure of the optional equipment on new cars.

You can get an idea of the role fleet buyers play by checking the "most popular" car color, as listed by the manufacturers. It is white. But you don't see many white cars on the road. The reason: white is simply easier to repaint—to become a police car, taxi, or transport pool vehicle.

Which options you choose will depend on the importance you attach to them.

RUNDOWN ON KEY OPTIONS

Here is a rundown of the major extra items.

Larger engine—adds about 5 per cent to your car's purchase price. It would give you more pickup and better performance, and may be necessary if you plan to tow a boat. But, all factors equal, bigger engines will use more gasoline and cost more to maintain (eight spark plugs, for example, versus six or four). Even the major fleet buyers, long holdouts for the larger power plants, have been moving to six-cylinder engines for most cars; and for subcompacts, four are usually sufficient.

The key factor is not in the number of cylinders an engine boasts, but the cubic inch displacement (or area) of those cylinders—the bore and stroke.

Even with air conditioners, automatic transmissions, power steering, and brakes, you usually don't need an eight-cylinder power plant for most driving, but you may need one with more "cubes."

Automatic transmission—another 3 to 5 per cent of purchase price. This is one which engenders controversy. Old-timers who learned to drive with the manual shift, or "straight stick," believe automatic transmissions are threefold money wasters: they cost more to begin with; they eat gasoline; and they are costlier to repair.

In addition, purists feel they rob the driver of "control." The ultimate, these traditionalists maintain, is "four on the floor"—four-speed forward manual shift (plus one in reverse). As much as 15 per cent better gasoline mileage is claimed for straight sticks.

The other side of the argument is that millions of you can't drive a manual shift car well, so the automatic transmission is not only a convenience, but a fuel saver.

If you can drive a straight stick and plan to keep your car more than four or five years, forget the automatic. But if you trade annually, or often, go for the automatic. It holds value at resale time. (See pages 357–60 for gas-saving tips.)

Air conditioner—10 per cent added to purchase price. In Maine, no; in Florida, yes. Elsewhere, maybe. Again, high resale value retention, but prone to breakdown, a contributor to car overheating, a fuel waster, and a weight-adder. Check the car's ventilation system (some are notoriously bad, others fairly good). If you can do without the air conditioner, try—you always can add a "hang-on" unit later, for not much more than the cost of the original equipment air conditioning. On top of this an air conditioner almost demands tinted glass— which tacks on another 1 per cent or so to your purchase price (and can reduce nighttime vision). It also may put you into a bigger engine and the need for power steering.

Power steering and brakes—another 4 to 6 per cent onto your bill. On big cars, these items have become almost a necessity to handle the heavy engine and other options. But with Detroit chopping huge chunks of weight from its cars to meet new federal fuel economy standards by the mid 1980s, the need for these items may be somewhat reduced.

These power options will neither stop you better, nor help you steer more precisely. They just enable you to do both with less effort; and power steering is a help in tight-place parking. The decision will lie in the relationship between your weight and that of the car.

Remote control outside mirrors—less than 1 per cent of car cost. Take two, they're small. The electrically controlled types of the past were prone to failure, but newer versions are more reliable and they are a definite safety feature. If the car you want doesn't have them, buy them from a discount accessory store.

AM radio—2 per cent of car value, and overpriced at that. For about the same money, you can get an AM/FM version and install it yourself or have it done. Some versions have stereo and tape-deck capability and other models now also have that biggest of all fads of the 1970s—citizens band radio.

CB radio—a few words about CB—citizens band radio—which some people call "children's band." In theory, it is marvelous. In the country and in rural areas—and in cases of emergency—it is useful. In the city, it is a shameful disappointment.

Many sets are so cheap—in every sense of the word—that virtually anyone can afford them; and those who can't, steal them. Everyone talks ad nauseam, making meaningful urban-area transmissions difficult. Even the emergency Channel 9 often is cluttered with "skip" transmission—beams bounced off the atmosphere and back to earth several times. The forty-channel sets provided some relief, but not much. So-called "single sideband" versions are a definite improvement. They provide eighty additional channels and increased transmission range (ten to fifteen miles on flat land, against four to five with the regular AM sets), but in the late 1970s these sets suffered from the opposite problems—not enough people monitoring these channels and talking on them as opposed to too many on the AM bands.

The Federal Communications Commission, which is supposed to be in control, has virtually abdicated its responsibility, and the CB wavelengths were chaos as the 1970s closed. Some CB users resorted to illegal linear amplifiers to overpower their messages through the airwaves; but as more and more people tried such tactics, the confusion was merely compounded—everybody talking louder and nobody able to listen.

In sum, buy a cheap CB set, install a magnetic roof mount for your antenna, and use it for emergency transmissions only. Your costs should be about 1½ to 2 per cent of the purchase price of the car.

Rear-window defoggers and wipers—2 to 3 per cent of vehicle purchase price. An excellent safety feature for hatchbacks and station wagons.

Vinyl roof—3 to 3½ per cent of purchase price—a useless item, despite everything you may hear about appearance and resale value. Difficult to keep clean; a vinyl roof also marks a used car as a possible former police cruiser or taxicab, as these are used to disguise the holes made by the taxi and police light-and-siren mountings.

Power windows—another 3 per cent or so of a car's purchase price, and another waste of money. They are failure-prone, use electricity, and can be a child safety hazard.

OTHER OPTIONS

There are almost limitless additional options, both factory-installed and "after market" items which are strictly a matter of individual judgment. A warning, though: for the do-it-yourself enthusiast, many of the add-on items require you to drill holes. This is fine if you intend to keep the car until it goes to the junkyard. But if you expect to trade it in every two or three years, these add-ons can make your car look like a dart board inside and out.

Computers—in the late 1970s, Detroit manufacturers had climbed aboard the computer bandwagon, with the luxury makes beginning to offer "on board" electronic gadgets which tell you everything you ever could want to know about your car—from how much fuel you are using at any given minute to how long it will be until you get to your destination.

Computers for cars will become more efficient and less expensive each year. When they reach the level of 2½ to 3 per cent of car cost, they probably will be worthwhile. Essentially, they measure fuel use, time, and distance—and spray statistics from these three bases. Some are hooked to key vehicle components to alert you to the condition of your car: from battery charge to ignition timing to the amount of air in your tires.

Air bags—in the late 1970s air bags were not generally available to the public, but they could be by the early or mid 1980s. They have been the center of intense controversy, with the government and most segments of the insurance industry lined up in favor, the auto manufacturers against.

Even their basic costs are a matter of heated dispute, and data about their upkeep is a mass of misunderstanding. The automobile industry, this time, seems at least to have logic on its side—with the claim that other forms of "passive restraint" e.g., *automatic* seat belts, are better and cheaper.

Some small foreign cars already have these automatic safety harnesses available. They work with pulleys and springs when you open and close the car doors and early models are extremely unsightly. The air bags, in contrast, are stowed compactly, virtually out of sight.

But one experienced automotive journalist who "tested" an air bag during its early stages of development pronounces the bags themselves "a distinct safety *hazard.*" If they deploy unexpectedly, incorrectly, when a car is in traffic, the odds are high they will *cause* an accident, he says.

"I took my pipe from my mouth, doffed my hat, removed my eyeglasses—and *bang.* It was like being hit by Muhammad Ali. I was stunned and dazed for seconds and would not have been able to control a car during that time."

Granted, he says, they would *save* lives. But, with millions upon millions on the road, some would go off unexpectedly. And even the costs of bags, as estimated by their proponents, would add far more to the expense of the car than passive safety harnesses. In addition, the cost of rearming them after they had accidentally misfired would come to almost as much as installing them in the first place. Finally, they would *not* give protection against sidewise, or "T-bone" crashes, as would the passive safety harnesses. With air bags, you still would need lap belts.

Trim and moldings—a wide range of costs. Carpeting, color-co-ordinated upholstery, reclining seats, clocks, vanity mirrors, interior trim, and other inside items are strictly articles of individual preference.

A nice item available on a few models is individually folding rear seats, so you can make half your car a load-carrying station wagon (or bed). A similar fold-down *front* seat is an item which should become available as Detroit moves to satisfy consumer demand for versatility in travel.

The popularity of the hatchback—really a station wagon that looks like a sedan—attests to the public's desire for a double-duty or triple-duty vehicle.

One item you should *never* pay for: the fake-wood outside panels on station wagons. They can add to the car's weight, rust faster, chip easier, and dent quicker. Laugh at the dealer when he tells you he will "throw them in" for nothing on a particular model he is pushing. (On used cars, they may even hide collision damage, as vinyl roofs hide taxis and squad cars.)

"Shopping" for a Dealer

At least as important as picking the right car with the right options, and buying at the right time, is shopping for a dealer. In the long run, it could be *more* important.

• Stick to dealers in your own neighborhood. You can reach them fast and they can't duck you easily. If, though, you choose to buy a new car from a dealer some distance from your home, try to estimate what it would cost in fuel alone to go back and forth for repairs, servicing, warranty work. Don't ignore the cost of time lost from work.

• Also stick to members of the National Automobile Dealers Association and dealers who are franchised by the major automobile manufacturers (the auto manufacturers will give you the names and addresses of such dealers in your area if you ask them). The key advantage of dealing with a franchise dealer is that you can ask the manufacturer to put the screws on him if he fails to honor the warranty, fails to make repairs he has promised, etc.

• Ask your neighbors and friends for guidance on local automobile dealers.

Find out not only whether a dealer has a reputation for offering a fair deal but also whether he follows through by delivering the car when he promises to, by reliable servicing, by honoring warranties. How long must his customers wait for routine servicing and for emergency repairs both in and out of warranty? What days—and hours—does the repair shop operate? Saturdays? And evenings? Will the dealer pick up and/or return your car if you need this type of convenience? Is his advertising honest or does he claim "fantastic savings"?

• Read and compare the warranties the manufacturer offers at the dealership. Have the warranties explained to you, for warranties have changed substantially in recent years and undoubtedly will continue to do so. Ask the dealer if you can buy an owner's manual and warranty for the models you are interested in purchasing, then take them home and read them.

THE DEALER'S PROFIT

It is difficult to determine the dealer's markup on a car—from wholesale to retail. It usually ranges between 15 and 25 per cent, depending on the make, size, and model car in question. But this does not equate with dealer profit. He has his own overhead to consider: so, just because you can get the "tissue" price on some car from a computer car sales service, from a leasing company, or from some car magazine, don't assume the best deal is one $50 to $75 above this tissue price.

The manufacturers offer dealers so-called holdback percentages, based on the number of cars they sell from one model year to the next. Sales contests also provide extra income to dealers, as do kickbacks from financing companies and insurance brokers. (See pages 328–38 on saving money in your car insuring and financing.)

Accessories, too, provide another bargaining element for dealers. His markup may be 50 to 100 per cent on such items; but, again, the dealer overhead—rent, salesmen's salaries and commissions, light and heat, as well as advertising—all must be factored.

A dealer must make a profit—and he'll make it one way or another, if not on the sale of the car, then on its servicing.

Thus, it is reasonable to expect that you will pay more for your car if you buy it from a midtown, big-city dealer rather than from a franchised outlet in a suburban or rural area. But if you live in a big-city, midtown area, the convenience to you in getting the car serviced may be worth the extra price.

DICKERING FOR A DISCOUNT

There are few hard rules about the discount you should expect. For if you are like most car buyers, you have a used car to trade. Thus, it is often difficult even to determine the true discount you are getting.

Don't fall for the gimmick the salesman may use of whipping out a used car price book from his inside coat pocket to "prove" to you that he is giving you $100, $200, or $500 "over what the book says." Such "books" are a dollar a dozen and their quotations generally have no relationship to reality. (More about trade-ins later.)

The best tactic is to tell the dealer you have not made up your mind whether to trade your old car or not—that you may keep the car as a "second" or sell it yourself. *Stick first to the price of the car you want to buy.*

Don't commit yourself, either, to whether you will be financing the car through the dealer, or buying your insurance from him. Determine what the purchase price of the car alone will be—then ask him what that will involve in monthly payments, how much would be required as a down payment, what the cost of insurance would be.

When you have made your decision to buy, get a written sales agreement which has been approved by the sales manager, and read it with utmost care before you sign. Have all blank spaces crossed out or marked *void* by the dealer. On extra charges for such services as "preparation" or "undercoating" of the car, keep in mind that preparation (an item often costing between $35 and $150) is included in the advertised retail price of all U.S. cars and undercoating should not cost much more than $35 to $40.

And make sure any oral promises the salesman has made to you regarding special servicing or adjustments to the car are included in the sales contract before you sign it.

Even if your car is in stock, on the dealer showroom floor, make certain exactly *when* it will be delivered. If, for some special reason, you are ordering the car for future delivery, note on the contract that delivery time is "of the essence." If delivery is to be more than a few weeks away, and your deposit is a substantial one, be sure that you get interest on your money in the interim. But again, the best buy is a car in stock—even if you have to shop a half-dozen dealers *in your area* to find one that meets your requirements.

WARRANTIES—AND HOW TO COMPARE THEM

As emphasized in the analysis on the costs of owning and running cars, maintenance costs can be a significant factor in your overall auto outlays—averaging almost 15 per cent of total expenditure over the life of the vehicle, though these outlays are lower in the early years, higher in the later ones.

Getting all you are entitled to under your warranty, therefore, is an important element in reducing your costs. Manufacturers carefully calculate the costs of their warranties—*and build these charges into the prices they charge for their vehicles.* They *expect* you to collect on your warranty.

Of course, they don't *tell* you they expect you to collect. But some manufacturers stress the liberality of their warranty in their advertising. So, pay the closest attention to a car "feature" which could be important you. So vital is this aspect that you will find a full analysis of it on pages 1207–9 in the chapter on your rights.

SPECIAL RULES FOR BUYING A NEW ECONOMY CAR

DOWNSIZING OF CARS YEAR BY YEAR

There's no mistaking the downsizing of cars to achieve federal fuel economy standards and to help make at least some pretense that prices are not rising as much as dollar statistics suggest. Each year's models are smaller, lighter, use more plastic, aluminum, and glass in place of steel, carry fewer eight-cylinder engines.

But if you're in the market for a new economy car, are you aware of the yardsticks by which to make a critical assessment of this car in terms of your own needs? Have you ever awakened to the fact that you have bought a car that isn't quite what you need only after you have taken delivery—and it is too late to correct your mistake?

If you have made that commonplace error, it can be not only burdensome but also extremely expensive should it reach the point where it involves trading in your new car for another.

To begin with, what is the definition of an economy car?

One booklet listed three criteria in the late 1970s.

(1) It seated four or more persons.

(2) It had a suggested list price of $4,400 or less. This was exclusive of optional equipment and destination charges.

(3) It had an Environmental Protection Agency (EPA) rating of 22 miles per gallon or more for combined city/highway driving.

Many automobiles on the market meet this definition.

But with manufacturers retiring many models each year (as always), the automobiles meeting the criteria also will be constantly changing. What's more, not all models within the above lines meet all the criteria for an economy car.

Don't try to zero in immediately on the "best" car for you. This haste will put you under too much pressure, tend to confuse you, and will place emotion ahead of reasoning. The result often will be that you'll choose the wrong car.

Instead of placing your emphasis on finding the cars you like, place it on eliminating those you don't like. By narrowing your selection to those cars "you can live with," you give yourself a wide choice and are almost sure to choose one you will like.

HOW TO BUY AN ECONOMY CAR YOU CAN LIVE WITH

Key Rule One: Don't assume the car with the most miles per gallon is automatically the most economical. This is wrong. The initial purchase price is generally the most important factor in determining the economy of an economy car—usually much more important than miles per gallon. The reason: you also must take into account sales taxes and finance charges, which multiply the differences between two cars.

Let's say, for instance, that the sales tax in your area is 6 per cent and you intend to finance your car at 12 per cent simple interest for three years. Each additional $100 in the price of your car will cost you almost $127—$100 plus $6 tax plus $21 in interest. Thus, a $300 difference between two models might really be a $380 difference; a $500 difference is $634; and a $1,000 difference is $1,267.

If the more expensive economy car gives you better gas mileage, can it pay for itself through lower fuel costs? Probably not.

Take one car that gets 22 mpg and another, costing $300 more, that gets 30 mpg. At 15,000 miles a year and 85 cents a gallon for gas, you would have to drive the more expensive car for more than two years before you would break even.

The difference in cost of gas between 36 and 40 mpg, at 15,000 miles a year and 85 cents a gallon, is $35. If you pay $300 more for the 40-mpg car, you would have to drive it more than nine years to recover your extra investment.

Key Rule Two: Do *not* buy a new car on your first trip to a dealer—even though this may have been your procedure in the past, you like the current ads about the car, and it's a quick, easy way. Instead, make at least three trips to auto dealers: one to become familiar with the car; two to test-drive the car seriously; and three, only after you already have made your choice at home, actually to buy the car.

Make a list of economy cars, so you don't overlook any.

Consider only those cars whose dealers are convenient to your home or place of work. Service and parts are important, so eliminate any inconvenient dealers. (Also, of course, avoid a dealer with a bad reputation for service or any other essential.)

Decide just what kind of body configuration and equipment you want. Do you need a four-door model because you're in a car pool? Or do you need a two-door model because you have young children? Do you need a trunk because you carry valuables that must be kept out of sight? Or do you need a hatchback because you carry heavy loads? And do you need an automatic transmission because one of the drivers in your household can't operate a stick shift? Make your firm decisions on these points before you even visit a dealer.

You well might want: radial-ply tires, which can give superior traction and last longer than conventional tires; a day-night inside mirror, which improves rear vision (and reduces driving fatigue) at night; reclining seats, which enhance driver comfort; and a rear window defogger/defroster, which is a major safety aid in damp or freezing weather.

But options which while desirable are not essential would include: body side moldings, cloth upholstery (but choose vinyl if you have small children), armrests, intermittent windshield wipers, clock, five-speed manual transmission, tinted window glass, rear window washer-wiper, and opening rear side windows. Nearly all these are desirable, though, and are standard or available at extra cost on most economy cars.

Weigh, too, the relative merits of the trunkback and the hatchback (or liftback)—and make your choice entirely on the basis of your needs. If it doesn't matter to you, you will have many more cars from which to choose. As for front-wheel versus rear-wheel drive, decide that based on how the car rides and handles.

BASIC TESTS BEFORE BUYING A NEW ECONOMY CAR

Your first trip to various dealers will be for basic self-education only. You would not buy a new car on this trip. You shouldn't even drive one.

• Bring along anyone who will be paying for, driving, or riding in your new car. But leave your small children at home. This self-education trip will take the better part of a whole day—and it would be neither wise nor fair to your children to drag them along. They actually could be a major drawback.

• Even though you won't be driving any of the new cars on this first trip, you will be busy. For you will be finding out the availability of the equipment you want, judging the styling and interiors of these cars, collecting brochures, getting a general idea of prices, and forming an impression of each dealer.

• Perform at least the following four tests, as part of your strategy of eliminating cars that aren't right for you.

TEST No. 1 is based on your pretrip decisions regarding equipment and configuration. Find a salesperson and ask about aspects you deem essential: air conditioning, automatic transmission, four doors, two doors, hatchback, trunkback. If what you want is not available, cross that car off your list and move on to the next auto dealer on your list.

TEST No. 2 is far more subjective. Do you like the car's styling? If not, ask to look at other versions with different trim or colors. If you still find nothing you can live with, cross that car off your list.

TEST No. 3 is to try out the inside, if you find the car that is available with the equipment you want and you can live with its looks. Sit behind the steering wheel, make yourself as comfortable as you can, critically appraise what you see and feel. Rate the steering wheel position, seat comfort, headroom, elbow and knee room, foot room, accessibility of gauges and controls.

TEST No. 4 centers on the dealer, assuming the car has passed the first three tests. Is the salesperson trying to move you into a more expensive car? Are the new economy cars shunted off to a corner? If so, that could mean neither economy cars—which you want—nor you, a potential owner, is important to that dealer. If this is the case, then cross that dealer off your list.

• Of course, once you start asking questions, a salesperson may try to make a deal with you on the spot. Resist. Don't say, "Just looking," but instead say, "I'm shopping around." In this way, you inform the salesperson that you're a serious customer.

• On your way out, pick up literature about the cars that interest you. Write down the sticker prices for the cars and the options you like and want to buy.

• Visit as many dealers as possible on this first self-education trip. When you return home, you will find that you will have eliminated cars you can't live with and dealers that appear unsatisfactory. And you will have literature and rough prices on the cars that really interest you.

• Now you're ready to think seriously about what you have accomplished. Certainly, you don't want to go back out that same day to test-drive any cars. Wait awhile. Meanwhile, study the sales brochures to learn what is available in terms of optional equipment and trim. Don't assume equipment is not available because it isn't in a brochure. Call the salesperson to find out if it is a dealer-installed item.

Almost surely, when you started your hunt for the "the best economy car in the world," you had eight or ten or maybe even more models of cars under consideration. Merely by the four tests you have applied on your first self-education trip, I'll wager you have pared down that list—and perhaps now only three or four remain.

These are the three or four cars you'll test-drive on trip No. 2. And from these test drives, you'll find the one that you believe is just right for you.

THE FINAL CHOICE OF THE BEST ECONOMY CAR FOR YOU

You have now visited several dealers for basic self-education only. By applying four key tests, you probably have narrowed down the initial number of new economy models from which you might have made a final selection to, say, three or four.

On this, your second trip to visit the dealers offering these few models, you should test-drive the cars still under consideration, appraise their passenger and cargo specifications, get firm prices.

But you still won't make a final decision. So you should leave your checkbook at home and resist all lures.

Try to test-drive a car that is equipped similarly to the automobile in which you are interested. And don't drive it just around the block. Tell the salesperson that you're a serious customer and need to drive the car far enough to make an informed judgment. Then drive the car as you normally drive and on the kinds of roads you normally use. For your goal is to find out how well it fits your particular needs.

Let's say your choices have been narrowed to three cars. Each of these three has passed the first four tests outlined in the previous section. Now while test-driving each, you'll be rating the car on tests 5 through 13. To summarize each of these tests:

(5) Gauges and controls: are they visible and easy to use while driving?

(6) Visibility: can you see easily while changing lanes or parking the car?

(7) Steering effort: is it acceptable even when the car is stopped?

(8) Ventilation: do you get enough air with the windows closed and vents open?

(9) Noise: can you carry on a conversation in a normal voice at surface street speeds? At highway speeds?

(10) Acceleration: do you have enough power to keep up with traffic in view of the way you drive?

(11) Braking: have you confidence in the power of your brakes during normal driving?

(12) Ride: is it comfortable on the kind of roads you usually use, keeping in mind that a slightly firm ride is generally more comfortable on long trips than a soft ride?

(13) Handling: does the car go where you want it to go when you turn the steering wheel?

Rate each car on each of these points with a simple "like," or "don't like." This can be extremely revealing. And when you finish the drive, ask yourself whether you feel a sense of relief or regret when you shut off the engine.

Don't expect a car to score perfectly. If, on balance, you believe you can live with a particular car, based on its road test, then go on to evaluate the interior.

(14) Front passenger room: enough for the person who normally will be your passenger?

(15) Rear passenger room: What is the ease of entry? Is there enough room for the people who normally would be your backseat passengers? And if you have small children, might they outgrow the back before you're ready to get a different car?

(16) Cargo: hatchback—can you easily load or unload cargo without hitting your head on the hatch? Will your favorite suitcase fit behind the rear seat? (Don't guess; try it out.)

(17) Cargo area: trunkback—does the trunk lid swing up out of the way for easy loading? Will the trunk accept what you usually put into a trunk—bags of groceries or a big suitcase?

Obviously, none of these tests requires any technical skill on your part. You're evaluating the cars based on your own needs and likes. Beyond a few items of equipment you are ignoring specifications.

For whichever economy cars remain in the running after test 17, get firm prices that include all the optional equipment you want as well as tax, license, and registration. This is your total cost, not counting finance charges.

Now, which car is best for you? If only one car remains, that's it. If more remain, you might choose between the one that is lowest-priced and another you prefer for other reasons.

How to Finance Your Car

You have located the car you want to buy and arrived at a fair price. Now you are shopping for the best possible deal in financing the car—for I'm assuming that you, like two out of three new car buyers and half of used car buyers, plan to buy on time. On top of steep interest rates on automobile loans, and the ever-increasing prices of the cars, financing costs also are being hoisted by the trends towards longer and longer repayment periods (ranging as long as five years in the late 1970s on a new car); lower and lower down payments (often only 20 per cent); and larger and larger loans (the other 80 per cent). In the late 1970s the *average* new car loan was for more than $4,000. The *average* monthly car payment was more than $120, and typical interest—paid and lost—was $1,200 to $1,500 over the term of the loan.

THE BEST WAYS TO SHOP FOR AN AUTO LOAN

Here, therefore, are your best ways to shop for the best deal in financing your car:

• Ask the dealer from whom you intend to buy the car exactly what financing terms he'll offer. Don't consider *any* deal unless the total financing charges, over the full life of the loan, are spelled out clearly in writing—including the amount of the cash down payment, the unpaid balance to be financed, and the true annual percentage cost. This detailed disclosure is required by the Truth in Lending Law: be warned if it isn't made.

• Ignore such slogans as "easy payment terms" until you know exactly what these terms actually mean in dollars and cents.

• Plan to make the biggest down payment you can—if possible, at *least* one fourth to one third of the purchase price—and try to repay in the shortest period you can manage. Of course, your monthly payments will be larger this way than if you stretched out the loan, but you may save hundreds of dollars in interest.

Study this stark table showing what you pay in finance charges on a $1,000 loan extended for twelve, twenty-four, thirty-six, forty-two, forty-eight, and sixty months.

$1,000 Loan

RATE	12 MONTHS	24 MONTHS	36 MONTHS	42 MONTHS	48 MONTHS	60 MONTHS
8%	$ 43.86	$ 85.45	$128.11	$149.83	$171.82	$216.58
9%	49.42	96.43	144.79	169.47	194.48	245.50
10%	54.99	107.48	161.62	189.31	217.40	274.82
11%	60.58	118.59	178.59	209.34	240.59	304.55
12%	66.19	129.76	195.72	229.58	264.02	334.67
14%	77.45	152.31	230.39	270.64	311.67	396.10
16%	88.77	175.11	265.65	312.48	360.33	459.08
18%	100.16	198.18	301.49	355.10	410.00	523.61
20%	111.61	221.50	337.89	398.49	460.66	589.63
24%	134.72	268.91	412.38	487.53	564.89	726.08

Even before you get the facts on financing a car through your car dealer, visit your local bank or, if you belong to one, your credit union. Ask the loan department what terms the bank or credit union will offer. Make sure such variables as the down payment you intend to make and the period (in months or years) during which you will repay the loan are the same when you compare each lender's terms.

In general, the most expensive sources of automobile credit are new and used car dealers, the automobile finance companies which often work with them, and small loan companies. The least expensive sources are credit unions, which usually charge the lowest rate of true annual interest and which tend to lend relatively large amounts toward purchase of new or used cars; commercial banks, which charge auto loan interest rates generally comparable to those of credit unions; and your life insurance company, if you have a policy with a cash value against which you can borrow, at the lowest rate of all.

By all means, put up collateral—securities you own or other assets or a savings passbook—if this will reduce the net cost of your loan to you.

• Find out what provisions are offered by each lender for prepayment of the loan. Will you get a full or nearly full refund of future finance charges if you are able to repay the loan more rapidly than you have planned? Is there a penalty for late payments? What are your rights in the event of repossession—such as fair warning before this takes place? Does the contract include an "acceleration clause," making all payments due immediately if you fail to make a payment on time?

• Shop for automobile insurance separately. Don't merely accept the package offered by an automobile dealer, for very possibly you will find that your regular insurance agent will offer the same coverage at a lower cost. Avoid being pushed into a costly credit life insurance provision. This would pay off the car loan in the event of your death, but the cost of credit life insurance tends to be relatively far greater than that of your regular life insurance—which should be sufficient to pay off your smaller debts.

CHECK LIST FOR COMPARING CAR FINANCING COSTS

Here's a check list which will show you how to figure and compare the dollar cost of financing your car:

	LENDER A	LENDER B	LENDER C
Price of the car, including taxes, options, and all other extras			
Minus down payment			
Minus trade-in allowance			
Amount to be financed			
Amount of monthly payments			
Number of monthly payments			
Total amount of monthly payments			
Total dollar cost of auto loan			

It cannot be stressed too strongly that you should make your *auto purchase,* your *financing* and your *insurance* deals *separately.* Not only is financing through a dealer almost always higher than via other sources, but often you can find yourself in the three-in-one tie-in package: you finance for four or five years, so you must have full insurance for that length of time—and the full multi-year insurance premium is tacked on to the "front end" of what you borrow. You not only pay your insurance premiums ahead of time (putting money in the pocket of the insurer early) but you are paying interest on those insurance payments, which you needn't have been paying in the first place.

It takes longer, but shop separately, and first, for your loan and your insurance.

INSURING YOUR CAR

THE RISE IN INSURANCE COSTS

Automobile insurance—covering collision, fire, theft, and other property damage, as well as liability for injuries you may cause to others—has been the fastest-growing element of your car's ownership and operating costs in recent years.

The premiums for this protection zoomed far beyond other inflationary increases during the 1970s, more than doubling in one recent three-year period. In the past, insurance was pegged at less than 15 per cent of overall expenditures. Today that ratio is more than 20 per cent—and your protection coverage now ranks second only to the car's depreciation as the single most expensive element of automobile operation. It's even ahead of gasoline in recent years!

And these rate hikes have come at a time when you were assured that you might expect actual insurance cost reductions, or at worst only moderate boosts in premiums, as a result of so-called no-fault laws put into effect in many states— revised rules under which every insured accident victim is paid for lost wages, medical expenses, and other direct economic losses, no matter whose fault the accident was.

These promised savings have never materialized.

A study in the late 1970s showed that insurance rates literally were chaotic. And if car owners think they had it rough, truck operators had it even rougher.

For instance, a truck operator based in Manchester, New Hampshire, making regular delivery runs to Fort Lauderdale, Florida, and back, was charged $948 for liability insurance alone (not fire, theft, or collision) on just the tractor, or cab section, of his eighteen-wheel combination tractor-trailer rig. Yet if this trucker switched his headquarters from New Hampshire to Fort Lauderdale, and made the same round trip between those two points, the same number of times with the same loads, his annual premium for the exact same coverage would jump to $1,596 a year—68 per cent more.

To a lesser degree, car owners are the targets of similar mindless penalties.

The insurance industry laments that the glowing promises of the no-fault proponents simply have not been realized because trial lawyers have watered down all proposed no-fault legislation to next to nothing.

OTHER INSURANCE COMPLAINTS

Second only to the public dismay at the soaring insurance costs is the outcry against the fine print of the insurance policy. "You're covered for everything except what happens to you" has long been a national joke among insurance buyers.

Here you may be getting a little relief: a number of companies have introduced "plain talk" policies that tell you in understandable English exactly what coverage you have, and have not. These "translations" may stand alone, or accompany the old-style legalistic language.

CRASH REPAIR PRACTICES

Many insurance companies themselves say that the most frequent complaints they receive concern crash repair claims. Most states now have laws which specify that:

• An insurance company cannot turn down a claim on the basis that it isn't covered in the policy unless it informs you of the specific policy provision which excludes your claim.

• The company must acknowledge receipt of your claim within ten working days unless the claim is actually paid within that period. Also you must get a reply from the company within seven working days on all communications regarding your claim which call for a reply.

• Investigation of your claim must begin within fifteen working days of the company's receipt of it. You also must be furnished with any statements, forms, or other papers you need to process your claim.

• If your car is "totaled," you have the choice of taking a replacement auto or a cash settlement based on the actual cost of buying a comparable car of like kind and quality in your local area.

• Insurance companies must pay the amount of money finally agreed on or authorize necessary repairs no later than ten working days from receipt of such agreement by the company. And if additional time is needed to investigate your claim, the company must so advise you and give the reasons the additional time is needed.

PUSH FOR FEDERAL CONTROL

Despite the fact that the state-by-state no-fault insurance laws have not worked as was anticipated, pressure continues for a countrywide, federal no-fault system.

A Department of Transportation study in the late 1970s was devastating to the old "fault" system. Under this traditional method, DOT said, victims with serious losses received far less than they actually lost and they often received it much later than they should. Ironically, the government said, victims with the *least* losses often recovered *more* than they had lost, largely because the insurers pay to be rid of the nuisance of the claim.

In blunt summary, under the "fault" system, about 20 cents of each premium dollar goes for legal costs, 44 cents to the victim. Under no-fault, 5 cents on each premium dollar goes to the lawyer, 60 cents to the victim. More benefits can be paid under no-fault because of the elimination of many unnecessary lawsuit expenses and of overpaying of small, nuisance claims.

DOT concludes "the existing [fault system] ill serves the accident victim, the insuring public and society. It is inefficient, overly costly, incomplete and slow. It allocates benefits poorly, discourages rehabilitation and overburdens the courts and legal system."

A national no-fault automotive insurance system well may be emerging in the early 1980s. And it may be everything its proponents claim—providing all things to all people, fairly, justly, promptly, and efficiently.

But the threat remains: lawyer-lobbying, industry influence or simply bureaucratic bungling well may have slashed the effectiveness of the national system, as happened to the state-by-state approach.

HOW TO REDUCE YOUR INSURANCE COSTS—MAYBE

You are caught in a bind in your approach to cutting back your insurance premium outlays:

(1) Because inflation has increased the costs of the car you are insuring, and also has increased the size of the awards which injured people are collecting, you must keep raising your maximum coverage limits.

Thus, you, the motorist, are hit with a double whammy; the inflation spiral means it is costing you more simply to retain the same maximum coverage on liability; and your higher car costs mean you are paying additional dollars to cover property damage insurance.

(2) The higher awards being handed down by judges and juries mean you

must hike your maximum liability coverage, producing still more in increased premium charges.

Your best escape clause is the "deductible." This is the dollar amount which you, the policyholder, decide that you can afford to pay yourself—the amount for which you, in effect, decide to "insure" yourself.

A rule of thumb in the auto insurance industry has been that your auto insurance deductible should amount to slightly more than one week's pay. Back in 1945, the average weekly salary for a typical worker was calculated by the Bureau of Labor Statistics at $44.20. A $50 deductible range was considered about right.

But over the decades since, while the average weekly wage has moved steadily higher, many drivers still carry a $100 collision deductible. A more realistic application of the rule of thumb would place the deductible for the average worker at between $250 and $500.

Another rule of thumb is that there should be a close relationship between the purchase price of your car and the amount of your deductible. In 1950, the average selling price of a new car was under $2,000, so a $100 deductible represented about 5 per cent of the value. If this rule of thumb of 5 per cent were applied today, it would raise today's deductible to $275 or $300.

Here are approximate savings that you could attain on your physical damage coverage by raising your collision deductible from $200.

To $250—a saving of about 10 per cent;

To $500—a saving of about 35 per cent;

To $1,000—a saving of about 50 per cent.

And if your deductible is still at $100, any increase from that level would of course give you even greater savings.

On your comprehensive coverage if you raised a $50 deductible to $100, you would save about 20 per cent on the premium.

Also, when you obtain insurance with a higher deductible, the U. S. Government shares a portion of your risk. The reason is that the portion of the loss you pay in excess of $100 is allowed as an itemized deduction on your income tax return and thereby reduces your taxable income.

If you're driving a car that's more than three years old or worth less than $1,000, consider dropping collision coverage entirely. No matter how much damage is done in an accident, you usually cannot collect more than the actual cash value of the car. This may not be enough to repair the damage.

Meanwhile, inflation has boosted court settlements to such a degree that everyone driving should carry a policy which provides for payment of up to $100,000 per person for injuries and up to $300,000 for total accident damage liability. Many Americans with modest incomes now have policies which call for a $500,000 to $1 million limit.

The costs for such expanded coverage are relatively small—and could be more than offset by the increase you put into effect on your deductible.

SIXTY-FIVE OR OVER? CUT YOUR AUTO INSURANCE!

If you are among America's mounting millions of citizens who are sixty-five years of age or older, and you also drive your own car, you well may be overlooking an important area for saving money in your automobile insurance.

In many states, you, a driver of sixty-five or over, are entitled to lower auto insurance rates. Even in states where you can't get lower rates, you may be able to cut your insurance premiums because your life-style now reduces your exposure to accidents and thus alters your insurance needs.

Rating systems used by the major auto insurers in the United States vary from company to company. State Farm Mutual, largest auto insurer in the nation, offers to policyholders sixty-five or over rates that are generally 5 per cent lower than its rates for adults under sixty-five. In a few states, rates for the sixty-five-and-over are about 10 per cent less.

You, an older driver, are by no means necessarily a safer driver than a young adult—despite the lower insurance premiums available to you. In fact, liability claims from older policyholders exceed those from adults under sixty-five.

But the key to the lower rates is that claims payment rates for comprehensive and collision coverages on cars owned by the sixty-five-and-over are substantially less than claims rates on cars owned by other adults.

The net result works out to a lower premium for the sixty-five-and-over in most states.

As for the lower premiums for you, in a state where you are entitled to lower rates, the explanation here is that you may be less exposed to accidents—particularly if you retire from work—and no longer drive to and from work or use your car in business.

Insurance companies base their rates partly on how far you drive to work and your car's total mileage each year. Your premium may be slashed if and when you notify your insurance agent that you're not driving to work or your own business any more.

What you save varies from one insurance company to another and from state to state. If you have been commuting between 30 and 100 miles each week, and you stop driving, your rates may go down 10 to 15 per cent. Or if you have been driving more than 100 miles a week to and from work, your rates may go down 20 to 25 per cent.

You also may get a lower rate if you drive your car less than 7,500 miles a year—a group including many sixty-five-and-over couples who do not travel extensively by car. For instance, if you formerly drove more than 100 miles to and from work each week and, if after your retirement, your total annual mileage falls below 7,500 miles a year, your premiums may be reduced by more than 30 per cent—a savings not to be underestimated.

Ask your auto insurance agent if you are entitled to lower insurance premiums at your stage of life and according to your present life-style. He'll advise you what's best in your situation.

But don't try to lie. Unless your agent knows you're driving less, you won't get the lower rates to which you may be entitled. Your agent can tell you precisely how much you could save by either eliminating your collision and comprehensive coverage on an old car or by raising your deductibles no matter what your car's age.

And of course, your insurance agent will know whether your company (or any other) gives lower rates to drivers sixty-five-or-over in your state.

Insurance regulators are also moving to force the insurance companies to revise their premium rating standards for drivers—particularly those rates based on sex and marital status.

The insurance commissioners believe that premium surcharges for young, single males, for example, should be revised, even though insurance company statistics show that such drivers generate more and higher claims.

The latest trend is to base premiums more on mileage driven and upon driving experience. This trend may lower insurance costs substantially for some drivers while raising them for others.

COST-CUTTING CHECK LIST

Go over the following analysis with your insurance agent if you have any reason to believe you are not now getting the full advantages of discounts and reductions available to you.

• Decide first what types and amounts of coverage you need, then check the costs of the coverage you want offered through auto dealers and from reputable insurance agents and firms. One good approach is to solicit bids for your business from several reputable insurers. Reason: rates for liability coverage alone can vary as much as 50 per cent from one insurer to the next in a given area.

Use this chart to make cost comparisons:

		Rates Quoted		
COVERAGE	AMT. OF LIMITS	Co. A	Co. B	Co. C
Liability	. . ./. . ./. . .	___	___	___
Medical payments		___	___	___
Personal injury protection		___	___	___
Uninsured motorist				
Collision	. . . deductible	___	___	___
Comprehensive	. . . deductible	___	___	___

• Find out if such "extras" as towing and temporary car rental costs are included in each package.

• Check the reputations of dealers for financial soundness in *Best's Insurance Reports* and try to stick to dealers with a *Best's* rating of A or A+. This is only a guideline; many reputable dealers have lesser ratings.

• If you are a student, enroll in a recognized driver training course to qualify for a 5 to 10 per cent premium cut. Nearly fourteen thousand schools in the United States now offer these courses. In addition, the National Safety Council has launched a "Defensive Driving Course" whose graduates in some states are being offered substantial premium reductions.

• If you are a student age sixteen or over with a high (B or better) scholastic average, you may be eligible for a "good student" discount of up to 25 per cent. You also may get a substantial discount if you attend a school more than 100 road miles from home or wherever the family car is kept.

• Explore, if you are a young driver, the possibility of getting a "restricted" policy, using your family's coattails as a form of financial security.

• If you change your commuting habits—switch from a car to a train or bus— notify your insurer at once so he can reduce your premium rate accordingly.

• If you are an older person, ask about special policies and discounts offered by most companies based on your age bracket's good driving record. In many states, the typical discount for drivers over age sixty-five is 5 per cent. (See pages 334–35.)

• If you drive your car fewer than 6,500 miles a year, check whether you're eligible for as much as a 10 per cent rate cut.

• If you quit smoking or drinking, find out whether your company offers reductions for non-smokers or teetotalers.

• If you work for a large company or are a member of a union, social, or professional group, check whether you can get low-cost insurance for your group. This *alone* can cut your own premiums 15 per cent or more.

• Check carefully what's offered by a *reputable* mail order insurer; savings could run to 15 per cent.

• If the dealer from whom you are buying a car offers you collision or comprehensive insurance as part of the deal (to protect himself or the firm which is financing your purchase), find out whether your local insurance company or agent will offer you a lower-cost deal.

In almost every instance, you'll find that, with common-sense shopping, you can beat the dealer price. Also, as noted in the previous section on buying your car, the dealer may tie in your insurance and your financing—and you could wind up paying advance premiums of up to five years, and interest on those advance premiums as well.

• If you already have health insurance, make sure you are not taking on medical payments coverage which duplicates the coverage in your group or individual health insurance policy. Today, more than four out of five Americans are covered by medical insurance, and some auto insurance policies rule out duplicate payment if your health insurance policy already fully covers you. (On the other hand, you might want to *increase* your medical payments coverage if you regularly drive a group of children to school or fellow commuters to work.)

• If you move from one state to another, inquire immediately about auto insurance rates, for these rates vary widely in the United States today. For example, the cost of bodily injury liability insurance on a recent-model four-door sedan driven by a thirty-year-old married man with a clean driving record in Bismarck, North Dakota, was only one quarter as much as the exact same coverage in New York City. Comprehensive coverage in Bismarck for this same man and vehicle was two fifths of the New York City premium.

• If you're a farmer or rancher and use your car or pickup truck only on and around your farm or range, check on your eligibility for a farmer's auto insurance discount.

• If you're buying a new car, keep in mind that rates on a "muscle" or high-performance car may run 20 to 50 per cent higher than average. If you buy an inexpensive or low-powered car, though, you will be charged a lower-than-average premium.

• If you are unmarried and you insure your car in your family's name, stating that you are the principal driver, you are likely to pay a lower insurance premium than if the car is registered in your name and you are listed as the sole driver.

• If you are a family head, insure all the family cars under the same policy; a second family car generally can be insured at a discount of about 20 per cent on the grounds that two cars in one family are likely to be exposed to less risk than two single cars would be.

• And save by paying your premiums annually, if your company bills that way.

• Inquire about any less-well-known discounts which your insurance company might offer—for instance, discounts of up to 20 per cent for models with bumpers that meet certain damage-resistance standards.

• Don't file collision claims which are just over your deductible or you may lose your "good driver" discount.

• Leave your car outside the city limits; your rates won't be as high if you can show you don't bring your car into a city. If you park your car in a garage, tell your agent; this could qualify you for lower rates than regular on-street parking.

• If your car is more than three years old, or a jalopy worth less than $1,000, you may find it's not worth it to carry collision insurance at all.

You also might simply make your coverage a little less comprehensive. Normally, comprehensive insurance protects you not only against fire and theft but also, if you wish, against a whole list of other perils including flying or falling objects, explosions, vandalism, earthquakes, windstorms, hail, water, floods, civil commotions, riots, and collision with a bird or animal. To illustrate the possible savings, if you were paying a $200 annual premium for full comprehensive coverage as the 1980s neared, you might have paid only $60 a year for insurance against fire and theft only.

The important point to remember about automobile insurance is that it is intended to protect you against a financial catastrophe, especially if you do not have other means of protecting yourself against such a catastrophe.

Automobile insurance (and this also goes for other types of insurance) was *never* intended to help you budget. It was never designed to pay for small repair bills for which you ought to be able to budget routinely. Common sense should urge you to trade off a higher deductible for a higher upper range of liability coverage.

A typical car owner carries at least a minimum 10/20/5 (see "Liability Limits," page 341) auto liability insurance policy—the minimum required under state financial responsibility laws. (Some states require 15/30/5 or even 20/40/10.) But if you should be found responsible for a fatal accident, the jury verdict against you easily could amount to $50,000, $100,000, or even $1 million and up.

Here, then, is a table showing you the typical—minor—cost of raising your present bodily injury liability coverage to meaningful levels.

COVERAGE	ASSUMED YEARLY PREMIUM COST
$ 25,000–50,000	$100
50,000–100,000	110
100,000–300,000	120
500,000–1,000,000	135

IF YOUR INSURANCE IS CANCELED

You have not had an auto accident and your driving performance generally has been good—but suddenly your auto insurance policy is not renewed. Or suppose you do have a rotten driving record and you're having trouble getting any insurance coverage at all. What should you do?

Countless millions of you have been exposed to the frustrations of these typical auto insurance problems. If this includes you now or in the future, here's what you should do:

If your policy is not renewed, first contact the agent or salesman who sold you the policy and find out why. In many instances the non-renewal may have nothing to do with your driving record. For instance, the agent may no longer be doing business with that company or the company may have withdrawn from your area. You then may find the agent already has switched your policy and you have no problem at all.

If you learn that the non-renewal was for cause and feel this is unwarranted, write the company. In most states an auto insurer is required to provide an explanation if you, the policyholder, ask for it. If the non-renewal is related to a change in your credit standing, you have the right to know the name and address of the credit rating bureau so you can check your credit file and correct any misinformation that may have crept into it.

If you find erroneous information about you or your driving record in the insurer's file, it is essential for your own benefit that you correct it. If, on the other hand, the non-renewal had nothing to do with your personal characteristics, this information will be helpful when you seek coverage from another company.

IF YOU'RE A BAD RISK

Among the strikes against you when you go to buy auto insurance today in addition to your accident or conviction record—if it's a bad one:

> your age—if you're under thirty;
> your race—if you're non-white;
> your residence—if it's in a major city.

If you're an American under twenty-six years old, and particularly a single American male, you may be paying a penalty of as much as four times the automobile insurance rates being paid by other drivers.

You pay so much more for automobile insurance simply because your age bracket has the highest accident rate in the nation. Traffic accidents, in fact, are responsible for one half of all deaths of Americans between age fifteen and twenty-five.

If you have trouble getting any auto insurance, shop around. Many insurers have companion companies that specialize in insuring those with a higher-than-average risk exposure. If your insurance agent is unable to get coverage for you, you must be placed in an "assigned risk" category, a "pool" required to insure "poor risk" drivers. States usually require companies in the plan to keep bad risks at least three years. Most drivers can get regular insurance after a three-year good driving record.

The rates charged for insurance in assigned-risk pools are far higher than in the regular market in many states. Drivers with poor records, though, always pay higher rates whether they are in or out of a risk pool.

In shopping for high-risk insurance coverage, watch out for the gypsters. Beware of advertised rates which are suspiciously below those charged by other insurers in your area for your risk category.

If you question the legitimacy of *any* high-risk mail order insurer (and note: *most* are legitimate and do offer insurance below rates charged by insurers with elaborate offices and sales organizations), inquire about the insurer's reputation at your State Insurance Department or State Commissioner of Insurance office. And check *Best's Insurance Guide* for the record of financial soundness of any high-risk mail order company with which you're considering doing business.

If all else fails, and if your previous policy has been canceled for reasons you consider to be unfair—send a written complaint to your state insurance commissioner, with copies to your local Better Business Bureau and also your congressman. And find out what limitations (if any) your state may put on auto insurance cancellations.

The Bafflegab of Auto Insurance

ADJUSTER   Employee or agent of an insurance company whose job it is to help settle auto insurance claims by deciding the extent of financial loss in an accident, and also the extent of the insurance company's liability.

APPRAISAL   Estimate of the amount of loss sustained by a car in an accident—which becomes the basis for a settlement by the insurance company.

ASSIGNED-RISK PLANS (or AUTOMOBILE INSURANCE PLANS)   Plans in operation in all fifty states, the District of Columbia, and Puerto Rico, which sell bare-bones protection to drivers who cannot otherwise get liability coverage.

BAD RISKS   Individuals whom the auto insurance industry labels such bad drivers, with such bad accident records or such poor statistical odds of keeping out of an accident, that they are required to pay extra-high insurance premiums—even assuming they can be insured at all through regular channels.

BODILY INJURY LIABILITY INSURANCE   Pays damages and legal costs if your car kills or injures people in an accident and only if the driver of your car is at fault.

CANCELLATION   Termination—by you or by your insurance company—of your auto insurance policy before it actually expires. Rules for cancellation of auto insurance by the company should be spelled out in the insurance contract.

CLAIM   Demand by an insured individual for the amount of his or her loss insured and covered by the insurance policy. A *claimant* is the person making a claim.

CLASSIFICATION   Categorization of insured individuals according to the extent of risk they represent—statistically—to the company. Taken into account are the individual's occupation, age, similar factors.

COLLISION INSURANCE   Insurance which pays for damage to *your* car if you collide with another car or object, or turn your car over. If an accident is clearly the other fellow's fault and if he has liability insurance, his policy probably would pay to have your car repaired or replaced. However, if there's no way to prove whose fault the accident was, or if the other person involved isn't insured, collision insurance helps cover losses.

COMMISSIONER OF INSURANCE   (or SUPERINTENDENT OF INSURANCE or DIRECTOR OF INSURANCE)   Key official in your state whose job it is to oversee and enforce the state's auto insurance laws.

COMPREHENSIVE INSURANCE   Insurance which pays for damage to your car from a variety of mishaps other than collision, including not only fire and theft, but also damage from missiles, falling objects, larceny, explosion, earthquake, lightning, windstorm, hail, water, broken glass, flood, malicious mischief or vandalism, riot or civil commotion, and collision with a bird or animal. Comprehensive insurance also covers the cost of renting a car if yours is stolen.

CREAM   The best drivers—statistically speaking—and, therefore, also the best auto insurance risks. These pay the lowest premiums and include Americans over sixty-five, women over age twenty-five, and middle-aged family men.

DEDUCTIBLE INSURANCE   Coverage under which a policyholder agrees to pay up to a specified sum in each claim or accident toward the total amount of the insured loss. The higher the deductible, the lower your premium.

DOC (Drive Other Cars) INSURANCE   Coverage which protects you, the driver, against liability or bodily injury or property damage while you are driving a borrowed or a company car.

FINANCIAL RESPONSIBILITY LAWS   State laws under which car owners are required to prove they are financially responsible—a requirement most people meet by owning a certain minimum dollar amount of auto insurance. Such proof is required either to register a car or to preserve your right to return to the road after you have had an accident.

FULL COVERAGE   Coverage for the full amount of covered losses, without any deductibles.

GUARANTEED RENEWABLE   Insurance policy which the covered individual may renew up to a certain age (e.g., sixty or sixty-five) or over a certain specified numbers of years.

LIABILITY INSURANCE   Protection against claims in the event you injure or kill someone else—or damage his property. This insurance covers legal expenses and also protects others driving your car with your permission, and it protects you and members of your family when you drive someone else's car with his permission.

LIABILITY LIMITS Maximum amount for which you are covered by a given policy—frequently expressed by a succession of three numbers separated by slashes, designating maximum coverage for bodily injury and for property damage. For example 10/20/5 means insurance protection of up to $10,000 payable to any one accident victim in an accident caused by you; up to $20,000 in protection for *all* victims in such an accident; and up to $5,000 in insurance protection against property damage caused by your car to other cars, other people's garages, etc.

MEDICAL PAYMENTS Coverage of a wide range of "reasonable" medical or funeral expenses within a year of an accident not only for the car owner but also for reasonable expenses of any other people who are injured or killed in his car. Medical payments coverage also applies to the policyholder and members of his family while riding in or being struck by any other car. Payment is made no matter who caused the accident.

NO-FAULT Type of automobile insurance which an accident victim is automatically compensated for part or all of his medical costs, wage losses, and other expenses associated with the accident by his own insurance company, without regard to who caused the accident. But such programs are usually widely modified, so many victims can sue other drivers who seem to be at fault, under a variety of conditions.

NON-OWNERSHIP AUTOMOBILE LIABILITY Liability coverage for loss or damage caused by you while you are driving a car not owned by you.

PAIN AND SUFFERING Vague, albeit very real, category of claim in auto liability lawsuits for financial compensation to cover intangible losses such as fright, mental anguish, emotional shock, etc.

PROPERTY DAMAGE LIABILITY INSURANCE Insurance which protects you if your car damages another person's property, and if driver of your car is at fault. This usually means the other person's car, but it also can mean Japanese gardens, garages, lampposts, telephone poles, and buildings.

RISK Insured person or thing. In the case of your automobile insurance coverage, you and your car are the principal "risks."

SAFE DRIVER PLAN Widely used system under which insurance rates are adjusted up or down according to your own driving record.

SCRAP VALUE Estimated value of a car which has been involved in an accident if it were sold as junk.

TOTAL LOSS Car which has been so badly damaged that it is not considered to be worth repairing.

UNINSURED MOTORIST INSURANCE Insurance, sometimes called family protection, which covers you, all members of your family, and any guests in your car for bodily injury losses when an uninsured or flagrant hit-and-run driver causes the accident. This type of insurance also pays medical bills and income loss due to bodily injury if the insurance company of the other driver, who caused the accident, goes bankrupt. And it covers you and all members of your family who are injured by uninsured or hit-and-run drivers while you are walking or riding on bicycles. Payments are limited to the required liability minimums in your state. In some states, this insurance does *not* pay for bodily injuries.

UNSATISFIED JUDGMENT FUND   An alternative, in a few states, to uninsured motorist coverage, for this is a fund against which you may file a claim if you are hit by an uninsured motorist.

TRADING YOUR CAR

In most instances, an important element in buying a new car involves trading in your secondhand auto. You can do this in one of two basic ways: by trading your car to the dealer from whom you are buying the new one, or by selling the car directly yourself.

SHOULD YOU DO IT YOURSELF?

If you want to sell your used car on your own, you'll save the cut of 10 per cent or more a car dealer would tack on as his profit. But you'll have to do your own advertising and selling. And you'll have to find out, too, what is a fair price for the car—considering its make, model, warranty status, age, looks, and mechanical condition.

Consider the fact that you may have to pay a higher finance charge on your new car if you sell your old car on your own. If, for instance, you keep your $1,200 used car for a time-consuming sale to a private individual, you'll raise the amount of the new car loan by $1,200. This could boost the finance charge by $234 over a three-year period on a 12 per cent loan.

Also, if you live in a state where trading an old car for a new one reduces the sales tax on the new one (you pay sales tax only on the cash amount you pay the dealer), recognize that you'll have to get a higher price from an individual to make up the loss of this saving. For instance, the sales tax saving from trading a $1,200 car in a 6 per cent sales tax state would be $72; you would have to get $1,272 for the car on the open market to get a deal equal to a trade-in.

In addition, when you sell your own car, you are, in effect, becoming an auto dealer yourself, assuming many responsibilities under new buyer protection laws. For you, now, are no longer a buyer, but a seller, in an era of caveat *vendor,* or let the *seller* beware.

ACTING AS YOUR OWN DEALER

But more and more of you are assuming the role of being your own auto dealer. Of the 13 to 15 million used cars retailed each year, estimates are that at least one fifth are sold directly by their owners.

And the savings? The average dealer markup from wholesale to retail on used cars is about 22 per cent (and may reach 50 per cent including refurbishing and transportation if the car is auctioned from dealer to dealer). If you split the average markup, both the seller and the buyer come out $350 to $500 better for a typical recent-model car.

There are other dangers and drawbacks in private selling, too. For one thing, you now risk going to jail if you tamper with the odometer, under the 1978 Anti-Rollback Law.

WHAT PRICE TO ASK

How much should you, as a private seller, charge for your car? One way to get the answer is simply to study the newspaper ads for several weeks to see what cars of similar make and mileage are bringing.

Refer to the previous section on depreciation and calculate your car's basic wholesale price. Then add on to that the rate at which inflation has eroded your dollar's value since then. The average new car purchased for personal pleasure driving is kept an average of 5.2 years (against just 2.4 years for the business car). So assume your car has depreciated 80 per cent or so. Subtract that amount from your car's original purchase price and you have your raw wholesale value.

Add to this the inflation that's taken place in the time you've had the car. Then check its mileage. The depreciation figures apply to cars driven an average of 10,000 miles a year. If your car is five years old and has gone only 40,000 miles, it is 10,000 miles "younger" than it should be, and you can add still more to its selling price.

How much? Again, figure your overall costs per mile and take about 6 per cent of that figure. For instance, if your costs per mile average 31 cents, your per-mile add-on figure will be just 2 cents a mile. Multiply that by your 10,000-mile difference and you have about $200 to be *added* to your wholesale costs. (Of course, if your car has 60,000 miles on it, you subtract that $200 from your wholesale price.)

Now look at your maintenance costs. Over a five-year period, your per-mile upkeep expenses should have totaled about 10 per cent of your overall operating expenses—about $1,250 at prices prevailing in the late 1970s. If you've spent *more* than that—for example, recently bought another set of tires, a new battery, adjusted the brakes, etc.—you can add that to your price. If you've spent less, subtract it.

With your resulting figure, add 10 to 12 per cent as your profit.

(See pages 379–83 for more on selling your car—yourself or to a dealer—in the later section on *when* to get rid of your used vehicle.)

If you decide to trade your car or sell it on your own, these do's and don'ts will help you get a better price.

Do:

wash the car;
polish it;
touch up paint and chrome;
clean stains from upholstery;
vacuum the interior;
wash floor mats;
clean out trunk, glove compartment, and other storage areas;
check all fluid levels (gas, water, oil, transmission and brake fluid) to insure proper operation during a test drive;
check tires and adjust pressures;
replace any burned-out light bulbs.

In addition to using the obvious classified ads in local or regional newspapers or shopping throwaways, try all free or inexpensive methods of advertising when you put your car on the market: word of mouth, notices on bulletin boards, classified ads in company newspapers, a prominent sign on the car, a "trading post" announcement on your local radio station. Be sure to include times and telephone numbers at which you can be reached by prospective buyers.

When you arrange meetings with possible buyers, try to accommodate their preferences for times. Be honest, but not apologetic, about your car. Do not permit a demonstration drive if your car is not insured for other drivers or if the prospective buyer cannot show you his driver's license.

Be firm about the price, assuming it is the book value range. You may come down to a lower price if the buyer looks right, but don't begin by indicating the price is flexible.

If a buyer needs time to arrange financing, insist on a binder payment of 5 to 10 per cent of your asking price before you agree to hold it for him. And accept payment only in the form of cash or a cashier's check.

Don't:

- invest in a new paint job—it will only cost money and raise suspicions in a potential buyer's mind of what you may be trying to hide;
- invest in major repairs—it's too late for them, and you will be able to recover only a small fraction of their cost;
- spend money on little details a potential buyer may well shrug off: a clock that doesn't run, a window that sticks, that sort of thing.

Whether you are selling your used car to a private buyer or to a dealer, the above rules will help you get the proper value for it, and help you hold down your important depreciation cost for your car—the difference between what you paid for it and/or what you sold it for—as low as possible.

Curbing Your Auto Repair Bills

By the late 1970s, you, America's motorists were spending between $45 and $50 billion each year to maintain and repair your automobiles—about 20 per cent the total $225 billion in annual outlays for all car costs.

This high percentage stems from the very nature of auto repairs—which are done on an individual basis, whereas the car itself is mass-produced.

As a result, it would cost four times as much to rebuild an auto from the ground up, according to insurance data, than it required to produce the complete car in the first place. Put even more bluntly, if a car suffers 25 per cent damage, repairing it would cost as much as you paid for it new—probably more, in view of annual inflationary cost increases.

MAINTENANCE COSTS—BY AGE OF CAR

What should your automobile's repair and maintenance expenses amount to each year? If you drive a typical 10,000 miles annually, here are figures for each year on an average 1977 intermediate sedan, along with their percentage of the total, since inflation will undoubtedly boost the dollar amounts relentlessly higher and higher.

YEAR	COST	% OF TOTAL	YEAR	COST	% OF TOTAL
1	$161	5.5%	6	$292	10.0%
2	231	7.9	7	308	10.5
3	244	8.3	8	347	11.8
4	256	8.7	9	380	13.0
5	268	9.1	10	446	15.2
			TOTAL	$2,933	100.0%

Of course, if you drive greater distances each year, your costs will be higher . . . fewer miles and they'll be lower. Also, there will likely be "bulges" and contractions from year to year if major purchases are made—such as for tires—or postponed. These figures and percentages are just averages. And, they are figured in "constant" dollars, meaning unadjusted for inflation.

HOW STATISTICS CAN DECEIVE YOU

Some studies—the U. S. Government's among them—say that maintenance charges are even lower in your car's early years than private figures show, and higher later on. But the Federal Highway Administration maintenance cost figures are obtained simply by "checking the service managers of major automobile dealerships in the Baltimore area." The figures I'm using are national averages published by major fleet operators.

On top of this, the manner in which some government figures are presented masks the potential savings of keeping your car longer—perpetuating the trade-in-sooner myth.

These statistics are calculated on the assumption that newer cars are driven more miles each year than older ones—14,000, 15,000, and 16,000 miles annually in the first years of a car's life, but dwindling to just 4,000 or 5,000 miles every twelve months in the final years of a vehicle's service.

Aside from the fact that these statistics may be a fluke (the large number of new cars which go into high-mileage fleet service may distort the use pattern) simply presenting them on a *per-mile* basis in this manner lowers the overall *per-mile* expenses in the early years (since the fixed costs are spread over a larger number of miles then) and raises the *per-mile* outlays later on (when the fixed expenses are spread over a smaller mileage base).

Whether you use 10,000 miles a year, 15,000 or even 25,000, you get a more reliable picture of your cost savings by using a constant annual mileage from year to year rather than employing the varying mileage method—which may, itself, be a statistical mirage.

WARRANTIES HELP

If you are lucky, you may not need any major auto repairs until your car has gone 12,000 miles or more. And your repair bills will be paid for through your warranty before then. After that mark, though, you well may face a parade of minor repairs: brake relining; reconditioning of brake drums; possibly an alternator overhaul; replacement of cylinders, hoses, shock absorbers, muffler and/or other parts of the exhaust system, batteries and numerous smaller parts of the electrical system ranging from headlights to the voltage regulator and ignition coil. You're also likely to be confronted with a variety of problems involving the various pumps—water, oil, and fuel—that help keep your car running.

If you keep your car past the 50,000 milestone, you almost surely will need some major repairs—a transmission overhaul or even a whole new transmission, a "valve job," involving extensive repair or replacement of your engine's valves and related parts. At this point, too, the likelihood also becomes all too real that you'll have to have your car's engine overhauled or even replaced at a cost of hundreds of dollars. Some of your car's complex options—air conditioning, power windows—also may start to fail.

Or if you are in a costly collision at any stage of your auto's life, you may face big-ticket repairs running into hundreds of dollars.

Larger cars, obviously, will be more costly to fix; smaller ones will require less outlay. Standard-size vehicles in the late 1970s cost only about two thirds of the intermediate expenses in the list above, larger models required 12 to 15 per cent more.

In the early 1960s, Detroit auto manufacturers entered a "warranty war" which led to guarantees on various parts of vehicle for up to five years or 50,000 miles, at no extra charge.

The companies soon back-tracked on such largesse. But as the 1980s began, the auto makers again introduced longer warranties, this time on an "optional" basis. For specified sums, a buyer could purchase an optional extended warranty for varying periods and mileage, up to three years and 50,000 miles.

Most of these warranties require a "deductible" for each visit to the dealer. You pay the $25 to $50 "deductible," and the warranty takes care of the rest. The warranty covers only the original buyer and it must be purchased at the time you buy the car.

HOW TO SHOP FOR AN AUTO MECHANIC

• Start shopping for repairs *before* you need them. It's too late when your car conks out and you need service at once. Make a plan of action now; have a list of places you would take your car should you need minor repairs, major repairs, simple maintenance, etc.

• Check with your friends and acquaintances on their experiences with local auto repair shops.

• In states which license auto repair facilities, stick to the licensed establishments.

• Make a deliberate choice between your new car dealer, repair boys in local gas stations, independent general mechanics who do not sell gas, and shops in specialties such as brake relining, muffler replacement, or wheel alignment—and recognize you do have these four alternatives.

For instance, if you like the dealer from whom you bought the car and have come to trust him, his shop is probably your best bet. He is apt to give you good, fairly priced service in the hope that you will also buy your next car from him. And he probably will be familiar with your car's quirks and will have ample stock of the parts the car is most likely to need. But if the dealer from whom you bought seems not interested in servicing, go elsewhere.

Convenience is the key advantage of a local service station—and you easily can establish a valuable relationship with a station if you buy your gas there and take your car to the station for regular servicing. Here too, look for the proprietor who considers his service area a major part of his gas station operation. Many gas stations are not equipped for complex repairs, though, and—as a result—generate customer complaints.

Your third alternative is the independent mechanic whose earnings depend primarily on repairs and servicing, his ability and reputation. The independent, though, may not be as conveniently located as a gas station, may not be able to do repairs on as short notice as an automobile dealer—and may not have as complex a line of special tools and parts as the dealer.

For some types of work—such as muffler replacement or brake lining—you may be able to save money by patronizing a specialty shop which does a large volume of repairs in these areas and which has accumulated all the special equipment, parts, and expertise needed to perform them. But carefully check out the reputation of any outside specialty shop before you turn your back on your regular mechanic. And remember that these shops are sometimes highly skilled at selling you repairs you don't need.

• Whatever type of establishment you choose to patronize for repairs, note whether the mechanic and/or owner solicits your repeat business. The competent, honest shop will want you back. Its mechanics will schedule work with as much regard for your convenience as possible; will explain as much about the repairs your car needs as you seem capable of absorbing. They will take the time to make a careful diagnosis of your car's problem instead of casually informing you, "That sounds like your 'whatzit' and will cost fifty dollars to fix." They even may tell you the work you thought you needed isn't necessary until later—or isn't needed at all.

• Try to find a place where you can talk face to face with the man who will actually work on your car. In many shops, the customer sees only a person who writes work orders for the mechanics to follow. This fellow is primarily a salesman, rather than a mechanic. He well may be working on a commission basis, so that the more repairs and parts he sells you the more he earns. If you speak directly with the mechanic, you're less likely to be talked into unnecessary or inappropriate service. Also, two-way communication is much clearer than a few words scrawled on a service order. And the mechanic is likely to feel more responsibility toward the job if he has discussed it with you personally.

If an establishment won't let you indicate you're willing to pay for the time he spends talking to you, go elsewhere.

• Consider taking a course on auto mechanics at a local extension college, night school, or similar place. Even if you never work on a car, it will help you to evaluate the mechanical competence of others.

• Be your own mechanic whenever possible, if you're capable and so inclined. First you'll save money—most obviously on simple repairs, for which you pay a skilled mechanic the same hourly rate as for complicated ones. With a little practice, you'll also be assured that what you do is done right. Most important, you'll become better acquainted with your car's workings and will be less easily baffled or intimidated by a serviceman if a breakdown occurs on the road.

DO IT YOURSELF—AND SAVE

In some areas, do-it-yourself auto service centers, which rent repair bays and tools (at $5.00 to $6.00 or so an hour, depending on the equipment you use), make it easier to do at least some of your own work. They may even provide free advice if you run into problems. If there is no such facility in your area, there may be one soon: the idea is catching on fast. Savings, even after rental fees, can run to 75 per cent on some jobs.

Of all the motorists in the United States, 47.5 million are maintenance do-it-yourselfers for at least some repairs, but fewer than 1 per cent are women. We usually offer the excuse "lack of know-how."

Yet there is absolutely no justification whatsoever for our ignorance when eliminating unnecessary expense can help you cut your car costs so substantially. And actually, the auto parts manufacturers are now launching a major drive to attract us.

They are writing their ads directly to us in newspapers and magazines; putting on do-it-yourself instruction classes the nation over, many "for women only"; simplifying their how-to instructions. Auto parts also are being made increasingly available in supermarkets, drugstores, discount houses, and department stores, where women represent the majority of customers.

The amounts of money you can save, first by proper auto maintenance and second by doing much of it yourself, are significant.

The two top jobs performed by do-it-yourselfers are installation of antifreeze and changing engine oil. Changing the engine oil yourself will not only save you labor charges but also will help you cut the cost of the oil because you can shop for the best price.

Other popular installations in descending order are: air filter, spark plugs, oil filters, windshield wiper blades, batteries, headlights, oil additives, V-belts, mufflers.

OTHER WAYS TO SAVE ON REPAIRS

• Look for reasonably detailed estimates on repairs which also indicate what work may be optional. A good repair shop will itemize parts on its bill and the parts which mechanics have taken from your car will be available for you to inspect and keep (if you wish). And although labor probably will not be itemized among repairs—very difficult to do and would cost more than it is worth—the mechanic can estimate the proportion of his time devoted to each job.

• Give preference to shops willing to warrant their work. For instance, some dealers will now guarantee repair work for 4,000 miles or ninety days.

• If you suspect you have been overcharged for any parts, demand to see the suppliers' parts price list—giving both wholesale and estimated retail prices on parts of every description. To this you must add labor costs, of course. If a mechanic refuses to show you his copy of this book, be warned. You may have been gypped this time. Start looking at once for another shop to patronize the next time you need service. (A good repair shop will return old parts replaced to you as proof the work was done.)

• Once you have found a mechanic or service repair station you feel confident will give you honest, skilled, and reliable service, stay put. Many service stations automatically separate their customers into either regular, bread-and-butter business or once-in-awhile customers. And understandably enough, they tend to provide better treatment for the regulars—a great help when your car won't start on a bitter subzero morning.

• Whenever possible, make an appointment in advance for work you want done. This makes your mechanic's job easier, more profitable, and ultimately more economical for you.

• Try to avoid scheduling work on Mondays or Fridays, the busiest times in any repair shop.

• When you ask for a tune-up, or any other collection of procedures customarily lumped under one term, be sure you and your mechanic know exactly what you mean. There are nearly as many definitions of a tune-up as there are mechanics.

• When you discuss your problems with a mechanic, describe symptoms rather than giving your opinion on what needs fixing. Your view will tend to prejudice even a good mechanic and can lead to a wrong diagnosis.

• If you cannot wait to see the mechanic, leave a note on your windshield, describing what you want done if you have particular services in mind, and problem symptoms if a diagnosis is necessary. Leave your name and phone number, and leave instructions such as: "Call me before making additional repairs."

• Whenever you deal with the service writer in a large shop, make your own list of what you want done, date it, and sign it. The service writer can staple your list to his to have your signature. This will protect you from having additions made to the service order after you leave and will permit you to refuse to pay for work you did not request.

HOW AND WHERE TO SHOP FOR BIG-TICKET REPAIRS

How can you tell if, say, a new transmission or an engine overhaul is really needed?

A transmission overhaul is among the first big, costly repair jobs your car is likely to need—and it's a job that easily could pit you against some of the biggest swindlers in the auto repair business today. This is a reconditioning of the unit which transmits the power that moves your car from the car's engine to its wheels. Among the key symptoms of trouble are: puddles of fluid on your driveway; erratic gear shifting or refusal to shift at all; engine racing between shifts.

But these symptoms do not necessarily mean you need a complete transmission overhaul costing from 3 to 7 per cent of the car's purchase price! Erratic shifting can often be corrected by adding fluid or by quick and inexpensive repairs; leakage of transmission fluid frequently can be corrected for less than 2 per cent of the car's cost.

To find out just what kind of transmission work is required, a mechanic *must*, at a minimum, road-test the car and make a close inspection. In some instances, he must disassemble the transmission to determine exactly what is needed. For this diagnosis, you must expect to pay a reasonable fee. Beware, though, of the repair shop that will refuse to reassemble your transmission without being paid a whopping amount. Check into this with care *before* the shop takes apart your whole transmission.

Steer clear of any outfit which advertises a transmission overhaul at a flat rate —especially a ridiculously low rate of, say, less than 2 per cent of the auto's cost. Don't be misled by claims that your transmission needs only an "adjustment." Most modern automatic transmissions cannot be adjusted at all, and even in older ones little adjustment is possible. Don't be taken in by a mechanic who shows you metal filings in the bottom of your automatic transmission case and says you need a complete overhaul—some metal filings are a normal result of using the transmission.

Also, be just as cautious about a "valve job"—another category of big-ticket auto repairs which can cost up to 4 per cent of the car's original price or more. Although a rough-running engine, lack of power, and declining gas mileage are symptoms of poor valves, here too they may be signs of other problems as well. A properly performed compression test is a *must* for a correct diagnosis of sick valves. Be suspicious of any repairman who says you need a valve job without doing this test.

Now, what about an engine overhaul? If your car's performance falls off drastically, a complete engine overhaul may become necessary at a cost of as much as one fifth the car's initial cost. But as an alternative to an overhaul, you might buy a rebuilt engine. Assuming the engine has been properly rebuilt by a qualified factory, it is virtually the equivalent of a new engine, and factory-rebuilt engines are commonly referred to as "new." The costs of the engine overhaul and the rebuilt engine will be about the same, but the rebuilt engine usually can be installed a lot faster than the repair shop can perform an overhaul. Your old engine will normally be taken in trade, rebuilt, and later sold to someone else—which certainly should warn you to be sure the engine you are buying is actually *rebuilt* and not simply used.

"Motor exchangers" deal in rebuilt engines and some of these offer a worthwhile service at fair prices. But the motor exchange business is loaded with unscrupulous fringe operators who resort to just about any lure you can name to get your patronage and your money. Here is a sampling of the myths they use to trap you:

MOTOR REPAIR MYTHS

Myth No. 1: "Your motor can be replaced for a low flat rate." You, the customer, are told over the phone that the cost of a motor for your car will be "$149.80, exchange." The conversation quickly switches to where and when the operator can pick up your car. What he does *not* tell you is that there will be an additional charge of $50 for such items as installation, gaskets, oil, perhaps a "federal tax." Nor are you told of the $35 to $40 charge to be made if your engine block turns out to be damaged "beyond repair." Nor does the dealer mention that the $149.80 price omits a lot more parts you need just to make your car run. Upshot: after the old motor has been removed, you discover you must pay $238 for other parts and accessories, for a new total of $387.80.

Myth No. 2: "Make no down payment; take eighteen months to pay." Few motor exchanges extend their own credit. In most cases, you must pay cash for your repairs and arrange your own loan with a financial institution.

Myth No. 3: "We can give you one-day service." Under ideal circumstances, an engine can be installed in one day, but it doesn't happen very often. You must be prepared to wait several days until space becomes available in the shop or while your loan application is being approved.

Myth No. 4: "You get a 10,000-mile guarantee in writing." But nothing is said about the time limit on this guarantee—which may be as short as thirty days.

Avoid repair shops which give you bargain-basement estimates on accident repairs; they also may do low-quality work and your insurance company is almost surely willing to pay the cost of a decent job.

Be warned: once your car is in the shop and is being dismantled, you're over the barrel.

THE QUICK AND DIRTY TRICKS AWAY FROM HOME

What if your car unexpectedly grinds to a halt on a trip, hundreds or even thousands of miles from your home where you know nothing about the local service stations and there's no Better Business Bureau to call?

Although most service stations on the road are no more anxious to swindle you than those near home, some "last chance" stations actually specialize in "skinning the dude"—especially along stretches of the nation's 42,500-mile interstate highway system. They may try to sell you an oil change or a new oil filter by flashing a dipstick covered with "dirty" oil (all oil in a car looks "dirty" after a few minutes of circulation in the engine). Or some swindlers will actually slash your tires ("honking") while you aren't looking in order to sell you new ones. Or they will refuse to remount tires they have removed until you agree to buy a new set (at an exorbitant price, of course).

Or they will tell you your tires have dangerous "flaws" and must be replaced. The gullible itinerant may not only get talked into buying an expensive set of new tires, she or he also will leave the "old" still good tires behind. While your car is jacked up for new tires, they may wobble the front wheels as "proof" you need new ball joints too—but all suspension systems are designed to have some looseness when the weight is off the wheels.

Among their other quick and dirty tricks:

  draining the acid out of a battery cell, replacing it with plain water, then
    "proving" the battery is dead by a hydrometer check;
  bending windshield wiper blades and pointing out you need new ones;
  "boiling batteries"—putting an alkali such as baking soda or Alka-Seltzer in

a battery to make it foam and appear damaged or dead or pouring soapy water on the top to produce the same appearance;

"short-sticking it"—pouring "oil" from an empty can;

"short thumbing"—or not pushing the dipstick all the way in;

"the liquid smoke trick"—inducing smoke from an engine by spraying it with chemicals;

puncturing radiator hoses;

slashing the fan belt;

switching ignition wires around to make the engine run roughly or not at all;

bending wires on the alternator to make the red warning light glow;

squirting oil on the engine to simulate a leaking fuel pump or oil pump;

filling the gas tank from one pump and charging the higher amount registered on an adjacent pump;

altering amounts or adding sums to the credit card slip after you leave—or imprinting blank bills with your card to be filled in after you have gone.

Then there are "freeway runners"—advance men who hang around exits shouting friendly warnings of wobbly wheels to terrified travelers and thereby forcing them to head for the nearest service station, where, of course, collaborating con artists are waiting.

HOW TO AVOID THE TRICKS ON A TRIP

To avoid these fast-buck maneuvers, stand by and carefully watch all operations performed at any service station whose reputation is unknown to you.

If you suspect your oil has been incorrectly checked, ask to have the check repeated.

Watch the gas tank filling operations.

Don't leave your car unattended, and if you must, even for a few minutes, lock your doors.

If you want to use the rest room, lock your car and do so *before* you even talk to the service people about your car's problems.

Check the credit card slip for the correct amount before you sign and save your copies to check your bill at home before paying. Never let your credit card out of your sight.

Have your car checked regularly for possible trouble spots: e.g., tire tread, fan belt, battery, ignition and other electrical equipment, radiator hoses, spark plugs, brake fluid. Without fail, have this checkup done *before* you leave home for a long automobile trip.

Experts, in fact, say that if you're going to put on the miles—6,000 or more round trip—install a complete new or almost new set of tires before you go and take along a spare with as much tread as your regular tires. When you're pulling a camper, another two good spares are a must for the camper, if they're an odd, hard-to-get size.

If all precautions fail and you begin to suspect you are in trouble on a trip, heed the warning signals your car is putting out. *Stop early.* You will save the cost and nuisance of having to be towed off the highway. You'll also have a chance to shop around, rather than being forced to accept the services of whatever shop the tow truck delivers you to.

Make sure your travel budget earmarks at least $200 for automobile emergencies far from home and that you carry adequate oil company credit cards.

Generally, the rules for finding reliable service on the road are the same as the ones you would use at home, but you'll have to substitute advice from the local Better Business Bureau and chapters of automobile clubs for the advice of friends. An additional tip: try to find a repair shop which is a member of the Independent Garage Owners of America. Members subscribe to a nationwide guarantee plan which provides that any member garage will make good on work done improperly by another.

OTHER COST-SAVING MAINTENANCE TIPS

Auto manufacturers over the years have introduced a series of improvements which have moderated the costs of maintenance for most motorists. These include better rust-proofing, longer intervals between lubrication, longer-wearing radial tires (about which, more later), electronic ignitions, disk brakes, and such seemingly unimportant items as an automatic parking brake release and a visual coolant recovery system, which saves antifreeze by cutting down boil-offs and preventing damages from overheated engines.

Take advantage of these items in selecting your car or in buying optional equipment.

Save on maintenance by purchasing a six-cylinder rather than an eight-cylinder engine—or a four, rather than a six—as suggested on pages 315–21, the new car purchase section. Smaller engines not only keep the purchase price of the car lower, they also produce savings on maintenance.

Do your driving, if possible, in moderate weather—both extremes of summer heat and winter cold can add to your car operating costs.

In the summer, your air conditioner will have to work harder, wasting gasoline. In winter, you use more gasoline at extremely low outside temperatures and winter driving involves such extras as antifreeze, undercoating, rust-proofing, and snow tires.

In addition, winter weather also tends to chew up windshield wiper blades, requires more windshield washing fluid (admittedly trivial), and, too, tends to deaden batteries.

THE COSTS OF CORROSION

Countless thousands of cars ten to fifteen years old are still giving their owners good service and showing little evidence of structural deterioration. Equal numbers less than ten years old are in junkyards because rust has eaten away their bodies or weakened their frames. Between the extremes are uncounted thousands more which have sustained varying degrees of structural decay—some merely unsightly, others actually a threat to life and still on the streets.

Any car can rust. This prime enemy of metal has shortened the effective life of hundreds of thousands of vehicles. It's a problem that defies a cheap remedy because you, the auto owner, frequently fail to recognize the problem until too late.

But it can be averted—and the need for preventive maintenance becomes more urgent as automobile sheet steel gets thinner in many cars.

In some economy imports, for instance, the gauge of the metal is just over three times the thickness of the metal in a soup can. Sheet-metal thickness in some economy cars and imports is down to .032 inch against a consistent .037–.040 inch previously.

Treatments for the *interior* (unseen areas) within the walls of your auto's body can run from 2 to 4 per cent of your car's purchase price. Treatments for the exterior or outer surface can add 3 per cent to your car's initial cost. However, in merely a three-year span, a car which has been treated in the snow belt can be worth 8 to 15 per cent more than an untreated car, government experts claim.

You are misled if you believe that traditional optional auto undercoatings prevent corrosion, say industry leaders. This undercoating serves primarily as a sound deadener. Moreover, the skill in applying a rust retardant is equal to or greater than the compound used.

"No rust-proofing compound will protect surfaces caked with dirt, flaking, rust, water-soaked crevices, or missed areas," says the Corrosion Engineers Association. "If not thoroughly applied, the protection will not be achieved. The results are no better than the skill of the mechanics."

For your own protection, check the firm's reputation with your local Better Business Bureau before having your car rust-proofed. Note the clauses in the warranty, particularly in regard to subsequent responsibility for exterior rust.

THE COSTS OF CONSUMERISM IN CARS

On balance, there is no doubt that government regulatory agencies have done a good job of automotive safety, durability, emissions and damage control. But the cost of these advances has not been minor.

By some calculations, the price of this regulation is approaching 4 per cent of overall automotive ownership and operating costs—tens of billions of dollars each year.

One respected automotive expert has stated, only partly in jest, that proposed government programs will, in the 1980s, force the manufacturers to build a car which gets 50 miles per gallon and is safe in crashes at speeds of up to 50 miles per hour—"at a cost of $50,000 per vehicle."

In reply, it is easy to ask: what is a single human life worth?

The proper question is not what my life is worth to me, or what your life is worth to you, but what my life is worth to you, and yours to me.

Too, it should be noted that our years of highest national inflation have coincided with the years of highest ownership and operating cost increases for our cars and trucks—the backbone of our transportation and distribution system.

In their haste, some overzealous government officials have made costly errors, too. The ill-fated seat-belt interlock system (under which the car could not be started until seat belts were fastened) is one example of "do-goodism" gone bad.

Also, safety bumpers were supposed to reduce damage in low-speed collisions; but insurance premiums have continued to soar, despite these new bumpers.

Perhaps the ultimate in terms of "bum raps" was the furore created when an Oldsmobile buyer complained because his car was delivered with a Chevrolet engine, rather than the Rocket 88 he expected in his Oldsmobile. State law-enforcement officials all over the country leaped on this one.

But, in truth, the practice of putting an engine in various makes and models of one manufacturer's cars has been commonplace in the auto industry for decades. The interchangeability of parts has been one factor in helping keep costs down and in improving the efficiency of Detroit's power plants.

The Olds advertising was simply too successful: the engine never powered a rocket, nor did it have anything to do with a piano keyboard. It was purely an advertising hyperbole—which caught the public's fancy.

But when law-enforcement officials learned that the practice had been going on for years, their embarrassment only spurred them to redouble their efforts—bringing recompense to a small number of auto buyers, at the expense of all of us.

The lesson is this: what may be good in small quantities is not necessarily beneficial in large measure. A government agency created to fight a real wrong may continue to seek other wrongs to justify its continued existence, in a variation of Newton's First Law: A Body in Motion Tends to Remain in Motion.

All levels of government certainly must watch the abuses of business—and labor. The press must watch the abuses of all three. And, as consumers, you must keep your eye on everyone, and your hands on your wallets and pocketbooks.

The consumer movement has made giant strides in the automotive field—and in no area more outstanding than calling attention to car defects and in making cars better and safer in the first place.

While it may seem incongruous in these days of $20-to-$25-an-hour labor rates and $3,000 to $3,500 upkeep costs over a vehicle's lifetime, even in normal use, maintenance costs as a *percentage* of total operating expenses actually have dropped by almost 25 per cent over the last quarter century.

But still, Detroit makes many mistakes, as indicated spectacularly by the "lemons" produced and the large number of cars recalled under government programs.

RECALLS AND LEMONS

Under today's regulations, if the car you buy turns out to be a lemon, you now have significant rights, rights under which you may "revoke" your ownership of the car, get your money back or another new car, or have major defects repaired free even though your manufacturer's warranty has expired.

For example, after you have given the dealer who sold you the car a "reasonable" number of chances to fix it, and if the problem "substantially impairs" the car's value to you, you have a right to demand the replacement or your money back.

Although many of you mistakenly believe you're stuck with a lemon so long as the dealer continues to try to repair the defects, this just isn't so.

Here are tips on what to do if you find yourself in the unfortunate position of owning an automobile dud:

• From the very first day, keep records of all defects which appear in your car. Note, for instance, if it consumes excessive amounts of oil, record how much you add, when, and the odometer reading when you add it.

• Have the service manager at the repair shop initial each of the defects he has "fixed" and be sure to write down the dates of service appointments you make to correct the car's problems.

• Give the dealer a "reasonable" number of chances to fix your car and then if he doesn't or can't fix the problem and if the defect truly slashes the car's value to you, exercise your right to demand a replacement or your money back.

• Note that except when you have a full warranty, you must officially give back your car to the dealer to get a replacement or a refund. This process is called "revocation of acceptance."

• Note also that you must notify the dealer that you are giving up ownership of the car by delivering it to him and submitting to him a letter listing the exact reasons why. You must inform him as well that you are canceling your insurance and registration. Do all of this as soon as the problems start to develop.

• If you financed your car through the dealer, inform the bank or finance company that you will not make any more payments until the problem is resolved. If you got your loan directly from a bank or credit union, inform the bank or union where the car is. You might wish to continue making these payments to avoid the chance of being sued for the balance.

• Before taking any of these steps, study the *DownEaster's Lemon Guide* a booklet outlining your rights and responsibilities in this area and reporting to you about lemon owners who got unstuck. Send $1.00 to the Bureau of Consumer Protection, State House Office Building, Augusta, Maine 04333.

HAS *YOUR* CAR BEEN RECALLED?

Are you among the tens of millions of automobile owners in this country driving a car that is potentially a threat to your safety and to the safety of others on the road?

You well may be—for more than one out of every ten cars being driven today has been recalled for inspection but has never been brought in for possible manufacturer repairs.

Even worse, most of you, the drivers, aren't even aware of it.

Your failure to reply to a manufacturer's recall notice may be due to the fact that you bought your car from a used car dealer who may or may not have been told by the original owner of a recall notice. A car may pass through the hands of two or three owners in this period of frequent resales. The original owner may have been notified of the recall, but the odds are slim that the manufacturer can track down a second or third owner.

Not all the unchecked cars on the road are unsafe, of course. But manufacturers want to focus on cars that are defective and have them fixed before the owners and others are killed.

Until the 1970s, there was no law requiring manufacturers to pay for the repairs, although most of them did so voluntarily. Since some of these repairs were expensive, it is entirely possible that many of the original owners decided to accept the risks rather than pay the bills. Or by the time the buyer of the new car had been notified, he may have already sold his car. In fact, that car could have been resold many times.

Under the law as the 1980s begin, manufacturers must pay for the repairs of safety-related defects. In some instances, the car owners may request that the automobile assembler replace the car after paying differences in depreciation.

What, then, should you do, if you have bought a used car and want to be certain it's not on any recall list, or are about to buy a used car and also wanted to be sure about its status?

Call the Auto Safety Hotline of the National Highway Traffic Safety Administration—a nationwide facility—which has been set up for the specific purpose of helping you find out whether or not your car has been recalled for possible safety repairs. (Dial (800) 555-1212 for information on *all* toll-free numbers.)

Should it be determined that your car has been on a recall list, the NHTSA will send you a copy of the recall report with a postcard preaddressed to the appropriate manufacturer. The law requires manufacturers to maintain a list of all cars within the recall group that have been brought in to be checked and they are required to pass on the information to the owner of the car. This way, you, the car buyer, know whether or not to take your car into a dealer for a checkup.

You also can use the Hotline to report car problems which the NHTSA will then pass on to the appropriate manufacturer to obtain for you every consumer aid within the agency's authority. Reports which are safety-related will be relayed immediately to the department's investigative, enforcement and/or legal divisions for proper follow-ups.

Take advantage of the advances impelled by consumerism to help you handle the problem of lemons and recalled cars with manufacturing defects. Detroit has built into its automobile prices the expenses of complying with these laws, just as it has built into its price to you the cost of warranty repairs and service.

By taking advantage of all the advances to which you are entitled, you can help keep down the costs of your car's upkeep.

How to Increase Your Gas Mileage

YOUR MOST ECONOMICAL SPEEDS

You need not be an expert to increase your gas mileage as much as 30 per cent above the average.

To measure your gas consumption, have your tank filled so you can see gasoline in the filler pipe, record the odometer reading, and drive until the tank is nearly empty. Then refill the tank and again note the mileage reading. Divide the miles you have driven by the number of gallons in the second fill-up; this gives you your mileage per gallon. Repeat this process several times to give an accurate result, since variable factors such as head winds can substantially change the mileage you get from a single tankful of gas.

Now:

• Make a habit of driving smoothly and steadily. Jackrabbit starts gulp gasoline, as do high speeds and quick speed changes.

• You'll find you do your most economical driving at about 45 to 50 miles per hour, at a steady speed in a straight line in dry weather and no wind. At 50 mph you get about 100 per cent of the car's potential under these conditions; at 60 mph your fuel efficiency drops by about 20 per cent; and at 70 mph, it's down by 35 per cent from optimum levels. But slowpokes suffer "erosion" of fuel efficiency too: the 40-mph driver loses about 12 per cent from the optimum.

• Keep your tires inflated to two or three pounds above the lowest recommended pressure listed in the owner's manual.

CHECK LIST OF FUEL SAVERS

• In winter, keep your gas tank as full as possible to reduce condensation of water vapor in the tank and the risk of subsequent freeze-up of the fuel line.

• Instead of wasting gas on prolonged warm-ups in winter, start off slowly and increase your speed as the engine warms up.

• In winter or summer, turn off the engine whenever it is not needed to move the car. A minute of idling uses more gas than it takes to restart. Idling usually uses nearly a gallon of gas an hour, increases pollution, and may clog your engine.

• Don't fall for what one expert calls "additive madness"—the slew of "new," "scientific" products which you simply pour into your gas tank or oil supply or clip onto your motor and which are advertised in glowing phrases ranging from "Run your car half on gas, half on air!" to "Drive up to 700 miles on a single tank of gas!"

• Aren't there, then, any "aftermarket" items which can really help us get more miles per gallon? Yes:

A first item is a comprehensive shop manual. This will make it possible for you, if you're at all handy, to keep your car in proper tune. Another item is a "vacuum gauge," an accessory which will tell you when you are applying more gas pedal pressure than you need to, consistent with the most economical operation of your car. And one gasoline additive which does have merit in cold, wet winter climates is gas line antifreeze, which prevents water condensed in your gas tank from freezing and blocking the fuel line.

• Under no circumstances try to extend your weekend cruising range by having necessary fuel tanks installed in the trunk of your car. A car's trunk is among its most vulnerable areas, and in a rear-end collision a trunk-mounted gas tank might rupture and cause a fire. In addition, federal Environmental Protection Agency rules make it illegal for an automobile dealer to install an accessory gasoline tank that does not meet present evaporation control standards. The fine could be up to $10,000.

Also, if an auto dealer is found tampering with any of the emission control devices on new cars, the same fine could be the punishment. And if you, the motorist, either remove the devices yourself or have them removed by an independent mechanic you're possibly liable too.

On top of the possible fine, you face a stiff complete engine rebuild bill if you are to gain anything. The reason is that present emission systems are functional parts of the engines and the simple removal of one or two components might actually result in a decrease in mileage or not improve it at all.

WILL YOU GET THE MILEAGE YOU EXPECT?

The driving patterns and habits of each of you vary so widely that you must not count on achieving the mileage claimed for any car. You could get more—and you could get less than the government figures say or the tests by independent consumer organizations or automotive magazines indicate.

If you buy a small car, will you always save on gas?

Not necessarily. Your own driving habits—smooth, even driving, anticipating stoplights and slowing down gradually, avoiding rapid accelerations, driving at or slightly below the 55-miles-per-hour limit, etc.—will have a significant impact on your car's consumption of fuel.

Many factors—including your car's weight; engine size; whether it is automatic or manual; the number of cylinders and fuel systems it has—combine to account for the wide range of fuel efficiency.

There are different-size sedans, station wagons, two-seaters, and light-duty trucks. Within each category of car, there will be different savings in gas.

The condition of your engine will also change your fuel efficiency. More than half of all car engines are operating inefficiently, according to one estimate. New York City's Bureau of Motor Vehicle Pollution once tested twenty-five of its own department vehicles reported to have been maintained to manufacturer's specifications. Almost two thirds of the cars required a new air cleaner; 62 per cent needed new spark plugs; half required new points; and about one third needed new positive crankcase ventilation (PCV) valves.

With proper servicing, these cars could return an average of 8.2 to 25 per cent more gas mileage—and some cars could give even more mpg.

For instance, *cars with the new emission controls need to be tuned regularly*. If not maintained, the controls may slash your gas mileage up to 25 per cent.

A dirty air filter can cost you another mile per gallon at 50 mph. Oil and air filters should be replaced at least as often as your car owner's manual says. If you permit either filter to become clogged, you are wasting gas.

Misfiring spark plugs can reduce your mpg by 10 per cent. Check the spark plugs every 7,500 miles (or, if you are a do-it-yourselfer, every 5,000 miles). You may not be able to notice that the spark plugs misfire slightly, but they can penalize you by shooting unused gas out the exhaust pipe. Cleaning and regapping the spark plugs will cost the do-it-yourselfer about the same as paying to have a new set installed.

Improper front-wheel alignment will cost you another .3 mile per gallon—and prematurely wear out your front tires.

OTHER GAS-SAVING TIPS

• Consider buying radial tires (see pages 362–63). These could give you ½ to 1 mile per gallon extra, in addition to their other benefits.

• Be sure your brakes are adjusted properly. It may seem obvious, but some brakes are improperly adjusted and actually put a drag on the car wheels.

• Don't carry unnecessary luggage. For every additional 100 pounds you carry, you may reduce your mileage two tenths of a mile per gallon.

• Finally, consider seriously the purchase of a car with a manual shift, rather than an automatic transmission, especially a four-speed forward gearbox. The car salesmen may tell you that your resale value will suffer—and this may be true, to a degree. However, especially if you intend to keep your car at least five, six, or seven years—as you should—the loss in resale value will be minimal. (See pages 317–18 on options.)

It can be more of a chore to drive, but true professional drivers insist they have greater control of a car with a manual shift than one with automatic.

Most important: studies indicate that you can improve the fuel efficiency of a car by 15 per cent with the *proper* manual shifting, a saving of 3¾ miles per gallon on a car which gets 25 miles per gallon with automatic transmission.

The drawback: if you don't shift properly your savings could be zero. But a standard transmission usually costs less than an automatic, so you have saved money on the purchase price of the car—and thus on depreciation—right away and your mileage savings are extra.

How to Stretch Your Tire Dollar

THE ELEMENTS OF TIRE SAVINGS

Our annual bill for tires in this country had reached the $10 billion range by the late 1970s. We are buying replacement tires for our cars at an annual rate of about 187 million. And this is on top of the 55 to 60 million tires with which the new cars we buy already are fitted.

If you drive a typical 10,000 miles a year, your annual tire bill for *each* car in the family easily can average $75 or $100. If you live in an area in which you go through snow tires at a relatively rapid rate during the winter, your bill easily can be even more.

Your tires, and the air inside them, are your most important single item of armor between you and the road—or the telephone pole, or the pedestrian, or the onroaring trailer truck. Ask any professional racing car driver and he will confirm that the amount of performance *and* protection you get from your car depends to a very considerable extent on the way in which you choose and care for your tires.

Thus, if you fail to shop carefully and if you fail to take proper care of your tires, you will greatly increase your tire costs, year in and year out—not to mention the risks to your life implied by defective, ill-chosen, or abused tires. And if yours is a two-, three-, four-, or more car family, you can multiply your extra costs—and your risks—by this figure.

Do not take your tires for granted.

Do not assume that your tires are safe unless and until you have taken all the steps and precautions reasonably in your power to make sure that they are safe.

Do not assume that the tires which happen to be attached to the new car you are about to buy are really suitable for *your* personal driving habits and needs.

These may be fine for the "average" driver but they may not be fine for *you*. And in many ways greater safety translates into greater economy in the long range.

How do you judge a tire which is on sale for $20 against one carrying a $100 price tag?

How can you, the amateur tire buyer, plow your way through the complex language of tire sizes and plies, cords and studs, belts and biases, treads and retreads —to find the best deal? How can *you* cut *your* tire bill without sacrificing any vital aspect of safety?

TIRE BUYING RULES

• No matter whether you are buying tires as an option on a new car or as a replacement for tires already on your car, your *best* guide to the *best* deal is a reputable and conscientious dealer.

This is a fundamental rule in every area of purchasing—as this book surely has underlined. A conscientious dealer will make an honest effort to sell you the type of tires best suited to your driving needs. He will make no bones about the cost difference between, say, whitewall tires and plain black ones. He will not try to sell you superduper (and supercostly) sports car tires if "sporty" just isn't your automotive style. He will honor his tire warranty, which also will save you money in the long run.

In general, the most reliable dealers are franchised dealers of nationally known and advertised brands of tires, large mail order retailers, and established automobile service stations. Probably your best guide to a satisfactory dealer is a satisfied customer; query your car-owning friends about their experiences with tire dealers in your area.

• Shop locally among reputable dealers, service stations, etc., and compare prices. Look for legitimate tire sales they may be having.

• Compare prices *and* warranties. Is mounting included? Sales tax? Balancing? How many miles—or months—does the warranty cover? Is there a lifetime guarantee against road hazards? Today, some manufacturers will pay part of the price of a new tire if you accidentally run over an old muffler or a beer bottle and their tire does not survive intact.

TIRE TRAPS—AND HOW TO AVOID THEM

• Do not, if it's at all possible, buy tires when you're in a hurry. An unscrupulous tire salesman operating along some desolate stretch of the interstate highway system may ask any price he wants to replace your blown-out tire.

• Steer clear of vague, extravagant performance claims which some tire salesmen continue to make. For example, "Stops 25 per cent quicker." (Quicker than what—a train?)

Or "50 per cent more traction." (Again, than what—ice skates?)

Or "Safety tested at 130 mph." (Just what does that *prove?*)

Such claims are utterly meaningless.

• Look out also for the unscrupulous tire dealer who advertises huge but misleading discounts. As with many other types of merchandise sold through this lure, the "original" prices may be sure fiction. Moreover, with tires, warranties are based on list—not sale—prices. Thus, when you get a discount from the advertised list price you must discount the guarantee by a like amount.

• Do not permit yourself to be pulled in by such come-ons as "Buy three tires and get the fourth free!" Real tire bargains do exist, and you may be able to find them shopping carefully. But use your common sense: no profit-minded businessman is going to give anybody a free tire.

The extravagant claims, the misleading bargains, the fictitious price cuts—the above are the main tire traps in which you easily could lose money. But there are other pitfalls.

• When you buy new tires, insist that the dealer register your name and address and the identification numbers of every tire. This is required by federal law to enable tire companies to recall tires in the event a safety defect is discovered. Many dealers, though, continue to violate this law and, as of now, riding herd on the dealer is your *only* way of being warned if you have a potentially dangerous tire.

Tire designations such as "first line," or "premium," are strictly subjective claims of tire quality. New national tire-quality standards now rate tires according to high-speed performance, traction, and tread wear.

Additional objective information is molded into the sidewall of the tire: size; maximum permissible inflation pressure; brand name and manufacturer's code number; composition of the cord; number of plies (sidewall and tread); the word "radial" if the tire is a radial type.

A final point: *do not,* once you have decided which tires you want to buy, automatically permit the dealer from whom you are buying to put the tires on your car—*until* you know what he will charge (if anything) for this service. Exorbitant tire-mounting fees can wipe out any savings you may have achieved in the tire purchase—and then some. If the charge is more than a couple of dollars per wheel, simply take the job to another service station.

RUNDOWN ON TIRE TYPES

Now, how do you find the best type of tire for *your* budget and *your* driving habits and *your* car? To help guide you through today's maze of jargon and baffling labels, here is a brief rundown on the major types of tires available today:

Bias ply tires: generally the least expensive available, have cords which wrap around the tire at an angle, tend to ride the most smoothly, and handle well at moderate speeds. Their disadvantage is they may wear out more rapidly than other types of tires.

Belted bias ply tires: cost somewhat more than plain bias ply, but they wear longer; have a reinforcing belt of glass fiber or some other material running around the tire beneath the tread, which helps to reduce tread scuffing, and thus permits longer wear but at a cost of a somewhat harsher ride.

Radial ply tires: the highest-quality tire available today; have special plies running straight across the treads, tire-chain style, and a stiff belt (sometimes made of steel) beneath the tread; wear long, handle very well, are capable of improving gas mileage by 3 to 5 per cent. (See pages 357–60 on gas-saving tips.) Although one of the most costly categories of tires, their quality, safety features, and the "hidden" gas economy they allow make them the top premium tire.

WHICH IS LEAST EXPENSIVE FOR YOU?

Use this rough guide to make your own price comparisons as you shop:

A radial ply tire will last about 40,000 miles.

A belted bias ply tire will last about 25,000 miles.

A good bias ply tire will last 15,000 to 20,000 miles.

You can figure out the tire cost per mile in each category depending on the going prices in your area but you may be surprised to discover that the "premium" radial ply tires are the least expensive—particularly when you include your gasoline savings over a distance of 40,000 miles.

The major factors to consider in choosing your tires are: the type of car you drive, the amount of 60 mph (or over) driving you do, the type of roads you ride on, the type of loads you carry in your car, the number of miles you cover during the year, and how you handle your car—in terms of starting, stopping, and cornering.

UNIFORM GRADING REGULATIONS

Uniform tire grading regulations being adopted in the late 1970s did not give us a definite answer on which tire is best or precisely how a certain tire will perform. Too much depends on where you live, how you drive, what type of driving you do, other factors. But the standards do give you some basis for deciding which tire is best suited to your needs and pocketbook—and thereby help you comparison-shop.

All three major types of tires—biased, belted bias, and radials—are likely to be graded according to how many miles they will last (*treadwear*), how well they will stop on a wet road (*traction*), and how well they can withstand heat (*heat resistance*).

Treadwear will be graded by number. A grade of 60, for instance, means this type and brand of tire control (tested on a government test course in Texas) lasted for at least 18,000 miles. A 100 tire should give you about 30,000 miles of wear; a 150 about 45,000 miles; a 200 about 60,000 miles or more.

When tire shopping, this treadwear label will help you note that a 120 grade will probably give you about 20 per cent more mileage than, say, a 100 grade tire. But it's no guarantee, for a tire's life-span depends on such factors as the climate where you live, road conditions, how and what you drive.

The same basic biased tire might last for 17,000 miles in Washington, 10,000 miles in Salt Lake City, closer to 28,000 miles in Michigan.

Traction will be graded by A, B, or C, with C representing lowest traction performance. A grade of B would tell you that the tire's ability to stop on a wet road is average, while A would say its traction performance is better than average. Here, too, it's impossible to be precise because traction varies according to a car's size, speed of travel, wetness of road, etc.

Although you may care most about how long a tire will wear, the traction standards serve as a vital check on excessive treadwear or durability. Generally, a longer-lasting tire is made of harder rubber which reduces its traction. The softer a tire, the better its traction but the shorter its usable life. The traction grade is a safeguard against development of a tire with great treadwear which would also skid easily.

The *heat-resistance* standard is a variation of the existing high-speed performance rating. It is also noted by letters. A grade A tire should withstand heat better than a grade B or C, but most will probably carry the lowest rating, except racing car tires.

SNOW TIRES

Snow tires are available in all major tire types. In snowy climates, snow tires more than pay for themselves through reduced accident risks and towing charges.

Usually, the open, heavier treads have better traction in snow and mud but build heat and wear poorly on dry pavement, so be guided in your choice of tread style by the prevalence of snow where you drive most.

Some snow tires can be bought with steel-jacketed tungsten carbide studs. Studs significantly improve traction on hard-packed snow or ice but they decrease traction slightly on wet or clear roads or on ice at subzero temperatures. Thus they are *not* a good buy if you do most of your driving in the city or on main roads in a climate where snow does not stay on roads long. Also studs are much more effective on radial ply tires than on any other kind. However, studs are illegal in several states, so check before you buy.

OTHER TIRE HINTS

You must now also decide what size, how many plies, what type of cord material you want.

The three types of tires—bias, belted bias, and radial—are produced from a multiplicity of materials in addition to rubber, nylon, fiberglass, rayon, and steel.

To confuse matters even more, the types come in a wide range of sizes with varying types of guarantees.

• Never choose as a replacement a smaller-size tire than those the car came with.

• Use tires of the same type or construction on all four wheels unless the tires are designed for special performance (such as snow tires).

• Pair a single new tire on the rear axle with the tire having the most tread depth of the other three.

• Limit your speed for the first 50 miles to under 55 miles per hour to give your tire a break-in period and to permit the many complex elements in the tire to adjust to one another and function as one integral unit.

• Periodically rotate your tires and check the inflation levels to maintain them at top efficiency and extend their usefulness—sometimes well beyond their guaranteed mileage.

• Buy the size recommended in your car owner's manual or, in the case of snow tires, at most one size larger.

For the majority of uses, two plies of modern cord materials are sufficient. Federal tire standards rate tires according to their load-carrying ability, a far more useful yardstick than a statement of the number of plies. The total load capacity of four tires should be equal to the weight of your car, fully loaded.

Caution: Do *not* combine radial tires with bias or belted bias tires on the same axle. If you buy the radial tires (or wide tires) buy four if you can; otherwise put a pair on the drive wheels first, and a pair on the rolling wheels later.

WHAT ABOUT RETREADS?

Retreads now account for one of every five replacement tires sold in the United States for passenger cars. What's more, 98 per cent of the world's leading airlines are using retreaded tires. In addition, many trucks—from the smaller pickup and delivery units to the biggest eighteen-wheel tractor trailers—are major users of retreaded tires, as are many government vehicles.

Since 70 per cent of the cost of a tire is the casing, the average cost of a retread to you is about half the cost of a comparable new replacement tire—a money saver, indeed.

Retreads also have a true cost/performance edge. A good retread will deliver the same mileage as an equivalent new tire, making its cost per mile much lower.

An undamaged casing, properly retreaded, is no more likely to fail than a new tire. And warranties now being offered on retreads are similar to those available on new tires.

How can you buy retreads most safely?

Again, the most fundamental of fundamental rules comes first: *buy from a good dealer, who gets his retreads from a shop which does quality work and inspects used tires carefully before retreading them.*

Have your own used tires retreaded, since you know how they have been used (or abused) to date. If you go this route, shop for a good recapping firm. An excellent way to avoid the risks of poor-quality work is to deal with firms which also do fleet work—e.g., for taxi companies or government agencies.

If you deal with a reputable recapper, and *if* the quality of his work is indisputable, you can consider retreads as good as new tires and thus save a substantial amount on your tire bill. Caution: Tires for passenger cars should *never* be retreaded more than once, and a reputable firm will refuse to do so.

Fundamental is to know when your tire is becoming dangerously near-bald and should be changed. The answer: when the tread is less than $\frac{1}{16}$ of an inch thick. Tires with less than this amount of tread are fifty times more likely to have flats or blowouts than those with proper tread—and about 90 per cent of tire trouble happens in the last 10 per cent of tread wear.

On your own, you can tell when it's time to retread a tire by watching for the small wear-indicator bars that appear horizontally across the tire's face when the tread is too low. Another method is to insert a Lincoln's-head penny *upside down* into the tread and if the top of Lincoln's head shows, there is not enough rubber left for safe driving. If there still is $\frac{1}{16}$ of an inch of tread left, and the tire isn't damaged, you can turn it over to a dealer for retreading.

How to Cut the High Cost of Accidents

WHAT DO ACCIDENTS COST?

An important, but often overlooked, expense of owning and operating a car is the cost of accidents. This category is not classified separately, but it is a major item in any case—boosting either the amount of your automobile insurance premiums or your maintenance and repair expenses.

The annual death toll from highway accidents dropped sharply in the mid-1970s as our driving mileage decreased during the oil embargo and its aftermaths, and as a result of the 55-mile-per-hour speed limits. But as driving increased again, so did highway deaths.

In recent years there have been at least 20 million car and truck accidents on U.S. roadways annually, involving at least some property damage. Furthermore, in every twelve-month period there are between 1½ million and 2 million more serious crashes—involving either death or disabling personal injury. These rates have persisted despite the various government-mandated safety and damageability design changes imposed during the 1970s.

In any given year, therefore, your odds of having some type of accident in your car are about one out of five, and the chances you'll be in a death or disability wreck are one in fifty.

Now, of course, this doesn't mean that in five years of driving you are bound to be in at least one fender-bender, nor that even in fifty years of driving you are certain to be in a highway crash causing death or disability.

The statisticians have an unchaperoned ball with figures such as accidents. First, note that your odds depend on the mileage you drive: the greater your mileage, the bigger your chances of a collision—mild or serious.

Then, too, the odds are new each time you take the wheel; obviously, you could drive 50,000 miles a year for fifty years and never suffer even a dented door. But still, the *odds* are that sooner or later you *will* suffer some type of highway mishap.

If you are a fatalist, so be it. But keep in mind that if you buy a used car (as most of us do for our personal driving; see pages 383–99 on used car buying) you stand a good chance of buying a fixed-up wreck, or one not so fixed up. (More about the odds against you in the used car section.)

HOW TO REDUCE YOUR ODDS ON AN AUTO ACCIDENT

What can *you* do to reduce the odds that you'll have an auto accident?

• At the very beginning, when you are looking for a new or used car, comparison-shop for safety features—just as you comparison-shop for operations, comforts, economies. Ask car dealers you visit to give you the federally required free rundown on the safety aspects of each car you are considering—ranging from acceleration and passing ability to tire reserve loads and stopping distance.

• Before you buy a car, new or used, check whether the model and make you want has been the subject of a federal safety recall—and if so, for what reason.

• If you receive a recall notice on the car you already own, don't ignore it, take in your car *immediately* for the suggested repairs and/or adjustments.

• Don't try to sidestep your state's motor vehicle inspection laws—e.g., by sweet-talking an inspection station into overlooking such hazardous problems as too worn tires or a burned-out headlight or brakes on the blink. Have the recommended (and, remember, legally *required*) repairs performed promptly—and be grateful the problems have been spotted before they can kill you.

• *Drinking* may account for as many as half of all fatal car crashes today. Although the ideal rule is "If you drink, don't drive," this may be unrealistic for many. Thus, an alternative rule, offered by the National Safety Council, is: take no more than one normal drink per hour—and do not drive until at least one hour after the last drink.

• Don't drive when you're overly fatigued or in an angry or depressed mood. These conditions frequently lead to *fatal* accidents.

• At night don't try to guess what may be beyond the reach of your headlights: most cars going at 60 mph cannot stop within this range.

WHAT TO DO IF YOU ARE IN AN ACCIDENT

If you are involved in *any* auto accident, even if the other driver involved is completely at fault, admits it, and promises to have his insurance company pay for all damages, call the police.

Although no laws may have been violated, that is always a possibility; and, regardless, a policeman is a trained, impartial observer.

Next, call your insurance agent. The other driver's verbal promises to you are worthless. He or she could have a change of mind at any time and even turn around and claim it was you who caused the accident.

Follow up this call with a registered letter to the company writing your insurance, stating that you have been in an accident and giving your policy number as well as the name of your auto insurance agent.

This rule holds even in cases in which visible damages are minimal and in which reporting the accident may end up costing you more in hiked premium rates than the expense of just having the car fixed yourself. Reason: should the accident turn out to be more serious than it first appeared (e.g., if the other driver later develops signs of whiplash injury), you may lose the benefit of your insurance coverage because you did not report the accident within the prescribed number of days.

Also in order to *collect full benefits* due you on your automobile insurance, you may be required by the company writing your policy to report any accident in which you become involved within a certain limited period of time. If you don't report, the insurance company may be able to disclaim any and all legal responsibility in the affair.

KEY RULES FOR ACCIDENT SITUATIONS

Do you know what moves you must make in order to be confident you'll collect the full amount of insurance actually due you?

The most practical step is to ask your insurance agent or the police to give you a copy of the accident report they would require you to fill out in the event of an accident. Then keep this form in the glove compartment of your car.

Or copy the composite form you'll find at the end of this section.

• After you have stopped your car, check to see if there are any injuries needing medical attention, set up some kind of system to route other vehicles around the accident area, and call the police, exchange driver's license and registration numbers. Take down the other person's name and address plus the make, model, and year of the other car. Exchange telephone numbers and the names and addresses of your respective insurance companies and/or agents.

• Get the names and addresses of:

all other drivers involved in the accident;

the insurance companies of these drivers;

two or three witnesses (if you fail to get their names, at least get their license plate numbers so you can track them down later if you need to).

• Write down the name, badge number, station number, and jurisdiction of the policeman who arrives at the scene of the accident.

• Make accurate notes on the following circumstances surrounding the accident:

The date, place, and time.

Weather conditions—Rain? Snow? Fog? Sleet? Clear?

Road conditions—Icy? Dry? Wet? Slushy?

Any evidence of physical injury to either party.
Whether either or both cars were under—or out of—control.
The car seats in which passengers in the other car were sitting.
How fast you—and the other car—were going at the time of the accident.

Where on the road each car was (e.g., on his own side of the road?).
Whether there is evidence of either driver being drunk (encourage a breath test for *both* of you when the police officer arrives if there's any question about this aspect).

Whether the other person's driver's license lists any relevant restrictions—such as a requirement that he or she wear glasses while driving (obviously particularly important if you noticed that the other driver was *not* wearing glasses when the accident occurred).

• Make your own notes even though the policeman or state trooper also is taking lengthy notes on the same topics.

• Make a sketch of the cars and placement of people and cars involved in the accident in relation to each other as well as to the road. If you have to move your car from the place it was hit, make marks on the road indicating the original position.

• If you should have a camera with you, snap a few pictures of the accident, the people involved, details of the damage.

• *Do not* disclose the extent of your insurance coverage.

• *Do not* confess guilt, even at the scene of an accident you have caused, and do not pledge to have everything taken care of by your insurance company.

• *Do not* sign any waivers of liability or any assurances that you have not been physically injured. Such injury might not become evident for days or even weeks.

• *Do not* attempt to answer by yourself letters or telephone queries from the other party involved in an accident. Send all along to your insurance agent to handle.

If the accident is a serious one—particularly one involving injury to others—consult a lawyer. But avoid the services of any lawyer who claims he can win an unusually large settlement, the proceeds of which he might split with you. And if it's a serious or complicated accident resign yourself to staying in the area awhile —even if it's far from home. It'll be cheaper than trying to resolve difficult problems by long-distance phone.

• Go to two or three reputable auto body shops and compare estimates for properly repairing your car. Steer clear of any repair shop which offers to jack up its estimate—and later its bill—to cover the cost of your deductible. The shop which goes in for this type of cheating may not stop short of compromising the quality of its work on your car.

• Keep a record of your substitute transportation costs while your car is being fixed: the costs to you of renting a car, or taking taxis, or whatever.

• Make a copy of these rules and keep the guide in the glove compartment of your car. Otherwise you'll more than likely forget most of the important ones when and as you do get involved in an accident.

• Also keep in your glove compartment the insurance identification card your insurance agent may have given you—listing his office phone number and also the name of the company insuring you. This card may include the addresses and phone numbers of branch offices—most useful information if you smash your car up a few hundred miles from home.

ACCIDENT REPORT FORM

Policyholder and Driver

Name of policyholder _____ Policy number _____

If married, name of husband or wife _____

Home address _____ Phone _____

Business address _____ Phone _____

Occupation _____ Employed by _____

Driver's name_____ Address _____ Phone _____

Driver's license number _____Years driving experience _____

Driver's age _____

Relation to policyholder _____

Who authorized him to drive? _____

Names of occupants of policyholder's car _____

_____

Policyholder's Automobile

Make _____ Year _____ Body type _____ Model _____
State license number _____ Motor number _____ Serial number _____
Name of holder of auto loan, if any _____
Name of owner if other than policyholder _____
Address _____ Telephone _____
Car garaged at _____

Details of Accident

Date of accident _____ Time _____
Where accident occurred _____
City _____ State _____
Purpose for which car was being used _____
Was driver on errand for owner? _____
Where may car be seen during day? _____
Name of claim representative handling claim _____
Name of insurance firm _____
Direction my automobile was going _____
What side of street? _____ How fast? _____ Speed limit _____
Were headlights on? _____ Signals? _____ Condition of street _____
If object collided with was moving, in what direction? _____
How fast? _____ Which side of street? _____
Any signals given? _____
If an automobile, were lights on? _____
Was either driver violating traffic regulations? _____
Was accident investigated by police? _____
What department and precinct? _____
Were any charges brought? _____ Against whom? _____
Give full account of accident, including direction of all vehicles involved and traffic controls present (draw a diagram): _____
_____
_____

Personal Injuries

Name of injured person(s)   Address   Age   Occupation
_____   _____   ___   _____
_____   _____   ___   _____

Situation of Each Injured Person

Driver _____ Pedestrian _____ Rider in your car _____
Rider in other car _____
Describe injuries _____
_____
Name, address, and phone number of physician called _____
_____
Where was injured person taken? _____
Were there seat belts in your car? _____
If so, were they in use? _____

Damage to Property of Others

Name and address of owner of damaged automobile or other property _____

_____

Home phone number _____ Business phone number _____

Name of other party's insurance company _____

Policy number _____

Make of auto _____ Year _____ Body type _____ Model _____

Describe damage _____

Estimated repair cost _____

Name of driver of other car _____ Age _____

Address _____

Driver's license number _____ State registration number _____

Occupants of other car _____ Address _____

_____

Where can other car be seen? _____

What was said between you and other driver? _____

_____

Is claim being made against you? _____

Are you making claim against other party? _____

Damage to Your Automobile

Date of damage _____

Description and damage—itemize parts damaged _____

_____

Estimated cost of repairs (attach estimate) _____

If car was stolen, were police notified? _____

Officer's name and number _____

Give make, size, and mileage of tires stolen or damaged _____

_____

Age of convertible top _____

Purchase date and warranty of battery _____

Witnesses to Accident

Name _____ Address _____ Telephone number _____

_____

Date of report _____ Policyholder's signature _____

Your Car Breaks Down . . .

Even if your car is not in a traditional accident, you are very likely, sometime in your driving "career," to suffer a breakdown on the highway. How can you minimize the risk of these costly events—which, by themselves, could result in an accident?

WHAT WOULD YOU DO IF . . .

You're moving along in your car at a good speed down Chicago's Outer Drive when the throttle sticks in an open position. Suddenly, you are rapidly overtaking cars.

What do you do?

You're caught in the heart of a big traffic jam en route to the San Francisco airport when your car's engine overheats.

What now?

You're driving in the middle lane of fabulous Highway 684 in Westchester County, New York, when your drive shaft drops.

What next?

At some time during our driving lives, most of us will come up against at least one emergency situation involving a malfunction of our car or truck. If not handled promptly and with a clear head, the result could be serious injury or worse.

To minimize the chance of accidents caused by your auto's malfunction, the best way, of course, is to keep your car in safe running condition.

PREVENTING BREAKDOWNS

Periodic checkups are imperative to save you time, money, the life of your car and you. Include routine safety checks on such items as fan belts and hoses, the exhaust system, brakes, steering assembly, related components, wheel alignment.

Always carry a fire extinguisher, auto jack, spare tire, warning devices or flares, a flashlight—all in good condition. Know where the fuse panel is and maintain a supply of fuses, too.

Make certain safety checks automatically before driving: tires which are low in air; looseness in steering or pulling to right or left; an oil pressure light that is slow to go out, indicating a potentially serious engine problem.

But the most serious emergencies are those that require stopping on the highway. To illustrate:

(1) A dropped drive shaft, one of the most dangerous problems of all. The problem doesn't occur often, but when it does (as it did to me on Highway 684), it happens suddenly.

On cars with front-mounted engines and rear-wheel drive, the drive shaft is that long tubular device beneath the auto, connected at one end to the transmission and at the other to the rear end differential. It transfers power from the transmission to the rear end to turn the rear wheels and propel your car. The connections on the drive shaft at the front and back are called universal joints. When one of these fails, the drive shaft can drop to the roadway. The most serious hazard to the driver is failure of the front joint.

Most important, slow down before pulling over from the road to prevent the drive train from digging into the road's surface.

Have your service facility examine and lubricate your car's universal joints regularly and check for possible looseness in the joint assemblies or in the bearings.

A warning sign: universal joints become noisy before failure. Watch for severe vibration throughout the vehicle at all speeds.

(2) Throttle sticking. If this occurs on the open highway and there is distance between you and other traffic, tap lightly on the accelerator pedal a few times to see if it springs back to a normal position. If this fails, try to pull the pedal up with the toe of your shoe. Don't reach down with a hand.

If you must slow down or stop quickly, turn your ignition to "off" (not "lock") and apply the brakes. Don't pump the brakes. Guide the car off the road.

(3) Overheated engine. If you notice steam or liquid coming out from the front of the car, pull off the road, turn off the engine, and let it cool. If you can't pull off and the engine has not reached the critical overheat point (note needle movement of the gauge), certainly turn off the air conditioner. In stop-and-go driving, shift into neutral while stopped. During long waits in traffic, increase the idling speed lightly (making sure, of course, that you're in neutral when you do it). Never remove the radiator cap and risk burns before letting the engine cool.

(4) Driving through water in heavy rain or snow. Drive slowly to avoid stalling or loss of steering control. After moving through water or heavy slush, apply your brakes lightly while driving to dry out the linings and other components.

BAD WEATHER AND YOUR DRIVING

Road conditions are an important cause of vehicle breakdowns and highway accidents. Heed the radio and television "travelers' alerts" and try to stay off the road when the weather is bad. Winter is especially costly in terms of highway breakdowns and accidents. Be doubly cautious of venturing out on the highways during the cold-weather months.

WINTERIZE YOUR CAR

If you are traveling in the colder climate of our country during October to March, make sure your car is thoroughly prepared for the trip—even short journeys.

• If your car requires antifreeze—either for driving in your own area or going on a trip to a cold climate—buy it early.

• The same foresight applies to snow tires. If your old ones are fairly worn, snow tires with new, deep lugs on the tread can make the difference between go and no-go when the snowdrifts pile up.

• Invest in a couple of new rubber inserts for your windshield wiper blades. Wiper blades must be in better condition for winter driving than for normal summer use because they must clear away the salt spray thrown by the wheels of cars ahead. Make sure the blades pivot as they wipe.

• Have your car's heater checked. After a summer of no use, the heater water control valve sometimes clogs. Clean it out or replace it.

• Have the defroster action checked at the same time as the heater. Be sure the vents have not been plugged by dash trash during the summer. If the heater control valve is not clogged but little heat comes through, check the engine's thermostat.

• And even if you have the best and newest wiper blades, they need help from the windshield wipers. Fill the windshield washer fluid container with a non-freezing cleaning solution and make certain the washers operate properly and are correctly aimed.

• If any brake is acting with more enthusiasm than the one on the opposite wheel, have it fixed before you have to drive over a slippery road, to protect you from losing control of your car while braking.

• Recheck the age of your battery. Is the water level sufficient and does it have enough charge? If water is below the plates in any one cell, it may merely be waiting for winter's weather to let you down. The battery posts and cable clamps should be cleaned. If any cables are frayed or have broken strands, replace them with cables at least as big in diameter as those provided by the vehicle manufacturer, to assure better charging.

• Unless your car has an electronic ignition system, new ignition points are good insurance for winter starting. A complete tune-up now will help assure you more reliable starting and economical running through the winter as well as save on gasoline use.

• If you live in or plan to visit really cold country (for skiing or other winter sports or holiday reunions, etc.), use of lightweight or multi-viscosity oils in your engine crankcase will help relieve the starter drain on your battery. A thorough lubrication will keep corroding salt water out of lubricated components.

• Replace any missing weather stripping and plug or patch holes in the floor pans or body before the cold air and carbon monoxide come whistling in.

• Have your steering alignment checked. This is always important, and on slippery roads proper alignment will keep your car going in the direction you intend.

WINTER DRIVING TIPS

Once your car is in shape for cold-weather driving, and you are under way, here are additional tips to help you avoid breakdowns and accidents.

(1) *Start your car slowly and easily.* As soon as your wheels begin spinning or sliding, they have lost more than half of their potential traction.

(2) *Stretch out your following distances substantially.* It takes nine times as much distance to stop on snow as it takes to stop on dry pavement.

(3) *Drive more slowly in winter than in summer,* test the surface occasionally by braking on a straight stretch with no cars near you. Don't jam on the brakes; instead, pump the brake pedal rapidly.

(4) Since *prevention* is more effective than any cures for getting stuck, fight the urge to drive downhill into a slippery place, such as a parking lot, if you're not sure you can get out. Find ways not to drive when conditions are really bad.

(5) If you do get stuck, get out and look over the situation before you do anything else. You may find that scattering a *handful of sand* is all you need.

(6) Also if you do get stuck, *"rock" back and forth,* going as far as you can forward before you start spinning, then reversing gears and repeating the process. This easy technique could avert having to call out a tow truck.

(7) *Turn your front wheels as little as possible* when getting unstuck; they roll most easily pointing straight ahead. And use a snow shovel as an instrument of

prevention as well as a cure. A mere five minutes of shoveling can save you an hour of spinning.

(8) To get started on a cold morning, first *turn off your car lights, radio, and other accessories.* This will increase the amount of electrical power available to your starter. Try, too, to avoid using these when your engine is not running; they wear down a battery fast.

(9) *If you do have trouble starting your engine, crank it no longer than thirty seconds at a time,* with a minute or two of rest between times. Also, give up trying to start the engine as soon as it is evident it won't catch without some kind of repair. Running a battery down to zero charge drastically shortens its life.

(10) *Instead of wasting gas on prolonged warm-ups, start off slowly and increase your speed as the engine warms up.* Idling a cold engine creates pollutions, fouls the spark plugs, clogs the engine with sludge, forms corrosive acids in the engine oil, and dilutes the oil with unburned gasoline.

(11) *Be gentle when you're freeing wiper blades* (exposed variety); the rubber may tear if you abruptly pull them away from the windshield. Handle frozen recessed windshield wiper blades with hot water. This trick also will work on exposed wiper blades but don't use it on a frozen lock—the water will just freeze.

(12) *And carry an "emergency kit"* to help you cope. Key items to include: a windshield scraper with snow brush; a small snow shovel; a sack of sand in your trunk; tire chains; booster cables (but use only if you know exactly how or you can ruin your battery); jack, plus flat board to use on such soft surfaces as snow; flashlights, plus spare batteries; flares, windshield de-icer; gas line antifreeze.

Final note: another antidote for frozen gas lines is to keep your gas tank as full as possible.

THE UNSEEN COST OF CAR THIEVES

Car theft is another unseen cause of rising auto costs. Vehicle thefts add roughly $2 billion a year to our annual automobile ownership and operating costs by raising the premiums you and I pay for our theft and comprehensive insurance.

BASIC WAYS TO PROTECT YOUR CAR

• Be wary of superbargains in Johnny-come-lately car lots. Be leery of any sale being made in the street. If you innocently buy a stolen car, you will have little chance of recovering your investment; if such a car is traced to you, you'll have to give it up, of course, so it can be returned to its rightful owner.

• Do not tempt a car "window-shopper" by leaving suitcases, gift boxes, obvious valuables within sight inside the car. At a minimum, keep your stereo tapes in the glove compartment or elsewhere out of sight. You might also "mark" your stereo players and tapes—and record these "fingerprints" to help you establish your ownership if they're stolen later and traced.

• Mark your engine, transmission, and other valuable accessories not bearing identification numbers with your initials—to help police recover the items if they're stolen and to identify them as yours.

• Identify your car by dropping your business card in the slot between the door and window or by scratching your initials in some hidden place. This will help you particularly if the engine numbers and other identification have been tampered with.

• Park in lighted, well-trafficked areas—preferably near a streetlamp or lighted store window. Most thieves won't risk working on a locked car in the light. At home, lock your car in the garage if you have one; many cars are stolen right in their owners' driveways. If you lack garage space for all your cars, put the most desirable ones inside and block the driveway with the others.

• If you leave your car in a public garage or parking lot, do not be definite about when you will pick it up. Dishonest attendants can easily steal new equipment from your car and replace it with old parts when they know how much time you will be away. Double-check your mileage to make sure it's the same as when you parked the car. This will reveal whether thieves have driven your car while you were away to a spot in which they could switch equipment.

Assuming your state laws do not force you to keep the car's title and registration certificate in the glove compartment, leave them home or carry them on your person. Pro auto thieves steal these documents, then forge them for their own use.

• Keep your car locked—both doors and windows. If you're afraid of locking yourself out—with your keys accidentally left inside—carry a second set of car keys with you. Do not "hide" extra keys, though, in what you consider safe places but to which thieves turn at once: under a seat, fender, floor mat, the hood, the like.

• Always take the keys out of your ignition. Even when you're on a brief errand, remove your keys. Never leave your engine running. By always removing your keys you'll not only reduce the chances of having your car stolen but also eliminate the possible hazard of being faced with liability charges if your stolen car later becomes involved in an accident.

• If your car breaks down or runs out of gas, continue to follow the rules on locking your car and taking out the keys. Just because you can't start your car doesn't mean a thief can't.

A variety of gadgets—some inexpensive, some costly—are on the market which will help discourage the car thief. These range from simple hidden ignition switches that prevent your car from being started normally, all the way up to electronic gadgets which sound your horn periodically if the doors of your car are opened, somebody sits in the driver's seat, or the car is moved.

Other devices cut off the fuel to the carburetor after the thief has driven a few hundred feet, while still others consist of steel "crooks" which attach to the steering wheel so the car cannot be turned.

None of these devices—repeat, none—will stop a dedicated car thief. If he wants your car, he may roll a truck up at night and push your auto inside, then drive off.

But the longer it takes a thief to get your car, the less likely he is to steal it. Many thefts are by youngsters intent only on a joyride; and if your car is not easy to steal, they'll move to another vehicle which is. Time is their enemy and your ally.

More than 30 per cent of the million cars a year which are stolen are never recovered. That's over 300,000 cars a year; and that, in turn, means that you are paying for those cars, through your insurance premiums.

IF YOUR CAR IS STOLEN

But let's say that, despite all your defenses, your car is stolen. If or when this happens, you will find out at once that the police, your insurance company, and possibly the National Automobile Theft Bureau will ask you to supply critical information necessary to trace your car.

Will you at that moment have the essential data at hand—some twenty items including detailed information on your car, license, insurance, bank or finance company?

To help you be prepared, here is a form developed by the American Mutual Insurance Alliance which you should fill out *now* so that you will have all the facts on file for ready reference. You might carry a card in your wallet which gives all this information—to speed the search for your car if it is stolen.

Vehicle Information
  Make _____ Year _____
  Model _____ Body style _____
  Vehicle identification number _____ Color (upper/lower) _____
  Type and size of engine _____ Type of transmission _____
  Ignition key number _____ Trunk compartment key number _____
  Repair work, dents, secret marks, or other peculiarities which would help identify vehicle
  _____
  _____

License Information
  License number (and state) _____ Year license expires _____
  City registration number _____

Additional Information
  Insurance company _____ Policy number _____
      Agent _____
  Bank or finance company holding title _____
  _____ Account number _____
  Purchased (new/used) from _____
      Address _____ Date _____
  Optional equipment or other items usually kept with auto (list serial numbers)
  _____
  _____

Now here is another form, also developed by the AMIA, for your use immediately after the theft. This information will provide a permanent record of the facts surrounding your case and will be helpful in co-ordinating efforts to find your car.

If Your Car Is Stolen

Date of theft _____ Place of theft _____

Time of theft _____ Speedometer reading _____

Personal items in auto when stolen _____

_____

_____

Law enforcement agency contacted _____

   Date _____ Complaint number _____

   Officer investigating theft _____

Insurance company contacted (date) _____ Claim number _____

   Claims representative _____

Auto recovered at _____ Date _____

   By (law enforcement agency) _____

Condition of car (list damage) _____

_____

_____

PARKING AND GARAGING

PARKING: CAN BE HUGE EXPENSE

In New York City, *daily* parking charges at downtown garages in the late 1970s ran as much as $10 to $15. For a commuting businessman this could mean a monthly cost for parking his car in Manhattan of $200 and up! Even at less expensive garages, typical monthly parking charges in New York ran from $100 to $150—one third of the cost of your car, per year.

Although you probably think of your car primarily as "wheels in motion," the fact is it is *parked,* on the average, more than 95 per cent of the time. If you are a regular automobile commuter in a major U.S. city today, your yearly parking costs probably run between $500 and $1,500, your daily charges between $2.50 and $10. Parking, in sum, can be a huge part of the cost of owning a car for millions of city and suburban families.

If today's parking costs seem exorbitant to you, tomorrow's charges will be even more so. The reasons are a cinch:

• In virtually every big U.S. city, land costs are soaring—along with demand for space to build offices, stores, apartment buildings, hospitals. City parking lots are being erased by these more lucrative uses of land.

• Parking also has become a major burden at suburban shopping centers, hotels, airports, hospitals, universities. What was once free parking is being replaced by monthly charges to growing numbers of students, doctors, others. As high a proportion as 75 per cent of leading U.S. colleges and universities are now slapping parking charges on students: the argument is that a car takes up the same amount of space as a seminar room for twenty students.

"Free" parking downtown surely is doomed to disappear altogether—along with all on-street parking in densely populated areas. Even in suburban towns, street parking is being banned—and in some cases monthly charges are being assessed for street parking.

TEN WAYS TO SAVE ON PARKING CHARGES

(1) Form a car or van pool and arrange a monthly contract with a downtown garage under which it won't matter whose car is parked each day. Quite a few garages will do this for you and some will provide movable plastic stickers so carpoolers can take turns during the month. In some cases, a car pool can be less expensive than public transportation.

(2) Shop for a garage a short distance from the central business district. A daily walk of as little as five or six blocks can mean as much as a 20 per cent cut in your parking charges.

(3) When you drive downtown for shopping, find out which of your favorite stores offers free or reduced-rate parking. Merchants of all types across the country have arrangements with parking companies to provide free or reduced-rate parking for customers.

(4) If you're commuting alone, do so, if you can, with a compact car: these often qualify you for preferential garage rates because they can be slipped into spaces which are too small for the larger cars.

(5) If you are renting a car from a company which also owns parking facilities, check what parking benefits you might get as part of your rental agreement.

(6) Be careful about adding steep charges to your bill by taking your car in and out of a long-term parking garage; taxis might be cheaper.

(7) Compare monthly and daily parking costs. Monthly rates might come out cheaper even if you don't use the garage every day.

(8) Seriously consider parking your car at a low-cost facility at the edge of the city and taking a bus, subway, or train from there to the office. Such facilities are being expanded and made more convenient in response to gasoline shortages.

(9) Avoid all extra charges by obeying the rules of the garage. For instance, if the garage requests you leave your key in the car, do so, and thereby avoid possible penalty charges.

(10) Be sure your brakes are in top-notch condition to avoid damage due to an accident in the garage.

Note: In figuring your car expenses, even if you do *not* commute, you have a "garaging" cost to consider—the expenses of your own, at-home garage. Part of your payments on your mortgage, tax, and insurance, your maintenance and repairs, goes into the garage. (See pages 308–9 for how much this type of garaging may be costing you.)

When Should You Trade in Your Old Car for a New One?

WHY YOU CAN KEEP YOUR WHEELS LONGER

How long you keep your car is one of the key factors in determining what it will cost you. Sell it too soon, you lose money; keep it too long, you may lose, too.

But the odds greatly favor keeping your car as long as possible. Your car *should* last fifteen to twenty years, *if* you care for it properly; and it *should* hold up for 100,000 to 150,000 miles, *if* your driving habits don't abuse it.

In the past, the traditional wisdom was that a car should last ten years or 100,000 miles, whichever came first. Traditional wisdom also held that the age and mileage limits probably would roughly coincide—that you'd average about 10,000 miles a year for each year of the decade that you drive the jalopy.

However, in the late 1970s several developments began to undercut this wisdom. First, the Anti-Rollback Odometer Law, which went into effect in 1978, produced evidence that many people who sold cars—dealers, wholesalers, auctioneers, even individuals—rather routinely had been turning back the mileage on car odometers.

Thus, when a car was sold, the 50,000 or 60,000 or 70,000 miles its odometer had recorded would be rolled back to read 20,000 or 30,000 or 40,000 miles. So when the old buggy literally started to "fall apart" in its ninth, tenth, eleventh, or twelfth year, with 90,000 or 100,000 on its clock, people concluded that the odometer was accurate and that—therefore—most cars would last "only" about 100,000 miles.

Unrecognized was the fact that when the car was sold—perhaps two or three times—the odometer had been rewound by 10,000 to 40,000 miles.

In addition, people awakened to the phenomenon that big trucks routinely roll as many as 100,000 miles a year. True, these trucks usually got top maintenance and tender loving care, since they each could cost $60,000 to $75,000 to buy new. And, true, they would have major engine overhauls every 150,000 miles or so. And, granted, they were made of heavier-gauge steel and their components were of sturdier, heavier-duty stuff than were cars'.

But 500,000, 600,000, sometimes 750,000 miles as a truck's lifetime—six, seven, eight, nine years of useful truck life? That had to force a reappraisal Cars were smaller, lighter, and usually less well maintained; but still, they obviously were going farther than had previously been thought.

PROGRESS FROM DETROIT

Furthermore, Detroit was making progress in building its cars. Components were lasting longer and did not have to be repaired or serviced quite as often. As a result, maintenance costs—while rising in *absolute* terms as the national inflationary spiral went on and on—actually were declining as a *percentage* of total outlays. (See pages 344–45 on car maintenance.)

Finally, auto analysts dug more carefully into some key figures First, they looked again at the so-called "scrappage" or "junker" figures Traditionally, the analysts had considered any car registered in one year but not reregistered the next had been junked or scrapped.

But, they concluded, this was giving a false picture. What about those 300,000 cars per year which were stolen and never recovered? These cars were not just "disappearing." They were being shipped to South America or South Africa or some other area—by professional auto thieves—to be resold and rerun tens of thousands of miles more.

MISLEADING STATISTICS

In addition, some statistics on automobile ownership had been presented in a manner that made them misleading; other statistics were just plain incomplete, or wrong.

Government studies "showed" that newer cars were driven greater distances each year than older ones. For example, assuming the national annual mileage average for all cars on the road was 10,000 miles, the government studies showed that in the first year a car would go about 15,213 miles.

Each year, according to these studies, the annual mileage would drop, as the car aged. In its second year of life it would go only 12,900. By the time the car was ten years old, the figures purported to show, it was going only 5,400 to 5,500 miles every twelve months.

While the figures may be true, as a statistical *average,* they undoubtedly stem from the fact that cars are traded (two or three times in each car's lifetime); or that a car kept in one family is put to different use at different times in its life.

As a new "first" car, a vehicle may be driven more and farther than normal. Then, as the auto is replaced and becomes a "second" car, its mileage might drop. Or, if the car is sold, its second owner may drive it less than the original buyer did. This latter situation is highly probable considering that the majority of Detroit's new car output each year goes into government or business "fleets," into smaller business car pools, or into other non-personal service. Such "fleet" cars regularly run 20,000 to 30,000 miles a year; and thus, they are traded relatively soon—after two and a quarter to two and a half years, with a total of 50,000 to 55,000 miles recorded on their odometers at their time of trade-in.

Cars bought new for personal use, though, are kept some 5.2 years before they are traded—an ownership period more than twice as long as that for the non-personal autos. However, the personal cars are driven only about half as far each year as fleet cars; so they, too, have about 50,000 to 55,000 miles on them when they are sold.

WRONG SELLING DECISIONS?

The bottom line in all this is that buyers of new cars seem to trade them when they have been driven between 50,000 and 55,000 miles—regardless of the ages of the cars in years.

Is this a wise election for owners of personal cars to make? Perhaps. The majority, at least—business and personal users, both—apparently think so. But for purely economic reasons, it does not make sense for you, as a private individual.

The *depreciation* element in a car's cost is highest in its early years, lowest in the later ones. Maintenance, on the other hand, is lower when the car is young and grows higher as the vehicle ages.

In addition, financing costs are higher in the early years—and virtually non-existent later, since few loans are for more than four years, even today. Also, insurance costs are cut by 40 to 60 per cent in later years; with the car loan paid off, and the car depreciated substantially in value by the end of the fourth year, many people drop their fire, theft, and collision coverage, retaining only the liability portion of their policies.

Here is a table of car costs—by percentage of the ten-year totals—which illustrates exactly how car costs fluctuate from year to year *assuming travel at a constant number of miles each year*.

Year-by-Year Car Cost

YEAR CAR AGE	DEPRE-CIATION	LICENSE, FEES, ETC.	INSUR-ANCE	INTER-EST	MAINTE-NANCE	GAS, OIL, LUBRICA-TION, ETC.	ANNUAL TOTAL
1	8.0%	0.24%	2.8%	1.8%	0.8%	2.6%	16.24%
2	6.5	0.24	2.8	1.7	1.1	2.7	15.04
3	5.0	0.24	2.8	1.6	1.2	2.7	13.54
4	2.0	0.24	2.8	1.4	1.3	2.8	10.54
5	1.2	0.24	2.0	—	1.4	2.8	7.65
6	1.0	0.24	2.0	—	1.5	2.8	7.54
7	0.6	0.24	2.0	—	1.6	2.8	7.24
8	0.5	0.24	2.0	—	1.7	2.8	7.24
9	0.4	0.24	2.0	—	1.9	2.9	7.44
10	0.3	0.24	1.9	—	2.2	2.9	7.53
10-YEAR TOTAL	25.5*	2.4	23.1	6.5	14.7	27.8	100%

*To make your own table, calculate your car's actual purchase price (not the net after trade-in, but the sticker price, less true discount, plus delivery and taxes). To find your true purchase price, obtain your old car's basic wholesale price, if a trade was involved, from a used-car price guide. Subtract the wholesale price from the allowance you received, then subtract this in turn from the retail price the dealer quoted you for the new unit, including delivery and taxes. When you have this figure, subtract $100 as the car's "junk" value, then divide this by .255 to get "100%." Multiply this "100%" figure by the percentages listed for each category in each of the years. You'll have your approximate expenditures in each category for each year—excluding inflation increases for your later years of car operation.

This table assumes a constant 10,000 miles a year over a decade of car operation. The "conventional wisdom" might still hold if the car should be traded after the seventh or eighth year, when costs stop dropping and start inching up.

However, in that case, even unrealistically assuming no inflation, you would start again at the top of the scale, with the new car costing more than double its seven-to-ten-year average outlay.

WHY YOU TRADE TOO SOON

Many car owners think in terms of a "cash flow" set of expenses. Your insurance and monthly payments stop or drop drastically when your loan is repaid after the third or fourth year.

For a year, perhaps two, you are pleasantly surprised at the "extra" money you seem to have. And since the figures in the table are averages, subject to fluctuation, you may get by for a year or so without being hit with a significant maintenance outlay.

Then, maybe in the fifth or sixth year, when the battery, tires, and valves all go at once, or perhaps when the car suffers a major fender crushing, you look at the "heap" and say, "It'll cost me more to fix it than to buy a new one," so you start shopping.

Repairs might be estimated at $600 to $800. The dealer says he'll "give" $500 for the old heap. (In reality, of course, he's discounting the new car by $300 to $400.) So, for an additional $200 to $300—on top of the $600 to $800 you have mentally budgeted for the old buggy's repair—you have $1,400 to $1,500 available as your down payment on the new model. That's about 25 per cent of the total cost of a new car; your car for which you paid $4,000 seven years before now goes for $6,000.

And you start the cycle again. Only this time, your monthly outlays for the first four years are even higher than during the early years of the previous car's life.

That's inflation.

By repairing that six- or seven-year-old buggy and driving it another three to five years, you could still get $400 or so for it when you do trade and you would have had those extra years of relatively low-cost driving.

Of course, the old car won't *look* as nice as a new model. And you'd be (understandably) apprehensive about its being able to travel long distances without a breakdown. But from a strictly financial point of view, you could be making the right decision by keeping the car.

In real life, you'll probably "compromise": buy a new car *and* keep the old one —almost tripling your real outlays.

SHOULD YOU BUY A USED CAR?

If you studied the table on page 382 on when to trade your car, you may have leaped to the conclusion that you should never buy a *new* car.

Actually, most of you who purchase cars for your own personal driving, rather than for business-related travel, do just that: buy used cars instead of new ones. For the best way to save money on your automobile is to drive a new car until it becomes a used car—or buy the car used in the first place.

SECONDHAND WOES

In almost any given year, half again as many used cars are sold as new. In recent years, secondhand car sales have been running 13 to 15 million annually, against 7 to 10 million new models sold. Some three out of every four cars purchased for personal driving are used units, rather than current-year models.

But if buying a new car requires care and knowledge, it is a cinch compared to entering the jungle of the used car. This is a world of its own, loaded with frauds and misrepresentations, most of them flourishing precisely because the typical buyer is seeking to save money.

The statistics are against you, even if you get exactly what you pay for. You are, almost literally, playing a game of roadway roulette. Consider these facts:

• In the late 1970s, Americans were spending $25 to $30 billion a year to buy used cars.

384 SYLVIA PORTER'S NEW MONEY BOOK FOR THE 80'S

- Some 50 per cent of the used cars sold were retailed by franchised new car dealers.
- Another 30 per cent of the used units were sold by used-car-only dealers.
- The remaining 20 per cent of the used buggies were sold privately—by individuals trading with each other.

The *average* markup on a used car—from its true whoesale price—is 22 per cent, and this margin can rise to as high as 50 per cent if the car is wholesaled from one dealer to another, across state lines, perhaps via a used car auction.

This used car markup contrasts with an average of 12 to 15 per cent dealer margin on *new* cars. Thus, you, a shopper for a used car, start off behind the eight ball, with risks on a used car far higher than on a new one.

A used car may have been in an accident, unlikely in the case of a new model.

A used car may have 20,000, 30,000, or 40,000 more mileage behind it than its odometer shows, again an unlikely condition for a new car.

A used car may have some manufacturing defect—or be a lemon built on a Monday morning after a holiday at the factory—and if the initial owner, armed with a warranty, couldn't get it repaired properly, how well do you think you will fare?

TAXIS AND POLICE CARS

Use a modicum of common sense. Since a decent car will be costing its owner less each year, why should he sell it? It could be a lemon. It could have been in an accident. It could have suffered abusive driving. It might have been in a flood. Or the owner may have simply "driven it into the ground," spending little or nothing on its repair—leaving you, the new owner, to pay not only the normally higher maintenance costs which older cars are subject to, but also the earlier upkeep costs the first owner didn't make. *Plus* the penalties stemming from that earlier improper maintenance.

To make the point even stronger, even if none of these circumstances took place, there still is the possibility of a rolled-back odometer. Despite the 1978 Anti-Rollback law (making rollback artists subject to $50,000 fines and up to a year in jail) odometer "spinning" continues—though at a slower pace than in the past. The real change is that the spinner is charging more, and you are picking up the tab.

What's more, the spinning which *is* taking place probably is more flagrant now than it was before. With both penalties and profits up, the spinback might as well be 30,000 miles instead of 10,000.

Traditionally, the nemesis of the used car buyer has been the taxi or police car. These units often travel 50,000 to 100,000 miles *a year* and it is rough mileage: extremely high speeds, sharp turns, running over curbs, much stop-and-go travel, twelve-to-eighteen-hours-a-day use, inadequate maintenance.

So if you are in the market for a relatively recent-model used vehicle, especially if it is an intermediate- or standard-size vehicle (which taxi firms and police favor), your odds are high that your car will be an ex-hack or former squad car (one study shows the odds to be one out of six for one- and two-year-old domestic units).

If you add to this scenario a car with heavy-duty suspension, battery and alternator and throw in a vinyl roof (perhaps to hide the holes made for the lights and siren mountings) you simply are asking for trouble.

THOSE "LATE-MODEL EXECUTIVE CARS"

How many advertisements have you seen for "late-model, low-mileage executive cars"? At least a few, I'll wager. Think. With more than half of all Detroit's annual output going to some sort of non-personal use, and 15 per cent to the major, high-mileage fleets—with the statistics showing that fleet cars are driven on the average twice the number of miles as personal cars—and with these fleet cars traded about twice as often as personal cars, what does that do to your odds of buying a high-mileage unit if you are shopping for a late-model, one-to-three-year-old car?

Caveat emptor, caveat emptor, caveat emptor.

Buyer beware, buyer beware, buyer beware.

ARE YOU BUYING A WRECK?

Now, superimpose your accident statistics onto these figures for high-mileage units: one car out of five in some sort of accident *every year, if* all cars traveled the same distance every year. But those fleet cars, police units, and hacks go twice as far each year as the overall average. That means almost *two* chances out of five that these cars will have suffered a highway hang-up.

For two-year-old cars, it's more than three chances out of five—as the statisticians figure these things. And those are just the *averages*. Common sense tells you that the chances are high that a car which *has* been in an accident will be traded.

Admittedly, this is an area of speculation.

But put yourself in the driver's seat of a car which has been in a wreck, especially an early model still covered by collision insurance.

Keep in mind that statistic cited earlier that it costs four times as much to repair and rebuild a complete car than the car cost in the first place. It means that a car with 25 per cent damage will be considered totaled. The insured owner will get the price of a new car. The old one will be junked.

Says who?

That car with 25 per cent damage is "free" to somebody—the insurance company, the body repair shop, or the dealer. What a temptation to "repair" it halfway and put it on the used car lot for a $300 to $500 profit. Perhaps inadequately repaired, perhaps dangerously *un*repaired.

Nobody would be that heartless?

Again, look at the statistics.

In a typical year during the 1970s, an average of about 8 million domestic cars were sold. Factoring in the steep percentage of high-mileage cars, it means that in the first three years of a car's life, more than 450,000 of these cars will have been in *serious* accidents—wrecks causing death or disabling personal injuries. And accidents which are *that* serious certainly can be expected in most cases to do rather severe damage to the car, as well.

How many of those cars are *not* reregistered after three years? Again, the statistics! Only about 250,000 of them. Presumed junked. Thus, about 200,000 of these recent-model cars in serious wrecks *are* returned to the road—at least this many.

If you also factor in the cars stolen and never recovered—and therefore presumed to be not reregistered, but rather shipped overseas for sale—then add another 50,000 to 60,000 units to reach the total.

Altogether, about a quarter million one- to three-year-old seriously damaged cars return to the road, via used car lots, each year!

USED CARS COST LESS

So much for the bad news. If things are all that black, why do three out of four of you purchasing cars for your personal use—over 13 million Americans each year—buy used cars rather than new ones?

Price.

The purchase price of a used car ranges from about 20 per cent under that of a new one for a year-old model—to about 90 per cent under the new car cost for a jalopy seven years old. The average saving is about 60 per cent.

What's more, the total ownership and operating expenses for a secondhand auto are some 10 per cent to 55 per cent less than costs for a new car and they average about half the new car's costs for similar use.

But be on guard: if you like to trade your car annually, don't buy a used one. The dealer markup is higher on used units, your depreciation is relatively high, and it is simply uneconomic.

To take the greatest advantage of used car savings, buy a car that is one to three years old and keep the car for three years, or longer.

The biggest savings can be made on recent-model cars, since they suffer the greatest depreciation. For example, a new car driven 10,000 miles a year for three years might be purchased by a secondhand buyer and driven another three years for another 10,000 annual miles. The operating costs for the second owner would be only about half what the car cost the original owner.

If you bought the same car *third*hand—now six years old with 60,000 miles on it—and in turn drove it another three years for 10,000 miles a year, your costs would be about one third those paid by owner No. 1. Assuming you don't get a lemon, an abused car, or one in a wreck, and that the mileage on the odometer accurately registers 10,000 miles a year, your best bets are one-to-four-year-old cars which you, in turn, keep until you junk them.

CONSTRUCTIVE RULES FOR USED CAR BUYING

So you decide to spin the wheel and take your chances.

How do you go about shopping for a good, reliable used car? Here are constructive rules:

Shop for your dealer first. You are buying his honesty and integrity. He should be a local dealer, one who has a new car franchise, preferably with a franchise for the same make car you intend to purchase used.

Do *not* buy from a used-car-only dealer. The reasons:

The odds that you will get a high-mileage car which has been wholesaled are much higher.

The chances that the dealer sold the car to its previous owner are less, and the chances that he sold it to its original owner are nil, since he doesn't sell new cars.

Thus the likelihood that you will obtain any data about the car's previous use is greatly reduced.

Cars which have been wholesaled are often cars which could not be retailed, the "dogs"—the ones in accidents, abused, with high mileage, stolen, former taxis or squad cars.

The chances that the used-car-only dealer will have adequate repair facilities are less, since he does not have to repair new cars under warranty and does not have the benefit of factory-supported training for his service employees.

Consider buying directly—either from an individual, preferably one you know, or from one of the major fleet operators, now increasingly retailing their better used units.

Buying from an individual (unless he is a car dealer, policeman, or taxi driver) gives you a better chance of getting a car which has been in personal use.

You also know where he lives and can inquire about where he operated the car and, generally, under what conditions.

He may have his records of maintenance and repairs which he can show you.

Too, there is less possibility that he will have rolled back the odometer. Odometer spinning *is* against the law, as we have noted, but it is still being done. Private individuals, especially car buffs, certainly can spin odometers, just as dealers can, but the odds are higher that they haven't.

BUYING FROM A FLEET OPERATOR

If you buy from a fleet operator—such as the lease-rental companies—you also know who has owned the car, and that it has *not* been in personal use. But you know you are *not* getting a taxi or police car with extremely high mileage, either. Furthermore, some of the fleet operators are providing detailed maintenance records and any damage repair data.

True, the car you get will be a business-use car and, year for year, the mileage undoubtedly will be higher than for a car which has been only in personal service. But it won't be *that* high. Same-year and year-old rental units, for example, will generally have 12,000 to 25,000 miles recorded and you usually can bet it will be accurate. These firms have national reputations to protect and they are so big that the federal government is always scanning their operations.

In addition, the same-year and year-old rental car probably will be in better shape than many units because although perhaps eighty to one hundred persons have driven the car in its nine-to-fifteen-month-use life, it has been washed and cleaned eighty to one hundred times too, and has had dozens of maintenance checks.

The leased cars, and those in other fleets, are in a somewhat different category.

A leased car generally has had only one driver, not eighty to one hundred. It may be only one year old, but more likely it is two or three years of age. It probably has 20,000 to 25,000 miles on it for each year of use. And, it may or it may *not* have been well maintained.

The company (or leasing firm) could have been responsible for its maintenance; or the individual driver could have had that responsibility, either under a non-maintenance lease or under a company reimbursement plan.

Another factor enters into the maintenance that a fleet or other non-personal car received: namely, was the driver responsible for the resale value? Some companies make the driver take—or share—resale losses, others do not. Some leases are written so the driver can "walk away" at the end of the contract, some are set up so he participates in either a profit or a loss, depending on what the car brings when it is resold.

A fleet operator may not tell you what arrangements he makes with his traveling representatives, but a leasing firm should give you information on the previous driver. If it won't, go elsewhere. In general, beware if the lease has been a non-maintenance, closed-end contract (meaning that the driver was responsible for upkeep, but not responsible for loss on the resale value).

As the 1980s neared, federal authorities were zeroing in on used cars as their next target for consumer protection. The Feds want regulations requiring that a used car buyer be told what type of service the vehicle has previously seen and whether or not key components of the car are in working order.

These requirements would, of course, help you, as a used car *buyer*. But they also could mean that you, as a used car *seller*, would have to tell customers about repairs, previous use, and damage. These new restrictions probably would exempt anyone selling fewer than six cars a year from the proposed controls.

BUYING THROUGH A DEALER

When shopping for the franchised new car dealer from whom you expect to buy your used car, choose him carefully, only after thorough investigation. Look for one who is a member of a local, state, or national car dealers' association. Query friends on their experience with local dealers and follow their recommendations. Don't go too far from home, or servicing problems could become a real nuisance. Study dealers' ads in your local newspapers and on local TV programs. Are the ads *reasonable* and *believable* to you? If not, don't deal. Also, check your local Better Business Bureau, which is likely to have a bulging file of complaints on certain local used car gypsters and deceivers.

• Check your local new car dealers to see whether they also have their better trade-in cars for sale—frequently backed by warranties they are prepared to honor in their service shops (they usually sell their lemons to used car dealers).

• Avoid, if possible, shopping for a used car during the peak summer season when millions of other Americans are competing against you to buy a used car for vacation travel.

• Consider as *part* of the purchase price the total finance charges, immediate repairs for which you know you must pay, optional equipment, sales and other taxes, insurance. But don't, when you approach a dealer, announce that you have, say $1,000 or $2,000 and want to know what he has in that price range.

• Choose—if you are trying to find the best bargain in strictly dollars-and-cents terms—a relatively recent compact or other lower-priced model with comparatively few complicated extras over an older, higher-priced model with a lot of extras. The latter well may mean stiff repair costs later.

• Consult the National Automobile Dealers Association's *Official Used Car Guide,* or, on the West Coast, *The Kelly Auto Market Report (Blue Book),* listing current average retail car values for most U.S. and foreign models, makes, and years. These guides, which your dealer or the loan department of your local bank should be willing to show you, dramatize the fact that prices for a given car can vary as much as $500, depending on whether its condition is "extra clean," "clean," "fair," or "rough."

But these "guides" are published by and for dealers, so don't take them as gospel. Refer to pages 399–400 on how to price your used car if you are selling it; and remember that prices also can vary by as much as $500 for a similar car in similar shape—in different areas of the country.

Keep in mind, too, that your direct fleet sellers will generally be $300 to $500 under the competition.

• Consult, also, *Consumer Reports,* which regularly rates used cars as well as new ones and can serve as a valuable guide to used car bargains. Get a copy of Consumers Union's pamphlet entitled *How to Buy a Used Car,* which gives details on twenty tests you should run on any used car you are considering buying. Also get Car/Puter's *Auto Facts—Used Car Prices,* available from Davis Publications, Inc., 229 Park Avenue South, New York, New York 10003. And look over *Motor Trend* magazine's yearly issue devoted exclusively to used car buying.

• Don't fall for the salesman's well-worn come-on, "I'm losing money on the deal." How could the dealer stay in business if he does that?

• Take into consideration that fact that a new car's value drops 50 to 60 per cent during the first two years of its life owing to depreciation—although on certain imported cars, "hot" domestic lines, and specialty cars, the rate of depreciation tends to be lower because of less drastic year-to-year style changes. This suggests that a well-cared-for-two-to-three-year-old car may be a good buy.

• Test-drive any car which seems to meet your needs—or get a trusted mechanic to test-drive it for you. Try it out in a variety of traffic conditions; on a dirt road as well as a paved superhighway; on a hill as well as on the level.

• Hire a mechanic or diagnostic clinic to check the motor, brakes, clutch, transmission, other vital parts, and expect to pay $25 to $50 for this service—well worth it, even if the check results in your *not* buying the car.

Get a signed statement that the odometer is accurate, now required by law. If the statement says the odometer is wrong, don't buy the car—no matter what reason is given for the odometer error. And even after you get the statement that the odometer is accurate, take it with a grain of salt. A *better gauge* of how many miles a used car has been driven is to multiply its age by *15,000 (miles per year).* Check the driver's seat for wear. Does the mileage on the odometer equal interior wear? If not, be suspicious of the odometer.

• Heed these guidelines and clues to how much a used car has been used:

The original tires on a car which has been driven 15,000 miles or less may still have good tread. But by 25,000 miles the tread will probably be well worn. As a clue to whether or not the tires are the originals, check to see if all four are of the same brand and similar serial numbers.

At 25,000 miles, the battery may have been replaced. Look for a sticker with a guarantee date.

At 30,000 miles you'll see considerable wear on the brake pedal, and if this or the floor mat has been replaced the car probably has gone more than 40,000 miles.

Another clue to a car's age is its most recent service stickers, giving the mileage at the latest lubrication and oil change. If these have been torn off, that alone should beg the question: "Why?"

• Although many used cars are sold "as is," try to get a guarantee that the dealer will pay in full for all necessary repairs within thirty days of the time you purchase the car. Or perhaps you can get a written guarantee that will protect you against major repairs, or a pledge that the car will pass state inspection. If you do settle for the more typical fifty-fifty deal in which the buyer and seller share the repair costs for the first thirty days, keep in mind that a wheeler-dealer might try to double the repair charges so that you would end up paying the full cost instead of half.

• Ask a dealer if he will give you the name and address of a car's previous owner (some will)—and query this person on possible problems, defects, or advantages of the car. If the former owner turns out to be a traveling salesman, this could serve as a warning to you that the car may have been driven an unusually large number of miles. Or it could turn out to be the proverbial "little old lady."

Important note: In some areas, a contract to buy a used car is not binding if you are unable to move it off the lot—even if you have bought a car "as is."

• Do not assume that because a used car bears an inspection sticker it's in good mechanical fettle. Normally, state inspection laws cover brakes, steering, tires, horn, windshield wipers, headlights, brake lights, etc.—but the laws do *not* cover in any sense the condition of the engine or transmission. And in many states it is easy for a dealer to get a sticker from a friendly mechanic who has made only a cursory inspection. The dealer himself may even have an inspection license in states where private mechanics hold state inspection licenses.

• Some of the direct fleet operators are now offering warranties and even financing help, so check prices with them if one is near you.

• If you buy a used car from a private individual, try to pay no more than 10 per cent over the wholesale price. And try to get a money-back guarantee to cover you if the car fails to live up to the way in which it was represented to you. (See pages 399–400 on selling your own car for help in figuring what you should pay if you are buying from an individual direct, rather than selling direct yourself.)

• Make notes on each car which interests you—including the year, make, model, and vehicle identification number—so you can identify it if you return to the dealer. Take a notebook along when you inspect cars on each lot and when you test-drive.

• Compare the deals offered on a comparable car by several local dealers and choose the best for you.

• Shop among local lenders for the best financing terms as carefully as you shop for the car itself. As with new car buying, do your insurance and finance shopping first—and separately. A dealer won't hold a car without a sizable deposit while you shop for insurance and money, especially if the car is a "good deal."

CHECK LIST FOR BUYING A USED CAR

The following check list for buying a used car is exhaustive. With it at hand, it would be difficult for you to go wrong! The guide is adapted from *Family Financial Education for Adults* and was prepared by L. W. Erickson of the Graduate School of Education, University of California.

I. Preliminary Check on the Lot (Exterior)

A. Paint
   (1) Is it faded, scratched, pitted, or peeling? Does it need repainting?
   (2) Pry up rubber on door edges; look for difference in paint spray on moldings. If car has been repainted, look for other signs of overhaul.

B. Body
   (1) Look to see if sheet metal is dented or scratched in several places.
   (2) Probe door bottoms and fender joints for signs of rust. A "rusted-out" car has little value.
   (3) Look for paint overspray or damaged metal on underside of trunk lid. (Lid may have been wrecked.)
   (4) Open and close all doors to see if they are sprung or sagging.
   (5) Check fit of hood and trunk lid to see if they latch easily.
   (6) Check door handles for looseness, indicating hard use.

C. Glass
   (1) Is windshield cracked or scratched by wiper blades? A damaged one may fail state inspection.
   (2) Work windows. Note whether excessively loose or stiff.
   (3) Check windows for cracks.

D. Chrome
   (1) Are bumpers and molding rusted or pitted?
   (2) Molding missing or loose?
   (3) Bumper bent, crooked, or loose?
   (4) Grille badly damaged or rusted?

E. Tires
   (1) If car's mileage is said to be less than 20,000 all tires should be of the same make, similar serial numbers—and evenly worn. If they are not, mileage is probably over 20,000.
   (2) Measure tread depth. New tires have $\frac{9}{16}$ inch; worn-out tires, less than $\frac{1}{16}$ inch.

(3) Note chafes, tears, and bulges: all indicate replacement is needed.

(4) Look for front tires showing uneven wear: means front end is out of alignment.

(5) Heavy wear on rear tires could mean "rubber burning" by dragster.

F. Suspension

(1) Does car sag on level ground? Could mean one or more weak or broken springs.

(2) Bounce front of car. If it continues to bounce when you release it, shocks are worn.

(3) Stoop directly in front of car about 20 feet away. If front wheels lean inward at top, they need alignment.

(4) Grasp the top of a front tire and vigorously push it in and out. Clunking sound means worn parts in the front-end assembly.

G. Leaks

(1) Look under the car near the engine and transmission. Oily spots on the ground indicate leaks that may be costly to repair.

(2) See if ground or frame beneath radiator is wet with water.

(3) Inspect the inner side of all wheels. Dark areas indicate leaking brake cylinders or grease seals.

H. Chassis

(1) Look at the frame for weld marks or heated areas—indicating repairs made after an accident.

II. *Preliminary Check on the Lot* (*Interior*)

A. Upholstery

(1) Generally dirty?

(2) Seats or backrests torn or frayed?

(3) Springs in seats sagging?

(4) Armrests missing or frayed?

(5) Door panels torn or frayed?

(6) Overhead lining torn or frayed?

(7) Sun visors missing or frayed?

(8) Are there high-water marks anywhere—on fire wall or in trunk, indicating flood damage?

B. Dash

(1) Paint scratched or pitted? Car had hard use.

(2) Dash freshly repainted? Car may have been a taxi or police car. Reject such cars.

(3) Glove compartment door loose, sprung, or won't latch?

(4) How is oil pressure gauge? It should read high on starting, then drop to middle of dial at a fast idle as engine warms. If indicator type, light should go out on starting. If gauge isn't normal, engine bearings may be worn.

(5) Does fuel gauge register?

(6) Check ammeter. It should show charge at fast idle, or if indicator type light should go out on starting. If not operating there may be trouble in generator or regulator.

(7) Is water temperature gauge working?

(8) Are light switches broken? Check dome and backup lights.

(9) Does ignition switch stick?

(10) Are heater and vent controls stiff or inoperative?

(11) Is windshield wiper control stiff or inoperative?

(12) Check radio. Working?

(13) Check clock, if any. Working?

(14) Are knobs missing on any dash controls?

C. General

(1) Is horn working?

(2) Are directional signals working?

(3) Is steering wheel safe? Gently rotate it. More than two inches of play before the wheels respond is unsafe.

(4) Is seat adjustment stuck or broken?

(5) Are floor mats torn or worn?

(6) Are pedals worn more than mileage indicates? Or are they new pedals?

(7) Is foot switch for dimming headlights working?

(8) Does brake pedal sink slowly under steady foot pressure? This indicates a leak in the hydraulic system or worn master cylinder. Check leaks again as previously suggested. Spongy feeling means air in system, needs attention.

(9) Open door and look to rear of car while you race the engine. Blue smoke from exhaust means a ring job is needed.

III. *Preliminary Check on the Lot* (*Engine*)

A. Engine idling

(1) Examine engine for oil leaks or rust on block. Look closer for cracks in such areas. Be wary of a "steam-cleaned" engine. A dirty one will at least show you what might be leaking.

(2) Is head cracked or welded? If so, new one is probably needed.

(3) Are manifolds cracked or warped? Repairs needed.

(4) Is engine idling too fast? Have idle speed reduced, as fast idle can cover irregular engine operation or tendency to stall.

(5) Is throttle linkage bent or worn, keeping engine from returning to normal idle after being raced? (Can be dangerous.)

(6) Is there sputtering sound when engine is raced? Often indicates clogged jets or worn accelerator pump in carburetor.

(7) Is air cleaner missing or damaged?

(8) Are there sounds of knocking, grinding, squealing, or hissing? All are potentially expensive.

(9) Are there regular clicking noises in engine with hydraulic valve

lifters? Could be tip-off that lifters may have to be removed, cleaned, or replaced.

(10) Is alternator noisy? Signals worn bearings.

(11) Are there traces of gas or oil on fuel pump? Diaphragm may be worn.

(12) Is water pump leaking or noisy?

(13) Is radiator hose leaking?

(14) Are there rusted areas on radiator? Or is it leaking?

(15) Do you see oil or bubbles in coolant? Could be internal crack in block.

(16) When you kneel beside car, do you hear sputtering sounds? Could indicate dangerous pinholes in muffler or loose connection to exhaust pipe.

(17) Is tail pipe rusted or kinked?

B. Engine off

(1) Is oil level very low? Car may be an oil burner or a leaker. Recheck for blue smoke in exhaust and oil drippings under car.

(2) Are there water droplets on oil dipstick? May indicate internally cracked block.

(3) Is oil pan dented? Look carefully under recent-model cars.

(4) Is fan belt worn or frayed? On a low-mileage car, a worn belt suggests the mileage has been set back.

(5) Is distributor cap or case loose or cracked? If so, replacement is needed.

(6) Are ignition wires brittle or cracked?

(7) Look for bulging battery case or cell tops, loose or cracked terminals and cell connectors, which mean battery is about finished.

(8) Remove wire from center of coil and crack engine for ten to fifteen seconds. Starter should turn engine over quietly and smoothly.

(9) Listen for clanking sounds or broken teeth on flywheel gear while cranking engine as above. Entire flywheel may have to be replaced.

(10) With coil wire still removed as above, crank engine. Uneven cranking may indicate unequal compression caused by a burned or sticking valve.

IV. *Road-testing the Car*

A. Brakes

(1) Is pedal low? Brakes need relining or adjustment.

(2) Do brakes pull car to one side when applied?

(3) Do brakes grab or chatter, squeal or scrape?

(4) Does hand brake hold on hill?

B. Steering

(1) Does car wander or drift from side to side on straight, flat road?

(2) Is there a loose, uncertain feel of steering wheel?

(3) Make a series of S-turns on a quiet road. Is it hard to steer on quick

turns or when parking? Could be a defective pump or merely a slipping drive belt.

    (4) Does steering wheel bind on tight turns?

    (5) Do front wheels shimmy above 40 mph on smooth roads? Wheels need balancing.

    (6) Do front wheels shimmy on rough roads at low speeds? Front end needs work.

C. Standard Transmission

    (1) With hand brake set and transmission in second gear, slowly release clutch pedal and depress accelerator. Engine should stall, or clutch is slipping.

    (2) Check clutch pedal free play. Pedal should move 1 to 1½ inches before it begins to disengage clutch. If it doesn't clutch, facing may be worn.

    (3) Drive a block or more in each speed range and listen for all sounds of chipped gears.

    (4) Depress the clutch pedal. Lever should move easily into all ranges and there should be no clashing of gears.

    (5) Check for slipping out of gear while driving. This means transmission is worn.

    (6) Check on noisy transmission. This means bearings are worn. (Some dealers have been known to put sawdust in transmissions to keep them quiet temporarily.)

D. Automatic transmission

    (1) Is transmission jerky when engaged in low or reverse?

    (2) Do shifts take place smoothly?

    (3) Does transmission squeal, whistle, or whine? Trouble may be imminent.

    (4) Can you hold a park position on a hill?

    (5) Does selector lever move easily? If not, linkage may be bent or out of adjustment.

E. Rear axle

    (1) Run car at 20 mph and listen for metallic clanking or grinding noises that indicate wear or damage. You will hear these noises better down a narrow street lined with buildings.

    (2) Alternately depress and release the gas pedal to jerk the car while in motion. Clicks or thumping sounds mean too much play in power train parts.

F. Engine

    (1) Reduce speed to about 15 mph in high gear or drive range, then accelerate moderately—not hard enough to downshift automatic transmission. Sputtering, hesitation, or backfiring indicates poor carburetion, valves, or ignition.

G. Wheels
   (1) Open windows slightly on your side and listen for crunching sound of chewed-up wheel bearings. Don't confuse the sound with sound of clicking wheel covers. Remove covers if you are uncertain of origin.
   (2) Check for bent wheels by watching them while friend or dealer drives car.

H. Frame
   (1) Watch car from behind as it is driven; wheels should track.
   (2) Drive car through water, then on dry pavement. You should see only two lines from directly behind the car; if you see four, the frame is bent and the car should be rejected.

I. Speedometer
   (1) Is speedometer working as it should? As measure of speed and mileage.
   (2) Does needle flutter or vibrate?
   (3) Is there a ticking or grating sound, indicating a kinked or very dry speedometer cable? If so, it needs oiling or replacement.

V. *Final Inspection Back on the Lot*

A. Last checks
   (1) Recheck the engine to see that nothing has opened while on road.
   (2) Hubcaps missing?
   (3) Wiper blades missing or deteriorated?
   (4) Cigarette lighter missing or inoperative?
   (5) License plate brackets missing or damaged?
   (6) Spare tire useless, flat, or missing?
   (7) Jack and lug wrench the correct ones for car?
   (8) Wheel lugs missing or threads stripped?
   (9) Radio antenna missing or bent?
   (10) Keys work in all locks? Check inside door locks.
   (11) Courtesy lights and switches on door pillars working?
   (12) Serial numbers agree with dealer's papers? Have dealer rectify any error and prove title before you buy, or you might drive out with a hot car. At a minimum, you will have trouble at state inspection stations.

This is a long list, and even a used car zealot might not have the time to follow it. But study it, and try to keep in mind as many of its points as you can.

USED CAR BUYING TRAPS—AND HOW TO AVOID THEM

Whenever you enter the market for a used car you become a target for one of the slickest groups of high-pressure promoters in our land. And you well may turn into a victim unless you are aware of the pitfalls.

To warn you and guide you, here is a short "dictionary" of today's most widespread car traps, come-ons, and gyps. Read and remember!

Doping. You are told that the used car you want has been completely "reconditioned" and your test drive seems to confirm this claim. But within a few days it develops a host of mechanical problems, for the dealer has used a variety of methods which temporarily—but only temporarily—disguise the car's faults.

The "almost new" car. This may be a bargain late-model "leftover" car which may have been used as a demonstrator. Or it may be a last year's model advertised by mail at the unbelievably low price of, say, $1,999. The catch with mail order cars is that they often turn out to be repainted taxis or police cars, which may have been driven 100,000 miles or more. You would not be able to tell this from the odometer reading.

Bushing. Here the new car dealer hikes the price after you have made a deposit —or he lowers the generous trade-in allowance he has offered to keep you from shopping around. You can avoid bushing by insisting on a signed statement promising a refund if the car is not delivered on the specified terms and at a specified time.

Packing. This means heaping extra charges—special fees, exorbitant finance-insurance charges, the like—on top of the purchase price. In some cases the dealer gets a rebate from the finance company. Make sure there is no packing *before* you sign any deal.

The balloon note. In this deal, you pay relatively low installments at the start and a fat lump sum at the end. Although the only deception here is if the dealer fails to tell you about the "balloon" at the end, you are caught if you cannot meet the final payment.

Bait and switch. Cars are advertised in such tempting terms as "below cost," "below wholesale," etc. *But*—and this will be your warning—when you arrive at the lot you find that the advertised car is not available. The ad has been used as bait to get you to the lot, then switch you to another, costlier deal.

Macing. In this racket, you are the victim of a used car dealer to whom you have sold, on your own, your used car, at a favorable price to you. The dealer pays you a small amount of cash and the rest of your purchase price in notes or a postdated check. At its due date, the check turns out to be worthless. Or, by the time the notes mature, the fly-by-night operator has flown and the notes also turn out to be worthless paper.

Odometer tampering. To the expert, it's no problem to crank an odometer back tens of thousands of miles. Use the rules on pages 389–90 to figure out on your own how many miles a car has been driven.

The highball. This is part of the bushing racket—in which a new car dealer makes a fantastically attractive-sounding trade-in-offer and thereby halts your efforts to comparison-shop. However, when it comes time to deliver your new car, the dealer suddenly starts uncovering flaws in your old car—all of which diminish the sum he's actually willing to allow you on it for the trade-in.

The lowball. This is the opposite side of the above trap in which a dealer quotes an unrealistically low price for a new car as "insurance" that a prospective customer will return to his showroom after he has made the rounds of other local dealers. When you return, though, the quote inevitably expands to a more realistic level.

"Would you take . . ." You park your car on a street, go away, and then return to find a card under your windshield wiper which says, "I have a buyer for your car. Would you take $1,500 in trade for a brand-new ————? Call or bring in your car today." If you follow up, you will discover that the price of the new car has been jacked up so it more than makes up for the overgenerous trade-in offer; or the promised trade-in allowance has been somehow diminished to a realistic sum. This one is pure misrepresentation.

The basic rules for avoiding all of these traps are:

(1) Deal only with a respected, reliable local, franchised new car dealer.

(2) Or shop newspaper ads by private owners for low mileage, one-owner cars, other pluses pinpointed in the preceding pages.

(3) Or deal with a reputable, national fleet sales organization.

(4) Resist the temptation of questionable "bargains."

(5) Have a qualified mechanic or automotive clinic inspect any used car you are considering buying.

(6) Read and understand any contract before you sign it.

(7) Shop among several sources of used cars to find the best deal for you.

(8) Try to get the longest warranty available, with the dealer responsible for paying in full for all needed repairs.

(9) Be sure, if reconditioning has been done, that the warranty spells out the details—and whether the car is guaranteed to pass state inspection.

THE ODOMETER LAW

One important consideration in used car buying is the 1978 amendment to the Motor Vehicle Information and Cost Savings Act (Public Law 92-513 as amended by P.L. 94-364, Sections 409, 412, and 413). Unofficially, this is the Odometer Anti-Rollback law, effective in 1978.

This revised act—which also, by the way, regulates sales of gas-guzzling cars—provides for $50,000 fines and one-year jail terms for anyone convicted of spinning back odometers on used cars. And it requires every seller of used cars—including you—to sign an Odometer Mileage Statement certifying the true distance a car has traveled, or stating clearly that the car's odometer is wrong and why.

Some states have had odometer laws for more than a decade. California adopted the first in 1968, New York followed the next year, other states joined later. In 1972, the federal government itself passed an anti-rollback law. But the regulations often were mere hand-slappers, convictions were difficult to obtain, punishment was usually minimal. So spinning continued, although spinners charged more—with rates climbing from $5 to $10 a car in the 1960s to $25 to $50 in the late 1970s in states with tougher statutes.

"Spinning was something even the best dealers had done routinely on virtually every high-mileage car they retailed," said one industry executive (who wants to remain anonymous for obvious reasons). But my informant continued:

"The game in 1978 changed drastically. Some dealers are still seeking the services of a spinner, but they are being far more cautious and the rollback artist is charging even more. A dealer today may actually sell his used units to a spinner and then repurchase them as lower-mileage models at $400 to $500 markups."

One result of this higher spinner cost: in the 1970s, used car prices climbed half again as fast as new car prices.

The threat of jail has changed the ways of other dealers, though, for they know FBI agents are checking used car lots in major cities and mingling with buyers and sellers at auto auctions.

Another result: newspapers are carrying classified ads heralding recent-model cars with 50,000, 60,000, or even 70,000 miles of use—the actual totals.

Several companies now market to dealers a high-mileage "warranty" program —enabling the dealers to offer service contracts good for six months or 6,000 miles on cars with 60,000 to 100,000 miles of use, providing the cars are not more than five years old.

New car operating costs also are being affected by the anti-spin crackdown.

When odometers could be readily rolled back, mileage didn't count and trade-in allowances were based almost entirely on age and appearance. As the 1980s approach, the trade-in allowance can vary as much as 2 cents a mile for travel over or under the typical 10,000-mile-a-year average (and will go up as car costs rise). This, naturally, increases or decreases the initial owner's depreciation costs.

• Still, if you are shopping for a used car, protect yourself by assuming any used car has run at least 20,000 miles a year during its first four years of use.

• Assume, too, that taxis and police cars may run 50,000 to 100,000 miles in a single twelve-month period.

• Figure that the newer the car, the more likely it is a high-mileage unit. (Cars in non-personal service are traded an average of every *2.4* years, but private owners keep theirs *5.2* years.)

• Since the car dealer is the professional and you are the amateur, expect the worst until otherwise indicated. Bring a non-related friend on your used car shopping tour, ask lots of questions, take plenty of notes.

• Find out the name of the original owner. Does the owner live nearby? Beware of out-of-state cars. Can you see the maintenance records? How much did the dealer spend on repairing the car, and why? (Major fleet operators will willingly show these records.)

Ask, ask, ask! The odometer rollback law is a great leap forward in protecting you as you go used car shopping. But you still must be wary. Odometer spinning never will be stopped completely.

BECOMING A DEALER YOURSELF

Selling your old car yourself when you buy a new one . . . Buying directly from a private individual (or fleet operator) rather than from a dealer . . . What are the advantages (and disadvantages) of this direct trading, both ways?

PRIVATE SELLING

With the odometer law, the advantages of private selling are diminished somewhat—if only because you, as the car dealer, must comply with an additional law, and face a stiff fine or jail if you don't.

As an amateur, rather than a professional, you won't be assumed to be violating the law willfully, but the possibility of penalty remains: and you, as the seller this time, must beware.

A private seller must provide any buyer with a statement certifying the odometer is correct—or if wrong, why. Get a copy of the required statement from a dealer or check your state motor vehicle agency.

How much should you charge for a car you sell?

(1) Estimate the purchase price by subtracting 10 to 15 per cent from list cost (including preparation and delivery), then add back local sales taxes.

(2) Take into consideration that a car depreciates 30 to 32 per cent from its purchase price its first year; 24 to 26 per cent its second; another 18 to 20 per cent its third; 7 to 8 per cent its fourth; 3 to 5 per cent annually fifth through seventh; 1 to 2 per cent for years eight to ten.

(3) But inflation pushes up auto prices each year. So you must find the consumer price index for the year you bought the car and for the current year—the year in which you intend to sell it. Divide the current index by the index in the year of purchase, then multiply the car's wholesale price by this factor.

(4) For mid-size cars, add about 1 per cent of your per-mile costs for all mileage under the yearly average; subtract the same amount for all distance over the average. Thus, for a five-year-old intermediate traveled only 40,000 miles, the trade-in wholesale value should be *increased* by this factor. For 60,000 miles, it would be *lowered* by the same factor.

(5) Finally up the total by 10 to 11 per cent for your profit as a private seller. This comes to about half the normal car dealer's markup, and you are thus splitting the traditional profit margin with the direct buyer, to compensate him for his added time in dealing with an amateur.

Of course, the car's condition is a key factor. For instance, maintenance, service, and repairs on a five-year-old, 50,000-mile intermediate should have been about 30 per cent of the car's purchase price during this span. Whatever was not spent by the original owner eventually will have to be spent by the second buyer.

SHOULD YOU LEASE OR RENT YOUR CAR?

WHAT IS LEASING? AND RENTING?

With the costs of owning and running cars (and trucks) continuing to soar, increasing numbers of you are discovering that you may not need to have legal title to your auto at all in order to enjoy its benefits.

Instead, following a trend started by corporations, you are leasing and renting your wheels. The two terms—leasing and renting—really are interchangeable, but the terms usually refer to different periods of temporary use.

Within the business, *renting* refers to short-term use of somebody else's buggy: a day, a week, a month, or several months. *Leasing* generally refers to longer-term arrangements: six months to several years.

Under both types of agreement, you use a vehicle which actually belongs to somebody else, under a variety of conditions.

THE GROWTH OF LEASING AND RENTING VEHICLES

Founded more than sixty years ago when the motor vehicle itself was in its infancy, leasing and renting began to surge in 1960 and in the 1970s continued to outpace the automotive industry which spawned it. One major automobile company executive has forecast that by the end of the 1980s almost 40 per cent of U.S. passenger car output will be earmarked for lease-rental use.

Still another Detroit official has remarked: "Leasing is the wave of the future; we might just see the day when ownership is old-fashioned."

Most experts feel the lease-rental business will continue expanding at the 14 to 16 per cent growth rate of the past ten to twenty years, putting revenues over $30 billion starting in the 1980s.

In the decade of the 1970s, the number of lease-rental units on the road more than doubled and their revenues nearly quadrupled.

More than one car in every five which rolled off U.S. assembly lines—over 20 per cent of them—entered lease-rental service in the late 1970s. (Only a tiny per cent of imported makes became lease-rental units, though.)

Leasing of cars by individuals has paced the boom.

During the 1970s:

- *individual* car leasing nearly tripled;
- *passenger car fleet leasing* almost doubled;
- and *short-term auto rentals* climbed only slightly less.

Hertz, Avis, National, Gelco, and Peterson, Howell & Heather are generally regarded as the leaders in the car fields, while Hertz, Ryder and U-Haul are the biggest in trucks. Others operate on a regional or local basis. Some national concerns confine their business primarily to cars, or to trucks; and some specialize in leasing, others deal primarily in renting. Hertz operates in all four major segments of the business: car renting, car leasing, truck renting, and truck leasing.

Some place the total number of companies in the business as high as fifteen thousand outlets—ranging from automobile dealers who rent or lease only a handful of vehicles each to major banks and retail chains specializing in car leasing. The number of banks in the business has grown rapidly, especially in the so-called "open end" car leasing sector. As the 1980s began, car dealers themselves increasingly were turning to leasing, too.

WHICH LEASE FOR YOU?—A VARIETY OF LEASES

Within the four major segments of the business, an almost infinite variety of lease or rental contracts is written to meet almost any vehicle need you may have. Under a so-called "open end" or "finance" lease, for example, the lessee assumes any gain or loss when the vehicle is sold at the end of the lease term. With a "closed end" contract, on the other hand, the lessor has the responsibility for the profit or loss.

With a "full maintenance" lease, the lessor provides complete service of the vehicle; with a "non-maintenance" contract, the lessee usually is responsible for keeping the vehicle running.

One agreement may cover a huge fleet of jumbo tractor-trailer combinations for a giant corporation while another involves one individual leasing a single subcompact passenger car. One form of agreement could include fueling, maintaining, garaging, insuring, and administering a nationwide fleet; another type of contract might call for little more than financing a single vehicle.

At one extreme, a car lease can be little more than a buy-and-sell contract under which the lessor agrees to purchase a car for a specified price and dispose of it after a certain period, for a fixed fee.

At the other end of the scale, a lease can include a "full maintenance" agreement, which calls for the leasing company to license and insure the car, pay for tires, parts, batteries, servicing, inspections, and cost reporting.

A contract may include insurance and licensing, but no operating or maintenance work; another agreement may specify a maximum number of miles that can be driven—per year or over the duration of the lease—or it may permit limitless mileage. The driver may remain responsible for any difference in estimated and actual trade-in value at the end of the lease, or the leasing company may assume that responsibility.

Monthly lease payments vary with lease terms. Without considering gasoline and oil use, the lease payments for two identical automobiles could differ by as much as one third for leases of the same duration.

OPEN OR CLOSED LEASES

Perhaps the most common consumer misunderstanding of car leases is the difference between closed-end and open-end lease contracts. These terms do *not* refer to whether the lease is for a definite or indefinite duration; they relate to whether the lessor (the leasing company) or the lessee (you the driver, or your employer) stands to gain or lose on the sale price of the car at trade-in time when the lease expires.

With a *closed-end* lease, the lease company takes the car back with no further obligation on the part of the driver. The car is then sold at prevailing used car prices. The lease company takes the profit or loss.

Under an *open-end* lease, the lessee is responsible for any gain or loss on the sale of the car at lease end—over or under a price specified at the time the lease is signed. Open-end contracts can "save" you, the lessee, a significant amount each month during the lease period; but you also could "lose" this, or more, at the end of the lease on the trade-in.

It is in this area of resale value on an open-end lease that the greatest consumer misunderstanding lies.

It is difficult enough for car experts to predict any given vehicle's resale value two to three years from the day the lease is written; it is almost impossible for a consumer to do so accurately.

Closed-end contracts can confuse any unwary individual, too. Most agreements in this category state that the driver must return the car in good condition at lease end, "ordinary wear and tear" excepted. You, the lessee, must make sure what constitutes "ordinary wear and tear."

COSTS OF LEASING VS. OWNERSHIP

The range of leases makes it difficult to generalize on their costs, just as variations in purchase and use of a car make calculation of average ownership expenses complex. You, as an astute buyer, may purchase your car for just $125 over dealer cost. You may equip it with the most popular accessories to enhance its resale value; and you may drive it in such a way that you obtain the maximum price on a trade-in, so your depreciation cost is low. Your car may turn out to be a "peach"—as opposed to a lemon—or you may be handy at mechanical repairs, so maintenance expenses are below average. Your insurance premiums may be less than normal. You may be in an ultra-high income tax bracket so your after-tax interest rate on the car purchase money is reduced. You may be able to buy parts and accessories at discounts. And you may drive almost exclusively on business, so your tax deductions will be high.

But this is an ideal. Unless you are this expert—and this lucky a car buyer—a lease usually will cost you only slightly more than buying your car on the installment plan.

Nothing is cheaper than paying cash—even when you factor in your lost interest on the money you withdrew from savings to make that cash payment.

MAINTENANCE LEASE INCLUDES REPAIR COST PROTECTION

While full-maintenance leasing is not as popular as non-maintenance arrangements, more than one quarter of a million cars are under some form of partial- or full-maintenance agreement.

Many drivers opt for this type of contract because of the additional convenience and protection it provides. Under this sort of arrangement, the lease company handles the servicing, repairs, tire replacement, battery, and other upkeep.

The motorists' variable per-mile maintenance costs become "fixed" charges covered by the monthly lease payments. The lessee's variable costs are reduced to the basic per-mile gas, oil, and other service station expenditures and outlays he would have under ownership as well. See pages 305–12 for information on "fixed" and "variable" car costs.

A maintenance lease can be considered a form of insurance against a lemon which could produce for you abnormally high repair bills, since extra costs of a maintenance lease are based on the lease firm's average upkeep expenses.

THE MILEAGE FACTOR IN LEASE SELECTION

If you plan to drive 20,000 to 30,000 miles a year, the full-maintenance, closed-end lease—which gives you walk-away privileges at the end of the contract—probably is the contract to write.

In the 15,000-to-25,000-miles-a-year category, a *non*-maintenance closed-end lease may be the best buy for your situation; while in the 10,000-to-15,000-miles-a-year bracket, you probably should select a *non*-maintenance, *open*-end—or so-called "finance"—arrangement. Under such a deal, your lower mileage will usually mean that your car is worth more, with inflation what it has been, at the end of your contract. And you'll participate in any profit the leasing company makes on the sale of your car at that time, thus, in effect, reducing your monthly payments—on an *ex post facto,* after-the-contract-is-over basis.

In recent years, the leasing companies have been making their agreements far more flexible. You can include insurance coverage in the arrangement—or leave it out. You can get partial-maintenance contracts, covering specific items such as tires and batteries at the lease company's volume rates, or "free," or receive other specific upkeep equipment and service.

There even are contracts which protect you against any loss on the resale of the vehicle at the end of the lease, but allow you to collect a part of the gain if your unit brings a higher-than-agreed-upon price.

RECORD-KEEPING BENEFITS

One cost factor you should not overlook—especially if you use your car for business for a significant portion of its annual mileage—is record-keeping.

Your calculations of your actual extra auto expenses can be extremely complex, especially figuring depreciation. With a lease, your income tax record-keeping is automatically done for you: you just add up the monthly statements.

In addition, with ownership, you must calculate the cost of interest lost—either on the full purchase price if you are paying cash, or on the amount you withdrew from savings for the down payment. (If your old car's trade-in covered your down payment, keep in mind that you could have sold that old buggy and deposited the proceeds into your savings account.)

Interest lost is *not* a deduction for you for tax purposes if you own your car. With a lease, though, you in effect obtain that deduction, while at the same time you keep your money in your bank account drawing its interest.

Those of you who are sophisticated business and professional people also should investigate organizing a group to buy your cars and lease them back to yourselves for investment-tax credit and other depreciation benefits.

It is our monstrous tax code that makes finaglers and connivers of so many Americans, but until this monster is brought under control, do not ignore the potential advantages tax regulations and loopholes create.

WHAT ABOUT RENTING?

If your annual driving is under 10,000 miles, you still may be able to take advantage of the lease-rental business—via short-term renting.

In the past, of course, you probably have rented a car at some time *in addition to* owning one: for a special vacation trip, in a strange city, or hiring a station wagon to cart a kid to college. (More on the latest wrinkles in car rentals on pages 423–24.)

But have you ever considered short-term car renting *instead of* ownership? Under certain circumstances, it could produce significant savings.

ADVANTAGES FOR CITY DWELLERS

If you live in a city, drive a typical intermediate, make the national 10,000-miles-per-year norm or less, keep your car the usual three to four years and don't commute in it, you might save more than 10 per cent of your annual car expenses by selling your car and renting a substitute for your vacations, weekend trips, and occasional weekday visits.

And the *lower* your annual mileage, the more money you may be able to save by renting. Even if you drive a *five*-year-old car, renting could be less expensive —provided your annual mileage is under 7,500. And for anyone silly enough to be garaging and insuring a *ten*-year-old auto in a big city, you can rent a brand-new model and drive it 5,000 miles a year—still at less than your current owner-ship costs for that jalopy.

At the other end of the scale, if you're a city resident and trade in your car *every* year, you could drive a rented one as many as 14,000 miles annually and be ahead of the money game. Or if you drive the more typical 10,000 miles each year, you could save 20 per cent every twelve months by renting instead of trading in annually.

These were late 1970s comparisons of ownership vs. rental costs in major cities throughout the country, using prices charged by the top rental firms—which have convenient locations, current-model cars, and other benefits.

The off-brand, out-of-the-way rental firms, which often specialize in two- or three-year-old cars, could provide even greater savings.

The key, of course, lies in the fact that car ownership cost in a city is well above the national average, because of higher insurance and garaging expenses, which can add at least 25 per cent to the countrywide averages.

Using the figures and guides provided in the earlier sections on car ownership and operating costs, calculate your specific auto outlays. Then check back on your driving patterns.

Since you live in the city, you probably do not use your car to commute; you take public transportation, or hoof it, or, possibly, take a taxi.

Your car sits either on a street or, more probably in these days of high urban crime rates, in a parking lot or inside a garage.

Your insurance expenses are undoubtedly at least one quarter above the national norms.

Too, you probably use your car primarily on weekends, for vacations, or for a periodic weeknight trip.

If this is your own driving pattern, you're a prime candidate for renting rather than owning.

TREND TO "DRY" RENTAL RATES

In many cities, your savings could be even more, because you get the added advantage of lower weekend rental rates (unless you live in a top tourist area). The comparisons are for regular rates charged by the premium-price companies.

The comparisons give you a station wagon for a two week, 1,400-mile vacation jaunt, plus a car for the other fifty weekends of the year—with up to 175 miles of travel each trip, figured at regular per-mile rates. In most cities, even the "majors" do not tack on the per-mile extra charge on weekends, increasing your potential savings. And the "minors" with their older cars almost never do so.

The calculations were done at the so-called "dry" rates which the entire car rental industry is moving toward, rather than the traditional "wet" rates. Explanation: you pay for the gasoline and are *not* reimbursed for it when you return the car under the dry rates. With the old-style wet rates, gasoline is included in the price charged, and if you buy fuel on the road, you are reimbursed—through reduction of your bill—when you return the car and show your fuel purchase receipts.

In the comparisons, gasoline thus has been eliminated from both sides of the calculations, since you'll be paying for it whether you own or rent the vehicle.

HOW DO YOU SPOT TRUE CAR RENTAL BARGAINS?

Whether you are renting a car in your hometown, or in a distant city for business or for pleasure, how do you tell the best deal? It's never a cinch, but with an understanding of car costs, the comparison of various rental rate structures will be easier for you.

No matter what the "special" is, your basic problem is calculating the expected *total* price.

Your key is your own estimate of the miles you will travel—and how long you will be gone.

The selection almost always comes down to the differing costs between a flat rate and one which combines cost-per-day plus cost-per-mile.

Especially if you are renting in a distant city, make sure you have with you a nationally recognized travel-and-entertainment credit card (one issued by one of the giant specialists in T&E cards, or by bank groups, or a card supplied by the rental company from which you are renting the car).

You are not simply charging the $50 to $150 cost of the rental, but the price of a $5,000 to $8,000 car. The renters want to be sure you are financially responsible and will return their auto.

If you don't use an acceptable credit card, you may have to post a big deposit. If you rent cars often, you might be wise to get a rental-company card, since this also will enable the renting company to fill out the rental agreement in advance, eliminating the need for you to stand in line and give the counter clerk such facts as your driver's license number, what sort of insurance you require, and the type and size car you need.

OTHER RENTAL TIPS

• *Comparison-shop by checking rates* through toll-free phone numbers, inquiring at air terminal rental counters, and investigating the local Yellow Pages.

• *Give the clerk or operator full details* about your mileage plans, drop-offs, destination. A "drop-off" is the privilege of picking up the car at one location and returning it to another. Ask which of the many deals is best for you. The major companies are competing—and their employees have been told to serve you efficiently.

• *Compare equipment* as well as rates. If you'll need specific equipment, such as a rack for skis, book early. As for getting the precise model you request, read the fine print to find out what are restrictions on your choice, loopholes for the company, the like.

• List any other member of your family who will be driving the car, on the rental contract.

• *Examine the car* for dents, a lost hubcap, similar defects, before driving away. Insist that the attendant note the defects on your contract. Be sure there is a spare tire and jack as well.

• Note whether the mileage on the speedometer checks with your rental form. Make sure that the needle on your gas tank reads "full." If you are operating on a dry rate contract, find out how much the rental company charges you for gas you used and did not replace at the time the car is returned. You may save money by filling up just before you turn in the car.

• Ask the company if you are entitled to any grace period. Some car rental offices will give you a few hours of "free" time when the car is due—an assist if you are under pressure to get your car back in time.

• If you are making your own car rental reservations, request a confirmation listing as much of the price and type of car awaiting you as possible. The rental firms want to accommodate you, but your request may be subject to the availability of the car you want at the price you mention. These are facts that you should firmly understand before you start on your trip.

• If you're en route to warm weather in either the South or the West, getting a car as part of a package may be the least expensive deal, particularly if the car is part of the land package in conjunction with a tour-basing air fare.

BIG OR SMALL FIRM?—PROS AND CONS

Why pay up to twice the car rental rate and mileage charge from a big-car, big-name company when far less expensive deals might be made around the corner?

Item: Frequently, the biggest companies offer newer cars with newer tires than do the smaller companies. But this does not necessarily mean that the cars rented out by big-name companies are always safer or significantly more trouble-free.

Item: The bigger companies have hundreds or even thousands of offices across the United States—usually in the most convenient places such as airports, downtown hotel lobbies, etc. And you can make car reservations over toll-free telephone lines from anywhere in the country.

But the lower-cost car rental companies usually will deliver a rental car to you quickly if you call them, often on a direct-line telephone from an airport or hotel lobby—or, in some cases, also on a toll-free line from wherever you are. They also are frequently willing to let you drop off a car wherever you want when you are ready to return it, for a small charge or no charge at all.

Item: The bigger companies tend to keep their offices open for longer hours than do the smaller companies, and to offer you a long list of travel assistance. But smaller companies often will make special arrangements for off-hour needs or returns and also will provide you with maps, directions, etc.

Item: The bigger companies will let you drop off a rental car at another U.S. city—either at a small drop-off charge or at no charge. In this case, the smaller companies may not have an office at your destination.

HOW WELL INSURED IS YOUR RENTED CAR?

Basically, there are three types of financial protection you, the driver of a rented car, need: insurance to cover damage to or loss of the car (collision and comprehensive); insurance to protect you against financial loss arising from property damage or bodily injury sustained by others (liability); and insurance to provide medical payments in case you, the driver, are injured in a crash.

In most cases, your rental car company provides adequate insurance to cover theft or collision damage to the rented vehicle. Contracts issued by the leading companies usually make available a "full collision waiver" for which you are charged an additional amount (about $2.50 a day as the 1980s neared). By paying this extra charge, you are relieved of all financial responsibility for collision damage to the vehicle you rent.

If you do not wish to pay the extra charge, an optional plan is available. Under this plan, you, the renter, assume financial responsibility for damage to the car up to a certain stipulated total, usually $200 to $250. Damages in excess of this amount would be the responsibility of the company that rented that car to you.

What choice you make between these two options depends on your own needs.

For some of you, the full waiver of liability which gives the renter "first dollar" protection against collision damage will be worth the extra charge.

Or you may be among those willing to assume the risk of damage up to a limit of $250 or so, in much the same way as you assume the standard deductible clause in your personal auto policies.

If your job requires that you regularly rent cars for business purposes, you probably should choose the less costly option and assume the first $250 of liability. You thereby save the $2.50 a day extra charge for full coverage.

But if you rent a car only occasionally, the full coverage provision probably is worth the charge. The reasoning here is that, if you rent a car during an occasional business or vacation trip, you may be driving in a strange city where you are unfamiliar with street and traffic conditions. At such times, the likelihood of an accident is greater than normal—and the added $2.50 a day gives you the extra protection you need.

Even more significant than insurance on the rented vehicle is insurance against bodily injury to others and against damage to autos and property belonging to others. Most reputable nationwide car rental agencies provide substantial amounts of liability insurance with limits up to $100,000 for any one person killed or injured and $300,000 for all persons killed or injured in one accident. Property damage liability (which includes damage to the other car or cars) generally is set at a $25,000 limit. In some instances, overall limits are even higher.

Some rental companies, however—particularly those that do not operate on a countrywide basis—may carry only the bare minimum limits set by state law. Some states have extremely low limits for any one person killed or injured in one accident.

Considering the size of recent court awards in death and injury cases, these limits are clearly inadequate. Once the rental company's insurance limits are exhausted, you, the renter-driver, may be held legally responsible to make up the difference.

The third area in which you may need financial protection is in coverage for medical payments and other expenses, should you be injured in an accident. Since standard coverage provided in rental car contracts generally does not cover you for your own injuries, some rental agencies offer personal accident insurance at an extra fee which covers you and your passengers for accidental death or injury. The insurance extends from the time you rent the car until you return it.

If you are traveling to foreign countries, you will come up against special problems. A driver involved in an accident in Canada may face arrest unless he can show his auto insurance is adequate. When driving into Canada, you need a card to show Canadian officials that you have adequate coverage. You need similar proof in many European countries. Proof is normally furnished by the rental company.

In Mexico, you must purchase insurance from a Mexican-owned company. Representatives of these firms are located in U.S. border communities. The rental car company may require you to buy the insurance before releasing the car to you.

FINAL HINTS ON RENTING

There is no doubt that the "off-brand" rental firms—including an increasing number of car dealers—can provide less expensive rental cars. But there are pitfalls.

Especially if you are away from home dealing with a cut-rate firm, check carefully all aspects of the transaction. Often, even with major firms, a small-town outlet will be run by a franchise. His sign may proclaim that he is Hertz, Avis, National, Budget, etc., but he is really Honest John, the local Ford, Chevrolet, or Chrysler dealer—or even a used-car-lot operator.

Your leverage with him, if something goes wrong, is obviously far less than it is with a corporate-owned and company-operated facility in a major city or at a metropolitan airport.

When you book your out-of-town reservation, ask if the outlet is corporate or franchise. If it is a franchise, check to see whether your confirmed reservation is really confirmed, or whether it is what the rental agencies call a "pre-sell," under which the reservation is made and *then* the local outlet is notified.

That outfit may or may not have the car. All rental agencies overbook just as the airlines do. They argue that they must, because so many call and double- or triple-book, then change their plans or never show up at all. It has been said that the real test of management is the quality of its reservations computer program—telling it how many of what kind of cars it will need where and when, how many renters will keep their cars longer than they say they will—and how long.

One major company has a computer program which can tell, for example, just how many cars will be needed at, say, Los Angeles Airport next Fourth of July. One recent year the computer, almost six months in advance, hit the number of reservations down to a single car.

The major firms, of course, keep some cars in reserve, but it is poor management to keep too many as backups. And if there is an unexpected surge in demand, you could be out of luck—especially with a franchisee in a smaller town, where the next car to be returned might be several days from when you expected to pick one up.

When you look for bargains, keep in mind that the smaller firms are often "off-airport." You may have to hike several miles (or take a cab) to pick up your vehicle, or wait until a driver is free to bring the car to you. Your "economy" rental may turn out to be dirty, old—and even in a state of disrepair. Obviously, the price saving can be well worth some small sacrifices, but be sure you understand what those sacrifices may be.

OTHER WAYS TO SAVE—CAR AND VAN POOLING

Let's say you live in the area surrounding the community in which you work and you commute every day by car to and from your job. It's a common enough life-style both in suburbs and such auto-dominated cities as Washington and Los Angeles.

Now let's say your company buys a passenger van so that you and nine to fifteen other employees living along the same general route can commute via the van to and from work. You pay a monthly fee based on the operating cost of the vehicle. One employee in the van pool drives the van each day—in return for which the driver pays no fee and actually has personal use of the van on weekends.

Good deal, yes? It would slash your commuting costs, save enormous amounts of gas, almost surely reduce tardiness and absenteeism among all of you, quite likely boost your morale and camaraderie, too. And it would be just about the most comfortable and convenient way of commuting short of chauffeured limousine service.

Van pooling is a fast-growing form of commutation that has been sweeping the United States since the late 1970s—a system of mass transport praised by government, business, and participating workers.

What you can save from van pooling depends on: the cost of the van ride, length of your commute, previous operating and parking costs for your car, whether the need for a second car is eliminated. You also might save from less mileage on the family car and the possibility of reduced auto insurance rates.

And then there are potential benefits from lessening of tension involved in commuting, greater reliability of the van, the fact that your own car is released for other family members.

OTHER ROAD VEHICLES

RECREATIONAL VEHICLES

Although the energy problems of the 1970s slowed the rapid rise of recreational vehicles, by late in the decade the public's fancy for these roadway caravans had revived, reflecting their versatility and your own desire to have "a house on wheels."

Obviously, as a substitute for a car, these units are wildly extravagant—in purchase price and in virtually all aspects of operating costs, from fuel to insurance.

But the RV popularity stems from the fact that they are not substitutes for cars —they are substitutes for cars plus hotel and motel rooms in an era of increasing minivacations and the growth of all leisure activity.

WHICH TYPE FOR YOU?

If you are in the market for a recreational vehicle and if you are starting your hunt from scratch, here are the five basic types—a list you can use as a preliminary shopping guide:

Camping trailers: compact folding "cottage on wheels" which you tow with your own car. Typical campers sleep four to six, are equipped with bunks, kitchenette, and portable toilet.

Truck-mounted campers: in two variations—the slide-in camper which fits into the back of a pickup; the chassis-mount truck camper which is *permanently* mounted on a truck's chassis (with the truck bed and sides removed). "Truck mounts" have bunks, kitchenette, plumbing; are 6 to 11½ feet long.

Panel vans: converted from cargo and people-hauling units to miniature motor homes, with beds, kitchen, carpeting, and baths, some with "pop" tops, others "as is."

Pickup covers: simple structures with few, if any, built-in conveniences; attach to a pickup to create a sheltered space. Vans and pickups grew in popularity at an almost explosive rate in the 1970s.

Travel trailers: up to 35 feet long and 8 feet wide; pulled by your car; come with baths, kitchens, bedrooms. Largest travel trailer is the "fifth wheel" unit which is towed by a pickup truck by means of a special swivel hitch located directly above the truck's rear axle, making the huge unit easy to tow.

Motor homes: most luxurious, are comfortable carhouses in one unit; 20 to 35 feet long. Some are converted buses.

Then there's a whole new family of "fun" cars and specialty vehicles ranging from jeeps to snowmobiles.

SHOPPING GUIDES

Whatever type you choose, look for one which is convincingly described by the manufacturer as sturdy and stable in winds. If at all possible, test-drive on a windy day before buying. Many, if not most, recreational vehicles are unstable in winds and so flimsy they splinter in a rollover (frames are often wooden).

Don't spend a penny on buying until you have rented the equipment you think you would like best. You might properly rent more than one type before you settle on anything.

Buy a good, *used* unit when you begin: since many campers trade up to bigger units or different types as they go along, lots of good used equipment is for sale. Be sure, though, that an experienced mechanic checks the equipment—particularly the engine and transmission—before you buy. Don't buy a used lemon.

Finally, don't fail to count costs of owning and running a recreational vehicle.

These include registration and insurance (which often run more than the costs of registering and insuring an ordinary car); increased fuel costs of towing a trailer or driving a large motor home over costs of fueling a car by itself; extra garaging costs; extra maintenance and repair costs; financing charges and/or the interest you lose on your initial cash investment. Even a plush window van will cost about 75 per cent more to own and operate than a typical intermediate-size sedan.

Note: these units are trucks—and they *handle* like trucks. Do not assume you'll be able to operate them as you do your car; often they are unwieldy and you must learn to drive them; their acceleration and turning are sluggish; overall maneuverability, difficult. Fuel consumption: 3–10 miles per gallon.

MOTORCYCLES

In a word, don't.

If you are planning to become one of the nation's 5½ million motorcyclists, talk yourself out of it; and, certainly, don't buy one for your youngster. As someone aptly put it: "Don't buy your son a motorcycle for his last birthday."

Others consider the cycle as a form of insanity.

If you become a cyclist, you are just about the most unloved driver there is.

You will be forced to pay big premiums by insurance companies in order to get liability coverage and you will find it is far less comprehensive than similar coverage for an automobile. You will simply be unable to get certain coverages which are typical for cars—at any price.

The reason motorcyclists are getting so cold a shoulder from the insurers is that the danger of having a fatal accident is four times as great with a cycle as with a car.

So far as the insurers are concerned, the under-thirty age group is the worst—simply because the highest rate of motorcycle deaths is found in this group. Nearly seven out of ten motorcycle drivers involved in accidents are between the ages of sixteen and twenty-four.

Motorcycle insurance rates, like car insurance rates, vary from state to state and from area to area within the state, and from company to company too. If you can't get insurance from your regular auto insurance company, you'll probably have to seek out a company in your area which specializes in this type of insurance.

Insurance coverage for a motorcycle may differ radically from ordinary car insurance. Many liability insurance policies for motorcycles, for example, do not cover passengers on the cycle. Under many motorcycle liability insurance policies, coverage is limited to the owner-driver himself—and doesn't cover any other operators. Also, liability coverage may become invalid if a driver is speeding or racing. In addition, many motorcycle policies exclude coverage for medical payments for injuries to the operator.

It is vitally important to check with your insurance agent to make sure you know just what is and what is not covered.

Just how much more expensive is motorcycle insurance than car insurance? It depends on where you live, how old you are, what your own driving record has been, on a number of other factors. But here are a few general hints on how costs compare and how possible savings stack up:

If your cycle has an engine size under 200 c.c., it will cost relatively less to insure than one with a larger-sized engine.

If your cycle weighs 300 pounds or less, the premium for liability insurance coverage in most states will be about 60 per cent of the basic auto insurance rate. (In a few cases it will be only one half the car rate.)

But if you are an unmarried man under thirty years of age your cost of insuring this motorcycle will be about 150 per cent of the basic auto insurance rate—about the same rate an unmarried man in his mid-twenties would pay for insurance on his automobile.

If your cycle weighs more than 300 pounds you will have to pay double the rate for the smaller bikes—or about 300 per cent of the basic automobile insurance rate. This is approximately what an unmarried teenage boy would pay for insurance on a car.

On a motorcycle, you are traveling unprotected at highway speeds among vehicles far bigger and less maneuverable than yours. You cannot be seen as easily and your cycle, with only two wheels, is far less stable than the cars and trucks around you.

Again, don't.

THE BOOM IN BICYCLES

TIPS FOR BUYING BICYCLES

Do you remember (I do) when $20 to $30 was a standard price for a bicycle and $50 meant you were buying "all the extras"? Do you realize that a bike has now become one of the costlier pieces of equipment you can buy and that your spending for bikes passed the $1-billion-a-year level as the 1970s ended?

We are now buying more than 10 million bicycles a year and our bicyclist population by the late 1970s had crossed the 100 million mark.

Against this background, tips on how to shop for and save on a bicycle seem singularly appropriate for you—and you—and you. Here goes:

• Decide in advance how much a bike is worth to you and what kind is right for you. Your choices are:

Middleweights: weighing 50 to 60 pounds, costing $50 to $100 and rugged. They're one speed only and hard work to pedal.

Touring bicycles: miscalled "English racers," weighing 35 to 40 pounds, costing $75 to $150. Most have three speeds, are good for normal use, are your best buy if you're a casual cyclist.

Lightweights: racing bicycles, weighing less than 30 pounds, starting at $100 and climbing sharply from there. Have from five to fifteen speeds, with ten typical. Need fairly frequent maintenance, are tops in efficient pedaling for the serious cyclist.

Stores also carry a variety of children's bikes, "high risers" which look like motorcycles, folding bikes, three-wheelers for adults with poor balance, tandems, even unicycles.

• Test-ride any bike you're considering to see how it feels and "fits." A lightweight's turned-down handlebars will feel awkward at first, but it will be most comfortable for long jaunts. A way to test-ride is to rent one or more bikes before you buy.

• Get the correct frame size (distance from pedal crank to point where seat mounts) for you. The range is 17 to 24 inches. To get your size, subtract 9 or 10 inches from the length of your inseam, measured to the floor.

• Be sure your child's bike fits. Do *not* buy a big—but unsafe—bike that he'll "grow into." Just allow a reasonable range of seat and handlebar adjustment for some growth.

• Check the brakes before you test-ride. The bike may have a coaster brake on the rear wheel activated by back-pedaling, or caliper brakes activated by hand levers on the handlebars. A coaster brake takes longer to apply than calipers and is more difficult to service, but it rarely needs service and works better in wet weather. Dual caliper brakes will give you a quicker stop in dry weather, but they will be poor or worse when wet. Self-adjusting caliper brakes are a strong plus. Note: don't buy a child's bike with caliper brakes unless the child has a big enough hand to use them easily. Even some adults do not have strong enough hands for some caliper brakes.

• Also, while testing, find out how springy the frame is. A more rigid frame means less pedaling wasted. Guard against raw, sharp, or rough edges on any parts, even parts protected by guards and grips. On children's bikes, be wary of gearshift levers placed far back on the horizontal bar, "sissy bars" (high back on seat), small front wheels. The Bicycle Manufacturers Association thumbs-downed all these features some time ago as hazardous. Beware too of elongated "banana seats" (unless you prohibit riding double on them). Look for a red, white, and blue BMS/6 seal of certification on the post just under the seat of an American children's bike. This indicates that the bicycle meets the most recent standards of this organization. Note: no imported bicycle (even the best) can get this seal, and some excellent American bikes lack it too—so use it primarily as a guide to children's bicycles.

• Bikes, like cars, have options, or accessories. Although the cost of bike accessories is much less than car options, you'll still want to be discriminating in what you buy, for all add complexity and weight. Here are the most popular and useful:

Bell or horn: a bell is more reliable than a horn and doesn't consume batteries. Both will warn pedestrians of your presence, but neither will help you in your interactions with cars, unless you invest in a marine-type Freon-powered air horn.

Chain and lock: these are your first line of defense against bicycle thieves, who steal hundreds of thousands of bikes each year. The chain should be long enough to go through both wheels, the frame, and around a fixed object. It also should be hard enough to resist cutting by ordinary instruments. Your lock should be of equal quality.

Light: generator types eliminate the battery hassle but significantly increase pedaling effort when they're on—and go out when you stop. A small battery light which clips to your left leg is also a good idea, since it quickly identifies you as a cyclist by its motion. A taillight is as important for safety as a headlight.

Luggage rack or basket: they make a bike more useful for small errands and larger outings.

The list of possible accessories you can load onto a bike is long. It includes an odometer or speedometer (some types make a bicycle pedal harder; see a good dealer for recommendations); a tool kit; a tire patch kit; an extra inner tube; a water bottle for long trips; a kiddie seat for taking a small child along; an aerosol can of bike-chasing-dog repellent; special cycling clothes; and a protective helmet for areas with dangerous traffic.

To save money, buy a used bike—but if it's in good condition, expect to pay 75 per cent of the price of a new one. A low price for a good used bicycle is a warning that it may have been stolen. Inspect any used bike with care—or pay a qualified mechanic a few dollars to go over the bike for you.

• Assemble a new bike yourself—a job which will also save money by teaching you how to repair it. Have a competent repairman check your work to be sure you did it right.

• Be prepared to wait until the type of bicycle you want can be shipped to you: do not be talked into a more expensive model on hand. Few bicycle shops have any used ones, and bikes generally are in such demand that your choice may be very limited if you are not prepared to wait. You can, of course, widen your choice considerably by shopping around.

• If yours is a big family, you may be able to save literally hundreds of dollars over the years by letting your children earn the money for their own bikes, rather than providing them as gifts. An earned bike will probably last two or three times as long as a gift bike.

• After you have bought your bike, register it with the local police. Many communities impound unregistered bicycles, and, in any event, registration sharply increases your chance of recovering your bike if it is stolen.

• Check your homeowner's insurance to see if it covers a bicycle. If not, you can get a special policy at modest cost.

• And two final points: Don't set your heart on one bike as an absolute must. Until you get way up in the $300 price range, there is not that much difference between them. And in inexpensive bikes, a good dealer is your key to value, for he, rather than any manufacturer's guarantee, will stand behind your machine.

BIKE SAFETY

Bicycles, too, can require safety precautions. They are not in the danger category of motorcycles, or even cars. But you may not consider them to be dangerous at all, because of the relatively low speeds at which they travel. This is a mistake. Don't ignore precautions.

More than 1,000 persons are killed as a result of bicycle accidents each year and some 460,000 more are seriously injured, mostly in collisions with cars.

For your own protection when you buy:

Look closely at all potentially sharp edges. If you have a bike with sharp edges, file them down and cover them with heavy protective tape.

• Study all parts of the frame to be sure there are no *improperly welded joints* and no fracture due to bad handling.

• Watch out for *protrusions* which could cause injury to the thigh or groin.

• Check for *faulty* brakes and road-test a bike before you buy. If you buy a bike with hand brakes, be sure the levers can be easily moved, especially if the bike is for children with small hands.

• Consider *chain guards* a "must"—even if your bike's pedals can be rotated backward to release quickly any clothing that might get caught between the chain and sprocket.

• Test the *handlebars* for comfort and safe control. Handlebars ends should not be more than 16 inches above the seat surface when the seat is in its lowest and the handlebars are in their highest position.

• Select a bike that is *visible* from every angle and check for clearances: at least 3½-inch clearance between the pedal and front fender or the tire, and pedals that must not touch the ground when the bike is tilted at least 25 degrees on a turn.

• Inspect *tires for cushioning against potholes* and rocks and, again, check for braking (meaning a good tread).

• Avoid equipment which rises more than 5 inches above the rear of the seat and *do not* buy a bike that cannot be adjusted to fit and that is not firmly assembled. You should be able to straddle the bike with both feet flat on the ground and with no less than 1-inch clearance between the frame's top tube and the rider's crotch.

BIKE COURTESY

The bike boom has resulted in bicycling being in an awkward stage: it is off the sidewalks, and onto the streets and highways; but many cyclists still do not obey traffic signs.

There are now about 50,000 miles of bicycle pathways and more and more cities are designating bicycle lanes on their streets each year. If you, as a bicyclist, wish to avoid the type of regulations which has befallen the auto industry, make sure you are courteous and considerate.

A friend of mine in New York recently waited patiently and properly at a street corner on Park Avenue for the light to change—then waited again to make sure the automobiles had stopped before he started to cross at the crosswalk. He had taken only a few steps when he was hit solidly by a cyclist who was riding in the middle of the street—and running the light.

Both my friend and the cyclist went sprawling. Did the cyclist apologize? No. Instead, this self-centered individual cried angrily: "You walked right into me," as, indeed, my friend had, it never having crossed his mind that the bicyclist would disobey the lights.

Incidents such as this will only stimulate regulations against cycling. Be smart, be courteous, and obey the laws.

THE MOPED: A COMPROMISE

Faster than a bike, slower than a motorcycle, the moped is the half-breed cycle, a cross between motorized and leg-driven vehicles.

At one of the busiest and classiest shopping corners in New York City one day in the late 1970s I saw two attractive young women demonstrating a bicycle to which a motor had been attached. Along with a few dozen others, I stopped to look, listen, and consider buying the vehicle for short-distance, fuel-saving trips during this new era of major energy conservation.

On a highway out of the city that weekend, I watched a middle-aged man and woman pedaling similar motor-bicycles at a respectable speed of 35 to 40 miles an hour. They wore helmets, seemed comfortable and just as much at ease (if not more so) than the auto drivers going at 55 to 65 mph in the faster driving lanes.

The moped—a form of motor bicycle that swept over Europe in the 1970s—has finally put its wheels on the ground in the United States after a hard-fought campaign by its manufacturers.

It can be a boon for the short-distance driver, particularly the younger among you, eager to save money on fuel. *It can go as far as 200 miles on a gallon of gas.* It sells for *$400* to *$600* as the 1980s begin and maintenance costs are low. It can make its way through traffic jams with enviable ease.

Pollution is no problem. Emission levels have not been high enough even to warrant study by the Environmental Protection Agency. The noise level is below that of cars or motorcycles. Insurance costs as of the late 1970s were about $150 a year for a typical policy covering an adult driver.

As for further safety regulations, this question is being reviewed by government agencies. The tentative conclusion is that the accident pattern for mopeds is similar to that for motorcycles rather than bicycles.

While the motorized bike has long been very popular in Europe, it was only a few years ago that its European manufacturers decided we in the United States were ready for a low-gas means of transportation. Passage of New York State legislation for the moped (pronounced MOE-ped), toughest in the nation, is setting a guideline for other state regulations.

• Under the New York rules, a moped that can travel at *more than 17 mph* must be registered and carry insurance. Drivers of mopeds that can travel at 30 or more mph must be licensed and wear helmets.

• All drivers must be at least sixteen years of age. Mopeds not engineered for more than 17 mph are free of regulation.

In Bermuda, where the moped has been a standard vehicle for resident and tourist alike, accidents and rules have been minimal. In fact, the island some time ago loosened the ban on two on a bike, because it found accidents soared when new husbands anxiously looking back for the safety of their brides on separate bikes ended up in ditches along the narrow roads.

Even without the intensifying drive for energy conservation, a cheap motor-bicycle probably would have become a part of the U.S. transportation system. It has a use for short-distance commuting, assuming you are young and agile enough to ride a bike and handle the pedaling. It can get through urban traffic congestion without inviting heartaches among all nearby automobile drivers; a young homemaker easily could use it for many neighborhood chores.

BUSES: LEAVE THE DRIVING TO THEM

Each year for the past decade Americans have been taking some 400 million intercity bus trips, of which 60 million have been chartered group arrangements. These figures are, of course, in addition to the literally billions of short intracity journeys, usually for commuting purposes.

More than thirty thousand towns still depend on the bus for their sole means of scheduled transportation.

As the 1980s approached, bus lines were offering a variety of special fares to lure the single or family trip, with one-price tickets good "anywhere" in the United States within a specified period of time.

While these special fares have not been so widely publicized as the maze of special air-fare rates (see page 423), they do offer substantial savings to travelers, especially if you are taking relatively short trips of fewer than 500 miles.

In the promotion of these special fares, the bus (and train) lines are copying European travel promotions.

Convenience, flexibility, low cost—these have been the prime factors behind the popularity of the bus. In countless instances, people can't operate a car or can't afford one—because, say, of youth or old age, location, or income level. And even those who haven't had any special reason to take a bus have often preferred to "leave the driving to them."

Moreover, many buses are now equipped with reclining seats, individual reading lights, and lavatories. To add to their appeal, buses also have introduced airplane-style music and news via headsets; and a few buses boast miniature kitchen-bars which can serve drinks and snacks.

The very turnpikes which have made the automobile so popular also have been a boon to the bus. The flexibility of the bus hasn't been approached by the trains or planes because the buses follow the highways and the highways follow the people.

TIPS FOR BUS TRAVELERS

Here, in question and answer form, are tips for you, should you have to make a bus trip.

Q. *What about valuables and breakables?*
A. Carry them with you. Most companies will insure items up to $50 in value, free of charge, with added coverage available.

Q. *What about reservations and luggage on intercity trips?*
A. A reservation is not vital. During peak periods backup buses are ready. To avoid crowds, travel in midweek or midday. If you're in a hurry, check on express buses. Check luggage you can't carry on at the terminal about a half hour in advance. Be sure you have your identification tags on all luggage.

Q. *How do I find the right company for a charter?*

A. Ask your local college or athletic team: they use dozens of charters and know the good firms.

Q. *What are guidelines for prices on chartered buses?*

A. Prices are generally quoted in either of two ways, depending on the trip's distance. For local work of up to 50 miles in one direction, the price is quoted on a per-hour basis.

For trips of more than 50 miles in one direction, prices are usually quoted on a per-mile basis. In addition, there is usually an hourly charge if the trip goes over a specified number of hours because the driver must be paid, no matter whether the bus is moving or standing still.

Q. *What are the hidden cost pitfalls to look out for?*

A. Does the quoted price include tolls, parking charges, permits? Is the cost of the driver's lodging and/or food included if yours is an overnight trip? Check each of these items in advance.

Prices are usually higher on weekends, so consider scheduling your event during the week.

Order the bus to report as late as possible to reduce unproductive waiting time for the inevitable last-minute arrivals.

Use box lunches and save money.

Also, for your own comfort, make sure the bus you charter has sufficient baggage capacity for your luggage—particularly ski gear—and that the seating capacity of the bus itself is adequate.

AMTRAK: THE TWENTIETH CENTURY, LIMITED

Trains, like buses, are among the least expensive ways for people to travel today—and they also leave the driving to someone else, permitting you, the passenger, to relax, read, look out the window.

Trains also are a far more efficient means of transportation than cars and highways, and therefore are far easier on our fuel supplies: one railroad train can accommodate as many people as fifty cars. One track can replace twenty lanes of superhighway. A train gets twice as many passenger miles from a gallon of fuel as a fully loaded economy car.

The National Railroad Passenger Corporation, Amtrak—created by Congress as a quasi-public corporation early in the 1970s to help passenger trains stage a comeback—has helped bring this nearly moribund system of travel into the twentieth century.

Amtrak has:

Placed experimental high-speed turbo trains in service.

Ordered brand-new cars, including new Metroliners and a series of bi-level long-distance coaches, diners, lounges, and sleepers.

Upgraded the general quality of passenger trains, by picking the best two thousand passenger cars out of the more than three thousand formerly on the tracks, then refurbishing a number of these.

Installed a nationwide, centralized ticket and reservation system.

Begun building "satellite" train stations for suburban travelers.

Started the acquisition and refurbishing of old passenger stations.

Reintroduced long-haul sleeper routes in some sections of the United States— and started redesign of the cars to make them more efficient and comfortable.

Improved some connections on long hauls to reduce long waits for trains.

Made improvements on some trains in dining cars and other food service facilities.

Cleaned up many rest rooms so that, as one official notes, "the whole train no longer smells like a bathroom."

Made moves to ease buying of train tickets. You can pay for your ticket with American Express, a Master Charge, Diners Club, Carte Blanche, VISA, or a Rail Travel card. Thousands of travel agents can help you make arrangement for travel on the Amtrak system. You can order tickets by phone to be mailed to you and billed to your credit card.

Introduced a uniform ticket format across the country.

You can get reservations and information on Amtrak schedules by calling this toll-free number: (800) 523-5720.

Along with buses and airlines, in the final years of the 1970s Amtrak, too, began promoting "saver" fares—a variety of unlimited-mileage tickets to anywhere.

Ticket prices were based on the number of days for which the pass was valid rather than the miles to be traveled. So long as your trip took place within the time limits on your tickets—two weeks, three weeks, a month—you could theoretically go anyplace the system runs.

Amtrak operates to and from about five hundred cities throughout most of the country, and has affiliations with the Southern Railway, the last of the passenger lines remaining independent of the national system.

There are some loopholes in the Amtrak unlimited mileage tickets, though: the journeys must be interstate (this avoids competition with commuter schedules).

In addition to the unlimited mileage tickets, Amtrak also sells so-called "Tickets to Anywhere"—one way or round trip—during a specified time period for bargain prices. Stopovers are permitted so long as the stop is along a direct route between your starting point and your destination.

Despite Amtrak's efforts at upgrading, some trains, though, are traditionally late and cleanliness and service have been improved only marginally.

As 1980 neared, America's railroad system was far below its levels of service one hundred years ago and, seemingly, sinking slowly into oblivion as a means of passenger travel—local or long-distance.

COMMUTING BY TRAIN

Despite its much-ballyhooed efforts to upgrade commuter service, the nation's local rail system is no better than its long-distance runs and these local lines continue to lose business to both buses and cars.

Q. *How much can you really save if you use public transportation instead of your own car to commute from the suburbs to your job in a downtown city area?*

A. Not nearly as much as you probably think—unless, in addition to using the train or bus; you eliminate an automobile entirely from your transportation budget.

On the surface, the visible public transportation costs appear much less than the costs of owning and driving a car to work each day. But a study of daily commutation costs in seven major urban centers finds that six out of ten of the commuters continue to need a car to get from home to the train (or bus) stations.

Thus you, the commuter, still have the cost of owning and operating an auto, even if you only drive it to and from the station each day; and if the full costs of owning and operating your car are added to your commutation costs, the savings gained by using public transportation narrow significantly.

Just as one illustration, say you're commuting by rail from Northbrook, Illinois, to Chicago, about 25 miles away. Say you drive an average of 5 miles each way from home to station and back each day.

Now say you drive from the same suburban community to downtown Chicago and park downtown.

Taking the train could save you 75 per cent—in theory. But if the annual noncommuting costs of owning and operating the car you use to drive to the station are added, then your transportation costs as a train commuter jump to more than your costs of commuting by car alone.

Only if you eliminate the car from the family transportation budget and rely exclusively on public transportation do you, that Chicago commuter, save a respectable 70 per cent a year.

As another illustration, say you're commuting from Palo Alto, California, to San Francisco. Your public transportation costs come to less than one third of your private car expenses, which include downtown parking for those trips.

But if you, that Palo Alto commuter, could eliminate an auto from the family budget, your savings would mount to a respectable two thirds of your auto commutation costs.

Of course, there is a considerable lack of realism in assuming any family living in a suburban area could get along comfortably *without* a family car. There's more to an automobile's use than commutation, particularly in the suburbs.

BY AIR—"IT'S THE ONLY WAY TO GO"

If your time is limited and you're traveling a fairly long distance, a plane is the only way to go. If your funds also are limited and you're traveling a long way, a plane can be an economical form of transportation too. But how economical it will be will depend on your knowledge of and ability to take advantage of what has become a fantastic web of air-fare bargains, low-cost package deals, and travel discounts.

COACH—THE BASIC FARE

For more than a generation the basic "double standard" of airplane fares, for both domestic and overseas travel, has been first class and coach.

Every dollar of *coach*-fare travel was equal to from $1.33 to $1.67 of first-class accommodation. In the early days of post-World War II air travel, of course, "first class" was the only class. The planes were not big enough, nor the traffic heavy enough, to segregate the passengers.

As the aircraft became larger, though, coach travel was introduced—three seats abreast on each side of a single, middle aisle, as opposed to two seats abreast in the first-class section. Also, the rows of seats were closer together in the back of the plane—the coach section—than in the front, or first-class section. First-class passengers also were served free drinks, coach travelers had to pay for them.

In the days of piston-engine planes, when longer trips often meant long hours in the air, the advantages of first-class service were often worth the extra expense. But with the advent of the higher-speed jets, this advantage was reduced. You, the air traveler, took to sitting in the rear of the plane and buying your own drinks, more and more.

First-class sections dwindled in size, coach sections expanded.

Furthermore, to increase their utilization of planes, airlines began lowering fares for nighttime travel; and you, thrifty Americans, took to this cut rate, too.

With air routes and fares closely regulated in former days by the government, airlines competed with special promotional rates—for tickets purchased in advance, for travel on off-peak days as well as off-peak hours.

OVERSEAS AIR TRAVEL

As the jets got bigger, and faster, overseas travel became increasingly popular. To fill their planes, airlines introduced excursion fares, with a variety of stipulations—advance purchases, departures on certain days of the week only, trips to last a minimum and/or maximum number of days, journeys to be made only during certain months of the year.

Enter the charter.

The airlines had to fly certain routes to keep the franchises. They had to fly these schedules whether the seats were full or empty. And, often especially on off-hours, they were empty. I recall one late-night flight from Detroit to New York on a then new jumbo 707 when only eight of us aboard were paying passengers. Eight. We were actually outnumbered by the crew.

Charter flights don't have such problems. These operators can line up a group of travelers—or pseudo-groups—set a specific day, date, and time for departure, and fill the plane.

Obviously, with a guarantee of a capacity or near-capacity load, the price can be far lower than if you have to fly with your plane only 40, 50, or 60 per cent full. Certainly you can do it cheaper than if you are forced to fly with only eight paying customers on board.

The outcome became obvious: charter flight business—especially on overseas routes—began eating into the business of the scheduled airlines, even the bargain-basement excursion fares permitted under government regulations. Why pay hundreds of dollars more for a flight if you don't have to?

THE "SCHEDULED CHARTERS"

Toward the end of the decade of the 1970s, the United States Government reversed its generations-old policy: it began a trend toward deregulation of the airline industry.

The airline industry at this time is, as a result, undergoing the greatest changes in its history. Routes are being opened to additional carriers, increasing competition. At the same time, rates are being deregulated—leaving airlines free to cut the prices of their tickets, now sold on a charter-like basis.

Unlimited travel passes are being sold on airlines, as they are on buses and trains, again, with time, rather than distance, the prime criterion of price.

There is a bewildering variety of special requirements. In some instances tickets must be bought—and paid for—weeks in advance. In other cases there are no advance reservations at all. In some cases the traveler must spend from seven to twenty-one days away from his initial departure point; in other cases there is no limitation and a round trip may be made the same day.

Confusion and change are dominant: in some situations zigzag routings produce significant savings: in others, these are forbidden. Stopovers may or may not be permitted. For some rates, families must fly together. Package tours—in which your land charges for hotels, food, and car rental are included—may or may not be part of the deal.

SEE THE U.S.A. AND SAVE

Three late 1970s travel trends—cut-rate air fares, discount car rentals, and package hotel/motel rates—showed how you can save more than 50 per cent on your vacation, provided you plan properly, on a week-long coast-to-coast trip for two.

First, your air-fare savings. Major U.S. airlines may have as many as a dozen different rates between key cities of the nation. As the 1980s approached, American, for example, listed twelve round-trip New York to San Francisco fares, ranging from daytime first-class space to a nighttime, midweek "Super-Saver" ticket at a 58 per cent discount for literally fly-by-night Monday-to-Thursday trips made at least a week apart and paid for a month in advance.

Smaller but still significant savings were obtainable without reserve-in-advance or travel-duration restrictions. A round-trip day-coach rate saved almost 17 per cent under first-class costs, night coach saved 33 per cent.

Another step down the rate ladder was the excursion fare. With this, you bought tickets a week ahead of time and a Sunday had to come between your outbound and return flights. The weekend, nighttime excursion rate was 38 per cent under first class and midweek nights provided a 42 per cent saving.

The Super-Saver rates were the bargain basement of ticket sales. Daytime midweek and nighttime weekend Super-Saver tickets were half the first-class fare. The lowest charge—the 58 per cent saving—was the midweek nighttime Super-Saver cost. The actual ticket costs will rise with inflation, but the percentage of savings should remain the same.

Car-rental rates have also undergone changes. As the 1970s drew to a close, essentially you had three basic cost categories: the full regular *daily* price-plus-mileage charges, varying by car size; flat *weekly* unlimited-mileage rates; and the "Take-Off" prices—flat, unlimited mileage rates for extended *weekend* routes—good Thursdays through Mondays provided you keep the car two or three days (three-day minimum for Thursday rentals, two for Friday and Saturday pickups).

Figuring a typical 75 miles a day of driving, Take-Off rates cut 42 per cent from regular daily charges, more if you drive farther.

Third are the possible hotel/motel savings. In addition to traditional price spreads on different room sizes and savings for families sharing space, hotels and motels in the same chain in the same area may have standard "rack" rates for comparable rooms which vary by as much as 50 per cent depending on the hotel's distance from the downtown area. Also, in-season, off-season, or the be-tween-times "shoulder" season rates can vary another 15 to 40 per cent.

You can get quotes on these standard rack rates by calling the chain's local number in your city or its toll-free 800 number. If this isn't listed, dial the phone company's toll-free Information number, (800) 555-1212.

Furthermore, you can often find hotel/motel package rates—under which extras such as meals, drinks, sports, and shows may be included for one package price—at additional savings of 20 to 40 per cent. Travel agents and airlines themselves can often quote you package rates and make reservations for you, as will some national tour packagers.

The bottom line in vacation savings is this: a first-class trip for two, in season, including coast-to-coast flying, could cost over $2,100 in the late 1970s. The same in-season trip at fly-by-night, discount car and hotel package rates was as much as 37 per cent under the first-class fare. Off-season at an outskirts hotel with three-day car use at discount rates, the expense fell to just 45 per cent of the top rates, a 55 per cent discount.

SAVE EVEN MORE OVERSEAS

With the variety of travel rates in effect as this was written, you could save as much as 70 per cent on a week-long vacation trip to Europe or the Caribbean also, by planning ahead, sticking to your schedule, and sometimes by literally get-ting up early in the morning to buy your tickets.

For example, with off-season, pay-ahead fares, a seven-day budget tour of Britain cost a couple as little as 29 per cent of the typical on-season first-class prices in effect just a week earlier or later. Or, a one-week off-season Barbados stay was as low as 30 per cent of the top rates at a plushy place there in season.

Furthermore, depending on what's important, you could pick accommodations and flights almost cafeteria style at just about any price in between those limits.

Here's how a week's junket to Britain stacked up. More than a dozen New York–London fares were in effect, ranging from a $1,406 round-trip first-class ticket ($1,694 for the supersonic Concorde) down to $253 for off-season standby trips mid-October to April, an 82 per cent discount.

In between you could pick a traditional economy (coach) seat for 54 per cent of the first-class rate, 45 per cent off season. Excursion tickets were 35 to 43 per cent of the top fare, Advance Purchase Excursion 25 to 33 per cent of first class and Budget costs 22 to 27 per cent of the full fare. Beware, though, of weekend surcharges, which may add substantially to a round-trip flight for two.

The stand-by fare, a further saving, is usually just that—you get up early in the morning, go to the airport, wait in line to pick up your one-way tickets, then repeat the process for the return flight.

For your hotels, London-area rates as the 1980s approached ranged from $15 a night per person double occupancy to $60 in a superior spot—or as much as $80 to $110 at a place such as Claridge's. You had to add $7 to $10 a night at most places for on-season rates. Meals ran about $25 a day per person. Package tours saved you 5 to 10 per cent for week-long stays.

But the British Tourist Office says you could save still more by traveling to other British Isle places. Rooms at typical English country inns are 38 to 56 per cent of typical London prices at night, country food about 60 per cent of city rates a day, and rental cars comparable to U.S. rates for unlimited weekly mileage.

Plan on spending more in most other European countries. UN statistics showed London living costs were about the same as those in New York; but prices in Switzerland were half again as much, Paris about 30 per cent more, Bonn nearly 40 per cent higher, Rome about 10 per cent less. Currency fluctuations make overseas trips a gamble, but advance-pay plans can lock in rates for you. Hertz, for example, offers a 10 per cent discount on a car for a week in Britain and some other countries if you reserve and pay in advance in the U.S.A.—thus saving you money and also protecting against a further downward dollar-value plunge.

For a Caribbean vacation, the seasons change—"on" is mid-December to mid-April in most places there. And since even the farthest of the Caribbean islands, Barbados or Aruba, for example, are only about 2,100 air miles from New York, versus 3,450 New York to London, your week-long vacation to these tropical isles will be less overall.

As the 1980s approached, your round-trip New York–Barbados air tickets via advance-purchase, off-season budget-price midweek fares could give you a 71 per cent discount under first-class rates. (For a close-in destination such as San Juan, fares were about 33 per cent under those to Barbados or Aruba.)

Hotel rates ranged from as low as $6.00 per person a night double occupancy for an off-season week-long package at a small Barbados hostelry to $45 at a more expensive spot there. Comparable on-season cost 64 to 100 per cent higher. UN living cost data shows Bridgetown, Barbados, levels about equal to those in New York.

Rates for comparable Holiday Inn rooms on various islands range from 74 per cent of the Caribbean average in season at Ponce and 80 per cent in San Juan, Puerto Rico, to 40 per cent over the average in Guadeloupe. Car rental rates ranged from about the U.S. price to 50 per cent higher.

To achieve the savings *you* want shop at various travel agents and airline tour desks and make toll-free 800 calls to major hotel chains, plan far enough in advance, pay in advance, and stick to your schedule since there are hefty dollar penalties for last-minute changes.

You may not want to pay the price in time and inconvenience for a full 70 per cent saving, but you can make your own decision on how much to save.

DO IT YOURSELF

With the new lower rates and profusion of promotions, you probably will not be able to find a travel agent to do all your planning for you—except on the basis of standard coach (or first-class) fares.

It will be a do-it-yourself task—a challenge to pick the best and least expensive routes, carriers, and times to go.

One aspect that does *not* seem to have changed, though, in a generation of air travel: baggage. Travel light and take your belongings with you into the cabin if you can, rather than checking them. Baggage is still lost all too frequently. If it is on the same flight with you, claiming it at your destination will delay you fifteen minutes to half an hour.

PROTECTION ON BUMPING

According to the Civil Aeronautics Board (CAB), more than 150,000 airline passengers a year were being "bumped" during the late 1970s.

What rights do you have if you hold a confirmed reservation on a flight and are bumped against your will because the plane has been overbooked and is overcrowded?

If you are involuntarily bumped, the airlines must refund to you the full cost of your ticket to your destination or your first stopover. A stopover is more than just a change of planes; it is defined as a stop of more than four hours on domestic flights and more than twenty-four hours on international flights. Thus, if you are bumped from a New York to Los Angeles flight that has you changing planes in Chicago, say, the airline must refund the full cost of your New York to Los Angeles fare, not just the New York to Chicago portion. If you lose your seat involuntarily, the very least you must receive is $37.50, up to a maximum of $200.

If an airline fails to provide you with alternate transportation that brings you to your destination within two hours of your originally scheduled arrival time, it must refund you twice the cost of your ticket. The minimum you could receive in this case at the end of the 1970s was $75, the maximum, $400.

Under CAB rules, before anyone may be bumped against his or her will, the airlines first must ask for volunteers who agree to give up their seats in return for a payment at the discretion of the airlines.

There is no specified amount airlines must offer would-be volunteers. Compensation may vary from one flight to another, or even from one volunteer to another. Under American Airlines' volunteer system at the end of the 1970s, for instance, passengers on an oversold flight received a printed notice when they checked in. This notice disclosed that if they were willing to catch a later flight, they would receive a certain payment.

This payment could range from $25 to $100 depending on the airport, time of day, number of alternative flights available, other factors. Under American's system, all volunteers from a particular flight received the same compensation, but airlines may adjust their offerings to prospective volunteers as they see fit.

If no one volunteers, the airlines must follow boarding priority rules. These rules, or a summary of them, must be made available to passengers at all ticket counters and boarding points.

To avoid being among the bumped, your best protection is to check in early.

BOATS

The fundamental rules of buying, stressed over and over—and over—in this book, can easily be translated from area to area, and thus you can without difficulty translate them for yourself into the sphere of boats (or even horses).

BOATS FOR FUN

In our country in the late 1970s, boats numbered nearly 11 million—more than double the number of only two decades ago—and boating has become a multi-billion-dollar industry, with about one in five Americans now counted as a boater. Each spring, literally millions of boats change hands. Outboard motorboats costing from $3,000 to $10,000, new, are far and away the most popular type, and are familiar sights in every part of our country. Many of today's boats run over $100,000. And with maintenance, repairs, insurance, and a trailer to haul the boat or a marina, plus the frequently high cost of winter storage in or out of the water, a boat can become among the most costly possessions of an unwary family.

CHOOSING A BOAT

Before you do anything, study! Subscribe—for at least a year—to one of the major boating publications such as *Yachting* or *Boating*. If you get serious, add *The National Fisherman* to your list.

Purchase a copy of the boater's bible, *Chapman,* and read it from cover to cover. Regularly check the boating sections of your local newspaper and study boat—and marina and equipment—prices.

Your first decision will be—sail or power? Or a combination of the two, a motor-sailer? Your next judgment will be size. And remember, the costs of boats increase geometrically because you are talking not just length, but width (beam) and depth (draft). In short—capacity, or displacement.

If you are young and agile, a sailboat or motor-sailer is probably your best bet. Its size will depend on the size of your family. The bigger a sailboat, the more difficult it is to handle, and more expensive to operate, despite the sea stories you may have heard or read about transoceanic single-handed sailing. The bigger the boat, the larger the sail area—and the larger the sail area, the more grunting and heaving to raise and lower them.

So buy a boat the right size for you—not too small, not too large.

POWERFUL DECISIONS

If you decide on power, you must make a number of subdecisions. Outboard, inboard—or a combination "inboard, outdrive" or so-called sterndrive? Each type has its advantages and its drawbacks.

The outboards and sterndrives will give you speed (especially if you opt for twin engines rather than a single power plant). Twin engines give you a safety margin, too, in case one engine conks out. There are no gasoline stations open on the oceans or on our Great Lakes.

But, obviously, the more power you have, the costlier the boat will be—to buy and to run.

Then you will have to make up your mind about a planing, semi-displacement, or full-displacement hull. The planing hull is faster, but less stable. Displacement and semi-displacement hulls are slower, but usually stand up better to rough seas. *In boating, safety should be your prime consideration.*

If you elect more moderate speeds, you have additional choices to make. Gasoline engines or diesels? The diesels will cost more, but they are more fuel-efficient, and many boaters believe they are more reliable.

Water—especially salt water—and engines are natural enemies. Engine breakdowns are routine in boating, as are electrical failures. Murphy's Law is the constitution of the sea—Anything That Can Go Wrong, Will—and at the worst possible time. Many boating enthusiasts feel that Murphy was an optimist.

Another power-plant decision: salt-water cooling or fresh-water cooling? The latter is preferred by far for inboard engines; salt corrodes faster than fresh water. Also, air plays only a minor role in keeping your boat engine cool, unlike the dual air-water cooling system of an automobile. There are no fans on marine engines. Therefore, the liquid cooling system on an engine has tough work to perform—and is a frequent source of engine trouble. The fresh-water cooling system will reduce these troubles, but at considerable added expense.

BUYING A USED BOAT

Once you have priced new boats, you may quickly conclude that a *used* boat is your only practical choice.

Buying a used boat can be particularly tricky—and for this purchase, therefore, there are several special rules.

Under a typical cycle, a buyer's interest might first be grabbed by the fanciest styles; his attention would then be heightened by the flashiest accessories; finally, a transfer might be clinched by nothing more than the most colorful "cosmetics" added by an earlier owner (owners).

But this is not the way to buy a used boat. Instead what you, a potential buyer, should do is "kick the tires." What should govern your decisions is the same degree of caution that would be in order when you buy a used car—and that's caution! Specifically:

• Grasp from the start that used boats do *not* depreciate, as automobiles do, by a rule-of-thumb annual percentage and that some late-model boats, in fact, can grow in value. So comparison shopping is absolutely essential—after you have listed the basics you really want. Are you looking for a specific construction or type? Do you want the craft for day sailing or fishing? Inshore or offshore? What do you need in accommodations, speed, and size? How much do you want to spend—and no more?

As one general rule, the more experienced a boatsman you are, the less elaborate accommodations you will want, but the more safety equipment you will elect.

As another, a boat used inshore may be less sturdy than a boat used offshore or on the Great Lakes—*even once*. The latter must—literally—be strong enough to withstand being dropped into the water from 10 or more feet up *without any damage*.

• Check the hull once you have narrowed your choice to a couple of boats, for hulls determine the real value of a boat and you must inspect their safety. On wooden hulls, now all but outmoded, check that all butts, seams, and joints are tight. Also look carefully for rot—especially in corners where soft spots tend to "hide." With fiberglass boats, check the gel coat for cracking. Also check around the hull for any accumulation of slight cracks, for although this is primarily a cosmetic problem, a concentration of small cracks might indicate an impact area.

• When the boat is out of water, examine the keel and bottom for damage. Small gouges can be repaired easily but a badly mauled keel may have to be replaced. Inside the boat, check that hull fittings are sound, that hoses don't have cracks, that hose clamps fit tightly. Study the fuel connections, for a faulty hookup can cause a fire or even a major explosion. Check, too, the wiring and fuse systems for short circuits and improper insulation.

• A wise expense: pay an expert to help you, especially if you are new to boating.

• Make a list of the approved equipment the Coast Guard requires, under federal and state laws, for the area in which you intend to do your boating. This equipment usually includes fire extinguishers, life preservers, horns, proper lights, and sufficient ventilation. Be sure this equipment is still installed on the boat and is in top condition. Don't try to cut any corners on it.

• Be sure the boat is fitted with whatever anti-pollution devices (e.g., toilet holding tanks) are required locally, or wherever you intend to use your boat. These rules are in a state of flux.

• Check the installation and ventilation of the engine and fuel tank areas. Look for tank corrosion and leaks. You can get information on current ventilation requirements from your local Coast Guard office.

• Have the engine checked by a marine mechanic. When the salesman says the boat has "very little running time," does he mean the engine has given the previous owner trouble?

• Check the steering controls by rotating the helm from one limit to the other. Make sure the rudder or outboard motor moves without binding or requiring undue force. Then take a trial run. Does everything work? Does the boat perform as you expected? Is your "crew" satisfied?

• If you're in the market for a sailboat, inspect every inch of sails, spars, masts, and rigging. Check for abnormal wear, evidence of strain and compression cracks in the mast.

• And your personal inspection of these areas may well not be nearly enough. It may be more than worth your time and money to get the advice of a professional marine surveyor—particularly if you are spending more than $25,000 for the boat.

• In fact, if your purchase is into these high-dollar ranges, the advice of a professional surveyor whose interest is your interest would seem to me to be mere common sense.

THE COSTS OF UPKEEP

Boats, once purchased, cost far more to maintain than cars—even in relationship to their higher cost.

If your boat is of only moderate size, you'll need a trailer and winch to haul it to the water, launch it, and haul it out again.

Unless you live in southern climates, you'll have to take elaborate winterizing steps; and even if you leave your boat in the water year round, it will have to be hauled out periodically to scrape and repaint the bottom.

Marina costs are high—usually on a per-foot basis—and they have been rising rapidly for a decade.

Every accessory and maintenance item for a boat will be of higher cost than for its land-use equivalent, for the marine item must withstand the invasive properties of water, and often of salt.

It is not uncommon to pay one tenth to one fifth of your boat's purchase price, each year, for marina and upkeep costs on a powerboat. And while sailboat costs are lower (gasoline is needed only in small quantities for the auxiliary engine), sails and other rigging items are expensive—and less than permanent.

In short, boating is great fun . . . and costs great sums of money. Study and figure and save for a minimum of one year before you even attempt to decide what size and what type of boat you need and can afford.

Then, cut what you think you can afford by at least one third.

Only after this will you have a chance of enjoying your boat without also having nightmares about naming it *Bankruptcy*.

ENOUGH!

Of course, this chapter, lengthy as it is, merely covers the major forms of locomotion as the twentieth century enters its last two decades. Even now, there are parachutes and pogo sticks, roller skates and ice skates, snowshoes and cross-country snow skis. And more will be emerging before the twenty-first century comes alive.

But this is a "Money Book," not a "Money Encyclopedia." Enough!

8

THE ENORMOUS BURDEN OF
GOOD HEALTH CARE AND HOW
TO EASE THE LOAD ON YOU

What Your Health Bill Will Be

FASTEST-RISING OF ALL PERSONAL EXPENSES

The high cost of personal health in the United States had become a dominant political as well as economic factor in the lives of most American families by the late 1970s.

● Our spending on health care goods and services ranging from Band-Aids to open-heart surgery and cancer research had soared past $200 billion a year. For each of us, this represented an average health bill of close to $930 or nearly $3,720 for a family of four.

● The cost of health care services had increased since the late 1960s faster than any other type of personal expense—one and one half times the rate of rise in our overall cost of living. From the late 1960s to the late 1970s, hospital charges alone jumped four times as fast as the federal government's Consumer Price Index. Physician fees were three times higher.

● Hospital bills accounted for the lion's share of our total national health spending. By the late 1970s it cost an average of more than $200 to spend a day in a community hospital and at a growing number of hospitals the cost was from $250 to $300 per day. Some luxury private room costs went higher.

● Physicians' and dentists' bills, nursing home costs and drug costs—all were soaring.

HEALTH INSURANCE: CAN YOU AFFORD NOT TO HAVE IT?

A widow in Missouri is hospitalized with pneumonia. She needs round-the-clock nursing care for four days until she is out of danger. There are no complications and no surgery is required. She remains in the hospital for three weeks. Total cost: $4,100.

A New York executive has a moderately severe heart attack. The result is three weeks in the hospital, including one week in the intensive care unit. Total cost $7,000.

A fifteen-year-old Pennsylvania boy is severely injured in an automobile accident requiring more than four months' hospitalization, plus extensive skin grafts and cosmetic surgery. Total cost: $25,924.

A premature infant in Virginia receives intensive care over a nine-month period, including extensive oxygen, drug, cardiac and respiratory therapy as well as other services necessary to preserve its life. The bill tops $163,000, among the largest ever paid by Blue Cross of Virginia.

About 35 per cent of the claims for catastrophic medical expenses were exceeding $50,000 as the 1980s neared, the president of the Blue Cross plan in Virginia noted, adding that in addition to the impact of inflation, "medical science only recently has become equipped for the 'heroic measures' necessary to sustain life under extremely adverse conditions, and involving unusual and prolonged life-saving techniques."

How many, even in affluent America, can afford medical bills as astronomical as these?

Just because medical care today is so overpoweringly expensive and because we do not as yet have a system of national health insurance, you must regard some form of health insurance as absolutely imperative. What form you choose will depend on the organization from which you buy, the size and age of your family, where you live, where you work, a variety of other factors.

As a general rule, the simplest way to plan the best insurance package for your family is to decide which hazards are the greatest threat to you and to cover these with insurance. Then, to the extent you can afford it, begin to cover the less likely risks.

For instance, if you are a couple beyond childbearing age, it would be silly to buy a health insurance policy with maternity benefits. On the other hand, young people would be wise to include in their health insurance package a major medical policy to guard against the big medical bills that could result from automobile accidents, which constitute a major hazard for this age group.

FIVE KEY TYPES OF COVERAGE

Here is a rundown on five key types of coverage available today, whether you are covered under a group plan where you work or by an individual or single-family policy:

(1) *Hospital Expense Insurance.* This is the best-known and most widely held form. It provides benefits for varying periods of time, usually ranging from 21 days to 365 days or longer. It is offered by Blue Cross plans and by commercial insurance companies.

Benefits under these policies are used to pay for in-hospital services such as room and board, routine nursing care, and minor medical supplies.

In recent years, many Blue Cross plans have been offering coverage for such outpatient and out-of-hospital services as home care, preadmission testing, nursing home care, dental and vision care, prescription drugs, and a variety of diagnostic and preventive services.

(2) *Surgical Expense Insurance.* This coverage, offered by Blue Shield plans and commercial policies, is used to defray the cost of operations. Policies contain listings of surgical operations and the maximum benefit they will pay for each.

(3) *Physicians' Expense Insurance*. This coverage is almost always combined with hospital and surgical expense insurance, and the three form what is referred to as the "basic" coverage. Physicians' expense benefits usually cover a specific number of in-hospital visits to you by your doctor. Some policies provide benefits for home and office visits as well.

(4) *Major Medical Insurance*. This type picks up where basic coverage leaves off. It pays for most types of care in or out of hospital, with benefit maximums ranging to $250,000 and up. Blue Cross and Blue Shield plans offer this coverage too. These policies use a deductible, which is the amount you must pay before benefits start, and a co-insurance factor, which is a percentage of the total bill you also must pay.

(5) *Disability Insurance*. This type is used to replace earnings lost because of disability. Maximum benefits during disability can go up to $1,000, $2,000, or more a month, although the maximum is usually about 60 per cent of your gross earnings up to a stated maximum dollar allowance.

How to Shop for Health Insurance

HOW MUCH COVERAGE DO YOU NEED?

The most economical way to buy health insurance is to insure yourself and your family against the most serious and financially disastrous losses that can result from an illness or an accident. Your minor medical expenses should be met as part of your family's overall financial plan.

A general rule of thumb is that your basic benefit package should cover at least 75 per cent of your anticipated expenses from any illness or injury.

Other guidelines when you're shopping for health insurance are:

• If you are buying health insurance for the first time, look into the possibility of getting the coverage through a group—a union, an employer-employee plan, a fraternal organization. Group insurance costs 15 to 40 per cent *less* than the same coverage bought on an individual basis. Other advantages of group coverage: your coverage can't be canceled—unless and until you leave the group. You don't have to take a physical examination to qualify for coverage. And a pre-existing illness does not disqualify you, although there may be a waiting period to qualify for maternity benefits.

• Find out how many days in the hospital each policy you are considering buying will cover. This is one of the most frequent selling points used by insurers and prepayment plans—and one of the most *misleading*. All basic hospital policies, whether issued by Blue Cross plans or commercial insurers, express benefits in terms of days, with benefit periods of from 21 days to 365 days or more. But is it really necessary to buy 365 days of basic coverage? Government statistics show that the average length of stay in a hospital is just a little over seven days, and that only 3 per cent of all hospital confinements in the country last beyond 31 days.

• Also find out how much each policy pays per day and how the benefits are paid. Basic benefits are paid in two ways: Blue Cross makes payments directly to the hospital for services rendered to you; commercial insurers pay a specified dollar amount either to you *or* to the hospital. The Blue Cross arrangement is generally regarded as preferable to you as a policyholder because Blue Cross plans have direct contractual arrangements with hospitals which grant them (as bulk purchasers) discounts which are passed along to you. The service benefits offered by Blue Cross cover virtually all costs, whereas the specified dollar amount in the indemnity policies offered by the commercial insurers generally represent only a fraction of the costs incurred. There are, though, many exceptions in which both plans offer comparable benefits at comparable costs.

• If you already are covered by health insurance, be sure to keep this coverage updated. If your basic benefits are paid on an indemnity basis (i.e., the commercial insurers' approach), check *frequently* on the current medical and hospital costs in *your own area*. The rates for a hospital in, say, Mississippi, will be substantially less than for one in New York or California. If, in the late 1970s, you had a policy which paid $50 a day and you lived in an area where the average hospital cost was $150, you would pay the difference. Another point: in recent years hospital charges have been increasing sharply. Thus, if you had an indemnity plan that paid 80 per cent of the hospital charges in the year in which you bought it, chances are there has been steady "slippage" ever since. A mere two years later, your policy probably would cover only 50 per cent of the hospital charges.

THE MEDICAL CATASTROPHE: DO'S AND DON'TS

At today's medical prices, most of you would be plunged deeply into debt in the event of a really serious accident or illness. Every day throughout the country, newspapers carry horror stories telling of the enormous costs faced by families who have suffered this type of misfortune.

The insurance designed for this contingency is called the major medical plan, and if you are about thirty years old and if your family can afford the $175 or so per year it costs in premiums, it can certainly add to your peace of mind.

This type of insurance, like the others, is complex. In the thicket of terminology are such unfamiliar phrases as "inside limits," "co-insurance," "deductibles." Here are do's and don'ts which will make it easier to hack through this jungle.

Don't be dazzled by big benefit maximums such as $1 million and the like. Even with today's soaring medical costs, it's highly improbable that you'll ever have expenses at this level for a single illness or injury. Keep benefits such as these in perspective, just as you would if someone tried to sell you a policy covering undulant fever or being run down by a herd of buffalo at noon on Main Street. A more realistic ceiling for major medical benefits would be somewhere between $50,000 and $100,000 or even $250,000.

Do look into the possibility of getting this coverage through a group. As with your basic coverage, you can achieve big savings by insuring this way.

Do study the deductible and co-insurance features. For example, the usual co-insurance ratio is 75–25 or 80–20, with the 25 or 20 per cent being your share of the medical expenses. If you're willing to go along with the higher co-insurance percentage offered by one company over another, you may find your premiums proportionately lower.

Do study with care, too, what benefits you get from the way you set up your major medical coverage. You can do this in one of two ways: either as a supplement to your basic coverage or as a single-plan or "comprehensive" major medical plan.

As a general rule, the supplementary type of major medical insurance starts paying at the point where your basic hospital-surgical coverage stops. The "single-plan major medical" covers both basic and catastrophic expenses. Sometimes your deductible is absorbed by your basic coverage in one policy.

Other types of major medical insurance utilize what is known as a "corridor" deductible. That is the amount you must pay above your basic coverage before your major medical takes over. This is available on group health insurance only.

The deductible *applies separately to each family member* (in most cases, up to an annual maximum) for each illness covered by the policy.

Do choose the highest deductible your budget can take. Deductibles usually range from $100 to $1,000. If you feel you can afford to pay the first $1,000 toward medical bills out of your own pocket, the premiums will be lower than if you want to cover everything but the first $100.

And, by hiking your deductible, you can apply the savings you get through lower premiums to building up extra coverage in other areas that will give you an added dimension of protection.

MONEY-SAVING TIPS ON HEALTH INSURANCE

ELEVEN BASIC GUIDES

The following tips on health insurance could save you great aggravation *and* money:

(1) Hold on to any old disability policy you might have if your health is impaired. If you want to expand your disability insurance, keep your old policy and supplement it. Why not replace it? Simply because your present policy undoubtedly carries a lower premium, reflecting your younger age when you bought it. If your health is good, you may be able to get cheaper coverage, even though you are now older.

(2) Check whether a group or family policy has a conversion privilege, so that you can, if necessary, transfer your coverage to an individual basis—if, say, you leave an employee group for a new job, or you marry—without having restrictive waiting periods reimposed on you.

(3) At the same time, be sure you check whether any refund is owed to you on your previous policy.

(4) Investigate carefully how maternity benefits are paid, if you are a single woman and plan to remain so. Important changes are being made in response to changing attitudes about morals and sex discrimination. Some insurers are altering their hospital and medical coverages to keep up with the new attitudes: more

plans, for instance, are providing payments for unmarried women, including maternity benefits for babies born out of wedlock.

(5) Don't waste your money carrying duplicate coverage. It's possible you'll be able to collect on both policies—and maybe even make a profit on an illness—but many insurers are coordinating their payments to prevent this. Usually one policy, the first or primary one, is given preference by the company and the second policy will pay only that part of the medical bill not covered by the first. You'll find it increasingly difficult to beat the computers on this.

(6) Health insurance coverage for mental illness is becoming more readily available. Much of the time this condition is covered by major medical policies on a full-payment basis while the patient is hospitalized and with limited payments outside the hospital. But if you have a disability policy you may be able to collect under it. You're entitled to full payment of these expenses under many policies if you are totally disabled as the result of a mental condition—say, a nervous breakdown. If your disability is only partial, your payments will normally cover up to half of the out-of-hospital costs. Another approach to this type of benefit is a sort of "share-the-cost" plan for psychiatric treatment, either through a stated number of visits you make to the psychiatrist or psychologist or through a stated benefit ceiling for psychiatric treatments.

Many Blue Cross policyholders also have mental illness coverage. As the 1980s approached, the most widely held Blue Cross Plan contracts covering nervous and mental conditions provided up to 30 days in a general hospital—but some plans provided 120 days coverage and, at least one, coverage of 365 days. Outpatient services for nervous and mental conditions—treatment without being admitted to the hospital as a bed patient—usually were covered only under Blue Cross plan major medical contracts.

(7) Look into a little-known benefit now available in some disability insurance policies called "income insurance for the breadwinner's wife." This covers the cost of household help if she becomes ill or disabled.

(8) Although this may not be your problem, alcoholism is sufficiently widespread for you to become aware that many insurance policies and Blue Cross contracts cover alcoholics and will provide personal medical and social aid, often sending the alcoholic to a specialized rehabilitation center. And even those insurers which do not pay for such specialized treatment almost always cover treatment for alcoholism in their hospital and disability policies.

(9) Note at what age your policy covers your children. Children should be covered from birth and *not,* as some policies state, from the age of two weeks. It's the first two weeks in the life of your baby that are very often his or her most expensive medically. Some states have stepped in and now require coverage of newborns from the moment of birth.

(10) If you pay your own premiums directly, try to arrange to pay on an annual or quarterly rather than monthly basis. You'll save money by so doing.

(11) And one final reminder. Although it's important to know just what is covered under your health insurance policy, it's even more important to know what is *excluded* from coverage. Frequently excluded services include psychiatric care, extensive periodontal surgery, foot surgery by podiatrists, cosmetic surgery

care for pre-existing conditions. Knowing what's excluded won't help you pay for the condition if it arises, but at least you won't be in line for an unexpected shock at the worst possible time—when you're flat on your back.

HEALTH INSURANCE BAFFLEGAB GUIDE

ACCIDENTAL DEATH AND DISMEMBERMENT BENEFIT Payment to a beneficiary, usually through a disability income policy, when an insured person is killed or loses his sight or a limb in an accident.

BENEFICIARY Person who is designated in an insurance policy to receive a specified cash payment if the policyholder is killed by accident.

CLAIM Demand or application by a person covered by health or other insurance for financial benefits provided in his or her policy.

CO-INSURANCE Special condition, usually found in major medical insurance, in which you and your insurance company share costs. Typically, the insurer pays 50 to 80 per cent of hospital and medical expenses, and you pay the rest.

DEDUCTIBLE Share of the hospital and medical expenses which you, the insured person, must pay before your insurance policy starts paying.

DISABILITY ("INSURED SALARY CONTINUANCE") INSURANCE Coverage (often group) providing regular weekly or monthly cash benefits to help replace earnings you have lost if you become disabled from just about any cause. In some cases, payment is made for only a limited number of years, and in others, for life or until the disability ends.

ELIMINATION PERIOD Waiting period before benefits (e.g., disability benefits) begin.

FAMILY EXPENSE POLICY Type of health insurance policy covering you, your wife or husband, and your children.

HOSPITAL EXPENSE INSURANCE Insurance providing reimbursement of hospital care costs—usually including room and board charges, routine nursing care, anesthesia, surgical facilities, special diets, the like—for illness or injury.

INDIVIDUAL ("PERSONAL") INSURANCE Protection of individual policyholders and their families, as distinct from lower-cost group insurance which may be offered by employers, labor unions, or professional associations.

MAJOR MEDICAL EXPENSE INSURANCE Protection against the huge expenses implied by a catastrophic or very lengthy injury or illness. This type of insurance usually pays 75 to 80 per cent of "physicians" and hospital bills, after a deductible amount paid by the insured, up to a maximum which may range from $10,000 to $100,000, $250,000, or even $1 million. "Supplementary" major medical insurance builds coverage on top of basic protection through an ordinary hospital and medical expense policy. A "comprehensive" policy provides both basic and major medical insurance coverage and usually has a low deductible amount.

MEDICAL EXPENSE INSURANCE Payment, usually partial, of doctors' fees for non-surgical care in the hospital, but sometimes also at home or at the office. Medical expense benefits are sometimes included in hospital expense policies.

SUBSTANDARD HEALTH INSURANCE Policies issued to those who cannot meet normal health requirement of standard health insurance policies, usually involving a higher premium.

SURGICAL EXPENSE INSURANCE Benefits to help pay surgeons' fees and other costs of surgical procedures.

THE HEALTH MAINTENANCE ORGANIZATION—AN APPEALING ALTERNATIVE

PREVIEW OF THE FUTURE

The Blue Cross Association defines a Health Maintenance Organization as "an organized health care delivery system which promotes early detection and continuity of care through an arrangement holding a single organization responsible for assuring delivery of an agreed set of institutional and physician services to an enrolled population for a stipulated period of time in exchange for a fixed and periodic payment."

Mounting millions of Americans are now getting the opportunity to join these Health Maintenance Organizations—which, to put it in plain English, are organizations of doctors, hospitals, and others offering enrolling members a wide range of health services in exchange for a flat fee paid in advance, usually monthly or quarterly.

HMOS—ON THE MOVE

If you work for a company with fifteen or more employees—or for a state or local government subdivision with twenty-five or more employees—and if you receive health benefits, your employer is required to offer you the alternative of joining an approved Health Maintenance Organization, assuming there is a qualified HMO in your area.

You would thereby join more than 7,300,000 other Americans across the nation who as the 1980s approached already were members of these medical care groups in which you prepay your medical bills—and in return, get a type of one-stop, one-bill health care.

One major advantage of the HMO type of health care delivery system is that it brings together into a single organization the physician, hospital, laboratory, and clinic so that patients can get the right care at the right time.

More important, the economics of the HMO idea is tilted toward maintaining health because the organization will get only the fixed payment regardless of the number of hospital admissions, surgical procedures, or other medical treatments provided.

Thus, there is the motivation to keep you well, to give you necessary checkups and health education, to avoid unnecessary operations, hospital stays, and unnecessary tests. A number of studies have shown that members of HMOs use 30 to 50 per cent fewer hospital days and operate at a cost 10 to 30 per cent under the traditional fee-for-service health care providers.

There may not yet be an HMO in your area, of course, although at the end of 1978, there were more than two hundred programs (not all, however, federally approved), operating in thirty-six states. But your chance to join an HMO unquestionably will increase as more and more HMOs gain federal qualification.

To suggest the trend, as the decade ended, hundreds of groups were planning or beginning to form HMOs. The nation's Blue Cross plans—which most of us associate only with payment of hospital bills—have become more and more active in creating HMOs and were involved in close to seventy operational HMO programs. These are being offered to subscribers by Blue Cross plans as alternatives to the traditional type of health care coverage.

Just what do HMOs offer that might warrant your considering them as alternatives to more familiar types of health care? Typical is the following package:

• The full cost of as many as 365 days of hospitalization, including room and board, drugs, laboratory tests, ambulance, anesthesia, radiotherapy, physical therapy, and all physicians' and surgeons' services.

• Up to 504 hours of private duty nursing, with no charge for general nursing care.

• Outside of the hospital, such key services as unlimited doctor visits as well as home visits, specialist care including consultations, physical checkups, eye examinations, laboratory and X-ray tests, maternity and well-baby care, immunizations, physical therapy, plaster casts and dressings, emergency care, hemodialysis, etc. —just about every conceivable type of health care you might need or want.

The heart of the Health Maintenance Organization is revealed in its name— preventive care. The emphasis is on keeping you well so that the need for hospitalization is held to a minimum and limited to instances where it is absolutely essential.

And indications are that HMOs succeed in doing this.

In a northeastern city, for instance, the average length of stay in the hospital was 4.8 days for one Blue Cross HMO plan and 5.6 days for a second HMO plan. In comparison, the average hospital stay for the regular Blue Cross plan subscriber was 6.8 days.

But what about costs? HMO coverage is more expensive than traditional care merely because of the comprehensiveness of the care provided. Premiums vary according to the number of benefits provided and the length of hospitalization covered as well as the HMO's location.

AN HMO FOR YOUR COMMUNITY?

The government's administration of the Health Maintenance Act of 1973 was lackluster for years, but as the decade ended, the White House began actively pushing the development of HMOs because of their cost-saving potential. On the private front, many Blue Cross plans and private insurance companies are promoting HMOs or tying in their coverage with existing organizations.

What might you expect?

Services. Virtually all you might need—with such exceptions as dental care, long-term psychiatric care, rare and expensive types of care for the few at the expense of the many. Or you might be asked to pay nominal fees for each visit to the doctor or for outpatient prescription drugs. Also excluded are medical services covered or provided by others—such as workers' compensation, employment physicals, and accident insurance.

Fees. If you're a family of four, a monthly payment ranging between $65 and

$125 at the close of the 1970s. If you're an individual, a monthly cost ranging between $26 and $50.

KEY QUESTIONS TO CONSIDER

Let's say a group in your community is considering setting up an HMO. What basics should the plan include? Here are key questions you—and everybody else involved in launching an HMO—should ask:

• Is there strong emphasis on such aspects as primary preventive care and health education?

• Are you, a consumer, involved along with health practitioners in determining the planning and delivery of services?

• Is the HMO cooperating with state and local planning agencies to avoid duplicate facilities and services and, thus, unnecessary costs?

• What mechanisms are there to permit continual assessment of the system as a whole, to tell how well it is working?

• What review-evaluation techniques are there to maintain a high quality of service—e.g., peer review by doctors and others? The new problem-oriented patient record system? One of the key requirements under the law is an "ongoing quality assurance program."

• Are there provisions for hospital and doctor emergency services both inside and outside the area? Is there referral to specialists and superspecialists? Who pays how much for the costs of these services?

• Are there incentives to cut health care costs to patients?

SHOULD YOU JOIN AN HMO?

Let's say that a local medical group, hospital, university, or other organization is setting up an HMO. Or the Blue Cross plan to which you subscribe is offering an HMO-type plan as an alternative to your regular coverage. Or your employer offers you the option of switching from your regular health insurance coverage to an HMO.

Costs and coverages vary all over the place—but costs easily can run $800 to $1,300 or more a year for a family. Should *you* join an HMO under these circumstances? How can you tell whether or not it is a bargain for you? Here's your guide:

• Read with utmost care all the literature on the plan, what's covered and what's excluded, how long the coverage lasts.

• Check the monthly premiums and the extra costs you'll be required to pay for non-included items, deductibles, etc.

• Compare these totals with the amounts you've been paying in health insurance premiums, doctor bills, out-of-pocket cash, costs of services not covered or only partially covered in your present insurance, including that provided by your employer.

• Find out the arrangements for choosing and keeping a physician.

• Investigate the provisions for prescription drugs outside the hospital. Does the plan cover these or offer a way you can save when you buy? (Some HMOs have their own pharmacies.) And what about prosthetics and medical appliances?

• Check other subscribers' opinions. If they are already in a plan, are they satisfied with the medical attention?

• Find out what hours full HMO services are available and what the procedure is for care in evenings and over weekends.

• Ask whether the outpatient services and facilities you use most—physicians' offices, lab facilities, pharmacy—are under a single roof. Is this roof located conveniently for your family?

• Make sure preventive care services are stressed—early disease detection via diagnostic screening, periodic physical checkups, appropriate immunization.

• Investigate what hospital accommodations are provided—private, semi-private? Are such extras as special-duty nursing and private room included if your physician thinks they are essential?

• Are there age limits in the plan—such as when a son or daughter reaches age nineteen? Or marries?

• What medical facilities are included in the hospital to which you would go—such as coronary care, radiation therapy? What exclusions, if any, are there for health handicaps?

CHECK LIST FOR HMO SERVICES

Here is a check list of "basic" services, most of which an HMO is required to offer under the 1973 HMO Act. Use it to judge the comprehensiveness of any HMO, but also weigh it against your own list of health priorities:

physicians' services (including consultant and referral services by a physician);

inpatient and outpatient hospital services;

medically necessary emergency health services;

short-term (not to exceed twenty visits), outpatient evaluative and crisis intervention mental health services;

medical treatment and referral services (including referral services to appropriate ancillary services) for the abuse of or addiction to alcohol and drugs;

diagnostic laboratory and diagnostic and therapeutic radiology services; home health services; and preventive health services (including voluntary family planning services, infertility services, immunizations, well child care from birth, periodic health exams for adults, children's eye and ear examinations).

HEALTH MAINTENANCE BAFFLEGAB GUIDE

Do you know the difference between a Health Maintenance Organization, a Health Co-op and a Health Care Provider? What "capitation" payments are as opposed to "fees for service"? The meaning of a "prepayment plan" for health services? This is the jargon of this unfolding system of health care—soon to become a language you must be able to understand.

CAPITATION FEES Payments to anyone providing health care of a certain amount of money per month, for each patient for whom the practitioner provides a certain specified range of services.

CATASTROPHIC COVERAGE Health insurance with a high deductible—payable by you—but also a high ceiling ($50,000 to $250,000) so catastrophically costly care would be paid by the plan.

COMPREHENSIVE HEALTH CARE Generally includes, both in and out of hospital, the whole works. Specifically:

preventive care—e.g., periodic physical checkups, immunizations, various diagnostic tests at appropriate intervals; counseling, e.g., diet, exercise, etc.;

primary care—or medical care by a family doctor or general physician, aimed at maintaining or restoring good health, up to the limits of the physicians' capabilities;

specialty care—by board-certified specialists for complicated illnesses;

rehabilitation for patients who have suffered from disabling accidents, strokes, mental breakdowns (plans usually exclude illnesses and injuries which require permanent medical maintenance);

extended care—in nursing homes and other facilities—for non-permanent chronic conditions needing medical attention.

DUAL CHOICE Setup in company-offered plans in which you are allowed to choose between two alternative plans (typically, fee for service or a prepaid group practice plan).

FEE FOR SERVICE A sum of money paid by the patient for each individual service performed by a practitioner.

GROUP PRACTICE Organized delivery of health care, by a group of two or more physicians with a prearranged system for sharing income. Some groups are highly specialized (representing a single specialty); others cover a variety of specialties. Most groups charge a fee for each service rendered.

HEALTH CARE PROVIDER A hospital, clinic, or other institution, such as an HMO or prepaid group practice plan, providing health care services.

HEALTH CO-OPERATIVE A health plan involving ownership and board participation in the plan by the members of the plan.

HEALTH MAINTENANCE ORGANIZATIONS Typically prepaid group practice with dual goals of comprehensive continuous health care and more health care per dollar and with stress on early disease detection and prevention. More than 7.3 million Americans now enrolled getting comprehensive high-quality and preventive health care.

MEDICAL INDIGENT Person not legally poor but likely to become poor instantly if hit by expensive illness.

MULTIPHASIC SCREENING Battery of tests and exams to determine person's state of health and detect signs of illness. Tests usually performed by specialists in lab work, with interpretation by doctors.

PEER REVIEW Ideally, formal review of medical decisions or procedures by an outside doctor or group of doctors with equivalent training and experience *and* in possession of essential data in each case. Typically, peer review covers quality and appropriateness of care, and charges for medical service.

PREPAYMENT Health plan concept pioneered by unions—via Blue Cross—in which the subscriber pays a given sum in advance in the event that insured health benefits are needed. Payment is made in advance and limits the individual's liability as against paying for each separate service after it has been performed with unlimited liability.

Millions of Americans belong to some type of prepaid group practice plan. The cost of health care in these organizations has been less because doctors and hospitals maximize the use of facilities, personnel, etc. There are built-in incentives for preventive health care (immunizations, physical checkups) and against overuse of costly hospital facilities. Many problems are handled on an outpatient basis rather than by admission to a hospital where care is extremely expensive. The frequency of elective (non-obligatory) surgery tends to be far less in prepaid group plans since surgeons do not have any financial incentive to perform operations.

HIGHER QUALITY DENTAL CARE AT LOWER-LEVEL COSTS

WHAT TO LOOK FOR IN A DENTIST

Every year, tens of millions of U.S. families move to new areas and while they may "settle in" quickly, most avoid selecting a dentist until an emergency hits. When that happens and the person stricken is in acute pain, the choice usually is made with haste and often results in unsatisfactory or incomplete treatment.

With more than 120,000 dentists in the nation in the late 1970s, of whom about 90 per cent were in private practice, you can establish a relationship with a dentist who will be concerned about your overall as well as your oral health. You can find a dentist who will not only care for your teeth and gums but also look for conditions in your mouth that may require special treatment and suggest an appropriate dental or medical specialist for you.

But since dental care is such a highly personalized consumer service, it will take time to find that practitioner—and you may have to meet several dentists before you find one with whom you can have a long-lasting, beneficial relationship. How do you begin?

• Inquire at a university's dental school about practitioners in your community.

• Ask at a nearby hospital with an accredited dental service or consult with your family physician or local pharmacist.

• Check the latest American Dental Association Directory, containing a complete list of association members, at the nearest public library, or contact the local dental society for the names of dentists listed in its referral service.

• Ask friends and co-workers which dentists they use and what their experiences with these practitioners have been. But don't blindly accept the responses of others as your guide. Instead, evaluate the names critically, learn about their work and performance records.

• Avoid dentists who are fast on the "pull."

Look for a dentist who believes in prevention and make sure the dentist you have puts a high priority on prevention of dental disease.

• If an extraction is proposed, consider getting a second opinion from another dentist. A qualified, confident dentist will be not only in favor of this consultation but also may advise it.

• Learn from your first visit whether the dentist will be thorough. Note whether he takes your dental and medical history, including name and phone number of your physician; whether he inquires about any allergies you may have; whether you are under medical care for such problems as diabetes or hemophilia; whether he takes a full mouth series of X-rays before starting any treatments; whether he tries to teach you how to avoid and prevent oral disorders.

• Don't be embarrassed to request information about his fees and payment plans and get an advance written estimate for non-routine work. Competent dentists are willing to discuss their fees, give detailed explanations, itemize their bills, and describe their services.

• Ask for a bill itemizing services, rather than one marked "for services rendered." Computerized billing is error-prone, so if you suspect an incorrect charge, question your dentist.

• If you hold some form of dental insurance, check in advance which services will be covered, which won't be, what percentage of your fee will be paid by the policy. If insurance is involved, take the essential documents with you.

• Ask the dentist at this introductory session about arrangements for: emergencies when you have no appointment but need immediate care; emergencies that occur outside of office hours; backups by another dentist or emergency referral service.

• Look for other signs of good dental practice. Does the dentist put a lead apron on you for your protection while taking X-rays? Does the dentist take pride in the appearance of the office and waiting room? Use modern equipment and treatment techniques? Give advice on care to follow between visits? Are you told how you will feel after a treatment session so you can plan your appointments (no romantic date on the day of oral surgery?). When and what you may eat?

• Don't be alarmed if your dentist refers you to a specialist for some phase of treatment—orthodontic care, root canal therapy, periodontal treatment, children's very special problems.

• Choose a conveniently situated dentist, to eliminate lengthy trips to and from the office, if you can. Select a practitioner who does not require unreasonable waiting time for an appointment and who sends reminder notices when it is time for your checkup. And if your appointment time is not honored on a regular basis, go to another dentist who is better organized—taking your dental records with the assent of the one you are leaving.

• Be sure your dentist's personality makes you feel comfortable and secure. You should be able to communicate with ease.

• Don't cut corners, for in terms of oral health, initially high expenditures can easily turn out cheaper in the long run. A simple extraction, for instance, can cause more problems and eventual dental work than having the tooth saved through marginally more expensive root canal therapy. Beware of so-called bargains in dental care. Avoid cut-rate opportunities and assembly-line dental operations.

• If you have reason to believe a dentist has performed inadequately or irresponsibly, talk and try to work out a mutually agreeable solution. If this measure fails, contact your local dental society, insurance carrier, or local consumer agency before seeking legal help. Most cases are mutually and satisfactorily resolved through dental society "peer review committees."

WHAT HAS HAPPENED TO DENTAL COSTS

In a letter which could have been hailed as a top accolade in the inflationary atmosphere of the late 1970s, President Carter wrote the president of the American Dental Association:

"While seeking deceleration in the medical care sector, we note favorably the more moderate behavior of dentists' fees which have increased at significantly lower rates than physicians' fees and most other medical care prices . . . We recognize that this more moderate trend in dentists' fees is in part related to substantial increases in dentist productivity and the relatively greater responsiveness of dental fees to competition."

A few statistics confirm the White House's assessment.

• In the ten-year span between the late 1960s and 1970s, the overall rate for consumer services was up 94 per cent, dental fees were up 85 per cent, physicians' fees zoomed more than 100 per cent, and semi-private hospital room rates skyrocketed 200 per cent.

• As the 1980s neared, you, an average American, paid 0.6 per cent of your personal income for dental services, virtually the same percentage as ten years and twenty years previously.

• As a percentage of total health care costs, dental expenses have actually been declining—from 10.9 per cent in 1950 to 7.5 per cent in 1960 to 6.5 per cent in 1970 to 6.3 per cent as the 1980s approached.

And all this has occurred while the cost of maintaining a dental practice has soared, fringe benefits for employees have risen rapidly, outlays for supplies and services have climbed substantially—and, in fact, average expenses for operating a dental office have ballooned 100 per cent since 1967.

How come? How has the profession achieved this record of holding the line while all other health costs have exploded?

(1) Greater productivity. Dentists now treat 43 per cent more patients and handle 18 per cent more patient visits than a decade ago—and the key reason is due to the auxiliary personnel they employ. A dentist with a full-time assistant raises his productivity by around one third, while a dentist with a hygienist and a full-time assistant can boost his productivity by 100 per cent. On top of this is the development of modern instruments which speed up the dentist's work as well as make the patient's visits more comfortable.

(2) Preventive dentistry, which has cut back on the patient's need for extensive reparation and restorative treatments. Frequent exams equal fewer major dental problems, since disorders are diagnosed early when they can be corrected more easily.

(3) Still another factor in moderating dental care costs has been the fact that 95 per cent of all these costs are paid privately, compared with 45 per cent government funding of other aspects of health care. Dentists want any national health plan to include dental care, particularly for children. But they want to focus the use of limited public funds (coming from taxes) only to those unable to afford dental services and stress that these dental services should be provided through a private system of delivery while benefits should be administered in the private sector.

But whatever lies in the future, the recent past does underline the bright fact that dental care costs have indeed risen less in proportion to other health costs than you probably have believed.

PREPAID DENTAL INSURANCE

As the 1970s ended, more than 48 million workers, their spouses and their families had dental insurance—a method of prepaid dental care providing eligible employees and their dependents with a broad range of benefits and one of the fastest growing fringe benefits in the United States. The coverage has spread among 170 insurance and service plans, through more than 14,000 employee and union groups throughout the country, and was heading toward the 60 million mark. The momentum was unmistakable.

The need for this insurance as a spur to preventive care has long been obvious. Only half the population visit a dentist as often as once a year, and half of this group go only for emergency treatment. Tooth decay affects 95 per cent of those with teeth and some 56 million teeth are extracted each year; 51 per cent of all adults have no teeth left at all by the age of sixty-five.

There is a key distinction between medical and dental insurance. Medical insurance is geared to treatment after illness strikes, while dental insurance promotes regular treatment as a way to minimize serious, costly problems later. Furthermore, if you are ill or involved in an accident, you usually have no choice but to accept medical treatment. Most dental care can be postponed for a long time before severe discomfort occurs. This tends to create heavy expenses in the initial years of a dental insurance plan, when new participants quickly take care of neglected restorative and maintenance problems.

Dental insurance plans are extremely varied. While most plans provide for such basic and routine service as emergency treatments, exams, X-rays, cleaning and fluoride applications, such coverage as restorative work, oral surgery, root canal treatments, orthodontics adds to premium expenses. Dental costs in a hospital are rarely included, nor are cosmetic treatments.

Methods of reimbursement in prepayment plans also vary. Most common is the "usual, customary and reasonable" basis (UCR), under which individual dentists charge their usual fee for a particular service, and the insurer reviews and verifies the charge. Some UCRs have a deductible amount that must be paid by the participant before benefits start.

Others have a co-insurance or co-payment provision, under which a portion of the fee is paid by the beneficiary, the balance by the plan. Under a few plans, the patient pays a decreasing share of his dental bill if he visits the dentist regularly.

Another reimbursement format is a table of allowances listing actual dollar limits for each covered service the plan will pay. A third means gives beneficiaries direct payments from the company with the dental bill itself determining reimbursement.

Whatever the format, many plans call for precertification or predetermination before a dentist proceeds with work exceeding a specified amount (usually $100).

The cost of the insurance is as variable as the different programs available and, of course, rests on the type of services, methods of reimbursement, and the company offering the plan. But a monthly charge for individuals in group plans ranging from $9.00 to $20 was typical at the decade's end whether payment was made by employer, employee, or both.

In view of all the achievements in increased care and reduced costs, prepaid dental insurance is still in its infancy. It well may be that by the end of the 1980s, dental insurance will cover almost everyone and we'll be on the way to good oral health for all.

HOW TO BE A WISE DENTAL CONSUMER

If you are a typical American, you probably will need the services of a dentist more frequently than those of a physician during your lifetime. For that reason alone, there is no wise substitute for regular checkups and a thorough program of preventive home care.

So protect your teeth by dutiful regular checkups, proper brushing and flossing, a healthy diet and oral hygiene.

Your teeth were meant to last a lifetime.

YOUR MEDICARE BENEFITS

WHO IS ELIGIBLE

Medicare has two parts: Part A, the Hospital Insurance; and Part B, the Supplementary Medical Insurance.

For Those 65 and Over. Just about everyone reaching sixty-five who is eligible for Social Security benefits as a worker or as the dependent or survivor of a worker is automatically eligible for Part A, the Hospital Insurance part of Medicare—and whether or not he or she continues to work. In effect, at sixty-five, you have a paid-up hospital insurance policy financed out of a portion of the Social Security deductions that have been made from your paychecks (or the paychecks of the family breadwinner) over the years.

For the rare person who reaches sixty-five but is not eligible for Social Security benefits, a special provision makes it possible to get Medicare hospital insurance coverage, but this person must pay the full cost of his or her protection.

Part A of Medicare helps pay for medically necessary hospital care and for required post-hospital care in a skilled nursing facility. In addition, it will pay for up to one hundred home health care visits following hospitalization.

Part B of Medicare, the Supplementary Medical Insurance which covers doctor bills and a wide variety of other medical expenses, is different from Part A. First, it is voluntary; you don't have to take it. Also, it is financed partly out of the premiums you start paying when you become covered and partly out of general federal revenues. Your monthly premium rate rises as medical care costs go up. But since 1972, the increase has been limited by law to the percentage by which Social Security benefits have been increased since the last time the Part B premium was raised.

If you are on the Social Security benefit rolls, the Part B premium will be deducted from your monthly benefit check. If you are not collecting Social Security benefits because you or the breadwinner are still working, or if you are not eligible for Social Security benefits, you will be billed quarterly for your premiums.

For Those Under Sixty-five. Medicare benefits are also available to certain people under sixty-five:

(1) Persons who have been collecting Social Security disability benefits for at least two years; and

(2) Men, women, and children who have chronic kidney disease and need dialysis treatments or kidney transplants. Some 3.5 to 4 million of our nation's disabled under sixty-five are now eligible for the same Medicare benefits as those sixty-five and over.

WHEN YOU GO TO THE HOSPITAL UNDER MEDICARE

There is a deductible amount for which you are responsible the first time you are admitted to the hospital during a benefit period.* This deductible amount—which is equivalent to the average cost of one day's hospitalization under Medicare—is adjusted periodically to keep it up-to-date with rising costs.

Any Social Security office can give you information as to the current amount of the deductible. It equaled $160 in January 1979. Except for the deductible, Medicare covers virtually all your hospital expenses for the first sixty days of hospitalization in a benefit period. (Only about 3 per cent of people sixty-five and over stay in a hospital for more than sixty days.)

If you use up your sixty days of hospitalization, you become responsible for paying a co-payment for the sixty-first to the ninetieth day of your stay. The co-payment is equal to one quarter the amount of the hospital deductible at any given time.

If you should ever need to use more than ninety days of hospitalization in a

* A "benefit period" begins the first time you are admitted to a hospital as a bed patient under Medicare. It ends and a new benefit period begins after you have been out of a hospital, skilled nursing facility, or rehabilitation institution for sixty consecutive days.

benefit period, you may draw on an additional reserve of sixty hospital days and pay a co-payment that is equal to one half the amount of the deductible for each day used. You get only sixty of these reserve days in your lifetime.

Note: Your doctor bills for services provided to you in the hospital are covered under Part B, the Supplementary Medical Insurance part of Medicare.

WHAT IS NOT COVERED BY YOUR MEDICARE HOSPITAL INSURANCE

Medicare will not pay for hospitalization that is not medically necessary, even if your doctor recommended your admission. Also, Medicare payments will end if your stay is longer than need be. In addition Medicare does not cover the following:

- Private duty nurses.
- The first three pints of blood.
- Extra charges for a private room unless needed for medical reasons.
- Charges for TV rental, radio, or telephone.

Medicare can generally help pay your bills only if the hospital is what is called a "participating hospital," which most U.S. hospitals are. But in an emergency, care in a non-participating hospital can be covered if it was the closest hospital equipped to handle the emergency.

Care in a foreign hospital is not covered except for care in a qualified Mexican or Canadian hospital and then only in three situations:

(1) You are in the United States when an emergency occurs and the Canadian or Mexican hospital is closer to your home than the nearest U.S. hospital that could provide the care you need;

(2) You live in the United States, but a Canadian or Mexican hospital is closer to your home than the nearest U.S. hospital that could provide the care you need;

(3) You are en route to Alaska (but not vacationing in Canada) and an emergency requires your admission to a Canadian hospital.

CARE AFTER HOSPITALIZATION

In a Skilled Nursing Facility. If you no longer need to be in the hospital, but still require skilled nursing care or skilled rehabilitation services on a daily basis (and for the same condition), your hospital insurance can help pay for up to a hundred days of inpatient care in a Skilled Nursing Facility in each benefit period. To be eligible, you must have spent at least three days in a hospital and be transferred to the skilled nursing facility within fourteen days of your discharge from the hospital.

Medicare will pay for the first twenty days in full. From the twenty-first to the hundredth day, you are responsible for a co-payment that is equal to one eighth of whatever the hospital deductible is at the time. It is unlikely that you would require the covered level of care for a stretch of a hundred days. But if you should leave the Skilled Nursing Facility and have to return later, you will not have to spend another three days in the hospital before going back. You may use any days you have left—so long as you need the skilled nursing or rehabilitation services on a daily basis for the same condition as before.

The Skilled Nursing Facility will bill Medicare. You don't need to send in any forms.

Health Visits at Home. If, following your confinement in a hospital for at least three days, or in a Skilled Nursing Facility after hospitalization, you need further skilled nursing care or therapy on a part-time basis, Medicare can pay for up to a hundred visits during the year following your discharge from the hospital or Skilled Nursing Facility.

To qualify, your doctor must set up a home health plan for you within fourteen days of your discharge from the hospital or Skilled Nursing Facility and you must be housebound.

Note: Under Part B of Medicare, you also are eligible for one hundred home health care visits. But you get the Part B home health care visits (provided, of course, that you are signed up for Part B) whether or not you have first been hospitalized. They can be used if you don't go to the hospital at all, or after your hundred Part A home health care visits have been used up.

For both types of home health visits, the home health agency will send in the bills. You don't need to do any paperwork.

Be warned, however, you may be charged for any non-covered services performed in the home—for example, general household services, preparing meals, shopping, or assisting in bathing, dressing, or other personal needs.

PART B—YOUR DOCTOR BILL INSURANCE

The main services covered under Part B—the Supplementary Medical Insurance part of Medicare—are doctors' services, in the home, the doctor's office, or the hospital, clinic, skilled nursing facility, or nursing home. But Part B also covers speech pathology services, outpatient physical therapy, hospital outpatient services, the rental or purchase of wheelchairs, hospital beds, and other medical supplies, independent laboratory services, and, with limitations, ambulance transportation and the services of chiropractors and podiatrists.

There is a deductible under Part B, too. As of the late 1970s, you are responsible for the first $60 in covered expenses in each calendar year. (The $60 can be made up of any combination of services covered under Part B.) After you have met the $60 deductible, Medicare will pay 80 per cent of the reasonable charges for covered services over and above that $60.

The Medicare carrier in each area of the country determines what are the "reasonable charges" for covered services and supplies based upon an annual review of the actual charges made by practitioners in the area during the previous year.

HOW DOCTOR BILLS ARE PAID

There are two methods of getting Medicare payment of your Part B bills and generally it is up to the doctor to decide which method will be used. If at all possible, persuade the doctor to use the so-called "assignment method."

The "Assignment Method." If the doctor agrees to the "assignment" method, he sends the bill to the Medicare carrier, saves you, the patient, the paperwork, and commits himself ahead of time to accepting the "reasonable charge" as total charge for his services. The Medicare carrier will send the doctor a check for 80 per cent of the reasonable charge, minus any part of the $60 annual deductible that the Medicare beneficiary has not yet met.

All that the doctor can bill the patient for is the remaining 20 per cent (plus any part of the $60 deductible still owing). In effect, the doctor agrees to reduce his charge if it turns out to be higher than the amount the Medicare carrier determines to be the "reasonable charge."

"Direct Payment." Under the alternative method of "direct payment," the doctor bills the Medicare patient and the patient sends in the Request for Payment to the Medicare carrier. Under this method, there is no limit on the doctor's total charge. The Medicare carrier will send the patient a check for 80 per cent of the "reasonable charge," but if the bill is for a greater amount, the doctor can collect from the patient. And that can be not only for the remaining 20 per cent, but also for the full amount by which his bill exceeds the reasonable charge.

At one time, more than two thirds of all Medicare doctor bills were being sent in under the assignment method—but after Medicare administrators put a ceiling on reasonable charges to try to restrain escalating program costs, the rate of assignment fell to less than half of all bills.

Increasing numbers of our elderly are finding they owe the doctor more than they expected, increasing numbers are discovering they must fill out claims forms —and errors are soaring. Many do not even know about the assignment method of payment. Some doctors don't tell patients about it; others may have a sign in the waiting room: "I do not accept assignment."

You may not want to change your physician, but at least ask him if he will take an assignment. Your physician may if he understands you are in poor financial circumstances, or if you are infirm or have a problem with your sight.

If, though, you must send in your claims to Medicare, here are tips to help you avoid delay in getting your check for reimbursement.

Tips to Speed Your Payments. • Make sure your physician gives you a fully itemized bill, or if not, that he fills out all items in the bottom part of the claims form.

• Check whether your itemized bill includes the diagnosis of the illness or injury for which you were treated; a listing of the charges for each service provided by the doctor; such details as the address of the doctor's office, doctor's name, address of the laboratory, hospital, or clinic where you received tests or treatment.

• If you received ambulance services or medical supplies, be careful to give the name and address of the ambulance service or the supply company.

• Fill out all the spaces on the form where you are asked for your name, address, the insurance number, sex. An astounding percentage overlook these details.

• If you run into a special problem filling out the form or getting an itemized bill from your doctor, ask for help at your Social Security office. See your phone book for address and phone.

Bills for Other Part B Services. When services or supplies covered under Part B of Medicare are furnished by a hospital, a Skilled Nursing Facility or home health agency, the organization usually will make the claim for payment.

Other suppliers of medical equipment or services have the same options as doctors:

They can agree to use the assignment method, thus saving you the paperwork and also committing themselves to charge no more than the "reasonable charge";

Or they may elect to bill you and leave it to you to collect the portion of the bill that is covered by Medicare.

The Request for Payment Form. The same form is used no matter which method of payment is selected. It is called a Request for Payment Form, or Form 1490. All Social Security offices and most doctors' offices have copies on hand.

Do not forget that before any Part B payment can be made, your record must show that you have met the $60 annual deductible. To get the information on the record, as soon as your bills for covered services amount to $60, send the bills to your Medicare carrier with a Request for Payment Form.

If your bills for any year amount to less than $60, Medicare cannot pay any part of your Part B bills for that year. But any expenses you have in the last three months of the year can be counted toward the next year's deductible. So even if your medical expenses have amounted to less than $60, send in the bills for covered expenses in October, November, and December.

You can send in your Request for Payment either before or after you have paid your medical bills.

Explanation of Benefits Notice. Medicare will send you a notice after a Medicare bill has been submitted—whether you send it in or whether it is sent in by a hospital, skilled nursing home, doctor, or supplier. It will show what services were covered and what charges were approved, how much was credited toward your deductible and the amount Medicare paid.

If you find anything questionable about it—if, for instance, it lists a service you didn't receive—report that fact to the Medicare carrier that sent you the notice or to your Social Security office.

If you have other health insurance to fill in Medicare gaps or to pay the deductibles and co-payment amounts, you will need the Explanation of Benefits notice to send in with your claim for the supplementary insurance payment. The insurance company or Blue Cross and Blue Shield plan must know what Medicare paid before they can pay the amount due on your supplementary policy.

What to Watch Out for in Mail Order Health Insurance

NOT THE BEST HEALTH CARE INSURANCE

Americans are now investing hundreds of millions of dollars each year in mail order health insurance—lured by aggressive advertising, no-strings-attached benefits, and purportedly low monthly premiums.

Most experts, however, do not regard this type of insurance as the best way to finance your basic health care.

As just one illustration, one survey disclosed the companies which sell this insurance return only 40 cents of each premium dollar in the form of benefits—

compared with an average of close to 92 cents on Blue Cross policies. Even the better state lotteries return more: about 45 cents on the dollar.

KEY GUIDES

If, therefore, you are thinking of buying a mail order policy, obey the following guides:

Consider this coverage as strictly supplementary. Most of these companies advertise benefits of $100 to $125 a week. But if you don't have an adequate basic health insurance plan, $100 a week will provide picayune protection in an era when your hospital costs alone can come to more than $200 *a day*. Also, though they may offer benefits for as long as a hundred weeks, and this may unduly impress you, remember the average hospital stay is less than eight days.

Study the advertisements carefully. Sometimes enthusiastic copywriting implies that the policy can deliver more dollars than it actually will. For instance, one major company in the mail order health insurance field has an ad which contains this paragraph near the beginning of the text:

"How long could you stay in the hospital without worrying about the pile-up of daily expenses? Who will pay for the expenses of costly X-rays, doctor bills, drugs and medicines? And how about the expenses at home—rent, food, telephone and others that just go on and on? With expenses like these could you avoid having your savings wiped out and your family life upset?"

Then the following paragraph makes the statement (italics added): "Wouldn't it be comforting to know *these problems* could be solved by your Extra Cash Income Plan . . . the plan that gives you $100 a week IN CASH . . ."

The implication is that this plan, which offers approximately $14.29 per day, will solve the problems of X-rays, drugs, medicines, doctor bills, rent, food, telephone, and all the rest when, in actuality, such an amount would not even pay for more than a fraction of the hospital bill itself, let alone all the other bills.

Be wary of direct-mail pieces which contain approaches such as: "Dear Friend: I know that YOU DON'T DRINK. Because of this I can offer you the Blue Chip (Green Comet; Silver Bullet) brand new hospitalization plan that will pay you $100 a week EXTRA CASH . . . As a non-drinker, why should you be forced to pay as much for health insurance as people who drink? Our actuaries say that non-drinkers take better care of themselves, so doesn't a non-drinker like you deserve a lower rate? . . ."

A mail order piece such as this is a mass-merchandised catchall unrelated to actuarial realities, for there is no way for the company issuing the piece to know whether you, the addressee, are in fact a non-drinker. In addition, there has been no study by the nationally known Society of Actuaries to support the contention that non-drinkers are better health insurance risks. In many instances the premium charged may even be higher than for a policy from a company which does not use this type of gimmickry.

Buy whatever insurance you do decide to take only from a company licensed to do business in your own state. This is a fundamental rule.

Because the mails and mass-circulation advertising cross state lines, the ads you see easily may be those of a company which is unlicensed in your particular state. This can increase your difficulty of collecting in the event of claims. By purchasing this insurance you not only deprive yourself of the protection of your own state laws but also, if a dispute arises over a claim, you may have to go to the state where the company is based to bring suit. You can find out whether or not a company is licensed in your state simply by phoning or writing to your state insurance department.

Since premiums usually are paid monthly, take the trouble to learn what would be your leeway should you inadvertently permit a lapse in payment. The usual grace period is ten days, or, if you pay the premium weekly, seven days. Be on guard: since companies usually do not issue reminder notices, you are obligated to keep track of your payments yourself. If a policy lapses because of non-payment, a new round of waiting periods may be installed.

Analyze the exclusions and waiting periods. Many policies, for example, exclude coverage if the hospitalization results from mental illness. Some policies use large type to state NO WAITING PERIODS, but in the smaller type use a phrase which restricts this significantly.

Another key point: there's nothing special about the advertised tax-free benefits of the payouts. Most health insurance payments are tax-free. And, unlike regular health insurance policies, *premiums* on this type of policy may not be tax-deductible.

CHECK LIST FOR READING MAIL ORDER ADS

There are no direct federal controls over mail order health insurers and until recently most state regulatory insurance departments have been grossly understaffed and reluctant or unable to crack down on misleading ads that could conceal loopholes or exaggerate benefits. Use this check list to your own advantage when you read an ad:

What's covered: Are illnesses as well as accidents covered? What illnesses are excluded? Many policies exclude payments for treating such conditions as alcoholism, pregnancy, miscarriage, mental disorders, and some policies exclude cancer, tuberculosis, or heart disease. Most will cover you only if you are actually confined to a hospital, but not if you are being treated in the hospital's outpatient department.

Waiting periods: When do you begin to receive benefits? If you've had an accident, you can probably collect from the first day you're in the hospital. In the case of illness, however, the waiting period may be from three to eight days, with an average wait of six days. Moreover, eligibility for sickness benefits often does not begin until the policy has been in force for thirty days. And there is usually also a six-month waiting period for coverage of certain specific diseases such as tuberculosis, diabetes, hernia, cancer, or heart disease.

"Pre-existing" conditions: Among the most agonizing loopholes in many of these contracts are the provisions covering "pre-existing" conditions. In one policy, this small-print clause reads:

"No claim or loss incurred after two years from the date of this policy shall be reduced or denied on the ground that a disease or physical condition not excluded from coverage by name or specific description effective on the date of loss had existed prior to the effective date of coverage of this policy."

At first glance, this may look like a helpful provision aimed at protecting *you* the insured. But what it really says is that for the first two years your policy is in force you can't collect for any condition you had when you first took out the policy—even if you weren't aware of the condition at the time. Incidentally, one factor helping to hold down the costs of these policies is the high number of claims rejected because of pre-existing conditions. Some companies routinely reject from one half to four fifths of policyholders' claims for this reason.

Benefits paid: Don't be dazzled by the advertised lump-sum figures of $100 a week or $600 a month. Instead, figure what the policy would pay you *per day*. A payment of $100 a week comes to $14.29 a day; $600 a month works out to $20 a day.

And what would be your chances of collecting the sums advertised? Say an illness keeps you in the hospital for eight days and your policy has a six-day waiting period before you can begin collecting benefits. You collect for only two days or, in the case of the $600-a-month policy, a total of $40 for your eight-day hospital stay.

And to collect the maximum $39,000 over a five-year period some ads promise, you would have to be virtually a basket case.

Premiums: A 25¢ or $1.00 "introductory premium" may look inviting but that's just for the first month and typical premiums are $5.00 or so a month thereafter. Rates also may be sharply hiked later or the contract may call for higher premiums at age sixty-five. So, if you're in doubt, write the insurance company and ask for a complete schedule of premium payments.

Enrollment period: Is there a deadline for applying? Often a "limited enrollment period" is advertised and this may create a sense of false urgency. The deadline also may serve to prevent you from making inquiries, since it may leave you only two or three days to enroll. (One company's ads, published on January 3, specified an enrollment period ending midnight, January 6. The company advertised again on February 22, again specifying a three-day enrollment period.)

Renewability: How long will the policy stay in force? Under what conditions can it be renewed—or canceled? You well may get the impression that policies may be renewed indefinitely. But the catch here is that rate changes or policy cancellations may occur as long as they are made statewide or apply to all policyholders of your "classification." This is subject to wide interpretation: it could, for example, mean people of your own age group. Raising premiums statewide is by no means uncommon. If the rates are raised to prohibitive levels, that alone could in effect force many to drop their policies.

This is merely a brief sampling but surely it warns you to read a health insurance ad with healthy skepticism and to check with your state insurance department if you have any doubts or questions.

And I emphasize again the first guide: never buy this type of policy as a substitute for the broader types of hospital policies which pay virtually your entire bill and which can be supplemented by extra coverage available at moderate additional cost.

WHAT IF YOU'RE DISABLED?

SOURCES OF HELP

What would you do if you became, through some tragic accident, permanently and totally disabled? Could *your* family survive on the average Social Security disability benefit?

Long-term disability insurance, like major medical coverage, also is being overlooked by the vast majority of Americans. Only about one in three of us has any private disability insurance protection. And even in the cases of those who have the insurance, the monthly benefit is often inadequate and the term that benefits are paid is too short to be meaningful. (The average disability lasts five years.)

Disability insurance (often called loss-of-income insurance) pays cash benefits designed to help replace earnings you have lost because of disability up to a maximum of about 60 per cent of your gross earnings. The policies begin paying benefits anywhere from a week following the start of the disability to six months later. They pay benefits from as few as thirteen weeks to as long as a lifetime.

There's little point in trying to insure yourself privately against the loss of your entire income because you will have other sources of disability income which will make up much of the difference.

For example, your employer well may have some form of wage-continuation policy which will keep income flowing in for a number of weeks or months after you have become disabled.

Or your union contract may include certain sick-leave benefits.

There also are state workers' compensation payments for job-connected disability.

There's Social Security: you're eligible for benefits in the sixth month of disability, so long as the disability is severe enough to keep you from working in any substantially gainful activity and is expected to last at least twelve months.

Look into all these sources plus any veterans' benefits for which you think you might be eligible.

WHAT YOU SHOULD KNOW ABOUT SOCIAL SECURITY DISABILITY BENEFITS

HUGE NUMBERS COLLECTING BENEFITS EACH YEAR

"How bad must my husband's blindness be to qualify him for Social Security disability benefits?" the letter began in a handwriting which wiggled with emotional distress. "My husband has been laid off because of his failing eyesight. He isn't even trying to get another job and he says he can't get disability benefits." Then the letter continued with an urgent plea for guidance.

The answer to this question of the understandably distraught wife is that:

Blindness is defined in the Social Security law as either central visual acuity of 20/200 or less in the better eye with the use of corrective lenses, or visual field reduction to 20 degrees or less.*

In the late 1970s, close to three million disabled Americans plus more than two million of their dependent wives and children were collecting about $12.8 billion in Social Security disability benefits each year. A full four out of five men and women in the age brackets from twenty-one to sixty-four are "insured."

In all likelihood, *you* can count on monthly cash benefits in the event that a severe and prolonged disability keeps you from working. And, in addition, disabled workers who have been collecting Social Security benefits for at least twenty-four months also are eligible for Medicare hospital and doctor bill benefits (see "For Those Under Sixty-five" in the preceding section "Your Medicare Benefits," for details on this coverage).

FACTS ABOUT BENEFITS

Because so many of you do not understand the requirements that may qualify or disqualify you, the need for greater knowledge is enormous. Here, therefore, are key facts about these benefits:

Q. *How do you qualify for disability benefits?*

A. In addition to qualifying as "disabled," you must have earned twenty quarters (five years) of coverage during the ten years before you were disabled and be fully insured. If you become disabled before age thirty-one, you will need less work credit—only half the quarters between the age of twenty-one and the time you are disabled, with a minimum of six quarters. Payments begin with the sixth full month of your disability. You must provide the names and addresses of doctors and hospitals involved with your medical treatment and you must accept rehabilitation.

Q. *At what age can you start collecting benefits?*

A. At *any* age under sixty-five if you qualify as disabled. A disability can be mental or physical, but it must be "medically determinable" and it must be expected either to result in death or expected to last (or have lasted) at least twelve months. Also, with few exceptions, it must make you unable to do any substantial gainful work anywhere in our economy.

Q. *What about wives and children of disabled workers?*

A. While you are receiving benefits as a disabled worker, payments to your dependents can be made as follows:

Each unmarried child can get a monthly benefit if he or she is under eighteen (this is in addition to your benefit); if he or she is a full-time student age eighteen through twenty-one or suffering from a disability which began before age twenty-two. Stepchildren and adopted children similarly qualify.

Your wife can get up to 50 per cent of your full benefit, too, if she's caring for a child eligible for benefits (except that she can't collect if the only eligible child

* If a worker's visual impairment falls short of this test, consideration may be given to his age, education, training, and work experience to determine whether or not he is disabled.

is a full-time student between eighteen and twenty-two). Or she can collect, if she is sixty-two, a reduced benefit, even if there are no children entitled to benefits. At sixty-five, she can collect 50 per cent, the full wife's benefit.

A husband sixty-two or older also can qualify for benefits—50 per cent benefit at age sixty-five, less if benefits begin earlier.

Q. *How much of a benefit would you get?*

A. Disability benefits, like your retirement benefits, are based on your average monthly wages. If you are under sixty-two, the total benefits paid to you and your dependents may be reduced if you are receiving workmen's compensation.

Q. *What if a disabled worker with an impairment not expected to improve wants to try going back to work? Does he continue getting benefits for a transition period?*

A. If you return to work, your benefit may continue to be paid during a trial work period. If, after testing your ability to work, it is decided that you are able to hold a substantial job, your benefit will be paid for an "adjustment period." After that, you're on your own.

Q. *Why is there a waiting period of five full months before a disabled worker can begin to receive benefits after applying?*

A. Because usually there are payments made by the employer, a group insurance plan, a private health insurance policy—or, if the injury occurred on the job, by workers' compensation.

Q. *What are the key types of disability for which workers are now receiving benefits?*

A. In the late 1970s, diseases of the circulatory system (heart disease) ranked first. Emphysema was next and schizophrenia was third.

Check any questions with your nearest Social Security office. You'll find the address under "Social Security Administration" in the phone book. If you can't leave the house, a Social Security representative will come to you. Telephone or write or have a friend do this for you. These are your rights.

WHAT'S YOUR WORKERS' COMPENSATION WORTH?

THE HIGH COST OF WORK ACCIDENTS

When a coal mine disaster hits the front pages, as one does with heartbreaking frequency, our attention is riveted on the tragedy of fatal on-the-job accidents. Yet headlines such as these only touch the tip of the accident iceberg.

Each year, about 13,000 Americans lose their lives in on-the-job accidents. Each year, workers suffer a startling 2.3 million injuries on the job.

Merely in economic terms, the cost of work accidents and injuries was over $20 billion a year in the late 1970s, double the total for as recently as 1972. This included lost wages, medical costs, damages to equipment and materials, delays in production, insurance, etc.

Injuries are a daily fact of life in today's most hazardous industries: coal mining, longshoring, roofing, and sheet metal work, meat and meat products (especially cutting and handling), mobile home manufacturing, lumber and wood products, construction.

Workers' compensation, formerly known as workmen's compensation, for job-related accidents, illnesses, and injuries is the oldest form of social insurance in the United States—dating back to 1908 when Congress set up a program under the Federal Employees Compensation Act to cover certain federal employees in hazardous occupations. State after state followed with its own workmen's compensation law until, today, all fifty states have programs of their own, with the coverage paid for completely by the employer and employees getting these free benefits through private insurance, self-insurance, and state insurance funds.

Today the yearly dollar outlay of workers' compensation benefits is in a neck-and-neck race with the massive Social Security disability program.

However, the rules vary widely from state to state and there also is a wide variation in the proportion of lost wages which are replaced.

In recent years, there has been a solid trend toward liberalization of the laws across the land.

Among the significant liberalizations:

Employees of smaller and smaller firms are being brought under the workers' compensation umbrella. The number of states with compulsory coverage is rising and the trend in more and more states is toward including at least some farm and domestic workers. More states are providing benefit limits which increase along with the statewide wage scale.

Limitations on the amount of reimbursable medical, surgical, and hospital expenses are being eliminated. Compensation periods for permanent disabilities—such as loss of limb—are being stretched out. More states are providing complete coverage for occupational diseases. Injured employees are often being given a free choice from a panel of recognized physicians and specialists. There has been a steady succession of hikes in benefits. Every state now has a retroactive pay provision covering the waiting period before normal workers' compensation benefits begin.

The potential importance to you of this coverage must not be downgraded: glance back at those figures on how many workers are injured and killed in on-the-job accidents.

QUESTIONS AND ANSWERS ON BENEFITS

But do *you* know what your workers' compensation coverage is worth to you? Are you aware of how much this insurance would pay if a serious accident befell you while working?

Q. *How many of us are covered?*
A. Between eight and nine out of ten workers.

Q. *Who's eligible?*
A. Covered workers who are partially or totally disabled as a result of an accident or injury on the job—regardless of blame.

Q. *Who isn't covered?*

A. It varies from state to state but among the occupations with large numbers of non-covered workers are agricultural work, domestic work, work for religious, charitable, and non-profit organizations, "casual" labor, self-employed, workers in small firms.

Q. *How much do benefits run?*

A. Normally, maximum benefits are between 60 and 80 per cent of the predisability wage and often there's a dollar ceiling on benefits. In several states there's an extra allowance for workers who have dependents, which brings typical benefits to 60 to 65 per cent of the amount of take-home pay.

Q. *What types of benefits does the program pay?*

A. Three types. The biggest chunk goes to make up for income loss due to disability incurred on the job. The next biggest chunk goes for medical costs. The rest goes for death benefits paid to the worker's survivors. Included in the program are hundreds of millions of dollars in "black lung" benefits paid by the federal government to coal miners suffering from pneumoconiosis—a serious lung disease which comes from inhaling coal dust—and to their dependents.

Q. *How long are benefits paid?*

A. Most state programs pay benefits as long as the disability lasts. Note: More than one in six of our civilian working-age population has some kind of limitation on his or her ability to work because of a chronic disability or health condition.

Q. *Who pays for the workers' compensation program?*

A. In most cases, employers pay insurance premiums either to state insurance programs or to private health insurance carriers or they insure employees themselves. The average cost to employers in covered employment is about 1 per cent of payroll, although costs range in some states up to nearly 3 per cent.

Q. *Can you collect both Social Security benefits and workers' compensation benefits at the same time?*

A. Yes, if the combination does not exceed 80 per cent of your predisability monthly earnings. Beyond that, Social Security payments are trimmed to keep the total at the 80 per cent mark.

Q. *What about private health insurance benefits?*

A. There's usually a provision that private health insurance won't pay for any medical conditions covered by the compensation law. But if your employer has "long-term" disability insurance for employees, this will make up the difference if workers' compensation provides a smaller amount.

Use the above guidelines to help you find out whether the *total* amount of benefits you and your family would get if you, the breadwinner, became disabled would or wouldn't be adequate to meet your family's needs. Also include company insurance, Social Security, your savings and investments.

PRIVATE DISABILITY INSURANCE COVERAGE

WHAT WOULD IT COST YOU?

Let's say you use the guidelines in the preceding section, check your various benefits, and come to the firm conclusion that your benefits would be seriously inadequate in case of need.

How much would it cost you to buy supplementary private disability insurance —to add to your protection from Social Security, worker's compensation, and other sources?

If you get a private individual policy providing $100 a week for up to two years, it'll probably cost you $75 to $115 a year. If the coverage lasts up to two years, your annual premiums probably would be between $110 and $140. And typically there is a thirty-day waiting period before any private disability insurance benefits may begin.

With this as a yardstick, you can compute what the coverage you need will cost, keeping in mind that the longer the waiting period the less your premium cost will be. Also, the longer the benefit continues, the more your cost will be.

CHECK LIST FOR COVERAGES

Check with care these points about private disability coverages:

(1) How is "disability" defined in your policy or the policy you are considering buying? Generally, these policies state that you must be "totally" disabled before benefits are paid.

Your policy may have a variation of this definition:

"Unable to engage in any gainful occupation for which the policyholder is suited by education, training, or experience."

(2) What is the difference in benefit periods for an accident and for an illness? For instance, the same policy might provide benefits for two years for sickness and five years for an accident.

(3) What waiting period is appropriate for you? Take into account the length of time your regular earnings would continue, as well as all the other sources of income, then decide whether you should accept a seven-, fourteen-, thirty-, ninety-day waiting period—or longer.

MAKING DEDUCTIBLES WORK FOR YOU

As in major medical insurance, the best way to save money in your disability coverage is to select the highest deductible your budget can stand. In this type of insurance, the deductible amount is expressed in terms of the waiting period. By extending the waiting—or, as it is called, the "elimination"—period before benefits start, you can cut your costs and either save the money or use it to build up your protection. Since you're less likely to have major medical and disability coverage than you are to have basic protection, it's probable that you'll work out some combination of these.

Here's how you can juggle the deductible to your advantage:

One major medical policy offered by a large insurer would provide a twenty-eight-year-old man with $25,000 maximum coverage for himself, his wife, and two children, with a $500 deductible, at a cost of about $262 per year.

If he raised this deductible to $1,000, he could get a policy which would cut his annual premium to about $162. Then with the money saved, he could buy a short-term disability policy which would pay him $600 a month for two years after a thirty-day waiting period.

By lengthening the waiting period, the policy can be changed either to cover a longer term of years, or to provide a higher benefit.

HOW TO SLASH YOUR MEDICAL BILLS

There was no hope for anything more than a slowing of the pace of rise in medical expenses as the decade of the 1980s neared.

But there are many ways you can cut your own costs. Below you will find fundamental rules that you could translate into big savings for yourself and family—without in any way jeopardizing your health.

SHOP FOR A HOSPITAL

In shopping for health services, perhaps the most difficult area is the hospital. You can't merely pick out one and walk in. Invariably, unless you're an emergency case, you must be admitted by a physician who is affiliated with the hospital.

Few of the one out of every seven Americans admitted to a hospital each year, I'm sure, even thinks about "shopping" for a hospital. But it can be done.

The easiest way would be to telephone each hospital in your city or nearby area until you found the one with the lowest daily rate. But the trouble with this approach is that the hospital you pick in this manner may not be on your doctor's affiliation list, so you'll have to get another doctor. And chances are the institution with the lowest rate is a municipal or "city" hospital. You may not regard municipal institutions with the same esteem you have for private voluntary community hospitals. Private health insurance usually does not cover any tax-supported hospital where no charge is being made for service.

You'll find that your physician is probably affiliated with more than one hospital. If he doesn't have strong feelings about admitting you to a particular institution for a particular reason (if the hospital to which your physician wants to send you is the only one in town with a cobalt radiation unit and you need cobalt radiation treatment, you have little choice in the matter), then bear these points in mind:

• *Do* select the hospital on your physician's list that is a teaching institution and also has a strong research program. If a hospital has affiliations such as these, it has resources of revenue and talent not normally open to other community hospitals which are supported almost exclusively by taxes and patient charges. This is also the facility that will give you the greatest range of diagnostic and treatment resources.

• *Don't* confuse bigness with best. Depending on your condition and the type of treatment you need, maybe a smaller hospital would provide you with less hurried and more personal tender loving care—a difficult item to put a price tag on.

• *Do* check whether your state regulatory agencies can help steer you toward a lower-cost hospital. For instance, in Pennsylvania a few years ago, the state's insurance department published a "Shopper's Guide to Hospitals." This guide compared costs charged by the 101 hospitals in the Philadelphia area—and found that the *daily* charges varied by as much as $50.

• *Don't,* unless it means a big sacrifice to you, go into the hospital on a Friday. A large-scale study a while ago showed that the day of the week you go into the hospital is the single largest factor in determining how long you'll stay there. Admissions on Friday, the study disclosed, resulted in longer stays than admissions on any other day. The reason: the hospital is not fully staffed on weekends and if you go in on a Friday you'll have to wait until Monday before all the necessary laboratory and other diagnostic tests can be performed. Meanwhile, you well may be paying $200 or more a day for your "hotel room."

The study also revealed that the *shortest* average length of stay was found for patients admitted on a Tuesday.

If you have an indemnity-type health insurance policy which leaves you with part of the hospital bill to pay out of pocket, getting out just a day or two earlier can be a considerable relief to your budget. In fact, it has been estimated that if we could cut the average hospital stay by just one day from its 7.2 days in the late 1970s, the nation could save $1 billion annually.

• *Do* ask your doctor if it's possible to have some of your routine lab tests done *before* you're admitted to the hospital. An increasing number of hospitals participate in preadmission testing programs of this type. More than two out of every three Blue Cross plans will pay benefits for this type of visit to the outpatient department, and many insurers also pay through diagnostic riders to their contracts.

And finally, *do,* unless you feel you absolutely must have complete privacy, take a semi-private room, for it is far less expensive than a private room. Many hospitals will charge less for a four-bed semi-private room than for a two-bed room and it's becoming easier to get exactly what you want. Also, semi-private accommodations are usually paid for in full by Blue Cross.

HOW TO CHOOSE A PHYSICIAN

Choose him (or her) carefully—for his reputation in the community, the type of practice he has developed, and his availability. If you are a newcomer in the area, the local city or county medical society will supply you with the names of physicians from whom you can make a choice. You may want to become acquainted with several before deciding.

But don't make your selection solely on the recommendation of a local medical society. Membership in these organizations tells you only that a doctor is licensed to practice and has paid his dues. Also don't assume that because a doctor is well known in his community he is good. He may be prominent for reasons other than medical skill.

One clue to his competence will be his membership on the medical staff of a good hospital, especially a hospital affiliated with a medical school. If so, you can be well assured that he's above average.

Your doctor may practice medicine alone, in a group, or in a large clinic, but he should be a person who knows you and your family and is interested in your *health,* not just your illnesses.

He will keep a permanent record of your medical history.

He will know your background and be better able to tell promptly if anything is wrong.

He will control a key portion of your medical spending, simply because he will determine what drugs you will buy, whether or when you must go to a hospital, whether or when you must see a specialist. And when you must consult a specialist or go to a hospital, he will save you money by making sure you do not repeat costly, time-consuming tests. He also may save you money by referring you to a nurse practitioner for routine health problems.

THE FAMILY DOCTOR—A CLASSIC MEDICAL PRACTICE BECOMES A NEW SPECIALTY

Say you are a woman who suffers from chronic headaches. You might have a brain tumor—or merely need a night out once a week.

Or say you're a man with stomach problems. You might have an ulcer demanding an operation—or merely need a less tension-creating job.

Or say your young son is anemic. He may need medication—or perhaps you, his parents, need counseling on nutrition.

A properly trained family physician can treat 89 to 90 per cent of all medical complaints. In the other one out of ten cases, he (or she) will know to which specialist to refer you and he will stay on the case interpreting the specialist's findings for you, the patient. He looks at you, the whole person, not part of you. More than that, he considers your whole family, and interactions among the various members which may affect the health of any one of you.

Without the family doctor as your entry to the health care system, we are lost in a confusion of specialists, often forced to self-diagnose our own ailments and make our own selection (right or, just as often, wrong) of a specialist.

Yet today, there is only one family physician for every four thousand Americans, against a ratio of one for every thousand of us forty-five years ago. This does not mean that our medical education system is not producing enough physicians. Counting all M.D.s (specialists, researchers, administrators, educators), the ratio of doctors to population is about the same today as it was in 1932. But 75 per cent of those doctors in 1932 were practicing family medicine, while in 1977 less than 20 per cent were on the front line of this type of care.

Against this background, the American Academy of General Practice was created in 1947 to identify the changing pattern of American medical education and the effect on the delivery of medicine in the country. In the late 1950s, a concept began to take form: the development of a new medical specialty that would update the classical general practitioner and create a specialist in family medicine.

The Academy spent years working with the American Medical Association and others to outline the parameters of the new specialty.

In 1969 the American Board of Family Practice was created and the new specialty was on its way.

The core of Family Practice is a unique educational system. To become a diplomate of Family Practice, a doctor must take a three-year residency in Family Practice and pass a board certification exam, not once, but every six years, thus requiring that he stay current with the changes in medicine. Family Practice is the only medical specialty with such a mandatory recertification requirement. The residency program is not tied to the hospital but set apart in the community. The doctor in training has his own office and sees healthy patients whom he seeks to keep healthy.

The response has been astounding. More than three hundred approved Family Practice residency programs have been created in association with general hospitals and medical schools, with over five thousand young doctors currently in training in the late 1970s. There are now divisions of Family Practice in virtually all U.S. medical schools. Over 40 per cent of new medical students are opting for Family Practice, against less than 20 per cent choosing this in the 1950s and '60s.

Most significant, the number of family physicians who have graduated from the residency programs is starting to matter—four thousand since 1971. The goal of the American Academy of Family Physicians is to have sufficient numbers distributed evenly throughout the population so that every one of us can have a family doctor. This goal is attainable within fifteen years.

And the goal might be achieved even earlier if interest continues to expand and the residency program can be extended.

Originally developed in rural areas, Family Practice is now beginning to have an impact in major cities, too. Chicago, for instance, had seven Family Practice residency centers in the city itself, with more in suburban communities as the 1980s neared. In industrial Ohio, Columbus had four while Akron, Dayton, Cleveland, and Toledo had three each.

The need is there; the means for satisfying the need are at hand; support would be abundantly available if you knew, as you do after reading this, what is being created. The day when every American again will have access to the long respected and beloved G.P. (in a new suit and carrying an updated but still mysterious black bag) is nearing.

DON'T WAIT TO SEE YOUR PHYSICIAN UNTIL YOU'RE ILL

If you try to save money on medical bills by not seeing the doctor until you are seriously ill you will defeat the purpose of preventive medicine—the *only sound way* to preserve your health. And it will be more expensive in the long run, for once a disease process has started, it often lasts longer, costs more to cure.

Emergencies are always more expensive, whether the crisis involves the family car, the household plumbing, or your health. And if you are rushed to a hospital emergency room, you really may compound your misfortune—financial as well as physical.

AN OUNCE OF PREVENTION

Item: Diseases of the heart are the predominant killer in our land, accounting for more deaths each year than any other disease, and, worse, their prevalence is rising. From an economic point of view alone, the cost to us of caring for heart disease is estimated at above $3 billion a year.

But the incidence of heart disease could be slashed right now by an enormous 50 per cent with the use of available improved diagnostic techniques and early identification.

Item: Cancer will strike 53 million Americans (one in four) living today; at any time, more than one million persons are under treatment for cancer and a startling fact is that more school children die of cancer than of any other disease. Again, strictly from an economic point of view, the cost to us of caring for cancer patients is estimated at $900 million a year.

But early detection and treatment could sharply reduce this cancer toll, especially certain forms of cancer—and lung cancer particularly could be greatly cut by control of smoking.

About 35 million of us have definite high blood pressure, and another 25 million have borderline hypertension—a total of 60 million people with the risk of developing blood vessel disease with subsequent heart attack, stroke, or kidney failure and premature death.

But much can be done to control hypertension through early detection, treatment, and control of diet and smoking. Premature deaths and disability could be drastically curbed. There is proof in the statistics for the years after 1972 when the federal government and many public and private organizations joined in a national blood pressure education program. During the five-year period just before the start of the program, the death rate from strokes went down, but by only 9 per cent. During the next five years, the stroke death rate dropped by 21 per cent and deaths from hypertension-related diseases have continued to decline sharply. Also, the decline in hypertension-related deaths is occurring at a faster rate among those in younger than in older age groups. This means that more early and premature deaths are being prevented.

A few years ago I was hit by a case of pneumonia (brought on by my own failure to heed clear warnings that I was "sinking" under my work pressures and by my own stupid refusal to obey my physician's orders to "slow down!"). I didn't need new procedures or drugs; all I needed was to follow rules long known and of proven value.

And that will be true in millions of other cases—quite probably yours. For instance, some 14,000 Americans still die each year of communicable diseases, yet the means of prevention are readily at hand, if used. Respiratory diseases can be disabling and fatal; yet they can be controlled with easy change in life-styles (including non-smoking). Diabetes is easy to detect and can be controlled, and avoiding obesity can help prevent onset of the disease.

Venereal disease can kill and disable and is actually on the increase; yet VD can be eliminated with the application of known techniques, if properly used.

As for smoking, its ties to greater risks of coronary heart disease, cancer, chronic pulmonary infections, etc., need no repetition here. Suffice it to say that if smoking were eradicated, today's annual 72,000 lung cancer deaths could be cut 60 per cent!

A quarter century ago, insurance companies offered no coverage for preventive medicine in the absence of a disabling sickness or injury. Today, of the eighteen companies writing more than half of all health insurance coverages, most offer coverages for the costs of preventive medicine without evidence of the presence of a disabling sickness or injury. The shocking point, though, is that there is little buyer demand for the protection. You, whether from ignorance or apathy, are turning down a benefit that could be of such great help to you. Ask your company, your union, your own insurance agent for guidance.

Meanwhile, help yourself by studying the following key guides to health maintenance, put together by the American Health Foundation, a non-profit organization dedicated to the concept of preventive medicine.

• Don't start smoking; if you do smoke, quit; if you can't quit, cut down and smoke only low tar and nicotine cigarettes.

• Know your normal weight and maintain it.

• Have your blood serum cholesterol level checked and keep it within normal ranges by eating low fat foods.

• Have your blood pressure checked regularly; 50 per cent of all Americans don't! Work to lower it if it is high.

• Don't drink in excess; exercise regularly. Have a physical exam before attempting a rigorous exercise schedule.

• Have a periodic health checkup, and maintain a personal health record of your weight, cholesterol, and blood pressure levels, so you are aware of risk trends.

REGULAR CHECKUPS?

But the need for a physical examination every twelve months is being questioned. According to Dr. Keith W. Sehnert, Director of the Center for Continuing Health Education, at Georgetown University, "What you need is regular screening to discover what is normal for you. It's a matter of establishing baseline data on your blood pressure, hemocrit (blood chemistry) cholesterol, electrocardiogram, and chest X-ray. Then, if something goes awry, it shows up."

If you are well, not on regular medication (this includes the Pill), have no specific complaints or symptoms, and have established your baseline tests, Dr. Sehnert's schedule for you would be:

> age 50–60, every two years
> " 40–50, every three years
> " 30–40, every five years
> " under 30, every five years

If you have known medical problems, examinations should be on at least a yearly basis, or more often as your physician directs. Mr. Donald M. Vickery, co-author with Dr. James F. Fries, of "Take Care of Yourself: A Consumer's Guide to Medical Care," goes beyond this and calls the need for the annual checkup a "myth." It is a fact that the elaborate "executive physical," made popular a few years ago by large corporations is slowly being discontinued. There are few advantages to be gained from the "routine checkup," in Dr. Vickery's view, if you follow good health habits—cut out smoking, exercise regularly, and watch your diet, and use alcohol with moderation. The important points to check on:

• "A regular "pap" smear," if you are a woman over twenty-five; also, breast self-examination every month after you are twenty-five.

• During adult life, a blood pressure check every year or so.

• A test for glaucoma after age forty if there is a family history of glaucoma.

• Skin tests for tuberculosis or chest X-rays for the same purpose (but not as desirable because of radiation) every three to five years; more frequently if you have definitely been exposed to the disease.

• Urinalysis, urine cultures, tests for blood in the stool after age thirty and sigmoidoscopy after age fifty are screening procedures that have value in particular circumstances; take your physician's advice on these.

Physical examinations that turn up negative findings serve a worthwhile purpose by bringing together the doctor and patient from time to time. So health screenings should not be judged solely by the amount of disease detected, says Professor Anne Somers of the College of Medicine and Dentistry of New Jersey. Professor Somers, a well-known proponent of prevention, emphasizes that an essential part of a physician's job should be to help you understand the risks and benefits of your life-style and to make informed trade-offs.

Professor Somers and Dr. Lester Breslow, of the University of California, have developed a schedule of preventive steps, called a lifetime health monitoring program, with specific types of examinations or tests at key points in each person's life, beginning with prenatal counseling along with life-style histories and counseling. They are urging that it be adopted by unions, employers, and health insurers and hope to have it included in any National Health Insurance program.

HOW TO SHOP FOR A PHYSICAL EXAM

If your physician recommends a complete physical what should you expect?

"Any medical history that fails to explore your life-styles and living habits such as smoking, drinking, occupational stress, and nutrition—and thereby identify risk factors which may predispose you to medical problems—is *worthless.*"

This statement comes from the New York-based Life Extension Institute which has been in the "physical examination business" for sixty-five years.

The LEI's personal-medical history questionnaire asks all clients such questions as: Do you use a seat belt in your car? How much coffee do you drink? How much alcohol do you consume? Did you have a vacation last year?

The questionnaire—a relatively new system called the "Health Risk Profile"— was pioneered by a team of physicians at the Methodist Hospital of Indiana in Indianapolis. The answers, which are processed through a computer, indicate your risk in the future of developing a major disease by appraising your living habits now—rather than by assessing actual symptoms which may not appear until the disease has become incurable.

For instance, treatment for a possible heart attack should begin with the appearance of high cholesterol, high blood pressure, cigarette smoking, obesity, plus a genetic predisposition to the disease, *not* with the *appearance of chest pains.*

The Health Risk Profile (which, in the late 1970s, cost only $15 for the questionnaire, computer processing, and a medical interpretation) is only one earmark of a careful physical exam today.

The Life Extension Institute also provides a self-administered Emotional Assessment Exam.

To sort out the complete, fairly priced medical exam from the incomplete, overpriced physical, here are other guidelines:

• After the physical, is there a follow-up system to determine whether any proposed treatments are working?

• Is there a health educator on the staff or any evidence of health education activities?

• Is there a personal, unhurried consultation with the physician, discussion of key problems and "precursors" and counseling on how to deal with the problems?

• Are you permitted to have a copy of your medical record, including not only the results of your tests and medical observations by the examiners but also any computer printout analyzing the questionnaire you filled out and your exam's findings?

• If the exam is given at a group practice or clinic or a Health Maintenance Organization, is there a peer review system under which doctors monitor each other's work?

• Is the staff oriented toward prevention vs. acute care? Are they members of such organizations as: the American Board of Preventive Medicine, which certifies physicians to specialize in this field, sets up training criteria and offers periodic exams; the American College of Preventive Medicine; the American College of Physicians; the Society of Internal Medicine? Have the physicians been certified by the American Board of Internal Medicine?

• How stable and reputable is the group practice or the clinic? Who is behind the operation, who runs it, how long has it been there? Watch out for today's rapidly expanding "mass" operations, including health spas and fly-by-night "physical factories."

• Are all X-rays and electrocardiograms interpreted by those who have had special training in the fields? Is the laboratory properly certified by a state, local, or, in some cases, federal agency? Does the lab subscribe to outside quality control services such as the program of the American College of Clinical Pathologists? Are there subprofessionals on the staff—to help physicians expand their services without compromising quality?

Some final warnings: inquire about costs of proposed lab services and be wary of excessive numbers of tests.

If you suspect lab charges are excessive, ask the physician for a detailed report on costs of services. As the 1970s closed, a reasonable total charge for a twelve-channel blood chemistry was $10–$15; for a urinalysis, $3.00–$5.00; serology, about $5.00; blood count, $3.00–$5.00; chest X-ray $15–$25; EKG, $15–$25. Prices of services should be easily obtainable.

If you feel you can't afford the full physical recommended for you, ask for advice on what corners you can cut.

And a special caution on "life insurance exams" for which the company may pay as little as $10–$12.

This type of exam is designed to pick up only "big" problems, such as hypertension. It meets the company's needs, but not necessarily yours.

HOW MUCH SHOULD A PHYSICAL EXAM COST?

The key point to grasp at the start is that there is absolutely no standard, "accepted" definition of the physical exam.

But the Life Extension Institute, which as the 1970s closed, had done more than 4 million physicals in its sixty-eight-year history and which performs physicals and related preventive health services for thirteen hundred organizations plus eighteen thousand individuals each year, has established general guidelines. Below is what you should look for in a physical, what you should expect to pay for it, and how to judge the individual or organization performing it.

(1) A physical exam can take from one hour to a full day—and in a few cases even two or three days.

(2) Costs of a "complete" physical ranged, as the 1980s neared, from $100 to $300. But if you're healthy and younger (under thirty-five), you probably can get away with an abbreviated physical, costing between $35 and $50.

(3) First, a personal and family medical history should be taken. Then, if you are under age forty, here are items which should be covered in a complete physical:

A chest X-ray; "hands on" examination, including measurement of height, weight, blood pressure, pulse, examination of eyes, ears, nose, mouth, throat, dental hygiene, neck, chest, heart, lungs, abdomen, genitalia, skin, spine, bones, muscles and joints, lymph nodes, nervous system, rectal exam; for women, pelvic exam, Pap smear, breast exam. Also, an electrocardiogram (unless symptoms suggest special problems, a single EKG to be used as a "base line" should be sufficient for the under-forty); pulmonary (lung) function test; vision and hearing tests; basic blood tests including complete blood count, blood sugar cholesterol, and triglycerides, chemical profiles showing the adequacy of functioning of key body systems such as liver, kidney, thyroid, and pancreas; serology (to detect venereal disease); urinalysis (sugar, albumin, microscopic exam).

(4) Expect to pay at least $100 for the above complete exam. For the younger person, such a complete exam is probably not necessary every year.

(5) If you are over age forty your exam should include among others, at least these additional tests:

Proctosigmoidoscopy (visual exam of lower bowel); electrocardiogram (yearly); tonometer test for glaucoma.

(6) In the late 1970s each of these extras cost $35 or so.

(7) If your age, family history, or symptoms suggest that you may be in the high risk category for heart disease, you should also be given, in addition to the electrocardiogram, some kind of cardiovascular risk analysis.

Depending on your own medical circumstances, you can add on and on to this list—but this is enough to suggest the scope.

(8) The exam should include updating of your immunizations and a legible

record of the status of your protection against tetanus, polio, etc.—plus dates for re-immunizations.

(9) You also should get a personal medical history exam with indications of your emotional states and living habits—serving the same purpose as the Life Extension Institute's Emotional Assessment exam.

(10) Don't shortchange yourself on this exam. But don't permit yourself to overspend for tests not needed in your age/health bracket or to be grossly overchanged because you don't know what the various aspects of a physical should cost.

ALWAYS DISCUSS YOUR PHYSICIAN'S FEES WITH HIM

Fees are not inflexible, and physicians frequently adjust their charges to meet your financial situation. Be sure, though, to discuss fees at your first meeting; do *not* wait until after you receive the bill. If you decide a medical fee is unreasonable after a service has been provided, the first step is to negotiate directly with the doctor.

Be particularly careful to discuss fees at the start with a specialist, who may be very expensive but who also may reduce and stretch out payment for his charges to fit your budget.

GO TO THE DOCTOR'S OFFICE

House calls are not only more expensive but also less efficient. Without office equipment and a trained staff, your physician cannot perform a complete examination. (Of course, chronically ill, confined patients can be seen only at home.)

What's more, a house call may not be adequate for the doctor and he'll ask you to come to his office for further consultation. Result: two fees instead of one.

Reserve house calls for real emergencies.

USE THE TELEPHONE

This saves money and also makes good medical sense. A family doctor who has examined you regularly is familiar with your health history. Consequently, he often can advise you over the phone about minor health problems. For anything that seems to be serious, he will ask you to come to his office to be examined.

But call the doctor only when you have adequate reasons—and confine discussions of your appointments and other routine matters to his nurse.

FOLLOW YOUR DOCTOR'S ORDERS

Just as a commonplace illustration, have you ever been told to take off ten pounds and get more exercise? Did you do it? If you refuse to follow the expert advice you solicit and pay for, you are throwing your money away.

YOUR COMMUNITY HEALTH RESOURCES

DON'T OVERLOOK THEM!

All around you are a great number and variety of community health services. They are available to you, and they could mean considerable savings to you over the long term. Don't overlook them!

These resources range from your public hospitals and clinics to volunteer ambulance services, local blood banks, visiting nurse service, rehabilitation and mental health counseling, vocational rehabilitation and retraining programs. In addition, there are special services, such as free screening and immunization programs, especially if you live in a highly populated area. The list of these services is almost endless, combating health problems ranging from deafness to drug abuse, and fighting illnesses ranging from alcoholism to venereal disease.

On top of your community resources are other facilities backed by labor groups, private foundations, business organizations, and social service agencies. And don't forget government programs. As one illustration, the Veterans Administration conducts a large-scale national program of medical care and rehabilitation services.

Your Department of Health is the place to go to start finding out what services you might use. Every state has one, and so do many cities and counties, although in some areas you may find this function is fulfilled by a health officer instead of a department. In any event, the Department of Health or the health officer will be able to refer you to the health services that are available through the department or through private agencies.

SAMPLING OF SERVICES

Here are some of the areas of special services you might need or want which are there for your asking:

Abortion	Drugs
Adoption	Family Planning
Aging	Food stamps
Alcoholism	Handicapped children
Ambulance service	Heart disease
Arthritis	Hemophilia
Birth defects	Kidney disease
Blindness	Leukemia
Blood banks	Maternity care
Cancer	Medicare and Medicaid
Cerebral palsy	Mental retardation
Child placement	Nursing and homemaker services
Chronic illness	Prescription emergency services
Convalescent care	Rehabilitation
Day care	Speech handicaps
Deafness	Unmarried parents
Dental services	Venereal disease
Diabetes	Welfare services

How to Slash Your Hospital Costs

FORCES PUSHING HEALTH COSTS UP-UP-UP

Health care costs continued to climb relentlessly year after year through the decade of the 1970s—with hospital bills jumping 12 to 15 per cent and physicians' fees rising on average by 8 per cent per year. What are some of the forces behind these ever-escalating costs?

Inflation by itself accounted for close to half the annual rises in medical costs. Hospitals are paying out more and more in salaries (which represent about two thirds of their budgets) and more and more for gas, electricity, food, other goods and services they routinely buy. In one recent year, for instance, the cost of patient gowns rocketed 40 per cent, disposable surgical caps 70 per cent, sutures 35 per cent!

But other also important forces are:

• Inappropriate use of services. Because of a shortage of physicians in many areas, hospital emergency rooms are increasingly being used as general health facilities, reported "A Handbook for Consumer Participation in Health Care Planning," a pamphlet prepared by the Blue Cross Association to help orient new consumer members of local health planning organizations, called Health Systems Agencies.

In fact, patient visits to emergency rooms soared 35 per cent in a four-year span—and these visits are twice as costly as a visit to a physician's office. Yet, the irony of it is that while many hospital emergency rooms are jammed, many hospital beds are either empty or occupied by patients who should not be there. And on top of this construction continues—not of ambulatory or outpatient facilities, but of new hospitals or additions with even more unnecessary beds.

• Excess beds. "The oversupply of beds results in pressures that encourage unnecessary admissions and prolong the length of stays. "Even if beds stay empty," the consumer handbook said, "there is the cost of maintaining them," far above the cost of an occupied bed.

• Institutional productivity. Much more could be done than is being done to improve hospital management in areas such as budgeting, scheduling of patient admissions, more efficient use of personnel.

• Defensive medicine. In the last few years, the proportion of X-ray and lab tests has soared. Many of these tests are superfluous, are done because physicians want to have "proof," if they are sued, that they were not negligent, or because hospital "routine" may require doctors to order certain tests, even if they were done before admission.

• Expensive medical technology. The past decade has been marked by enormous technological advances . . . new surgical procedures to replace arteries, heart valves, knee and hip joints . . . sophisticated equipment, such as the kidney machine . . . the CAT (computerized axial tomography) scanner, a technological miracle which combines a computer with an X-ray machine to produce superdetailed, three-dimensional views of any cross section of the body.

While the scanner may provide additional diagnostic information with less discomfort and risk to the patient than other procedures, it is not yet clear whether or not this information leads to a better outcome for the patient.

One point is clear, though. With the machines costing between $400,000 and $600,000 each in the late 1970s to purchase and about $300,000 annually to operate, their very existence easily can lead to their use—and abuse—in even minor cases. For about $200-plus per scan, the machines can yield hefty profits for hospitals and physicians. This explains why their sales have pushed scanners from about 250 in 1976 to an estimated 1,200 just two years later in hospitals and radiologists' offices.

According to the consumer handbook, the Washington, D.C., Blue Cross and Blue Shield plans learned several years ago that hospitals and physicians' groups in the area were planning to buy seventeen scanners—at a cost of close to $7 million—although six to eight scanners were deemed adequate for the patient population there.

A Virginia hospital, in applying for permission to buy a scanner, claimed it would charge $220 per scan—or more than three times its anticipated cost—to make up for the losses it incurred in providing obstetrical and emergency care and for its loss in revenue due to the opening of another hospital in the area.

The local Health Systems Agency disapproved the application, but was overruled by the state health planning council, which, like other state bodies of its kind, has final say on spending.

SOME WAYS TO CUT COSTS

About two thousand hospitals throughout the United States are now boasting that they offer some form of outpatient surgery. In many, if not most cases, a patient can be in and out of a hospital before dark.

The cost of same-day surgery is between 20 and 50 per cent of the cost of staying a day or two in a hospital.

An estimated three out of ten medical procedures could probably be performed as effectively, and certainly more economically, outside the hospital or on an outpatient basis. Yet, not all U.S. hospitals are using this cost-reducing measure to the fullest possible extent—not by any means.

How many hospitals offer seven-day-a-week hospital care—reducing the high cost of entering a hospital on Friday, among other obvious beneficial cost reduction?

How many actually offer self-care facilities for patients who aren't very sick—who, for instance, are undergoing diagnostic tests, diabetes care, preparation for surgery, stroke rehabilitation—and who are perfectly capable of looking after many of their personal domestic needs and doing without costly nursing care?

How many hospitals have genuine consumer representation on their boards or effective consumer complaint mechanisms—e.g., ombudsmen—to bring the people who are paying the bills and who could make valuable contributions into the system?

We still are paying only a pittance for home health services (visiting nurses and home health aides homemaker service agencies). Yet, it's a well-established fact that home health care costs only a fraction of hospital care and often is superior.

We still are paying only relatively small sums for preventive, outpatient services vs. inpatient and acute care.

We still are flagrantly underemphasizing preventive health, prenatal care, patient education, immunization, efforts to promote occupational health and safety.

We still are making far too small an effort to train and use assistants, nurse practitioners, family health workers, and others who can assume a major part of the workload of a fully trained physician.

We still have made only baby steps toward development of comprehensive pre-paid health services and organizations, and salaries for medical personnel and only baby moves away from the costly fee-for-service system which encourages runaway costs.

We still haven't made a real effort to promote the development and/or application of standards of appropriateness of various type of care—for instance, elective and other surgery, lab tests, hospitalization, home care, visiting nurse care.

We still have done little to combat the irrational differences in aggregate fees and payments to family physicians against pathologists; pediatricians and psychiatrists against neurosurgeons and general surgeons. What is the justification for the giant difference in payments to surgical specialists and family physicians?

HSAS—HOW YOU CAN GET INVOLVED IN COMMUNITY HEALTH CARE DECISIONS

A venture in consumer participation in health care planning is now under way, which—if it can be made to work—could not only greatly improve our health care delivery system but also smooth the way for whatever national health insurance system is eventually enacted.

The experiment takes the form of Health Systems Agencies (HSAs) which are planning agencies set up under 1974 law to identify the health needs of their communities and to create programs to meet those needs at the most reasonable cost.

The Health Systems Agencies also are responsible for approving proposed capital expenditures for medical facilities and equipment in the area—so there will be no costly and unnecessary duplication and care will be made available to men and women who may not now receive it.

Although mandated by law, these HSAs are not government agencies. They are non-profit corporations or public planning bodies in which ordinary citizens are given a much bigger role in health care decisions in their communities than ever before.

The governing board of each HSA must be composed of a majority of consumers who live in the area—up to 60 per cent. At least 50 per cent of the board, also residents of the area, are to be "providers"—meaning physicians, dentists, nurses, hospital administrators, individuals working for other health care institutions, or for professional schools and in the allied professions.

But consumer participation in HSA activities is not limited to the governing board. There also is an important place for consumers on sub-area advisory councils, committees, and task forces and as monitors of how the HSA is doing its job. For instance, in northeastern New York, more than 150 planning volunteers contributed over 6,000 hours to produce the first proposed Health Systems Plan for the area in the late 1970s.

Now—right now—is the time for you to become involved.

All HSA meetings must be public and all must be announced well in advance in local newspapers.

CAN HSAS CURB HEALTH CARE COSTS?

Although still young, HSAs are demonstrating that they can put a lid on health care capital spending. Across the United States in the late 1970s, fifty of the sixty-nine Blue Cross plans had representatives on HSA boards. A full thirty-three plans had "conformance clauses" with hospitals, supporting decisions of local HSAs regarding further expansion, construction, equipment. Exercising these clauses, the plans have blocked or delayed expenditures in Ohio, Maryland, Chicago, Kansas City, Washington, D.C., and Pennsylvania, many others.

But not any of their efforts—by the new consumer-dominated Health Systems Agencies, nor certainly the familiar Blue Cross plans—has a chance of success without your active support.

• Learn about and honestly participate in local health planning activities. You will get valuable tips by writing your local Blue Cross plan or The Blue Cross Association for its booklet, "A Handbook for Consumer Participation in Health Care Planning."

• Volunteer to serve on the governing board or on one of the sub-area councils of your local HSA. Be aware of what's happening in your own community. If a hospital or hospital expansion is needed, support it. If it is not needed, oppose and stop it.

If you act, you can contribute to curbing your own health care costs. If you do not act, your failure will result in all of us paying more and more for health care, directly or indirectly—as taxpayers, patients, health insurance subscribers, and employers.

"PAT"

Whenever you have had to have an operation in the past, you almost surely have had to go into the hospital at least two to three days before the operation to undergo laboratory tests and have the tests evaluated. Result: unnecessary over-use of scarce and costly hospital beds, inconvenience, lost time away from work or home.

This procedure—which may involve hundreds of thousands of hospital patients on any given day—soon may be obsolete for many types of surgery. To replace it across the country is a program called PAT—Pre-Admission Testing. Under this innovative program, your diagnostic lab tests and X-rays are done in the hospital's outpatient department before, rather than after, your admission for surgery with Blue Cross coverage paying for the tests to the same extent it would have paid if you had been in a hospital bed.

Pioneered by the nation's Blue Cross plans back in the 1960s, the program was slow to catch on. As recently as 1970, only one in three Blue Cross plans paid for these outpatient diagnostic tests. As the 1980s neared, though, because of the Blue Cross organization's increasing emphasis on paying for outpatient care, eight out of ten of the plans provide some form of preadmission coverage to more than 58.3 million subscribers and their dependents.

PAT has been reported as cutting hospital inpatient stays by an average of 1.4 days—suggesting annual savings exceeding $1 billion.

Typically, PAT works this way:

Your physician decides you need elective surgery and schedules it for, say, a Wednesday. Instead of checking into the hospital on Monday or Tuesday, as in the past, you go to the hospital Monday and get your X-rays and appropriate lab tests done on an outpatient basis. You then return home or to work and do not check into the hospital until Tuesday evening or early Wednesday. Meanwhile, your doctor has your test results in hand.

PAT's advantages are obvious. It:

• Cuts your hospital stay, which reduces your total hospital bill and which, in turn, helps slow the seemingly never-ending upsurge in health insurance rates;

• Conserves benefit days of inhospital coverage for future use.

• Frees hospital beds for patients who really need them, also forestalling the expense of building new beds and new hospitals;

• Permits scheduling of tests so the tests do not interfere with your job and family responsibilities and do not keep you away from your office and home any longer than essential;

• Relieves physicians of the pressure of getting both testing and treatment completed on patients in a hurry, in order to make beds available for other seriously ill patients. (One Pennsylvania hospital reported that its potential bed capacity had risen by eleven beds with PAT and that the length of stay for elderly patients had been cut by more than two days.)

What kinds of tests are covered by preadmission testing? Generally, laboratory, X-ray, electrocardiograms, metabolism, and other tests health insurance plans would normally cover on an inpatient basis. And although PAT is used most frequently in elective (non-emergency) surgery cases, it also is applicable to obscure and rare medical conditions requiring extensive testing before hospital treatment seems indicated.

This is merely one of the relatively new cost-cutting techniques, many of which you can apply to reduce or at least moderate the soaring costs of hospital care.

Ask about PAT! Use it!

WALK-IN SURGERY

In an era of fast-food outlets and drive-in banking, why not walk-in surgery? Why not, indeed—and this has become one of the fastest growing phenomena in the medical field. With walk-in surgery—or in-and-out or same-day surgery—you enter the hospital in the morning, have your operation, go home before the day ends. Ordinarily, the operation might have kept you in the hospital at least two or three days.

You save time. You save money. By eliminating the need to occupy expensive bed space and many customary expenses that go with hospitalization, this quick procedure may cost you one third of what the same operation done the traditional way would cost.

Pioneered in 1961 at Butterworth Hospital in Grand Rapids, Michigan, walk-in surgery grew slowly at first, then took off. As the 1980s approached, about three thousand hospitals offered this type of care.

In addition, a new form of free-standing health facility (with names such as "surgicenter") has come into being to provide walk-in surgery exclusively. There were about thirty to forty of these facilities in existence as the decade ended, with as many as a hundred more said to be in the planning stage.

Of the more than forty types of operations that can be done on a one-day out-patient basis, the most frequently performed is the dilation and curettage (D&C).

Others include tonsillectomies and adenoidectomies, hernia repairs, removal of cysts and other growths, hemorrhoidectomies, biopsies, skin grafts, therapeutic abortions, vasectomies, cataract removals, and various kinds of plastic and ortho-pedic surgery.

Generally, patients selected must be in reasonably good health and not too old —in order to minimize the possibility of complications which could come in the absence of the prolonged observation that follows conventional surgery.

With this precautionary preadmission screening, the record for walk-in surgery has been impressive.

You, the patient, are watched closely immediately after the operation and you may be kept in the recovery room for, say, an hour or two. Patients undergoing some operations, however, have been able to check in and out of the hospital or clinic in as little as three and a half hours. Walk-in surgery is particularly beneficial for children, for it eliminates the psychological trauma that is often triggered by an overnight stay in the hospital.

What about the possible dollar savings?

Verticare, Blue Cross of Southwest Ohio's same-day surgery program, es-timated savings of $250,000 during its first twenty-four months of operation. In addition, the 1,273 patients receiving treatment under the program saved an es-timated 4,121 hospital days.

As walk-in surgery proves itself, increasing numbers of health insurance plans from coast to coast are providing coverage for it. Blue Cross plans already offer this benefit. In New York City over 100,000 Blue Cross plan subscribers annu-ally receive benefits for same-day surgery; in Boston, the number is 25,000 subscribers; in Phoenix, another 25,000.

It cuts costs because it eliminates the hotel part of the expense, such as room and board, and the hospital can then also be used more effectively, for beds go only to those patients requiring full hospitalization.

HOME HEALTH CARE

Home health care programs, too, are taking hold from coast to coast as one of the "newest" solutions to runaway hospital costs (although, in actuality, home care is the oldest form of care there is).

With home care, you, the patient, may receive an early discharge from the hos-pital to continue your treatment or convalesce at home. You may be provided with a hi-lo hospital bed, an overbed table, and any other needed medical equip-ment and supplies. Many of the same services you would get in the hospital are available at home. For instance, under a physician's supervision, a nurse and physiotherapist may visit you, if you are a patient, twice a week to administer drugs, check blood pressure, and give therapy. If necessary, an ambulance can pick you up periodically and deliver you to the hospital for more detailed checkups or for X-ray therapy.

And not only does home care get you home if you're convalescing or chronically ill. You may find the quality of care at least as high as that at a hospital. The care at home may be much more preferable for psychological reasons alone.

In any case, your use of home care is optional—and not every patient is accepted for home care. Screening and evaluation determine the suitability of the home and consider the nature of the illness. Most cases are orthopedic (fractures), cardiovascular, and cancer, but also included have been emphysema, arthritis, the like.

Home care programs for the elderly also may be an alternative to nursing home care. For with hospitalization costs continuing to soar, nursing homes incapable of accommodating the swelling ranks of applicants, and an overburdened society unable to help families threatened with dissolution, the homemaker-health aide is filling a big vacuum.

It was back in 1947 that the modern concept of home care was pioneered by New York's Montefiore Hospital. It was a revolutionary concept, for it was not limited to the indigent or elderly chronically ill, but was open to all types of patients and was a broad community-coordinated program calling on many forms of skills.

As recently as 1963, though, there were only 250 agencies in the United States with coordinated home care programs. As the 1970s neared, such programs were provided by about 2,200 home health agencies—most visiting nurse associations, but also other community organizations, hospitals, and health departments.

The savings to individuals are and can be enormous. In Rochester, New York, as an illustration, the $25 home care cost compared with $200 for inhospital!

The savings to the hospitals and insurance plans in terms of services and beds are equally enormous. And incalculable are the benefits in emotional-psychological terms. As one Delaware patient put it: "While I'm still far from well, today I'm celebrating my thirtieth wedding anniversary here at home with my husband. I am really getting 'tender, loving care' from my family and my fine home care nurse and doctor."

ON SURGERY: GET A SECOND OPINION

You (or a relative or friend) have been advised to have a gall bladder operation—or perhaps a tonsillectomy, hysterectomy, hernia repair, some other type of elective surgery—meaning an operation of non-emergency nature.

Should you have that operation—often at considerable cost and pain—not to mention the risk of even minor surgery?

Before you do, consider these startling findings:

• In one out of four cases in which subscribers to Blue Cross and Blue Shield of Greater New York were advised to undergo elective surgery and sought second opinions, the consultant recommended against having the operation.

• Of the obstetrical-gynecological cases (such as hysterectomies) studied, 28.6 per cent of the recommendations of the first physicians were not confirmed.

• Of the orthopedic cases, the first physicians were contradicted in 33.2 per cent of the cases, and of the ear, nose, and throat (mostly tonsillectomies) cases, 26.6 per cent.

These findings are not necessarily conclusive. But the high proportion of disagreement does add some credibility to the growing concern that much surgery is unneeded.

An estimated 2.4 million unnecessary operations, causing nearly 12,000 deaths, are performed annually at a cost to the public of about $4 billion, a congressional committee charged several years ago. There is startlingly widespread agreement among experts that there is more surgery in the United States today than there ought to be. There are many thousands more surgeons than we need, and excess surgeons lead to excess surgery.

Studies in California, Kansas, Maine, Vermont, and elsewhere seem to bear this out. In one Vermont community, for instance, there were twice as many appendectomies as in a nearby community that was apparently similar in every relevant respect.

Although challenged as wildly exaggerated, these statistics have led a growing number of Blue Cross, Blue Shield, and other health insurance plans to offer to pay for second and even third opinions on recommendations for elective surgery. In New York, in fact, state law now requires all health insurance plans to offer this option.

Typical of how the programs work is the Greater New York Blue Cross and Blue Shield plan, with 5.5 million subscribers. Under this program subscribers call a referral center and are given the names of three board-certified specialists in their area to choose from—specialists selected at random from 1,700 co-operating surgeons. The plan pays for all charges, and even for a third opinion, if the first two do not agree. But the subscriber is under no obligation to accept the opinion of the consultants and is covered by insurance even if the operation is against the advice of the consultants.

The program saves money. For each operation not performed on a subscriber, the health insurance plan saves $1,500 in hospital fees alone.

Yet relatively few of you as yet take advantage of the free second opinions.

While the reason may be your faith in your own physician, it's also likely that you are not aware of the second-opinion option. Learn now if you are covered by this program so you can get another opinion when you are advised to undergo surgery.

In fact, even if you are not covered for it, get this opinion for your own safety and to protect your pocketbook.

MORE COMPETITION ON THE WAY

In the late 1970s, consumers were spending an estimated fourteen cents out of every dollar on health care and drugs. No drain on your pocket book has been more subject to inflationary pressure.

As physician fees, hospital costs, and health insurance premiums have contin-

THE ENORMOUS BURDEN OF GOOD HEALTH CARE

ued to rise alarmingly, consumers' need to be able to shop for the best bargains has intensified.

To assist you in this effort, the Federal Trade Commission (FTC) launched an across-the-board attack on private regulations that keep health care prices high and prevent you from getting information you need to stretch your medical care dollars.

As the 1980s opened, the FTC had:

• Issued a complaint against the American Medical Association, the nation's largest association of doctors. The agency charged that sections of the Principles of Medical Ethics restrict price competition among doctors and hinder physicians from soliciting business by advertising or other means. As a result, the complaint alleged, prices of doctors' services have been fixed or tampered with, and consumers have been deprived of the benefits of competition and information necessary to the selection of a physician. An administrative judge has ruled in the FTC's favor. He declared the AMA's ban on physician advertising illegal. He noted, too, that the AMA's restrictions have discouraged—and in some instances eliminated—new methods of health care.

• Filed a similar complaint against the American Dental Association and four state and county dental societies.

• Launched an investigation of doctors' control of Blue Shield plans. The FTC staff argues that health insurance plans controlled by doctors have little incentive to keep fees down and to stimulate alternative methods for delivering health care services. Blue Shield plans provide medical and surgical coverage for over 40 per cent of all Americans. In doing so, they set payment levels for doctors. In most cases, these levels are set by the doctors who control the individual Blue Shield plans across the country. A trade regulation rule governing doctor influence over Blue Shield plans may be proposed during the 1980s.

• Done a simple but intriguing study showing that in those parts of the country where health maintenance organizations have gained a strong foothold, competing Blue Shield and commercial health insurance plans provide lower rates and broader coverage than elsewhere. As a result, the agency is investigating whether physician groups have tried to restrain competition from HMOs through boycotts and other subtle and not so subtle pressures. The Commission has accepted one consent decree preventing a Blue Shield plan from boycotting physicians affiliated with HMOs.

• Begun to examine whether doctors unduly control non-doctors' efforts to provide alternative and often cheaper health care. A similar investigation is under way involving the delivery of dental care.

• Charged that the Indiana Dental Association encouraged its members not to co-operate with health insurance companies' cost containment programs. The Association agreed to stop inducing its members to frustrate such cost-cutting efforts.

• Started working with state insurance commissioners and others to develop sound cost disclosure plans for life insurance, an area of unparalleled consumer confusion. The plans will enable consumers to shop wisely for the best insurance values that meet their needs.

These are just a few of the actions the FTC had initiated to check spiraling health care costs. As the next decade unfolds, these and other efforts could help curb the shrinking value of your health care dollar.

How to Slash Your Drug Bills

NINE BASIC HINTS

(1) Take only the drugs and medications prescribed or recommended by your doctor. And be sure that your physician knows what other drugs and other over-the-counter medicines you may be taking—whether prescribed by him or by another doctor or dentist. Such drugs can interact in ways that could cause serious problems for you.

(2) Urge the pharmacist filling a prescription to follow your doctor's instructions at the lowest possible cost. But *do not* decide on your own to substitute a generic equivalent for a trade-name drug—assuming you are now taking one of these drugs or one is prescribed for you. Let your physician make the decision.

(3) Ask your physician to steer you to drugstores in your area which offer quality drugs at the lowest cost. The American Medical Association is now urging physicians to do this as a matter of course.

(4) Shop the drugstores recommended to you, for the variations can be astounding. As a general guide, discount drugstores will fill prescriptions at lower cost to you than regular drugstores. Co-op pharmacies are scarce, but if you can find a co-op, it may pay you to compare its services and prices with other pharmacies.

(5) Don't buy non-prescription drugs in large quantities unless they are really needed. A thousand-tablet aspirin bottle may seem more economical than a small size, but aspirin—and many other medicines—deteriorate with time. On the other hand, if you suffer from a chronic illness that calls for the use of prescription drugs over a long period, your doctor may prescribe in relatively large quantities and this may result in some savings.

(6) Ask your pharmacist how to store your medicines to avoid deterioration. Temperature, humidity, and other storage conditions may vary with different drugs.

(7) Get "starter" supplies of drugs from your physician. Most doctors may request samples from drug firms and here you save in two ways: you get your initial supply free and you can try out the medication for its effectiveness before you buy a larger supply.

(8) Make sure you're not paying a professional charge for a non-prescription over-the-counter drug. Sometimes physicians recommend drugs which can be sold without prescriptions. But if the drugs are handled as regular prescriptions, the pharmacist will charge his usual fee. Ask your physician if the drug is a prescription item at the time he gives you the slip from his pad. If there's any doubt in your mind, look for the legend on the label.

(9) Don't waste money buying the most expensive brand of aspirin, as it is a specific chemical compound. (Aspirin tablets are required by law to meet the

standards of strength, quality, and purity set forth in *Pharmacopoeia,* a book of drug standards recognized by the Federal Food, Drug and Cosmetic Act as an official compendium. Aspirin must be packaged and labeled in the manner prescribed in this book. But reject any aspirin if there is a vinegar-like odor when you open the bottle. A chemical compound called acetomenophen is now commonly used as a substitute for aspirin in some situations, because it does not cause the stomach reactions some people get from aspirin. However, although the new drug can reduce fever and pain, it is not considered effective in reducing the inflammation of arthritis.

READ DRUG LABELS AND SAVE

If you are among the 23,000,000-plus Americans age sixty-five or over, your spending for medicines and related products has now soared close to an average of $100 a year—more than double the spending on medicines and related products of those aged nineteen to sixty-four.

If you are in the sixty-five-and-over category, you represent 1 per cent of the population but you receive 25 per cent of all prescriptions written by physicians —and as the above statistics dramatize, you spend far more per person than any other age category for the purchase of medicines. Moreover, Medicare does not cover any part of the cost of self-administered drugs taken when you are not in a hospital or nursing home.

But, if you are buying prescription drugs and over-the-counter medicines, you may derive some comfort from the Bureau of Labor Statistics estimate that these costs rose only 25.8 per cent between the late 1960s and 1970s as against an 86.1 per cent upsurge in living costs generally. But you're also using the services of a physician and you well may have had to go to the hospital too—and in that same ten-year span, the medical care portion of the Consumer Price Index soared 109.3 per cent. The squeeze from all three sources at the same time is what has been hurting you so much.

Yet, even in the face of the appallingly heavy burden on this age group, millions of our elderly men and women least able to carry the load are wasting huge sums because of ignorance, misunderstanding, or just plain carelessness.

One study by the U. S. Food and Drug Administration disclosed that less than half the public even read non-prescription labels, although most believe the labels "contain enough information to tell them how to use the product safely." According to another FDA study, consumers rank labels at the very bottom of the sources of information about new non-prescription medicines—behind advertising, and recommendations of friends, relatives, druggists, and doctors. According to still another study of hospital outpatients ranging in age from seventeen to seventy-eight, physicians discovered a "surprisingly wide range of interpretations, a high frequency of misinterpretations, and a significant potential for therapeutic failure" because of the inability of the patients (of average income and educational background) even to interpret and follow correctly the label directions on prescription medicines.

This is obviously dangerous as well as wasteful. Thus, to protect your health and pocketbook:

• Always read the labels carefully—once when you pick up the container, and again when you are ready to take the proper amount of the medication. Pour liquid medicines so you do not smear the directions. Never transfer medicine to another unlabeled container. If you have any doubts about directions, check with your doctor.

• Keep an accurate count of your daily dosage (so you'll not have to ask yourself whether or not you took your two-o'clock pill or whatever by measuring out each day's dosage when you get up in the morning. Put the dosage in a separate container on which you have copied the original label. Don't experiment and take only the recommended dosage of both prescription and non-prescription medicines.

• Don't waste what may be an extremely expensive medicine—such as an antibiotic—by discontinuing its use because you feel better. If you don't take the medicine for the recommended number of days or even weeks, you'll probably get sick all over again and have to spend money for a new series of pills.

SPECIAL DRUG TIPS FOR THE ELDERLY

If you are sixty-five years of age or older, and you are typical of the millions spending a far, far greater proportion of your disposable incomes for drugs than any other segment of our population, here are special tips designed for *you*, to help reduce your medicine bills to a sensible minimum:

(1) Ask your pharmacist or physician for additional instructions if you do not fully understand the directions for taking whatever medicine has been prescribed.

(2) Always keep in mind that caffeine, nicotine, alcohol, and some foods can affect the way medicines work. Be sure to inquire whether you should avoid using any foods, beverages, or other medicines while taking your prescription.

(3) If you have difficulty opening safety-type containers, ask the pharmacist for an easy-to-open container. The law permits the pharmacist to dispense your medicine in an easily opened bottle only if you or your physician ask specifically for this. Of course, keep medicines out of the reach of children at all times.

(In the late 1970s, a federal judge ordered a nationally known drug company to recall 1.5 million bottles of popular vitamin tablets because many adults were unable to put the child-proof caps on properly. This marked the first such recall under the Poison Prevention Packaging Act.)

(4) Call your physician at once should any new symptoms or side effects occur while you are taking the drugs.

(5) Never mix different tablets and capsules together in one container. Keep each medicine in its own container and make sure that the container bears the correct label. This is especially important while you are traveling.

(6) Never swap medicines with someone who believes he or she has the same condition that you have. It can be extremely dangerous to take prescription medicines prescribed for someone else.

(7) Each time you leave your physician's office or your pharmacy, ask yourself and answer the following questions:

• What are the names of each of my medicines?

• What is each medicine supposed to do to help me in my condition or to ease my discomfort?

• Exactly how and when should I take the medicine?

• Is there anything special I should be doing or I should avoid doing while I'm taking these medicines?

• Are there any side effects for which I should be on the alert and which I should report to my physician immediately?

If You Need Help with Mental Health Problems

About one in ten persons in the United States will at some time develop a form of mental or emotional disorder requiring professional care. On any given day of the year, nearly 400,000 persons are in state, county, and private mental hospitals.

The American public spends literally billions of dollars each year on the treatment and prevention of mental illness; the economy loses many more billions because of the decreased productivity of mental patients. Over all, it's a problem costing more than $20 billion a year in our country alone.

CHOOSING A MENTAL HEALTH PRACTITIONER

If you are looking for a mental health practitioner, your search probably will be undertaken during a time of great personal stress and an illness emerging in forms ranging from mild depression to a severe psychotic episode.

Of every three admissions to public and private mental health facilities, two will be to tax-supported public mental health facilities, even though these facilities comprise less than half the facilities available. Of total admissions in the past, 47 per cent have been to inpatient services, 50 per cent to outpatient facilities, 3 per cent for day treatments.

The highest rates of admissions have been and will be in the wage-earning adult category, with those between twenty-five and forty-four years of age accounting for 38 per cent of admissions. Running a close second will be the youngest members of our population: 36 per cent under twenty-four years old. With advancing age, admissions drop substantially—to a rate of just 5 per cent for those over sixty-five.

Since these totals do not include Americans receiving mental health care from a family physician, nursing home, private therapist, or at a general hospital without a formal psychiatric unit, an informed estimate is that an enormous 12 million Americans are now receiving traditional "medical" mental health services.

If you're among the millions seeking a mental health practitioner, you almost surely will be utterly befuddled by a dizzying array of titles, licenses (given by the state in which the professional practices), and certificates (bestowed by professional organizations or training institutes). Here, therefore, is a guide to titles practitioners can hold, the type of help offered, the costs.

(1) Most states license a mental health professional according to the degree he or she holds. For instance, a psychologist will hold a Doctorate in Psychology; an M.S.W. has a Master's Degree in Social Work; a psychiatric nurse is an R.N. with

a Master's Degree in that specialty; a psychiatrist is an M.D. who has completed a psychiatric residency at an accredited institution. These are definitions of the National Institute for the Psychotherapies, a New York-based institute representing professionals in many fields of therapy.

(2) Be wary if you see the term "licensed psychotherapist" or "licensed psychoanalyst" on a practitioner's stationery. Professionals may refer to their therapeutic work as psychotherapy and frequently call themselves psychotherapists but "psychotherapist" and "psychoanalyst" are broad, general terms, not licensed titles.

(3) The term "certified" psychotherapist is legitimate, though. This means that after receiving the basic degree, the practitioner has done postgraduate work at a training institute which usually takes four more years of part-time study and supervised clinical practice. At the end of this training period, he or she can properly claim to be a certified comprehensive psychotherapist or, in the case of a psychoanalytic institute, a certified psychoanalyst.

Typically, the more training the professional has, the better the quality of the care you will get. But, of course, there are other factors to be weighed when you are choosing a mental health practitioner at this critical moment in your life.

SELECTING THE APPROPRIATE TYPE OF TREATMENT

The most important thing to look for on your first visit to any health care professional is the feeling of being understood, of having made emotional contact.

Since this initial visit can be traumatic, you should be able to discuss dollars-and-cents issues freely, to ask straightforward questions about the therapist's methods and credentials.

The therapist may have a fixed fee. If it is too high for you, he or she may refer you to another in your price range—or, perhaps, agree to work with you on a sliding scale basis. Often, a therapist with a fixed fee will make allowances for your special circumstances or needs.

In addition to the fee, what about the therapist's policy on missed sessions? Some therapists require you to pay for a missed session unless you give twenty-four hours' notice of cancellation. Also at the start of your therapy, decide how you will handle vacations—both yours and the therapist's. And how will any of the therapist's increases in fees be taken care of? If you are paying up to the limit of what you can afford, this can be a crucial question.

Also, what about the method of payment? Will it be every month, or at the conclusion of each visit? Do not be startled if your therapist requests payment at each visit.

"Psychotherapists probably have a tougher time than most collecting fees," reported the newsletter *Psychotherapy Economics,* after a special study of fees. "The main reason is that their fees, and any discussion about them, tend to become intertwined with the therapy process."

Because this is so touchy an issue with both your therapist and you, have it clearly spelled out before you even begin.

Finally, ask to which professional organization your therapist belongs. For instance, a social worker would be listed with the National Association of Social Workers, a psychiatrist with the American Board of Psychiatrists.

Probably, though, the most befuddling aspect of psychotherapy is the wide range of techniques—"modalities"—available.

• Psychoanalysis, originated by Sigmund Freud, and the analytical psychology of C. G. Jung are perhaps the best-known systems. Psychoanalysis, explained the board chairman and founder of the National Institute of the Psychotherapies, emphasizes "obtaining an insightful and penetrating connection between the individual's present-day psychological difficulties and problems . . . unsuccessfully dealt with in the formative years of life."

• Behavior therapy concentrates on changing destructive behavior patterns— for instance, curing such irrational fears as claustrophobia (fear of enclosed places).

• Gestalt means "the whole," and its emphasis is on experiencing the here-and-now more freely and spontaneously.

• Integrative therapy is specifically tailored to your needs, can reduce the length of treatment and thus the cost.

• Primal therapy takes you back to your earliest memories, especially the traumatic ones, encourages you to relive them consciously and let them go.

• Transactional analysis (originated by Eric Berne, author of the best-selling *Games People Play*) clearly identifies your three personality states—parent, adult, or child—to help you change your behavior relatively quickly in the way you wish.

• Group therapy can include any of the above systems, or a combination of several. It provides a laboratory where group members can practice being connected with themselves and others, allows for direct expression of both positive and negative feelings in the group.

"The difference in techniques can be filtered down into two basic approaches," according to Al Yassky, Ph.D., founder of the Mental Health Help Line in New York. "There is cognitive 'thinking' therapy with an emphasis on figuring things out. This would include psychoanalysis and transactional analysis. Then there is feeling therapy which would include primal and gestalt."

And there are many other therapies which work on triggering your emotional responses to help you to overcome your mental illness. Here I've covered just a few of the many techniques offered.

HOW MUCH MONEY AND TIME ARE INVOLVED IN TREATMENT?

How much you can expect to pay and how long your treatment will last depend on your condition and the treatment chosen for you.

The fee for your initial psychiatric consultation would depend on the time involved and might be slightly more than the hourly therapy charge. A majority of patients will be treated in less than twenty sessions. For some, longer-term psychotherapy will be needed. For a few in psychoanalysis the number of sessions may range from three hundred to five hundred, although this depends on the patient and the progress, and the span for you could vary considerably from these totals.

A GUIDE TO FEES

If you're paying $1.00 to $5.00 at a public clinic for mental health therapy, you're probably not getting the best care available. Psychotherapy is a field in which experience counts for a lot, and at low-cost clinics, you're likely to get professionals who may be very bright but who are usually inexperienced.

But if you're paying $50 a session or more—which patients in big cities were paying in the late 1970s—you are not getting proportionately better care than if you are paying, say, $35.

The fee structure in the late 1970s for mental health care broke down as follows, according to *Psychotherapy Economics:*

• 6 per cent of all psychiatrists and psychologists charged $25 or less per session;

• 20 per cent of psychiatrists and psychologists charged $50 or more per session;

• the largest proportion—36 per cent—charged $40;

• for group sessions, the average fee was $20 per person per session (usually for 1½-hour sessions);

• but 6 per cent of the reporting professionals charged $10 or less, while another 6 per cent charged $30 or more;

• fees set by MSWs (professionals with a Master's Degree in Social Work) and others ran somewhat lower than psychiatrists and psychologists; as the 1980s neared, 3 per cent charged $40 or less per private session; 19 per cent charged $25 or less; only 4 per cent charged $45 or more; and not one was in the $50 range.

Obviously any kind of private psychotherapy is expensive, even for one session a week. The highest-priced psychiatrists can cost you $200 a month or more for private sessions, the lowest-priced in this category were running $80 to $100 a month. For group sessions, the least costly was about $40 a month or less with an MSW.

If your limited income requires it, you can spend as little as 50 cents per session at community mental health clinics.

But there are disadvantages: overcrowding may necessitate shorter treatment; you usually cannot choose your own therapist; there is not much choice in the form of treatment; and if there is any choice, treatment is usually decided for you.

Nevertheless, public mental health facilities offer qualified, usually young, therapists and produce excellent results.

Private facilities—either clinics or institutes—frequently operate on a sliding scale system for payments, although the bottom of this scale is nowhere near as low as the public facility. The $10 to $45 range of fees for private and $10 to $25 range for group treatment, commonplace as the 1980s approached, make them essentially middle-class facilities. (Generally, a clinic is a facility offering therapy exclusively, while an institute trains therapists and sometimes does research.)

Before you start a program of treatment at either a clinic or an institution, ask at least these specific questions:

• What can you honestly afford and what are the fees?

• If a sliding scale is offered, what are the special rates and do they fit your finances?

• Do you qualify for a special low rate at the National Institute for the Psycho-therapies and other institutes because you are an eligible student or retired?

• Who are the therapists at these places? Graduate students studying for advanced degrees? Postgraduates in training with the institute? Psychiatric residents?

• In addition to the training background of the therapist, are you compatible and do you feel you'll work well together?

• By what criteria are therapists assigned to patients? Are you free to choose another therapist if you don't feel comfortable with the first?

• What is the range of treatments (modalities, or "schools" of therapy) at the institute? Some institutes are specifically set up to practice only one therapeutic treatment; others are fairly comprehensive. This availability of choice can be exceedingly important to you if you are not sure what kind of treatment you want or you need.

WILL HEALTH INSURANCE HANDLE PART OF THE TREATMENT?

Since the cost of care by a mental health professional is no trifling matter, the issue of your insurance coverage becomes vitally significant to you—one of possibly 12 million who will be seeking medical mental services each year.

In general, only group policies cover psychiatric help. It is extremely rare for a policy covering you as an individual to provide this type of care.

Should you have to be hospitalized, Blue Cross will cover a specific number of days of care in most cases, with thirty days most common, but some Blue Cross plans covering more. After release, if you hold a major medical policy, this policy will help you with the cost of your outpatient care.

Since policies and state regulations vary greatly, check at once with your Blue Cross plan or insurance company about any particular mental health care you are receiving and the extent of its coverage.

Medicare: If you are sixty-five or over and eligible for Social Security benefits, or collecting Social Security disability benefits, then you probably are eligible for Medicare coverage. But Medicare covers care by a psychiatrist only—that is, an M.D. The setting is not an issue; it can be office, clinic, or institute. Visits to a psychiatrist's office are coverable up to $250 a year.

Query your Medicare office about details.

Medicare covers hospitalization for psychiatric reasons, but the extent of coverage varies, depending on whether you are admitted to a general hospital or to a psychiatric hospital.

Care in a general hospital is covered in full for the first sixty days except for a hospital deductible, which is equivalent to the average cost of one day's care. For the sixty-first to the ninetieth day of a stay in a general hospital, the patient is responsible for a copayment equal to one quarter of the deductible amount.

Should a Medicare beneficiary use up the entire ninety days of hospitalization in a benefit period, he or she may draw upon a reserve of sixty additional days but will be responsible for paying a copayment amount for each day used that will be equal to one half the deductible amount.

You pay the same deductible amount and copayments if you are admitted to a psychiatric hospital, but Medicare will pay for no more than 190 days of care in a psychiatric hospital in your lifetime. Once you have used those 190 days, Medicare won't pay for additional days in a psychiatric hospital even if you have some of your sixty reserve days left, or even if you are in another "benefit period."

There is another rule, too, that affects you if you are in a psychiatric hospital at the same time you become eligible for Medicare. Any days that you were hospitalized in the fifteen-day period before your Medicare eligibility began must be subtracted from the days you could otherwise use in your first benefit period.

A "benefit" period begins when you are first admitted to the hospital under Medicare and it ends after you have been out of a hospital or other institution providing skilled nursing or rehabilitation services for sixty consecutive days.

Medicaid: If you are receiving any form of social assistance such as welfare, or if you are under twenty-one or over sixty-five, live in a city such as New York, and ordinarily earn enough income to maintain yourself except when illness occurs, you may be able to receive assistance under the Medicaid program. The same applies if you are between twenty-one and sixty-five and handicapped; you also may be eligible for assistance under Medicaid.

All psychiatric care is covered under this program in full, if the provider of care meets certain state eligibility requirements. Care by a private psychiatrist in his or her office is coverable if the psychiatrist has an M.D.

Care in an institute or clinic by an M.D., Ph.D., or M.S.W. (Master's Degree in Social Work) or other professional is coverable if the institute or clinic is state-certified and, in addition, there is a certified psychiatrist on the staff.

For full information on all these technical but so vitally important dollars-and-cents details, consult your local Medicaid office at your earliest feasible date.

Some final basic rules and guides:

• The extent of mental illness is far greater than most of you even suspect, with on top of the millions of Americans now receiving traditional "medical" mental health services, millions more desperately needing the care but either unaware of where to go or how and fearing they cannot afford the help.

• Fees for mental care vary widely, with an impressive range of fees in existence and costs flexible enough to cover almost any valid need.

• Just as fees can be adjusted to fit your income and circumstances, so mental health care facilities are so varied that they too can be adjusted to meet your needs. You can be treated at public or private facilities; in private sessions or in group therapy meetings; you can get treatments daily, weekly, monthly, or however you and your chosen therapist agree is best; you can go to a clinic or an institute or, of course, to an individual professional at an office, nursing facility, or hospital.

• Even more varied is the type of treatment available to you. And costs as well as your individual mental illness may play a tremendous part in the decisions you make here.

• The time to find out all the facts is before your illness progresses to the point where decisions on your treatment are taken out of your hands.

IS IT POSSIBLE TO SHOP FOR THESE SERVICES?

Yes, it *is* possible to shop for psychiatric services.

By checking with your local health and welfare departments, religious leaders and others, by just looking in the telephone directory, you will discover the range of low-cost psychiatric services available in your community. And they may be of great money-saving value to you.

HOW TO BEAT OUR $50 BILLION HANGOVER

THE STAGGERING BURDEN

The United States today is suffering from a national alcoholic hangover which claims thousands of lives and is costing a staggering $40 to $50 billion a year.

Of this, the National Institute on Alcohol Abuse and Alcoholism estimated in a special report to Congress $20 to $30 billion is the price our economy pays for lost work time; $13 to $14 billion for health care and medical payments, and over $5 billion for auto accidents.

More than 10 million Americans (one in ten over the age of eighteen) are suffering from the disease of alcoholism, according to the National Council on Alcoholism—and most of our alcoholics are not on skid row, but at work, at least some of the time.

Absenteeism is two and a half to three times as great for alcoholics as for non-alcoholic workers. Alcoholics average three times as much sick pay as others, and their accident rates also are much higher. Many alcoholic workers lose a full month of working days each year.

Even more devastating is the towering problem of "on-the-job absenteeism"—where an alcoholic employee may fritter away hours each morning recovering from a hangover or sleep off a multi-martini lunch in the local movie house.

Moreover, alcoholism is everywhere and does not respect corporate names or job descriptions. An estimated 45 per cent of the alcoholics in this country are professional or managerial workers; the typical alcoholic has been at his job twelve years; he is between the ages of thirty-five and fifty-four, the key productive years; his alcoholism has been present but unrecognized for years.

If you are the typical alcoholic, you are almost surely spending tremendous time and effort trying to disguise your problem so cleverly that neither you nor your company will become aware of its seriousness. Yet the cost of your illness to you *and* your company (and, of course, also your family) may be enormous—in terms of loss of time, mismanaged business deals, bad decisions, missed promotions, etc. And continued drinking not only can get you fired from your present job but also can become a towering barrier in your search for another.

Whether or not *you* admit you are an alcoholic, you have at least one enormous incentive to seek help—and that incentive is your desire to hold your job.

WHERE DO YOU FIND HELP?

A first step is to inquire whether your employer offers counseling and/or rehabilitative services to employees. Hundreds of companies do, although most of these programs reach only a small number of alcoholics.

Your best single source of help is Alcoholics Anonymous, which for years has been carrying the alcoholism problem almost single-handedly—and, incidentally, very successfully. Today AA is available to virtually all who wish to use its services, with 32,000 local groups in 92 countries. AA's key resource is an army of over a million of recovered alcoholics who stand ready, around the clock, to give free help to anyone with a drinking problem. AA meetings are now being held not only in churches and synagogues and regular meeting halls but also in such places as airplane hangars and at state reformatories.

Other sources of help have been multiplying too. To be specific:

• The National Council on Alcoholism, set up in 1944, has 190 affiliates around the country which provide information, referral, and other services. Its headquarters office in New York City is operating a pilot employment counseling program for recovered alcoholics. Similar services may in time be offered by the NCA affiliates, as well.

• Since the National Institute on Alcohol Abuse and Alcoholism was set up in 1970, dozens of local programs have been set up and funded to treat alcoholics. The Institute's National Clearing House for Alcohol Information can provide you free-of-charge with a State-by-State listing of facilities where treatment for alcoholism is available. Write: P. O. Box 2345, Rockville, Maryland 20852.

• More and more general hospitals are now treating alcoholics. A few have set up special alcoholism services.

• City after city has been setting up a variety of alcoholism programs.

• Blue Cross and other insurers have begun to add hospitalization and also outpatient benefits for alcoholics.

• The military services, too, are beefing up their programs for alcoholic servicemen.

CARING FOR OUR ELDERLY

WHAT WOULD YOU DO?

What would you do if this problem came before you—or a member of your family?

You, one of your parents, a grandparent, or other close relative or friend is over sixty-five:

faces increasingly severe medical, nutritional, living, and other problems;

knows that something has to be done—but is uncertain as to just what;

and is worried about the costs as well as terrified about the unspoken agony of change.

By the late 1970s, 11 per cent in the United States were over sixty-five, one in every nine, and that number may increase by another third—by 8 million—by the end of the century. *Between the late 1960s and late 1970s, spending for the elderly grew from one fifth to one third of the federal budget—from about $40 billion to $153 billion. These were the amounts being spent for Social Security, Medicare, and Medicaid payments, federal retirement, and other benefits.*

Once it was customary for elderly persons no longer able to live alone or with families to enter a safe decent place to live where medical care was available. With the cost of nursing home care now running into five figures annually per person, families are giving second thoughts to that "solution."

Throughout the United States an increasing range of services is being made available for elderly people—and an urgent search is on for better services at less expense.

The shocking estimate is that perhaps 10 per cent of the elderly are institutionalized too soon because of lack of knowledge of available alternative facilities.

According to a report of the Congressional Budget Office in the late 1970s, home health care and day care services were available to between 300,000 and 500,000 persons. At the most conservative estimate, the demand for home health care exceeded the supply by 1.5 million people. The demand for personal care homes, sheltered living arrangements, and congregate housing also far outshadowed the estimated need. By the most conservative measurement, over 1 million persons were not being served.

THE ALTERNATIVES AVAILABLE TO YOU

What then are the choices available to you if you are facing the agonizing problem?

Home care program: An elderly person remains at home, receiving homemaker assistance, outpatient medical care—and, if and when needed on a temporary basis, emergency admission to a full-care institution. (See pages 482–83 for more information about home health care.)

Day hospital and treatment centers: This is a new concept, which enables older people to remain at home with all the advantages of geriatric and general medical facilities. The trend is growing.

Apartment residences: There are several throughout the United States. Kittay House in the New York area is a pioneering experiment in independent living with a service package including two daily meals, weekly maid service, other assistance.

Homes for the aged: These are run by voluntary, non-profit agencies, with the largest institutions offering the broadest range of services. All residents share the high overhead, in part, but not every resident needs all the services available.

Proprietary or profit-making residences: These provide similar services to apartment residences operated by institutions—rooms, meals, programs. Such homes usually do not provide medical services. As a result, their costs often are less.

Even though Medicaid and Medicare pay the bills for a majority of nursing home residents, it is essential that you become aware of your alternatives. For instance, in recent experiments, this thought-provoking pattern has emerged:

First, the elderly person uses the home care program; then the apartment residence; then, as required, he or she moves to intermediate or extended nursing care. Ask yourself:

Can this person truly benefit from institutional living? Is he or she capable of adjusting to special requirements?

NEW WAYS TO CARE FOR THE ELDERLY

You're among countless millions of Americans if you have an elderly parent or relative who is not sick enough to be in an expensive nursing home but yet needs care now and then. As an indication of the scope, health authorities estimate that the vast majority of the 23 million Americans over the age of sixty-five have some kind of illness, ranging from minor arthritis to total incapacity.

What can you do to minimize the costs to you? Plenty. But you must know where and to whom to turn—and thus, the following rundown of relatively inexpensive (or even free) community programs to which the elderly can now turn for help.

• Under the sponsorship of the United Hospital Fund, Project Ezra goes into tenements on New York's Lower East Side to seek out old people not receiving needed medical care. About eighty such people were being visited weekly by medical teams. Can your community use this as a model?

• Under Tele-Care, a nationwide system, volunteer callers make daily phone calls to people who live alone. One call by a volunteer at Herrick Memorial Hospital in Berkeley, California, saved the life of an elderly diabetic who had gone into a coma after she had given herself too much insulin. Can you copy this?

• In many cities, people suffering from Parkinson's disease, disabilities caused by a stroke, etc., can enroll in group programs, such as those at Baltimore's Mount Sinai, which provide day care, rehabilitation services plus meals, transportation.

• "Meals on Wheels" delivers well-balanced cooked meals at modest cost to shut-ins too sick or disabled to cook or shop. The volunteers also report any problems to local hospitals.

One of the really great results of the Older Americans Act of 1973 is the Nutrition Plan for the Elderly. It is more than just a hot meal program; it also provides a place for the elderly to meet and talk with others. In some cases, this is even more important than the meal. Friendships—even marriages—have developed out of these contacts and many older Americans have become volunteers, cooks, transportation assistants, and outreach workers and thereby have been brought back into the mainstream of society.

As of the late 1970s there were more than a thousand nutrition projects serving meals at 9,166 centers in every state. About 85 per cent of the meals were being served at the centers and the remainder to the homebound. The nutrition centers were located at senior centers, in religious facilities, housing complexes, restaurants, and other facilities. Sixty-seven per cent of those served meals were in low-income categories, but elderly people in all income levels are eligible to participate and are expected to make a contribution toward the cost of their meals if they can afford it.

• To help the elderly fill out the often bewildering forms involved when receiving Medicare, Medicaid and/or health insurance benefits, Boswell Memorial Hospital in Sun City, Arizona, conducts monthly seminars. This is an easy one for you to adopt.

Then there are the special home-care programs designed to keep elderly citizens out of nursing homes and hospitals. By the late 1970s, there were more than 3,000 programs, providing 2 million home care visits a year to people of all ages —not only by physicians but also by registered nurses, physical therapists, and psychologists.

As an illustration of what's being done—and what you might use as models for your own community or neighborhood—the Chelsea Project of New York's St. Vincent Hospital took care of elderly patients in their homes for about one quarter the average cost of nursing-home care. The saving to the community: almost $500,000 per year.

As another, regular doctor's visits provided for elderly, chronically ill patients through Los Angeles County-USC Medical Center. Some seventy resident physicians and ten staff doctors were available seven days a week, twenty-four hours a day. In one year alone, physicians made approximately ten thousand house calls in a fifty-mile area.

Finally, four hospitals and two skilled nursing services in Tucson, Arizona, successfully cooperated in providing a unique system of day-care services for hundreds of older people. About 94 per cent of the participants would be in nursing homes if the program didn't exist.

The Johns Hopkins Hospital in Baltimore trains families so that they can take in old people with health problems—so the old people can live in a home setting instead of going to a nursing home.

The "care-givers" learn to provide basic care in about six or eight classes and then are paid for their services. They are taught basic nursing skills, the importance of diets, the arrangement of living quarters for the convenience of all those living with the family, and the emotional needs of the patients.

After training, the care-giver, the individual or the family taking in the patient, comes to the hospital and meets the patient. The nurse on the floor gives special instructions about the care of that patient. The homes and the applicants are checked out, of course, and the Fire Department inspects the home for safety and general cleanliness.

The families are free to choose which patient they will care for and the patient can choose whether or not he or she wants to be cared for by a particular family or person. A social worker and a nurse make follow-up visits to the home and the patient comes back to the hospital for clinic appointments.

The central point is that as many as four out of ten of the elderly now in nursing homes *don't need round-the-clock nursing services*. More workable home-care programs could prevent the sending of as many as 2,500,000 elderly Americans to nursing homes, save at least $200 million a year now being spent on these homes.

Start out by asking your physician, hospital, or social service agency what home-care programs are available in your community. Many are covered by Medicare, Medicaid, Blue Cross, and other insurance carriers, and local welfare agencies.

Fill in the gaps by using programs mentioned in this report as models for your own care systems. Copy, refine, remold.

Help your parent or relative live in comparatively good health with a sense of personal dignity. And do it at a low cost.

SHOPPING FOR NURSING HOMES

But let's say that like millions of other deeply troubled Americans, you've tried just about everything to ease the physical and mental limitations of your aged loved one: group housing programs, day care centers, visiting nurses, therapists, homemakers and home health care aides, outpatient care, "meals on wheels" to your loved one's home.

Finally, you're faced with the brutal task of finding a nursing home that will give your relative or friend affectionate and top-notch care. But you're far more frightened about this than you would have been a few years back, before the scandalous revelations in the late 1970s about nursing home abuses, the unscrupulous actions and outright cheating of proprietors, the high costs concealing horribly inadequate care.

What can you, what should you do?

First, you must learn thoroughly the kinds of nursing care available to you and conditions under which Medicaid and Medicare will pay the costs and to what extent.

Nursing home costs in a single year as the 1970s ended projected to be a shade over $15 billion. Between 1960 and 1979, nursing home revenues increased 3,000 per cent!

The Medicaid program by itself continued to account for roughly one half of nursing home industry revenues. The share paid by Medicare was small by comparison—only 3.3 per cent. Private contributions accounted for 43 per cent.

You'll find homes that specialize in personal care, others that focus on health and nursing care, still others that cater to residents with a wide range of needs.

Barely will you find the home's services clearly defined in the name of the facility. For instance, two frequently used terms in the professional health care field are "skilled nursing facility" and "intermediate care facility"—terms springing from the U. S. Government's Medicaid and Medicare programs under which bills for a majority of nursing home residents are paid.

To be more specific, Medicaid pays for an intermediate care facility, which caters to those who need health care service plus some nursing supervision along with assistance in eating, dressing, walking, and other similar essentials. There is no reimbursement from Medicare for intermediate care.

Medicaid also pays for care in a skilled nursing facility where round-the-clock services are available. A physician must approve this type of care for an applicant to be eligible for this phase of the Medicaid program.

Medicare will assist in paying up to a hundred days in a skilled nursing facility after a patient has spent at least three days in a hospital and a physician has recommended admission with ultimate Medicare approval. The patient must, however, require skilled nursing or rehabilitation services on a daily basis.

Medicaid may pick up charges after a hundred days for those eligible for both programs.

When either Medicare or Medicaid is involved, the U. S. Government sets standards for services, safety, and sanitation. States must obey the federal guidelines for inspection and certification of nursing homes receiving reimbursement under either program. All other nursing homes come under state inspection and approval standards.

If a patient is eligible for Medicaid payment, seek a home certified for intermediate care or a skilled nursing facility. If a patient is eligible for Medicare, look for a home certified as a skilled nursing facility. Many homes are certified in both categories and are eligible for payments under both Medicaid and Medicare.

• In shopping for a nursing home, ask to see the facility's licenses and certificates. Examine them. Are they current?

• Since all states require licenses, avoid any home that isn't licensed. Also avoid any home where the administrators fail to produce a current license on your request.

• Check whether the home is approved by the Joint Commission on Accreditation of Hospitals, a non-governmental group which inspects hospitals and nursing homes. The JCAH certification is a good indication of quality, although not necessarily a certain one.

• Make a list of homes in your area, getting names from your health department, medical society, senior citizens organizations, social service groups, Social Security office, clergyman, physician, hospital, nursing home association, and welfare office. Check with friends who have had experiences with any home, good or bad.

• Make preliminary calls to the homes, asking about participation in Medicare, Medicaid, state inspection. Visit and meet the owner or administrators, check on licenses, details on charges not covered by basic rates, status of coverage if an admission is projected under Medicaid and/or Medicare.

• Inquire about specific medical care, hospital association, physician availability, medical record bookkeeping, therapy, fire safety, and accident prevention facilities. Do not use a home that has not been inspected and cleared for fire safety in the past year.

"INTANGIBLE" FACTORS IN NURSING HOME CARE

"You can't teach people to be kind. It has to be there to begin with." With this seemingly simple but actually profound observation, an outstanding administrator of one of the nation's better nursing homes zeroed in on a major intangible involved in finding the proper nursing home for a loved one whom you must sign into a nursing facility.

The care of aged patients is heavy labor and it is difficult to find top-notch professionals to take on this backbreaking task. The burden of the disoriented and confused individual is often heartbreaking for any assistant. The combination of a tough and often emotionally destructive job can upset even a sympathetic aide. And while the irritation of overloaded aides cannot be condoned, it is easily understandable.

Thus, the "intangible" factor of innate kindness. And thus the search by progressive nursing homes for programs to help patients not lose touch with reality and to check any regression.

• As for you, the relative or friend in charge of the brutal task of finding a nursing home that will provide loving and high-level care, choose one in a location that will be convenient for visitors. Visitors are vitally important.

• Also take into consideration whether the patient prefers the country to the city or vice versa.

• Note the physical setup, check the rooms. Each should open into a corridor and have a window. If it is a semi-private room or room with four beds, there should be a drapery for privacy, a nurse call bell and drinking water at hand. Essential are a reading light, drawer space, and a closet.

• Do not underestimate the point of compatibility with roommates. If a roommate is a moaner, for instance, the other patient could have trouble sleeping.

• Rooms should be designed wide enough for wheelchairs. Toilet facilities should have the same provisions. Check for grab bars near the toilet. Is there a nurse call bell within reach? Are there non-slip floors in the bathtub or shower?

• Find out if the facility has an isolation room for anyone with a contagious disease. Special purpose rooms should be set aside for physical exams or therapy.

• Hallways should be wide enough to permit two wheelchairs to pass. Handgrip railings on either side are a "must."

• Try the so-called sniff test for odors associated with lack of cleanliness or inadequate care of the patients.

• Investigate the dining room, visit the kitchen, check for proper refrigeration facilities and usage, examine the menus.

• Does your loved one want the service of a private family physician? This may be a factor in your home selection. Is the home close to the hospital to which the family physician is attached? How often does the nursing home's own physician visit? Is there a doctor always on call for emergencies? What about arrangements for dental services? Podiatrists? Specialists in eye care? What do these services cost in addition to the basic charges?

• Check the ratio of nurses and aides to patients. A ratio of three to one would be considered very good. Since the aides are in most frequent contact with patients, inquire about the training program, ongoing training, performance evaluation.

• Investigate the rehabilitation program, therapy treatment, social services. What about the availability of hair grooming, other services of this type? These can be enormously helpful.

• Look carefully into safety features, fireproofing, attractiveness of surroundings.

• Tour the facilities during the mornings, afternoons, evenings, and all meal times. Be thorough.

• Recognize that the more services that are needed, the greater will be the financial burden. Get the facts straight on basic charges and additional costs of extras. Be sure you understand Medicaid and Medicare benefits. If your loved one is ineligible for any government financial help, make sure you know all the angles about any private health insurance coverage and whether any costs of nursing home care are included.

None of this will be a welcome experience for any of you. But the sooner the questions are asked and the sooner you have the correct answers, the easier will be the emotional trauma of separation as well as the unavoidable financial load.

WHERE TO COMPLAIN

If you have a complaint about a nursing home, for whatever reason, tell it to:

(1) The nursing home administrator.

(2) Your local Social Security district office. It functions as a clearinghouse for complaints about all nursing homes, whether or not they receive government funds.

(3) The patient's case worker or the county welfare office if the patient is covered by Medicaid.

(4) The state Medicaid Agency if the home is certified for that program.

(5) The state Health Department and state licensing authority.

(6) The nursing home ombudsman if such an office has been established in your community.

(7) The state board responsible for licensing nursing home administrators. (Get address information from the welfare department.)

(8) Your congressmen and senators. (Address congressmen at House of Representatives, Washington, D.C. 20515; senators at United States Senate, Washington, D.C. 20510.)

(9) Your state and local elected representatives.

(10) The Joint Commission on Accreditation of Hospitals (875 North Michigan Avenue, Suite 2201, Chicago, Illinois 60611) if the home has a JCAH certificate.

(11) The American Health Care Association (1200 15th Street, N.W., Washington, D.C. 20036) if the home is a member.

(12) The American Association of Homes for the Aging (1050 17th Street, N.W., Washington, D.C. 20036) if the home is a member.

(13) The American College of Nursing Home Administrators (4650 East-West Highway, Bethesda, Maryland 20014) if the administrator is a member.

(14) Your local Better Business Bureau and Chamber of Commerce.

(15) Your local hospital association and medical society.

(16) A reputable lawyer or legal aid society.

TEST YOUR CHANCES OF STAYING ALIVE

REVEALING QUESTIONS

How often do you exercise? Daily, three times a week, weekends only, rarely or never?

How much do you smoke? Not at all, five cigarettes a day, one half to a pack, two packs or more?

What's your weight as against your height and age?

What are your cholesterol and triglyceride levels? Your blood pressure?

Do you drink an average of more than three ounces of alcohol daily?

Have such between-meal snacks as potato chips, peanuts?

When was your last physical checkup?

The medical bill for circulatory diseases in our country is now an almost unbelievable 10 per cent of our national bill for all illnesses. At the top of all killers in the United States are diseases of the heart and blood vessels.

The loss to the nation in terms of income and productivity from deaths caused by heart attacks tops $1 billion a year, with half of it lost in the top-productive age group of forty-five to sixty-four. The bulk of the loss to the nation in terms of income and productivity from persons becoming ill of heart conditions and unable to work also is in the most productive age group of forty-five to sixty-four. The convalescence period can stretch to many months.

The economic costs involved in heart and blood vessel diseases alone—not to mention the emotional and other costs—are vast. What's more, our costs are jumping instead of sinking. We are actually falling behind other nations in keeping our men alive longer.

You surely are aware of the danger of a high-cholesterol level, although this is not the terrible bugaboo it has been pictured. New discoveries in another blood fat—triglycerides—have added a second warning device, with the two comprising what are called blood lipids. In some patients cholesterol is found to be relatively normal, while blood triglyceride count is dangerously high. (Question to you: Has your physician ever had your triglyceride count checked? Interpreted it with your cholesterol level?)

During the German occupation of Scandinavian countries, when butter, milk, and cream became scarce, the incidence of coronary artery diseases went way down. But the disease rate went way back up after World War II when these foods again became abundant—"pretty good proof on a large scale," say physicians, "that there is something to dietary control."

Stress aggravates high blood pressure and circulating blood rate—high-risk factors in heart diseases—but exercise lowers them.

And sex is also a very good exercise.

We can't do anything about any adverse family histories we may have, but we can do a great deal about every life-shortening activity or life-lengthening hint. Just by honestly answering the few revealing questions in the quiz alone, you're helping yourself to stay alive.

HEALTH HOAXES

Down through the ages mankind has been plagued by the charlatan with his claim of being able to heal the sick, rejuvenate the aged, to make that which is drab a thing of beauty forever. In fact, health hoaxes extend so far back into history that they appear on the first known written medical record, the Ebers Papyrus (circa 1500 B.C.), which contained a prescription for preventing baldness. This ancient Egyptian remedy included, among other things, fats of the lion, hippopotamus, crocodile, goose, serpent, and ibex.

It didn't work—and not because anything was left out.

Things have not changed so much in the 3,479 years since this old Egyptian gyp. Today, we are still under a constant bombardment of come-ons, exaggerated advertising, gimmicks of dubious value, and pure-and-simple fraudulent claims, ranging over a wide area of products which affect your health.

Following is merely a sampling of what to watch out for. If it serves only to put you on guard against a hoax in the health sphere, I will have accomplished my aim.

DIET COME-ONS

You are young, you are in normal health, you want to look attractive—and you are overweight. It is to you that ads such as these are directed:

"I lost 54 pounds of ugly, dangerous fat!! . . . in only THREE short months!! without a doctor, a diet or calorie counting."

"A definite weight loss of 10–20–50 pounds, even 100 pounds or more may be accomplished in a short time."

The ads go on to claim that you, the overweight person in normal health, may continue to enjoy such foods as cream of mushroom soup, malted milks, spaghetti, pizza, and french toast—and still lose significant amounts of weight in "a short time." A key to these amazing achievements is a "miraculous formulation" involving pills for which you pay "only" $20 for a 120-day supply.

Then comes the fine print, along with the pills for which you have already paid a substantial sum. As it turns out, the spaghetti isn't really spaghetti, the pizza contains no pastry, and the malted milk must be made with skim milk or buttermilk.

Thus it is to you that this warning must also be directed:

Any claim of a cure for overweight which does not even mention dieting is fraudulent. No type of diet pill or program available today can achieve significant, permanent weight loss within a specified period unless the use takes strict dieting measures as well.

Tens of millions of overweight Americans are spending hundreds of millions of dollars a year on an unprecedented array of gadgets, gimmicks, pills, and potions to help them lose weight. Thousands of U.S. physicians are now devoting part or all of their practices to the problem of obesity. No one knows just how much money is being wasted on useless weight reduction schemes or how many of the obesity doctors actually manage to achieve major long-term weight reduction for their patients.

But it is known that the Food and Drug Administration in Washington has year after year seized millions of doses of multicolored "rainbow pills" used in weight reduction schemes on the grounds that they are either useless or dangerous. And the FDA and the American Medical Association have declared over and over that many of today's so-called diet pills may cause serious side effects. As just one illustration, in the late 1970s, the FDA warned dieters that the use of a shocking number of liquid protein supplements had been linked to the deaths of women. Although the precise cause of the deaths was not determined, a dozen of the women had been dieting under medical supervision. Although no deaths had been reported among women trying to lose weight on solid protein diets, the prestigious *New England Journal of Medicine* cautioned that the solid-protein, low-carbohydrate diet might be no less risky.

You cannot lose weight on a diet of whiskey and whipped cream.

You cannot expect reducing pills to have any long-term effect—without the usual dietary restrictions and change in your eating habits.

You cannot "melt away fatty tissue" by wearing special tight-fitting plastic belts, blouses, and slacks.

To be blunt: there is no such thing as "effortless" reducing. Loss of pounds is directly dependent on using up more calories by exercise than you consume in food and drink.

Calories *do* count. For any major weight reduction program, you should enlist the help of a physician.

If you are among the millions with a problem of overweight, here are four fundamental rules for facing your problem and avoiding the many useless weight reduction programs now available:

(1) Avoid all "miraculous" formulas and high-powered pills recommended by *anybody*.

(2) Stay away from all gimmicks such as "slimming underwear" and vibrating machines if they are advertised as capable of achieving a permanent loss of X number of pounds in X number of days, weeks, or months.

(3) Be suspicious of any weight reduction schemes involving special pills, "diet cocktails," or self-hypnosis if they do not also involve a lowering of your calorie consumption.

(4) In sum, if you have an overweight problem, consult your physician or your psychiatrist and follow your doctor's advice—which easily might include the suggestion that you join a respected local weight-reduction club or organization operating under medical supervision.

"STOP SMOKING"

A three-day supply of a new product which is supposed to help you stop smoking costs close to $3.00 a package at my local drugstore. If you complete the entire four-week program recommended in the directions, your total investment might add up to $20 or more.

This is a big bargain if you manage to quit smoking, of course. If you are a three-pack-a-day addict, you will spend many hundreds of dollars a year to support your habit—and you can add hundreds of dollars more to this if your spouse chain-smokes too. Also, today's non-smoker may be eligible for non-smoker life insurance at considerable savings in premiums.

Would-be non-smokers are now spending tens of millions of dollars to buy the products of today's "Stop Smoking Industry"—ranging from pills to gum, lozenges, "pacifiers," stop-smoking books, etc.

Are you among the majority of U.S. smokers who, according to the U. S. Public Health Service, have made at least one serious attempt to quit smoking? How much money have *you* spent on stop-smoking products—or on losing bets with other would-be non-smokers?

If you are gulping sugar pills and concoctions of ordinary spice such as ginger, licorice, clove, coriander—as well as pharmaceutical preparations—to stamp out your cigarette craving . . .

If you are taking up fake cigarettes—dubbed "smokes" or "adult pacifiers" which contain such non-nicotinic ingredients as menthol crystals, cabbage, lettuce, or just flavored cigarette paper—to keep your nervous hands busy and permit you to "smoke without fear" . . .

If you are falling for suggestive stop-smoking phonograph records . . .

If you are devouring no-smoke tablets and how-to-stop-smoking pamphlets . . .

Here are a few straight guides for you:

Despite the welter of new labels, there are no really "new" substances on the market to help you stop smoking. Old ones simply have been dressed up or combined to appear new.

The three standard types of anti-smoking medications now available are: the nicotine substitute (e.g., lobeline sulfate), which alleviates cigarette craving; substances which make smoking taste unpleasant (e.g., silver nitrate); and local anesthetics (e.g., benzocaine), which numb the mouth and reduce desire for the puffing part of the smoking ritual.

Many of these products do, in fact, help you quit smoking temporarily. But none does the job permanently without a generous dose of will power on your part. Most are harmless, but a few cases of nausea, stomach pain, and loss of appetite have been reported as side effects.

A far more effective and more economical approach could be the Stop Smoking clinic. The programs at the better clinics are drawn up by physicians and psychologists. Most conduct regular meetings and seminars, some patterned on the highly successful Alcoholics Anonymous concept. You may or may not pay a small fee to attend the meetings.

QUACK MEDICAL DEVICES

If you have a naggingly painful disease or if you become seriously ill, you could well join the millions of Americans who each year spend billions of dollars for all forms of medical quackery—most of it for worthless and possibly dangerous gadgets and machines.

To illustrate with one horror story, tens of thousands have fallen for a contraption claimed capable of diagnosing and treating conditions ranging from cancer to chicken pox and jealousy—on the basis of a single drop of blood from the patient. When federal officials ran their own test, the machine failed to detect the fact that it was being fed blood samples from a turkey, a pig, and a sheep rather than from three children. Nevertheless, once a "diagnosis" had been made, the practitioner arrived at a special "vibration rate" for each patient and treated the patient's disease by radioing back into the patient the supposedly "normal" vibration rate. For those unable to visit the practitioner's office it was said that healing vibrations could be broadcast to reach anywhere on earth.

To illustrate with another equally shocking tale, suffering Americans have paid as much as $475 for an elaborate machine claimed to be able to cure cancer, diabetes, heart disease, and a wide variety of other serious conditions by "attuned color waves" shined on parts of the body. The primary medical qualification of the machine's inventor was an "honorary M.D."

To illustrate with still another, desperate Americans have paid large sums to another practitioner who claimed he could diagnose and cure anything from double vision to a "bone" in the colon—simply by using an elaborate-looking radio device.

Then there are devices—for which trusting (or despairing) souls among us have actually spent money—which "charge" your body with electrical energy and determine the "wavelength" of your cells so that the wavelength can be rearranged to restore your health and magnetize or demagnetize you depending on your needs.

There's even a machine which can, in the words of its inventor, "straighten out people who walk lopsided." Most quack devices are fitted with impressive-looking dials, switches, buttons, flashing lights, other space-age trimmings.

Why do countless thousands of Americans, including the intelligent and well educated, fall every year for this unbelievable array of quack gadgets and machines?

The victim of a devastatingly painful, progressive, or fatal disease often will find a quack cut-and-dried diagnosis and sure "cure" completely irresistible—and the very fact that we are living in an era of such medical "miracles" as laser surgery, heart transplants, cardiac pacemakers, nylon arteries, and artificial kidneys has made the machines of the quacks believable. What's more, federal regulation of medical devices has not kept pace with the proliferation of the devices—even legitimate ones.

Thus, basically, it comes down to this: you must protect yourself and your friends and relatives (particularly if they are aged) from the medical quacks.

And your basic protections are:

Stick with a legitimate, trained, medically qualified physician.

Avoid any quick, easy "secret" machine.

Be acutely skeptical of any electronic wonder or formula advertised by a practitioner who claims that the medical establishment is afraid of the "competition" of his sure cure.

CANCER QUACKERY

Today, more than half of all cancers can be cured if they are diagnosed in time and treated properly by surgery, radiation chemotherapy, or a combination of these. In many types of cancers, such as skin or cervical cancer, the odds are even better: the vast majority of cases can be cured if they are detected early and correctly treated.

Yet thousands of cancer victims continue to refuse or postpone to a fatal degree legitimate treatment and to seek instead the services or elixirs of the cancer quack. Too frequently huge sums are spent by frightened elderly citizens who are already on the brink of bankruptcy and who may not have the disease to begin with.

Why? The key reasons, says the American Cancer Society, are the cancer victim's fear of incurability, fear of the high cost of treatment, fear of the prospect of radical surgery, fear of radiation treatment. In view of the number who develop cancer in our country and the odds on survival, many people are quite understandably quick to suspect its dread presence.

The cancer quack can be a devastatingly expensive economic drain as well as a devastatingly dangerous physical threat. Thus, here are the key guides to spotting the quack.

First, you must know that any qualified specialist will invariably conduct standard tests for any cancer at a recognized hospital or clinic and he will plan a course of therapy according to the results of these tests.

But the quack will:

• Neither perform recognized tests nor be associated with a recognized hospital or clinic—although the tests he does perform will invariably produce a diagnosis of cancer. He very well may advise against biopsy to verify cancer, using the excuse that "it will only spread the cancer."

• Boast that he has many well-known patients, including politicians, lawyers, movie actors, writers, etc. (This, incidentally, may be perfectly true.)

• Produce testimonials from former patients who claim he has cured their cancer. No reputable doctor advertises accomplishments or boasts in print about his famous patients. And, if you look behind the testimonials carefully, you may find those quoted died shortly after they authored the glowing accounts of their cures.

• Claim, when challenged to put his treatment to a scientific test, that he "won't get a fair trial" because the medical establishment is prejudiced against his method. Or he may challenge the medical establishment to test his product—then either fail to deliver a sample or insist on designing the test conditions himself.

• Insist, perhaps to help justify the high cost, that his cancer cure is "secret"— something no reputable member of the medical community would do for obvious reasons.

Until a universal cure or cures for cancer are found, our most potent—and also least expensive—weapons against this dread disease are regular medical checkups and awareness of the seven widely published cancer warning signals.

THE PSYCHOQUACK

If you are a relative or friend of one of the nation's 5 million mentally retarded citizens, you are acutely aware of the heartbreaking, frustrating search for effective treatment of this most widespread and debilitating of all medical problems. You also must be aware of the extent to which parents of the retarded are tempted by the mental health quack, both here and abroad.

There are no hard figures on how many tens of millions of dollars Americans are spending each year to line the pockets of quacks, unqualified psychotherapists, and untrained marriage counselors. But in the past, parents of retarded children have been reported to be laying out $1,000 apiece to have their children injected with worthless serum. In other forms of pseudo-professional treatments by fringe practitioners, ex-mental patients have been recruited as "adjunctive therapists" to treat other patients, "nude psychotherapy" has been practiced by borderline psychotherapists, and any number of quacks have managed to persuade parents that their retarded child's problem actually was an allergy, a vitamin deficiency, a low blood sugar level, or some other condition which could be treated relatively easily.

The mental health quack today is often difficult to detect by an average citizen, who probably doesn't know the difference between a psychologist, psychiatrist, psychoanalyst, and psychotherapist. Many of the fringe practitioners are forming quasi-medical organizations, adopting scientific jargon, and using a smattering of accepted therapeutic techniques.

Why the upsurge in this form of quackery? How can you tell a quack from a non-quack in this field?

A first reason why mental health quackery (and particularly quackery aimed at the retarded) is thriving now is the simple fact that there is a growing market for the treatment of retardation. Every year in our country an estimated 3 per cent of all babies born are retarded babies.

Another is that the rate of spontaneous "cures" ranges up to two thirds for some types of mental disturbances. Thus, even the quack can claim a high percentage of successes which would have occurred anyway.

Still another reason is the severe shortage of qualified mental health professionals in the nation. Waiting lists at mental health facilities are frequently long; treatments are often stretched out over months or years and seldom result in what could be termed complete "cures." This frustration alone may easily translate into an open invitation to the fringe practitioner to move in.

Finally, state laws today are grossly inadequate in the regulation of practitioners in this field. There are still many areas of the United States in which an utterly unqualified person can legally hang up a shingle designating himself a psychologist, psychotherapist, or marriage counselor.

To protect yourself against the psychoquack, *beware of anybody who:*

- offers services for which his or her training is obviously inadequate;
- makes exaggerated claims, not backed up by the medical literature, about their treatments;
- uses articles in the popular press, frequently written by the person himself, as advertisements for his treatments;
- touts his treatments as more "natural" than other kinds of treatment;
- turns directly to threats and lawsuits rather than debate in professional circles as an answer to criticism;
- offers to administer various treatments outside the United States because the "cures" are banned in this country.

In sum, always deal only with qualified physicians and other trained mental health personnel.

ARTHRITIS "CURES"

Would you pay $200 or more to sit in a "uranium tunnel" at an arthritic "clinic" in the Midwest (actually an abandoned uranium mine)?

Or would you buy a "magic spike" containing less than a penny's worth of barium chloride for over $300 and wear it as an arthritis cure?

Or attempt to treat your painful joints by bathing them in colored light with a gadget consisting of a light bulb and a plastic lampshade? Or try to help your arthritis simply by attaching a metal disk to a joint, then placing a cylinder, connected by a cord to the disk, into cold water? Or would you risk taking a powerful drug developed in another country and banned in the United States because its side effects include internal hemorrhaging and mental derangement?

Perhaps you would, if you were suffering enough from this often excruciatingly painful disease. For the fact is that today's extraordinary array of nostrums and devices promoted as capable of curing or relieving arthritis seems to be as tempting as ever to the victims, who include the well educated and well-to-do as well as the ignorant and poor.

Unproved "bootleg" drugs and devices are coming into this country via a thriving underground network of quackery, dispensed sometimes by the patients themselves. Americans are traveling, by the planeload, to other countries for arthritis "cures" banned here.

In some cases, potentially useful and legitimate treatment is delayed because the arthritic sufferer is so involved with quacks. Also the quacks are aided by the fact that in rheumatoid arthritis, the most serious form of the disease, pain comes and goes intermittently, so over the years the quack can frequently claim success.

The copper "arthritis bracelet" staged a spectacular comeback in the 1970s with countless hundreds of thousands of Americans spending from $1.00 to $10 to $100 for this form of copper jewelry on the claim that it will help prevent and/or cure this disease. Although precise statistics are unavailable, this single slice of the "anti-arthritis business" accounted for tens of millions of dollars in annual sales and covers copper jewelry ranging from tie clips to cuff links, from bracelets to anklets.

And this occurred despite the fact that the Post Office Department, the Federal Trade Commission, and the Food and Drug Administration repeatedly condemned as fraudulent any claims that copper bracelets would cure arthritis (although admittedly, in most cases, no written claims are actually made). Also utterly phony are any claims that two copper bracelets, one worn on each wrist or each inner sole, create a special therapeutic "circuit."

Nevertheless, just because arthritis now affects one out of every seven Americans and the number of sufferers is growing by 1 million a year, any suggestion of relief is immediately seized upon by millions and immediately mounts into big-time money.

The total economic cost of arthritis is approaching a record $15 billion a year, estimates the Arthritic Foundation of New York—in the form of medical care costs and wage losses, lost homemaking services, and premature deaths. On top of this the "hidden" costs—in the form of spending on worthless arthritis "clinics" and treatments—are approaching $950 million, almost four times the yearly costs in the 1960s.

As you would expect, financial outlays for fake cures and phony treatments swell with the number of arthritis sufferers. Worthless cures tagged by the Arthritis Foundation now cover white metal and plastic "electrogalvanic" bracelets; expandable "magnetic" bracelets; special electrical vibrators; hyper-immune milk; high-priced "magic spikes" containing a few pennies' worth of various vitamins, laxatives, and ointments; bootleg drugs illegally imported here from Mexico and Canada.

I will not downgrade one tiny bit the anxiety of a person suffering from great pain or a terminal illness to try anything at any cost in the hope of relief or cure. But the tragedy is that you might delay legitimate diagnosis and treatment, you might waste the most precious time as well as money in your commitment to quacks.

The bright fact is that we are at a moment in medical history when nearly three out of four cases of crippling arthritis can be headed off by early detection and proper treatment. The merciful prospect is that we are near major breakthroughs in drugs to treat arthritis.

Thus, if you are among the 31.6 million sufferers or close to an individual who is, heed these warnings:

• Be wary of any person who uses "testimonials" from former patients as a lure and avoid "home cures" not prescribed or at least approved by your own physician.

• Don't postpone conventional treatment or abandon an ongoing program so you can patronize an unconventional course of therapy.

HEARING LOSS—AMERICA'S MOST WIDESPREAD MALADY

• The most widespread malady in the United States today is loss of hearing—affecting more Americans than heart disease, cancer, blindness, tuberculosis, venereal disease, multiple sclerosis, and kidney disease put together. More than 15 million Americans are afflicted and at least one out of every fifteen of us is involved, according to the National Institutes of Health.

• Of the total, a full 3 million are school-age children. The malady is more prevalent among the elderly, however, with about half of the millions needing attention over the age of sixty-five. What's more, the problem is getting worse—if for no other reason than the fact that we are living longer and deafness among the elderly is growing.

• Yet, we pay less attention to this disability than to any other ailment. Millions refuse even to admit that they have any impairment; others know it but ignore it; still others fail to follow up on treatment that could be of immense benefit to them. An estimated 11,500,000 Americans suffer from uncorrected hearing loss; most could be helped by available medical, surgical, or amplification treatment.

• This is much more than an intensely personal problem. It has major economic-social implications, for hearing loss directly costs our nation at least $500 million annually, estimates the Department of Health, Education, and Welfare, just for the education, management, and compensation of those with impaired hearing. The same HEW study puts the yearly loss of earnings due to communicative disorders at a massive $1,750,000,000!

If you suspect you are afflicted:

(1) Recognize that nearly everyone with uncorrected hearing loss can benefit from medical, surgical, or amplification help.

(2) Find out what kind of hearing loss is your problem. There are two major types—conductive and sensorineural, or "nerve," hearing loss. Conductive hearing loss can often be traced to wax blocking the ear canal, infection of the tissue lining the middle ear. You will find that conductive hearing loss often can benefit from medical or surgical help.

(3) If yours is "nerve" loss, though, your problem is in the inner ear and caused by damage to the hair cells, nerve fibers, or both. This type is generally not medically correctable and is most commonly helped by a hearing aid. More than 95 per cent of all hearing aid users have a sensorineural hearing loss.

(4) Your first step is to consult a physician, preferably an ear specialist—called an otologist or otolaryngologist. The specialist will diagnose the cause of your hearing loss and may be able to help you medically or surgically.

(5) If a hearing aid appears to be the answer, your doctor probably will refer you directly to a hearing aid specialist or first to a clinical audiologist, who is trained to measure hearing and to help rehabilitate and counsel you if you have a loss.

(6) When you are referred to a hearing aid specialist, be sure he is reliable. While most states have licensing regulations which establish qualifications and standards for hearing aid specialists, check whether the specialist will: stand behind the product he sells; clearly define for you the guarantee or warranties; be able and willing to provide quick and efficient repair of your hearing aid when necessary.

HOW TO SHOP FOR A HEARING AID

The standards, manufacture, labeling, and dispensing of hearing aids finally were brought under federal regulations in the late 1970s. Issued by the Food and Drug Administration, they required:

• A statement from a physician that a hearing aid may help a patient. This is necessary for the purchase. (The FDA estimated in 1977 that more than 10 million with hearing impairment never had medical evaluation.) The supportive medical evaluation must have taken place within six months before the purchase of a hearing aid.

• While buyers eighteen years of age and older may waive the medical evaluation, a hearing aid dispenser must not encourage a prospective buyer to do so. There are approximately 1,200 hearing aid models in the market place. Older people account for 60 per cent of the market; children make up another 12 to 13 per cent; the balance are sold to people between eighteen and sixty-five.

• Manufacturers to provide for each model of hearing aid a detailed brochure telling you what the aid will and will not do; how it works; how to use it. The brochure must make it clear that an aid can only amplify sound; it cannot restore hearing or prevent further hearing loss.

• A hearing aid dispenser to give you a brochure to read before completing a sale. The brochure must warn you to consult promptly with an ear specialist or other physicians if any of these problems appear to exist: dizziness, ear deformity, pain, or fluid damage, rapid onset of hearing loss, foreign body in the ear.

• Sellers of hearing aids to keep records for three years after the sale, including the medical statement or waiver.

But the fact remains that hearing loss can result from a number of conditions and diseases for which a hearing aid may not be helpful. And no matter how tight the federal regulations, you bear the ultimate responsibility to protect yourself:

(1) First, above all, visit a physician for an evaluation. This is necessary because hearing loss is only a symptom of a disease. In some cases, it might even be caused by a tumor. Or your condition might be improved by drugs, surgery, or even a change in diet. An audiologist may recommend further testing. Or you may be referred directly to a hearing aid dispenser.

(2) Comparison shop for an aid just as for any other product. Compare full costs, including one year's service.

(3) Check warranties. Manufacturers usually guarantee an aid against factory defects or breakdowns for two years. All dealers must now give you a thirty-day trial period, during which you may return an unsatisfactory hearing aid and get most of your money back. (The dealer may keep up to $50 per aid.)

(4) Before you buy, try this self-test: How is the sound quality? Does it help you understand speech in quiet places? In noisy places? Is the aid comfortable? Are the controls easy to operate?

(5) Recognize the differences in costs and complexity. Hearing aids cost an average of $350 apiece in the late 70s.

(6) To check on reputable dealers, contact your local Better Business Bureau; the National Hearing Aid Society, 20361 Middlebelt, Livonia, Michigan 48152, or a nearby local or state chapter of the society. Or write or phone toll-free the Better Hearing Institute, 1430 K Street, N.W., Washington, D.C. 20005, (800) 424-8576.

(7) As the 1980s approached, about forty states had licensed hearing aid dealers. Ask the National Hearing Aid Society or the Better Hearing Institute (addresses above) whether your state is among them. If so, find out whether the dealer from whom you are considering buying your aid is licensed.

LIFE-SAVING MEDICAL EMBLEM

"I was driving home from work, hit an icy spot and crashed into a pole. The police pulled me from what was left of the car. On the way to the hospital, they found my Medic Alert bracelet saying I am a hemophiliac and diabetic. Thanks to the warning on my Medic Alert emblem, I am alive today. The doctors were able to know immediately what blood type I have and attended to the diabetic shock." Letter from a Medic Alert member.

"I was admitted to the hospital for severe migraine and dehydration with petit mal seizures and was totally incoherent. Although a friend had taken me to the hospital, he was unable to provide my medical history. My bracelet gave the admitting physicians the necessary information for immediate treatment as well as Medic Alert's phone number to receive additional information on my particular medical needs." Another testimonial from a member with epilepsy and allergies to drugs.

"When I was in San Juan, Puerto Rico, I had an epileptic seizure on the street. The police started to take me to jail—they thought I'd been taking drugs—when they noticed my Medic Alert bracelet. I was immediately taken to the hospital." Still another letter from one of the hundreds of thousands of members of Medic Alert Foundation International, a non-profit, charitable organization which for over seventeen years has been helping to save the lives of people whose specific medical needs are not apparent.

You may be one of the 40 million Americans—one in five—who run the risk of receiving inappropriate or incomplete medical treatment during medical emergencies. That's the astounding total, says the American Medical Association, who flirt with death because they do not wear emergency medical identification.

A well-known corporation president is dangerously allergic to penicillin, for instance. He insists his Medic Alert bracelet has saved his life at least twice. Hospital emergency rooms often receive patients who are unconscious or are in a state of shock and are unable to communicate. Since physicians cannot elicit essential emergency information, they follow the most expedient medical treatment to help save their patient's life.

But, if the patient is allergic, the administering of a particular drug could be precisely the wrong measure. Or, again through no fault of the physician, life-sustaining medications may not be provided to those with congenital diseases.

There are more than two hundred reasons why people should become members of Medic Alert, or a similarly respected organization. In descending order, the top six reasons are diabetes, allergy to penicillin, taking anticoagulants, wearing contact lenses, neck breather, and epilepsy.

The system includes an emblem—worn on the wrist or around the neck—which has the internationally recognized caduceus and the words Medic Alert emblazoned in red on the outer side. On the reverse side are engraved the member's hidden medical situation (up to four lines), his or her file number, and the phone number of Medic Alert's emergency answering service in Turlock, California. Emergency personnel throughout the world can call this twenty-four-hour number collect to obtain additional information on the patient. There is a backup wallet card too. The emblem is internationally recognized, is registered in forty-one countries in addition to ours, and the foundation has affiliate organizations in fifteen foreign nations.

If you're traveling, the system does give you the security that language barriers will not prevent proper medical treatment, should you need it fast.

With this kind of lifeguarding service, it is not surprising that hundreds of medical and civic organizations have endorsed it—including the American College of Emergency Physicians and the American Nurses Association. In fact, Nevada

Blue Shield provides a complimentary lifetime membership to its subscribers if the subscriber's physician requests it.

The cost of lifetime membership is minor. If you are among the one in five who needs the service, write to Medic Alert Foundation International, Box SP, Turlock, California 95380.

How to Shop for Eyeglasses or Contact Lenses

who does what in eye care

Hazel Johnson has spent $500 and bought seven pairs of glasses and she still cannot see as well as the doctor she went to promised she would. With 52 per cent of Americans using prescription eyewear today, there are hundreds of thousands of Hazel Johnsons around. You well might be one of them.

"I'm tired of the fuzzy world I live in," says Mrs. T. Nicks. To her, the hardships of poor vision far outweigh the money and time she has wasted trying to find the proper eyeglasses.

"I will need a seeing-eye dog in another year unless I find a doctor who knows and cares," adds Mary Steele—a comment that goes to the heart of the problem of knowing how to find quality vision care and eyewear.

Q. *Do you know the difference between an optometrist and an ophthalmologist? Almost 50 per cent of our population doesn't, and many don't even know what kind of doctor they go to for eye care.*

Ophthalmologists are doctors of medicine (M.D.). They concentrate on treating eye disease with drugs or surgery, also prescribe glasses, and some fit contact lenses as well.

Optometrists hold the doctor of optometry (O.D.) degree, requiring a minimum of six or seven years of college and professional-level education. They examine eyes to diagnose vision problems and detect eye diseases. They prescribe glasses, contact lenses, low-vision aids, and sometimes vision therapy for such problems as crossed eyes, lazy eye and learning disabilities.

Q. *How do you know if you are going to "a doctor who knows and cares"?*
The best way to tell is by the examination you get.

It should take thirty to sixty minutes, involve a battery of tests to determine: your eye health; your ability to see sharply and clearly at near and far distances; the ability of your eyes to work together as a team; your ability to change focus easily from near to far and vice versa; the presence or absence of such common vision problems as nearsightedness, farsightedness, or astigmatism. If you are over thirty-five or your health history indicates it, a glaucoma test, too.

The basic cost of your first office visit can be quoted in advance and you should find out the costs and what the basic exam covers. The total cost of your exam often cannot be quoted in advance, because the first tests may lead to others.

When your vision exam results in a lens prescription you take your written prescription to an optician—a technician who fills doctors' prescriptions—or you can get your glasses from an optometrist who acts as a buffer between you and the optical lab and can require the lab to redo your glasses if the lab makes an error.

Q. *How should you order glasses?*

Ask yourself: do you want the fashionable oversize lenses, and can your prescription be ground into them without distorting your vision? Your doctor can give you the answers. Do you want glasses or plastic lenses? Plastic lenses are much lighter but they require more careful handling and scratch more easily than glass.

Do you need tinted lenses for comfort or for sunwear? Lightly tinted fashion or comfort lenses will not double as sunglasses. Nor should they be worn while driving at night.

Q. *What about prescription sunglasses?*

Most of us who wear glasses need sun protection, but you well may find the clip-on sunglasses cumbersome, heavy, unsightly, and sometimes damaging to the surface of prescription eyewear.

Prescription sunglasses should screen out 75 to 90 per cent of available light. They should be made of quality glass or plastic, be of a medium or dark gray or green tint, and be large enough to keep light from getting around them. Frames should be sturdy and comfortable, with sidebars that do not interfere with your side vision.

If you work outdoors or on or near water or snow, you will need the type of tinted glass lenses that screen out both ultraviolet rays and infrared rays. Or you might want to try coated "mirrored" sunglasses which are great against intense glare.

If you are typical, you will get adequate protection from tinted glass or plastic lenses that screen out ultraviolet rays; the sun-sensitive sunglasses that grow darker in sunlight; or, for glare, polarizing lenses.

KNOW-YOUR-EYEGLASSES QUIZ

The prescription lens industry has soared into the multibillion-dollar range in recent years as the number of us wearing prescription lenses—both in eyeglasses and in contacts—has reached more than half of all Americans; technological breakthroughs have vastly broadened the contact lens field; and prices have been fluctuating widely, both up in eyeglasses and down in contacts.

This quiz will help guide you to buy the right type of help for you and to pay the least price for the most quality.

Q. *What about bifocals and trifocals?*

If you are getting bifocals or trifocals, you must be certain your prescription is placed precisely in the right spots within the lenses. If it is not, you may have difficulty seeing and you will be adding to your risks of an accident while you are walking, using stairs, or driving.

You can help avoid this problem by telling your doctor your tasks that involve seeing both on and off the job. Do this at the time he or she is giving you a thorough eye exam. In this way, the lenses can be designed to meet your needs. The traditional placement of the near prescription on the bottom and the distance prescription on top may not be satisfactory for you.

Be extremely wary of multifocal glasses advertised at appealingly "bargain" prices.

Often, those prices cover only a standard bifocal lens, which may not meet your needs. Some optical shops have been known to change the type of bifocal lens the doctor prescribes to a poorer quality and less expensive type without telling the consumer, warns the American Optometric Association.

Q. *Can you have your new glasses mailed to you?*

You can—but don't. Pick up your new glasses yourself, for they must be adjusted to your head and face. If you are not looking directly through the optical center of your lenses, you may experience distorted vision and a pulling sensation in your eyes. Multifocal wearers may find it impossible to wear maladjusted glasses.

Q. *What about ready-to-wear glasses?*

Ready-to-wear reading glasses sold without a prescription for $5.00 to $10 a pair in some department stores will be a waste of money for most of you. These mass-produced glasses are simple magnifying lenses mounted in frames.

The glasses just will not work in the overwhelming majority of cases, because both lenses are identical. Seventy-five per cent of all of us wearing glasses need different lenses for each eye.

They never correct astigmatism, which causes blurred vision in about 75 to 80 per cent of all Americans who need eyeglasses. They come in only one size (people's heads do not). The size refers not to the frames but to the distance between the optical center of the two lenses.

Q. *Is it wise to shop for glasses or not to shop?*

By comparison shopping, you almost surely will find a far larger selection of frame styles than in your doctor's office. You probably will save money.

But the big advantage, I repeat, in getting your glasses from your doctor is that the doctor stands between you and the optical lab which fills your prescription. If your prescription is filled incorrectly—which happens more often than you might suspect—the doctor has the leverage to require the lab to redo your glasses. The doctor represents much more business to the lab than you do.

Q. *What about group vision care plans?*

Mounting awareness and concern about the need for eye care and the costs involved have spurred many consumers, labor unions, and companies to consider group vision care programs. And it is highly likely that these group programs will become part of the fringe benefit demands of powerful unions as the 1980s progress.

By eliminating or reducing the cost factor, these plans make it possible for you to receive the vision care you otherwise might neglect—care which easily can be translated into enormous dollar as well as health savings for the individual, the companies involved, and the economy as a whole.

Group programs, though, will not wipe out the need for you to know how to find that "doctor who knows and cares" about you and your individual problems. It always will be up to you to judge the quality of the care you receive.

SHOULD YOU BUY CONTACT LENSES?

More than half of all Americans (52 per cent) now wear prescription lenses— with eyeglasses still the overwhelming choice. But contact lenses are rapidly gaining in popularity, with the number of contact lens wearers approaching 14 million in the late 1970s, the percentage of wearers more than triple the level of a decade ago, and annual spending on contact lenses up to a third of a billion dollars.

What's more, as the contact lens industry has boomed, prices have been falling —in contrast to increases in the prices of eyeglasses. You could buy the least expensive hard contacts, for instance, at a price of less than $100, as the 1980s neared.

The range in hard contact lenses was from a low of $99 to $350 a pair; the range in soft lenses, from $150 to $450.

So wide was the spread in prices for contacts and eyeglasses, in fact, that restrictions on the advertising of prices were lifted specifically to spur competition that would force down charges.

If you're a typical contact lens wearer, you're a woman between the ages of seventeen and twenty-four. But with new technological developments and advances in contact lens design, materials, prescribing and fitting, the appeal of contacts is broadening to young men as well as to people over age fifty.

Of all contact lens wearers, 73 per cent are female; nearly half are age seventeen to twenty-four; another third or so are in the twenty-four to forty-four bracket; approximately 10 per cent are forty-five or older. Today's ratio of female contact lens wearers is around 60 to 40 against 80 to 20 a short time ago.

By the end of this century, an estimated half of the 100 million Americans who wear eyeglasses will have switched to contact lenses—hard or soft, or a new mix in between. Technological breakthroughs are accelerating. Semi-hard and soft tinted bifocal lenses are being tested by the industry for more comfortable fit and better vision. Studies are well under way, too, for contact lenses that can be worn twenty-four hours a day and for a lens material that will permit the eye to breathe normally through the lens itself.

Your growing acceptance of contacts has resulted in a surge of mail order sales, but mail order contact lenses may damage your eyes. A slight deviation from a perfect fit can cause the lens to ride incorrectly. So minute are the measurements that you may have to return for several visits after you receive new lenses for adjustments. These visits and individualized instructions plus practice in applying, removing, and caring for the lenses should be included in the total cost of the lenses to you.

With mail order lenses, you may have no one to whom you can go back to check the lenses.

Computer programs are being developed to select lens designs based on vision performance and eye measurements. The computer helps doctors "try out" a lens design on a computer model of the patient's eye. An immediate feedback can suggest modifications before prescribing the actual lens specifications.

It was only thirty years ago that lens experts began working with hard plastic lenses. The soft plastics were introduced in the late 1950s, came to market as recently as in 1971. Now as new discoveries speed up, millions more will be turning to these lenses.

But be on guard!

Before buying, get all the facts.

Make sure you can wear contacts successfully.

Ask the doctor's policy concerning patients who cannot, for whatever reason, adapt to their new lenses.

Find out in advance what the total fee will be for your contacts and what the fee covers (how many tests? followup visits? what about cleaning equipment? insurance against loss or damage?).

BEWARE OF "BARGAINS" IN CONTACT LENSES

Since all professionals now can advertise their services, daily ads in newspapers the nation over are trumpeting bargains in eyeglasses, in general, and in contact lenses, in particular, which seem almost unbelievable in comparison with prices to which we have become accustomed. But are all these bargains really bargains?

To find out for yourself, weigh each of these points with great caution before you buy:

• Does a $99 price for contact lenses include a complete eye exam by a licensed eye specialist?

• Are all essential accessories included (solutions, cases, the like)?

• Are you given individual instruction in the art of applying lenses or are you taught these steps in a group?

• Are the lenses tested on your eyes before you accept them, to make sure you are being helped to get correct vision and to obtain maximum comfort?

• Is there an extra charge for alterations?

• Is a physician available to see you in an emergency, or is there a long wait, and if a doctor is not available, who makes the adjustments that might be imperative?

• Are all necessary follow-up visits included in the initial fee? Over what period of time?

• How long has the firm selling the contacts been in business, and has it established a reputable name in that period?

• Are there any additional charges after the initial fitting of your contact lenses?

The answers should be implicit in these hard-hitting questions.

You may be deeply impressed by the sharp reductions in the costs of both soft and hard contact lenses—but you may not be aware that most of the cost for lenses is absorbed by professional fees and allied services—and that the actual cost of the lenses themselves is a relatively small part of the total charge to you.

If you ask your prescribing doctor for a cost breakdown, you will become acutely aware that low costs advertised by some high-volume optical shops and mail order firms are for the lenses alone and that these prices are about the same as those charged by highly responsible physicians providing you with full services.

Before your contacts are prescribed, your entire health history should be in your doctor's records, for certain ailments—allergies, diabetes, high blood pressure—can affect the results of your vision tests. So can certain prescription and non-prescription drugs you may be taking.

Your eyes should be thoroughly examined for signs of eye disease and other abnormalities that might preclude your wearing contacts. This means an examination of the exterior of your eyes and lids as well as the interior of your eye where the natural state of your blood vessels may be seen. If symptoms of other diseases are detected, you should be referred to another health care professional for additional tests and treatment, if needed, and your prescription for contact lenses should be delayed until all signs say it's okay to go ahead.

Your eye coordination and eye muscle function should be checked to make sure your eyes are working together as a team.

If you are over thirty-five, or if other symptoms of your case history in general indicate a need, you should be given a tonometer test for glaucoma.

The quantity and quality of your tear flow should be carefully checked; your eyelid tension and corneal sensitivity should be tested; your blink rate and depth should be observed; the ability of your eyes to change focus easily from near to far and vice versa should be determined.

To any ophthalmologist or optometrist among you reading this, my warnings may sound sickeningly simple—almost akin to a kindergarten teacher's lessons to pupils in the first week of school. But the blunt fact is these warnings are desperately needed by Americans seeking bargain-priced eye care. You risk not only throwing away your money on "bargains" that are useless but actually harming your eyes.

SUNGLASSES VS. FUN GLASSES

Of equal concern to you—either a misinformed or uninformed consumer—is the distinction the industry makes between sunglasses and fun glasses. It well may be that you are paying for protection you don't need or are not getting the protection you are paying for. These guides may be of valuable help to you.

Sunglasses contain lenses made of prescription-quality glass, prescription ground and polished. Fun glasses, which are made with plastic lenses, do not filter out infrared rays, as contrasted with optical glass filters.

Often, fun glasses are lower priced. But as frames have been styled up for high fashion and become key fashion accessories, fun glass prices have climbed rapidly. Frequently, their lens colors—ranging from pastels to bright blues and yellows—are not necessarily the best for your protection.

When buying sunglasses:

(1) Select a neutral gray or sage green for best color perception and minimum color distortion.

(2) Don't buy a cheap frame. Examine it with as much care as you would give to the purchase of regular eyeglass frames. Sunglasses must withstand months of outdoor use and abuse.

(3) Test your glasses at the store before buying. Hold the glasses to an overhead fluorescent light which reflects on the inside of the lens. Move the glasses so that a reflection travels across the lens. A wavy or distorted lens will not do.

(4) Look into a store mirror while testing the glasses. You won't be able to see your eyes with top-quality sunglasses.

(5) After selecting your sunglasses, pretend you're at the beach, on the golf course or tennis courts by swinging your head to make sure they don't slip.

WHAT TO DO ABOUT YOUR EYE CARE WHEN YOU TRAVEL

If you wear prescription glasses or contact lenses, make a vow right now that you'll carry a spare pair of glasses or contact lenses with you the next time you go on a vacation or even a short business trip.

If you don't have spares, get from your ophthalmologist or optometrist a written copy of your current lens prescription and take that prescription with you.

And if it becomes necessary for you to get expert eye care while you are a long way from home, check for guidance on what to do and where to go with members of a state association or a local society. You'll usually find these listed in the Yellow Pages of the local phone book. By no means, go just "anywhere."

Having suffered through long evenings of not seeing a theater stage because I need glasses for distance and had forgotten to put a pair in my purse before I left for the theater, I have trained myself to carry extras on every trip. But millions of Americans ignore this easiest solution and then find themselves in a miserable plight without a replacement for their prescription lenses when they're hundreds or thousands of miles away from home and their ophthalmologist or optician.

So obey these vital words of caution:

If you have to replace your prescription lenses while you're in a strange city, have them evaluated by your own physician or optometrist as soon as you get home. The purpose: to make sure that the glasses meet your exact prescription.

When not in use, keep your prescription glasses in the case provided for them. Vacation casual living makes it all too easy for you to toss around your glasses—and your glasses can become hazardous rather than helpful to you if they become scratched, dirty, or misaligned. This is because the precision light control built into your prescription lenses can be upset by dirt and scratches.

And if you suffer an eye injury while on vacation or on a business trip, go at once to the nearest hospital emergency room for treatment. Any delay in caring for an eye injury could result in permanent eye or vision damage.

9

EDUCATION AFTER HIGH SCHOOL —AND HOW TO FINANCE IT

Costs Continue Relentless Climb

Until the early 1970s, a college education was considered essential in the workplace—a *must* for those who wanted to qualify for jobs in many professions. But as the 1980s neared, Department of Labor reports on occupational demand in the future confirmed a trend toward more jobs that do not require four years of college: service and clerical workers, technicians and paraprofessionals. The demand for teachers, journalists, and lawyers is declining, while the search for physicians, dentists, and engineers remains powerful. The career your child wants, his or her special interests, and your financial position, will determine the type of college, vocational, or trade school that's best.

Whether it's a four-year university program, a public two-year college around the corner, or a job training program at a trade or technical school, the cost of education after high school continues its relentless climb—up about 6 per cent a year.

Families in lower-income brackets have always worried about paying the bills, but if you're a family making $30,000 a year or more, you also are feeling the school squeeze now.

At the close of the 1970s, average costs at private colleges ranged from $3,900 to over $9,000. At proprietary schools (trade and vocational) the cost for a nine-month program was about $4,900.

To afford these prices will take some careful financial planning—and the earlier you start, the better your children's chances of being able to attend the college or school of their choice.

The central element in affording a college or technical education is the motivation of you and your family—primarily motivation to seek out good information so you can avoid making decisions based on myths or misconceptions.

The first consideration should be the education your child wants—and don't let the price tags scare you away from certain types of schools and colleges. If you do, you won't be giving yourself or your child a fair chance.

Why? Because more and more families each year are applying for and *getting* money from government and private student financial aid programs to help them pay college bills. There are many possibilities to explore. The earlier you begin, the less you risk overlooking important sources of assistance.

A few revealing facts about financial aid as the 1980s approached:

(1) At some colleges as many as 80 per cent of the enrolled students were getting some form of financial aid to help pay the bills.

(2) Over $12 *billion* was available from all sources—federal and state governments, colleges, and private agencies—*specifically* to help millions pay for colleges, vocational and trade schools they could not afford on their own.

(3) Costs varied widely at different schools and colleges, but your share of the costs remained the same. Your eligibility for financial aid is greater at schools with higher costs. So if you are asked to pay $1,500 toward total costs, don't worry about the $3,000- or $8,000-a-year price tag. With financial aid, the "net" cost to you is still $1,500!

WHERE TO BEGIN YOUR HUNT FOR AID

Since federal, state, and college financial aid programs help most who apply, that's where you should start your search for information.

Your key to getting money from these sources is *proving you* need it. You don't have to be poor, but you must demonstrate that you can't pay total costs on your own.

Essentially, there are three steps in estimating your chances for most financial aid.

• Find out about costs at the schools or colleges that your child wants to attend. Include estimates for *all* expenses—tuition and fees, room and board (even if your child lives at home), books and supplies, transportation, and personal expenses.

• Estimate the amount you might be asked to pay toward those costs (your "share" of costs).

• Determine the amount of financial aid you would need by subtracting your share from total costs. Usually, you are eligible for financial aid equal to the amount you need.

STEP 1: FINDING OUT ABOUT COSTS

In the late 1970s, students at public colleges offering four-year educations were paying about $3,250 if they lived on campus. And at a few public colleges, expenses were hitting $4,500.

At private four-year colleges, the average was over $5,500 if the student lived on campus. And at some private colleges, expenses were exceeding a shocking $9,000!

Commuters at private four-year colleges were paying about $4,900. At public two- and four-year colleges, total costs for commuters averaged $2,500 and $2,700 respectively.

Costs at trade and technical schools varied according to the length of the educational program. On the average, a nine-month program at the close of the 1970s cost between $4,400 and $5,000—and this increases each year at about the same rate as college expenses.

Study the chart below to see how much four years at a state university will cost when your child is ready to attend. This chart, prepared by the Oakland Financial Group of Charlottesville, Virginia, also will tell you how much *you* would have to save each year to be able to pay the bills on your own. These price tags are almost double if your child chooses a private college.

State University

AGE OF CHILD	4-YEAR COST	ANNUAL SAVINGS REQUIRED*
1	$47,380	$ 1,570
2	44,660	1,610
3	42,150	1,660
4	39,770	1,710
5	37,530	1,780
6	35,420	1,860
7	33,000	1,930
8	30,710	2,010
9	28,940	2,140
10	27,270	2,300
11	25,690	2,500
12	24,200	2,760
13	23,110	3,160
14	22,090	3,720
15	20,840	4,500
16	19,660	5,800
17	18,550	8,420
18	17,500	16,220

* Rounded

At the end of this chapter (pages 551–53), you will find a sampling of resident expenses at private and public four-year colleges in the late 1970s. It was excerpted from "Student Expenses at Postsecondary Institutions," available for $5.00 (prepaid) from The College Board, Publications Orders, Department C12, Box 2815, Princeton, New Jersey, 08541, one of the best guides of its kind and revised annually. It includes average costs at about 2,700 two-year and four-year institutions.

HOW TO COMPARE COLLEGE COSTS

After you have made the basic choice of what type of college or school you want to attend and in what state, write to the institution for details. Ask each for catalogs and all available material on local living costs, financial aid programs, and the like.

Then, using this material and your own estimates of other costs, make out financial work sheets to give yourself an idea of what a year's total expenses will be. If you're careful, you'll come very close to the actual amount.

Three tips: Add 7 per cent a year for the second year, 15 per cent for the third year, and 23 per cent for the fourth year to take inflation and other price-boosting factors into account. *Don't underestimate,* and thus invite a rude shock later on. *Remember* your eligibility for assistance is greater at schools with higher costs.

COLLEGE-EXPENSE WORK SHEET

Use the following college-expense work sheet to estimate and compare college costs.

ANNUAL EXPENSE ITEM*	COLLEGE A	COLLEGE B	COLLEGE C
Tuition			
All fees (student activity, library, application, breakage, etc.)			
Room and board			
Books			
Equipment and supplies			
Laboratory charges			
Travel to and from school			
All other travel			
Recreation and entertainment			
Clothing			
Laundry, dry cleaning, etc.			
Dues for fraternity or sorority			
Grooming (cosmetics, haircuts, etc.)			
Health expenditure (incl. insurance premiums)			
Snacks, cigarettes, etc.			
Church and charity contributions			
Your capital expenditures, prorated annually (car, bicycle, record player and records, musical instruments, sports equipment, etc.)			
Miscellaneous current expenses			
Total annual estimate			

* If you are a married couple, see Chapter 2, "Budgets Are Back In Style."

STEP 2: ESTIMATING YOUR SHARE OF TOTAL COSTS

All financial aid sponsors expect you and your children to contribute something toward college expenses, according to your ability. If you have built up savings over many years for this purpose, you will be asked to use some of these funds.

If your children are young enough, it may be possible to save enough through long-term planning, periodic investment, discipline, and dedication to get a head start on college costs. Your children, too, could begin to save especially for this purpose. In fact, when the time comes to apply for some help from financial aid programs, your children will be asked to contribute between $500 and $800 a year from summer earnings and other assets.

The amount you are asked to pay often depends on the results of "need analysis" performed by such national organizations as the College Scholarship Service (CSS) of the College Board. You will complete a *confidential* Financial Aid Form reporting your income, debts, expenses, assets, number of children in the family and in college. Be sure to include any unusual financial circumstances that strain your resources, such as expenses related to a family member's handicap.

The "need analysis" results will be sent to financial aid directors at colleges you name, who might adjust these results especially if you have new facts to present.

PROTECTION FOR YOUR ASSETS

Don't think that the need analysis system will require you to wipe out your assets to pay for college or technical school.

According to the College Scholarship Service, the need analysis system analyzes family assets—cash savings, equity in the home, securities owned, etc.—to get a more complete picture of the family's financial strength. It is generally agreed that the possession of assets allows the family to be more flexible in the use of its income.

A major portion of your assets will be protected in the need analysis system. The amount untouched can range from $10,000 to $40,000 depending on your age and other factors. After this "asset protection allowance," only 12 per cent of your remaining assets are considered in determining your ability to pay for college.

Here are some ball park figures from the CSS that applied in the late 1970s. They represent the amount a two-parent family with one child in college might be able to pay for one year of college. Look for the figure that corresponds most closely to your situation in amount of assets, income before taxes, and number of people in your family.

If you have more than one child in college at a time, you will have to pay a slightly higher total. As a rule of thumb, find the appropriate amount of your share of costs in the table above, *divide* it by the number of children in college, and *add* about $100 or $200 more *per child*.

Note: These are just suggested contributors. By no means do they bind any college to provide the balance of the costs. They do give you a general indication of what financial efforts are expected from the student and his or her family. They also indicate what financial help many colleges are trying to provide you or your child via scholarships or grants, loans, and student jobs.

TIPS ON WHAT YOU WILL PAY

• To get a closer estimate of what you will be asked to pay, you can use the work sheets in *Meeting College Costs,* a free booklet available from the College Scholarship Service. Ask your high school counselor for a copy.

A Guide to Need Analysis, Academic Year 1979-1980

EXPECTED PARENTS' CONTRIBUTION

NET ASSETS:	$10,000				$20,000				$30,000				$40,000			
FAMILY SIZE:	3	4	5	6	3	4	5	6	3	4	5	6	3	4	5	6
Income before taxes:																
$ 8,000	0	0	0	0	120	0	0	0	380	70	0	0	650	330	30	0
12,000	530	220	0	0	740	430	140	0	1,000	690	400	80	1,270	950	670	340
16,000	1,190	810	520	200	1,360	1,010	720	400	1,710	1,310	990	670	2,120	1,650	1,280	930
20,000	1,960	1,520	1,180	790	2,200	1,720	1,340	990	2,700	2,130	1,690	1,290	3,270	2,620	2,100	1,620
24,000	3,040	2,430	1,950	1,510	3,360	2,720	2,190	1,700	3,930	3,290	2,690	2,110	4,490	3,850	3,250	2,590
28,000	4,200	3,570	2,990	2,380	4,520	3,890	3,310	2,660	5,080	4,450	3,870	3,220	5,640	5,020	4,440	3,790
32,000	5,280	4,670	4,100	3,470	5,600	4,990	4,420	3,780	6,160	5,550	4,980	4,350	6,730	6,110	5,550	4,910

NOTE: The figures above are parents' contribution figures which assume:
1. Two parents, one with income.
2. One dependent child in undergraduate postsecondary education.
3. No business and/or farm assets.
4. Age of main wage earner is 45 years.
5. 1977 U.S. income tax schedules; joint return, standard deduction.
6. No Social Security benefits.
7. No unusual medical, dental, casualty, or theft expenses.
8. No other unusual circumstances.

• If your child isn't yet a high school senior, you might want to do some early planning. A new program—the Early Financial Aid Planning Service—can give you a computerized estimate of your eligibility for aid from several different sources, plus a comprehensive picture of your family's financial situation in relation to costs and aid funds. It also outlines some steps to help you develop your own personal financing strategy. Ask your counselor for more information or write to Early Financial Aid Planning, Department 1978, Box 2843, Princeton, New Jersey 08541. This service is not for parents of high school seniors.

STEP 3: DETERMINING YOUR NEED

Now that you know the basics about costs and the amount you might be asked to pay, calculating your need is simple. Just use this table to see how much financial aid you might need at colleges with different costs.

College	A	B	C
Total costs			
Minus your share of costs	—	—	—
Equals the amount you need	=	=	=

Sometimes eligibility depends on factors in addition to your need for money, such as whether you are a part-time student.

If for some reason you might not qualify for assistance on a "need" basis, see pages 539–44 for other cost-cutting strategies.

WHERE THE MONEY COMES FROM

Merely by following the steps and suggestions in the previous pages you probably know by now how much you'll need from other sources to pay for education after high school.

There are hundreds of scholarships, grant and loan programs to help you pay for education, and many have different requirements, application procedures, and average amounts they award. The following will help you look for money in places that are right for you. But these steps take time, so start early.

• Start investigating the major possibilities first, such as federal and state government programs, which help more people than any other single source of funds, mainly because there are *billions* of dollars set aside for this purpose. Later you can check out smaller programs designed for the few people who meet special requirements.

• Most of the big financial aid sponsors give out their money *through the colleges*.

• And colleges themselves have their own money to supplement federal and state financial aid awards.

Applying to major sources was simplified recently in the late 1970s, so that now you can fill out just one form to apply for all federal programs, college aid, and many state programs.

Regardless of the source, most financial aid comes in three basic forms: *scholarships and grants,* which don't have to be repaid; *loans,* which must be repaid, but often at low interest and after leaving school; and *jobs.*

Read the descriptions of each program to understand how to apply, and what obligations you would assume in terms of repayment and work. In the end, you probably will wind up with an aid "package" that combines grants, loans, and jobs. When you receive award letters from different colleges and schools, compare them to see which offers the best package for you.

FEDERAL GOVERNMENT PROGRAMS

All three types of financial aid are given out by the federal government, although grants are the most desirable because they don't have to be repaid.

BASIC EDUCATIONAL OPPORTUNITY GRANTS (BEOG)

As a first step, colleges will probably ask you to apply for a Basic Educational Opportunity Grant, since this is the largest of all programs, helping over a million students a year.

The Basic Educational Opportunity Grant (BEOG or Basic Grants) Program has about $3 billion for distribution to students. The money can be used at any college or school and does not have to be repaid.

Eligibility for a Basic Grant depends on your family's financial circumstances. The ceiling on awards may be as high as $1,800 a year, or half the total cost of attendance (whichever is less). But the average grant is about $950.

College students at all levels—freshmen to seniors—who are half- or full-time students are eligible. You can use Basic Grants at all types of colleges—two- and four-year, public and private—as well as proprietary (private, vocational, and technical) schools. If you have a high school equivalency, you are eligible too.

You're almost sure to qualify if your family's annual income before taxes is less than $25,000 a year. Families at $25,000 can expect about $200 in grants.

When you complete a Financial Aid Form for other programs, check the appropriate "yes" box for entering the Basic Grant program. It doesn't cost extra, so you have nothing to lose.

The Basic Grants information center has set up a toll free number for more information: 800-638-6700. Or write to P. O. Box 84, Washington, D.C. 20004.

THE SUPPLEMENTAL EDUCATIONAL OPPORTUNITY GRANT (SEOG)

This program had $370 million available in the late 1970s for students who needed it. Awards range from $200 to $1,500 a year, up to $4,000 for a four-year program and $5,000 for a five-year program. The amount of the grant may not exceed one half of the total cost of college, or one half of the total aid provided.

Colleges match the SEOG amount with grants from their own funds, loans, and/or jobs. More details are available from the college financial aid director.

COLLEGE WORK-STUDY PROGRAM

College financial aid directors provide summer and part-time jobs (subsidized by the federal government) for students with "demonstrated need" as part of the financial aid package.

By working about fifteen hours a week while attending classes, or more during breaks and summer, your child can earn about $1,300 per year.

This program (which should not be confused with co-operative education) is aimed strictly at promoting employment to help students get through school. The jobs are not necessarily related to the anticipated careers for which the students are studying, but in some cases they are career-geared.

Here's how it works: the government provides up to 80 per cent of the salaries of those students who qualify for jobs on campus or by nearby employers; the latter must be non-profit, non-religious, and non-political.

More than 800,000 students and over 3,000 institutions participate in the College Work-Study Program. Your college is probably one of them.

Many governmental agencies are also taking part in the work-study program as employers. There's a whole range for you to investigate. For instance:

• The Civil Service Commission hires students during summer periods in a variety of specialties, including such esoteric fields as oceanography.

• The U. S. Weather Bureau hires students to train in meteorology.

• The Army, Navy, and Coast Guard all have co-operative programs and hire undergraduate technical students in engineering, mathematics, science, and accounting.

Other agencies involved include the Federal Aviation Agency, the Federal Communications Commission, the National Aeronautics and Space Administration, and the Departments of Commerce, Agriculture, and Interior.

The federal "academic apprentice" program is operated very much like other co-operative education programs in that students alternate study and work periods. It will give you a chance to earn while you learn, and may give you a clue as to whether you would enjoy government work later on.

For information, contact the Civil Service Commission or those government agencies that have departments in your specialty. If you have any questions, check with your college placement office.

NATIONAL DIRECT STUDENT LOANS (NDSL)

NDSL loans are given by colleges, but 90 per cent of the money comes from the federal government.

Financial aid directors determine who is eligible and the amount to be loaned. There's a maximum of $2,500 for students in the first two years of a program, and a total maximum of $5,000 for the bachelor's degree. If you are a graduate or professional student, you can borrow up to $10,000.

Students enrolled at least half-time can qualify for NDSL funds. Repayment and interest (3 per cent per year) do not begin until nine months after you stop your studies. In some cases, all or part of the loan can be canceled if you enter certain fields or the armed forces.

GUARANTEED STUDENT LOAN PROGRAM (GSLP)

Federal legislation in the late 1970s opened up availability of these loans to all students by removing the income ceiling (formerly $25,000) for eligibility. Now just about every student would qualify for interest subsidy. As a result, the federal government anticipated a 60 per cent increase in one year in the number of students who would apply—from 1 million to 1.6 million students.

Guaranteed student loans are available to half-time or full-time students through banks, savings and loan associates, insurance companies, pension plans, credit unions, and some colleges.

They can borrow up to $2,500 a year, or a total of $7,500 for undergraduates, and repayment begins nine to twelve months after leaving school. The interest: 7 per cent.

Students at many vocational, business, trade, correspondence, and technical schools also are eligible for guaranteed loans.

CAUTION ABOUT LOANS

The cliché that "ignorance is bliss" was never less appropriate or more disastrous than it is in the case of loans. Especially loans to college students!

The appallingly high rate of defaults on student loans—from 13 to 18 per cent in the late 1970s—spurred the U. S. Office of Education into tightening up its collection procedures and cracking down on those who don't pay.

In one recent year, $600 million in bad debts were found in the National Direct Student Loan Program, and $300 million in the Guaranteed Student Loan Program. This money, when repaid, goes back into the loan programs for other students who need to borrow.

Many reasons have been given for the massive student loan defaults, including student dissatisfaction with the schooling they receive, breakdowns in communications between students and lending institutions, and laws that protect an individual's privacy but which impede the government's ability to locate defaulters.

Representatives of national student groups claim that the real problem is the absence of consistent, accurate, and clearly stated information to students about their obligations to repay student loans.

Loans play a major part in paying for education after high school. The default record is harmful to everyone.

Now, more than ever, it pays for your child to investigate his or her obligations carefully before signing a contract.

STATE PROGRAMS

Whether or not you qualify for financial aid from federal programs, apply for help from your home state. Some states have become key sources of financial aid —even for families with incomes over $15,000 a year.

The State Student Incentive Grant program (SSIG), through which the federal government matches the state grant to students, has become an increasingly important source of help since 1972. In the late 1970s, all fifty states shared over $64 million in SSIG funds—and the total is rising every year.

SSIG will award you, a student, up to $1,500 a year, but grants generally average $500.

You'll probably have to prove your need for this money, too. To save time, and reduce the number of forms you fill out, ask the state scholarship agency, school counselor, or college financial aid director if you can use the same form that you used to apply for federal and college money.

When you contact the state scholarship agency in the capital city about SSIG and other opportunities, ask at least the following questions:

• Can part-time and half-time students get awards?
• Can the money be used at both private and public colleges?
• Can grants be used at colleges out of your home state?
• When is the application deadline?
• What are the requirements for eligibility?

SCHOLARSHIPS AND GRANTS FROM PRIVATE SOURCES

Scholarships and grants always are the most eagerly sought type of financial aid —whether the giver is government, colleges, corporations, foundations, cities, states, or civic organizations—for the simple reason that these do not have to be repaid.

Thus, if you count on getting either one from a private source, while ignoring the major public programs described earlier, chances are you will be bitterly disappointed.

Sure, there are many specialized scholarships knocking around, for would-be organic vegetable growers, future rodeo ropers, pottery majors, prospective missionaries, direct descendants of Union soldiers who served in the Civil War, etc. But only a fraction of all who need money ever qualify for these. Furthermore, the amounts involved are so small they barely touch real-life financial needs.

Be suspicious of any claims you may have heard that millions in scholarships "go begging" each year. This kind of information may be traced to commercial firms that use computers to search for scholarships, matching the needs, interests, and qualifications of students against huge banks of details on the scholarships actually available to them today.

I would never downgrade any effective scholarship matching service—computerized or otherwise! I certainly won't claim that every penny of available scholarship money is actually being used, particularly those "funny funds" for students with special backgrounds.

But I will quarrel with the implication that huge sums of scholarship money are being wasted because students and parents just don't know where to find them.

It is not true. The students who are in college now are up against the biggest scholarship squeeze in our history—and this by itself has made them excellent, if not expert, scholarship fund sleuths.

PRIVATE SCHOLARSHIP SHOPPING LIST

There are scholarship sponsors you *should* contact which do not fall under the category of "funny funds." The major national sources are the National Merit Scholarship Corporation and colleges themselves—especially heavily endowed private colleges.

• The National Merit Scholarship Corporation, which awards more than $15 million through the Merit Program each year, is the largest, best known, and most widely sought private scholarship source in the United States today. More than a million students take the combined PSAT/NMSQT one-hour and forty-minute test every fall in high schools across the nation both for guidance purposes and in competition for one of these scholarships. But only about 4,700 outstanding students ever get one. The scholarships range in value from $250 to $1,500 a year for four years, with financial need the yardstick determining who gets the $1,500. Some winners simply get one-shot stipends of $1,000. About 18,000 high schools in the country give the test, so you might as well try. See your guidance counselor.

There is one added dividend here. Even if you're not one of the lucky winners, you could be one of the 50,000 who receive special commendations and citations because of your test scores. These might help you when you look for financial help elsewhere.

• Labor unions also now award large numbers of scholarships. Check with either your union or the union your parents belong to.

• Corporation scholarships are a worthwhile source of funds, so don't overlook them. Many businesses now offer scholarships for children of employees. Some companies award scholarships to students who have no connection with the company.

• Trade associations often have their own scholarships for children of members.

• Tuition paid by the company. Education provided by employers—from on-the-job training to tuition aid for outside schooling—is a fast-growing trend. The 7,500 largest U.S. companies spend over $2 billion a year on it; the federal government, over $880 million for its civilian work force. Over 90 per cent of the firms responding to a recent Northwestern University Endicott Survey reimbursed some or all of their employees' tuition costs for graduate education. Though most require that the courses be job-related, 7 per cent said they don't have to be.

• Civic and fraternal organizations sponsoring scholarships range from the American Legion posts or auxiliary units to the Elks, Lions, Masons, Parent-Teacher Associations, and Daughters of the American Revolution. In most instances scholarships are for young men and women living in the community in which the organization is located.

• Other sponsors include the Boy Scouts, 4-H Clubs, Chamber of Commerce, Jaycees, Junior Achievement, a wide range of religious organizations.

• Minorities often can get help from national organizations that offer scholarships and/or special counseling and referral services. A few are: ASPIRA Educational Opportunity Center, 216 West Fourteenth Street, New York, New York

10011 (Puerto Rican); Bureau of Indian Affairs, Higher Education Program, Box 8327, Albuquerque, New Mexico 87108; League of United Latin Citizens, National Education Service Centers, 400 First Street, N.W., Washington, D.C. 20001; National Association for the Advancement of Colored People, 1790 Broadway, New York, New York 10019; National Urban League, 55 East Fifty-second Street, New York, New York 10022.

• Women, too, have options in addition to the usual sources of student aid. Athletic scholarships for women soared in the late 1970s. About 500 colleges and universities offer more than $7 million for this purpose! The Business and Professional Women's Foundation in Washington, D.C., has programs for women only, and some foundations award grants to colleges and universities, which then select the women to receive the awards.

• You can get more details on opportunities for minorities and women from *Selected List of Postsecondary Education Opportunities for Minorities and Women*, available free from the Department of Health, Education, and Welfare, Office of Education, Regional Office Building 3, Room 4082 Washington, D.C. 20202.

• Handicapped students should check with the State Department of Vocational Rehabilitation.

• Professional associations are worth following up, and if you already have plans to enter a specialty after you finish college, check with the professional associations in your future specialty for the financial aid they may offer. Many try to stimulate young students to enter their fields through scholarships and fellowships.

• ROTC scholarships are being awarded to students at hundreds of colleges in most states of the United States. These scholarships are aimed at students wanting to pursue careers as officers in the military services. In most programs, your full costs of tuition, books, and fees—plus a monthly allowance for living expenses—are covered. In return, you, the student participant, must commit yourself to a military career. In the Army, though, you can retire after only twenty years of service at one half your base pay. To apply, contact the appropriate military service or the ROTC office at the participating college of your choice. Application deadlines in most cases are in November and December.

This is only a sample. Any complete list of scholarships available in this country today would be so extensive that it would make a book of its own.

"HIDDEN" SCHOLARSHIPS

Are you aware that Social Security benefits are a major source of income for many students? Could it be that you're among the many qualifying for such benefits today but you don't know it?

All of you who are unmarried full-time students qualify for this Social Security program, which can be a major income supplement to help you meet college costs —if you are children of deceased, disabled, or retired workers. Check at once at your nearest Social Security office.

And do you realize that veterans' educational benefits are now being paid to hundreds of thousands of college students—and tens of thousands of veterans' wives, widows, and children are also receiving college benefits? These benefits represent more help to students than all scholarships at all U.S. colleges and universities put together.

Under the Veterans Readjustment Benefits Act of 1966 (also known as the "GI Bill"), single veterans who were at some time on active duty between February 1955 and January 1, 1977, were being paid $311 a month in the late 1970s if they attended an accredited college or other educational institution. Married veterans were getting as much as $370 a month. Married veterans with one child were getting up to $422 a month—and $26 for each additional child. Stipends were reduced for veterans studying less than full-time. For example, the monthly benefit for a single half-time student was $156 ($185 for a married student).

You, as a veteran, can get these "scholarships" not only to attend college but also to complete high school if you have not already done so; or to attend business school; or to enroll in a wide variety of vocational training programs. There are provisions for farm co-operative training and 90 per cent reimbursement programs for correspondence school and flight training. If you have difficulty with your studies, the VA will pay for tutoring (up to $69 a month). Veterans in apprenticeship or on-the-job training programs in the late 1970s were eligible for beginning stipends of $226 per month if single, or $254 per month if married and more if there were children.

In addition, under the so-called Junior GI Bill, if you are a wife, widow, widower, or child of a veteran who died or became permanently and totally disabled as a result of his military service, you can get similar monthly stipends to attend college.

And if you're already enrolled in a VA educational program, you can get extra allowances if you agreed to work up to 250 hours for the VA (up to $725 as the 1980s neared).

HOW TO GET A GRADUATE FELLOWSHIP

A single year of graduate study now costs a staggering $6,500 to $10,000. A Ph.D. may cost $25,000 to $30,000 or more, on top of as much as $24,000 for undergraduate schooling.

Obviously the vast majority of you cannot afford such sums, even though you may be acutely aware of the potential long-range return on the investment. You must have financial help. Fellowships, which have jumped to an average of about $3,000 a year today, are a major solution.

However, the number of fellowships is diminishing and competition for graduate fellowships is fierce, particularly in the sciences and particularly for the fattest fellowships. There are only a limited number of fellowships available to the non-genius with a serious interest in higher education. For him or her, the emphasis is on loans and jobs.

So, if you are considering graduate study and need a fellowship to help support it, here are five basic rules for finding and applying for one:

(1) Consult your graduate study adviser and professors in your major department on kinds and sources of fellowships and on institutions you might want to attend. Write the graduate school of each university to which you intend to apply

and ask what financial assistance is available. The universities administer not only their own fellowship funds but also many of the government and private foundation funds as well.

(2) Find out all the financial details of each fellowship for which you think you might qualify. Exactly what does it cover: tuition? travel? the full year? or only the academic year? Will the funds be tax-free? Are there special allowances for dependents?

(3) Focus on three or four fellowship sources, and confine your efforts to those for which you think you really qualify.

(4) Fill out application forms neatly, concisely, thoughtfully, and correctly. Pay special attention to your statement on why you want a fellowship and how you intend to use it. Include with your application all supporting documents which may be required, letters of recommendation, special tests, academic records, financial information, etc.

(5) Get your application in on time. Deadlines for some fellowships are as early as the fall of your senior year in college. Preparation of your applications can easily take as long as six months before the deadline.

OTHER COST-CUTTING STRATEGIES

Let's say that you do not qualify for financial aid in the form of a scholarship or grant, a job through the College Work-Study Program, or a special loan. What can you do to cut the costs of going to college?

You still have several options.

• Try to get credit by examination which will reduce the number of credits for which you must pay while you're in college.

• Check out the special payment plans that more and more colleges are developing to help families that can't meet the costs.

• If your child has decided on a career, investigate the possibilities of a cooperative education program.

• And finally, investigate the various loans (other than special government loans) described on pages 544–47 which might meet your needs.

SHOPPING FOR COLLEGE

You can cut the costs of education after high school simply by your choice of a college.

The least expensive alternatives are a public two-year college and a state college in your own state where you live at home.

In ascending order more costly possibilities include:

A state college in your own state where you live away from home.

A state college out of your home state, where you live in the dormitory or off campus.

A private two-year college where you live at home.

A private four-year college where you live at home.

A private four-year college where you live away from home.

If your child's choice is a proprietary school (trade or vocational school), which prepares students for a particular business position, skilled trade, semi-profession, personal service, recreational activity, or some other occupational training, see the guides on pages 554–58.

To illustrate how choice of college affects cost, consider two well-known universities in one state: the University of Pennsylvania, in Philadelphia, and Pennsylvania State University in University Park (the central part of the state). Both are major coeducational institutions; both are highly respected for their faculties and programs.

As the 1980s approached, the University of Pennsylvania cost you about $8,600 for a year. This included all educational and living expenses for a student living away from home. For the same year, if you were a resident of the state and had chosen Pennsylvania State University you would have paid about $4,050 for all your expenses.

If you found the two institutions both offered you comparable programs for the purposes of your studies, and you chose the state university, your annual savings would have been $4,550.

However:

If your child attends a public or state college *outside* his or her state of residence, you might pay extra charges ranging from $200 to $2,000. When added to regular tuition and fees, those extra charges for out-of-state students slash the savings usually associated with attending a public college.

While your child will save money by commuting to school from home instead of residing on campus, the difference generally will not be more than $600 a year for students attending the same type of college.

BARGAIN EDUCATION

Other ways to slash your college costs are through a telescoped, three-year degree program, through credit by examination programs, or through an "external degree program."

Many colleges offer different ways to earn a four-year degree in less time. The options are ordinarily open only to the ablest students, because you must not only take on a heavier load of courses but you must also, normally, attend classes during the summer. This obviously reduces your ability to earn money to meet college expenses. Nevertheless, the possibility of paying only three years of tuition and living expenses for a college degree, combined with the time saved, make three-year degree programs a very attractive deal financially.

Here are some ways to do it:

• *The College-level Examination Program* permits you to cut the college costs by demonstrating your knowledge of a subject in an examination. CLEP exams are given monthly at 1,000 different locations throughout the United States—and more than 1,800 colleges and universities grant credit toward degrees to those who score high enough on the tests.

Before you decide to take CLEP tests for college credit, check with your college on its CLEP policy.

For details write to CLEP, College Board Publications Orders, Box 2815, Princeton, New Jersey 08540. Home study courses which might not by themselves qualify for college credit can help you toward a college degree if they enable you to get a passing score on the appropriate CLEP tests.

(Caution: If you are in the market for home study courses, heed the warnings on pages 562–63, "Beware: Home Study Gyps.")

• *Advanced Placement Examinations* can help you slash the costs of college and increase the lifelong earnings potential of your son or daughter. If you are the parent of a high school student enrolled in an honors program or college-level course, look into this. Many high schools offer special courses to able students in subjects covered by AP exams.

Each year more and more high school students take AP exams to verify their college knowledge in advance. In the late 1970s, 95,000 students in 4,300 schools took the tests each year. Satisfactory exam grades earned them course exemptions, college credits, advanced standing, or placement at just about every top college and university in the nation.

With AP benefits, these students were able to go right on to more challenging courses, enrich and diversify their programs, take double majors, enroll in graduate courses as undergraduates—all choices greatly enhancing their earning power after graduation.

If your child can enter college with some credits for college-level work in high school, this might cut the costs of a college education 12 to 25 per cent.

If your child graduates early and enters the job market ahead of time, this alone can be worth $12,000 or more in income.

Advanced Placement exams are given in May each year, and high schools register students in March and early April.

For more information about Advanced Placement, write to Advanced Placement Program, Box 300, The College Board, New York, New York 10019. Also ask individual colleges about their Advanced Placement policies.

In an *external degree program* you do your regular college studies off campus. It's a unique form of low-cost education with particular appeal if you must maintain a job while you study. It also opens up many new opportunities for millions of you—housewives and others—who might never have a chance otherwise to get a degree.

If you, a student, live and study at home, your education may cost only about half as much as the cost of an on-campus education. One large program of this kind is New York State's Empire State College, where costs for New York residents ran only $1,067 for a recent twelve-month year for freshmen and sophomores and slightly higher for juniors and seniors. Another is the New York Regents External Degree Program, which is unique in its willingness to grant a degree to an applicant who has not followed any prescribed program of study—if he can demonstrate his ability in his field.

The degree you get through one of these external degree programs *is not a cut-rate mail order diploma in any sense.*

It is the same high-quality, specialized degree granted the normal way by a given institution. Despite the fact that these programs still are not traditional, they do offer you great potential—if you are capable of studying independently.

SPECIAL PAYMENT PLANS

When my brother John was attending medical school in the depression years of the 1930s, there was only one way he could finance it: through high-interest education loans, cosigned by the most financially respectable friends we had. These loans were renewed . . . renewed . . . renewed . . . until many years later, after John had graduated from med school, returned from World War II, and was earning money as a physician, he was able to repay the debt out of his current income.

It was a clumsy, monstrously expensive way to meet the costs of his education but it was the best we could do. John got his education and became a physician and surgeon. His loans, although stretched out over a long period, were finally and honorably repaid. Both goals were achieved and that's all any of us cared about.

In the 1970s, a "new" idea for financing a college or graduate school education is a revolutionary refined version of John's makeshift plan. The idea has various names: "the Yale plan"; "deferred tuition"; "tuition postponement"; "pay as you earn" (or "PAYE"). But fundamentally the student does in the 1970s what John did in the 1930s; he or she postpones paying at least part of the tuition until the years after graduation, when he is earning money and can manage it out of his own income.

Yale was the pioneer in the experiment, and other colleges have developed their own variations. A national tuition postponement option plan, patterned after Yale's program, is very much a possibility, if not a probability, in coming years. But a national tuition postponement plan remains in the future. Here, meanwhile, are the key features you'll find in most of today's plans:

• The schools borrow the funds from private sources such as banks. Because of the caliber of the borrower and because the loan is a single large transaction, rather than a lot of little ones, the interest charges are comparatively favorable. These charges are certainly much lower than you would be charged for a conventional loan at the same institution.

• The student defers tuition by getting a loan from this fund. Then, after graduation, he repays what he has deferred.

• Repayment is geared to the graduate's income. Some will pay back more than the cost of their respective loans; others a bit less, depending on their income level. Essentially, this means that those fortunate enough to earn more money in later life will help pay toward the education of those who earn less. Students can borrow to meet the cost of their education without losing the opportunity to take low-paying but possibly challenging jobs after graduation.

COLLEGE CO-OP PROGRAMS

Co-operative Education Programs, under which students alternate periods of study with periods of work in *their field of study,* are not new. Massachusetts Institute of Technology has offered one in the Department of Electrical Engineering and Computer Sciences since 1917.

These programs are multiplying, however. Some 200,000 college students at more than 1,000 colleges in the nation are now using these programs to earn an estimated $450 million during the school year. Both students and colleges are satisfied with the results.

In fact, MIT added a new Engineering Internship Program in its School of Engineering in the late 1970s. Students can earn a combined bachelor's and master's degree in five years, working three summers and one graduate term. The amount the student earns depends on how much the employing company pays for the student's particular level of expert knowledge or special skills.

At some schools such as Antioch and Boston's huge Northeastern University (one of the pioneers in the co-operative education movement) participation in the co-operative education program is *mandatory*.

Although the programs differ from place to place, the basic aim is the same: to spread the burden so that the student shares the financial responsibility with parents and/or the college. Most plans also spread tuition costs as well, simply by requiring five years to earn a degree instead of the usual four.

At Northeastern, more than 15,000 full-time students were enrolled in some forty-six different degree programs in a single year and at the close of the 1970s, also worked for more than 2,000 employers across the nation. Here's how the five-year Northeastern study schedule works:

As in most plans of this type, the freshman year is spent in regular, full-time, on-campus study. During the next four years the student alternates between three months of school and three months working in a paying job. He is paired with another student so that the job is covered full-time throughout the year without a break. At the end of five years the graduate has his degree, plus about two years of relevant job experience—and that's a priceless plus these days.

The college usually will find the job for you and the position will be related in some way to your field of study. When the job market is tight, you may not be able to count on getting just the kind of job you had in mind, and business cutbacks may also temporarily cut down on your selection of jobs. But these cycles run their course in time. Employers also are showing increasing sympathy to the needs of students and willingness to employ them on a temporary, part-time basis.

How much can you earn in a co-op program? The *average annual* earnings of these students in the late 1970s were approaching $4,500—usually higher than the earnings of students in the more traditional type of program.

Most co-op students can earn an average $170 per week during work assignments. Thus, if you live at home during the work periods, you should be able to earn and save on living costs.

At Philadelphia's Drexel University, the tuition, fees, and room and board in the late 1970s were approximately $18,800 for the traditional four-year course, and $22,290 for the five-year co-op plan also offered by the university.

A student working during the school year (excluding summers and vacations) under a federal work-study program can earn perhaps $5,600 over four years. This leaves a tab of $13,200 to be paid. In contrast, as a co-op student in Drexel's business program, you can earn about $13,500 by working during four of the five years you are studying. This leaves only $8,700 for the co-op student to pay over five years. In addition, both students would be able to work during summers and vacations, adding perhaps another $1,500 toward college expenses.

And don't underestimate the *intangibles* of co-op education:

You well may find the work experience gives you a heightened sense of responsibility, more confidence in your decision, on-the-job training related to your field of study, and greater maturity.

For a free list of colleges offering co-op programs write: National Commission for Co-operative Education, 360 Huntington Avenue, Boston, Massachusetts 02115.

LOANS

HOW TO SHOP FOR AN EDUCATION LOAN

For vast numbers of you there will be an unprecedented number of scholarships, grants, low-cost government loans, and special payment plans offered by colleges to help you and your child.

But what about the millions of you who aren't considered needy enough by federal, state, or university standards to qualify for a scholarship or a "special" loan?

What about parents in the higher income brackets who suddenly face the staggering drain of a college education for two or more children?

Confronted by the steep and rising costs of education after high school more and more families are turning to commercial banks, savings and loan associations, insurance companies, credit unions, and other lending plans with a wide variety of repayment terms and interest costs.

If you think you need a loan—*after you have explored other cost-cutting strategies* (see pages 539–44—you must learn to find your way through the maze of loan plans. How? You must shop—as vital in this sphere as in all others. You must shop for a college loan as you would for a mortgage or any major personal purchase.

Here, then, are basic rules for finding the best deal:

• As I urged you at the start of this chapter, first draw up a total budget for all anticipated college costs—including tuition, board, room, books, clothes, transportation, spending money. Divide this amount by the total number of semesters of school attendance.

• Decide how big a debt you can handle and don't exceed your limit.

• Figure out (honestly) how long you will need to repay the loan.

• Submit your calculations to at least two or three different lenders and ask what monthly payments would be required—including any charges for insurance.

• Compare the bids. The lowest monthly charge will be most favorable to you—assuming equal repayment periods, equal loan amounts, and equal insurance charges.

A LIST OF LOANS AVAILABLE TO YOU

The most desirable loans are the National Direct Student Loans and Guaranteed Student Loans (see pages 533–34).

Other loan possibilities, starting with the least expensive, are:

(1) A college loan involving low interest on the loan, which is repayable starting sometime after graduation.

(2) A low-interest loan through a civic or religious group.

(3) A deferred-tuition plan offered by a number of schools.

(4) A loan from a credit union, if you're a member.

(5) A bank or insurance company loan.

(6) As a last resort, a finance company loan.

Now the details . . .

LOANS FROM COLLEGES THEMSELVES

Hundreds of colleges and universities are now offering long-term loan programs of their own to students. Almost all of these are bargains in terms of low interest rates and tolerable repayment schedules.

You'll find that the amount of money available through these loans does not begin to compare with the huge sums available from other sources. But if you're lucky enough to borrow through a school's own program, most of your financial worries will be minimized from the beginning.

Loans made to:	Students.
Loans made by:	College itself. May be short-term emergency loan. Or may be in co-operation with federal government for long-term. Or may be a long-term loan under a postponed tuition plan.
Amount of loans:	Varies widely. Can be small if short-term emergency loan or can run into thousands of dollars.
Interest rates:	Also vary widely, no fixed rate, but always compare very favorably with rates charged by commercial lenders.
Repayment:	Starts at graduation or a year thereafter if ordinary college loan; can be stretched out over a very long period. Repayment is likely to be deferred for as long as the student is in graduate school.
How to apply:	Go directly to the financial aid officer at your college.

UNITED STUDENT AID FUNDS

The largest private guarantor of student loans today is the non-profit United Student Aid Funds (845 Third Avenue, New York, New York 10022), supported primarily by foundations and private business contributions. The USAF is not only a major participant in the Government Guaranteed Student Loan Programs, in its role as the administrator of a number of state programs; it also has a separate guaranteed student loan program with many hundreds of colleges and universities participating in all fifty states. The key characteristics of these loans are exactly the same as previously described for the government Guaranteed Student Loan Program (see page 534).

LOANS FROM CIVIC ORGANIZATIONS

Sources of college loans that are frequently overlooked but that might be ideal for you are local civic groups. Or perhaps your best bet would be a labor union or a church group.

Whatever the group, before you turn to a commercial lender, check into organizations such as these in your town. You well might find that one or more of them have substantial low-interest loans available to students.

Loans made to:	Students.
Loans made by:	Organizations sponsoring the loan program: Rotary, Lions, Kiwanis, PTA, labor unions, churches, employers, etc.
Amount of loans:	Vary, depending on the financial resources of the organization and the student's need.
Interest rates:	Comparatively low against the money market at the time of loan.
Repayment:	Generally deferred for a while after graduation but also varies, according to the agreement between lender and borrower.
How to apply:	Consult your high school guidance counselor, your community center, your church, similar likely sources for information on what loans are available and your eligibility.

LOANS FROM PRIVATE FINANCIAL INSTITUTIONS

If you can't develop other alternatives to finance your college education and must go the commercial loan route, do not hesitate to do so.

If a loan—even a long-term debt of thousands of dollars—is the difference between going to college and not going, consider it among the best investments you ever made.

Loans made to:	Parents, guardians, or students—usually the adults and students of legal majority age.
Loans made by:	Commercial banks, savings institutions, finance companies, credit unions, other financial sources.
Amount of loans:	Not specifically limited, if the borrower has demonstrated ability to repay or satisfactory collateral. This is, in short, an ordinary personal loan for education purposes. Maximum, though, is usually $8,000 to $10,000. Funds usually given to borrower in lump sums at start of each semester.

Interest rates: Vary depending on state of money market, area of country, caliber of borrower, term of loan. Generally rates are relatively high against levels of the money markets at the time—and a minimum "service charge" may be added.

Repayment: Terms vary and depend on deal agreed upon but a period of six to eight years is fairly typical and repayments often start at the end of the first month of the loan's life.

"Special" college loan sources: Then there are private lending companies which specialize in education loans. Some offer special arrangements—"budget" plans, revolving credit accounts under which borrowers may repay loans in installments and prepay whenever possible, etc. The plans might involve a fee for joining, monthly service charge, insurance premium, possibly a cancellation charge, possibly other fees, too.

The costs of each and all of these plans should be carefully compared—a chore you will find made easier by the Truth in Lending Law, which requires the lenders to disclose all important details of the charges to you.

A major company specializing in education loans is: The Tuition Plan, Inc., 575 Madison Avenue, New York, New York 10022.

QUESTIONS TO ASK EACH LENDER

What is the simple interest rate on your loan? Remember, by law, this rate must be disclosed.

What extra charges are involved?

How much may your family borrow for each child?

Can the lender terminate the plan? Under what conditions? Does it have to give you notice before cancellation?

Can you, the borrower, terminate the loan before the expiration of the contract? How much notice are you required to give? Are there any prepayment penalties involved?

Is there an age limit above which a parent will no longer qualify for the loan?

What other restrictions are there?

SOURCES OF INFORMATION ON THE GUARANTEED STUDENT LOAN PROGRAM

ALABAMA
Regional Administrator
Student Financial Assistance
Office of Education, Region IV

50 Seventh Street, N.E., Room 404
Atlanta, GA 30323
(404) 881-3106

ALASKA
Alaska Commission on Post
  Secondary Education
Division of Student Financial Aid
Pouch F, State Office Building
Juneau, AL 99801
(907) 465-2962

ARIZONA
Regional Administrator
Student Financial Assistance
Office of Education, Region IX
50 United Nations Plaza
San Francisco, CA 94102
(415) 556-1630

ARKANSAS
Student Loan Guarantee
Foundation of Arkansas
Suite 515, 1515 West Seventh Street
Little Rock, AR 72202
(501) 371-2634

CALIFORNIA (See Arizona)

COLORADO
Regional Administrator
Student Financial Assistance
Office of Education, Region VIII
Federal Office Building, Box 3608
Nineteenth and Stout Streets
Denver, CO 80294
(303) 837-4128

CONNECTICUT
Connecticut Student Loan Foundation
25 Pratt Street
Hartford, CT 06103

DELAWARE
Delaware Higher Education Loan
  Program
c/o Brandywine College
P. O. Box 7139
Wilmington, DE 19803
(302) 478-3000 Ext. 34

DISTRICT OF COLUMBIA
D.C. Student Loan Insurance Program
1329 E Street, N.W.
Washington, D.C. 20004
(202) 638-1020

FLORIDA (See Alabama)

GEORGIA
Georgia High Education Assistance
  Corporation
9 La Vista Perimeter Park, Suite 110
2187 Northlake Parkway
Tucker, GA 30084
(404) 393-7253

HAWAII (See Arizona)

IDAHO
Regional Administrator
Student Financial Assistance
Office of Education, Region X
1321 Second Avenue, M.S. 136
Seattle, WA 98101
(206) 442-4156

ILLINOIS
Illinois Guaranteed Loan Program
102 Wilmot Road
Deerfield, IL 60015
(312) 945-7040

INDIANA
Regional Administrator
Student Financial Assistance
Office of Education, Region V
300 South Wacker Drive
Chicago, IL 60606
(800) 621-5434

IOWA
Regional Administrator
Student Financial Assistance
Office of Education, Region VII
601 East Twelfth Street, Room 360
Kansas City, MO 64106
(816) 374-5875

KANSAS (See Minnesota)

KENTUCKY (See Alabama)

LOUISIANA (in-state residents)
Louisiana Higher Education
   Assistance Commission
P. O. Box 44127
Capitol Station
Baton Rouge, LA 70804
(504) 389-5491

LOUISIANA (out-of-state residents)
United Student Aid Funds, Inc.
845 Third Avenue
New York, NY 10020

MAINE
Maine State Department of Education
   and Cultural Services
Augusta, ME 04330
(207) 289-2475

MARYLAND
Maryland Higher Education Loan
   Corporation
2100 Guilford Avenue
Baltimore, MD 21218
(301) 383-4150

MASSACHUSETTS
Massachusetts Higher Education
   Assistance Corporation
1010 Park Square Building
Boston, MA 02116
(617) 426-9434

MICHIGAN
Michigan Higher Education
   Assistance Authority
309 North Washington Avenue
Lansing, MI 48902
(517) 373-0760

MINNESOTA
Higher Education Assistance
   Foundation

1100 Northwestern Bank Building
55 East Fifth Street
St. Paul, MN 55101
(612) 227-7661

MISSISSIPPI (See Alabama)

MISSOURI (See Iowa)

MONTANA (See Colorado)

NEBRASKA (See Iowa)

NEVADA
State Department of Education
Carson City, NV 89701
(702) 885-5700 Ext. 270

NEW HAMPSHIRE
New Hampshire Higher Education
   Assistance Foundation
143 North Main Street
Concord, NH 03301
(603) 225-6612

NEW JERSEY
New Jersey Higher Education
   Assistance Authority
1474 Prospect Street
P. O. Box 1417
Trenton, NJ 08625
(609) 292-3906

NEW MEXICO
Regional Administrator
Student Financial Assistance
Office of Education, Region VI
1200 Main Tower
Dallas, TX 75202
(214) 655-3766

NEW YORK
New York Higher Education Services
   Corporation
Tower Building, Empire State Plaza
Albany, NY 12255
(518) 474-7061

NORTH CAROLINA
North Carolina State Education
  Assistance Authority
P. O. Box 2688
University Square West
Chapel Hill, NC 27514
(919) 929-2136

NORTH DAKOTA (See Colorado)

OHIO
Ohio Student Loan Commission
50 West Broad Street, 8th Floor
Columbus, OH 43215
(614) 466-5659

OKLAHOMA
Oklahoma State Regents for Higher
  Education
500 Education Building
State Capitol Complex
Oklahoma City, OK 73105
(405) 521-2444

OREGON
State of Oregon Scholarship
  Commission
1445 Williamette Street
Eugene, OR 97401
(503) 686-4166

PENNSYLVANIA
Pennsylvania Higher Education
  Assistance Agency
Towne House, 660 Boas Street
Harrisburg, PA 17102
(717) 787-1932

PUERTO RICO
Regional Administrator
Student Financial Assistance
Office of Education, Region III
26 Federal Plaza, Room 402
New York, NY 10022
(212) 264-8746

RHODE ISLAND
Rhode Island Higher Education
  Assistance Corporation
187 Westminster Mall, Room 414
P. O. Box 579
Providence, RI 02901
(401) 421-4964

SOUTH CAROLINA (See Alabama)

SOUTH DAKOTA (See Colorado)

TENNESSEE
Tennessee Student Assistance
707 Main Street
Nashville, TN 37306
(615) 741-1346

TEXAS (See New Mexico)

UTAH (See Colorado)

VERMONT
Vermont Student Assistance
Vermont Federal Savings Building
5 Burlington Square
Burlington, VT 05401
(802) 658-4530

VIRGINIA
Virginia State Education Assistance
  Authority
Suite 311, Professional Building
501 East Franklin Street
Richmond, VA 05401
(804) 786-2035

WASHINGTON (See Idaho)

WEST VIRGINIA
Regional Administrator
Student Financial Assistance
Office of Education, Region III
P. O. Box 13716

3535 Market Street
Philadelphia, PA 19101
(215) 596-1031

WISCONSIN
Wisconsin Higher Education
   Corporation
123 West Washington Avenue
Madison, WI 53702
(608) 266-2897

WYOMING (See Colorado)

AMERICAN SAMOA (See Arizona)

GUAM (See Arizona)

TRUST TERRITORY (See Arizona)

VIRGIN ISLANDS (See Louisiana,
   out-of-state residents)

COSTS AT SELECTED PRIVATE AND PUBLIC COLLEGES, LATE 1970s

NAME AND LOCATION	TUITION, FEES	ROOM, BOARD	OTHER EXPENSES	TOTAL EXPENSES
Private Colleges				
Beloit College, Beloit, Wis.	$4,585	$1,680	$ 850	$7,115
Bennington College, Bennington, Vt.	6,590	1,830	850	9,270
Boston College, Chestnut Hill, Mass.	4,070	2,175	1,155	7,400
Brandeis University, Waltham, Mass.	5,175	2,180	725	8,080
University of Chicago, Chicago, Ill.	4,512	2,538	760	7,810
*Colgate University, Hamilton, N.Y.	4,870	1,900	750	7,520
Dartmouth College, Hanover, N.H.	5,289	2,430	827	8,546
Duke University, Durham, N.C.	4,535	2,200	745	7,480
Emory University, Atlanta, Ga.	4,095	1,796	1,111	7,002
*Fairleigh Dickinson University, Rutherford, N.J.	3,113	1,752	735	5,600
George Washington University, Washington, D.C.	3,350	2,200	850	6,400

Name and Location	Tuition, Fees	Room, Board	Other Expenses	Total Expenses
Private Colleges				
Howard University, Washington, D.C.	$1,765	$1,786	$ 967	$4,518
Johns Hopkins University, Baltimore, Md.	4,630	2,255	1,300	8,185
Knox College, Galesburg, Ill.	4,384	1,640	900	6,924
Loyola University, New Orleans, La.	2,400	1,850	1,075	5,325
Massachusetts Institute of Technology, Cambridge, Mass.	5,265	2,570	915	8,750
*Northwestern University, Evanston, Ill.	5,025	2,100	700	7,825
*Oberlin College, Oberlin, Ohio	4,463	1,840	475	6,778
University of Richmond, Richmond, Va.	3,400	1,500	900	5,800
Sarah Lawrence College, Bronxville, N.Y.	5,550	2,450	1,090	9,090
Tulane University, New Orleans, La.	4,546	2,150	575	7,271
Vassar College, Poughkeepsie, N.Y.	4,733	2,125	900	7,758
*Xavier University, Cincinnati, Ohio	2,600	1,610	770	4,980
Public Colleges				
Arizona State University, Tempe, Ariz.	550	1,930	1,060	3,540
University of Florida, Gainesville, Fla.	710	1,962	885	3,557
*Indiana State University, Terre Haute, Ind.	868	1,343	764	2,975
University of Maryland, College Park, Md.	842	2,085	700	3,627
*University of Michigan, Ann Arbor, Mich.	1,150	1,900	1,120	4,170

NAME AND LOCATION	TUITION, FEES	ROOM, BOARD	OTHER EXPENSES	TOTAL EXPENSES
Public Colleges				
*Ohio State University, Columbus, Ohio	$ 975	$1,707	$ 693	$3,375
University of Texas, Arlington, Tex.	440	2,030	1,130	3,600
University of Virginia, Charlottesville, Va.	910	1,700	760	3,370

* Indicates data are for the 1978–79 academic year.

VACATION COLLEGES

When millions of younger Americans across the land throw off the burdens of the school year at summer's start, countless numbers of their parents simultaneously make plans for school to begin.

A phenomenon began sweeping the nation in the late 1970s and it is now an "in" thing for adults to couple the annual summer holiday with an intellectually refreshing course or two at college.

Its name may be "vacation college" or "alumni college" or some similarly revealing title—but under each program, a university or college offers both old graduates and new students the chance to mix education with fun and games.

Swimming? Tennis? Golf? Drama? Dance programs? Music? Nightly dining out? Yes, it does sound like an ideal vacation at a posh resort—but during the summer ahead as you read this, it just as easily may be courses on campus plus a relaxing holiday. Many colleges also invite you to bring the family by providing child-care facilities, special children's programs, or a combination of both.

What's more, the non-competitive courses often are led by some of America's leading intellectuals, teachers, authors, etc.

To top it all, you get excellent value for your dollars: tuition is comparatively low for seven-day, seven-night sessions, and in addition, you get an air-conditioned room, double occupancy, and hall bath in a university dormitory, linen service, use of all the school's recreation facilities, a welcoming party, a week-long course, and field trips. You and your family may eat in the budget-oriented university cafeterias to minimize your food bills—or may attend a college with a plan that includes prepaid dining facilities.

If you are intrigued by this concept of a vacation at college, first decide in what area you'd prefer to spend your holiday weeks. Then write the director of admissions at the various schools in that region, inquiring what each offers. *Lovejoy's College Guide* is a good reference for college listings. You can get a copy at most public libraries.

CHOOSING TRADE OR VOCATIONAL SCHOOLS

JOB MARKET NEEDS SHIFTING

The needs of the job market are shifting toward vocational and away from a general academic education. The attitudes of you, as adults, as well as of you, as young Americans, are undergoing dramatic changes in favor of vocational work.

A natural result of these forces: vocational schools are becoming increasingly accepted and more popular than ever before.

These privately owned schools—also called *proprietary* schools—are supported entirely by student tuition and fees. They are in the education business, and are operated to make a profit. In fact, it well may be that the annual revenue of private vocational schools will exceed $5 billion by 1985.

This doesn't mean you won't get the education and training necessary for certain careers, but it *does* mean you must have a clear understanding of what they do and whether they can give you the education you want.

WHAT ARE THEY?

Proprietary schools provide education and training in specific areas, with courses related directly to the career field. Unlike colleges and universities, they do not offer liberal arts courses to supplement the training. But they do give you, a student, experience with the equipment used in the field and an exposure to actual working conditions.

Not all proprietary schools deal in the technical trades. In fact, they run the whole range—from art, music, drama, and dance to X-ray technology and cosmetology, thus covering a wide range of single-purpose career educational programs. You must have a high school diploma—or the equivalent—to enroll in most of the programs.

The length of courses varies as much as the courses themselves—from a few months to four or more years. At the end, a certificate or degree is usually awarded.

A major training area in which proprietary schools have surged in importance recently is the education of *paraprofessionals*. These workers are equipped to handle those aspects of a professional's work that do not require full professional training.

Paraprofessionals in law, medicine, accounting, engineering, education, and library work, for example, can complete their formal education for these jobs in one or two years. Occasionally, on-the-job training will suffice, but usually it supplements schooling.

CHOOSING A SCHOOL

Let's say you or your child—along with roughly 3 million others in this country—want to attend a private vocational, trade, or technical school.

How do you select one out of the more than 10,000 in the United States today?

First, do your homework before you decide! And start by answering one vital question:

What do I want to get out of this training?

Once you know, then find out whether specific schools can prepare you for that career, whether there are jobs in the field you want, and whether the school will help you find those jobs.

Find out if the school is licensed or accredited. This will tell you whether it has met the appropriate educational and business standards and has been officially recognized by agencies responsible for such approval.

This information is especially pertinent if you will need money from federal financial aid programs to help you pay the bills. (See pages 525–34 for information on costs.)

Schools *must* be accredited to participate in federal aid programs: licensing is not enough. If you attend a school that is not accredited, you will *not* get financial aid.

Accreditation. To be accredited, proprietary schools volunteer to be reviewed by independent teams of educational experts. And they must meet the various requirements established by the agency that will evaluate the school's educational programs, faculty, and facilities.

The National Association of Trade and Technical Schools, which operates its own accrediting agency, specifies five areas in which their schools must demonstrate quality. Keep them in mind for each school you consider.

• *Goals and objectives* must be clearly stated and visible. (Make sure these come across in any printed materials you receive.)

• *Instructors* and other staff such as counselors must be qualified—that is, they must have demonstrated proficiency and work experience in the field. The evaluation team also looks for a satisfactory faculty ratio so students can get the educational attention they need.

• *Courses and facilities* (labs, etc.) must be up-to-date so students can be prepared to compete in the job market.

• *Job placement services* must be offered.

• Success in placing students in the industry for which they've been trained must be demonstrated. Also, these students must have been placed at the level for which they were trained.

If you need financial assistance, find out if the school you're interested in is eligible to award you financial aid funds.

To be eligible, the school must be accredited, but only about 25 per cent of the 10,000 proprietary schools in the country are.

To find out which they are, get a copy of *Accredited Institutions of Postsecondary Institutions* from your library. It's published by the American Council on Education. Or you can write to:

U. S. Office of Education
Division of Eligibility and Agency Evaluation,
Department of Health, Education, and Welfare
Washington, D.C. 20202

or

Council on Postsecondary Accreditation
One Dupont Circle, Suite 760
Washington, D.C. 20036

If you want to check out a school's eligibility for use of Veteran's Benefits, write to the Veterans Administration regional office in your area.

Licensing. Proprietary schools (non-collegiate vocational, trade, and technical), I repeat, are businesses. Because of this, they *must* be licensed to operate by the state agency. This type of approval is not as difficult to get as accreditation. Nor is it voluntary. It's more like a business permit, and the requirements schools must meet have nothing to do with their educational programs.

When you investigate different schools check for both licensing *and* accreditation, since you must know if it has a solid business reputation as well as a quality educational program. If the school you're considering has had a questionable business track record with previous students, the state licensing agency (usually found within your state's Department of Education) is likely to know about it (list attached).

ARE JOBS AVAILABLE?

This question is critical. And you must search for the answer yourself, especially if you think special training in a proprietary school will gain you entrance into the job market.

If jobs in the field you want are decreasing, it's better to find out before you've spent the time (maybe several years) and the money (maybe several thousand dollars) being trained for a job that's almost impossible to find.

Don't rely on a school's claims of plentiful job opportunities in your field of interest! Here's why:

Recent fraud and abuse audits by the Department of Health, Education, and Welfare show that some of the more aggressive proprietary schools have sophisticated systems to use federal financial aid money to beef up their student enrollment, *regardless of job availability in the field they specialize in.*

One chain of cosmetology schools in Pennsylvania, faced with declining enrollments, increased its student body from 181 to 1,700 in four years. Also during that time, the number of accredited cosmetology schools nationally grew from 200 to 1,069, enrolling some 78,000 students.

How did they do it? Partly by luring students with the promise of federal financial aid to help them pay for their education. The Cosmetology Accrediting Commission admitted that the availability of federal funds to these schools "opened the floodgates."

Oh sure, the students probably received aid money.

But were the jobs there when they finished?

A revealing fact that might provide the answer: there's no apparent correlation between the growth in the number of cosmetology students (and schools) and the need for cosmetologists in the United States!

Over $1.5 million in federal money was used at the Pennsylvania cosmetology schools alone—making up 68 per cent of all tuition charges collected by those schools.

Cosmetology schools have now been the target of intensive audit by the Department of Health, Education, and Welfare.

To learn more about available jobs, talk to counselors at your local, state, or private employment agency. A free publication called "Occupations in Demand," published monthly, lists the high-demand occupations in many areas and cities. You'll find it at public service employment agencies, many schools, libraries, and community agencies.

Check whether your independent findings match up with claims made by the schools you're considering.

GETTING HELP FINDING A JOB

Accredited proprietary schools must have services to help you get a job, and must prove that they've done so successfully for other students.

Beware if any school makes any excessive claims—*guaranteeing* you a job, for example.

Most states have enacted laws prohibiting job guarantees because this has been an area of vicious and widespread abuse.

One of the best ways to find out about a school's job placement success is to contact recent graduates of the school you're examining. Ask for a list of names and addresses, especially of graduates in the area you hope to be a part of when you're ready for your future occupation.

Don't hesitate to get in touch with these graduates. Probe into the training they received and the jobs they found.

If at all possible, speak to their employer (or someone knowledgeable in their employer's company)

Did the school provide these graduates with the skills the employer needed?

Were those skills up-to-date?

What are the employer's future needs likely to be?

Would the employer have preferred to train these workers himself?

How does the salary of a vocational school graduate compare with that of an on-the-job trainee?

Which route provides the best means for advancement?

Don't ignore *The Occupational Outlook Handbook* issued by the U. S. Department of Labor. (See pages 583–84.) It's a prime source of information about jobs and the educational preparation they require.

OTHER WAYS TO AVOID A RIP-OFF

Aside from guaranteeing you a job, vocational schools have been prominent offenders (but not the only ones) in two other areas of widespread abuse—downplaying their dropout rates and omitting information about their tuition refund policies.

In fact, the Federal Trade Commission has proposed regulations to require these schools to return tuition to students on a pro-rata basis when they drop out. The FTC hopes this rule would give vocational schools more incentive to screen prospective students, and once admitted, to monitor their progress. (See pages 1241–42.)

To be safe, be your own investigator:

• Ask the admissions officers how many students actually finished the course you're interested in, particularly if you're planning a correspondence course. If you can't get the facts here, be suspicious. If you still want to consider that school, try to get more information from the students.

• Be sure you have a clear picture of the school's refund policy. If you quit after completing only half of the prescribed classes, will you owe the full tuition or will you get half your money back? If less, how much less? Do not permit yourself to be among the huge numbers who sign a training contract, drop out after a few courses, then discover they owe the school a lot more money than they expected. This has become an open scandal.

• Finally, study the school's catalogs closely. Compare the vocational school's offerings with those of your nearby community college, adult education programs, public high schools, state vocational training programs, and on-the-job training programs offered by business and industry.

• Since other types of educational institutions are tax-supported, they may offer similar courses of training in the fields you are seeking of equal or even better quality.

• Check out specific schools with the state licensing or approval agency, usually found within your state's Department of Education. If the school you're considering has had a questionable track record with its students, this agency is likely to know about it. (List of state agencies for vocational schools follows.)

• Write the National Association of Trade Technical Schools, 2021 K Street, N.W., Washington, D.C. 20006, for its directory of schools it has accredited. Ask also for its brochure "How to Choose a Career—and a Career School." Both are free.

STATE AGENCIES FOR VOCATIONAL SCHOOLS

Following are the names, addresses, and telephone numbers of the statewide agencies responsible for postsecondary institutions that offer vocational-technical training in forty-eight states and the District of Columbia.

Governing boards are indicated by (G), coordinating boards by (C).

ALABAMA
Alabama State Department of
  Education
Postsecondary Division
817 South Court Street
Montgomery 36104
(205) 832-3340   (G)

ALASKA
Board of Regents
University of Alaska Statewide System
Fairbanks 99701
(907) 479-7312   (G)

ARKANSAS
Department of Education
Division of Vocational, Technical,
  and Adult Education
Arch Ford Education Building
Little Rock 72201
(501) 371-2165   (G)

CALIFORNIA
California Advisory Council on
  Vocational Education
708 Tenth Street
Sacramento 95814
(916) 445-0698   (C)

COLORADO
State Board for Community Colleges
    and Occupational Education
State Services Building
1525 Sherman Street
Denver 80203
(303) 839-3071   (G)

CONNECTICUT
Board of Trustees for State
    Technical College
165 Capitol Avenue
Hartford 06115
(203) 566-3976   (G)

DELAWARE
Delaware Technical and
    Community College
P. O. Box 897
Dover 19901
(302) 678-4621   (G)

DISTRICT OF COLUMBIA
District of Columbia Commission
    on Postsecondary Education
1329 E Street, N.W.
Washington, D.C. 20004
(202) 347-5905   (C)

FLORIDA
Florida Department of Education
Division of Vocational Education
Knott Building
Tallahassee 32304
(904) 488-8961   (C)

GEORGIA
Georgia Department of Education
Office of Vocational Education
237 State Office Building
Atlanta 30334
(404) 656-6711   (C)

HAWAII
University of Hawaii
Bachman Hall
2444 Dole Street
Honolulu 96822
(808) 948-7461   (G)

IDAHO
State Board of Education and Board
    of Regents of the University
    of Idaho
650 West State Street
Boise 98720
(208) 384-3216   (G)

ILLINOIS
Illinois Community College Board
518 Iles Park Place
Springfield 62718
(217) 782-2495   (C)

INDIANA
State Board of Vocation and
    Technical Education
401 Illinois Building
17 West Market Street
Indianapolis 46204
(317) 633-7673   (C)

IOWA
Department of Public Instruction
Grimes State Office Building
Des Moines 50319
(515) 281-5331   (C)

KANSAS
State Department of Education
Vocational Education
120 East Tenth Street
Topeka 66612
(913) 296-3951   (C)

KENTUCKY
State Department of Education
Bureau of Vocational Education
Capital Plaza Tower
Frankfort 40601
(502) 564-4286   (G)

LOUISIANA
State Department of Education
Division of Vocational Education
Department of Education Building
P. O. Box 44064
Baton Rouge 70804
(504) 389-2312   (G)

MAINE
Department of Educational and
   Cultural Services
Bureau of Vocational Education
Education Building
Augusta 04333
(207) 289-2621   (G)

MARYLAND
State Department of Education
Division of Vocational-Technical
   Education
P. O. Box 8717
Baltimore-Washington
   International Airport
Baltimore 21240
(301) 796-8300   (G)

MASSACHUSETTS
Board of Education
Bureau of Postsecondary
   Occupational-Technical Education
182 Tremont Street
Boston 02111
(617) 727-5738   (G)

MICHIGAN
State Board of Education
P. O. Box 30008
Lansing 48909
(517) 373-3373   (C)

MINNESOTA
State Department of Education
State Board for Vocational Education
Capitol Square Building
550 Cedar Street
St. Paul 55101
(612) 296-3994   (G)

MISSISSIPPI
State Department of Education
Division of Junior College
P. O. Box 771
Jackson 39205
(601) 354-6962   (C)

MISSOURI
Co-ordinating Board for Higher
   Education
Department of Higher Education
600 Clark Avenue
Jefferson City 65101
(314) 751-2361   (C)

MONTANA
Board of Public Education
State Capitol
Helena 59601
(406) 449-3126   (G)

NEBRASKA
Nebraska Co-ordinating Commission
   for Postsecondary Education
301 Centennial Mall South
Lincoln 68509
(402) 471-2331   (C)

NEW HAMPSHIRE
State Department of Education
Division of Postsecondary Education
163 Loudon Road
Concord 03301
(603) 271-2722   (G)

NEW JERSEY
Department of Education
Division of Vocational Education
225 West State Street
Trenton 08625
(609) 292-6340   (C)

NEW MEXICO
Board of Educational Finance
Legislative Executive Building
Santa Fe 87503
(505) 827-2115   (C)

NEW YORK
Regents of the University of the
   State of New York
State Education Department
Albany 12234
(518) 474-5880   (G)

NORTH CAROLINA
State Board of Education
Department of Community Colleges
Education Building
Raleigh 27611
(919) 733-7051   (G)

NORTH DAKOTA
North Dakota State Board of Higher
   Education
State Capitol Building
Bismarck 58505
(701) 224-2960   (G)

OHIO
Ohio Board of Regents
30 East Broad Street
Columbus 43215
(614) 466-5810   (C)

OKLAHOMA
Oklahoma State Regents for Higher
   Education
500 Education Building
State Capitol Complex
Oklahoma City 73105
(405) 521-2444   (C)

OREGON
Oregon Department of Education
Division of Community Colleges
942 Lancaster Drive, N.E.
Salem 97310
(503) 378-8609   (C)

PENNSYLVANIA
State Board of Education
Box 911
Harrisburg 17126
(717) 787-5530   (G)

RHODE ISLAND
Rhode Island Junior College
   State System
400 East Avenue
Warwick 02886
(401) 825-2188   (C)

SOUTH CAROLINA
State Board for Technical and
   Comprehensive Education
Rutledge Building
1429 Senate Street
Columbia 29201
(803) 758-3171   (G)

SOUTH DAKOTA
State Board of Vocational Education
State Office Building ⚹3
Pierre 57501
(605) 224-3423   (G)

TENNESSEE
Department of Education
Division of Vocational-Technical
   Education
200 Cordell Hull Building
Nashville 37219
(615) 741-1716   (G)

TEXAS
State Department of Education
Department of Occupation
   Education
201 East Eleventh Street
Austin 78701
(512) 475-2585   (G)

UTAH
State Board of Regents
807 East South Temple Street
Salt Lake City 84102
(801) 533-5617   (G)

VERMONT
Vermont State Colleges Board of
   Trustees
322 South Prospect Street
Burlington 05401
(802) 864-0241   (G)

VIRGINIA
Community College System
P. O. Box 1558
Richmond 23212
(804) 786-2231   (G)

WASHINGTON
Commission for Vocational Education
Airdustrial Park
Olympia 98504
(206) 753-5662　(G)

WEST VIRGINIA
State Department of Education
Bureau of Vocational, Technical,
　and Adult Education
B221 State Capitol Complex,
　Building 6
Charleston 25305
(304) 348-2346　(C)

WISCONSIN
Wisconsin Board of Vocational,
　Technical, and Adult Education
4802 Sheboygan Avenue
Madison 53702
(608) 266-1207　(G)

WYOMING
Community College Commission
New Boyd Building
1720 Carey Avenue
Cheyenne 82002
(307) 777-7764　(C)

Beware: Home Study Gyps

Today more home study courses are available by mail than you could possibly find at any of the nation's largest universities. Home study has truly come of age in the United States—a great force in upgrading the educational-economic status of millions, and a potent weapon in our nation's struggle to overcome skill shortages.

But as legitimate, worthwhile home study courses have gone into a record boom, the racketeering fringe has expanded too.

For instance, the appeal of Empire State College and the New York State Regents External Degree Program has encouraged some major colleges and universities in the state of New York to grant thousands of degrees through off-campus extension centers. A study in the late 1970s suggests that many of these newly established extension centers are academically deficient, operating with "inadequate facilities, counseling and other services." This type of situation might exist in other states. So before you decide on an extension college where you would earn an off-campus degree (either graduate or undergraduate) check carefully.

Use the same guidelines as for choosing a trade or technical school, and be suspicious of a school that uses any high-pressure sales tactics.

• If you have any doubt whatsoever about the value of a home study or extension course you have seen advertised, check its reputation with the local Better Business Bureau, Chamber of Commerce, or state Department of Education.

• To find out what legitimate courses are available to you in the field you wish to pursue, consult a high school or college guidance counselor.

• Get a free list of accredited, reputable home study schools from the National Home Study Council, 1601 Eighteenth Street, N.W., Washington, D.C. 20009.

• As for correspondence courses offered by accredited colleges and universities, a similar list entitled "Guide to Independent Study Through Correspondence Instruction" is available from National University Extension Association, Book Order Department, P. O. Box 2123, Princeton, New Jersey 08540. ($2.00)

• You'll also find useful information on choosing a correspondence school in

"Tips on Home Study Schools," a pamphlet available from the Council of Better Business Bureaus, Inc., 1150 Seventeenth Street, N.W., Washington, D.C. 20036. (Single copies free with self-addressed, stamped envelope.)

WHERE TO GET ADDITIONAL HELPFUL INFORMATION

Here is a sampling of free or inexpensive publications which should be of extraordinary help to you as you pursue this subject by yourself.

• "Meeting College Costs." College Board. (Free from high school counselors, updated annually.)

• "Need a Lift?" American Legion, P. O. Box 1055, Indianapolis, Indiana 46206. (50¢)

• "Don't Miss Out." Octameron Associates, P. O. Box 3437, Alexandria, Virginia 22302. ($1.25)

• "Selected List of Postsecondary Education Opportunities for Minorities and Women." Carol Smith, Department of Health, Education, and Welfare, Office of Education, Regional Office Building 3, Room 4082, Washington, D.C. 20202. (Free)

STUPID WASTE OF OUR SCHOOLS

Of all the stupid moves we, as citizens, made in the murderous era of spiraling living costs during the seventies, one of the most stupid was our shameful waste of our public schools throughout periodic vacations, weekends, and the summer months.

While our property taxes skyrocketed almost out of sight and intolerably squeezed homeowners in areas across the nation to the point of spectacular rebellion, most of the schools financed and maintained by these taxes were closed for a startling 50 per cent of the time!

While during Christmas-New Year's vacations, countless millions of our elderly, lonely, handicapped, poor, and other needy were yearning for places to meet and share their meals and thoughts, our handsome, beautifully landscaped elementary and high schools were shut tight. While during summer, millions more sought places to improve their skills, learn new skills, find ways to meet today's problems, most of these schools again were closed down as usual.

Our public schools are to an appalling degree unused for long periods of time —representing an abuse of schools and an extravagance that in this era America simply cannot afford.

The cost of supporting our elementary and high school system has tripled during the past ten years. But the overwhelming majority of the schools still are used only five days a week, nine months a year, and are restricted to the formal education of Americans between the ages of five and seventeen or eighteen. A stranger to the American educational system might understandably deduce that human learning begins in early September at the age of five and terminates (for all except the lucky) in June at the ages of seventeen to eighteen.

Meanwhile, there is an ever-mounting need for further education of the older

American—ranging from vocational training to retirement preparation and planning, consumer education, nutrition, music, arts, crafts. It must be increasingly clear to all thinking Americans that learning is a lifelong process, among the human being's most basic needs—and not the process that begins at five and ends a few years later.

What's the answer? The answer is community education schools—the use of our idle public schools to serve all of us.

And this answer also will help slash our local tax bills by avoiding the need to build and maintain additional expensive facilities, by keeping more real estate from falling off local town tax rolls, and incidentally by reducing vandalism in and around the schools. (Experience has demonstrated in a fascinating way that around community schools with all the facilities for full-time, year-round use to help young and old, vandalism becomes negligible.)

The whole concept of community education is gaining acceptance at the federal, state, and local levels at a speed that may come as a revelation even to the knowledgeable. As of last count, there were hundreds of school systems involved in implementing community education on a planned, organized basis. There is an expanding national network with centers for community education development headquartered mostly at colleges in a majority of our states.

Instead of being used to a puny one third of their potential, our traditional schools could become community schools and be open to all ages, twelve months a year, twelve to eighteen hours a day, seven days a week—and be used to their full potential. Instead of taxpayers getting a 25 per cent return on their investment in schools and paying in addition for many other duplicated services, we would be getting a full return on our investment plus interest through more and better organized services.

You and your own community can broaden your schools in a thousand and one ways—using them for purposes ranging from rehabilitation to special feeding programs for those who need them; from meeting places for the elderly especially to special outings for those who could not leave their homes otherwise. Whatever you do to use your schools more fully will all be plus.

10

YOUR LIFETIME FUTURE IN A JOB, CAREER, OR BUSINESS OF YOUR OWN

Your Own Choices Will Create Your Career

If you are thinking of "choosing" your occupation in terms of one great, momentous decision, your thinking is obsolete. It will *not* be one crucial decision; it will be a continuous process.

Your career outside the home will be made up of all the individual job choices you will make over the course of your working life, *as well as* whatever *education and training* you get *to prepare yourself* for those occupations. Your choices will create your future in a continuous building process.

All your education, training, and job choices may add up to one career, or two or three careers or even more! If you make all your choices within one occupational area or field—for example, health, communications, transportation, or manufacturing—generally it would be said that you have a career in that field. But you *may* make your choices in more than one field and have multiple careers, or you may create distinct but related careers within the same occupational field during your lifetime—for instance, as a nurse who studies to become a nursing practitioner and then studies to become a doctor. Within each major occupational field and industry, there are literally hundreds of related jobs with which to build your career. If you are a younger American, it's increasingly likely that you will have at least three or four careers in your lifetime, each of which will be the result of many, many individual choices.

Your career choices are not made in a vacuum. A multitude of factors over which you have little or no control can shape the nature of your choices. Technological advances can create new jobs even as they destroy old ones. . . . Changing needs and desires of America's citizens are reflected in the pool of available jobs, where the pool is and its size. . . . Access to training and educational opportunities affect your decisions. . . .

But the most important point for you to grasp and never forget is that *you yourself make your choices. You* build your career.

So how do you begin to build a future given the ever-changing nature of the job market and the enormous range of occupational possibilities?

The first step is: get information—information about the nature of U.S. industries and the job market they create, information about specific occupations, information about the best way to prepare yourself with education and training to get the jobs you want, information to help you with the job-hunting process.

Now study where the jobs are and will be, given these basic assumptions. . . .

BASIC ASSUMPTIONS

The United States Labor Department's Bureau of Labor Statistics is the source of the employment projections quoted throughout this chapter. The BLS based these projections on the following major assumptions:

• Our country will maintain today's system of government and institutions.

• Current social, technological, and scientific trends will continue, including the values we place on work, education, income, and leisure.

• No such major catastrophe as widespread or long-lasting energy shortages or global war will significantly alter our nation's industrial system.

• Trends in the occupational structure of industries will not change radically.

• Our economy will reach and maintain "full employment" (5 to 6 per cent jobless rates) by the mid 1980s.

So, given these basic assumptions . . .

WHERE WILL THE JOBS BE?

TRUE OR FALSE?

• The fastest growth in government jobs in the years ahead will be jobs in federal agencies.

• Most workers in the United States work for companies producing goods.

• Increasing automation in the office will slash the number of jobs for office workers.

• Good jobs for high school graduates will shrink dramatically as more and more employers demand that workers have college degrees.

• Jobs in agriculture will dwindle nearly to zero because of mechanization of farm work along with the virtual disappearance of small farms.

If you answered "true" to *any* of these questions, you were wrong. If you answered "true" to most of them, you flunked! Let's take the questions one by one:

• There will be considerable growth in the number of government jobs. But *almost all* of the growth is projected to occur at the *state and local levels,* not the federal level.

• Over 65 per cent of the United States work force today is producing *services* —medical, banking, insurance, writing, advising, planning, etc.—making ours the first service-dominated economy in world history. The vast majority of the new jobs now opening up are in the services: some 13.9 million new service jobs are predicted by 1985. In contrast, manufacturing, mining, and construction jobs (the goods-producing industries) are expected to gain only 4.5 million workers in the same period.

• Automation in the office has reduced opportunities for certain types of workers but has sharply increased demand for other important categories ranging from business machine operators and copying machine repair people to computer programmers, tape librarians, and tape perforator typists.

• Despite the stress on college education in the early 1970s, three out of four jobs will be open to people who have not completed four years of college— including high school dropouts as well as high school graduates. More and more training is being required of young people, but it is not necessarily college training. In fact, the Bureau of Labor Statistics predicts that the number of *college graduates* entering the work force will exceed openings in jobs college grads have traditionally filled *by 2.7 million* between the late 1970s and 1985!

• The decline of the small farm has been accelerating for more than a century, and by 1985 our entire food supply probably will be grown by a minuscule 3 per cent of the labor force. However, some new agricultural occupations are opening up in big "agribusinesses" which employ large numbers in fields ranging from stenography to surgery. And more and more farmers are going to college to learn biology, soil science, engineering, agronomy.

REVOLUTION IN THE U.S. WORKPLACE

Can you define the following occupational fields?

Cryogenics
Fiber-optics
Geomagnetics
Pattern recognition

These are some of the job categories and occupational specialties that are appearing on the U.S. job landscape.

Here are brief definitions of each:

Cryogenics: study and use of super-cold temperatures, ranging from 100° F. below zero (the temperature of dry ice) to nearly 460° below zero ("absolute zero"). Cryogenic temperatures are used today for making liquid air, liquid natural gas, and for fast-freezing certain foods.

Fiber-optics: use of transparent fibers made of glass or other materials to transmit light along curves and around corners. The technique is now being used to light otherwise inaccessible places such as inside the human body.

Geomagnetics: study of the earth's composition (geology) through the measurement of irregularities or disturbances in its magnetic field.

Pattern recognition: study of how to recognize patterns, especially when the patterns are hidden, incomplete, or partially obscured (e.g., in images, facts, concepts, information, etc.).

Just the strange sound of the above job titles underscores the extent to which whole new occupations are emerging under our eyes, while old occupations— ranging from the elevator operator to the railroad foreman—are disappearing.

KEY TRENDS IN JOBS AND CAREERS

Here are other key U.S. employment trends to watch for in the years directly ahead. Let them guide you not only in your initial career choice (if indeed you make such a "choice") but also in any of your deliberations over a second career.

- Demand for professional and technical workers—and especially for the latter —will continue to be strong.
- Increasingly, scientists and engineers will assume leadership of U.S. corporations.
- And manufacturers, under pressure from consumers and government regulatory agencies, may hire some workers to attend to social and environmental as well as strictly technical considerations—e.g., pollution controls, accident-proofing of cars, factories, toys, and homes.
- Physicians also will be moving toward outpatient care and comprehensive, continuous health care for groups of people for whom this care has not previously been available, such as the urban poor and those living in isolated rural areas. (And for the "haves" as well.)
- Today's "minorities"—especially women and blacks—will continue to find new and better jobs as companies vie with each other to eliminate discrimination.
- Part-time jobs will open in many fields, creating new work opportunities for students, young mothers, older workers.
- Expanded vocational rehabilitation programs will boost job chances for the handicapped, the retarded, and ex-criminal offenders.

What message does this sampling of employment trends shout to you? This above all:

Before you settle on any career choice, at least scan the literally hundreds of different occupations which will be open to you in the years ahead. Find out which jobs within each occupation or field seem to interest you. Then check the most promising job opportunities in each occupation. Then, and only then, zero in on choosing a career path to follow.

CHANGES COMING IN YOUR WORKWEEK

One further vitally important trend in the U.S. workplace is a reshuffling of your workday, workweek, and work year.

Thousands of Americans are now moving to a four-day, forty-hour week, and unions are pushing for a four-day, thirty-two-hour week. Thousands of companies already are on some kind of rearranged week, and the federal government as well as many industrial corporations and services are experimenting with different "flextime" plans. This is a trend certain to prevail in the years directly ahead.

The variations of work patterns are endless. Workers and employers may come around to "negotiating" their schedules and thus getting far more out of each other than they do now. One trend is toward the "gliding" workday, with workers arriving and departing when they choose within a twelve-hour day: the only requirement being that they work a certain number of hours a week.

Some plans call for "core" hours of work by all employees, with arrival and departure time left to choice.

As for the advantages of extended time off, it can be a real antidote to on-the-job boredom—by permitting a worker to recharge his physical and mental abilities periodically. Moreover, many people find they can do things with extended periods of leisure that they cannot manage otherwise.

Experiments in a rearranged workweek are, in fact, part of a broader trend toward great employment flexibility which already is well under way. Flextime combined with part-time work could be a means of opening job opportunities to more people while maintaining or increasing productivity. The shorter workweek also is expected to meet the needs of many older Americans to remain active as well as leave people more time to devote to community affairs, volunteer work, and continuing education.

Since the trend seems relentless, it is only common sense to start preparing now for the time when the five-day, forty-hour workweek gives way to "4-40" (four days, forty hours) and then swings into "4-32." (How have you handled yourself on previous three-day holidays?) Look into the fascinating choices in volunteer work, the absorbing possibilities of second careers in services starving for you, the many deeply satisfying alternatives in the vast expanse of non-work.

Killing time is suicide on the installment plan.

FLEXTIME—A GREAT WAY TO WORK

At Control Data, 25,000 employees have the option of setting their own working hours within certain specifications. Flextime, as this rapidly growing way of work in the United States, Europe, and Russia is known, "has positively affected productivity, absenteeism, tardiness, employee morale, travel time to and from work, and employee leisure time," says a personnel official at this giant American corporation.

At Hewlett-Packard, more than 30,000 employees have the option. "It is now such an accepted part of HP's personnel policies that we no longer are looking for reasons to justify it," says an HP spokesman who volunteers that HP imported the idea from West Germany and was among the U.S. pioneers in the concept.

At Occidental Life of California, flexible hours are considered a way of life and 3,500 employees are "flexing," reports a vice-president of personnel. "Our employees value this approach as mature individuals who appreciate having additional control over various aspects of their working lives."

And at Keyboard Communications, a word-processing firm headquartered on Long Island, the company's president credits flextime as responsible for Keyboard's rapid growth. "In most urban areas, companies have an enormous problem getting and keeping qualified office personnel. The better people are in the suburbs, so our offices are in the suburbs. We cater to the obligations of these people by giving our staff enormous latitude in setting hours."

This is just a random sampling of U.S. companies that have embraced the flextime concept. Just since the mid 1970s, the number of firms using flextime has doubled, says an American Management Association study. More than 6 per cent of all United States employees are now on flextime, excluding the self-employed and others who traditionally set their own hours. And the study's authors predict the trend will accelerate.

Among other United States companies offering flextime are Nestle, Sears Roebuck, Metropolitan Life, and Continental Oil. Also using the system are some federal agencies—such as the Department of Health, Education, and Welfare, where 70,000 are flexing.

How does it work? While there are variations, the basic structure is simple. The total workday is known as bandwidth and can run from 7:30 A.M. to 6:30 P.M. Inside this are core times, when you have to be on the job—say, 9:30 to 11:30 and 2 to 3:30—and the rest is flextime. How you use the flextime is up to you, providing you put in the required number of hours.

What's the objective? To reduce the stranglehold that the clock has on you. It can help you get the kids off to school, avoid peak rush hours on the highways, make a better train available, keep a hairdresser or dental appointment at lunch, arrange a game of tennis before or after work, etc.

Of course, there are drawbacks—management difficulties in scheduling of work hours and in communicating with employees, to name just two. And a recent survey by the non-profit Administrative Management Society, located in Willow Grove, Pennsylvania, also identified as important disadvantages: accommodating employees whose output is the input for other employees; employee abuse of flextime programs.

But even companies that feel flextime is not for them agree its popularity is spreading—and its use will grow.

As Vladlyen M. Livshits, a Soviet engineer who pioneered a flextime project in Kohtla-Järve, U.S.S.R., put it simply: "It humanizes work."

WHERE WILL THE JOB OPPORTUNITIES GROW FASTEST?

First, here are the U. S. Labor Department's projections for growth in major occupational categories until 1985:

FIELD	PER CENT CHANGE 1976–85
Professional and technical workers	+18%
Service workers (except private household), e.g., hospital attendants, policemen, waitresses	+23%
Clerical workers	+29%
Sales workers	+17%
Craftsmen and foremen	+22%
Managers, officials, proprietors	+21%
Mining (a new growth field)	+39%
Operatives (assemblers, truck drivers, bus drivers)	+17%
Non-farm laborers	+11%
Farm workers	−34%
All occupations	+19%

Here, even more specifically, is a list of occupations with job requirements projected to 1985:

OCCUPATION	ESTIMATED EMPLOYMENT 1976	AVERAGE ANNUAL OPENING TO 1985
Business administration and related professions		
Accountants	865,000	51,500
Engineers		
Electrical	300,000	12,800
Mechanical	200,000	9,300
Civil	155,000	8,900
Industrial	200,000	10,500
Health service occupations		
Registered nurses	960,000	83,000
Licensed practical nurses	460,000	53,000
Physicians, M.D.s and D.O.s	375,000	21,800
Veterinarians	30,500	1,800
Pharmacists	120,000	8,900
Medical laboratory workers	240,000	20,000
Dentists	112,000	4,800
X-ray technologists	80,000	6,300
Dental assistants	135,000	13,500
Teachers		
Kindergarten and elementary school teachers	1,364,000	70,000
Secondary school teachers	1,100,000	13,000
College and university teachers	593,000	17,000
Technicians		
Engineering and science technicians	586,000	29,000
Draftsmen	320,000	16,500
Other professional and related occupations		
Lawyers	396,000	23,400
Programmers	230,000	9,700
Social workers	330,000	25,000
Librarians	128,000	8,000
Home economists	141,000	6,100
Systems analysts	160,000	7,600
Managerial occupations		
Managers and assistants (hotel)	137,000	7,000
Bank officers	319,000	28,000

OCCUPATION	ESTIMATED EMPLOYMENT 1976	AVERAGE ANNUAL OPENING TO 1985
Clerical and related occupations		
Stenographers and secretaries	3,500,000	295,000
Bookkeeping workers	1,700,000	95,000
Cashiers	1,250,000	92,000
Typists	1,000,000	63,000
Bank clerks	456,000	36,000
Stock clerks	490,000	25,000
Telephone operators	230,000	232,000
Shipping and receiving clerks	440,000	23,000
Office machine operators	163,000	7,700
Receptionists	500,000	38,000
Electronic computer operating personnel	480,000	531,000
File clerks	270,000	16,000
Bank tellers	310,000	36,000
Sales occupations		
Retail trade sales workers	2,725,000	155,000
Wholesale trade sales workers	608,000	41,000
Manufacturers' sales workers	362,000	17,600
Insurance brokers and agents	490,000	27,500
Real estate sales workers and brokers	450,000	45,500
Securities sales workers	90,000	5,500
Service occupations		
Private household workers	1,125,000	53,000
Gasoline station attendants	420,000	14,800
Waiters and waitresses	1,260,000	71,000
Cooks and chefs	1,065,000	79,000
Cosmetologists	534,000	30,000
Police officers	500,000	32,500
Guards	500,000	63,300
Fire fighters	210,000	8,300
Barbers	124,000	8,100
Bartenders	261,000	17,800
Building trades		
Carpenters	1,010,000	67,000
Painters and paperhangers	425,000	27,700
Plumbers and pipe fitters	385,000	30,000

Occupation	Estimated Employment 1976	Average Annual Opening to 1985
Building trades (CONTD)		
Operating engineers (construction machinery operators)	585,000	41,000
Electricians (construction)	260,000	13,700
Bricklayers	175,000	7,500
Sheet metal workers	65,000	2,600
Mechanics and repairmen		
Automobile mechanics	790,000	32,000
Farm equipment mechanics	66,000	4,000
Appliance service workers	144,000	7,000
Industrial machinery repairers	320,000	30,000
Aircraft mechanics	110,000	5,200
Air-conditioning, refrigeration, and heating mechanics	175,000	17,400
Truck and bus mechanics	145,000	6,900
Telephone installers and repairers	110,000	4,000
Television, radio service	114,000	6,700
Office machine service workers	58,000	3,400
Other craft occupation		
Foremen (blue-collar worker supervisors)	1,445,000	79,000
Driving occupations		
City bus drivers	81,000	1,400
Truck drivers (long-distance)	467,000	15,400
Forklift operators	360,000	14,600
Other operative occupations		
Assemblers	1,100,000	70,000
Insulation workers	30,000	29,000
Welders and arc cutters	660,000	33,800
Machine tool operators	508,000	22,000
Waste water treatment workers	100,000	10,400

JOB PASSPORT FOR TOMORROW'S WORLD: A FOREIGN LANGUAGE

Teaching, law, and veterinary medicine once were considered sure and safe careers. But all three fields are overcrowded today. If you train for a job that looks great in the early 1980s, how can you be certain it will even be in existence twenty, or even ten, years from now?

The answer: you can't be certain. But whether you're a young student selecting your college major, a parent trying to guide your children, or one of the growing numbers of adults seeking a second career, there is one move you can make that will enhance your chances for just about any career.

Learn a foreign language.

With a language skill added to your other skills, you might double your chances of getting the job you want. There are more openings for an auto mechanic who also speaks Arabic, an electronic radio expert who knows Japanese, a chef (even a woman chef) who understands French. It even could be that a foreign language would be more useful to you during the next ten years than a college diploma, for whatever the shape of tomorrow's world, you can be sure it will be increasingly international. Consider how international it already is.

• One American in six now owes his/her employment to foreign trade.

• Many of the five hundred largest U.S. corporations earn more than half of their profits overseas.

• More and more Americans are finding jobs in the United States as "local nationals" for foreign-owned companies. Foreign companies in the late 1970s invested more than $30 billion directly in businesses here and needed these "local nationals."

• A full 43 per cent of the chief executive officers who have assumed their positions in America's hundred largest corporations since the mid 1970s have had overseas experience—and there are increasing numbers of ads for executives "fluent in . . ."

• The fourth largest Spanish-speaking country in the world is the United States. We're close to becoming bilingual.

Some basic guides if you're thinking of gaining or improving language skills:

(1) The most popular language with Americans is Spanish, but German, Japanese, and French are useful, too, since these are the languages spoken in top business cities.

(2) Whatever language you choose, speak the language yourself in give-and-take discussion with a teacher so you can become fluent. Don't rely solely on books and records. At world-famous Berlitz, which numbers more than half of the "Fortune 500" companies among its clients, private lessons cost around $15.00 each while classes cost from $7.00 to $9.00 as the 1980s began.

(3) If you must learn a language in a hurry, a Berlitz "Total Immersion" (TI) course will bombard you with the "target" language for nine hours a day, including lunch, five days a week. TI can give you a high degree of fluency in only four to six weeks, and varies in cost with the language being taught. Such major languages as French, Spanish, and German are cheaper to learn than unusual languages like Urdu or Tagalog.

But while enrollments are rising at language schools, university enrollments in several basic languages have declined 30 per cent in the past several years, and fewer than 2 per cent of high school graduates in the late 1970s had any competency in a foreign language.

We're even more inferior in our cultural knowledge of other countries. Fewer than 5 per cent of teachers now being trained are required to take intercultural courses for certification. The percentage of international items featured on U.S.

commercial TV networks is the lowest out of one hundred nations surveyed by UNESCO. Fewer American correspondents are abroad now than at any time since World War II.

Is it so surprising that in a survey a few years ago of high school seniors, 40 per cent thought that the late Golda Meir was president of Egypt?

And it is against this background that you should weigh the judgment of one executive that "a person who speaks two languages is worth two people."

YOUR EDUCATION AND YOUR CAREER

The long-term trend has been toward more and more education to qualify for most jobs, higher and higher degrees to aspire to the very top in many fields, lower and lower esteem for the less-than-college-educated individual.

Do these ever-rising educational requirements reflect real job requirements—or merely "creeping credentialism"?

Some of both. Specifically:

The U. S. Bureau of Labor Statistics estimates that between now and 1985 the demand for professionals will increase at twice the rate that demand rises for all other workers. But it also estimates that the number of college graduates entering the job market between 1976 and 1985 will exceed by 2.7 million the kinds of jobs available that college grads traditionally have filled. This means that large numbers of college graduates may have to downgrade their expectations. In fact, this downgrading already is well under way. Moreover, as the demand for paraprofessionals has soared, particularly in the health, education, law, and environmental fields, so has the number of two-year colleges and/or job-training opportunities—points not to be overlooked or underrated.

Meanwhile, the oversupply of certain Ph.D.s has been balanced by real shortages of skilled craftsmen and technical support personnel in many areas. As we pushed back the limits of scientific and academic knowledge, we tended to undervalue craftsmanship. Dropouts who took up carpentry or pottery were among the first to rediscover that working with one's hands could be deeply satisfying. Now educators and economists realize the urgent need to give status to those who have manual talents. (In pay, many craftsmen, such as electricians, carpenters, plumbers, already more than compete with high-paying white-collar jobs. It's how society has viewed the craftsmen that is different.)

Does this mean guidance counselors will stop encouraging students to go to college? No. But it does mean counselors will increasingly endeavor to persuade overanxious parents of something many young people have long suspected: college isn't for everyone and this is nothing to be ashamed of.

It also means that the educational systems of the future must be designed to turn out fewer specialists and more generalists in both the "humanities" and the sciences so that young people will be able to shift among a number of different professions. For example, a young man or woman interested in children might train simultaneously for child care, recreation, mental health, and education, in order to be able to step into whichever field most needs his or her talents at a given time.

And it means that training programs, apprenticeships—in fact, all forms of occupational training—will come in for more serious consideration than ever before. Says a noted educator: "We are going to have to make the same resources available for the would-be hairdresser as we are doing for the Ivy League collegian."

What, then, will be the new status of education? More than ever, education for its own sake will be a prime concern in this country. Colleges already are expanding efforts to make their educational facilities available to the community at large, enabling professionals (and paraprofessionals) to keep abreast of change and to enrich all those leisure hours that are coming, as the workweek shifts from five to four and eventually three days. "Lifelong learning" for occupational advancement and personal enrichment will become the norm.

Yes, the pay will remain somewhat higher for the college graduate who can find work, and it usually will still take a degree to get to the very top. But a college degree is no longer a guarantee of employment, whereas certain crafts, paratechnical and paraprofessional areas are crying for help. Graduates of two-year colleges whose pay scale is lower and who do a perfectly adequate job are even now preferred in many areas where the B.A. had become a bloated requirement.

In essence, what all this says to you is:

Read the projections in this chapter and other occupational guides with two points always in mind. First, our society is changing faster than ever before, reacting to technological breakthroughs with unpredictable impacts on the job market. And second, where evidence is unmistakable that work exists to be done, such as in preserving our environment, the key factor in determining how many jobs will be available for the trained worker will depend on the future reordering of our national priorities.

Against this background, it is no more than common sense to try to start with as broad and sound an education as you can get: to choose your general field of work as late as you can to give yourself as much and as varied a training in that field as possible. Then you will enter the job market supported by the widest range of capabilities from which you can only benefit.

Good Occupations for College Graduates

You will find most of the details on which jobs require which levels of training in the current edition of the United States Labor Department's "Occupational Outlook Handbook" or in another guide, "Occupation Outlook for College Graduates." Both of these are well worth the $5.00 to $8.00 the United States Government charges for them. Look for them in your school guidance office or library.

An edition of the "Occupational Outlook for College Graduates" in the late 1970s predicts that overall job prospects for a wide range of college grads are grim. Many will be forced to take jobs that previously have not been filled by degree recipients. Some occupations, however, are exceptions to this general rule. Would-be accountants, bank officers, computer programmers, engineers, and physicians, for instance, face good job prospects.

But you don't have to confine yourself to these fields. The Labor Department's books provide information on more than one hundred occupations. You will find descriptions of what the work is like, the qualifications and training required, the working conditions, earnings, chances for advancement, and job prospects until 1985.

Following is a summary for a sampling of the many occupations listed:

Accountants: employment, 865,000; annual openings, 51,500. Employment expected to increase about as fast as average as managers rely on more accounting information to make business decisions. Graduates with four-year accounting degrees will be in greatest demand.

Architects: employment, 49,000; annual openings, 3,100. Employment expected to rise about as fast as the average for all occupations. Competition for jobs likely. Prospects are best in the South and in states without architectural schools.

Bank officers and managers: employment, 319,000; annual openings, 28,000. Employment expected to increase faster than average as rising costs of new technology and services require more officers to provide sound management. Good opportunities for college graduates as management trainees.

Chemists: employment, 148,000; annual openings, 6,300. Employment expected to grow about as fast as average as a result of increasing demand for new product development and rising concern about energy shortages, pollution control, and health care. Except for positions in colleges and universities, good opportunities should exist.

College and university teachers: employment, 593,000; annual openings, 17,000. Despite expected employment growth, applicants will face keen competition for jobs. Best opportunities in public colleges and universities. Persons who do not have a Ph.D. will find it increasingly difficult to secure a teaching position.

Dentists: employment, 112,000; annual openings, 4,800. Employment expected to grow about as fast as average due to population growth, increased awareness of importance of dental care, and expansion of prepayment arrangements. Opportunities should be very good.

Economists: employment, 115,000; annual openings, 6,400. Employment expected to grow faster than average. Master's and Ph.D. degree holders may face keen competition for college and university positions but can expect good opportunities in nonacademic areas. Persons with only bachelor's degrees likely to face brutal competition.

Engineers: employment, 1,133,000; annual openings 56,600. Employment expected to grow slightly faster than the average for all occupations. Good employment opportunities for engineering graduates in most specialties. Some openings also available to graduates in related fields.

Foresters: employment 25,000; annual openings 1,100. Employment expected to grow about as fast as the average for all occupations as environmental concern and need for forest products increase. However, applicants likely to face keen competition.

Geologists: employment, 34,000; annual openings, 2,300. Employment expected to grow faster than average as domestic mineral exploration increases. Good opportunities for persons with degrees in geology or related scientific fields.

Health services administrators: employment, 160,000; annual openings, 16,000. Employment expected to grow much faster than average as quantity of patient services increases and health services management becomes more complex.

Historians: employment 22,500; annual openings, 900. Employment expected to grow more slowly than average. Keen competition expected, particularly for academic positions. Persons with training in historical specialties such as historic preservation and business history have best opportunities.

Kindergarten and elementary school teachers: employment, 1,364,000; annual openings, 70,000. Competition for jobs expected as enrollments continue to decline until early 1980s. Re-entrants will face increasing competition from new graduates.

Lawyers: employment, 396,000; annual openings, 23,400. Employment expected to grow faster than average in response to increased business activity and population. However, keen competition likely for salaried positions. Best prospects for establishing new practices will be in small towns and expanding suburbs, although starting a practice will remain a risky and expensive venture.

Librarians: employment, 128,000; annual openings, 8,000. Although employment expected to grow, field is likely to be somewhat competitive. Best prospects in school and public libraries away from large east and west coast cities.

Life scientists: employment, 205,000; annual openings, 12,000. Employment expected to grow faster than average due to increasing expenditures for medical research and environmental protection. Good opportunities for persons with advanced degrees.

Manufacturers' sales workers: employment 362,000; annual openings, 17,600. Employment expected to grow about as fast as average because of rising demand for technical products and resulting need for trained sales workers.

Mathematicians: employment, 38,000; annual openings, 1,000. Slower than average employment growth expected to lead to keen competition for jobs, especially for academic positions. Opportunities expected to be best for advanced degree holders in applied mathematics seeking jobs in government and private industry.

Newspaper reporters: employment, 40,500; annual openings, 2,100. Slower than average employment growth and rising number of journalism graduates expected to create major competition for openings. Best opportunities for bright and energetic persons with exceptional writing ability on newspapers in small towns and suburbs.

Physicians and osteopathic physicians: employment, 375,000; annual openings, 21,800. Employment outlook expected to be very favorable. New physicians should have little difficulty in establishing new practices.

Physicists: employment, 48,000; annual openings, 1,100. Although employment will grow more slowly than average, generally favorable job opportunities are expected for persons with advanced degrees in physics. However, persons seeking college and university positions, as well as graduates with only a bachelor's degree, will face strong competition.

YOUR LIFETIME FUTURE IN A JOB, CAREER, OR BUSINESS   583

Programmers: employment, 230,000; annual openings, 9,700. Employment expected to grow faster than average as computer usage expands, particularly in accounting and business management firms. Brightest prospects for college graduates with degrees in computer science or related field.

Registered nurses: employment, 960,000; annual openings, 83,000. Employment expected to grow faster than average. Favorable opportunities, especially in some Southern states and many inner-city locations. Nurses may find competition for higher paying jobs and for jobs in some urban areas with large nurse training facilities.

School counselors: employment, 43,000; annual openings, 1,500. Employment expected to grow more slowly than average as declining school enrollments coupled with financial constraints limit growth.

Secondary school teacher: employment 1,111,000; annual openings, 13,000. Keen competition expected due to declining enrollments coupled with large increases in supply of teachers. More favorable opportunities will exist for persons qualified to teach vocational subjects, mathematics, and the natural sciences.

Social workers: employment, 330,000; annual openings, 25,000. Employment expected to increase faster than average due to expansion of health services, passage of social welfare legislation, and potential development of national health insurance. Best opportunities for graduates with Master's and Ph.D. degrees in social work.

Statisticians: employment, 24,000; annual openings, 1,500. Employment expected to grow faster than average as use of statistics expands into new areas. Persons combining knowledge of statistics with a field of application, such as economics, may expect favorable job opportunities.

Systems analysts: employment, 160,000; annual openings, 7,600. Employment expected to grow faster than average as computer capabilities are increased and computers are used to solve a greater variety of problems. Excellent prospects for graduates of computer-related curriculums.

GUIDES TO OCCUPATIONS AND CAREERS

Now that you've had a chance at least to scan the state of the job market as the 1980s approach and what the nation's top experts think will be its shape in the future, how do you go about preparing for it?

KEY POINTERS FOR YOU

• First and most obviously, study the full range of options and combinations open to you—and the range is vast indeed.

If you were asked to list, in a reasonable period of time, all the occupations you could think of, I'll wager you would name fewer than 50. Yet the United States Labor Department's *Occupational Outlook Handbook* describes more than 800 occupations—many of them not even in existence a few years back. And the United States Government's *Dictionary of Occupational Titles* lists approximately 40,000 different job titles!

The *Occupational Outlook Handbook* should be your primary source in exploring your job/career options. This publication (revised every two years) provides details on each occupation—what work it involves, salary ranges, projected number of job openings, education and training requirements, and sources to which you can write for more information. The *Handbook* is available at most schools and libraries, but it is worth the price to buy your own from the Superintendent of Documents, United States Government Printing Office, Washington, D.C. 20210. It also can be ordered from Bureau of Labor Statistics Offices in eight major cities: Atlanta, Boston, Chicago, Dallas, Kansas City, Philadelphia, New York, and San Francisco. (You also might want to order a subscription to the *Occupational Outlook Quarterly* magazine, which, as the name implies, comes out four times a year, with updated employment projections and special job-related articles.)

Surely it is already obvious that an excellent place to launch your information search is the public library, which often has a good selection of occupational materials. Your school, local college, and junior or community college libraries and school counselors' offices are other top-notch sources. Don't overlook professional and trade groups (a listing appears in this chapter) as occupational information sources and you also might try asking local corporations for information on the types of trained workers they need. (Your local state employment service office, which is part of the U. S. Employment Service, also offers a wealth of career information and can give you local as well as nationwide job opening information.)

If you live in one of the nine states (Alabama, Colorado, Massachusetts, Michigan, Minnesota, Ohio, Oregon, Washington, and Wisconsin) that have computer-assisted occupational information systems (OIS) funded by the United States Department of Labor, be sure to use them. These systems, which use microfilm and audiovisual and printed materials to help you get access both to statewide and national career and occupational information, can be "gold mines." If you live in one of those states, ask your local state employment service office about where you can get access to OIS materials. Or write to the Division of Career Information Services, Employment and Training Administration, U. S. Department of Labor, 601 D Street, N.W., Room 9122, Washington, D.C. 20213.

• Don't, though, make the mistake of abandoning a career goal you genuinely want just because your choice isn't among the fastest-growing occupations. Simply accept the likelihood that you will have to face stiff competition—and possibly a certain amount of job insecurity too. Explore the new careers, for you may find there an unsuspected offshoot of your dream career.

• Understand thoroughly the extent of education and training that may be required—and available—for any given occupation. Today's machinist, for instance, must have a solid foundation in mathematics. Today's top-notch secretary must know how to operate a range of new office machinery, possibly must know a foreign language or have a secretarial specialty (such as law or medicine). Today's plumber needs at least a high school diploma to qualify for a job, and additional on-the-job training has become a minimum requirement.

• Recognize that, whatever occupation you choose, broad general knowledge ranks in importance with the specific education directly related to the occupation. In this era's rapidly changing job market, flexibility is crucial.

• Keep open your chances to change careers throughout your whole working life. The choice of an occupation is not a single decision. Rather, it is at least a ten-year process, I repeat and re-emphasize, involving a long-term strategy which could include several different careers. This holds for the physicist as it holds for the pipe fitter; both can anticipate a continuous process of training and re-education throughout their working lives.

• Think of your career as a "gift box" inside you. It's yours to unwrap and unlock and pursue—not anyone else's.

GUIDES FOR PARENTS

As for you, the parents of a young person beginning his or her career hunt, here are six "do's and don'ts" to guide you on counseling your children:

Don't force your own occupational choice on your child. The idea that your son must be a doctor because you are or wanted to be one is ridiculous. A career choice involves much more than intelligence. It involves the child's values, attitudes toward work and life, emotional maturity.

Do be understanding if your child is in no hurry to choose a career. Even if he or she drops out of college in the second year, it could be a sign of wisdom. Be supportive as your child explores the occupational options open to him or her.

Don't try to drive your child to "get ahead." The young generation has watched their parents become great "career successes"—at the cost of discontent, divorce, alcoholism, absentee fathers. Relax. You've had your chances to make your choices. Let your kids have the same.

Do understand that your home is the single best source of values and that your attitudes toward work generally can be a real and important influence. Stress the values you cherish.

Don't plague a child who does not have the required intellectual equipment to become a professional or even to complete college. You'll only create impossible conflicts for him or her.

Do realize the enormous range of job opportunities open to your child even if he or she does not go to college.

OPTIONS FOR OPT-OUTS

What if your goal is a career in farming? Organic gardening? Leather working? Running an organic food store? Weaving or wool spinning? Or a job as a waiter in a Greenwich Village coffee shop? Or driving a taxi in San Francisco? Or delivering newspapers in Denver?

Perceptible numbers of you have rejected America's long-standing occupational values of money, security, success, challenge, position. You turned your backs on the standard careers which I have listed in previous pages, and traded well-paying jobs you could perform excellently for non-paying jobs in conservation, political campaigns, consumer organizations.

If you are a college dropout and especially one who hates competition, computers, machines, executive authority, the profit motive, you well may already have become an emigrant to the backwoods where the preferred occupations are homesteading and manual crafts.

But there are other alternatives for you, the young humanist, in blending such fields as engineering with social consciousness, technology with ethics.

Perhaps you have seen the old vocational aptitude tests on which you found such questions as "Would you rather read novels to a blind old lady or repair a broken garbage disposal unit?" If you checked the former, you were classed as preferring the social service type occupations; the latter, as a budding scientist. It could be that one of the choices on tomorrow's tests will turn out to be "scientific social service" (that is, repairing a garbage disposal unit for a blind old lady). The tests already are being rewritten to include that sort of option.

A LIST OF CAREER INFORMATION SOURCES

Even the preceding smattering of clues to a random sampling of career fields must dramatize how vital it is to your whole future to get as much information as possible about any occupation that intrigues you before you even begin to commit yourself.

Here is a list of trade and professional groups, government agencies, and other organizations that can provide you with information about specific fields:

ACCOUNTANT
American Institute of Certified Public
  Accountants
1211 Avenue of the Americas
New York, NY 10036

ADVERTISER
American Association of Advertising
  Agencies
200 Park Avenue
New York, NY 10017

American Advertising Federation
1225 Connecticut Avenue, N.W.
Washington, DC 20036

AEROSPACE ENGINEER
American Institute of Aeronautics and
  Astronautics
1290 Avenue of the Americas
New York, NY 10019

AGRICULTURE AND AGRICULTURAL
  RESEARCH
Office of Personnel
U. S. Department of Agriculture
Washington, DC 20250

AIR CONDITIONING AND
  REFRIGERATION MECHANIC
Air Conditioning and Refrigeration
  Institute
1815 North Fort Meade Drive
Arlington, VA 22209

AIRPLANE MECHANIC
Air Transport Association of America
1709 New York Avenue, N.W.
Washington, DC 20006

Aviation Maintenance Foundation
P. O. Box 739
Basin, WY 82410

ANTHROPOLOGIST
American Anthropological
  Association
1703 New Hampshire Avenue, N.W.
Washington, DC 20009

APPAREL INDUSTRY
International Ladies' Garment
  Workers' Union
1710 Broadway
New York, NY 10019

Apparel Manufacturers Association
1440 Broadway
New York, NY 10018

American Apparel Manufacturers
  Association
1611 North Kent Street, Suite 800
Arlington, VA 22209

APPLIANCE SERVICEMAN
Association of Home Appliance
  Manufacturers
20 North Wacker Drive
Chicago, IL 60606

ARCHITECT
The American Institute of Architects
1735 New York Avenue, N.W.
Washington, DC 20006

ASTRONOMER
American Astronomical Society
211 FitzRandolph Road
Princeton, NJ 08540

AUTO MECHANIC AND BODY REPAIR
Automotive Service Industry
  Association
230 North Michigan Avenue
Chicago, IL 60601

National Automobile Dealers
  Association
2000 K Street, N.W.
Washington, DC 20006

AUTOMOTIVE ENGINEER
The Society of Automotive Engineers,
  Inc.
400 Commonwealth Drive
Warrendale, PA 15096

Automotive Service Councils, Inc.
188 Industrial Drive, Suite 112
Elmhurst, IL 60126

BANKER, BANK TELLER
American Bankers Association
1120 Connecticut Avenue, N.W.
Washington, DC 20036

BIOCHEMIST
American Society of Biological
  Chemists
9650 Rockville Pike
Bethesda, MD 20014

BIOLOGISTS, OTHER LIFE SCIENTISTS
American Institute of Biological
  Scientists
1401 Wilson Boulevard
Arlington, VA 22209

BRICKLAYER
International Union of Bricklayers
  and Allied Craftsmen
815 Fifteenth Street, N.W.
Washington, DC 20005

BUSINESS MANAGEMENT
The American Management
  Associations
135 West Fiftieth Street
New York, NY 10015

CARPENTER
United Brotherhood of Carpenters
  and Joiners of America
101 Constitution Avenue, N.W.
Washington, DC 20001

Associated General Contractors of
  America, Inc.
1957 E Street, N.W.
Washington, DC 20006

CHEMICAL ENGINEER
American Institute of Chemical
  Engineers
345 East Forty-seventh Street
New York, NY 10017

CHEMIST
American Chemical Society
1155 Sixteenth Street, N.W.
Washington, DC 20036

Manufacturing Chemists Association
1825 Connecticut Avenue, N.W.
Washington, DC 20009

CHILD WELFARE WORKER
National Association of Social
  Workers
1425 H Street, N.W., Suite 600
Southern Building
Washington, DC 20005

CITY PLANNER
American Institute of Planners
1776 Massachusetts Avenue, N.W.
Washington, DC 20036

American Society of Planning Officials
1313 East Sixtieth Street
Chicago, IL 60637

CLERICAL WORKER
United Business Schools Association
1730 M Street, N.W.
Washington, DC 20036

State Supervisor of Office Occupations
  Education
State Department of Education
State Capitol (of your state)

COMPUTER OPERATOR,
  PROGRAMMER, SYSTEMS ANALYST
American Federation of Information
  Processing Societies
210 Summit Avenue
Montvale, NJ 07645

Association for Systems Management
24587 Bagley Road
Cleveland, OH 44138

Institute for Certification of Computer
  Professionals
35 East Wacker Drive, Suite 2828
Chicago, IL 60601

CONSERVATIONIST
The Conservation Foundation
1717 Massachusetts Avenue, N.W.
Washington, DC 20036

The Wildlife Society
7101 Wisconsin Avenue, N.W.
Bethesda, MD 20014

The Wilderness Society
1901 Pennsylvania Avenue, N.W.
Washington, DC 20006

The Nature Conservancy
1800 North Kent Street
Arlington, VA 22209

National Wildlife Federation
1412 Sixteenth Street, N.W.
Washington, DC 20036

Society of American Foresters
5400 Grosvenor Lane
Washington, DC 20014

Soil Conservation Service
U. S. Department of Agriculture
Washington, DC 20250

National Parks and Conservation
  Association
1701 Eighteenth Street, N.W.
Washington, DC 20009

American Public Works Association
1313 East Sixtieth Street
Chicago, IL 60637

National Audubon Society
950 Third Avenue
New York, NY 10022

COOK, CHEF
Educational Director
National Institute for the Food Service
  Industry
120 South Riverside Plaza
Chicago, IL 60606

Culinary Institute of America
P. O. Box 53
Hyde Park, NY 12538

The Educational Institute
American Hotel and Motel
  Association
1407 South Harrison Road
East Lansing, MI 48823

DATA PROCESSOR
American Federation of Information
  Processing Societies
210 Summit Avenue
Montvale, NJ 07645

DAY-CARE WORKER
Day Care and Child Development
  Council of America, Inc.
622 Fourteenth Street, N.W.
Washington, DC 20005

DENTIST AND DENTAL ASSISTANT
Division of Career Guidance
Council on Dental Education
American Dental Association
211 East Chicago Avenue
Chicago, IL 60611

American Dental Assistants
  Association
211 East Chicago Avenue
Chicago, IL 60611

American Association of Dental
  Schools
1625 Massachusetts Avenue, N.W.
Washington, DC 20036

Division of Dentistry
Public Health Service
U. S. Department of Health,
  Education, and Welfare
9000 Rockville Pike
Bethesda, MD 20014

DIESEL MECHANIC
International Association of
  Machinists and Aerospace Workers
1300 Connecticut Avenue, N.W.
Washington, DC 20036

DIETITIAN
The American Dietetic Association
430 North Michigan Avenue, 10th
  Floor
Chicago, IL 60611

DIRECT SELLING
Direct Selling Association

1730 M Street, N.W.
Washington, DC 20036

ECONOMIST
American Economic Association
1313 Twenty-first Avenue South
Nashville, TN 37212

EDUCATION (TEACHING CAREERS)
National Education Association
1201 Sixteenth Street, N.W.
Washington, DC 20036

American Council on Education
One Dupont Circle, N.W.
Washington, DC 20036

ELECTRICAL CONTRACTING
National Electrical Contractors
  Association
7315 Wisconsin Avenue
Bethesda, MD 20014

ELECTRICAL-ELECTRONIC
  TECHNICIAN (RADIO AND TV)
Electronic Industries Association
2001 Eye Street, N.W.
Washington, DC 20006

ELECTRICIAN
International Brotherhood of
  Electrical Workers
1125 Fifteenth Street, N.W.
Washington, DC 20005

Edison Electric Institute
90 Park Avenue
New York, NY 10016

National Joint Apprenticeship and
  Training Committee for the
  Electrical Industry
1730 Rhode Island Avenue, N.W.
Washington, DC 20036

ENGINEER
National Society of Professional
  Engineers
2029 K Street, N.W.
Washington, DC 20006

Engineers Council for Professional
  Development
345 East Forty-seventh Street
New York, NY 10017

FAMILY AND HOME ECONOMICS,
  NUTRITIONIST
American Home Economics
  Association
2010 Massachusetts Avenue, N.W.
Washington, DC 20036

FARMER, AGRICULTURAL RESEARCH
  WORKER
Office of Personnel
U. S. Department of Agriculture
Washington, DC 20250

FLIGHT ATTENDANTS
Air Transport Association of America
1709 New York Avenue, N.W.
Washington, DC 20006

FOOD SCIENTIST
Institute of Food Technologists
Suite 2120
221 North LaSalle Street
Chicago, IL 60601

FOREIGN SERVICE
Director, Foreign Service Recruitment
Board of Examiners
Department of State
Washington, DC 20520

FORESTER
Society of American Foresters
5400 Grosvenor Lane
Washington, DC 20014

U. S. Forest Service
U. S. Department of Agriculture
Washington, DC 20250

American Forestry Association
1319 Eighteenth Street, N.W.
Washington, DC 20036

GEOGRAPHER
Association of American Geographers
1710 Sixteenth Street, N.W.
Washington, DC 20009

GEOLOGIST
American Geological Institute
5205 Leesburg Pike
Falls Church, VA 22041

GEOPHYSICIST
American Geophysical Union
1909 K Street, N.W.
Washington, DC 20006

Society of Exploration Geophysicists
P.O. Box 3098
Tulsa, OK 74101

GOVERNMENT JOBS
U. S. Civil Service Commission
Bureau of Recruiting and Examining
Room 1416A
1900 E Street, N.W.
Washington, DC 20415

HEALTH
Division of Careers and Recruitment
American Hospital Association
840 North Lake Shore Drive
Chicago, IL 60611

National Health Council
Health Careers Program
1740 Broadway
New York, NY 10019

Health Resources Administration
Bethesda, MD 20014

Program Services Department
American Medical Association
535 North Dearborn Street
Chicago, IL 60610

HOSPITAL ADMINISTRATOR
American College of Hospital
  Administrators
840 North Lake Shore Drive
Chicago, IL 60611

Association of University Programs in
  Health Administration
One Dupont Circle, N.W.
Washington, DC 20036

American Public Health Association
Division of Program Services
1015 Eighteenth Street, N.W.
Washington, DC 20036

HOTEL-MOTEL WORKER
The Educational Institute
    American Hotel and Motel
    Association
1407 South Harrison Road
East Lansing, MI 48823

The Council of Hotel, Restaurant and
    Institutional Education
11 Kroger Executive Center, Suite
    219
Norfolk, VA 23502

INSTRUMENT REPAIRMAN
Instrument Society of America
400 Stanwix Street
Pittsburgh, PA 15222

INSURANCE UNDERWRITER OR CLAIM
    EXAMINER
American Council of Life Insurance
1850 K Street, N.W.
Washington, DC 20006

Insurance Information Institute
110 William Street
New York, NY 10038

American Mutual Insurance Alliance
20 North Wacker Drive
Chicago, IL 60606

JOURNALISM
The Society of Professional Journalists
Sigma Delta Chi
35 East Wacker Drive
Chicago, IL 60601

American Newspaper Publishers
    Association Foundation
Box 17407
Dulles International Airport
Washington, DC 20041

Journalism schools at major
    universities (e.g., Columbia, New

York City, University of Missouri,
Columbia)

LAWYER AND LEGAL ASSISTANT
    (PARALEGAL)
Association of American Law Schools
One Dupont Circle, N.W., Suite 370
Washington, DC 20036

Information Services
The American Bar Association
1155 East Sixtieth Street
Chicago, IL 60637

LIBRARIAN
American Library Association
50 East Huron Street
Chicago, IL 60603

LICENSED PRACTICAL NURSE
National Federation of Licensed
    Practical Nurses, Inc.
250 West Fifty-seventh Street
New York, NY 10019

National League for Nursing, Inc.
10 Columbus Circle
New York, NY 10019

National Association for Practical
    Nurse Education and Service, Inc.
112 East Forty-second Street, Suite
    8000
New York, NY 10017

LIFE INSURANCE SALES WORKERS
National Association of Insurance
    Agents, Inc.
85 John Street
New York, NY 10038

MACHINIST
The National Machine Tool Builders
    Association
7901 West Park Drive
McLean, VA 22101

National Tool, Die, and Precision
    Machining Association
9300 Livingston Road
Oxon Hill, MD 20022

MASON
International Union of
  Bricklayers and Allied Craftsmen
815 Fifteenth Street, N.W.
Washington, DC 20005

MEDICAL LABORATORY WORKERS
American Society for Medical
  Technology
5555 West Loop South
Bellaire, TX 77401

American Medical Technologists
710 Higgins Road
Park Ridge, IL 60068

Accrediting Bureau of Medical
  Laboratory Schools
Oak Manor Office
29089 U.S. 20 West
Elkhart, IN 46514

MEDICAL RECORD LIBRARIAN
American Medical Record Association
875 North Michigan Avenue, Suite
  1850
Chicago, IL 60611

MEDICAL TECHNOLOGIST AND
  MEDICAL TECHNICIAN
American Medical Association
Department of Allied Medical
  Professions
535 North Dearborn Street
Chicago, IL 60610

American Society for Medical
  Technology
Suite 200
5555 West Loop South
Houston, TX 77401

METEOROLOGIST
American Meteorological Society
45 Beacon Street
Boston, MA 02108

MINERAL INDUSTRY WORKER AND
  MINING
Chief, Division of Personnel

Bureau of Mines
U. S. Department of the Interior
Eighteenth and C Streets, N.W.
Washington, DC 20240

MUSEUM WORKER
American Association of Museums
1055 Thomas Jefferson Street, N.W.
Washington, DC 20007

MUSIC TEACHER
Music Educators National Conference
1902 Association Drive
Reston, VA 22091

National Association of Schools of
  Music
11250 Roger Bacon Drive
Reston, VA 22090

NATIONAL PARK SERVICE WORKER
National Recreation and Park
  Association
Division of Professional Services
1601 North Kent Street
Arlington, VA 22209

NURSE'S AIDE
Division of Careers and Recruitment
American Hospital Association
840 Lake Shore Drive
Chicago, IL 60611

NURSING
Career Information Services
National League for Nursing, Inc.
10 Columbus Circle
New York, NY 10019

Department of Nursing Education
American Nurses' Association
2420 Pershing Road
Kansas City, MO 64108

OCCUPATIONAL THERAPIST
American Occupational Therapy
  Association
6000 Executive Boulevard
Suite 200
Rockville, MD 20852

OCEANOGRAPHER
International Oceanographic
 Foundation
3979 Rickenbacker Causeway
Virginia Key
Miami, FL 33149

American Society for Oceanography
Marine Technology Society
1730 M Street, N.W.
Washington, DC 20036

American Society of Limnology and
 Oceanography
Great Lakes Research Division
University of Michigan
Ann Arbor, MI 48109

OIL INDUSTRY
American Petroleum Institutes
1801 K Street, N.W.
Washington, DC 20006

OPTOMETRIST
American Optometric Association
7000 Chippewa Street
St. Louis, MO 63119

PAINTER
Painting and Decorating Contractors
 of America
7223 Lee Highway
Falls Church, VA 22046

National Joint Painting, Decorating,
 and Drywall Finishing
 Apprenticeship and Training
 Committee
1709 New York Avenue, N.W.
Washington, DC 20006

PAPER INDUSTRY
American Paper Institute
260 Madison Avenue
New York, NY 10016

PATHOLOGIST
American Society of Clinical
 Pathologists/Board of Registry
P. O. Box 4872
Chicago, IL 60680

American Medical Association
Department of Allied Medical
 Professions
535 North Dearborn Street
Chicago, IL 60610

PHARMACIST
American Pharmaceutical Association
2215 Constitution Avenue, N.W.
Washington, DC 20037

American Association of Colleges of
 Pharmacy
Office of Student Affairs
4630 Montgomery Avenue
Bethesda, MD 20014

PHOTOGRAPHY
Photographic Arts and Science
 Foundation
111 Stratford Road
Des Plaines, IL 60016

PHYSICIAN
Association of American Medical
 Colleges
One Dupont Circle, N.W.
Washington, DC 20036

Council on Medical Education
American Medical Association
535 North Dearborn Street
Chicago, IL 60610

PHYSICIAN'S ASSISTANT
American Medical Association
Department Allied Medical
 Association
535 North Dearborn Street
Chicago, IL 60610

PHYSICIST
American Institute of Physics
335 East Forty-fifth Street
New York, NY 10017

PLASTERER
International Union of Bricklayers
 and Allied Craftsmen
815 Fifteenth Street, N.W.
Washington, DC 20005

Operative Plasterers and Cement
Masons International Association of
U.S. and Canada
1125 Seventeenth Street, N.W.
Washington, DC 20036

PLUMBER, PIPE FITTER
National Associations of
Plumbing-Heating-Cooling
Contractors
1016 Twentieth Street, N.W.
Washington, DC 20036

United Association of Journeyman
and Apprentices of the Plumbing
and Pipefitting Industry
901 Massachusetts Avenue, N.W.
Washington, DC 20001

POLICEMAN
International Association of Chiefs of
Police
11 Firstfield Road
Gaithersburg, MD 20760

POLLUTION CONTROL
Water Pollution Control Federation
2626 Pennsylvania Avenue, N.W.
Washington, DC 20036

Office of Personnel
Environmental Protection Agency
Washington, DC 20460

PRINTING AND PUBLISHING TRADES
Graphic Arts Technical Foundation
4615 Forbes Avenue
Pittsburgh, PA 15213

National Association of Printers and
Lithographers
570 Seventh Avenue
New York, NY 10018

Printing Industries of America, Inc.
1730 North Lynn Street
Arlington, VA 22209

American Newspaper Publishers
Association

11600 Sunrise Valley Drive
Reston, VA 20041

American Photoplate-makers
Association
105 West Adams Street, Suite 950
Chicago, IL 60603

PSYCHIATRIST
American Psychiatric Association
1700 Eighteenth Street, N.W.
Washington, DC 20009

National Association for Mental
Health
1800 North Kent Street
Rosslyn Station
Arlington, VA 22209

PSYCHOLOGIST
American Psychological Educational
Affairs Office Association
1200 Seventeenth Street, N.W.
Washington, DC 20036

PUBLIC HEALTH WORKER
American Public Health Association,
Inc.
1015 Eighteenth Street, N.W.
Washington, DC 20036

PUBLIC RELATIONS WORKER
Career Information Service
Public Relations Society of America
845 Third Avenue
New York, NY 10022

RADIO AND TELEVISION
National Association of Broadcasters
1771 N Street, N.W.
Washington, DC 20006

REAL ESTATE AGENTS AND BROKERS
National Association of Realtors
430 North Michigan Avenue
Chicago, IL 60601

RECREATION WORKER, THERAPIST
National Recreation and Park
Association

1601 North Kent Street
Arlington, VA 22209

RESPIRATORY THERAPIST
American Association for Respiratory
  Therapy
7411 Hines Place
Dallas, TX 75235

SCIENTIST
Scientific Manpower Commission
1776 Massachusetts Avenue, N.W.,
  6th Floor
Washington, DC 20036

SECRETARY
National Secretary's Association
2440 Pershing Road, Suite 610
Kansas City, MO 64108

SOCIAL WORKER
The National Association of Social
  Workers
1425 H Street, N.W., Suite 600
Washington, DC 20005

Council on Social Work Education
345 East Forty-sixth Street
New York, NY 10017

SOCIOLOGIST
The American Sociological
  Association
1722 N Street, N.W.
Washington, DC 20002

SOIL SCIENTIST
The American Society of Agronomy
677 South Segoe Road
Madison, WI 53711

Office of Personnel
U. S. Department of Agriculture
Washington, DC 20250

SPEECH PATHOLOGIST
American Speech and Hearing
  Association
9030 Old Georgetown Road
Washington, DC 20014

STATISTICS
American Statistical Association
806 Fifteenth Street, N.W.
Washington, DC 20005

TAX WORK
Chief, Recruitment Section
Internal Revenue Service
Washington, DC 20224

TEACHING
National Education Association
1201 Sixteenth Street, N.W.
Washington, DC 20036

American Federation of Teachers
1012 Fourteenth Street, N.W.
Washington, DC 20005

TECHNICIAN
Engineer's Council for Professional
  Development
345 East Forty-seventh Street
New York, NY 10017

TELEVISION-RADIO SERVICEMAN
National Alliance of Television and
  Electronic Service Associations
5908 South Troy Street
Chicago, IL 60629

TILE SETTER
International Union of Bricklayers
  and Allied Craftsmen
International Masonry Apprenticeship
  Trust
815 Fifteenth Street, N.W.
Washington, DC 20005

Tile Contractors' Association of
  America, Inc.
112 North Alfred Street
Alexandria, VA 22314

TOOL AND DIE MAKER
International Association of
  Machinists and Aerospace Workers
1300 Connecticut Avenue, N.W.
Washington, DC 20036

Skilled Trades Department, United
  Automobile Workers of America
8000 East Jefferson Avenue
Detroit, MI 48214

National Tool, Die, and Precision
  Machining Association
9300 Livingston Road
Oxon Hill, MD 20022

VETERINARIAN
American Veterinary Medical
  Association
600 South Michigan Avenue
Chicago, IL 60605

VOCATIONAL REHABILITATION
Social and Rehabilitation Service

U. S. Department of Health,
  Education, and Welfare
330 C Street, S.W.
Washington, DC 20201

WELDER
The American Welding Society
2501 Northwest Seventh Street
Miami, FL 33125

X-RAY TECHNICIAN
The American Society of Radiologic
  Technologists
500 North Michigan Avenue, Suite
  836
Chicago, IL 60611

How to Look for—and Get—a Job

You have just graduated from high school or college. You are now ready to look for your first full-time job.

Or you are currently stuck in a dreary, dead-end position—and yearning to escape to another, more challenging and interesting job.

Or you are a well-paid, middle manager, approaching forty, working for a firm with a declining market share and falling profits.

Or you are a woman with skills that the market place needs but all your recent experience has been in the home where you have reared your children to school age. You are determined now to return to an outside job.

How do you begin your job hunt? How do you apply? How do you get ready for job interviews? How should you prepare yourself to succeed? How do you write a résumé and what information should it include? How, in sum, do you sell yourself to prospective employers?

STAY EMPLOYED

Above all, first resolve to keep the job you have until you find a better one. Don't resign on principle, quit in a huff, or slack off your performance because you despair.

Continue to do your job as best you can while you plan your departure on your terms.

Always retain as many options as possible, including a good reference if you need it. Remember, you are most employable when you are employed.

AN INVENTORY OF YOURSELF

Before you begin to pursue specific job openings, look hard and honestly at your personality and career. Alone, at ease, in a quiet corner, and with deliberation, make a thorough inventory of your interests, experience, and skills. Write it all down, including random thoughts, recollections, and fantasies. (This inventory, incidentally, will be a valuable fund of information for you when you later prepare your résumé.)

Here are key areas to explore and key questions to think about.

YOUR SKILLS, TALENTS, AND ABILITIES

What are you really good at?

Have you special qualities which you bring to a job? Leadership? Flexibility? Perseverance? Imagination? Organization? Compassion?

What are your special abilities? To analyze and simplify difficult problems? To supervise numerous subordinates? To be patient with details? To work with children, old people, sick people?

YOUR ACTUAL WORK HISTORY

List all the jobs—including summer jobs, campus jobs, and volunteer jobs—you have had, along with the nature of your duties at each. What aspects did you like and dislike about each? Why did you take and why did you quit each? Or if you were fired, why, honestly why? Where did the job lead? What was the next rung up the ladder? Were you qualified for it?

YOUR EDUCATION

Which schools, colleges, and technical training courses have you attended? When and for how long? What were your key courses? What subjects did you most enjoy (and least enjoy) and why? What degrees, scholarships, and special honors did you earn? What were your extracurricular activities? How might these count as job skills? What did you learn? What is the market for the knowledge?

YOUR "OUTSIDE" ACTIVITIES

What serious hobbies do you have that might relate in any way to a job? What volunteer jobs have you held? These cannot only serve as a form of work experience and training but also be a key clue to your real interests.

Are you, for example, good at drawing? Painting? Cooking? Caring for children? Can you play a musical instrument? Or sing well? Do you speak a foreign language? Have you traveled widely—within or outside the United States?

YOUR PHYSICAL CONDITION

Are you in good physical shape or handicapped in any way that might limit your ability to work? If you do happen to have a major handicap, there are many special schools, courses, and rehabilitation programs to help you—and the employment service or the Vocational Rehabilitation Administration can steer you to them. How can you turn your handicap into an asset, an experience or understanding that others lack?

YOUR FINANCIAL POSITION

Do you have an adequate financial cushion to fall back on if you are entering or considering a job or career field involving high risks of layoffs, cutbacks, etc.?

Can you afford to take the time now to find a job that is really suitable to you? Can you manage a period of relatively low, entry-level wages into a new occupation? Calculate how many months your savings will cover minimum monthly expenses.

YOUR CAREER GOAL

What types of jobs, activities would you like to be doing now? What type of work do you think you would like to be doing a year or five years from now? Does this long-range goal suggest added training you should consider getting now? Is your present career field truly one in which you want to remain indefinitely? Or is now the time to consider a Big Switch to another field?

YOUR INTERESTS

What do you really want out of the work you choose to do, the job you choose to take, the career you choose to follow? Money? Security? Status? Power? Challenge? Fun? Usefulness? Adventure? Social contact? A chance to change the world in some meaningful way? Recognition for your achievement?

Your goals and values may differ greatly from the norms and averages—but whatever they may be, think about them, sort them out, decide what's really important to *you*.

CONSIDER JOBS A LEVEL ABOVE THOSE YOU HAVE HELD BEFORE

Now study your personal inventory. What kinds of jobs can you list that would use your talents and skills to their best advantage?

With your completion of your inventory of yourself, you have begun an intelligent job hunt.

YOUR RÉSUMÉ

Your next step in this vital "how to" section is to write your résumé—your key to getting your foot in your prospective employer's door.

From the inventory of yourself you have prepared, select and organize with utmost care the facts that will help most to sell you. Keep the résumé concise and uncluttered—no more than two pages long and, of course, have it neatly typed. Include all of the following items of information about yourself, more or less in this order:

NAME
ADDRESS
MARITAL STATUS
DEPENDENTS, IF ANY
CONDITION OF HEALTH
EDUCATION: Give data on highest degree first, then work backward. List name and location of school, degree, date awarded, major study, honors, if any.
WORK EXPERIENCE: List your last employer first, including name, address, length of service, and type of work performed. Make this section impressive. If a job was title but little action, skimp on the details. If your duties were greater than

the title, describe them in detail with such words as "organized," "initiated," "established," "supervised," "managed," or "operated." Always stick to the facts but present them to reflect most favorably on you and your accomplishments.

GENERAL: List other relevant experience, such as memberships in community or other organizations, special skills or unusual accomplishments, volunteer activities.

REFERENCES: Optional, but if you include them, give three or four persons whose names, positions, or achievements will reflect favorably on you. Of course, get permission to use their names, and give their addresses.

Your résumé should be as perfect as you can make it. Write it six times before you finish. After each rewrite, forget it for a day and then come back to it. Start fresh a couple of times. By the time you finish, you'll have an excellent product.

Writing a résumé for five or ten years hence is not a bad way to plan your career, either. Planning what you want to be able to write about yourself in 1990 may be a good way to start accomplishing it in 1980.

For samples of effective résumés and more pointers on how to write one, get a copy of "Merchandising Your Job Talents," free from the U. S. Department of Labor, Manpower Administration, Washington, D.C. 20210.

SOURCES OF HELP FOR JOB HUNTERS

With your inventory of yourself clearly in your mind and your résumé typed, you are ready to start looking for the best possible jobs in your chosen career field.

You need an inventory of job prospects. Here are some tips on looking for leads.

• Be thorough in your search. Keep records. A 3×5 card system will be good enough. Include the firm name, address, phone, nature of business, job you would like, name of contact, and any other information that will be useful to you in an interview. President's name, background, products or services, subsidiaries, and financial position of the firm. Enough to show that you have done some homework and have some interest in the company and its business.

• Fit the sources you use for leads to your skill and pay levels. Don't look only or primarily in a small, non-urban, general circulation newspaper if you are a computer programmer with five years' experience looking for a supervisory position at $30,000 per year.

• If you can relocate, look into geographic areas with major concentrations of the industries offering the kind of job you seek. Examine growth rates of firms and industries. A regional plan commission, the state economic development commission, or the regional office of the United States Department of Labor can perhaps help with this information. Get some figures on projections for jobs in a specific area over the next ten years.

• Never be afraid to try the unusual. Try a thoughtful letter to a chief executive officer about your knowledge or suggestions for some aspect of his business. If you get no reply, what have you lost?

While it's useful to try the unusual, never overlook the obvious.

• Visit your local public library. Check for . . .

. . . Help-wanted advertisements in both local and regional newspapers. But understand that most of the best jobs are not advertised here.

. . . Trade publications and professional journals. Near the back you will usually find a small section of help-wanted ads. But don't overlook the news sections as a source of leads also. Most have a "Who's News" column about people on the move in the industry. When executives move, there is change. Change is opportunity. Also look at the "New Development" column and see what firms are doing new things.

. . . While at the library, ask for the latest reports on the recent and planned economic growth for the region. Try to get specific projections for jobs in major categories. If not available, the two hours you spend won't be wasted if you make some notes for observations to mention in your interviews.

• If you are looking for firms by type of product or service, don't overlook the local or nearest big-city Yellow Pages for a current list of firms with addresses. The local library probably has both. While at the library, look at *Standard & Poor's Business Directory*. It contains a wealth of information about firms nationwide and lists their executive officers.

• Local offices of the state and federal employment service listed in the phone directory often will have jobs in the private sector.

• If you want a job with the local, state, or federal government, civil service is usually a must. This often means special application forms and procedures—check with the government agency that interests you for details about its application process.

• For members of a profession in your town, check with professional or industry associations. Ask for a list of members and any information they have on current availability of jobs.

• Large corporations usually maintain management training programs. Make a list of the largest employers in your area. Again, check your local public library.

• Read newspapers and business publications with a different eye. Look for new developments in industries and companies that are making changes.

• Discreetly let your colleagues and friends know that you are looking around. Usually, by the time you get this far, your employer will have some hint that you are dissatisfied. So your looking around will probably not come as a great shock and will alert him to the fact that you are serious about moving up or on. He may even make an offer to keep you.

• But try to avoid getting a job because of family or friends. That puts you in their debt and you lose some of your independence and stature before you even start. Sell yourself on your own merits. Sooner or later you will have to. You may as well develop the skill early.

• Consider a "situation wanted" ad in your local newspaper. Make sure it is eye-catching, accurate, and enticing. Write it several times, like the résumé. Show it to friends and colleagues.

• Ask for help from your high school or college guidance counselor, whose advice you may have spurned while in school.

• And use the U. S. Employment Service, undoubtedly the biggest and best among free job placement facilities, with more job listings in more different occupations than any other single job source in the United States today. The USES has more than 2,000 offices throughout the country offering many new and/or specialized services for job hunters.

If you are a professional, use the many branches of the employment service that have national registers for professional occupations ranging from anthropology to economics and library science.

If you are a young American in a low-income bracket, investigate the USES offices' special programs for high school dropouts, including counseling as well as referral to training and job opportunities.

If you are a worker who is willing to take a job in some other city or state, use the USES' nationwide computerized job bank, which has details on job openings throughout the United States.

If you are interested in training programs, ask the USES to pinpoint programs appropriate for you.

HOW TO USE A PRIVATE EMPLOYMENT AGENCY

The help-wanted ads placed by the nation's thousands of employment agencies are a primary source of jobs to which millions of job seekers turn. Many agencies specialize in particular career fields, but most attempt to match any job hunter with the job he seeks.

Employment agencies must be licensed in almost all states. Many states fix legal ceilings on the fees employment agencies may charge, and many regulate their practices. But, typically, fees charged by non-executive employment agencies run about one half of the first month's salary in the $400-a-month range, or 5 to 10 per cent of the first year's salary. Frequently, too, you must pay the fee— normally over a period of several months. And the fee is figured as a percentage of your base salary—not your take-home pay.

Here are the basics for dealing with an agency.

• First, make sure you are dealing with an agency. Look for the word "agency" in the ad. Many job counselors charge an advance fee for a service but do not have jobs available. Many schemers place help-wanted ads when, in fact, they are looking for suckers to make a cash outlay. Advance fee model schemes selling photographs and head sheets are a good example. Neither of these is an employment agency.

• Determine who pays the fee and under what terms. An employment agency never charges you a fee unless you accept a job. For some lesser skilled jobs, an agency may require a deposit or registration fee prior to sending you out for an interview. But it is refundable if you do not accept the job. If the agency advertises "fee paid," then make sure the job offer you accept has a fee paid by the employer, not you. If the agency claims "never a fee to the applicant," then all fees should be paid by the employer.

In many states the law allows the agency to collect some of the fee from you if you quit a "fee paid" job after you have accepted it but before you have been on the job a specified number of months. Get the details in writing in the contract.

• Verify whether the agency's advertised job is actually available.

Most of the ads and the agencies are legitimate. But be wary of a bait ad by either employer or agency. Time is more than money when you are looking for a job. It is energy and hope. You can't afford to lose time, money, or hope to an agency or employer that lures you in with an ad claiming "Assistant to the President . . . $300 per week, no skills" and then switches you to a switchboard operator opening at $145 per week.

Here are a few tips to protect yourself from those agencies that advertise deceptively.

• Watch the ads for several days or weekends. If the same ad appears day after day and week after week offering the same unbelievable job, it may not exist.

• Be realistic. Secretaries, administrative assistants, and clerks rarely start with four weeks' vacation. Bookkeepers at a travel agency don't start with travel benefits that include much "free travel."

• Be inquisitive. Ask for as much information over the phone as the agency will give you. Expect details quickly once you get to the agency.

• Be organized. Keep the ad you answer. Write out your questions in advance of the agency interview so you forget nothing.

• Watch out for cute language in the ad that fails to describe job duties, the necessary skills, required experience but instead stresses benefits.

• Don't be misled into confusing the type of business the company operates with the job description. A law firm may need a switchboard operator but the ad should not read "top lawyer needs assistant to work with clients. . . ."

• Do not return to an agency that advertises jobs that do not exist or refers you to a firm that is not seeking employees.

HOW TO GET THE MOST BENEFIT

To help you get the most benefit from any private employment agency:

• In advance, find out precisely how much the fees will be and by whom and how they will be paid. Find out in advance what the agency's policy is in the event the job falls far short of your expectations within days after you begin working. If the policy is to refund your money if the job goes sour, find out what the time limit is for your eligibility for a refund. These details should be in writing.

• No matter how "ideal" the job is portrayed to you, take the time to look it over with the utmost care. Since the typical employment agency earns its fee only if it places you in a job, there's a real "incentive" to sell you on any opening that happens to be available—whether or not it suits your career objectives.

• Don't be swayed by such scare tactics as a warning about how tight the job market is or an implication that, with your limited skills and talents, you're lucky to get any job.

• Make sure you read and understand any contract before you sign it—and make sure you get your copy of it.

• Be direct and straightforward. Don't hide adverse aspects of your record (a recent firing, a previous physical or mental illness). But don't volunteer adverse information or understate your own abilities. Facts are subject to interpretation and you are entitled to present yourself in the best light.

• Don't give references who you have not confirmed will put in a good word for you.

• Communicate and co-operate with the agency as your job hunt proceeds. Let the agency know how each interview went, whether or not you got the job.

• Understand that advertised salaries reflect a budget, not an obligation to pay a specific wage or the top of the range. Ask the minimum when you call the agency if the ad does not specify.

• Jobs may be placed with several agencies and ads may appear in several newspapers. Inquire about availability before you go to the agency. Also ads are called in to a newspaper days before the ads appear. The job may be gone when you read the ad. A reputable agency will tell you that and offer something else if another job is open.

• If your state requires licensing, make sure you deal with a licensed agency. Find out what the requirements are to get and hold a license and what recourse is available if you need it.

• If in any doubt, assure yourself about the credentials of an employment agency, check with your local Better Business Bureau and with the National Association of Personnel Consultants, the industry's self-policing organization (1012 Fourteenth St. N.W., Washington, D.C. 20005). The National Association of Personnel Consultants (NAPC) has over 2,000 member firms nationwide, and all of its members subscribe to a strict code of ethics. NAPC will send you a directory of its member firms that includes a discussion of industry practices of employment agencies operating where you live.

• Keep your résumé on file with the agencies that serve your field. This is highly advisable, because then if you need the agency's assistance, you'll find you have the first opportunity to consider openings that are exactly right for you.

Of course, you must be concerned about how confidentially the agency will treat your résumé and convey this concern to the agency. Mistakes do happen. An employer could learn that one of his employees is looking for work through an error by the agency.

But confidentiality is violated far more commonly when workers run into their counterparts at meetings and speak thoughtlessly. Personnel people make very few mistakes along these lines. An agency can't violate a candidate's confidence and survive.

• Use an agency particularly if you want to relocate to another city. Agencies exchange information and they can save you travel costs and vacation time.

• Use an agency to coach you on interviewing techniques. The agency may have an insight into an employer's personality and history of treating employees. And if you, the applicant, get several offers the agency can help you make a decision.

• Do not, though, make what has been called the "worst mistake"—namely, going to agencies to look for a "job." You should have a career plan. The agency's counselor is not a vocational counselor. The counselor will help match the applicant's skills with the employer's needs, but before you, the applicant, go to an agency you should have decided on your career objectives.

• While you're holding a job and well protected, learn which agencies serve your field. Don't wait until you are looking. Keep your résumé updated in the agency files and keep in touch. That way you'll know what's going on, when there's a lot of movement among your peers, what the salaries are.

• Know your agency and develop a relationship with the counselor in whom you have confidence. Check out the agency before giving any confidential information. You can do that among your peers. Never meet an employment agency representative any place other than in the agency's office. This is not only plain common sense for your own safety but also gives you the chance to see how the agency operates and how reliable its staff is.

• Work with only one or two quality agencies and develop a rapport, a feeling the agency is doing everything it can for you and treating you as an individual. If you put yourself in the hands of a good agency, you can accomplish more than by hitting the pavement. If you lack confidence in the agency's feeling for you, go elsewhere.

• If you're a high-level executive suddenly on the job market, you may find it tough to reach a search firm (see pages 641–44) because these firms generally are not geared to help those who approach them, and they do not store up potential candidates for searches they don't have. They don't even respond to letters. Employment agencies are far more approachable and although, of course, they don't provide the degree of services a search firm does, you may find they can help you more than you realized.

YOUR LETTER OF APPLICATION

Next, here are the rules on how to write a covering letter of application to a prospective employer:

• Address your letter to a specific individual—the head of the personnel department, the camp director, the person in charge of the department, or whomever; double-check the spelling of his or her name before you make a final copy.

• Apply for a specific job—not just for "anything that is available."

• Keep your letter to one page; let your résumé (which should be attached to this letter of application) give the details.

• State what you have to offer your employer and state it clearly, concisely, neatly. Avoid jargon, gimmicky or flowery language.

• After you have written a draft and edited it to cut out unnecessary verbiage and to correct any spelling mistakes, etc., retype it neatly on 8½ × 11-inch bond paper. Or, if you can't type, get someone who can to do this for you.

• Do not send a duplicated letter to several employers. This is insulting because it suggests an "assembly line."

• Do not give details on the former salaries you may have earned.

• Be sure to include an accurate return address for yourself—including your telephone number and zip code.

• Make—and keep—a carbon of each letter you write, for reference in the event an employer responds positively to your application.

- Enclose a business-size stamped self-addressed envelope.
- If you are looking for a summer job, apply early. Christmas vacation isn't too soon.
- Keep in mind that your letter of application is your prospective employer's first impression of you; it's his sole initial guide to your sense of neatness, your personality, your capacity for organization of thoughts, plans, etc.
- If the employer sends you an application form in response to your letter, fill it out neatly and completely—and follow all directions on extra documents requested, references, deadlines, etc.

You might use the following as a "model" for your letter of application:

150 W. Ask Street
Anywhere U.S.A. 12345
Anytime, 1980

Dr. Timothy Street
Thistown Health Clinic
55 Wentworth Avenue
Seattle, Washington 98107

Dear Dr. Street:

This is my application for a job as a health aide, which I learned about through the employment service office.

My goal is a career in the field of medicine and I am seeking experience in community work—the aspect of medicine which interests me most. I have worked with disadvantaged people in volunteer jobs during the past three summers, both in the city and on an Indian reservation.

My résumé and a stamped return envelope are enclosed. I am prepared to come for a personal interview at any time. If you wish to know more about my qualifications, please tell me what additional information to submit.

Thank you for your consideration.

Sincerely yours,

JANE DOE

HOW TO HANDLE A JOB INTERVIEW

Your first face-to-face meeting with your prospective employer—the job interview—will be your best single chance to get (or lose) the job you are seeking. It also will be an excellent opportunity to get real-life impressions of what it might be like to work for his or her company. Heed, then, these guidelines on job interviews:

Before the interview, find out as much as you can about the company—e.g., the goods and services it sells, its business philosophy, its size and financial standing, its markets, its problems, its competition. You might study the firm's annual report to guide you with this advance research.

Clearly organize in your mind what skills or talents you want to stress, and what you think you can contribute to the company.

Be able to tell the interviewer why you want to work for this particular company.

Take along extra copies of your résumé—just in case the copy you have already sent has been mislaid. Also take, if you are, say, an artist or a writer, examples of your work. And take copies of any letters of recommendation you may have.

Pay attention to such amenities as neat appearance, civilized grooming, and punctuality. Whatever generation you belong to, the odds are strong that your would-be employer belongs to an older and more conservative era. At the same time, do not overdress for the interview. Do not permit your girl friend, boy friend, relative—or anybody, for that matter—to come along on the interview. Your interviewer is interested solely in how you act and react on your own.

Avoid being vague, overly aggressive, or wordy. Stress your qualifications without exaggeration. Listen carefully to the interviewer and follow the conversational directions he or she sets. Answer questions briefly and naturally.

Have a fairly good idea of what salary you expect to earn. *But let the interviewer bring up the subject of money.* And be as flexible as you can when you discuss salary—particularly if you find that your expectations are significantly above prevailing rates in the area or at the interviewer's particular company.

When the subject of pay does come up, be sure you give proper value to fringe benefits such as company-paid health insurance, pension plans, vacation time, year-end bonuses, etc. These easily could add tremendously to the straight dollar pay you receive.

Do not hesitate to ask the interviewer questions about the company or about the job for which you are applying. Asking good questions not only may get you interesting answers but also will give the interviewer further clues to your enthusiasm for and knowledge of the company and your prospective job.

Don't criticize former employers, discuss your domestic or financial problems (unless specifically asked about them), make promises you can't keep, talk in monosyllables, stare at the ceiling, drag out the interview. And don't panic. Your world won't come to an end if you miss out on this particular job.

Find out, if you can, whether you will be expected to take any intelligence, ability, aptitude, personality, or other tests at the time of your job interview and approximately how long they will take. Leave plenty of time for this procedure. When you are actually taking the tests, carefully listen to (or carefully read) whatever instructions you are given—especially the rules covering time limits.

• If the employer does not definitely offer you a job or indicate when you will hear about it, ask when you may call to learn of his decision.

• If the employer asks you to call or return for another interview, make a written note of the time, date, and place.

• Thank the employer for the interview. If the firm cannot use you, ask about other employers who may need a person with your qualifications.

• It's a good idea to send a follow-up letter to thank the employer once more for the interview, especially if the employer indicated that he had not come to a decision. The follow-up thank you letter gives you an opportunity to restate your interest in the position the employer has available. If you can do the job and want it, say so!

• Think of each job interview as a learning experience. After the interview ask yourself how the interview went and how you can improve for your next one. You might ask yourself: What points did I make that seemed to interest the employer? Did I present my qualifications well? Did I pass up any clues to the best way to "sell" myself? Did I learn all I need to know about the job? Did I talk too much or too little? Was I tense, too aggressive, not aggressive enough? How can I help myself do well the next time?

Finally, study the following key reasons given by employers for rejecting job applicants—in descending order of importance. Learn from these reasons what to do to help yourself. The list is based on a study by Northwestern University's director of placement, Dr. Frank C. Endicott:

Poor personal appearance.

Inability to express oneself clearly—poor voice, diction, grammar.

Lack of interest and enthusiasm—passive, indifferent.

Failure to participate in activities.

Overemphasis on money.

Poor scholastic record—just got by.

Unwilling to start at the bottom—expects too much too soon.

HOW TO ASK FOR—AND GET—A RAISE

Few workers who are not members of powerful, aggressive unions plan a strategy to get a pay increase. Fewer still successfully carry out their plan. But you can. Here's how.

(1) Know your worth. Compare the quality and quantity of your work with those around you. Do you come in early and do you stay late? Are you always quick to do what is asked? Do you often initiate improvements and offer suggestions? Are you always dependable and co-operative?

(2) Make lists of your best work characteristics, the functions you carry out, your major contributions in the last year, and special projects that are your responsibility.

(3) Find out when your boss prepares departmental budgets. Asking for more money at the wrong time will get a polite, "Yes, but if you had come in last month . . ." Plan to see the decision-maker early in the budget-making period. Get an appointment if necessary. But try to take advantage of one of the boss's free moments. Simply state, "I'd like to talk for a couple of minutes about something important to me." No good supervisor will refuse.

(4) Limit your talk to three or four minutes, with four or five major points. Most important, rehearse what you plan to say several times during the preceding week. Anticipate an objection, though you probably will get none. Have arguments ready to reinforce and illustrate your points if need be. Don't ex-

pect an answer on the spot and don't pressure. Never back your boss into a corner on a raise. You'll lose. Give him time to digest what you say and get back to you at his pace. Always stress your value and worth to the firm. You'll be surprised how it works.

WHERE TO GET JOB TRAINING

The range of occupational training opportunities in the United States today is broad and attractive—and in many cases the training is accompanied by very respectable pay checks.

Where will you find these opportunities?

CONSIDER AN APPRENTICESHIP

Consider one of the oldest but once again rapidly growing ways to acquire important job skills—apprenticeship. This type of training, which permits you to earn while you learn, is open to women as well as men. Hundreds of women, in fact, now are being trained in fields ranging from plumbing to aircraft mechanics, carpentry, fire fighting, machining sheet-metal work, pipe fitting, shoe repair, jet engine assembly, cheese making, embalming, computer repair, and even as purser-pharmacist mates on oceangoing vessels. By the late seventies, hundreds of thousands of apprentices were being trained each year in some 450 trades ranging from stained-glass window making to musical instrument repair, photography, and leatherworking.

As a general rule, apprenticeship training programs run from one to six years, but the average is three to four. You, the apprentice, learn on the job, under the guidance of an experienced craftsman who probably was an apprentice himself some years ago. You also can expect to spend a few hours a week in a classroom —technical instruction will be an important part of your apprenticeship. Local vocational schools and community colleges often provide this instruction, sometimes using home study courses.

Apprenticeship programs are run by employers, often as a joint labor-management effort. The programs generally are registered with the United States Department of Labor's Bureau of Apprenticeship and Training, or with your state's apprenticeship agency. The programs usually are open to you if you are at least sixteen years of age. Applicants must be physically able to do the work of the trade, and some trades require an entry examination.

For some trades—but not all—applicants must be high school graduates or have earned a General Educational Development (or equivalency) certificate. There often is an upper age limit for applying to these programs, but veterans may add their years of honorable service to this upper age limit to extend their eligibility.

Starting apprentices usually earn 40 to 50 per cent of the going pay to journeymen in their trade or craft (journeymen are those who have satisfactorily completed apprenticeship training). Apprentices usually are granted pay raises every six months until the end of their training period when the pay scales reach

80 to 90 per cent of the current rate paid to journeymen. In addition, there may be valuable fringe benefits such as paid vacations and holidays, health insurance and pension plans.

Journeymen wage rates vary by geographic area within the same trade. But if, for example, journeymen electricians in your area were being paid $9.50 an hour in the late 1970s, your starting apprenticeship pay would be $4.75 an hour and increase by certain percentages every six months until you were being paid $8.08 per hour for your last six-month training period.

Moreover, if you are a veteran who is eligible for benefits under the Veterans Pension and Readjustment Assistance Act of 1966 and amendments, you will receive from the VA starting monthly training allowances, the size of which will depend on your number of dependents. This allowance decreases as the apprenticeship period progresses—but the sums you receive are *over and above* the amounts you receive from your employer.

If you want to pursue an apprenticeable trade, these are your best sources of information:

• Bureau of Apprenticeship and Training, United States Department of Labor, 601 D Street, N.W., Room 5000, Washington, D.C. 20213. BAT, as it is called, can send you a booklet called "The National Apprenticeship Program," which provides an overview of hundreds of apprenticeable trades.

• Apprenticeship Information Centers operated in over forty states as part of the United States Employment Service. AIC staffers can provide you with details about apprenticeable trades in your area (such as entrance requirements and dates of open application), arrange for you to take an aptitude test for the craft that interests you, and generally provide guidance. Write for a list of AICs from the Apprenticeship Information Center Program, U. S. Department of Labor/USES, Room 8118, 601 D Street, N.W., Washington, D.C. 20213.

• State Bureaus of Apprenticeship and Training or State Apprenticeship Councils. See state government listings in your telephone directory for these, or ask your local state employment service office.

• Human Resources Development Institute, AFL-CIO, 815 Sixteenth Street, N.W., Washington, D.C. 20006. HRDI will provide information on building trades apprenticeship programs across the nation. (Women are encouraged to apply!)

• The Urban League LEAP (Labor Education Advancement Program), 500 East Sixty-second Street, New York, New York 10021, and the Recruitment Training Program, 162 Fifth Avenue, New York, New York 10010, operate outreach activities to help minorities enter apprenticeships in many locations across the United States.

THE EMPLOYERS' EDUCATIONAL SYSTEM

Apprenticeship is just one form of on-the-job training. You will discover there are myriad other training and educational opportunities in the working world for employees.

In fact, the governmental and private employers of this nation spend literally *billions* of dollars each year on the training and development of you, the employees. No one actually has measured by anything approaching scientific methods precisely how much is spent on employee education and training each year, but observers of the field agree that it is huge—probably in the neighborhood of $30 billion to $40 billion annually when the costs of training facilities, instructor staffs, employee wages, and training equipment are taken into account.

Employee education generally takes two forms—on-the-job training that an employer provides to his employees "in-house" (within the corporation); or education and training furnished by major corporations at large training centers they own and set aside for the development of their employees; and education and training opportunities offered "out-of-house," or away from employer-owned facilities (at colleges, community colleges, technical schools and universities, through correspondence courses, or through seminars and workshops offered by management development firms and professional associations.)

In this last case, the training and education often is at the employee's initiation —you may want to study for a degree to advance your career. One recent study by American Telephone and Telegraph found that 95 per cent of the major U.S. corporations studied had educational assistance programs for their employees that allow workers to study in the fields of their choice, with their employers footing the bill for some portion of their tuition and other course costs. Do not neglect the existence of "tuition reimbursement" plans, as they are known, when you weigh the relative merits of working for a certain company. And when looking for a job, consider what in-house training and education opportunities are provided by a potential employer before you make a final job choice.

For more information about the employers' educational system, write to the American Society for Training and Development (Suite 400, One Dupont Circle, Washington, D.C. 20036), the professional organization of employee educators.

CO-OPERATIVE EDUCATION

Still another way to get job training is through a co-operative education program—a system in which you, a student, attend high school or college for a semester (or other period of time), then work a semester at a paying job in a field related to your study program. The result is a degree plus valuable on-the-job experience plus a significant amount of pay during the year. Many schools offer this type of program. See "College Co-op Programs," pages 542–44 for more details.

FEDERAL JOB TRAINING PROGRAMS

If you are poor and without a job, or if you earn little money in an unskilled job, go to your local state employment service office and ask if there is a CETA program that could help you learn new skills.

The Comprehensive Employment and Training Act (CETA) provides legal authority for an enormous range of job training programs funded by the United States Government that operate throughout the nation. Most of the CETA programs are run by "prime sponsors," usually states, and fairly large cities and counties. The state, city, and country prime sponsors—there were 450 across the nation as the 1980s neared—receive federal dollars to run their programs, which they design to meet the needs of people living in their area, especially those who are poor and without jobs.

Some of the basic kinds of programs available from city, country, and state governments under CETA are:

• Classroom training (for specific job skills, remedial education or English as a second language).

• On-the-job training (offered by both public and private employers to provide entry-level job skills or to upgrade skills of workers for jobs requiring higher skills).

• Work experience (short-term and/or part-time work with a public or private non-profit organization to improve work skills).

• And public service employment (temporary jobs within state and local governments to provide needed public services and help prepare the worker for higher-level occupations).

Most of these programs pay you wages while you learn the skills that will help you get a better job.

The United States Department of Labor gets money under CETA too and uses it to run programs for people who have special needs or who might require extra help to get a job. Because so many young people do need help in getting work skills, some of the large programs serve them.

One of the major youth programs is the *Job Corps,* which offers entry-level training in fields such as clerical, automotive, health care, food service, and electronics assembly for young people from low-income families who are between the ages of sixteen and twenty-one. The young people live at Job Corps Centers (there were more than sixty around the nation in the late 1970s) learning "basic" language and math skills in addition to receiving job training and career counseling.

For more information about this program, write to the Job Corps, U. S. Department of Labor/ETA, Room 6100, Patrick Henry Building, Washington, D.C. 20213.

COMMUNITY AND JUNIOR COLLEGES

A major source of occupational, vocational, and technical postsecondary education is offered by the two-year community and junior colleges of the United States. These institutions, the vast majority of which are public, number well over a thousand nationwide. There is at least one in every state and the District of Columbia.

Programs offered by the community and junior colleges generally are extremely responsive to the needs of people living in their immediate area, and local employers and unions alike often participate actively in the development of programs they offer.

The vocational/occupational/technical types of programs offered by these schools are designed to lead directly to employment in a specific established or emerging field, and lead to a certificate, diploma, or associate degree. Typically they offer training in such fields as: data-processing technologies; health services and paramedical technologies (dental hygiene and medical records); engineering technologies (including automotive, diesel, and welding programs); business and commerce technologies (including restaurant management, accounting and communications); and public service technologies (such as recreation and social work, police and fire science). Of course, the community and junior colleges also offer programs designed for students who plan to continue their postsecondary education at a four-year college or university, so there's something to be said for the broadening effect such programs have on all students at these institutions.

In recent years, the community and junior colleges have been experiencing unprecedented growth, as the nation's economy has demanded occupational skills of workers with more than a high school education but less than that provided by four-year institutions. It's likely that a community or junior college is highly visible where you live, but if not ask your high school counselor.

Also consult the *New York Times' Guide to Continuing Education in America* (Quadrangle Books, $12.50 hardcover, $6.45 paperback), probably available in your library. Compiled by the College Entrance Examination Board, it describes more than 2,000 schools in the United States especially suited to continuing education. Look at the *Directory of Postsecondary Schools with Occupational Programs,* 1973–74, an excellent listing (although somewhat dated) from the U. S. Government Printing Office, Washington, D.C. 20402. It, too, is available in many libraries.

If you have trouble finding a community or junior college, write to the American Association of Community and Junior Colleges, Suite 410, One Dupont Circle, Washington, D.C. 20036, to learn about institutions in your state.

TECHNICAL AND TRADE SCHOOLS

Private business, technical and trade schools are scattered throughout the United States today that offer you an enormous array of job training opportunities.

Among the typical courses of study that you can get at these postsecondary schools are: automotive mechanics; data processing; printing; medical secretarial or legal secretarial; dental assisting; office machine repair; fashion design, illustration and merchandising; and drafting. Often a private trade and technical school offers training in one occupational field, but with specialized courses of study for the different kinds of jobs found within it.

Start shopping for schools by writing for the free "Directory of Accredited Private Trade and Technical Schools," published annually, with quarterly supplements, by the National Association of Trade and Technical Schools, 2021 K Street, N.W., Suite 315, Washington, D.C. 20036. (NATTS also can send you some excellent free brochures about choosing careers and career schools. Also, write for the free "Pocket Guide to Choosing a Vocational School" from Consumer Information, Pueblo, Colorado 81009.)

See pages 554–63 for more vital links in this area.

IF YOU ARE A WOMAN

YOU PROBABLY HAVE OR WILL HAVE A PAID JOB

If you are a woman between the ages of eighteen and sixty-five, the odds are greater than fifty-fifty that you now hold a paid job. The chances are nine out of ten that you will work or have worked for a prolonged span at some time during your life. Women have been job seeking in such enormous numbers since the end of World War II that the growth in their employment has been described by experts as the single most important development of the twentieth century!

In fact, the percentage of women in the labor force has been steadily rising, while the percentage of men has been falling! Women have, in truth, brought about a revolution in the United States work force.

Even if you are married, you are just about as likely to be holding a job as not; more than four out of ten of all married American women were in the United States work force as the 1980s began. The two-paycheck family has become a dominant factor in the American way of life. More than 27 million husband-wife families—nearly three out of five—had two or more wage earners in the late 1970s; 84 per cent of these were families in which both the husband and wife worked.

Inflationary pressures in the form of a continuous price-wage spiral, higher levels of educational attainment, deep changes in social attitudes, rising expectations of job success fueled by government efforts to eliminate sex discrimination—all these have contributed to this overwhelmingly significant change in our society—and there will be no turning back, no retreat.

If you have children, the chances also are that you're working, either full- or part-time. More than half of the millions of working wives have children under age eighteen. Even the mothers of very young children work; in the late seventies, 5.5 million working mothers had children under age six and the numbers of young working mothers will continue to grow, too. As the 1980s neared, the labor force participation rate—the per cent of the population in the labor force—for women ages twenty-five to thirty-four (those of you most likely to have young children at home) was more than 61 per cent!

Although the birth of children historically reduced your paid work-life expectancy by more than ten years, you'll probably work in a paying job for more than twenty-five years during your lifetime.

And if you are not married, or you do not have any children, it's even more likely that you are working. More than half of all single women are in the labor force—as are three out of four divorcees and one in five widows.

As a general rule, the more education a woman has and the older her children, the higher the odds she is in the labor force. Nearly 60 per cent of the wives who have completed four years of college are in the nation's work force.

WOMEN WORKERS AND FAMILY INCOME

Like men, women work primarily because they need to earn money. For most, the question of working purely for personal fulfillment simply is not the issue.

Almost all of the 11 million-plus single working women and the nearly 8 million women workers who were widowed, divorced, or separated in the late seventies were working to support themselves and—in the latter cases—often their children too. These are all women who must work because they do not have husbands to support them.

But as already documented, wives and mothers work too. For a great many of these women, financial need also is the compelling force keeping them in the labor market. These wives—many of them with young children—need to work to keep their families afloat because their husbands are unemployed or to raise the family's standard of living. On average, wives' earnings contribute 25 per cent to family incomes with the wives' contribution to family income ranging from roughly 40 per cent for those who work full-time all year, down to 12 per cent for those who work less.

Many need to work because they are what the Labor Department calls "female heads of families"—women with young children to support and no husband to help. There were more than 8 million families in the United States headed by women in the late seventies.

Moreover, survey after survey has shown that a very large percentage of the women who are not in the labor force would like to work if they thought they had a chance at a job. These women don't actively look for work (and are therefore not counted as being "in the labor force") because they think racial or sex discrimination would bar them, or they lack skills, or they have family responsibilities that keep them at home. Many would go to work if decent day-care facilities were available.

The income level for families with children under age eighteen and headed by women, however, is low. When we talk about people with low incomes in the poverty class in our society we are often talking about them. Until the situation of these women can be vastly improved by upgrading their skills, expanding their job opportunities, abolishing sex discrimination in pay levels, and providing adequate child care, our welfare problem will continue to plague us and millions of our children will continue to grow up on a hopeless treadmill of poverty.

For information on how to fight job discrimination on account of sex see chapter on your rights (Chapter 28).

GET READY NOW FOR THE "EMPTY NEST"

But what if you're among the many, many mothers who want to stay at home with your young children, and who are financially able to do so? Fine—but, at the very least, realize now that your children, too, will grow up and leave home. And when they do, you, the full-time mother, will be a still young, vigorous woman. What will you do then?

For several years my husband and I lived what economists call an "empty nest"—an economic unit that has become enormously significant in our society, the family in which both parents are alive and the last child has left home. Over one third of all husband-wife families in the United States, ages forty-five and older, have no children under eighteen living at home.

Now that I have lived this story and learned its true dimensions, I cannot urge you too strongly to start preparing for your empty nest early in your life! Start before you are married and even have a nest of your own.

The empty nest is very much a phenomenon of modern times. At the turn of the century the average American family never knew an empty nest; typically, the father died before the last child left home. A half century ago, if an empty nest did develop, it lasted only a year or so, until one spouse died. But now, as a result of trends toward longer life-spans, smaller families, and concentration of childbearing before the age of twenty-six, an empty nest in the United States will last an average fourteen years or more. Some couples may spend thirty or forty years together between the time when the last child leaves home and the death of either spouse.

The number of empty-nesters is impressive enough and growing rapidly—but the reasons they are so important stretch far beyond numbers alone. Specifically, this unit includes:

• The most affluent of all age groups. When the typical empty nest occurs, the husband is at the peak of his earning years. Although this group represents one tenth of our total population, it gets one fifth of our annual personal income.

• The least debt-burdened of all age groups. By the time the nest empties, most parents have slashed their debts, and the overwhelming majority own their own homes. They are financially "free" to an unprecedented degree.

• Consumers who are eager buyers of leisure time and luxury items of all types. Here are the big spenders for foreign travel, eating out, costly clothes and cars— all the goods and services they had to forego while bringing up the children.

• Devoted buyers of small packages of almost everything. There are still tremendous gaps in goods and services designed for the small adult family unit.

• And most important, a towering percentage of working wives. Among women in their middle years (in their forties and over) the non-working wife is the exception!

The economic implications of all these points are clear—and equally unmistakable should be the message to you, as a girl in school, a young bride, a mother of babies or teenagers. If you are still in school, remain there until you have achieved the education to get and hold a job that interests you. If you are a young bride or young mother who chooses not to work temporarily, keep your education up-to-date. If you are a mother of teenagers, refresh your training to be ready to go to work part- or full-time.

Abysmally lost is the wife who does not have something to occupy herself when the nest empties. Don't wait to find out for yourself how true this is: prepare now to avoid the experience.

BASIC CAREER GUIDES

Let's say you are a young woman planning for a career in today's challenging era, or a not-so-young woman seeking to enter the work force for the first time or to re-enter it. What basic guides could I give you to help you fulfill yourself as well as make a significant contribution to your family and to the national economy?

• Before you decide on your career, study the enormous range of occupations available in today's world of work. *Do not limit yourself* to exploring fields where women have traditionally worked—many of the traditional "women's work" jobs are those that are the lowest paid of all and that offer the least upward mobility, or chance to advance. Look at information on *all* fields—especially those in which growth is likely to occur—and relate your interests and abilities to the requirements for employment. For example, if you have done well in math and science courses, you could consider an engineering occupation. By the late seventies, the demand for women and minorities in this growth field had pushed up dramatically the salaries they could command for these normally well-paid jobs. Keep in mind, too, that experts predict skill shortages during the eighties in many technical jobs.

• The general guides to occupational information appear earlier in this chapter —use them! But also seek information specifically about opportunities for women.

• The American Association of University Women (AAUW) publishes each year, with regular updates, a listing of professional groups that offer job information about their fields and employment aid to women which includes the names and addresses of specific people in those groups to write or call. (AAUW, 2401 Virginia Avenue, N.W., Washington, D.C. 20037, "Professional Women's Groups"—a modest charge per copy.)

• Catalyst, a national nonprofit organization launched to help women choose, start, and advance their careers, offers self-help materials for personal planning and career information materials. It also can provide you with a list of affiliated resource centers serving women across the country. Write and ask for the Catalyst publication list (14 East Sixtieth Street, New York, New York 10022).

• Also write to Wider Opportunities for Women, Inc. (WOW), 1649 K Street, N.W., Washington, D.C. 20006, for a directory that lists employment counseling and advocacy organizations for women.

• And the National Center for Educational Brokering, whose affiliates serve many women by helping them match their needs to educational offerings, can send you its "Directory" (NCEB, Office for Research, Publications and *Bulletin*, 405 Oak Street, Syracuse, New York 13203).

• Set your career goals as high as you dare, or think about how you might upgrade your goals within a given field you've already picked. For example, if you're thinking about becoming a nurse, ask yourself whether you might qualify for training as a nursing practitioner or a doctor.

If you want to become a secretary, consider upgrading to a high-paying specialty such as court reporter or medical, legal, or bilingual secretarial work.

And if you've already trained for a specific job but are not satisfied with your occupation, consider a new one for which you could prepare by building on the skills you already have.

• Make a long-range plan to meet the requirements for the occupation you choose. Your immediate goal may be to complete your education and training. If you're a student, stay in school until you've prepared adequately for the job you want. If you interrupt your education, pick it up on a part-time basis while you're an active housewife. Today hundreds of colleges and universities—including community colleges and university extensions—offer "continuing education programs" for adult women. In many cases, class schedules are geared to the hours you're likely to be free from domestic duties.

• If you're already working, inquire if the company for which you work offers tuition assistance for continuing education or training in your job or for another occupation you may want within the company. Educational assistance from employers is one resource many women neglect to tap.

• If you received professional training or graduate education before you married and left the labor force, do everything possible to keep that training up-to-date while you're at home. Maintain your membership in professional associations. Subscribe to, and read, technical journals in your field. Attend any seminars or lectures in your field which you can. Keep in touch with other members of your profession. Use your education and practice your skills through part-time jobs or volunteer work in your field.

• Part-time jobs are becoming more popular with employers, as are flextime arrangements (see pages 573–74) that allow you to tailor your working hours. If you have children at home, these are good alternatives to a full-time job.

• Explore the possibility of studying at home—via correspondence courses, adult education programs, educational television, independent study—then taking examinations leading to a high school diploma or giving college credit toward a degree. Ask your local board of education, community college, or state employment service for details on high school equivalency examinations. Or write to Educational Testing Service in Princeton, New Jersey, and ask for a copy of its $3.00 book, "How to Get College Credit for What You've Learned as a Volunteer." You'll find information on home study approaches to a college education on pages 562–63.

• Financial aid sources may be found in a booklet entitled "Selected List of Postsecondary Education Opportunities for Minorities and Women," available from the United States Department of Labor, Women's Bureau, 200 Constitution Avenue, N.W., Washington, D.C. 20210. The booklet, prepared by the United States Department of Health, Education, and Welfare, offers detailed information on various sources of scholarships and loans, many just for women.

• When you're free to take a full-time job, don't just "take a job." Look for work in the field in which you were originally educated or trained. If it requires more training or retraining, get it. Or if you want to start over on a new career, do that.

• Consider creating your own job tailored to your free time. Some of the businesses you could operate out of your own home are bookkeeping for small firms, typing, catering, making and selling jewelry, caring for and training pets, repairing home appliances, child care, and operating a roadside market. To get started, write for these free booklets from the U. S. Small Business Administration (1441 L Street, N.W., Washington, D.C. 20416). "Home Business–Small Business Bibliography ⚹2"; "Small Marketers Aid ⚹71—Check List for Going into Business," and "Small Marketers Aid ✕150—Business Plan for Retailers." These guides can help you determine your qualifications and requirements for success.

JOB GROWTH AREA FOR WOMEN: SALES

Note: At the end of the 1970s Schieffelin & Company, the nation's largest privately owned wine importer, employed a woman as brand manager for its prestigious Marquis de Coulaine wine.

Note: Merrill Lynch, the largest financial services company in the United States, was at the same time actively recruiting women brokers in all its three hundred branches across the nation.

Note: Pitney Bowes, one of the country's top manufacturers of business systems and mailing equipment, reported that 11.1 per cent of its 2,700-person sales force was female, up from a mere 3.4 per cent as recently as 1974.

If you are a career-oriented woman, concentrate as never before on sales as your entry into the business community. Today, the traditional roles for women in sales (in real estate, in retail stores) have been vastly expanded. You are just as likely to be selling manufactured and wholesale merchandise, stocks and bonds, consumer goods and consumer services. And while we, the women, have a long way to go before we come even near to parity (only 20 per cent of all manufacturing and wholesale companies employ women sales representatives and less than 10 per cent of all sales representatives are women), our progress is indisputable.

Are you the right person for sales? Honest answers to the following questions will give you the guidance you seek.

• Can you handle rejection, cope with occasional "dry spells"? You must be able to handle the inevitable no and keep yourself going when sales aren't good.

• Can you work effectively without supervision, arrange your own schedules, make your own customer calls? If you like being in business for yourself, you may find no limit to your career.

• Can you fit into an area that interests you? Do you feel comfortable about the products and the company that makes them? A growth area is definitely marketing. You would be wise to get solid marketing skills before going into the sales end.

• Can you handle whatever travel may be required? How will your travel affect your family relationships?

If you are deeply concerned about your earnings potential, the only square answer is that it can vary widely—and can go very high.

And how do you prepare for a career in sales?

While few companies require a college degree, many women who are successful in selling urge you to go to college to get a bachelor of arts degree, or to study business administration.

For more information on sales careers of women, write to the Women's Bureau, Department of Labor, 200 Constitution Avenue, N.W., Washington, D.C. 20210, or to Catalyst, 14 East Sixtieth Street, New York, New York 10022.

ANOTHER HOME HEALTH CARE PLUS—JOBS

If you are a middle-aged woman in good health, looking for part-time (or full-time) employment but without any special education, background, or skills, investigate the great opportunities you may find in the booming field of home health care.

If you are a younger woman—in your twenties, say—and you also have few technical skills but are seeking a job that will pay fairly well and could be unusually satisfying, you, too, should now look into the job of a home health care aide.

Home health care programs are sweeping across the nation, are being hailed as one solution to runaway hospital costs as well as a welcome alternative to institutional care for the countless numbers of Americans who do not require constant nursing or personal attention.

As recently as 1958, there were only a few thousand home health care aides in the United States. In 1975 the total was up to 60,000, according to the Labor Department's *Occupational Outlook Quarterly*.

But as the 1970s closed, the need for these aides was projected at a whopping 300,000.

It is estimated that there is only one home health care aide in our country for every 4,709 persons. Sweden, by contrast, has one for every 101 persons.

What's more, the need will climb ever upward as home health care services become an entrenched part of our entire health care delivery system and our elderly population expands. Also contributing to the need for this occupation is the prevalence of such chronic illnesses here as diabetes, hypertension, arteriosclerotic heart disease, cerebral-vascular disorders, arthritis, neurological problems, malignancies, and other long-term, partially disabling illnesses that can be treated at home—and treated far more cheaply and often far more successfully than in traditional institutions.

Pay for home health care aides varies considerably, depending on the size of your city or town and its prevailing wage scale, whether you belong to a union, whether you work for an agency or organization with career ladders, etc. Generally, pay is in a range well above the minimum wage, with the precise figure determined by your qualifications and experience.

Benefits vary even more than wages. Some health care agencies offer no benefits at all, while others offer a full package of holidays, vacation, sick leave, health and life insurance, retirement plans, etc. While some agencies hire only "on call" hourly workers with no benefits, many agencies employ aides on a full-time or part-time basis with numerous benefits and a minimum number of hours guaranteed.

If you were a typical full-time home health care aide in the late 1970s, you were guaranteed thirty-six hours of work a week; earned more than the minimum wage, depending on your length of employment and level of responsibility; had one to three weeks paid vacation each year, depending on your number of years of service; one day of sick leave a month; were paid for major holidays and were eligible to participate in pension and health insurance plans.

If you were a typical part-time employee working a regular schedule, you were guaranteed twenty hours of work a week; received the same hourly pay as full-time employees and similar benefits allocated according to the number of hours you worked. A few agencies also allocate vacation and sick leave to those of you who do not have a guaranteed minimum hours of work or a regular schedule.

As an aide, your occupation will have superior status to jobs that do not require a high school education. You will be an important member of the health team since your regular reports on a client's condition will be the basic information used to reassess the services needed. You will have a desirable degree of independence and self-direction in carrying out your day-to-day duties.

Helpful to you will be courses in home economics such as meal planning and family living. Some agencies require you to have a year's experience working as a nursing aide in a hospital or nursing home. As a college student you even might find this an excellent summer job, leading you into other better-paying health care jobs.

A WIFE'S WORTH A MILLION, AT LEAST

Donald Johnson, a timber manager in Grants Pass, Oregon, won $375,000 from a New York jury in the late 1970s deciding a suit he had brought against Pan American Airways and KLM Royal Airlines as "just compensation" for services he and his children lost when his wife, Beverly, was killed in a historic collision of two jets in the Canary Islands in 1977.

Johnson had sued for $1 million, and in my judgment, even that would have been modest compensation for the multitude of services Beverly had performed.

The American housewife who stays at home and is paid $000.00 a week for taking care of her husband and youngsters a minimum of twelve to fourteen active hours a day, seven days a week, is a dwindling species. But she still numbers in the millions and her performance of at least twelve different occupations without any pay in dollar terms—and even in the face of scorn from her job-holding sisters—cries out for recognition. Her contributions can be easily translated into a minimum of 99.6 hours of hard work a week, at least $18,862.48 a year at merely the $2.90 per hour minimum wage in 1979.

As the senior vice-president of Jefferson Standard Life Insurance Company, among the fifteen largest stock life insurance companies in the United States, headquartered in Greensboro, North Carolina, put it to me, "Even in Greensboro, a widower will be lucky to find a suitable housekeeper for four to five dollars an hour, or even more, depending upon the specific duties involved." And in Greensboro, pay scales are much lower than wages demanded by houseworkers in, say, New York, Chicago, San Francisco.

If you sew a magnificent wardrobe for yourself and if you're a (nonpaid) housewife, all that counts toward the nation's output (gross national product) is what you spent for materials, trimmings, thread, etc. Not a penny of your contribution in labor is included. But if you had bought that same wardrobe, every dollar you spent—a giant part of the cost reflecting the labor involved in sewing the clothes—would be included in GNP.

In sum, "you" are nonexistent! Our GNP is, as a result, grossly understated, more misleading than revealing.

You, this U.S. housewife, may start your hard working day as early as 5 A.M., to get the kids off to school and your husband off to work. If you're lucky, you may finish twelve to fourteen hours later. You have no guarantee of a vacation at any time; you may receive little, if any, appreciation from your own family or others.

My life as a working-for-pay woman is much more rewarding than yours.

Outside of the obvious fact that this is unjust and wildly discriminatory against you, what else does it mean?

(1) It underlines again that "wife insurance" is among the most neglected fields in insurance in this era. If you, a wife and mother, were to die prematurely and leave young children as well as a husband, it would cost him from $20,000 to $25,000 just to replace your regular services (love and devotion not counted). It is no more than common sense for a wife to be insured so that her major services could be replaced, if necessary. (See page 942.)

(2) And if you're a working wife and mother, wife insurance is equally vital for you, so your earnings can be replaced to help keep your home going, educate your children, maintain your family's standard of living.

(3) As for your contribution to our GNP, that *must* be recognized by development of a conservative total representing the non-paid services of the wife and mother—when (and if ever) we finally tackle the task of revising this crude barometer.

Below is Jefferson Standard's compilation of the jobs a non-paid wife performs and what she might conservatively be paid weekly.

JOB	HOURS	HOURLY	WEEKLY VALUE
Nursemaid	44.5	$ 2.90	$129.05
Housekeeper	17.5	4.00	70.00
Cook	13.1	4.00	52.40
Dishwasher	6.2	3.75	23.25
Laundress	5.9	3.75	22.13
Food buyer	3.3	5.00	16.50
Chauffeur	2.0	5.00	10.00
Gardener	2.3	5.00	11.50
Maintenance man	1.7	3.75	6.38
Seamstress	1.3	5.00	6.50
Dietitian	1.2	10.00	12.00
Practical nurse	0.6	5.00	3.00

It adds up to 99.6 hours a week, $362.71 in pay a week, $18,862.48 a year. And it's so understated, it's nonsense.

Imagine what our GNP would swell to if we counted in just the $362-plus a week being earned by tens of millions of women!

Use the following chart to figure *your* worth as a housewife in *your* area, at current wage rates:

JOB	HOURS PER WEEK	LOCAL RATE PER HOUR	YOUR "VALUE" PER WEEK
Nursemaid			
Housekeeper			
Cook			
Dishwasher			
Laundress			
Food buyer			
Chauffeur			
Gardener			
Maintenance man			
Seamstress			
Dietitian			
Practical nurse			
TOTAL			

HOW TO FIND A DAY-CARE CENTER FOR YOUR CHILD

If you are a typical young family with small children, an absolute *must* before you, the mother, can take even a part-time paying job is a good nursery school, baby-sitting service, or day-care facility at a cost you can afford.

If you could find a top-notch day-care center, it could be a boon not only to you but also to your child—for if it's top-notch it will be well staffed, well equipped, well populated with other children, and well supplied with a variety of cultural-educational stimuli.

Where and how do you find good child care arrangements? What are the costs likely to be? (One factor that will help you with costs is the tax credit for child care expenses, which allows you to reduce the income tax you owe the Internal Revenue Service by fairly substantial amounts. Watch for the instructions to be part of the tax forms the IRS sends to you, or pick up a form around tax time from your local post office. Also check to see if your state, city, or county also permits deductions for child care. Some do.)

• Start by checking your would-be employer's day-care facilities. Many, many companies—ranging from hospitals to factories, baby food companies, and government agencies—have set up day-care facilities. In most cases you pay a modest sum each week.

• If you are considering taking a job in a hospital, weigh the presence or absence of day-care facilities before you choose a particular institution. Hundreds of hospitals have day-care centers today—as a way to attract nurses and other health service workers who otherwise might be housebound. And hundreds more are in the process of setting up such facilities. Almost all have opened their doors just within the past few years.

• If you work for the federal government, check with the several agencies that now have day-care centers—including the Department of Labor, the Department of Agriculture, and the U. S. Office of Education.

• Make inquiries at local civic and religious organizations about available day-care facilities run by these organizations or by other agencies.

• Certainly canvass with care the wide variety of private day-care combinations —including nursery schools, baby-sitting services, communal care, informal child care agreements among neighbors.

• If you're a college student, investigate whether the college you're attending (or plan to attend) has some type of low-cost day-care facility.

• If you're a member of a labor union, check whether your union runs a day-care center.

• Look among available publicly supported preschool programs—particularly any federally financed programs aimed primarily at preschool-age children from lower-income families, but not always segregated along economic lines.

• Use these sources of guidance and information on child care services for you and in your community:

The Day Care and Child Development Council of America, 622 Fourteenth Street, N.W., Washington, D.C. 20005 (it has an extensive set of publications).

The local chapter of the National Organization for Women.

• Ask your library to help you get a copy of *The Early Childhood Education Directory* (New York, R. R. Bowker Company)—a descriptive compendium of more than 2,000 nursery schools, federally financed centers, and day-care centers throughout the country.

• If you can't find decent day-care facilities at a cost you can manage in your home community, try pooling your own ideas, children, time, skills, with those of other neighbors and friends who are working mothers. Share out-of-pocket costs —and rotate responsibilities among you. Or try to hire, at least part-time, someone who has been trained in this field and launch a "parent co-operative."

• Another alternative is to try to find a conscientious college student willing to trade bed and board, say, for looking after your small children part-time. You might even be able to track down an au pair foreign student through an agent specializing in making arrangements for such young people to live in your home —for a small sum per week plus room and board.

Here are the key questions to ask about any day-care center to which you are considering entrusting your child and to which you may be committing yourself to pay substantial fees, charges, or tuitions:

• Is the center a professionally staffed, decently equipped place in which your child is likely to learn something? Or is it merely a baby-sitting service?

• What are the center's hours—and does it operate five, six, or seven days a week? Is this schedule convenient for you?

• Will your child be permitted to "try out" the center for, say, a couple of weeks before he or she is committed to sign up for a longer period?

• Do toys, equipment, and the layout of the center itself appear to add up to a safe place to be and play and learn?

• Is a doctor and/or nurse on call—especially if the center is a relatively large one?

• Is the center licensed by the state or some other public agency? (Most licensed centers are listed in the Yellow Pages of your telephone book.)

- What meals and/or snacks are offered and is their content of real nutritional value?
- Who and how many are on the staff—and what kind of training (if any) have they had in early childhood education?
- What is the child-to-teacher ratio? An adequate ratio would be around eight or ten children per teacher.
- How varied are the activities and experiences to which your child will be exposed?
- What are daily or weekly charges? Are there special rates for half days and for second or third children from a single family? Is there a special charge for lunch? If fees are based on your family's ability to pay, just what would that mean?
- Is after school care provided?

IS IT REALLY WORTH IT?

Every word in this section surely must shout to you my own profound conviction that "it" is worth it indeed.

Every line in this discussion surely must disclose how intellectually and emotionally committed I am to the right of a girl and a woman to have her own career and the importance of this to her own sense of values and dignity. And surely my own life underlines how I have translated my beliefs into reality.

But you may want to calculate the advantages strictly in financial terms.

Okay. Let's say your before-tax salary was $175 a week and that deductions for various federal, state, and Social Security taxes and for group health insurance amounted to $43.82. That would leave you $131.18.

Then deduct $2.00 a day for transportation to and from work, $2.50 a day for lunch, and $15 to $20 a day for the baby-sitter or day-care services.

Next figure that the extra clothes, personal-care costs, and other personal items will be about $7.00 a week.

Then try to estimate the higher household expenses you're likely to have, such as more expensive convenience foods to save you cooking time. Say these come to $15 a week.

The total comes to $41.50 a week, meaning $85.32 will be deducted from your $175 paycheck. This leaves you $89.68 a week, or a little more than half of your before-tax pay. And your husband may argue with even that figure for income tax reasons, although the child care tax credit may help a bit.

But I cannot say it too strongly: the amount left is *not* the key point! What *is* the key is that, if you want to work, you should. If you want to take extra training to upgrade your job and your pay, you should.

To estimate *your* own costs, fill in this chart—and weigh the total against your own paycheck.

GROSS WEEKLY SALARY $_____

Deductions:
    Federal income tax   _____
    State income tax   _____

State disability _____
Social Security _____
Group life insurance _____
Group health insurance _____
Pension plan _____

Total deductions _____

Amount of take-home pay $_____

Weekly Expenses:
Transportation _____
Lunches _____
Child care _____
Personal grooming (including extra
   cleaning and laundry) _____
Extra clothes _____
Dues (professional, union, etc.) _____
Household help _____
Added household expenses
   (convenience foods, paying for
   things you might have done
   yourself, etc.) _____

How to Play "Success Chess"

YOUR LIFETIME JOB GUIDE

"At what ages," asked Terry, a twenty-nine-year-old investment banker obviously destined to climb the success ladder, "is it entirely okay for you to change jobs frequently in order to test yourself on what you want to be and do?"

In what age range, both of us then debated, should you be finding the industry in which you want to spend your future years and should you be moving from job to job within that industry in order to build up your skills and experience?

By what age should you have definitely located your own industry, be set to move vertically toward the job goals you have concluded are right for you?

Spurred by Terry's penetrating questions, I went to one of the top executive recruiting and management training firms in the world—charging, for counseling on a single job, fees ranging up to $3,000 for an individual, $30,000 for a corporation.

Since it's highly unlikely you'll have the opportunity—not to mention the fee —to ask such a firm in person for specific advice about jobs, I did the asking for you.

Important note: The advice that follows applies as much to "Theresa" as to "Terry." In fact, the experts at this firm went out of their way to emphasize that the guides are for young women as well as for men.

Now here are six practical guides to job success this firm developed over years of helping to mold the careers of famous industrialists.

(1) In the first five years of your job career—say, from age twenty-two to twenty-eight—try to find out what you want to *do,* what you want to *be.* Don't hesitate to make several job changes, for you are testing yourself. As a young man or woman, ask yourself: "What do I want out of life? What do I want to do?"

In these years young men or women who are unmarried are generally more successful than married individuals, because they can more easily move around on their own or more easily be moved by their firms.

(2) Also, in the twenty-two to twenty-eight age range, concentrate on finding the industry in which you want to stay.

The future top leaders are to an impressive extent the ones who were set in their own industry in their twenties and who then moved within it to gain know-how.

(3) At the age of thirty, stop and think hard. Take the time to sit down quietly and write out some answers to yourself on such questions as these: Where do you want to live? Where would you and your spouse be happiest? How much annual pay will you need to earn ten or fifteen years from now to meet the standard of living you want? You'll have a much clearer concept of your goals after you've honestly made this effort to "know thyself"—which well may be among the hardest tasks you'll ever undertake.

(4) For the next ten years—say, to age forty—prepare yourself deliberately for what you want to be. Grade yourself on these qualities for success: drive, responsibility, health, good character, ability to communicate, ability to think, ability to get along with people, ability to keep your perspectives (i.e., recognize your responsibilities to society even while you're watching your competitors in business).

(5) In the forty to forty-two age bracket you'll hit a treacherous phase of "cyclical restlessness" when you may mistakenly change jobs because you're looking for the "greener grass." Be on guard: again, quietly check up on your goals.

(6) After age forty-five, start consolidating—use the years to broaden your objectives, achieve fulfillment, lay the basis for a rewarding new life after you leave your company.

Brief as this guide is, it's loaded. And it also has given you one of the most significant job hints of your entire career if it challenges you merely to find your answers to those two deceptively simple questions:

What do you want out of life?

What do you want to do?

WHAT MOVES TO MAKE

Now let's say you are in your thirties—into the decade during which you should be preparing yourself for what you want to do and be.

Let's say, too, that you have found a new job as a well-paid middle executive in an aggressive fast-growing corporation. The promise of rapid promotion into the upper corporate ranks was part of the deal—as long as management believes you deserve a promotion because of your superior performance in your starting position.

What moves can you make at this stage to boost your chances of stepping up the corporate ladder as rapidly as possible? Here are nine—drawn up by a top authority in the field of executive behavior:

(1) Keep open the widest possible set of options or of future opportunities to alter your behavior. It is less important to know exactly where you are going than to keep your options open. When you see that you are being stereotyped, make a move either within or outside the company to break the stereotype.

(2) Avoid loss of career time. Do not waste this precious commodity by working for an immobile superior. The chances are greater that you will be blocked by such a boss, for a shelf-sitter is more likely to stay than be replaced.

(3) Become a crucial subordinate to a mobile superior. When he moves you'll move, since you are as important to him as he is to you.

(4) Aim for increased exposure and visibility, and make sure you are traveling the right kind of "route" in your company. If manufacturing men tend to inherit the presidency and you are in sales, think very hard about whether or not you have gone as far as you can go up the management ladder.

(5) Practice "self-nomination" for top jobs. Let those who do the nominating for key posts know that you want a bigger job or at least want to learn how to qualify for it.

(6) Make sure that if you leave your company you do so on your own terms, and always leave on the best of terms.

(7) If after long and serious deliberation you decide to quit, rehearse the move ahead of time. Avoid being counted among the executives who have fired their corporation in the afternoon and rehired it the next day. Instead, write out your resignation, put it in a safe place in your desk, and let at least a week go by before you submit it.

(8) Look upon the corporation as a market rather than a place in which you simply work for a living. The market is for skills, and skill is best determined by your real achievements and performance.

(9) Have faith that if you can succeed in one thing you can probably succeed in another, even without having climbed a single rung on a corporate ladder.

FIVE CLUES ON PROMOTIONS

Now study the following five clues on promotions offered by other experts on the subject of executive advancement:

(1) The great majority of promotions to top executive spots are made from within the firm; significant numbers of these, however, were employed by their companies for only a relatively few years.

(2) The average age of newly promoted company presidents and chief executive officers is now in the early to mid forties.

(3) Virtually all newly promoted company executives are college graduates and more than one in three holds an advanced degree. Among those holding B.A. degrees, most majored in business or engineering, and among those with master's degrees, most are in business.

(4) The top four rungs of the corporate ladder from which executives are being promoted today are operations-division management, finance, marketing, and administration.

(5) The least likely corporate specialties from which businessmen are now promoted to top jobs are public relations, manufacturing, international, and research and development.

THE DIVORCED EXECUTIVE AND HIS CAREER

• A $100,000-a-year executive found his career at a giant blue-chip company just about ended when he told his wife he wanted a divorce. She immediately enlisted the wives of his superiors to convince their husbands that he was not worthy of the company's confidence. She did this even though at stake was not only his career but also his subsequent alimony payments to her.

• Another divorced executive who was uncomfortable with his life at an old-line company said he took a new position paying $90,000 a year for which he was recruited by an executive recruiting firm only after he checked and discovered that the new company president was himself divorced. This made the climate more comfortable.

• One divorced wife said to her then-executive husband, "I can compete with any woman, but not with your career."

"At least 50 per cent of the executives we screen for client assignments are divorced or separated," says the president of a New York-based executive recruiting firm. "The stigma of the divorced man has practically disappeared." There are still a few very conservative companies that silently subscribe to the theory that if "a man can't manage his own affairs, how can he handle company business?" But attitudes have changed dramatically in this area.

Divorce has long been accepted in U.S. society and, as always, this cultural change has followed into the business fabric.

What is the prime advantage of being a single, highly paid executive in a big company (earning on average between $55,000 and $75,000 a year as the 1970s closed)?

Recognition by top management that you are able to move quickly in a given situation. As a single executive, you are considered unusually hardworking, ambitious, flexible. If there's a key problem that needs instantaneous action in an out-of-town branch, the single man often can move right in and tackle it until it's solved.

"Of course, this very quick and deep commitment to work might mean he's a workaholic, which could have contributed to the breakup of his marriage," said the executive recruiter. "Ironically, this characteristic might also have contributed to his job success."

Workaholics aren't necessarily better executives, but they usually do get a lot of work done. They can drive their subordinates crazy, just as they probably did their wives and kids.

And the worst disadvantage of being divorced or single?

The view (still held by some, although clearly obsolete) that a single man doesn't need as much money as his married counterpart, or that he doesn't need as much of a raise in salary. This attitude is difficult to fight.

As for the problems of married men compared with singles, both in general are much the same. An unhappy single man is no better a manager than an unhappy married man. Nor is a happily married man a better manager than a happy single person. And the single man is not necessarily a heavier drinker than his married counterpart, more of a woman-chaser, or more conservative or radical in his business practices.

If you're changing jobs or searching for new opportunities and if you're divorced or single, some key guides for you are:

• Don't volunteer your marital status. But if asked, answer the question honestly and openly.

• Be direct and brief about your current status.

• Don't volunteer why you got divorced. It's no one's business but yours.

• Don't criticize your former wife or complain about excessive alimony or other payments.

• Express concern about the welfare of your children, and of your former wife, too.

• If you plan to remarry, let that be known in advance.

A provocative finding is that most divorced executives remarry much sooner than expected. Is it that company life is still much more comfortable for a married man than a single person? Or do the frustrations of corporate life make the need for a comfortable home environment all the more imperative?

And what about divorced women executives? "We don't come across them often," says the executive recruiter, "so I really can't say."

(But I can. The pros, cons, and problems are about the same for women as for men.)

TAILORED PAYCHECKS

KEY TRENDS IN COMPENSATION

The "tailor-made paycheck" is becoming ever more widespread, permitting you, an individual employee, to shape your own paychecks (so much cash, such and such a pension deal, this or that type savings or stock purchase plan) according to your own individual wants and needs. For example:

If you're in your late twenties, at the start of your career, married, with young children and loaded with debts, what you need from your employer is all the current cash income and protection against death or disability you can get. What you don't need is a retirement income plan to which you are required to make fat contributions.

But if you're in your late fifties, around the peak of your taxable earnings and free of many family burdens, what you need is assurance of a lifetime retirement income for you and your wife. What you don't need is more current cash income on which you'll pay more taxes.

COMPENSATION GEARED TO YOUR AGE

Let's take a more detailed specific example of a middle-income manager called John Jones.

In his late twenties, Jones holds an accountant's position in an industrial corporation which pays him $21,000. Married and with three children, he finds it hard to keep up with his mounting family obligations despite several raises. Though his life insurance program is barely adequate, he complains of being "insurance poor." His requirements at this stage are easily defined.

He needs all the cash income he can command plus protection for his family. Thus, salary compensation, medical coverage, life insurance, and disability income protection are key elements in his pay package, with a minimum of employee contribution requirements.

Consider Jones fifteen years later, in his mid forties, holding a higher job paying $35,000. Now one son is in college, another is a year away, his teenage daughter is having expensive orthodontic work, his debts and tax obligations are higher, and his auto insurance bill is painful. He still needs all the cash he can command.

But he needs to be able to count on the cash regularly. Thus, bonus dollars in lieu of salary dollars offer little attraction because of their uncertainty. And though various forms of protection continue important, he must start building toward a retirement income in the years he has left at work.

Now consider Jones at fifty-seven, earning $45,000 in a job he'll almost certainly keep until retirement. His expenses have declined but his peak earnings have been cut by peak taxes and he still is far from achieving his retirement fund goal. Social Security (an increasingly important source of retirement income) will help, but his most urgent need now is additional retirement income from his company's program.

The idea of "tailored paychecks" (or "cafeteria compensation") is becoming ever more widespread. But as company management explores their use as a powerful and sensible motivating force, you, the middle manager, will increasingly reap the benefits of a personalized pay package custom-designed for you.

AND "PERKS"

On top of all the cash compensation, the fringe benefits, and the tailoring of paychecks to meet the individual's changing circumstances comes a long list of "perks"—perquisites—for executives: use of company hotel rooms and resort facilities; use of company planes and company autos; medical care; personal money management, etc.

In many cases the perks are old-fashioned, tax-loophole frivolities. In others they are highly imaginative incentives to executives.

(P.S. One "extra" which virtually no executive enjoys is overtime pay. No matter what the rules for premium pay for overtime work under the federal wage-hour law, these men and women work sixty, seventy, eighty hours a week or more for no extra pay at all. Why? They love what they do, they want to work, that's why!)

Shop for Fringe Benefits, Too!

ROUTINE DEDUCTIONS

You're not at all atypical today if as much as one third of your pay or even more is "missing" by the time you receive your check. And you're not at all atypical if, aside from the large chunk you pay for taxes, your deductions cover a dozen or more different items offered by your employer as a fringe benefit at lower-than-usual cost or as a convenience to you.

Here is a partial list of goods and services for which deductions from paychecks are now routinely being made: federal and state income taxes; Social Security (FICA) and Medicare taxes; life insurance premiums; health and disability insurance; dental insurance; contributions toward company profit-sharing plans, and stock purchase plans; purchase of U. S. Savings Bonds; homeowners insurance premiums; personal catastrophe liability insurance premiums; repayments to credit unions for many types of loans.

A key attraction of fringe benefits rests on our income tax structure. If your employer simply increased your pay so that you could buy your own life insurance, health insurance, etc., you would have to pay income taxes on your fatter paycheck. But if he offers these as fringe benefits you get the coverage without paying increased taxes. Moreover, your employer can get a better buy on many fringes (such as group health insurance) than you could get as an individual for yourself.

The extent to which increases in fringe benefits have entered and are continuing to enter crucial wage negotiations involving millions of workers dramatizes this fundamental and yet still startlingly understated point: in a mounting number of cases, improvements in fringe benefits are becoming as important as—or even more important than—cash pay hikes themselves.

For the majority of U.S. workers in the economic mainstream fringe benefits are a real blessing. But for the have-nots in our society they are a potent source of discontent. Reason: the "fringe binge" perpetuates the gap between those who are eligible for valuable fringes and those who are ineligible—because they are unemployed, employed part-time, or work for marginal employers who cannot finance the extras.

Nevertheless, focusing strictly on the "haves":

• As the 1970s ended, if you were an average U.S. worker, for every $1.00 you were earning in regular pay, you were getting another 30 cents or even more in fringe benefits. That translated into an extra $3,000-plus in fringes for every $10,000 of yearly pay.

• In the late 1970s, if you were typical, you were receiving more than $1.00 an hour in the form of "hidden" pay which didn't appear on your regular dollars-and-cents paycheck, against only 25 cents of "hidden" benefits in the late 1940s.

• Fringe benefits have been increasing in recent years at two to three times the rate of increase in cash wages and salaries; the growth has been a hefty 10 to 12 per cent a year.

To help you compare your benefits with what others are receiving and to help you shop for benefits as you compare one prospective new job with another, here is a brief rundown on key benefits and trends today:

PAID VACATIONS AND HOLIDAYS

Typical in the seventies was a two-week vacation plus at least six to eight paid holidays. But this norm is rapidly becoming three weeks and ten to twelve paid holidays after just a few years of service.

Also the typical employer grants employees the equivalent of another two weeks' "vacation" in the form of a couple of coffee breaks each day.

The trend is toward ever-lengthening vacations as well as vacation splitting—permitting you to divide your vacation into chunks. Moreover, a growing number of companies are switching to the four-day (but still forty-hour) workweek—giving you no fewer than fifty-two long weekends during the year.

GROUP INSURANCE

Nearly all U.S. companies now make at least a minor contribution toward some type of insurance for their employees. Health and life insurance are the most common but the trend is toward group automobile insurance, and even group homeowners insurance. The typical company-paid policy is canceled when you move to another job, but often you can convert your group coverage to a low-cost individual policy if you do so within a stated period of time.

The new trends in health insurance are toward increasing amounts of major medical coverage for catastrophic illness, outpatient psychiatric care as well as in-hospital care, dental bills and eye care, yearly physical exams. A few employers provide coverage for totally disabled dependents and make prescription drugs available at bargain prices. For more details on health insurance coverage and costs, see pages 437–41.

In life insurance, the trend is toward substantial group coverage not only for workers themselves but also for their wives and children.

EDUCATIONAL BENEFITS

Many employers today will pay the full costs of further education and training —even programs lasting as long as a year. In a few cases employers also are offering college scholarships for workers' children.

MOVING BENEFITS

A growing minority of top U.S. corporations will pay at least part of your mortgage interest costs when you are reassigned to a new post in a new location. Many also will extend a low-cost loan to you to help you with the down payment on this new house. Virtually all companies will pay at least some of your direct moving expenses.

TIME OFF TO VOTE

The overwhelming majority of firms make some time-off arrangements for employees—both hourly and salaried—to vote. The usual thing is to give workers whatever time is needed "within reason." Only a dwindling minority says "no time off," on the basis that their employees have ample opportunity to get to the polls on their own time. Incidentally, most states now have laws providing for time off to vote, and many require that time off with pay be provided.

SPECIAL INVESTMENT PLANS

Under these plans, which vary widely from employer to employer, employees may invest regularly in company stock, in government bonds, in securities of outside companies, or in mutual funds. See pages 1010–12 for more details.

DIVIDEND REINVESTMENT PLANS

See pages 1007–8 for full analysis.

PROFIT-SHARING PLANS

Today, millions of workers—both white- and blue-collar—participate in private corporation profit-sharing plans often as an alternative to private pension plans, and thousands of new plans are being set up annually. In some, profits are distributed as periodic bonuses to employees. But in the vast majority of plans funds are held in trust until you, the employee, quit or retire. A key advantage of the typical "deferred" profit-sharing plan is that you pay no federal income taxes on your cut until you actually withdraw it from the profit pool. These plans are being set up by smaller and smaller companies. Employees are becoming eligible to participate in them and to withdraw their full funds after fewer and fewer years of service. The plans can build up into retirement nest eggs for some employees running high into the six figures!

NEW "EXTRAS"

After reporting its findings in a recent every-other-year survey of fringe benefits in private industry, the U. S. Chamber of Commerce suggested that we stop labeling them "fringe" benefits. The Chamber has a point. For here is a sampling of extras already offered by some companies.
- Free or reduced-price meals in company cafeterias.
- Paid membership in clubs, professional and trade associations.
- Medical help for alcoholic and drug-abusing employees.
- Discounts on company products and services.
- Free or low-cost day-care services for preschool children of employed working mothers.
- Free or nominal-cost use of company vacation and recreation facilities.
- Free retirement counseling to middle-aged workers in such areas as financial planning. Medicare benefits, how to turn a hobby into a part-time job.
- Financial aid for adoption expenses—to parallel maternity benefits.
- Fat bonuses for valuable employee suggestions.
- And free flying lessons . . . paternity leave for expectant fathers . . . time off for working mothers to consult with schoolteachers . . . company-paid legal services . . . taxis to and from work . . . free parking . . . employer-paid funerals (about the last word in paternalism!). . . .

And this is not all.

EXOTIC BENEFITS

Here's an abbreviated list of some of the exotic fringe benefits that knowledgeable students of this type of "pay" are predicting for the decade of the eighties and beyond:

● Free concert and theater tickets at regular intervals.

● Use of company computer facilities for your own purposes.

● Loans via employer credit cards which you'll repay by deductions from your
paycheck.

● Company-run private schools for your children—particularly if you live in an
area where public schools are below average.

● Free financial advice from experts paid by the company for which you work.

Before 1985, many experts think, fringe benefits might include coverage of
more than 50 per cent of the costs of home nursing care for the employees, maternity benefits for the unwed as well as the wed, and subsidized homes in com-
pany-owned retirement communities.

But, of course, towering above all other fringe benefits is the private pension
plan—next to your salary, quite likely your most important single point of comparison between Job A and Job B.

It's so important, in fact, that it demands a key place in the chapter on planning for your future financial and personal security. And that's where you will
find full details on pensions.

You can roughly approximate your total compensation by filling in the blanks
below and adding up the figures. If you don't know the specific amounts spent on
your share of the following fringe benefits, ask your employer.

TOTAL REAL PAY

Major medical insurance	$_____
Dental insurance	_____
Other health/hospitalization insurance	_____
Disability insurance	_____
Life insurance	_____
Pension plan	_____
Profit sharing	_____
Savings plan	_____
Services paid by your company (parking, meals, physical exams, health club)	_____
Discounts on company products	_____
Club memberships	_____
Financial counseling	_____
Tuition allowances	_____
Bonuses	_____
Other benefits	_____
Value of benefits	_____
Pay	_____
Total annual compensation	$_____

Do You Like Your Job?

JOB SATISFACTION GAINS ON MONEY

Of the more than 95 million jobholders in the United States as the 1970s closed, an alarmingly high proportion of you were deeply discontented with your everyday work lives. Despite all the fringe benefits, pay hikes, company attempts to provide an atmosphere of "team effort" via company parties, picnics, etc., you continued to feel restless, even alienated. The "extras" become meaningless when you spend eight hours (or more) a day on an activity which you find boring, frustrating, and without any real value.

Why? Because you have so little to say in the work assigned to you. You sense that your opinions and recommendations are not welcomed or respected by management, and thus you lose interest or concern about your work.

A cartoon that appeared some time ago gets to the heart of the problem. It shows a company president seated behind his desk, talking to an employee. The caption has the president saying, "We do live in a democracy, Perkins, but here we operate under an authoritarian regime."

The problem involves more than unhappy workers. It spreads out to the fundamental issue of increasing productivity—a prime essential to curbing inflation and promoting economic stability in our land. Discontented employees can be a drain on the efficient running of any business; people are a successful organization's most important asset as well as the largest single budgetary expense of most businesses. The goal is to make the cost pay off.

What, then, might be some answers?

Giving employees more active—and real—participation in management decisions regarding their jobs, so you become much more than just another cog in the wheel.

U.S. industry is moving far too slowly toward this goal. In Europe, "participative management" has been widely used for many years. But in our country, although the present work force is better educated, more affluent, and brings to the job greater expectations for advancement, only minor changes have occurred in authoritarian managerial practices. Among basic guides:

• You, an employee, should not be asked to participate when your suggestions will not influence the final decision. Token participation is destructive. You can legitimately be asked for your counsel, but not your consent. The objective is to assure you the right of an effective role in the decision-making process.

• In inviting your frank expression of opinion, your bosses run the risk of hearing things they might not want to hear. If top management is surprised by your opinions, there has been a dangerous barrier to good communication. Management must be prepared to respond, to give and to take.

• The value of your opinions can only be rated by how well informed you are, and you are likely to be much more informed about your own jobs than the key executives in the boardroom. When you are invited to make a decision, you develop an "ego-investment" in making it work. A reason you may be so bored is that you have so little to say in the work you do.

• You, too, should try to develop a better attitude toward your employer, as you learn the organization's basic goals and how it expects to achieve them. And this will happen as your supervisors concentrate not on "controlling" you, but on understanding what motivates you and in watching your performance.

In sum, your resentment stems from a fact that management in the United States has too long ignored—namely, that you want recognition and satisfaction in your work, not just periodic raises in pay.

The traditional management practices of the past still may be acceptable to older workers accustomed to thinking solely in terms of money rewards. But you, the younger workers, do not share those same material values. Money is important of course, but so is your life-style. The sooner business realizes this, the faster will be our progress toward the society we all want so deeply.

SHOULD YOU QUIT YOUR JOB?

Here are fifteen questions which will reveal to you your own feelings about your job:

(1) In the last couple of months have you thought that you would like to quit or change jobs because you do not like the work itself?

(2) Do you feel that your work is monotonous, that the work itself provides no basic interest?

(3) Do you like the work itself that you are doing?

(4) Do you feel your work is checked too much?

(5) When you are away from work, do you think of your job as something you look forward to?

(6) Do you feel your job is a dead end as far as a work career is concerned?

(7) Do you find your work interesting enough to talk about it with people outside your work situation?

(8) Do you feel that your job is a place where you can continually learn something worthwhile?

(9) Do you find your job less interesting than, say, six months ago?

(10) How often are you fed back information about things that go wrong in a way embarrassing or awkward for you?

(11) How often do you feel that putting in effort to do your job well is not worth it because it really won't affect anything in the long run?

(12) How often do you feel that some parts of the job you do really do not make sense?

(13) How often do you find yourself wishing that you could take up another type of work because the work itself is not interesting?

(14) How often do you feel that you are just marking time, just putting in time at your work?

(15) How often do you feel that putting in extra effort is just looking for more problems?

Your answers just to these fifteen questions will indicate the scope of your dissatisfaction with your job.

And will your answers also determine whether you should switch jobs? At the very least, they will give you something to ponder very, very hard.

DO'S AND DON'TS ON QUITTING

Say you are a young middle-management executive earning between $20,000 and $25,000 in a subsidiary of a giant corporation and say three men and a woman in your own age bracket are ahead of you. Say you have just made a New Year's resolution to get out of this box now and find another job with better prospects for advancement. What should you do?

• Don't quit! Keep your present job while you look for another, for in addition to giving you income and a sense of security it will prove to a would-be employer that you are making the move voluntarily.

• Do get firmly in your own mind that this job change may be just one link in a lifelong chain of job changes. For if you are a man or woman twenty years old, you can expect to make more than six job changes during the remainder of your working life. Even at age forty you can still expect to make more than two job changes, and even at fifty you can expect at least one more job change.

Of course, these are only averages, calculated by the Labor Department. Some of us will work at one job all our lives, some will make many more than the average number of changes. Nevertheless, the averages underline the extraordinary degree of job mobility in this country—despite the holding power of fringe benefits, pensions, seniority rights. Executive "dropouts" have become almost as commonplace as high school dropouts.

We're changing and upgrading our jobs and careers as never before in history. We're shopping continually not only for higher pay but—often more importantly —for more fringe benefits such as better pension plans and longer vacations; for a better chance to advance; for a more appreciative boss; for a way out of the big city rat race; for greater on-the-job excitement and adventure; for a chance to learn more; for an opportunity to do our bit to better the troubled world in which we live.

• Don't answer in your own name any "blind" ad (one giving only a box number and not identifying the company). Instead, have a friend cover for you by signing a third-person letter describing your qualifications to help you remain anonymous if the ad was placed by your own company. Do not have a job counselor, recruiter, or employment agent answer for you, for the recipient may get the impression that money is changing hands and this will destroy your letter's impact.

• Do prepare on your own—and with no professional help—a résumé of your career, your qualifications, your objectives. (See earlier in this chapter for rules on résumés.)

• Don't be thrown off base if your employer discovers you are job hunting and, in fact, do accept that you are taking this risk and your employer is likely to find out. This emphasizes the importance of having your campaign planned in advance—so you will be well on your way to something new by the time your plans are discovered.

• Do, if you know of employment agencies that others have found responsible and effective, register with them and leave your résumé. The company hiring you probably will pay the fee. If yours is a highly specialized field, you may be able to locate an agency specializing in finding jobs in this field.

• Do register, too, with your nearest state employment agency, which offers free job finding and/or counseling. Many branches of this agency now have specialized job placement services for executives and professionals. They also can steer you to further job training opportunities if appropriate.

• And you may find of vital help the U.S. computerized "job banks" listing job openings in your field in many nearby states or even throughout the country. Ultimately the job banks' computers will be linked nationally and the network will be able to provide comprehensive information on all major national job markets—for professionals, technicians, managers, and others.

• Do also send a covering letter and résumé to executive recruiters who work at your salary level. This is admittedly a long shot but certainly worth the price of a postage stamp. (You can get a list of responsible recruiting organizations from the Association of Executive Recruiting Consultants, 30 Rockefeller Plaza, New York, New York 10020.)

WHAT IF YOU LOSE YOUR JOB?

"My husband is an advertising account executive in his early forties, earning $40,000 a year. We have a daughter halfway through college and a son who is a senior in high school and will be entering college next fall. We have a large house in southern Connecticut and my husband commutes to New York City by his car or train. I am president of the local garden club.

"For the past year or so we have been spending every cent coming into this house and are just barely managing to scrape up enough a year for our daughter's college tuition, fees, and expenses. A couple of months ago we committed my husband's next year-end bonus (usually $2,500 or more) to a skiing vacation in Switzerland in January and made a down payment on a charter flight.

"We had been planning to sell some of our mutual fund shares at a profit to pay our son's freshman year college costs but the shares are now selling for much less than we paid for them and we hate to sell and take the loss.

"Last evening my husband came home and told me that, because of a sharp drop in his agency's profits, this year's bonus is being canceled and all executives are also being asked to accept a 20 per cent pay cut. Moreover, he said it would be only realistic for us to consider that his job is in serious jeopardy.

"What if he loses his job? Where do we go for help? What can we do?"

Answer: Don't panic!

INTERVIEW YOURSELF

Many young executives are—or have been—in exactly this same bind. The bind may be in the form of a layoff, outright firing, a pay cut, a "vacation without pay," a merger, forced "early retirement," or corporate bankruptcy.

But in every case it means you (and here I'm writing to both and either of you) must at least think about finding a new job—sooner or later. In every case, also, it should mean taking a penetrating new look at yourselves—as a husband, as a wife, as partners—and at both of your ways of life.

Sure, it may have been years since you've pounded the pavement to find a job.

Sure, the threat of losing your job comes at a moment when you've become accustomed to spending to the hilt and even overspending, and when you're faced with an ever-rising cost of living.

Sure, you may be confronted with a job market that is riddled with irrational prejudices against "older workers" in their fifties and even forties.

But why not turn this emergency to your own advantage?

Whether or not this is precisely the moment to make a job switch, at least ask yourself: Is your job one that you find truly rewarding? Or do you feel trapped in it? Has it become overspecialized or too narrow in scope? Are you bored? Frustrated? How did you get into your present career in the first place—and do the reasons still make sense to you?

Think hard about yourself. Interview yourself: prepare a synopsis of your own past career, your qualifications, your goals. Decide whether or not you like this man who is you. In short, are you "doing your thing"?

A new, second career in mid-life can be a glorious adventure. In fact, I cannot overemphasize my earlier message that you should expect and welcome the prospect of two or even three entirely different careers during the course of your working lifetimes.

For facts on your unemployment insurance rights, see Chapter 28 on your rights, pages 1238–40.

"HIDDEN" RESERVE

But quite possibly you, the wife and marriage partner, are the biggest "hidden" financial reserve. If you, this non-working wife, are no more than average, you are entirely capable of earning a paycheck from a part-time or full-time job. In fact, the threat of your husband's job loss easily could turn out to be a blessing for you, by forcing you to consider the benefits of going outside your home to work, particularly if your children are on their way out of your nest, and the need for you to be at home during the daytime hours will soon disappear.

If you are like many of the women I know, you would like to return to work but you don't know how—and you're afraid.

Okay. Use your husband's crisis as your catalyst and with his blessing (if he's an understanding man, he'll be happy to give it) start moving back into the job world. (See pointers in this chapter.)

WHY?

In any event, and whatever financial resources you fall back on to ease the blow of being fired, you, the husband, should make a real effort to find out why you were the one (or among those) to be fired, laid off, sent on an unpaid vacation, or whatever. Don't be unduly brutal with yourself, but be as honest as you can be. The answers and reasons could be valuable clues to help steer you into a new career direction or toward a different type of employer.

Were you really able to work smoothly and effectively with co-workers as well as your boss and those working under you?

Was your interest in the job really sincere and enthusiastic?

Were you flexible enough to welcome—and use—new facts and techniques affecting your bailiwick?

Were you willing to learn on the job?

Were you up to the demands of your job? And, on the other hand, was the job big enough for your talents and energies?

MERGER!

Or perhaps you were dismissed from your job because your company merged with another company and a certain number of heads inevitably had to roll.

For you who may face this prospect—and millions of men and women will indeed face it in coming years—here are profoundly important warnings which almost surely will startle you:

The more successful you may be as an executive in your present job the less likely you may be to advance in a new company created by a merger.

Higher-placed executives are not necessarily the ones who will be in on merger discussions or the ones who will necessarily come out on top.

Those top executives who have a basic sense of security and who are good leaders and administrators are not necessarily the most likely to exercise good business judgment on behalf of themselves when a merger occurs.

Nine out of ten executives are psychologically unprepared to cope with the aftermath of a merger.

A QUIZ TO PROTECT YOURSELF

How do you use this information to help yourself in a merger? Study this quiz. Use the answers to protect yourself against weakness in a future merger.

(1) Did the new owner buy your company for management talent, including yours?

(2) Are you the key executive in a profit center of vital interest to the new management?

(3) Are you flexible enough to: (a) report to a new group of executives; (b) function in a new organization setup; (c) do things "their" way?

(4) Are your executive skills transferable within the new structure?

(5) Was your company acquired for non-management reasons, special financial advantages, manufacturing facilities, distribution structure—of which you are a part?

(6) Is your salary high in relation to the compensation scale of the purchasing company?

(7) Is your salary high relative to the market place for your job outside the company?

(8) Is your future duplicated in the parent company?

(9) Were you publicly against the merger?

(10) Are you in a staff position?

(11) Are you a "self-made" man with long tenure?

If you answer yes to the first five questions and no to the remaining six, you are in a strong position in a corporate merger. If your answers are off—on even three or four points—look out!

GUIDE FOR EXECUTIVE JOB HUNTERS

What's the difference between an "executive search firm," an "executive job counselor," and an employment agency? Who pays for each type of service—you, the executive seeking a new job, or your new employer?

These are vitally important questions to which you must have the correct answers if you are to avoid some perilous traps in the labor market today. To name just one: the unscrupulous "career counselor" who promises a high-paying job which he cannot deliver, but for which he still charges a fee amounting to thousands of dollars.

Therefore, following is your guide to . . .

WHO DOES WHAT IN EXECUTIVE SEARCH

Executive search firms, executive recruiting firms, and management consultants are frequently all grouped as "headhunters," since they always are on the lookout for marketable executives.

The difference between them and the executive or career counseling firm lies in the key question: "Who pays?"

Executive search firms come under many different labels:

• Management consultants often will find new executives for their client companies. The employer always pays, usually a retainer plus a fee based on the time needed to conduct the search and the salary paid for the position.

You, the job seeker, should never pay.

• Executive search or recruiting firms search out, screen, and evaluate prospective executives for their clients. The employer pays a flat fee plus as much as 25 per cent of the executive's annual salary.

• Employment agencies often have search divisions. The agencies usually are licensed by the state, but fees for executive positions are not normally regulated by law. The fee may be paid by either the employer or the job seeker but only on placement. Clarify this before agreeing to any contract.

It is customary for all the above firms to collect a fee from the employer.

Executive career counselors, though, collect a fee in advance of providing their service from the job seeker. Contrary to what their ads may imply, they are not obligated to place a client but only to consult, counsel, or advise. You, the client, pay in advance in stages with no guarantee of placement.

Beware!

The fee ranges from $100 to $200 for the first phase to $2,000 or $3,000 or more for the full three- or four-phase service. More caveats on this later.

HOW TO USE AN EXECUTIVE SEARCH FIRM TO ADVANTAGE

Any executive recruiter considers himself a professional. Make sure you are ready for his realistic judgment. Since the only things he initially sees of you are the résumé and covering letter, make sure both are perfect. (See previous section in this chapter on preparation of résumés.) Never forget: you are *not* his client; the employer is. Therefore, don't expect to be treated like a client.

You may not even get an acknowledgment of the résumé. Your phone calls will be bothersome. You will not be able to drop by unexpectedly and have an interview. Wait for the recruiter to get in touch with you.

If you hear nothing after three months and are still in the job market, send in another résumé. Many headhunters don't keep résumés that come in unsolicited.

An excellent guide to search firms is the *Directory of Executive Recruiter,* available for $10 prepaid from Consultants News, Templeton Road, Fitzwilliam, New Hampshire 03347. It lists 1,400 search firms in the United States and abroad with cross-indexes by management function, industry, and location.

Or write to Association of Executive Recruiting Consultants, Inc., 30 Rockefeller Plaza, New York, New York 10020, for its membership list.

BEWARE: EXECUTIVE COUNSELING TRAPS

You, the job-hunting executive, answer a "career counselor's" newspaper ad which claims "placement, not consultation, and no initial charge." After a brief pitch at the firm's office, in which a smooth salesman name-drops you into confiding in him, the salesman says, "Why don't you go home and bring your wife back for the next interview? After all, this is a family affair."

Your wife accompanies you on the next visit and the salesman now aims a special pitch appealing to her desire (blatant or buried) for her husband to earn more money.

"Mr. A., like your husband," the spiel goes, "was fired just a few weeks ago from a $50,000 job. But we managed to find him a $70,000 job in no time."

You, who have just lost your job, now lose your resistance. You're like the victim of an unscrupulous fast-talking funeral director just after a member of the family has died. You sign a lengthy contract.

Counseling sessions are set up which include aptitude testing and psychological profiles. Expensive résumés are prepared and mailed out indiscriminately to dozens of companies.

The résumés and sessions may—or may not—result in a job or better salary. The "counseling" may be next to useless. In the words of one victim, "The psychological evaluation was a farce. The counseling amounted to bull sessions."

If you do get a job, you probably will have to get it on your own and it won't be at anything like the salary level you have been led to believe you'll achieve.

But you are induced to pay $2,000 for the contract before you get a job or even a single interview.

To avoid this trap:

• Steer clear of any job counseling firm that leads you to believe it is also an employment agency or makes extravagant claims or promises. Use your informed skepticism.

• Check out the reputations of any firms with which you are considering a relationship and ask for, then follow through on references from former clients similar to yourself.

YOUR LIFETIME FUTURE IN A JOB, CAREER, OR BUSINESS   643

- Do not sign a contract before you have asked a lawyer to read it and before you are satisfied that the firm is reputable and will actually provide you with services you need at a fair price.

- Get those definitions and the facts straight on this whole befuddling subject of job assistance so you know where you're going and what to expect.

- Shop with care for job advice. Consult friends or others who have dealt with the agency or firm whose advice you would like to buy. Also ask officers of your former employer for guidance.

- Contrast the claims in the advertisements, promotional literature, and the verbal sales pitch, on the one hand, and the contract on the other. You will find that the first will refer to "placement, jobs, success, satisfaction, and earnings," but the contract will mention words like "consult, advise, attempt, prepare," and will usually have in the fine print a statement that "we are not an employment agency and cannot guarantee employment or placement." Sometimes the firm will offer a "guarantee" that will require you to work with them until you are satisfied. Common understanding of "satisfaction" is getting a job. But who can wait four, six, or eight months for a paycheck?

- In investigating any of these firms, ask for the names of executives with similar skills and backgrounds that the firm has helped to find a job similar to the one you are seeking. See what you get. Or ask the firm for two numbers: the number of clients from whom they have collected advance fees in the last year and the number they have directly helped to find a job. In many cases, the company will claim confidential information in response to all such requests. But ask what you will! If answers are your requirement for doing business, so be it.

- Never sign a "fine print" contract before you have read it several times at your leisure. Take a copy home with you. Read it out loud to your spouse. Note the phases of the program and the cutoff points for a partial refund, if any. What functions must the counseling service carry out before each phase is completed and you lose the right to a refund of that portion of the fee?

- Also, contracts can be modified to meet the needs of both parties. You do not have to accept the requested terms. If both parties cannot agree, they do not do business. Negotiate. You may learn more about selling yourself in that process than you learn from the counseling service.

TEN QUESTIONS TO ASK

You will protect yourself if you get satisfactory answers to these ten key questions about any career counseling firm with which you are considering doing business:

(1) Just what obligation am I incurring? What is the cost? Paid when?

(2) How long has the firm been active in this business under current management?

(3) How competent is its staff in executive guidance—and what are the qualifications? What are the firm's résumés like?

(4) What is the firm's record of success or placement and what are the names of satisfied client-executives? Can I check them myself? How soon did they get jobs? What jobs did they get?

(5) What are the names of satisfied employers with whom it has placed personnel? Can I verify this?

(6) Has the firm's advertising accurately described services offered? Is the promotional literature different from the contract?

(7) Does the contract cover all aspects of the agreement? Have I read it several times?

(8) Are additional promises in writing and signed by an officer of the firm? Does he have authority to obligate the firm?

(9) What provisions are there, if any, for a refund? Are there phases of service tied to a partial refund?

(10) What service period is covered by contract? Can I wait that long?

JOB-HUNTING TIPS FOR THE OVER-FORTY-FIVE

You're out of a job. You are in your late forties or older. You are being turned down by employer after employer as "overqualified" or "inexperienced" in whatever the specialty is. You're told over and over again that you "shouldn't have any trouble finding a job," as you're ushered out the door of your interviewer. But in your heart you know the towering obstacle is your age alone.

For your rights if you are hit by job discrimination because of your age, see page 1237. But always, no matter what, remember these do's and don'ts for improving your job-getting chances.

DO'S AND DON'TS

Don't apologize for your age or for minor disabilities or insignificant physical limitations.

Don't dwell on your need for a job.

Don't underrate yourself in your résumé or interview. Shoot as high as you think reasonable in your pay and status.

Don't hesitate to remind a prospective employer who may throw the old myths at you—for instance, older workers are slower workers, less flexible, weaker, more prone to absence and illness—that numerous objective studies prove precisely the opposite. Older workers' attendance and motivation records are likely to be better than those of younger workers; older workers are less likely to job-hop; the productivity of older workers compares favorably with that of younger workers; the learning ability of an individual in his or her fifties is approximately the same as that of a sixteen-year-old. Do the reminding in terms of your own work history.

Don't fail to register with your state employment office. Many of these offices have specially trained counselors to help those in your position. And even if your local office does not offer such services, it is still required to give you an equal crack at any job opening listed.

Do check the nearest federal Job Information Center (these centers are located in dozens of U.S. cities) for advice and information on federal job opportunities. Another good public source of help: your state Agency on Aging.

Do inquire about any federal government programs through which you might find appropriate training, leading to a good-paying job.

Do check whether there is any private employment agency in your area specializing in helping middle-aged and older workers find jobs. One such agency, Mature Temps, Inc., is backed by the non-profit American Association of Retired Persons, based in Washington with offices in several other major cities. Check into whether there is a "Forty-plus Club" in your area and whether it has anything to offer you. Also touch base with such organizations as the Chamber of Commerce, YWCA, and private temporary employment agencies.

Do ask your trade association or professional association for job advice, and look into professional journals in your field for job leads. Ask your former business colleagues for guidance.

Do approach all employers who you think might have use for your services and go straight to the top people in these companies or agencies or organizations to present your qualifications.

Do keep active, both at home and outside. Keep up social contacts and volunteer for a public service organization that needs your help. You never can tell when volunteering will lead to a paid position with an organization that deals daily with a variety of business people at a relatively high level. A trade association would be ideal. A consumer complaint handling agency or a community and business improvement organization could be productive.

It's easier said, I know. It's even somewhat unrealistic, I admit. But *do,* above all, keep your confidence!

HOW TO USE AN EMPLOYMENT AGENCY—AS AN EMPLOYER

If you're an employer planning to use an employment agency to find the best men or women available for jobs you have open, how do you go about it so you get top results? Or if you're an unemployed worker seeking to find the job you want through an employment agency, what are the rules for you? There are guidelines, ways to avoid past errors and get what you need in the shortest possible time, but where do you find those rules and guidelines?

(1) Before you even call an agency, agree with all who are involved in the hiring on precisely what skills and personality are needed for the position that's open. Be specific to the agency. For instance, don't say "management engineer," for in one company that might mean a project engineer, in another someone in charge of processes. Always be sure the agency understands what you are looking for.

(2) Ask the agency if the salary you have in mind is realistic. Too often it is not—and this slows down the search.

(3) Learn how the agencies work, especially their relationship between their counselors and job candidates. The counselors know many people not actively looking who might be perfect for the job, but who are reluctant to answer a blind ad.

Any recruiting effort that doesn't tap into this pool of prospective employees eliminates some of the employer's brightest prospects.

Make an effort to know the agency very well. Treat it as a consultant, even though you're working on a contingency basis. Think of it as part of your personnel department, get the agency people into your office, so they can understand what the work is like, the positives and negatives.

(4) Use only one or a very few agencies to fill the position, so the agency will work harder for you. If you have tentatively chosen an applicant but want to see a few more, be frank with the agency and it usually will co-operate.

If an agency knows, say, that it's competing with a half-dozen to a dozen others, it might send in anyone just to keep its hand in—a waste of time for you and for the agency. Certainly do not use an agency to check the market if you have no hiring plans; your company may as a consequence find it hard to get co-operation when you really need it.

(5) For specialized technical positions, give the agency suggestions of companies who may be employing the kinds of workers you need. Also, tell the agency the type of personality you are looking for, not only the skills and work experience. If maturity or articulateness is required, this should be explained to the agency. In brief: be honest. Don't let a prospective employee assume that the atmosphere in your company is different from what it actually is, based on your company's past reputation.

(6) It could be, if yours is a hard-to-fill position, that you should make special arrangements with the agencies you have chosen. At least explore the advantage of making such an arrangement. The agency, for instance, might use search techniques, but work primarily on a contingency basis. You, the employer, might agree to pay the cost of advertising or provide an incentive to be applied toward the agency fee if the agency fills the job. You, the employer, and the agency might work co-operatively with a search firm.

And let the agency help sell the candidate you want on taking the position. This help can be of enormous value—and the agency probably will offer to help persuade the applicant's spouse to relocate, if this is needed.

SHOULD YOU GO INTO BUSINESS FOR YOURSELF?

WHY BUSINESSES FAIL

If you go into business for yourself in the 1980s, the odds are fifty-fifty you won't survive two years.

Each year hundreds of thousands of new, small businesses close their doors, in good times as well as bad, in periods of economic stability, as well as phases of great unrest.

Why?

The reasons underlying the failure in an overwhelming nine cases out of ten are the manager's incompetence, inexperience, ineptitude, or a combination of all three.

The apparent causes may seem entirely different: a slump in sales because of economic recession, heavy operating expenses eating up revenues, a poor location with no foot traffic, increased competition, or excessive fixed costs, for example.

But why did sales slump? Or operating expenses eat up revenues? Or no foot traffic come in the door? Because of the boss's incompetence or inexperience. All other explanations for business failure can be bunched into that minor 10%—including neglect, fraud, disaster.

Should this discourage you from realizing the American dreams of going into business for yourself, of being your own boss? No! But surely it shouts a warning to you to prepare yourself thoroughly, to formulate carefully your objectives, evaluate your risks, measure the likelihood of failure, and tabulate the savings you can afford to lose.

A QUIZ TO SUCCESS

Ask yourself and honestly answer all these questions. Write out the answers and read over them in a week. Let your family and friends in on your plans and ask their frank, objective advice about your abilities and your proposal (even though the appraisals may hurt.)

• Have you worked recently in a business like the one you want to start? Have you run the business or closely watched someone else run it?

• Does your business evolve from your previous experience? Or is it a departure, a new activity in which you have little or no experience?

• Are you willing to work long hours with no guarantee of a paycheck? Have you done it before? Do you regularly work overtime without any guarantee of extra pay?

• Do you know how much money you will need to get your business started? How much can you personally put up?

• Do you know how much bank credit you can get initially on your name alone? How much more on the business? How much from your suppliers, the people from whom you will buy? Where can you borrow the rest? Will you worry to the point of anxiety about the money you borrow? Have you managed debt before?

• Have you made an educated estimate of the net yearly income you can expect to get from this enterprise (count your salary and a reasonable return on the money you put into the business), and can you live on less than this amount so you can use some of it to help your business grow?

• Do you know the good and bad points about going it alone, having a partner, or incorporating your business?

• Have you talked to both a lawyer and a banker about legal and financial aspects of your plans?

• Have you tried to find out whether businesses like the one you want to open are doing well in your chosen area and elsewhere?

• Do you know what kind of people will want to buy what you plan to sell? Do people like that live in your neighborhood and do they need an outlet like yours?

• Have you talked with other business people in the area to see what they think of the type of business you want to start?

• Are you timing your move right, thus giving yourself every chance to succeed financially—in terms of demand for the goods and services you want to sell, availability and cost of credit, quantity and quality of competition already lined up against you?

• Do you have a real interest in people—both the prospective employees who will be working for and with you and the customers who will buy from you?

• Are you capable of delegating authority and responsibility to those capable of handling it?

• Can you fire someone? Perhaps a friend that helped you initially but is not working out now?

• Are you a good, sensible planner—financially and otherwise—since your profits will depend largely on your capacity for planning, promotion, cost measurement, and a good sense of product and service?

• Do you know the local zoning and licensing rules covering the type and size of business you want to launch?

• Have you totaled the income you are sacrificing by going into the business? The income from the job you will give up? The loss of interest income on money withdrawn from your savings account? If the family will work in the business, have you totaled the money they would make if they were working on the outside? Have you weighed the loss of leisure time that you and perhaps family members will suffer? The income that you won't receive and the value of everything you will sacrifice to determine the cost of this opportunity?

Have you answered yes to every question? If so, okay, you seem a good risk.

If you have answered with even one no, back up and think again. For this suggests you have a lot more preparing to do.

Whatever your answers to this sampling, write for the Small Business Administration's pamphlet "Checklist for Going into Business." Available from the SBA, 1441 L Street, N.W., Washington, D.C. 20416. Your tax dollars make the booklet available. Get a copy and study the pamphlet with great care.

If you are buying an existing business, study the "Business Opportunities" section of your local newspaper. See if alternate possibilities to the plan you already have in mind seem worth checking through. Also, compare the prices asked for businesses in the field that interests you with the price being asked for the business you think you want to purchase.

Follow this check list:

• Visit the premises, several times at different times of day and on different days.

• Talk to customers.

• Talk to other businesses in the neighborhood.

• Survey the area for several blocks around.

• Inspect books, records, and title to the business.

• Secure a non-competition clause from the seller.

• Learn the position of the business in its market. Is the market growing or declining?

• Comparison-shop as you would for anything else—except even more thoroughly.

• Make sure you find out the real reason why the owner wants to sell.

A SURVIVAL TIMETABLE

Don't get so caught up in the often frantic day-to-day activity of starting a business that you forget to look at whether or not you are likely to survive. You may have lots of customers and make lots of sales and still go broke if your expenses are not in line. Before you actually open the doors to your business, make a diagram setting some criteria for success and survival. Keep the criteria in your head and check the table once a month to see how you are doing. Criteria for success and survival vary greatly among different types of businesses. If you have the capital to use to cover expenses, you may hold out longer than if you started on a shoestring. On the other hand, if you are not going to succeed, it's common sense to get out fast with minimal losses. Compare your performance with other businesses in the same area offering the same product or service. Write the relevant criteria for your business with your financial backing on a table like this:

TIME	CRITERIA FOR QUESTIONABLE SURVIVAL	CRITERIA FOR LIKELY SUCCESS
First Month	Little foot traffic; few calls or letters; if they come in, they don't buy; if they buy once, they don't buy twice.	Active foot traffic; people coming in, calling, writing, and coming back with friends. Sales volume picks up every day.
Third Month	Promotional campaign brings some sales, but little repeat business. Revenues cover only one third of operating expenses. No referral business.	Building some referral and repeat business. Revenues almost cover operating expenses during the best weeks.
Sixth Month	Revenues increasing slightly but by year end, capital will have been used to cover operating deficits.	Revenues are covering expenses. Biggest season ahead.
First Year	Revenues barely covering expenses during peak months of biggest selling season. No cushion to fall back on. No more capital available to cover operating deficits. No revenue for pay increases. Promotional campaigns bring "one sale" customers; no repeat business.	Revenues covering expenses. Rebuilding capital. Revenues sufficient for pay increases and slight expansion. Some left over for me.

Of course, mold these generalities with specifics that apply to your business.

But put some survival numbers on paper! Modify them as you go along. Measure your progress against survival requirements, so that you will have the peace of mind of knowing the chances are excellent you will survive or the assurance of knowing when to pull the plug, cut your losses, and get out.

FUNDAMENTAL RULES

Now, ask your friends and objective observers—a lawyer, banker, casual acquaintance at your office—to judge you, too, against the following fundamental rules for success in launching any new business:

Know thoroughly the line you're going into and don't kid yourself about your own know-how.

Be sure you have well-rounded experience—in selling, purchasing, producing, whatever—or that you can get others to fill in your gaps.

Provide yourself with ample cash and access to credit to carry your business through the first, most vulnerable years. Be sure to budget ample sums for start-up advertising and promotion costs, for buying stocks, for extending credit to your customers.

Ask the appropriate trade association in the field in which you want to work for ideas and leads on companies that may be for sale. One catalogue of these associations, which you may be able to find in your library, is the *Directory of National Trade Associations*.

Go to the nearest branch of the Small Business Administration for further guidance on buying a business. The SBA publishes several vitally important booklets, available free or for little cost.

Do not even attempt to buy or launch a business without the help of a competent lawyer, a competent accountant—and the appropriate officer at the bank with which you do business.

Is Franchising for You?

ANOTHER WAY TO GO INTO BUSINESS

In the late 1970s, more than 468,000 businesses in the United States were franchises selling an eye-popping total of more than $280 billion of goods and services to Americans.

The upsurge in franchising during the entire decade of the seventies mirrored changes in America's life-style faster than many other elements of the business community. For franchise offerings often are ahead of a developing trend and often fade rapidly as a trend turns into a fad and disappears. Franchising offers quick but not always stable and permanent growth.

Many franchisers that were offering a new style of restaurant two decades ago, the fast-food eatery, are now operating vast franchise networks of established businesses that are in the mainstream of the transient, mobile, automobile-dominated American life-style of this era. But as that life-style changes—as it will —so will the fortunes of the franchise empires built on it.

Among the most rapidly growing franchises in the 1980s will be:
• Automotive products and services
• Beauty and health services
• Business aids and services
• Convenience grocery stores
• Day-care centers

- Drugstores and pharmacies
- Educational products and services
- Entertainment and leisure time activities including recreation and travel
- Fast-food establishments
- Medical and custodial home care services
- Nursing centers
- Real estate brokers
- Rental and leasing services
- Security services
- Tax preparation services

Fast but risky growth that is not necessarily stable or permanent is a common feature of franchise operation.

Franchising is *not* for just anyone! Many victims of a franchise failure learn that lesson only after they have lost their life savings in an ocean of red ink. (See Your Rights, page 1242, for information on new protections for franchises.)

Among the most eager and most vulnerable investors in franchises are:

Financially strapped family breadwinners needing to supplement their regular income;

Unemployed men in their forties or fifties who are suffering from job discrimination;

Elderly individuals and couples seeking to boost their meager retirement income;

College students needing a means to help pay today's high college cost.

Is franchising a business for you—the man or woman whose experience has been limited until now to working for others? The answer is a resounding "no!":

- Unless you realize it is easier to lose money than to make it in a franchise operation;
- Unless you choose a reputable, well-capitalized, well-managed operation;
- Unless you have enough capital to cover your initial investment and carry you through at least the first six months;
- Unless you first do a lot of "homework" about yourself as well as the business;
- And unless you are on the alert for the fraudulent operators who have in the past infested franchising.

QUESTION AND ANSWER GUIDE FOR POTENTIAL INVESTORS

Q. *Exactly what is a franchise?*

A. A franchise is a license for you (the franchisee) to sell a brand name product or service owned by a firm (the franchiser) in accordance with the owner's marketing methods. For this license you, the franchisee, pay a fee and a percentage of the gross. The franchiser should have a continuing relationship with you and a vital interest in your success. Therefore, the franchiser should provide you with assistance, training, and usually some advertising in addition to the product or service.

Q. *What type of operation should the amateur choose?*

A. None. Franchising is not for the amateur. Most legitimate franchise offerings don't want amateurs and will not allow you to buy their valued name. If you, as an amateur, are eagerly wooed to pay up-front money, this may be a come-on and *the key* to a rip-off. If it's too easy to "qualify" as a franchisee, watch out! The only qualification may be your up-front money.

Q. *What type of operation should you choose?*

A. Only one in which you have some experience. Your own business should be an evolution, not a departure, from what you have done in the past. If you are a bookkeeper, don't buy into an auto transmission overhaul franchise which demands a mechanic and managerial skill you don't possess. Always choose an area with an established and growing demand. Avoid being the last or the first franchisee, avoid old products that have been on the market too long to have any growth left for them, and avoid the fads that are popular this month but were not around last month and may not be around next month. Sure, it's tough to know what is a fad, and what is the new consumer growth item—but *you* must proceed with the maximum guidance you can get and with great caution. As one illustration: several years ago, trampoline franchises were hot businesses. But the fad died quickly and most of the franchises flopped.

Q. *What are your abilities?*

A. A central point never to forget: a franchise will not magically endow you with abilities you do not already have even though you are eager to learn. There is no way that a retired letter carrier can become an entrepreneur in two weeks. A degree in physics is not necessarily a passport to a successful art gallery or nursing home.

Q. *What sort of investigation should you make?*

A. Here is a check list of sources:

(1) The newspaper carrying the ad. How long has the firm been advertising? Does the newspaper extend credit for advertising? (If not, what kind of financial base does the franchiser have that could convince you to pay $10,000 up-front if a large newspaper requires cash with the order?)

(2) A good public or business library. Examine newspapers and trade periodicals. *The Wall Street Journal* is essential reading for people in business. There are few good publications aimed at franchisees. But *you are not going into the franchise business.* You are going into the fast-food business, the auto repair business, the real estate business, etc. Read the trade publications in the industry you are joining. Subscribe to a few before you buy a franchise.

(3) The current issue of Franchise Opportunities Handbook published by the U. S. Department of Commerce. Write for a price list to the Superintendent of Documents, U. S. Government Printing Office, Washington, D.C. 20402. Also, it is worth the $5.00 price to get a copy of "Investigate Before you Invest" from the International Franchise Association, 7315 Wisconsin Avenue, Suite 600 W, Washington, D.C. 20014.

(4) Past and present franchisees. Select them yourself from among all the firm's franchises and write as well as visit them. Go over the franchise check list with them (see pages 654–56, point by point). Be wary of any franchiser unwilling to

supply you with a complete list of past and present franchisees and their addresses.

(5) The major suppliers and trade creditors of the franchiser. Investigate the quality of the products and services, the length and level of satisfaction of the business relationships.

Q. *How should I evaluate the contract?*

A. Carefully and thoroughly. Be specifically on the lookout for inconsistencies between claims in the promotional literature, advertisement, and sales pitch on the one hand, and the written words of the contract on the other. *Anything* that you rely on from the company should be clearly stated in the contract. Here is a check list that covers some of the most common inconsistencies.

(1) Site selection, lease negotiation, and store design.
(2) Financing, long and short term.
(3) Equipment purchasing, financing, and maintenance.
(4) Promotion, public relations, and advertising.
(5) Accounting assistance, including cost analysis and control.
(6) Centralized purchasing and resultant savings.
(7) Training, both initial and follow-up for management and employees.
(8) Legal advice. (Insist that your own lawyer evaluate the franchise offering.)
(9) Resolution of disputes by conveniently located impartial third parties.
(10) Resale provisions.

If there are inconsistencies, these are the danger signals of franchise fraud. Look further. Make sure they are all clarified before you decide to go ahead with the agreement. Have an experienced franchise attorney look over the contract and other material before you sign. Before you go to the attorney, examine all documents thoroughly yourself and have specific questions for him to zero in on. Assume nothing; question everything. Leave no inconsistencies unclarified.

Q. *What about the franchise fee?*

A. Virtually all franchising operations require an initial fee, or "front money." Requirements in the late seventies ranged from $2,000 to $45,000 with a few higher. But a legitimate franchiser also requires that you have a sufficient pool of liquid capital not only to buy the franchise, but also to keep it going for several months. Don't expect to be in the black from the beginning. No new business, franchise or non-franchise, ever is. If the franchise promoter is more interested in getting your up-front fee than in making sure you have liquid capital or established financing, walk away fast.

Q. *What about profit potentials?*

A. A franchise should produce a net pre-tax profit of at least $15,000 a year— just to make the investment worthwhile. But don't expect a big annual income from a small franchise investment. The franchisers have a good idea of what their kind of operation will gross and net and they scale their franchise fee accordingly.

Q. *What will the legitimate franchiser do for you that you couldn't do for yourself?*

A. Sell you a recognized brand name product or service built up by national or regional advertising; provide established selling, advertising, and public relations techniques; offer experts who will help you get started; finance you or help you obtain credit in addition to what you must contribute: guide you in selecting a satisfactory location; sell you equipment and supplies at a fair price because the franchiser bought in volume at discount prices, and offer the training you and your employees might need to make a success from your franchise.

If a franchiser you are considering does not offer you all of these fundamentals in return for your cash, beware!

FRANCHISING CHECK LISTS

Here is a check list developed by the Council of Better Business Bureaus, designed to lead you, a prudent investor, to sufficient information to make an informed decision and commitment.

General

(1) Collect information on both the franchise and the type of product or service. Continue your search for several months using numerous independent sources. (See the sources check list on pages 652–53.)

(2) Double- and triple-check everything the company tells you with independent sources. Note whether you get the same answer to all questions listed below from several sources.

(3) Keep a notebook. Take notes of all of your conversations. (If you can't make an orderly, timely, thorough evaluation of a business opportunity, what makes you think you can run a business?)

The Company

(4) What is the corporate name? Are you paying your franchise fee to a separate corporation set up specifically to sell franchises or to the founding company turned franchiser? Beware of professional franchise salesmen that may be brought in to set up a franchise sales corporation and sell many franchises quickly. There may be no continuing relationship that is essential to success as a franchiser.

(5) How long has the franchiser been in business? How long selling franchises? How many franchises has he sold in each of the last five years? Of these, how many are still operated by their original purchasers?

(6) Who are the principals of the firm? What businesses were they associated with for each of the last ten years? Get company names, addresses, and check them out.

(They should ask similar information from you. Why shouldn't you get it from them? This one question, if accurately answered and if you thoroughly check out the answers you get, will almost always keep your money out of the pockets of franchise crooks.)

Are the principals experienced in this type of business service, or are they specialists at franchise sales?

(7) What is the company's financial strength?

Get a copy of the annual report and certified financial statement. Check banking references, trade creditor references, and lines of credit with financial institutions. (Learn the lingo here. When a bank tells you the firm has a "medium four-figure balance, non-borrowing account" that means that the firm has between $3,000 and $7,000 in the bank and the bank does not extend credit. If the bank does not extend credit, why are you paying $9,000 in advance? Aren't you extending credit?) How long have these financial arrangements been established? Longevity is often more important than dollars in the bank.

(8) What are the franchiser's plans for future development? Are they written? Do they appear reasonable in light of recent past expansion and management and financial resources?

(9) Check the firm and the owners with your local Better Business Bureau. Don't be lulled by the fact that the company has no complaints against it. That is only relevant if the company has been in business in the local area for several years. Franchise complaints often never surface at all, and when they do, it is frequently two years after the cash outlay.

(10) Is the franchiser licensed in the state? As of the late 1970s, fifteen states required a franchiser to register with the state and provide a disclosure statement to potential franchisees. Read the law in your state. If your state does not require licensing, check the provisions of the law in a state that does. But don't drop your guard and be lulled into a false sense of security simply because a franchiser is licensed. Licensing is not protection against fraud, let alone business failure. Under a Federal Trade Commission franchising trade rule, you will be provided with information on potential franchisees. (But like the Interstate Land Sales Disclosure Act, the FTC rule will not eliminate fraud and will do you no good if you fail to study carefully the disclosure statement.)

(11) How selective is the company in choosing franchisees? Ask to see the names and addresses to back up the numbers. Many claim they are selective and that the qualifications are tough. But often the qualifications are not written and the main one seems to be ability to pay the up-front fee.

The Product or Service

(12) What is the quality of the product or service? Comparative shop as your future customers will. How does the franchiser's offering compare?

(13) Is it a staple, a fad, a luxury item? If a luxury item, are income levels right for it in your area? If a fad, will it be a best seller long enough for you to get your money out plus a profit? If a staple, is there enough demand for your added competition? If a seasonal item or service, will you be ready to tap the first major selling season shortly after you open?

(14) How well is it selling now? In the recent past? Over the last several years? How long has it been on the market in your area?

(15) Is it priced competitively and packaged attractively?

(16) Where is your competition?

(17) Would you, your family, friends, and associates buy the product on its merits?

The Sales Area

(18) Is the territory well defined?

(19) What are the provisions for territorial protection?

(20) Is it large enough to offer large enough sales potential?

(21) What are its growth possibilities?

(22) What is its income level?

(23) Are there fluctuations in income?

(24) What is the competition in this area?

(25) How are nearby franchisees doing?

The Contract

(26) Does the contract include all claims, written and oral, by both parties?

(27) Are benefits and obligations for both parties balanced?

(28) Can it be renewed, terminated, or transferred? Under what conditions?

(29) Under what conditions can the franchise be lost?

(30) Is a certain size and type of operation specified?

(31) Is there an additional fixed payment each year?

(32) Is there a per cent of gross sales payment?

(33) Must a certain amount of merchandise be purchased? From whom?

(34) Is there an annual sales quota?

(35) Can the franchisee return merchandise for credit?

(36) Can the franchisee engage in other business activities?

(37) Is there a franchise fee? Is it equitable?

(38) Has your lawyer examined it? Does your lawyer know anything about franchising?

Continuing Assistance

(39) Does the franchiser provide continuing assistance?

(40) Is there training for franchisees and key employees?

(41) Are manuals, sales kits, accounting system supplied?

(42) Does the franchiser select store locations? Is there a fee?

(43) Does he handle lease arrangements?

(44) Does he design store layout and displays?

(45) Does he select opening inventory?

(46) Does he provide inventory control methods?

(47) Does he provide market surveys?

(48) Does he help analyze financial statements?

(49) Does he provide purchasing guides?

SOURCES FOR ADVICE ON JUDGING A FRANCHISE

Here are the names and addresses of the organizations most likely to be able to give you practical advice or assistance in judging a franchise today:

International Franchise Association
7315 Wisconsin Avenue
Bethesda, MD 20014

Council of Better Business Bureaus, Inc.
1150 Seventeenth Street, N.W.
Washington, DC 20036

Small Business Administration
1441 L Street, N.W.
Washington, DC 20416 (or any of the SBA's field offices)

Office of Minority Business Enterprise
U. S. Department of Commerce
Washington, DC 20230 (or any of the Commerce Department's field offices)

GYPS AGAINST SMALL BUSINESS

If you run a small business, you are the target of swindlers swarming all over the United States. Market place realities mark you as a more likely sucker than the gullible consumer: fierce competition for customers; growing anxiety on the part of business to avoid offending minorities of any type; an extraordinarily large swing of individuals from the role of the untrained, unhappy employee to the coveted ranks of "my own boss"; weak laws and even weaker enforcement.

The most successful schemes that bilk small businesses of hundreds of millions of dollars are the simplest.

To detect these gyps and protect yourself, you must be constantly on guard against the commonplace rip-offs—and this holds whether you are a small store-keeper or executive or bookkeeper. Here are the top and rapidly growing schemes to watch out for:

THE DIRECTORY INVOICE

You get an invoice for $75, $299, or $750 for a listing in a trade directory with impressive words in its title—such as "Global Worldwide," "Universal Hemisphere," or whatever.

The bill touts the directory as including the leading business and professional firms in the United States and urges payment for the renewal order on receipt of invoice. You are a conscientious bookkeeper, promptly pay the total asked. But in its gyp (not honest) form, your firm never ordered the ad, never advertised in the directory before. The publisher's office is a P.O. box. Neither the listing nor the directory will be printed.

Simple and petty? Simple, yes. Petty? No way!

It's impossible to be precise about how many millions of dollars are taken from businesses each year by this one scheme. Some experts estimate 5 per cent of firms that are solicited pay, with a single solicitation totaling hundreds of thousands of dollars. As fast as one scheme ends, a new one pops up. Many even manage to stay within the law.

But it's not much of a law. The promoter can select his own disclosure. Under a 1977 law, postal regulations require "a solicitation in the guise of an invoice" (the official name of this con) to disclose in big type: "This is a solicitation for the order of goods or services, or both, and not a bill, invoice, or statement of accounts due. You are under no obligation to make any payments on account of this offer unless you accept this offer." But the con man also may use the old disclosure required since 1972, with similar language although some variation in type size.

So to protect yourself against phony invoices:

• Check the authorizations. Just because the invoice says "AUTHORIZED by Henry Smith, V.P." doesn't mean it was.

• Double-check an invoice addressed to "Accounting Dept." for quarter or half ads.

• Look for a company or executive name that is misspelled, a wrong title, or an executive listed who has been promoted or is dead.

• Suspect any invoice requiring a check to be sent overseas. England, South Africa, and Germany often seem to be used as bases for invoice frauds. Compile a list of your subscriptions and directories. Keep it handy. If the name is not on your list, don't pay the invoice.

• Investigate who is behind that P.O. box or mail drop. Ask your supplier for any P.O. boxes they use. Cross-reference the box to the name. Don't send a check to a box not on your list.

• Don't be intimidated by an invoice. Take your time.

• And whether you get ripped off or just receive a phony invoice, *complain*. Contact your local postal inspector or Better Business Bureau. Ask for an affidavit for reporting "look-alike invoices." Send it with the material you received, including the envelope in which the invoice came, to Postal Inspection Service, Fraud Branch, U. S. Postal Service, Washington, D.C. 20260.

Swindlers specializing in small business gyps are creative, clever, sophisticated con men. Vow that you will not be among their victims in the 1980s. Use the information in these pages to help you detect the biggest schemes before they catch you.

CHECKWRITER SWINDLES

Have you, owner of one of this country's millions of small businesses, warned the receptionist who sits near your office entrance how to handle a checkwriter swindler if this crook walks into your office? Have you thoroughly discussed with the person who handles advertising solicitations in your shop, office, or plant how to recognize a minority advertising solicitation fraud?

No? Then you're an easy mark for these rip-offs which are hitting new highs each year—victimizing you as well as countless hundreds of thousands of others.

To illustrate, in the scenario for the checkwriter maintenance fraud, a couple of repairmen will walk into your office, brush by your trusting receptionist with the glib claim, "We have been called to repair your office checkwriter." They examine the machine, report it needs bench work, and take it with them. Within a few hours, you, the business owner, get a phone call informing you the work will cost $150. Or perhaps the claim will be that your machine is beyond repair and you will be offered a rebuilt model at a "special" price.

You counter with, "But I have a service contract." The answer: "Not with us, sir." Only then do you discover that these men are not from the legitimate service company with which you have dealt for twelve years, but are from ZYX Checkwriter Co., Downtown, U.S.A. "It'll be $150 plus pick-up and delivery charge. . . . Total $210 . . . in cash."

In the checkwriter forgery insurance variation, you get an agent's invoice for, say, the $95 premium for the renewal of your "forgery and alteration policy." You pay it. A few weeks later, you get a bill for the extension of the policy for a "full thirty-six months." You call the toll-free customer service number to learn that this is not the company with which you have insurance. This imposter has used a look-alike invoice and a local post office box to deceive you into buying duplicate insurance coverage. You order cancellation because you do have bona fide coverage. The phony mail-order agent says, "That was just a sales gimmick. Your company's policy is illegal in your state."

To protect yourself:

• Have two people in your office authorize payments to vendors for service.

• Prepare and keep at hand a list of firms with which you have service contracts, the date of the last visit and by whom. Record the full name and address of the service company on the equipment.

• If a phony service company victimizes you, notify the district attorney at once. If a forgery insurance invoice swindler hooks you, write to your local postal inspector.

MINORITY ADVERTISING RIP-OFFS

In the minority advertising solicitation rip-off, the pitch will be a phone call from a person claiming to be with a committee for interracial, etc., etc., harmony and adding, "Your firm has been checked out by our inspectors and approved because of your commitment to equal opportunity. As a measure of your continuing good faith, we are confirming your $750 contribution to our annual program. . . ."

If you reply you can't manage a contribution of that size, the promoter will bargain you down to some amount—even $25.

The pitch is typical. No matter what questions you ask, you will get no answers because there was no inspection, there are no inspectors. If you persist, there will be implied threats about reporting your lack of co-operation to the "Equal Opportunity Division."

Or instead of a phone call, your bookkeeper may receive an invoice for, say, $298 and a newspaper tear sheet with your company's name listed among hundreds saying "we support equal opportunity." Or there may be just an invoice and a note confirming your "order."

Don't pay the invoice. Hang up the phone. This type of high pressure pitch is the give away that an unscrupulous promoter is operating a minority advertising scheme. The legitimate concern for equal rights has been twisted by these con men into schemes that have been and are phenomenally successful.

A California company operating in the early to mid 1970s used more than thirty different names and mail service-post office box addresses! The misrepresentations ranged from organizations dedicated to job training for minorities to aiding handicapped workers to promoting equal opportunity employment. The promoter finally was convicted of twenty-three counts of mail fraud, sentenced to a five-year prison term and a $15,000 fine. He reportedly had raked in more than $2 million.

PHONY "POLICE" PITCH

Your business phone rings in the middle of a busy afternoon.

"Hello, I represent the National Police Something-or-other. We are calling to renew your ad in our journal, which will help with the National Police Investigators Something-or-other's law enforcement program. We are working to keep the two-man patrol car and to get legislation to protect widows of police officers. We are sure you will want to renew your support of your local police organizations. Our full-page ad is $800. . . ."

You finally settle on an ad of one-eighth page for $75.

"I'll send an officer around to pick it up."

You vaguely remember a similar call from the group last year. "It's for a good cause. . . . Why not . . . ?"

Because while some of these calls are 100 per cent bona fide, most of the time the call is not for any "good" cause except to line the pockets of a for-profit promoter contracting with a "police" group to raise money for them. A huge bite, as much as 60 per cent or more, goes to the for-profit fund raiser. He may get even more to cover his "expenses."

The minor balance goes to the "police" group—with the implication that the group is supported by, connected with, or at least endorsed by the local or state police department. But what the fund raiser wants you to think is just not so!

Police as a rule do not solicit ads. In New York City, for instance, the police commissioner has warned local businesses that police are not selling ads. In Rochester in upstate New York, the fire chief has publicly declared that a group selling ads for a fire-fighter magazine had no connection with the fire department and that the ad sales did not benefit firemen.

But the fund raiser relies on the name alone to convey the impression that a connection exists. The group may be loosely connected with a police union, may do a little lobbying, may hold a convention. But try to find just what it does.

To protect yourself, require in writing:

• A request for your financial support on the organization's letterhead, along with a list of the Board of Directors and a statement of the purposes of the organization.

• The latest annual report including an audited financial statement, plus a report on how much of your money goes to the fund raiser and how much goes to the programs that you do want to support.

• A list of current activities that the organization conducts or supports with names and addresses.

• A clear answer to your question whether you can volunteer your time instead of giving money. (That will sting the phonies!)

Any legitimate organization will gladly send you this information. Many will welcome you as a volunteer. But not phonies . . .

OFFICE SUPPLY CON

Now say you are a purchasing manager in a Midwestern manufacturing company. You get a call on your return from lunch:

"Hello, I'm Edward Jones with Elegant Office Supplies of Nowhere, Ohio. James Wilson, the vice-chairman of your board, suggested I call you. My father recently passed away and I'm closing out his office supply business. I am offering some first quality supplies at a fraction of their original cost. You can save hundreds of dollars."

You then are offered a list of brand name office supplies at "low" prices. You agree to take a small shipment, perhaps a dozen ball-point pens to help him out. You will be billed.

Now the pitchman goes to work. Instead of a dozen ball-point pens, you get a dozen gross. Instead of quality brand names at bargain prices, you get off-brand or defective products at exorbitant prices. You won't buy again, but these schemers don't live on repeat business, want only a one-shot sale.

Become familiar with the countless variations of this gyp:

"By error we printed your firm's name on a large supply of pencils . . ."

"With cutbacks in the schools, we have supplies that they don't need that we can offer you at less than our cost . . ."

"We are liquidating office supplies for (some company just headlined as bankrupt) and can offer . . ."

Con men frequently tie their pitch to the bankruptcy of a well-known giant corporation.

The so-called bargains could be purchased cheaper from regular stores, and the name brands rarely, if ever, are. Yet the schemes are so successful that some operations run from the same locations for years. One company ordered by both the Federal Trade Commission and the United States Court of Appeals to stop its deceptive practices is still in business today using the same tactics!

ADVERTISING PROMOTION SWINDLES

A stranger walks into your small importing business and offers to sell you a full-page ad in a guide distributed to several hundred college bookstore buyers in the fall. The ad costs $375, you supply the artwork. You flip through the book, see some familiar names. The salesman suggests you think it over, he'll be back tomorrow.

You call his office, an efficient girl answers, explains that he is out but will return your call. He does.

You check with some friendly competitors. They have signed up recently but since the catalog has not gone out, don't know how it will pull. You decide to go ahead, phone to say you will send a check. The salesman offers instead to pick up your check.

While you think this odd, you sign the contract, give the salesman the check and the artwork.

Autumn comes—but no catalog. You call, get a friendly answer, leave a message, but no return call. Nor does your next call get a reply. As you look through the contract, it hits you.

The contract has no delivery date, no number of bookstores, no geographic area, no minimum number of copies, no method for verifying delivery. You check with your friendly competitors, who also have received no sample catalog, no return call, no orders.

You call the local Better Business Bureau, learn your experience is typical. "A BBB survey of one hundred colleges on the list turned up not one bookstore buyer who remembered receiving the catalog, despite the repeated mailings claimed by the company," says a BBB investigator. "The promoter has been doing this for three years. The case was referred to law enforcement agencies but none has acted."

Now you know you should have:

• Obtained a copy of last year's directory, checked with some of the advertisers to learn their experience, checked with some college bookstores to see if they use the book.

• Insisted that you mail the check. (Personal pickup avoids the use of the mails and may evade the postal inspectors.)

PHONY "DISCOUNT CARDS"

Another phony promotion involves advertising discount cards. Most of these discount card plans are completely honest and good for the merchant and for us, the consumers. But some are crooked, smear a great theory by their execution of a program prompting participation by merchants (usually small ones) in a customer discount plan and then never following through on any promise.

The usual gyp: you, a local businessman, pay several hundred dollars to be listed in a directory that is never published or on a discount card that is never printed and distributed.

• Check the track record of the company behind the promotion. In what cities has the firm recently operated? Get names, addresses, and do inquire about their experiences.

• Don't rely completely on the credibility of the local business sponsor. A large business also can be conned!

• Weigh the cash outlay in terms of probable results. How much more business will the promotion need to create in order to pay for itself? What other advertising costs this much? Have shops similar to yours found this promotion worthwhile?

"SPACE BROKER" GYPS

A third swindler in this category is the ad space broker who not only lifts your classified ad from a general circulation newspaper but also then gives you a phony pitch on why you should advertise with his particular outfit.

• Watch out for circulation overstatements by space brokers representing numerous ethnic newspapers.

• Be on guard against a variation of the old phony office supply con. You authorize one insertion at $17 but then get a bill for "One insertion . . . full week . . . $119."

• To protect yourself, get a circulation report from the Audit Bureau of Circulation or a verified circulation statement.

• Realize that this space broker is not the newspaper. Take careful notes on the claims these brokers make, then check with the newspaper. You well may get two wildly different stories.

• Inquire at a local public library where the paper mentioned is supposed to circulate and find out if they even have heard about it, much less have a file on it.

• Never forget the basics: don't buy supplies over the phone from strangers; don't accept pledges of big business gains from pitchmen who want your money up front; don't hand-deliver checks to strangers; use the mails and alert the postal inspectors to complaints; always double-check any claims, particularly the most alluring.

THE SCAM

The scam is a hit-and-run swindle designed to make a big killing all in one shot from countless thousands of small business victims—and then to scram.

If you're lured into a scam, you, the victim, get nothing—not defective office supplies, not a police certificate to put on your auto's windshield in the hope of avoiding a parking ticket, not even the illusion (albeit totally erroneous) that you are helping minority workers by contributing to a phony civil rights organization. Just zilch, with the exception of a sock in the bank account.

To illustrate with a New York City-based scam from the late 1970s:

Reliable Sales Company (that is the real name but it wasn't) set up shop in April 1977, at 2 Penn Plaza in Manhattan, a fancy-sounding address which the promoters obtained from a space rental firm for $75 a month. The scam operators had some artwork made up and catalogs printed, then contracted for a mailing of 18,000 catalogs in late May—early June to retailers across the nation, primarily drugstores and camera shops. The catalogs offered consumer goods of every description—cosmetics, crayons, cologne, cameras, clocks, TVs, cat food, crackers, candy bars, coffee makers, calculators, etc.

Hundreds of items were priced at up to 50 per cent *below* normal wholesale prices. Under the terms of purchase, a minimum order was $250, with no price changes if orders were in by June 20, the "extended sale date"; a deposit of 25 per cent was required with all orders, but if you paid in full with the order, you could deduct 2 per cent from your check; shipping charges were 5 per cent of the gross order. And the firm's return policy was generous:

"All merchandise carries a complete guarantee and is returnable for a full refund if dissatisfied for any reason."

There was only one hitch: what was returnable to whom? Nothing was ever shipped! Reliable Sales was gone from its prestigious New York City address before the end of June 1977. In July the U. S. Postal Inspectors obtained arrest warrants for the principals, but they had skipped from their Manhattan apartments. As of this writing, their whereabouts are still unknown!

And the retailers were merely half the intended victims. The other half were

suppliers, for the company sent out hundreds of orders for merchandise to manufacturers, jobbers, wholesalers, covering products ranging from motorboats to diamond rings—all to be delivered by June 25 to the firm's warehouse.

Payment was to be C.O.D. The warehouse turned out to be the ground floor of
a tenement in Queens, New York, which the firm had rented a few days before.
The long July 4 weekend was obviously the target date for the two halves of the
scam to come together with a potential take of several million dollars.

Although quick work by the local Better Business Bureau and the postal inspectors foiled a big take, the principals were tipped along the way—and the law
could not collar them.

Don't get caught in either half of a scam:

• Automatically suspect bargain prices. How can this company offer me such a
bargain—and why should it?

• Ask your normal supply channels what they know about the company and
call telephone information in the firm's city to find out if the firm has a new listing. Often, phone operators can tell you if the listing is less than three months
old.

• Investigate addresses. "Reliable" could not have had a warehouse at 2 Penn
Plaza. Where then? Get an address and check it.

• Ask manufacturers you trust if they have heard of this "wholesaler" and
request references. "Reliable" did not have any good references and refused to
supply any when requested. It had five bank accounts in different New York City
banks, none open more than a few months. Longevity is often more revealing
than a balance.

• Look for inconsistencies in the catalog. Since when is a "dealers' confidential
price list" mailed unsolicited with a bulk mail permit? The catalog offers every
type of consumer goods, yet describes the firm as "wholesaler to the trade." What
trade?

• Don't underrate your own creditworthiness by believing their line about shipping on "open account" only after you have established your credentials. Why
should a mail order solicitation insist on having your money up front?

STEALING FROM THE BOSS

"Stealing from the boss is a remarkably attractive activity. I can build a much
better case in favor of stealing than against it."

This would be a startling judgment from any reputable citizen. It is particularly
so, coming from an industrial security expert who counsels some of the nation's
biggest retail chains on employee theft motivations and how to combat white collar crime.

The magnitude of business crime in the United States today staggers the imagination. It's estimated at $125 billion a year. And of this huge amount, $44 billion
for white collar crime is by far the biggest single element.

And call it what you will—shoplifting, employee theft, management fraud, inventory "shrinkage"—business crime is here to stay. What's more, moan and
groan as you may, you and I will carry the load because the retailer has no option

but to pass on to the consumer the cost of crime and crime control. The cost of retail store security ranged from a high of 8 cents per sales dollar in big city stores to 2 cents per dollar in suburban stores in the late 1970s.

Why is stealing from the boss so popular? Because it:

• Enriches you, a very good reason indeed. At the least, it permits small luxuries. And if you're a good thief, you can vastly enhance your style of living—house, club, car, etc.

• Provides some of the kicks or excitement psychologically essential to a sense of well-being. Most jobs are boring.

• Makes you a warmly accepted, committed member of a brotherhood who depend on each other and protect each other. "Don't spoil it for the rest of us," said an advertising executive to a new executive being initiated into the practice of big expense padding.

• Equates you with the boss himself, if the boss prides himself on his slyness and deceptions.

• Restores the self-pride and self-esteem that the boss might have undermined by criticism or snobbishness.

• Restores to you money that was stolen from you when you weren't paid overtime or didn't get an expected raise or bonus.

• Is not considered a crime at all, for if nobody gets hurt and you get helped, no harm is being done.

• Is easy, for basically nobody cares if you steal. Most of the time, nobody even misses whatever it is you stole.

Although some of the above must be tongue in cheek, the causes of employee dishonesty tend to fall into two groups: causes that provide the psychological environment inviting the crimes; causes that offer the opportunities.

• To combat the first group, consider changing the work environment so that it would discourage theft;

• To combat the second, organize your loss-prevention efforts far more efficiently.

Job enrichment programs might help provide the kicks that rechannel energies away from dishonesty to other exciting activities—a sports team, participation in an employee arts and crafts show, a lottery, contest, etc.

Make sure your employees are not underpaid. Just as important, make sure they feel they make a difference and have a responsibility to perform. Job enrichment programs are no substitute for competent, open, forceful management.

When the company becomes "us" to the employees instead of "them," there is a new switch and a new meaning to the phrase "Don't spoil it for the rest of us." That phrase becomes a force for honesty, not dishonesty.

Another critical step in achieving the "us" or "we" identification is the establishment of a series of policies that say:

(1) Dishonesty on the executive level will not be tolerated;

(2) Cheating customers, vendors, and employees must be out of the question;

(3) Promises to employees must be specific and clear, and met in timely fashion;

(4) Offending executives must be made aware of how, by manner or state-

ment, they injure the pride of employees and discourage identification with the company.

A continuing demonstration of "caring" about dishonesty is crucial, over and beyond actual preventive controls.

It well may be that unless business does take steps to minimize internal dishonesty, you and I soon will be spending 10 cents of every dollar just to clothe and feed the thieves!

BEWARE: "BUSINESS OPPORTUNITIES" SWINDLES

Fraud is illegal. But like so many other laws, the anti-fraud laws cry out for enforcement. As a wary investor looking for a legitimate business venture, your best protection is your own informed skepticism. Question everything; assume nothing. Don't get caught in the web of deception and fraud con men often spin around these schemes.

A CLASSIC SWINDLE—RACK ROUTE

A "rack route" is simply numerous display racks distributed among several locations on a route. You, the distributor/investor, buy the merchandise and collect the money. At least that's the theory. The reality is often a nightmare that starts with an ad such as the one below you will see in the 1980s in the "business opportunities" classified columns of your local newspaper:

> PART-TIME/FULL-TIME . . . P/T 5–6 hours weekly nets to $700 monthly . . . F/T 50 hours weekly nets to $7,000 monthly . . .
> $2,800 part-time investment secured by inventory fully refundable has unlimited growth opportunity with potential earnings to $100,000 per year. This national public company has outstanding success record since 1954 and is seeking reliable individuals to service company secured routes. An opportunity to own your own business and become part of a multimillion-dollar market. This is no get-rich-quick scheme or a pyramid but a solid year-round business.
> NO SELLING, NO OVERHEAD, IMMEDIATE INCOME . . . No experience necessary; we train. Simply check stores weekly and restock what has been sold . . . LIMITED OPENINGS AVAILABLE. MAKE THE AMERICAN DREAM A REALITY. OWN YOUR OWN BUSINESS TODAY . . . Write or call . . .

An ad of this sort—the above is a composite for a "rack route"—shouts "Fraud!" It has, though, deep appeal to men and women searching for ways to solve their income problems by going into business for themselves. Business opportunity rackets will continue in the top ranks of white collar swindles in the 1980s.

Thus, beware these earmarks of a "rack route" gyp:

• Inconsistencies. The ad says that one can realize an immediate income and advertises that, while no experience is required, earnings can go up to $100,000. How can this be if "no selling is required" and the investor isn't paid a wage or a salary?

A "business" is a going concern, an active enterprise, but what's really involved in this case is a static inventory of goods for resale—and you're the only one to do the selling. The salesman will tell you that the merchandise will "sell itself" from the "high traffic" locations his locations specialists will provide. Don't believe it!

• Appeal to flattery. This usually comes in the initial letter you get from the company in which there are flattering references to "your talent and your experience in your job" plus your capacity to "bring profit to your company way above your own present pay." Few people who have just lost their jobs will stop to consider how presumptuous are these statements by an unknown correspondent who doesn't know them personally.

• Pressure to act quickly. This is evident in the phrases "limited openings available" and "own your own business today."

• Claims of ease of operation of business. All you need do is "check stores weekly and restock." That's ridiculous.

• Exaggeration. The ad is saturated with impressions of instant wealth, and the promotional literature when it arrives also suggests almost automatic acquisition of this wealth. "A few hours each week and you are on your way to a whole chain. . . ."

What's wrong with this operation?

The earnings are simply not there—and it's not because you're not working hard enough. They're just not there.

The product is frequently inferior. For instance, if you're selling cosmetics, you may have been stuck with last year's colors or antiquated packages. While the claim is that no selling is involved, the product doesn't sell itself and your income is dependent on the sale of the product.

The service you get from the promoting company is inferior: late delivery or no delivery, no maintenance when you need it.

The misrepresentations begin to manifest themselves. The implication that the promoter is connected with, or endorsed by, a nationally known company just isn't true.

To avoid being taken in by this racket:

• Ignore the flattery. Be honest about your own qualifications. Do you really know anything about merchandising? Are you really a good enough salesman to develop and maintain successful relationships with twenty or more retail merchants in widely separated, distinct businesses?

• Verify the claims made to you with at least two independent sources.

• Call the local Better Business Bureau. Frequently the BBB will have a report on the company. But don't let a complaint-free BBB file convince you to drop your guard. If the firm has been active only a few months, the absence of complaints means nothing.

• Talk to the man behind the operation, not the front man or a salesman. There are hundreds of salesmen for these schemes and they move from one scheme to the next, not caring what they sell or what they say. Give the BBB not only the company's name but the promoter's name as well. Ask for résumés for the owners and officers of the company. Do they show a stable background or a string of business connections and disbanded ventures? Promotions come and go but the promoters remain the same.

A TRENDY SWINDLE—ENERGY SAVINGS

Business opportunity rip-offs are often fadish. In the 1980s you will be suckered by schemes in solar energy, home insulation, energy savings, commodity exploration, and artifacts reproduction.

Here is how a typical energy savings come-on might start:

"Earn up to $45,000 full-time, $15,000 part-time per year. Become a foam insulator. A Million Dollar Energy Industry. No Insulation Experience Needed. Training Program. Equipment Included. $6,000 Investment. We Are Seeking Full- or Part-time Dealers. Exclusive Dealerships."

This ad appeared in August 1977, in a major metropolitan newspaper in New York City. In September 1977 the promoter agreed to delete the earnings claims. By October 1978 the company's phone number had been disconnected. Again, some fact and some fiction blend to create deception.

The energy industry *is* a million-dollar industry.

But were there any distributors with this company that made $45,000 full-time, $15,000 part-time per year?

Is it realistic to think that you can go into the highly competitive "million dollar" energy industry with "no insulation experience needed"?

And what happened to the training program? How limited must this firm's capitalization have been if they were established in 1977 and were out of business by October 1978? This was not a $6,000 investment" as claimed. This was a "6,000 high risk capital for new venture . . . little likelihood of success or recovery. . . ."

Throughout the 1980s there will be dozens of these offers which claim you can make a lot of money in the energy savings business. But the promoter will want both your energy and your savings up front.

THE VICIOUS SWINDLE—PYRAMID SELLING

Perhaps because of all the grossly ineffective law enforcement action in the late 1960s and 1970s, the endless chain selling scheme is still around. Even though they swindled thousands of hopelessly naïve victims out of hundreds of millions of dollars, few pyramid promoters went to jail. Nationwide pyramid cons have disappeared but regional ones continue. Here is the bait:

Help Wanted Male/Female . . . College Graduate 15M to 25M Caliber . . . Executives/Managers on the Way Up . . .

> Our company has openings in mgt.
> positions recently created through our
> northeast expansion. Must be self-starter
> and have leadership capabilities. No exp.
> necessary. We will train . . .
> For interview, call . . .

Or you are walking through a suburban shopping center when a limousine pulls up and the rider in the front seat asks you if you would like to make $45,000 a year in an executive position. He invites you to a local hotel to learn about the company, but won't give a detailed job description or even the company name.

This apparent route to a successful venture of your own sounds so attractive, seems a way to avoid ever again being dependent on someone else's fortunes for a paycheck.

But don't fall for it! This composite ad highlights still another "business opportunities" fraud. Here are the major earmarks of this one:

• Inconsistencies. What "college graduate" with "no experience" will be handed a $20,000 paycheck? What "management position" requires "no experience"? Any man or woman intelligent enough to have completed college will be unable to reconcile the claims. And any thoughtful person will wonder why any successful company has to advertise this way for executives and managers.

• Incongruities. Legitimate $20,000 management positions usually aren't advertised in the general help-wanted male/female columns but in the business sections of newspapers and specialized business publications.

• Appeal to flattery and to status. That's implicit in the "college graduate" lure and in the "must be a self-starter and have leadership capabilities" requirements. Don't we all think we are self-starters and potential leaders?

What are the pitfalls of accepting a ride in that limousine?

That limousine driver is not offering any job, let alone one that pays $15,000, $25,000, or $45,000. Instead, he wants $1,000 or maybe $5,000 of your money. Here's how it works:

Promoter P offers A and B the chance to buy distributorships at $1,000 each, which will give A and B the "exclusive" right to sell "distributorships" to others for $1,000 each and to sell certain products to the public. Each $1,000 that A and B receive from their sales of distributorships, though, must be divided with P, perhaps on a 50-50 basis. In theory, A and B can realize $500 on each distributorship they sell and can completely recover their initial $1,000 by selling only two distributorships each. P has received not only A's and B's $1,000 each, but also $500 for each distributorship A and B sell.

But obviously, the number of investors needed to keep the scheme going is out of reach. Say each distributor has to sell eight other distributors, then each of these eight has to sell eight more: 64 . . . 512 . . . 4,096 . . . 32,768 . . . 262,144 . . . 2,097,152 . . . Whether you win depends on your place in the pyramid.

It all started a half century ago in the 1920s when Charles A. Ponzi invented an alluring fraud. Variations of the Ponzi scheme still are around as the 1980s begin under which "investors" are paid off with cash coming in from new "investors."

The best way to protect yourself against a Ponzi scheme is to recognize its ear-marks the instant you hear or read about it.

Here is an illustration of how a representative Ponzi scheme works, as prepared by the Securities and Exchange Commission:

Investor A gives Promoter P $1,000 on P's promise to repay $1,000 plus $100 "interest" in ninety days. (What a quick return, a "once in a lifetime" opportunity!) During the ninety days, P makes similar promises to investors B and C, receiving $1,000 from each of them. At the end of the first ninety-day period, P offers to pay A the $100 "interest" and to return his original $1,000. He also invites A to "reinvest" the $1,000 plus the $100 for a similar or even higher return at the end of another ninety days.

Thereafter, A, believing that he can receive this whopping return on his investment, is likely to bring other investors, eager to get in on this sort of deal, to P.

P thus collects a pool of money from which he can draw to pay the comparatively few who ask for a return of their money. P may operate the scheme for quite a while before either disappearing with the so-called investments or disclosing the news that the investments have gone down the drain.

The central factor in the inevitable collapse of a Ponzi scheme is that there really is no significant source of income—other than the new, unsuspecting, naïvely greedy investors.

Similarly, the best way to protect yourself against a "pyramid" scheme—a business variation of the familiar "chain letter"—is to recognize its earmarks in advance.

And despite tightened government regulations and warnings piled on warnings about pyramid schemes, the racket continues to thrive and remains one of the nation's most vicious business opportunity swindles. Just how vicious? Read these conclusions in a memorandum of decision by a United States judge.

"The Securities and Exchange Commission attributes a host of false statements, actions and omissions to G [the company], K and S [individuals] in particular. Before discussing the more blatant particular misstatements and omissions, it seems clear that the totality of the carnival-type Opportunity and Step-Up Meetings, the 'Jack-up' objective and the 'fake it 'til you make it' approach to selling constitutes a manipulative and deceptive device. . . .

"The psychological selling techniques employed by G successfully duped many innocent, though unwise, investors into parting with funds, often borrowed, which they could ill-afford to invest even in far safer enterprises. . . .

"There is evidence in the record that G's promoters sincerely hoped that the retail enterprise would be successful and that consequently their franchisees would prosper. Nor can it be said efforts were not made to implement the retail end of the business. These factors, however, do not mitigate the fraud perpetrated on the public investors. However strongly the promoters of an enterprise may believe in its potential, prospective investors must still be dealt with fairly and the unadulterated decision to invest or not must be theirs alone. The cornerstone of any contractual arrangement is the agreement of the parties, concluded without over-reaching. While the profit of the defrauded may in private litigation absolve the defrauder from damage in actions brought to protect the public interest, it is of no moment.

"Moreover, any notion of good faith by G promoters is belied by the huge overrides, totaling 18%, they took notwithstanding that G had never earned a cent from retail operations.

"It would take pages to list all the untruths, half-truths and unrealistic projections and predictions contained in the presentations and literature associated with G. Among the more frequent and flagrant violations . . . which the court finds established by the evidence are the following:

Misrepresentations

"1. An investment in G was guaranteed.

"2. G would accumulate and distribute 8,000–10,000 retail customers to its franchisees.

"3. G was already operating in New York City, Buffalo, Poughkeepsie, Montreal, Canada, and New Jersey.

"4. G would begin retail operations in June 1972."

Omissions

"1. G's management was receiving override equalling 18% of gross franchise sales.

"2. Certain G executives had received franchises for 'services.'

"3. None of G's incorporators or key executives had any managerial experience in the retail food industry.

"4. No retail commissions were to be paid during the 'pilot program.'

"Each of the misrepresentations and omissions listed above was material in that a reasonable investor would have unquestionably considered them important in making the decision to invest in G or not.

"While negligence alone suffices as a standard for liability in enforcement proceedings, the misrepresentation and omissions found here were made or withheld either with actual knowledge or with reckless disregard for the truth.

"The evidence reveals that the guarantees were adopted and touted by G with reckless disregard for its ability to honor them. No sinking fund was established, no insurance taken out and, more importantly, officials knew that 53–58% of funds received from franchise sales were being immediately paid out in various commissions, leaving less than 50% for working capital.

"Similarly, the projections concerning the commencement of retail operations and the promise to distribute thousands of retail customers were made without regard to G's ability to realize them. The representation relating to the geographical scope of G's operation was *known* to be false when made.

"While there was no proof in the case that the omissions listed above were deliberately withheld from prospective investors, in view of their obvious importance, the court concludes that the failure to make them known to prospective investors was in reckless disregard of the duty to disclose."

So said the judge. What happened to the promoters in this real case?

Five persons were indicted: two were acquitted; one was dismissed from indictment due to illness; and two were convicted of multiple counts of mail fraud. Of the two convicted, one was sentenced to a year and a day in jail and the other to eighteen months.

As of the late 1970s, neither had reported to jail! It is likely that when the appeals end and the jail terms begin, each will be eligible for parole in a few months.

Did the penalty fit the crime? You be the judge. The promotion grossed over two and a half million dollars (that's $2,500,000) in a short span of two years from more than 800 persons, each parting with between $3,000 and $5,000. None got any money back.

Beware the pyramid!

The prospective investor is pressured to invest on the spot. The "opportunity" meeting the investor attends is so emotionally charged that if he hasn't left his checkbook at home he may sign away his savings right there.

The investor can never make the money predicted by the advertiser, because in fact there are never enough people in a community to sustain the pyramid, or the chain-selling method, indefinitely.

Millions of dollars have been lost on these pyramid or chain schemes in the last two decades—$44 million to one flimflam empire alone.

Government regulations against certain pyramid operators have been tightened. But the pyramid selling racket continues to flourish and the promoters continue to lure victims through ads and solicitations on the street. So, to protect yourself:

• Get the details on any help-wanted ad over the phone, and if details are sketchy, just forget it. If this were a valid help-wanted offer, the person answering the phone would want to discourage unqualified applicants, not intrigue you. Don't even bother going to the personal "interview."

• If you do go to a personal interview, leave your checkbook—and your enthusiasm—at home. Don't sign anything, no matter how pressured you are.

• Be suspicious at once of any help-wanted ad that does not pay a wage or salary, that does not disclose selling is involved, and that does require an investment. This is all wrong! The advertiser is deceiving the medium as well as you.

• Since a pyramid or chain letter scheme depends on an ever-growing rate of recruitment for its success, beware of high-pressure meetings in which salesmen try to extract a hefty fee in exchange for your entering their business. Many such meetings are held in motels, indicating a lack of roots in a particular community; the principals in the firm can—and probably will—be gone as soon as they have saturated the community.

• Be sure the basis of the company's promotion is the retail sale of a product, not the unending recruitment of other distributors. And beware if the entrance fee is way out of line when compared to the business. Why should you pay $5,700, for instance, simply to acquire the right to sell $200 vacuum cleaners door-to-door?

• Note whether the company stresses (if at all) the time, effort, and frustrations involved. No sales enterprise—which is what these offers usually are—is an easy business.

• Ask the nature of the limitation (if any) of the sales personnel to be recruited in your community. Will the company allow only one salesman per county, for example, or is it a meaningless restriction, such as one salesperson per 7,000 people in the state?

• Check if there is a provision that the company will guarantee any products ordered but not sold will be bought back by the firm for a certain percentage of the price you paid.

• Consult consumer organizations in your area to determine if any litigation involving the company is taking place or if similar companies have had difficulties with the law.

• Willingly spend the money to consult a lawyer if you are the least bit suspicious of the enterprise—and you should be if the company uses high-pressure tactics and makes fantastic income projections. A fee of $100 now could save you thousands of dollars over coming months.

• Never sign any agreements until you have given yourself several days to cool down and consider the proposal. If the company pressures you to join using "it's now or never" as a sales pitch, accept that as a warning to make it never!

Why the most vicious swindle? Because as one would-be investor plaintively characterized this touted business opportunity, it's "pure and simple, just an invitation to cheat my friends."

THE MOST ENDURING SWINDLE—VENDING MACHINES

Come-on ads for vending machines have been commonplace since World War II. They will continue on in the 1980s as most enticing lures for the unwary. Vending machines are everywhere. The suckers will think an ad like this is the way to become a vending machine king:

"Four distributors wanted, immediate income, 8 hours a week nets you from $5,000 to $15,000 a year. Part-time or full-time. Get in on the ground floor of this automatic merchandising opportunity. Large national concern looking for a few highly motivated self-starters to operate established routes in this area. Minimum investment, $3,500 secured by inventory. Written buy-back agreement. After this, you can't say that you never had your chance to make it. Call us for information . . ."

This hypothetical ad is similar to ads you'll see now in most business opportunities columns all over the United States. More often than not, it is an invitation to be taken in. The "automatic merchandising" program turns out to be vending machines or perhaps merchandise racks. The "national concern" is really a group of promoters looking for people with savings to "invest" in an inventory of merchandise. The merchandise—vending machines or display racks—offers none of the "security" touted in the ads.

The con man makes his money by selling the machines and merchandise to the victim. Only in theory does the company make its money on the reorders of the merchandise that the investor puts in to satisfy consumer demand for the merchandise.

In fact, there is no consumer demand. The investor ends up with the machines or racks and a garage full of hot dogs, soup, lipstick, panty hose, whatever.

Why don't law enforcement agencies do more? A few are interested. As for consumer agencies, they usually are restricted to civil actions, which are rarely effective against business opportunities swindlers. And a criminal prosecutor has to prove intent to defraud beyond reasonable doubt to obtain a criminal fraud conviction. That's difficult.

So what can you do? If you are victimized by one of the schemes, write in detail to the nearest office of the U. S. Attorney—and help him eliminate that specific fraud.

If you have seen the ad in a newspaper, write to the publisher, make your complaint as specific as possible: list dates, places, names, who-said-what. The publisher should be grateful for the help you give in eliminating this fraud.

You must practice prevention; there is no cure.

• And to start with, don't be taken in by unbelievable claims. Ask yourself: if it's so easy to make so much money, why does the company have to advertise in a newspaper? Why am I getting $15,000 a year for a $3,000 investment? Why doesn't the company make that money for itself?

• Never believe a claim by a vending machine salesman unless it's in writing on company letterhead signed by an officer of the firm. Then you verify it independently by your own investigation. Check out the claims with other investors by writing to them. Get their written replies.

• Ignore the salesman's flattery. Be honest about your own qualifications to run a business. Admit your own limitations. Are you really a good enough salesman to develop and maintain successful relationships with thirty or more retailers where these machines and racks will be located?

• If the promoter boasts of a nationally known manufacturer in his sales pitch, check with the manufacturer to be sure the company in fact endorses the promoter. If it doesn't, be warned right there. And don't be impressed by companies with high-sounding words such as "international" or "general" in their names.

• After the salesman has finished his pitch to you, talk to the men behind the operation. Verify what the salesman has told you. Visit the company at their place of business. You may learn they don't even have a place of business.

• A final tip: have more faith in your own experience than in a promoter's promise. Enlightened skepticism can help you hold on to your lifetime's savings.

THE IN-YOUR-LIVING-ROOM SWINDLE—MAIL ORDER DISTRIBUTORSHIPS

"Make big profits! Become an authorized distributor. Sell Special Formula gasoline additive—the hottest selling item in the automotive direct selling field. Manufacturer-endorsed.

"Guaranteed free luxury motorcar if appointed state franchise director . . . Free samples available. Send $10.35 . . .

"Good only for orders received in next 10 days. Bigger discounts if order rushed."

Then appears a table showing that your cost for six units is $24.50, on which you make a profit of $7.00. But if you buy three dozen units at a cost of $92.50, you make a profit of $90.

The telltale signs of fraud, as exemplified by this ad, are:

• "Creative" accounting. That table is very clever, for who's going to buy $24.50 of goods to make a $7.00 profit when he can make approximately 100 per cent if he goes up to $92.50?

• Exaggerations. A "free luxury motorcar" if one sells enough cans of gasoline additive? Even a cockeyed optimist should have trouble believing that one. "Manufacturer-endorsed"? "The hottest selling item in the field of automotive direct selling"? Hardly . . .

• Pressure. The implication is that you must act at once or you're barred. The offer will last for only ten days. The pressure is intensified in follow-up letters to the sucker.

• Duplicity. There are "free samples" offered to the skeptical—but the "free" samples cost $10.35.

• Ease of operation. This is not in the composite ad, but it is in the letter the potential investor receives, assuring him that "you don't have to be a salesman in order to rake in those profits. Those unique formulas, together with the endorsement from the luxury motorcar, practically sell themselves."

How do you avoid being taken by this business opportunities swindle—as in the others preceding?

• Verify the claims for the product. Check out the endorsements from manufacturers referred to in the literature. Ask the company representative for the name of a person at the manufacturer's office to whom you can talk and with whom you can discuss your doubts. Do not permit yourself to be turned away.

• Ask the promoter for names and addresses of other distributors. Contact them to find out how much money they have made selling these products under current market conditions.

• Find out how many of these distributors have been in operation for more than a year. A year should be long enough to determine whether or not the business can be a success.

• Discuss the investment and operation of the business with your own family, your lawyer, your local banker.

• Never forget that a written guarantee is only as good as the company behind it. If the company offering "full refund" isn't in business, the offer is worthless.

From these five illustrations, you can carry away the guides to protect you from all other variations of business opportunities rackets.

WHAT ABOUT WORKING AT HOME?

A POWERFUL TREND

Still another way to "be your own boss" is to work at home—even if you're working for some relatively distant employer. And there is now a powerful and underestimated trend in this country toward doing just that.

You well may be among the millions who could do so if you really wanted to. The switch could be a real boon if, say, you are a young mother who can't leave the house but still have plenty of spare time; if you are a businessman who could easily switch your office to your home and who detests the daily commute to the big city; if you are a shut-in for any reason; if in your work you spend virtually the whole day on the telephone and could easily use the phone just as well at home as at the office.

Today, millions of Americans work at home, part- or full-time, and the list of jobs you can perform without going to an office is lengthening daily. Some work from elaborate home offices, fitted with typewriters, electric calculators, dictating machines, filing cabinets, and other office equipment. Others manage to earn a living from a bedroom card table.

Of course, some people simply can't work at home. Your job, for instance, may involve the use of expensive specialized equipment available only in an office. You may need to confer frequently—and face to face—with others in your office. Or you might be subject to destructive distractions at home from children, social telephoning, visiting neighbors. Or you might not have the essential discipline to set up and stick to a productive work schedule. Or you may be unproductive without the stimulus of a busy office.

But for many of you the advantages far outweigh the disadvantages. Anybody who works at home can save substantial sums of money by not having to pay commuting costs, eat lunches out, keep up an office wardrobe, lose hours of work time battling traffic.

If you are a working mother, a job at home may save substantial sums on baby-sitting fees—which when combined with other typical expenses of working mothers often chew up 40 to 50 cents or more of your pay dollar.

A further advantage lies in the substantial income tax deductions that can be claimed for the bona fide costs associated with the portion of your house you use as an office, the cost of business equipment, business telephone calls, etc.

SAMPLING OF "AT HOME" CAREERS

Following are some of the jobs being performed, at least in part, at home. Study them carefully to see if this could spark a desired new trend in your own life.

In journalism-publishing: foreign language translation, proofreading, copy editing, technical writing, artwork, copy writing—and, of course, the usual writing of books, magazine articles, feature stories, newsletters.

In education: many assistant teaching jobs such as correcting test papers, tutoring in remedial reading and other key subjects, music and art instruction, child day care, vocational counseling, speech therapy.

In scientific and technical fields: inventing, engineering and scientific consulting, computer programming, a wide assortment of individual projects in chemistry, mathematics, and other disciplines, appliance repair.

In health and medicine: physical and occupational therapy, the practice of medicine, dentistry, psychiatry.

In radio and TV: disc jockeying, film editing, filmmaking, script writing.

In advertising: literally thousands of small ad agencies are operating out of private homes in this country today.

Also: architecture, art, law, insurance and real estate, interior decorating, investment management, sewing, cake baking, public relations, many kinds of research, accounting and drafting. And this is only a random selection. There are dozens of others.

If the idea of working at home appeals to you, analyze your interests and/or your present job. You can tell as well as anyone what the potentials are.

Before you decide to go ahead, check the local zoning rules and also any restrictions that may be included in your own deed (or rental lease) against at-home business operations. These limitations could be a temporary obstacle—but that's all they can be *if* "working at home" is what you really want.

BEWARE: "EARN MONEY AT HOME" SWINDLES!

But precisely because so huge a number of you secretly wish you could work at home, the crooks and gypsters can make fortunes exploiting your yearnings.

"Fortunes?" you ask. "Yes, *FORTUNES!*"

One New York-based homework schemer grossed over $1 million in a little over a year advertising an envelope-stuffing scheme with the claim "How I made $35,000 in just one day at home in bed with the flu." Many of you may remember the ad appearing in national magazines and featuring an open suitcase filled with money. For thousands of you, that money was yours.

Here's a profile of the victim.

Let's say you are a young mother who is staying at home to care for your infants. Let's say, too, that you're finding it increasingly tough to get by on your young husband's paycheck; quarrels about money are starting to undermine your marriage, and thus you're desperately seeking ways to supplement your family's income.

You are now a perfect setup for the "work at home" swindlers.

Here is a sampling of the most common forms making the rounds—along with the catch in each case and rules for spotting outright gyps.

Come-on: The ad in your favorite women's magazine reads:

> Homeworkers needed to address postcards. Earn $50 a week.
> We furnish everything. Send for information.

Scheme: Promoter is selling "instructions"—not offering employment—despite the fact that he lures you through the help-wanted columns. If you're a "double victim," you'll pay for postcards as well as instructions. You make money only if the cards you send actually bring in orders. In a typical case, a homeworker spent a total of $25 for instruction, 250 postcards, and postage. Total revenue (from two orders): $2.50. Loss: $22.50.

Come-on: Ad in your monthly home hobby/do-it-yourself magazine:

> Assemble at home fish lures or artificial flowers. Reap big
> money from piecework. New line-sewing jeans. Write for details.

Scheme: Promoter offers no employment. Again, he's selling instructions and in all probability overpriced equipment and precut materials. He has no intention of buying the goods you make unless they're "up to standards" and, of course, they never are. Often, victims spend hundreds of dollars on heavy equipment at grossly inflated prices in the belief that the promoter will furnish enough work to cover the equipment costs. Such work never materializes and you're left with enough unassembled fish lures to last several lifetimes.

Come-on: A local paper might carry this ad in "help wanted":

Earn $75 a week selling local press mentions to individuals and companies at $1 to $5 each. Write for details and instructions.

Scheme: "Instructions" cost up to $15 (often shoddy, badly mimeographed, unprofessional), and you must subscribe to the newspapers yourself. You also must find your own markets for your clips.

Come-on: An ad in the local paper reads:

Grow worms for us and earn $10,000 to $14,000 in your basement. Modest investment.

Scheme: The so-called modest investment is actually $2,950. The promoter is trying to convince you that because some commercial companies are making a lot of money in worm farming, you can effectively compete and make the same kind of profits with a sizable cash outlay. What you are likely to end up with is a basement full of worms. Worm farm promoters will cite a variety of lucrative markets for your product, including fishermen, zoos, fish hatcheries, school biology classes. Some promoters were recently claiming Israel and Japan were buying worms for soil conditioning.

Like so many schemes, they combine fact and fiction to defraud you.

The fact that there is a market for your product does not mean that you can reach that market. And if you reach the market, it doesn't mean you can sell your product at a profit. But what is certain is that you parted with nearly $3,000 and all you have is a "can of worms."

Come-on: A direct mailing to your home offers you the opportunity to participate in a new service:

Test consumer products in your own home. We pay you up to $10 each for the opinions you give us on the products we send you. And you keep the product. Send $15 good faith deposit for first product.

Scheme: The "good faith" deposit is nonrefundable, the products are of little or no value, and the "up to" hedge on the $10 means you probably will get next to nothing for your time, trouble, and $10. Legitimate market research companies do not operate in this manner and do not require "good faith" deposits or registration fees.

Come-on: You get a mailing piece which includes the statement that "thousands of our members already know . . . that finder's fees are truly the easiest way to make money . . . just send us our membership fee of $125 for our library of finder's fees opportunities . . . ."

Scheme: According to the law enforcement agency that investigated this matter, the promoter was not able to substantiate the number of members that he claimed had made money from finder's fees. The promoter inflated his membership costs and was involved in a scheme to make himself rich, not provide any legitimate business opportunity for his members to act as business brokers.

OBVIOUS EARMARKS OF A FRAUDULENT SCHEME

There are many, many more—all the frauds feeding on your need, greed, gullibility, and ignorance. Like anything else, there is no easy way to make a lot of money at home. And anybody who has found a way will not advertise it, much less sell it for a few dollars! Here are the most obvious earmarks of the fraudulent scheme:

• Up-front money, as little as $5 perhaps. This may be for "instructions." Never pay up-front money.

• Ads slanted to imply the offer of home employment when in fact the advertiser is selling something, not hiring.

• A promise of huge profits or big part-time earnings.

• A profusion of vague "testimonials" to the deal.

• A requirement that you buy expensive instructions and equipment—even before the promoter gives you details of the deal.

KEY QUESTIONS ABOUT ADS

Here are the key questions to ask about any ad you see in your local newspaper or that comes to you through the mails regarding homework deals.

• Will you be paid by the firm and, if so, how much? If you will not be paid by the firm, where will the promised earnings come from?

• Are you expected to pay any significant sum to buy "instructions"—before you can get into business? (If so, consider this a warning signal to stay away from the deal.)

• Who will be your customers and who will be responsible for lining them up—the company or you?

• Is the product or service in which you are supposed to invest—either time or money or both—one for which you will manage to find a market close to your home? Would you buy and use the product?

• If commissions are promised as payments for your efforts, what assurance do you have that such commissions actually will be paid? A vague promise that comes through the mail from a company unknown to you is hardly adequate insurance.

• Is the company willing to give you names and phone numbers of other people who have invested in its instructions or products so that you can query them about their experience in the real market place? How much money did these people make on the deal? (Disregard any and all "testimonials" quoted in ads if you cannot check them out personally.)

Finally, and especially if "fantastic profits" for "easy work" are offered, in combination with a requirement that you invest substantial sums of money for instructions, materials, etc., find out whether the firm is trying to buy your services or—much more likely—sell you a bill of goods.

If still unpersuaded about the silliness of paying money in advance to "work at home," contact your local Better Business Bureau, the nearest office of the U. S. Postal Inspection Service or Federal Trade Commission, or your local consumer protection office.

Do not take another step toward any deal without informed assurance it is legitimate.

11

DRESS WELL ON LESS

Finding Your Way Around the Clothing "Supermarket"

Shopping for clothes in this era is somewhat like shopping in a supermarket. It's up to *you* to determine the various ingredients needed to create a wardrobe to your taste, and then to search the shelves and racks for sizes and styles to suit you, your way of life, and your budget. After you have reached a tentative decision, your best information will come from labels and your own ability to check and recognize quality. Salespeople (if you can find them) often are untrained and inexperienced, and far more concerned with closing a sale than with answering your questions or helping you to dress appropriately and attractively.

Clothes labels, as one skeptic put it, frequently look "like inventory lists in a chemical factory." Today, in addition to natural fibers—wool, cotton, linen, silk —there are hundreds upon hundreds of manufactured fibers and blends, more than three dozen mechanical and chemical fabric finishes, and thousands of construction and processing techniques, along with countless trade names.

On the minus side is the blunt fact that it's easy to be confused by continually changing technology. And, if you choose wrong, you probably won't be able to get your money back or even a replacement.

On the plus side are the far more important facts that:

There never has been a greater variety of clothing styles, fabrics, finishes, and desirable features available.

The price range is also the broadest ever.

Federal laws protecting you against mislabeling are the most varied and strictest in history.

And there's a wealth of information you can use to help you shop for and buy clothes for yourself and your family.

In the following pages, you'll find some of this "wealth" broken down into the most valuable nuggets that *you* can use to plan your—and your family's—wardrobe, and to shop for clothes to fill them.

THE FUNDAMENTALS

SHOP FOR WHAT'S RIGHT FOR YOU

Your clothes speak for you before you've uttered a word: "I'm an individual." "I'm part of the crowd." "I'm someone to be reckoned with." "I'm creative." "I'm organized." "I'm up-to-the-minute." Or "I don't care how I look."

Most people want a wardrobe with enough versatility to make more than one statement, depending on the audience, activity, occasion, or maybe even a mood.

A good way to achieve this versatility is to establish one or two color themes and start with the most flattering basics you can find—perhaps separates to mix and match—and the best quality you can afford. These basics are simple, classic designs that stay in style and last several seasons and are *real* clothing bargains. To them, you can add the most alluring fashion craze or way-out accessories.

Since top-quality and durability aren't musts for items that will go out of style quickly, you don't have to spend a fortune to update or change the look of your basic wardrobe. Similarly, once-in-a-rare-while clothes, such as a special holiday skirt or shoes bought to go with just one outfit, can be selected more for effect than for wearing ability.

BUY CLOTHES THAT FIT YOU PROPERLY

This will add to the life of your wardrobe as well as to your comfort and good appearance.

Don't make the common error of buying sizes that are *too small* for you on the assumption that you're about to lose ten or fifteen pounds! If you can't get a really good fit, it's usually best to buy a size slightly *too large*. Generally it's easier to take in than to let out.

Use the following table, prepared by the Money Management Institute of Household Finance Corporation, Chicago, Illinois, as a guide to size ranges used by most clothing manufacturers for women's clothes. Note that, in addition to regular sizes, some types of clothing may be marked "tall," "medium" or "average," and "short" or "petite."

SIZE CLASSIFICATION	SIZE RANGE	FIGURE TYPE
Junior Petite	3–15	For figures 5'1" or shorter. The neckline and armholes are smaller and length from shoulder to waist and from waist to hemline is shorter than a Junior.
Junior	3–17	For figures 5'1½" to 5'5½" with a higher, smaller bust, narrower shoulders, and a shorter waistline than the Misses.

Size Classification	Size Range	Figure Type
Misses Petite	8–18	For figures 4'11½" to 5'2" with a longer waist and a fuller bust than a Junior Petite. Smaller neckline and armholes than a Misses.
Misses	6–22	For the well-proportioned figure 5'2½" to 5'6½". Hips moderately larger than bust and normal to low waist.
Misses Tall	10–22	For the well-proportioned figure over 5'7½".
Half Sizes	12½–26½	A mature Junior. Fuller throughout the bust, back, and shoulders, and shorter-waisted than the Junior.
Women's Sizes	34–52	The mature, more developed Misses figure. Fuller in the back and shoulders and longer-waisted than the Misses.

And use the following chart, published in *Your Clothing Dollar*,* as your guide to standard children's sizes, corresponding to body weight, height, and other measurements:

	Size	Weight	Height	Chest	Waist	Hip
Infants' and Babies'	(Months)					
	3	13	24	17		
	6	18	26½	18		
	12	22	29	19		
	18	26	31½	20		
	24	29	34	21		
	36	32	36½	22		
Toddlers'	(Years)					
	1	25	31	20	20	
	2	29	34	21	20½	
	3	34	37	22	21	
	4	38	40	23	21½	
Children's	2	29	34	21	20½	21½
	3	34	37	22	21	22½
	4	38	40	23	21½	23½
	5	44	43	25	22	24½
	6	49	46	25	22½	25½
	6X	54	48	25½	23	26½

* Household Finance Corporation, Copyright 1978.

Body measurements for the sizing of apparel for girls

SIZE	WEIGHT	HEIGHT	BUST	WAIST	HIP
7	60	50	26	23	27½
8	67	52	27	23½	28½
9	75	54	28	24	29½
10	83	56	29	24½	31
12	95	58½	30½	25½	33
14	107	61	32	26½	35

Body measurements for the sizing of apparel for boys

		SLIM		REGULAR		HUSKY	
SIZE	HEIGHT	CHEST	WAIST	CHEST	WAIST	CHEST	WAIST
6	46	23½	20½	25	22½	26	24½
7	48	24½	21	25¾	23	26¾	25
8	50	25½	21½	26½	23½	27½	25½
9	52	26	22	27¼	24	28¼	26
10	54	26¾	22½	28	24½	29	26½
11	56	27½	23	28¾	25	30	27
12	58	28½	23½	29½	25½	31	27½
13	59½	29¼	24	30½	26	32	28
14	61	30	24½	31½	26½	33	29
15	62½	30¾	25	32¼	27	34	29½
16	64	31½	25½	33	27½	35	30
17	65	32¼	26	33¾	28	35¾	30½
18	66	33	26½	34½	28½	36½	31
19	67	33¾	27	35¼	29	37¼	31½
20	68	34½	27½	36	29½	38	32
21	69	35¼	28	36¾	30	38¾	32½
22	70	36	28½	37½	30½	39½	33
23	71	36¾	29	38¼	31	40¼	33½
24	72	37½	29½	39	31½	41	34

STUDY CLOTHES LABELS

Someday there may be one comprehensive label to tell you everything you want or need to know about an article of clothing. Until then, you must search at least a bit—but you will find vital information on many different tags, labels, and stickers.

The price tag usually will tell you the size, will give the retail price of the item (without local taxes), and may tell you the number of pieces included.

The size may be printed or stitched to clothing. Errors can occur, though, so it's wise (whenever possible) to try on each item before you buy it.

A manufacturer's and/or designer's label may be sewn almost anywhere on clothing, inside or out. This can be especially helpful if you've had either a good or bad experience in the past with other items carrying the same label.

A decade ago, a shopper had to have the equivalent of a special dictionary to translate the hundreds of trade names given to manufactured fibers into generic terms. Today, you're assisted by the United States Textile Fiber Products Identification Act. Under this law, all textile products must contain the following information on the label or tag:

- the *generic name* of the fibers (cotton, polyester, etc.), listed in order of predominance by weight;
- the *percentage* of each fiber weighing 5 per cent or more of the total;
- the *name* (or registered number) of the manufacturer or seller;
- the *country* from which an imported fiber comes.

In addition to the above, wool products, under the Wool Products Labeling Act, also must tell you what type of wool (virgin wool, reprocessed wool, reused wool) has been used, and the percentages.

Because care of clothing is important to its appearance and durability, the United States Federal Trade Commission has ruled that labels giving *care instructions* be permanently attached by manufacturers to most wearing apparel, and provided by fabric companies on labels that home sewers can stitch into seams of items they make.

These care instructions are to include the manufacturer's recommendations for cleaning or laundering, drying, and pressing or ironing (if needed), along with warnings against products and procedures that may cause damage, such as chlorine bleaches, excess heat, or the use of certain solvents.

Use your common sense when following these care instructions. But sometimes even a healthy dose of that won't help. Most manufacturers do not actually test each garment, and rely heavily on guidance from fabric makers. According to a spokesman for the International Fabricare Institute, a trade group representing launderers and dry cleaners, with research facilities in Silver Spring, Maryland, the method a label recommends "often actually damages the clothing."

For example, synthetics labeled "professionally dry-clean only" too often shrink. Laminates may stiffen and peel when cleaned by standard procedures used by most professional dry cleaners. Water spills, steam used in cleaning, and even perspiration may cause color bleeding. Clothes labeled "wash hot" wash well in home washing machines, but are damaged in the hotter wash cycle of commercial machines.

In contrast, some manufacturers are overly cautious about the information they put on their labels; a garment with "dry-clean only" on the tag may actually be machine-washable.

If your clothes are damaged after you've followed care instructions, return them with the sales receipt to the store. A reputable store should refund your money and return the item to the manufacturer. And clothes manufacturers, subject to FTC penalties for failing to comply with regulations, may label their garments more accurately if you besiege them with returns.

And, while reforming their care labels, you, a consumer, well might wonder why more manufacturers don't stencil information to clothing, or attach care labels to side seams, for most labels haphazardly sewn at the back of the collar can curl up and tickle the wearer to the point of annoyance after laundering or cleaning.

To supplement government-required labels, fiber producers, dyers, yarn and fabric makers, finishers, and clothing manufacturers will sometimes attach additional tags or stickers to clothing or packages, listing features and benefits, and offering more detailed care instructions.

Read this information carefully, too, to learn as much as you can about each article of clothing—fibers, yarn, fabric construction, dyes, finishes, care—and what each implies in durability, upkeep, cost, and appearance.

Fibers: These are the basis of yarn and largely determine a fabric's properties: warmth, wear, appearance, care, etc. They may be natural (cotton, silk, linen, wool—including hair, such as mohair, rabbit hair, or cashmere). They may be man-made (such as rayon, nylon, polyester, acrylic, etc.). Or they may be blends (combining natural and/or man-made fibers).

Yarns: Fiber strands are laid or twisted together to make yarns, from which fabrics are woven or knitted. Staple fibers are short and must be spun into long strands before being twisted into yarn. Cotton, linen, and wool are staple fibers. Filament fibers are continuous, and can be either laid or twisted together. Silk and man-made fibers are filament fibers, but they also can be cut short and handled like staple fibers. The strength, thickness, and texture of fibers, the number used, whether they're laid or twisted, and how tight the twist, are among factors that determine appearance, features, and wearability of a yarn.

Construction: The three basic types of fabric construction are woven (usually the closer the weave, the better the wear), knitted (loops provide a natural stretchability and wrinkle resistance), and non-woven (fibers are matted together with heat, pressure, and possibly chemicals). In addition, one of the three basic types of fabric may be used as a backing for another type (as in some bonded or laminated fabrics) or for a "plastic" (such as vinyl or polyurethane, which are used for man-made leathers).

Woven fabrics can be given the stretchability of a knit with fiber, yarn, or finish. Look for details on the label if you're buying a stretch fabric that's woven: comfort-stretch for every day, action-stretch for sports and exercise. A stretch fiber (spandex) or yarn construction (similar to a coil) may prove more satisfactory for your needs than a finish which may wash or dry-clean out.

Knits can be stabilized to the level of a woven fabric with a backing, lining, or by double-knitting. Many variations within each type of fabric construction create an almost infinite array of textures, designs, and weights from which clothing designers—and you—can select.

Color: Dyes can be added at almost any point in fabric production, from the moment when chemicals are mixed together to create man-made fibers until after fabric has been woven or knitted. Fiber- and yarn-dyed fabrics, generally considered stable, are easily recognized in checks and plaids, because colors are as clear on the underside of the fabric as on the surface. Vat-dyed yarns and fabrics are also considered stable. Fabrics printed only on the surface can be spotted quickly: although colors may be labeled "fast," prints may fade in time from abrasion.

There are many variables in dyes (some are absorbed by, others are bonded to yarn), and selection of the right dye for each fiber and quality control in the coloring process depend on the manufacturer. Check labels carefully for specific information, such as "sun- or perspiration-fast," "fade-resistant," or such warnings as "wash separately."

Finishes: A wide variety of temporary and durable finishes improve or add desirable features to fabrics, aiding appearance, comfort, ease of care, and protection from a wide range of possible problems. Most will boost the price of fabric and therefore of clothing, and some will require special care, but benefits can outweigh any added cost or attention. Among finishes available are those that:

• Alter appearance—adding or subtracting shine; brightening, drabbing, or fixing colors; improving drapability or softness; increasing crispness or body; reducing static; changing texture, etc.

• Increase comfort—providing a smooth "lining" for rough fabrics or thermal insulation; increasing moisture absorbency; repelling water; creating stretchability, etc.

• Simplify care—minimizing or eliminating wrinkles and ironing, such as wash and wear and permanent press (which also retains pleats and creases through both wear and laundering); increasing soil resistance; providing soil release, etc.

• Offer special protection—against spots, stains, shrinkage, moths, mildew, fading, etc. The United States Flammable Fabrics Act requires fabrics used in making children's sleepwear (up to size 14) to be flame-resistant. Pay special attention to labeling to learn whether the flame-resistant finish is temporary or durable, and carefully follow care instructions.

At home, save all information tags from new garments, mark them for identification, and file them in an indexed box kept near the laundry area, along with the sales receipt, extra buttons or darning yarn the manufacturer may have provided, and scraps of fabric left over (if alterations were made) for later patching.

Don't remove care labels that are sewn in.

Your best safeguard against clothing rip-offs is to buy from reputable retailers and clothing manufacturers, who will heed your complaints, and, if justified, will make refunds or exchanges. Having tags and the sales slip handy will make your case much stronger.

PLAN YOUR WARDROBE WITH MORE THAN ONE PURPOSE IN MIND

For instance, in men's clothes, a top-notch buy is a raincoat with a detachable lining. Without lining, it can double as a topcoat in mild weather. With lining, it can get you through the coldest weather. Women's raincoats with detachable linings can be equally good buys.

Another bargain is a tweed suit with a coat which can double as a good-looking jacket to wear with slacks.

And either a man or a woman can buy a flannel suit with pants that can be worn with other jackets or jackets that can be worn with other pants.

LOOK FOR GOOD WORKMANSHIP

Consumers Union, the most prestigious consumer testing laboratory in the field, publishes in its monthly *Consumer Reports* and its annual "Buying Guide" issue excellent reports of controlled tests on standard clothing brands—from diapers to dinner jackets. You'll benefit from these reports on durability, color-fastness, appearance, laundering ease, quality of workmanship, etc., and learn exactly what to look for when you shop.

Specifically:

Seams should be smooth (no "puckering"), wide enough to let out if necessary, properly finished to prevent fraying.

Hems should be even, properly bound with tape, securely fastened, invisibly stitched, deep enough to permit lengthening.

Stitching should be even and close together.

Buttonholes should be sewn through on both sides of the cloth.

Linings—of the fabric and pockets—should be firm, closely woven, and made of a material which will not stretch or shrink.

Zippers, snaps, and decorative trim should be firmly attached and properly placed.

AVOID IMPULSE BUYING

If you need a spring raincoat, don't stop off at the section reserved for bathing suits and buy a bikini at top price. (And don't laugh, I've done this sort of thing plenty of times and I'll bet you have too!) The same goes for "bargains" which have no place at all in your wardrobe. They are not bargains to you if you don't need or really want the items.

And this applies equally to a variety of clothing accessories which you may find tempting in the store but which you didn't even dream of wanting until you spotted them.

MAKE A CLOTHING BUDGET—AND STICK TO IT

Clothes are among the most flexible of all your budget items, but as a general guide, below are a few national "averages" from the Bureau of Labor Statistics in Washington:

• On the average, out of each $1.00 a United States family spends on everything, about 9 cents goes for clothes and shoes. The share rises to more than 10½ cents when the cost of clothes upkeep is included.

• Our annual national clothes and shoes bill in the late 1970s ran about $370 for each man, woman, and child.

• Typically, clothing costs triple to quadruple between the ages of one and eighteen.

• On the average, women spend $3.00 out of every $5.00 of the family's clothing dollars. But these are merely averages and almost certainly they do not apply to you. Only you can set your own clothing budgets, priorities, and preferences. In your clothing budget:

Make room for luxuries as well as for necessities.

List all the items you must have and then the luxury items you'd like to have. Ask yourself what kind of clothing you need: for work at your job away from home; for sports and leisure-time activities; for social occasions. Just the listing will help you pinpoint the necessities you can appropriately buy at minimum prices and you then can apply whatever amounts you have saved to your luxury purchases.

TEN WAYS TO SLASH YOUR CLOTHING BUDGET

You can truly slash your clothing costs—and be better-dressed than ever—by learning and following these ten specific guides:

(1) *Buy clothes off-season*—and achieve savings running to a sensational 30 to 50 per cent. March is the best time to buy ski outfits, for instance. January and August are good months to buy furs.

There are three major periods for storewide clearance sales: after Easter, after July 4, and after Christmas. These are excellent times to pick up clothes as well as a long list of other items—although you may run into shortages of styles, sizes, and colors if you don't shop as early as you possibly can in the sale (if possible, the day it begins).

List the clothing items of standard styles which you know you will need during the next six to twelve months. Study and use the clothing bargain calendar which follows.

Budget your cash and your credit so you have the funds to buy the items you need and want during the clothes-buying bargain seasons.

Your Calendar

Back-to-school clothes—August, October
Bathing suits—after Fourth of July in July and August
Children's clothing—July, September, November, December
Coats (women's, children's)—April, August, November, December
Costume and fine jewelry—January
Dresses—January, April, June, November
Furs—January, August
Handbags—January, May, July
Hats (children's)—July, December
Hats (men's)—January, July
Hosiery—March, October
Housecoats—April, May, June, October, November
Infants' wear—January, May, July
Lingerie—January, May, July
Millinery—February, April, July
Men's and boys' suits—April, November, December
Men's shirts—January, February, July
Piece goods—June, September, November
Shoes (boys' and girls')—January, March, July
Shoes (men's and women's)—January, July, November, December
Sportswear—January, February, May, July
Toiletries—January, July

Of course, bargains also turn up at odd times through the year because of special circumstances—a store going out of business or into business or moving, an anniversary celebration, an unusual holiday, etc. You can always use these opportunities to buy items you know you'll need later.

A warning is necessary at this point, though: watch out for those "going out of business" sales on clothes. They can be phonies—and you can spot one if the sale has been going on for months or even years.

(2) *Buy certain items in quantity*—and save 10 to 30 per cent.

If, say, you can buy one pair of stockings or panty hose or one pair of socks, a single run or hole can mean a total loss. But if you buy six pairs of the same type and color, you can match what is left and prolong the useful life of each item. (You can cut one leg out of a pair of panty hose when it runs, then one leg out of another pair, and wear both "good legs.") Buying in quantity is particularly practical if yours is a large family. Much clothing is sold on a "three for X dollars" basis.

(3) *Buy standard sizes.* If you're buying a man's sport shirt you will save by buying a small, medium, or large size. The price goes up when you buy shirts in more detailed neck and sleeve sizes. This principle holds for socks, gloves, and many other types of clothing—men's and women's.

(4) *Find and patronize a variety of clothing sellers.*

• Chain stores and catalog houses are particularly good for such staples as jeans, underwear, shirts, athletic socks, sneakers, boots, pajamas and nightgowns, scarves, belts, and work clothes. The larger ones commission major manufacturers to produce items to their specifications in sufficient volume to mean savings of from 10 to 20 per cent. When ordering by mail, be sure to include postage charges, which continue to swell.

• Check discount stores, including army-navy stores and co-ops, for special buys. Oversupplies, slightly irregular items, manufacturers' closeouts, and imported copies of popular American clothing are among the articles they may stock. Typically they are self-service, cash only (occasionally they accept a bank credit card), but savings range up to 25 per cent of the usual retail price.

• Factory outlets may offer excellent bargains. These no-frill, self-service, usually cash only clothing stores sometimes sell overruns of their own products, seconds, name-brand clothes made by others (with or without the manufacturer's label), or arrange to have garments made by contractors. Located in low-rent areas, most allow try-ons, but do not handle alterations, or, if they do, charge extra. Savings offered can go as high as 40 per cent.

• Thrift shops, clothing exchanges, and resale shops, sometimes operated for the benefit of a charitable organization, can be a bargain hunter's treasure troves. Next-to-new secondhand clothes and leftover clothing from retailers and manufacturers, frequently in least popular sizes, are offered at a fraction of the original price, and usually at much less than cost.

• High-fashion discount outlets, usually found only in or near large cities, are a delight if you have a champagne taste and a beer budget. Top designers, retailers, and manufacturers get rid of samples, display and fashion-show garments, overstocks and overruns at these stores. To supplement the "good" merchandise, outlets may also carry lesser "bargains," so you need an ability to separate the wheat from the chaff. And since the best merchandise is usually snapped up soon after it arrives, it may take several visits before you find what you want. Loehmann's (New York and several other cities) and Filene's Automatic Bargain Basement (Boston) are among the better-known stores of this type. Discounts can range from 10 to 50 per cent.

• Specialty stores and boutiques offer appealing value if your time is limited and you are willing to pay for preselection and personal attention. These stores offer a limited amount of clothing for a specific "type" of customer: tall men, large women, children, teenagers, devotees of certain designers, etc. Or they may offer a specific type of merchandise: handbags, lingerie, tennis fashions, etc. for a broader spectrum of people. Because these stores buy in limited quantities, most sales consist of end-of-season leftovers or slightly soiled or damaged clothing.

• Department stores in this era consist of a number of specialty shops and boutiques under one roof, and similar merchandise may be carried in more than one department at different prices, depending on what type of customer each department is trying to attract.

At certain times (see pages 48–51, 690), there are storewide sales; at others, individual departments hold their own sales. Some stores devote an entire department just to price-reduced merchandise year-round, supplementing marked-down clothing with special purchases and items brought in from branch stores.

Don't assume that a department store basement is the home of bargains; it may or it may not be.

Do assume that merchandise stocked and displayed near entrances, elevators, and escalators is geared to impulse buying.

Retailers measure their successes and failures in sales per square foot of floor space and constantly strive to top last year's figures by moving around departments, getting rid of merchandise that doesn't sell quickly, setting up new shops within the store, and creating excitement with promotions, fashion extravaganzas, bazaars, fairs, one-night-only sales for charge customers, and whatever else their imaginations can conjure. Merchandise bought for promotion purposes and quick sale may offer excellent buys *if* you need the items.

The clout of stores affiliated with large buying offices is considerable. Look, too, for "store brands."

Learn the various departments of your stores, but don't be surprised when they move or change.

(5) *Don't try to carry colors, sizes in your head.* If you've ever arrived home proudly with a new navy-blue belt for your old navy-blue dress to discover that the belt has a purplish cast and the dress a greenish one, or if you've confused sock and shoe sizes, you'll want to set up a little shopping file to carry with you. It can be as simple as an envelope taped to the last page in the address or appointment book you carry, as casual as a list tucked in your wallet, as elegant as a card case bought just for the purpose. The point is to keep your, and the family's, sizes together with snippets of fabric in a handy place. The bits of fabric can be carefully cut from seams or hems, but if there isn't a quarter inch to spare, you can match a spool of sewing thread to the color, and take along a few yards. With a shopping file for reference, you can buy more confidently at no-returns sales or when you spot something that looks just right.

(6) *Look without prejudice at clothing seconds.* As a general rule, the bigger the flaws in clothing seconds, the greater will be the price cut. The key point you must consider before buying seconds is whether the flaw is "basic" or simply on the surface. Will the blemish significantly reduce the item's usefulness, attractiveness, or durability? Can the defect be easily and inexpensively repaired? If the answers are favorable to the purchase, it could be an extraordinarily good one for you.

(7) *Steer away from frills, especially on utility items.* As an illustration, a sweater with a lavish belt or fur collar will be far more costly than the same sweater without the extras. The simple sweater also will be more useful, for the simpler it is the more occasions you'll be able to wear it (and the more you'll be able to dress it up or down on your own).

(8) *Match prices against utility.* For instance, if you have young children, the mortality rate on playclothes will be exceedingly high. Thus it's smart to get them at rock-bottom prices. You can extend this rule to a wide range of clothing purchases for every member of your family, particularly in sports clothes. And, incidentally, remember this rule when you're shopping for your husband. Don't push him into the latest "peacock revolution"—wild frills, rainbow-colored shirts, newfangled shaped suits—if that's not where he's at.

(9) *Buy children's clothes by size, not age.* Buy according to your child's height and weight. Buy clothes which have room for growth as your child grows (i.e., deep hems and pants cuffs, adjustable straps on overalls and jumpers, elastic waistbands, raglan sleeves). Buy clothes which are durable and don't show wrinkles and dirt too readily. And don't impose your adult tastes on your child.

(10) *Use credit plans with caution.* You can easily overspend with easy charge plans. You also may miss sales opportunities in other stores because you're still paying off old bills to the store in which you have the revolving charge account. But if you have charge accounts at various stores you'll often get advance notice of special customer clearances—and you can use those clearances to get bargains.

Many department stores and clothing shops hold private "courtesy days" sales for charge-account customers a week or so before advertising them widely to the public. If you have charge accounts, you'll be on the stores' mailing lists and you'll have first pick of the sale items.

When you are fully aware of the advantages as well as the pitfalls of store credit plans you can use them for your own benefit. See Chapter 16, "How to Borrow Cash and Use Credit," for details on department store charge accounts.

Six Rules on Dressing for Work Away from Home

Where you work and what you do determine how you'll dress on the job. These rules apply to both men and women:

(1) Unless you're in the fashion world, avoid imprisoning yourself in the latest styles, or even being in advance of any new clothing trend. Wait and see which trends "stick" before making a significant investment.

(2) Look around at what others wear at work, and take your cue from your

boss rather than employees on your own level. How you dress won't determine your chances for promotions—but it can hinder your advancement.

(3) Test the wrinkle resistance of any garment you choose for a full day's wear at work by crinkling part of it in your hand at the store to see if it returns quickly to its original shape. If it doesn't, pass it up. This doesn't doom you solely to the purchase of polyester double knits; there are many marvelous fabrics that won't crush or muss, including a wide variety of wools, cotton blends, and silk and linen look-alikes.

(4) Be sure any garment you intend to wear all day long is comfortable. Thus, when you try on clothes, sit down, raise your arms, and bend over—preferably in front of a mirror. Also consider temperature: heating and air conditioning that can't be adjusted make "layering" desirable. When it's cool, can you add a vest, sweater, or jacket? If it's steamy, can you peel down appropriately?

(5) Every job has its own special clothing limitations or requirements you must heed. For instance, in an office where ink, carbon paper, and dusty files are handled, white and light colors usually are impractical. Full skirts or pants, flowing scarves and ties, and loose sleeves are safety hazards near heavy machinery in a plant. A job that requires a lot of standing or walking means giving first consideration to shoes and hosiery. The business man or woman who must attend many black-tie banquets will want to budget evening wear as part of his or her working wardrobe. The traveler must consider the ease of packing and versatility for varying weather conditions.

(6) When in doubt, buy quality for greatest economy, and don't try to assemble an entire wardrobe in one shopping spree. It's far wiser to invest in one good and becoming suit or dress and add parts and accessories than to settle in a hurry for two or three outfits that are just so-so.

How to Buy a Sewing Machine

With roughly 45 million home sewing machines already in use and with hundreds of thousands being added in our homes each year, let's assume *you* are now in the market for a sewing machine—either a new one or one to replace your aging model. How should you shop? What type of machine should you buy?

Make up your mind how you will use your machine before you buy. If you'll be doing only utilitarian sewing, then you'll need only a basic, inexpensive machine, without many frills. If you love to create fancy things with a lot of embroidery, you may want a machine with all today's built-in features, which can cost hundreds of dollars.

Decide what you want your new machine to be able to do. Take a sewing course first if you do not know and rent a machine while you do it.

If you are a beginner, you might start with a basic portable machine that has straight, reverse, and zigzag stitching capabilities and which may be available for less than $100. These are neither heavy-duty machines nor do they have a long anticipated life-span. They are basic models, so try several before deciding which machine suits your needs. As an alternative, you might buy a secondhand or reconditioned machine from a dealer you are sure you can trust and learn on that one. (You may even decide to keep it indefinitely.)

Most sewing machine dealers will give basic operating instructions for your new machine even if it is a less expensive brand. Both the manufacturers and authorized dealers of the European machines are especially eager that you learn to take advantage of every feature on your new machine. One manufacturer even has a learn-by-doing instruction book. The new owner, under the supervision of the dealer, makes her own samples of each sewing technique and puts them in the instruction book for future reference. The fabric for the samples, also provided by the manufacturer, comes with the machine.

Stick to a well-known brand sold by a company which has an extensive network of sales and service dealerships throughout the country. If properly used and cared for, even a medium-priced sewing machine may last your lifetime.

Off brands, or "private labels," are a particular problem in the sewing machine business. If you buy an off brand in Los Angeles, and later move to New York, you probably will find that you are unable to locate a dealer who handles that brand; therefore, service and parts are for all practical purposes unattainable. A dealer in New York may handle exactly the same sewing machine you have but sell it under his own name. He is reluctant to accept your machine for service because he cannot tell from the outside whether he has the parts or can get them.

The two most wanted features in more sophisticated sewing machines are the zigzag and stretch stitches. There are zigzag attachments available for less expensive straight stitch machines: these attachments, though, move the fabric back and forth (as opposed to the built-in zigzag where the needle moves back and forth), they cannot handle all fabrics, and they are inconvenient and inefficient. The zigzag feature is invaluable for mending, sewing with elastic, making buttonholes, overcasting, and reinforcing what might otherwise have to be done by hand.

The least expensive zigzag machines usually come with manually insertable cams that allow you to do some decorative stitching. Higher in price are automatic machines, which contain pattern cams or built-in disks that can be "dialed," as well as additional cams that can be inserted. Highest of all in price are new electronic machines, which, instead of cams, contain solid-state circuitry which permits "push-button" stitch selection.

Don't be pushed into a decision beyond your needs and budget. Buy a machine with a zigzag or stretch stitch only *if you really intend to use them*. Start basic and trade up as your needs and skills increase.

A portable sewing machine will save you $30 or more over a cabinet model, assuming you have a permanent surface—possibly an old desk or kitchen table—so the machine always will be easily available. The salesman may tell you a cabinet is a must so that dust won't get into the machine. But the dust argument is nonsense, because if the portable doesn't come with a cover, all you need do to solve the dust problem is to whip up a simple dust cover as your first project—something like the covers used for office typewriters or your toaster. It's a lot less expensive than purchase of a bulky cabinet.

However, though a sewing machine cabinet does add to the original investment, it can save money in the long run.

First, by making the setup task easier, you well may sew more often—especially mending and maintenance sewing. Or you may use an available hour rather than wait for a full evening or day for sewing.

Second, a cabinet will add to your comfort—less eye strain tension, aggravation—and thus tend to produce better results.

Third, a cabinet is safer—less danger of dropping, knocking over—and thus protects your machine.

With either a portable or a cabinet model, be certain:

> It is a comfortable height for you to work on.
> You sit with center of your body in front of the needle.
> Leg room is adequate for you.
> Controller is comfortably positioned.
> Table leaf is well supported.
> Cutout holds machine level without wobbling.

Most sewing machine manufacturers suggest to their dealers a demonstration technique—and the better ones include the demonstrations of how the machines work on various commonly used fabrics. By all means, take advantage of the demonstrations; ask for them.

Be suspicious if your sewing machine dealer demonstrates a machine *only* on the very stiff cotton fabric that all dealers use. This fabric cannot show the shortcomings or the advantages of the various machines you may be considering. Remember that you will probably be sewing on many different fabrics, from soft nylon tricots (many dress fabrics are nylon tricot) to bulky wools, corduroys, or fake furs.

The most convincing sales demonstrations are those that show the performance of a machine on many different types of fabric, such as sweater knits, double knits, Lycra, nylon tricot, bulky wool or corduroy, leather, various stretch fabrics, and also problem fabrics. You may think you won't use all these, but how can you be certain now what fabric you will wish to sew on next year or the year after?

If your sewing machine dealer does not have any "real fabric" bring some of your own (bring some anyway!) and try the machine yourself.

Once you buy, use the machine. Your complaints will be handled more equitably early in your ownership than later. Don't grumble to yourself or your friends for a year before you tell the dealer of your dissatisfaction.

BEWARE: SEWING MACHINE TRAPS

Be particularly wary of the gypsters who operate on a grand scale in the area of sewing machines. A dealer, for example, may pass off inexpensive foreign-made machines as American-made by stenciling the names of well-known American machines on them, or by obliterating foreign-origin markings. Others may misrepresent old, well-known machines as being rebuilt by the manufacturer when actually they've only been given a once-over-lightly cleaning by some backroom mechanic. Some imply in their ads that a sewing machine is zigzag-equipped—but not, as you later discover, at the advertised price.

Some insist that their fabulous sewing machine offer is "good for today only" —to keep you from going out and comparing prices. Some give you (or send you) a discount in the form of a "check" for, say, $150—made payable to you but as yet unsigned. However, the price of the sewing machine well may have been jacked up so that it more than covers the discount. Or you may be a second-prize winner in a contest—entitling you to receive a sewing machine *only* if you buy an overpriced cabinet. Or you may be given the "opportunity" for a "free" sewing machine—and pay *"only"* $79.50 for a ten-year service contract. But the catch here is that most machines don't need much—if any—servicing within the first five years and you are still paying $79.50 for the machine, no matter what the disguise is.

Or it may be a "repossessed" sewing machine which has not actually been repossessed. Or the claim may be that the price charged is only the very low amount of the "unpaid balance"—which, by no coincidence, turns out to be just about what the machine is worth.

Beware these traps. And if you unluckily fall into any one, check your nearest consumer protection agency at once to find out your rights under federal and/or state law or regulation.

CUTTING YOUR CLOTHES CARE COSTS

Buying (or making) clothes is only part of your investment in your wardrobe. Over the long run, an even larger chunk of your money may go to the cleaning, washing, storing, and repairing of many items in your wardrobe.

How do you keep *these* costs to a minimum—and at the same time make your clothes last as long and look as good as possible?

TIME-TESTED TIPS

To save money and keep your wardrobe looking better for a longer time, here are tried and trustworthy tips:

Wear washables (or old clothes) for dirty jobs—digging in the garden, preparing food, housecleaning, painting, washing the dog, repairing the car.

Protect good clothes—with smocks, aprons, overalls, napkins, bibs, or towels when near splashable or spillable items. Roll up sleeves before washing hands. Apply perfume, cologne, hair spray, and makeup before dressing. Always make sure deodorant or anti-perspirant is completely dry before putting on clothes. Consider the use of dress shields. Nail polish, remover, and lighter fluid can damage some fibers seriously, so handle them with special care.

Prepare when bad weather threatens or actually arrives by wearing a raincoat or cape and boots or shoe covers, carrying an umbrella. Roll up trouser legs (or tuck them into boots) before splashing through puddles or wading through snowdrifts; protect your handbag or briefcase by carrying either one in a plastic shopping bag.

Be careful about where you sit or lean to make sure your clothes aren't smeared with wet paint, grease, oil. Beware especially of chewing gum, bits of candy, or cigarette ashes on seats, of dust and dirt on revolving doors, turnstiles, and stairway railings.

Be sensibly cautious about what you put in your pockets—pens that might leak, heavy keys that may poke a hole through them, colored items (such as matchbooks and advertising flyers) that can rub off dye, candies or makeup that might melt. Don't overstuff pockets to a point that can tear seams, stretch clothes out of shape, and even wear fabric thin.

Look out for items that will snag or discolor clothes—a jangly bracelet or sharp ring that will catch in a knit; a dark bag or briefcase that can rub off against a light jacket, polished shoes that will smudge pants legs or skirt when legs are crossed, or even a bright handkerchief, scarf, or costume jewelry that may not be color-fast.

Check clothes immediately after removing them—for rips, spots, loose buttons or snaps, torn hems—and take care of problems as soon as possible. Mend small rips before they become large ones; tighten buttons before any fall off (which may mean replacing several buttons); spot-clean using the appropriate cleaner and technique for both the spot and the fiber of the garment. (If in doubt, check your dry cleaner.) Never press soiled or spotted clothing; heat may "set" stains and make them impossible to remove.

Launder or dry-clean soiled clothes as soon as possible. Cover clothes not worn frequently, or seasonal garments (be sure they're clean!) to prevent them from getting dusty, and brush clothes that are uncovered frequently. Once dirt has set in a fabric, it's hard to remove. Dirt also may attract moths and insects.

Hang up clothes at once after taking them off, using suitably shaped wood or plastic hangers (wire ones bend out of shape and can distort a shoulder line or may leave rust marks). Sweaters and other knit garments are best folded and placed on a shelf or in a drawer so that they won't stretch.

Leave damp clothes outside the closet until they're completely dry. Clothes hung in the closet should be separated so that air can flow around them and they don't crush each other. Zip zippers; button buttons. If sleeves are wrinkled, stuff them with tissue paper. Make sure collars, cuffs, pleats, and creases are straight.

Keep your clothes closet cool and dry; install a dehumidifier if you live in a high-humidity area.

Immediately clean or polish and place trees in shoes just worn. Shoes can then be stuffed with tissue paper and stored in shoe bags or boxes.

Hang a pomander ball in the closet to help keep air fresh and fragrant. This old-fashioned, long-lasting closet sachet is easy and inexpensive to make: stud a small firm orange with whole cloves until the rind is completely invisible. Mix together 1 teaspoon ground cinnamon and 1 tablespoon orrisroot powder in a paper bag, and drop in clove-studded orange; shake gently until orange is coated with the powder. Tie bag closed and put pomander in a dark, dry, cool place to "cure" for a week. Remove from bag and tie ribbon around it, using straight pins to hold ribbon if necessary. Hang on small nail or hook in back of closet. (Note: several pomander balls can be made at the same time, and those not used immediately can be wrapped tightly in plastic film to preserve the fragrance. And they make nifty gifts!)

In home washing and drying of permanent-press fabrics and clothes with stain-resistant finishes, load your washer only to about 80 per cent capacity and remove the clothes from the dryer just as soon as they are dry.

Slash your dry-cleaning bills by using self-service dry-cleaning machines for the appropriate garments. These machines are especially valuable for children's winter jackets, woolen sweaters, and most of a long and varied list of items for which delicate hand pressing and steaming aren't necessary.

Follow clothes care labels when you iron. And remember that letting clothes simply steam awhile in the bathroom while you take a shower often will do the ironing for you.

Iron lightweight handkerchiefs and scarves (as well as fabric napkins and place mats) effectively by plastering them to a smooth wall, like the tile or glass around bathtub or shower, while they're sopping wet. Tape corners with strips of cellophane or masking tape to keep them from peeling off as they dry.

Also study the care labels on washing stretch fabrics. While most of these fabrics can be washed, the kind of fiber, the weave or knit, the color, and the finish may dictate the method and temperature to be used—and these will be indicated on the labels. (Be particularly careful with your stretch ski wear, which often can't even be washed, much less machine-dried.) Dry your stretch fabrics in a tumbler dryer, set at the correct temperature for the fabric. If you don't have a dryer, lay the garment flat and block it if necessary to ensure that, when dry, the garment comes back to the correct size. Never hang a garment to dry if it has lengthwise stretch. Never wear a damp stretch garment; it will lose its shape. Don't hang stretch garments for long periods even if dry. Store the garments flat in a drawer or on a shelf.

Twelve Ways to Reduce Your Shoe Bills

Each year we buy an *average* of three to four pairs of shoes per person. Sneakers, slippers, galoshes, other footwear push the total to more than 1 billion pairs of shoes a year. Our annual footwear bill averaged more than $175 per family as the 1980s neared.

With the guides that follow, though, you can spectacularly reduce your shoe bills—and you'll also find you're enjoying your shoes far more.

(1) Obey the rules for a proper fit: make sure that your big toe doesn't reach the tip of the shoe when you're standing, that your little toe lies flat in the shoe, that the heel fits snugly, and that the sides don't yawn. (Poorly fitting shoes can impose the "hidden" extra cost of podiatrists' bills.)

(2) Don't buy shoes by size alone. A size 8 may fit perfectly in one style but not in another. Have each pair fitted.

(3) Shop for shoes in the middle of the day. Typically, the human foot swells 5 per cent with exercise and this swelling can obviously make a big difference in how a shoe fits.

(4) Economize on shoes you won't wear frequently, such as women's shoes

dyed to match an outfit. Don't economize on work shoes or hiking shoes: the savings won't be savings if the shoes aren't comfortable or if they wear out quickly.

(5) Save money in men's shoes by buying those with composition soles and heels, usually no more expensive and actually more serviceable than leather.

(6) Choose simple, traditional styles. A simply styled shoe may cost one third less than its high style counterpart. And stick to darker colors, which look better for a longer time than lighter colors.

(7) Buy children's shoes at least a half size larger than is indicated by the measurement. But sturdy, well-fitting shoes are vital for children, so economize only on style. Use the following chart to guide you on how rapidly children's shoe sizes change as they grow up.

Rate of Change: Children's Shoe Sizes

AGE OF CHILD	SIZE CHANGES EVERY
1–6 years	1–2 months
6–10 years	2–3 months
10–12 years	3–4 months
12–15 years	4–5 months
15 years and older	6 months or more

(8) Don't misuse shoes by, say, wearing them out in the rain. Polish shoes regularly to protect them against dirt and bad weather. And note: few shoes can survive a washing machine.

(9) If your shoes become wet, stuff them with paper, dry them away from direct heat with a soft cloth, and rub them with a light film of mineral oil.

(10) Change your shoes at least once a day to give them a chance to "rest" and dry out from foot moisture. If you do this, two pairs of shoes will outlast three which are not alternated during a day.

(11) When buying, look for: smooth, soft linings and smooth inside seams; stitching which is not too close to the edge of the shoe sole; flexible "uppers" and evenly trimmed edges; good material; reputable brands from a reputable retailer.

(12) Buy shoes for yourself and children during the seasonal sales—using both the winter and summer sales for maximum savings.

THE ABCs OF BUYING FURS
(or "How to Sound like a Fur Authority Without Really Being One")

You know the type: she has just bought a raccoon coat and now she's the world's greatest authority on *all* furs, ready to advise friends, acquaintances, strangers, and *you* on what to look for and "where to get it wholesale."

Don't listen to her! It's impossible to compress years of fur-buying knowledge and experience into a few days, weeks, or even months, and "wholesale" usually means a reduced price on something not good enough for a store.

The best approach to buying furs is to ask yourself a few basic questions before you set out on your shopping trip, and then put yourself in the hands of a reliable furrier.

ASK YOURSELF

"Where and when do I plan to wear the fur?"

If your answer is "everywhere" and "anytime," you'll want something sturdy. This generally (though not always) means shorter- rather than longer-haired. However, longevity is crucially affected by the quality of the fur and how you treat it.

If you're looking for something in which to cuddle at football games, or can afford to shrug off practicality, that's a different matter entirely.

Be candid with the salesperson if you want the best advice.

"What kind of fur will look best on me?"

Forget the fable that you have to be skinny to wear fox, or over thirty to wear mink. Try-ons in front of a three-way mirror are full of pleasant surprises and the only reliable way to answer that question. It's wise to have at least a vague idea of color, so that the fur complements the rest of your wardrobe, but keep an open mind.

"How much can I afford?"

As the 1980s neared, you could get a marvelous curly-lamb jacket for under $300—or an opulent sable for $25,000 or even more. Determine a general price range, and then look for the best quality (and style for you) within that range. Better a superb muskrat than a poor mink!

A FEW FACTS

There are five hallmarks of a good fur:
(1) Bright luster
(2) Uniform color
(3) Density
(4) Silky texture
(5) Soft, pliable leather

When you're buying fur from a reliable furrier, there's no need to be concerned with whether the pelts are from a male or female animal, whether they come from an endangered species (they won't), or workmanship. Look at the general appearance of the fur and lining, but, most important, study the way *you* look wearing it. The selling price usually includes alterations, but it's sound to check the set of the shoulder seams and the weight of the coat, which usually can't be altered.

LANGUAGE OF FUR

A fur label always tells you the true name of the animal, the country of origin if outside the United States, and how the fur was processed. If it's entirely or partially made of tails, paws, bellies, sides, flanks, or gills, the label also will tell you that.

(1) Basic fur terms include:

Pelt: The skin, including either or both underfur and guard hairs.

Underfur: The short thick hair next to the skin.

Guard hairs: Longer, stiffer, smoother hairs that protect an animal from rain and other elements.

Grotzen: The central back, long spinal region of a pelt.

(2) The words used in *processing* fur also are handy to know:

Let out: To retain the beauty of the pelt of a small animal, the skin is "let out" diagonally. This decreases the width and increases the length.

Let in: To make skins shorter and wider, pelts are cut into strips and joined with other matched skins.

Glazed: This process, applying a special fluid and steaming it into the fur under pressure, brings out the fur's clear, lustrous beauty. A fur may be reglazed from time to time.

Sheared: Fur is cut to even off or shorten underfur and guard hairs.

Plucked: Guard hairs are removed.

(3) *Coloring* terms are helpful, too. Coloring may be used for uniformity; to bring out natural tints, tones, and shades; to add luster and highlights; to change color completely. They include:

Bleached: Natural color is lightened: light and white furs often are bleached to remove streaks or spots.

Tip-dyed: Only the ends of hairs are dyed.

Tipped: Leather side of a pelt has been dyed; this does not change the fur color, however.

Natural: Fur has not been colored in any way.

Mutation: A mutation occurs when the offspring differs radically from its parents. Fur ranchers breed mutations in foxes, minks, and nutria to produce exciting new colors. *Mutations are natural.*

FUR CARE

Furs should be worn! They thrive out of doors. They are for enjoyment, and shouldn't be buried in a closet.

Have furs professionally cleaned at least once a year, more often if they show soil or spots.

Put them in storage during the warm months.

Take them to your furrier the minute a repair is needed.

Do give fur "breathing space" in a closet (and don't cover it with a bag). Hang it on a padded hanger; if you've come in out of the rain or snow, let fur dry on the hanger (away from a radiator) before putting it in the closet.

Don't abuse fur with unnecessary friction, such as a shoulder bag strap. Don't comb or brush it (a good shaking is all it needs), and never pin flowers or jewelry to fur. Perfume, cleaning fluid, and hair spray can damage fur, so avoid using them near or on it.

IF YOU FEEL YOU'VE BEEN GYPPED

First discuss your misgivings with the furrier.

If still unhappy, write directly to the manufacturer, or, if you don't know the manufacturer's name, contact the Federal Trade Commission, Division of Furs and Textiles, Washington, D.C. 20580.

If you can provide the registration or identification number (which will appear on the bill of sale), both the manufacturer and the fur can be identified.

The FTC won't protect you from buying a poor fur, but will protect you from deceit about the identity of a fur.

12

JEWELRY AND BEAUTY —FROSTING ON THE CAKE

JEWELRY

NOT A NECESSITY—OR IS IT?

Jewelry is not a clothing necessity. Or is it?

In the late 1970s, Americans had adorned themselves with an estimated $6 billion worth of *fine* jewelry, more than half of it sparked with diamonds of varying sizes and quality. Fewer than 10 per cent of these diamonds and other stones were "investment" gems (see pages 1168–73). Additional millions were being spent on *costume* jewelry.

Even when our long-ago ancestors dressed in leaves and skins, we know they wore jewelry: rings of bone, amber, ivory, and flint; necklaces and bracelets strung with choice shells, stones, and carvings; braided rushes and grasses.

Throughout recorded time, jewelry has played an important role in helping us proclaim our status—separating royalty from commoner, the married and engaged from the single, the rich from the poor, the old from the young.

Symbols for schools, colleges, fraternities, religions, political parties, peace, ecology, and women's rights in the forms of pendants, pins, and rings speak for us as loudly as words.

And individual pieces of jewelry have long been worn as "personal trademarks": the late author Fannie Hurst was never without her dramatic calla-lily pin; in the seventies, designer Pauline Trigère always wore a turtle in some form; and actress Arlene Francis' much-copied diamond-heart pendant necklace became almost as famous as she is.

For most of us, jewelry is a fashion accessory, worn to brighten ears, fingers, wrists, ankles, necks, or clothing. We would rather wear it than put it in a vault. If it's expensive, we expect to enjoy it for many years, perhaps pass it along to our children and grandchildren or even sell it in a pinch, for jewelry has long been a popular form of portable wealth. We don't want to lose it, have it fall apart, or go out of style. In brief, we want our money's worth!

TEN TIPS FOR BUYING FINE JEWELRY

(1) Consider carefully whether the piece you're about to buy is a long-term "fashion investment" or a fad that might better be bought in costume jewelry. The fashion director for the nation's largest retailer of fine jewelry suggests this basic (and classic) wardrobe of fine jewelry, noting that it can be mixed or matched and that—as fashions change over the years—you can add pieces and supplement it with costume jewelry:

• 3 gold chains of different lengths, weights, and designs (one of which might be sparked with diamonds)

• 2 (or more) pendants, one of which could be jeweled and convertible to a pin

• 1 pearl necklace
• 1 pair of diamond stud earrings
• 1 pair of pearl earrings
• 1 pair of gold earrings, such as hoops
• 3 gold bangle (or gold chain) bracelets of different widths and designs
• 1 gold watch (a classic such as the "tank" watch)
• 1 "important" gold pin, possibly set with diamonds
• 1 jeweled pin
• 3 or 4 small pins (stickpins, scatter pins, bar pins) to wear singly or group together

• 1 jeweled ring, 1 gold ring; assortment of bands, with or without stones

For additions, the jewelry expert suggests:

• Neck ornaments—More chains, pendants; colored beads (such as jade, peridot, tourmaline, amber); and, if you're really flush, a diamond necklace.

• Earrings—Gold studs, drop earrings, as well as sapphire, ruby, and/or emerald studs. Stud "jackets," which slip around studs, make this type of earring especially versatile.

• Bracelets—More chains and/or bangles; a pearl bracelet; a circlet of diamonds; and a gold or gold-and-diamond evening watch.

• Rings—Another jeweled ring; more bands of different widths and designs.

• Pins—A large pin that separates into two smaller ones; additional scatter pins that can be clustered are useful accessories.

(2) Although platinum, silver, and other precious metals are used for fine-jewelry settings, gold is by far the most popular and practical because it is malleable, won't tarnish, and is available in a variety of colors. Always check the karat markings when buying gold:

An item marked 24K (24 karats*), or 999, is 100 per cent pure gold. However, pure gold is generally considered too soft for practical use in jewelry, and since ancient times, gold has been alloyed (combined) with other metals. (See pages 1158–59.)

---

* Stones are weighed in *carats;* the percentage of pure gold is expressed in *karats;* and both words are derived from "carob." Many centuries before the birth of Christ, precious gems and metals were measured on a scale balanced against carob seeds. Today a carat is approximately 200 milligrams.

Each karat represents 1/24 part of pure gold: finest gold jewelry is usually 18K (eighteen parts pure gold and six parts of another metal). Most American-made gold jewelry is 14K (fourteen parts pure gold and ten parts other metal). By Federal Trade Commission regulation, no domestic jewelry can be stamped with percentages rather than karats.

The different colors of gold are determined by the other metal(s) with which pure gold is alloyed. Gold alloyed with copper has a warm reddish color; gold alloyed with nickel or palladium results in the white gold frequently used as a setting for diamonds.

In addition to its use in fine jewelry, gold is also used in costume jewelry. When the term *gold-filled* is used, it indicates that a layer of (at least 10K) gold has been mechanically bonded to a base metal. This layer must constitute at least 1/20 of the total weight of the finished metal piece. *Gold-plated* means that 10K or better gold has been electrolytically electroplated to base metal. Watch cases are frequently gold-filled or gold-plated.

(3) In addition to the intrinsic value of materials used in fine jewelry, other factors determine its cost: design, workmanship (including whether it's hand-wrought or machine-stamped), and the retail markup.

Check workmanship carefully to make sure that fine jewelry will hold up: make sure chain links are invisibly soldered closed; run your fingers over the piece to assure there are no rough edges to catch and snag clothing. Make sure fastenings not only close tightly, but that there are backups—safety chains, guards, and catches. Gems should be firmly set (never glued), and they must be rechecked from time to time. Earring posts or clips should be solidly attached; pearls and beads should be strung with knots between each one so that a break doesn't scatter them all to the winds; rings should be sized exactly to your fingers and heavy enough so that they don't bend when pressed.

(4) Many fine jewelry designs are copyrighted, and for these you usually pay a premium price. Successful copyrighted designs are, however, almost always adapted (but not always successfully!) by other manufacturers. If you wait a short while, you may be able to find a less expensive version of a piece of jewelry that you adore but can't afford when it's first introduced. Elsa Peretti's "Diamonds-by-the-Yard" design for Tiffany in the 1970s is an example of a successful copyrighted piece that was adapted successfully by others. (An exception is the copyrighted designs on which *any* manufacturer must pay a royalty, such as replicas of Snoopy, Little Orphan Annie, or Mickey Mouse.)

(5) The store with the fastest turnover in fine jewelry generally offers you the best "values," although it may not have the unique or valuable pieces you're seeking. Inventory for a jewelry store (or for the fine jewelry department of a larger store) is a sizable investment; the markup must cover not only the usual cost of doing business, but also must give the retailer a fair return on the funds he has invested. Jewelry stores with many branches and jewelry departments in larger stores (many of which are operated by outside specialty chains) frequently are able to offer a considerable price edge, both because they save by buying in quantity and because they can ship slow-moving items to their other stores where they may sell more quickly.

(6) Beware of "bargain" jewelry stores. Whether you buy jewelry from a neighborhood shop, from a major jewelry chain, or from a department store, make sure of the store's reputation. Unless you are a jewelry expert yourself, and few of us are, you have to rely completely on the store for information on what you're buying.

(7) Get the facts in writing! Any reliable jewelry store or department will willingly describe the item you're buying in detail on the sales check. Ask for specifics: What is the karat of the gold? How many carats do the stones weigh? What are they and how many are there? If you're buying diamonds (other than tiny ones), be sure that color and clarity gradings are noted, and that the cut (round, pear, marquise, emerald, etc.) is described. If you plan to insure your jewelry, you'll need this information.

(8) If everything you admire is way beyond your capacity to buy, consider substitutes. Semi-precious stones and synthetic gems set in gold and combined with precious stones make excellent fashion investments. For the price of a small emerald ring, you can—for example—buy a sizable chrysoprase encircled with tiny diamonds. White sapphires are considerably less expensive than diamonds and, unless you're a purist, man-made sapphires, rubies, emeralds, and diamonds can't be detected from the real thing except under a jeweler's loupe!

(9) Buy slowly. If you can't afford a yard of diamonds, buy a chain with a single diamond—and then add more stones as you can afford them.

(10) Trade up. Some stores offer to give you full retail-price credit on selected jewelry pieces if you later trade them in for more expensive items. If a store tells you that it has this policy, and that what you've bought can be traded later, get the information *in writing* on the sales check—spelling out whether this applies only to the stones or also to the setting.

COSTUME JEWELRY

Jewelry made of any material other than precious metals and precious or semi-precious stones is generally considered "costume jewelry," although the prices for these items can far exceed prices for some "fine jewelry," and some costume jewelry may incorporate semi-precious stones as well as be set in silver.

Costume jewelry may imitate the real thing, be "frankly fake," or use totally different materials: plastic, wood, shell, clay, glass, fabric, enameled metal, papier-mâché, etc., for infinite variety and effects.

"Stones" are frequently set in gold-filled, gold- or silver-plated metal or silver. The intrinsic value of materials usually doesn't have as great an influence on price as design and workmanship.

If you see an inexpensive piece of costume jewelry that you do like, buy it! Just make sure that it won't harm your other clothing—that colors don't rub off or run, and that sharp edges won't snag or tear fabrics. Before you buy an expensive piece of costume jewelry, however, investigate the same workmanship details as you would for fine jewelry. In addition, look for even "coatings"—pearl, paint, enamel, etc.—to assure yourself they won't peel off easily. And consider materials in context with their use, remembering that rings and bracelets get harder wear than pins, necklaces, and earrings.

JEWELRY CARE

Whether you have a drawer full of jewelry or just a few pieces, and whether it's fine jewelry or costume jewelry, a compartmental jewelry box is a good investment—to guard chains from tangling, keep pairs of earrings together, and prevent knocks and scratches.

Take fine jewelry to a jeweler for occasional buffing, polishing, and professional cleaning, and to see that stones and fastenings are secure. Costume jewelry usually can be cleaned with a sponging of warm soapy water, after which it should be thoroughly dried.

Because of its value, keep your fine jewelry in a home (or bank) safe. Burglars are just as clever about finding hiding places as you are!

UNDERSTANDING TODAY'S WATCHES

Close to 70 million Americans buy or receive a watch each year, and if you are among them, the odds are three to one that it was purchased in December.

The watch may have been a $15 stocking-stuffer or a special $100,000 collector's item, a workhorse or an ornament, a one-and-only or an addition to a wardrobe of timepieces, but it probably cost in the neighborhood of $35.

Buying a watch continues to require more and more know-how.

A WATCH IS NOT ALWAYS FOREVER

Price is not the sole determining factor of a "good" watch. The same basic watch movement may come in a wide range of prices, depending on the case, dial, bracelet, and special features offered with it.

Like any item with moving parts, a watch needs special care.

Unless you have selected a pin-lever watch, which does not lend itself to service, a watch should be cleaned and serviced at least every two years, should be kept away from extreme temperatures, and generally should be treated with respect.

Except for installing a battery, don't try to fix it yourself if anything goes amiss, and never take a watch apart "just to look."

Even if you buy one encased in precious metal and studded with gems, the finest watch in the world eventually will need repairs. Assuming you are not preserving it for its future value as an antique, there will come a time to consider replacing the inner workings rather than having it fixed, especially when parts are no longer available.

Check the guarantee carefully to see what is covered and for how long when you buy a watch, and keep the sales check with the warranty for future reference.

And just a few additional commonsense rules will help maintain it in top condition.

• Keep your watch away from powder, perfume, loose tobacco.

• Even though you have bought a water-resistant watch, don't risk wearing it in the swimming pool or shower. Why test it?

• If you have a mechanical hand-winding watch, wind it once a day, preferably after you get up, and wind it with thumb and forefinger after you have taken it off your wrist.

• Don't take even the smallest chance of overwinding. Play safe and stop winding the watch when you sense that the tension is close to the maximum.

• Don't expose your watch to overly vigorous treatment, even if it's supposedly shock-resistant.

THE HIGH PRICE TAG ON YOUTH AND BEAUTY

TEN WAYS TO LOWER IT

The beauty industry is considered recession-resistant by many security analysts.

The reason: given only a few dollars to spend on yourself, odds are you'll hand them over for a beauty product or service—lipstick or hairdo, shaving cream or haircut.

"If my hair's a mess, I feel downright dowdy—no matter what I'm wearing," moans the impeccably dressed, svelte vice-president of a major department store chain, who couldn't look dowdy if she tried.

Her statement echoes the feelings of American women (and men†), who were spending an estimated $7 billion a year on beauty services and products in the late 1970s, approximately $5 billion of that in beauty salons and barbershops, and unknown additional millions of dollars on beauty books and periodicals, exercise machines, scales, and other beauty-allied products.

If beautifying yourself takes a big bite out of *your* budget, here are ten ways to nibble away at the prices you pay:

(1) Do some of the work yourself. "The works" at your favorite beauty salon can make you feel, as well as look, like a million! Most salons won't object, however, if you go for a cut and styling having just shampooed your own hair (a saving of from $1.00 to $5.00 or more, depending on the salon). And if you have one of the popular wash-and-wear styles, you can even forgo blow-drying or setting after a cut—an additional saving of from $3.00 to $15 or more!

(2) Watch for specials. Many department store beauty salons (others, too) have "specials" on slow days (generally during working hours, early in the week) and in certain months. January and February, for example, are traditionally "perm sale" months, and late summer–early fall "make-over packages" (hair styling, facial, makeup) are often real bargains to put you in a mood for clothes-shopping. Watch newspaper ads for these offers, or give your hairdresser a supply of addressed-to-you cards so he or she can drop you a line when a sale is in the offing.

Watch, too, for cosmetic and toiletry sales: during periods when product sales lag (after Christmas, for example), you'll find excellent buys.

(3) Be a guinea pig. Volunteer to be a "model" at a hairdressing (or barber) school. Putting your locks at the mercy of an unlicensed student who is practicing can be risky: however, instructors need models on whom to demonstrate various

† A survey in the late 1970s by *Modern Salon*, a beauty-services trade publication, reveals that 76 per cent of the 153,000-plus beauty salons in the United States now cater to men as well as women, and that 54 per cent of these salons are doing 25 per cent or more of their business with men!

haircutting, perming, and coloring techniques, and you're usually assured first-rate work.

Similarly, advanced hairdressing schools, attended by already licensed stylists who are taking brushup courses, offer great bargains: for a small service fee (sometimes without charge) you can get a new style by either an instructor or a professional hairdresser-student.

Check the Yellow Pages for beauty schools in your city. Also, if you hear that a big salon is about to open in your area, ask if the salon will need "models" for stylist training.

(4) Try before you buy. Salons and stores selling cosmetics often have "aestheticians" or "demonstrators" who will cheerfully (and without charge) turn you from ugly duckling to swan with the hope that you'll buy every product they use for the transformation. Since they usually work on commission, I'm not suggesting you get beautified for a big date without buying anything, but if you're in the market for a new eye shadow and lipstick anyway, why not plan to take advantage of their expertise; you can see how what you're buying will look, learn how to apply it—and have a professional makeup session at no cost.

Also, take advantage of samples and "trial sizes" of new products used as come-ons by many cosmetic and perfume manufacturers.

(5) Consider alternatives. Your great-grandmother probably softened her hands with pharmacy-mixed rosewater and glycerine, and shampooed her hair with liquid castile or green soap. These products are still available in many drugstores. You don't *need* expensive perfumed and prettily packaged creams, lotions, and potions to be beautiful.

Many dentists agree that brushing your teeth with a paste of bicarbonate of soda, salt, and water is as effective as most toothpastes. Mayonnaise (bottled or homemade) works as well as any hair conditioner on the market; unflavored gelatin dissolved in boiling water has few equals as a setting lotion.

For your skin, lanolin is a fine lubricant; witch hazel is a splendid astringent; and the lightly beaten white of an egg, smeared on your face until dry and then rinsed off, makes a time-revered "firming masque."

If your hair style requires frequent salon visits, consider an easier-to-care-for "do." Streaking, frosting, and highlighting let you have the fun of being a blonde without biweekly root touch-ups, and a gentle perm may make blow-drying or setting unnecessary.

(6) Check prices carefully. A department store may have two beauty salons: one offering head-to-toe pampering, the other (usually geared to a younger clientele) offering only the basics. The price difference can be substantial. Similarly, prices at a trimmer-snipper-type salon usually will be more modest than those at a full-fledged beauty department. If prices aren't clearly posted in the salon, don't be too embarrassed or intimidated to ask—and compare.

One trap into which many women (and men) fall is the "whatever you think best" syndrome. There you are, head full of suds, when the shampooer tells you casually that you're about to get a wonderful special bee's knees conditioning rinse.

Say "halt" until you find out what it does *and* what it will cost! The little extras at a salon can add up to a big ticket. If the bee's knees rinse is a must, perhaps you can buy it at the salon and use it at home; product cost is considerably less than 10 per cent of the price of a beauty salon service.

(7) Scout for store brands or name brands at discount. Absolutely convinced that a certain $25-a-jar night cream is totally responsible for her peaches-and-cream complexion (although she should be thanking her lucky genes!), one New York model made a discovery that cut her night-cream expenditures almost in half! She was near tears when her local drugstore temporarily ran out of the "miracle" wrinkle preventer and she proceeded to look for it elsewhere. Her first stop: a nearby discount store. Her night cream was nowhere in sight, and expecting to be told he'd never heard of it, she timidly asked a stock boy whether the store carried it. From inside a closed cabinet, he immediately pulled out a $25-size jar —marked $14.99!

The moral of this tale: shop for cut-rate prices on products you can't live without, and don't assume that everything is on display. Ask!

If you're not hooked on a particular brand, consider store brands. Large drug and department stores (many of which are parts of groups or chains) frequently carry the most popular cosmetic and toiletry products with their own brand-name labels—at considerable savings. These products may even be made by the same manufacturers who make name brands. Differences are usually slight: fragrance, color, and, of course, packaging.

(8) Buy in quantity. Twelve exercise classes for the cost of ten, a box of eight cakes of hand soap for the price of six sold separately, special beauty salon rates for groups of four or more—all add up to savings.

Find out if and how you can save by buying in quantity, including large sizes of items you use a great deal.

(9) Gift (or purchase) with purchase. Cosmetic manufacturers hate them; stores love them. You may—or may not—benefit from the highly competitive promotion gimmick of GWP (gift with purchase) or PWP (purchase with purchase). The way this works is that you buy an expensive brand-name product and receive (or can buy at cost or less), for example, a nifty travel bag filled with sample sizes of the manufacturer's other products. The manufacturer is delighted to have you sample the products and hopes you'll return to buy them in regular sizes; it's the extra that makes him wince. Each merchant wants you to buy that brand at his store, so insists that the manufacturer offer a (frequently exclusive) superbargain. If you were going to buy the expensive brand-name product anyway, and want—or can use the gift—you'll probably get a good buy. Otherwise, forget it.

(10) Avoid beauty charlatans. There are many around ready to take your money. Beauty products and services—even plastic surgery—won't work miracles. No known products can eliminate baldness, erase wrinkles, increase your bust six inches in a month, reduce your weight by twenty pounds in a week, or win you the love of your favorite movie star overnight.

Read ads, booklets, pamphlets, and packages carefully to make sure you aren't inferring performance promises that are merely implied.

Be wary of mail-order beauty bargains, club plans, and door-to-door salesmen and -women.

Beauty products taken internally—like special vitamins, protein supplements, diet pills—can be hazardous to your health, and should be used only with your doctor's approval. Others—such as scented feminine hygiene sprays, products "enriched with" vitamins, eggs, milk, etc., and skin bleaches—are considered by most legitimate beauty and health authorities to be simply a waste of money.

A week at a pleasant beauty spa can make you feel, even look better. But investigate the place carefully before you spend your money. Brochures can be deceiving, and you may find yourself living a Spartan existence in a remote area for the cost of a deluxe European vacation.

Common sense tells you that a facial will brighten your complexion by removing "dead" skin on the surface; cleverly applied cosmetics will create an illusion; a good haircut will give you a becoming, easy-care style; proper diet and exercise will improve your figure.

"Wishful thinking" sells beauty products and services, however.

Before you buy, determine whether a promise given *can* be kept.

Sometimes it can—but, unfortunately, often it can't.

Common sense can be your best guide. Let it be!

13

HOW TO SLASH THE COSTS OF
YOUR VACATIONS IN THE 1980'S

DE-REGULATION OF AIR FARES

With the opening of the 1980s, the traveling public and the airline industry are geared for the still utterly unforeseeable impact of the momentous action taken by the Civil Aeronautics Board when, in the late 1970s, it permitted United States airlines to cut fares by as much as 70 per cent without CAB approval. Even in an era of dramatic changes in commercial aviation, so drastic a move toward freedom from regulation by a federal agency made history.

It was only after intense and prolonged debate that the CAB finally adopted its amended policies. Under these policies now governing your air travel:

Ceiling fares on coach trips are set at the levels of September 1978.

Airlines have the discretion to cut their normal fares by as much as 50 per cent in all domestic markets.

On some of their flights (40 per cent of their seat miles a week), cuts of up to 70 per cent are permissible.

To remind you of how great are these changes, deep discounts had in the past generally been available to you only on capacity-controlled restrictive fares.

The policy for the 1980s has further ramifications to you as a traveler. It has abolished the prescription that first-class fares be set at a certain percentage above coach.

As a result airlines can set first-class fares at *any* level above coach fares. For some of you who travel first class the cost of flying your favorite airline actually could increase, therefore—despite the potential giant cuts. In addition, carriers may boost fares from 5 to 10 per cent on a large part of their route system, depending on the amount of competition on their system.

The CAB's action, which is only beginning to be felt by the traveling public, put pricing decisions and the consequences of those decisions back in the hands of the market place and the carrier management.

Previously, airlines had been forced to compete for passengers on the basis solely of schedules and amenities (the biggest steak).

Probably one of the greatest benefits to accrue to you, the air traveler, as a result of the Board's action is elimination of the bewildering array of air fares that always has defied public understanding.

While airlines still are fighting jammed telephone reservation lines as hundreds of thousands of air travelers seek answers to questions on the multitude of discount fares that have been built up over recent years, the CAB's action ultimately should wipe out the problem of complicated fares.

The industry is trying to work its way out of the maze of Discover America excursion fares, Unlimited Mileage fares, Freedom Excursion fares, Visit U.S.A. fares, Super Coach fares, Super Saver fares, etc., etc. They held out such airline lures as (if you can believe it!) round-trip travel at night except on weekends in seats purchased thirty days before departure if the return trip is made a week to forty-five days later!!

At one airline, the in joke was, "We have a new slogan: a fare a day on TWA."

At another major carrier, a horrified efficiency expert found nineteen fares between Los Angeles and Chicago alone!

The sweeping action of the Board in de-regulating plane fares must take a long time in producing overall results. However, you already are seeing the effect in the form of lower fares for long-haul markets and the elimination of many of those nightmarishly confusing discount fares in favor of generalized peak and off-peak pricing.

LIBERALIZED PUBLIC CHARTERS, TOO

A second benefit now emerging in ever fuller measure for you, the traveling public of the 1980s, is the adoption of new liberalized charter regulations. These have replaced most current charter forms with a single form called "public charters."

Liberalized features of the new charter form include:

—No advance purchase requirement.

—No minimum stay requirement.

—No restrictions on discount pricing.

—No minimum size group.

—An end to open-ended round-trip charters.

The prohibition on open-ended round-trip charters is an important protection for the airline traveler.

Charters were responsible for nine out of ten complaints logged against agents and tour operators by the Office of the Consumer Advocate of the CAB in the late 1970s. Inherent in the problem was the infancy of the mass charter market, which really only began to take off in the middle of the decade. Horror stories spread about charter passengers sleeping at terminals overseas, about unexpected cancellations and defaults, about charters that took bookings and then never even got off the ground.

But now under the CAB rules, if you are a charter passenger, you may be able to cancel your reservation if:

• there is an alteration of departure or return date;

- the origin or destination city is changed;
- you are assigned a hotel other than the one named in the operator-participant contract;
- the price of your tour is hiked 10 per cent, whether all at once or in smaller chunks. No increases would be allowed after the tenth day before departure.

Should you be advised of a major change by the charter operator, you have seven days in which to cancel and you are entitled to receipt of a refund seven days after cancellation.

The bulk of all those confusing "alphabet soup" special regulation charter names no longer exist to befuddle you. Gone are such names as Advance Booking Charters (ABCs), Travel Group Charters (TGCs), Study Group Charters (SGCs), Inclusive Tour Charters (ITCs), and One-Stop-Inclusive Tour Operators (OTOs).

You can, though, still take affinity group and single-entity charters due to the specialized nature of the groups to which they appeal.

ASK!

If you are a traveler bound on a charter tour overseas, here is basic advice before you fly—*ask!*

—Ask who is the tour operator and what is his reputation.

—Ask what are the cancellation privileges and options available if the tour is canceled at the last minute.

—Ask if the tour operator is bonded or there is an escrow account—required by the CAB.

—Ask what penalties and refunds you can expect if you cancel your trip. Penalties can be substantial—up to 90 per cent of the tour price. Unless you cancel by a certain date, you may not be entitled to a refund.

—Ask at what kind of hotels you will stay. Don't misconstrue the European term for "first class" as being the best, for example. On the Continent this really describes establishments that are several grades below the top, which is "superior deluxe." You can check out your hotel in the *Official Hotel and Resort Guide.*

—Ask what the package includes.

—Ask what is extra. Transfers? Baggage handling at airports and hotels? Sight-seeing? Admissions? All meals?

If you run into problems on a tour that went wrong, you have recourse for complaints. Write the CAB, Office of the Consumer Advocate (1825 Connecticut Avenue N.W., Washington, D.C. 20428) or the American Society of Travel Agents (711 Fifth Avenue, New York, New York 10022).

You also can sue the operator in small-claims court or file a civil suit if the amount is large. In addition, you may find the office of your city or state consumer protection agency helpful as well as your state attorney general.

CAUTION ON MEDICATIONS FOR TRAVELERS

All those who travel for a living—airline crews, entertainers, reporters such as myself—know that as a traveler you must be prepared for the worst.

Carried as standard for a traveling medicine chest: aspirin; vitamins, including B complex and C, the latter to compensate for body loss under stress; antibiotics; antacid; Lomotil or paregoric for symptomatic relief of that ancient malady—turista.

You also may want to include antihistamines, salt tablets, and possibly quinine.

Carry your medicines in duplicate—some on your person and some in your luggage. Carry a copy of any prescription you are required to take written in generic terms as well as the drug itself. Brand names of drugs may not be recognized in other countries.

Local health authorities will advise you on any immunizations you will need.

Consider a Medic Alert emblem if you have a special medical history with chronic conditions or allergies. Membership in the organization provides a twenty-four-hour phone number for physicians you can call for information or crucial assistance. The service is available for a $10 contribution to the non-profit, tax-deductible Medic Alert Foundation. Request an application form before mailing your contribution by writing the Foundation at Box 1009, Turlock, California 95380.

Before departure, also obtain a list of English-speaking doctors the world over in return for a contribution to the International Association for Medical Assistance to Travelers (IAMAT), 350 Fifth Avenue, New York, New York 10001.

In addition, Intermedic, 777 Third Avenue, New York, New York 10017, offers a *Directory of Participating Physicians* with fees that are fixed for the initial office visit or hotel call.

In many areas with socialized medicine (for example, Sweden and Great Britain), health care is free to the visitor.

You might arrange, too, for some form of trip cancellation insurance in the event you become ill before departure or on the trip.

And don't forget to pack that extra pair of eyeglasses.

THE HANDICAPPED TRAVELER

Millions of Americans have disabilities—temporary and permanent—that restrict their vacations. Advance planning can eliminate much of the trouble.

As the 1980s begin our government has adopted a more enlightened attitude about the problems of the handicapped in traveling. A new era is emerging for the disabled vacationer.

The United States Travel Service of the Department of Commerce reports that a growing awareness of the special needs of handicapped travelers has opened previously closed doors if you are in a wheelchair or have other physical disabilities.

Several government publications on travel facilities for the handicapped are available. These include *Travel Tips for the Handicapped, Access Travel,* and *Access Guide to the National Parks.* You may obtain the pamphlets from the Consumer Information Center, Pueblo, Colorado 81009 (free).

To aid you in your planning, here's what airlines, buses, and railroads offer you in services.

(1) *Airlines*—The Federal Aviation Administration mandates each airline to have a policy for the handicapped traveler approved by the FAA.

Make your reservations early.

Describe the nature of your disability. Many airlines provide attendants to assist in boarding and at the terminal.

When transporting your own wheelchair, be sure you have attached your name and address.

Arrive at the airport early. This will enable you to board ahead of others.

Safety regulations require that canes and crutches be stowed, so you will have to relinquish them while on board.

Advise the airline in advance if you plan to bring special equipment such as oxygen.

(2) *Buses*—Greyhound has a "Helping Hand" program and Trailways offers a "Good Samaritan" package—both to enable a handicapped person to travel with an attendant for the price of a single ticket.

You must provide a certificate from a physician noting that an attendant's services are required to qualify.

You can get more information by contacting the Director of Customer Relations at Greyhound Lines, Greyhound Tower, Phoenix, Arizona 85077; phone (602) 248-2920; or Continental Trailways, 1512 Commerce Street, Dallas, Texas 75201; phone (214) 655-7900.

(3) *Railroads*—Amtrak has put into service new cars with special facilities for the disabled.

Blind passengers, in company with an attendant, can get a 25 per cent discount on the regular one-way fare by presenting a certificate from the American Foundation for the Blind.

You can get detailed information about rail facilities for the handicapped by calling Amtrak's toll-free number, (800) 523-5720, and asking for the Special Movements Desk.

TIME YOUR VACATION OFF-SEASON

If you take a trip to Rome during the Thanksgiving holidays, you well may save 20 per cent on a double room at one well-known luxury hotel as against the price you would pay during the packed, pushy, peak tourist summer days.

If you rent a car for an Irish holiday in October, you'll save even larger percentages as against the sum you would pay for the same car during the summer— and you'll enjoy additional savings on plane and boat fares, hotel rooms, meals, local transportation, entertainment.

If you take a three-week package tour of eight European countries starting in October, you well might pay $100 less than the same tour would cost you in June–August.

And if you are planning a week's skiing vacation this winter, you'll save 20 per cent or more on hotel accommodations just by waiting until late in the ski season, when the snow will be just as skiable, but the influx of skiers and après skiers will have slowed to a snowplow's pace.

Timing is at the very core of saving money on your vacation—either in the United States or abroad. What's more, since millions of you now have the privilege of taking your vacation whenever you wish during the year, this is a major money-saving weapon you can use at your discretion and to whatever extent you want.

You might even split your vacation into two holidays, taking advantage of bargain off-season rates at traditional summer resorts, then repeating your move and taking advantage of off-season rates at traditional winter resorts.

A key fact is that in many resort areas across the United States the weather is far more trustworthy in off-season than it is at the season's height. May and October are particularly glorious months in many foreign lands.

As a general rule, the expensive "high season" in the Caribbean runs from mid-December until mid-March. In Europe, it's more or less the reverse: the high season begins with June and runs to (or, in some cases and places, through) September. A short "shoulder season" with intermediate prices sits between the high and low seasons.

SAVE BY GOING WHERE THE CROWDS ARE NOT

But even if you must take your vacation during the peak weeks of summer, you can save by heading for the less-crowded areas and by avoiding the well-known paths.

Don't squeeze yourself into the popular national parks, or visit a jammed resort. Head for one of the less crowded western Canadian provinces, the wide-open spaces of Montana or Idaho, or a remote section of Upper Michigan. Or go to New York City while New Yorkers are off summer-vacationing themselves. Miami and the Florida Keys offer reduced summer rates (though increasing numbers of tourists are discovering the fact). The ski towns of Colorado don't have as many summer visitors as winter skiers, yet their year-round weather and accommodations are delightful.

You also will be extra smart in midsummer if you avoid day-by-day travel, and instead find a single resort or hotel which can accept your reservation for a week or two.

SAVE ON A PACKAGE PLAN

Another key way to save is by buying a vacation "package." Many hotels in resort areas advertise special rates for stays of a weekend or a week or more. Often these are part of a transportation package with the airline or railroad serving the resort. Travel agents can suggest literally hundreds of good, money-saving packages.

Or if you are buying a tour, consider a package, too, on unescorted standard-itinerary tours sold by tour operators. Included in the flat, low price will be your air ticket, hotel room, and certain sight-seeing expeditions. You pay only for meals and extras and you decide how you'll spend most of your time.

Ask your travel agent about the many other ways you can cut your vacation costs today. (See pages 419–27, 723–25.)

How to Save on Shopping Under United States Customs Limitations

If you plan to do your Christmas shopping at cut-rate duty-free shops, be warned: there are many limitations imposed by U. S. Customs.

Check the current maximum in exemptions at the time of your trip (based on fair retail value of each item in the country where acquired) which may be brought in free of duty subject to limitations on liquors and cigars.

There are strict rules on exemptions.

—The articles must be obtained for your personal or household use.

—The articles must be brought with you at the time you return to the United States and properly declared. If you purchase items and leave them for alterations or other reasons, their value cannot be applied to your exemption when shipped at a later date.

—You must stay abroad at least forty-eight hours. This time limitation does not apply if you are returning from Mexico or the U. S. Virgin Islands.

—You cannot use the exemptions within the preceding thirty-day period.

You may bring back one quart of liquor if you are twenty-one years old or older.

If you return directly from the U. S. Virgin Islands, American Samoa, or Guam, you may receive a higher customs exemption based on fair retail value of the articles in the country where acquired.

If you cannot claim the exemptions because of the thirty-day or forty-eight-hour limitations, you can bring in duty-free articles acquired abroad for your personal or household use if the retail value is not over $10.

You can send bona fide gifts of not more than $10 in fair retail value where shipped to your friends and relations in the United States duty-free—provided the same person does not receive more than $10 in gift shipments in one day.

You pay no duty at all on original oil paintings, stamps, coins, books, or on antiques more than one hundred years old. Trademark restrictions curtail the number or amounts of certain items you may bring home—particularly watches, perfumes, clocks, and cameras.

If you buy an automobile abroad and want to bring it back with you, you'll have to pay duty, of course—although under most circumstances you and other members of your family may use all your individual exemptions to reduce the value of the car for duty purposes. The rate of duty on a passenger car in the late 1970s was 3 per cent of the "dutiable value," as determined by the customs inspector.

For more details on customs regulations, request the following pamphlets from the U. S. Customs, P. O. Box 7118, Washington, D.C. 20044:

U. S. Customs Trademark Information;
Know Before You Go;
Customs Hints for Returning U.S. Residents; and
Importing a Car

How to Shop for a Vacation Tour

In recent years scandal after scandal has erupted across the front pages of the nation about "bargain" vacation tours. If you were a victim, you found many real costs hidden in the small print; or your costs were vastly increased when omitted essentials were included; or your deluxe accommodations were marginal at best; or you, a single, discovered too late that you had been booked into a double room with a stranger. Or many, many times your departure was at an abysmally "off" off-hour.

But in strictly economic terms, the package tour *is* the least expensive way to take a vacation, particularly a vacation abroad, today.

Just what is a package tour? It is not, as you might think, always a highly organized, closely timetabled tour during which the tour members eat, tour, sightsee, practically sleep together, and are herded in and out of places and countries with stopwatch precision.

Some travelers, primarily older couples, single persons, and inexperienced travelers, may prefer the security of the traditional escorted group and require only that the relatively small group fly together to and from their destinations.

A tour package does have, though, a predetermined price, number of features, and period of time. Within those limits, you, the traveler, can do whatever you please when you please. The greatest advantage to the traveler is that the cost of the land tour arrangements and air fare in the package is far less than the costs the traveler would otherwise pay for each item separately.

But how do *you* avoid the traps? How do *you* shop for a tour?

Obviously, the prime rule—which I cannot repeat too often—is to deal only with an airline or tour operator or travel agent you have checked thoroughly and are confident is honest, reliable, and well established.

Obviously, it's no more than common sense to phone a couple of airlines, car rental firms, and the like to double-check whether the price of the tour you want really represents a saving over booking your vacation yourself or through a travel agent.

Now, use this check list to help you decide what you want from a vacation tour, to compare one tour against another, and to alert you to possible hidden costs.

Price: What's the total, including taxes and other extras, for the accommodations you want? If the tag says from "$198," will this minimum give you the comforts you need?

What's included: How many meals are provided each day? Fixed menu—or a la carte? Who pays tips for porters and tour guides? Who pays the hotel bills? For sight-seeing buses and guides? For theater tickets? For transfers between airports, train stations, and midtown? For transportation to your hotel? Is air fare included? If a rented car is part of the package, who pays for gas, a very costly item in most foreign lands? Typical *exclusions:* one or two meals a day, porters' tips, airport taxes, laundry and valet costs, taxi fares, snacks, excess baggage costs.

Accommodations: What type and class of hotel rooms are offered? Are the hotels named? Is there a clause permitting the tour operator to book you into substitute hotels for those named? Is the stated price for double occupancy? If you're traveling alone, is there a supplementary charge for a single room? Are such basic amenities as a bathroom included? Is the hotel's location convenient to where you're likely to be spending your time?

You'll save a lot of money by not bolting from the "package" to higher-cost hotel rooms. But if you prefer fancier surroundings, find out from the airline or tour operator the conditions and costs of trading up, if you so desire.

Terms: When do you have to pay for the tour? Is a deposit required and, if so, how much? What are the conditions for getting a refund if you cancel out or change your vacation plans? If you're paying on the installment plan, what annual interest rate is charged on the outstanding balance and how does this rate compare with the rate you might get on a loan from your bank or savings institution?

Your companions: How many other people will be along? Will they be interesting company for you—if you must be in close quarters (such as a bus) for long periods? Is there a theme for the tour to attract people with interests similar to yours?

Timing: How far in advance must you sign up? Choose a departure date and itinerary? Make a deposit? Pay in full?

Free time: How much will you have in each place you visit? Can you duck out for an afternoon or a day or two without being left behind, if you so wish? What's the likely pace of the tour? Will you be up to it? (As a general rule, if you travel more than nine or ten hours a day or more than 250 miles a day, you well might find your trip exhausting.) Will local guides shepherd you on certain legs of your trip and supplement your regular guide?

Find out these details *before* you sign up!

WHAT A TRAVEL AGENT CAN (AND CANNOT) DO FOR YOU

Let's say you are planning your first major vacation trip—either in the United States or abroad—and you have a general idea where you want to go and what you want to do. But you know absolutely nothing about costs, schedules, hotel accommodations. Just what could a travel agent do for you at what (if any) cost? How and where do you find a suitable travel agency?

A good travel agent should be well supplied with air and boat schedules; rates and costs for various types of travel; details on tours and group arrangements, schedules of festivals and other special events, hotel-motel room rates, cruise information.

A knowledgeable travel agent can:

• Guide you in applying for a passport and/or visa, alert you on immunizations you'll need for travel abroad, fill you in on customs rules and regulations.

• Sign you up for almost any kind of group tour (including tours the travel agency itself is putting together and selling).

• Make almost any kind of reservation or buy any kind of tickets for you—hotel, motel, plane, train, theater, ballet, bullfight, etc.—although many travel agencies do not sell bus and train tickets or short-haul air tickets or freighter accommodations.

• Sell you traveler's checks and counsel you on how to get the best deal when you change money abroad.

• Steer you to bargain vacation packages—including transportation, hotel rooms, car rentals, meals, etc., off-season deals, places which cater to and offer cut rates to families traveling with children.

• Tell you what are the "on" seasons, the "off" seasons, and the "shoulder" seasons in between—in various parts of the world.

• Advise on tipping customs, what kind of clothes to take, what kind of weather to expect, good restaurants.

• "Tailor-make" a trip or tour for you and your family—to fit *your* tastes, *your* interests, *your* budget. This type of trip is known in the travel trade as an Independent Inclusive Tour (IIT) and this category is further divided into the Domestic Independent Tour (DIT) and the Foreign Independent Tour (FIT).

How much do travel agents' services cost you, the traveler? How and by whom are these costs paid?

The bulk of travel agents' costs are paid by the airlines, steamship lines, railroads, hotels and resorts, tour operators, in the form of commissions. But you, the customer, well may be charged for such extras as:

> certain telegrams and long-distance telephone calls;
> reticketing;
> making reservations in certain foreign hotels;
> short-stay hotel reservations.

Many travel agents also charge you for arranging a special, fancy custom-designed trip abroad.

Okay, now that you know what travel agents do—and don't do—how do you find a good one?

Get recommendations from friends and others who have been customers of a travel agency with which you are considering doing business.

Try to find a travel agent who has himself (or herself) traveled in the area where *you* intend to go—and ask just how extensive the travel was.

Take time to *visit* the travel agency. How thorough and "personal" is the agent's interview with you to discover your travel needs and wants? What "extras" are offered—i.e., reading list on the countries you intend to visit?

Discuss your budget as well as your travel tastes frankly.

Ask if the agency is a member of the American Society of Travel Agents. (This is only a clue, since many reputable travel agencies are *not* members.)

Do not be misled by the size of a travel agency, for this is *not* necessarily an indication of the quality of its services. Good ones come both large and small.

Note whether the agent seems genuinely interested in steering you to travel bargains or whether he or she tries to push you into more expensive ways to "get there" than you can afford (remember, travel agents are paid commissions based on the cost of the accommodations). If the latter, go to another agency.

If you are booking a tour being sold by the travel agency, nail down details on deposits you'll be required to make, policies on refunds and cancellation fees. Each agency sets its own rules in this area and if the agency fails voluntarily to spell out the rules, *ask* what they are. You may lose 100 per cent of whatever amount you have paid toward a tour—if this is the written policy of the tour operator and/or travel agency selling the deal. The loss could include even air fares you've paid for overseas tours.

If a travel agency promises to make refunds for cancellations you have made for valid reasons, find out just what constitutes valid reasons.

If a "slight" penalty is to be imposed in the event you cancel, check just how slight is "slight."

If you ask a travel agent to draw up a special itinerary for you, find out in advance what the costs will be, whether you'll be required to make a deposit, and, if so, how much. The charge for a custom-planned trip can be as high as 25 to 50 per cent of the value of the package—if the planning involves a lot of the agent's time, thought, and expertise.

Consider purchasing some form of trip cancellation insurance. You will be partially or fully reimbursed—depending on your policy—if you have to cancel the trip. Shop around for cost and coverage; they vary. Some companies also will write baggage insurance in connection with trip cancellation insurance. You can get trip cancellation insurance through a travel agent although the agent may carry only one company's insurance, however.

If you have any suspicions about a travel agent with whom you're considering doing any substantial amount of business, check the agency's reputation with the local Better Business Bureau.

DO-IT-YOURSELF TRAVEL PLANNING

If you are booking on your own into one of the large hotels and hotel chains, use their toll-free telephone reservations number. You'll get an instant answer by phone or a letter at times by return mail to confirm your reservation.

If you are making your own airline reservations, ask any major airline to advise you on other airline schedules as well as on special rates offered by all airlines. Most will freely do so.

Call Amtrak for most U.S. rail travel. The toll-free number throughout the United States for reservations and information: (800) 523-5720. More than five thousand travel agents around the world also are authorized to sell Amtrak tickets. In Canada, contact Via Rail Canada, P.O. Box 8116, 1801 McGill College, Montreal, Quebec, Canada, H3C 3N3.

The two best-known domestic bus lines are Greyhound and Trailways. Both have offices located at Eighth Avenue and Forty-first Street, New York, New York 10014 (the New York Port Authority bus terminal).

Most of the key steamship lines have headquarters offices in New York City.

Look into the wide array of overseas travel information available from each major country's government travel office in New York (and, in some cases, in other cities as well).

Write the state Tourist Information Bureaus in the states you want to visit within our borders or the U. S. National Park Service, Department of the Interior, Eighteenth and C Streets, Washington, D.C. 20240.

Go to the nearest passport office for guidance on how to apply for a passport. In some cities and towns which have no passport office, this information is now available at the U.S. post office along with passport application forms; elsewhere, get the information and application forms from the clerk of a federal or state court or from your county clerk's office.

For details on international auto registration certificates and international driver's licenses, check the local affiliate of the American Automobile Association. And if you're a member of this organization, use its facilities to help plan your trip—including information on roads under construction and speed traps; maps; itinerary recommendation; regional guides to motels, restaurants (with ratings and tourist attractions).

Check your automobile insurance to be sure it covers you in all states you will visit. (Failure to take care of this would be very costly in the event of an accident.) If you will be traveling in Canada, ask your insurance company for a Canada Non-Resident Inter-Province Motor Vehicle Liability Insurance Card, required to prove your coverage to provincial officials. In Mexico, auto insurance laws are very strict. U.S. insurance is usually not valid for more than forty-eight hours after entry and you will need a more expensive Mexican policy for longer stays. *Be sure* to look into the car insurance problem *before* you leave home.

Study at least a couple of travel guides and books, which you can borrow from your library or buy at a bookstore. (Some have coupons which will buy you discounts for various tourist services.) Among the best ones:

Fielding's Travel Guide to Europe and many other Fielding guides (William Morrow).

Frommer's *Europe on $10 a Day* and other $10 and $15 a Day Guides (Simon & Schuster).

Fodor's *Europe* and other Fodor Guides (McKay).

Let's Go: Europe, a Student Guide (Harvard Student Agencies, Inc., distributed through E. P. Dutton & Co.).

The Mobil Travel Guides (Simon & Schuster).

Rand McNally Guidebooks: *Road Atlas, Travel Trailer Guide, Guidebook to Campgrounds, Campground and Trailering Guide, National Park Guide, Ski Guide.*

Woodall's *Parks and Campgrounds* (Woodall Publishing).

The Michelin Guides to France and other European countries and Michelin's *Green Guide to New York City* (Simon & Schuster).

A to Z Guides by Robert S. Kane (Doubleday).

Blue Guides (Rand McNally).

AAA Tour Book, one for each region of the United States; also *Eastern and Western AAA Campground Guide*—all available to AAA members only.

The Official Student Travel Guide (International Student Travel Conference; 1560 Broadway, New York).

Whole World Handbook—A Student Guide to Work, Study, and Travel Abroad,
1980–81 Edition, 205 East 42nd Street, New York, New York 10017.

1001 Sources for Free Travel Information (Jens Jurgen, Kings Park, New York
11754).

PanAm's New Horizons World Guide and other PanAm guides to the United
States, Canada, South America, European countries, Africa, Asia, the Middle
East, and the Caribbean.

And finally the most important rule for all do-it-yourselfers: *plan ahead,* just as
far ahead as you possibly can.

Do's and Don'ts for Cutting Your Hotel Bills

If you're a typical American today, your spending for hotel and/or motel bills
will run into hundreds of dollars a year. So will your spending for food and drink
away from home—on long weekends, holidays, vacations.

If you're typical, you'll also "waste" as much as $2.00 of every $10 you spend
simply because you do not know the basic do's and don'ts for saving on your
hotel and motel bills:

Do, when you make a room reservation, ask for a room by price category.
(Most hotels have three categories: economy, standard, and luxury.) If you want
the minimum rate, ask for it. Virtually all good hotels now provide radio, TV,
phone, air conditioning—and if the hotel isn't full, many will give you better than
minimum room accommodations even though you pay the lowest rate.

Don't underestimate the cost of room service. There usually is a room-service
charge added to the bill the waiter gives you and the prices on the room-service
menu usually are higher than prices for the same or similar items in the hotel
coffee shop. Room service is a luxury which makes sense when you're on a special vacation, but it can add many dollars to your bills if you are a frequent traveler.

Do be careful about check-out time. If you want to stay an hour or two after
check-out time, notify the manager or assistant manager directly, and unless your
room is needed at once, he'll probably allow you to stay without charge. But if
you stay as long as three hours after check-out time, the hotel may charge you
$5.00 extra, and if you stay into the evening hours, you may be charged for a full
extra day.

Don't, if you're traveling with your family, fail to inquire about the "family
plan" that many hotels feature. It's ridiculous to pay for an extra room when—
for no charge or for at most a nominal fee—the hotel will provide a folding bed
which can be set up in your room. And this rule may apply to kids into their
teens. Also, many hotels have special meal-ticket programs which will cut down
on your family's dining bills.

Do take advantage of the toll-free electronic reservations systems which most
large chains provide. By doing so, you can save the expense of a phone call or of
a wire ahead to hotels in other cities you are planning to visit.

Don't, if you are driving your own car, ignore the extent to which overnight

728 SYLVIA PORTER'S NEW MONEY BOOK FOR THE 80'S

parking fees can throw your budget out of line. Make sure the midtown hotel you choose offers free parking either on the premises or nearby. Even in New York City, major hotel chains park cars without charge. Frequently, however, a charge is made each time you take your car out of the garage.

Do find out in advance if the hotel at which you're planning to stay is on the regular route of an airport bus or limousine. If it isn't at one of the regular stops, you'll have the added expense of a taxi to get you to your destination.

Do take another look at famed old downtown hotels which you may bypass because you assume they're too expensive. To meet the competition of motor inns, airport and suburban hotels, many of these great establishments have cut their rates. You may be concentrating on saving a tip or two by staying in a motel, but as one great hotel man remarked, "I could never understand why anybody would want to spend $2.00 more for a room to save 25 cents on a tip."

Don't pay for the use of a hotel or motel swimming pool, sauna, gym, etc. (which may add $1.00 to $2.00 to daily room rates) if you don't intend to use the facilities.

And *do,* finally, try to plan your travels around the hotel package deals—off-season bargains, weekend plans, family specials—I've underlined in the preceding pages.

WHOM AND HOW TO TIP

The old guideline for restaurants, resort hotels, taxis, etc.—tip 15 per cent of the bill—has been firmly upped to 15 to 20 per cent of the total if you want to be known as generous.

The old rule for *porters* carrying your luggage also has been upped from 25 cents a bag to a minimum of 50 cents, and frequently $1.00 is the minimum if you want to avoid scowls and recriminations from the porter.

The minimum tip for *taxi drivers* in big cities is 25 cents—which works out to 25 per cent of a $1.00 fare.

Of course, many travelers still tip well below these levels—and a surprising number of skinflints don't tip *anyone any* percentage at all. But tipping remains an economic institution in this land, and so:

The hotel doorman: Tip him 50 cents when you arrive, if he carries your baggage to the registration desk, $1.00 if you have three or more bags. Give him 25 cents each time he finds you a taxi—but give only a "thank you" if he merely waves forward a cab waiting in front of the hotel.

The bellhop: Tip him as you tipped the doorman, increasing your tips if your luggage is very heavy or cumbersome. Whenever he delivers anything give him 25 cents even if it is just a newspaper costing 10 cents. If he has paid for the item, of course, reimburse him.

The wine steward: Tip him 10 to 15 per cent of the cost of the wine, at the end of the meal.

Room service: Tip 50 cents each time an item is delivered. But tip $1.00 if the waiter brings ice and drink mixers and $1.50 to $2.00 if he brings a whole tray full of soda, glasses, ice, and other drinking equipment. When you have a meal sent to your room, tip as you would in a restaurant—15 to 20 per cent of the check.

Valet: Tip 50 cents per delivery. If you give the valet a rush order, though, or ask for extraordinary service—say a suit pressed and back within the hour—give him $1.00.

Chambermaid: You need not tip her if you spend only a night or two at a regular commercial hotel, but it's increasingly recommended that you leave her 50 cents a day if you stay longer. Leave the money in an envelope addressed "For the Chambermaid in Room ———" at the reception desk the last day of your stay and tell the housekeeping department you left it. Tip her $1.00 to $2.00 if you have a cocktail party in your room or suite, involving a big cleanup job for her. In a resort hotel, the standard minimum tip for the chambermaid is 50 cents per day for a single person, $1.00 per day for a couple, more for special service.

Travel abroad: Even if a substantial service charge has already been added to your hotel or restaurant bill, the trend today is toward adding another 10 per cent to the total rather than just leaving the small change. The trend also is toward personal distribution of the money to make sure the chambermaid, doorman, waiter, or others who have served you actually get the tips. And the trend too is for tipping above and beyond these percentages for any extra special services— for tips frequently are the sole source of income for service personnel in Europe and elsewhere abroad.

At a resort hotel—including those operating on the American plan (all meals included) or modified American plan (breakfast and dinner included)—a service charge of 15 per cent or more may be added to your total bill. If it isn't, tip your dining-room waiter 15 per cent of your restaurant bill. You'll probably find details on how much of your daily room rate is for your meals in the hotel directory in the dresser drawer of your room, but if not, ask the assistant manager or social director for pertinent facts. Tip bellboys 50 cents for each bag they carry and tip your chambermaid and pool boy 50 cents each per day per person, as you leave. Tip your resort's hairdresser 15 to 20 per cent.

Visiting friends: If there is a housekeeper or cook who helps make your stay more gracious and comfortable, you, as a visiting couple, might properly tip at least $1.00 to $2.00 a day as a "thank you."

P.S.: Perhaps as you grumble and struggle over whether to tip 10 per cent or 15 per cent or 20 per cent or whatever, you might remember that, by one definition, "TIPS" were originally intended as a means "To Insure Prompt Service." This reminder might help guide you to the right amount for the right persons.

AND TIPPING ON WINTER CRUISES

Let's say you are now making plans for your first winter vacation on a cruise ship. You've read all the brochures on what to wear, what to see, what to do. But one angle I'll wager you've missed is: whom to tip how much. Even if you already have been on every type of winter holiday, I'll bet you have made plenty of inadvertent tipping blunders.

Here, too, tipping expectations are being revised sharply upward in many instances from the old 10 to 15 per cent range to a new 15 to 20 per cent range—and employees who never were considered eligible for tips suddenly are turning up on the lists. Following, therefore, you will find up-to-date rules for cruise-ship tipping:

Tip your dining-room steward and your room steward or stewardess a minimum of $1.00 each per day per person. Thus, if you are a couple on a two-week cruise, tip a total of about $30. If your cruise lasts a week or less, tip at least $10 for each steward—at the end of the trip.

Tip the deck steward 50 cents a day or about $2.50 to $3.00 a week. Tip the headwaiter in the dining room a couple of dollars, plus $1.00 or $2.00 each time he performs some special service for you. Tip the bartender 15 to 20 per cent each time you are served a new drink. Tip the telephone operator $1.00 or $2.00 if she puts through complicated ship-to-shore calls for you.

On shore, tip tour guides 50 cents to 15 per cent of the cost of the tour if it's a half-day tour, $1.00 if it's a full-day tour. Tip the men who carry your luggage in U.S. ports at least 35 cents per bag—even if the dock is plastered with "no tipping" signs.

Don't tip the cruise's social director; or the person who leads calisthenics; or the purser or other ship's officers; or customs men in port. If you are in doubt, ask for guidelines from your travel agent, the cruise director, or the ship's purser. The excursion agent on board your ship can tell you if tipping is expected anywhere ashore.

SAVE BY HOSTELING

One of the very least expensive ways to "see the world" today is to use the world's extraordinary network of youth hostels. These are inexpensive dormitory-style accommodations providing shelter, bunks, or beds, and often some sort of kitchen facilities. Fees in the United States are typically $2.00 to $5.00 per day for lodging; abroad, fees are somewhat lower.

There are some 4,500 hostels today in 50 different countries, and the youth hosteling organizations offer a long list of special bargains to hostelers. You can go hosteling by foot, canoe, bike, public transportation, or car. You can go alone, or with friends, or with a group and trained leader.

Typical cost of a thirty-day American Youth Hostel tour within the United States in the late 1970s was in the $350 to $500 range and in the $1,250 to $1,500 range for tours abroad. Included were: transportation from a specified departure point; all costs of accommodations and food; insurance; leadership; and transportation back to the original departure point. *Not* included in this price were: equipment you must have (generally simple camping gear); spending money; cost of passports; bicycle shipping; transportation to or from trip starting point; AYH membership dues; and an emergency fund which must be deposited with the trip leader for unexpected expenses (unused amounts are returned).

Hostelers on a National Group Trip must be at least fourteen years old or must have completed tenth grade. For Hawaii, hostelers must be sixteen years old. For all trips, hostelers must be in good physical and mental health as certified by a physician. On International Trips campers must be at least sixteen years old or have previously completed a National Trip. There is no upper age limit, but most trips are intended for young travelers in good physical condition. A few, however, are for adults only.

Your passport to hostels throughout the world is a pass issued by AYH.

A junior pass in the late 1970s (for people under age eighteen) cost $5.00; a senior pass for older hostelers cost $11; a family membership covering children up to age eighteen cost $12. Only individual passes—junior and senior—can be used outside the United States.

For detailed information on trips and applications for passes, write American Youth Hostels, AYH National Campus, Delaplane, Virginia 22025.

Bus Passes and Bike Trails

Another way to cover a large territory on your vacation—at very low cost—is to go by bus. You can now get a special type of bus ticket, similar to the well-known Eurailpass, which will give you virtually unlimited bus travel in the United States and Canada for sixty days. Greyhound calls its version Ameripass and Continental Trailways calls its ticket Eaglepass, but both cost about $225 for thirty days and about $325 for sixty days. This worked out to $6.00 to $8.00 a day in the late 1970s—a clue to how great a bargain the passes really are.

Your only limitations in using either pass are: you may not take more than four round trips between any two points; neither pass is valid during the peak summer travel months.

More than 150,000 miles of routes in forty-eight states and Canada are yours to choose from, and Greyhound's pass also gives you a variety of discounts up to 20 per cent on hotels, car rentals, tours, and other services. Greyhound's pass may be used on the Trailways system where Greyhound does not provide service and vice versa. But it is most convenient to buy your pass from the line which serves your travel plans best.

An increasingly popular way to go camping—or just to sight-see at your vacation destination—is by bicycle. You can even combine it with bus travel. Bicycles are proliferating and it is becoming easier all the time to find places to combine this sport with camping. The Bureau of Outdoor Recreation, U. S. Department of Interior, estimates that there will be more than 200,000 miles of bike routes in the United States by the end of this decade. Ohio, for instance, has more than a half-dozen biking routes running through the most scenic areas of the state, and more are being laid out all the time. The average length of these routes is about 30 miles and all are marked by standard bikeway signs. (*Ohio Is Happening Along Bikeways,* from the Ohio Department of Development, Box 1011, Columbus, Ohio 43216, describes the trails.)

Or you can ride through Indiana's covered-bridge country on a bikeway running through Parke County. A longer trail is the towpath of the old Chesapeake and Ohio Canal from Georgetown, D.C., to Cumberland, Maryland—184 miles Or you can ride 320 miles on the Wisconsin State Bikeway from the Mississippi River to Lake Michigan.

Many more trails are being planned for the future; most spurred locally, but some of them with financial help from the federal government. But you don't have to wait for official designation of trails. With a little help from cycling clubs and friends, plus some practice and experience on your own, you'll be able to choose the most enjoyable routes yourself from highway maps and government topographic maps.

Also, send for *The AYH North American Bike Atlas,* which describes sixty one-day trips throughout the United States and one hundred one-week to one-month trips throughout the United States and one hundred one-week to one-month trips in Canada, Mexico, and the Caribbean ($2.45; American Youth Hostels, Inc., AYH National Campus, Delaplane, Virginia 22025).

Try combining hostels, state and private campgrounds, perhaps a friendly farmer or two, and even an occasional motel. You'll surely find you can work out literally hundreds of real cycling adventures almost anywhere in the country—at astonishingly low cost. (The rules on how to *buy* a bicycle are in Chapter 7, "Getting to and from—by Wings, Wheels, and Water.")

MONEY-SAVING GUIDES FOR CAMPING TRIPS

During most of the summer weeks each summer, tens of millions of you go off on camping trips and in the process spend more than $1 billion on travel trailers alone, plus hundreds of millions on camping equipment, plus millions more on getting to and from the camping grounds, on overnight fees, and on other expenses.

Until recently, camping in the United States meant stuffing a sleeping bag, some warm clothes, a few cooking utensils, and first-aid equipment into a rucksack, slinging it over your back, and heading for the hills. But today the typical camper travels in a fully equipped trailer or motor home, cooks on gas stoves instead of campfires, watches TV instead of beavers. Today's typical campsite provides creature comforts ranging from hot showers to hair dryers, clothes washers to canteens.

Obviously, camping has become a significant factor in the outdoor recreation industry and also a potentially whopping expense to the individual camper or camping family.

As one measure of camping's spectacular growth just in this decade, the Rand McNally *Campground and Trailer Park Guide* listed more than 20,000 campgrounds in the United States and Canada (with more than 600,000 individual campsites), up from 10,000 campgrounds listed in 1961. Rand McNally also counted thousands of camping areas specifically set up to accommodate travel trailers, with more than 400,000 separate sites for recreational vehicles.

If you're the back-to-nature type and really prefer to rough it, you and your family can go on a camping trip by foot or by canoe in any one of thousands of national and state parks for as little as $100 a week,* assuming you don't go too far from home and you already own basic equipment such as cooking utensils, sleeping bags, and backpacks. Even if you have to rent these basics, the total cost

* All of these figures prevailed in the late 1970s.

for a family of three or four needn't run over $200 a week. But if you prefer the "motel in the wilderness" type of camping, involving rented travel trailers, overnight fees at private campgrounds, electricity and gas bills, etc., costs can rise to $300 or more a week.

If you're considering taking your first camping expedition, your best bet is to avoid an outlay of hundreds of dollars to buy trailers, tents, etc. Rent them instead. Buy as little as possible until you find out whether or not you like the whole idea of camping and, if so, what style of camping you enjoy most.

If you decide to go the recreational vehicle route, you can choose from a wide range of travel trailers, campers, motor homes, etc.—at an even wider array of prices. (You will find the money-saving guides on buying recreational vehicles on pages 410–12.)

Another possibility is a U.S.- or foreign-made small camper which you can rent for about the price of renting a car at an airport. This type of camper will sleep four people and has the full range of kitchen equipment and other camping gear. The vehicles are available in many major U.S. cities and throughout Europe.

Here are more tips if you prefer to rough it:

The federal government offers a $10 Golden Eagle Passport card which will admit you and any passengers in your car to all areas of the national park system and give you the use of most facilities and services provided by the National Park Service during the year. (A free version, available to citizens more than sixty-two years old, also gives a 50 per cent discount on all special user fees on all federal lands—not just the national parks.)

Get your pass at any national park, at most national forests, or from any first- or second-class post office. Also write the U. S. Superintendent of Documents, Washington, D.C. 20402, for brochures entitled *Camping in the National Park System, Fishing in the National Park System,* and *Boating in the National Park System* (modest cost for each).

If you're inclined toward a really "wild" camping experience, full of educational information about the wild areas you visit and the ways to get there, it is hard to beat the package wilderness tours offered on a non-profit basis by several large conservation outdoor sport associations.

• If you are camping in a national park, choose your campsites carefully. Each year, more than 50 million people somehow squeeze themselves into fewer than 1 million campsites. In the process, many areas become overused, while some are underused. The name of the game, of course, is to find the latter.

• Be on the lookout for the creation of new national parks on the very edges of major cities. The current proposal of the Interior Department is to make 1 million park acres easily accessible near every city of 250,000 or more people.

• But even before these new areas are created, study the areas close to your home carefully. Often you'll find little gems of wilderness in the midst of urban areas, unfrequented by crowds whose urge to escape leads them to overlook their immediate neighborhood and to travel as far as possible. If you find one of these, restful camping may be yours for very little money and travel time.

• If your interest extends beyond camping to the more exacting sports—such as mountaineering, rock climbing, white-water canoeing, or scuba diving—you'll need special instructions as well as special gear. First-aid courses are also valuable if you plan to do much camping. You can get this training most economically from experienced friends or from local clubs, who usually share their knowledge willingly and without charge.

Nationally known groups, such as the Sierra Club or the Red Cross, are sound non-profit alternatives though they may charge for direct expenses. There are also dozens of commercial schools, whose reputations and costs are usually easy to check through knowledgeable devotees of the sport.

TOURISM AND ENERGY SHORTAGES

Tourism is defined as travel 50 miles or more one way, in any form of transport, for any purpose other than commuting for work. It is a vital part of our country's life-style, employing 4 million people and accounting for $60 to $65 billion of spending each year (food, lodging, public transportation, fuel, auto operating costs, entertainment, sight-seeing). It is a labor-intensive, service industry, and in every state tourism is vital to our economic well-being (we take in each other's washing). In three states—Florida, Hawaii, and Nevada—tourism is the leading industry. In six others—California, Texas, Pennsylvania, Illinois, Michigan, Ohio—tourism brings in more than $1 billion annually. In seven other areas —Maine, Alaska, Arizona, Washington, D.C., the Virgin Islands, Puerto Rico, and Guam—the dependence on the travel dollar is extremely heavy.

Not only for your own physical and mental well-being, but also for your nation's welfare, the thing to do in this era of energy shortages is to plan your vacation so that, with the use of 75 per cent of the energy you consumed before the shortages emerged, you can enjoy 10 per cent of your life-style.

Here, therefore, are tips on travel designed specifically to help you conserve energy:

• Investigate with much more care than you formerly did fly/drive, bus/drive, rail/drive, fly/sight-see packages. Be as flexible on dates and routing as you can and use public transportation where feasible.

• Fly/drive vacations now come in all types and sizes, involving rental cars and hotels. Nearly all the airlines have them. Check with a reputable travel agent for pertinent details.

• "Take me along" vacations are booming. For the very simple reason that it saves money, families are planning their vacations around convention and business trips.

• If you like national parks, you'll have no trouble getting to the park by bus these days as well as rail. And buses within the parks have been vastly improved too. There are two hundred park systems located within 100 miles of a metropolitan center—involving the use of a bus rather than a tankful of gas.

• Hotels and motels are offering minivacations and "escape weekends" to people within 100 miles at up to 50 per cent discounts. Most major attractions are within 100 miles of airports or rail terminals or can be reached by bus.

• When traveling by air, be much more flexible on dates, avoid Fridays and

Sundays if possible. On routing, adjust your schedule if need be and don't insist on non-stop.

• Let your travel agent make one booking, and have a confirmed reservation. Avoid double booking—which means you are depriving someone else of a seat.

• Investigate Amtrak, especially for family travel and short-haul business travel. Railroads and motor coaches are the most economical users of fuel.

• Discover your own area close to home by motor coach. Travel in groups. Avoid congested areas by private auto. On these trips, you really waste gas because of traffic tie-ups and idling motors.

• Take buses to the airport, get there early, avoid gas-eating traffic jams, try not to meet friends at the airports.

• Forget haphazard touring. Do not plan an auto trip without a plan. Know where you want to go, when. Buy guides, know your wayside itinerary, make reservations.

• Now the universities are trying to lure us with vacation and travel opportunities on college campuses and surrounding areas. Mort's *Guide to Low-Cost Vacations and Lodging on College Campuses* (Check prices in bookstores or from CMG Publications, Box 630, Princeton, New Jersey 08540) describes the great recreational and cultural facilities of 180 colleges in the United States and Canada which formerly have been enjoyed mostly by students but now are open to all of us at a fraction of commercial recreational, food, and lodging prices.

You need only make relatively easy adjustments. Try them, you'll even like them.

The Wilderness Society operates dozens of tours ranging from hiking, backpacking, and canoeing to horseback riding in wilderness areas throughout the United States. Emphasis is on getting to know the wilderness in a non-destructive way. (For information, write to the Wilderness Society, Western Regional Office, 4260 Evans Avenue, Denver, Colorado 80222.)

The American River Touring Association runs an extensive program of river touring in many distant parts of the world as well as in the United States. Prices in the late 1970s ranged from under $100 for weekend trips to up to $1,500 to $2,000 and more for international expeditions of from fifteen to twenty days.

The Sierra Club, the oldest and one of the largest (180,000 members) wilderness conservation clubs in the United States, sponsors hundreds of wilderness outings each year, including river trips (by raft or canoe), hiking/backpacking trips, and saddle trips. You may be continually moving or operate in a more leisurely fashion from a base camp. Many trips are specifically designed as family trips. You can write the Sierra Club for a publication describing the entire year's trips at 530 Bush Street, San Francisco, California 94108. Chapters also organize a regular schedule of local trips throughout the year at very low cost.

14

SEX ... AND ... MONEY

"Mingling Singles"

As the 1980s approached, close to 600,000 women in the under-twenty-five age bracket were living "alone" and loving it—more than double the number who were so living at the start of the decade. As for young men, the number of men under twenty-five living "alone" had nearly tripled from early 1970 to the late 1970s. And there were more than 4 million men and women in the under-thirty-five age group living "by themselves."

But were they living alone? Of course not! They were mostly "mingling singles"—young couples who had (temporarily, if not permanently) rejected the whole concept of a marriage with the attendant "nuisances" of ceremony and formality. Their substitute was a commitment without the legal ties so traditional in the United States and most other nations throughout the world.

Several states permit common-law marriage if both partners are free from other legal ties. Simply by the acknowledgement of married status over a period of time, common-law marriage is recognized in some states. In others, vows said in private are valid. And in still others, it is clearly illegal for members of the opposite sex to cohabit, even though today it's customary to wink at these laws.

A commitment is . . . a commitment, not to be taken lightly, even though to some it may appear to be rather a *noncommittal* arrangement!

In California, for example, where common-law marriage is not recognized, a precedent was set in the late 1970s: after a couple who had lived together openly for quite a while broke up, the woman sued (and won) her share of community property, as though they had been married.

If you are living with a member of the opposite sex to whom you are not married, *check now* with a lawyer to determine how you should establish your status clearly, especially when leases, insurances, wills, and other legal documents are concerned.

From a practical viewpoint, you also would be wise to keep accurate records of what's yours and what's his or hers, so that—should you decide to part—there need be no wrangling, and ownership of property is clearly defined. Until a lawyer tells you otherwise, beware of signing papers jointly (even Christmas cards), sharing major purchases, and letting people think of you officially as "Mr. and Mrs."

For "mingling singles" budgets see pages 38–40.

HOW MUCH DOES IT COST TO GET MARRIED?

To the casual observer, weddings may appear to be definitely on the decline and young women may seem to be scorning legal ties and to be delighting in having illegitimate children. But well publicized as that image may be, it is just not the picture of the average young woman today. The fact is that no matter how casual (sloppy) you are in dressing, no matter how vehement and vocal you are about living according to your own ideals and goals rather than your parents' traditions, when it comes to your wedding, Miss America, you want a formal gown, attendants, and as elaborate a reception as your family can afford. Out of every five young brides, *Bride's* magazine reports, four choose a traditional, formal wedding. Out of every five, more than four brides still receive a diamond engagement ring.

THE STAGGERING BRIDAL MARKET

Marriage itself is a powerful force in the U.S. economy, with more than 2 million marriages a year accounting for an estimated $12 billion-plus in annual retail sales and services.

If you are merely an average first-time bride and groom, with an average number of relatives and friends to be invited to your wedding, according to statistics gathered by *Modern Bride,* you will spend, roughly, $650 on wedding and engagement rings, $1,500 on a wedding reception (including $250 on a wedding dress), $1,250 for a honeymoon, trousseau, and luggage, and close to $3,500 on furnishing your first home. And that doesn't even take into consideration what others will spend on gifts for you, and such major expenditures as a new home, apartment, car, insurance.

FIGURING OUT WEDDING COSTS

Although cost is hardly the romantic part of a wedding, it's of bread-and-butter concern to the people who pay the bills after the bells have rung. Traditionally, the bride's family is responsible for both the wedding ceremony and the reception; the groom's family gives the rehearsal dinner; bridesmaids give a party for the bride, and ushers give a "bachelor party" for the groom. But today many weddings are limited to a ceremony and reception with the groom's family and even the bride and groom themselves sharing the cost of the reception.

How can you determine what *your* wedding will cost?

Obviously, prices vary widely—starting from the moment you agree to get married until you've settled down to married life—depending on where you live, what type of wedding you plan, and how many people you invite to share your happiness.

Among the expenses to consider are:

- *Engagement:*   engagement ring*
  announcement party
  engagement portrait photograph

- *Wedding:*   stationery (including invitations, announcements, thank-you notepaper, at-home cards, and special items such as cake boxes, matches, and cocktail napkins)

  flowers (for site of the ceremony, bridal attendants, mothers* and grandmothers,* ushers*; reception table arrangements, cake table, other areas where the reception will be held; bride's bouquet* and going-away corsage*; groom's boutonniere)

  photography (wedding portrait and candids, including cost of prints for parents, grandparents, attendants, friends, and relatives)

  music (for both the wedding and the reception)

  catering (including food, liquor, waiters, bartenders, wedding cake and "extras")

  bride's dress, headpiece, and veil

  attendants' dresses and headpieces

  groom's outfit*; ushers' outfits*

  rental fees (church, reception hall; canopies, awnings, carpets, and other equipment for both wedding ceremony and reception)

  special fees (clergy or ceremony official,* sexton, soloist, organist)—and, of course, the wedding license* and (in most states) blood tests

  wedding rings for the bride* and groom (if it's to be a double-ring ceremony)

  gifts for attendants (bride's and groom's*)

  transportation (limousines, rental cars, taxis, parking)

  hotel accommodations for attendants and out-of-town guests

Not included in this check list are the bride's present to the groom and vice versa, trousseau clothes, hairdressers' costs, taxis, tips, and the many other extras (such as rice-bag favors) that can quickly add as much as 25 per cent or more to the total cost.

* Asterisked items are traditionally paid for by the groom or his family.

GET IT IN WRITING!

The first-time bride and groom compress a tremendous amount of planning, shopping, and buying into a few short, unusually busy months. In addition to planning the wedding, they are (or should be) thinking ahead to a honeymoon, furnishing a new home, and setting guidelines for their life together.

You can avoid many unpleasant moments by making all your wedding plans—clearly spelling out *all* arrangements—on paper and carefully reading every word before signing.

As you go down the check list, don't just guess at the prices or accept rough estimates. Don't assume that the experts with whom you're dealing have your best interests at heart. Weddings are big business, and once the word is out that you're getting married, you'll find people coming to you: musicians, photographers, caterers, insurance agents—whoever feels there's some money to be made.

TWELVE RULES FOR BUYING ENGAGEMENT AND WEDDING RINGS

Since you, the young husband-to-be, are, almost by definition, inexperienced in this field and since the occasion is in itself a temptation to splurge, you are likely to make costly errors. What rules are there to guide you?

(1) Do not spend more than three weeks' salary or 6 per cent of your annual income for the diamond ring.

Comparative-shop thoroughly for rings with your prospective mate—especially if diamonds are involved. Diamond prices skyrocketed in the 1970s under heavy speculative pressures, so set your price ranges in advance and between yourselves, agree on a maximum.

(2) Just because the tendency to overspend is so great on this occasion, protect yourself by telling the jeweler this agreed-upon price range as soon as you enter the store. If he is a reputable merchant, he will not try to talk you into buying in a higher price category.

(3) Try to buy your jewelry for cash, but if you must buy on credit, make sure you thoroughly understand all the terms: carrying charges, legal warranties, insurance coverage. And before you accept the financing deal offered by the jeweler, check on whether you can get more favorable terms at a local bank or credit union.

(4) Insure your jewelry. Diamonds, pearls, and rubies can and do fall from their mountings and they can be lost or stolen. And whether you're buying with cash or on credit, find out the store's policy on guarantees and return of merchandise.

(5) Make sure you select a reputable and knowledgeable jewelry merchant. Ask your friends and relatives for guidance and check too with your local chamber of commerce or Better Business Bureau on a merchant's reputation.

(6) As soon as you enter a store, ask to speak with the expert in stones. At most stores, the manager or his assistant will be the expert.

(7) Learn the four basic characteristics of precious gems: color, clarity, cut,

and weight—of which, despite common misconceptions, weight is the least important and color is the most important, followed by clarity and cut.

(8) Consider buying the stone and mounting separately. And if you're buying a truly gem-quality diamond, consult a gemologist, who will know more than just the basic C's of cut, clarity, color, and carat, and will be able to grade the stone.

(9) Seek quality merchandise guaranteed by established and reputable jewelers. A precious stone should (and in some cities must) carry a written guarantee from the merchant; insist on it.

(10) Take your expensive mounted stone back to the store periodically for inspection of the mounting and polishing.

(11) Steer clear of any merchant who offers ridiculous "bargains," and be on guard against fictitious savings claims, unreasonable discounts, and the "I'll let you have it for . . ." pitch.

(12) Walk away from any jeweler who directs you to a specific appraiser and choose your own. If what you've bought and what your appraiser tells you you've bought don't agree, return the stone or ring for a refund fast. Also, investigate trade-in arrangements. Despite the sentimentality of an engagement ring, many women trade in their rings some years later and some retailers guarantee the price, which is usually more than the value, on the trade.

STATIONERY

Etiquette books devote whole chapters to wedding invitations, RSVP cards, announcements, and how to word and address them. Choose the style of invitation that best suits you (and that includes handwritten notes). If the wedding ceremony or reception is off the beaten path, include a little road map.

Invitations generally should be ordered three months ahead, so that they are ready for mailing three or four weeks before the wedding. When you order them, get everything in writing:

• Delivery date of invitations (you can request envelopes in advance so that you can address them at your leisure);

• exact wording (and be sure you proofread carefully to make sure that names are spelled correctly, the day of the week and date correspond, addresses are complete and accurate);

• style and color of engraving or printing (and which will be used; thermography—raised printing—is much less expensive than engraving);

• size, weight, and color of the paper for invitation, envelope, and any enclosures.

At the same time you order your invitations, order notepaper for thank-yous, and any printed wedding specialities you may wish to have—such as cake boxes and cocktail napkins or matches.

But don't be pressured into little gimmicks (swizzle sticks, balloons, garters). They're there to tempt you, but you must carefully weigh their cost against whether you really need or want them.

PHOTOGRAPHS

One or more of your relatives or close friends may have movie cameras and may want to take all the photographs for your wedding book. Thank them graciously and say no. If you're spending $2,000 or $3,000 on a once-in-a-life-time party, it isn't unreasonable to spend $500 for a *professional* photographer, too.

Avoid referral photographers—either those who have called you when they heard you were getting married, or those suggested by the caterer, musicians, or florist (who are probably getting a cut).

Select an established photographer with a local studio, who will still be around five or more years from now should you decide to order an extra print. Visit the studio in person, examine the photographer's work (especially wedding party shots, family groups, and candids).

If you're having engagement and/or wedding portraits made, you may get a special package price, but make sure the photographer is good at both portrait work and candids. Again, once you've agreed on a price, get everything in writing, including:

• The name of the photographer who actually will hold the camera (no substitutes, please), with the exact times, dates, places he is to be.
• All terms of payment: minimum order (and what it includes), amount of deposit, whether there's a penalty for late return of proofs, when final payment is required (before or after you receive finished pictures).
• Cost (and size) of additional prints.
• Whether an album is included (it's usually less expensive for a photographer to supply the album than to buy one yourself, but make sure you have the privilege of "editing" the album, and see what it looks like before committing yourself).
• Specifics about the photographs: black and white or color prints; transparencies; slides; 8mm film; etc.
• Before the wedding and reception, be sure to outline pictures you want taken, together with the names of special guests that should be singled out for photographs.

FLOWERS

You clearly specified white lilacs, and you are crushed when you see gladiolas instead. Did you get a confirmation of your order in writing? Or did you leave the flowers to the caterer or church or hotel? If you really care (and most brides seem to), you'll want to specify exactly what flowers, leaves, and containers you want used, exactly how many arrangements are needed, how large they should be, where they are to be placed, what type of ribbon (if any) will adorn bouquets and corsages, and exactly where and when the flowers are to be delivered.

To keep flower costs in line, find out what blossoms are in season, and consider renting flowering plants to decorate church or reception room. In lieu of more traditional floral arrangements as table centerpieces at the reception, fresh fruit and fruit blossoms attractively arranged in baskets have their practical side; they can be carried home by family and guests for future enjoyment.

MUSIC

If you're being married in a church or temple, consult with the clergy member for suggestions, and possibly restrictions, about music. Traditional selections sometimes can be supplemented by a special arrangement that has personal meaning to the bride and groom. The clergy member can also suggest organists, soloists, cantors, and ensembles who have sung or played at other weddings. Plan the music carefully, and confirm in writing exactly who will provide music, the exact pieces to be included, and the cost. A fanfare of trumpets may seem a dandy idea, but if you're using musicians who are members of the local union, you may find you're paying them for a whole evening's worth of trumpeting even though the wedding lasts less than an hour.

At a reception, almost anything goes! Some hotels and banquet rooms do not permit outsiders, however. Before signing up your favorite group or band, check. Also consider whether instruments will have to be rented (piano movers can be very expensive), and whether the sound system is appropriate. If you have no preset ideas about who should play, the caterer can give you two or three suggestions, but hear them all before signing on the dotted line.

To economize a bit, don't rule out the use of records or tapes, but do hire a professional to provide the sound equipment and to play the recordings. Also, make the musical selections yourself.

When you receive confirmation about the music in writing (and insist on that), make sure that possible overtime charges are included in case exuberant parents want to continue the party on into the wee hours.

WEDDING FINERY

If yours is to be a formal wedding, order the men's clothing, bridesmaids' gowns, and your own dress well in advance. Keep a copy of all measurements you give the rental firm. Get a written pickup or delivery date on the receipt. Phone or visit the firm several days prior to the wedding to make sure your order is on schedule. If you have gowns custom-made, get written details of the fabric, color, trim, and a swatch of fabric.

It's preferable to deal with a firm you know, but if you can't, ask:

• How long has the firm been in business at the same location?
• What similar-sized wedding parties has it outfitted recently?
• What is the size of the dress shop staff?
• How many other weddings will it be serving the same week as yours? Insist on a delivery date that allows for corrections.
• Is all the work completed in-house?

And don't overlook accessories; you'll want to make sure that shoes, gloves, jewelry conform by reminding attendants in writing what to bring, or by providing them yourself. The groom traditionally supplies gloves and ascots or ties for the ushers and best man, too.

TRANSPORTATION

The logistics of getting bride, groom, families, attendants, and special guests from out of town to a ceremony, from the ceremony to the reception, and back home again (or off on a honeymoon) require special planning. So does parking near the church or temple and/or at the site of the reception. Chauffeur-driven limousines are the easiest, but most expensive, solution. Imaginative, but not necessarily practical, are double-decker buses or horse-drawn carriages. Even if you enlist family and friends, make sure that drivers know whom they're taking where —and when.

CATERING—PUT IT IN WRITING!

Finally, you must make arrangements for the reception (and possibly wedding) with a caterer or hotel or banquet hall.

Check the credentials of the caterer, and comparative-shop for prices.

Leave *nothing* to verbal agreements. When you are close to making a decision, tell your choice that, before you make final arrangements, you would like to visit a wedding the caterer is handling.

If you're holding the party at a private or community club, hotel, restaurant, or banquet club, ask whether there is a rental fee for the space—in addition to other costs.

Among points to consider:

• Date and hours—are they available? If there's another event scheduled immediately before or after yours, look elsewhere.

• Number of guests—is the size appropriate?

• Type of party—do you want a buffet meal, sit-down dinner, cocktails and hors d'oeuvres, punch and cake? Get prices for all.

• How many waiters will there be? bartenders? And what are their overtime rates if the reception lasts longer than expected?

• Determine the location of the receiving line, dance floor and bandstand, rest rooms, cloakroom, dressing rooms for bride, groom, and attendants, parking facilities.

• Specify brands of liquor and wine—and exactly when each will be served, and how much.

• Does the caterer provide entertainment or a master of ceremonies? Unless you know the act, you may want to hide under a table with embarrassment!

• Exactly what linens, silver, china, and glassware will be used? If you're shown elegant service pieces, make sure they are described—and specified—in the contract.

• From candles to cake knife, make certain that every last detail is mentioned, and priced.

WHAT HAPPENS IF PLANS CHANGE?

If you become ill, or the wedding is postponed or canceled for any of a number of reasons, what then? When contracting for products and services, make sure that written agreements specify what you do (or don't) have to pay for if you don't take delivery, and by what date you must give notification before your commitment is uncancelable.

Changing your mind at the last minute can be very expensive!

THE HONEYMOON AND ITS EXPENSES

After the vows are said, the next major expense is the honeymoon, usually paid for by the husband.

There are so many variations on honeymoon expenses that to get an idea of costs I must invent a mythical couple. Okay, you're invented: you're an average groom and you're submitting typical questions.

Q. *How long is the average honeymoon trip?*
A. About nine days.

Q. *What is the average cost?*
A. It was about $720 in the late 1970s. Outside the United States (excluding Canada and Mexico) the average cost was well over $1,000. A survey of *Bride's* readers indicates they travel an average of 1,980 miles on a honeymoon trip.

Q. *How do honeymooners in the States travel?*
A. Most couples go by car, about 30 per cent fly, the rest use rail or sea transportation.

Q. *What about a honeymoon abroad?*
A. In this case, you should have at least two or three weeks to make it worthwhile. If you get in on a special cut-rate deal, though, your transportation costs will be slashed. Your expenses in other countries are subject to enormous variation.

Q. *What about honeymoon costs in big cities?*
A. Again, the costs of honeymooning in such cities as New York, New Orleans, San Francisco, etc. vary immensely, but if you are a typical couple spending a week or so in one of these cities, you should expect to spend $500, $1,000, or more.

HOW TO SAVE ON YOUR WEDDING AND HONEYMOON

How can you save money and still have the wedding and honeymoon you want? Here are six tips:

(1) Consider having a home wedding, an obvious major money-saving area. Make your reception simple. The completely open bar is giving way to a controlled serving of wine, champagne, or punch.

(2) Have a cocktail buffet instead of a sit-down dinner. It can be just as satisfying and will be much cheaper.

(3) Or consider the services of a "wedding palace"—a professional catering establishment which provides bells-to-bonbons wedding packages at various price levels.

(4) Choose a wedding dress that you can use for other occasions or even consider renting or borrowing a dress.

(5) Also select dresses for your attendants which they can use for other occasions, and the same goes for the costumes of the mothers.

(6) For your honeymoon, work with travel agents on package deals—and take advantage of bargain flights if you're going abroad. If you're renting a car, make it a compact. Plan ahead and, if feasible, make your reservations well in advance to take full advantage of any money-saving offers.

RULES FOR BUYING WEDDING GIFTS

You need not spend nearly as much for wedding gifts as you think. Nor do you need to waste nearly as much time and effort as you do. Having learned over the years the value of expert guidance in this wedding minuet, I pass along to you my key hints on wedding gifts:

• Find out if and where the bride has registered for gifts and take advantage of the bridal registry to give her what she needs and wants. You can buy almost anything at a bridal registry now, for the concept has been broadened to include furniture, carpeting, and bedding as well as silver, china, and stemware.

• Decide at the start how much you want to spend and don't fall into the trap of spending too much in order to impress the bride's friends or to "repay" her family for a gift to your child. The gift-for-gift idea is costly, and in bad taste.

• Buy with an eye to the bride's life-style. What are her tastes, profession, plans? Will she live on a campus, in a city or suburb? In a private home or apartment? How does she dress?

• Stay away from "the most original gift in the world," for these are the gifts most often returned or exchanged.

• If you're a relative, resist overstressing your own tastes when the bride is registering her patterns and gift choices at her favorite store.

• If you're the bridegroom, be sure you, too, respect your bride's selections.

• Find out how sophisticated a cook the bride is. Be sure that the set of gourmet cookbooks or the case of rare wine you may offer is a respectful reflection of her interest (rather than yours) in the art of cooking and dining.

• When in doubt, buy quality silver; it probably will continue to rise substantially in value in coming years.

AFTER THE WEDDING IS OVER

You've set up your home and furnished it; your thank-you notes are written; you've talked to your insurance agents, notified the Social Security Administration of your marriage (and name change), rewritten your wills, and changed the beneficiaries on company pension and profit-sharing plans.

In all likelihood, you'll continue to work (80 per cent of all brides work either full or part time, and 95 per cent will stay on the job at least for a while after the wedding)

Although you're not in the mood to contemplate such endings at this stage, the odds are almost 50-50 that your marriage will end in divorce. Whether or not it does, be prepared!

A Bride's Guide to Credit

You are about to establish credit standing as individuals as well as a husband-wife team. The following are twelve fundamental guides for women particularly:

(1) Open both checking and savings accounts at your bank in order to create financial identities. While these accounts in themselves do not build your credit history, they lead you to other lines of credit, such as bank credit cards, overdraft checking privileges, automobile loans, personal loans, mortgages, etc.

(2) Speed up your credit-building process, if you so desire, by taking out a small loan from your bank in your own name and then pay it back promptly. This transaction will be recorded in your favor, as an individual woman and wife, at the credit bureau.

(3) Buy some appliance or other product you want on the installment plan and open charge accounts at retail stores, again in your name, and here, too, be extra careful about your repayments. All this activity will establish your name at the bank and local credit bureau as a good credit risk.

(4) While you are building your credit rating, obey the basic limits on prudent borrowing. As one rule of thumb, the American Bankers Association suggests that not more than 10 to 15 per cent of your income should be used to repay loans—not counting your mortgage payments.

(5) As soon as you qualify, get a free credit card from your bank and use it as another loan device. When you use your card, you have at least thirty days before a payment comes due, and usually the period is even longer. During that time, you are using the bank's money, and if you pay your bank card bill in full each month, you won't pay any interest on this credit.

(6) Double-check to see whether your bank does indeed not charge you if you pay within the thirty-day limit, for some banks have started charging a monthly administrative fee even on accounts paid in full within the stated period. On the part of your bill not paid within the time limit, you will be charged 1½ per cent interest per month, or 18 per cent a year.

(7) Do use your credit cards to take advantage of unusual bargains. (Say, for instance, you grab a $350 air conditioner on sale at $300 and extend your credit card payments for three months. Even with the 1½ per cent per month interest on the balance, you still will realize 75 per cent of the savings you achieved by seizing the bargain while the price was right.)

(8) Take advantage, too, of overdraft checking—a credit tool that lets you write checks for more money than you have in the bank without fear that the check will bounce. The amount of overdrafts you'll be permitted to make will be based on the credit history you are now establishing, and the charge will be about 1 per cent a month or 12 per cent interest a year. (The average overdraft in the United States today is about $1,000.)

(9) As a working wife, your creditors must consider the combined income of both you and your husband when you apply for credit—and that goes even if

your work is only part time. Be sure your banker does not discriminate against you because of your sex.

(10) Become fully informed about the federal laws now in effect which forbid lenders from forcing you to reapply for credit, or impose new conditions when you get married. If you had a credit-worthy history before you were married, it is still valid now that you have become a wife and, quite probably, assumed your husband's last name. (See pages 1218–19 on your rights as a borrower.)

(11) If you want to keep your credit accounts separate from your husband's, just write your creditors, tell them your new name, and explain that you will continue to be as credit-worthy as before. The credit bureau and bank then will maintain independent histories of your credit standing.

(12) As a wife, use your own personal first name for credit account purposes —not your husband's first name. Credit under your husband's first name is merely an extension of his credit, and does nothing to establish your independent credit history for the future.

THE LOW COST OF NOT HAVING A BABY (OR HAVING FEWER OF THEM)

THE NEED FOR FAMILY PLANNING

Family planning permits couples to say whether and when to have a baby. Some couples have religious or other reasons that may dispose them against certain methods of family planning; but most will endorse the principle that planning of some sort is desirable if children are to be properly cared for and families not strained to the breaking point.

GETTING LOW-COST OR FREE HELP IN FAMILY PLANNING

Where do you get family planning help?

• Your best source of clinic care is Planned Parenthood, which in the 1970s had 191 local affiliates operating more than 750 medically supervised clinics in forty-three states plus the District of Columbia. Fees vary around the country, and often are based on your income. However, *no one is ever turned away because of inability to pay.*

In San Francisco in the late 1970s fees ranged from $29 down to $10 for a year's services relating to contraception, including follow-up visits for any complications. A month's supply of pills cost $2.00 while other contraceptives cost much less than their usual retail price. In New York City, Planned Parenthood's fee for pregnancy detection was $15. Fees are adjustable and deferred payment may be worked out. The fees are never more than the patient can afford.

• For the location of the PP affiliate nearest you, check the white pages of your telephone directory or contact the organization's national headquarters at 810 Seventh Avenue, New York, New York 10019; telephone (212) 541-7800. The telephone directory's Yellow Pages sometimes show referral or service listings under "Birth Control." And your county medical society will usually be able to give you the names of private doctors offering birth control services in your area.

• If your income is limited, you should be able to get free or low-cost service from government-subsidized family planning clinics run by PP, county health departments, county hospitals, and neighborhood health centers. Medicaid recipients are eligible to receive free family planning services and supplies in most states.

• Some private hospitals also run family planning clinics, as do many community clinics and group practice plans. Inquire at facilities of this type or ask your regular physician for assistance.

Important note: An increasing number of private physicians and clinics (including Planned Parenthood) will provide birth control services, on a confidential basis, to minors upon their own request. Such physicians and clinics may offer treatment and services without charge. In some, however, parental consent is still required.

Finally, along with birth control services, many all-purpose outpatient clinics and health centers have been opening up and offering a whole spectrum of health services for women.

CONTRACEPTION: COMPARING THE OPTIONS

METHODS AVAILABLE

A full dozen methods of contraception are available today: some obtainable without a doctor's prescription or advice; others requiring a prescription and medical consultation and follow-up.

When choosing a method, the factors to consider are your personal preferences, psychological or religious attitudes, and individual medical history. But many of you looking for a suitable means of contraception know very little about the available methods—how they work, how effective they are, what side effects they may have, what health problems may be related to their use.

Here is basic information on the contraceptive methods most widely used today. It is beginning information only, to help you understand the choices. Discussion with your physician can help you make a selection.

It is essential that you realize no method of contraception is 100 per cent effective and that you must use the method correctly to make it as effective as possible. Other factors also contribute to failure: diaphragms that have been improperly fitted, intrauterine devices (IUDs) that can be expelled without the woman being aware of it, a foam or jelly that might be used too long before intercourse.

Effectiveness figures in the following methods are expressed in terms of pregnancies per 100 woman years, which means the number of women out of 100 who would become pregnant in one year using the method. If no contraceptive method were used 60 to 80 women out of 100 would become pregnant.

A wide range of effectiveness is shown for some methods because people differ in how well they use them. For example, a method may be more effective when used by thirty-year-old college graduates but less effective when used by teenagers in high school.

THE PILL

Prescription Required

"The Pill" refers to any of the oral contraceptives. The most widely used contains two female hormones, estrogen and progestin, and is taken twenty-one days each month. Another (sometimes called the "minipill") contains progestin only and is taken every day. You should be sure you receive from your druggist, doctor, or person who gives you the pills an FDA-required brochure that explains the use, benefits, and risks of the product in greater detail.

Effectiveness

Effectiveness depends on how correctly the method is used.

Of 100 women who use the combination estrogen and progestin pill for one year, fewer than 1 will become pregnant. Of 100 women who use the progestin-only pill (minipill) for one year, 2 to 3 will become pregnant.

Advantages-Disadvantages

Advantages. The combination pill is the most effective of the popular methods for preventing pregnancy.

No inconvenient devices to bother with at time of intercourse.

Disadvantages. Must be taken regularly and exactly as instructed by the prescribing physician.

Side Effects

Side effects may include tender breasts, nausea or vomiting, gain or loss of weight, unexpected vaginal bleeding, higher levels of sugar and fat in the blood. Although it happens infrequently, use of the Pill can cause blood clots (in the lungs, brain, and heart). A clot that reaches the lungs or forms in the brain or heart can be fatal. Pill users have a greater risk of heart attack and stroke than non-users. This risk increases with age and is greater if the Pill user smokes.

Some Pill users tend to develop high blood pressure, but it usually is mild and may be reversed by discontinuing use. Pill users have a greater risk than non-users of having gallbladder disease requiring surgery. There is no evidence that taking the Pill increases the risk of cancer. Benign liver tumors occur very rarely in women on the Pill. Sometimes they rupture, causing fatal hemorrhage.

Health Factors to Consider

Women who smoke should not use the Pill because smoking increases the risk of heart attack or stroke. Other women who should not take the Pill are those who have had a heart attack, stroke, angina pectoris, blood clots, cancer of the breast or uterus, or scanty or irregular periods. A woman who believes she may be pregnant should not take the Pill because it increases the risk of defects in the fetus.

Health problems such as migraine headaches, mental depression, fibroids of the uterus, heart or kidney disease, asthma, high blood pressure, diabetes, or epilepsy may be made worse by use of the Pill.

Risks associated with the Pill increase with age, and as a woman enters her late thirties it is generally advisable to seek another method of contraception.

Long-term Effect on Ability to Have Children

There is no evidence that using the Pill will prevent a woman from becoming pregnant after she stops taking it, although there may be a delay before she is able to become pregnant. Women should wait a short time after stopping the Pill before becoming pregnant. During this time another method of contraception should be used. After childbirth the woman should consult her doctor before resuming use of the Pill. This is especially true for nursing mothers because the drugs in the Pill appear in the milk and the long-range effect on the infant is not known.

INTRAUTERINE DEVICE (IUD)

Prescription Required

The IUD is a small plastic or metal device that is placed in the uterus (womb) through the cervical canal (opening into the uterus). As long as the IUD stays in place pregnancy is prevented. Although how the IUD prevents pregnancy is not completely understood, IUDs seem to interfere in some manner with implantation of the fertilized egg in the wall of the uterus There were five kinds of IUDs available at the start of the 1980s—Copper-7, Copper-T, Progestasert, Lippes Loop, and Saf-T-Coil. IUDs containing copper (Copper-7 and Copper-T) should be replaced every three years; those containing progesterone (Progestasert) should be replaced every year.

Effectiveness

Effectiveness depends on proper insertion by the physician and whether the IUD remains in place. Of 100 women who use an IUD for one year, 1 to 6 will become pregnant.

Advantages-Disadvantages

Advantages. Insertion by a physician, then no further care needed, except to see that the IUD remains in place (the user can check it herself but should be checked once a year by her doctor).

Disadvantages. May cause pain or discomfort when inserted; afterward may cause cramps and a heavier menstrual flow. Some women will experience adverse effects that require removal of the IUD. The IUD can be expelled, sometimes without the woman being aware of it, leaving her unprotected.

Side Effects

Major complications, which are infrequent, include anemia, pregnancy outside the uterus, pelvic infection, perforation of the uterus or cervix, and septic abortion. A woman with heavy or irregular bleeding while using an IUD should consult her physician. Removal of the IUD may be necessary to prevent anemia.

Women susceptible to pelvic infection are more prone to infection when using an IUD.

Serious complications can occur if a woman becomes pregnant while using an IUD. Though rare, cases of blood poisoning, miscarriage, and even death have been reported. An IUD user who believes she may be pregnant should consult her doctor immediately. If pregnancy is confirmed, the IUD should be removed. Although it rarely happens, the IUD can pierce the wall of the uterus when it is being inserted. Surgery is required to remove it.

Health Factors to Consider

Before having an IUD inserted, a woman should tell her doctor if she has had any of the following: cancer or other abnormalities of the uterus or cervix; bleeding between periods or heavy menstrual flow; infection of the uterus, cervix, or pelvis (pus in fallopian tubes); prior IUD use; recent pregnancy, abortion, or miscarriage; uterine surgery; venereal disease; severe menstrual cramps; allergy to copper; anemia; fainting attacks; unexplained genital bleeding or vaginal discharge; suspicious or abnormal Pap smear.

Long-term Effect on Ability to Have Children

Pelvic infection in some IUD users may result in their future inability to have children.

DIAPHRAGM (WITH CREAM, JELLY, OR FOAM)

Prescription Required

A diaphragm is a shallow cup of thin rubber stretched over a flexible ring. A sperm-killing cream, jelly, or foam is put on both sides of the diaphragm, which you then place inside your vagina before intercourse. The device covers the opening of the uterus, thus preventing the sperm from entering the uterus.

Effectiveness

Effectiveness depends on how correctly the method is used. Of 100 women who use the diaphragm with a spermicidal product for one year, 2 to 20 will become pregnant.

Advantages-Disadvantages

Advantages. No routine schedule to be kept as with the Pill. The diaphragm with a spermicidal product is inserted by the user. Can be inserted up to two hours before intercourse.

No discomfort or cramping, as with the IUD. No effect on the chemical or physical processes of the body, as with the Pill or the IUD.

Disadvantages. Must be inserted before each intercourse and stay in place at least six hours afterwards.

Size and fit require yearly checkup, and should be checked if woman gains or loses more than 10 pounds. Should be refitted after childbirth or abortion.

Requires instruction on insertion technique. Some women find it difficult to insert and inconvenient to use.

Some women in whom the vagina is greatly relaxed, or in whom the uterus has "fallen," cannot use a diaphragm successfully.

Side Effects

No serious side effects.

Possible allergic reaction to the rubber or the spermicidal jelly. Condition easily corrected.

Health Factors to Consider

None.

Long-term Effect on Ability to Have Children

None.

FOAM, CREAM, OR JELLY ALONE

No Prescription Required

Several brands of vaginal foam, cream, or jelly can be used without a diaphragm. They form a chemical barrier at the opening of the uterus that prevents sperm from reaching an egg in the uterus; they also destroy sperm.

Effectiveness

Effectiveness depends on how correctly the method is used. Of 100 women who use aerosol foams alone for one year, 2 to 29 will become pregnant. Of 100 women who use jellies and creams alone for one year, 4 to 36 will become pregnant.

Advantages-Disadvantages

Advantages. Easy to obtain and use.
Disadvantages. Must be used one hour or less before intercourse. If douching is desired, must wait six to eight hours after intercourse.

Side Effects

No serious side effects. Burning or irritation of the vagina or penis may occur. Allergic reaction may be corrected by changing brands.

Health Factors to Consider

None.

Long-term Effect on Ability to Have Children

None.

VAGINAL SUPPOSITORIES

No Prescription Required

Vaginal suppositories are small waxy "tablets" that are placed at the opening of the uterus just before intercourse. Note: very few vaginal suppositories are intended for birth control. Ask before you buy.

Effectiveness

No figures available, considered fair to poor.

Advantages-Disadvantages

Advantages. No devices needed.

Disadvantages. Must be inserted fifteen minutes before intercourse. If placed earlier, they may become ineffective. If placed later (too close to intercourse) the suppository will not have time to melt and will be ineffective.

Side Effects

No adverse side effects.

Health Factors to Consider

None.

Long-term Effect on Ability to Have Children

None.

RHYTHM METHOD

The woman must refrain from sexual intercourse on days surrounding the predicted time of monthly ovulation or, for a higher degree of effectiveness, until a few days after the predicted time of ovulation. Ways to determine the approximate time of ovulation include a calendar method, a method based on body temperature, and a mucus method. Using the calendar method requires careful record-keeping of the time of the menstrual period, and calculation of the time in the month when the woman is fertile and must not have intercourse. To use the temperature method, you must use a special type of thermometer and keep an accurate daily record of your body temperature (body temperature rises after ovulation). To use the mucus method you, the woman, also must keep an accurate daily record of the type of vaginal secretions present. The temperature method or the mucus method used alone or concurrently with the calendar method are more effective than the calendar method alone.

Effectiveness

Effectiveness depends on how correctly the method is used. Of 100 women who use the temperature method for one year, 1 to 20 will become pregnant. Of 100 women who use the mucus method for one year, 1 to 25 will become pregnant. Of 100 women who use for one year the temperature or mucus method with intercourse only after ovulation, fewer than 1 to 7 will become pregnant.

Advantages-Disadvantages

Advantages. No drugs or devices needed.

Disadvantages. Requires careful record-keeping and estimation of the time each month when there can be no intercourse.

To use any of the three methods properly a physician's guidance may be needed, at least at the outset.

If menstrual cycles are irregular, it is especially difficult to use this method effectively.

Dissatisfaction because of extended time each month when sexual intercourse must be avoided.

Side Effects

No physical effects, but because the couple must refrain from having intercourse except on certain days of the month, using this method can create pressures on the couple's relationship.

Health Factors to Consider

None.

Long-term Effect on Ability to Have Children

None.

CONDOM

No Prescription Required

The condom is a thin sheath of rubber or processed lamb cecum that fits over the penis.

Effectiveness

Effectiveness depends on how correctly the method is used.

Of 100 women whose partner uses a condom for one year, 3 to 36 women will become pregnant.

Advantages-Disadvantages

Advantages. In addition to contraception, may afford some protection against venereal disease.

Easily available. Requires no "long-term" planning before intercourse.

Disadvantages. Some people feel the condom reduces pleasure in the sex act.

The male must interrupt foreplay and fit the condom in place before sexual entry into the woman.

The condom can slip or tear during use or spill during removal from the vagina.

Side Effects

No serious side effects. Occasionally an individual will be allergic to the rubber, causing burning, irritation, itching, rash, or swelling, but this can easily be treated. Switching to the natural skin condom may be a solution.

Health Factors to Consider

None.

Long-term Effect on Ability to Have Children

None.

FEMALE STERILIZATION

The primary method of sterilization for women is tubal sterilization, commonly referred to as "tying the tubes." A surgeon cuts, ties, or seals the fallopian tubes to prevent passage of eggs between the ovaries and the uterus. Several techniques are available. With one new technique, the operation can be performed in a hospital outpatient surgical clinic with either a local or general anesthetic. Using this method, the doctor makes a tiny incision in the abdomen or vagina and blocks the tubes by cutting, sealing with an electric current, or applying a small band or clip. Hysterectomy, a surgical procedure involving removal of all or part of the uterus, also prevents pregnancy, but is performed for other medical reasons and is not considered primarily a method of sterilization.

Effectiveness

Virtually 100 per cent.

Advantages-Disadvantages

Advantages. A one-time procedure—never any more bother with devices or preparations of any kind.

Disadvantages. Surgery is required. Although in some cases a sterilization procedure has been reversed through surgery, the procedure should be considered permanent.

Side Effects

As with any surgery, occasionally there are complications such as severe bleeding, infection, or injury to other organs which may require additional surgery to correct.

Health Factors to Consider

There is some risk associated with any surgical procedure, which varies with the general health of the patient.

Long-term Effect on Ability to Have Children

Procedure should be considered non-reversible. Once the surgery is performed successfully, the woman cannot become pregnant. There have been exceptions, but they are very uncommon.

MALE STERILIZATION

Sterilization of men involves severing the tubes through which the sperm travel to become part of the semen. The man continues to produce sperm but they are absorbed by the body rather than being released into the semen. This operation, called a vasectomy, takes about half an hour and may be performed in a doctor's office under local anesthetic. A vasectomy does not affect a man's physical ability to have intercourse.

Effectiveness

Virtually 100 per cent.

Advantages-Disadvantages

Advantages. A one-time procedure that does not require hospitalization and permits the man to resume normal activity almost immediately.

Disadvantages. Although in some cases a vasectomy may be reversed, it should be considered permanent.

The man is not sterile immediately after the operation—usually it takes a few months. Other means of contraception must be used during that time.

Side Effects

Complications occur in 2 to 4 per cent of cases, including infection, hematoma (trapped mass of clotted blood), granuloma (an inflammatory reaction to sperm that is absorbed by the body), and swelling and tenderness near the testes. Most such complications are minor and are treatable without surgery.

Studies by the National Institutes of Health show that vasectomy does not affect a man's sexual desire or ability.

Health Factors to Consider

None.

Long-term Effect on Ability to Have Children

Procedure is considered non-reversible. Once surgery is performed successfully, the man cannot father children. There have been exceptions, but they are very uncommon.

WITHDRAWAL (COITUS INTERRUPTUS)

This method of contraception requires withdrawal of the male organ (penis) from the vagina before the man ejaculates so the male sperm are not deposited at or near the birth canal. The failure rate with this method is high and it should not be considered effective for preventing pregnancy.

DOUCHING

Use of a vaginal douche immediately after sexual intercourse to wash out or inactivate sperm is completely ineffective for preventing pregnancy.

SOURCE: U. S. Department of Health, Education, and Welfare; Public Health Service, Food and Drug Administration, Office of Public Affairs, 5600 Fishers Lane, Rockville, Maryland 20857, HEW Publication No. (FDA) 78-3069.

COMPARATIVE COSTS OF CONTRACEPTIVE METHODS

The cost of preventing pregnancy can range from zero to more than $500, depending on the method you choose. Terminating a pregnancy also may cost you nothing, depending on your financial circumstances. However, using effective contraceptive methods is to be preferred to abortion for a variety of reasons—medical and personal as well as economic.

The method you choose to plan and space the birth of your children should depend largely on the factors already outlined. Still, you probably will wonder how the costs of the various methods compare, so here is a rundown.

The following chart summarizes the longer-range costs (1979) of each major type of birth control—annually and over a lifetime. Sexual activity one hundred times a year is assumed, over a period of thirty years during which fertility is an issue. It also is assumed that any checkups and follow-ups relating to using each method will not be counted as an "extra" cost. Gynecology exam costs not related to contraceptive use are not included in this table.

METHOD	FIRST YEAR COST	LIFETIME COST
Rhythm (calendar method)	No Cost	No Cost
Withdrawal	No Cost	No Cost
Condom*	$35 to $125	$1,050 to $3,750
Foam	$22.50 to $39.50	$675 to $1,185
Diaphragm†	$42 to $54.50	$804 to $879
IUD†	$40 to $100	$620 to $1,559
Pill†	$67 to $136	$2,210 to $4,080
Sterilization		Male: $50 to $250
		Female: $650 to $1,120

STERILIZATION

Sterilization, or permanent contraception, may well be the most costly method of birth control in terms of initial outlay. However, even a payment of $500 for the procedure could be less than the cost of the Pill taken over, say, a fifteen-year period. If your insurance covers sterilization, out-of-pocket costs to the patient may be only $100 or even less.

Sterilization also has the advantage of being virtually failproof. The failure rate for sterilization (male or female) is a minuscule .003 pregnancies for each 100 woman-years of use.

The male operation—the vasectomy—can be done in a doctor's office in only twenty minutes and costs about $250, although there are the usual variations above and below this. Fees at vasectomy clinics range from $150 down to zero, depending on the economic circumstances of the family involved. For the sake of the patient who may have some postoperative discomfort, doctors often schedule vasectomies on a Friday or Saturday so the patient is able to avoid missing time from work.

For a female, the most common surgical procedure, tubal ligation, as the 1980s neared, cost an average of $500, plus the charges for the one- to five-day hospital stay that this procedure usually entails. (The operation itself seldom takes more

* Assumes 35 cents for plain latex; $1.25 for membrane (skin).
† Includes annual checkups after first year.

than twenty to thirty minutes. With today's charges for a semi-private room this could easily bring your total cost to between $650 and $1,120, not counting such "extras" as operating-room charges.)

To shave some of these costs and also for convenience, you may want to have the operation performed while you are in the hospital for the delivery of what you have decided will be your last child. Your recovery from the operation should take little time more than the usual recovery time from childbirth—perhaps an additional day or two.

In a few areas, female sterilization is now being done on an outpatient basis by a technique known as laparoscopy. With total time in the hospital reduced to less than twelve hours, costs are somewhat lower. Hospitals using this technique charge from $400 to $500 for the procedure, covering both the doctor's and hospital fees. Planned Parenthood's Laparoscopy Clinic in Syracuse charges $375—which includes the total package: surgeon's fee, operating room, initial fee, etc.

If you want further information or if you have trouble in getting a sterilization operation, contact the Association for Voluntary Sterilization, a nationwide organization, headquartered at 708 Third Avenue, New York, New York 10017; telephone (212) 986-3880. Or contact your local Planned Parenthood affiliate.

BASIC FACTS ABOUT ABORTION

When contraceptive measures fail or are not used, abortion is the only means of stopping an unwanted pregnancy. At one time abortion was a risky, costly procedure that was usually done illegally. Today, however, costs and risks have plummeted and the number of legal instead of illegal abortions performed in the United States has been soaring at a spectacular rate.

The 1973 landmark U. S. Supreme Court decision, in effect, ruled that no state may restrict a woman from getting an abortion for any reason during her first trimester (twelve weeks) of pregnancy. The ruling also specified that states could intervene in the second trimester only to protect the health of the woman— through medical regulations covering the licensing of the facilities and persons involved. Although a number of state legislatures have contested this Supreme Court decision, these challenges had not reversed the fundamental trend (as of the late 1970s) toward abortion on request—by unmarried and married women.

In the late 1970s an estimated 700,000 American women were undergoing legal abortions each year, compared to only about 6,000 in 1966, the year before Colorado became the first state to rewrite its restrictive law.

Costs, however, still remain a significant factor, although they are now generally far below what people were forced to pay in years past for an illegal abortion. They range across the nation from zero to $500, depending on the span of your pregnancy, your financial status, and, of course, the type of hospital, clinic, or office in which the abortion is done.

Here were typical charges in the late 1970s:

• At a New York state-licensed clinic or city hospital, an early abortion (done during the first twelve weeks of pregnancy, usually by vacuum aspiration or "suction") cost $140 to $175. This was generally also the top fee at similar facilities throughout the country.

• At a New York City voluntary (non-profit) hospital, the same procedure generally cost $200, while at private hospitals through private physicians, the fees began at $350 and varied greatly, depending on the individuals involved.

• Early second-trimester abortions (fourteenth to sixteenth week of pregnancy) at some hospitals and clinics are now being performed by "D&E" (dilation and evacuation), another vaginal method. Costs for this service may range as high as $300, according to the medical facility or anesthesia used. Late second-trimester abortions (sixteenth to twenty-fourth weeks) may be performed by saline injection, which induces labor. These are not only more risky but also cost more, since they may require a few days' hospitalization. You can count on paying at least double what you would have paid for an early abortion, with all-inclusive fees starting at a minimum of $350, but generally reaching totals significantly higher than this.

Since it may be difficult to get an abortion in some hospitals, communities, or states, you may have to add transportation and other travel expenses involved in getting to a place where you can have the operation.

How to Shop for—and Reduce the Costs of—an Abortion

• First, and above all, consult your family doctor or obstetrician or family planning clinic, and the sooner the better! *Avoid* profit-making abortion referral agencies which you may have seen advertised in your newspaper; you should *not* have to pay for a referral. Keep in mind that the cost and complexity of an abortion go up sharply after the twelfth week of pregnancy. Late abortions, it has been found, are three to four times more likely to result in complications than early abortions.

Keep in mind, too, that when you have missed one menstrual period you could be up to four weeks pregnant. If you've missed two periods, you may be as many as eight weeks pregnant. (Weeks are calculated from the last menstrual period, so actually at a missed period the week count is four.) Also, you should wait a full two weeks after a missed period to get an accurate reading of your possible pregnancy. Tests may show a false negative before this. If you have doubts about the reliability of your pregnancy test, repeat it to be sure the result is accurate.

If your doctor or clinic is unable or unwilling to arrange an abortion, call your local hospital and ask for a recommendation of a qualified physician or a specialist in obstetrics and gynecology ("OBG"). Also helpful may be your city or county public health department or medical society.

• Or you can look under "Birth Control" in the Yellow Pages of your telephone directory. In addition to local independent agencies such as women's groups or college counseling services, you also may find chapters or affiliates of such nationwide, non-profit organizations as Planned Parenthood, the Clergy Consultation Service, and Zero Population Growth (ZPG). The referrals and pregnancy counseling services of Planned Parenthood and the Clergy Consultation Service often are free.

• If none of these three organizations has an office near you, you can contact them at their central office or referral services:

Family Planning Information Service of Planned Parenthood, 380 Second Avenue, New York, New York 10010; telephone (212) 677-3040.

National Clergy Consultation Service, 55 Washington Square South, New York, New York 10012; telephone (212) 254-6230.

Zero Population Growth of New York, 52 Vanderbilt Avenue, New York, New York 10017; telephone (212) 697-3877.

These agencies, as well as others, also provide information on such alternatives to abortion as placing the child for adoption.

Quality is the most important factor in choosing the best abortion service. You may find you've been penny-wise and pound-foolish if you let cost considerations alone guide you in choosing. A phone call to any of the above organizations can help you make an informed decision, or you can call the National Organization for Women (NOW) in Chicago or its local office in your area.

Here are additional guides:

Whether you are dealing with a private doctor or with a clinic, make sure that you know what your *total* cost will be, including hospitalization (if necessary), medication, lab work, and checkup exam (usually two to three weeks after the abortion). Special medication, for example, may be necessary for Rh-negative patients. Not all doctors and clinics will volunteer this information. Then you may want to compare the range of charges elsewhere.

Agree on the payment terms before the operation, especially if you have to travel. In most cases, full payment is required in advance, particularly if you are a transient. Personal checks are generally not accepted. Some hospitals, however, take VISA or Master Charge.

If you are a woman in severe financial distress, ask an abortion-referral agency for suggestions of doctors and clinics who will perform abortions at reduced or no cost. Many states no longer pay for Medicaid abortions.

INSURANCE COVERAGE

FOR ABORTIONS

Abortion coverage is generally found within the maternity provisions of group health contracts. However, the coverage may be restricted. It can be spelled out in the contract itself. Single women may be covered. Daughters of insured workers may not be covered. A waiting period may be applied to married women and daughters who are covered. Usually conception must have taken place during the contract period. The size of the benefits may be very small, etc.

So far as Blue Cross and Blue Shield are concerned, in most local plans hospital and surgical expenses for abortion are covered. But there may be conflicts in coverage by Blue Cross (for hospital expenses) and Blue Shield (for surgical costs). For example, a Blue Shield plan may cover abortion while the Blue Cross plan in the same area does not.

In general, however, where a local Blue Cross plan offers obstetrical benefits, any abortions performed would be considered obstetrical benefits and covered according to the provisions of the specific contract. Where obstetrical benefits are restricted to family contracts, wives and single female dependents (usually those under nineteen years of age) would be covered.

Some Blue Cross plans now offer such coverage to all persons—including single women and dependent children—on all contracts. In fact, the Blue Cross Association has adopted a policy requiring its member plans to make abortion coverage available to all subscribers (including single women and female dependents) enrolled in *national* contracts—i.e., people belonging to large groups which include employees in more than one state.

Under this expanded benefit, new women enrollees who become pregnant no longer have to wait nine months before becoming eligible for coverage for a legal abortion. *But* it is *not* automatically included in national contracts—only to those specifically requesting it. Similar riders are available on a local basis, but again, only to those groups who want to include it as a benefit. Check your plan to see if and how your abortion is covered *before* you obtain one.

FOR STERILIZATION

Some Blue Cross policies also cover sterilization in a hospital for contraceptive reasons or for reasons of medical necessity—including vasectomy, tubal ligation, and the newer laparoscopy method. In a few areas, however, you are covered only after a specified waiting period.

Blue Shield may cover the cost of office vasectomies and in states where this is so, Blue Shield may pay from one third to one half of the fee for the procedure. Blue Shield covers sterilizations performed in a hospital, for either sex. Since there are wide variations in these and other health insurance contracts, you must check your *own coverage,* to be sure of the extent to which you are protected.

Medicaid—which covers eligible low-income families and individuals—pays for sterilization for medical reasons in all states with Medicaid plans (as of the late 1970s, Arizona had no Medicaid program).

But a fundamental point as the 1980s neared was that coverage for costs was "fragmented." In the words of a nationally acknowledged expert on the subject, Charlotte F. Muller, Associate Director, Center for Social Research, City University of New York, "group health insurance . . . has made an incomplete adaptation to legalization of abortion, and has done little to promote or underwrite contraception . . ."

Or putting it in blunter words, *you* still are mostly on your own.

TAX TIPS ON BIRTH CONTROL PILLS, ABORTIONS, STERILIZATION

If you practice some form of birth control, virtually all your expenses now qualify as medical expenses that you can take as part of your itemized medical expense deduction. This includes: birth control pills you buy for your own personal use through a prescription provided by your physician and the costs of an operation for an abortion or sterilization, male or female, undertaken voluntarily, assuming the operation was legal under the applicable state law.

How Much Does It Cost to Have (or Adopt) a Baby?

All signs are now pointing toward substantial and continuing moderation in procreation. A first reason is that you are postponing your marriages—and, therefore, you are shortening your childbearing years. A second is that more women are now attending college for longer periods of time, and taking full-time jobs. And a third powerful force slowing our population growth rate is, I submit, the high cost of having babies and bringing them up.

Rundown on Costs of Having a Baby

It's not news to you that baby costs of every kind have been spiraling upward —primarily obstetricians' fees and hospital charges. In addition, we are going in for ever more expensive nursery supplies and other "baby equipment." So steep have been the increases that, according to the Health Insurance Institute, as the 1980s neared, the total cost of having a baby passed the $2,600 mark. That included only costs through the baby's first week at home.

Biggest expense of all is, of course, hospital care. In the late 1970s a single day in a short-term general hospital cost more than $145, and the average hospital stay in maternity cases is now about four days. Delivery room, nursery room charges, and other items count as "extras."

Next biggest cost is the layette for the baby—which easily can total more than $700. The layette includes a basic wardrobe for the baby plus a full range of nursery items, baby furniture, bathing equipment, etc.

Third biggest item is medical care—covering an obstetrician's services, usually offered as a complete package, through the delivery and hospital stay; plus a circumcision fee; plus the cost of a pediatrician's newborn baby care while the baby is in the hospital. Most obstetricians now charge about $400, but some charge $600, $800, or more.

Finally, the cost of a typical maternity wardrobe is calculated by the Health Insurance Institute at about $300.

The grand total adds up to well over $2,600 as the 1980s begin. And under certain circumstances the cost can run even higher. For example:

If you stay in a private room at a fashionable big-city hospital it easily might have cost more than $200 a day in the late 1970s, bringing this part of the cost to $800—far above the rate for a multiple-occupancy room.

If the birth is complicated, if the baby is born with special problems calling for surgery, extensive transfusion, or other special treatment, or if the birth involves caesarean section, the hospital part of the cost could skyrocket. Today about one in twenty babies is born by caesarean section, involving an average hospital stay of eight days, versus four for a normal delivery.

Hospital and physicians' services for a caesarean delivery tend to run about 50 per cent higher than the costs for a normal delivery. About one in twelve newborn babies must be temporarily confined in a glass "isolette"—involving extra charges. Rh blood factor complications at birth also can boost expenses.

If you have twins, this obviously will greatly increase your bills, although some department stores promise to give you a second set of everything if you have twins.

Or you may require expensive extra drugs, use of a fetal monitor, and medications somewhere along the line.

Or your hospital may slap on an extra fee of $150 or more for preparation of the delivery room and sharply increase its rates for nursery accommodations—in many cases to $75 or more per day.

Or if you have a boy you may find that in addition to a circumcision fee there frequently is a circumcision "setup" charge of $12 or so.

In the maternity clothes department, your costs will rise if your baby is born in winter (or early spring) and you need to buy heavy wool or knit clothes instead of lightweight ones. Or you well may decide you need more than two everyday dresses and more than one dress-up dress over the five-to-six-month period when you will need special maternity clothes.

And if you insist on elegant new christening clothes, you'll have no trouble spending $50 to $150 just for a dress.

Ten Ways to Cut the High Costs of Motherhood

But aren't there some circumstances under which the costs of having a baby might be greatly reduced?

Yes. For instance, a second or third child costs a lot less than the first baby—simply because you already have most of the baby and maternity clothes, nursery things, etc. on hand. If you live in a small town or in a rural area, the expenses are likely to be a lot lower than in a big city. Mothers who breast-feed their newborn babies don't have to invest in special formulas.

Here are ten specific ways in which you can cut the high costs of motherhood:

(1) Before you make an arrangement with a specific obstetrician, discuss fees fully and frankly. In your initial consultation ask about fees for prenatal examinations and care, delivery, probable costs of such common complications as breech birth and caesarean section. If you feel you simply cannot afford the fee scale, say so. If the physician isn't willing to reduce the fee, ask him to refer you to a less expensive colleague. It's a perfectly reasonable and legitimate request, so don't be shy.

(2) Go home as soon as sensibly possible after your baby is born, and alert your obstetrician to your desire to do this. You will be more comfortable at home, and the cost of hiring a practical nurse or home health aide at from $35 to $50 a day is far less than the cost of a hospital room. Although the American Hospital Association estimates that the average hospital stay for having a baby is

about four days, some hospitals have shaved this to under three—and some new mothers pack up and go home after only a day or two in the hospital.

(3) Take advantage of all maternity benefits in your health insurance policies or prepaid health plan. A typical policy today contributes from $200 to $350 toward hospital and doctor bills—about half the total—and some policies also contain coverage for costly complications at birth.

(4) Check the coverage your employer (or your husband's employer) provides via group health insurance. If your company does provide group health insurance with a private insurer, chances are three out of four that maternity benefits are included. And the trend here is toward expanded maternity coverage.

(5) Carefully look into the health insurance provisions for your baby-to-be as well as yourself. Does such coverage begin at birth? When the baby is discharged from the hospital? Or when? Whatever the provisions, notify the insurer as soon as your baby is born.

(6) Investigate midwife services or maternity clinics in your neighborhood, generally associated with large teaching hospitals. Although such clinics are often geared to the needs of low-income people or special obstetrical problems, many are open to all—and these alternatives almost invariably offer services at far lower costs than the typical hospital. For more information contact the National Association of Parents and Professionals for Safe Alternatives in Childbirth, Box 267, Marble Hill, Missouri 63764.

(7) In selecting a hospital, find out how room rates are levied. A few hospitals do not charge maternity patients arriving late at night for a full day, but instead charge for part of a day. And if you can, accept a semi-private room; it will be considerably less expensive than a private one.

(8) Eliminate the utterly unimportant, but expensive at-home frills: fancy toys, nursery lamps, bottle warmers, heated plates, bath tables. Let your affluent friends and/or grandparents-to-be come up with such expensive items as dress-up baby clothes.

(9) Check secondhand stores, discount houses, and nationally recognized charities for good, used nursery furniture and other baby equipment. Tell your friends and relatives what you really *need* as baby presents—and don't hesitate to accept what relatives and friends might be happy to pass along.

(10) Explore and compare the costs of signing up for a diaper service versus buying disposable diapers versus buying cloth ones and doing them in your own washing machine.

CHECK LIST FOR YOUR OWN BABY COSTS

You can spot other areas in which you could achieve significant savings simply by going over the following detailed check list of new-baby equipment, on which the $2,600 plus in costs is based.

COST IN YOUR AREA

HOSPITAL AND MEDICAL CARE

    Four days' hospitalization   _____

    Labor and delivery-room charge   _____

    Nursery charges, four days   _____

    Circumcision setup charge   _____

    Obstetrician's fees   _____

    Circumcision fee   _____

    Pediatrician's newborn care   _____

    TOTAL   _____

BABY'S WARDROBE

    4 to 6 shirts   _____

    3 to 4 gowns   _____

    1 to 2 sleeping bags   _____

    3 to 4 stretch coveralls   _____

    4 to 6 receiving blankets   _____

    4 to 6 dozen diapers   _____

       (if not using diaper service)

    Diaper pins   _____

    Sweater or shawl   _____

    4 waterproof panties   _____

    Booties and bootie socks   _____

    Bunting   _____

    TOTAL   _____

NURSERY ITEMS

    6 fitted crib sheets   _____

    4 waterproof sheets   _____

    5 waterproof pads   _____

    3 crib blankets   _____

    1 blanket sleeper   _____

    Comforter or quilt   _____

    1 mattress pad   _____

    Bassinet or carrying blanket   _____

    Crib   _____

    Crib mattress   _____

    Crib bumper   _____

    Diaper pail   _____

    Portable baby seat   _____

    Wicker changer with drawers   _____

    Nursery lamp   _____

    Vaporizer   _____

    Baby carriage   _____

    TOTAL   _____

FEEDING EQUIPMENT   COST IN YOUR AREA

    8 to 12 8-ounce nursers   _____

    2 to 4 4-ounce nursers   _____

    Extra nipples, caps   _____

    Disposable nurser kit   _____

    Sterilizer kit or separate formula utensils _____

    Bottle and nipple brush   _____

    Hot plate   _____

    Bottle warmer   _____

    2 to 3 bibs   _____

    TOTAL   _____

BATH ITEMS

    Bath table or tub   _____

    4 washcloths, 2 towels   _____

    Lotion   _____

    Baby oil   _____

    Cream   _____

    Powder   _____

    Sterile cotton and swabs   _____

    Baby shampoo   _____

    Bathing cream or liquid   _____

    Petroleum jelly   _____

    TOTAL   _____

MISCELLANEOUS

    Baby vitamins   _____

    Sweater set   _____

    30 disposable diapers   _____

    Baby care book (Spock paperback)   _____

    Diaper bag   _____

    Brush and comb   _____

    Diaper service
      (first week—70 diapers)   _____

    Crib mobile   _____

    Rectal thermometer   _____

    Baby scissors   _____

    Car bed or seat   _____

    Birth announcements   _____

    TOTAL   _____

MATERNITY CLOTHES	COST IN YOUR AREA
3 dresses	_____
2 skirts	_____
4 tops	_____
2 pants	_____
2 slips	_____
3 bras	_____
1 girdle	_____
4 panties	_____
TOTAL	_____

TOTALS	
Hospital and medical care	_____
Baby's wardrobe	_____
Nursery items	_____
Feeding equipment	_____
Bath items	_____
Miscellaneous	_____
Maternity clothes	_____
GRAND TOTAL	_____

Copy this table on a separate sheet of paper, study it, share it with your friends. Just having this detailed list will help you curb, cushion, and cut the costs.

One final note: *prepare* yourself for the expenses and make up your mind right now that, no matter how much you save on these items, your baby will cost more than you anticipate. So do your best to manage your expenses properly, and you'll come through with your financial banners flying.

AND IF YOU ADOPT A CHILD?

No rundown on the cost of a baby would be complete without at least a footnote on the costs of adopting a child. And adoption not only has become a widespread practice among childless and zero-population-growth-conscious couples, but is being done by increasing numbers of single American women as well.

The cost of baby clothes and equipment will depend on the age of your child. But the above itemized list will guide you on how much these might run if you adopt a babe in arms.

In most states, no charge is made for adoption if you adopt a child through an approved social welfare agency, or a private one that is state-recognized. Private adoption agencies, though, charge fees ranging from $600 to $1,700 or charge on a sliding scale depending on family income. In relatively rare instances a licensed adoption agency may charge as much as 10 to 11 per cent of the husband's gross yearly income. Normally there is no need to hire a lawyer. However, some states *require* that you hire one. In this case, fees in the late 1970s ran between $80 and $400 and occasionally to as much as $800.

If you go the route of "black market" adoptions—usually arranged by lawyers outside normal channels and often without benefit of careful matching and screening of child and parents-to-be—you do so strictly at your own risk and probably at a very high cost in dollars and cents too.

Among your best sources of information on adoption are your local community welfare council, your state or local welfare department, reputable local adoption agencies, the U. S. Department of Health, Education, and Welfare's Office of Child Development.

A key source of information on adopting children from foreign countries is International Social Service, Inc., 345 East 46th Street, New York, New York 10017.

The best place to inquire about children with special problems who need adoptive homes is ARENA (Adoption Resource Exchange of North America), 67 Irving Place, New York, New York 10003.

The Soaring Costs of Rearing a Child

WHERE THE MONEY GOES

Of each child-rearing dollar being spent by a moderate-income north central city family of four, the U. S. Department of Agriculture calculated in an exhaustive study in the late 1970s:

26 cents goes for food
9 cents goes for clothes
32 cents goes for shelter
5 cents goes for medical care
1 cent goes for education
16 cents goes for transportation
11 cents goes for "all other"

Child-rearing costs vary widely from large family to small family, from city to country, from one part of the United States to another, from income level to income level—but in general:

• The yearly cost of rearing one child is approximately 15 to 17 per cent of family income.

• The costs of supporting an eighteen-year-old are 30 to 45 per cent higher than for a one-year-old.

• The costs of providing food and clothes for a growing child tend to rise at a much faster clip than other aspects of the child's support.

WHAT THE MOTHER "LOSES": THE HIDDEN COSTS

What's more, the enormous sums alone represent only the *direct* costs of rearing a child—food, clothes, schooling, etc. There also are such hidden costs as the lost earnings you, a homebound mother, accept by not taking a paying job outside the home.

The Commission on Population Growth and the American Future in 1969 counted a full $40,000 in these "lost-opportunity costs" for each mother assuming she stayed home until her youngest child reached age fourteen. These figures would be much, much higher today.

And these lost-opportunity costs skyrocket along with the educational level of the mother. The mother who remained at home until her youngest child reached age fourteen "lost" earnings totaling $58,904 if she had a high school diploma, $82,467 if she had a college degree, $103,023 if she had a postcollege education, the Commission found. (By now, these totals are grossly underestimated.)

Another fascinating point: the loss in income tends to be greatest in cases of premarital conception. (About one in three couples in the very low income brackets experiences premarital pregnancy.) Reason: if she has the baby, the mother usually has less opportunity to complete her education or job training before the child-rearing process begins, or to work and build a nest egg during the early years of marriage. Also, the husband's education or training may have to be cut short to support his family.

According to one national study, among families in the under-$15,000-a-year bracket, those who experienced premarital pregnancy averaged approximately $800 a year less in income than those whose children were conceived after marriage.

On the opposite side, your costs of child rearing will surge even more if you send your children to private schools, Ivy League colleges, summer camps, or on summer expeditions to Europe. Or if you give your children automobiles when they reach sixteen or seventeen. Or if you must pay the high cost of orthodontia. Or even if you give your youngsters their own home encyclopedia.

Further, since the long-term trend of prices is ever upward in this century, this will be reflected in ever rising costs of rearing children. On top of this, the preferred living *standards* of children will keep climbing along with the standards of their parents—from their preferences for food to their choices of entertainment, transportation, personal care. What "everybody else" has today is a lot more and a lot better than what anybody else ever had before.

So You Want a Divorce . . . Can You Afford One?

A "GROWTH INDUSTRY"

At a cocktail party a while back, I overheard a conversation between a stockbroker and a divorce lawyer. The broker complimented the lawyer on being in a "growth industry." And even though the divorce rate in the United States appeared to be leveling off as the 1970s ended and actually may be heading for a decline in the 1980s, divorces have indeed been in a long-term upsurge. Just consider:

• Of every ten marriages in our country, four end in divorce, with teenage marriages *twice* as likely to be broken by divorce as marriages of men and women in their twenties.

• Of the 4.5 million Americans marrying in an average year during the 1970s, an estimated 1.8 million of them eventually go through the emotional and financial agony of a divorce.

• Even if the divorce rate levels off, about 1 million marriages in our nation will be breaking up every year, according to population experts, and 40 per cent of all children will live in a single-parent family at some time before they reach age eighteen.

• The reasons for a possible reversal in the long upswing in the divorce rate are by no means clear. It could be that since men and women are waiting longer to wed, today's marriages presumably will be more durable. Or it could be that many couples simply dispense with marriage altogether and live as "mingling singles," thus erasing any breakups from public records and making the marriage-divorce figures misleading. Or it could be that the experience of living together before marriage improves the odds on a successful marriage.

Whatever the qualifications about the future, the broker's remark was not only arresting but also quite perceptive.

CAN YOU AFFORD A DIVORCE?

No matter what your income bracket, when considering divorce, you *must* ask yourself bluntly, "Can I afford one?" The cost of an uncontested divorce entails legal fees which may be moderate—a separation agreement will increase the costs —and the costs zoom up from there, if the action is contested or if a legal fight develops. The cliché that "two can live (almost) as cheaply as one" becomes acutely pertinent if you are contemplating a divorce, for the simple reason that the same amount of money must cover all the costs of two households instead of one, unless the wife is or can become truly self-supporting. In most cases, both of you must be prepared to cut your former standards of living. In the sage words of one lawyer, "There is only one pie and no matter how it is sliced, the portions become smaller."

DOWNWARD TREND OF LEGAL FEES

Although the economic impact of your divorce will almost surely be drastic, there have been important recent developments in the area of attorneys' fees, which in contrast to the inflationary trend of most expenses, can (and should) substantially reduce the cost of obtaining a divorce:

(1) A Supreme Court decision in the late 1970s permits lawyers to advertise, and some do advertise "uncontested divorces" at extremely low fees. While a lawyer ideally should be chosen on the basis of personal recommendation rather than from an ad in the newspaper, the element of competition already has impelled many lawyers to charge more moderate fees.

(2) Some states allow inexpensive "do it yourself" divorce kits as an alternative to hiring a lawyer, and there never has been a specific prohibition against going to court without a lawyer.

(3) Local bar associations do not uniformly have your interest in mind, but several bar associations have established panels of qualified divorce lawyers under the umbrella of a "legal referral service" to help you, an average citizen,

obtain legal assistance at a moderate cost. As the 1980s neared, over 250 such referral services were operating from coast to coast. One which had an excellent record was established by the Joint Committee of the Association of the Bar of the City of New York and the New York County Lawyers Association. The fee for a half-hour consultation was $15, an amount well below the cost of running a law office. Subsequent services, if needed after the initial consultation, were more realistically priced.

ALIMONY AND CHILD SUPPORT

Obviously, the major divorce expense is for alimony and child support. It is hazardous to generalize because no divorce is "typical" and guidelines vary in different parts of the country. A rule of thumb is that you, a husband without children, may be expected to pay between 20 and 25 per cent of your gross income as alimony. If your marriage is of short duration, though, and your wife has a good, well-paying job, she would be entitled to only nominal, if any, alimony.

If there are children involved, your alimony and child support package may go as high as 40 per cent of your gross income. In the past these amounts have been greater, but the flood of women into the work force and of jobs that provide steady incomes on which they can support themselves has reduced some ex-wives' need for large alimony payments.

In addition, some courts have become more sympathetic toward the sometimes crushing economic burden of alimony upon the husband.

Still another factor in the trend toward lower alimony and child support awards and settlements has been the realization that if the husband's obligations are too great, he often will default and even disappear.

Courts have a broad discretion, however, and will be guided by the facts of each particular case. Most divorces do end up in a negotiated settlement rather than in an award by the court. If the husband and wife are each represented by competent counsel, the separation agreement usually will be in line with what the lawyers expect a court would do.

The separation agreement generally is incorporated into the divorce decree and also may contain an "escalator clause" based on increases in the cost of living (consumer price) index or the husband's income. A key difference between a negotiated settlement and a court-imposed award is that the former usually cannot be changed. However, child support is subject to modifications by the court even if the separation agreement provides to the contrary. The theory is that children are "wards of the court" into whose best interests the court always can inquire, despite the existing contractual arrangements between you, their parents.

TAX CONSEQUENCES

An alternative to periodic alimony payments is a lump sum settlement. Lump sum payments, however, are *not* tax-deductible to the husband and taxable to the wife (the tax consequences of periodic alimony payments). The lump sum payment is not considered a gift. Therefore, if you, the husband, make the transfer in property other than cash, you, the husband, would be required to pay a capital gains tax on the difference between its cost and its fair market value. Also when considering a lump sum settlement, you must realize that if your former wife uses up the money and is likely to become a public charge, the courts in some states will award alimony to your former wife, regardless of the fact that she had traded periodic payments for a lump sum.

ALIMONY FOR HUSBANDS

Alimony traditionally has been viewed as payments from a husband to a wife, but as the 1980s neared, more than half of the states permitted a husband to receive alimony from you, his wife, if your financial circumstances warranted it. The remaining states will now be required to make similar provision for the husband because of a decision in the late 1970s by the United States Supreme Court.

In sum, the concept of alimony is changing from what once was an absolute right on the part of a wife to a pragmatic arrangement based upon personal economics.

While alimony is tax-deductible to the spouse who pays it, and child support is not, husbands in high tax brackets often arrange to pay an unallocated amount as "alimony" (instead of "alimony and child support") to wives who are in lower tax brackets. Thereby they obtain a major contribution by the government to their financial obligations. The Supreme Court has held that this is a perfectly legal loophole.

"HIDDEN" COSTS

In addition to legal fees, alimony, and child support, there are the so-called "hidden" costs of divorce. Who gets the family house? How are stocks, bonds, and other assets to be divided? What about life insurance? The high cost of medical care? The cost of a college education?

Family House

The family home often is a middle-class family's most valuable asset. Usually the wife gets possession until the last child moves out, at which time the house is sold and the proceeds are divided. However, if there are substantial assets other than the family home and the divorce is amicable, it is not unusual for the husband to deed the house to his wife. In either event, watch out for this pitfall:

Can the wife manage the increased expenses of maintaining the house out of her income, even when augmented by alimony and child support from her husband?

Stocks, Bonds, and Other Assets

If these assets are jointly owned they are usually divided equally by the husband and wife. Although assets acquired during a marriage once belonged to the person in whose name they were held, as the 1980s approached, three quarters of the states had statutes providing for a 50-50 split.

Even in the majority of states which have equitable distribution statutes, inherited money and money or other assets acquired before the marriage in general are excluded from divorce settlements.

Life Insurance Policies

Under the usual separation agreement, the husband's obligation to pay alimony and child support ceases upon his death. Therefore, in all situations in which there are insufficient capital assets to fund continuing support, life insurance becomes an absolute necessity, at least until the children become self-sufficient. Most states have lowered the age of majority to eighteen; many, though, still require child support payments until age twenty-one. The details of the insurance must be spelled out in the agreement, and it is imperative that there be a provision for annual disclosure and verification that the premiums are being paid and that there is no borrowing against the policy.

Medical Care

Because of the high costs of hospital and medical care, a separation agreement should provide for Blue Cross-Blue Shield and major-medical insurance for the benefit of the children. Often these items are fringe benefits of either spouse's employment as far as the children are concerned—but a divorced spouse will not be covered under the other spouse's group health insurance.

A separation agreement also may specify that expenses not covered by insurance—such as orthodontia, cosmetic surgery, and psychiatric treatment—will be undertaken or partially paid for by the husband.

College Expenses

A seasoned attorney representing you, a wife, undoubtedly will advise you to obtain a definite commitment in the separation agreement for your soon-to-be former husband to pay for as much of the college education of the children as possible, especially if it appears that your former husband intends to remarry and raise a new family. The attorney for you, the husband, on the other hand, usually will advise you to resist such an open-ended commitment especially in view of the ever increasing costs of a college education. The result is a matter for serious negotiations, based upon the circumstances of each case. The problem is compounded by the realization that a college education is roughly the equivalent of what a high school diploma once was. Thus, graduate or professional school is becoming the name of the game.

Yet it's an unusual separation agreement in which the husband undertakes such a significant additional commitment, especially if the children are still relatively young.

MORE ON COSTS, TRAUMA, AND LAWYERS

Despite the progress toward lower legal fees, they remain of great importance to the cost of divorce, especially if the divorce is contested or even if both parties agree to a divorce but cannot agree upon the terms of the financial settlement. If litigation is involved, attorneys' fees can run up to $15,000, depending in part upon (1) the duration and intensity of the controversy; (2) whether there is a custody fight; (3) your individual income brackets. You must face several difficult decisions in this area:

(1) If you can come to an agreement on your own without the intercession of lawyers, fees may be as low as $150, including disbursements, but not including a separation agreement. In simple situations, a separation agreement may not, in fact, be necessary.

(2) However, the tortuous question is: "When is a divorce and/or separation so simple that it requires no negotiations between lawyers?" By the nature of their responsibilities to their clients, lawyers cannot and should not represent both sides. The lawyer who does his (or her) job properly should be an advocate for you, the client. He is required to, and presumably will, negotiate on your behalf unimpaired by feelings of guilt, intimidation, or other blind spots which often will hamper you if you attempt to negotiate your economic futures between yourselves without the aid of counsel. In this context, no divorce should be wholly uncontested.

(3) To avoid the expenses of hiring separate lawyers to negotiate as well as to perform the somewhat ministerial duties of obtaining an uncontested divorce, another option is to obtain the services of an intermediary with a background in psychological counseling. The problem here is that the disadvantages of the adversary system (principally the discomfort of confrontation and the substantial expense involved) may be outweighed by the therapist's imperfect attempts to serve two masters, or even worse, succumbing to the human temptation to play God.

(4) Even if you decide to proceed by the conventional route of each of you engaging separate lawyers, there is no reason to accede to open-ended charges of "whatever the traffic will bear." You should openly discuss fees with your lawyer at the start, and if they appear to you to be too high, you are free to consider other alternatives. Not everyone needs a "bomber" or should be required to pay a retainer of up to $10,000.

(5) You also might consider whether you should agree to a flat fee or an hourly rate. If you decide on the hourly rate, obtain an estimate of the anticipated number of hours your case will take. A lawyer's hourly charges vary, depending on experience, professional standing, and the section of the country in which he practices. Hourly charges can range from as little as $20 an hour to as high as $200 an hour. In large cities, most hourly rates will be within the $50-to-$100-an-hour range.

(6) And then—"who pays the legal fees?" In the past you, the husband, were customarily expected to pay all fees, including those of your wife's lawyer, except if your wife had her own independent assets or income, or if she was the spouse pressing for the divorce. In the late 1970s, though, the trend was toward a gainfully employed wife's paying her own attorney's fees. The prior practice, in fact, placed lawyers in the uncomfortable conflict-of-interest position of taking money from the adverse party.

OTHER NEW TRENDS IN DIVORCE

Grounds

The national trend has been toward no-fault divorce, thereby reducing the need for evidence on such harsh grounds as adultery, cruelty, or abandonment.

One result of the no-fault trend is practically to eliminate the need for "migratory divorce mills" where no-fault divorces could be obtained on the basis of an overnight stay in such places as Mexico, Haiti, and/or the Dominican Republic.

Ownership of Property

By the late 1970s about three quarters of the states had enacted some form of legislation providing for equitable distribution of property acquired during marriage, thereby reducing the advantage of the spouse in whose name the property happened to have been held.

Flexible Maintenance

Legislation providing for equitable distribution of property also changed the concept of alimony.

The characterization "maintenance" is used, whereby the courts have the discretion to relate the payments to a retraining period which would enable the dependent spouse to find remunerative employment.

Custody

More husbands are obtaining custody than ever before, but there is still a judicial bias in favor of the wife, especially when the children are young. The custody changes which ostensibly put fathers on an equal footing with mothers, unfortunately, have been used by many husbands as a weapon by which to intimidate their wives into accepting either inadequate financial support or the threat of a custody fight.

Joint Custody

Although this development has worked in special situations, many lawyers and psychologists view it principally as a compromise to salve wounded egos—creating more problems than it solves.

Mingling Singles

After the experience of divorce, more and more women with children are understandably reluctant to enter into a new legal entanglement. Instead they decide to establish a "family" relationship outside of marriage. However, alimony often ceases when even this informal arrangement becomes known—and the ex-wife also becomes vulnerable to a custody fight by her ex-husband, who may be "aggrieved" over the effect her new life-style might have on the children. Nevertheless, courts still are reluctant to take a child away from the custodial parent unless the circumstances are extreme.

Living together as unmarried singles is indisputably on the rise. What happens when singles separate? Some courts say that a separated person may be entitled to what has become known as "palimony."

Grandparents' Visitation

Until recently, grandparents were victims without a remedy of bitter marital disputes after which the custodial parent (or, in the event of the death of a parent, the surviving parent) excluded the former in-laws from his or her new life, and barred them from visiting their grandchildren. Recognizing that such a situation is among the most heartbreaking results of a broken marriage, several states now give grandparents the right to apply to the court for reasonable visiting rights even over the objection of the custodial parent.

NO SUBSTITUTE FOR PLANNING IN ADVANCE

The economic and psychological costs of divorce can be, and all too often are, devastating. Recent trends in divorce costs and divorce arrangements plus sound advice may ease the situation somewhat.

But there is no substitute for *planning for economic survival in the event of divorce in advance of marriage*. This planning could range all the way from vocational education to (unromantic as it may seem) a premarriage contract along the lines of a partnership agreement.

TRACING ABSENTEE FATHERS

There soon will be no place to hide for husbands, ex-husbands, and/or fathers who skip out of supporting their families. Whether they flee from the nation's wealthiest areas or our worst slums, federal and state officials have geared up to track down fathers who leave their families and duck child-support payments.

That's bad news for these men. But it's good news for us, America's taxpayers, for it must lead to a sharp reduction in our welfare caseloads.

For years, welfare agencies and administrators have struggled with the costly problems of fathers who desert their families or who never marry the mothers. But in the late 1970s, under an amendment to the Social Security Act providing for the Child Support and Establishment of Paternity program, the government's authorized Parent Locator Service began assisting local welfare departments in tracking down absentee fathers. Through this, the cost to taxpayers of supporting children of errant fathers could be trimmed by as much as $1 billion a year.

An estimated 4.8 million American men had left their families and had failed to provide child support as the decade of the 1970s closed. We, the taxpayers, are burdened with a bill of many billions a year under the Aid to Families with Dependent Children program.

All mothers applying for welfare must, by law, name the father of the child except in cases involving rape, incest, and adoption or in certain situations that might endanger the child. Federal records from the IRS, Social Security, and the Defense Department are made available to local welfare departments to help locate the fathers.

The Parent Locator Service, as part of a computerized project, tracks down fathers who have disappeared. Requests coming into the Washington-based facility are reaching thousands a month. The PLS has located about 70 per cent of the fathers to date.

A return of $5.00 for every $1.00 invested in the program is projected in a study for the Health, Education, and Welfare Department. Even a $3.00 to $1.00 recovery rate would more than make the program worthwhile, the HEW study points out.

A recovery of $100 million a year is expected in New York, New Jersey,

Puerto Rico, and the Virgin Islands alone, for parents can no longer desert with impunity and assume that someone else will pay the cost of supporting their children.

Federal employees and military personnel, the latter previously free of garnishment of pay, are now subject to the law.

Title 4-D of the Social Security Act, as amended, provides for a central locator service and reimburses the states for enforcement actions they are mandated to take. This introduces a combination of new inducements and penalties.

The U. S. Treasury is bearing 75 per cent of the cost of finding deserting parents and fathers of children born out of wedlock. The states are obligated to help track down and recover support funds from such parents if they change residence to another state.

An early benefit is the increased co-operation of unwed mothers to establish paternity with the putative father accepting his obligation for child support without a paternity trial. And many fathers do have the capacity to pay but the states have not had the machinery or the perseverance to go after them, especially if they cross state lines.

If a state doesn't do what is required, it is assessed a 5 per cent penalty against the welfare fund (which can be hefty). New Jersey, for instance, gets 50 per cent of its welfare costs from the federal government.

The system may be used by families not on welfare. All families must be provided with the same services no matter what their incomes, if the families so request. In this category, HEW reimburses states for 75 per cent of the locator costs but allows the states to charge the families for an amount not to exceed the cost of the remainder of the services.

The law authorizes federal district courts to act. Regional offices of the HEW will be monitoring performances and programs, providing technical assistance and assessing penalties. And the return to us may be $5.00 for $1.00.

15

YOUR PERSONAL BANKING BUSINESS

COMPARISON SHOPPING AMONG FINANCIAL INSTITUTIONS

You easily may be befuddled by the array of financial institutions serving you today and the myriad of new services they offer. It isn't easy figuring out how to earn the most on your savings and where it's cheapest to open a checking account.

The once clear-cut functions of commercial banks and "thrift" institutions—credit unions, savings and loan associations, and mutual savings banks—have blurred. America's financial institutions have become increasingly similar in the services they offer and intensely competitive for your patronage.

For instance, many commercial banks, savings and loan associations, and credit unions offer what amount to interest-bearing checking accounts. At your commercial bank, this account may take the form of a prearranged transfer system, enabling you to have money moved automatically from your savings to your checking account when you pay your bills. At your S&L or credit union, you may accomplish the same objective with a negotiable order of withdrawal account (NOW) or a share draft account. No matter what it is called or how it is triggered—by telephone or writing a check—the important "plus" for you is that all your money is earning interest until you spend it.

But this very trend toward "sameness" makes many *differences* between the same *type,* as well as among different *classes,* of financial institutions. Major banks throughout the United States, for example, compute interest on savings accounts in more than fifty ways.

Checking account fees at different institutions can cost you little or nothing or as much as $80 a year.

Because costs and services can vary so widely and advertising tends to emphasize "free" gimmicks and "convenience" rather than conveying information that you can use to comparison shop, you need objective help to figure out the best deal for yourself.

Say you have just moved to a new town and you must have the services of a financial institution so you can get cash, pay bills, start a savings account, or arrange for a small loan. Where do you start? How do you weigh the virtues of bank "A" against those of bank "B" or against those of an S&L or credit union?

Or perhaps your present bank has just informed you that it's raising its checking account fees. Should you switch to another institution or merely take advantage of another type of program that your bank offers?

What's more, although you take for granted such traditional financial services as prepaid bank-by-mail envelopes, "free" checking, nearby branches, comprehensive statements, etc., banks and other institutions are cutting back on such routine amenities.

Why?

Because of higher costs coupled with your demand that deposits, including checking account funds, earn interest.

The rule of the game in the 1980s is that just about everyone and every service must pay its own way. While your bank or S&L still may offer "free" copying and notary services or travelers' checks, the chances are such extras will be tied to some requirement, such as maintaining a minimum balance in your savings or checking account.

Thus, it's silly and costly to channel your family's banking business to institution "A" simply because it offers you "free" money orders or "free" checking accounts. Don't allow such lures to mislead you.

Always keep shopping. View today's banks, S&Ls, and credit unions as little more than financial supermarkets. If the service or products in one becomes shoddy, don't hesitate to look elsewhere.

Compare which of the following institutions seem most important to you, then make up your mind:

Savings: Are a wide variety of savings plans offered? Are time deposit plans, savings certificates, other forms of savings programs available in addition to regular "passbook" accounts?

Interest: Is your institution's rate of interest on savings and checking accounts the maximum allowed? How frequently is interest compounded and credited on savings and checking? What kind of interest penalty will you have to pay if you withdraw money early from a time or savings account?

Availability: Are there any restrictions on withdrawals should you require your money in a hurry? Could your deposit be "frozen" without your being aware of it? What are the legal restrictions on withdrawals—if any?

Insurance: Are your deposits federally or state insured? With most deposits covered by the Federal Deposit Insurance Corporation (FDIC), the Federal Savings and Loan Insurance Corporation (FSLIC), or the National Credit Union Administration (NCUA), or state insurance corporations, they almost certainly are. But be sure.

Checking: Is the institution's rate of interest on checking, NOW, or share draft accounts competitive? What are the minimum balance requirements necessary in order to earn interest? How many free items, or checks, are you allowed to write each month? How much is the service charge? Does the institution offer a non-interest checking account? Can you get an automatic line of credit with checking?

Loans: How do the financial institutions compare on availability of credit—ease, lack of red tape, speed? And how do they compare on interest rates, other terms, range and availability of auto and similar loans? Does the institution run loan sales, offer interest rebates, provide preferential rates if you borrow against savings?

Mortgages: Are they easy to get? Are you charged a fee by the institution for originating a mortgage for you? Are mortgages available for co-operatives, condominiums, summer homes? Does the institution offer alternative mortgage plans —reverse annuity, variable interest, graduated payment plans, etc.? Is there a prepayment penalty if you pay off your loan early? Is interest paid on escrow accounts?

Trust Department: Has this department good junior as well as senior staff so that there will be continuity of trust services? Can you check the department's record on its investments to find out how it performed for other clients over a prolonged period?

Convenience: Does the financial institution have a branch or cash dispenser or twenty-four-hour automated teller near your home or office? Are late evening or weekend services provided? Are the teller lines long? Is there easy access to the institution's office? Is the service friendly and personal? How frequently do you receive statements, and do they include an accounting of all your loans, checks, savings, etc.?

Extra Services: Do you need or want these in light of the fact that all financial institutions are charging or beginning to charge you for the services you use? Interest-paying Christmas club? Help with your income tax forms? A travel service? Automatic bill-paying?

Continuity: If you do stay with the institution with which you've done business for a long time, will you receive preferential treatment—mortgage money when mortgages are high, other special and valuable favors of this nature?

Electronic Services: Does the financial institution offer automatic transfer from savings to checking? Are automatic bill payer and payroll deposit and deduction services available? Does your institution provide check guarantee services through computer terminals located in stores in your area? Can you "talk" to the institution's computer to help with bill-paying or just to figure out where you stand financially?

WHAT EACH FINANCIAL INSTITUTION IS

All types of financial institutions today offer long-term mortgages, credit cards, savings instruments of varying maturity, checking accounts in one form or another. This movement toward uniformity, begun in the mid-1970s, continues but it is not yet complete. The following is a rundown of the major services provided by financial institutions as the 1980s approached.

COMMERCIAL BANKS

Also known as banks and trust companies and community banks.

Our country's roughly fifteen thousand commercial banks still remain our foremost financial "department stores," offering you almost every service and convenience a borrower or saver might seek.

At the corner commercial bank, you may get unsecured installment loans, saving instruments of varying denominations at varying rates of return and maturities; checking accounts; mortgage and home improvement loans; credit cards, debit cards, a whole new range of electronic banking system services; consumer loans for automobiles, appliances, and furniture, as well as student, personal, and farm loans; trust, investment, estate, and investment brokerage services.

Virtually all bank deposits are insured by the Federal Deposit Insurance Corporation (FDIC) in Washington.

While banks in general are at the top of the consumer credit and savings market, some are business-oriented; others concentrate on consumer borrowers.

As of the late seventies, banks are restricted by law to paying lower interest on savings accounts than other types of financial institutions.

This is changing.

SAVINGS AND LOAN ASSOCIATIONS

(Also known as building and loan associations, co-operative banks, savings associations, and homestead associations.)

If you are a typical customer of a savings and loan, you use the institution as a haven for your savings rather than a source of loans. S&Ls have five savers for each borrower because they have in the past been allowed by law to pay slightly more interest than banks. If you borrow, you usually seek a long-term mortgage loan from the S&L, which traditionally has played a key role in home financing.

But more and more, S&Ls are broadening their services to include: direct deposit of Social Security checks into a customer's account, Individual Retirement Accounts and Keogh Plans (see Chapter 18), passbook loans to customers with money on deposit; automatic account deductions for such bills as mortgage and insurance premium payments.

There are roughly five thousand S&Ls in the United States, classified as insured or uninsured, federally chartered or state chartered. Savings in federally chartered S&Ls are insured by the Federal Savings and Loan Insurance Corporation (FSLIC). Insurance for state-chartered institutions is optional, but most institutions provide savers with this protection. Privately insured associations may pay more interest on deposits than federally chartered S&Ls.

As the 1970s ended, state and federally chartered S&Ls in a number of states could offer what are essentially interest-bearing checking accounts, known as NOW or Negotiable Order of Withdrawal accounts. Associations in other parts of the country soon also will offer the interest-bearing checking accounts in some form.

MUTUAL SAVINGS BANKS

Since these were established in the early part of the nineteenth century, mutual savings banks have provided customers with some of the services of both commercial banks and of savings and loan associations. This holds true today.

In some of the seventeen states in which they operated as the 1980s opened, mutuals are virtual duplicates of commercial banks, offering you checking account services, bank credit cards, low-cost life insurance policies. The services are not uniform, however.

Like S&Ls, in the past the big attraction of mutual savings banks has been the slightly higher interest they were allowed to pay on savings. This higher rate vis-à-vis commercial banks applied to long-term certificate accounts, too. In exchange for the higher return on longer-term certificates, you, the saver, agreed to "freeze" your money in the institution for a specified period and, depending on the account, to make a minimum deposit. This differential well may be erased in the 1980s.

CREDIT UNIONS

Credit unions are non-profit savings and lending co-operatives made up of individuals with a common bond, such as place of employment, professional associates, area of residence, membership in a union, religious group, etc. Governed and run by members, credit unions have specialized in offering reasonably priced credit and often higher interest on savings than other financial institutions. They deal exclusively with households and individuals.

CU members are shareholders, not depositors, and they receive dividends on shares, not interest on deposits. Credit unions, at this date, are exempt from federal taxation. All federally chartered CUs are insured under the National Credit Union Administration. Many of the state-chartered institutions have the same federal insurance or state insurance.

While continuing to emphasize consumer loans and some financial counseling, CUs recently have been granted new powers. Among them is the right to offer members longer-term mortgage loans, savings certificates, credit cards, and the equivalent of interest-bearing checking accounts, known as share draft accounts. Some CUs, too, have started to be involved in establishing such electronic banking devices as automated teller machines and point-of-sale terminals.

Whether or not a particular credit union offers these or other services depends on the decisions made by each CU's directors, as well as rapidly changing state and federal regulations.

YOUR CHECKING ACCOUNT

I remember, and I am sure you do as well, when a checking account was just that and nothing more. Your only option was to choose between a regular and a special account. But now the choices are so numerous they are almost mind-boggling.

The reasons lie first in the introduction of computer technology into the banking industry, making it possible for you to conduct much routine business with a plastic transaction card or turn bill-paying over to your financial institution almost entirely. Second, the increased competition among S&Ls, banks, and credit unions has broadened your options.

The purpose of a checking account or its equivalent NOW or share draft account is to give you a convenient and safe way to handle relatively large amounts of cash and to transfer money to other people. Of every four American families, three have at least one checking account, and more than 90 per cent of payments in this country are by check. (Still, about 25 per cent of households have no checking accounts and rely heavily on money orders.)

Despite all the talk about ours becoming a "checkless society," millions of you are reluctant to give up the accounts. You are familiar with checks; you rely on the proof they provide of to-whom-you-have-paid-how-much-and-when, and you like their stop-payment and "float" features. Thus, checks remain very much part of our financial transaction system.

To open a checking account, go to your bank or "thrift" institution's New Accounts Department, fill out a signature card, decide what type of account you want (or can afford) to open, and make your initial deposit. In some states, you must be at least eighteen or twenty-one years old to open an individual account. Otherwise, you may open a joint account with a parent or relative.

Before you investigate the different types of checking accounts or their equivalents available to you, figure out roughly how many checks you write each month. If you are average, you write fourteen to twenty-two. Consider your income, credit card use, and other factors that might affect the size of your deposits and your average and low monthly balance.

If you have had a checking account before, glance through your checking account statements of the past few years. When you have some idea of your check-writing habits and the size of your balance, calculate the interest you would earn on your balance if it were in a savings account. Estimate this figure according to the lowest rate paid by any savings institution in your area. A $500 minimum balance, for example, at 5 per cent interest, translates into a loss of about $25 in interest during one year.

It generally costs a financial institution between 10 and 30 cents to process a customer's check. To cover this and to make a profit, most institutions impose service charges and/or minimum balance requirements on you, a customer, and invest the money you leave in your accounts.

While computerized banking is supposed to cut an institution's check-processing costs by as much as 80 per cent, the systems are costly to put in place—one automatic teller can cost up to $50,000—and must be used heavily if savings are to be obtained. So usually (but not always), you'll have to pay some fee to maintain a checking account.

There are two main traditional types of checking accounts—regular accounts and special accounts.

REGULAR CHECKING ACCOUNTS

• In a regular checking account, you normally must keep a certain minimum balance—usually at least $100 and quite possibly $300 or more. Some banks state their requirement in terms of a person's "average" balance, while others look at the "low" balance. *The average balance* is more favorable to you, the customer.

As long as you maintain the required balance, many banks will permit you to write as many checks and make as many deposits as you please without paying any monthly service charge. However, if the amount in your regular checking account falls below the minimum, you may have to pay a monthly charge of $2.00 to $3.00 or more. Or the bank may levy a maintenance charge for your account each month, in addition to the required minimum balance. Still other banks will let you write a certain number of checks and make a certain number of deposits before any service charge is made.

Clearly, institutions which charge no maintenance or per item fees and have no minimum balance requirements are your best bargains.

Some banks which do not offer such low-cost checking to everyone, do make it available to older citizens, certain civil servants, persons on direct payroll deposit system, students, or other special groups.

Generally, a regular checking account is the best choice for you if you write a relatively large number of checks each month and can maintain the required minimum balance in your account.

The key point about any checking account that requires a minimum balance is that you are paying the bank a fee equal to at least the interest you could earn on the funds if they were kept in a savings account. For every $100 you keep in a checking account just to meet the bank's balance requirements, you give up at least $5 a year in interest.

Still, if you write more than four or five checks per month a regular checking account is usually the most economical type. If you choose it and it requires a minimum balance, try to maintain your deposit above the minimum to avert a monthly penalty charge.

As the 1970s ended, most commercial banks could transfer funds automatically from your savings accounts to cover a check or meet a minimum balance if you had requested and signed up for the service. This provided you with a protection against bounced checks (which generally cost you between $7.00 and $10) and not meeting a minimum balance requirement. The fee for this automatic service ranged between 25 cents and $1.00. The service also allowed you to collect interest on deposits longer.

To determine the cost of regular checking, multiply the monthly maintenance fee you are charged by 12. Add to it any charges for deposits and checks, plus 5 per cent of the minimum balance you are required to maintain. The result is the yearly cost of regular checking.

SPECIAL CHECKING ACCOUNTS

• With a special checking account (or "economy" account), you do not have to keep a minimum balance. However, you usually must pay a flat monthly service charge plus another 10-cent or 15-cent fee for each "item" processed. Some institutions count only checks as items, while others include both checks and deposits. Some even count each separate check listed on a single deposit slip as one "item."

To figure the annual cost of special checking, add up the number of checks you write each month. Multiply this figure by the cost the bank charges you per check. Add in the monthly maintenance charge and multiply the result by 12.

NEW, EXCITING VARIATIONS

Your other alternatives to traditional checking accounts include:

• *Bill-paying services:* Funds can be directly transferred from your savings accounts to cover such regular bills as mortgages or insurance premiums. Until then your deposit earns interest. You must give the institution initial authorization or telephone each time you wish a payment to be made or arrange each month to send the bills you wish paid.

• *Overdraft accounts,* also called automatic lines of credit: Some institutions simply will tack the "overdraft" feature to your regular checking account. Others will issue to you a special set of overdraft checks.

• *Electronic transfers:* Some institutions enable you to make deposits, withdrawals, move money from one type of account to another or make transfers directly from your account to a merchant's account through use of a computer terminal and a transaction card. For details, see pages 794–96.

• *Share drafts:* These are essentially interest-bearing checking accounts offered by credit unions. Interest is paid, however, generally on amounts deposited in your account by the tenth or twentieth of each month, provided they remain on deposit for the quarter. Credit unions usually do not charge their members any fees for this type of account. They keep their processing costs down by sending you statements quarterly, not monthly, and by not returning your canceled checks. Each share draft in your book of drafts is backed by copy paper, so you have a copy of every check as you write it.

• *NOW Accounts:* NOW or negotiable versions of withdrawal accounts are other "thrift" institutions' versions of interest-bearing checking accounts. It is likely the accounts will spread to other types of institutions early in this new decade and throughout the country.

NOWs could both hurt and help you, depending on several factors—for instance, your check-writing habits and how much money you keep in your account. If you are accustomed to writing many checks while holding low balances, you could end up paying more in service charges than you receive in interest. Say you have a NOW account with an average balance of $200; your bank pays 3 per cent interest, so your yearly interest payment is $6.00. If the bank charges $12 a year service fee, plus 11 cents per transaction, and you write fourteen checks a month, your total service charges would amount to $30.48 annually. Thus, the net cost to you of a 3 per cent NOW account would run $24.48.

In short, if institutions offering NOWs decide to charge you more for the services they provide, you could receive pennies in interest while spending dollars in service fees.

Of course, competition among different types, as well as the same class of institutions, for your household funds may hold service fees down. Institutions also may decide to cut back on services or they could raise the cost of borrowing money, so you, as a borrower, would subsidize savers.

When considering a NOW account, weigh (as you would with any checking account) your check-writing and deposit habits. Take note of any service fees the institution may charge and estimate whether these may exceed the interest you will earn. If they do not, then a NOW may be a sound choice, because in addition to its interest-earning feature a NOW enables you to avoid the costs involved in switching funds from savings to checking.

• *Telephone transfers:* Financial institutions may permit you to move money from your savings to your checking account merely by making a telephone call or transfer your funds automatically (once you have authorized them to do so). You, in effect, create your own interest-bearing checking account. Most of your funds earn interest until you need to pay a bill. There may be some time constraints, or fees may be charged for this service. An institution, for example, may require you to phone before noon if you want funds transferred that same day. Fees vary.

• *Money orders:* Traditionally money orders have been considered "the poor man's checking account," and completely secure. While the first part of this notion is generally correct, the latter is not, as large numbers of unfortunate Americans discovered when a big private money order company went bankrupt in the 1970s. Money orders, except for those issued by the U. S. Postal Service and insured banks, can be risky instruments. As a result, a few states now require or are working to require that all such payment instruments sold in their states be insured. No federal agency at the end of the 1970s regulated money orders nationwide. Until this occurs, one state superintendent of banks warns, "Money order purchasers are to a degree playing Russian roulette."

• *Money-market funds:* Some money-market funds, a category of mutual funds (see page 1059) which invest in highly liquid securities, allow you, a customer, to write checks on your accounts. Often there is no charge for this service but the amount of your check must be $500 or more. Unlike your treatment with regular checking accounts, you continue to earn interest until your check clears. Accounts are not insured, however, and, say, in the event of forgery, you may not have some of the legal rights that you have against a bank.

RULES FOR WRITING AND ENDORSING CHECKS

Millions of Americans do not know the basic rules for writing, endorsing, and depositing a check. Do not permit yourself to be among them—for you may be unwittingly courting the bank's refusal to honor your checks—or even inviting costly check-doctoring by a professional earning a living in this craft.

Heed these main do's and don'ts on writing checks:

Do date each check properly. A bank may refuse to accept a check which is dated ahead, or hold it until its date is reached. The bank's reasoning is that if the check were charged to your account before you expected it to be, it might cause other checks you wrote to bounce.

Don't leave any spaces between the dollar sign and the amount of the check you are writing, or between the amount you spell out in the middle line and the word "dollars" at the end of that line. Or, if you do leave such spaces, draw lines across them.

Do make sure each check is numbered properly—for your own bookkeeping purposes.

Don't alter the way you sign your checks (e.g., by adding your middle initial) once you have decided on a standard signature.

Do, if you are a married woman, sign checks with your own first name, plus your married name—"Mary Dowd," *not* "Mrs. Jack Dowd."

Don't use "Mr.," "Miss," or "Mrs." as part of your signature.

Do fill out the middle line ending with the word "dollars" in this format: "Five and 50/100," or "One hundred and fifty and no/100." If you write a check for less than $1.00, be sure to put a decimal point between the printed dollar sign and the amount of the check—followed by the word "cents." On the line where you write out the amount of the check, write, for example, "Only 95 cents," and cross out the word "dollars."

Don't use somebody else's check unless you punch a hole in at least one number of the special magnetic code which usually appears at the lower left-hand corner of the check. Inking it out won't do the trick with today's electronic check-"reading" devices; if you don't actually cut out this account number, you risk having the check charged against your friend's account. (Technically, you can write a check on any surface from a paper bag to an eggshell, but banks shudder at this sort of eccentricity.)

For the identical reasons, don't lend anyone one of your checks. Because of the indelible symbols, your pre-imprinted check will be sorted according to its magnetic coding and charged to your account even if someone else, with no dishonest intentions at all, has crossed out your identifying number and name and written in his own.

Do endorse a check only on the back of the left-hand side (the perforated side, in one type of checkbook), *exactly* as your name appears on the front of the check. If this is not your usual signature, add the correct signature below your first endorsement. Of course, if your address is on the check too, you need not include this—or the "Miss," "Mrs.," or "Mr." which may also be included.

Don't ever underestimate the importance of your endorsement or forget that your endorsement on someone else's check means you would be willing to cover the check yourself should the bank for any reason refuse to honor it.

A blank endorsement—your signature only—means you transfer the ownership of the check to the person holding it at the time. This person may then cash it.

An endorsement in full—or special endorsement—means you sign a check over to someone else by writing on the back of a check "Pay to the order of" this person or organization.

A *restrictive endorsement* should be used on checks you wish to deposit by mail. You write "For deposit only" over your signature. Or, if you give someone a check which has been made out to you or cash, you write "Pay to the order of ———" and sign your name beneath this.

Do deposit all checks you receive as soon as you get them. Not only is it a big bookkeeping nuisance for the person who has issued the check if you keep it for a month or more, but many banks refuse to honor checks which are two or three months old—unless they are "reauthorized" to do so by the payer.

Don't write checks out to "cash" unless you yourself are cashing them at a bank, supermarket, or elsewhere. Such checks are negotiable by any bearer and leave you with no record of how the money was spent.

Do record on your check stub the key facts about every check you write This includes the date, check number, payee, amount, and the purpose of the check if the "payee" notation doesn't make that evident. The best way to make sure you don't forget to record this information is to do so *before* you write the check itself.

And *don't* ever, ever give signed blank checks to anybody whom you do not trust completely; blank checks are as good as cash—unlimited amounts of it, for that matter. As a matter of fact, it's risky ever to sign a blank check!

KEY QUESTIONS ABOUT WRITING CHECKS

Now here are additional questions you almost surely would like to have answered—leading logically from the rules covered in the preceding pages.

Q. *When you deposit a check from another bank, how long should you wait for it to be cleared before you can safely draw checks against your deposit?*

A. If the other bank is in the same city, allow at least three days for the check to be collected. If the bank is out of town, allow five to fifteen days depending on its location. When it's important for you to know exactly when a check will actually be credited to your own account—so you won't risk having any of your own checks returned—ask one of your bank's officers about the particular check.

Q. *Is it legal to write a check in pencil?*

A. Yes. But it's obviously dangerous since anyone could erase the amount and substitute a larger one. Write all checks in ink.

Q. *May a check be dated on Saturday, Sunday, or a holiday?*

A. Yes. The folklore to the contrary is wrong. However, since some people who believe the folklore may refuse to accept the check, it's generally safer to date it on a previous day.

Q. *What happens when you make the mistake of writing one amount in words and another amount in figures?*

A. Some banks pay the amount which is spelled out, but many more return the check.

Q. *Should you ever erase or cross out anything on a check?*

A. No. Even if you initial the change, the bank often will not honor an altered check. And knowing this, you should never accept or cash an altered check yourself.

Q. *How long does a check remain valid?*

A. Technically, a check is good for six years. In actual practice, though, most banks consult with the payer before honoring a check which is more than six months old and many, I repeat, do this after only two or three months.

Q. *Will your bank give you a new check if you spoil one for which you've already paid?*

A. Yes.

Q. *How do you stop payment on a check?*

A. You can, for a fee of $4.00 to $9.00, stop payment on any check you have written simply by *telephoning* your bank's stop payment department and giving the details, including: the date, amount, name of payee, check number, and the reason for stopping the payment. Then immediately confirm the order in writing.

The bank will issue a stop payment form which you must complete and which the bank will keep on file—to be sure your intention *not* to have the bank honor your check is properly carried out.

When you stop payment, be sure you notify the payee—the person or company or organization who was to have received the amount of money you specified on the check.

As a general rule, *don't* send a check in payment unless you are willing to have it honored. Stopping payment itself won't damage your credit rating but not paying your bill—unless it's in dispute—will.

GUARDING AGAINST CHECK FORGERIES

What would you do if you suddenly discovered your checkbook has been stolen and that a professional forger was using *your* name to write check after check against your account?

Do not dismiss the question, for check forgeries have been climbing at an alarming pace in recent years. As a simple precaution against becoming another victim, you should at least be aware of a few of the forger's favorite techniques.

Typically, the forger will find out when your bank mails out monthly statements and will loot your mailbox at that time. Armed with samples of your signature, a good idea of the amount of money you keep in your account, and the number of checks you usually write during the month, he will start raiding your account. You may not discover the damage until *his* canceled checks start coming home to you.

Or the forger may simply "raise" a carelessly written check of yours, by hiking the amount from "one" dollar to "one hundred" or "six" dollars to "sixty," or "twenty" to "seventy"—at the same time subtracting this amount from your account.

Here are a few key rules to protect yourself against check forgery:

• Guard your checks as if they were cash. I re-emphasize, in many ways, they're *better* than cash, since they can be written out for any amount.

• Notify your bank *immediately* if you lose even a single check, not to mention your entire checkbook. Note: Forgers frequently will steal checks from the *back* of your checkbook to postpone detection, so flip through your whole checkbook now and then as an added precaution.

• Notify the bank if you fail to receive your bank statement within a couple of days of the usual time.

• Reconcile your bank statement promptly each month and glance at each returned check for evidence of any tampering or forgery.

• Report any such evidence to the bank immediately. Banks normally are insured against such losses.

• Learn and obey the rules I've already given you for writing checks.

• Destroy all old checks if and when you change your name, address, account number—or become formally separated or divorced.

• Avoid the sweeping illegible "executive" signature—or a hand-printed signature. This is much easier to forge than a clear, freely written two-name signature with connected letters.

HOW TO PROTECT YOURSELF AGAINST CASH-MACHINE CONS AND ERRORS

Electronic banking devices—automated tellers, "money-matic" machines, "24-hour banking centers," cash dispensers, the like—are still relatively new. Even their developers have not grasped all of the problems which financial institutions and you, their customers, may encounter with them.

The machines are neither totally fail- nor fraud-proof.

In California a computer error put more than $30,000 into a savings account of a cafeteria worker. The man quickly withdrew the money and disappeared. As 1980 neared, he still was being sought on charges of grand theft.

• In Washington, D.C., a "money-matic" machine went on the blink one weekend and dispensed money to customers seeking withdrawals. The computer recorded the account numbers but not the amount of money each person withdrew. Some customers would or could not recall how much money they had withdrawn.

• In New York City during the introductory phase of some twenty-four-hour banking center terminals, some customers left their machines before they had shut down. On one occasion an observant con man noted a customer's identification code and, with the machine still running, he stole $1,000. The bank reimbursed the customer for his loss and has corrected the system so this type of electronic theft cannot happen again.

To avoid these and other types of electronic banking mishaps:

• Request a personal demonstration and explanation from a responsible bank official of how the computer device operates. This will eliminate any worry that you will operate the machine incorrectly and will make sure that the services the new technology provides will really be a convenience, not a headache. Most institutions accept liability for mechanical malfunctions and fraud if neither is due to your negligence.

• Do not write your personal identification number or code on your transaction card or anywhere else where it might be observed, stolen, or misplaced. This would be an example of negligence, so memorize your code or number. With some systems, if you forget your code or number, you must select a new one. Not even the financial institution keeps a record of it; it's totally confidential. Other systems, however, do keep track of such identification numbers or codes and will remind you of them if you supply proper identification.

• Do not lend your transaction card to anyone, and do not tell anyone your personal identification code or number.

• When using a computer terminal, be sure that the machine has turned itself off and that you have your card before you walk away.

• Depress all keys of the machine firmly and slowly to make certain your message gets across correctly. Most systems are designed to operate relatively slowly so even as a first-time user, you won't become confused and you will be able to keep up.

• Ask for and keep the receipts of the transactions that you have made. Study these receipts as soon as you get them to be certain that you didn't push the wrong buttons or the computer didn't make an error. Once you know your receipts are accurate, you have records against which you can compare your monthly statements and with which you can resolve any disputes.

• Make an entry into your checkbook after you have completed each transaction. Because you can make deposits, withdrawals, or transfers from savings to checking or vice versa so quickly, it is easy to forget to make the proper notations in your checkbook. But the entries are vitally important if you are to know how much money you have in your account.

• Avoid using cash dispensing machines located in low-traffic areas late at night or at other odd hours. Although many computers have cameras strategically located nearby for your protection, don't make yourself an easy target for a crook who demands your card and code.

• Check your balance periodically on the computer to make sure that its record of your balance squares with your own. Make allowances, however, for any checks or deposits which may be outstanding. Not all systems are connected directly to the institution's main computer. Some terminals may record your transactions on magnetic tape or in other ways. This tape is periodically pulled from the machine and then fed into the institution's central recording facility. These machines do not automatically credit your deposits or withdrawals but act as a kind of overnight banking mailbox.

• Mainly because of this time lag, many systems limit the amount of money you can withdraw at any one time—say, $100 every three days. Some machines issue receipts which tell you when you can next make a withdrawal. If you need more money than this—for example, you will be traveling and know you'll need $300 every week for the next month or two—your bank often will upgrade your withdrawal limit on your request. The bank's willingness to do this will depend, of course, on your status as a customer, its policies, and the technology of its particular electronic system.

• Many computers have attached telephones which you can use to discuss problems with a "live" bank official or consumer representative. You don't have to wait until you get your monthly statement to discuss any discrepancies or problems.

NEW PROTECTIONS FOR ELECTRONIC BANKING CUSTOMERS

Under the Electronic Funds Transfer Act of 1978, consumers have some protection in the event their EFT transaction card is lost or stolen. But warning: you must notify the bank or other institution which issued you the card *at once.*

If you believe your card has been lost or stolen or if you think money is missing from your account, and you contact the bank within two business days after learning of the loss, you are liable for no more than $50.

If, however, someone uses your card without your permission you could lose as much as $500 if you fail to notify the institution within that time, and it can prove that it could have prevented the loss if you had informed it.

Also, if your monthly statement shows transfers that you did not make, and you don't notify the institution within sixty days after your regular statement was mailed to you, you may not get back any money you lost if the institution can show that if you had contacted it, it would have prevented the loss.

If you are traveling or hospitalized and cannot notify the institution of the unauthorized use of your card, these time periods may be extended.

The law also permits institutions to send you unsolicited EFT cards providing they can't be used until your identity is verified and the card is validated. You must also be told the following:

• how to dispose of the card if you don't want to use it.

• what your liability is in the event your card is lost or stolen and whom you should contact if that occurs.

• the type of electronic fund transfers that you can make and what you might be charged for such transactions.

• any limits on how often you may make transfers or how large they may be.

• whether you have the right to stop payment of a preauthorized transfer and, if so, how to go about it.

• whether or not you have the right to receive documentation of fund transfers.

• whether or not the institution has methods for resolving errors, what they are, and your rights under them.

• the circumstances under which a financial institution may disclose information about your account to such third parties as credit bureaus or government agencies.

• and finally whether or not the institution is liable to you for failing to make transfers that you have requested.

HOW TO BALANCE YOUR CHECKBOOK

As Chapter 2, "Budgets Are Back in Style," stressed, the monthly ritual of checkbook balancing should be assigned to whichever member of the family is the more deft at it and the more willing to do it *as soon as possible* after each bank statement comes in. An arbitrary decision that this chore should automatically go to the man in the family is downright foolish—if he has neither a flare for nor an interest in it. Whoever gets the job can use this chart to guide you on the key steps to balancing a checkbook:

1. Your own checkbook balance	
2. Minus service charges appearing on your bank statement	
3. Your own new checkbook balance	
4. Balance in the bank's statement	
5. Plus recent deposits not yet recorded in bank statement	
6. Minus value of all outstanding checks — those not appearing on bank statement	
7. New bank statement balance	

This last total—item 7—should agree with item 3, your own "new checkbook balance." If it does not, go back and follow these steps:

(1) First compare the amount of each canceled check with the amount appearing in the bank statement. Make a notation after each check on the bank statement as you go.

(2) Now arrange the stack of checks in order of check numbers—which will permit you not only to recheck the amounts against those appearing in your own check records but also to tell immediately which ones are missing.

(3) Compare the amount of each check with the amount you have written on each appropriate stub—and check off each entry in your record as you go.

(4) Compare, and verify with a notation, all the deposits you have made and recorded with the deposits recorded on the bank statement.

(5) Add up, in the appropriate space provided on your bank statement, the amounts of all checks you have written which have not yet appeared on your statement and subtract this total from the balance appearing at the end of your bank statement. Make sure the amounts on the checks agree with the amounts recorded on your check register.

(6) Add to the statement balance the total amount of deposits you have made to your account which do not appear on the bank statement.

(7) Subtract any bank service charges appearing in your statement from the balance which appears in your checkbook. Do this in your checkbook as well.

The revised totals for the bank statement and for your checkbook balance should agree to the penny.

But don't panic if they still don't agree. Here's what to do:

Recheck your original math in your checkbook. The bank's math is usually correct since it was probably done by a machine. However, errors of other sorts are entirely possible.

Recheck the balances you carried forward from page to page in your checkbook.

Double-check to be certain you have subtracted *all* outstanding checks from your bank statement balance—including those still missing from previous statements.

Double-check to be certain all the canceled checks which came with your statement are included in your checkbook record—and that you haven't forgotten to note *any non-checkbook checks* you may have written during the period of the statement.

If your accounts *still* don't balance, and you're completely stymied as to why, take the whole business to the bank and ask for help. You'll probably be given this help without charge—but don't delay. There is always the possibility, though remote, of sleight of hand with your bank balance—and the sooner any type of thievery is pinned down, the better your chance of avoiding financial losses. Most banks expect to be informed of a possible error within ten days.

Your Savings Account

HOW MUCH MONEY SHOULD YOU KEEP IN A SAVINGS ACCOUNT?

How much money should *you* keep in a savings account?

• The rule of thumb in Chapter 2, "Budgets Are Back in Style," is that your emergency fund should equal at least two months' income.

• Many of the major financial institutions of the country would call my total far too low, would recommend your reserve in the form of "liquid assets"—cash or its equivalent—should total three to six months' income.

• But the vital point which erases any apparent disagreement is that your own special financial circumstances must be the crucial factor deciding whether your emergency reserve can safely be as low as two months' income or should properly be equal to six months' earnings.

So how much should you keep in an emergency fund? For the answer, ask yourself these questions:

How many circumstances can you think of in which you might require really large sums of cash, literally at overnight notice?

What types of unexpected financial emergencies might conceivably befall you or your family? (A disabling accident, job layoff, big auto repair job.)

What share of the estimated costs of such emergencies would be covered by your other forms of financial protection such as major medical insurance, life insurance, other types of insurance, disability and survivor's benefits under Social Security, U.S. savings bonds you might have stashed away, stocks, mutual fund shares, bonds, other investments, benefits from your employer?

What emergency financial help could you realistically expect from parents, other relatives, or your employer?

Could you, the non-working wife, move into a paying job fairly readily—if need be?

If the family breadwinner should lose his or her job tomorrow due to a layoff, merger, or other development, how long would it probably be before he or she could find a comparable job in his or her field of training?

How big a financial nest egg in cash do you need to *feel* financially secure?

Are you preparing for big-ticket expenses and purchases in the months ahead —e.g., a down payment on a house, a new baby, a long-planned vacation, a big outlay to go into business for yourself?

The amount you really need as an emergency reserve will depend on your honest answers to these questions.

It well may be that *if* you're a young couple with no children and a modest income, the *maximum* you should keep is $1,000 to $1,500 in a regular savings account. And in some cases even less would be realistic if you have other safe financial reserves which you could readily tap.

For your emergency cash reserve—whatever its amount or wherever you deposit it—should be precisely what its name implies. It should be protection against unexpected financial emergencies. It should be no more nor less than that.

KEY FORMS OF SAVINGS ACCOUNTS

Within any single financial institution, you may choose between a variety of savings accounts, each one tailored to fit particular needs, each account with special advantages, and each with disadvantages. You must select the one which best fits your requirements.

In general, these will be offered to you:

Passbook Savings Accounts

Have complete flexibility. Your money is always instantly available. You may deposit or withdraw any amount at any time.

Interest you earn on this type of "liquid" savings will be the lowest among the major types of accounts. Commercial banks by law paid the lowest rates on passbook savings accounts in the mid-1970s—one of their key disadvantages.

"Liquidity" of this type of account is the highest, the best of all types of savings outside of your checking account or cash in your hand. Liquidity denotes the ease and speed with which you can convert your funds into cash, and the amount of interest you can earn on your savings tends to be lowest where the degree of liquidity is highest.

Interest is usually compounded annually, semi-annually, or quarterly, and in some cases daily.

These accounts are federally insured or state insured in almost all cases up to $40,000 for each account held in a different name (a joint account can be insured separately from the individual accounts of those sharing the joint account).

Funds in this type of account can be used as collateral for personal bank loans.

A tally of your savings balance may be kept in a passbook or reported periodically to you in computerized statements mailed by the financial institution holding your account. The passbook itself is being gradually phased out.

Time Deposit Open Accounts

Form of savings account in which you must leave your savings with the institution for a specified period of time in order to obtain the higher interest rate offered on these deposits. (Has many names. The trick name depends on the institution.) Note: you can usually withdraw the interest but not the principal.

Minimum initial deposits required, usually ranging from $500 to as much as $5,000.

While you can usually—but not always—add funds to this type of account or withdraw interest at any time, notice of thirty to ninety days is frequently required for withdrawal of the principal, with the actual interest you receive depending on how long you maintain your account.

Insurance features the same as for Passbook Savings Accounts.

Consumer Certificates of Deposit

• These are the certificates of deposit for individuals with savings of under $100,000. They are a medium for your most liquid funds—assuming you are confident you will not need to cash in your certificates before they mature.

• In the late 1970s, consumer CDs were available in denominations from $100 to as high as $5,000 to $10,000.

• Maturities ranged from ninety days to six years or more with the interest rate the highest paid on any savings account.

• Notice of withdrawal was required and a penalty imposed—in form of reduction of interest—in the event of prior withdrawal.

• Insurance features and all the rest identical with other forms of savings accounts.

On top of these basic forms of savings accounts, financial institutions are developing new savings programs or variations of older ones. As a banker remarked, "In my midwestern youth, our small-town bank had only two different devices to help me save. Today, that bank has nine variations and larger banks have still more." Just to indicate the scope, ponder these variations:

• *Monthly memo savings*. The bank lets you set a goal in total dollars, then it develops a savings plan to fit and determines what monthly deposits you need to make to meet the goal. Every month the bank sends a statement to the depositor reminding him that he "owes" the account a deposit of X dollars. The top of the statement can be detached and used as a deposit slip, with an attached pre-stamped envelope.

• *Assorted interest*. On many savings accounts, especially higher-interest time accounts, larger banks offer several options on payment of interest: interest can be credited to the time account, the regular savings account, the checking account, or mailed out on a quarterly basis.

• *Special savings withdrawal*. In one midwestern city, several banks have together installed a special-purpose computer system to provide instant savings withdrawal transactions for customers. Through an on-the-line system of ninety keyboard terminals, the teller keys in a savings account number and dollar amount any time a customer wants to make a withdrawal and gets a green, yellow, or red light response for Yes, Maybe, or No.

• *Quick deposits*. More and more banks have quick deposit boxes for savings so customers needn't stand in the teller line. There also has been great improvement in teller line traffic, drive-in and walk-up windows, expresslines, etc.

• *Safe deposit boxes*. Some banks give customers free use of safe deposit boxes if their savings accounts run a certain size. Other special promotions are widespread.

• *Insurance*. Based on the depositor's age and the size of his account, this program makes term insurance available at what amounts to a group policy rate or less.

The mutual savings banks in New York, Massachusetts, and Connecticut also sell low-cost life insurance over the counter. It is inexpensive insurance because it is sold directly to you—at the bank itself or by mail—and there are no salesmen's commissions to add to its price to you. Many savings banks now also sell shares in a no-load, no-redemption-fee mutual fund. (See Chapter 22 on investing in mutual funds, for details on no-load funds.)

Most credit unions provide life insurance without charge to you if you put your savings in the credit union.

Treasury Rate Certificates

At the end of the 1970s, many financial institutions were offering twenty-six-week saving certificates with interest rates pegged to those the U. S. Treasury was paying on its short-term securities.

The minimum deposit you, a saver, had to make to obtain such a "money market" certificate was $10,000.

If you went to a commercial bank or thrift institution, the amount of interest you could earn roughly equaled that paid on the previous week's U. S. Treasury Bills.

The short maturities on these new certificates demanded that the owners be on the constant alert to the due dates for rolling over the certificates into new paper, so you would not forfeit valuable interest by permitting an interruption in the payment schedules.

In addition, the interest that savers earned on the "money market" certificates was subject both to state and federal taxes, whereas that earned on U. S. Treasury securities was subject to federal taxes only.

WHICH TYPE OF SAVINGS ACCOUNT IS BEST FOR YOU?

You can decide which savings account is best suited for your personal needs and goals only when you know the variety of accounts available. In brief, you may choose among these major types:

(1) *An individual account*. This may be opened by only one person—adult or minor—and you are the sole owner, the only person who can draw on the account. You can open this type of account with a small deposit.

(2) *A joint account*. Two of you may open this type—usually a husband and wife. Either of you may deposit funds in the account and either of you may withdraw funds from the account. In the event that one of you dies, the balance will be payable to the survivor.

(3) *A voluntary trust account*. You may open this type in trust for your child or another person. You will control the account during your life—after which it will be payable to the person you name as beneficiary. You have the right to change the beneficiary of this account at any time.

(4) *A fiduciary account*. If you are appointed an administrator, executor of an estate, or a guardian of another person, you may open a fiduciary account for the funds entrusted to you.

(5) *An organization account*. If you belong to an organization which collects dues or fees and which therefore has funds to safeguard and if you are in charge of the funds, you can open an organization account. The organization might be a club, your church, your lodge, a mutual benefit society, or any other non-profit organization.

(6) *A school savings account*. Your child may open a regular school bank savings account with insignificant deposits—and as he or she learns how to save and the virtues of saving, this tiny account may grow to become your child's regular savings account with a respectable deposit balance.

HOW CAN YOU FORCE YOURSELF TO SAVE—GRACEFULLY?

One way to save money is through a "loose money" system. Put aside at the end of each day all the change you have left in your pocket—or only all of your quarters, or even all your single dollar bills. Once every week, faithfully deposit your little hoard in a nearby bank or savings association. In just over eighteen months, the dollar-bill approach helped one family make the first payment on a piece of land in the exurbs for a weekend cabin.

Another way to build a nest egg is to save all windfall money—dividends, inheritances, bonuses, cash gifts, tax refunds. Put this money in your savings account the instant you get it. Don't even cash the check or do more than peer at the amount of cash in a gift envelope. Don't give the temptation to spend the windfall the slightest edge.

A third excellent way to save is to authorize your bank to deduct a specified percentage from your paycheck automatically when you deposit the paycheck in your checking account and to transfer this percentage to your savings account. Make it 10 per cent, if you can manage, or 5 per cent—but make the transfer automatic and regular. The automatic, regular feature is the secret, as stressed over and over in Chapter 2, "Budgets Are Back in Style."

Or maybe you will decide the best approach for you is an automatic deposit of X number of paychecks each year entirely in the savings account. For instance, you might decide to save every tenth weekly paycheck or the first check of every quarter of the year. Or if you're paid on a semi-monthly basis, you might decide you can manage to put away two or three full paychecks a year.

Or you might find a periodic "Nothing Week" is your best deal. During this week you would not spend any money on dinner out or stop at the bar on the way home from work or go out to the movies or go bowling—or whatever. You would eat inexpensive foods at home, read books, or look at TV—and add at least $25 to your nest egg.

Or surely you could save the money you formerly used for, say, cigarettes. I, for one, am saving more than $400 a year on this item alone since I quit.

And there are all sorts of tricks, of course. You might put, say, $50 in your savings account on every national holiday or family birthday. Or you might add an agreed-upon amount whenever you break a family rule. Or add that agreed-upon amount whenever you enjoy a particular pastime.

You can easily figure out your own approach, once you make up your mind to adopt one.

You'll save if you force yourself to by some method. Then you'll build your nest egg if you'll put the program on an automatic basis. You can't lose by trying this. You can only win.

WHAT IS "HIGHEST" INTEREST ON SAVINGS?

By law, banks and other financial institutions must state clearly in their advertisements the *true* annual interest rate they pay on savings—if they make any reference at all to interest in their ads—as well as any special conditions for getting the full interest rate.

But clear as this seems, it still leaves plenty of room for befuddlement. In fact, in this area of interest earned on savings, "highest" may not be highest at all— and the institution which advertises the top stated rate of interest on your funds may not actually be paying you the top total of dollars on your funds.

So much more than the stated rate of interest is involved. Far more revealing than the percentage which stands out in the ad may be what is not even included in the ad. How often is the interest promised you compounded—so that your interest earns interest? When does your deposit start to draw interest? Is there any penalty for frequent withdrawals or any bonus for no withdrawals for a specified period?

Banks compute interest in more than fifty ways and many don't readily disclose what method they use. You may think you are getting the best interest deal but you might be able to do significantly better at another institution a block away. You may think you are handling your savings sensibly, but you actually may be cutting your own return by the way you deposit and withdraw funds. Here are five questions you should be able to answer.

(1) What is the institution's policy on the compounding of interest? The more frequently interest is compounded the more interest your savings earn. A rate of 6 per cent paid once a year is a straight 6 per cent—or $60 per $1,000 of savings. But a rate of 6 per cent paid to you every quarter is higher, because the interest credited to your account is added to your original amount every quarter and then the stated rate is paid on the bigger sum. A rate compounded every month comes out to still more and a rate compounded every day is most. The larger your savings and the longer you maintain your account, the more the factor of "compounding" matters.

(2) When does your savings account start to earn interest (or dividends)? Under a policy most favorable to you, the institution will pay interest on your account from the day of deposit to the day of withdrawal. Also, under a most favorable policy, the institution will pay interest on all funds you keep in your account during the interest period. Under a least favorable policy, the institution will pay interest only on the smallest balance you have in your account during the interest period.

(3) When is interest credited to your account? On the first of each month? At the end of each quarter? At the end of June and December? Or just at the end of December? This is of major importance, for under the policies of many institutions, if you withdraw funds before the stated interest payment date, you will lose all the interest owed to you on these funds, for the interest period. When you withdraw funds, try to schedule the withdrawal immediately after the date for crediting interest.

(4) Is there any "grace period" during which you can withdraw funds around the interest payment date without being penalized by loss of interest? If so, how many days of grace are you allowed in which to withdraw funds and still be entitled to the interest the funds had earned? Also find out if there is a grace period after each interest payment date during which you can deposit funds and have them earn interest from the payment date. Pertinent too is whether the period of

grace includes every calendar day or just business days. A period of grace which includes only business days will be longer than it appears offhand.

(5) What about penalties for frequent withdrawals? And what about payment of an interest bonus if you make no withdrawals for a specified period—say none for one year? Both penalties and bonuses are fairly commonplace.

Any reputable financial institution should automatically answer these questions (and others which may bother you). With the answers, you then may make an intelligent decision on where to keep your cash nest egg.

HOW DOES A SAVINGS ACCOUNT GROW?

Compound interest means that you are earning interest on the interest paid to you as well as interest on your own deposits.

Say you can deposit $5.00 to $50 a month. How will your savings grow at 5 per cent a year interest, compounded semi-annually? Here's how much:

HOW SAVINGS GROW	$5 MONTHLY	$10 MONTHLY	$15 MONTHLY	$20 MONTHLY	$25 MONTHLY	$50 MONTHLY
6 months	30.44	60.88	91.31	121.75	152.19	304.38
1 year	61.64	123.28	184.90	246.54	308.18	616.37
2 years	126.40	252.81	379.17	505.57	631.97	1,263.94
3 years	194.44	388.89	583.26	777.71	972.15	1,944.30
4 years	265.93	531.85	797.69	1,063.62	1,329.55	2,659.10
5 years	341.03	682.06	1,022.98	1,364.01	1,705.04	3,410.09
10 years	777.58	1,555.16	2,332.48	3,110.06	3,887.64	7,775.28
15 years	1,336.40	2,672.80	4,008.76	5,345.15	6,681.55	13,363.10
20 years	2,051.73	4,103.47	6,154.53	8,206.26	10,257.99	20,515.99

Or say you have $5,000 in cash to deposit in a savings account. How much will this sum grow at varying interest rates over the years, if compounded quarterly? Here's that answer:

How a $5,000 Deposit Will Grow

INTEREST RATE	AFTER 1 YEAR	AFTER 3 YEARS	AFTER 5 YEARS	AFTER 10 YEARS
5.00%	$5,255	$5,804	$6,410	$8,218
5.25	5,268	5,847	6,490	8,423
5.50	5,281	5,890	6,570	8,634
5.75	5,294	5,934	6,652	8,849
6.00	5,307	5,978	6,734	9,070

Or say your objective is to save a specific sum—anywhere from $2,000 to $20,000. If you save X dollars a month, how many years will it take you—at Y interest compounded continuously—to achieve your goal?

The following compilation answers this one.

Start by setting your savings target in total dollars and years (the left-hand column). Follow across to one of the other columns and see how much you should save each month in order to reach your goal—at varying interest rates.

Or start with a rough idea of how much money you can put aside every month. Then look in the left-hand column to see what size nest egg you're aiming for.

Savings Time Table

If you want this amount:		Save this much each month at the interest rate of:	
		5%	5¾%
$ 2,000 in	1 year	$162.20	$161.53
	3 years	51.39	50.78
	5 years	29.28	28.70
$ 4,000 in	1 year	$324.40	$323.06
	3 years	102.78	101.56
	5 years	58.56	57.40
$ 6,000 in	1 year	$486.60	$484.59
	3 years	154.17	152.34
	5 years	87.84	86.10
$ 8,000 in	5 years	$117.12	$114.80
	10 years	51.28	49.21
	15 years	29.78	27.93
	20 years	19.36	17.72
$10,000 in	5 years	$146.40	$143.50
	10 years	64.10	61.51
	15 years	37.23	34.91
	20 years	24.20	22.15
$12,000 in	5 years	$175.68	$172.20
	10 years	76.92	73.82
	15 years	44.67	41.90
	20 years	29.04	26.58
$14,000 in	5 years	$204.96	$200.90
	10 years	89.74	86.12
	15 years	52.12	48.88
	20 years	33.88	31.01
$16,000 in	5 years	$234.24	$229.60
	10 years	102.56	98.42
	15 years	59.56	55.86
	20 years	38.72	35.44
$18,000 in	5 years	$263.52	$258.30
	10 years	115.38	110.72
	15 years	67.01	62.84
	20 years	43.56	39.87

If you want this amount:		Save this much each month at the interest rate of:	
		5%	5¾%
$20,000 in	5 years	$292.80	$287.00
	10 years	128.20	123.03
	15 years	74.45	69.83
	20 years	48.40	44.30

NOTE: This table was prepared by the Continental Bank of Chicago. It is based on three assumptions: (1) Deposits monthly are made at the first of the month; (2) periodic deposits are monthly and are the same amount as the initial deposit; and (3) interest is compounded continuously.

COMPUTER TECHNOLOGY CHANGES OUR FINANCIAL HABITS

The introduction of computer technology in the United States has dramatically changed the way you regard and conduct your financial affairs. As of the 1980s, in cities across the nation:

• You, a shopper, may pay for goods and services at retail stores by using a plastic card inserted in an electronic terminal. Your savings or checking accounts are charged electronically. You carry less cash.

• You, a bank customer, may deposit or withdraw cash at any time of day or night by using your cards in an unattended "robot" teller.

• You, an employee, may have your paychecks deposited directly into your checking or savings accounts. Your employer makes the deposits by delivering a magnetic tape to the depository institution.

• You, a family money manager, may pay monthly installments on your mortgage or loans or utility bills by preauthorized charges to your deposit accounts or by phoning your instructions to your bank, savings and loan, or credit union.

• Electronic banking or electronic funds transfer system (EFTS), as it is called, already is revolutionizing the way you manage your banking affairs. Many of your routine financial tasks—bill-paying, deposits, withdrawals, etc—will be made easier. Banking could become more impersonal and automatic. You probably will conduct most everyday financial transactions without ever setting foot in the office of a financial institution.

ELECTRONIC FUNDS TRANSFER SYSTEM—ITS MEANING TO YOU

The changes that EFTS has brought will mean greater convenience to you, the customer. What is not so obvious is the savings that the system is designed to offer the financial institutions themselves. The institutions could save a minimum of $10 billion a year by slashing check-processing costs and eliminating the need for additional branch offices.

Whether or not these savings will be passed along to you, the borrower or saver, is far from certain. You are likely to find depository institutions charging you for the individual services they perform—bill-paying, transfer of funds from savings to checking, etc. The day soon may come when U.S. financial institutions will make more of their money from service fees than from lending or investments.

Equally uncertain, as the 1980s unfold, is precisely what type of responsibility both you and your depository institution will be required to assume for the accuracy, safety, and confidentiality of any electronic transactions. (See pages 794–96.)

Despite these big unknowns, financial institutions will continue implementing EFTS and offering you an array of new services.

Below is a sample of these increasingly common offerings. When deciding whether or not you want to take advantage of them, be sure you know what they will cost, what the alternatives are, and who is liable for any errors or foul-ups—you or the institution.

(1) *Automatic bill-paying:* Many banks, savings and loan associations, and credit unions will automatically pay such routine monthly bills as utility charges, insurance premiums, or mortgage payments.

(2) *Automatic line of credit:* The line of credit is a preapproved, unsecured amount of credit which essentially serves as overdraft protection on your checking account or as a means of financing purchases. The line of credit becomes available to you either through your regular checking account or a special checking account. If the credit is part of your regular checking account, you may write checks for more than your balance, up to the limit of the line of credit. The amount of credit forwarded to your account can be in standard denominations, such as $100. Once you have drawn on the credit, it is treated as a loan on which monthly payments must be made. There is usually no charge for the line of credit until you actually use it. If yours is a special checking account, the line of credit is the balance of the account. You receive a book of special checks to use against the predetermined maximum credit amount. Some of these accounts permit you to write the check for any amount. Others provide checks for specific amounts, say, $250 (as with travelers' checks). This service also may be available in conjunction with NOW (Negotiable Order of Withdrawal) accounts, essentially interest-bearing checking accounts, and credit union share draft accounts.

(3) *Automatic savings:* A financial institution will automatically transfer specified amounts of money at regular intervals from your checking to your regular or special savings account, just as it deducts payments for loans and bills. The institution also will invest these funds in United States Savings Bonds or designated mutual funds. If you have a trust account, you may have the dividends or interest from your investment automatically deposited into your savings account.

(4) *Telephone transfer:* Upon your request by phone, an institution will move funds from your savings to your checking account or vice versa if you ask for this service in advance. Some institutions may even move money from savings into checking automatically whenever there are not enough funds to cover a check.

(5) *Automatic payroll service:* Some institutions will perform a company's regular payroll services. The company and each employee have accounts at the institution. Once it records all employees and your salaries, it will deposit your earnings directly into your accounts, after making appropriate deductions for federal, state, and Social Security taxes. You, the employee, receive no paycheck but only a deposit slip indicating your salary, taxes withheld, net salary, and credits to your checking, savings accounts, or to your loan balance.

(6) *Direct deposit service:* This rests on the same principal as the automatic

payroll system, but usually is done for paychecks, Social Security, and pension checks going to a number of individual accounts at various institutions.

(7) *The transaction card:* The transaction or debit, access or asset card is the foundation of EFTS. It looks like a plastic credit card but often is magnetically coded to your bank, S&L, or credit union accounts through a computer system. The card permits you access to your accounts from a remote computer terminal. Some nationwide credit cards also are magnetically coded to permit access to your accounts. These cards frequently are used in conjunction with special identifying codes known as personal identification numbers (PINs).

(8) *Automatic teller machines (ATMs):* ATMs are computer terminals which provide access only to the customer's accounts. You, the customer, operate these machines with push buttons like those found on a telephone and with the magnetically coded transaction card. By pushing the buttons, you can get cash from your checking or savings account, deposit money into your accounts, move funds from one account to another, or even make loan payments. ATMs most commonly are attached to the financial institution itself, but more are being located at remote locations of greater convenience to customers.

(9) *Check verification:* These cards, held by customers, are inserted into a computer terminal in a grocery or department store by the salesperson. The bank tells the merchant via the computer whether there are adequate funds in the customer's account to cover the check. The system is designed to protect stores against bad checks.

(10) *Point-of-sale terminal (POS):* These terminals are found at stores. They permit you to pay for your purchases by immediately having money withdrawn from your account and transferred to the store's account. The debit card, which activates the POS, acts like an electronic check—one which neither bounces in the traditional way nor "floats" (the time—two to three or more days—it takes for a check to clear).

(11) *Push-button telephone banking:* Still experimental as the 1980s neared, this system involves attaching a small box, essentially a computer terminal, to your telephone. Your phone becomes an ATM, giving you access to your accounts at the push of the phone's buttons.

(12) *Travelers' checks via credit cards:* Under one American Express Company program, you may use your magnetically coded American Express card at ATM machines in airports around the country to obtain travelers' checks. The cost of these checks is automatically deducted from your checking account, not charged to your American Express account. Your bank must agree to participate.

How "Safe" Is Your Money?

It is almost impossible for most Americans to conceive of what it must have been like before the federal government insured bank and savings association deposits—to imagine the tragedy when an innocent family's lifetime savings disappeared in the crash of the trusted bank on the corner.

But ponder what it is like now:

In recent years, a fair number of banks failed—several of them frighteningly large institutions but *in no case did a depositor lose a single penny of his or her in-sured deposits.* The system has worked superbly well, there has been no worry—much less panic.

In recent years a fair number of savings and loan associations also failed—*but not one depositor in an institution federally insured lost one penny of his or her insured funds either.*

Today, 97 per cent of our banks are insured by the Federal Deposit Insurance Corporation in Washington. The insurance fund, contributed to by nearly four-teen thousand member banks throughout the nation, totals many billions of dol-lars. On top of this FDIC has authority to borrow as much as $3 billion addi-tional from the U. S. Treasury.

As for us, 99 per cent of all bank depositors' savings and checking accounts are FDIC-insured, and as of the late 1970s most of the funds we had on deposit in insured banks were covered up to a $40,000 limit.

In a recent year, too, about 4,200 federal and state-chartered savings and loan associations—out of a total of roughly 5,400—were insured by the Federal Sav-ings and Loan Insurance Corporation in Washington. The FSLIC's fund also to-taled billions and covered more than 96 per cent of the savings in insured associa-tions. The vast majority of associations not covered by the FSLIC are backed by state insurance funds.

In the late 1970s, all federally chartered credit unions were insured by the Na-tional Credit Union Administration—a total of approximately 13,000—and many of the 10,000-plus state-chartered credit unions were also federally insured. Other of the credit unions not protected by federal insurance have opted for other insurance alternatives and some states have mandatory laws for federal in-surance.

It's not a perfect system for depositors, but it's coming close, and the perform-ance record has been great.

Q. *What are the chances your bank might fail?*

A. Very slim indeed. In contrast to an average of 588 bank failures a year in the 1920s and an average of 2,277 in the 1930–33 period, bank failures averaged only five a year between the 1940s and 1970s among all banks, and only four a year for insured banks. The record has been similar for insured savings and loan associations.

Q. *Are only savings and checking accounts insured?*

A. No. These other types of deposits also are insured: Christmas savings and other open-account time deposits, uninvested trust funds, certified checks, cashier's checks, bank travelers' checks, and all other deposits "received by a bank in its usual course of business."

Q. *If you have both a checking and a savings account, is each insured up to $40,000?*

A. No. All deposits under your own name are added together and this total is insured up to $40,000.

Q. *What if you have, in addition to your own accounts, a joint account with your husband?*

A. Your joint account, with your husband or child, is insured separately for up to $40,000.

Q. *Are accounts kept at different banks insured separately?*

A. Yes. However, if you keep separate accounts at separate branches of your bank, all of these are considered as a single bank for the purposes of deposit insurance.

Q. *Are certificates of deposit covered?*

A. Yes. But they are not insured separately if they are held in the same bank at which you have other deposits in the same name.

Q. *My firm has some of its pension plans fund in an insured bank. Is my interest in the plan insured?*

A. Yes. Your interest in the plan is insured up to $40,000 regardless of any other accounts you may have at the same bank.

Q. *How and when would you be paid in the event your bank failed?*

A. You might be paid, probably within a week of the date your bank closed, by an FDIC check which you could then either cash or have deposited in your name in another insured bank. Or, more likely, your funds would be transferred to a new bank under new management, and become available to you within a few days. The payment period might be more prolonged in the case of a savings association failure, but the payment period of the FSLIC has generally been comparable to that of the FDIC.

Q. *Who pays for the insurance coverage on deposits?*

A. FDIC member banks, which are assessed approximately 1/30th of 1 per cent of their total deposits. Savings and loan associations pay higher assessments.

Here's a brief table to give you an idea of how much money you, a couple with one child, could keep in a single bank or savings and loan association, fully insured:

INDIVIDUAL ACCOUNTS

Man:	$ 40,000
Wife:	40,000
Child:	40,000

JOINT ACCOUNTS

Man and wife:	40,000
Man and child:	40,000
Wife and child:	40,000

TESTAMENTARY REVOCABLE TRUST ACCOUNTS

Man (as trustee for wife):	40,000
Man (as trustee for child):	40,000
Wife (as trustee for husband):	40,000
Wife (as trustee for child):	40,000

IRREVOCABLE TRUST ACCOUNTS

Man (as trustee for wife):	$ 40,000
Man (as trustee for child):	40,000
Wife (as trustee for husband):	40,000
Wife (as trustee for child):	40,000
TOTAL:	$560,000

It's most unlikely anyone would keep this total in cash in a financial institution, but you can actually have *insured* savings of as much as $560,000 in one institution!

To get 100 per cent protection against the remote possibility of a bank failure, follow these two fundamental rules:

1. *Don't* keep more than the legal maximum in your individual accounts of all types in any one financial institution or its branches.

2. *Do* bank only with a federal- or state-insured institution. All insured institutions advertise this fact, so take the time to make sure your institution is properly insured.

But be reassured. Banking is among the more tightly regulated and closely scrutinized industries in the nation. And legal steps are continually being taken by federal and state regulatory agencies to make the system ever more failure-proof.

SHOULD YOU RENT A SAFE DEPOSIT BOX?

You almost surely own a collection of records and valuables which *should* be stored in a bank safe deposit box—particularly in this period of soaring numbers of home burglaries and in view of the fact that many types of documents are very difficult if not impossible to replace.

Today, it costs only $15 to $25 a year to rent the small (typically 2 or 3 by 5 by 22 inches) safe deposit box most people find adequate. In some areas the cost is less. And, assuming you use the box to store such income-producing property as stocks or bonds, the rental charge is deductible from your federal income tax.

To be specific, you *should* rent a safe deposit box and put into it your valuables, hard-to-replace or irreplaceable items, including:

Any stock or bond certificates or bank savings certificates which you do not keep at your bank or with your stockbroker.

Insurance policies—except life insurance policies, which should be kept in a more accessible place in the event of your death.

Property records, including mortgages, deeds, titles.

Personal documents such as birth certificates, marriage licenses, divorce papers, citizenship papers, adoption papers, diplomas, business contracts and agreements, important legal correspondence and income tax records, passports, military discharge papers, and trust agreements.

An inventory of all household items of any value, giving the cost and purchase date of each item as a reference in case of fire or theft. This inventory should include photographs of furs and jewelry and fine pieces of art and furniture; serial numbers of TV sets, stereo sets, etc.; details about valuable coin or stamp collections you keep at home; jewels, collections of stamps or coins, heirlooms which you seldom wear or use or refer to.

A copy of your will—but *not* the original, which should be filed at your lawyer's office, kept in the hands of an executor, or in some similar protected but accessible place. Frequently a bank safe deposit box is sealed by state law for a specified period after the box owner's death.

Should you, as a married couple, own a safe deposit box jointly? How do you arrange for someone besides yourself to get in the box if need be?

The advantages of joint ownership of a safe deposit box are strongly offset by the disadvantages. You may squabble—when it comes to removing the box's contents—over which of you owns what. Or if a lawsuit is brought against one of you, this would tie up the property of the other—if it's in a jointly owned safe deposit box. As for what happens when *one* of two renters dies, ask your lawyer what are your own specific state laws covering this aspect.

Instead of joint ownership, you might authorize the other (or a lawyer or trusted relative) to serve as his or her "agent" if necessary. The first spouse keeps the keys and, technically at least, owns the entire contents of the safe deposit box. If the second spouse has valuables or important records of her or his own, there is no reason why this partner shouldn't have a separate box.

Once you make the decision to rent a safe deposit box, here are further rules for you to follow:

Make a list of what is in your box and put the list in a safe place at home. Your list should include: an identification of each valuable in the box; serial numbers and dates of stock or bond certificates, insurance policies, etc.; written appraisals of jewelry; the date you put each item in the box; the date you remove any item; the date of your most recent inspection. Keep this inventory up to date.

Collect receipts or other papers which prove you own the items in the box and put them in a safe place outside the box. Then you will have the essential papers should the box ever be destroyed or burglarized (most unlikely but possible).

Check your homeowner's insurance coverage to find out if it covers the contents of your safe deposit box, and, if so, to what extent it insures you against loss. Also, check the agreement you sign or have signed with the institution from which you rent your box to find out if the agreement includes clauses which limit your protection. For instance, are you prohibited from putting cash or diamonds in the box?

Keep each other (husband and wife) informed about the location of your safe deposit box, the number of the box, the contents of the box, the place you keep the keys.

Of course, the odds are overwhelmingly against any loss of the contents of your safe deposit box due to a robbery or some other catastrophe. This is obvious from the way boxes are built and the location of the vaults. And remember, *nobody* but you, the box holder (and any agent you may name), has keys which can open the box.

HAVE YOU FORGOTTEN MONEY YOU OWN?

In New York State alone in one year in the late 1970s, $123 million in "unclaimed or abandoned property"—most of it money forgotten by its owners (maybe you?)—was left in savings and checking accounts.

But this "unclaimed property" also included credit balances left with department stores, uncashed gift certificates, unclaimed payroll checks and dividends, uncashed airline tickets, travelers' checks, money orders, forgotten insurance benefits, utility company deposits and bonds, jewelry, coins, and cash left in long-abandoned safe deposit boxes.

In California, the total came to $15 million; in Illinois, to $11 million. Florida collected about $750,000 a year in unclaimed property; Wisconsin, close to $650,000; Alabama, about $1 million. Minnesota received almost $3 million in unclaimed property in fiscal 1978.

For many states, if not most, unclaimed property represents the largest source of revenue, next to taxes! In the late 1970s, about forty-five states had laws requiring banks, retail stores, and other businesses to turn over unclaimed property to the state after a certain number of years, usually seven but sometimes as long as twenty years. The state then holds the property in perpetuity for the owners. But since most owners or their heirs never claim their property, the individual state gets the funds.

Now, a drive is under way in many states to step up enforcement of unclaimed property laws.

The states deny that their more aggressive compliance and collection effort is a revenue-raising device. They insist it's an important service to you, the consumer.

But returning abandoned property to its owner (you?) isn't easy. Officials send notices to the owners' last known addresses and regularly publish ads in newspapers, listing owners' names. Business, banks, and insurance companies often do the same before they turn over the property to the state. But most owners of the unclaimed property never learn about it. The ads are too thick with names, and Americans move so often to so many far-apart areas.

In Minnesota, late in the 1970s, the state treasurer traveled to different parts of his state two to four times a month, bringing with him a list of abandoned-property owners whose last known addresses were in that particular county. Local reporters frequently ended their stories or broadcasts with lists of a hundred or so names of people with unclaimed property worth $100 or more.

Up to 75 per cent of the individuals whose names were so displayed ultimately reclaimed their goods or money. The return rate from another list published in a Minnesota TV magazine ran close to 50 per cent.

A legal but distasteful fringe development of this information campaign was the emergence of operators who scan the state's unclaimed property files (open to the public), copied down names, located the owners, then demanded a fee for reminding the owner that he or she owned an abandoned savings account or, say, payroll check. The operators can't be stopped but they are strongly opposed.

The biggest volume of unclaimed property, though, remains in the hands of the federal, not your state, government. No one knows precisely the value of the property—uncollected tax refunds, bonds, farm subsidy payments—but state officials want it turned over to their treasuries for eventual distribution to the proper owners.

Legislation was, in fact, being proposed to require such a federal-state transfer —or, at the very least, to require the U. S. Government to try to inform citizens it is holding their property.

Think hard. Can it be that I'm writing about you? I once saw in an abandoned property ad by a New York savings bank, the name of the bank's own president!

16

HOW TO BORROW CASH
AND USE CREDIT

INTRODUCTION

Should you borrow money now?

Of course you should—if you have sound (to you) reasons for doing so.

Is this the *right time* for you to borrow money?

Of course it is—if your reasons for borrowing are sound and your chances of repaying your debt within a tolerable period of time are good.

"Of course" always will be the answer to both these questions assuming your debt is for goods or services you feel you need or want, your loan is in line with your income, you have a plan for regular repayments.

There are two distinct sides to the possession of money: one is saving it, the other borrowing it. In our economy, both sides are crucially important to our financial health as a nation and as individuals. And both sides make vital contributions to our financial well-being as a nation and as individuals.

It is no exaggeration to say that almost uninterrupted buying on the installment plan or with a credit card has become a way of life in American homes to a point where a hefty percentage of the families we consider as representing the "ideal" in our nation are never out of debt and another hefty proportion seldom are.

That was, in fact, one of the most provocative findings that emerged from a survey I made a few years ago of the finalists in the "Mrs. America Pageant"—all outstanding women, bright, talented, good-looking, superb homemakers. What leaped first from their answers was how knowledgeable the women were, how acutely aware they were of money management, how devoted they were to budgeting, even "strict" down-to-the-penny keeping of the household accounts. And what leaped next from their answers and impressed me even more was the extent to which installment buying was an essential part of their family lives.

As one contestant put it to me: "We find that the best way to obtain major items is to maintain planned debt, purchasing one major item at a time for a cost which will fit into our budget and including interest as part of that cost." In the words of another, "We consider it worth the interest cost to use someone else's money and have earlier use of a product."

THE SIZE OF THE CREDIT MARKET

Over the past thirty years the number of Americans owing installment debt has soared and so has the amount each one owes. The increases have been far greater than the population growth and much more than the rise in our take-home pay.

As of the late 1970s, more than one quarter of our disposable personal income, the money we have each month to spend, was being earmarked to repay installment debt. More than one out of every two U.S. families today owes some type of loan, in addition to the mortgage on their homes.

And it's all but certain that you have some installment debt if—

• you are between eighteen and thirty-five;

• you are married and the head of a family;

• you have children in their teens, or younger;

• your income is in the low to middle range of the medium-income brackets, roughly $10,000 to $30,000 a year in the late 1970s.

IS ANYTHING WRONG WITH BORROWING?

I do not find the modern attitudes toward debt any cause for alarm. I see nothing wrong with paying money to use "someone else's money." I approve of "planned debt," which really is a kind of thrift. And, to an important degree, payments on an installment loan are merely replacing many old-time cash payments—like the money Americans used to dole out to the iceman or the cash we paid to the corner laundry.

In fact, I'll go beyond this and submit that the fundamental reason Americans have been borrowing so much today is precisely that they have had so much. This has intensified your desire to satisfy your aspirations rather than simply to finance your needs. And this in turn has led to unprecedented borrowing to achieve your aspirations at once.

Another factor is your increased financial security—through health insurance, Social Security, unemployment compensation, retirement pensions, employee savings and stock plans, ownership of stock and mutual funds, life insurance, etc.— and, very important, the income of the working wife. All these economic cushions are helping to make obsolete the traditional goal of protection against a "rainy day."

A third similarly subtle factor is the increased regularity of your income, which strengthens your capacity to take on responsibility for repaying installment debts. This development stems from the fundamental fact that our economy is now dominated by the service industries—and employment is much steadier in a service-oriented economy than in a predominantly industrial society.

Other factors include: the huge amounts of financial assets you as families are building up, primarily in your homes; the dramatic extension of credit to include unsophisticated as well as sophisticated borrowers, primarily through credit cards; the youthful hunger to acquire, instantly, all the things that other families have; and finally, the tendency of lenders to extend credit to borrowers at much younger ages than ever before.

And, of course, behind all the factors is the basic change that inflation has created in your attitudes toward being in debt and toward the goods and services that you appropriately may buy on time.

Perhaps as fundamental as any point is this: you, today's American, are far less interested than past generations in your legal total ownership of your toasters or automobiles or refrigerators. Instead, you are far more interested in the toasting services of that toaster, the transportation services of that automobile, the cooling service of that refrigerator. You are less and less impressed with owning things, more and more interested in the proper use of things. The growth of leasing and renting, not just of cars, but of a wide variety of other goods and services, is further testimony to this trait.

The Right and Wrong Reasons for Borrowing

Even in this era of high inflation, the cheapest way to buy any thing or nonthing is to buy it for cash. You always save money when you do this, for there are no extra charges added to your purchase price. As a buyer for cash, you can shop around for the best buy. Also, as a buyer for cash, you don't tie up future income, you are well aware of how many dollars you actually are spending, and you are not tempted to overbuy. The reason that retailers dangle the lure of "easy credit terms" before you is that the lure does work. It does encourage you to buy more. It does increase the retailer's sales.

But when you borrow to buy some things or non-things, you get the privilege of enjoying the purchase while you pay for it. You can start using at once something you need or want instead of being forced to wait until you can accumulate the savings to finance its purchase. Your buying on credit can teach you thrift. The discipline forced on you by your installment payments can spill over and encourage you to develop excellent saving habits. Many types of credit charge accounts are more convenient than cash or checks. Credit can be a crucial assist in a financial emergency.

To me, the advantages of buying on credit far outweigh the disadvantages of the cost of credit and the possible extravagance, provided, of course, that your reasons for credit-buying are sound and that you indulge in this type of purchasing with sensible moderation.

THE RIGHT REASONS FOR BORROWING

Regardless of whether you are equally convinced at this point, for the moment assume you agree that borrowing money—in the form of cash, or in the form of goods and services—is right for you if your reasons are right.

What might those reasons be?

(1) You are establishing a household or beginning to have a family. Either of these major events in life will take a lot of money—and it's in these, your early years, that you should learn how to use credit wisely and to the best advantage for yourself.

(2) You must make some major purchases. Few Americans can buy a car out of cash on hand and few can buy furniture or appliances that way either. These big-ticket items are traditionally bought with credit. As for a house, virtually all of us borrow to finance that key purchase of our lives. (See chapter on your home, 183–93.)

(3) You are faced with a genuine emergency and have not as yet had the opportunity to accumulate a sufficient emergency cash fund. Borrowing to meet emergencies is about as valid a reason as there can be.

(4) There are attractive seasonal sales or specials on which you can save money if you can use a charge account or a time-payment plan or get a low-cost loan from a financial institution. This assumes that the items on sale are ones you really want or need.

(5) You need money for college or other education expenses. This also is a top-notch reason for borrowing either by the student or by the parents. In fact, borrowing for college is the normal thing in America in this era. (See education chapter, pages 525–28 for details.)

(6) The price of an item you need in the future is heading sharply higher and it is ridiculous for you not to try to beat the price rise by borrowing the money to buy it now, and then repaying with cheaper dollars.

THE WRONG REASONS FOR BORROWING

(1) You haven't a reasonable prospect of repaying the loan, but you are going ahead anyway and borrowing because you need the money or want the goods or services. Or you are borrowing to the very hilt of your capacity to repay, which means that even a minor miscalculation on your part could force you to default.

(2) You are buying something impulsively and are primarily attracted to the purchase, not because the product is of good quality and reasonably priced, but because the payment terms seem so easy and you are offered a long time to pay up. This is self-deception of the most dangerous kind from your personal financial point of view.

(3) You are charging purchases solely to boost your morale. Some individuals try to beat the blues with an extravagant shopping spree. Doing this on credit can bring an ever bigger attack of melancholy when the bills—with interest—finally come due.

(4) You are using credit to increase your status. Charging a purchase does allow you to pay for things while you're enjoying them. But credit alone can't raise your standard of living. Over the long run, if you "can't afford" certain items on your present income, you can't afford to buy them on credit.

(5) You are overusing credit generally and failing to maintain an adequate cash reserve. People who do this also tend to live hand to mouth with their cash. They build up little or no savings fund to use during medical or other emergencies. So even if they are able to repay regular debts on schedule, any unexpected financial reversal can be their complete undoing.

(6) You are using credit against the expectation of future salary increases or windfall cash. When your income is on the rise, it's tempting to figure that your

next raise is a cinch. But if you go ahead with major credit expenditures and then don't get the extra money, your budget can get very, very tight in a hurry.

(7) You are borrowing to gamble on some exceedingly risky venture—as distinct from borrowing to invest in a worthy enterprise you have thoroughly investigated. Borrowing to buy stocks or real estate or invest in a small business deal is entirely in order, particularly if you are young enough to recoup if you lose. But borrowing to gamble is begging for trouble—and the very fact that you have to borrow means that this is not extra money you can afford to lose.

(8) You are living so far beyond your income that you have to borrow to meet your current bills. On pages 873–76, analyzing how much debt is too much debt, you'll find several guidelines on the safe limits for borrowing. Suffice it to say here that when you must pile up debts just to manage your day-to-day living, you are headed for financial disaster.

(9) You are borrowing to buy something that will be used up or worn out long before you have made the final payment for it. This caution is exceedingly flexible, though, and you must use your common sense in applying it to yourself.

For instance, it might make sense to take out a twelve-month installment loan to pay for this year's vacation, for even though you would still be paying off the loan after the vacation is a memory, it could be worth it if you wouldn't have any vacation otherwise. But it would not make sense to take a two-year loan for this year's vacation, for in this case you would still paying off this year's vacation when next year's vacation time rolls around.

Another illustration of this point (9) is borrowing to pay for college and education or special training courses. You well may be paying off a loan years after you've completed your education, but the value of your education will endure years and years after that. In this case, the value of your purchase is without time limit and cannot be measured by the yardsticks which we use for material goods. But precisely the opposite is borrowing to pay for an exceedingly expensive gown. Buy this sort of gown for cash if you have it, and if this is your deep desire. But borrowing to buy it? That's financial stupidity.

Loans for such purposes—long-term installment debts for items which will be worn out or used before the loan is paid—are called "garbage debts." Remember the plaint of Willy Lohman, in Arthur Miller's *Death of a Salesman*. He wanted, just once, to be able to buy a new car which would not fall apart before his final payment was made.

THE BASIC DO'S AND DON'TS OF CREDIT

No matter where you go for credit and no matter how many different types of loans you take out in the years to come, the basic do's and don'ts of credit will remain the same. Below you'll find them in the form of a simple check list to which you can refer again and again to make sure you are obeying these most fundamental of all credit rules.

Do always keep in mind that credit costs money. When you borrow you are, in essence, renting money—and just as you must pay when you rent an apartment or a car, so you must pay when you rent money. Anything you buy on credit will cost you more than the identical item bought for cash.

Do shop for credit as you shop for any other important purchase and buy your credit on the most advantageous terms to you. You can compare credit terms much more easily today than before the Truth in Lending law went into effect in 1969. Compare the price of any item bought for cash or bought on the installment plan. Find out whether it's cheaper for you to borrow from a bank or credit union and then buy the item you want for cash—or whether it's better for you to finance the purchase at the store or dealer's. (If you can meet the credit terms, it will *almost always* be cheaper, for example, to borrow from a bank or credit union than from the retailer, the dealer, or a small loan firm.)

Do check with care the maximum amount of credit you can soundly and safely carry. You can do it against the guidelines you'll find in this chapter, and you also can check your credit status with a responsible loan officer at your local bank, consumer finance office, credit union, other lending source. This officer is in the business of "selling" money—and nothing else—and he will want to make sure the person to whom he is selling the money is in a sound position to pay back.

Do ask lots of questions about the credit deal you are being offered, if you have any doubts at all. Insist on a written statement from the salesman showing you all charges plus the cash cost before you decide on buying.

Do ask yourself: would you buy the item for this amount of money in cash if you had the cash in your wallet or purse right now? Would you buy as expensive an item as the one you are considering if you had to put down the entire sum in cash now? In short, have you taken the proper time to make sure that this is a good purchase for you in view of the time it will take you to pay for it?

Do study your installment contract with utmost care and be sure you understand it before you sign it. When you sign, get a copy of the contract and keep it in a safe place.

Do keep receipts of your payments in a safe place.

Do pay off one major installment debt obligation before you take on another. Stagger your debts; time them; don't pile them one on top of another.

Do make sure that, in the installment deal you sign, all your monthly payments are roughly equal and make sure this applies particularly to your last payment. Avoid the danger that you'll be faced with a very big final installment ("balloon" payment). (See "The Great Pitfalls of Credit" later in this chapter.)

Do have the courage to say no to an installment deal if any of the above warning signals are flying—any of them.

And do continue saving regularly as you buy on credit. Even if you can save only a small amount each week, save it. For it's the regularity of savings and the discipline of the installment payments that will be the foundation of your own and your family's wealth.

Don't buy any item or service from any seller unless you have checked his reputation and have confidence he is a responsible retailer or dealer or whatever. Before you pledge to pay a specified part of your earnings for a protracted period, use your common sense and make sure you are dealing with a reputable businessman conducting a reputable business at a reputable place and that you can come back to him should your purchase turn out to be a lemon.

Don't buy anything you don't need or want—certainly not for credit. Learn how to handle high-pressure selling.

Don't carry several charge accounts that are seldom or never paid up. Revolving accounts make it very easy to maintain a permanent debt. But pay off each account periodically, for without this kind of self-discipline, revolving balances tend to grow ever larger (and more expensive) over periods of time.

Don't use your debts to establish your budgeting "system." Although some people would have no financial system at all if it weren't for their stack of bills, wise use of credit means month-by-month planning—not this sort of upside-down method.

Don't ever buy any thing or non-thing on credit without consulting your spouse or other person with whom you may be sharing financial responsibility and making sure that the two of you think the purchase is worthwhile. You must agree on any major purchase or you'll have great difficulty meeting the discipline of installment payments.

Don't be in any hurry to sign any installment contract or agreement.

Don't make the mistake of thinking you can get out of an installment debt simply by returning the merchandise you bought to the seller.

What you may have done when you bought the item is to sign two contracts: one for the actual appliance purchased and the second for the money to finance the purchase. This second loan contract will usually be sold immediately by the dealer to a finance company or bank, which then becomes what the lawyers call a "holder in due course." The bank or loan company has no ability to correct any defect in the item you have bought, and little interest in doing so either.

Under new legislation, you may have some protection in these situations, if the retailer from whom you bought the appliance also arranged for the loan for your purchase. But recognize that you are now dealing with third parties. You must go through the loan company to get the dealer to repair your TV set, dishwasher, or other appliance.

Don't rely on verbal warranties or pledges of the salesman, his boss, or even the owner. Get the promises in writing. But don't assume that because you *do* get it in writing, the promises will be honored. Under the Magnuson-Moss Warranty Act, there has been a vast improvement in disclosure of warranty terms to you, but little improvement has been made in compelling the companies who issue the warranties actually to fulfill them.

Don't buy any item on credit which does not have a value that will outlast the installment payments. This is an extension of the flexible wrong reason No. 9 for borrowing. The key word in this rule is "value."

Don't buy anything on credit of which you will tire before you finish the installment payments. You might really ponder this "don't" when buying your four-year-old an expensive and easily breakable toy game on a twelve-month payment plan.

Don't ever borrow money from a loan shark—even if you are desperate for the cash. In fact, the more desperate you are for the money, the more insane it is for you to commit yourself to pay back interest rates ranging to 1,000 per cent a year and more for the money. This way lies financial disaster.

Don't sign any loan contract that contains blank spaces that could be filled in to your disadvantage.

Don't co-sign a loan for anyone unless you have complete faith in that person's ability and willingness to repay the loan. For if the borrower whose note you co-sign defaults on the loan, you are responsible for paying off the entire indebtedness.

And, above all, *don't* borrow unless you will be able to *continue* to save regularly, too.

How to Establish a Credit Rating

A young army veteran, with a wife and two babies, was recently turned down for a mortgage which he needed to buy a new home in eastern Texas. The reason: information at the local credit bureau showed him to be a bad credit risk. Astonished, the veteran visited the credit bureau and discovered that the reason for his credit troubles was that his former wife had run up a lot of unpaid bills just prior to their divorce. The veteran explained that under the separation agreement his estranged wife had signed a full year before she ran up the bills, she was legally responsible for all her debts, and his credit record had been wrongly damaged. His credit record was cleared and he got the mortgage he needed.

The ease with which Americans can open a charge account, get a new credit card, or take out a bank loan is directly dependent on the voluminous dossiers in the files of 2,500 credit bureaus throughout the United States and of large numbers of local merchants' associations on virtually every borrower. The bureaus freely exchange this information. They sell it to retailers, banks, other lenders, credit card companies, corporations, etc.—and a credit report almost surely will be obtained on you when you apply for a job or insurance or credit.

The consumer credit reporting industry processes from 125 to 150 million credit reports each year. Just one computerized credit reporting company says it maintains 30 million files, enters 4 million "pieces of information" on individuals each month, services 14,000 subscribers, and maintains on some individuals as many as 35 to 40 open accounts on which credit performance is reported.

Credit bureaus do not "rate" how good or bad a credit risk you are. They simply collect, from merchants with whom you have credit, public records, other sources of information on you which can be used in turn by banks, merchants, etc., to decide whether to grant you credit. The information ranges from your name, address, occupation, employer, and earnings to your former employment and earnings record, your marital history, your moving habits, your repayment patterns on previous loans, and records of any court proceedings against you.

The lenders then decide, on the basis of information provided by the credit bureau, whether or not you are a good credit risk. The guidelines vary from lender to lender, of course. A department store may be satisfied if you are in the habit of repaying charges within thirty to sixty days, while a bank may demand that, with very few exceptions, you repay bank loan installments on the due dates.

Or lenders may summarize their policies by telling you they are rating your application in terms of the "Three C's" of Credit. These Three C's are your:

Character: your personal characteristics, revealed through factual records, which indicate how you are likely to perform as a borrower. These would include your honesty, sense of responsibility, soundness of judgment, your trustworthiness.

Capacity: your financial ability to repay the loan. Your capacity would be judged on the basis of the job you hold, the amount of money you earn, the length of time you have held this or a previous job, your prospects in this or another job.

Capital: your assets which can serve as banking—collateral—for your loan. These assets would include your home, bank accounts, stocks and bonds, a car or cars, jewelry, valuable paintings, other tangible property.

These three qualities of Character, Capacity, and Capital form the foundation of any credit rating for you, as an individual or as a family.

To get even more specific, here are points that every lending officer will tick off when considering your application for a loan and your rating as a credit risk.

Your Employment Record: How long have you worked for the same company —although not necessarily in the same office or plant of the company?

A prime consideration is the stability of your employment. It is up to you to prove your trustworthiness by showing you have not been a job-hopper who might once again leave for a job far away from your present one when, say, less than half your loan payments have been made.

Your Previous Loans: Have you ever paid off a loan before? The theory is that, if you have repaid a loan on time before this one, you will repay this loan, too. If you have defaulted on any previous loan, the danger is you'll default again. You'll almost certainly have a poor credit rating if you have any record of defaults or of repossession of items you have bought because you didn't maintain your payments or of suits for being delinquent in payments.

Your Home: Do you own your own home? Or have you lived in the apartment in which you now live for some time? If the answer is yes to either question, it's a sign that you probably are trustworthy.

Your Charge Accounts: Have you a record of paying your charge accounts regularly? If so, this will be a plus mark for you because it will indicate your sense of responsibility and your ability to repay.

Your Checking or Savings Accounts: Do you have either? If so, and particularly if they are at the bank to which you may be applying for a loan, this will be a great help.

Now here are six potential black marks on your credit rating:

(1) If you can't identify yourself. Surely you will have one or more of these: a driver's license, birth certificate, Social Security card, draft card, union card.

(2) If you have a "floating" address. This might be a furnished room in a

rooming house or a transient hotel, a post office box number, a mail address in care of a friend. You might offset this, however, if previously you had lived in one place for a long time.

(3) If your employment is in an exceedingly unstable industry or profession and your own job is also basically volatile. If you're a ballet dancer . . . have a strictly seasonal job . . . are in a very restricted field . . .

(4) If, in some states, you are under twenty-one or eighteen and have no adult to co-sign for you. However, many stores do extend credit to teens without a co-signer anyway, for as a group they have turned out to be good credit risks.

(5) If you apply for a loan at a bank or small loan company or other financial source far from your residence or if you have a record of dealing extensively with numerous small loan companies.

(6) If you are planning to go into the armed services before your loan is repaid. Under these circumstances, the lender almost surely will demand that a co-signer guarantee your loan repayment.

Under laws enacted in the late 1970s, it is much easier for a woman to get credit. In fact, lending institutions are now required to carry a wife's credit history under her own name, as well as that of her husband, if she requests it. (See pages 1218–19.)

But some lending organizations are engaging in other practices that can restrict credit. For example, banks—and some insurance companies—are turning down loans (and policies) simply because you have the wrong zip code, live in a particular neighborhood. And living *habits* are being used as criteria for establishing "character." If you are offending the "traditional" mores of society (using drugs, for example, keeping late, loud hours, or sharing your apartment with a member of the opposite sex), your life-style could be a factor in whether you are granted, or denied, a loan. (See pages 1213–21 on "Your Rights as a Borrower.")

WHAT IS THE DIFFERENCE BETWEEN CREDIT REPORTS AND INVESTIGATIVE REPORTS?

A regular credit report is compiled and maintained by a credit bureau for the purpose of helping consumers obtain credit. The credit bureaus do not make use of outside investigators, who are sometimes used in insurance reporting.

The information normally accumulated in your credit record consists of identity information, including your name, address, marital status, and Social Security number; present employment, which includes the position you hold, length of employment, and income; your personal history, such as date of birth, number of dependents, previous address, and previous employment information; credit history information including your credit experiences with credit granters; and public-record information which credit granters feel is important to know.

An investigative report consists of much more information—including data about a consumer's character, general reputation, personal characteristics, or mode of living. The information usually is obtained through personal interviews with the consumer's neighbors, friends, or associates or with others with whom the consumer is acquainted.

Credit bureaus do not normally compile this type of report, although an employment report made by a credit bureau will often contain some investigative information.

Both types of reports are subject to errors and one-sided presentations which can unfairly deny you credit and damage you in other ways. But you now have protection against such damages. (See pages 1221–27 on your rights.)

And because you have not been late in an installment payment or have not been turned down for a loan or credit application, don't assume your credit is excellent. If you have applied for a credit card and received no answer, for example, suspect that there is an unfavorable entry in your record. Or if you are turned down for a job, or not called back for a second interview, be equally suspicious.

Check your records, and correct any errors, *now,* before a financial emergency arises. And recheck every two or three years. Then, if you need money fast, you'll be more likely to get the loan quickly.

THE BASIC TYPES AND MATURITIES OF LOANS

THE SINGLE-PAYMENT LOAN

This is precisely what its name implies: a loan you must repay in one lump sum. A single-payment loan may be a demand loan, meaning there will be no set time when you must repay but you will be obligated to pay back what you owe when the lender asks you to. Or the single-payment loan may be a time loan, meaning your loan will have a fixed maturity date and you'll have to pay back every penny on that prefixed maturity date.

Some single-payment loans call for the repayment of the amount borrowed in one lump sum, on demand or on a certain date, but also require that you pay interest on the amount borrowed periodically—monthly, quarterly, or annually.

A single-payment loan is usually made against collateral, meaning that you must put up certain valuable assets, such as your stocks, bonds, insurance policies, etc., to guarantee the loan repayment. The primary drawback of the single-payment loan is that you do not have periodic payments on it and thus you are not disciplined into reducing the loan month after month until it is all paid off. Instead you are faced with the entire repayment on a single date.

THE INSTALLMENT LOAN

This also is precisely what its name implies: a loan you must pay off in specified amounts at periodic intervals.

Usually you repay an installment loan in equal amounts every month over a period from twelve to sixty months. Usually, too, the interest cost is figured on the total amount of your loan.

In addition to these two basic types of loans, there are three major maturities on loans: short-term, intermediate, and long-term.

THE SHORT-TERM LOAN

This is the type of loan you use most frequently either to buy goods or to obtain cash or to finance everyday services.

For instance, you're using short-term credit when you buy a big-ticket appliance on the installment plan or with a credit card and promise to pay off within twelve to thirty-six, forty-eight, or even sixty months for autos. You are also using short-term credit when you get a cash loan—single-payment or installment payment—and promise to pay off within three years. Whether it's "cash" credit or "sales" credit, whether it's "installment" credit or "non-installment" credit, whether it's a "demand" loan or "time" loan, you're using short-term credit if you pledge to repay within a period ranging from as little as thirty days to five years.

THE INTERMEDIATE-TERM LOAN

This is the type of credit you use most often when you are financing major improvements or major repairs on your home. The maturity of this type of loan ranges from five to seven or even to ten years or more for boats, home improvements, or household furnishings.

THE LONG-TERM LOAN

This type is implicit in its name. A familiar example is the real estate mortgage, extended over a period ranging from twenty to thirty and thirty-five years or even more—and repayable in regular installments at fixed intervals, usually monthly, during the life of the loan. Of course, you may get a long-term loan for other purposes but the mortgage is the best illustration of this category.

YOUR SOURCES OF LOANS IN CASH

If you want to buy a new TV set, you don't just walk into the first TV store you pass and buy it. You look around, decide which model you prefer, then shop for the dealer who offers the set you want at the most favorable price to you.

Okay, you want to buy money.

Whatever the reasons—whatever goods or service you want to buy or whatever you want to build or finance—you need more money than you're earning each week or are able to commit for this single purpose. Whatever the amount—$500 or $2,500 or $5,000 or whatever—you are about to borrow (buy) money and pay the interest rate (price) asked by the lender (seller).

You live in a highly competitive economy, though, and the price of money in this competitive economy, like the price of everything else, will vary considerably. There are many sources for cash loans. Many compete for your patronage on the basis of price, convenience, service. Many also compete by specializing in specific types of loans. Many of them—such as your parents, other relatives, or friends— are simply "there." But never forget this key point: you easily can pay a price (interest rate) hundreds of dollars a year more than you need to pay by going to a lender who is not the best *for you*. You easily can cheat yourself disgracefully by not shopping for your money.

Let's approach this vital aspect of your financial life in the simplest way possible. To begin with, here are your sources of loans in cash.

THE "INSIDE" SOURCES

Your sources of a loan fall into two broad, general categories: "inside" sources and "outside" sources. The inside sources are the people close to you, the ones who know you—your parents, other relatives, friends, your employer or even business associates.

The second category covers the outside sources—the broad spectrum of the financial community, ranging from traditional commercial banks to savings banks, savings and loan associations, small loan companies, credit card companies, employee credit unions, your life insurance company, your stock brokerage firm, pawnbrokers—and even loan sharks.

First, the "inside" sources.

PARENTS OR OTHER RELATIVES

Your parents or other relatives could be your best, easiest source of low-cost or no-cost loans. Assuming they have money available and are eager to help, your search for a cash loan may end right here.

Typical maximum you may borrow

That depends on your relatives' affluence, their attitudes toward lending you money, your needs, your relationships, etc. In short, obviously there is no "typical" maximum.

Typical annual interest rate

Yours could be a no-interest loan or you could insist on paying the same interest rate you would pay another lender (say, what you would pay the bank on the corner). I opt strongly for paying an interest rate and also for matching at least the minimum you might be charged by an outside source of credit. But this is your loan negotiation and again the obvious point is there is no "typical" charge.

Typical maximum maturity

There is no typical maximum maturity, and, just because most loans made by the parents would have no maturity date, the loan might drag on and on. This lack of a definite maturity can be both an advantage and a disadvantage.

Advantages

There is no legal pressure on you to meet regular monthly payments, even if you do have a moral, if not contractual, responsibility to try to pay back the loan as soon as you can.

Your parents may have a sympathetic understanding of the reasons you are borrowing and be eager to help you.

Disadvantages

The embarrassment of having to ask your parents or other relatives for financial help.

The very lack of pressure on you to repay may make you lazy about repaying and the debt could continue hanging over your head much longer than it need to or should.

The amounts you borrow may be too large or too small, because the personal relationships will affect your judgments on both sides.

FRIENDS

A loan from a close friend or a group of close friends with sufficient extra cash and interest in you to be your loan source is in the same general category as a loan from your parents or other relatives.

This applies even though your friends may be backing you in a venture they think is as exciting and promising as you do and even though there is a stated or implied pledge on your part to let them share liberally in any profits you make, for presumably you are also making the same explicit or implied pledge to share the profits with your own relatives. And if you aren't, you should.

Typical maximum you may borrow

None. See above.

Typical annual interest rate

Also none. But I repeat it's only common sense to insist on paying roughly the same interest rates you would pay the local bank.

Typical maximum maturity

None. However, again I suspect your friends will work out a maturity date of some sort—and if they don't, you work it out.

Advantages

In general, the same advantages that apply to a loan from parents or other relatives apply to loans from close friends. But I warn you: a loan from friends easily can corrode your friendship even if you pay it off promptly.

Disadvantages

The same disadvantages apply to these loans as to loans from relatives.

ADVANCE AGAINST SALARY OR LOAN FROM EMPLOYER

Most employers are reluctant to advance a salary paycheck or to make a personal loan. This generality, though, by no means applies to all employers, and in fact many corporations have special departments through which employees may borrow money with a minimum of red tape. Also your boss may be an acceptable loan source for you if yours is a close friendly relationship in a small office.

But an advance against your future salary—say your next two paychecks delivered right now—means you will face two empty pay periods some days hence.

Typical maximum you may borrow

This varies so widely from corporation to corporation and small business to small business that it would be a disservice to be specific. Also, in a small business, the maximum will depend on the business' profit picture, the employer's financial position, your relationship with the employer, your reasons for borrowing, and on and on.

Typical annual interest rate

Usually the same interest rate that you would be charged if you went to a bank for a loan. However, I know of no employer who charges interest on a salary advance. Other conditions of the salary advance are subject to private negotiation between the employer or the corporation personnel manager and the employee.

Typical maximum maturity

Usually six months to a year although, again, this maximum varies widely among both large and small businesses.

Advantages

The money is there.

Your employer may be a most sympathetic lender if he knows and approves the reasons you are borrowing.

The interest rate and repayment period will be among the best available from all sources.

An advance on your salary is simply borrowing in advance money due you in the future and involves no more than that.

Disadvantages

Borrowing money from your boss can hurt your relationship with him and place you in a sticky position.

This loan may permit him to ask and find out things about your personal financial life which you would prefer he not know.

If you take an advance on your salary, you may not be able to swing the payless pay periods and you may have to go to outside sources for cash after all.

THE "OUTSIDE" SOURCES

During the 1970s, the inevitable trend toward elimination of our country's crazy-quilt pattern of money institutions grew ever more powerful—and with this trend will come benefits—and pitfalls—for all of us.

Traditional separations of functions are breaking down, "new traditions" are being established. As the 1980s began, commercial banks had begun to pay interest on checking accounts, while savings banks had also entered the checking account business with such devices as "negotiated orders of withdrawal," and both credit unions and savings and loan associations had broken down the barriers as well.

Employee credit unions are competing with commercial banks and savings banks. Even stock brokerage firms are offering what amounts to savings and checking accounts, in the form of "money funds," and these brokers are also actively soliciting their customers to take out loans against their stock portfolios. Credit card companies are offering loans, too.

While the financial community is in this state of flux, it becomes even more important for you to shop for your loan, for the best price and the best terms.

COMMERCIAL BANK

For most of you a commercial bank will be the most convenient loan source of all. For at this bank, which is probably a mere city block or two from where you live in town or only a couple miles away if you live in the suburbs, you may get the widest variety of loans including:

Personal loan

You may apply for a personal loan, repayable in one lump sum at its due date, or you may apply for an installment loan repayable in regular monthly installments over a period of twelve, eighteen, twenty-four, or thirty-six months.

Automobile loan

You may apply for an automobile loan to finance your new or used car. These loans usually are repayable in installments ranging from twelve to forty-two or even forty-eight to sixty months. Many automobile dealers as well as other merchants help the customer arrange for bank installment financing right in their showrooms.

Check loan

You may get money simply by writing a check, assuming you qualify. Your bank automatically enters the "loan" on your monthly statement of checking account transactions—when you write the special or overdraft check.

Mortgage and home improvement loan

You may get home improvement loans with intermediate maturities under which you can repair, remodel, expand, and generally improve your home. And you may get a long-term mortgage through which you may finance the purchase of your home in the first place.

Secured loan

You may get a loan quickly and comparatively inexpensively simply by putting up collateral to back your pledge to repay the loan. You can arrange to repay this loan in monthly installments. Your collateral may include your stocks or bonds or mutual fund shares or savings account passbook or the cash surrender value of your life insurance policy.

Student loan

Banks offer several types of student loans—some government subsidized, some not.

Credit card loan

You, the owner of a bank credit card, may use your card to buy goods at stores participating in the bank's credit card plan. The bank bills you monthly, and you, the borrower, pay interest on the unpaid balance you owe on your purchases.

Or you may use your bank credit card to borrow a limited amount of cash. (See special section below on credit cards and segment on "ready-credit" plans.)

Typical maximums you could borrow as 1980s opened

$10,000–$15,000 on a personal loan; $8,000–$10,000 on an auto loan.*
$75,000–$100,000 on a mortgage loan. *
$15,000–$20,000 on a home improvement loan. *
$2,500 a year on a federal-state guaranteed student loan.
$1,500–$2,000 on a check loan.
$1,500–$2,000 on a credit card plan.*

Up to the amount in your savings account on a passbook loan and up to a specified proportion of the estimated value of the collateral you put up to back a secured loan.

Typical annual interest rates were

So flexible and variable from year to year and loan to loan and area to area that no "typical" figure has meaning to you for long. However, here were typical rates as of the late 1970s:

Personal loan:	12–18%
Automobile loan:	
New car	10–14%
Used car	12–18%
Check (overdraft) loan:	10–16%
Mortgage loan:	8–12%
Home improvement loan:	10–15%
Passbook loan:	8–12%
Secured loan:	10–16%
Federal-guaranteed student loan:	8%
Credit card loan:	12–18%
Education loan:	9–12%

With inflation an acute problem during much of the 1970s, the interest rates listed above may vary considerably, up or down, depending on the state of the economy and where you live. However, they are a useful relative guide to com-

---

* Although these are typical amounts in most cases, banks are not in any way limited to making loans in these amounts.

mercial bank practices. The general rule is that unsecured loans cost more than secured loans, and the type of security affects the rate on secured loans.

Typical maximum maturities†

Three to five years on personal loans, auto loans, secured loans.

Five to ten years on home improvement loans.

Up to thirty or thirty-five years on first mortgages and three to ten years on second mortgages.

Up to twenty-five to thirty years on refinancing mortgages.

By regulation, up to ten years after graduation on student loans.

Advantages

Simplicity: you fill out an application and a financial statement, have an interview with the loan officer, and quite likely your cash loan is approved within twenty-four hours.

Objectivity: you can get a loan whether or not you are a depositor at the bank and, although of course bank practices vary widely, generally you will qualify for a loan if your credit rating is okay and your income will enable you to handle the monthly payment.

Relatively inexpensive: rates on bank loans compare favorably with rates from most other loan sources and so do bank loan maturity terms.

No extra or hidden fees or charges; under the law, there must be full disclosure of terms.

Since co-makers are not usually required, you need not appeal to friends or business acquaintances to endorse your note.

When you have fulfilled the terms of the loan, as prescribed, you have established a valuable credit reference.

Disadvantages

The requirements—your personal financial standing, credit rating—are sometimes more rigid than other lenders may demand.

You will be penalized if you take out an installment loan and don't meet your monthly installments on schedule. The penalty is often a flat fee of 5 per cent, plus interest, for each delinquency. State laws generally prescribe allowable charges for delinquency.

READY CREDIT (THE LOAN IN ADVANCE)

How does this form of credit work? Who qualifies for it? When is it economical to use it and when not?

Ready credit is an automatic line of credit offered by your bank or credit card company. In some cases its reserve is an extension of your checking account. In others the reserve may be kept in a separate account involving special checks. Usually the reserve is between $500 and $2,500, but it may run up to $5,000 or more.

In either case, the overdraft check or special check you may write becomes a

† Rates listed are typical, but actual maximums are set by each bank.

loan as soon as it reaches your bank. In either case also, the typical interest rate, including credit life insurance, is 1 per cent a month on the basis of the daily outstanding balance, which works out to a true annual interest rate of at least 12 per cent. Typically, no interest charge is made unless and until you actually use your special line of credit, and the interest charge stops when you repay the amount you have withdrawn from your reserve.

"Ready credit" is granted by a signed agreement to qualified customers, and the requirements for eligibility are generally stricter than those for ordinary bank loans because it is unsecured credit and, once granted, is available year after year to the responsible borrower. It may be canceled at any time by the bank, however.

As an illustration of the costs involved at 1 per cent a month interest (12 per cent a year annual rate) let's say you overdrew your checking account by $100. If you repaid the amount one month later, the cost to you would be $1.00. If you repaid the total after one week, the cost would be 23 cents. If you repaid it in one day, the cost would be 3 cents.

Under what circumstances is it to your advantage to use this type of credit and when is it a disadvantage? Here are the answers:

• If you spot a major bargain, an appliance selling at a big discount, for example, you probably would save by using the overdraft plan. Here, the amount of interest you would pay would be comfortably covered by your savings on the appliance, assuming you repaid the special loan within a few weeks or even a few months.

• If an emergency arises on a weekend, or when you are far from home, a reserve credit line may be the easiest and surest way to raise emergency funds.

• If you are a chronically bad bookkeeper, the interest on a reserve credit line might be less costly to you than a pile of service charges for department stores or for overdraft checks. It might also save you the tremendous embarrassment of bouncing checks.

• If you are self-employed or if your income goes into sharp but temporary dips, this credit may provide you with enough peace of mind to make it worth the interest you pay.

To save on interest expense, a fundamental guide is that your line of ready credit should be strictly for short-term purposes and your overdrafts should be repaid as quickly as possible. Thus, "ready credit" is not usually the right type for you when you're paying longer-term debts—financing a car, a planned home improvement, your college education. Banks offer other types of loans more appropriate for these purposes and generally at lower interest rates.

CREDIT UNION

A credit union may be the ideal answer to your borrowing problem if you have access to one and the union is efficiently managed.

Few, if any, regular lending agencies have the credit union's advantages of low operating costs, tax exemption, and often free office space, clerical and managerial help, too. Thus, naturally no other type of lender can afford to make loans at the low rates credit unions charge or can compete with the credit unions on service to borrowers.

Credit unions usually are formed by members of a closely knit group—such as employees of a business firm or members of a labor union, club, or lodge—and their purpose is implicit in their name. The union extends credit to its members when the members need the help.

There are now more than 22,500 credit unions operating in offices, churches, professional organizations, and communities across the country, chartered under federal or state laws. Moreover, if there isn't one around and you are part of a well-defined group, it is not too difficult to form one of your own. You can get help and precise rules for creating a credit union with either a federal or state charter by writing to CUNA, P. O. Box 431, Madison, Wisconsin 53701.

Credit unions specialize in small personal loans, particularly to a member faced with a sudden emergency. Credit unions also can make automobile, mortgage, and home improvement loans.

Recent changes in the obsolete Federal Credit Union Act of 1934 significantly broaden the type of loans that credit unions can make to their 30 to 35 million members, and the maximum loan amounts that credit unions can offer have been substantially raised.

Typical maximum you can borrow

The maximum a credit union member could borrow used to be $2,500 on your personal signature, but under the new legislation, there is no restriction. Individual credit unions, though, impose various maximums on the different types of loans they make.

Typical annual interest rates

Usually the lowest of any major category of lender, often ¼ per cent below the prevailing rate in your area for the type of loan you are seeking, and sometimes there is an even greater reduction.

Typical maximum maturities

These limits, too, have now been broadened, and maximum maturities on personal loans can go as high as twelve years, can range up to fifteen years on home improvement loans, and on mortgage loans can be as high as thirty years.

Advantages

The interest rates may substantially undercut rates charged by other lenders. A credit union is probably the cheapest borrowing source available to you.

You are dealing with fellow workers or friends or lodge members who have in common a special interest in the financial welfare of all credit union members.

Disadvantages

You must be a member to borrow. This means not all of us have the opportunity to borrow through one of these co-operatives.

You may hesitate to reveal your borrowing needs and financial problems to the committee of fellow workers who must approve your loan request.

SAVINGS BANK OR SAVINGS AND LOAN ASSOCIATION

Savings banks exist in only seventeen of our fifty states, mostly in the Northeast. Savings and loan associations exist in all states and number about 5,000; but in most they are given power to lend primarily for the purchase of home and for home improvements.

Both types of savings institutions specialize in mortgages and home improvement loans. (Savings and loan associations are authorized to make mobile home loans and educational loans, too.) Savings banks also frequently make personal loans.

Typical maximum you may borrow

Up to 100 per cent of your passbook savings total for passbook loans.
Up to $10,000 for personal loans.
Up to $100,000 for mortgages.
Up to $25,000 for home improvement loans.

Typical annual interest rates

Slightly less than a commercial bank for passbook loans and home improvement loans; about the same for other types of loans.

Typical maximum maturities

One year for passbook loans and up to three years for personal loans.
Up to twenty-five to forty years for mortgages.
Up to ten years for home improvement loans.

Advantages

Although you are borrowing your own money when you make a passbook loan, your net cost is far less than on any regular installment loan and you are disciplining yourself into maintaining your savings.

Savings institutions specialize in mortgage and home improvement financing. Their rates are competitive and their services superior.

Disadvantages

Really none.

LICENSED SMALL LOAN COMPANY

Over the years, leading small loan companies throughout the nation have spent countless tens of millions of dollars to advertise their willingness and readiness to extend financial aid to you, the little fellow. They have boasted that they exist to help solve your emergency problems and the littler you are the more welcome you are. Their very name—small loan company—inspires the trust of the would-be borrower. (Other well-known names are "consumer finance company" and "personal finance company." All have the same appeal.)

There is no doubt that these companies have filled and do fill an important place in our financial structure. You will note from the interest rate range below that the small loan companies charge a comparatively high rate of interest—but there are explanations. For one thing, they borrow part of their own capital from banks so they themselves are paying a high rate of interest to get the money to lend in turn to you. For another, small loan companies lend to individuals who do not have top credit ratings and who well might receive a flat no from a local bank. Inevitably, they have to write off a number of these risky loans or spend considerable money and time collecting the money due them.

Small loan companies specialize in personal and automobile loans and offer both single-payment and installment loans. As for security, the usual requirement of the small loan companies is nothing more than your promise to pay; i.e., your signature. Under certain conditions, they also ask additional security in the form of a chattel mortgage on your household furniture, to make sure that you will honor your debt.

If, though, you have a questionable credit rating and do not have a regular source of income, the small loan company may demand that a qualified friend co-sign for your loan. If you, the borrower, then fail to meet your payments, your co-signer will become responsible for the unpaid balance of your loan.

Typical maximum you may borrow

$500 to $1,500—with the actual limits (some are higher) depending on state law.

Typical annual interest rate

State laws generally prescribe interest rate ceilings but rates often are two to three times higher than bank interest charges.

Typical maximum maturities

One to three years.

Advantages

Frequently you can obtain a smaller loan from a small loan company than from a bank. You may even borrow just a few dollars if that is all you need.

The small loan companies are not as selective as banks. They can take greater risks just because they charge higher rates.

As the charge is based on the unpaid balance of your loan, you pay only for the credit you actually use.

Suits for collection are less frequent, the small loan company often preferring to tack extra interest onto the loan for delinquencies, since the rates are relatively high.

If you have a grievance against a small loan company, you may take it to the state banking department and get advice and help at no expense.

You also may take a gripe about a small loan company to the Consumer Affairs Center of the National Consumer Finance Association, 1000 Sixteenth Street, N.W., Washington, D.C. 20036. Telephone (202) 638-1340.

Disadvantages

The interest rates are much higher than those charged by full service commercial banks.

The maximum amount you can borrow is often less than you can get from banks and less than you need.

You may not be able to get the loan without a co-signer.

TUITION LOAN SPECIALISTS

Tuition loan companies are actually small loan institutions, some of which deal exclusively in loans to parents to pay tuitions for their children at private schools and colleges. They may be subsidiaries of national "small loan" firms, or they may be independent companies.

Usually, a school or college has arrangements with at least one tuition loan company, and when your child is accepted by the school, you are sent loan application forms to complete along with your registration contract.

The school and the loan company make it simple and easy for the parent to borrow the money—often too simple and easy. For tuition loans can be extremely costly, with the lending institution realizing as much as 32–40 per cent true annual interest on its money. When you consider that the tuition loan company has excellent security on its loan—the school will not "graduate" the student or supply his or her grades or transcripts of records—the true interest rates are extremely high.

Typically, you, as a parent, can borrow one to four years of tuition and repay the loan in one to seven years or even more in some cases. But you must realize that you usually will be paying interest on the full amount of the loan even though the tuition loan company may not forward the money to the school until much later. You will not, if you pay cash, have to forward the full year tuition all at once, but semester by semester. A bank loan, therefore, or even a credit card loan, or some "ready credit" arrangement with a bank or credit union is almost always significantly cheaper than the tuition loan company's interest rates.

Many of the better schools also have their own "tuition budget" plan, under which, for a nominal annual fee, you make monthly payments for ten to twelve months of the year, rather than two or three lump sum payments at the beginning of the semesters or trimesters.

This arrangement is the least expensive of any. When you and your child are "shopping" for schools, a key question should always be what, if any, type of tuition-payment plan they have. Since you will be paying $20,000 to $30,000 over a period of years, at charges in effect in the late 1970s, a tuition-budget plan could save you literally thousands of dollars in interest payments.

If you do decide to deal with a tuition loan company, though, you can expect that the advantages and disadvantages of a loan from a small loan company will apply.

Typical annual interest rates

Anywhere from 16 to 36 per cent true annual interest, based on the time the tuition loan company turns the money over to the school.

Typical maximum you can borrow

As much as 100 per cent of your youngster's tuition, room and board charges (costs of books and other school fees usually are not included).

Typical maximum maturities

Up to seven years for a loan covering the entire four-year tuition.

Advantages

Loan is usually relatively easy to obtain, and you need not worry about tuition payments. It's almost always a "mail-order" arrangement so you don't have to approach your local lending institutions.

Disadvantages

Interest rates are almost always higher than you could obtain elsewhere; tuition loan company usually has an arrangement with the school, so that if you default, your child may be embarrassed, perhaps even dropped from school for non-payment of the scheduled charges.

LIFE INSURANCE COMPANY

This may be your indisputably number one source for money. In fact, it is a source I suggest you check before you turn to any other. After a period of two or three years the premiums you have paid on a regular life insurance policy (not a term policy) become a prime cash asset. Your insurance company will then lend you your cash surrender value directly at a specified and relatively very low interest charge.

Typical maximum you may borrow

Generally up to 95 per cent of your life insurance policy's cash surrender value. And since every year the cash value of your policy increases, every year the total you may borrow increases, too.

Typical annual interest rates

This will depend on what your insurance contract states. For older persons, whose policies have been in effect many years, your interest rate may be as low as 5 per cent, but policies issued more recently may have provisions calling for loans at 8 per cent and higher. You must check this rate with far more care than ever before.

Typical maximum maturities

None.

Advantages

The loan is a cinch to get. You merely ask your company to send you the loan forms, fill them out, return them, and the cash is yours.

The interest charged is low by today's standards—a flat rate on the unpaid balance of your loan without any extras or hidden charges. Usually the company will collect the interest you owe at the time you pay your premiums: quarterly, semi-annually, or annually.

You are not held to any specified time for repayment. This may be an advantage if you cannot take on the burden of regular payments right away.

Disadvantages

The amount of your loan decreases the face value of your life insurance policy —which means, of course, that you're temporarily undercutting the protection of your family.

The absence of a specified time for repayment might lull you into maintaining the loan indefinitely, thus continuing to pay interest indefinitely and decidedly increasing the overall cost of your loan.

YOUR STOCKBROKER

Another loan source is your own stockbroker, provided, of course, that you have stock, leave the certificates at the brokerage house "in street name," and have, or open, a "margin" account.

You can borrow up to a specified percentage of the current value of any stocks you own (usually 40–60 per cent), depending on the regulations in effect at the time. In this case you are arranging a single-payment loan and paying interest monthly or quarterly on the amount you have borrowed.

The interest rate is flexible, being ½ to 1½ per cent above what is called the broker's loan rate. This rate in turn is usually pegged in relation to the so-called prime rate, the rate at which bankers lend money to their largest and most credit-worthy corporate customers.

The traditional use of such "margin" loans is to enable stock market investors and traders to buy stock without paying the full market price, just the 40 to 60 per cent part-payment, with the rest being "financed" or "margined."

Recently, though, brokerage firms have been soliciting their margin customers to borrow money and take it in cash. It works this way: say you have 100 shares of five stocks, each stock worth $100 a share on a given day. Your portfolio is thus worth $50,000. If the margin percentage then was 50 per cent, you would be able to borrow $25,000. The interest rate would depend on your broker's policy and the current broker's loan rate.

The interest would be deducted from the funds in your brokerage account, or, if these funds were insufficient, you would be billed.

There are dangerous drawbacks in borrowing from your stockbroker, though. If the price of the stock declines, you could be required to advance substantial sums on short notice to "cover" your position. The same thing might happen if margin requirements were increased to a higher percentage. In addition interest costs may fluctuate widely, and recently rates have soared in short spans of time.

Typical maximum you may borrow

Varies from a normal 40 to 60 per cent of the value of your stock portfolio.

Typical annual interest rates

Fluctuating: range from ½ to 1½ per cent above the broker's loan rate, which in turn varies with the prime rate established by banks.

Typical maximum maturities

None, so long as your stock does not decline in value and the margin rates remain the same.

Advantages

Quick and easy, provided you have an adequate portfolio and have set up a margin account. A single call to your broker is enough to produce a check for the amount you want. Also, though interest rates vary, they are generally low, since the money is partially (40–60 per cent) secured. No amortization required.

Disadvantages

Many. Your interest rate can fluctuate widely. The margin requirements may be increased, forcing you to put up additional cash (in effect, pay back part of the loan) on extremely short notice. The market may drop rapidly, again producing margin calls for quick cash at short notice, just when economic conditions may be putting the squeeze on you from other directions, too. The fact that you do not have a regular schedule to amortize the loan may lead you to postpone repaying it.

INDUSTRIAL LOAN COMPANY

The "industrial" part of this source's name stems from the fact that the companies make loans mostly to industrial workers—not to the industrial corporations employing them.

Industrial loan companies fill a gap between the commercial bank and the small loan company. They make a wide variety of loans, ranging from a regular personal or auto loan to a second mortgage on your home.

Typical maximum you may borrow

Up to $10,000 on personal loans.
State laws prescribe limits on second mortgages.

Typical annual interest rates

Comparatively high compared to banks, but the companies may make loans at lower interest rates than small loan companies.

Typical maximum maturities

One to five years on personal or auto loans.
Ten years on second mortgages.

Advantages

They can make larger loans than small loan companies and might charge lower interest rates.

They will accept a wide variety of your possessions as collateral, ranging from your home to pieces of your furniture.

They might lend you money when you do not have a sufficient credit rating to get a loan from a bank.

Disadvantages

Interest rates are higher than charged by banks.

Industrial loan companies frequently insist on co-signers—which means you must ask your friends or business acquaintances to guarantee the repayment of your loan and this you may hate to do.

That interest rate of up to 18 per cent a year if you are not careful about paying.

The temptation to overuse this source of credit just because it's so easy.

ANOTHER MORTGAGE ON YOUR HOME

With the prices for houses climbing in recent years even faster than the inflation rate, an increasingly popular loan source is another mortgage on your house.

Assume you purchased your house twenty to thirty years ago, perhaps for $20,000 to $30,000. Today it may be worth $75,000 to $100,000. Furthermore, your original mortgage may be paid off or nearly so by now. You have, in effect, $70,000 to $90,000 "equity" in your home—some $60,000 to $75,000 of which you can again borrow against.

Depending on your circumstances, you can do one of two things: you can refinance your present mortgage, or you can take out a second mortgage. But, beware, both these courses of action have subtle but serious drawbacks. First, the second mortgage.

SECOND MORTGAGE COMPANY

These companies do precisely what their name implies: lend you money against your home on a second mortgage so you can meet your pressing obligations. On top of the first mortgage you are carrying to finance your original home purchase, you take out a second mortgage for a given period of time and then use the money raised from the second mortgage for purposes which may have nothing whatsoever to do with your home.

But this can be an exceedingly expensive source for money—and an unsound borrowing method, too. The interest stated on your mortgage may not seem high, but the extra charges can multiply the actual rate you are paying. At the same time, your second mortgage may run for years—meaning you'll be paying for the money long after you have forgotten the purpose for which you borrowed. And this, you will recall, breaks one of the cardinal rules for borrowing.

Typical maximum you may borrow

Up to $25,000 or 85 per cent of the equity you have in your home.

Typical annual interest rates

The legal maximum in the state plus "charges" which, I repeat, can build up to startlingly high percentages.

Typical maximum maturities

Three to ten years.

Advantages

Quick way to raise funds for just about any purpose.
Repayment can be strung out over a number of years.

Disadvantages

A second mortgage can add a financial burden undermining your entire investment in your house in bad times.

You take on a relatively long-term debt—three to ten years—to purchase a product or service that may have a much shorter life.

You could, without realizing it, commit yourself to paying an excessively steep rate for the money.

YOUR OWN HOME MORTGAGE

You may get a second mortgage on your home and raise substantial sums from other lenders besides a second mortgage company, of course. Or you may refinance your mortgage, take out a new mortgage with a new long-term life and new interest rate, to raise hefty sums. This you may do through the institution that gave you your first mortgage or through another bank, savings association, or an individual investor.

The trend toward borrowing on your own home to raise money for non-home purposes exploded in the 1960s and 1970s and the trend is apparently here to stay. What this represents, in effect, is the dramatic development of a twenty-to-thirty-year installment loan. The long-term mortgage is the vehicle through which money is raised for everything from college costs to pleasure boats.

Typical maximum amounts you may borrow

Depends on your deal.

Typical annual interest rates

The going rate for first mortgages.

Typical maximum maturities

From ten years up to original life—twenty, twenty-five, thirty years—of first mortgage, depending on age of the property.

Advantages and disadvantages

This trend toward using the home mortgage for purposes far removed from the original purchase of the home is so powerful that it demands more than a few short sentences stating the pros and cons. Thus read the following real-life illustration with care:

Mr. H.B.A. is a successful lawyer in his forties who bought a $50,000 house in a suburb near New York fourteen years ago with the help of a 6 per cent mortgage. H.B.A. now has one son in college, another entering this fall, and an extremely popular teenage daughter. In addition to tuition fees, he therefore has suddenly developed a wallet-emptying list of new "necessities": a car for the boys, a swimming pool, new terrace furniture, etc.

So H.B.A. recently refinanced his mortgage and raised $22,000 in new cash to be repaid over a twenty-year period. He has bought the car for his boys, he is decorating the terrace, and he is about to build the swimming pool. To him, this is an excellent deal—a way to borrow "instant cash" on the most painless repayment terms.

But right as the deal seems to H.B.A., it's wrong from a strictly dollars-and-cents viewpoint. For H.B.A. is breaking that fundamental rule of sound finance: he is "borrowing long to buy short." Years after his son's auto will have been junked, he'll be paying interest on the loan to purchase it. By committing himself to pay interest over a twenty-year period, he'll end up paying far more on this loan than he would have paid on a two-or-three-year loan at twice his borrowing rate.

That's H.B.A. Now let's take you as an illustration. Say you borrow $3,000 on a conventional installment loan, pay 9 per cent interest, agree to repay over a two-and-a-half-year period. Your true interest rate is almost double 9 per cent, or about 16.4 per cent. Your monthly repayment will be $122.50. Your total interest cost will come to $675 ($3,000 × .09 × 2.5 = $675).

Or say you borrow $3,000 by refinancing your mortgage over a twenty-year period. Your interest rate is a simple 6 per cent a year. Your monthly repayment will be only about $21.49. But over the twenty years the 240 monthly payments will total $5,158.30—an out-of-pocket interest cost to you of $2,158.30. In addition, you'll pay at least $250 for closing costs.

In the first case, your interest cost is $675. In the second, it's $2,408.30 —more than three and a half times as much.

(See the section in this chapter on knowing your true interest costs for a more complete discussion of interest charges.)

THE ROLE OF INFLATION

At this point, financial super-sophisticates among you might point out that over the past ten years the inflation rate in the United States (and in countries throughout the rest of the world the situation has been similar or worse) has been about 100 per cent or so. Stated another way, it means the dollar today is worth about half of what it was ten years ago!

If the same rate continues for the next ten years, the $3,000 will be worth about $1,500 and those $21.50 payments will be the equivalent of under $11. Assuming that your salary just keeps pace with inflation, your payments will be cut by more than 50 per cent long term.

But inflation does not take place all at once. Rather it erodes your dollar's value over the years. Furthermore, those closing costs are up front. If you don't have to pay them in a lump sum in advance, it will take you a year just to repay the loan fee.

Certainly, our inflation of recent years is largely responsible for our increasing tendencies to borrow and finance our purchases, rather than to pay cash. Both long-term and short-term borrowing have their places. But borrowing long to buy a short-term item never makes sense no matter what the inflation rate.

Now I can summarize the pros and cons, confident that you grasp the nuances. The easy appeal of refinancing a home mortgage to obtain cash for non-home equity purposes is undeniable but it glosses over the tremendous difference in interest costs. Like other financing methods that on the surface seem easiest and least expensive, this one turns out to be among the hardest and most costly.

RURAL FAMILY LOANS

If you are a farm family living in a rural area, you may be able to get a rural family farm or home loan at a comparatively low interest rate through a nearby production credit association. These are co-operative associations created to assist in providing credit for people living in rural regions—and you also may be able to get a loan to finance your farm or farm-related business or other enterprise.

You'll get details on these loans and your possible eligibility for them from the production credit association serving your area or from the Farm Credit Administration, 490 L'Enfant Plaza, N.W., Washington, D.C. 20578.

PAWNBROKER

The pawnbroker is not the worst of all loan sources but he's close to it. He certainly must be classed as a source of last resort for the desperate borrower. You'll not only pay an enormous annual interest rate on small loans; you'll also be able to borrow only a fraction of the auction value of the asset you pledge as collateral. And to get your funds, you'll have to turn over your property (which you may badly need) to the pawnbroker for the life of the loan.

Your loan usually will have a very short life and in many parts of the country you must redeem your collateral within thirty to sixty days or it becomes the property of the pawnbroker, who may then offer it for sale. A pawnbroker's terms underscore how limited are the options of the desperate borrower. The person least able to afford horrendous interest rates always is the one who pays them.

Typical maximum you may borrow

Up to 50 per cent (but possibly 60 per cent) of the auction value of the asset you pledge.

Typical annual interest rates

Three to four times higher than rates on personal loans charged by most major lending institutions.

Typical maximum maturities

180 days, possibly with the privilege of a 180-day extension.

Advantages

You have complete privacy, need not give any information about yourself or your financial circumstances. The pawnbroker doesn't care who you are so long as he's assured the asset you are pledging isn't stolen property.

You can borrow money at once against your possession and, if you need the cash in a matter of hours, this can be a crucial factor.

If you are in a very volatile profession—the theater, say—you can get periodic loans by pawning and redeeming the same asset over and over again.

Disadvantages

It's an excessively expensive way to borrow.

You do not have the use of your asset while the loan is outstanding—and you might need that asset to earn an income (a musical instrument, for instance, or a typewriter or special tools).

You can borrow only a small percentage of the value of your assets.

LOAN SHARK

Absolutely at the bottom of any list of loan sources is the loan shark—in every way an evil source, lending money to the desperate, innocent, and ignorant at sinfully high and openly illegal rates. He is a racketeer charging usurious rates for money and threatening punishment if the repayment is not on schedule.

A typical deal might be "7.50 for 5"—$7.50 for $5.00 borrowed until payday next week. That may seem only $2.50 in interest on your $5.00 loan, but it's actually 2,600 per cent a year, and that's a hellish rate by any yardstick. Moreover, the loan shark usually will try to keep you from repaying the entire sum you owe, for if part of your loan remains outstanding at all times, he can build up the interest you owe to ever higher totals. At the same time, he threatens you with punishment ranging from broken bones to death itself for failure to repay.

Yet the brutal fact is that the loan shark continues to thrive. Even though the Truth in Lending law forbids the collecting of debts by violent means, loansharking is a multibillion-dollar business dominated by organized crime. Even though there are many alternative sources for loans, these crooks can and do get away with charges running 1,000 per cent, 2,000 per cent, or more a year, and a conservative estimate is they are bilking the poor out of more than $350 million each year.

How do you spot a loan shark? Be suspicious if he:

does not show his state license prominently;

dates a loan prior to the time you get the money;

asks you to sign the papers before the figures are filled in;

requires more than one note for one loan;

refuses to give you a copy of the papers you signed or receipts for payments;

requires you to buy expensive insurance.

Get legal advice immediately if, when you attempt to repay part of a debt, the lender says you must repay the entire principal or none.

Appeal to local or state legal authorities at once if, when you admit to the lender that repayment is difficult, he sends you to someone else who seeks another fee in addition to the interest owed.

If a reputable lender's plan for repayment seems too difficult for you, turning to a disreputable lender will only intensify your problem.

Typical maximum amount you may borrow

None.

Typical annual interest rates

500 to 2,600 per cent.

Typical maximum maturities

None.

Advantages

None.

Disadvantages

Endless. The loan shark as a source for money is truly unspeakable.

CREDIT CARDS

Bridging the area between loans for cash and credit for other goods and services (which in effect also are loans) is the credit card—the plastic foundation for our increasingly cashless society in this country.

First, the basics about a credit card.

WHAT ARE THEY?

What a credit card is: this is an identification card (usually plastic) permitting you, the holder, to charge a wide variety of goods and services simply on your signature. You agree to pay for all you charged either once a month or over an extended period. If you make only a partial payment on your account, your account is automatically treated as a loan and interest is charged.

If you have an airline card, you use it to charge air trips; an oil card, to charge gas and other purchases at a gas or service station; a travel and entertainment card, to charge travel and all sorts of hotel, restaurant, and entertainment bills the world over. This card is an automatic charge account at all the participating businesses in the plan to which you belong and may give you charge accounts at thousands of places.

If you have an all-purpose bank credit card, you also have automatic charge accounts at all the businesses participating in the bank's plan, which can include thousands of places all over the world.

The card issuer gets a record of what you have charged from the business at which you have charged a purchase of goods or services. The issuer then bills you, the holder of the card, once a month for the total of your charges. You write one check a month covering what you owe. If you don't pay off within twenty-five days on a bank credit card, your account also is automatically treated as a revolving account and finance fees are added on the unpaid balance.

You are expected to pay for charges on travel and entertainment cards upon receipt of a bill unless it is a major item which may be paid for in installments set up at time of purchase. If you haven't paid your debt within sixty days after receipt of your bill, you must pay a late charge and your card may be revoked.

WHO ISSUES CREDIT CARDS?

Credit cards are issued by a variety of organizations ranging from local department stores to national retailing chains, from the telephone company to airlines, from car rental concerns to oil companies, from hotel/motel chains to local banks, from local restaurants to international travel companies—and, of course, from the giant firms specializing in credit cards alone.

In general, the credit cards fall into three broad categories: (1) single-purpose cards; (2) multipurpose travel, food, and entertainment cards; and (3) bank credit cards.

Single-purpose cards issued by all kinds of businesses—oil companies, motel chains, telephone companies, car-rental agencies, department stores, and the like. You pay nothing for them, and they allow you to charge merchandise or services, paying when billed. If you don't pay promptly, you will be charged interest, typically amounting to 1½ per cent a month. The aim of this kind of card is to encourage you to buy only from the company that issued the card to you. With most of these single-purpose cards you receive a receipt at the time you charge your purchase and a duplicate receipt when you receive your monthly bill. This helps you with your bookkeeping records since the separate receipts can be filed in their proper categories—by category of goods or services and chronologically.

With some cards, you get quantity discounts depending on the total amount of your purchases each year. This is an advantage to many business concerns who arrange for their employees to have these credit cards. Purchases by all employees then count toward the discount the company using the credit card receives. In addition, some firms (such as car rental concerns, for example) keep computer records of your preferences, and other data on you, to speed the completion of the transaction.

Some of these "single-purpose" cards, however, also enable you to charge services with related organizations. For instance, an oil company credit card will enable you to charge at a national hotel/motel chain (and vice versa). Others serve as identification to allow you to cash small-denomination checks when you are away from your hometown.

Food, travel, and entertainment or multipurpose cards, like Diners Club, Carte Blanche, and American Express. These are used mostly by businessmen and women, although anyone may apply. Holders of these cards pay a yearly fee— usually $20 to $30—to the issuer, and then can use the card in thousands of business places. Bars, restaurants, hotels, and expensive shops are this kind of card's best customers. Usually card holders are billed within thirty to sixty days and are expected to pay on receipt of the bill. No interest is charged if payment is prompt. But interest is added if your payment is delinquent by sixty to ninety days.

Frequently the so-called T&E (travel and entertainment) cards offer members additional services or opportunities, such as group life and health-and-accident insurance; free travel insurance if, for example, you charge your air or rail travel on their card; group discounts to businesses for high-volume usage.

These cards, too, provide individual receipts at the time the goods or services are charged and again with each monthly bill.

Bank credit cards, of which Visa (formerly BankAmericard) and Master Charge are the best known. All operate in much the same way. The bank issues you a card after checking your credit rating. There is no fee. You then may use the card in place of cash at any shop, restaurant, service station, or other business participating in the plan. The shop will turn the charge slips over to the bank, which will accumulate them until the end of the billing period. If you pay the bill within the time specified—usually twenty-five days from the date of billing—the use of the credit card is free. After that a service charge of 1 to 1½ per cent a month is levied against the balance.

The bank credit cards do not provide separate additional receipts each month, as do the single-purpose and T&E cards, so if you do not recognize a charge, you have to write to the bank credit card company.

HOW DO YOU GET A CREDIT CARD?

In the past, many organizations sent credit cards unsolicited in the mail. But now, since a person receiving such an unsolicited card is not responsible for charges made against it, this practice has stopped.

Still, credit cards today are widely—and often easily, perhaps too easily—available. You can obtain an application at virtually any commercial bank in the country—for either Visa or Master Charge. The T&E card applications are obtained from any merchant honoring the card. You simply complete the forms and mail them to the company, Diners Club, Carte Blanche, or American Express. The single-purpose cards are available from the companies that issue them, and their retail outlets carry application forms.

THE ADVANTAGES AND DISADVANTAGES OF CREDIT CARDS

Use of credit cards has been growing at a fantastic rate as both the bank credit card companies and the travel and entertainment card firms vie for your business, as do the companies issuing single-purpose cards.

The modern credit card started in the 1950s and was, initially, issued primarily for use in restaurants. Quickly, though, its use spread to other areas, hotels, airlines, car rental firms.

Today, virtually every retail outlet in the country has some type of credit arrangement, often through a credit card. Doctors and dentists take Master Charge and Visa cards, as do some traffic courts.

The credit card has rapidly replaced other forms of short-term installment loans and credit. With these "plastic passports" to free spending, you can now use credit cards to pay for:

tooth extractions, tombstones, and taxi rides;

driving lessons, diamonds, and dog kennel fees;

ambulance service, apartment rent, and auto license fees;

music lessons, movie admissions, and marriage costs;

and savings bonds and scuba diving instructions, church tithes and college tuition, garbage removal and psychiatric care . . .

In the late 1970s, over 12,000 banks were participating in credit card plans and more than 75 million bank credit cards alone were in circulation. About 6 million travel-entertainment cards are in use. So it goes, for we are far into the era of plastic credit.

If you know how to handle your credit cards, they can be a tremendous convenience. They can help you keep detailed tax records for your travel and entertainment expenses. They can allow you to charge these costs anywhere in the world—without paying any interest. They can be a magnificent substitute for cash everywhere, a major benefit if you travel a lot. (And Americans lose more than $2 billion a year in cash, says the American Express Company.)

Of if you are among the millions who have all-purpose bank charge cards, you can greatly simplify your budgeting problems by paying for hundreds of dollars' worth of purchases of every kind with a single check at the end of the billing period. You can achieve substantial savings by buying an item on sale even if you're low on cash. You can order goods easily by mail or telephone—and also return merchandise with a minimum of trouble. And any arrangement that can give you the use of big amounts of cash for as long as twenty-five days without interest (from date of billing), as with bank charge cards, is advantageous to you.

CASH LOANS BY CREDIT CARD

Credit cards, such as Master Charge and Visa, issued by banks throughout the country, are usually used to purchase goods and services on credit, but they also can be employed to secure cash loans.

There are a variety of plans under which you can obtain cash on your credit card. Some call for specific loan applications; others supply special checks you write to "trigger" loans. Still others automatically transfer money to your checking account any time you write an "overdraft" check—what used to be called a "rubber" check which would "bounce," or be returned for insufficient funds. Today, though, you are encouraged to do this, provided, of course, that you have arranged for the fund transfer ahead of time. Otherwise, your check will bounce as it has in the past.

You should be aware, though, that when you "buy" the use of money in this way, on your credit card, you don't get the twenty-to-twenty-five-day "grace" period as you do on the purchase of goods and services before interest starts. When you buy money this way, interest starts immediately.

In addition to the bank credit card loan plans, the so-called travel and entertainment cards, American Express, Diners Club, and Carte Blanche, also have introduced credit card loan plans.

Typical maximum you may borrow

$500 to $5,000 at any bank honoring the card.

Typical annual interest rates

Interest is not charged on any balance if paid within normal cycle from purchase date-billing date to repayment time—usually a span of twenty-five to thirty-five days from the date of billing.

Then interest accrues only on balances "rolled over" or unpaid after fee billing time allowance.

Annual rate of interest charged ranges from 12 to 18 per cent.

Typical maximum maturities

One to two years.

Advantages

It's quick, "easy," convenient credit.

You don't have to ask anyone directly for a loan; you just use your own previously established line of credit and get it.

At a few banks you even can get an instant $50 to $100 loan simply by slipping the bank's magnetically coded plastic card into a machine.

Disadvantages

See previous sections on the drawbacks of credit that is too easy to get. The very simplicity of this type of credit can induce impulse purchases, lure you into overbuying.

MAIL-ORDER AND PHONE-ORDER CREDIT CARD SALES

One significant side effect of the great growth of credit cards has been the increase in "mail-order" sale of appliances and other department and hardware store items via catalogs and promotional brochures. Your oil company credit card, for example, may be used to buy dinnerware or clothing or jewelry through the mail, on the installment plan. Furthermore, traditional "mail-order" firms— which once required a check or money order to accompany your "mail order," now accept your order via phone, often cross-country through a toll-free "800" line, creating, in effect, nationwide "phone-order" firms. These firms often are physically located in states that have low sales taxes, or none at all.

Furthermore, these firms are not required to collect sales tax on goods shipped out of their state. You, the receiver of the goods, are supposed to do that. But do you? As a result, mail- and phone-order firms, which do not have to maintain local outlets, either, frequently can sell for less.

Beware, though! Mail-order selling presents many pitfalls, and it is difficult to apply pressure to a firm that may be hundreds or thousands of miles from home.

HOW DO YOU USE CREDIT CARDS?

Do you have at least three credit cards, most of them good only at a particular store or chain of stores?

Do you use at least one of these cards regularly?

Do you think of your card or cards primarily as a source of credit, and in only a secondary way as a convenience?

Do you write more checks than you used to, despite your use of the cards, too?

Do you have a basic, nagging fear that credit cards make it too easy for you to buy things you do not really want or cannot honestly afford?

Do you, as a result of this basic fear, tend to think of your cards as an evil—a necessary evil, but still an evil—and not as a good thing?

If you answered yes to every one of these probing questions, you are typical of today's credit user, according to one comprehensive study of the subject. Few Americans tend to think of credit cards as a good thing, whether they use them or not. Fully 75 per cent of all respondents said that credit cards made it too easy to buy things.

Now, check where you, a credit card owner, fit in the wide range of users analyzed.

• If you have a higher-than-average income and higher-than-average education, you're more likely to be a card user than those with lower incomes and educations. Income is the major determinant of credit card use.

• If you are a young family and have children, you are more likely to use cards than other groups and more likely to incur debt on your cards than other groups. Another determinant of credit card use is related to the age of the family head.

• If you live in the suburbs, it's probable that you are an active credit card user, while families living in central cities or rural areas are least likely to use such cards.

• If you use your cards to buy clothing more than any other category of goods, you're typical. On both bank and store credit cards, clothing is the most frequent type of purchase.

CREDIT CARDS—CONVENIENCE AND LOANS (FREE AND OTHERWISE)

The big bank credit cards are making their greatest inroads in the area of retail installment credit.

Credit card users fall into two broad categories. One is those who use the card as a convenience, rather than carrying large amounts of cash or writing great numbers of checks each month. These users pay their credit card charges promptly within the twenty-to-twenty-five-day period required, and incur no interest charges. In effect, they have a free short-term loan.

The second broad category use the credit card's revolving installment loan features, virtually never completely paying off their obligations, incurring interest charges every month, and, in effect, budgeting their payments over a long-term period.

Several years ago one major bank attempted to impose a flat fee on what it called "free riders" who paid their bills promptly, avoiding interest charges. There was such an outraged reaction, however, that this proposal was shelved.

In fact, the prompt-payers were *not* "free-riders." The bank gets its money in two ways: through the purchaser who elects to pay for his acquisitions on the installment plan, paying interest; and, second, through the merchant, who pays a fee to the bank for acting as a sort of bookkeeper and collection agency.

These fees range up to 4 to 5 per cent a month on the charges processed. Although the bank does perform services for the merchant, the bank is, in effect, collecting "interest" of 48 to 60 per cent a year, from the merchant.

• If you're in any income group below the very top, you most likely use your card to obtain credit, and this is the most important use you make of the card. You see your card as another instrument for taking on installment debt and you treat your card debt like an installment loan—paying a little each month, generally the minimum allowable monthly payment.

• But if you're in the higher income group you use your card as a convenience —and whatever debt you incur on the card you attempt to pay off as quickly as you can, thus obtaining a free short-term loan along with the convenience you also gain.

According to a recent study, fully one third of you pay off your bank credit card charges, in full, within the "free" twenty-five-day period, thus avoiding the interest charges.

• And no matter what your special group, you write more checks than families who do not use cards.

What are some of the fundamental implications of all this? One prime implication is that, although all credit cards are substitutes for money or checks in transactions, they are not pushing us toward a "checkless society"—as was so widely forecast and is still so widely believed.

Another prime implication is that our consumer debt pattern is being changed by the addition of credit card debt to other types of consumer debt.

The use of credit card debt is most pronounced among higher-income families, who often have no other consumer debt and certainly could borrow at less than an 18 per cent annual rate. But these families aren't taking on long-term debt; they're using the cards as convenience and they pay off the debts quickly.

And a third implication is that most of you are using your eminent common sense in handling your credit cards—recognizing their dangers as well as their allure. Most Americans are indeed their own best money managers.

SHOULD YOU USE A CREDIT CARD?

As a general rule, you should—at any income level—if you have shown in the past that you can handle credit responsibly and that you will use your card as a convenient budgeting and record-keeping tool rather than a license to overspend.

As a general rule, though, you should not use cards if you're a habitual impulse buyer who frequently buys unnecessary things; if you're habitually late in meeting payments; if you've never managed to live comfortably within your income. And you should certainly shy away if, on top of all these characteristics, you do not have a steady income.

Here are the ways to use any credit card to your best advantage.

• Accept only those cards that you actually need and want and will use fairly regularly. For most of you in the middle-income bracket, one bank charge card and maybe a couple of oil company cards for gas are enough—although if you are in business you may find a travel-entertainment card helpful as well.

• Treat every purchase you are planning to charge as you would a cash purchase. Ask yourself: Do you really want and need the item? Can you really afford it? Can you repay the charge comfortably and on time?

• At the beginning of each month, decide on a maximum total of charges you'll be able to repay easily. Stick within that limit and repay the charges promptly to avoid any finance charges.

• Keep all your receipts until you receive your statement to check your spending and your totals against the statement for errors, which can easily occur (due, say, to no more than a clerk's bad handwriting).

How to Protect Your Credit Card

In just a matter of days in the 1970s:

• Three Long Island housewives went on a shopping spree, billed $16,000 worth of merchandise to stolen credit cards.

• A Pittsburgh gambler was arrested with $10,000 in his pocket—most of it refunds from airline tickets he had bought with other people's credit cards.

• A credit card thief posing as a health center operator ran up bills of more than $10,000 at gas stations by promising attendants health courses in his non-existent health center if they would make out phony bills against the credit card and give him cash.

These are not extreme examples, and the warning to you is implicit if you own a credit card or department store charge plate. Criminals have invaded the credit card field. Millions of cards are now being lost or stolen each year and are being used by thieves and other fraudulent operators to run up millions of dollars in unauthorized charges.

Fraudulent use of credit cards on sizable amounts is now a federal crime and the Truth in Lending law forbids the mailing of unsolicited credit cards.

The Truth in Lending law now also provides that a card holder is not liable for charges on a stolen or lost card if the issuer has failed to inform him that he is otherwise liable for up to $50 per card, or has failed to supply the holder with a self-addressed, prestamped notice to use if a card is lost or stolen. Your maximum liability in the case of unauthorized use of any credit card that has been stolen from you is $50 for each card. This maximum holds even if you fail to discover the loss for a considerable period of time and even if you fail to notify the issuer promptly. The law also provides that all cards must bear your signature, photograph, or similar means of identification.

But you also must take steps on your own to protect yourself. Here's what to do:

• As soon as you've finished reading this, go over every card you own. Make sure you have destroyed all you do not need. Cut unwanted cards in half and throw them away.

• Make a list of all credit cards you decide to keep with the names and addresses of the issuers and the account numbers. Keep this list in a safe place but not in your wallet.

• Sign each new card this minute. This will force anyone trying to use the card fraudulently to forge your signature on store bills, restaurant checks, etc.—no problem for the professional card-abuser, admittedly, but a definite deterrent to an amateur.

• Check your credit card collection every couple of weeks. If any card is missing, inform the issuer immediately—first by phone, then by letter or telegram in which you refer to your call. Some issuers now have twenty-four-hour answering services for just this purpose. Although there is a federal $50 limit on your liability, it applies to each card you own.

• Never lend your card to anyone else. This is a violation of your contract with the issuer.

• Make sure your card is returned to you each time you use it. Among the major suppliers of credit cards to fraudulent users are dishonest employees of legitimate establishments.

• Don't leave your credit card in the glove compartment of your car. This is one of the first places a professional credit card thief looks.

• Don't underestimate the value of your card because it's made of plastic. Consider it the equivalent of cash and at least as tempting to a thief as cash.

• Don't leave credit cards lying around in your office or hotel room any more than you would leave a stack of cash lying around. Instead, keep your cards securely in your wallet or purse.

In sum, either give up the advantages of owning credit cards and return to cash-check living or treat these cards with the respect that they—as the equivalent of cash in your wallet or purse—deserve.

OTHER CREDIT SOURCES FOR GOODS AND SERVICES

When you have a telephone in your apartment or house, make a number of phone calls, receive a bill, and pay the bill after you have made the calls, you probably have been using credit (unless, of course, you have a deposit with the telephone company, as often is required these days). Instead of a loan in the form of cash, you are getting credit in the form of the service provided to you by the telephone company. The same goes for an electric light bill or a gas bill or doctor bill or dentist bill.

You receive the service. The service is unmistakably, indisputably worth money. You do not, however, pay for the service, usually, until thirty days or more after you've taken advantage of the service. This is credit.

When you open a charge account at a local store, buy goods you want or need, use the goods, receive a bill the month after your purchase, and pay the bill usually at least thirty days later, you have been using credit, too. This time the credit is in the form of the goods provided to you by the store. This is credit just as much as a loan in cash is—with the vital distinction that the loan comes via goods given to you with the clear understanding that you will pay later under an agreed-upon schedule.

When you sign a charge account agreement, you have applied for credit. When you have filled in the lines of the application form asking about your income, outstanding debts, assets, family responsibilities, etc., you have in effect done the same thing you do when you fill out an application for a cash loan.

Similarly, when you sign a retail installment contract to buy an important product—TV set, furniture, kitchen appliances, a car—this too is a loan in the form of credit for the merchandise you are buying on time. The contract spells out the terms you, as buyer, and the merchant, as seller, agree upon. You, the buyer, do not own the goods until after you pay for them, and if you do not meet the terms of your contract, the seller may take back (repossess) the goods.

After you've signed an installment contract, you may receive instructions in the mail that you are to make your payments not to the merchant who sold you the TV set or auto or furniture, but instead to a bank or finance company. This means simply that the merchant has sold your contract or "paper" to the financial institution named in order to replenish his cash so he can continue offering installment contracts to other customers. That's all it means—just that you must make your payments to the financial institution that took over your contract.

Here are the types of credit you can get today in the form of goods and services and examples of these credit sources.

SERVICE CREDIT

Sources: utility companies; physicians; dentists; hospitals.

What it is: this is the free credit you use to get vital services such as utilities and professional help. You pay for the services only after you have taken advantage of them. Your debt is usually payable within thirty days after the service has been rendered.

Again, though, many physicians, dentists, hospitals, and clinics are switching to one or the other (or both) of the big national bank credit cards.

CHARGE ACCOUNTS

Sources: department stores; other types of retail stores.

What it is: an open (thirty-day) account is an account in which the store accepts your promise to pay for the goods you buy, usually within thirty days of your purchase.

A revolving account is one in which the store states a maximum amount of money you may owe the store at any one time. The limit is decided when you open the account and is based on your income and credit rating. You in turn agree to pay a stated amount on your balance every month and to pay interest on the unpaid balance you owe.

A budget account or flexible account is an account in which your monthly installment payments to the store are based on the size of your account balance and interest is charged on the unpaid amount. For instance, if your account balance is $100, you might be expected to make monthly installment payments of $25 each.

A coupon credit plan is an account in which you are given "credit coupons" which you may use in the store as cash while you pay for the coupons over, say, six months. This eliminates a monthly billing to you and the nuisance of detailed bookkeeping by the store.

Here, too, many retail outlets and even major department stores have either switched to a national bank credit card completely, or accept the bank credit cards if a customer does not have a charge account with that particular store.

RETAIL INSTALLMENT CREDIT

Sources: Department stores; appliance stores; furniture stores; automobile dealers; hardware stores; sales finance companies; door-to-door salesmen of big companies selling books, magazines, cosmetics, hardware items, etc.

What it is: this is the credit you use when you buy such big-ticket items as automobiles, vacuum cleaners, other household appliances, encyclopedias, the like. You usually make a down payment and then sign a contract to pay off within a period ranging from a few months to as much as five years in regular weekly or monthly amounts which you and the seller agree upon and which are stated in your contract. The retailer adds a finance charge to the cash price of the article, and you, the buyer, do not own what you have bought until you have completed your payments.

Sales finance companies specialize in auto loans but also finance such big items as boats, mobile homes, major home appliances.

Interest Rate Charges

The primary purpose of the 1969 Truth in Lending law, the landmark aid in consumer financial protection, is to help you understand just how much it costs you to borrow money either in the form of cash or in the form of goods and services.

That is why the law makes it mandatory for the lender or merchant to provide complete information to you. The theory is that, once you have this information and you know how much the credit costs, you will be in a position to judge whether or not it is worthwhile for you to borrow—and if you decide it is, you will be able to compare the costs at various sources.

Despite the law, though, most borrowers are still in an interest rate labyrinth. Even sophisticated borrowers admit they are still befuddled by the various ways interest charges are stated. As for most amateurs, they readily confess they are lost in the maze. Shockingly, a study made years after Truth in Lending became law disclosed that only two out of three borrowers knew what interest rate they were paying on their used-car loans. Even more shocking, one in seven didn't even know the rate of interest they were being charged on their home mortgages! This is something like buying a house without bothering to inquire about the price.

Thus, I think the easiest way to guide you through this labyrinth is to pretend the law doesn't compel disclosure and to take you through a series of fundamental questions and their answers.

Q. *What is the annual percentage rate?*

A. The annual percentage rate (APR) is the key yardstick by which you can measure and compare the costs of all types of credit. It is the basic interest rate you pay when you borrow—essentially a simple annual rate which relates the finance charge to the amount of credit you get and to the amount of time you have the money. With this information, you can compare financial terms offered by competing lenders, regardless of the terms of the loan or the amounts of credit offered or the difference in state laws.

When you know the annual percentage rate and the finance charge, you know the cost of borrowing money.

Q. *What is the finance charge?*

A. This is the total of all charges you are asked to pay to get credit. Among the charges that must be included in the finance charge are interest, loan fees, finder's fee, service charge, points, investigation fees, premiums for life insurance if this is required, amount paid as a discount.

Some costs are not part of the finance charge, though: for instance, taxes, license fees, certain legal fees, some real estate closing costs, other costs you would pay if you were using cash instead of credit.

Q. *If I borrow $1,200 for twelve months at a dollar cost of $6.00 per $100, or $72 for the year, what rate of interest am I paying?*

A. That depends on your terms of repayment. If you repay the total amount of $1,200 plus $72 at the *end* of the year, your interest rate is a simple 6 per cent. But there are other ways of figuring interest, which raise the rate.

With a basic electronic calculator so inexpensive these days, you easily can determine true interest rates. In this case you simply divide your $72 interest by the $1,200 you borrowed. The answer is ".06," which represents the simple 6 per cent interest stated.

This is known as the "add-on" method of loan interest calculation.

HOW INTEREST AND REPAYMENT "COMPOUND" THE PROBLEM

Suppose, however, that you pay that same $72 up front, on the day you take out the loan. In effect, you do not get the full $1,200; you receive $1,200 *minus* the $72, or $1,128. In this case what is the true interest rate? It is 6.38 per cent—$72 divided by $1,128. This is known as the "discount" method, a misnomer.

Now, here are more complex, but still "do-able" examples, with an inexpensive calculator, reflecting the real world of "renting" money.

Again, let us assume you borrow $1,200. But you repay the money in twelve monthly installments of $106 each, a total of $72 interest. In this case, though, your interest rate is far more than 6 per cent—about 10.9 per cent in reality.

How is this figured? You don't have use of that full $1,200 for a complete year. You are steadily reducing the amount of the loan so that, in effect, you have the use of only little more than half the original amount over the full term of the loan.

The more expensive calculators will solve your "true interest" problems for you almost automatically; but you can do it yourself even with an inexpensive one.

First, multiply your monthly payments by the term of the loan, in this case, twelve months. You get $106 times 12, or $1,272. Your loan was $1,200, so, as before, your interest is $72. However, you are not paying $6.00 in interest each month. You must follow what is called "The Rule of 78s."

To understand this, remember that with a twelve-month loan, you have the use of the full amount of money—$1,200—for only *one* month, and you are paying back one-twelfth every month. So, you have the use of all of your money—*12*/12 of it—for only *1*/12 of the time. The next month you have the use of 11/12 of it (plus your first month's interest and less your first repayment) for 1/12 of the time; until the final month, when you have the use of about 1/12 of your money— $100, approximately—for 1/12 of the time.

You must add 12, plus 11, plus 10, and so on, down to 1. The sum is 78. Therefore, the full interest on a twelve-month loan is 78/78. In the first month you pay 12/78 of the interest; in the second, 11/78 of it, and so on down to the twelfth month, when you pay 1/78 of the interest.

THE COMPLEX CALCULATIONS

Using this Rule of 78s, note that 12/78 comes to 15.38 per cent of 78/78. (12 divided by 78.) Multiplying your $72 interest for the year by .1538 you get— roughly—$11.08 as the *first* month's interest.

If you wish to do the calculations for all twelve months, you simply repeat the process, using 11/78, 10/78, and so on, down to 1/78 in the final month. For example, in the second month you divide 11 by 78 to get 14.10 per cent of the $72, or $10.15. By the twelfth month, you have monthly interest of just 92.31 cents (1 divided by 78 equals 1.28 per cent, times $72 equals 92.31 cents).

Going back to your $1,200 loan for $72 interest per year:

In that first month that you've had use of the full $1,200, the interest has run your true debt to the lending institution up to $1,211.08. You then pay them $106. Therefore, in the second month you will be paying interest on $1,105.08 ($1,211.08—106=1,105.08). Your second month's interest was $10.15. If you divide that $10.15 second month's interest by what you owe—the $1,105.08—you get the second month's interest *rate,* 11.02 per cent. The way you do this, incidentally, is to divide $10.15 by $1,105.08 to give you the *monthly* rate of 0.918 per cent. You then multiply this monthly rate by 12 to get the true *annual* rate, for the second month, of 11.02 per cent.

By the time the twelfth and final month of your loan comes around, the interest has dropped to 92.31 cents and the amount outstanding to roughly $105.08, for an interest rate then of 10.54 per cent. The average amount outstanding is about $661 and the average interest then becomes just under 10.9 per cent. The actual amounts will vary because the "Rule of 78" is not precise. Some months have thirty-one days, others thirty, etc.

But, from this, you can understand the principle, and get fairly precise answers.

The following tables show you your loan interest on both the "add-on" and "discount" methods of calculation, for one-year, two-year, three-year, and four-year loans.

Interest Rate and Payment Data Table

One-Year Loan

RATE PER $100 PER YEAR	ADD-ON INTEREST RATE % PER YEAR	YOU RECEIVE	PAYMENTS PER MONTH	TOTAL RE-PAYMENTS	DISCOUNT INTEREST RATE % PER YEAR	YOU RECEIVE	PAYMENTS PER MONTH	TOTAL RE-PAYMENTS
$ 4.00	7.3	$100.00	$8.67	$104.00	7.6	$96.00	$8.33	$100.00
4.50	8.2	100.00	8.71	104.50	8.6	95.50	8.33	100.00
5.00	9.1	100.00	8.75	105.00	9.6	95.00	8.33	100.00
5.50	10.0	100.00	8.79	105.50	10.6	94.50	8.33	100.00
6.00	10.9	100.00	8.83	106.00	11.6	94.00	8.33	100.00
6.50	11.8	100.00	8.88	106.50	12.6	93.50	8.33	100.00
7.00	12.7	100.00	8.92	107.00	13.6	93.00	8.33	100.00
7.50	13.6	100.00	8.96	107.50	14.6	92.50	8.33	100.00
8.00	14.5	100.00	9.00	108.00	15.7	92.00	8.33	100.00
9.00	16.2	100.00	9.08	109.00	17.8	91.00	8.33	100.00
10.00	18.0	100.00	9.17	110.00	19.9	90.00	8.33	100.00
11.00	19.7	100.00	9.25	111.00	22.1	89.00	8.33	100.00
12.00	21.5	100.00	9.33	112.00	24.3	88.00	8.33	100.00

Two-Year Loan

4.00	7.5	100.00	4.50	108.00	8.0	92.00	4.16	100.00
4.50	8.4	100.00	4.54	109.00	9.1	91.00	4.16	100.00
5.00	9.3	100.00	4.58	110.00	10.2	90.00	4.16	100.00
5.50	10.2	100.00	4.63	111.00	11.3	89.00	4.16	100.00
6.00	11.2	100.00	4.67	112.00	12.4	88.00	4.16	100.00
6.50	12.0	100.00	4.71	113.00	13.6	87.00	4.16	100.00
7.00	12.9	100.00	4.75	114.00	14.7	86.00	4.16	100.00
7.50	13.8	100.00	4.79	115.00	16.0	85.00	4.16	100.00
8.00	14.6	100.00	4.83	116.00	17.2	84.00	4.16	100.00
8.50	15.6	100.00	4.88	117.00	18.4	83.00	4.16	100.00
9.00	16.5	100.00	4.92	118.00	19.7	82.00	4.16	100.00
9.50	17.3	100.00	4.96	119.00	20.9	81.00	4.16	100.00
10.00	18.2	100.00	5.00	120.00	22.2	80.00	4.16	100.00
11.00	19.8	100.00	5.08	121.00	24.9	78.00	4.16	100.00
12.00	21.6	100.00	5.17	122.00	27.7	76.00	4.16	100.00

Three-Year Loan

4.00	7.5	100.00	3.11	112.00	8.4	88.00	2.78	100.00
4.50	8.4	100.00	3.15	113.50	9.7	86.50	2.78	100.00
5.00	9.2	100.00	3.19	115.00	10.9	85.00	2.78	100.00
5.50	10.3	100.00	3.24	116.50	12.2	83.50	2.78	100.00
6.00	11.1	100.00	3.28	118.00	13.4	82.00	2.78	100.00
6.50	12.0	100.00	3.32	119.50	14.7	80.50	2.78	100.00
7.00	12.8	100.00	3.36	121.00	16.1	79.00	2.78	100.00
7.50	13.6	100.00	3.40	122.50	17.4	77.50	2.78	100.00
8.00	14.5	100.00	3.44	124.00	18.8	76.00	2.78	100.00
8.50	15.4	100.00	3.49	125.50	20.3	74.50	2.78	100.00
9.00	16.3	100.00	3.53	127.00	21.8	73.00	2.78	100.00
10.00	18.1	100.00	3.61	130.00	24.9	70.00	2.78	100.00
11.00	19.5	100.00	3.69	133.00	28.2	67.00	2.78	100.00
12.00	21.2	100.00	3.78	136.00	31.8	64.00	2.78	100.00

Interest Rate and Payment Data Table (continued)

Four-Year Loan

RATE PER $100 PER YEAR	ADD-ON INTEREST RATE % PER YEAR	YOU RECEIVE	PAYMENTS PER MONTH	TOTAL RE-PAYMENTS	DISCOUNT INTEREST RATE % PER YEAR	YOU RECEIVE	PAYMENTS PER MONTH	TOTAL RE-PAYMENTS
$ 4.00	7.6	$100.00	$2.42	$116.00	8.7	$84.00	$2.08	$100.00
4.50	8.4	100.00	2.46	118.00	10.1	82.00	2.08	100.00
5.00	9.2	100.00	2.50	120.00	11.3	80.00	2.08	100.00
5.50	10.1	100.00	2.54	122.00	13.4	78.00	2.08	100.00
6.00	10.9	100.00	2.58	124.00	14.1	75.00	2.08	100.00
6.50	11.9	100.00	2.63	126.00	15.6	74.00	2.08	100.00
7.00	12.5	100.00	2.66	128.00	17.1	72.00	2.08	100.00
7.50	13.5	100.00	2.71	130.00	18.6	70.00	2.08	100.00
8.00	14.4	100.00	2.75	132.00	20.3	68.00	2.08	100.00
8.50	15.2	100.00	2.79	134.00	22.0	66.00	2.08	100.00
9.00	15.9	100.00	2.83	136.00	23.8	64.00	2.08	100.00
10.00	17.7	100.00	2.92	140.00	27.7	60.00	2.08	100.00
11.00	19.2	100.00	3.00	144.00	31.9	56.00	2.08	100.00
12.00	20.7	100.00	3.08	148.00	36.7	52.00	2.08	100.00

Monthly Payments Rounded to nearest cent, producing slight variations to total repayments.

SHOPPING FOR YOUR MONEY

What leaps out of these tables is that your actual dollar payments can vary considerably, depending on the length of your loan and how the interest is figured, in addition to *the actual amount you are borrowing.*

To illustrate how you can use these tables in typical buying situations—so that you can shop for your loan as well as your item purchased—say you wish to buy a $6,575 car. The total comes to 65.75 "hundreds."

You are quoted a rate of $7.50 per hundred per year "add-on" interest for a four-year loan. Checking the table, you see this is 13.5 per cent true annual interest and that you'll be repaying about $2.71 per month for every $100 borrowed. Your total monthly repayments for your 65.75 "hundreds," then, will come to $178.07—65.75 times your monthly per-hundred repayment. (It's *not* $179.18 because the tables are rounded; your actual monthly repayment is, in the case of a four-year loan, $2.7083333, etc., the $130 divided by the 48 monthly repayments. The rounding off of payments may *seem* insignificant, but the difference, even in the case of this four-year car loan, is worth noting and on a 30–40-year home mortgage on a $50,000–$75,000 home a ½ cent difference per hundred in monthly repayments could amount to thousands of dollars.)

In our example, though, the $178.07 monthly repayment on the car loan adds up to $8,547.50 in total repayments, so total interest paid is $1,972.50—those total repayments less the $6,575 car loan.

Now, however, let's say you continue your shopping for money. A second financial organization quoted you a rate of $7.50 per hundred per year *"discounted."* Checking the table, you see that your monthly repayments per hundred are much less, just $2.08 rather than $2.71. But you also see your true annual interest rate is far higher—18.6 per cent versus 13.5 per cent under the add-on method (both rounded).

Why? First, understand that you don't get that $6,575 if you borrow 65.75 "hundreds." You receive only $70 for every $100 you borrow; thus you have in your hands only $4,602.50. You are $1,972.50 short. Familiar figure? Yes. Your interest. It was taken out *in advance*, remember. "Discounted," to use the technical term. You really need 92.92857 of those "hundreds" ($6,575 divided by $70). Therefore, your monthly repayments are each $195.68, your total repayments are $9,392.86, and your total interest amounts to $2,817.86—a full $845 more under this "discount" method than you paid under the add-on formula.

From the tables you also can see the advantage of taking out loans for shorter terms. At the $7.50 per hundred add-on rate for three years, rather than four, your interest is just $1,479.38, though your monthly payments are $223.75. At two years, the interest is down to $986.25, although monthly payments are still higher, $315.05. For one year, interest is a mere $493.13, but monthly payments top $589.

OTHER QUESTIONS AND ANSWERS ABOUT INTEREST

Q. *Is a 6 per cent interest rate ever a simple 6 per cent annual rate (or 8 per cent or 9 per cent)?*

A. A 6 per cent annual rate is 6 per cent simple annual interest if you borrow the $100 for one year and repay it one year later with the $6.00 added on—or a total of $106 in a single payment.

A 6 per cent mortgage also is a true 6 per cent a year, for you are paying the 6 per cent on the declining balance of your mortgage, not on the original total.

Q. *What if I'm charged interest monthly on my unpaid balance?*

A. If you're charged monthly on the unpaid balance you owe, then:

¾% per month	is 9% simple annual rate
⅚	is 10
1	is 12
1¼	is 15
1½	is 18
2	is 24
2½	is 30
3½	is 42

Q. *How can I compare the dollar cost of different ways of charging interest?*

A. Take as an example a $500 loan to be repaid in twelve monthly installments. If the rates charged are:

• 1 per cent per month on the unpaid balance, the dollar cost will be $33.09.

• 6 per cent annual interest on the unpaid balance, the dollar cost will be $16.40.

• 6 per cent annual interest "add-on," with one lump-sum payment at the end the dollar cost will be $30.

If the payments are spread over eighteen months, each payment would be smaller, but the total dollar cost would of course be higher. For example, at 1 per cent per month on the unpaid balance, the cost over eighteen months would be $48.84 compared to $33.09 for twelve months.

Q. *Why does the percentage rate on an installment loan for twelve months sound so much higher than the dollar charge?*

A. Because the dollar charge is applied to the total amount of money you borrow, but on an installment loan you do not have the use of the money for the twelve months and this increases the percentage rate charged.

Q. *If I pay back a twelve-month installment loan in six months, will I get back half the interest added to my loan?*

A. No. You will get back less because in the first six months you've had the use of most of the loan funds, so it is only fair that you pay more of the interest in the first six months than in the last.

To illustrate go back to "The Rule of 78s." In the first month of your twelve-month loan, you have the use of 12/12 of the money. In the final month of your twelve-month loan, though, you have use of only 1/12 of the money.

Your rebate of interest on your installment loan will be figured on the basis of the "Rule of 78s" formula.

In the first month of your twelve-month loan, you pay off 12/78 of the interest; in the second, 11/78 of the interest; in the third, 10/78 of the interest, and so on to the last month, when you pay 1/78 of the interest.

Now, say you pay off your twelve-month loan at the end of the sixth month. You have already paid off 12/78, 11/78, 10/78, and on through 7/78. The total of $12+11+10+9+8+7=57$. What's left is 21/78—or about 27 per cent of the interest initially added on to your loan. And that 27 per cent, not 50 per cent, is what your rebate would total.

It is a complicated formula and you need not puzzle over it. But in the case of the $500 one-year loan at 6 per cent with monthly repayments of $43.03, at the end of six months you would have repaid $258.18 of the total $516.40 you would have owed, with interest, by year's end. But you would get back only $4.43 of that $16.40 interest; you would owe $253.79 to pay off the loan early.

Q. *What about the charges on bank credit card and revolving credit accounts?*

A. Finance charges on these accounts are usually expressed as a percentage of the unpaid balance per month, as of the billing date. This is a simple monthly rate, which is then multiplied by 12 to give you the annual percentage rate, as listed above—e.g., ¾ per cent a month on the unpaid balance equals 9 per cent a year.

Q. *Why is the rate on credit card accounts higher than the rate on a simple installment loan?*

A. The main reason, say the banks, is that the amounts are smaller and the monthly processing expenses are higher. Generally, the monthly processing on a regular installment loan involves only one operation—recording the monthly payment. With a credit card account, the bank or retailer, etc., must make a record of the charge every time the card is used, total the charges at the end of the billing period, compute the interest on any unpaid balance, make up a bill, mail it, and record your payment.

Q. *How are mortgage rates quoted?*

A. Mortgage rates have been traditionally described in terms of simple annual interest rates. However, if points, a finder's fee, or certain other charges are required, these now—under the Truth in Lending law—must be included in the finance charge. These "extras" make the true annual rate appear slightly larger than before the law went into effect.

Q. *Why are mortgage rates lower than rates on installment loans?*

A. The average cost to the lender per dollar loaned is lower for a mortgage loan because mortgage loans are substantially larger than most other types. Their sheer size helps to offset the monthly processing expenses, permitting the lender to pass the saving on to the borrower in the form of a lower interest rate.

Q. *What can I do when no credit charge is quoted at all?*

A. This is illegal. But, for illustration, let's say a sewing machine is offered to you at $100 and you can pay for the item in twelve monthly installments of $9.00 for a year. Multiplying the monthly payment by 12 will give you $108. You are therefore paying $8.00 or a 14.45 per cent true interest rate for the equivalent of an installment loan of $100.

How to Hold Down Your Borrowing Costs

How can you, an attractive credit risk, hold down your cost of borrowing?

Throughout this section I have dropped in rules on this and you will find more hints for mortgages in the chapter on housing pages 183–93 and more rules for automobile loans in "Getting To and From" pages 328–30. But the guides below are the most fundamental of all and go across the board for all types of credit. Whatever repetition you note can only help underline their value to you.

(1) On any type of purchase on time, always keep in mind that the most expensive way to borrow money is to make a small down payment and to stretch out the life of the loan for the longest possible period.

(2) Thus, to save interest on any type of loan—from appliance to auto or mortgage—make the largest down payment you can manage and repay in the shortest period that's feasible for you. Unless you buy the pessimistic view that the United States will never be able to curb inflation, in which case the only way to protect yourself is to borrow as much as you can so you can pay back in dollars of dwindling value, you cannot dispute this rule's logic.

(3) Try to include a clause in any long-term loan contract giving you the privilege of prepayment of your loan at no penalty to you or at the lowest possible penalty. This will give you leeway to renegotiate your loan at more favorable rates when and as interest rate levels decline or to pay it off entirely. (Note, though: refinancing costs must be considered, and minimum loan charges are often set by policy and sometimes law.)

(4) On the other hand, don't pay off loans you might have outstanding at dramatically lower rates than now prevail. Just keep up your regular required payments and invest your extra cash so it earns more money for you than you're paying out on your old loans.

(5) Beware of ads for big-ticket items on "easy" repayment terms, and if the ads are befuddling despite Truth in Lending law requirements, use the formulas I've given you for determining how much you are paying on a true annual basis.

(6) Always keep in mind that any "instant cash" plan will be comparatively expensive to you. Whether it's a multipurpose credit card or an automatic line of credit at your bank, or any newer plan, the point is you'll almost surely end up paying more for this instant cash than you would for a traditional loan.

(7) In general, during periods of high interest rates, borrow only the exact amount you need. Borrowing more will mean paying peak interest rates for the extra cash. Borrowing too little will mean returning for another loan and paying extra processing costs.

(8) Offer the best security you can. A loan secured by top-notch collateral almost always may be obtained at a cheaper rate than a loan backed only by your signature. You lose nothing. You get back full possession of your asset when you pay off your debt.

(9) Before you borrow or buy on time, use whatever free credit you can get. For instance, use your regular twenty-five-to-thirty-day credit card grace period and thirty-day charge account as much as you can. If you buy at the start of the billing cycle, you won't be billed for about thirty days, and then you have another thirty days to pay. If you have several credit cards, note when their billing cycles close and buy just before those dates. Often merchants are late in processing the paper work on your credit card purchases, giving you as much as fifty-five to sixty days free "credit" on what you buy.

(10) Before signing the papers on your next loan, check whether you are being charged for credit life and credit accident insurance. If such a charge has been made, think *three* times before accepting it. Such insurance is usually not obligatory, though many people think it is. For younger people especially, such insurance is highly overpriced, running to $700 or more on many auto or consolidation loans.

(11) In shopping around for bargain credit, don't overlook the occasional "money sales" or similar features offered by commercial banks. For regular bank customers who already have savings, checking accounts, and the bank's charge card, installment credit may be offered at ½ to 1 per cent less than the normal interest rates, if you let the bank deduct the monthly repayment directly from your checking account. A warning, though: some banks also have you sign a form that ties up your savings account, too. If your savings equal or exceed your loan, what you borrow is then, in effect, fully collateralized, and you should get a far more substantial reduction in your interest charges in such circumstances.

And if you have a number of small loans outstanding, ask your bank whether you would qualify for a "clean-up" type of loan at a lower rate. If so, by all means take advantage of the lower rate.

To dramatize it again, on that $6,575 car discussed previously, a difference of just 1/10 of 1 per cent of true annual interest would cost you almost $15–$17 on a four-year loan, a 1 per cent difference more than $150–$160 at typical rates.

THE GREAT PITFALLS OF CREDIT

Truth in Lending has not eliminated the credit tricksters and racketeers—and the likelihood is no law will ever wipe them out. As for us, it would be ridiculous to claim that even an excellent education on credit would be sufficient protection for the vast majority of Americans—particularly since eight out of ten Americans admit they are unable to find their way through what one observer once called the "wonderland of credit where percentages multiply and divide at will, where finance charges materialize on command and fees are collected on the way out."

Do you know how to read the fine print on a complicated installment sales contract? Do you even understand the bold-type statement of interest charges required under the Truth in Lending law? How, then, can you, the ordinary borrower, detect hidden interest charges, protect yourself against unsuspected loan costs? One very good way is by becoming aware of the great pitfalls of credit—and, by this awareness alone, learning how to avoid these yawning traps.

Many of the tactics listed are illegal; and new laws are regularly making others illegal, too. But this does not mean that the practices have stopped.

"DEBT POOLING"

No matter what your plight, avoid commercial debt poolers, who simply lump your debts together, collect one regular payment from you—then charge you as much as 35 per cent of your debts for this "service."

Debt pooling, or "prorating" or "debt adjusting" or "debt liquidating," for profit is now barred in a majority of our states and the District of Columbia. But it still thrives in many parts of the country, and you must be on guard.

Specifically, a "debt adjuster" may say to you: "If installment payments or past-due bills are troubling you, let us consolidate and arrange to pay all your bills, past due or not, with one low monthly payment you can afford." If you accept this offer, you will turn over part or all your income to a firm and your debts supposedly will be paid out of the income on a prorated basis. The basic difficulty with the arrangement is the fact that almost never is the plan carried to fruition. Either the creditors won't accept the plan or you, the debtor, find it impossible to live with the expected payments. Some "consolidators" simply pocket the money and never pay your creditors. As a consequence, the only thing you, the debtor, obtain is an expansion of your original debt because of the fee you must pay to the adjuster. The service charges are steep in debt consolidation and, typically, your whole first payment may be taken by the company for these charges—without a penny going to your creditors.

Debt adjusting or debt pooling has nothing to do with legitimate credit counseling services—nor should it be confused with legitimate bank or credit union debt consolidation loans. The debt adjuster merely takes the debtor's money with the understanding that he will make the payments to the creditors—after absorbing a substantial portion of the debtor's funds as payment for his services. He adds to the debtor's problems with excessive charges and makes no effort to offer financial counsel or budget guidance. In some cases, he leaves the debtor with far too little money to live on.

"SEWER SERVICE"

Let's say that you, a consumer committed to periodic payments on an installment loan, lose your job and subsequently default on a payment. Under the law, if a creditor wishes to sue you for payment, he is required to serve you a formal notice of the impending lawsuit.

But let's say you never receive the notice—quite likely if you are among the nation's millions of unsophisticated borrowers. If so, the next blow well may be a "default judgment" against you, the equivalent of a decision that you, the debtor, are at fault before you consult a lawyer and find out your rights, not to mention go to court.

"Sewer service" is the colloquial name for this technique, formally known as a default judgment, which is widely used by unscrupulous debt collectors to deprive the gullible low-income borrower of his or her legitimate rights. To summarize what happens: the summons or other legal document which the creditor is supposed to deliver to the debtor is simply chucked into any dead-end receptacle (thus, "sewer" service). Unless you manage to get the judgment set aside, you are automatically stamped as liable and may be legally bound to pay whatever the creditors say you owe and you may lose your right to defend yourself in court, no matter what the facts may be.

Sewer service is the least expensive way for an unprincipled creditor to force payment of a debt. It is used not only to collect payments on installment debts but also to deprive tenants of their rights to contest eviction by landlords.

This is a flagrant attack on your most basic rights. If it happens to you, complain immediately to a law enforcement agency and also to the court where the judgment was entered. Get a lawyer to move to set the judgment aside. If you can't afford a lawyer, tell the clerk of the court you want to make a motion to set aside a default judgment for lack of service and ask him for advice on how to file the necessary papers.

Don't take this lying down!

"INCONVENIENT VENUE"

"Inconvenient venue" is another technique designed to deprive debtors of their legal rights. Under this procedure, the creditor simply files suit against his victim from a branch, affiliate, or lending institution hundreds of miles away from the debtor's home. Again, the victim has no feasible means of defending himself against the suit.

"CONFESSION OF JUDGMENT"

Ranking with the most vicious of all ways in which debtors are being trapped is the "confession of judgment" clause appearing in so many installment sales contracts. In effect, this clause is a built-in confession of guilt should the borrower miss a single monthly payment unless, in many instances, he can come up with the entire amount he still owes. By signing the contract he has waived whatever legal rights he otherwise may have had in advance—and the creditor can move in to collect at once. Frequently, too, the first a debtor knows that such a judgment has been made against him is when he receives a notice that his property is being put up for a sheriff's sale within days.

Confession of judgment is legal in only a few states, but this technique is still being illegally used to some extent against consumers in many other states as well.

Of course, it is reasonable for lenders to insist that they be protected against default and, of course, there are explanations for each of these clauses. But this technique is an outrageous deprivation of the rights of the individual.

Even if you signed a confession of judgment, under recent Supreme Court decisions you may be able to have it set aside if you can show that you didn't understand the clause when you signed it and didn't have legal advice.

HARASSMENT

Harassment is the "normal" means, in countless cases, of collecting small debts and past-due installment payments. And you need not be a ghetto resident to come up against this: it can happen to you, whoever and wherever you are.

• A typical cornered debtor may first receive a flood of dunning notices from debt collection agencies with names that sound in some cases very like those of government agencies. The letters will threaten legal action and serious damage to the debtor's credit rating.

• In addition, the debtor may be subjected to repeated telephone calls at all hours of the day and night, not only at his home but also at his job.

• The caller may falsely represent himself as a lawyer, a policeman, a private detective. Or he may hint that he works for a government agency.

• He may call a debtor's neighbors, relatives, wife, even his children. He also may call the debtor's employer, a tactic that easily can lead to the debtor's losing his job.

Whatever the tricks, the harassment usually succeeds in frightening a debtor into "settling" his debt—even though the debt may have been imposed on him through fraudulent, illegal means and even though he may have a sound, legitimate, legal defense against the creditor who is harassing him.

As you might expect, laws have been passed to control this sort of viciousness. The Federal Trade Commission has proceeded against some unfair debt collection methods, and new investigations are being conducted to check on law violations. In Massachusetts debt collectors are licensed by the state, and a collector may lose his license if he calls you late at night, informs your employer that you owe money, or indicates on an envelope that you have not paid your bills. In New York City a regulation forbids creditors (or their lawyers or collection agencies) to "communicate or threaten to communicate with an alleged debtor's employer" without first obtaining a court judgment against the debtor. And the Federal Consumer Credit Protection Act makes it a federal crime for a creditor or his representative to use violence or threats of violence to collect debts.

But none of it is enough. Neither the new laws nor regulations are curbing, much less wiping out, the problems of debtor harassment.

REPOSSESSION

You buy a used car loaded with options for $3,600, including 18 per cent interest on your auto loan, fees, insurance, etc. You pledge to pay $130.15 a month including interest for three years.

After one year and over $1,560 in payments, you fail to meet a due date. A while later your car disappears from your driveway. A lending company which bought the note for your car from your used-car dealer has simply sent his "repo" man to your home. He has crossed the wires of your car to get it going and has driven off.

Repossession of automobiles, as well as of many other personal items, is a widespread and entirely legal practice used against the delinquent—particularly low-income—debtor in the United States today.‡ It also may be only the beginning, for the lender may then turn around and sell your repossessed car back to the original dealer for an amount to be credited to you. This resale price, if the participants are unprincipled, may be a rigged bargain sum of, say, $500 for your car. You are now sued for the remainder you still owe. You're also liable for extra charges.

You thus not only have no car but you also have a debt equal to more years of payments! And now the used-car dealer may in turn resell your repossessed car to another buyer for $1,500. Of course, cars are repossessed without such tactics—but a shocking number do involve deceit, fraud, and perjury, too.

Automobiles are only one category of consumer goods subject to repossession today. Another not untypical situation is repossession when the consumer buys a set of furniture on time, then defaults on a single payment. The seller or the holder of the installment loan contract may confiscate the entire set and then sue to collect the remainder of the debt, plus charges and fees. Many corrupt ghetto merchants, in fact, make a living selling goods over and over in this manner. Their profit depends on default in payment and a chance for resale—not on the original sale itself.

To crack down on these practices, laws are being urged at both federal and state levels which would permit creditors either to repossess their goods or to sue for payment of the debt—but not both. Meanwhile, the only protection you, the debtor, have is your own awareness of the pitfall.

"HOLDER IN DUE COURSE"

An elderly woman bought a hearing aid for her son, involving a fat down payment and an installment loan for the balance of her purchase. When the device failed to work, she took it back to the seller, who agreed to send it to the factory for repair. But when she returned again to pick up the hearing aid, she found that the seller had gone out of business—and had sold her installment loan contract to a local lender.

Incredibly, this woman remained under legal obligation to repay the loan plus stiff interest charges—despite the fact that her son still had no hearing aid.

This legal quirk—called the "holder in due course" doctrine—was once the most vicious of all consumer credit traps.

Under the holder in due course doctrine, an unscrupulous used-car dealer or other retailer would lure naïve consumers into buying a long list of products or services on time. He would then immediately sell the contract to a finance company. The product would turn out to be a lemon, or it would be badly damaged, or it needed servicing under the warranty, or it would not even be delivered. And

‡ However, the U. S. Supreme Court has ruled that certain repossession practices which have been widely used violate constitutional guarantees. The Court ruled that no item may be repossessed unless the buyer is notified that the matter is in court and given a chance—in formal hearings—to tell his side of the story.

the seller would flatly refuse to replace or repair the product. Nevertheless, the financial institution that owned your loan contract would sternly remind you that he was "in the business of financing, not repairing furniture or cars." If you refused to make payments as they came due, you could have been sued for the remainder of the loan, payable at once. Or, as an alternative, the finance company would repossess not only the item in question but also other personal goods.

Among the goods and services most frequently involved in holder in due course problems were: vacuum cleaners, furniture, carpeting, sewing machines, "lifetime" series of dancing or judo lessons or health spa visits, major appliances, home improvements.

In many cases the basic conditions under which the sale was made—for instance, the "referral" scheme, in which you were led to believe you'd get a product free if you referred a specified number of other customers to the seller—were fraudulent. But once your loan contract was turned over to a finance company, any rights you might have had to challenge the original terms of the deal also went out the window. Frequently, too, the finance company was far, far away.

Both the state and the federal governments have taken steps to outlaw the "holder in due course" practice. Under legislation passed in the 1970s, if the merchant who sells the goods or services also arranges for the installment loan, the finance company that bought your "paper" installment agreement from him cannot fall back on the holder in due course doctrine. It has been wiped off the books.

While federal and state governments are giving increasing attention to these credit abuses, your best defense is knowledge of what is and what is not legal. Every government service costs money, and the government itself is often startlingly inefficient, shockingly inadequate. It is one thing to have laws, quite another to have them enforced in an era of lethargy, and worse, on the part of many bureaucrats.

Fundamentally, it will be less expensive for you—in what you pay in interest charges and in what you pay in the way of taxes—to know what should and should not be done than to rely on some government agency to help you.

AND ALSO BEWARE THESE TRAPS!

The add-on clause. Avoid the contract in which the seller keeps title to a whole list of items you are buying on credit until all payments have been completed (for instance, a fourteen-piece set of furniture). A single delinquent payment could permit the seller to repossess the entire set, even though you have paid all but a few dollars of the total. This gimmick also permits the installment seller to add purchase after purchase to your original installment contract. Then just one delinquent payment could permit the seller to repossess your whole collection of purchases.

The balloon contract, which provides for a final payment that is considerably larger than the previous monthly payments. If you are not aware of this and are not prepared to meet the final payment, your purchase may be repossessed before you can produce the money. Or you may be compelled to refinance at disastrously disadvantageous terms to you. Balloon payments are illegal in some states today because they are widely used to trick you into buying—at low initial monthly costs—things or services you cannot afford.

An acceleration clause. In this case, default in one single payment—or in some instances, the fact that you have lost your job—can make all other payments due at once. If you are unable to pay the total balance, your purchases could be carted away for resale and you still may not be absolved of all future liability.

Obscure provisions in your credit contract which stipulate you must buy extra items you may not want. These clauses are frequently buried in the contract so you don't realize they are there until after you have signed.

Exorbitant extra charges and "processing fees," adding substantially to your borrowing costs. A lender might list such charges separately to deceive you with seemingly very low loan rates.

Life insurance, or even disability insurance, is a gimmick widely used to inflate charges. Almost always the retailer who insists on such "protection for you" is getting a commission as an insurance agent. Furthermore, the rates for such insurance (essentially a decreasing face value term insurance contract) are exorbitant. If a merchant or bank insists on making insurance a part of the installment loan, take your business elsewhere.

How Much Debt Is Too Much Debt?

WHO RUNS UP TOO MUCH DEBT?

Who are the individuals and the families who get caught in an intolerable debt squeeze? Can we draw a fine but critical line between a healthy, bearable load of loans and an unhealthy, unbearable load?

The overextended credit individual is usually a faceless vexation in our society, according to a revealing study by a University of Wisconsin professor some years ago, who then drew this detailed portrait of the overextended credit family:

• The family is young, has more than the average number of children and an average income.

• The parents are easygoing, carefree, and impulsive, have "limited pleasure postponement mechanisms" and rubber wills when confronted with high-pressure salesmen.

• Although the husband, in most cases, is satisfied with his job, one in three wives is dissatisfied with her husband's pay.

• The family doesn't read anything, not even the daily newspaper. TV is the major communications medium in the family's life, and TV disproportionately influences the couple's buying decisions.

• The parents tend to blame their plight on vague, unavoidable "circumstances" or superficial backbreaking straws such as pregnancy, temporary loss of job, buying a car—and thus they feel their troubles are not really their fault.

• Neither husband nor wife assumes clear responsibility for managing the family's finances. Even among the couples who think they are sharing money management responsibilities, there is little indication of joint decision-making. As one husband remarked, "We don't quibble about it. If either one of us wants to buy, we buy!"

• The family moves from house to house more often than the average U.S. family.

Most consumer debts are adequately cushioned by our incomes and savings, our financial assets, and our earnings potentials. But there is a minority always in deep financial trouble—in the eighteen-to-twenty-four age bracket, and in the under $10,000 bracket, particularly.

Also increasingly prone to getting into (and staying in) deep financial trouble is the single-person household, especially those headed by women and by an individual who has been divorced, separated, or widowed.

The crucial difference between sound and unsound borrowing is whether or not you are carrying too much debt at any one time. Okay, then, how much debt is too much debt?

WARNING SIGNS OF DEBT TROUBLE

Deep and prolonged study has gone into this question—and there is considerable disagreement on the conclusions. However, the following are clear warning signals that you're moving dangerously close to the debt borderline and may be crossing it.

• You are continually lengthening the repayment periods on your installment purchases and putting down smaller and smaller initial payments. At the same time, your interest charge load is mounting just because you are sinking deeper and deeper into debt for longer periods.

• What you owe on your revolving charge accounts also is climbing steadily. You're never out of debt to the local stores at which you have revolving charge accounts.

• Before you have finished paying last month's bills this month's are piling in. You're always behind these days in your payments and you're now regularly receiving notices that you're delinquent. You might even get an occasional notice threatening repossession or legal action against you—something that has never happened to you before.

• Slowly but unquestionably, an ever-increasing share of your net income is going to pay your debts.

• You are so bedeviled by so many separate bills coming at you from so many sources each month that you turn to a lending institution or lending agency for a loan to "consolidate" and pay off all your debts and leave you with just this one big consolidation loan to meet. But you continue to buy on credit—thereby adding more new bills on top of your one big debt you must pay each month.

• You are taking cash advances on your credit card to pay such routine, regular monthly bills as utilities, rent, even food.

WHAT LIMITS SHOULD YOU SET?

Here are three different guidelines, drawn up by respected economists and money managers, of what your installment loan debt should be, exclusive of your home mortgage:

• Do not owe more than 20 per cent of your yearly after-tax income.

• Do not owe more than 10 per cent of the amount you could pay for out of your income within the next eighteen months.

• Do not owe more than one third of your discretionary income for the year—meaning the income you have left after you have paid for the basic needs of food, clothing, and shelter.

You can see that these guidelines give you a wide range of "acceptable" debt levels. But, in fact, any one of them may be too high, or too low, for you—depending on your income.

Obviously, a family in a high income bracket with relatively low expenses for basics such as shelter, food, and other essentials might easily be able to afford well over any one of those guidelines.

The "discretionary income" approach is the soundest. If you are in a relatively low take-home income bracket (or have extremely high expenses for "basics" such as home, tuition costs, and other fixed monthly charges) the formula permitting you to spend one third of this discretionary amount on installment payments could be too high.

The real test involves planning: figuring out what your actual expenses have been for *regular* outlays over the past several years (whether these outlays are for basics or not), since they reflect your *pattern* of spending.

You may, for example, have high commutation costs, an expensive hobby, or steep charges for medical or dental attention.

Furthermore, regardless of how much installment debt you decide you can *comfortably* incur, if you cannot also save a substantial portion of your income *every* month—at least 5 per cent of your take-home pay—then you should not be borrowing at all.

You should have an emergency fund in the bank, a life insurance program, and a regular savings plan to build a retirement income nest egg.

This is the ideal, of course. Fewer and fewer families are able to meet it. Nevertheless, these are fundamental economic facts.

Finally, in deciding how much debt your family can handle, ask yourself: how stable is your family breadwinner's job and income?

What is the chance of a layoff in his or her occupation and in your area? Is he or she eligible for unemployment compensation? How much? How long would this finance your needs? If both husband and wife work, your job security is obviously better than if there is only one wage earner in the family. How many protections does your family have against other disasters besides unemployment—insurance coverage for your home, health and life pension credits, savings and investments, equity in your home, etc.?

HOW TO MAINTAIN OR RESTORE A GOOD CREDIT RATING

How do you keep up a good credit record? Or restore one if it has gone bad? Here are the key rules:

• Avoid overloading yourself with installment debt. Note those guidelines on how much debt is too much debt for you and abide by them!

• Aim for and maintain a rainy-day fund in cash or its equivalent equal to two to three months' pay.

• Be truthful when you apply for credit and repay all your debts as agreed. But if you find you are unable to meet one or more payments on time, go to the creditors involved, explain your circumstances, and try to work out a more practical repayment schedule. The problem could be merely that payments on a loan or a purchase fall due on the twelfth of the month, though your paycheck doesn't arrive until the fifteenth.

In some cases, of course (too many), your credit rating can suffer because of an inadvertent human error. Wrong data is put in a computer. Your payment isn't credited properly. A bill goes astray in the mail. There is a dispute over a defective product, and the merchant elects to "write it off" rather than settling with you—but he enters into your record that you have not paid what you owed. (See pages 1221–27, "Your Rights to an Honest Credit Rating.")

Check *regularly* on your credit rating; and take action, immediately, if you are denied credit, or if your application for credit is simply not processed.

If you have legitimate payment problems, though, there are still actions you can take to avoid your credit rating being tarnished unduly.

WHAT IF YOU FIND YOU'RE OVER YOUR HEAD IN DEBT?

Bill W. is an appliance serviceman, forty years old, married to Ann, who has a job at the post office. Together, they earn close to $23,000 a year, and because their two children are now teenagers, they recently bought a new home in a small midwest city on a $36,000 mortgage.

Bill and Ann are widely admired for their carefree way of living, and Bill's friends frequently ask for his sensitive, prudent financial advice, wishing that they, too, could afford a new home, two cars, at least two vacations a year.

But, unknown to their friends (and not fully realized by Bill and Ann either), their total monthly expenses now top $2,500, they owe a startling $32,283 to eighteen creditors, and they're going deeper into the red each month by $658.49.

In sum, this couple—so respected for its financial common sense—is flat broke.

"When I went shopping at Christmas for clothing and presents," said Ann, "I assumed the only way you could get them was with a plastic card. Cash was unheard-of."

"We really tried to make and stay within a mental budget, but it never seemed to work when it came time to pay the bills," added Bill. "In nine years, I can't recall more than two or three times that we seriously discussed our spending habits, let alone what we were saving. It all went unsaid somehow."

Who is this American who gets over his or her head in debt?—particularly at the Christmas holiday season?

It's *you*.

You may be a $50,000-plus executive working for one of America's top five hundred giant corporations. Or you may be a family receiving welfare.

Consumers coming to an office of the Consumer Credit Counseling Service of

Greater New York for budgeting advice range across all income, age, and social classes.

In fact, you're merely typical of a consumer over your head in debt if this is your profile:

- head of a four-person household in your mid thirties;
- a gross annual income of around $13,600;
- debts averaging $7,600 to nine creditors;
- spending roughly $360 more per month than you earn.

At least one out of every twenty Americans is in serious financial trouble, well beyond the point at which you can hope to repay your staggering debts on your own.

WHERE TO GO FOR HELP

Even if you are over your head in debt, the statistics indicate that you can be saved from financial disaster.

It's estimated only about one in six families can*not* be helped by credit counselors, because their problems are psychological or legal or because they are "credit drunks" who simply are not willing to try to solve their problems. However, without counseling service, today's huge annual personal bankruptcy toll easily might be 50 per cent higher than it is.

The fact is, says the Family Service Association of America, "people do want help—desperately—but they don't know where to go, and until recently there hasn't been anywhere to go."

So what if you find you are over your head in debt?

- Start at your local bank: more and more banks are offering formal or informal debt counseling to overburdened customers.

- If your bank (or credit union or consumer finance company) can't or won't help, write to the National Foundation for Consumer Credit, 1819 H Street N.W., Washington, D.C. 20006, for the address of one of the hundreds of existing Consumer Credit Counseling Services nearest to you. These non-profit organizations, backed by local banks, merchants, educators, and others, are set up to provide financial counseling to anyone, but offer special help to overextended families and individuals in an effort to find ways to get them out of trouble.

- Check the nearest Family Service Agency. Hundreds of Family Service Agencies across the nation either offer financial counseling or can refer you to some agency offering such counseling. If you don't know which agency offers such help in your area, write the Family Service Association of America, 44 East Twenty-third Street, New York, New York 10010.

- Other sources from which you may get some form of debt counseling include:

    legal aid societies;

    your labor union's community services counselors;

    your employer's personnel department;

your church;

the Army and Navy also maintain debt counseling services to assist service-men and their families.

• Do everything possible to avoid such extreme measures as repossession, litigation, or having your account turned over to a collection agency. However, if any of these is threatened, go to your credit granters first, explain what happened, and in many cases they will be willing to extend your payment schedule. Or they may refer you to a reliable local credit counseling service.

• Consider refinancing your loan to extend its term and reduce your monthly payments. This will, of course, increase the interest charges, but it may be a small price to pay to get through a critical financial period.

• On mortgage loans, try to arrange with your bank to make alternate payments, every other month, for six months, a year or more, or see if the bank will let you pay only the interest for a period of time. (Try, though, to avoid refinancing a mortgage at higher interest rates.)

If all else fails, however, you may want to consider "the ultimate solution," financially. Bankruptcy.

How to Go Bankrupt

Let's say all efforts and plans to bail you out have failed. The debt counseling service hasn't been able to come up with a plan your creditors will accept. No consolidation loan is available. The only option left seems to be bankruptcy.

If so, here are your final two "outs":

(1) "Chapter XIII." This method of debt reorganization is provided for under Chapter XIII of the Federal Bankruptcy Law. Under Chapter XIII, debtor, creditors, and a referee—all supervised by a federal judge—get together to work out a way for the debtor to pay his debts on an installment basis.

This is known as the wage earner plan, because it protects the wages and essential property of a debtor who wants to stay away from straight bankruptcy by repaying his or her debts from future earnings.

Whether rooted in puritanism, pride, or ego, the general attitude toward bankruptcy is negative and you well may find it difficult to live with. But there are other than social aspects to be considered. Your friends who co-signed your loans may turn into bitter enemies as they "pay off" for you; the cost of going into bankruptcy may reach $500 to $1,000 or more; bankruptcy almost invariably is the blackest possible mark on a credit rating.

Here's how the wage earner plan works.

Either you, the debtor, get a written extension of your debts, with more time to pay them off in full; or, less commonly, you arrange a "composition" in which you pay off only a certain percentage of the amount you owe each creditor.

One half of your creditors must approve your filing of the Chapter XIII petition, at which time all interest charges usually stop. Your wages, personal property, your home and furniture, secured loans, particularly mortgages on real estate, usually are not included in the plan for distribution of your assets to creditors.

In addition to legal fees, which a Chapter XIII petitioner must pay to the law-yer who files the petition, there are filing fees of about $15 to $25 and a trustee's fee of up to 5 per cent of the debts, plus expenses.

You, the debtor, make your required payments, spread over three years, to the trustee, who then pays your creditors—thus making the federal government, in effect, a collection agency. An employer may agree to deduct the payment from a debtor's salary and forward it to the trustee.

There is no uniformity of application of Chapter XIII, and top legal experts deplore the fact that it is not more widely used.

Important note: if you successfully complete this plan, it will be considered a "plus" on your credit rating.

(2) Voluntary bankruptcy. Finally, there is the voluntary petition for straight bankruptcy. To do this you must put together a list of all your assets and liabili-ties and pay a $50 filing fee. Ordinarily, the rest is routine. Except for clothing, tools, a selected list of household goods, and other items depending on the ex-emption laws of your state, all your assets will be collected by the court and liquidated—and the proceeds will then be distributed among your creditors. Once you, the debtor, have been discharged by the court, your financial slate is clean—except for the bankruptcy record, which, no matter what you are told, will dog your footsteps for years.

THE BAFFLEGAB OF BORROWING

Many of the most crucially important terms to you in the sphere of credit al-ready have been exhaustively explained in the immediately preceding pages. But many other words you'll hear or read have not yet been put into simple language. You'll come across them frequently enough, though, and they are of sufficient im-portance to demand that they be as clearly explained as possible.

ACCELERATION CLAUSE   See page 873.
ADD-ON CLAUSE   See page 872.
ADD-ON RATE   See pages 864–65.
ANNUAL PERCENTAGE RATE   See page 861.
ASSETS   Everything you own that has monetary worth.
BALANCE   The amount you own on an account or loan at any given time.
BALLOON CONTRACT   See pages 872–73.
BORROWER   The person who borrows cash or who buys something on time.
CARRYING CHARGE   The charge you pay a store or any other lender for the privi-lege of having a period of time in which to pay for the goods or services you have already bought and which you may use in advance of payment.
CHARGE ACCOUNT   See pages 358–59.
CHARGE OFF   To declare a loss and remove a loan from the assets of a lender be-cause the loan cannot be collected from the dealer.
CHATTEL MORTGAGE   A legal document in which your personal property (chat-

tels) is put up as security for payment of your debt but generally is left in your hands so long as you keep up the payments as contracted.

CHECK CREDIT PLANS   Consumer loan programs similar to credit lines businesses have under which the loans are approved in advance and funds are available when needed. The consumer who has been approved for check credit may borrow up to a stated amount at any time simply by writing a check. As the loan is repaid, the credit limit returns to the stated maximum. See page 833.

CLOSING DATE   The day of the month on which credit accounts and monthly bills are calculated. Payments made after the closing date—or new charges or returns of merchandise—will not show on the bill you receive until the following month, when the next closing date will show subsequent payments, charges, and returns.

COLLATERAL   Anything of value that you have against which you may borrow money—for example, equity in an automobile, real estate, stocks and bonds, savings account passbooks, the cash-surrender value of life insurance policies. If you fail to repay your loan, the lender can take possession of whatever you have put up as collateral. Note: not all loans must be secured by collateral.

CO-MAKER OR CO-SIGNER   The other signer of a note when two people jointly guarantee to pay a loan. Parents often co-sign loans taken out by their minor children. Minors may not legally execute contracts.

CONDITIONAL SALES CONTRACT   Form of installment contract under which you do not legally own the product—say a car—until you've made the final payment. And you must make your payments even if you are not satisfied with the purchase. You cannot cancel your obligation by just giving back the product (car). Term no longer in common use in many areas.

CONSOLIDATE   To bring together several financial obligations under one agreement, contract, or note.

CONSUMER   Any person who uses goods and/or services for personal, household, or family purposes.

CONSUMER CREDIT   Credit offered or extended to a person primarily for personal or family purposes, for which a finance charge is imposed and which is repayable in installments. All consumer credit transactions divide into two types: (1) open-end credit, which includes revolving charge accounts and transactions through credit cards; and (2) installment credit, which is used by consumers to buy big-ticket items such as automobiles and appliances.

The one fact that consumer credit is used by individuals for personal and family needs distinguishes it from credit used for business, agricultural, or government purposes. Consumer credit usually refers to short-term and intermediate-term debt, thus excluding long-term home mortgage debt.

CONSUMER FINANCE COMPANIES   State-licensed companies that make installment cash loans to consumers.

CONSUMER LOANS   Loans to individuals or families, the proceeds to be used for personal consumption, as contrasted to loans for business or investment purposes.

CREDIT APPLICATION   A form that you must fill out when you want to use consumer credit. It usually contains questions concerning your present and previous places of residence, work history, present earnings, other credit transactions, and loans outstanding.

CREDIT CARD   See pages 849–57.

CREDIT CHARGE   See Finance Charge.

CREDIT CONTRACT   Usually a written agreement that says how, when, and how much you will pay.

CREDIT INVESTIGATION   An inquiry undertaken by a prospective lender or creditor to verify information you give in your credit application or to investigate other aspects about you which the creditor considers relevant to your credit-worthiness.

CREDIT LIFE INSURANCE   A type of term life insurance policy, required by some lenders, which pays off a loan in the event of the borrower's death.

CREDIT LINES (See Check Credit Plans):   Preapproved loan privileges made available by banks to big businesses that qualify and maintain specified minimum checking account balances.

CREDITOR OR LENDER   The person, store, company, bank, dealer, credit union, other organization, or person that lends money or sells things or services on time. Creditors are those to whom you owe money.

CREDIT RATE   The ratio—expressed as a percentage—between credit charges and the average principal amount.

CREDIT RATING (also Credit Standing):   An evaluation of your qualifications to receive credit based, in large measure, on your past record of meeting credit payments.

CREDIT RISK   The chance of loss through non-payment of debt. One considered less than credit-worthy.

CREDIT SALE   Any sale in which you are given time to pay for the goods you buy. There's usually an extra charge for the privilege of buying on time, and you usually pay for the goods in a series of installment payments which come due at regular intervals.

CREDIT SALE DISCLOSURE STATEMENT   The form a dealer must fill out giving you the essential details of your financing costs when you buy any product or service on the installment plan. This is required under the Consumer Credit Protection (Truth in Lending) Act.

CREDIT-WORTHY   Given a favorable credit rating and therefore entitled to use credit facilities.

DECLINING BALANCE   The decreasing amount that you owe on a debt as you make your monthly payments.

DEFAULT   Failure to pay a debt when due or to meet other terms of the contract.

DEFERRED PAYMENT   Future payment or series of future payments on a contract entered into sometime before the payment or payments are made.

DELINQUENT   A credit account that is past due and for which the debtor has made no satisfactory arrangement with the lender.

DISCOUNT (OR CASH CREDIT DISCOUNT)   Deduction of finance charges from the total amount of your loan before you, the borrower, receive the balance in cash.

DISCOUNT RATE   See page 860.

DOLLAR COST   A way of stating the cost of credit. It is the difference between what you receive as a loan or in merchandise and what you must pay back.

DOWN PAYMENT   Cash required at the outset of an installment sales credit transaction. Sometimes a used car, piece of furniture, or other durable goods will be accepted in place of part or all of the down payment.

DURABLE GOODS   Usually big-ticket things that are useful to you, the consumer, over an extended period of time, such as automobiles, furniture, appliances.

FACE AMOUNT   Total amount of your loan before deduction of finance charges.

FINANCE CHARGE   See page 859.

FINANCIAL COUNSELING   Expert advice on money and credit management.

FORFEIT   Lose or let go—as giving up to a creditor some security when you, the borrower, have failed to meet a contractual obligation.

HIDDEN CLAUSE   Any obscure provision in your credit contract that may stipulate requirements that may be against your interest—for instance, purchase of extra items you do not want.

HOLDER IN DUE COURSE   See pages 871–72.

INSTALLMENT   One of a series of payments to pay off a debt.

INSTALLMENT CASH CREDIT   Cash loaned directly to an individual and repaid in periodic payments (usually monthly) within a specified period of time.

INSTALLMENT SALES CREDIT   Credit through which an item of durable goods (a car, appliance) is bought and paid for in installment payments within a specified period of time.

INTERMEDIATE-TERM CREDIT   Credit that is extended for a period ranging from three to ten years.

LOAN RATE   The rate you are charged for borrowing money at a specific date for a specified period of time.

LENDING INSTITUTION   A bank, loan company, or other organization that lends money and makes money by advancing funds to others.

LICENSED LENDER   A lending organization authorized by license to conduct business in the state in which it is located.

LOAN SHARK   See pages 848–49.

LONG-TERM CREDIT   Credit that is extended for a period of ten years or more.

MARKET PLACE   Any place where a transaction is made or prices are quoted on goods or service.

MATURED   Fully paid up, fully carried out as to terms, completed as to time or as to contract.

MATURITY DATE (also Due Date):   Date on which final payment on cash loan or installment purchase is due.

MORTGAGE   A written pledge of valuable property to assure payment of a debt in case of default.

MORTGAGE CREDIT   Money owed for those borrowing for the acquisition of land and/or buildings (frequently, homes) and which is paid back over an extended period of time.

NON-INSTALLMENT CREDIT   A financial obligation that is repaid in a single lump sum.

NOTE   A written, signed promise to pay which lists details of the repayment agreement: where, when, and in what size installments, etc. A note can be transferred to a third party.

OBLIGATION An amount of money one is morally or legally bound to pay.

OPEN-END CREDIT OR REVOLVING CREDIT See pages 858–59.

OUTSTANDING The still unpaid part of a loan.

PAPER Nickname for a loan contract.

PERSONAL INSTALLMENT LOAN Money borrowed by an individual for personal needs which is repaid in regular monthly installments over a period of time.

PREPAYMENT PRIVILEGE The privilege, stated in loan contract, of repaying part or all of a loan in advance of date or dates stated in contract—with or without monetary penalty for the prepayment.

PRINCIPAL The amount of money you borrow or the amount of credit you receive.

PROCEEDS The actual amount of money handed to a borrower—after deductions for interest charges, fees, etc.

PROMISSORY NOTE A paper you sign promising to repay the total sum you owe on specified terms.

REBATE Return of a portion of a payment. For instance, you receive a rebate when you pay off your debt in advance instead of in the monthly installments you agreed upon. It then costs you less to borrow your money, because you are paying off in a shorter period.

REFINANCE Revision of a payment timetable and, often, revision of the interest charges on the debt also.

REPOSSESSION The reclaiming or taking back of goods which you have purchased on an installment sales contract and for which you have fallen behind in your payments.

REVOLVING CHARGE ACCOUNT See pages 858–59.

RIGHT OF RESCISSION Your right, guaranteed by the Consumer Credit Protection Act or various state statutes, to cancel a contract under certain circumstances (including cases in which you have put up an interest in your home as security) within three business days—without penalty and with full refund of any deposits you may have paid. The right to a "cooling-off period" is most frequently used in home improvements contracts, and the home improvement contractor must provide you with written notice of this right. It also applies, under a Federal Trade Commission rule, to sales made by door-to-door salespeople.

SHORT-TERM CREDIT Credit extended for a period up to three to five years.

SOLVENT Ability of the individual or group or organization to pay all of the debts owed. What the debtor owns is more than the total of the debts.

TERM The prescribed time you have in which to make installment or other payments, under your loan or credit contract.

TERMS Details and conditions of a loan (or other) contract: cash price, payment schedule, due date, etc.

THIRD-PARTY TRANSACTION A three-way transaction involving a buyer, a seller, and a source of consumer credit.

TITLE Legal ownership.

TOP CREDIT   Ready credit. See Check Credit Plans.

TRADE IN   Practice of trading in an old product for a new one. Trade-in allowance is the amount of money allowed for the article traded in as against the total purchase price of the article being bought.

TRUTH IN LENDING   Popular name for the historic Consumer Credit Protection Act of 1969. The law applies to virtually all consumer borrowing transactions to individuals which involve amounts up to $25,000.

UNPAID BALANCE   On a credit purchase, difference between purchase price and down payment or trade-in allowance. On cash loan, difference between total loan made and amount still owed (with charges included, of course).

UNSECURED LOAN   Loan extended solely on basis of borrower's ability and pledge to repay.

WAGE ASSIGNMENT   Clause in installment contract under which an employer may be requested to collect part of an employee's wages to pay off the employee's debt to the wage assignment holder.

WAGE EARNER PLAN   See pages 878–79.

WAGE GARNISHMENT   Classic legal procedure that creditors have used for generations to collect debts. Under "income execution" (its other name) a creditor gets a court order instructing the employer of the debtor to withhold a specified portion of his employee's wages until his debt is repaid.

17

WHAT RECORDS SHOULD YOU KEEP?
—AND HOW?

Are you among the millions of Americans—individuals and business owners—who are exaggerated savers of papers and records, receipts and canceled checks?

Do you know which of the many papers cluttering your home, or wasting valuable space in your office, are easily expendable and should be tossed out now?

Have you even a vague—much less clear and informed—knowledge of what records are needlessly overcrowding your filing cabinets or desk drawers and only confusing you?

No matter when you are reading this, it's an *excellent* time to update your filing system by getting rid of nonessentials. But while pamphlets and even books have been written to warn you what records to keep, little reliable guidance ever is given on what to discard.

As just one illustration, while you should keep checks and other receipts that may be needed for income tax purposes as proof of payment, it isn't at all important to keep all canceled checks. It's even silly.

In reviewing your own accumulation of records, don't overlook the fact that you often store more than one copy of the same record.

Overlooked, too, by many of you—individuals and businesses—is the need to transfer periodically records from your easily available files to inactive files in an out-of-the-way place.

DISCARDING RECORDS AT HOME

• Concentrate your efforts on the most important documents that may be jamming your drawers. You can create a family filing system that is efficient and exceedingly helpful with little equipment and modest outlay. Once you have screened out the nonessentials, a filing box containing manila folders and costing only a few dollars plus a small safe deposit box, also available at little cost and tax deductible too, will provide all the file storage space your home will need.

• Dispose of your weekly and monthly salary statements after you have checked them against your annual W-2 wage forms.

• Lighten your files by using a canceled check that relates to an entry on your return as your record. Unless you fear that the nature of a medical expense is ambiguous, for example, your canceled check to your physician is adequate evidence that you have paid for a specific medical service. Look into your files. How many physicians' statements have you been needlessly accumulating in your files from years gone by? Pediatricians' bills? Orthodontists' statements? Other bills that are clearly identified by your checks?

Caution: Don't throw out bills from the drugstore. The IRS may request proof of deductible drugs vs. nondeductible items such as cosmetics, etc.

• As a rule of thumb, dispose of your personal tax records after six years. Federal tax statutes make your tax return vulnerable to challenge up to three years if yours are normal circumstances. The six-year period is considered the time frame for checking returns on which income has been understated by more than 25 per cent.

• If you income-average, discard returns over five years old. The IRS usually retains personal returns for six years and can supply copies at a moderate cost.

• After you have recorded the year's total dividend payments, discard these papers on receipt of the annual dividend tally supplied by the company. Be sure, though, to retain a record of capital-gain distribution dividends because they must be reported for tax purposes when the shares are sold.

• Discard checks paid out for maintenance costs on your house. The only real reason to keep records on such costs as papering and painting is if you plan to sell your house soon. But keep permanent improvement records that add to the value of your property, such as the addition of central air-conditioning.

• Periodically check your warranties and guarantees, and if they're out of date, discard them. Throw out health maintenance certificates that have expired. Old Blue Cross/Blue Shield cards that you have accumulated from different employers (or as you have changed internal medical programs) can be a jumble of befuddlement—particularly if you must search your files in a hurry for a current validation.

DISCARDING UNNEEDED RECORDS AT YOUR BUSINESS

When a small business, of which I was a half owner, was transferred to its faithful employees recently and I was forced to go through its records, I was actually embarrassed to discover what a paper clutter had been accumulated while it was in my hands. In the files I found canceled checks dating back more than twenty years, job applications that had been turned down more than a decade ago, correspondence that had absolutely no relevance to 1978. Equally shocking, I found several copies of one contract, and that contract so out-of-date it was an antique. I think I need confess no more.

If you're also a typical owner of a small business, it's more than likely that your clutter is almost as bad (it would be unusual for yours to be as awful) as mine. Thus, as guidelines:

• In your office, one central file is adequate to protect a contract permanently, and there is no sense for other departments to be retaining copies as well. It's even more ridiculous to retain all the copies after the contract has expired.

But do not downgrade the fact that there are close to a thousand federal and state regulations covering retention of records. These vary widely on tax, unemployment, and workmen's compensation.

So caution: Before disposing of your unwanted and needless records, it would be wise to check with your state tax commissioner's office to be sure you do not go too far on discarding.

• Discard audit reports after ten years; audit work papers after three years.

• Get rid of general correspondence after five years; and eliminate classified documents—inventories, reports, and receipts—after ten years.

• Dispose of contracts twenty years after settlement. Also throw out requests for services and requisitions for suppliers one year after the end of the fiscal year.

• Discard accident reports, injury claims, and settlement papers thirty years after settlement.

• Eliminate from your files applications, changes, and terminations after five years. As for attendance records, seven years is long enough to keep them while employee activity files become mere clutter two years after they have been superseded.

• Dispose of employee contracts six years after termination. Get rid of fidelity bonds three years after termination.

• Garnishments can be eliminated after five years; insurance records for employees are needless eleven years after termination; time cards go into the discard heap after three years; and union agreements (according to the Walsh-Healey Act) may be thrown out after three years.

• Throw out your building and maintenance records after ten years, unless there are special reasons to do otherwise.

• Dispose of bids and awards three years after termination; price lists, when obsolete; purchase orders and requisitions, three years after termination; and quotations, after one year.

• According to the Code of Federal Regulations, you can destroy after four years employee withholding records, excise exemption certificates, excise reports in manufacturing, and excise reports at the retail level.

If you are a compulsive saver of papers, records, canceled checks, etc.—the way so many individuals are compulsive savers of string—you might try to "cure" yourself by buying a simple loose-leaf notebook and using it as a working tool to make your record system work more efficiently and reduce your frustrations. You can change the individual pages as you revise any part of your files, add or subtract subjects.

This can work for you as owner or manager of a small business just as it can work for you as an individual or a family.

And if you find that, at the start, parting with your records is just too bold a move—or you're afraid you might discard a paper the IRS or the courts or some agency will request the very next week—then at least double-check the records to divide them into current and background. Then clean out your active files by keeping only the current records in them; and move your background records to inactive files in another storage place.

Get a copy of "Keeping Records, What to Discard," by sending a postcard to

Consumer Information Center, Department 625E, Pueblo, Colorado 81009. It has some valuable hints and it's free.

How to Keep Your Own and Your Family's Health Records

If you have lived in one place and had the same physician all your life, you wouldn't have much need to keep your own health records. But if you're a typical American, you have moved your residence and changed your doctors or seen different specialists for specific health problems many times.

As a result, your health records almost surely have *not* kept up to you. And the only person who can maintain an accurate, complete medical history on yourself is you.

Here are the guides prepared for you by the Department of Health, Education and Welfare:

(1) Record any and all serious illnesses in your family background (heredity can play so vital a role in some diseases). Include the illness records of parents, brothers, and sisters on both sides of your family. List the histories of such diseases as cancer, diabetes, epilepsy, and heart conditions.

(2) If any of these relatives are deceased, record the causes and ages at the time of death. When discussing your own medical history, be sure you give this information to your new physician.

(3) Keep a regular record of fluctuations in your blood pressure and have your pressure checked every six to twelve months, so you'll be aware as soon as any significant changes occur.

(4) Record any and all injuries as well, for injuries from accidents may result in disabling conditions—or years later the injuries may be the basis of an illness, long since forgotten. Do not shrug off the potential for good in this injury record.

(5) Start your family's immunization program early in life, usually when a child is two to three months old. Keeping your immunization records up-to-date is an essential toward rearing a healthy family.

(6) Record the date of each immunization, so you will know when any family member needs a "booster shot" to renew his or her protection. Immunization against preventable diseases is not always permanent, warns HEW. Several childhood vaccines often may be combined in a single shot—for instance, measles, rubella, and mumps. Or other immunizations may require an initial series of injections over a span of weeks or months.

18

HOW TO ACHIEVE FINANCIAL INDEPENDENCE AND PERSONAL SECURITY IN YOUR OLDER YEARS

THE CULT OF YOUTH IS PASSING

The cult of youth which has so dominated our society for so long is passing. As the decade of the 1980s rolls on, "family planning" will focus not on children and babies but on planning for our elderly population—how to accommodate them, support them, limit the numbers of dependent elderly, maximize the potential of the non-dependents.

This is just one of the probable consequences of the drastic declines in the U.S. birth rate. In the past decade, for instance our crude birth rate dropped to fewer than 15 per 1,000 population, lowest in U.S. history. Our fertility rate, at 2.0 children per family, is actually under the zero population growth level of 2.1 children.

What's more, the trend is continuing. Young couples more and more are reporting intentions to have smaller families or no children at all. Easier abortion laws, later marriages, increased numbers of divorces, the tendency for more women to remain single—all are factors in the startling change.

ERA OF THE ELDERLY

The most obvious economic impact of ZPG will be on our marketing system for goods and services, for it will have to be geared to a stable rather than a soaring population. Other obvious economic implications are relief in pressures on our environment, a considerable easing of housing shortages, cutbacks in businesses catering to babies—ranging from obstetrics to diaper services, baby foods, and nursery schools. But far, far more fascinating are the implications for our elderly people. Among the specific forecasts of a major study by the Center for the Study of Democratic Institutions in Santa Barbara, California, coauthored by political scientist Harvey Wheeler and lawyer R. J. Carlson, are:

• A radical shift in emphasis from chronological age to "functional" age—not how old you are in years but how old you act and feel. Alongside this development will be not only tremendous new job opportunities for the elderly, but actually a new dependency on the elderly to perform a wide variety of public services. In the words of the authors: "The quality of public services will deteriorate if the talents of the elderly are not utilized."

• The formation of a new class of second-class citizens—the infirm "functionally elderly."

• New standards of beauty and morality which will be based on older rather than younger models (dizzying thought: wrinkles in fashion?).

• A complete overhaul of the present exclusive youth orientation of our educational system—with the big expansion in school enrollment in the future taking place in the thirty-and-over age bracket. In fact, says the report, a new educational boom will develop in high schools and at the post-high school level. "Colleges and universities will have to be redesigned with needs of the elderly uppermost in mind."

• "A new kind of revolutionary movement"—pressing for older Americans' rights in all spheres of life and led by the over-fifty because of their vast numbers and importance in our society.

These are just a few of the implications. I can think of dozens more: fundamental changes in both public and private pension systems, a growing gap between young workers paying even higher Social Security taxes and the elderly retired living on Social Security benefits, an enormous expansion in government medical care programs, a surge of population to warm-weather areas, and many more. So can you think of additional implications, I'm sure.

But the central point is that virtually everybody, including *you,* will be elderly one day. And then you will be forever glad that you planned now for your future financial and personal security.

PLANNING FOR YOUR RETIREMENT

How can you protect yourself against an older age threatened by poverty? A large part of the answer lies in one four-letter word: *plan!*

If you are in your twenties or thirties, retirement may seem too far off to worry about. It's tough enough to cope with the problems of everyday living. You also may feel that any money worries you may now have will somehow disappear by the time you reach retirement age. Or you may simply put off even thinking about retirement for year after year until it finally is directly ahead of you.

But the cold fact is that retirement planning is as important to you, the younger worker, as it is to the worker now reaching retirement age. For one thing, the earlier you start planning, the less it will cost you to amass the capital and income you'll need in your retirement years. Consider, for example, the lower cost of life insurance when you are younger, or the greater flexibility you have in saving and investing your nest egg.

What's more, today's younger American will need more financial resources than a person who is retired today. You well may spend as many as twenty to twenty-five years in retirement, almost twice today's retirement span.

Even today, a man retiring at age sixty-five can look forward to a life expectancy of another thirteen and one half years, and his slightly younger wife can expect to live an average of nearly twenty more years. So the sooner you start, the better the chances you will have of laying the groundwork for the comfortable, independent life you'll want in your retirement years.

Just how do you start planning? Begin by asking yourself two questions:

"Do I want to retire at sixty-five or sooner?"

"How much income and reserves will I need to live comfortably at that age?"

Before you can answer these two questions, you'll have to ask yourself just what kind of retirement life you want to lead, just what your future needs and wants will be.

You Don't Have to Retire at Sixty-Five!

Landmark legislation went on our statute books in the late 1970s raising the legal mandatory retirement age for most of us in the U.S. work force from the long-standing, artificially established age of sixty-five to a just as artificial but more realistic age of seventy.

The new retirement age covers tens of millions of us in private enterprise and state-local government jobs (with two limited exemptions for top business executives and tenured college professors). Also, the federal government's retirement age of seventy for most civilian employees was abolished with restricted exceptions.

No longer are you forced to leave your job at age sixty-five, no matter how good your performance, your health, and how eager you are to stay on.

Nor are you required to stay on after the discarded retirement age of sixty-five, if you neither need nor want the job or pay.

The choice is where it belongs—up to you.

Even before this historic adjustment took place, the pluses and minuses were debated with seemingly endless anxiety. Opponents forecast that shock waves would roll over the entire business, industrial, and academic worlds; pension plans would have to be rewritten (or at least renegotiated); many giant firms tried to work out systems and tests under which workers with inferior, if not downright negative, records still could be compelled to retire at sixty-five; the extent to which the burden on the Social Security system would be eased is still being calculated and recalculated, etc., etc.

One key concern is how their own peers, who may be jealous, ambitious, or whatever, can define and then accurately measure incompetence among fellow executives, and particularly professors.

Another is how to judge whether an employee is deteriorating physically or mentally to the point where he or she is slated to become a drag on the company

What is "deadwood" really? What is "competence" among top executives or professors who may be extremely unpopular but of undeniable value to their institutions?

How will younger workers respond when their promotions are delayed because those ahead of them in their categories are remaining on the job for longer periods?

What will be the impact on job opportunities for women and minorities, particularly, if the employment ranks are jammed?

Can workers truly keep performing at acceptable levels as they age?

An encouraging report, privately circulated by Prentice-Hall, suggested that "for many companies, keeping workers on the job until age seventy would pose very few problems."

Only three problems emerged as serious, the most serious being (1) the "delicate problem of dealing with reduced job performance among people who are only a few years away from retirement"; (2) increased costs due to absenteeism, benefits, etc.; and (3) "dealing with advancement for younger go-getters."

On the challenge of dissatisfied younger workers, possible solutions include: offering incentives or alluring bonuses to older workers to retire before age seventy; offering incentives to younger workers to stay with the company; revamping the company's compensation program to tie pay more closely to performance.

On the problem of jobs for women and minorities, few companies expect opportunities to shrink. Several corporations said, in fact, that they would make an extra effort to see that highly qualified minorities receive special advantages.

On the question of job performance, many employers said they would "tighten up" their policies to make sure employees in the older age groups are still working up to par.

A fascinating finding of Prentice-Hall was that while the mandatory retirement age is rising, the number of employees choosing to take early retirement also is increasing. Many of you would prefer to retire early if you can swing it financially.

No matter what your views as an individual, traditional discrimination on the basis of age alone is finally being eliminated from the law. Our society's attitude toward our elderly has been and is far more barbaric than the barbarians even dreamed of. I hail the step, although it is only one minor move forward. It has been so long in coming.

"Retirement Shock"

True tale: An Eastern machinery manufacturer found it increasingly difficult to recruit young, local residents. Even worse, a mounting number of younger employees were quitting. The company president was sufficiently concerned to call in an outside personnel consultant, who quickly discovered that retired employees were responsible. Despite liberal pension benefits, the retirees warned younger people in town not to work for the company if they wanted to avoid being treated as "just a name and address" after retiring.

True tale: A large utility filed a rate increase application with state authorities, anticipating that the required public hearing for approval would be routine. Unexpectedly, the application was opposed by an ad hoc committee of the utility's own retired employees, who felt they had been "discarded." The opposition resulted in considerable delay in the rate hike, in much unfavorable publicity, and led a chastened utility official to comment later, "A retired employee who is enjoying his retirement years is a living advertisement for his employer."

True tale: On a list of forty top stress producers, "retirement" ranks in a high ninth place—not far behind "death of a spouse"—a medical study a while ago disclosed. Not providing retirement counseling can be disastrous to the employee. And usually the company will be blamed for the trauma known as "retirement shock"—a stress-producing situation which recognizes no social or financial barriers.

Almost one third of our citizens over sixty-five live in poverty, yet many did not become poor until they became old. By itself, that flashes a red-hot signal of danger to all of us—and compounding it is the fact that there is a definite trend toward retirement at an earlier age than the traditional sixty-five. A recent study by West Coast corporate planners, in fact, predicts an average retirement age of fifty-five in two more decades—meaning that if current predictions on life expectancy hold and if you're an average worker now in your thirties, you can look forward to twenty-five years of retirement!

But "unexpected retirement or being unprepared for retirement can mean living without any framework," a retirement counselor pointed out at a seminar on "preparing employees for retirement" sponsored by the American Management Association. AMA is a non-profit educational organization which conducts worldwide management training programs for more than 100,000 business and government executives annually.

And the confrontation with retirement—which affects the top-level corporate executive as well as the assembly-line worker—the fear of idleness, loneliness, and deteriorating health, can affect an employee's job performance years before he or she actually retires.

Changes induced by retirement are more abrupt than those between other stages of life. And they occur when most people are least able in body and in mind to cope with change.

Putting it in simplest language, a company providing pre- and post-retirement counseling is simply using good business sense. Its retirement program will not only reduce the trauma of retirement stress but also will bring greater efficiency, higher employee morale, and, the AMA points out, "an added measure of valuable goodwill from the swelling ranks of retirees."

What might a thorough retirement program cover? At least these five points:

(1) Of course, finances—ranging from budgeting to investments, tax considerations, estate planning, and most particularly from the employee's viewpoint, crucial details on the company's pension plan.

(2) Health care, medical or geriatrics advice.

(3) Life-style adjustments, psychological factors, family relationships, housing arrangements such as selection of retirement location, climate considerations.

(4) Use of leisure time (hobbies, travel, educational opportunities, community services, second careers).

(5) And legal rights and responsibilities, ranging from sales of homes to writing wills to avoiding traps set by swindlers who concentrate on older people.

How Much Will You Need?

How will your total estimated income fit your actual financial needs during a retirement period which easily could stretch up to twenty years or more? The answer must rest to a large extent on your family's style of living, on the things and non-things you are accustomed to and would like to continue to have. But here are some guidelines for figuring your future retirement needs, so you can later calculate how big the gap is between your projected income and your actual future needs.

Some of your expenses will be higher.

For instance, your costs for medicine, both prescription and non-prescription, will average two and a half times higher than they do for younger Americans. With more leisure time, you may want to increase your spending on travel, dining out, entertainment, and hobbies.

On the other hand, many of the things that now figure in your budget will either cost less or cease to be at all important to you. By the time you retire the chances are that your home mortgage will have been paid off, or if you move to a smaller place, your overall housing expenses will be lower than they are now.

If you retire to a warm climate, your clothing needs also will be less, and your heating costs next to nothing.

When you reach age sixty-five, you will qualify for Medicare benefits, which could cut your costs for hospital and doctor bills. And these benefits are, of course, in addition to Social Security benefits.

By the time you retire, too, your life insurance policy may be paid up, or if it is not, you may find that you need less protection than you are carrying, which means a lower monthly premium cost or perhaps none.

The high cost of rearing and educating your children will be behind you. And your food costs will be lower, simply because the calorie needs of older people are less than those of younger people.

You also will be eligible, in retirement, for important money-saving tax breaks. Under the tax laws of the late 1970s, you could claim, if you were sixty-five or older by the end of the tax year, an extra exemption plus a second exemption for your wife if she was sixty-five and filed a joint return with you.

If you are sixty-five or over or are retired, you could get a retirement income credit which could cut your tax directly.

If you are fifty-five or older before you sell at a profit a home in which you have lived for three of the previous five years, you are eligible for significant tax benefits on the gain.

If you are in this age category, you well may get significant breaks on your property taxes.

Above and beyond tax breaks on your federal income tax, most states offer some type of exemption, special deduction, or reduction for retirees. To find out the rules, check with your state tax department.

Finally, many of the expenses formerly associated with your job, ranging from eating in restaurants to commuting costs, will be sharply reduced.

The basic point remains, though: the actual dollar amount of your financial needs in retirement will depend on your expected standard of living—in housing, dining, clothes, transportation, vacationing, giving. It also will depend on the level of property and state income taxes in the area in which you decide to settle.

It also will be crucially affected—and in an adverse way to you—by the degree of inflation in our nation in coming years.

You cannot ignore this inflation factor if you are to avoid the financial panic of discovering too late how drastically you have underestimated your future needs.

HELP FOR THE OVER-SIXTY-FIVE TAXPAYER

Q. *Which U. S. Government agency provides nationwide toll-free telephone assistance, toll-free TV phones and teletypewriters for the deaf, free information booklets (many printed in extra-large type for the partially blind), runs overseas seminars, and offers free walk-in counseling services (some designed particularly for those who don't speak English) for the elderly, handicapped, and low-income citizens?*

A. The Internal Revenue Service.

Why? Because our tax laws are so complex and change so frequently that even if you are more informed than most taxpayers, you may not be aware of all the deductions, credits, and exemptions to which you are entitled.

To whom is this of extraordinary importance? The millions of you who are sixty-five or over, for when you reach sixty-five or retire you are suddenly faced with a myriad of new federal income tax provisions.

What's more, if you're retired, your taxes are no longer withheld by your employer. Your income comes largely from pensions, annuities, investments, business activities, etc. not subject to withholding. The laws governing these forms of income are among the most befuddling in the tax code and require you to fill out several additional schedules as well as the long form 1040.

In addition, Congress has passed many special tax relief provisions for the elderly—as a result of which about 18 million of the 24 million of Americans considered older citizens currently pay no federal income taxes at all. You can receive levels of income tax-free which are roughly double the tax-free income levels for those under sixty-five.

Of every four older Americans only about one actually pays income taxes. If you are relatively well-off, with your income averaging close to $20,000 a year, under current law, you too are entitled to special treatment.

As just one illustration, you are granted an extra personal exemption. And tax preferences for you cost the U. S. Treasury billions annually.

But while many of today's measures ease and new proposals would further reduce the tax burden of millions of you, they are of little value unless you know they exist and how to take advantage of them.

The IRS distributes publications to assist older taxpayers. *Tax Benefits for Older Americans* is the main information booklet. It is free and you can get a copy at IRS and Social Security offices. The brochure carries sample forms illustrating many of the tax situations which you, an older taxpayer, will face.

PRECAUTIONS IN CALCULATING YOUR NEEDS

Obviously, no matter what your style of living, you must be coldly realistic in estimating your own needs.

• You must aim to have an emergency savings fund always on hand to take care of utterly unforeseeable emergencies. (See Chapter 2, "Budgets Are Back in Style.")

• You must have extra health insurance to supplement Medicare.

• And you must have some kind of "inflation cushion." If inflation continues to chew away at the buying power of your retirement income at an annual rate of say, "only" 5 per cent, and you expect to retire twenty years from now, you will need *165 per cent* more than you need today. This means that what you can buy for $3,000 today would cost you $7,950 in twenty years. For what your $10,000 buys today, you would need $26,500 twenty years from now. (See pages 4–6 for calculations of future prices at *other* inflation rates.)

FIGURING YOUR MONTHLY EXPENSES

Now, taking into account your own life-style and needs and allowing for inflation, figure your own monthly expenses now and after retirement on a work sheet that might look something like this:

Your Monthly Expenses

ITEM	WHERE MONEY GOES NOW	AFTER RETIREMENT
Food—including meals away from home		
Clothing		
Laundry, cleaning		
Transportation		
Car expense (including operating expenses and depreciation)		
Auto insurance		
Train or bus, other routine travel		
Housing		
Rent or mortgage		
Homeowners' insurance		
Heat		
Gas and electric		
Telephone		
Repairs, maintenance		
Lawn and garden upkeep		
Property taxes		
Household help		
Furniture and furnishings		

ITEM	WHERE MONEY GOES NOW	AFTER RETIREMENT
Medical care (not covered by insurance)	————————	————————
Medicare payments for doctor bills	————————	————————
Other health insurance premiums	————————	————————
Medicines	————————	————————
Dental care	————————	————————
Life insurance and annuity premiums	————————	————————
Vacation and travel	————————	————————
Education expenses	————————	————————
Savings	————————	————————
Newspapers, magazines, books	————————	————————
Personal allowances (including grooming, haircuts)	————————	————————
Contributions and gifts	————————	————————
Entertainment (movies, theater, etc.)	————————	————————
Hobbies and sports, club dues	————————	————————
Miscellaneous	————————	————————
TOTAL MONTHLY EXPENSES	————————	————————
TOTAL ANNUAL EXPENSES	————————	————————

As a rule of thumb, many retired couples find that they can live comfortably on roughly two thirds of their preretirement after-tax incomes. You, though, may be able to—or have to—live on less. Or you may want to live on more.

To determine where you stand, the next step is to calculate what your retirement income is likely to be.

HOW MUCH WILL YOU HAVE?

ESTIMATING YOUR RETIREMENT INCOME

Before estimating your retirement income, you have to estimate the age at which you will decide to—or think you will for some reason be ready to—retire.

What comes next will involve some arithmetic and paperwork, but this should not be difficult. The task is to make a list of all the sources from which you can anticipate retirement income.

• You can learn what you can expect in the way of Social Security benefits—most likely, the cornerstone of your retirement income program—in the section in this chapter called "What You Should Know About Social Security."

• Add to your expected Social Security benefits the amount of monthly income you can expect from your life insurance policies; annuities; and your company, union, or other pension program. These also are described in the sections that follow.

- Check such other key retirement income sources as cash savings, stocks, bonds, real estate. They are discussed in detail in various other chapters.

- Conservatively estimate the income you might get if you sold valuable assets you now own—art, stamp collections, your home, etc.—and reinvested the proceeds in various ways.

- Also very conservatively estimate what income you might get from a part-time job or business you are looking forward to having in retirement.

Just listing all these sources of income on the work sheet that follows will give you an idea of your expected total income. And that, along with what you have already estimated will be your future living needs, will give you a guide to how much more retirement income you should now be building to provide you with a comfortable standard of living later on.

Your Estimated Income

	MONTHLY	ANNUALLY
Social Security benefits (you and your spouse)		
Private pension		
Veteran's pension (if any)		
Any other military, civil service, or railroad retirement benefits		
Deferred profit sharing		
Income from annuities		
Income from investment of life insurance cash value		
Dividends from investments		
Interest from savings accounts		
Interest from bonds		
Capital gains from investments		
Income from property (e.g., rent)		
Payments on mortgages you hold		
Investment of capital from home sale		
Earnings from part-time job or self-employment		
Income from a business		
Other income from *any* source		
TOTAL		

PLANNING FOR YOUR PENSION

You are no more than normal if you shrink from the thought of growing old and shrink still further from the question of how you will be taken care of once you retire.

Most Americans simply assume that they will manage. They will get by, somehow they will be provided for. Why else have they been contributing to Social Security all these years? They assume, often unquestioningly, that the money taken out of their paychecks for a private pension plan will be returned to them at retirement.

The stark truth of the matter is that most of us can expect a dramatic drop in our incomes when we retire. Those without substantial savings, other assets, or family support well may face destitution.

Here are some of the reasons why:

• Less than half of the private work force is now covered by a private pension plan.

• Even among those who are covered, an estimated one third will never receive any payout from their pension plan. They won't work long or continuously enough to qualify. They may die before they collect. Or the plan might stop.

• But even if you should be lucky enough to receive a pension, the chances are it will not amount to much. In 1975, people sixty-five years old and over received private pensions that typically amounted to less than $200 a month. With Social Security payments to sixty-five-year-old workers retiring in 1979 averaging around $265 a month for individuals and $400 a month for couples, your prospects for a comfortable retirement aren't great.

• Your private pension benefits probably will not rise with the cost of living but will be fixed as of the date you retire and leave the plan. Increases in the benefits of retirees are generally not issues in collective bargaining, although employers sometimes voluntarily increase them.

• Not all pension plans are insured by the government insurance corporation, called the Pension Benefit Guarantee Corporation. Only plans under which you are promised a certain benefit (so-called "defined benefit" plans) are covered, and not all of them are covered. Plans financed by union dues are not covered. Neither are those with fewer than twenty-five employees set up by such professionals as doctors, lawyers, and performing artists.

• Even though your plan may be insured, not all of the benefits which you have been promised are covered by the government program.

By and large, pensions operate like insurance policies. Everyone pays in to protect themselves, but only a few ever draw benefits. The trouble with this model—trouble for you, the 40 million workers covered by private industry plans—is that while there is a chance you won't crack up the car or lose your house in a fire, you *will* get old, you *will* stop working, and you and your spouse will need a retirement income.

Take the time now, before you stare retirement in the face, to find out from your employer, plan administrator, or possibly your union the answers to these questions: How long do you have to work to qualify for a pension? If you leave the job for any reason and for any length of time, will you still get a pension? What size pension will you draw when you retire?

WORKING TO QUALIFY

You no longer must work a lifetime to earn the right to a pension—but by no means can you qualify for a pension overnight. On the contrary, first you must be covered by a plan; then if you are covered, you gain the right to a pension only after a substantial amount of time on the job. The requirements vary, and some plans are better, but most plans that promise workers a specific benefit require that they put in ten years with an employer contributing to the plan before they qualify for benefits.

Accumulating a decade of service with a single employer isn't easy today in view of the high mobility of the U.S. labor force. Labor Department figures in the early 1970s disclosed that only one out of four workers kept the same job continuously for ten years or more.

You should also know that if yours is a typical plan, there's a good chance that not all of your work for an employer will count toward the ten years you need to qualify for a pension. For example, your plan may not count early years on the job. Or if you were laid off or quit for a period, the years before your "break in service" won't count. Then too, if you start working under a plan when you are older, usually age sixty or above, none of your years may count.

To determine your chances of receiving a pension, find out if you are covered by your firm's plan. If so, how long do you have to work before qualifying to receive benefits? Will all your years of work count toward your pension? If you leave the job for any reason and for any length of time, how will your absence affect your chances of earning a right to a pension? Also find out what to do to collect your benefits if you leave your job before retirement age. What must you do before you retire to apply for your benefits? Try, if possible, to get the answers to these questions in writing from your plan administrator, boss, or possibly your union.

THE SIZE OF YOUR PENSION

What benefits does your plan promise you if you work until official retirement age? Quit? Get laid off or fired tomorrow? How is the amount of your benefit determined?

Most workers are covered by plans which pay benefits based on the number of years you are covered by the plan (which may not be the same as the number of years you have worked). These years are multiplied by a percentage of your salary during a particular year, or a percentage of your total average earnings, or a percentage of your earnings during the five years just before retirement to figure out your pension benefit.

Say you worked for ten years under a plan that provides benefits equal to 1 per cent of your final salary for each year of service that you had. If your final paycheck totaled $10,000 a year, your basic pension at age sixty-five would be about $83 a month or $1,000 a year.

But what if you retire early? Will you get any pension benefits and how much will they amount to? What if you are married and want your widow or widower to get a benefit? In both these situations your pension will be reduced. The reduction may be substantial. You should also check to see whether any benefits are paid if you are disabled.

One of the most important things you should find out is whether your plan is "integrated" with Social Security. Currently, firms with private plans may "integrate" or count part of your Social Security benefit when figuring out how much you will receive from your private plan.

Say your firm decides that your plan should provide an "integrated" benefit of 1½ per cent of your final average pay. You are an employee who has always earned the average wage, which in 1978 amounted to about $10,500 a year. If you worked for twenty years under this plan, your basic pension benefit would be about $3,000 a year.

If you retired in 1979 at age sixty-five and were single, your Social Security benefit could equal $5,000 a year. In figuring how much you'd receive in pension benefits, your firm might subtract 50 per cent (or more) of your Social Security benefit or $2,500 from $3,000. Thus, in this instance you'd retire with a yearly pension from your firm of only $500 or about $42 a month. If you had worked for fifteen years or less for the company, you'd get nothing from the plan. Your entire retirement income would come from your $5,000-a-year Social Security benefit.

In short, "integration" means lower-paid workers get less from their private pension plans than do higher-paid workers. The system is complicated and varies from plan to plan. Some are better for workers than others. If your plan is integrated, learn what this means in dollars and cents for you once you retire.

Ask how many employees in your company or division are slated to receive pensions. Ask what are the typical amounts which workers like you receive. Inquire if the plan has any provisions to hike postretirement benefits along with rises in the cost of living.

In addition, find out what size benefit—if any—you can reasonably expect to receive if your firm fails, changes owners or your plan terminates.

YOUR SURVIVING SPOUSE

Most of you working and covered by private pension plans believe that once you gain a right to a pension, it will automatically go to your widow, or widower, on your death. This is not the case. The pension system and the law do not consider an employee's pension joint property but view it as belonging to the employee alone.

When you retire, for instance, your pension will in most cases be automatically reduced so your surviving spouse can continue to get at least half of your benefits when you die. (You can sign a form stipulating that you don't want or cannot afford such a reduction. The size of any reduction depends on your age, your spouse's age and the details of your particular plan.)

Find out how much of a pension cut you must agree to accept if you elect this so-called "survivor's option." And if you die after you retire, how much will your surviving spouse receive? For how many years?

If you are still working and not ready to retire, yet you want to make sure your spouse gets some of your pension should you die, you can (under certain circumstances) opt early for a surviving spouse reduction. Find out how old you must be to take advantage of this chance to provide for your spouse. What if you were to die before this point or shortly after electing this option? Would your spouse receive anything, and if so what?

Since an employee's pension is viewed as his alone, there is little which gives a woman whose marriage breaks up any claim on her ex-husband's pension. However, in some states with community property laws, such as California, divorcées have been awarded a portion of future benefits.

Under Internal Revenue Service regulations, pension plans *may* require a spouse to have been married for one year on both the date her husband began to draw his reduced benefits and the date of his death. This rule, in effect, could make it impossible for a divorcée ever to collect a benefit even though her ex-husband opted for a reduction in his benefits in order to help provide for her.

Also, a divorced pensioner who wants to provide for his second wife could not do so, because they would not have been married when he began to collect his pension benefits.

Under the law, a retired worker whose spouse dies before him cannot reverse the reduction in his benefit and reclaim the full amount of his pension. Of course, some plans provide more than the law's minimum standards.

Find out what your plan provides for your spouse. Ask, too, about preretirement survivor's benefits, death or burial benefits or group term life insurance.

YOUR PENSION RIGHTS

Under the 1974 pension reform law, formally called the Employee Retirement Income Security Act (ERISA), all pension plan participants have these basic rights:

• To receive booklets giving you an explanation of your plan in "easy to understand" language. If you do not receive such a summary plan booklet, ask your plan administrator or employer for one. If you find that it is written in a way that is too complicated for you to understand, complain to the nearest office of the U. S. Department of Labor. Even if your plan seems simple enough, watch out for misleading language. "Eligibility" provisions, for instance, generally only tell you whether or not you are covered by a plan, not whether you are "eligible" to receive benefits. Too, the booklets often emphasize the terms and conditions under which you *will* receive a pension. They tend to downplay the circumstances under which you *won't* get a pension.

These booklets are *not* the final word on your plan. Many contain a disclaimer that says if there are any discrepancies between the language in the booklet and the plan's legal documents on file at the main plan office, you cannot rely on the booklet. The plan documents, not the booklet, prevail. Ask questions and insist on getting the answers in writing.

• To learn while you are working under the plan whether you are entitled to a pension. You have a right to learn how much you can expect to get and when. Make this request to your plan administrator. Make it in writing. You may obtain this information once a year.

• To be given a statement once you have earned the right to a pension and stopped working that tells you the amount you will receive. When you apply for your Social Security benefits (see pages 914–15), you will get a copy of this statement that will tell you how much you can expect to get at normal retirement age, usually sixty-five. It will *not* indicate by how much that amount will be reduced if you retire before that point or if you are married. When you reach retirement age, it will still be up to you to go back to your company and apply for your pension.

- To be told where your pension money is being invested, how well and by whom. You will receive a summary of this information annually. But if you want to know more details about how your pension funds are being invested, you have to ask, in writing, for a copy of your plan's full Annual Report. If you believe that your plan's funds are being invested in risky or improper ways, contact the U. S. Labor Department. (See Chapter 29, "How and Where to Get Help.")

- To go to court, if you believe that you have been fired or discriminated against so the plan will not have to pay you your pension.

- To be told the reason why a plan has decided not to give you a pension. If you believe that your claim for a pension was unfairly denied, you should ask the plan to review its decision. If that fails, you may sue in state or federal court.

HELP UNDERSTANDING PENSIONS

Pensions, in general, and individual pension plans, in particular, are complicated. Even pension lawyers and actuaries whose business it is to be experts argue endlessly over the meanings of various clauses in the pension law and their own plans. Don't be discouraged or put off if your own investigation into how your plan operates takes time and study.

There are a number of books and pamphlets, besides your own plan's summary booklet, that can help you. Here are a few of them:

- *Pension Facts*. The Pension Rights Center, a non-profit public-interest group specializing in pension matters, publishes a series of clear, simple fact sheets. *Pension Facts #1* explains what the 1974 pension reform law does and does not do for workers. *Pension Facts #2* focuses on women, the group most disadvantaged by the private pension system. You can obtain these fact sheets for 25 cents each by sending a self-addressed stamped envelope for each copy to the Center, Room 1019, 1346 Connecticut Avenue N.W., Washington D.C. 20036.

- *You and Your Pension*. This book by Ralph Nader and Kate Blackwell is a comprehensive description of how the private pension system works. Although it was written before the 1974 reform law was passed, it can give you good background material. It is available in bookstores (the publisher is Grossman, 1973) or for $1.00 from the Pension Rights Center.

- *What You Should Know About the Pension and Welfare Law* and *Often Asked Questions About the Employee Retirement Income Security Act of 1974* are two of several publications put out by the Labor Department. They are dry and rather technical but worth consulting. You can get them free through your local Labor Department office or by writing the Office of Procurement, Labor-Management Services Administration, U. S. Department of Labor, 200 Constitution Avenue N.W., Washington D.C. 20216.

SIMPLIFIED PENSION PLANS

If your employer has no pension plan, partly because of the hassle and cost of administering one, you might suggest he (or she) investigate Simplified Pension

Plans. The product of the Tax Reform Act of 1978, they are a great way to avoid ERISA paperwork.

Here's how the simplified plans work:

The employer makes contributions to an Individual Retirement Account in the employee's name. (See pages 910–12 for more on IRAs.) The maximum contribution is 15 per cent of the employee's pay, up to $7,500 a year. This is a big jump up from the $1,500 a year maximum that an individual can contribute on behalf of himself to an IRA.

The employer can deduct the full amount of the IRA contribution from the firm's taxes as long as the pension plan qualifies as non-discriminatory. This means it must cover all employees twenty-five and over who have worked for the firm in any three of the past five years, including part-timers. The plan may not favor owners or top management; it must contribute the same percentage of everybody's pay.

The employee does not have to pay income tax on what his firm contributes. And when it amounts to less than $1,500, the employee can add the difference to his IRA account and take that figure as a deduction.

A big advantage for employees is that with these simplified plans you are fully vested at once, that is, qualify for benefits. In traditional plans, an employee who leaves before he vests forfeits his pension benefits. The sum the firm contributed on his behalf remains in the fund and is used to pay the pensions of those workers who stay. In this way, employees who leave reduce an employer's future contributions to the plan.

Despite this advantage, employees should be aware that there is a disadvantage to simplified plans. As with regular pension plans, it is possible for employers to contribute a higher percentage of pay for higher-salaried staff. They may do this by deducting Social Security taxes from the amount contributed to an IRA. (See discussion of "integration," pages 904–5.)

The result might look like this:

	$10,000 SALARY/YR.	$60,000
Firm contributes 8 per cent of salary to IRA:	$800	$4,800
Minus: Social Security tax (1979)	613	1,404
Contribution	$187	$3,396
IRA contribution as per cent of pay	1.9%	5.8%

A SAFETY NET UNDER YOUR PENSION

Before the Pension Benefit Guaranty Corporation (PBGC) was established in 1974, it was just too bad for you, a worker covered by a private pension plan, if the benefits you were counting on for your retirement were wiped out because your plan went broke.

Today, the PBGC acts as a government safety net beneath the pension plan system. It protects covered workers in the same way the Federal Deposit Insurance Corporation protects bank depositors in the event their bank fails.

For the many workers whose plans have ended and especially for those whose plans did not have enough assets to cover their obligations, the guarantees the PBGC offers are vitally important.

You should realize, however, that the PBGC does not insure all types of private plans, only those called "defined benefit plans." Under these, an employer promises that once you retire, he will pay you certain fixed benefits based on the length of time you have worked.

Even with this type of plan, once the PBGC takes a plan over it is quite possible that your benefits will be reduced. The agency only protects what it terms "basic non-forfeitable benefits"—normal retirement annuities, certain early retirement benefits, disability benefits, and pensions for survivors. Generally severance pay, medical benefits, and life insurance are not included. There are limits, too, on the total non-forfeitable benefits that the PBGC can insure. If, for example, your plan folded in 1979 without sufficient assets, the maximum guaranteed benefits coming to you at age sixty-five would not exceed (1) your highest average salary for a consecutive five-year period or (2) $1,073 per month, whichever is less.

To find out if your plan is insured by the PBGC look at your summary plan description booklet that all plans are required to distribute. If yours is a plan paid for by union dues or if you are one of twenty-five or fewer employees covered by a plan set up by doctors, lawyers, architects, or similar professionals, it will not be insured. If you belong to a plan to which more than one employer contributes it is slated to become insured in July 1979, but this date may be pushed back.

Also, remember that if your plan stops before you have worked long enough to earn a right to a pension, your benefit will not be guaranteed. For more information about the PBGC's insurance program, write to its Office of Communications, 2020 K Street N.W., Washington, D.C. 20006, or call (202) 254-4817.

Getting the Retirement Income You Need

Whether the estimated retirement income you arrive at will be adequate will depend, of course, on your needs. If it is not adequate, several options are open to you.

One, obviously, is to do without certain things in your original retirement plan. Another is to beef up your income. Assuming you choose the second option, there are three stages in planning to get the retirement income you need.

(1) Accumulate as many resources as possible during your preretirement years. You can stint on some living expenses in this period in order to put more aside in savings accounts, mutual funds, growth stocks, high-grade bonds, or any of the other mediums analyzed in this book (see Contents).

(2) Use part of your current income and nest egg to buy an income for your retirement years. This income could come from life insurance, an annuity, or income-producing real estate.

(3) Plan on periodically withdrawing a portion of the capital in your nest egg during your retirement.

Also be alert to proposals in Congress that can help improve your retirement income situation—and make your views known.

DON'T MISS OUT ON KEOGH OR IRA PLAN

Q. *Why do so many millions of you fail to take advantage of superb tax shelter plans approved by the U. S. Government and specifically designed to help you accumulate money for your older years?*

Could it be that you simply don't know enough about the plans to establish them? Or that you don't know where to turn to get help? Or that it's just too much trouble to move on your own to benefit yourself?

Yet the facts are that the benefits you can derive from setting up one of the two types of tax-sheltered retirement plans created for you (Keogh or Individual Retirement Account) are both immediate and long-term; the earlier you arrange to participate the better off you and your family will be; and despite any of your concern about complexities, the procedures really are easy.

More specifically:

• The most immediate benefit you will realize from establishing a tax shelter for your retirement is on the contribution you make to the plan. That money goes directly into the plan and is freed from current income taxes.

To show how significant this can be:

If you are only in the 19 per cent income tax bracket and can contribute $750, you will save $143. Putting it another way, you will be able to invest an additional $143 a year toward your retirement nest egg.

If you are in the 50 per cent tax bracket, and you can contribute $7,500, your tax savings jump to $3,750 each year.

Another extremely important benefit of these tax shelters is that the money you put aside under the shelter grows tax-free. You pay no taxes on the dividends, interest, or capital gains earned during the years your funds are under the shelter.

Again, merely to suggest the significance of this, if you are an individual in the 50 per cent bracket and you contribute $7,500 a year for thirty years to a tax-sheltered account compounding quarterly at 5 per cent (a cinch to arrange), you will have $362,834 more for your retirement years than you would have had if you hadn't bothered to create a tax shelter. Quite a difference, yes?

• How big the difference will be will vary according to the number of years you have a plan until your retirement, the amount of money you contribute each year, the return you are able to get on your investment, and the tax bracket you are in each year.

And as your income moves up and you shift into a higher tax bracket (even if inflation robs you of the increased buying power of your extra dollars), the benefits of your tax shelter grow.

If you are self-employed, whether full time or part time, you should consider a Keogh plan, under which, at the end of the 1970s, you could set aside each year $7,500 or 15 per cent of your self-employed income, whichever was less. Your contribution into a Keogh plan is tax-deductible. There are no estate taxes on a Keogh plan if it is paid to your beneficiary over two or more taxable years.

You can start to collect your Keogh funds at age fifty-nine and a half, or earlier if you are disabled and cannot continue to work. You must start withdrawals by seventy and a half years of age, even though contributions can continue as long as you have earned income. And the money in your plan is not attachable if you suffer personal bankruptcy.

If you are an employee not covered by a company, government, or union-sponsored plan, an Individual Retirement Account (IRA) is for you. With an IRA, you could at the end of the 1970s set aside 15 per cent or a maximum of $1,500 of your annual earnings—and if you use a marital IRA to provide IRA benefits to your non-working spouse, you could set aside up to $1,750 or 15 per cent of your income each year, divided equally between you and your spouse. The deadline for establishing a new IRA or for making contributions to an existing IRA as of the late 1970s was the income tax payment date in April. Other provisions are generally similar to Keogh.

For a good free *Guide to Retirement Planning,* outlining details on Keogh and IRA, write Lord, Abbott & Co., *Retirement,* P. O. Box 666, Wall Street Station, New York, New York 10005. Also excellent is *A Shopper's Guide to IRAs and Keogh Plans: Choosing a New Plan and Evaluating the One You Have,* available for $2.25 from N.R.O.C.A. Press, Box 12066, Dallas, Texas 75225.

How Long Will Your Retirement Capital Last?

How long will your nest egg last? That will depend on the rate of return it is earning and the amount you withdraw each year. Conceivably, your fund could last indefinitely, as the following chart indicates.

If you retire with a nest egg of $100,000, you can make it last for one decade, two, three, or even longer. Just how long will be determined by the rate of return on your capital and the amount you withdraw for living expenses each year. Suppose, for example, you need $9,000 a year and your fund is earning a 7 per cent return; then your money will last twenty-two years. If your return equals or exceeds your withdrawals your fund will last indefinitely, as indicated by the symbol ∞. (Always keep in mind that the dollars will buy less in the market place than they are buying as you read this.)

ANNUAL WITHDRAWAL	YEARS YOUR FUND WILL LAST AT THESE ANNUAL RATES OF RETURN*					
	5%	6%	7%	8%	9%	10%
$ 6,000	36	∞	∞	∞	∞	∞
7,000	25	33	∞	∞	∞	∞
8,000	20	23	30	∞	∞	∞
9,000	16	18	22	28	∞	∞
10,000	14	15	17	20	26	∞
11,000	12	13	14	16	19	25
12,000	11	11	12	14	15	18

*Copyright 1971 by Medical Economics Company, Oradell, N.J. 07649. Reprinted by permission.

Of course, if your nest egg amounts to $50,000, you simply cut the annual withdrawal amounts in half and your money will last the same number of years shown in the chart.

What You Should Know About Social Security— Foundation of Your Retirement Program

A BASIC PROBLEM

Over decades of amendments, the Social Security law has become exceedingly complex, but the basic concept of Social Security remains simple. It is this: During your working years, you (employees, employers, and the self-employed) pay Social Security taxes—a percentage of earnings into trust funds. Then, in retirement, or in case of death or disability, payments are made from the funds to you, the worker and your dependents, or to your survivors.

The trust funds are not like a savings bank, with paid-in dollars held for you and returned on retirement with interest added. That kind of arrangement would require so huge a buildup of funds that the whole economy would be dislocated. And such a buildup isn't necessary in a government system that has continuity and can count on future generations of workers to contribute.

Instead, taxes are intended to bring in each year funds to pay benefits to those now on benefit rolls and to create just enough reserves to take care of contingencies. In effect, it's a pay-as-you-go system.

Collection of SS taxes began in January 1937, with the first monthly benefits paid in January 1940. From then until the mid-1970s—a span of almost forty years—the SS program was self-supporting. In almost every year until 1975, the system collected more than it paid out in benefits. The excess was invested in interest-bearing U.S. securities and the interest was added to the trust funds— separate funds maintained in the U. S. Treasury. Billions had been accumulated in the two cash benefit trust funds by the mid-1970s.

But starting in 1974, unemployment side by side with inflation wiped out huge totals. Part of the shrinkage in reserves was due to lost SS taxes that would otherwise have been collected had jobless and underemployed workers been getting paychecks. Part was due to galloping inflation; benefits to the millions on the rolls are automatically hiked to keep up with the cost of living and every 1 per cent increase in the inflation rate swells the annual benefit payout by hundreds of millions. In addition, all benefit payments in the future will be permanently higher because of past inflation and because the interest earnings lost by the trust funds due to shrunken reserves cannot be regained.

Had the jobless rate, instead of soaring, as it did, risen to no more than 5 per cent in that period, a Social Security Administration study shows, the cash benefits trusts funds would have grown by $25 billion between 1975 and 1981, instead of dwindling!

LONGER-RANGE PROBLEM, TOO

There was a longer-range financing problem, too, which would not even have hit until after the year 2000, assuming Congress did nothing to avert it. Congress did act, though, in its 1977 amendments. The two causes:

(1) A fluke in the benefit formula written into the law in 1972 which could have resulted in a large number of retirees in the twenty-first century receiving benefits higher than the top wages they had ever earned.

(2) The assumption that there will be a continued drop in U.S. birth and fertility rates.

In 1972, the law was amended to provide for automatic adjustment of benefits if and as prices rose moderately from year to year. (There was no anticipation of 1973–75's nightmare inflation!) The 1972 law additionally provides for the maximum taxable earnings under Social Security to rise as average wages rise from year to year.

But if you assume an indefinite continuation of a murderously steep rate of inflation, a strange situation would have resulted from the operation of these two provisions: benefits would run way ahead of wages and of the system's taxes from wages. This situation accounted for about half of the estimated long-range actuarial deficit of the system. (The 1977 amendments erased that problem.)

The other half of the projected deficit is based on that assumption about birth and fertility. If rates do continue dropping, there would, in the year 2010, be close to thirty Americans sixty-five and over for every 100 of working age. As the 1980s near, the proportion is 18.3 people 65 and over for every 100 of working age.

Predicting birth and fertility rates is risky—but even if these assumptions turn out to be accurate, there are offsetting factors. For instance, if the public cost of supporting the elderly went up, the cost of supporting and educating the young would be reduced. If fewer women were busy rearing children, more would be in the labor market and paying SS taxes. If fewer young people were entering the labor market, more elderly people could find jobs.

SOLUTIONS

Among the ways to provide additional financing for the Social Security programs are:

(1) Increase the SS tax rate and/or the SS taxable wage base substantially.

Under the law, the wage base goes up as average wages rise. Before 1979, only about 15 per cent of all workers had earnings above the wage base.

So, when and as the wage base is boosted, only higher earners and their employers are affected. If the tax rate is hiked, all workers—low as well as high income—are hit.

(2) General federal revenues can be drawn upon. Or provision can be made for other new sources of revenue—for instance, an earmarked tax on cigarettes or liquor, a value-added tax, or a surcharge on the income tax.

(3) Adding more workers to the SS rolls so more will be paying SS taxes is another way to increase revenues. However, nine out of every ten jobs already are covered by Social Security.

(4) As a last resort, benefits could be reduced, although no one ever has suggested reductions for those already on the benefit rolls. But there have been proposals for cutting back on some so-called fringe benefits and for lowering the "replacement rate" for workers retiring in the future. The "replacement rate" is

the ratio of Social Security benefits to earnings just before retirement of the individual.

(5) And of course, there could be many combinations of all these elements.

SOCIAL SECURITY AMENDMENTS HAVE PUT PROGRAM ON SOUND FOOTING

Each of these options has its advantages and disadvantages, of course. Congress, in December of 1977, corrected the fluke in the benefit formula that had contributed in part to the long-range financing problem. In addition, it provided for the infusion of funds to meet the short-range deficit—financing that will be enough to pay all benefits as they fall due over the next fifty years at least.

The size of the payroll tax scheduled in the law has been spectacularly increased; further increases well may cause a nationwide rebellion—and are definitely "iffy," as a result.

In addition, the maximum amount of earnings to which the tax applies is now geared to go up much more than in previous law. This so-called "wage base" is scheduled to rise under the 1977 amendments to such a degree that it, too, may undergo major revision. These tax and wage base increases will have their strongest impact on employees at the middle-upper-income levels, increasing their Social Security tax contributions substantially. Employers who will be matching the employees' contributions are also affected. Public reaction to reports of these increases in the tax rates and wage base has been, I repeat, predictably strong. Overlooked has been the fact that those who would be paying more would be getting more.

BENEFITS WILL BE KEPT UP-TO-DATE WITH PRICES AND LEVEL OF LIVING

In the past, Social Security benefits had been based on a worker's average earnings over his working lifetime, counting in the years at the beginning of his career when his earnings were low and also disregarding any earnings in excess of the wage base that he might have had in any particular year.

But if you are working under Social Security today, you are not paying toward benefits of the level being paid today. Your benefits will be based on your lifetime wage *updated* to reflect the level of living at the time you retire, become disabled, or die. If, for example, you are in your forties and earning an average wage of around $10,000 a year, you will qualify for a Social Security benefit of around $15,000 when you retire at age sixty-five. Your wife (or husband) will get an additional $7,500 based on your record of earnings.

Workers who pay Social Security taxes on the maximum amount of earnings that counts toward Social Security can look forward to benefits of about $21,000 a year—over $30,000 for a couple. This compares to the $6,036 payable to a worker attaining age sixty-five in 1979 after earning the maximum, or the $6,624 maximum payable to a worker reaching age sixty-five and retiring in 1980. People under forty will get even higher benefits. Once on the benefit rolls, your benefits will be kept up-to-date with the cost of living.

You therefore can be sure that your Social Security retirement protection and also your disability and survivors' protection will rise as the cost of living and the standard of living go up.

The chart below shows the benefits payable upon retirement at age sixty-five to workers of low, average, and maximum earnings under Social Security. The benefits payable to workers who become disabled and to the dependents and survivors of workers are similarly improved.

If you are over fifty-six years of age, you can ask the Social Security Administration to check your Social Security record and give you an estimate of what your monthly benefits would be at age sixty-two and at age sixty-five. Just ask your nearest Social Security office for a copy of a preaddressed postcard—No. 7004. When you get it, fill it in and add the words "Benefit Estimate" at the top. Put a stamp on it and mail it. You will receive the estimates directly from Social Security Administration headquarters in about six weeks.

Social Security is much more than a retirement program.

It provides benefits for your dependents while you are on the benefit rolls as a retired or disabled worker, and if you die, it pays benefits to your survivors to help replace your earnings.

It also helps with hospital and medical expenses when you reach sixty-five or are disabled.

Most Americans, including young workers, just starting out, can expect to collect more in Social Security benefits than they paid in taxes.

Projected Benefits for Persons Retiring at Age 65

CALENDAR YEAR OF RETIREMENT	EARNINGS IN PREVIOUS YEAR*			ANNUAL BENEFIT AMOUNT FOR WORKERS WITH FOLLOWING EARNINGS		
	LOW	AVERAGE	MAXIMUM	LOW	AVERAGE	MAXIMUM
1979	$ 5,271	$10,572	$17,700	$3,142	$ 4,932	$ 6,165
1980	5,682	11,396	22,900	3,375	5,315	6,699
1981	6,085	12,205	25,900	3,635	5,740	7,257
1982	6,475	12,986	29,700	3,485	5,438	6,809
1983	6,863	13,766	31,800	3,607	5,643	7,257
1984	7,258	14,557	33,900	3,841	6,010	7,798
1985	7,675	15,394	36,000	4,099	6,409	8,390
1990	10,150	20,359	47,700	5,451	8,519	11,509
1995	13,424	26,925	63,000	7,198	11,243	15,605
2000	17,753	35,609	83,400	9,519	14,870	21,427

*Low earnings are defined as $4,600 in 1976. Average earnings are $9,266 in 1976. Maximum earnings are defined as the top wages subject to Social Security taxes in a particular year. In each case it is assumed that the worker has had an unbroken pattern of earnings at the relative level indicated. The following increases in wages were assumed: 1977, 5.99 per cent; 1978, 8.10 per cent; 1979, 7.80 per cent; 1980, 7.10 per cent; 1981, 6.40 per cent; 1982, 6.00 per cent; 1983 and later, 5.75 per cent.

HOW MUCH YOU WILL GET AS A RETIREE OR DEPENDENT

• If you retire at sixty-two, your benefit amount will be reduced by 20 per cent to take account of the extra three years during which you will be receiving payments. The closer you are to sixty-five when you take your benefits, the smaller the reduction. At age sixty-three, for example, you could collect 86⅔ of your full benefit, and at age sixty-four, 93⅓ per cent. On the other hand, if you defer your retirement until after age sixty-five, you get an increase in your benefit amount—3 per cent for each year between sixty-five and seventy-two. So, if you work on until age seventy, you will get a benefit at least 15 per cent higher than if you had retired at age sixty-five.

• When you become entitled to Social Security benefits, your wife can collect benefits equal to 50 per cent of yours if she is sixty-five, or somewhat lower benefits as early as age sixty-two. (If the wife, because of her own earnings, is entitled to an amount more than 50 per cent of her husband's benefit, she gets the bigger benefit.)

• Your wife also can collect that extra 50 per cent if she is younger, if she has in her care dependent children under eighteen (or over eighteen, but disabled before age twenty-two).

Each unmarried child under eighteen (or over eighteen, but disabled) or a full-time student eighteen to twenty-two also is eligible for a benefit equal to 50 per cent of your full benefit. The maximum amount of benefits payable to a family is limited, however. In 1979, the maximum payable to the family of a man retiring at sixty-five was $880.70.

• As of the late 1970s, a special minimum payment for certain low earnings retirees who had thirty years or more of Social Security coverage was $230 a month; with twenty-five years of coverage, the special minimum was $172.50 a month. It will rise as cost of living rises after 1979.

The 1977 amendments made several other improvements in Social Security of which you should be aware.

(1) A raise in benefits, effective 1979, for 130,000 remarried widows. The result: a mounting number of marriages between elderly couples who have been living as "mingling singles" because marriage would cut their combined SS benefits.

Widows on the SS benefit rolls who remarried after age sixty had their monthly payments increased to the rate that would have been payable to them if they had not remarried. A widow sixty or over gets SS benefits equal to 71.5 per cent to 100 per cent of her deceased husband's SS benefit amount. The closer she was to sixty-five at the time she first took her benefits, the higher the percentage. But a wife gets benefits equal to one half her husband's Social Security benefit amount if she is sixty-five or older and a reduced amount if she is sixty-two to sixty-five at the time.

Under the old law, when a woman who had been receiving benefits as a widow remarried, she became a wife and therefore eligible for the smaller percentage although she had perhaps been receiving 100 per cent of her deceased husband's benefit as a widow beneficiary.

About 130,000 remarried widows on the Social Security benefit rolls in 1977 were known to have had their benefits reduced upon their remarriage. Other elderly widows, it also was known, had decided to forgo a marriage ceremony to avoid a cut in their SS benefits.

For the first group—the remarried widows—benefits were hiked starting January 1979 to the rate that would have been payable if they had not remarried. For widows sixty or over who remarried in 1979 or later, there will be no slash in benefits.

(2) If you're a remarried widower, you also became eligible for the restoration of your benefit rates in January 1979. But since most of you get benefits based on your own higher earnings records, remarriage has been less likely to force a cut in your payments.

(3) Another change in the law makes it possible for women, divorced after at least 10 years of marriage, to qualify for benefits at retirement age—either as divorced wives, or if their former husband has died, as surviving divorced wives. Until 1979 if you were a woman divorced before your marriage had lasted a full twenty years, you lost all rights to benefits based on your former husband's SS earnings record.

If you are an eligible divorced wife, you can begin collecting benefits when you are sixty-two. If you are an eligible surviving divorced wife, you can collect your benefits as early as age sixty.

If you are any divorced woman and you think you may be eligible for benefits under this provision, immediately contact your local Social Security office, so that you will not lose any of the benefits that are payable to you.

(4) Still another significant 1977 benefit improvement that is likely to be overlooked provides you with an added incentive to continue working past sixty-five. That was Congress' stated purpose.

Beginning in 1972, workers who delayed their retirement past age sixty-five earned a delayed retirement credit of 1 per cent per year (1/12 of 1 per cent per month). That credit was upped to 3 per cent a year for workers who reached sixty-five in January 1979 or later. The credits build up at the rate of ¼ of 1 per cent for each month that a worker between sixty-five and seventy-two does not collect Social Security benefits because he or she is still working.

The 1977 amendments also will give you, the surviving widow or widower, the benefit of any delayed retirement credits the worker has earned. Under previous law, the delayed retirement credits served to increase only the worker's own retirement benefit.

As Robert M. Ball, former commissioner of Social Security, noted: "The changes fit in with the need in the next century to have more people work past sixty-five and the need to have Social Security financing benefit from this additional employment of older people."

OTHER SOCIAL SECURITY BENEFITS

In addition to retirement benefits, monthly allowances will go to your survivors in the event of your death. You and certain members of your family also can collect important benefits if you become disabled. Or, if your income is very limited, you may qualify for benefits under the supplemental security income program. To illustrate the survivors' benefits:

• A widow who was first entitled to benefits at age sixty-five can receive a pension equal to the one her deceased husband would be collecting if he were still alive. If a widow begins drawing benefits exactly at age sixty, her allowance will be 71.5 per cent. If she is between sixty and sixty-five, her benefits will be between 71.5 per cent and 100 per cent depending upon how close she is to sixty-five. Widows may not start collecting benefits until they are sixty—unless they are disabled and aged fifty to fifty-nine, or have dependent children.

• A widow or widower under sixty-five caring for a young or disabled child can receive 75 per cent of the deceased spouse's primary benefit amount. Each dependent child, if unmarried, under eighteen (or eighteen to twenty-two if they are full-time students), or disabled before age twenty-two, also may receive 75 per cent of the deceased husband's full benefit, up to the current family maximum allowance.

• Benefits also may be paid to a surviving dependent parent or to a husband aged sixty-two or over or a widower aged sixty or over, or a disabled dependent widow or widower aged fifty or over.

• If you yourself are disabled—that is, suffering from a condition, physical or mental, which is serious enough to prevent you from working for twelve months or more—you can collect a disability benefit while you are under age sixty-five. Your wife and each of your young, dependent, unmarried children also could collect amounts equal to 50 per cent of your benefit, subject to a family maximum.

• Rehabilitation costs and services are available to disabled workers in the form of paid job training, counseling and placement, physical therapy, and money to buy work tools and equipment.

• If you are blind as defined by the law, you can qualify for disability benefits without having to meet the requirement of substantial recent work. Under Social Security regulations, a worker considered "industrially blind"—that is, with the visual acuity of 20-200 or less in the better eye, with corrective lens—is considered totally blind. So is a person whose visual field is limited to 20°.

SUPPLEMENTAL SECURITY INCOME

The federal supplemental security income program (SSI) is designed for aged, blind, and disabled persons with very limited income and resources. It replaces the state-federal programs of Old Age Assistance, Aid to the Blind, and Aid to the Permanently and Totally Disabled. SSI is administered by the Social Security Administration but is financed from general revenues rather than from Social Security trust funds.

The program guarantees a standard, nationwide monthly income floor for eligible individuals. If your present income is below the levels set by the program and you are otherwise eligible you will get a monthly benefit raise to bring your total benefit up to at least these minimums. In some cases, this SSI payment is augmented by an extra state supplement. This extra sum is either paid separately by the state or included in the federal supplement check.

To qualify for SSI benefits, individual beneficiaries may have cash assets of up to $1,500 and, for couples, up to $2,250. You may own your home, household goods and other personal effects, and an automobile—so long as these are only of "reasonable value"—and still qualify. Your relatives' income and assets do *not* count as yours; your eligibility for SSI benefits is determined without regard for their assets. If, however, you are married to an ineligible spouse, his or her possessions *do* count as yours. If you think you—or a relative or friend—may be eligible, contact your nearest Social Security office.

WHO IS ELIGIBLE FOR SOCIAL SECURITY?

You qualify if you work or have worked a required length of time at any job which is covered by the Social Security law—and that now includes most jobs. You also may qualify if you're self-employed. Railroad workers are, in effect, jointly covered by Social Security and their own separate retirement system. Most federal civilian employees, those who are covered by the civil service retirement program or other staff retirement systems, are not covered by Social Security, although there is mounting discussion of merging their separate retirement systems with SS. Other occupations (such as farm labor, domestic employment, and state and local government employment) and some types of earnings (such as tips and wages in kind) may be affected by special provisions of the law.

If you're not sure you qualify, inquire at your local Social Security office.

YOUR WORK CREDITS

To qualify for benefits, you also must build up a certain number of work credits. You get credit for a "quarter of coverage"—for each $260 in 1979 in covered annual earnings—up to a total of four quarters in a year.

If you're self-employed, you need net earnings from self-employment of at least $400 in a year before you can get credit for any quarters. Military service during the World War II and postwar periods may give you additional wage credits for each month of active duty.

Note: If you served in the armed forces during 1957–67 or are a survivor of someone who did, and are now getting monthly Social Security benefit checks, contact your Social Security office. You may, under amendments passed in recent years, be eligible for a higher monthly benefit.

In order for your widow and children to be eligible for survivor benefits, you must have at least one and a half years of work credits within three years before your death, unless you already have worked long enough to be fully insured

To be fully insured so that you and your family are entitled to retirement and all other benefits, you must, depending on your age, have anywhere from six to forty quarters or from one and a half to ten years of work credits, as indicated in the following tables:

FOR WORKERS BORN BEFORE 1929

If you were born before 1929, reach sixty-two, become disabled, or die in	You will need credit for this much work to be fully insured
1979	7
1981	7½
1983	8
1987	9
1991 or later	10

Workers born in 1929 or after will need forty quarters of coverage or ten full years of work in order to be fully insured for retirement benefits. The following chart shows how many years of credit they would need to be fully insured for the payment of all survivors' benefits.

FOR WORKERS BORN AFTER 1928

If you die when you are	You will be fully insured with credit for this much work
28 or younger	1½ years
30	2
32	2½
34	3
36	3½
38	4
40	4½
42	5
46	6
50	7
54	8
58	9
62 or older	10

Note: A person is fully insured if he has credit for a quarter year of work for each year after 1950 or after the year in which he reached age twenty-one and up to the year he reaches sixty-two, becomes disabled, or dies—whichever event occurs earlier.

To be eligible for disability benefits when you are thirty-one or older, you must be fully insured and must have credit for five years of work in the ten-year period ending with the time you become disabled. If you become disabled between the ages of twenty-four and thirty-one, you need credit for only one half the time between age twenty-one and the time you become unable to work. If disability starts before age twenty-four, you need credit for one and a half years of work in the three-year period before you become disabled.

You should know, too, that you do not automatically receive Social Security benefits as soon as you retire, become disabled, or a working member of your family dies or becomes disabled.

You must apply for these benefits at the nearest Social Security office.

IF YOU WORK IN RETIREMENT

Should there be any limit on how much you, an older person, can earn and still collect your Social Security benefits?

If so, how can a limit be set that will not penalize you if you work—and still be fair to other Social Security beneficiaries and to those of us who are working and paying Social Security taxes to finance the entire system?

These questions have been furiously debated since SS benefits first became payable. Back in 1940, under the so-called Retirement Test then in effect, an older person lost his entire SS benefit for any month in which his wages in work covered by SS amounted to one cent more than $14.99!

The law has been changed many times since, but the Retirement Test still remains—infuriating in its discriminations, inequities, and inconsistencies, unduly complicated by past attempts to improve and liberalize its provisions.

Why is there a Retirement Test?

Because, its defendants claim, the basic purpose of SS retirement benefits is not to pay benefits because you reach a specified age, but rather to replace the earnings you lose when old age cuts off or drastically reduces your earning power. The test was devised to measure whether that loss of earnings has occurred.

You do not have to stop work altogether to collect your benefits. If your earnings after you become eligible for benefits do not go over the "exempt amount" for the year, you get your full benefits for all twelve months.

The "exempt amount" rises each year as average earnings levels under SS go up.

The exempt amount for persons sixty-five or older was $4,500 as the 1970s closed and will rise by $500 steps each year until it reaches $6,000 in 1982 and will rise as the cost of living goes up after that. For retired workers who have taken their benefits before age sixty-five and for the dependents and survivors of workers who are under sixty-five, the exempt amount was set at $3,240 in the late 1970s and will rise over the years in tandem with the automatic cost-of-living adjustments in benefits.

Once you reach seventy-two, you get all your benefits no matter how much you earn. Without this provision (added to the law in the 1950s), those who work for good pay past age sixty-five might never receive any benefits despite their years of SS tax contributions. Beginning in 1982, you will be able to collect all your benefits as early as age seventy, no matter how much you earn.

If as an SS beneficiary under age seventy-two (or under seventy, beginning in 1982), you earn more than the exempt amount, you will lose $1.00 of benefits for every $2.00 by which your earnings for the year exceed the exempt amount.

THE "EDDIE CANTOR" RULE

When Eddie Cantor was invited to the TV spectacular celebrating his sixty-fifth birthday in January 1957, he never dreamed that he would be giving his name to a giant exception to the general rule that you forfeit benefits if your annual earnings exceed a specified total!

For this provision said that no matter how much you earn in a year, you would get your benefit check for any month in which you had wages that amount to no more than 1/12 of the exempt amount and you do not perform substantial services in self-employment.

Eddie Cantor received $2,000 for his appearance on the network broadcast in 1957, well over the exempt amount, which was $1,200 in that year. But since he did not plan to do any other work in 1957, he was eligible to collect his benefits for the remaining months of that year.

Approached by an enterprising U. S. Government public-information specialist, Cantor agreed to help publicize the then all but unknown exception—and also to remind Americans that Social Security benefits are an earned right, not welfare. He turned over his benefits to a favorite charity, a boys' camp at Surprise Lake, New York.

Millions of Americans became aware of the "Eddie Cantor" clause as a result of that 1957 publicity and a select group in each successive generation of retirees has taken advantage of it. But Congress did not design this exception to provide a bonanza for highly paid consultants, real estate salesmen, resort concession operators, technicians, and other specialists who upon reaching sixty-five can concentrate their work and earnings in one or two months and collect benefits for the balance of the year.

The exception was intended primarily for people who might retire in midyear or later, after earning substantial amounts, and would otherwise be unable to collect any SS benefits until the following year, even though they were completely retired. It also took note of the retiree who might be able to get an occasional job at good pay. For many years, an elite group of SS beneficiaries had been able to collect more benefits than contemporaries with the same or less earnings who were working year round.

No more!

Along with the drastic financing and other SS changes Congress enacted in 1977, it slapped a limit on the use of the Eddie Cantor clause. Now, you, an SS beneficiary, get the advantage of the exception only in your "initial year of retirement."

If you retire in the middle of the year, for example, and do not earn more than 1/12 the exempt amount during the remaining months of the year (and also do not perform substantial services in self-employment), you will be eligible for benefits for those months. It will not matter whether your earnings in the prior months of the year were way above the exempt amount.

But the next year will be a different story. You will have had your "initial year of retirement." If you have even one month in which you do not work after qualifying for retirement benefits, then you are considered to have had your "initial year of retirement."

Be careful, therefore, about setting your retirement date! Don't apply for benefits as soon as you are sixty-five if you plan to go on working. Try to plan for retirement early in the year. Also, you may want to wait to apply for your Medicare hospitalization insurance until you need it. An application for those hospital benefits, Part A of Medicare, is considered an application for retirement benefits and could kick off your initial year of retirement.

You can, though, apply for your medical insurance benefits under Part B of Medicare and start paying the premiums. That application will not start you on your initial year of retirement.

SOCIAL SECURITY AND WOMEN'S RIGHTS

In a unanimous decision in the mid-1970s, the Supreme Court declared a section of the Social Security law unconstitutional on the grounds that it discriminated against women workers—a ruling which primarily benefited men—and among men, mainly widowed fathers of young children.

The Court's decision represented a long overdue correction of an archaic assumption that "male workers' earnings are vital to the support of their families, while the earnings of female wage earners do not significantly contribute to their families' support." The "logical" extension of that now absurd assumption was that the surviving spouses of women workers who had paid their Social Security taxes were not entitled to the same protection as the surviving spouses of men workers who had paid their taxes.

With the rejection of that insulting premise—allowing widowers with young children to get the protection that widows with minor children have been getting—other Social Security provisions based on the same obsolete assumptions at last may also be on the way to oblivion.

Over the past forty years in which our Social Security system has been repeatedly modernized into a patchwork of amendments to the original law and court decisions, not one amendment has focused on the fundamental shifts that have occurred in U.S. family relationships and life-styles.

There has been no real challenge to the stereotypes which the framers of Social Security built into the law because those were the stereotypes in which they believed. There was the male family head—the breadwinner—and there was the housewife and, as a song of the period relates, "a boy for you, a girl for me." But even well before the law was enacted, these stereotypes were far from matching reality.

Women—and children—were employed in some of our earliest factories. The daughters of the poor were working in the mills of New England in the 1800s. Working wives and daughters were commonplace among immigrants to America. Women, black and white, labored on farms and plantations. In her book, *Enterprising Women,* Caroline Bird documents the enormous extent to which the wives of our Founding Fathers took over the running of their husbands' businesses and enhanced the family fortunes, while other women created products, provided services, filled a wide range of jobs outside the home to support themselves and educate their children.

Of course, giving the dependents of women workers the full rights enjoyed by the dependents of male workers is desirable and long, long overdue. But much more fundamental is the need to recognize that you—the American woman of the 1980s—do not fit neatly into either the category of lifelong housewife or life-long earner.

An overwhelming 90 per cent of all women work outside the home for pay during at least some part of their lives. More than 45 per cent—almost half—of our paid work force today consist of women. A full 60 per cent of all women working for pay are married and are half of a working couple.

Since the 1940 census (following the enactment of Social Security legislation), the proportion of women in every age group in the work force has soared. Among women thirty-five to forty-four, it has doubled; among middle-aged women forty-five to sixty-four, it has jumped two and a half times; among women over sixty-five, the number working for pay has more than quadrupled.

The trend born in the 1930s became increasingly powerful after World War II, when women, who had been actively recruited to replace men called up for serv-ice and to meet defense industry requirements, wanted to continue working.

Other forces since then have added strength to the development, called "the single most outstanding phenomenon of our century" by labor market expert and Columbia University professor Eli Ginsberg. Among them: college attendance and women's desire for careers; the move toward later marriages; the steady de-cline in the birthrate since 1957; growing acceptance of childless marriages; rising divorce rates; greater longevity; the family's need or desire for two incomes, not just among the poor, but among families wanting to send their children to college or to maintain what has become known as a "middle class" life-style.

Yet, despite all the lip service paid to equality for women in the work force, disproportionate numbers are still in low-paying jobs. Nearly two thirds of full-time, year-round women workers in the earlier years of the 1970s earned less than $7,000 a year, while more than three quarters of full-time, year-round male workers earned more than $7,000. And male workers generally do not have their working careers—and their Social Security records—interrupted because of fam-ily responsibilities (having children).

A woman will work after she leaves school and until she drops out of the labor force to have children. She may return to work when the children are of school age, or earlier—or later. Or she may become divorced. (One of every three mar-riages now ends in divorce, and in 1975 the annual number of divorces in the United States passed the million mark.)

A housewife's services for her family (maid, cook, laundress, child rearer, etc.) are not considered "work" for Social Security purposes. An estimate, so conser-vative it was ridiculous, placed a value on her services at $19,000 a year in the late 1970s, however.

A woman's absences from the paid labor force mean that there will be blanks in her Social Security record. The effect is to reduce the average earnings that will be the basis for figuring any retired-worker benefits due her in the future.

Women will continue to receive lower Social Security retirement benefits than men, says a recent Social Security report. "Only if some proposal to 'fill in' the gaps in women's earnings records is adopted will this situation change."

Nor will any substantial percentage of women have much in the way of private pensions to supplement their Social Security benefits. They are less likely to be in jobs covered by private pensions. And if they are in these jobs, if they do work for a company with a pension plan, the irregularity of their employment or the fact that they work part time may mean they will never qualify.

The Social Security program cannot be held responsible for the traditionally low wages paid to women, nor for the irregularity of their employment because of their responsibilities as homemakers and mothers. That would stretch "guilt" beyond all logic.

But the system can be restructured to take those factors into account and to make it less blatantly unfair to women.

A new concept that points the way for the restructuring has been proposed that would assume work in the home has an economic value and also that marriage is an economic partnership.

Couples could elect to have a share of the family income credited to each of their Social Security records, just as they now have the option of filing a joint income tax return.

You, a lifelong housewife, would therefore be able to build up your own Social Security record while you, the woman in and out of the paid labor force, would have a steady record of earnings, instead of earnings "gaps." And you, a divorced woman, would have a record of earnings to take with you from a marriage that had not lasted for at least ten years.

Not only do women workers feel the inequities in our Social Security system's treatment of them but the husbands and widowers of women workers also often suffer from the fallout of these provisions.

SOCIAL SECURITY'S INEQUITIES AFFECT US ALL

Item: Millions of women who have worked long enough to qualify for benefits as retired workers have been found to be entitled to higher benefits as dependents —although a wife's benefit at age sixty-five is only one half the amount of the retired husband's benefit (less if the wife is between sixty-two and sixty-five at the time her husband retires). This is because a woman worker gets her own Social Security benefit, but if it is less than the amount that would be payable to her as a dependent wife, the difference is added to her benefit total.

In effect, she gets the higher of the two benefits—but no more than she would have received if she had never worked outside the home and had never paid a cent in Social Security taxes!

The injustice of this is so apparent on the surface that I would insult you if I indulged in further indignant explanation. Suffice it to say that this happens in so many cases because of (1) the low wages paid to women generally and (2) the irregularity of women's employment (it is commonplace for a woman to drop out of the labor force to have children, and not return for a period—the absences which leaves blanks in her Social Security record).

Item: A married couple with both partners working can end up with smaller retirement benefits than a couple with the same total earnings, but where the husband was the only worker. And if one of the working couple dies, the widowed husband or wife will get much lower benefits than the surviving partner in the case of the couple in which only one was a worker for pay.

Difficult as you may find that one to believe, the Social Security Administration's files are choked with cases documenting the unfair fallout of the discrimination against women workers.

Item: A woman who is widowed before age sixty receives mother's benefits if she has in her care children under eighteen or an older, disabled child. If there is no severely disabled child, her benefits will stop when the youngest child reaches eighteen—unless she is already age sixty by that time or is age fifty or over and very severely disabled.

With what seems to me almost incomprehensible lack of realism, the law assumes that a reasonably able-bodied, middle-aged woman with no work experience can just move right out into the vast, indifferent labor market and quickly find a job that will enable her to earn enough to support herself.

These are merely a sampling of actual situations which should shock you into full realization of the inequities in the treatment of women under Social Security. And they are not limited to any one group.

In one way or another, they affect us all—homemakers, divorcées, elderly wives and widows, high-earning professionals, low-paid domestics, the wives of laborers, and the wives of executives.

BASIC REFORMS

Congress ordered that a task force study the situation of women under Social Security. The group recommended some basic reforms. It suggested, for instance, that a way be devised for considering a couple's income jointly for Social Security purposes, just as the couple does in filing a joint tax return. Just about every woman would eventually wind up with a Social Security earnings record of her own on which to collect Social Security benefits, and so would every man. Under the proposal:

• Married persons who elected to file joint income tax returns would each year be given Social Security credit for 50 per cent of the couple's combined earnings in work covered by Social Security.

• The W-2 forms that couples attach to joint returns and the returns themselves would give all the information needed to apportion the earnings to their individual Social Security records.

• They would pay no additional Social Security taxes on these earnings.

• Homemakers would be given their own Social Security records and would be brought into the system in their own right—instead of being able to collect benefits only as dependents of their employed husbands. A divorced homemaker would have an SS record to take with her into her new life instead of losing her rights to wife's or widow's benefits as she does now if she had not been married ten years at the time of the divorce.

• Men would receive advantages, too, because with SS records of their own, couples would both build eligibility for disability benefits.

• There could be a transition period to guard against unanticipated adverse effects, special provisions for women widowed under age sixty, other clauses to protect a newly widowed middle-age homemaker who has few marketable skills and who could not be expected to enter the labor market immediately.

There are many other details in this proposal and the proposals might not provide complete equity for women who never marry. But it is at least a basic springboard Congress can use to explore the concept's feasibility and merits.

And through public debate, this idea can be developed and improved. Surely the time has come for equality for women under Social Security. And surely the obsolete stereotypes of the American women built into the system cannot be condoned much longer.

THE BAFFLEGAB OF SOCIAL SECURITY

DISABILITY INSURANCE BENEFIT   Monthly benefit payable to a worker and his family if he has a severe physical or mental condition which prevents him from working and the condition is expected to last for at least twelve months. He also must have a certain required number of work credits.

LUMP-SUM DEATH BENEFIT   A one-time benefit paid at the death of a worker covered under Social Security.

QUARTER OF COVERAGE   See Work Credits.

RETIREMENT BENEFITS   Monthly benefits payable to a man or woman at age sixty-two (reduced benefits) or age sixty-five (full benefits) who has stopped working or is substantially retired as measured by the Social Security Retirement Test.

RETIREMENT TEST   Known also as the "annual earnings test" under the Social Security Act. This test is used to determine how much of a beneficiary's annual Social Security benefit will be paid. A beneficiary can earn up to the exempt amount in a calendar year and collect all of his Social Security benefits for that year.

SOCIAL SECURITY CONTRIBUTIONS (TAXES)   Percentage of your earnings paid into the Social Security trust funds—matched by your employer.

SOCIAL SECURITY TRUST FUNDS   The three funds into which Social Security contributions are paid: Old Age and Survivors Insurance Trust Fund, Disability Insurance Trust Fund, and Hospital Insurance Trust Fund. Social Security benefit costs are met out of these funds on a pay-as-you-go basis. The amounts kept in each fund are adjusted periodically by a special board of trustees.

SURVIVORS INSURANCE BENEFITS   Monthly benefits are paid to your survivors in the event of your death if you have had the required number of work credits. There also is a one-time lump-sum death benefit.

WAGE BASE   Amount of a worker's annual earnings which is taxed for Social Security.

WORK CREDITS   Also known as "quarters of coverage." To get monthly Social Security benefits a person must have worked under Social Security for a certain period of time. An employee earns credit for one-quarter year of work if he is paid a certain amount—$260 in 1979 and rising in the future as average wages rise. A self-employed person earns four quarters of coverage for any full year in which he earns at least $400 in self-employment income.

WHAT YOU SHOULD KNOW ABOUT LIFE INSURANCE

DO YOU NEED LIFE INSURANCE?

Make no mistake about it: the main purpose of life insurance—*and nothing does it better*—is to create an "instant estate" for your family in the event of your death.

It's not difficult to argue that you don't need any life insurance if:

You have no children or other dependent relatives.

Your wife is working—or is perfectly capable of returning to work tomorrow, as she did before you were married.

You are collecting substantial monthly Social Security benefits and believe that the benefits that will be paid to your widow are adequate. (A man age forty without dependent children may be in the maximum Social Security bracket as far as income is concerned, but if he were to die that year his widow would not be eligible for any benefits until she reached the age of sixty-two.)

Your company promises to provide you with a good-sized pension when you retire, with adequate benefits for your survivor when you die.

You have fairly comfortable savings or other assets.

If you are such a person, you represent a distinct minority. And the fact remains that nine out of ten U.S. families and seven out of ten individuals in this country—both young and old—have life insurance today. The average insured American family in the mid-1970s had policies of one type or another giving the family at least $37,900 of protection—or the equivalent of two years of take-home pay.

With what else but life insurance could you—on a relatively modest salary and little chance to save—provide the sizable estate that would enable your survivors to maintain some semblance of their accustomed standard of living, perhaps even assure your children of college educations?

Or, after the children are grown, give your wife a lifetime income and help her pay off the mortgage on the family home?

Consider, too, these key advantages life insurance offers the survivors of the average policyholder:

• Unlike the returns from many other assets, death payments from life insurance, under almost all circumstances, are not subject to federal income taxes to the beneficiary.

• If you die, the processing of your estate may take months, even years before the proceeds can be distributed. The value of your life insurance, though, becomes available immediately to your beneficiaries upon your death.

• It does not cost you a cent, as it may in the case of a will, to change the beneficiary of your life insurance or to revise the terms under which the proceeds will be paid.

Life insurance has certain other attractive features—what insurance men call "living values"—although they should be regarded as secondary to the primary purpose of protection.

• One value, though not inherent in all types of insurance, is savings. There are more rewarding ways to save than via life insurance. But many families find that the only way they can be disciplined into saving any money at all is through regular forced payments of life insurance premiums.

• Increases in the cash value of your policy contributed from the insurance company's earnings are tax-free—so long as you keep your policy in force.

• No matter how bad your credit rating, you are guaranteed the right to use the cash value of your policy as collateral for a loan from your insurance company and you may repay at your convenience, whenever you wish. However, if you are purchasing a new policy which provides cash values *first,* investigate with care the loan interest provisions. Some companies are now building into policies an 8 per cent or higher loan interest charge. Others continue to issue policies with much lower interest charges. This may mean a great deal to you in the future if you need to borrow on your insurance.

• If you get in trouble with your creditors, they'll have a lot harder time laying hands on the cash value of your life insurance than, say, the money you have in securities or bank accounts. This is simply because creditors' rights under the law are considerably weaker vis-à-vis life insurance than toward most other types of investments.

• As an investment, life insurance has obvious drawbacks—but it does promise to yield a stated total of dollars, whereas stock investments involve fluctuating totals of dollars.

• And certain types of life insurance will pay you a guaranteed specified lump sum or a specified income for life when you are ready to retire.

You cannot, in sum, reasonably argue that there are *no* good reasons why you should buy and hold life insurance. Much more to the point is how you, as a young family, should shop for life insurance—or how you can make sure your existing coverage is all you think it is.

HOW TO FIGURE YOUR LIFE INSURANCE NEEDS

To reach a proper decision on just how much coverage you need for your wife and children, answer these key questions:

(1) How much income would your family need for living expenses if you were to die tomorrow?

Many experts say that a young family with children would need 60 to 75 per cent of its present after-tax income. If you have no children or your children are grown, your wife might be able to get by on as little as 40 per cent of what you earned.

Another pertinent question here: if the wife of the family breadwinner died, how much would it cost to hire others to perform her duties?

(2) What resources are there to produce this income?

Add up your total assets, including equity in your home or business, savings accounts, stocks, bonds, property, etc., and estimate how much income all this could produce.

(3) What would your family receive from Social Security?

To find out just what your family would receive on the basis of your earnings, fill out and mail the card available at Social Security offices to get a record of your income credits together with instructions on how to estimate your expected future annual benefits.

(4) How much pension income—including veteran's pension—can you expect when you retire, and would any of this income be available to your spouse if you were to die?

(5) Do you have a group life insurance policy?

If so, what amount of benefits will it produce? Will it continue past retirement from your job, and could you afford to convert it into an individual policy if you left your present employer?

(6) Will your wife have any income of her own?

Does she now work or could she get a job and at what salary? A wife who has not held a job for several years might have to invest a period of time in training before she could qualify for a well-paying job. While working she might have to deduct considerable amounts for child care expenses, commuting costs, restaurant lunches, etc.

(7) Is there a mortgage on your home?

If your family sold the home, the proceeds could be used for their other needs. Otherwise, your insurance should also provide enough to cover the mortgage in the event of your death.

(8) How much will your children need for their college education?

With college costs going up year after year to eye-popping levels, enough money must be set aside or otherwise made available to cover this expense. (See pages 525–53.)

(9) Do you have any large debts outstanding?

Include in your calculations any money you may owe on auto or personal loans, installment payments, etc. These, too, would have to be paid off after your death.

(10) What cash would be needed immediately?

Your family may need money for "final expenses"—medical bills, funeral costs, minor debts.

Now add up everything your family will need for living expenses, your mortgage, college costs, debt clearance, other expenses. From this total, subtract the money that will be coming in from Social Security and other pensions, salaries, savings, investments and other assets, as well as any outstanding life insurance. The difference is the amount of insurance needed to enable your survivors to reach that income level of 60 to 75 per cent after tax, or to provide adequately for their needs.

Family needs differ depending on age and number of children. A reputable life insurance agent also may be able to offer you helpful advice on the amount—and types—of life insurance you need. But one industry rule of thumb is that a family needs at least enough life insurance to cover four or five times its yearly income. More specifically, a family with an annual income of $20,000 needs a total of $80,000 to $100,000 of life insurance.

HOW MUCH LIFE INSURANCE CAN YOU AFFORD?

How much life insurance can you afford?

Even though you find a fairly satisfactory answer to the nagging question "How much life insurance do you need?", there are no hard answers to help you answer this second question, any more than there were any "tight" rules of thumb to lead you directly to the answers to the first.

You must start by asking and honestly analyzing what are your family's values in terms of financial security—as well as knowing what budget your family has.

If, for instance, your family is thinking of its future, it will try to co-operate to find the means to afford the protection you all want more than another family that thinks in terms only of its immediate or short-term needs.

After analyzing your family income and how you spend it, you will be on your way to determining what you can budget for life insurance. And always keep in mind: there are no rules of thumb and any salesperson who tells you otherwise is to be avoided.

If your family maintains a visibly high standard of living, you may find allocating 1 per cent of your gross earnings to insurance a financial hardship (if you won't give up anything).

If your family has a more sober life-style, you may find allocating 5 per cent or more a reasonable share, even if the life insurance protection does mean additional sacrifice.

It comes down to your values.

No honest reporter can give you guidelines or recommendations that can be an adequate substitute for your own and your own family's thinking about your protection now and in the future.

Only in the privacy of your own home and without outside pressures can you determine what your needs for life insurance are and how much your family is willing to spend to cover those needs.

WHAT KIND OF LIFE INSURANCE FOR YOU?

With hundreds of different life insurance policy types, combinations, and options available today, deciding just what kind of insurance may be best for you can be a confusing experience. Some policies are designed purely for protection; others stress savings; still others, retirement benefits; and many give you a combination of these features.

It will help if you think of life insurance as falling into one of five basic categories:

(1) *Term insurance.* This is the simplest, least costly type of coverage. As the name indicates, it gives you protection for a specific term or period of time. Naturally, the shorter the period of coverage and the younger you are, the lower the yearly premium.

Term policies pay off only if you die during the period covered by the policy.

Like fire insurance, these policies generally have no cash or loan value. However, for young families with limited funds, they provide the best means of getting a maximum of protection. If you get *convertible term,* you have the option of swapping the policy for one of the higher-premium permanent protection plans without having to take another medical exam.

With *level term insurance,* the amount of insurance and your premium rate remain the same as long as your policy is in force or until it is renewed. This insurance is usually issued on a renewable basis for five or ten years, or on a non-renewable basis for longer periods or to age sixty, sixty-five, or seventy. At each renewal, the premium goes up to reflect the policyholder's increased age.

With *decreasing term insurance*—often used to cover such large debts as a mortgage—the amount of insurance declines a small amount from year to year until the policy finally expires.

(2) *Deposit term.* This type was developed by some companies to reward policyholders who maintain their insurance in force for a prolonged period.

Under a typical deposit term policy you are required to pay a deposit of $10 per $1,000 of insurance in addition to a low annual premium for the term coverage for ten years. The first-year deposit is returned, doubled, at the end of ten years. The doubled amount, guaranteed in the form of the tenth year cash value of the policy, represents a compounded interest return of 7.2 per cent. Under current tax rules—IRC Section 72 (e) (1) (B)—the interest on the return is tax-free to you. But should you let your policy lapse before the tenth policy year, some or all of the additional deposit is forfeited.

The blunt warning is, therefore:

This plan is neither intended nor recommended for individuals who do not feel reasonably certain that they can maintain coverage in force for the full ten years. It is, though, a plan of insurance uniquely designed to reward policyholders who maintain their policies in force for the required period.

The message is clear. *Do not buy* unless you believe you can meet this simple requirement. *Do investigate deposit term* at once if you are reasonably certain you'll hold your term policy for the full ten years. Your premium rates will be among the lowest on any form of term insurance. But before you buy deposit term and certainly before you replace any of your existing life insurance coverage with this policy, take these five steps:

(a) If you are advised to replace existing insurance with deposit term, obtain a written proposal of the suggested new program and send it to the companies which sold you the insurance you are being told to drop. Request the written opinions of the companies involved. Their answers well may be self-serving (which would be understandable) but their replies may help you focus on items that had not been clearly represented to you.

(b) Be sure you understand all the implications of a new contestable period in the event of your disability or death. This could be of crucial importance.

(c) Consider your investment-insurance goals. Do you wish to commit all your funds to equity programs for maximum yield or do you want to balance your investment program with reserve funds in a life insurance policy, even though the yield on this is low?

(d) If your answer is maximum yield, then double-check to be certain that the deposit term policy you buy does indeed give you a lower premium rate than regular term insurance.

(e) Obey the most basic rule of wise buying: compare costs before you buy! Just because you indicate confidence that you will hold your policy for a ten-year span, most companies issuing consumer-directed deposit term policies offer them at rates substantially lower than regular term insurance premiums. But some companies issue these policies at regular rates and pay very high commissions to their sales organizations on them. *Do not buy* deposit term unless you are sure you can meet the ten-year holding requirement. *Do weigh all its possible benefits* if you believe you will maintain the coverage.

(3) *Straight life (ordinary life or whole life)*. This type of policy is sometimes called a "bank account in an insurance policy," and costs considerably more than term because straight life must pay off, whereas a term policy may or may not pay off. The premium does not go up as you grow older, though, and you get permanent protection for your entire lifetime. In addition, your policy's cash value increases from year to year. By the time the policyholder reaches age sixty-five, the cash value usually amounts to more than half the face value of the policy. A key advantage of whole life insurance is that you, the owner of the policy, may borrow against its increasing cash value at any time, although you no longer can take very favorable low interest rates on life insurance loans for granted any more. In the late 1970s, most companies increased the loan interest provision to 8 per cent or more on new policies. Some companies still continue to issue policies with the low 5 or 6 per cent loan rate. Inquire about this loan provision when you are buying a new policy and thus avoid an unpleasant surprise in the future.

Moreover, a reasonably priced whole life policy is a useful device for those who require the mechanism of "forced savings."

You also have a number of other options with this particular type of policy. If you stop paying premiums, you can elect to continue to be covered in full for a specified period of time, or for a reduced amount of the policy's face value for the rest of your life. Or you can later cancel the policy and receive a cash settlement either in one lump sum or in the form of an income for a limited period of time, perhaps even for the rest of your life.

(4) *Limited-payment life*. In this variation of straight life, you pay premiums for only a specified number of years—usually ten, twenty, or thirty, or until you reach a certain age, such as sixty or sixty-five. Because of the limited premium-paying period, premiums are higher than for straight life policies. However, the higher premium builds up cash values correspondingly faster. Policies of this sort are favored by professional men, athletes, entertainers, and others whose earnings tend to be concentrated during a relatively short period.

(5) *Endowment*. This type of policy emphasizes savings and is designed for those who need not only protection for their dependents but, perhaps equally important, a specific sum of money—say, to provide funds for a child's college education or for a retirement income. Because of the emphasis on savings, cash value builds up most quickly in this type of policy. Consequently, it is also the most expensive.

There also are many variations and combinations of these basic types. A "family income" policy, for example, is a combination of permanent policy, usually straight life, and decreasing term insurance, and is a favorite of many couples with young children. With such a fifteen-year, $10,000 policy, the family will receive $10,000 plus $100 a month for ten years if the breadwinner dies five years after the policy is written. If the breadwinner outlives the fifteen-year family protection, the family still has a permanent policy for $10,000.

The "family plan" policy, which also combines straight life for the father with term insurance protection for the mother and children, simply covers the life of everybody in the family in varying amounts—all for one basic premium.

PRACTICAL EXAMPLES OF WHO NEEDS WHAT

For more guidance on how to pick the policies best suited to your needs consider these case histories:

Let's say you're twenty-five and just married. You started work a year ago after you finished college and your wife also is employed. Your income is $15,000 and your wife's income is $8,250 a year. You have a group life insurance policy through your employer which would pay your wife $15,000—one year's salary—in the event of your death. (You have no children yet, but plan to start a family soon.)

What type of individual life insurance should you have—if any? For what reasons?

Even though you are just starting out on limited resources, some life insurance experts say, you should invest in a straight life insurance policy with an option permitting you to buy additional insurance at later dates with no medical examination. This program would give you a means of continually increasing your insurance coverage as your family needs increase—and would at the same time provide a growing financial reserve in the form of increasing cash values. You may, if you need to, borrow against these cash values.

Or let's say you are a medical student, aged twenty-five, with a young wife, an infant child—and practically no income outside your summer earnings. The most practical type of insurance for you probably would be convertible term insurance covering the few years before you start to earn a big income, at which time you might convert to straight life, which covers you as long as you live and builds cash values as well.

Or let's say you are thirty, married and have two children, ages one and four. Your income is $30,500 a year. Your group insurance policy would pay a year's income, and you also have a straight life policy which you bought five years ago, prior to the birth of your first child.

Your primary need is for immediate insurance protection which would provide income for your wife in the event of your death while the children are dependent and would pay for your children's later education. You also should be creating some form of nestegg for emergencies.

To achieve these goals, consider buying a straight life policy with a twenty-year family income rider which would provide a monthly income to your widow from the date of your death to twenty years from the issue date. This income, when combined with your Social Security benefits (see pages 953–55), would provide for most of the average income needs of a young widow with children.

Also, under this policy your wife would receive, in the event of your death, the face amount of the policy—plus your previous insurance coverage, which could fairly easily be translated into an additional monthly income supplement.

Or say you're the type who is simply incapable of saving to supplement your anticipated retirement income. A more expensive retirement income or endowment policy, with limited life insurance protection in the meantime, might be your best means of forced savings.

Or say you want to be sure your children can afford college should you, the breadwinner, die in the interim. A life policy on your life—not theirs—would be the best bet.

Or say you're a disciplined investor capable of building a hefty nestegg and protection for your family. You might find sufficient protection in a straight life policy or term insurance providing a death benefit just covering immediate cash needs and death taxes.

Or finally, say you have no dependents, you don't intend to marry, and you do have liquid assets more than adequate to cover death expenses, small debts, and probable death taxes. Then it's hard to justify any life insurance program for you at all.

If any rules can be formulated from all this, they would be:

• As a young family, your vital interest is in immediate protection—not in the amount of life insurance you might be able to carry in your older years or in building retirement income or whatever. So buy life insurance as early as you can, but of the kind that will give you the most protection, even if it is only temporary.

• If your funds are limited, buy term insurance.

• Buy term insurance that is renewable and convertible. Later on, when you can afford the larger premiums, you can explore the advantages, disadvantages, and ways of converting your term policy to permanent insurance.

• If you're in your middle years, you might be best off starting with straight life for at least your long-run needs. But don't go for this higher-priced policy if it means straining your budget and cutting down on your regular savings program.

Instead of paying a high premium for straight life, what about buying a term insurance policy for a fraction of that premium amount and investing the difference in some other form of savings? Calculate how much interest or other income you would have to earn on such an account to outperform a straight life "savings account."

HOW TO FIND A "STRONG" INSURANCE COMPANY

• *Do not* assume all life insurance companies are financially sound! Instead, shop among the best 20 per cent of the companies available to you That's not being too choosy at all.

• To find a financially strong company, consult *Best's Insurance Guide* or

Best's Insurance Reports. Best's is the most authoritative insurance rating service available and you can find these publications in most public libraries.

Best's has five recommended ratings for life insurance companies:

(1) A+ and A (Excellent)
(2) B+ (Very Good)
(3) B (Good)
(4) C+ (Fairly Good)
(5) C (Fair)

• If you buy a low-cost insurance policy from one of the top companies, you will not necessarily have to pay higher premiums. In fact, many of the low-cost companies are among the financially strongest and many of the high-cost companies are among the financially weakest.

• And of course, also take into account the services and professional advice the company offers you.

HOW TO SAVE ON YOUR INSURANCE

If you are paying higher than standard rates for your life insurance because of medical considerations, and if your health has improved since your policy was issued, call your insurance agent, tell him you want your policies reviewed, and then apply to your insurance company for a reduction or elimination of the extra-risk premiums. Even if your health hasn't improved, you might be able to get a lower risk rating.

This is just one way to save significant sums on your life insurance premiums. But there are other ways either to slash your overall insurance costs or to free funds to buy extra, needed coverage. Here are some of them:

• Find out whether any club, association, union, professional or fraternal organization to which either you or your spouse belongs offers any low-cost group life insurance plan. In some group term insurance plans you can save as much as 40 per cent over the cost of individual coverage. Most of these plans taper off coverage as you grow older, and the insurance may end at age sixty or sixty-five.

Another big advantage of group coverage is that medical exams are waived.

• Consider reducing or even dropping some or all of your present life insurance coverage—and thus also slashing your premiums—*if* your children have grown up and are self-supporting, *if* the beneficiary you originally designated for your policy has died or become financially independent, *if* you have built up a substantial outside nest egg, *if* you have no debts. But before you drop any life insurance, be sure you're not likely to need the coverage again, for if you're forced to rebuy a policy later, you'll pay a considerably higher premium and, should your health deteriorate, you may not be able to get any coverage at all. (See "Handling Your Insurance at Retirement," directly below.)

• *Shop* for whatever individual life insurance coverage you decide on—not only among local agents but also, in certain states, at savings banks, which generally offer over the counter lower-priced policies than insurance companies.

• Pay your premiums in as few installments as possible to avoid extra charges. A policy with a $150 annual premium might cost you $156 if you paid it in two semi-annual installments. If paid quarterly, it might cost you a total of $159, and monthly, $162 for the year, or $12 more than the one-time annual payment.

• If you have several policies, reduce the frequency of payment on all of them and make it easier for yourself by staggering your payments so that they aren't bunched near each other.

• If there is some special reason why you prefer to pay your premiums monthly, ask your agent about a cost-saving "preauthorized check" plan under which your bank automatically deducts the appropriate amount each month to the life insurance company from your regular checking account.

• If you are paying a higher-than-usual premium because of the nature of your occupation when you bought the policy, and have changed occupations, inform your insurance agent of this fact and request a reclassification.

Only recently, millions of Americans were regarded as virtually uninsurable—including wild animal trainers, steeplechase riders, car racers, deep-sea divers, test pilots, submariners, and mine police. But all of these today are insurable. Today, even armored car drivers and chemists in nitroglycerin plants are regarded as "standard risks." And premium rates for workers in almost all "dangerous" trades have sharply declined. Key reasons: improved job safety and successful trials by the insurance companies which offered coverage to workers in these occupations.

Admittedly, if you are a steeplechase rider, trapeze artist, or a Grand Prix race car driver, you'll have to pay a somewhat higher premium to get life insurance. Similarly, private avocations are taken into account in calculating insurance rates. "A sky diver who won't open his parachute until he reaches treetop level would be rated as a pretty bad risk," says one top industry spokesman. But the key point is that almost all workers are insurable and almost all at a reasonable cost.

• It may be cheaper for you to add to an existing policy than to buy a completely new one. A decreasing term or family income policy, for example, will cost less as a rider to your regular policy than if bought separately.

• If you are a World War II veteran and have a GI term insurance policy, consider converting it to permanent government insurance, one of the best bargains ever offered veterans, even though the premium will be higher. Check with the nearest Veterans Administration office to see if the conversion is still possible in your case. (See Chapter 28, "Know Your Rights!—and How to Use Them," and Chapter 9, "Education After High School—and How to Finance It," for details on other veterans' rights and benefits.)

HANDLING YOUR INSURANCE AT RETIREMENT

When you reach retirement age—*and that's the latest date for doing this*—review and reevaluate all your life insurance policies in terms of your need for them and of your personal goals.

Do not be the least surprised to discover *you no longer need* your life insurance—for you no longer have a young family to protect. Your whole way of life has been drastically changed and straight life insurance simply doesn't fit into it.

When you took out your life insurance policies, you were forcing yourself to save out of your current income, but continuing to save after retirement is inconsistent with that concept. When you began your insurance program, you were intent on creating an instant estate for the benefit of your dependents in the event of your premature death. But when there's no need for protecting dependents this way, it's all wrong for any older person to deprive himself of a dollar to finance this protection.

You might cash in your policies and put the released funds to work earning more money for you—in a simple savings account or high-grade bonds or high-grade common or preferred stocks. Or you might put your insurance on a paid-up basis and relieve yourself of all further premium obligations.

Only if you are in the wealthier income brackets—in which life insurance could be an excellent way to pass on an estate or to provide cash for estate taxes—will you be told that it could be unwise to drop your policies. But this gets into a different area altogether.

IS YOUR LIFE INSURANCE UP-TO-DATE?

Now let's assume you already have adequate amounts of insurance—both group and individual.

As the preceding section on handling your insurance in retirement dramatized, it is vitally important for you to review your coverage at least every two or three years to make sure it is appropriate for your financial needs, geared to your rising or falling standard of living, realistic in terms of the number and ages of your children and properly tied into your other savings and investments.

Do both husband and wife know, for example, where all of your various family life insurance policies are now kept? The total value of all your life insurance protection—including veterans', fraternal organizations', group policies, credit life insurance, individual policies? The name and address of your insurance agent? Which members of the family are covered and for approximately how much? Are there children not covered? The amount and due date of premiums? Who are the beneficiaries of each policy? And the "secondary" or contingent beneficiaries—in the event both husband and wife are killed in a single accident? How benefits would be paid? The amount of cash values which have accumulated so far—against which loans could be made? If you've moved, does the insurance company have your new address?

Once you have the answers to these basic questions, explore these other important questions concerning your life insurance—and determine just where and just how big are the gaps in coverage:

What, if any, provision is there to cover the possibility that the family breadwinner might become disabled over a long period of time? Does your policy include a "waiver of premium" clause—a waiver of the obligation to pay further premiums in the event of total and permanent disability?

Does your policy contain a provision under which, if you for any reason fail to pay your premiums within the specified grace period (usually thirty-one days), the premium will automatically be paid by a loan against the cash value of the policy?

Does it also contain an "accidental death benefit" provision, often called "double indemnity," that doubles the amount payable if the insured dies accidentally? (Triple indemnity also is offered by some companies.)

Are your term policies renewable and convertible without your having to take another medical examination?

How much has the upsurge in the U.S. cost of living shrunk the actual buying power of your policies since you bought them? Have you made or can you make any provisions to offset this erosion? (See below.)

Do you meet the rule of thumb that you should have the equivalent of four to five years' pay in life insurance? You may need more of a cushion if you have several children, if you are loaded with debt, if your non-insurance financial protections are limited, and if you simply can't discipline yourself into saving. You may need less if your group coverage is extensive, if your wife is well trained for a job, if your debts are paid off, if your children have left the nest, if you have substantial savings and other investments.

How much income would all of your present life insurance policies provide when you retire—assuming you are using life insurance for this purpose at all? Add this income, figured on a monthly basis, to the amount you can expect from Social Security retirement benefits, from income on all your other savings and investments, and from your company pension.

If you own your business, is your life insurance adequate to keep it going should you die before you've trained a successor?

Is your designated beneficiary still the correct one—or should other dependents be added or substituted?

Should the wife be listed as the policyowner, even though it is written on the husband's life? If done validly, this could result in considerable savings in estate taxes. Get advice on this from your insurance agent, tax adviser, or lawyer.

Only when you have the answers to these questions will you know how much financial protection you and your family actually have. In this period of steep inflation, having these answers is absolutely vital to your financial security—now *and* later.

HOW INFLATION HAS ERODED YOUR LIFE INSURANCE

Q. *If you bought your life insurance policies to protect your family as recently as the late 1960s, are you aware of the degree to which the upsurge in the cost of living in the United States has shrunk your coverage just in the short span since?*

A. By a horrendous 70½ per cent! Just in one decade! And living costs are continuing to spiral upward—at intolerably high annual rates.

Q. *How long is it since you have put aside a quiet evening to discuss seriously with a trusted life insurance agent the adequacy of your life insurance in view of your pay hikes since the 1960s, your increasing obligations (children, a new home and mortgage, a job or business change of major importance, etc.) and the overall differences in your living style?*

A. If you're typical of most Americans, it has been years.

While the average insured family had $37,900 of life insurance as the 1980s neared, a new peak, and up a full $2,500 from 1976, it was equivalent to only twenty-four months of the average family's disposable income—or about two years of pay. To put against this, I repeat, the accepted rule of thumb is that an average family should have the equivalent of four to five years' pay in life insurance, savings, and other investments.

And you may need more of a cushion if you have several young children, if your non-insurance financial protection is limited, if you have only a modest amount in savings, and if you (typically) are carrying a heavy load of debts (in installment loans, other types of personal loans, a mortgage). You also may need less of a cushion than the rule of thumb suggests if your group coverage is extensive, if your wife also has a well-paying job or has easily marketable job skills should she need to go back to work, if your children are grown and on their own, if your debts are minor or paid off.

Q. *How much has the actual buying power of your life insurance policies been slashed since you bought them in 1967?*
A. The dollar which bought you 100 cents of goods and services in the market place in 1967 buys you only 50 cents worth of the same goods and services in the market place today.

If you consider the 1979 dollar as worth 100 cents today, and if you accept the "conservative" (but to me, intolerable) forecast of an inflation rate held to "only" 6 per cent a year, today's 100-cent dollar will be worth only 12½ cents in thirty-five years. If you are a young adult, that is when your insurance might be turning into an "instant estate" for your family.

Q. *How much income would all of your present life insurance coverage from all sources provide when you retire or when your family must get along without your contribution in earnings?*

How much does every asset on which your family can count for support add up to when you put together this life insurance income, figured on a monthly basis, plus what you can anticipate from Social Security benefits, from any company pension that seems safe, from income on your savings and other investments?

If you own your own business, is your life insurance protection adequate to keep the business going should you die before you have given a successor sufficient training?

Have you included all your dependents (or eliminated inappropriate ones) among your beneficiaries? Are your beneficiaries truly the ones you want to protect in 1988 as against 1968?

If you can answer satisfactorily all the questions in this report, your life insurance is up-to-date. If you cannot, get the answers now and put your instant estate in top-notch order.

SHOULD YOU SWITCH INSURANCE POLICIES?

If any insurance agent suggests you switch a policy you own—life or accident and health—for "a better one," the law in most states requires the agent to explain fully and clearly the differences between the policy the agent says you should cancel and the new one. If the agent doesn't make this "full disclosure" about the policies, he (or she) is breaking the law and could forfeit his license.

But even if the agent does tell you the differences there are many, many shadings to full disclosure—and you well may not understand what is being recommended. Even if you would be better off in some ways by switching, the disadvantages of changing might far outweigh the advantages the agent is stressing.

And even if you are persuaded by the arguments, heed this blunt warning: *in very few cases can changing insurance policies be advantageous to the policyholder*.

Unscrupulous insurance agents still do exist—although not on the scale of the past, when they thrived in the ghettos particularly. They still do sell to the poor and uninformed, then coax the ignorant policyholder into switching to other policies after only a couple of years—so that the buyer pays the front-end costs over and over again. There is still a real danger that you'll make a serious error in this area—if only because so many millions of you own so many more insurance policies and in such a wider variety than ever before.

There are, of course, many reasons why you might change a life (or accident and health) policy. But the most likely reason is that an agent advises you that another policy from another insurance company is a better buy. Here, therefore, are basic guides to weigh if and when a switch is suggested:

(1) Realize that with any new policy you are paying the full front-end costs all over again—just as you did when you bought your original policy. Most agents' commissions and company administrative costs come out of your first-year premium. If you've had your policy for several years, you've already paid these costs once. Don't duplicate them without extraordinarily sound reasons.

(2) Also be fully aware of the importance of the contestability clause in most life insurance contracts—under which your insurance contract can't be broken because of statements you made on the application after the policy has been in force for a period, usually two years (except, of course, for a misstated age). With a new contract, you start a new two-year contestability period. The person who switches policies frequently not only pays the front-end costs over again but rarely gets out of the contestable period.

(3) Find out precisely what will be the premium payments for your new policy and compare them with what you are paying. If the benefits are similar, your premiums probably will be higher—merely because you are older than when you bought the first policy.

(4) Be wary about the waiting period involved when a new policy is issued. All too often people apply for a new policy and let the old one lapse before the new policy becomes effective. The tragedy here is that the person may die in the meantime, with no insurance at all in force.

(5) As your best protection, deal with an insurance agent who represents a reputable company. If you're thinking about changing policies, ask his advice. If you're not satisfied with what he recommends, ask the company. Throughout the entire process, do not forget that it is the agent's duty under the law to disclose clearly all the facts to you before you switch any policy.

If, after all this, you feel you've been unfairly treated by the company or its agents, you do have a recourse. You can lodge a complaint with your state insurance commissioner's office at the state capital.

WHAT ABOUT WIFE INSURANCE?

Assuming you are convinced that you, the breadwinner, must have some life insurance to protect your family against loss of your income, the next question is: should the life of your wife also be insured?

Do you, Mr. America, realize how great would be the added expenses to you should the lady of your house not be around to share, plan, cook, clean, mother, drive, take care?

And do you recognize what would be the financial impact of the loss if she also is a working mother who contributes substantially to the household's total income?

Today, three out of four wives are covered by life insurance and the proportion is growing steadily. As a guide on whether or not the wife in *your* household should have life insurance, the key functions of "wife insurance" are to:

(1) Cover final expenses in the event of her death. Expenses of final medical and hospital care, funeral costs, and all other incidentals can now total $5,000 or more—enough to wipe out most family nest eggs and even put the surviving mate quite deeply in debt. (See Chapter 20.)

(2) Help care for the young children, for a fair period at least, and perform the other tasks that go with running a home. The cost of a competent housekeeper, or even regular cleaning help, can run into hundreds of dollars a month.

(3) Help meet the increase in income taxes which results from the husband's loss of his wife's personal exemption and the joint-return privilege.

(4) Cover the loss of the wife's contribution to the family income, if it represents a vital part of the family budget.

(5) And a mother may want to leave an inheritance to her children.

What sort of policy would be best?

In most cases term or ordinary life should fill the bill.

Term if the ability to pay premiums is limited, and ordinary life if your budget can accommodate a somewhat higher premium. Remember, term insurance, while low in initial cost, will require higher premiums every year or every stated renewal period.

It also terminates at some age, usually sixty-five or seventy, so if you desire permanent insurance consider ordinary life.

The fundamental point is that the loss of a wife and mother is a financial blow to the family as real—although not as readily measurable—as the loss of the husband and breadwinner. Wife insurance is one way to safeguard the family against this loss.

AND WHAT ABOUT INSURANCE FOR CHILDREN?

On their grandson's fifth birthday recently, a smart couple we know bought him as a gift a $10,000 straight life insurance policy—with the pledge that they will pay the premiums until the boy reaches twenty-five and will arrange to have the policy paid up immediately should they die before that date.

Young Dick's parents were less than delighted. "If any life insurance is to be taken out," grumbled the disappointed father, "it should be on my life, not Dick's."

"I gave that boy the best present I could think of," said the equally disappointed grandfather, "and neither my daughter nor her husband understood it at all."

Actually, both grandfather and father were right and wrong. The first and top priority in life insurance must go to adequate coverage for the breadwinner. And since Dick's mother hasn't earned a penny since he was born and the family is having a tough struggle on one paycheck in today's inflation, our friends could have been a little less original in their gift to Dick. And if they were determined to give a life insurance policy, it should have been to their twenty-five-year-old son-in-law.

On the other hand, our friends are doing their daughter, son-in-law, and grandson a tremendous favor by buying that policy so early in Dick's life. Since millions of you will be directly or indirectly affected by this tale, here are the key reasons why.

• You can buy basic insurance coverage on a child's life at extremely low rates.

• One of the forms to investigate is called the "jumping juvenile policy."* This policy provides $1,000 of insurance, per unit, until age twenty-one and then increases to $5,000 without any additional premium. In addition the increases in cash value each year are substantial, and when your son, daughter, or grandchild assumes the premium-paying responsibility, he may find that each of his payments is exceeded by the growth in the cash value of the policy.

• Among other types of policies designed for children and some of the features you should investigate are:

Guaranteed Insurability Option. This would guarantee the child the right to buy additional life insurance equal to the original amount at ages twenty-five, twenty-eight, thirty-one, thirty-four, thirty-seven, and forty. Thus an original $10,000 policy could provide a total of $60,000 in additional insurance.

Payor Benefit. This provision will waive the premium until the child is twenty-one years of age if the payor dies or becomes disabled.

• And, of course, this life insurance is protection for the parents should their child die.

How you apply this tale is up to you entirely. But at least you should know what's available and what others are doing, so you can reach an intelligent, informed decision.

One basic caution, though: don't invest in this type of coverage—or even in wife insurance—unless and until the family breadwinner is adequately insured.

WHAT YOU SHOULD KNOW ABOUT ANNUITIES

What They Are

Annuities are sold by life insurance companies, but they should not be confused with life insurance. You buy life insurance primarily because, if you die, you

---

* Juvenile insurance also might be valuable in times of emergency or to help finance the child's education.

want to have provided for those you leave behind. You buy an annuity primarily because you assume you will live and you want to have some sort of steady income to supplement what you'll get from Social Security, and perhaps your company pension, savings, other investments during your retirement years.

An annuity is a contract or agreement under which an insurance company accepts a given sum of money from you and in return guarantees to pay you a regular (usually monthly) income for a stated period or, more typically, for as long as you live. The amounts of the payments are based on your life expectancy, according to the mortality tables and how much money you put in. Since women tend to live longer than men, they normally receive smaller monthly incomes from annuities than do men for the same dollar input, but over a longer period of time.

Pros and Cons of Annuities

An annuity program frees you from the responsibility of money management or investment decisions, guarantees you a fixed monthly payment, and assures you that you will never outlive your capital. But it must not be your entire retirement program in an era of inflation.

Although an annuity can generate a good monthly return, you may be able to do much, much better by investing at a young age in, say, real estate, stocks, or other mediums.

It's simply not that easy.

New Types of Annuities

Single Premium—Deferred Annuity: This type of annuity has become popular in recent years as a medium via which interest earned on the investment is tax-deferred until later years. In addition, the yield provided by insurance companies is frequently competitive with other money instruments such as savings accounts, certificates of deposit, and government notes. It is issued on a load or no load basis, meaning that either the sales charges are paid by the purchaser (load) or absorbed by the insurance company (no load). The usual contract guarantees only 3 to 4 per cent yield but provides for extra payments of interest in excess of the guarantee on an annual basis. The amount of such excess is set annually by the company's Board of Directors. Withdrawal of investment before a certain stipulated time usually calls for some loss of the accumulated dividends.

Flexible Premium—Deferred Annuity: Designed primarily for the Individual Retirement Account market (see pages 910–11), this type of annuity requires annual payments which are tax-deductible if they meet the requirements of the Individual Retirement Act. The flexible feature permits you, the annuitant, to change or even skip annual payments. The yield on the accumulated funds will vary each year in accordance with the acts of the Board of Directors on payment of excess interest over guaranteed amounts.

WHAT'S YOUR RATE ON A LIFE INSURANCE LOAN?

Before you sign any contract to buy ordinary life insurance in the future, ask this crucial question and be certain you get an unqualified, clear, honest answer which you fully understand:

What interest rate will you be charged if you want to borrow against the cash value of your life insurance policy at any time you need or want to in coming years?

Will you be charged the cheap, bargain rates of 5 to 6 per cent with which you have long been familiar and probably take for granted?

Or will you be charged up to a hefty 8 per cent or more to borrow back your own money (the cash value of the premiums you have paid), which increasingly is becoming the norm?

The stable, low interest rate on life insurance policy loans has been one of the great selling points for ordinary life insurance over many years. It has been an advantage which observers such as myself have emphasized repeatedly to hard-pressed consumers, particularly during the mid-1970s era of double-digit interest rates on loans and hard-to-get credit.

It always has been cited by insurance policy salesmen.

There's no fooling around about this. In fact, the movement has reached the point where a mere handful of states still place a low statutory limit on life insurance policy loan interest.

The life insurance companies leading the drive have been among the nation's giants. They have argued that the low rates on policy loans deprive them of profits; charges to policyholders will be offset by "adjustments through dividends" paid to policyholders; many loans are taken out by borrowers not in economic need but seeking cheap money that they can reinvest elsewhere at higher interest rates.

But opposing the giants are life insurance companies which feel just as strongly that the boost to 8 per cent and above is an unjustifiable rip-off on policyholders, and that a retreat from the low borrowing rate concept would rob ordinary life insurance of a vital element. Say these executives: loans are generally taken because of need, not speculation; "debasing" this advantage of permanent life insurance will turn buyers to term insurance; what companies earn on their reserves is more than adequate to cover their loan rates; the policyholders are borrowing back their own cash, making this a 100 per cent guaranteed investment for the companies.

Be on guard! Do not take cheap policy loans for granted. Shop for loan rates. Recognize the differences can be of tremendous future importance to you. Insist that your insurance agent give you a straight answer on policy loan rates.

BUYING LIFE INSURANCE BY MAIL

If a life insurance sales agent has personally contacted you in the past year, you are in a minority of American households. A full two thirds of U.S. families have been utterly ignored—with the greatest decline in contacts concentrated among young, husband-wife families, traditionally the prime market for life insurance and the drop most apparent since the start of the 1970s.

The result? One is that buying of insurance by mail has been in a sharp upswing, for insurance companies that sell by mail have been saturating the market with print, broadcast, and mail ads. Another result is that premiums paid for insurance bought by mail have now punched through the $1 billion milestone.

Of course buying your insurance by mail has many advantages. Because the sales representations by their very nature are delivered entirely in writing, you can read and reread at your leisure in your own time, in your own home. You buy solely on the basis of what you see in writing, not on the persuasiveness of an agent's word. And while you must be extremely cautious about the responsibility of the insurance company with which you are dealing, and check with utmost vigilance, most insurance companies that sell by mail are licensed and are regulated by your state insurance department.

Insurance policies offered through mail, print, and broadcast media provide a wide range of life, accident and health, and casualty coverage. Hundreds of thousands of policies of these types are in force throughout the nation. Many of these policies are designed to supplement other insurance, providing the extra protection for expenses not covered by your existing insurance.

Q. *What generally should you look for?*

A. Ask yourself: Does this insurance fill your needs? Do you know what you are getting and not getting? Can you afford it?

Q. *What about buying accident and health insurance?*

A. You should understand what kinds of illness or injury are covered and what areas are specifically excluded from coverage.

Find out how many days of hospitalization the policy covers and if payments begin on the first day of hospitalization or if there's a waiting period. Usually, the longer the waiting period, the lower the premium (*but* the *average* hospital confinement is only seven days).

Check provisions under which your policy can be renewed. Many accident and health insurance policies are guaranteed renewable and cannot be canceled on an individual basis as long as premiums are paid on time. If there are provisions for increases in premiums or decreases in benefits at, say, age sixty-five, be sure you know them.

Find out about exclusions. Some policies may exclude payment for medical conditions that existed prior to the time you purchased your policy. Other exclusions might include confinement in a government hospital, mental or convalescent care.

Q. *How do you find out what policy is right for you?*

A. You must get some expert help here. A do-it-yourself life insurance program may be as bad as do-it-yourself medical care. Be sure the ad is explicit in describing the type of life insurance being offered ("term" or "whole" life).

Check whether your policy includes an option to buy additional life insurance in your later years without a physical exam, and note the specifically stated instances in which payment will not be made (such as death by suicide, acts of war, etc.).

Pay your insurance premiums annually (rather than quarterly or monthly), which will save you money.

Q. *How do you choose the right company for you?*

A. Ask your neighbors and friends about their experiences with individual companies on claims settlement, response to their communications, service to policyholders.

Ask your state insurance department if the company you are considering is licensed to sell in your state.

If you have any questions about a policy, ask the company to explain in writing or by phone to your satisfaction any aspect you don't fully understand.

PEOPLE FORGET

True tale: In the late 1970s a resident of Jersey City, New Jersey, borrowed—at 12.65 per cent interest—$1,500 from his local bank to finance some home improvements. He had forgotten that eight years ago he had elected to allow the dividends on his $30,000 ordinary life insurance policy to accumulate at interest —and his dividend account now contained $1,468.

Result: He was voluntarily forfeiting more than $100 a year in unnecessary bank interest charges. Reminded a month later during a routine visit from his insurance agent, he drew out the dividends, placed the money in the bank, and persuaded his banker to reissue the debt as a low-interest passbook loan.

True tale: A Denver resident, widowed for ten years, remarried at the age of sixty-seven, died five years later, and left his own widow nearly destitute. His life insurance had been made out to his wife. But he forgot that it had been made out to "my wife, Mary." His second wife's name was Hilda.

The $25,000 in proceeds passed to the estate of his first wife, who it developed, after making specific bequests to her husband and others had left the remainder of her estate to a favorite niece. The favorite niece received the $25,000.

People forget.

"And the thing that people most often forget," says the American Council of Life Insurance, "is that life insurance is a legal contract carrying all the force of law.

"The next thing they forget is that the passage of time can all too easily convert yesterday's wisdom into today's folly."

For many, many years, conventional wisdom has held that women, the major beneficiaries of life insurance, are incapable of managing their own financial affairs in widowhood. As a result, husbands often have elected to have the proceeds of their life insurance doled out to their widows in monthly installments.

Even during periods when the value of the dollar remains fairly stable, you, a policyholder, and you, the intended beneficiary, should examine this procedure with utmost care. But in eras of inflation, the consequences of deciding on the sufficiency of a fixed income can be doubly destructive.

A widow with, say, $50,000 of insurance could find herself strapped to an insurance income of $400 a month, with no way to reach the principal sum. Legally the money is hers. And just as legally the insurance company is bound by a contract which prevents her from drawing out any part of the principal in an emergency.

In response to anguished complaints of affected widows, many life insurers a while ago undertook lengthy and costly campaigns among policyholders who had elected the option, urging them to reconsider. Many policyholders did. Many who should have didn't.

There were an estimated 150 million policyholders in the United States in the late 1970s. If even 1 per cent of them have forgotten they have tied the hands of their beneficiaries this way, it means there are 1.5 million time bombs ticking away.

"It's really frightening," the Council emphasizes. "The income option can rescue people from paying unnecessary estate taxes. And if there are other assets a beneficiary can get at in an emergency, it's one way of being sure they can't outlive their incomes. But if it's used to insulate the widow from decisions about money, it's misused and can really hurt her."

If you doubt your beneficiary's ability to make sound decisions, leave a letter of instructions and suggestions. Or set up a life insurance trust. And certainly, insist that your wife learn the basics about handling money (while you're alive).

More shocking than the above are the instances of policyholders forgetting to tell their beneficiaries—or anybody else—that they have life insurance at all. Many forgotten term policies, for instance, would simply be carried in the records as having lapsed when, in fact, they had been in force and payable at the time of their owners' death—if a claim had been made.

The companies are ready to honor a valid claim years, even decades, after it was due. But if that claim isn't made, there's frequently no way of telling the difference between a lapsed policy and a lapsed memory.

LAPSED POLICY OR LAPSED MEMORY?

Each year millions of you buy life insurance policies for which you pay billions in premiums.

Among your reasons: As a man, because you wanted your home to be free and clear; or to be sure of ample funds for your children's education; or to be comfortable in later years. As a woman, to replace your value as a homemaker; or to replace the dollars you contribute to your home as a working wife; or if widowed or a separated head of household, to replace income vital to your children.

Yet, unless you act now—and that means today—many of those sound intentions may never be fulfilled. Why not?

The shocking answer is that an astounding number of you *never* make certain that the people for whom you are putting aside that money today will know about it in that distant tomorrow when you are not there to tell them.

Every year, millions of dollars in life insurance benefits that were meant for you go instead to the states as unclaimed personal property.

For thousands of you, that is money which could have been yours.

Life insurance companies, though, are obligated to turn this money over to the states after they have lost all hope of finding the rightful owners.

Before they do turn it over, the companies undertake exhaustive searches. One New York company, for example, has a ten-page itemized list of procedures for claims men to follow in tracking down the missing owners of "orphaned" funds. And life insurance files are loaded with successful searches.

But there also are those millions of dollars of failures they must ship each year to state treasuries—millions of dollars of promises unkept because you forgot to keep records.

Here's a sampling of letters received by the American Council of Life Insurance from individuals who believe they might be lost beneficiaries. The stories these letters tell could become the stories of your beneficiaries.

"My father was known to have carried a policy to protect my mother. She preceded my father in death and he had said only weeks before his own death that he was thinking of dropping this insurance. His effects were somewhat scattered and I was never able to determine what action was taken on this." A Kansas woman.

"When my husband died, I thought his insurance was $11,000 ($10,000 in my name and $1,000 in my son's). There were two policies missing, $2,000 each. I located the one which he had cashed, but cannot locate one for $2,000." A Pennsylvania widow.

"I'm writing in desperation. My husband always said I was protected, but would not discuss it." A Kentucky widow.

"In many of these cases, there never was a policy, or it lapsed, or was surrendered for cash. But not to know must be agonizing," says a Council spokesman. "And it's all so avoidable." His guides:

• Store your life insurance policies—including group insurance certificates—at home, preferably in a fireproof lockbox along with other key records (your will, instructions for heirs).

• In a separate letter, list the names of the companies with whom you are insured, the policy numbers, and the amounts. Leave this letter with your lawyer, store copies in your safe-deposit box and with a trusted relative.

• Inform your beneficiaries. Insist on this.

• Keep your records up-to-date. Note if you surrender a policy or let one lapse.

• Periodically re-examine your policies: your application, names of beneficiaries, settlement option, your action of dividends. If appropriate, make a change immediately and record it.

• Check out any policy you have dropped to be sure it has no value. Do not throw any away until you have checked the insurer.

• Notify your insurance companies when you move. The post office maintains records on new addresses for only about sixty days and since many insureds pay premiums annually or semi-annually, premium notices are returned frequently with the notation "not at address." The result: millions of insurance lapsed involuntarily each year.

One New York company maintains a staff that tries to locate such policyholders—but even after its staff calls the agent, employer, and family physician listed in the original applicaton, the staff still cannot locate 50 per cent of the company's policyholders who move and do not notify the company of their new addresses.

THE BAFFLEGAB OF LIFE INSURANCE AND ANNUITIES

ACCIDENTAL DEATH BENEFIT   Extra benefit, often added to life insurance policies, which is paid in the event of death by accident Often called "double indemnity," sometimes "triple indemnity."

ANNUITY   Contract under which you pay the life insurance company a given sum of money and receive in return a regular (usually monthly) income for the remainder of your life. A *deferred annuity* provides for the income payments to begin at some future date—e.g., after a certain number of years or when you reach a certain age. A *variable annuity* is one in which payments may fluctuate, often reflecting stock price changes.

BENEFICIARY   Person you name in your life insurance policy to receive the policy's proceeds in the event of your death. Also called "primary beneficiary."

BUSINESS LIFE (OR "KEY MAN") INSURANCE   Life insurance bought by a corporation or partnership on the life of a key executive.

CASH SURRENDER VALUE   Amount of money for which you can cash in your life insurance policy before it becomes payable by death or maturity.

CONTINGENT BENEFICIARY   One or more additional persons you name in your policy to receive all or part of its proceeds in the event the primary beneficiary dies before you.

CREDIT LIFE INSURANCE   Life insurance offered (and sometimes required) by lenders, providing for full payment of a home mortgage or other loan in the event the borrower dies.

DEPOSIT TERM   Special type of term insurance. (See pages 932–33.)

DIVIDEND   Refund of part of premium on a participating policy not needed by the company. Since it actually represents the refund of an overpayment, it is not taxable.

ENDOWMENT INSURANCE   Insurance in which the face value is payable at maturity to the policyholder if he is still living, or to his beneficiary if he dies before the policy matures.

FACE AMOUNT   Amount, stated on the face of the policy, that will be paid on the death of the insured or at maturity of the contract.

FAMILY INCOME POLICY   Policy which combines whole life insurance with decreasing term insurance and which pays your beneficiary a regular income for a specified period of time if you die before the end of that period. It also pays the full face amount of the policy at the death of the policyholder.

FAMILY POLICY   Life insurance contract covering all members of your family. Generally, such a policy provides whole life insurance on the family breadwinner and limited amounts of term insurance on his wife and also on present and future children.

GRACE PERIOD   Time span, usually thirty or thirty-one days after a premium is due, during which you may delay payment of your insurance premium without any penalty and without losing your coverage.

GROUP LIFE INSURANCE   Low-priced life insurance usually issued to employees by employers, or to members by their unions or professional groups, without a medical examination.

INDUSTRIAL LIFE INSURANCE   Insurance sold to individuals, usually in low-income brackets, in amounts of less than $1,000. Weekly or monthly premiums collected by an agent. Traditionally used to pay funeral expenses.

INSURED   Person on whose life insurance policy is issued.

LEVEL PREMIUM INSURANCE   A form of insurance in which the annual premium stays the same throughout the period over which premiums are payable.

LIMITED-PAYMENT LIFE INSURANCE Whole life insurance on which premiums are fully paid in a limited, specified number of years.

MATURITY Date when the face value of a policy becomes payable.

ORDINARY LIFE INSURANCE Individual life insurance, either or whole, which is sold in amounts of $1,000 or more. The proceeds can be in the form of a lump sum or as income or your policy can be converted to an annuity.

PAID-UP INSURANCE Insurance on which you have paid all required premiums. With reduced paid-up insurance, the plan for which you originally signed up remains in force, but the benefit amount is reduced, with no further premiums to pay.

PARTICIPATING INSURANCE Insurance on which the premium is somewhat higher than the actual cost of protection, but on which the company returns any amount it does not need in the form of policy dividends. Mostly sold by "mutual" life insurance companies. On *non-participating* life insurance, the premium you pay is calculated as closely as possible to the actual cost of the protection, and on this type of policy you receive no dividends. Sold by "stock" life insurance companies.

PERMANENT LIFE INSURANCE Any form of life insurance except term insurance. This type builds a cash value, which you can use as collateral to borrow from the insurance company, or which you may withdraw entirely by giving up the policy.

POLICY Printed document stating the terms of the contract with the life insurance company. This document should *not* be kept in your safety-deposit box, but rather in a safe place at home where your wife or other survivor can get at it quickly if and when she needs to.

POLICY LOAN Money you borrow from your life insurance company using as security the cash value of your policy.

PREMIUM Amount you pay periodically, usually once or twice or four times a year, or monthly (perhaps as a payroll deduction), for your life insurance coverage.

RENEWABLE TERM INSURANCE Temporary insurance which you may renew, for another limited period of time if you wish, when the original term of coverage runs out—even though you may have become "uninsurable" in the interim. However, your premium rates increase each time you renew your term insurance because you are older.

STRAIGHT LIFE (OR ORDINARY OR WHOLE LIFE) INSURANCE Insurance on which premiums are payable during your entire life.

TERM INSURANCE Relatively low-cost insurance which remains in force for a limited, specified period of time—usually five or ten years, or until you reach a certain age. Benefits are paid only if you die within this period of time. *Convertible* term insurance is guaranteed to be exchangeable for some other type of coverage, even if you, the policyholder, would not ordinarily be eligible for such coverage.

WHOLE LIFE (OR ORDINARY OR STRAIGHT) INSURANCE Insurance on which a lump-sum benefit is paid on your death. Also builds up a cash value based on premiums you have paid, and you may borrow against this amount at any time.

Premiums are payable either during your entire life (straight life) or over limited number of years (limited-payment whole life insurance).

VETERANS' PENSIONS

Another major category of retirement benefits is veterans' pensions. The conditions and amounts tend to change from year to year, as new legislation boosts and liberalizes these pensions. Pensions vary according to a veteran's income, the number of dependents he has, how severe his disability is, and his net worth.

But basically, VA pensions are reserved for veterans who are in considerable financial need, and so disabled that they are unable to pursue "substantially gainful employment." Veterans sixty-five and older are considered disabled for pension purposes.

Pension amounts are scaled according to need (as measured by the amount of other income available to the veteran). No pension benefits are payable if the veteran has sizable assets to draw on.

In the late 1970s, Congress made some major changes in the non-service-connected veterans' pension program, the first major amendments since 1959. Under a 1978 law, a single veteran was assured that his total income will be at least $3,500 a year; a married veteran can count on $4,651 per year with an additional $600 for each dependent child. Those veterans who need aid and attendance or are housebound get an additional allowance of $2,130 per year. Veterans of World War I and the Mexican Border War have another $800 added to their yearly rates—a belated acknowledgment that they never received the benefits of the GI Bill, such as educational assistance and home loan guarantees.

Under the new system, pension rates will be tied to the consumer price index and will be increased automatically as Social Security benefits are. Further, pensioners who receive Social Security benefits are protected from reductions in their VA pensions because of the cost-of-living increases in Social Security. In the past, it was possible for a veteran's Social Security benefit increase to be offset by a reduction in his veterans' pension.

VETERANS' BENEFITS

The Veterans Administration pays a dependency and indemnity compensation to widows of veterans who died while in service or from a service-connected disability, based on the husband's pay grade while he was in the service. In the late 1970s this ranged from $297 to $760 a month for a widow, with an additional $35 a month for each child under age eighteen.

If your husband died while on active duty (including training) or within 120 days after discharge and from a service-connected cause, there also is an award of a six months' death gratuity. This is a lump-sum payment of six times the veteran's monthly pay, but not more than $3,000 or less than $800, payable by his military service.

Under the law after the amendments of 1978, the surviving spouse of a veteran who died from non-service-connected causes could qualify for a Veterans Administration "death pension" in an amount sufficient to bring her (or his) income up to $2,379 per year; to $3,116 for a surviving spouse and one child; and with $600 added for each additional child. If the surviving spouse is so disabled that he or she is confined to the home, there is an extra allowance of $1,427 per year to cover needed aid and attendance.

These survivors' benefits, like veterans' pension benefits (see above), are to be increased to keep up with the cost of living.

There also is a burial expense grant of $300 for veterans whose death was not service-connected, and up to $1,100 if the death was service-connected. (See Chapter 20 "Funeral expenses—What to Do . . . How to Save . . . Where the Traps Are," for more details on veterans' death benefits.)

If the funeral director does not alert the VA insurance division of your husband's death, contact the nearest VA center.

Unremarried widows of men who served in World War II, the Korean war, or the Vietnam war and who died in service or from service-connected disabilities also may qualify for GI home loans and educational benefits. (See page 189 for more on the GI home loan program, and also pages 537–38 on financing an education.)

In addition, widows are entitled, until they remarry, to special preference when applying for civil service positions. If the widow is the mother of a veteran who lost his life or became totally disabled, she also is entitled to special preference.

For answers to other questions you may have, or assistance you may need, write, phone, or visit your nearest VA regional office.

WHAT EVERY WIDOW SHOULD KNOW

BASIC FACTS FOR WIDOWS

The thirty-nine-year-old husband of a young friend was recently killed in an automobile accident, leaving his widow with two preschool children. The husband, a dentist, had life insurance policies which paid his widow $60,000; credit life insurance which completed mortgage payments on the family's home; automobile insurance which bought a new car to replace the wreck in which the husband was killed, as well as funeral expenses. His dental practice was put on the market at $25,000.

The young widow received Social Security benefits, amounting to about $1,100 per month. She was confident she could manage on $1,450 per month. Her cash reserve of $85,000 would, therefore, be able to earn the extra $350 per month she would need and would contribute toward the education of her children.

This is not a typical set of financial circumstances for the nation's 575,000 young widowed mothers. Few young husbands have this much protection (including a salable professional practice) for their families.

Yet if you, an American wife, are typically five years younger than your husband, the chances are three out of four that you will wind up as a widow. Because females have a seven-year greater life expectancy than males, even if you are the same age as your spouse, there is a two-out-of-three chance that you will outlive your husband. And if you happen to be five years older than your husband, you have a 50 per cent chance of becoming a widow.

For your protection, you should be aware of the ways to handle the expenses that go with a final illness and funeral costs, and also with estates, wills, probates, and taxes. (See pages 984–92 on funeral expenses and how to control them, and pages 961–83 on what you should know about wills, estates, and trusts.) Equally important, you should take steps now to find out what Social Security, life insurance, and other survivor benefits your family could automatically count on and how to go about getting them. It is never too early for a wife and husband to talk about the financial resources that would be available if the breadwinner were no longer around.

HOW MUCH WOULD YOU GET?

If you are typical, chances are it wouldn't be very much. So, to make sure that you overlook nothing, run down this list of possible sources of funds for you:

Social Security

There is a tremendous general ignorance of how Social Security protects women and young people in our country.

• The maximum family Social Security benefit being paid to young widows with two children in the late 1970s was about $1,200 a month. This means that if your children are very young your family might receive an "inheritance" of benefits totaling as much as $200,000 during the entire period in which the benefits are payable.

• The full Social Security benefit is tax-free and continues to be paid until you remarry or until your children reach the age of eighteen unless a disabled child remains in your care, in which case your benefits may continue.

• If and when you remarry, your benefits ordinarily stop—but the children's benefits will continue to be paid and these benefits may amount to more than one half of the total.

• The total benefit begins to be reduced as each child reaches the age of eighteen (unless the child is disabled and has been before the age of twenty-two). After all children have reached this age, both widow's and children's benefits cease, unless there is a disabled child in the mother's care, in which case benefits for both may continue. However, if the children are full-time students, the children's benefits continue until they reach the age of twenty-two.

• Social Security also pays a lump-sum death benefit of $255 to all widows covered by the system who were living in the same household with the worker at the time of his death.

• For other categories of benefits that may apply to you or the children, see earlier in this chapter or contact the nearest social security office.

• Caution: all Social Security benefits must be applied for—none is automatic. And delay in applying can cause the loss of some benefits. To save valuable time, contact the nearest Social Security office as soon as possible after the death of your husband. Take with you:

(1) A certified copy of the death certificate.

(2) Your husband's Social Security number.

(3) A record of his approximate earnings in the year previous to his death and his employer's name (the W-2 form that accompanies the U.S. income tax form should suffice).

(4) Your marriage certificate.

(5) Your Social Security numbers and those of your dependent children.

(6) Proof of your age and the ages of any dependent children under age twenty-three.

Civil Service and Railroad Workers' Benefits

You also may be eligible for a survivor annuity benefit under the civil service retirement system if you are a widow or widower of a person who completed at least eighteen months of civilian service and, at the time of death:

the deceased held a position covered by the retirement system;
or
had accepted a reduced annuity with survivor benefits to his or her spouse.

If you are a widow or disabled dependent widower of a person covered by the civil service retirement system, you must have been married to this person at least two years before his or her death or be the parent of a child born of the marriage.

As a general rule, the amount of your widow's or widower's annuity is based on the number of years your spouse worked and on the salary your spouse earned during this period. Your annuity ceases if you remarry before age sixty.

Any unmarried children of your deceased spouse who are under age eighteen (or under age twenty-two if they are full-time students) or who are incapable of supporting themselves because of a disability which began before age eighteen also are entitled to annuities.

If you are the widow or widower of a person who worked for the nation's railroads for fewer than ten years, the railroad retirement credits earned by your spouse will be transferred to and counted toward your survivors' benefits under the Social Security program.

If your spouse had more than ten years of railroad employment, his railroad retirement credits will be combined with his Social Security credits (if any) and counted toward survivors' benefits under either the Social Security program or the railroad retirement program, depending on whether he had a "current connection" with the railroad industry when he died.

For further details on railroad retirement benefits, contact your nearest Social Security office or your nearest Railroad Retirement office.

Other Employee Benefits

If your husband worked for a private company or had his own business, he probably had group life insurance and perhaps was covered by a profit-sharing or pension plan. Most likely your husband's employer will notify you about benefits to which you are entitled. If not, contact the employer.

Be sure to check out: any accrued vacation and sick pay; terminal pay allowances; unpaid commissions; service recognition awards; disability income; credit union balance; and anything else that also may be due your husband. At the same time, ask whether you and the children are still eligible for benefits under your husband's hospital, surgical, and disability coverage and, if so, for how long.

Life Insurance

Your husband's insurance agent or company will tell you what information you have to supply with your claim. If your husband did not already decide on whether you were to get a lump-sum settlement or monthly income payments and if you have no immediate need for all of the cash you would get in a lump-sum payment, you have a number of settlement options. Generally, your options fall into these categories:

You may leave all of the money with the company and draw interest on it, with a provision that gives you the right to withdraw as much as you want at any time.

Or you may arrange to receive fixed installments on set dates over your lifetime or over an agreed-on period of time. Your insurance agent can discuss the pros and cons of these possibilities with you.

Finally, make sure to apply for any Medicare benefits due your husband—hospital or doctor bills he may have incurred and paid directly before he died but for which he did not apply for Medicare reimbursement.

A useful forty-page guide for widows and those who may be called to help widows in their financial affairs—covering everything from contacting the funeral director to life insurance, estate taxes, and probate matters—is *What Does She Do Now?* put out by the Life Insurance Management Research Association. If your insurance agent cannot give you a copy, write the Association directly at 170 Sigourney Street, Hartford, Connecticut 06105.

BEWARE: GYPS AIMED AT THE ELDERLY

Would you believe that a special tablet could be "effective for the treatment of run-down and weak conditions . . . loss of enjoyment of life . . . inability to be the man or woman formerly possible" as well as make it easier for you to endure noisy children, coated tongue, and gas?

Would you lay out money to buy mail order "electronic pulsators," "special stimulants," "geriatric elixirs," or any other chemical or mechanical product advertised as capable of restoring "lost vigor," reviving sexual activity, or even rebuilding sex organs?

I hope you wouldn't. As the late Dr. Alfred Kinsey put it: "Good health, sufficient exercise and plenty of sleep still remain the most effective aphrodisiacs known to man."

But as an elderly American, you are now the major target of an endless variety of fountain-of-youth promoters in this country. You also are the target of an endless variety of other types of gypsters attempting to bilk you out of your limited retirement income.

For tips on how to recognize health quackery, see Chapter 8, on the high cost of good health.

Even if you are not yet retired, you probably have elderly friends or relatives.

Surely you want to help them avoid the gyps which could seriously deplete their modest savings or slash their monthly benefit checks.

Here is a sampling of other widespread gyps and exaggerations aimed at our elderly population:

• In the dance studio racket, con men seduce lonely, elderly women into buying oversize packages of dancing lessons, payable in advance. In some cases, confused elderly widows agree to buy "lifetime memberships" in a dance studio, at a cost of thousands, even tens of thousands, of dollars.

• In the "vitamins forever" scheme, mail order houses of questionable reputation persuade the elderly to buy "subscriptions" to geriatric preparations but refuse to act on instructions to stop the cascade of pills.

• In another gyp, a phony "Social Security representative" offers to take over your benefit check and in return to prepare your taxes, pay your bills, etc. All too often, though, those offering such services take an unconscionable cut of cash for themselves—or even accept money for payment of income taxes but never file a return.

• In the sphere of often essential physical supports, hearing aids, eyeglasses, and dentures are advertised and sold through the mails to the elderly, without benefit of doctor's prescriptions or other data necessary for proper purchases. Or these vital aids are peddled by utterly unqualified, unlicensed promoters.

• In the world of finance, there always are the stock racketeers, who frequently are able to high-pressure older people into buying worthless securities just because the elderly are so pressed for money and eager to make an extra dollar.

CAN YOU FIND THE FOUNTAIN OF YOUTH?

One day fairly soon the intensive research now going on in the field of aging will make it possible for you to feel and look "young" into your oldest years. Imaginative experiments in the field of genetics are at last promising exhilarating answers to some of the most depressing—and unaesthetic—problems of old age.

When that day comes, the cures for face wrinkles and crow's-feet in women, for baldness and other embarrassing failings in men, will cease to be "secrets" and "miracles." Then the cures will be promoted and sold on the basis of their own proven worth. There will be no reason for phony testimonials and faked photographs. Then the real cures will cost only a fraction of what the worthless or near worthless treatments cost today.

It will come. And I hope it will come in time to matter to me. In the meantime, though, I (along with American women from coast to coast) will spend an all-time high total of tens of millions of dollars for a fabulous array of cosmetic gadgets, creams, and secret "methods" to turn back the clock. Simultaneously, it's quite possible that you, along with American men from coast to coast, also will spend record amounts for cures, rejuvenators, and other gimmicks to "slow" the aging process.

And we will spend these fortunes despite this brutally cold observation recently by a respected dermatologist at the University of Southern California in Los Angeles:

"With time and exposure to light, the skin loses its tensile strength—like an old worn girdle. No amount of massage has ever been shown to restore an old girdle."

Here, therefore, are warnings and guidelines to help you not waste money in two important areas of aging today: face wrinkles and balding.

• None of the facial creams, hormone creams, or so-called rejuvenating creams being sold today has been proven capable of safely preventing or removing wrinkles. This is because wrinkles are the result of permanent changes in and under the skin.

• Facial massage can temporarily improve circulation of blood to the skin but it cannot remove wrinkles.

• Facial saunas also may temporarily improve skin appearance by promoting hydration. But so will applying hot towels or coating your face with oily cream.

• Exotic-sounding face cream ingredients may slow evaporation of water from the skin and thereby temporarily improve its appearance too—but they cannot remove wrinkles either.

• Chemosurgery—or face peeling—can, though, in a limited number of cases, bring about a real improvement in the appearance of aging skin. But the treatment can be exceedingly dangerous. Like plastic surgery (which can successfully remove wrinkles), it should be attempted only by qualified physicians—not unqualified "wrinkle farms."

• On balding, the key fact is that 95 per cent of male baldness is of the "male pattern baldness" type, for which there is no known massage or special preparation cure. However, at least one effective, if tedious and costly, treatment has emerged for this type of baldness: hair transplants performed by dermatologists specializing in this field. In the other 5 per cent of baldness cases (called alopecia areata) regrowth occurs by itself in almost all instances. The "before" and "after" pictures promoting baldness cures, incidentally, are often of this type of baldness.

WARNINGS ON BUYING A RETIREMENT HOMESITE

Thousands of Americans have been lured by newspaper and magazine ads to invest now in a retirement homesite in California, Florida, Texas, New Mexico, Arizona, Nevada. Thousands are being invited and flown to retirement home developments by the developers, put up in motels for a weekend, wined and dined, bused around the developed parts of the development, shown "then and now" movies of the area to prove how rapidly it is growing, and subjected to a grueling hard sell.

Thousands have been persuaded to pay anywhere from $2,000 to $5,000 for a fraction of an acre, very often on or at the edge of the desert, at enticingly low monthly terms. I have no argument with your paying $2,000 or $3,000 or whatever for a homesite in surroundings which are likely to enrich your later years. I will even salute the farsightedness of the land tycoons who bought up huge tracts of land fifteen or twenty years ago for $50 an acre and who now can sell it for $8,000 to $10,000 or more an acre. I will argue, though, with touting these tiny parcels as great "investments."

There are millions of land parcels on the market today, so scarcity certainly won't be a factor driving up prices in the foreseeable future. In many cases all of the "investment" value—and then some—is being reaped by the developers. Whenever credit gets tight, many real estate development operations are forced to a halt, and then it's anybody's guess when the promised improvements will be completed.

Moreover, because of high-pressure sales techniques, a lot of people buy land they can't really afford. Included in the price are the promoters' high costs of advertising, bringing buyers in for the weekend, etc.

If you—or a friend or relative—are in the market for a piece of ground on which to build a retirement home, here are important rules to follow:

(1) Ask the Better Business Bureau in the area in which you are considering buying for a report on the promoter. Also ask for material to help you determine whether the price being asked is fair in comparison with the deals others are offering.

(2) Be sure the land seller gives you a "property report," not unlike a stock prospectus. The Interstate Land Sales Full Disclosure Act of 1968 requires anyone who is selling or leasing fifty or more unimproved lots smaller than five acres in interstate commerce (e.g., through the mails or advertised in nationally circulated magazines or newspapers) to furnish each customer with a statement giving "all material facts" about the land, including (but not limited to) the following:

- Name and location of developer and development.
- Date of property report.
- The distance to nearby communities over paved or unpaved roads.
- Taxes and special assessments you must pay.
- Existence of liens on the land.
- Whether the payments you make will be placed in escrow until you get clear title to the land.
- Existing and planned utilities and services, and their costs.
- The number of homes occupied at the time of the statement.
- Details of any obstacles to building on the land.
- The type of title you will ultimately get.

The development must file a similar statement with the Office of Interstate Land Sales Registration, an agency of Housing and Urban Development in Washington which can help you get your money back if any part of the property report proves to be fiction.

You, the buyer, have a "cooling off" period after signing the contract to change your mind about buying. The law permits you to waive this right if you personally inspected the property, so read the contract carefully to be sure you do not do so unintentionally. If you discover the facts have been misrepresented, you may sue for damages in a federal court. HUD can halt sales of land if it finds a property statement misleading, and if the courts find a promoter guilty of fraud, the penalty can be stiff.

If a developer who is covered by this act fails to give you the legally required property report, be on guard.

(3) In addition to getting this property report, find out if the state in which you are considering buying can give you the property report it requires developers to file covering subdivisions or land sold by mail. California and Florida

are two such states. A responsible developer will be willing to provide a report even if not required to by state or federal law.

(4) Find out how near or far the land is from roads, public transportation, churches, hospitals, refuse removal services, etc. If these are merely promised by the developer, make sure they are described in the sales contract.

(5) Before you sign any contract, have a lawyer or the local legal aid society go over it carefully.

(6) Inspect any retirement homesite personally—perhaps by combining this tour with a vacation—since you may spend ten, twenty, or thirty years of your life there.

(7) Most important, ask yourself these questions:

How do you envision your retirement home—surrounded by wide-open space and plenty of quiet and privacy, or in the middle of a busy community, surrounded by a lot of nearby neighbors?

How are you likely to spend your time? Hiking and fishing? Traveling frequently to other places? Attending theater, concerts, other cultural events?

How near do you want to be to old friends, children, and grandchildren in your retirement years?

A sunny climate, a big sky, and a patch of ground are not enough to make a happy retirement. (See Chapter 26, "Your Most Simple Guide to Buying Land.")

19

YOUR BASIC GUIDE TO WILLS, ESTATES, AND TRUSTS

Your Will

This chapter on wills is not intended to educate you in how to prepare your own will. Many of the general statements herein will vary in applicability from state to state. It is suggested that you consult a lawyer in your own state before drawing a will.

Who Should Have a Will?

To the threshold question of whether or not to have a will, the blunt answer is that next to your birth certificate and marriage license your will may be the most important document of your life. Yet an estimated seven out of ten in the United States die without leaving wills! About the only reason you should not have a will is if you are satisfied to die intestate (without a will) and have your estate divided and administered according to the state laws relating to intestacy. As an intestate:

• You would not have an executor chosen by you.

• The person who administers your estate would be determined by the law of your state. In many states your surviving spouse would have priority as an administrator over your children. That may be fine if your surviving spouse is the parent of your children. But suppose that your spouse is a step-parent who does not see eye to eye with your children by a former marriage. Even worse, suppose that in addition to your children by a former marriage you are also survived by children with your present spouse. These children would be favored by your spouse. Do you intend to treat your surviving children equally or do you want to perpetuate a family feud that will rage for years?

• And say you are survived by children, but not by a spouse. In most states the law says that each child has an equal right to administer your estate. That has divided an almost incredible number of families! The survivors draw up sides and fight bitterly and relentlessly to control the administration. This situation also applies when there is no surviving spouse or children but there are other family survivors entitled to administration.

• What happens if there is no one who is entitled by law to administration? The public administrator is then pressed into service. He is an absolute stranger to you and will administer your estate according to law but impersonally and with as much interest in your treasures as an indifferent salesman selling a pair of hideous shoes.

You are the master of your property and can dispose of it (with certain restrictions in the event of a surviving spouse or the amount that you can leave to charities) by will to anyone and in such amounts as you desire. You can reward those you love and eliminate the unfaithful. You can provide for friends or charities. However, if you die intestate, state law will decide the shares of your survivors. There can be no gifts to friends or charities, and if the law says that there are no surviving relatives close enough in kinship to inherit, the state will take all.

The tax consequences of dying without a will can be horrendous. For instance, your estate is entitled to a federal marital deduction on account of property left to a surviving spouse—which may require careful and expert estate planning.

Do you take full advantage of the marital deduction and increase your surviving spouse's potential taxable estate?

Do you provide income to your spouse for life, but with no option to dispose of the assets producing this income, and full tax? In this case the principal could go to your children without further taxes that might otherwise be required of your spouse's estate.

Do you sharpen a pencil and figure out your best options in dollars and cents? Not one of these options is available to you if you die intestate.

If you die survived by minor children and no spouse, do you want to designate their guardian? Or do you want your estate to pay for a bond for a court-appointed guardian or administrator and their attendant fees?

If you are the proprietor of a business, do you want it continued or liquidated? Are you concerned by the type of investment that your administrator will make according to law or do you want to leave some specific instructions? Do you have items of extreme sentimental value that you want to leave to particular friends or relatives and not sold to strangers? Can your family afford to have your assets tied up while the court appoints your administrator?

If none of the above matters is of any concern to you, then by all means die intestate.

ESTATE TAXES

Estate taxes combine both the certainties of death and taxes. The taxes are assessed by the federal *and* state governments on the value of property you leave behind—but the estate tax laws of states differ widely, and generally impose much smaller taxes than the federal estate tax laws. (The federal law also gives a certain amount of credit for estate taxes paid to states.)

In view of the great variation in state tax amounts, exemptions, and other circumstances, assume that such taxes exist and now concentrate on the federal tax aspects.

A fundamental warning on federal estate taxes. Forget any ideas you might have conceived prior to 1977! The Tax Reform Act of 1976 has made much traditional tax-thinking obsolete.

The starting point for the present estate tax calculation is your "gross estate," which is simply the fair market value of all property you own. Against this you are allowed certain deductions for funeral expenses, debts, and administration expenses to arrive at your "adjusted gross estate." Beginning with January 1, 1977, a "marital deduction" is then allowed for the value of your property which passes to your surviving spouse to the extent of $250,000 or 50 per cent of your adjusted gross estate, whichever is greater. A further deduction is allowed for bequests to charities. The remaining amount of your gross estate less these deductions is your "taxable estate" upon which a tentative tax is calculated at rates progressing from 18 to 70 per cent.

Against this tentative tax the estate is allowed a "unified" credit of $38,000 for decedents dying in 1979; $42,500 for decedents dying in 1980; and $47,000 for decedents dying after 1980. Finally, a limited credit for state death taxes is allowed to arrive at the federal estate tax amount.

The following illustration of the estate tax calculation assumes that the decedent died after 1980 owning property worth $470,000 all of which is left by will to the spouse.

GROSS ESTATE	$470,000
Less: Debts, funeral, and administrative costs (estimated)	—40,000
ADJUSTED GROSS ESTATE:	430,000
Less: Marital deduction (50% of adjusted gross estate is $215,000 which is less than $250,000)	—250,000
TAXABLE ESTATE	$180,000
TENTATIVE TAX ON TAXABLE ESTATE	$ 48,400
Less: Unified credit— post 1980	—47,000
Less: State death tax credit	— 880
FEDERAL ESTATE TAX	$ 520*

If the decedent in the above example has no surviving spouse, or children under twenty-one years of age, the federal estate tax would be $77,240, for the marital deduction would not be available. The following table shows approximate

* This amount will be somewhat larger if death occurred prior to January 1, 1981.

estate taxes for different-sized estates with and without the marital deduction for decedents dying after 1980 (earlier years' taxes are somewhat greater due to the escalating size of the unified credit):

SIZE OF ADJUSTED GROSS ESTATE	FULL MARITAL DEDUCTION	NO MARITAL DEDUCTION
$ 180,000	$ 0	$ 520
430,000	520	77,240
1,000,000	98,000	265,600

Once over the taxable threshold, estate taxes can be high indeed!

YOU NEED PROFESSIONAL HELP

If you do not now have a will or if your will was drawn prior to 1977 you need professional help, which means the help of a highly qualified lawyer. The law requires certain formalities in the execution of a will. If these formalities are ignored, even the most simple will may be void.

But say that you know the formalities. You have $350,000 of assets in your own name and your spouse has $350,000. You know that your spouse will take care of the children so you intend to leave $350,000 to your spouse and eliminate your children. You know that there is a marital deduction of $250,000 and the unified tax credit will take care of the balance. So you spend 25 cents for a form at the local stationery store, and with your knowledge of the formalities you draw a legal will in favor of your surviving spouse.

No taxes! No legal fees! Everything is quite simple!

Right?

Wrong!

You have now increased your spouse's potential taxable estate from $350,000 to $700,000 and your spouse will not have any marital deduction available. With competent advice, you would have arranged a trust with income to your spouse for life and payment of the principal to the children upon death of your spouse. A tax savings of about $60,000 would have been the result.

Or suppose you have assets of $250,000 and your wife has assets of $100,000. You decide to take advantage of the full marital deduction of $250,000 and leave your wife everything. You have managed to die without owing the federal government one dollar in estate taxes. However, your wife now has a gross estate of $350,000 on which her estate taxes, less the unified credit (after 1980), will approximate $52,000.

This tax on the wife's estate could have been avoided if you had used your full unified tax credit and by creating a trust with income to your wife for life and with principal payable on her death to your children in the amount of $175,000 and bequeathed to her the sum of $75,000 for which you would get a marital deduction. Again you have managed to die without owing the federal government one dollar in estate taxes. Your wife still has the income from $350,000 but she has a taxable estate of only $175,000. Applying the unified credit to her tentative tax the net is a zero tax liability for her estate as well as for your estate. Your tax savings would have come to $52,000.

Even if your spouse owns little or no individual property, you still can achieve substantial tax savings with proper planning.

How much does your lawyer charge for drawing a will with its associated planning? That will depend to a great extent upon the lawyer's standing in his profession, whether your will is complicated or simple, and the place of execution. The lawyer's overhead in New York City, for instance, is a lot higher than in a small town in Idaho.

Talk to your lawyer about the fee. Compared to the need for a proper will, the cost is relatively low. A simple will probably runs between $50 and $150. A complicated will with trust provisions will cost more.

You can save time if you will prepare and take to your lawyer a valuation of your assets and liabilities. Your assets should include real estate, cash in banks, stocks and bonds, life insurance, interest in a business, antiques and works of art, motor vehicles, pension or profit-sharing benefits and other assets over which you have the power of disposition. You should make it clear whether your assets are owned alone or jointly. And you also should provide the names, addresses, and ages of your relatives and beneficiaries.

You can change your will as often as you desire. But you cannot do this by drawing lines through sentences or by adding new provisions.

A change can only be effected by a new will or a codicil. You can destroy your will and die intestate but the destruction must be intentional and you should leave evidence of such intent. How can anyone ask you after you die whether the destruction was intended?

ASSETS WHICH CANNOT BE WILLED

You may find it strange, but there are certain assets that you own which you cannot dispose of by will.

Your insurance policies are usually payable to named beneficiary. However, the proceeds of those policies are added to your gross estate for tax purposes unless you do not "own" the policies. You generally own an insurance policy when you can change the beneficiary designation. You probably have named your spouse or children as beneficiaries of your policies and will save money on executor's commissions because the proceeds do not pass by your will. Again it is time to sharpen your pencil. Is your estate liquid? Will a forced sale of your assets to pay taxes, funeral expenses, debts, and administration expenses result in a loss? If immediate cash is required, it may be necessary to have some of your insurance payable to your estate. Any excess funds not essential for the above purposes will go to the beneficiaries named in your will.

Jointly owned property passes outside the will. This most commonly occurs with bank accounts and real estate. A familiar example of joint ownership occurs when a husband and a wife own their home, and the survivor takes title upon the death of the other. Part or all of such property may be added to the gross estate for tax purposes but no executor's commissions are payable on joint properties as they pass outside the will. The taxation of joint property is too complicated for this short treatment of the subject; discuss this in detail with your lawyer.

If your pension benefits are continued in some form after your death, you probably have named a beneficiary. Again this is an asset that passes outside your will. Whether or not the pension benefits are taxable depends on many complex factors. Likewise, if you have purchased U.S. savings bonds you have named a beneficiary and cannot dispose of them by your will.

You cannot dispose of property which you expect to inherit but which you did not in fact receive before your death. However, if your benefactor already has died and you are entitled to the property after an event such as the death of a prior life tenant your interest is deemed "vested" and you may dispose of it by will.

THE INGREDIENTS OF YOUR WILL

What kind of instructions and information should your will contain? There are certain standard ingredients which turn up in most wills.

(1) Your will must have been written clearly enough to permit a court to determine your real intent. There is a story—perhaps apocryphal—of the man who left his favorite niece an annual income in his will for "as long as she remains above the ground." When she died, her husband simply installed her in a mausoleum above ground and collected the money for the rest of his life.

(2) The opening paragraph of your will should identify you, the "testator," by name, give your place of residence, and state that you are knowingly making your will. Generally included in this opening statement is a clause that makes it clear that you are revoking any previous wills or codicils (additions or "amendments" to your will) you may have made. When you make a will, it ordinarily remains valid unless and until you revoke it.

(3) Next you generally would write a statement that directs the prompt payment of your burial expenses and all your just debts, taxes, and costs of administration. These are the first claims against your estate. Unless you specify otherwise, all the assets in your estate are regarded as a single pool of money from which these first-claim expenses are to be paid, and your executor must charge each beneficiary with a proportionate share of the cost.

(4) Then comes the core of your will—the provision for the distribution of your assets. A typical division is one half to your wife and one half to your children. Typically, you list first all the specific and general bequests, including charitable gifts you want to make. You may, for instance, want to leave a relative or friend a particular heirloom or some other part of your personal property, say one hundred shares of stock. This is known as a specific legacy. A general legacy is a bequest that does not designate the particular fund out of which it is to be paid. An example would be leaving, say, $1,000 to a housekeeper or someone else who has been of particular service to you. As a rule, general and specific legacies must be paid before residual legacies. What remains in your estate after all specific gifts of money or property have been made under your will is called your "residual estate." This usually is given to your principal heir. You must be

careful to limit your general and specific legacies because leaving too much in this fashion may not allow enough for your residual legates—the real objects of your bounty. In establishing the size of specific legacies, also keep in mind that if you suffer financial reverses and neglect to change your will, your residuary estate may be smaller than you intended.

Other major parts of your will include:

• *The name of one or more executors of your estate*—who will manage and settle your estate according to your instructions.

• *Provisions for some type of trust for your wife, children, or others*—if you feel such protection is necessary to keep your estate from being frittered away by financially inexperienced or irresponsible heirs. Trusts also can save on taxes. Because trusts are subject to many laws governing their organization and administration, though, they should not be set up without legal help!

• *The name of a trustee, if your will provides for a trust,* to manage and invest your trust assets for its beneficiaries.

• *The name of a guardian for your minor children*—to take care of them and their property. If you are survived by a spouse who is the natural parent, your appointment will ordinarily be ineffective. You should consider an appointment if your spouse has predeceased you or if you are concerned about the possibility that both of you may die in the same accident. You also may provide that your appointive guardian does not have to file a bond which is otherwise required in some states, and save the costs of such a bond.

• Burial arrangements—to spare your bereaved family the effort and complications of haggling over burial costs and decisions as to what type of funeral you'll have (if any). The more specific you are in stating your funeral preferences, the less burdened will be your family with the cost of such lavish, utterly unnecessary trappings as coffins fitted with innerspring mattresses. Ponder—in advance—that a funeral director is in the most advantageous position of dealing with survivors who are under great emotional stress and he also is well aware that the estate of a deceased is responsible for paying burial costs even before it pays taxes.

• Specific instructions—to guide your executors and trustees according to your wishes. You may want them to retain certain investments, to carry on your business or to liquidate it. If you are silent, they will be governed by the powers and duties laid down by statute or recognized by the courts. Such rules may not allow your executor or trustee the flexibility in handling your property that you may wish.

• Witnesses—at the end of your will is a section containing your signature, the date of your signature, followed by an "attestation clause." This clause contains the signatures and addresses of your witnesses and a statement properly certifying that they saw you sign the will. The witnesses must sign in your presence and also in the presence of each other.

Most states require two witnesses, but some require three. Even if you live in a state which requires only two witnesses, it is better to have three anyway. This will make it easier to probate your will after your death in the event, say, that you own real estate in another state which requires three witnesses to a will. A beneficiary of your will should never be a witness.

In fact, if you do make the mistake of having a beneficiary as witness, it could result in this person being partially or *totally* disinherited!

A common procedure for getting a will witnessed is simply to call in any two people who happen to be around your house when you sign your will and ask them to serve as witnesses. This is not the best practice. Your executor may not be able to locate these witnesses when the time comes to offer your will for probate. If your lawyer presides at the execution of your will, he will provide witnesses from among his associates or staff who can be reasonably easy to locate when your will is probated.

SIMULTANEOUS DEATHS

One of the most difficult problems confronting the courts is to determine the order of death of two persons involved in a common disaster. Many people believe that survivorship where no other proof exists is based upon sex, age, physical condition, and strength of the parties. That was true under the old civil law but no longer applies in most jurisdictions and in those jurisdictions survivorship must be affirmatively proved. In those states there is no presumption of survivorship. Length of time of survivorship is unimportant; one breath by the survivor is all that need be proved. Think of a shipwreck or death by carbon monoxide in a closed garage and you can see the difficulty of proof.

Assume that you and your spouse each have $150,000 in each of your names. You have made mutual wills in favor of the other which both provide that if there is no surviving spouse, your children get everything regardless of which spouse is deemed to have lived even one breath longer than the other.

But how about the IRS? If the IRS agent can show that one spouse lived one second longer than the other spouse, the temporary survivor will have a $300,000 estate with no marital deduction available. Estate taxes will be payable.

The IRS would get nothing, however, if neither spouse was deemed to have survived the other. Both estates would be $150,000 and not taxable. If, instead of children in the above example, each spouse's will made his or her brother the alternate beneficiary, one side of the family would get $300,000 and the other side nothing depending on the exact sequence of death.

To deal with such contingencies, most states have adopted a statute known as the "Uniform Simultaneous Death Act" which provides that where the devolution of property depends upon priority of death and there is not sufficient evidence that the persons have died other than simultaneously, the property of each person shall (except as otherwise provided) be disposed of as it would have been if that person had survived.

Even the Uniform Simultaneous Death Act may not cover all aspects of this question. One simple well-drawn paragraph by your lawyer will take the guesswork out of survivorship.

YOUR EXECUTOR OR TRUSTEE

Whom should you choose as your fiduciaries?

This is a vitally important decision. You can select your surviving spouse or a close friend who might waive executor's commissions otherwise allowed by law.

But is he or she truly informed about taxes, filings, investments, gathering assets, appraisals, payment of debts, accounting, tax audits, and many other functions?

An unsophisticated executor will, it is hoped, know enough to work closely with the estate lawyer, but there still may be pitfalls. Saving commissions with an inexperienced executor may turn out to be your greatest extravagance. You have too much to lose if he or she lacks knowledge and experience.

If you have a simple estate such as a home, cash in the bank, insurance, and a few securities, there should be little problem. A member of the family or friend can probably manage, with the aid of your attorney, without trouble.

If your estate is complicated or if you are going to establish trusts, you will need a professional. Your lawyer and your bank are ready to serve in that capacity. You can add a family member or friend as co-executor or co-trustee if that will make you more content but this may increase the commissions, too. A trust beneficiary probably should not be named as a trustee unless there is a co-trustee.

Executor's and trustee's commissions are fixed by statute or determined by the courts and are based on the size or complexity of the estate or trust. If you have two fiduciaries, the fees usually are doubled and in some states if you have three or more fiduciaries they will split three commissions.

If you choose a bank as your fiduciary, talk to the bank's representative first. Many banks will not accept the appointment if the estate is too small. If they do accept a small estate, many banks require a guarantee of a minimum commission.

PROBATE

The submission of your will in the proper court with proof of due execution and its acceptance by the court is known as probate. Probate may be challenged by persons who would benefit if a prior will was probated or under the distribution rules of intestacy if your will was proved invalid. This procedure is known as a will contest. Once your will is probated your named fiduciaries have legal power to act.

HOW ABOUT DO-IT-YOURSELF WILLS?

A young friend who was flying around the tumultuous Middle East hastily wrote to her older sister as she departed: "If the Arabs blow up the plane, then I leave everything to be equally distributed between you two (her sister and her younger brother). This includes my checking and savings accounts, my share in our property, whatever stocks are in the Merrill Lynch account, etc. Love, Mary." Hers is a do-it-yourself "will" at its utmost in simplicity—and illegality.

The probable outcome if Mary's plane did blow up: a large portion of her estate would be left to her husband (from whom she is separated but not divorced) and/or her father (who has no need whatsoever for Mary's financial assets).

You surely have seen simple do-it-yourself forms for filling out wills: they are advertised for a dollar or two. You've probably also heard of people who have handwritten their own wills and had these accepted by a court—even without having been witnessed.

But! Do it yourself at your own risk! If you make mistakes, they may be discovered when it's too late for anyone to fix them.

Responsible lawyers rarely use standard forms for a will. Objective sources also urge you to avoid them because the forms will channel your thinking in advance and, as a result, you may overlook vital aspects of your affairs.

Of course, laymen have written wills and there are some jurisdictions that will recognize a will in your own handwriting, with no witnesses. For soldiers or sailors in active service or mariners at sea, an oral will may be accepted if it is made within hearing of two witnesses. These wills, though, will be good only for a short time after discharge. And barring the most extreme circumstances, to handwrite or speak a will is most dangerous if only because whoever has to read the will eventually may not be able to decipher the writing, or the witnesses to an oral will may not remember accurately what was said.

You may be inclined to ridicule some of the legal formalities on which lawyers insist (for instance, fastening the pages with grommets so none can be detached or replaced, initialing each page and any correction, the ceremony with witnesses, etc.). But, says the Research Institute of America, consider the consequences of omitting some of these formalities:

• Where a handwritten will is allowed, no typewritten, printed, or stamped material can appear on the paper.

• A whole will can be voided by a page missing, replaced, or out of place.

• A change, addition, or deletion, not shown to have been made before you signed your will (as could be shown by initialing), may void a provision or the entire will.

• Any doubts about the witnesses having seen the testator or each other sign may be resolved by evidence that the same pen was used for the signatures.

• A will may become entirely void if any writing that disposes of property is placed after the signature. In any case, the added provision has no effect.

• You cannot void a will by writing "This will is void" at the end and signing your name. You must cancel with the same formality that you write the will—or destroy the documents entirely.

SHOULD A WIFE HAVE A WILL?

Definitely! Even if the wife owns absolutely no property of her own, she probably will inherit a portion of her husband's at his death and must have a will of her own for the redistribution of that property.

Too many families figure that, since most wives outlive their husbands, they will have plenty of time to make a will after their husbands die. But many men beat the statistical probabilities and, if the non-working wife of one of these men dies without leaving a will, the laws of intestacy can work just as much to the disadvantage of the children as if the family breadwinner had died without a will.

Another reason a wife should have a will is that she can name the guardian and/or trustee who will care for minor children and/or family property if both parents die at the same time. And this, in turn, can avoid bitter custody battles among relatives that almost always hurt the children both emotionally and financially.

Many married women fail to make a will because they feel that their property is "just not worth" the trouble of drawing a will—despite the fact that their belongings may include valuable jewelry, furs, paintings, and heirlooms, as well as insurance policies, stocks, bonds, and real estate held in their names.

Let me make the point unmistakably clear:

Every married woman should view her own will as equal in importance to her husband's. Then, to make sure benefits end up where both the wife and husband want them to end, the wife should have their lawyer prepare a will for her that does not conflict with the provisions of her husband's will.

Where Should You Keep Your Will?

Your will should be kept where it can be found immediately and easily by your executor when it is needed; it should not be kept where it can be stolen, forgotten, mislaid, or lost.

You certainly do not want it in a place where a disgruntled distributee can lay hands on it and destroy it.

Usually it is not wise to keep your will in your own safe deposit box because, on death, this box may be sealed—and sealed even though you hold the box jointly with another person. In this case, your executor would have to go to the court for permission to open the safe deposit box to find your will—an unnecessary annoyance at a terribly trying time. This is not true in all states. In some states the bank is authorized to open a safe deposit box and remove the will.

Keep your will in your attorney's safe.

Or if your executor is a bank or trust company, give it to your executor for safekeeping.

Have a copy in a safe place in your home and let your key beneficiaries know where it is. In some states you may file your will with the probate court and it will be sealed until your death. Due to administrative considerations this really is not good practice unless there are special reasons for filing.

Check List for Your Personal Affairs

You already have read that you should give your lawyer a list of your assets and liabilities to guide him in your estate planning. In addition, prepare a personal affairs check list which will assist your executor and attorney in handling your estate and inform them about where it is at all times. On this check list:

• List the names, addresses, dates and places of birth of yourself, your wife or husband, your children, your father and mother, your brothers and sisters.

• Write on separate lines and in clear detail:

• Your Social Security number and where your card is located.

• The location of your birth certificate and, if you have one, veteran's discharge certificate.

• If you have more than one residence, the address of each residence, the time you spend in each, where you vote, and where you pay income taxes.

• The date and place of your marriage and where your marriage certificate can be found.

• If you have been married previously, your deceased or former wife's or husband's name.

• If you are divorced, the place of the divorce, whether it was contested, who brought the action, where your divorce papers are. This will help your lawyer determine whether your former spouse has any inheritance rights remaining. If separated by agreement or court action, all the details and the place where your separation agreement can be found.

• Where a copy of any prenuptial agreement into which you entered can be found.

• Whether any of your immediate relatives are handicapped or incompetent.

• Other family information, such as the state of health of its members, whether you have any adopted children, marital problems, family feuds; "difficult" family members, if any.

• The names and addresses of others you intend to make your beneficiaries.

• If you are the beneficiary under a trust or have created a trust, where your lawyer can obtain a copy of the document.

• If you have the right to exercise a power of appointment under someone's will or under a trust, also where this document can be found.

A statement of your approximate income and general standard of living for the past several years.

• The name and address of your accountant if you have one.

• The place where copies of your income and gift tax returns may be found and the name and address of the person who prepared them.

• Name and address of your employer.

• Details of any employment contract or stock purchase plan in which you are enrolled.

• Whether you are entitled to a pension, profit-sharing benefit, stock options, or any other employment benefits. Give the name of the person who handles your company's fringe benefits plus information on how the benefits are payable on your death.

• Any union or unions to which you belong and appropriate details.

• Life insurance policies owned by you on your life; policies owned by others on your life (stating who pays the premiums on them); and policies owned by you on the lives of others. Also list annuity policies owned by you Include the name and address of each issuing company, name and address of your insurance agent, policy numbers, principal amount of each policy, the beneficiaries, and whether there are any outstanding loans against any of the policies.

• An itemization of all your real estate. Give the location of each property, its approximate value, the price you paid for it, any mortgages on the property and whether you own the property by yourself or jointly with others. Give the location of deeds to any property you own.

• The location and total of stocks, bonds, and other securities you may own, the name and address of your broker or brokers.

• A complete rundown of all your other assets, the approximate value of each, its cost basis, and location of each. This would include bank accounts, any business ownership, as well as your more valuable personal effects, such as jewelry, furs, art objects, and the like. (Don't overlook details of debts due to you).

• The location of your safe deposit box and the box key.

• A complete outline of your debts, including mortgages on your house or business, leases, and other obligations. Give the names and addresses of persons to whom you are indebted and the terms under which you are supposed to repay.

• The names and addresses of whomever you wish to name as your executors, trustees, and guardians.

• The name of your lawyer, his address, telephone number, and a list of your papers in his safekeeping.

• The name and address of any person to whom you have given power of attorney.

• The names of organizations—such as fraternal or trade societies—to which you belong. Make a special note here about any benefits which may be coming to your family from these organizations.

• If you have been in active military service, the branch and period of service and the date of your discharge.

• Funeral arrangements you prefer and any preparations you have made.

• In preparing your check list, consider once more:

• Have you married since you made your will? If so, call your lawyer, tell him so, and ask him what you should do about your will.

• If you have acquired a business interest, have you provided for its disposition at your death? No matter what the size of your interest, make a sound plan for its disposition. If your interest must be sold in a hurry to pay death taxes, it may be sacrificed—and your family may be badly hurt.

These questions are primarily designed to intrigue your interest. Your lawyer surely will bring up others.

How You Can Disinherit Members of Your Family

The idea of disinheriting your spouse or children may not even have crossed your mind. However, there are circumstances under which disinheriting a member of your family can be not only the most practical but also the most considerate thing you can do.

For instance, say one of your two children has become a huge financial success and is now worth many times the value of your estate. The other is disabled, unable to work, and badly needs all the financial protection you can offer. Your real-istic decision here well might be to "cut out" the wealthy son and leave all to the dependent one.

You may be able to disinherit one or more children simply by specifically stat-ing so in your will and giving your reasons for cutting them off. In many states an explanation is unnecessary, but advisable to show that this action was not due merely to oversight. You may avert a will contest by taking this precaution even if it is legally not required. In some states a child or his issue may under certain circumstances elect against an excessive charitable bequest.

In most states you may not completely disinherit your wife or husband unless such surviving spouse has abandoned you and such abandonment continues to date of death. Or there may be some other possible circumstances permitting disinheritance—all of which should be checked with your attorney.

Laws vary from state to state, but as a general rule a widow is entitled to one third or more of her husband's estate, and if he leaves her less than that in his will, the court may later grant it to her anyway.

Moreover, many states still recognize what is called the wife's right of dower. This means that she is legally entitled to the use of one third of her husband's real estate so long as she lives.

Some states give the husband a similar right to the real property of his de-ceased wife, known as the right of curtesy.

In states which have abolished the old dower rights, the wife may have the choice of going along with the provisions of her husband's will or renouncing the will and claiming the share of his estate that she would have received if he had died without a will. To illustrate: a man whose estate amounts to $120,000 at his death leaves his wife only $25,000 in his will. She could, in many states, choose to reject that sum and instead take one third of the estate, or $40,000—or possi-bly one half.

In still other states, however, a husband may satisfy the law by leaving his wife the minimum designated percentage of his estate in trust. She is then entitled to the income from this trust during her lifetime. When she dies, though, the princi-pal passes to whomever the husband has named in his will.

CO-OWNERSHIP OF PROPERTY

You may own property with another person in several different forms. Before buying property with another person find out from your lawyer which is the most advantageous.

TENANTS IN COMMON

This is the usual form of co-ownership. In most states, unless otherwise specified, it will be presumed that property in the names of two people creates a tenancy in common. In other words, a deed to John Doe and Richard Smith will be assumed by law to indicate a tenancy in common.

Tenants in common each own an undivided one-half interest in the whole property. Of course, if there are more than two owners, each owns a proportionately equal interest, unless they have agreed to some other formula. One party may own 75 per cent, but whatever his (or her) interest it is undivided. Each party may sell his share or dispose of his interest by will. The new owner will become a tenant in common with the other owners. Death of a tenant in common does not affect his property right from passing to whomever he chooses.

JOINT TENANTS

In this form of tenancy you also own an undivided interest in the whole property but upon the death of one joint tenant the entire property belongs to the surviving joint tenants (some states do not recognize this form of tenancy). Thus, you may have nothing that you can leave by will because your death could extinguish your interest in the property if you are the first to die. You have little that you can sell because you are basically selling a gamble that you will outlive the other joint tenants. This type of conveyance is sometimes employed by a parent who wants to keep property in the family line, thus: "to John, Harry, and Richard Roe, as joint tenants." The surviving Roe eventually will take all. Of course, all the joint tenants may get together and effectively convey good title to all the property during their lives.

Joint ownership is not only used for real estate, but also for bank accounts, U.S. savings bonds, etc. Talk to your lawyer about the legal effect of creating a joint tenancy. How much has each one contributed? Is there a present gift involved which requires the filing of a gift tax return? Will a gift tax return be required if the non-contributing tenant survives? If the non-contributing tenant withdraws funds from a joint bank account, is there a gift involved?

TENANCY BY THE ENTIRETY

This is a form of joint tenancy which occurs only when real estate is jointly owned by a husband and wife, say "John Doe and Mary Doe, as tenants by the entirety." In many jurisdictions the owning of property by "John Doe and Mary Doe" where John and Mary are husband and wife creates a statutory presumption of joint ownership as opposed to tenancy in common if the parties were not husband and wife.

COMMUNITY PROPERTY

Community property is another category of ownership, similar to jointly held property. The concept behind community property laws is that all property acquired by husband and wife after marriage is considered to be owned by them fifty-fifty—no matter whose name is on the deed or title to a given property. So far as the law in community property states is concerned, the family home is owned jointly by husband and wife.

Certain assets, known as "separate property," are excluded from community property. Examples: property which belonged to either spouse before marriage, or property acquired after marriage by gift or inheritance.

Community property is recognized in only a few states. If you live in such a state it is imperative to consult your lawyer on the law in your state.

JOINT OWNERSHIP BY HUSBANDS AND WIVES

Q. *Should husbands and wives own property jointly and will they avoid the cost of probate by so doing?*

A. While there are advantages and disadvantages, the bad probably outweighs the good.

(1) You have $50,000 in your own name and decide to buy securities for that amount in both names. If under your state law your wife is able to terminate the joint ownership and claim half of the proceeds, you have made her a gift of $25,000 for which a gift tax is payable unless part of the marital deduction is used.

(2) Instead of buying stock you put the $50,000 in a joint bank account. There is no present gift because you can withdraw the $50,000 at any time. But suppose your wife gets to the bank first? Her withdrawal for her use is a gift at that time.

(3) You have reconsidered and decided to invest the $50,000 in U.S. savings bonds in both names. There is no gift because you may outlive your wife. But suppose she digs them out of your vault, surrenders them, and keeps the proceeds? You have just made a taxable gift.

(4) You use the $50,000 as a down payment on a $200,000 home and have a $150,000 mortgage. You may elect to treat half of the down payment and the yearly payments on the mortgage as a present gift by filing a gift tax return. If you do not make the election when the property is bought, the law will make the election for you when the property is sold and you divide the sales price with your wife.

In considering the tax consequences of your gifts to your wife, keep in mind that the first $3,000 of gifts in each year is excluded. In addition, since 1976 an unlimited marital deduction is allowed for the first $100,000 of lifetime gifts to the donor's spouse. The next $100,000 of lifetime gifts is fully taxable and does not qualify for the marital deduction. A 50 per cent deduction applies to lifetime gifts to the spouse in excess of $200,000. It is unnecessary to analyze gifts made prior to September 8, 1976, because those gifts can now be disregarded and do not count against the marital gifts made after January 1, 1977.

If you think that the IRS has become your generous "friend," rethink! For what the federal government gives with one policy, it takes away with another. Although you can make the gifts as indicated here, when it comes time to settle your estate, your executors will have to subtract from your marital deduction 50 per cent of the value of your lifetime transfers (not including your $3,000 per year exclusion) when the amount of lifetime gifts is $200,000 or less. This is because the first $100,000 is free of gift tax. The second $100,000 of gifts is completely taxable without a marital deduction and for gifts in excess of $200,000 you are paying a tax on only 50 per cent of the value and therefore are taking the marital deduction on the other portion.

JOINT OWNERSHIP PRIOR TO 1977

If you and your wife owned property by the entirety prior to December 31, 1976, and have done nothing about it, hurry to your lawyer. You may be missing a major tax strategy. Your ownership for estate tax purposes goes back to the pre-1977 era when the survivor must show proof of contribution to the purchase price or face the prospect of paying tax on the full value. The Tax Reform Act of 1976 permits you to re-establish the tenancy by a completed gift to your spouse and only one half is taxed to the survivor. In deciding whether or not to make this gift, weigh the ultimate tax consequences and whether the end result will be an advantage or disadvantage.

ESTATES AND TRUSTS—BRIEF ANSWERS TO FUNDAMENTAL QUESTIONS

JUST WHAT IS AN "ESTATE TAX"?

Under federal law, an estate tax return must be filed for every estate with gross assets of more than $175,000 for the years after 1980 by your executor (or administrator) and any tax due on this return must be paid at the time it is filed.

This enhances the desirability of arranging your affairs in ways that will minimize the tax burden on your estate and beneficiaries.

Although the federal death tax is called an estate tax, a death levy imposed by the states may be called an inheritance tax, transfer tax, estate tax, or legacy tax. State death taxes vary so widely from state to state that there is no way to generalize on "typical" amounts—and they are imposed in every state except Nevada. The actual rate may depend, for instance, on the size of the estate or inheritance or the type of property involved or the closeness of the heir's blood relationship to the person who has died.

What's more, though some states allow roughly the same kind of exemptions and deductions that the federal government allows, they do not necessarily allow them in the same amounts. If a state exemption is lower, for example, you may have to pay a state tax even though you are not required to pay a federal tax. On top of this, both federal and state tax rates and regulations undergo frequent changes.

CAN YOU GIVE AWAY PROPERTY PRIOR TO DEATH AND AVOID ESTATE TAXES?

No. You will have to pay gift taxes which are assessed at rates equal to estate taxes under federal law. This is why estate taxes and gift taxes are said to be "unified."

But you may give away up to $3,000 per year to any person, and not pay taxes. If your spouse consents to having one half the gifts treated as made by him or her, your annual gifts may total $6,000 to each donee. Thus, a husband and wife with two children could give each of them $6,000 a year, or a total of $12,000 without gift tax consequences.

For other advantages of gifts made during your life, called "inter vivos gifts" by professionals, consult your attorney.

WHEN WILL YOU GET YOUR INHERITANCE?

As soon as the executor has been appointed by the court and has collected enough assets of the estates—such as cash in the bank—he can provide survivors with sufficient funds to meet immediate living expenses.

Certain other assets, such as proceeds from life insurance policies, also go to the beneficiaries almost immediately. If the estate is relatively small and thus not subject to taxation, and if there is no litigation or other complication, the proceeds often can be distributed within a year. But if it is a large estate, and if there are estate taxes to be paid, it may be several years before you can consider yourself "rich."

An executor may not distribute the proceeds of an estate until all the legal debts of the deceased have been paid. In most states, the way debts are uncovered is by giving notice to creditors and by requiring them to file their claims within a certain limited period of time. Notice is normally published in a local newspaper for the length of time required by statute; in most states the time limits for creditors to file claims against an estate range from six months to eighteen months after the decedent's death.

In some states a specific or general legacy is payable seven months after death and you may be entitled to interest if payment is delayed. You may not get it in seven months if the estate does not have enough liquid assets to pay funeral expenses, taxes, debts, and costs of administration. If you are a residuary legatee, you may have to wait until the estate is settled (two to three years) or until the death of life tenants if their interest precedes your enjoyment of the property.

Frequently, an estate's value is established for tax purposes as the value at the date of death. However, if the estate consists mainly of securities which have dwindled in value, the executor for estate tax purposes may want to take advantage of the optional valuation date, six months from the date of death. He cannot do this unless he maintains control of most of the estate's assets.

WHAT IS A TRUST?

A trust is an agreement under which the person who establishes the trust either by his will or by a legal agreement executed while he is alive gives property to a trustee to invest and manage for the advantage of the beneficiary. It is a highly flexible device that enables you to have a say in the use of your money after you have died as well as during your lifetime. Most trusts are established for the benefit of a surviving wife and children and most trusts remain in effect for some years. Trusts also can help save on taxes.

A typical provision is that only the income from the trust may go to one beneficiary, upon whose death the principal goes to another. Some trust agreements in addition contain an emergency clause which permits the trustee to invade the principal or part of it, if necessary, to provide for the education of a child or for other unforeseen needs such as major medical expenses.

Frequently a trust is used as a means of protecting beneficiaries against their own inexperience in managing financial assets. You may, for instance, want your wife to have the income from your property during her lifetime and your children to get the property later. Or, if you are a widower with children, you may want them to receive only the income from your property until they reach a given age (say thirty) and then to receive the principal outright.

Or a trust can be used to permit a desired standard of living for your family;

to educate a minor child;

to cover unexpected financial emergencies;

to provide a lifetime income for a wife or daughter or other relative;

to give a child his (or her) inheritance in installments;

to keep the child from squandering it all in a hurry and harmfully extravagant spree;

to provide for a favorite charity;

to achieve almost any type of personal or financial objective.

The organization, purpose, administration, duration, and eventual disposition of the principal of the trust are subject to many laws, and the laws governing your prospective trust depend on the state in which you live.

There are many different types of trusts—some fairly commonplace, others not so frequently established. You will find short definitions of the various types with which you might be concerned in the section "The Bafflegab of Wills, Estates, and Trusts" at the end of this chapter.

WHAT CAN BE DONE WITH LIFE INSURANCE?

If you own a considerable amount of life insurance you can create a life insurance trust and direct to whom and in what manner the proceeds from the policies are to be paid.

As an alternative, you can have the proceeds of your life insurance paid promptly upon your death simply by naming the beneficiary in the policy. This is most commonly done. And you or your beneficiaries may direct your insurance company to pay the proceeds in either a lump sum or a series of payments.

For instance, you can authorize the insurance company to make regular payments to your wife or children—including both the income and part of the principal—for a specific period of time.

A caution: should you direct that payments be made to your children and should you die while they are minors, a guardian may have to be appointed by the probate court to handle these proceeds. You can avoid this by a clause in your will authorizing your executor to receive the proceeds and handle them to the best advantage of the children.

Most life insurance proceeds must be included in computing the value of your gross estate for purposes of taxation, unless the policy was owned or controlled and paid for by a person other than the one whose life was insured.

But it is entirely possible for a man's life to be insured by his wife. Thus, if a wife takes out an insurance policy on her husband's life and has it registered in her name as owner, the policy will not have to be listed as an asset in the husband's estate and the wife will not have to share the proceeds with the tax collector.

THE BAFFLEGAB OF WILLS, ESTATES, AND TRUSTS

ACCUMULATION TRUST Trust in which the yearly income on the capital in an estate is added to the principal for a designated period of time—e.g., usually during a young beneficiary's childhood.

ADMINISTRATOR (ADMINISTRATRIX) Individual or institution appointed by the court to handle the estate of a person who has not left a will which names an executor or executrix.

ATTESTATION CLAUSE Clause at the end of your will containing the signatures and addresses of the witnesses and a statement that they saw you sign the will.

BENEFICIARY Person entitled to receive funds or property from an estate, trust, or insurance policy.

BEQUEST (OR LEGACY) Gift of personal property via a will.

CHARITABLE TRUST Trust in which the grantor stipulates that a certain portion of the trust be used for charitable purposes. A charitable trust may last indefinitely. All other types of trusts must have cutoff dates.

CODICIL Addition, or "postscript," to a will, drawn up separately, but with all the formality of the will itself.

CO-EXECUTOR (-EXECUTRIX) Another equal executor appointed by will.

COMMUNITY PROPERTY The concept in some states of fifty-fifty property ownership of property acquired by a married couple during marriage.

CONVEY To give or sell property to someone else.

DEATH (OR ESTATE) TAXES Taxes levied on your estate by the federal and state governments, with the amounts varying according to the size of the estate.

DECEDENT Person who has died.

DEVISE Gift of real estate by will.

DOMICILE Legal home, where person votes, pays taxes, etc.

ESTATE All assets and liabilities left by a person at death.

EXECUTOR Individual and/or institution you name in your will to safeguard the assets of your estate while it is being probated, and to distribute it according to your wishes.

EXECUTOR'S FEE Fee paid to the person or institution handling your estate— with the amount (or percentage of the value of the estate) usually set by state law.

GUARDIAN Person appointed to look after a person or property—e.g., a minor, until he or she is old enough to manage his or her own affairs.

HOLOGRAPHIC WILL Handwritten will—recognized as legal only under certain circumstances and only in certain jurisdictions.

INTER VIVOS GIFT A gift while the donor is still alive to which the donor relinquishes all rights and control.

INTESTATE Dying without leaving a will.

ISSUE   Children and direct descendants.

JOINT TENANCY (WITH RIGHT OF SURVIVORSHIP)   Ownership by two or more people of a piece of property, title to which passes completely to the last survivor.

LEGACY (OR BEQUEST)   Gift of property—especially money or other personal property—made under a will.

LIFE INSURANCE TRUST   Type of trust in which the assets are the proceeds of life insurance policies.

LIFE TENANT MARITAL DEDUCTION   Provision in our federal tax law designed to ameliorate the taxation of the same asset in two estates—at the death of the wife as well as at the death of the husband. It permits a husband or wife leaving a part of his or her estate to the surviving spouse to take a deduction for such amount to the extent of $250,000 or 50 per cent of the adjusted gross estate, whichever is greater. Thus, such property will be effectively taxed only in the estate of the last to die.

MARITAL DEDUCTION TRUST (see "Life Tenant Marital Deduction" above)   A trust which makes it possible to relieve from the burden of estate taxation, in the estate of the spouse first to die, certain property interests described as "deductible interest." These interests are not taxable as part of the estate of the first spouse, but rather as part of the estate of the surviving spouse. The surviving spouse receives all of the income from the trust; in some cases there is a right to invade the principal; and the surviving spouse must have the unqualified right to dispose of the principal of the trust in favor of himself or his estate. The residue of the estate may also be left to the surviving spouse in trust. This "residual trust" may provide for the payment of income to the survivor and contain provisions for invading the principal. It then will provide for the ultimate distribution of the principal. However, the principal of this residual trust is taxable to the estate of the creator of the trust, and not to that of the surviving spouse.

MUTUAL WILLS   Common arrangement executed according to an agreement in which husband and wife leave everything to each other. Frequently a further provision is that, when the second spouse has died, the estate is shared by the children. A reciprocal will is one which contains reciprocal gifts for and among the makers.

OPTIONAL VALUATION DATE   Date on which the size of your estate is computed for tax purposes can be either as of the date of your death or as of six months after your death—providing the assets are not disposed of in the interim—thus "optional" date. It provides a financial protection for the beneficiaries in the event of a sharp stock market slide, for if the value of the estate shrinks, the tax on it will be slashed too.

POWER OF APPOINTMENT   Equivalent of absolute ownership of part or all of a trust, since the person having this power may name the ultimate recipients of the assets of the trust.

PRENUPTIAL AGREEMENT   Agreement made prior to marriage—often one in which both spouses forfeit any interest in the other's estate.

PRESUMPTION OF SURVIVORSHIP   Clause in your will establishing a way to decide the order of death if both spouses die simultaneously.

PROBATE COSTS   Costs of administering an estate.

PROBATE COURT   Court in which estate settlements are made; in some states, estates are handled by a circuit court, orphans court, or surrogate's court.

PROBATING A WILL   Processing a will through a court in order to establish its validity.

RESIDUARY CLAUSE   Usually the key clause in your will since it covers the bulk of your "residuary estate"—typically, "all the rest, residue, and remainder" of the estate—after special, individual bequests of money and/or property have been covered.

REVOCABLE LIVING TRUST   Trust in which the income from the trust is paid to a beneficiary during his or her lifetime, and to his heirs or to some other person after he dies. This type of trust may be amended or revoked at any time during the grantor's lifetime. An irrevocable living trust cannot be revoked or amended without the consent of all beneficiaries involved.

RIGHT OF CURTESY   Husband's life interest in the property of his deceased wife.

RIGHT OF DOWER   Wife's life interest in the estate of her deceased husband.

SPENDTHRIFT TRUST   Trust in which only the income but not the principal may be touched by the beneficiary—no matter how urgent the demands or needs of the beneficiary.

TENANCY IN COMMON   Title held jointly by two people, usually unmarried, to a given piece of property—i.e., real estate—although each person keeps control over his individual share of the property. Either may sell or will his interest in the property independently of the other.

TENANCY BY THE ENTIRETY   Ownership by both the husband and wife in their home and/or other real estate.

TESTAMENTARY TRUST   Trust established by a will to take effect after that person dies.

TESTATOR   Person making a will.

TOTTEN TRUST   Way, often used by grandparents, to leave money to their grandchildren. The donor opens a bank account in the name of one person "in trust for" the grandchild or other beneficiary but retains control over the trust during his or her lifetime. The proceeds are part of the taxable estate.

TRUST   Property or money set aside for a certain person or persons to be managed by a trustee for the best advantage of the beneficiary.

TRUST DEPARTMENT   Department of a financial institution which is staffed with specialists in the administration of estates and in handling trust funds.

TRUSTEE   Individual or institution designated to oversee the handling and distribution of a trust fund.

WILL   Legal document—usually in writing and properly witnessed—which describes how a person wants his or her property to be distributed after death.

20

FUNERAL EXPENSES
WHAT TO DO . . . HOW TO SAVE . . .
WHERE THE TRAPS ARE

Would You Know What to Do?

Would you know what to do if suddenly confronted with a death in the family?

Are you aware that in the United States just the average cost of an ordinary funeral with the usual trimmings has now crossed the $2,000 milestone? "Death" has become a multibillion dollar industry, commonly involving distasteful ostentation and wasteful expenses. Each year countless thousands of families are plunged desperately and unnecessarily into debt because of these costs alone. Yet with intelligent planning the expenses connected with death need be only a small fraction of the $2,000 figure.

There are two immediate and closely related problems with which to cope at time of death:

CARE AND DISPOSITION OF THE BODY

You have several choices.

The least expensive is to donate the body to a medical school. Many educated, public-minded Americans do this. Sometimes a funeral service is held beforehand; sometimes the body is taken immediately to the medical school and a memorial service is held afterward. In that case there may be no funeral expenses at all. In most areas the medical schools pay the entire transportation costs.

Your next choice is cremation. This too can be carried out either following a funeral service or immediately after death, with a memorial service held later if desired. In the latter case no embalming or cosmetic work is required and a simple fiberboard container or a stretcher can be used, thus greatly reducing expense. You need not buy an urn for the ashes if you don't want to, and the crematory will provide a simple container without charge. (As stated previously, ashes may be sent by ordinary parcel post or the container may be carried in a suitcase.) The ashes may be scattered wherever you wish, with or without a ceremony. This may be done any time, even years later. Cremation is a clean, orderly way of returning the body to the elements and is steadily gaining acceptance.

Caution: While the actual cremation costs only around $100, funeral directors sometimes sell the family extra goods and services which can run up the bill into the thousand-dollar range, even without a funeral service.

If your family or your friends wish to build a box and take the body to the crematory themselves in their own conveyance you can do so in most states, but you first must take the death certificate to the county health officer and get a transportation permit. If a time lapse of more than a few hours is involved, or if the body is to be transported for a considerable distance, you can have the body embalmed by a funeral director or, less expensive, you can place a supply of dry ice in the box. (Embalming is mandatory if a common carrier, such as an airline, is to be used.) You must make sure in advance that the crematory will accept a body from a person who is not a funeral director. Some crematories are unwilling to do this, for fear of offending the funeral directors. Other crematories are quite willing.

Your last and most expensive choice is earth burial. As with other alternatives this can be carried out immediately after death, with a memorial service afterward, or can be done following a funeral service. Immediate burial is, of course, less costly.

OPTIONAL PROCEDURES FOR DISPOSITION OF THE BODY

These are shown below in ascending order of cost. The sequence may vary a bit with different localities and circumstances.

METHOD	COST
Bequeathal to medical school. Immediate removal of body, with memorial service to be held afterwards if desired.	Usually no cost.
Cremation. Immediate removal of body followed by memorial service if desired.	Small cost, if properly planned.
Bequeathal to medical school after a funeral service.	Usually more expensive. Depends on type of service.
Burial. Immediate removal of body followed by memorial service if desired.	May be either less or more than the above.
Cremation, after a funeral service.	Comparable to the above two methods.
Burial after a funeral service.	Most expensive of all.

(For concise, straightforward information on funeral costs and other vital facts on how to cope with the financial and emotional problems associated with death, order a copy of "A Manual of Death Education and Simple Burial" by Ernest Morgan. Cost: $2.00, plus 50 cents for postage, Celo Press, Burnsville, North Carolina 28714. It also includes directories of memorial societies, medical schools, eye banks and other tissue banks.)

ADDITIONAL POINTS

If you opt for bequeathal but plan to have a funeral service first, be sure the funeral director contacts the medical school to find out exactly what kind of embalming the school wants. Ordinary embalming usually is not acceptable.

If the body is to go immediately to the medical school, the school usually will make arrangements with the funeral director and instruct him.

If you wish the ashes returned from the medical school after the body has been used, be sure to let the school officers in charge know in writing.

If you choose cremation without a funeral service, ask that a simple fiberboard container, or the equivalent, be used instead of an expensive casket. Specify that no embalming is to be done, and no cosmetic work. The same applies to immediate burial. If possible, use a cemetery that does not require a vault or liner; these are costly.

If ashes are to be scattered, they should be pulverized first. The "ashes" consist of soft bone fragments which can be placed in a large bowl and pulverized with the handle of a hammer.

MEETING THE SOCIAL AND EMOTIONAL NEEDS OF SURVIVORS

The way these needs are met has an important impact both on the expenses involved at time of death and on the social and emotional well-being of the survivors.

All human cultures, and some animal cultures as well, have death ceremonies of one kind or another. Funeral directors point out, and correctly, that these ceremonies help meet the social and emotional needs of the survivors. It is important to remember, however, that the amount of money spent on death ceremonies bears little relation to the effectiveness of these ceremonies in meeting human needs. For example, a thoughtful memorial service held in a church, private home, or other meeting place at little or no expense can sometimes actually be more helpful than a costly funeral service.

There are two basic forms of death ceremony:

A funeral service is, by definition, a service held in the presence of the body. Because of the necessary time lapse between the hour of death and the meeting, it is generally necessary to embalm the body. It is common practice in our country to use a funeral parlor for the ceremony, though the funeral director can, if desired, bring the body to a church or other meeting place. Some funeral services are conducted with the casket closed, others with it open to permit viewing of the body. For purposes of viewing, the face of the person who has died is carefully prepared to appear lifelike. Whether the viewing of a lifelike body helps the survivors to accept the reality of death is an open question. Funeral ceremonies tend to be costly. Before ordering a funeral service be sure you are fully aware of exactly what services will be included and what each will cost.

Do not simply accept a "package deal"! Some states have laws requiring funeral directors to provide customers with a written rundown on all costs and charges and also prohibiting crematories from insisting that remains be put in a casket for cremation.

The other type of death ceremony commonly used in modern society is a memorial service. This is, by definition, a service held after the body has been removed. In a memorial service the attention tends to be focused on the life of the person rather than on the dead body. It offers, furthermore, greater flexibility in choice of location and in timing and programming. Since the body is removed promptly after death, no embalming or cosmetic work is required, a simple container can be used instead of an expensive casket, and other expensive goods and services become unnecessary.

The use of a memorial service often can cut the expenses of a death to a fraction of what otherwise would be involved. If well handled, it can in most cases serve the human needs just as well or better than a funeral service.

DEATH EDUCATION

Before you can deal wisely with the financial aspects of death, you must be able to cope effectively with the philosophical, emotional, and social aspects. In this sphere, death education plays a key role. This education should take place before death occurs or becomes imminent, but whenever it occurs, it is valuable.

Death education which is restricted solely to the philosophical, emotional, and social aspects, however, and which omits instruction in the financial aspects of death, is deficient and not achieving its full potential.

An important by-product of death education—if, indeed, not a central purpose —is to promote the maturity of the individual, whatever his or her age may be, with relation to himself or herself and to society, and to refine his or her motives and priorities.

When you have completed reading this chapter you will have had a significant session in death education. If you wish to pursue this further, the Ernest Morgan "Manual" (see page 986) will be a concise source of information and inspiration based on experience.

FUNDAMENTAL GUIDES

Be careful even of the advice given by your closest personal friends and dearest relatives. They may have the best intentions, but when in trouble you need help from people who have the full information and background to advise you.

If no prior arrangements have been made and if you are in a state of befuddlement, ask a sensible level-headed friend or relative, who knows what the family can afford, to help you with the arrangements. This person or these people will help find a licensed, reasonable funeral director who will co-operate in arranging for the type of funeral you want.

If a person dies at a distance and the body is to be shipped home, it may be transported in a private vehicle (assuming legal details are taken care of) or it may be sent by commercial carrier. Most airlines provide this service. Amtrak Express is less expensive and can provide service to some three hundred destinations

If the body is cremated near the place of death, the small container of ashes can be mailed by parcel post or carried in a suitcase.

Get advice—from your lawyer, minister, friends—on the arrangements you will make *before* you authorize any given mortician to remove the body from home or hospital. Obviously, once a mortician takes custody of a body, his bargaining power is multiplied. Note: Most large hospitals will keep a body for at least a day, and often longer, while you make arrangements.

If a bank or law firm is the executor of the deceased's estate, ask the appropriate officials to help arrange economical services.

If the funeral costs must be financed out of borrowed funds until any estate is settled, find out what interest rates will be charged by the funeral parlor or other lending source.

Check exactly what is included in the price tag on a casket. The casket alone? A complete range of services? Which? Don't permit a mortician to make you feel guilty or disrespectful if you try to economize.

● Steer clear of expensive frills such as costly "burial vaults" to enclose the casket, costing up to $150 or even more. Unless the cemetery requires these vaults, you can omit this expense altogether.

● If your family is in a serious financial squeeze, tell the facts to your funeral director. If he's reputable, he will make allowances for your circumstances.

● If you plan to buy a cemetery plot, find out if the cemetery participates in a nationwide Lot Exchange Plan under which, if you move to another area, you can trade one plot for another.

● If you want to donate your body (or part of it) for medical teaching purposes, transplants, etc., write to the medical or dental school of your choice and ask for details on how to go about it in your area. The above-mentioned manual lists names and addresses of U.S. medical schools and their rules covering bequeathal of bodies.

● Wait a few months or even years, until the shock is dulled and you've regained your balance, before you buy expensive markers or memorials.

Preplanning Saves Money and Minimizes Misery

By careful preplanning you generally can save 50 per cent to 75 per cent of the expenses with which you ordinarily are hit at time of death!

Equally important, the planning will help you accept the reality of death in advance so that when it does occur you will be able to cope with your own feelings more effectively. Then, too, the preplanning will help avert costly and painful misunderstandings within your family.

A practical way to preplan is to join a memorial society. You will find one of these co-operative, non-profit societies in 175 cities in the United States and Canada. You will be charged a one-time membership fee of $5.00 to $20 and your membership may be transferred from one city to another at little or no cost. The societies will provide you, a member, with the specific local information you need to plan effectively and in many cases they have advantageous contracts or agreements with funeral directors. As a member, you will normally pay from $150 to $350 for a cremation or a funeral. (Annual savings by the members run into millions of dollars.) Look for a complete list of the societies with their addresses in the Morgan Manual (see page 986) or send a self-addressed stamped envelope to the Continental Association of Funeral and Memorial Societies, 1828 L Street N.W., Washington, D.C. 20036, and ask for a list.

You also may preplan without a society if you are prepared to make the effort and check with local funeral directors. Choose one who will make the preferred arrangements in advance of the inevitable event. You may calculate the costs now (subject to future price increases) or even may finance them in advance. If you do pay an advance be sure the money is put in a state-supervised trust and you can withdraw it if and as you decide to cancel the arrangements.

ABOUT BURIAL LAWS

There is a good deal of confusion about burial laws. There are patent lawyers, divorce lawyers, and corporation lawyers but who ever heard of a burial lawyer? Some funeral industry practices are required by law; many are not, and funeral directors often are not sure which are which. Hence they often are mistaken in the legal information they give their clients.

Laws governing burial are meant to protect public health and safety, but they commonly have the added purpose of promoting the business interests of funeral directors. For example, some states have a law that only a licensed funeral director may transport a dead body and one or two states actually require embalming!

Most state boards which regulate the funeral industry are composed entirely of funeral directors. Regulations made by these boards acquire the force of law.

The laws and regulations are almost continuously changing, and their interpretation and enforcement vary considerably from time to time and place to place. In some cases non-existent laws are observed by funeral directors and their clients. In other cases, unreasonable or selfishly motivated laws or regulations are quietly ignored.

The average family is best able to cope with this situation if it is affiliated with a memorial society or burial committee which knows its way around.

FUNERAL BENEFITS—SOCIAL SECURITY, VETERANS, AND OTHER

A lump-sum death benefit is payable under Social Security upon the death of any worker who either is fully insured or has Social Security credit for as little as a year and a half out of the three years just before death.

This lump-sum death benefit of $255 may be collected by the surviving spouse even if there are no funeral expenses. If no spouse survives, it can be collected only to defray funeral expenses, or to reimburse persons who have advanced money for these expenses. It cannot be collected for funeral expenses if other specific provision, such as death insurance, was in force to cover those expenses. Hence any such insurance should be designated as "life insurance," not funeral insurance.

As in the case of other Social Security benefits, you must apply to get the payment. If a worker in your family dies, immediately get in touch with your nearest Social Security office.

Under the law, the lump-sum benefit is to amount to three times the worker's Primary Insurance Amount, but no more than $255. That $255 maximum has been in the law since 1954 and Social Security benefits have risen so spectacularly since then that the lump-sum benefit has become a flat payment of $255. Even the current minimum Primary Insurance Amount multiplied by three is more than $255.

Congress froze the maximum of $255 because of concern that increases would lead only to additional swelling in the costs of funerals. While in some quarters the belief is an increase in the maximum would not have the same impact on funeral costs as it would have had in earlier years, there also have been recommendations for the elimination of the lump-sum benefit altogether so that the money could be used to help finance other benefit improvements.

If the deceased person is a veteran, these are the key government funeral benefits:

• A basic $300 allowance will be paid toward the burial expenses of honorably discharged veterans, including veterans of peacetime service.

• Free burial will be permitted in a national cemetery in which space is available. Burial in national cemeteries is available, too, to an eligible veteran's wife or dependent children.

• For veterans who are not buried in a national or other U. S. Government cemetery, an additional "plot allowance" of up to $150 may be payable.

• If a veteran's death is service-connected, the total funeral expense allowance can go up to a total of $1,100.

• Headstone or grave markers will be available through the VA to the deceased, honorably discharged veterans.

You can get complete information on government burial benefits for veterans and their families at any VA office or veterans' service organization. Most post offices and funeral parlors are familiar with the benefits also, and can assist a beneficiary in applying to the appropriate government agency.

And there are many other types of death benefits.

For instance, some trade unions and fraternal organizations provide the payments for the families of their members. There are benefits for the survivors of any person who has been a railroad employee. Other employers may provide them as well.

If occupational factors were involved in the death, there may be Workers' Compensation benefits. There may be Automobile Club insurance; some auto insurance policies carry death benefits.

Depending on the circumstances of death, there may be liability insurance benefits. In some states, too, the families of state employees are entitled to survivor benefits.

And it is commonplace for the county to pay burial expenses for indigent families.

So many death benefits go unclaimed every year—usually not received by the persons most in need of them! Check out every angle with utmost care.

IF YOU ARE A DEPENDENT WIDOW

Don't make an investment of any sort until your mind is working more normally and you have had ample time to get the advice of competent objective advisers concerned only with *your* welfare!

Don't buy securities.

Don't make loans.

Don't convert your insurance policies.

Don't buy annuities.

Don't make any investment.

You have a limited amount of money. It is now more important than ever. Take your time, get the best advice available to you before you take a single step.

BEWARE: DEATH TRAPS

Survivors, particularly widows, are frequent victims of vicious swindlers—often men or women who seem friendly and honest, but really aren't.

A favorite device is to collect a non-existent debt owed by the deceased, or to deliver merchandise (say, a Bible) that was never ordered.

• Another favorite of these gypsters is to inform the survivor of a non-existent life insurance policy on which a final premium must be paid before benefits can be collected, or some other "valuable asset" requiring a final payment of some kind.

• Widows are prime prospects for bad investments, and, when asked, even representatives of reputable investment firms will at times recommend changing stock portfolios merely for the sake of the commissions involved.

Moral: Be cautious, go slow, consult an experienced member of the family or other trusted business advisers, neither pay any unfamiliar debt nor sign any document before careful investigation and before you have recovered your balance.

21

YOUR GUIDE
TO THE STOCK MARKETS

INTRODUCTION

Let's say that tomorrow you receive the news that you have a sweepstakes combination which gives you a chance to win from $50,000 to $200,000 net after taxes. Let's say your dream is to turn this into a million. How much of your possible winnings would you have to invest for how long, and in what ways, to reach this magic mark?

(1) You could invest $75,000 and be a millionaire within thirty years, if you could earn the 9.0 per cent a year which was the average rate of return on all common stocks listed on the New York Stock Exchange between the mid 1920s and the late 1970s. (The assumption was that you invested an equal sum of money in each stock each year and reinvested all your dividends.)

(2) You would have to put up $114,000 to become a millionaire in the thirty-year period if, instead, you put it into municipal bonds paying 7½ per cent (not the peak but fairly typical rate in the late 1970s).

(3) Or you would have to put up your entire $200,000 winnings plus $1,000 more—$201,000—to become a millionaire three decades hence if you invested in a passbook savings account paying the 5½ per cent rate prevailing in the 1970s, or $99,000 in 8 per cent long-term saving deposit certificates.

But let's come back down to earth: you're not due to win any wild contests or to get any financial windfall soon.

You may be, however, approaching your best earning years, or actually in them, and thus you may be ready to set aside fairly substantial sums. How much would you have to invest each year at 6 per cent to become a millionaire in one decade, two decades, three?

You could become a millionaire within thirty years by setting aside $12,649 a year if you could achieve the relatively commonplace yearly rate of return of 6 per cent—in stocks or bonds or real estate or some other investment medium.

You could become a millionaire within twenty years if you set aside $27,185 each year at 6 per cent.

Or you could become a millionaire in ten years if you invested $75,868 each year at 6 per cent.

These statistics were developed for me by the American Bankers Association and the New York Stock Exchange. They're drastically simplified, of course, since they do not take into account the inevitable tax bite on capital gains, dividends, or interest. And it's unrealistic to assume any set rate of return on stock or bond investments will continue indefinitely.

Nevertheless, a first key point is that, in today's society and at today's available rates of return on investments, it is within the realm of possibility that you can become the fabled millionaire. Right now, hundreds of thousands of American families have $1 million in assets. And there are several thousand families in the United States with assets of well over that.

A second key point is that the vast majority of these very wealthy have invested not with the goal of safety or liquidity or dividend income, but instead with the consistent aim of long-term capital gains. Most of the very wealthy look for returns of at least 10 per cent and usually 15 to 20 per cent a year in various types of enterprises, securities or real estate, or in the farther-out mediums of art works, antiques, commodities, etc.

A third key point underlined by the computations is that the faster you want to make your million the higher the return you must seek—which means the greater risk you must be willing to assume. The implication of this third fundamental point is that you must be able to afford to take the chance.

And a fourth point: not everybody aspires to be a millionaire. What most people want is an investment program that can help them reach some of their long-term family financial objectives: a comfortable retirement, a college education for the youngsters, perhaps a second home. For them, investing successfully can bring peace of mind and successful attainment of their goals even if they never come close to being millionaires.

WHAT ARE STOCKS?

When you buy stock of a company you buy part of the ownership of that company. If, say, you buy a share of—let's call it the Widget Company—in effect you buy a part of Widget's plant, its output, and everything that company owns.

If the Widget Company has 10,000 shares of stock outstanding and you own 100 shares, you own 100/10,000 or 1 per cent. As a stockholder you are normally entitled to vote in the election of directors and to participate in other company affairs. Each share has one vote and big companies have millions of shares outstanding and many thousands of stockholders. For example, the American Telephone & Telegraph Company in the late 1970s had 2.9 million shareholders; General Motors had almost 1.3 million; International Business Machines had more than 580,000; and General Electric had more than 545,000. If the company whose stock you hold grows and increases its earnings per share, the price of your stock should rise over the long run. The price also will fluctuate day by day based on ever changing supply-and-demand trends. It is a rare stock that stands still.

SHOULD YOU INVEST IN STOCKS?

Any well-balanced portfolio of investments should include stocks. But before you buy, consider these factors:

(1) *There is always an element of risk in stock ownership.* According to a survey of public attitudes toward investment conducted for the New York Stock Exchange in the late 1970s, most Americans resisted assuming the risks associated with common stock ownership. Whether because stocks have failed to keep up with inflation in recent years, disastrous previous experiences, or the attractiveness of other investments, stocks have plunged way down to ninth place—after life insurance, savings accounts, a home, and U.S. saving bonds—in investor popularity. The whipsaw, bull-and-bear markets of the late 1960s and 1970s have soured investors on the market. There is still money to be made in stocks, but you, an investor, must proceed with more caution than ever.

What degree of risk are *you* willing to assume?

(2) *Inflation is here to stay.* Stocks long have been considered a hedge against inflation. According to the Center for Research and Security Prices at the University of Chicago, an investment in a random cross section of stocks on the New York Stock Exchange from 1926 through 1977 would have increased in value to a degree giving you an average rate of return (before taxes) equal to 9 per cent a year compounded annually. To translate, an investment of $1,000 in 1926 compounded annually at 9 per cent would have grown to more than $80,000 in fifty-one years.

During bouts of extreme inflation, however, stocks may not be a good hedge. Late in the 1970s, the Dow Jones industrial average of thirty leading stocks was a numbing 8 per cent lower than its level ten years earlier! Investors who had taken for granted that an investment in the shares of America's largest companies automatically would keep up with inflation were disillusioned, disgusted, and determined to stick to a "never again" attitude.

Yet with proper research and timing, stocks can be excellent investments—even when the market as a whole does not keep pace with inflation. While many glamour issues on the New York Stock Exchange were declining in the late 1970s, for instance, smaller issues on the Big Board and on other exchanges were reaching new highs.

Often overlooked, too, is the fact that stocks are liquid investments. Real estate, while often appreciating faster than the rate of inflation, may be tough to sell. Other hedges, such as coins, stamps, art, and antiques, may be even more difficult to turn into cash (particularly when you need the money). Stocks, though, are readily bought and sold.

(3) *The economy is growing.* Inflation and recession may cloud the horizon, but the long-term trend of the U.S. economy is up. Stocks are a basic way for you to participate in this long-term economic growth.

The economic problems involved in energy and environmentalism, for instance, may adversely affect the stock performance of some companies. At the same time, these same problems create new opportunities for other companies. By buying shares in these corporations, you can participate in their future growth.

KEY, SELF-REVEALING QUESTIONS

Can you afford to invest? Purchase stocks only after you have adequate life insurance and sufficient savings in cash or the equivalent to help you through an unexpected financial emergency. If you do not have this extra disposable income, you cannot afford to invest in stocks.

Have you determined a specific investment goal? Set a goal suited to your needs before you invest and be faithful to it until your circumstances change. If your goal is income, you'll want one type of stock; if it is growth, you'll want another; and if it is, above all, security of principal, you'll want a third.

If you're a young person earning more than enough to meet your family's current expenses and have set aside funds to cope with financial emergencies, your objective normally will be growth. Therefore, you'll buy stocks that promise to grow in price along with the economy's growth over the years. You may take greater-than-average risks in the hope of getting higher-than-average profits. Although you may lose on a stock in which you speculate, you can afford the risk at your age; you have time to recoup.

Do you have the emotional temperament to own stocks? As the New York Stock Exchange itself says, "Many persons should never buy stocks. The individual who can be seriously upset by a slight decline in price or who goes off on a spending spree when prices rise is better off out of the stock market."

That leads into the confession that one of the most embarrassing questions frequently put to me is, "What do you think the stock market is going to do?" And, usually before I can open my mouth, the questioner adds, "Boy, I bet you get plenty of inside tips! In your position, you probably clean up . . ."

When I answer that (1) I don't get many tips and the ones I do get I invariably ignore, and (2) I don't clean up, and what's more, have absolutely no desire to—the mildest reaction is disappointment.

It is true, though, for because of my temperament—my emotional attitude toward speculating in the stock market—I don't feel comfortable taking stock tips. I haven't the temperament to be a gambler in Wall Street. I don't clean up because I don't even try to. But I don't go broke either.

Without my being particularly aware of it, my activities in the stock market reflect my own personality. And the purpose of this confession is to emphasize to you the vital point that if your aim is to be a serene as well as a successful investor the first thing you must do is analyze your own personality.

To be even more specific, don't buy—or sell—stocks because it seems the thing to do: in the stock market, "conforming" doesn't pay off.

Don't buy stocks of a type or in amounts that give you anxiety and concern. If you are so nervous about owning stocks that you can't take a trip without worrying about what is happening to your stocks, stay out of the market.

Don't try to beat the professional traders unless you are willing to study enough to become a pro yourself.

In short, follow the fundamental rule: "know thyself."

Can you and are you willing to invest your time? It takes time to become informed about the stocks which interest you. If you don't have this time you may find yourself acting in response to tips or rumors, which, however intriguing, are usually wrong.

You wouldn't dream of buying a house simply on the basis of how it looks from the outside. You would examine the inside thoroughly, check on the reputation of the builder, the quality of the construction, and a hundred other aspects. The same thoroughness must be applied to buying stocks, for along with buying a house, investing in the stock market may be among the most important financial decisions you make.

You also probably wouldn't dream of trying to trade in and out of real estate and pit yourself against the real professionals in this field. Again, the same rule must apply to stocks. In the long run, you, as a novice investor, will almost surely make out better than an in-and-out trader.

One of the best ways to select a stock is on the basis of your own familiarity with (and respect for) the company's products or services.

Do you have the advice of an experienced and reputable broker who can help guide you?

Do you expect too much too soon? Many inexperienced investors become fidgety when their stocks rise only a little or decline soon after they buy them. They refuse to allow time for their stocks to perform as expected. Millions who have taken short-term losses would have shown handsome profits if they had had more confidence in their own judgment and were willing to give their stocks a chance to move.

The overall caliber of hundreds of the stocks listed on the NYSE is sufficiently high to bail you out of your errors most of the time, assuming you have the courage and capacity to hold on. The odds on gain are heavily against the individual trading blindly in and out of the market and heavily for the individual investing for the long term.

Can you adhere to your investment objectives? Many investors pay lip service to the objective of long-term growth and ask their brokers to recommend stock to them that meet this criterion. Then they hear rumors and read stories about stocks that have doubled and tripled in a period of months. In envy and greed, they soon are badgering their broker to recommend speculative stocks in the hopes of also making tremendous gains. Be honest about your objectives. If you want long-term growth, buy and hold stocks that promise long-term appreciation. Don't be sidetracked into dangerously risky, speculative situations.

Are you fully aware that you buy stocks, not the stock averages? A common error of the amateur is to justify the holding of a "cat or dog" issue because the overall economy is growing or the stock averages are climbing. Even in the biggest bull markets, many stocks slide and, in this era's viciously selective and for so long deeply depressed market, what you own has been critical.

Do you have an overall family investment plan to protect you from falling into "hit or miss" investing? Most new investors overlook the importance of a diversified financial program that allocates funds to major types of investments— real estate (a home), stocks, bonds, etc., in addition to liquid savings in cash or its equivalent, life insurance, and similar vehicles.

There is no formula under which you can automatically put a proper percentage in each type of investment. The key point, though, is to avoid the error of "hit or miss" by diversification of your financial program.

What Causes Prices of Stocks to Change?

Once a company has sold its original stock to the public and the stock is freely traded in the market, the price of the stock will be set solely by what buyers are willing to pay for it and what sellers are willing to take. This is a classic case of how supply and demand operates in action.

Thus the market price of a stock is the reflection of the opinions of all the people who are buying or selling it. Among the key factors influencing the price people are willing to pay for a stock is the company's earnings. The more money a company earns, the greater the value attached to its shares. Obviously, selecting a profitable stock involves knowledge and judgment of the company behind it. How aggressive is its management? How popular are its products and services? What new products is it offering or planning? What about the industry in which it operates? Does it have a bright future? (The trolley car industry once was hot.) What about its competitors? How many and how strong are they?

Finally, what about the general business trend? Is it favorable or unfavorable to the industry in general and your company in particular?

What Are Dividends?

When a company earns a profit, it usually pays a part of its earnings in the form of dividends to its owners—its stockholders. Stockholders receive a certain amount for every share of stock they own. For example, if you own 100 shares of a company's stock and the dividend is $1.00 a share, you will get $100 in dividends. The rest of the company's earnings will be put back in the business.

The decision to pay a dividend on common stock and the amount of the dividend paid are determined by the directors of the company, who are elected by the stockholders. Many factors, including how much the company earned and how much should be retained in the business, influence the directors' decision about the dividend. Traditionally most companies distribute about 50 per cent of their earnings in the form of dividends. A study made in the early 1970s by the New York Stock Exchange showed that the 1,400 companies then listed on the Exchange paid out 51 per cent of earnings as dividends.

There are many companies that have paid dividends over a long span of years. In fact, on the New York Stock Exchange there are companies that have paid out some cash dividends to their stockholders every year for more than a hundred years. J. P. Morgan & Company has been paying dividends since 1840, the Singer

Company has paid dividends since 1863. Also, the New York Stock Exchange lists 170 companies that have paid cash dividends quarterly for fifty years or more.

How Big Are Dividends?

The size of a dividend will depend on what a company earns in any given year. Most companies try to pay dividends regularly each year at a fixed annual rate such as $1.00 or $1.50 or $2.00 for each share of stock. In good years the rate may be increased or an extra dividend declared at the end of the year. In bad years a company may reduce its dividend or eliminate it completely. Interestingly enough, there are some major companies with fine records that don't pay any dividends. They plow back all the earnings they generate for future developments of new products and services. So, while the dividend payment is important for many who are looking for a yield every year on their investment, it does not carry so much weight with other investors.

One important term used in connection with dividends is yield. The yield of a stock is the yearly dividend divided by the cost of the stock. For example, if you paid $60 for a stock that pays $3.00 a year in dividends, your yield is 3/60 or 5 per cent. If you bought a $50 stock and it pays $1.00 a year in dividends, your yield is 2 per cent.

On an overall basis, dividends in modern times have provided yields from as high as 7.8 per cent in 1948 to as low as 2.6 per cent in 1968. This is the median yield on dividend-paying common stocks listed on the New York Stock Exchange, but the range of yields on individual stocks can be very sizable in a given year. For example, in the late 1970s, when the median yield on all NYSE stocks was 4.5 per cent, 136 stocks were paying yields of 8 per cent or better while 166 stocks were paying yields of less than 2 per cent.

How Do You Find Out What Stocks Are Doing?

That's easy! Just look in the financial section of your newspaper for the latest daily reading of any stock market indicator it publishes and see whether that indicator is up or down. The Dow Jones averages and Standard & Poor's indexes are the most familiar of these market "thermometers." The New York Stock Exchange also publishes a composite index that includes all its listed common stocks. The American Stock Exchange publishes one too and the over-the-counter market has a composite NASDAQ index (see page 1005) which indicates the movement of stocks traded in this system. These indexes will tell you at once the price trends of large groups of stocks. In addition to these broad indicators, there are special indexes indicating how special industry groups—such as utilities stocks—have moved as a group.

If you are interested in finding out how a specific stock that you own or may want to buy is doing, you will find that most major newspapers publish detailed price information every day for stocks listed on the New York and American stock exchanges. They may also print condensed lists of stocks traded on regional stock exchanges and the over-the-counter market.

A chart showing you how to read a financial table follows.

Reading Newspaper Stock Tables

NEW YORK STOCK EXCHANGE TRANSACTIONS—DAY OF WEEK, DATE, YEAR									
YEAR				P.E.	SALES				NET
HIGH	LOW	STOCKS	DIV.	RATIO	100's	HIGH	LOW	CLOSE	CHG.
55	49¼	AT&T[1]	2.80	11	1362	51¾	51¼	51¾	—
9⅝[2]	6⅛[2]	AT&T wt[2]	—	—	1221	6⅜	6⅛	6⅜	—
75⅞	59½	Gen Elec	1.40[3]	19	1231	60½	57¾	59¼	−1¼
84⅝	70⅜	Gen Mot	4.45e[4]	9	797	71⅝	70⅝	71⅜	+½
78½	74⅝	Gen Mot pf[5]	5	—	15	75⅝	75	75⅝	+⅝
76⅞	59	McDonalds	—	63[6]	1048	60	58	59⅜	+¼
88⅞	77⅝	M.M.M.	1	34	444[7]	78⅜	77½	78⅛	−⅛
91	68¾	RCAcv.pf[8]	4	—	30	69⅞[8]	68¾[8]	69¾	+½
123¼	94⅞	Sears	1.40a	24	389	97⅝	94½	97[9]	+1⅝[9]

1. Abbreviated name of the corporation issuing the stock. The stocks listed are common stocks unless an entry after the name indicates otherwise.
2. Wt stands for warrant. As with stocks, the price range indicates the highest and lowest prices per share paid for this warrant on the Exchange during the year—in this case, $9.62½ and $6.12½.
3. Rate of annual dividend—for this stock, $1.40. This amount is an estimation based on the last quarterly or semi-annual payment.
4. Letters following the dividend number indicate additional information. Here, for example, the "e" designates the stated amount as declared or paid so far this year. Other symbols are explained in tables appearing in newspapers.
5. "pf" following the name indicates a preferred stock.
6. The price of a share of stock divided by earnings per share for a 12-month period.
7. This column shows the number of shares reported traded for the day, expressed in hundreds—for this stock, 44,400. This number does not include stocks bought in odd-lot quantities, that is, in quantities less than 100 shares for most stocks. The letter "z" preceding an entry indicates the actual number of shares traded.
8. The highest price paid for this security during the day's trading session was $69.87½—the lowest, $68.75. Cv. pf. stands for convertible preferred.
9. The closing price or last sale of the day in this stock was at $97.00 per share. And this, the closing price, is $1.62½ more than the closing price of the previous day—as indicated by the "+1⅝."

If the newspaper doesn't print price information on the stock in which you are interested, chances are the stock is not popular or widely held. In that case, call your broker and ask the price of the stock. He will have a wide variety of reference materials from which he can get the answer.

HOW DO YOU GET INFORMATION ABOUT STOCKS?

Whether you are among the tens of millions of us who already hold shares of publicly owned corporations and mutual funds or among the men and women who are considering becoming stockholders, most of you share this one characteristic: you want to learn more about the stock market and about individual stocks, but you don't know how to go about getting the information.

Okay, here are nine simple guidelines on how to inform yourself:

(1) Make an excellent start by enrolling in one of the courses offered through New York Stock Exchange member firms in major U.S. cities from coast to coast. Under this program, brokers offer lectures covering subjects such as: your investment objectives, investing for income, investing for growth, and methods of investing. Check with your local brokerage houses to find out what they have available and when they plan their next series.

(2) Take courses on investing at adult education institutions across the country. Investigate the sources in your neighborhood. Colleges and junior colleges in your area well may offer special credit and non-credit courses in investment. In New York, the New York Institute of Finance offers broad training in finance to both amateurs and professionals. Some of these courses can be taken by correspondence.

(3) Ask your own broker or investment firm for literature on specific companies and industries as well as on the general stock market. Several hundred New York Stock Exchange firms alone are now turning out more than 400,000 pages of investment research a year—much of it exceedingly helpful.

(4) Get free copies from a local NYSE firm of the Big Board's basic educational pamphlets. You will learn plenty from such publications as *The Language of Investing* and *How to Get Help When You Invest.*

(5) Write to the Publications Department, New York Stock Exchange, 11 Wall Street, New York, New York 10005, for an "Investors' Information Kit" providing basic booklets for $2.50 (cost at end of 1970s).

(6) Use your public library. You will find dozens of useful books written for the amateur as well as for the more sophisticated investor. On pages 1035–37 there is a bibliography of good books on investing that you might want to read.

(7) Read the business and investment news in your newspapers and subscribe to one or more specialized business publications—such as *Barron's, Forbes, Financial World,* and *The Wall Street Journal.* Keep up with trends in the economy as well as with developments in individual industries and companies.

(8) Learn by doing. For instance, you might begin learning through an investment club. These clubs are groups of people who share a common interest, get together usually once a month to discuss securities, and invest small sums contributed by each club member in stocks selected by the group. Brokers often serve as advisers to these clubs and many of the best clubs are members of the National Association of Investment Clubs. Write this association for advice on forming a club. (A separate section on investment clubs follows.)

(9) Check your local educational television stations to see whether any are offering, as some do, a program or programs on general business news and on the stock market.

Any of these moves will help you. All of them will help make you well informed and ready to continue your education on your own. When you make decisions based on facts and your study of available information—plus the help of a qualified broker or adviser—you have gone through the process which distinguishes investing in stocks from gambling.

Your decisions will not always be correct, far from it, but you will at least have acted in a mature, intelligent way. And, being intelligent, you'll not only learn from your mistakes but also translate them into successes.

WHAT IS THE NEW YORK STOCK EXCHANGE?

Although there are tens of thousands of different stocks, the ones bought and sold most frequently are traded on the floor of the New York Stock Exchange. The New York Stock Exchange has a history going back to 1792, well over 185 years ago, when a group of brokers gathered under a buttonwood tree on Wall Street to make up rules of conduct as to how the business of trading in stocks could be done.

Since that humble beginning, the New York Stock Exchange has become the leading securities exchange not only in the United States but also in the world— and many of the world's other exchanges are patterned after its activities.

The Exchange is located in a historic building at 11 Wall Street at the corner of Broad and Wall streets in New York and physically encompasses a trading floor about the size of a football field. On that floor in the late 1970s, more than 2,100 common and preferred stocks were being traded, worth almost $800 billion in market value. In these stocks alone, the number of transactions often equaled 50,000 a day. To handle these transactions, about 2,700 people were involved on the floor of the Exchange.

As the 1980s neared, the Exchange was an organization consisting of 1,366 members who had bought Exchange memberships (commonly called seats) for prices that varied in the past ten to fifteen years from $35,000 to over $500,000. Most of these 1,366 members represent brokerage firms whose primary business is carrying out the orders of other people to buy and sell securities. These brokers are paid commissions for executing the orders placed by their customers.

In the late 1970s, there were nine stock exchanges in the nation: the New York and American (also located in New York City, at 86 Trinity Place), and seven regional exchanges—the Boston, Cincinnati, Intermountain (in Salt Lake City), Midwest (in Chicago), Pacific (with trading facilities in San Francisco and Los Angeles), Philadelphia, and Spokane.

As the decade of the 1970s neared a close, the American, Boston, Midwest, New York, Pacific, and Philadelphia stock exchanges began operating the Intermarket Trading System (ITS), an electronic communications network. The system enables brokers representing public customers to reach out electronically to another participating exchange to obtain a better price on dually or multiply listed stocks. In effect, ITS links the nation's major exchange trading floors to create a nationwide trading environment.

The Intermarket Trading System was a response to securities legislation passed by Congress in the mid 1970s that called for the creation of a national market system for trading securities. While the national market system is supposed to encourage competition, Congress did not spell out how this should be done or how the system should be structured. As a result, it may be many more years before the government and the securities industry hammer out a system that fully satisfies the congressional mandate. Blueprints for such a system range from one not unlike today's system of stock trading to such extreme proposals as a fully computerized stock exchange that would eliminate trading floors and traders.

At the approach of the 1980s, however, the New York Stock Exchange still dominates stock trading. It does the bulk of trading in listed securities because of the high caliber of its markets in the shares of its listed corporations: AT&T, IBM, General Motors, General Electric, etc. To be listed on the Big Board, companies have to meet the highest existing standards. These standards involve earnings, assets, number of shares outstanding, number of stockholders, and number of stockholders who held at least 100 shares. The standards for listing on the New York Stock Exchange also are raised periodically.

The listing standards of the American Stock Exchange (known as the Amex) were deliberately established at a lower level—and to the Amex went many young, smaller corporations not yet seasoned enough to meet the NYSE criteria.

Most regional exchanges traded in stocks that also were listed on the New York Stock Exchange. In fact, 90 per cent of their volume came from issues listed on the NYSE. In addition, the regional stock exchanges traded in local stocks. For instance, stocks of Chicago-based companies were traded on the Midwest Stock Exchange.

What Are Unlisted Securities?

Stocks listed on recognized exchanges are called listed stocks. Huge numbers of stocks and bonds, however, aren't listed on any exchange at all and are bought and sold in what is called the over-the-counter market.

The vast over-the-counter market is not a place. It is a method of doing business: by private negotiation among securities broker/dealers who communicate via an immense communications network rather than use a trading floor on which to buy and sell securities.

It is a market which in volume and variety of transactions dwarfs the listed exchanges. And it is a market which not only has no market place; it also has no ticker tape and not even any rigidly fixed hours of trading.

Most bank and insurance company stocks are traded in this market. So are U. S. Government bonds, municipal bonds, and as of the late 1970s the securities of some large, well-known companies (Anheuser-Busch, Bekins Company, Ethan Allen, Noxell). But unlisted securities in general are those of small companies.

The over-the-counter market offers investors a broad variety of issues ranging from the most conservative to the most speculative. Here investors will find many attractive growth stocks of companies which have not yet become popular because they operate in a regional area rather than on the national scene. Here the stocks are given time to "mature" before they are listed on one of the exchanges.

WHAT ARE BULL AND BEAR MARKETS?

When a lot of people decide at about the same time to buy stocks, this increase in buying interest tends to push up the average price of stocks. If the price rise of these stocks overall is substantial and prolonged it is called a bull market.

When a lot of people decide at about the same time to sell stocks, their more or less simultaneous selling tends to push down the average price of stocks. If the price decline is substantial and prolonged it is called a bear market. If the price decline is both substantial and precipitous, we run into the possibility of a panic.

To be bullish or bearish, then, simply means to think that stocks will go up or down. The reason the term "bull" is linked with those who expect an uplift in prices is probably the tendency of a bull to lift and throw up an object with his horns. The bear is usually more cautious in his fighting tactics and tries to knock down his opponent.

WHAT ABOUT BROKERS? COMMISSIONS?

If you are to do your buying and selling of stocks through a broker, it is obviously of vital importance to you to choose one who can service your account properly. But don't create a tough and unnecessary problem for yourself by expecting the broker you choose to be right all the time. For he won't be—and when he is wrong, you may be tempted to follow the tips of amateurs who intrigue you by claiming they are making fortunes. This way often leads to disaster and every day a dismally large percentage of Americans do take this course. Even the most astute professional will not be right all of the time. In fact, in some periods, his advice will range from indifferent to downright bad.

Choosing and recommending stocks is not a science. It is an art. Your broker should be right enough of the time to help guide you toward your investment objectives and help you to enhance your assets. You should be able to trust his experience, research, and judgment and you should feel comfortable with him. That's all. It's *your* money, *your* investment program. And basically your nest egg is *your responsibility*.

Here are five key rules to follow in selecting a broker.

(1) Choose a firm that is a member of the New York Stock Exchange. Of course there are non-member firms that also rank at the top, but you are a beginner and you probably have no sound information on these. The New York Stock Exchange in the late 1970s had about 470 firms including nearly all the important firms doing business with the public, for an estimated 90 per cent of all the securities business in the country. Moreover, member firms of the New York Stock Exchange must meet the highest standards established to date—fulfill minimum capital requirements, undergo both an annual surprise audit by an independent CPA firm and spot financial checks by the Exchange. The member firm's brokers must complete a minimum training period of four months and pass an Exchange examination. These requirements give you at least some protection and it is only common sense to accept it.

(2) Examine the brokerage firm's commission schedule. Since May 1975 commission rates charged by exchange member firms have been negotiable. Until that time, exchanges determined the commissions brokerage firms could charge.

Now that brokerage rates are unfixed, you can and should shop for the best available terms.

Most brokerage firms charge small customers rates similar to the old uniform commissions—but several so-called discount brokerage firms have emerged. While they provide few, if any, of the services you may expect from a brokerage firm—research, investment advice, a broad range of products and services—they will buy or sell stocks for you for fees which are frequently much lower than those of the major firms.

If you are an investor who knows exactly what you want to do and expect your brokers merely to carry out your orders, these discount brokers can be money savers. If you are an investor who needs or wants advice, counsel, and investment information, traditional brokerage firms may offer more value.

(3) Shop around as you would shop around for any service as important as this. Ask your friends, business acquaintances, and local banker for recommendations on which broker might be the best for you—particularly important in the uncertain conditions of the late 1970s. Call at least three or four brokerage firms in your area and talk to the manager of each. Tell each one about your investment goals, the amounts of money you can invest, and ask whether he can assign someone to your account with whom he thinks you will have good rapport.

(4) Ask each firm for its recommendations of investments for a person in your financial position and for its research reports on the companies suggested. Incidentally, the person who will eventually be assigned to you may be variously called a registered representative, a customer's man, or an account executive—but you will call him your broker.

(5) Select your broker on the basis of your comparisons of the firms and their advice to you. Then give the broker all the pertinent facts about your financial circumstances and goals. The more he knows about your situation, the better he can advise you. Be frank and honest. Ask what you should reasonably expect in terms of capital gains and over what period of time. Find out how much service he can provide, how often you should expect him to call you, and how often he expects you to call him for information.

THERE'S A WAY TO BUY STOCKS
WITHOUT PAYING ANY COMMISSION

Q. *Would you like to build your portfolio of stocks or add to good stocks you already own without having to pay any brokerage commissions at all—not even the "bargain" commissions offered by discount brokers?*

A. Of course you would. And you can achieve this by accumulating your stocks through one of the dividend reinvestment plans offered by some nine hundred of the largest, most widely held corporations in the United States as the 1980s opened.

And not only do these plans permit you to reinvest your dividends on extremely favorable terms, but many also give you an option under which you can invest additional cash (over and above what you receive as the dividend payment) for the purchase of the company's stock under similarly favorable terms to you.

The dividend reinvestment part of this is not new. An estimated 1.5 to 2 million individuals and institutions already are participating in these so-called "original issue stock dividend reinvestment plans." It has been estimated that each year in the late 1970s between $800 million and $1 billion was reinvested by stockholders under these plans.

The benefits of the plans are undeniable:

• You are provided a simple, convenient, and economical way to invest relatively small amounts, at substantial savings in brokerage commissions and administrative costs.

• The automatic reinvestment is, in effect, forced savings—and most of us need this discipline to keep us from dissipating the relatively small amounts we would get in cash dividends.

• The automatic reinvestment also is a form of "dollar cost" averaging (see pages 1012–13), which means you buy the stock in price downturns as well as upturns and "average out" your purchase prices. It's a superb way to avoid buying only at peaks, as so many do.

• The compounding effects that result from this periodic reinvesting produce larger dividends as your investment grows which in turn are reinvested, etc.

Significant new twists also are being developed.

• Some companies have started offering shareholders a 5 per cent discount with the purchase of shares through dividend reinvestment.

• The cash option is even more significant because it permits you to invest additional cash in the stock at specified times (generally quarterly or monthly) and within specified limits (generally a maximum of $3,000 per quarter) without payment of brokerage commissions or any administrative cost to you. All your invested dollars go toward the purchase of shares, none for expenses usually involved.

You might build a diversified portfolio including many of our nation's leading companies simply by making modest original investments in these companies—and then taking advantage of the dividend reinvestment privilege and the "cash" option plan.

The companies find the programs beneficial, too (or they wouldn't be offering them). And you could, over a reasonable span of time, accumulate a substantial portfolio of leading U.S. stocks, without paying any brokerage commissions on the major part of your holding. Not bad!

BUT WHERE DO YOU FIND A BROKER WHO WANTS YOU?

Let's say you don't participate in a dividend reinvestment plan but you do want to start buying stocks. However, you don't know any brokerage firms in your area with which to open an account and you're not sure where to turn. What do you do?

You send a postcard including your name and address to PIO Directory, Public Information Office, New York Stock Exchange, Inc., 11 Wall Street, New York, New York 10005. You will receive by return mail and without charge a small pamphlet giving you the names and headquarters addresses of hundreds of New York Stock Exchange member firms which say they are willing and able to handle your small account—and listing what minimum requirements and criteria each firm may have.

In the late 1970s these firms had 3,500 branch offices in more than 800 cities in all 50 states, of which more than 1,000 or 33 per cent were located in 24 major U.S. cities. More than nine out of ten of them say they do not have a minimum dollar requirement for the size of any buy or sell order they will accept from you. More than eight out of ten (or about 2,000 branch offices) say they will buy for or sell to you any stock traded on the major stock exchanges at any price—with no minimum price-per-share limitations either.

What the NYSE is obviously trying to do with this free pamphlet is to counter in part at least the very negative publicity Wall Street has received for its attitude toward and treatment of the small investor in the past several years.

How Do You Detect a Swindler?

Another key rule to follow in selecting a broker is: explore each of the following questions about any person who suggests stocks to you, even a broker at what you believe is a highly reputable firm—and *if any answer is yes, beware, for these are frequently the earmarks of a swindler.*

Does he plug one certain stock and refuse to sell you anything else? The crook always has a specific stock to sell and he'll not bother with you if you request another stock or ask for written information about the company he's plugging.

Does he promise a quick, sure profit? The legitimate broker never guarantees that the price of any given stock will go up. Nor will he attempt to guarantee you against losses.

Does he claim to have inside information? Second only to outright fraud, alleged "inside information" has cost investors more money than anything else. Most tips are phony, and furthermore, if he truly does have inside information, there is always the possibility that at some future date he might be sued by other investors because he improperly obtained the inside information and you too might be liable in a lawsuit if you use the inside information.

Is he in a hurry and does he urge you to buy "before the price goes up"? The legitimate broker doesn't try to stampede you into action.

Can you check his reputation? The crook will have no references except perhaps forged ones which won't stand checking.

Employee Savings Plans

An excellent way to enter the stock market and start creating your securities nest egg is via your company's employee savings plan—if it offers one.

The fundamental mechanism of an employee savings plan is simple.

(1) A participant voluntarily contributes part of his or her salary through payroll deductions. The most common contribution is 3 to 6 per cent of one's salary.

(2) The company then matches all or part of the participant's savings with a company contribution. The average is 50 cents by the company for each $1.00 the employee saves, but in some companies the corporation contribution is higher.

(3) The company and employee contributions are put into an employee trust fund to be invested and later paid out to the employees. In some cases, part of the funds are placed in the company's own common stock, but usually the investments are in a wide selection of stocks similar to the range of a mutual fund portfolio. And, generally speaking, the company turns over the management of these investments to a professional management company which oversees them.

A majority of employees in companies offering these plans take advantage of them. Most save at the maximum rate their plan permits. And most stay in their plan until they leave their jobs or retire. There are many benefits. First, the company is automatically boosting the chances you will get a profit from the savings program by the amount of money it has put in to match your contributions. Second, you get professional management of your funds at no cost to you and you also get a diversification of a portfolio which helps make sure that, over the long term, the overall fund will grow. And third, there are tax advantages arising from the fact that your employer's contribution is not taxable income to you in the year in which it is made. You pay no taxes on this money and only pay taxes on the contributions when you finally draw out your nest egg on leaving the company or retirement.

A variation on this program is company stock purchase plans. Under these, the company helps encourage employees to buy stock in the company. In the simplest version, an employee signs up to purchase stock in the company through payroll deductions every month and is credited over the period of his or her participation with buying shares of the stock. The company usually picks up the bill for any commissions or other fees involved in the purchase of the stock and keeps all the records indicating how many shares of stock the employee owns. Obviously, if you are having $50 or $100 a month deducted from your paycheck to buy stock, you will wind up with fractional shares of stock and this is permissible under these company stock purchase plans.

Use one of these plans if you get the opportunity. They are a superb plus for any employee eligible to save and invest this way.

HOW TO START AN INVESTMENT CLUB

Let's say you feel that the only way you'll get started in the stock market is by being forced to invest a certain amount every month or so—and you want to do this via an investment club.

If so, you have plenty of company. In the late 1970s there were about 25,000 investment clubs across the nation with an estimated membership of more than 375,000. The majority of the clubs in operation for several years have been profitable, reports the non-profit National Association of Investment Clubs in Royal Oak, Michigan. Some 71,000 people belonged to clubs that were members of the NAIC and the track record on the investing of these clubs has in a surprising percentage of cases impressively surpassed the Dow Jones averages—not bad at all considering the fact that many professional managers of money didn't do nearly as well.

Basically, investment clubs are groups of ten, fifteen, or twenty people who work together, know each other socially, or belong to the same fraternal or business organization—and who then meet once a month to invest money regularly. In a sense, each club is akin to a small mutual fund with each club's members contributing $10, $15, $20, $25, or perhaps as much as $50 a month apiece into the club kitty for investment in stocks. Before stocks are purchased the club's members must make extensive investigations on the choices to be made.

If you are thinking of or are at the point of trying to start an investment club, you must recognize that you will be inviting a financial fiasco unless you know and manage your group according to the basic rules. Here are your ten guidelines:

(1) Limit your initial membership to ten or fifteen people. An investment club should be a long-term proposition and your members must be compatible not only personally but also in their attitudes toward investment.

(2) Understand, from the outset, that an investment club offers no avenue to instant riches. Instead, a get-rich-quick philosophy frequently is the cause for a club's failure.

(3) In an exploratory meeting with prospective members, try to arrive at an overall investment policy. For instance, what growth rate of your funds will you try to achieve? Will you invest every month?

(4) Set a reasonable goal for growth of your investments, including dividends and capital appreciation.

(5) Plan to invest a given sum each month no matter what the overall market conditions are. By buying shares of a selected company at both higher and lower prices, you average out the per-share cost over the long term.

(6) Plan also to reinvest dividends as they are issued.

(7) Aim for a diversified portfolio as protection against major swings in one segment of the economy or another. Strive, say, for shares in a dozen different companies per $10,000 invested.

(8) Seek guidance from well-qualified brokers, economists, security analysts, and established business publications. The amount of research and self-education members are willing to do and share with each other can mark the difference between a successful and an unsuccessful club.

(9) Before you formally establish your club, consult a qualified lawyer or tax adviser on how to get the biggest tax advantage for your club. Your club should have some legal status because brokers may refuse to do business with an informal organization. Usually, a partnership is the most economical form. If there are earnings in any given year, all members must report this on their income tax returns, of course.

(10) Also at the start, draw up a written agreement covering the club's investment policy; the maximum proportion any one member may own; which member will deal with the club's broker; how much information each will be expected to present monthly; what happens if a member wants to leave and wants to be paid

out for his or her shares. Also make sure when you establish your club how much each will be expected to contribute monthly—and make sure, too, that the amount is a comfortable sum for each member.

Follow these rules, consult the NAIC for more detailed guidelines—and the likelihood is that your club will be profitable. Incidentally, there are many NAIC publications that you will find useful when trying to decide which stocks to buy. For illustration, the NAIC has and will send you samples of a fifty-page investor's manual, stock selection guides, and a portfolio guide ($6.00).

The NAIC's address is 1515 East Eleven Mile Road, Royal Oak, Michigan 48068.

How to Beat the Stock Market Through "Dollar Cost Averaging"

One way you can beat any viciously fluctuating stock market, put your money to work, and sleep well at night is through "dollar cost averaging"—a stock-buying method that many institutional as well as individual investors use in a logical attempt to acquire a stock at a reasonable price.

First, let's assume you don't have any convictions about where the stock market is heading in the next several months—but you feel strongly that the long-term trend of the U.S. economy is upward and stock prices will be much higher on the average ten years, fifteen years from now.

Let's also assume you've accumulated some extra cash and you earn enough to be able to accumulate cash for investment from time to time. Okay:

(1) Decide now how much money you can comfortably invest at regular intervals.

(2) Plan to invest the same fixed amount at regular intervals in the future—say, the fifteenth of each month or the fifteenth of every third month or the fifteenth of every sixth month, etc. Don't get fainthearted and hold back purchases if the market drops.

(3) Keep this up over the long-term, so your shares can grow with the economy's growth over five or ten or more years.

(4) Ignore the day-to-day fluctuations in the market, for you aren't trying to guess the bottom. You're averaging out your costs and the fundamental uptrend of the market over the long-term should carry you with it.

Here's an easy example of dollar cost averaging with a hypothetical investment of $50 a month. The price swings have been exaggerated and commissions have been eliminated to make the illustration stand out.

Date	Invested	Price per Share	Shares Bought
Jan. 15 1980	$50	$25	2
Feb. 15	50	20	2½
Mar. 15	50	15	3⅓
Apr. 15	50	15	3⅓
May 15	50	20	2½
June 15	50	25	2
July 15	50	30	1⅔

As you can see, you have bought fewer shares at the higher prices, more shares at the lower prices—with equal amounts of money. The average price of your shares on the seven dates is $21.43 per share. But with your $350 you have purchased 17⅓ shares, so each share has cost you $20.19.

In this hypothetical case, you would be showing a paper loss in April 1980, but you would be nicely ahead by July 15 (your cost per share, $20.19; the market, $30).

You can, of course, lose even with this system if your judgment is so bad that you buy a stock that doesn't realize its growth potential or if you are forced to sell out when the market value of your accumulated shares is less than your actual cost. So you can't commit funds to dollar cost averaging that may be needed for other purposes.

But I'm assuming that you'll follow these easy—but absolutely essential—rules. If so, history shouts that over the long-term you'll come out well ahead.

INVESTMENT ADVICE—WHERE DO YOU GET IT?

Most investors expect, ask for, and get advice on buying and selling stocks from their stockbrokers. Most brokerage firms have research departments or access to professional research staffs and constantly feed their clients (you) with a stream of buy and sell recommendations. Some firms will even manage your portfolio on a non-discretionary basis—meaning you give the broker authority (discretion) to buy and sell without checking back for your approval. (Many brokers, though, shy away from such accounts.)

All you have traditionally paid for such services has been your commission fees—nothing more. But this is in the process of change—and this is just one of many great new changes taking place in the field of investment advice. Read on . . .

PROFESSIONAL INVESTMENT MANAGEMENT—TREND OF THE FUTURE

When my husband and I accumulated a nest egg to invest in securities some years back, we entrusted it to a small, little-known, but top-notch investment counsel firm in Wall Street. We paid the firm an annual fee based on a small percentage of our portfolio's overall total value each year. In return, the firm took over all investment decisions and worked to increase the size of the portfolio and, thus, the size of its fee. When the firm was dissolved about a decade later and we reluctantly terminated our relationship, we were spectacularly ahead of the Dow Jones average. We couldn't possibly have done as well devoting a few hours (if that) a week to managing our money.

This type of professional management for a fee is now in a renaissance and breaking into entirely new areas. The investment manager who supervises the funds of the small investor for a fee is one of the financial trends of the future in our country. Brokerage companies have taken over or set up investment management subsidiaries which are wooing accounts in the up to $25,000 range. Some established investment advisers are cutting the minimum account they'll manage for a fee to $10,000. And a growing number of banks are taking accounts as small as $10,000 (and even under) to manage. Until fairly recently banks were interested only in $100,000-and-up accounts.

Also new on the scene are a growing number of small investment counsel firms which accept accounts as low as $5,000. These are the so-called "minicounselors" and the likelihood is there will be hundreds servicing the small investor in a few years.

The reasons for this unexpected movement to serve the small investor aren't hard to find. The market declines of the 1970s made millions of small investors brutally aware of how atrociously unprepared they were to manage their own money. They were also bitterly disillusioned by the performance of their go-go mutual fund shares. Simultaneously, many brokerage firms discovered just how profitable it could be to handle the small investors' business. What's more, trading in and out of stock to make commissions on small accounts came in for universal condemnation.

Here are several key characteristics of the investment counsel firms.

The firm will take responsibility for your entire investment portfolio, will buy and sell on your behalf to achieve whatever goals are consistent with your needs, and will generally aim for enhancement of your portfolio's value. These firms make no commissions on your transactions. Their earnings come from the set percentage fee—usually 1½ or 2 per cent or a minimum dollar amount—you pay on your total portfolio and thus they profit most when you profit.

Your fee will be tied to the size of your account. A typical fee might be 2 per cent of the total, or 2 per cent on the first $10,000 and a smaller percentage on amounts above $10,000. Others might charge a yearly minimum of $250. Fees are usually payable annually, although you may arrange otherwise. Of course, the fees are deductible on your federal tax return if you itemize.

You pay your own brokerage commissions in addition to the fee you pay. Sometimes you can ask the investment adviser to put your trades through your own broker, but generally you open a brokerage account with a firm suggested by your investment adviser.

You receive a statement—usually monthly—of all transactions and a list of securities you own and a periodic report on the progress of your account.

You may open your account with cash or securities or both. You usually give your adviser a limited power of attorney so he can make discretionary investment decisions for you. All securities are bought in your name and you alone can withdraw capital or securities from your account. You may cancel the power of attorney at any time.

Generally, you give your investment adviser discretion to make investments for you without consulting you every time he wants to buy or sell something for your portfolio. Some advisers, however, do consult with clients in advance of taking action, and still others do not want a discretionary account setup.

You may close out your account at any time on written notice. You may have dividends credited to your account or sent to you. You may withdraw a given percentage of your funds on a regular basis and you also may tell your adviser what stocks or industries you want to avoid.

But the central point of this is that in most cases you have no control over what securities are bought and sold for you. Your adviser takes over once your objectives are set. He's paid a fee to help you achieve your investment goals.

Of course, there are many variations in the way investment counseling is developing. Under the usual bank setup, the bank sends you a list of its recommendations on securities to be bought and sold. You then indicate if you agree and send the buy and sell order documents to your broker for execution.

Under the way most minicounselors operate, each client has his own account with an average of from five to ten or twelve stocks, depending on the size of the account. Thus, if the minicounselor has given you some very good advice and you hold a cross section of excellent securities in your portfolio, your whole portfolio can grow rapidly in value.

Obviously, you can't expect the fancy treatment given someone with a million-dollar account. You will not have long personal interviews; you may talk to your counselor only on the phone and even then not too much; you will not receive a portfolio designed just for you; you will find that your portfolio is quite similar to other accounts that the minicounselor manages.

But there is nothing wrong with any of this, for presumably the stocks recommended to you are the stocks in which the firm has confidence.

How Do You Choose the Right Adviser for You?

(1) Decide at the very beginning what *your* investment objectives are: Long-term growth? Current income? Maximum safety? Compare your objectives with the stated investment philosophy (if any) of each of the investment management firms you are considering.

(2) Explore the credentials of each firm's officers and research staff. Where does it get its investment research? Investment counseling has been an unregulated field in the past with no established standards for the counselors. It's only recently that the SEC has moved to set up some sort of standards.

(3) Ask the firm to provide you with references against which you can check these credentials—and follow up on them. Check with local banks and brokerage firms. Do not hesitate to query other clients to whom you are referred. Question any friends or acquaintances who may have been clients or may have information.

(4) Pay particular attention to the performance records of the firm. How have the organization's actual accounts made out during the past five or ten years? (*Not* a selected "model" account!) If the firm hasn't been in existence that long, check back on the previous performance records of its individual members with other organizations. If the firm refuses to divulge its performance records, be skeptical about any of its claims.

(5) See what you can find out about the firm's performances in bear as well as bull markets. A firm should be able to demonstrate it has at least lost less than average in bear markets and surely gained more than average in bull markets.

(6) Make sure you differentiate between a firm's stated investment goal of a growth rate per account of, say, 10 to 15 per cent a year and its actual achievement.

(7) Try to interview personally at least one or two of the firm's officers and use this interview to discuss your investment goals and to ask such questions as these:

Are you permitted to specify the securities in which you want to invest? The answer should be no, or why pay your money for professional advice?

What is the procedure for withdrawing part or all of your funds to, say, meet an emergency? Can you do so immediately? How much, if any, of the fee is refundable if you cancel before completing a year?

How many different companies are in the portfolio of a typical account of the same size as yours? How often is your account reviewed?

At what intervals do you receive financial statements covering trading activity and progress reports on your portfolio? Who will have custody of your account?

(8) Before you make your decision among firms, compare the fees charged as well as their services and investment philosophies.

(9) Beware of any manager who pushes you to sign up. No reputable firm will use this type of hard sell. Take your time.

(10) But once you have selected a firm you consider competent, alert, and geared to your needs, don't try to second-guess the manager or push in turn. Let your investment counselor exercise the judgment you're paying for during a reasonable time span. Then reconsider, if need be.

WAY OUT ON THE HORIZON—
FINANCIAL SUPERMARKETS AND FINANCIAL PLANNERS

When the "financial supermarket" finally comes, it will be one of the most exciting developments on the U.S. financial scene: most, if not all, the major financial services you need available to you under one roof. And surely several emerging trends are telegraphing what is ahead.

Commercial banks are not only expanding their activities in the management of investment portfolios for both the little and the big fellow, they also are preparing income tax returns for a fee, aggressively promoting their extensive estate planning services, pushing innovations in paying of customer bills, creating new savings methods, and maintaining leadership in the overall lending field. Many banks are moving fairly close to one-stop financial centers even now.

Similarly, insurance companies are expanding the forms of insurance sold under one roof: life, homeowner's, health, etc. They are increasingly powerful factors in the making of personal as well as institutional loans. The insurance salesman who sells mutual funds is commonplace. Now an increasing number of insurance companies are planning stock brokerage subsidiaries.

Stock brokerage firms are studying the concept with utmost seriousness. Some brokers are diversifying by buying real estate and investment management companies. Many brokers now sell life insurance, some handle tax shelters (real estate, oil, and cattle deals). Although no brokerage firm is anything like a one-stop center, the giants are known to be working on it.

Still way out on the horizon is the organization which offers in one place *truly professional, high-caliber* assistance on services of such scope as: investment advice on stocks, bonds, mutual funds, other mediums; guidance on a sound overall insurance program; help in making out your income tax; financial planning for retirement; assistance in planning your estate and drawing up your will; bill-paying; on and on.

Why is the financial supermarket so easy to explain, so difficult to achieve?

The key stumbling block is the need for truly high-caliber professional experts. For such supermarkets can come into existence only when they are staffed by experts trained in each area, capable of giving you the assistance you want and guiding you, the individual. Although we have independent experts in each area, bringing them together in a constructive, profitable arrangement is something else again.

Another stumbling block is the establishment of standards for such a group, for in the long run this is imperative to protect the public. Several organizations are now at work to develop a professional category of "financial planner" and this should be a reality by the early 1980s.

Meanwhile, though, all over the country new small organizations are springing up to service on a completely different basis the overall financial needs of individuals. Their business takes a wholly different approach to the financial supermarket concept. These firms provide a broad range of financial counseling and advice to their clients but they usually *don't* offer any products.

What they do is analyze an individual's needs for insurance, savings, stocks, bonds, mutual funds; plan tax and estate strategy; and then come up with an integrated package of recommendations touching on about every aspect of the client's financial needs. But their work generally stops right there. If the client wants to follow the firm's recommendations, he does it through his own broker, insurance agent, banker, accountant, and lawyer.

The financial planning organization gets a fee for the master financial program it presents and doesn't try to make any commissions from the stocks or mutual funds the client buys or legal or accounting fees the client pays to implement the recommendations on estate planning and tax strategy.

So far, only a handful of organizations provide such services and their fees are steep. It is not unusual for a plan tailored to an individual's requirements and needs to cost $2,000 to $4,000. As a result, most customers for this service are wealthy individuals; in some cases corporations pay the costs of such programs for their executives and consider it an additional fringe benefit.

However, these new-breed financial planning organizations are working on ways to cut the cost of their services so they can serve the needs of the many millions of you who need professional help but can't pay such staggering fees.

On one side, there is growing interest by major financial institutions in developing financial supermarkets. On the other, there is the growth of professional financial planning firms offering comprehensive financial programs.

Between these, it seems clear that the professional assistance and variety of financial services available to you in the future will be vastly superior to any existing today.

STOCK MARKET LETTERS

If you don't want to go the investment adviser route, but want another source of investment advice besides your own broker, you might consider subscribing to one of the many stock market letters that are available. The letters range in quality from excellent to awful, so check with some of your business associates to get an idea of those that are highly regarded. The price tags on such letters can run from $25 to $1,000 a year and no one has yet proven that the price tag for such a market letter and the value of its advice go hand in hand.

One thing you should know: most market letter writers make their money from the *subscriptions they sell and not by using their own investment advice.*

HOW TO AVOID THE "GARBAGE" STOCKS

It is not only in so-called hot new issues that you find "garbage" stocks that should intrigue only the wildest gamblers—who know what they are doing and can afford the risks. You can find these unknown "growth" stocks outstanding in the over-the-counter markets and listed on the smaller stock exchanges too.

How do you, an average speculator-gambler, protect yourself from this garbage? How do you speculate-gamble intelligently?

Here are ten questions to ask yourself which when answered honestly will be a superb guide to this sort of speculation:

(1) Is this a high-quality stock in its own industry? It should be. It could be a dominant company in a small industry. Or it could be number one but still a small company in a big, fragmented industry. Whatever, it should be at the top.

(2) Does it have a record of solid earnings even in adverse times? How, for instance, did it make out in 1969–70, in 1973–74, in 1976–77?

(3) Has it a history of steady, solid growth? Buy a company with a history unless you're willing to admit you're in a wild gamble.

(4) Is the company's product or service sufficiently appealing to make customers willing to pay a good price for it? You can check this one out by your own willingness to pay for the products or services.

(5) Is the company saddled with long-term debt? It's okay for it to be aggressive in sales, but it should be conservative in finance. A well-managed, growing company should be able to pay off its debts.

(6) Is it paying a dividend? It probably should *not* be. A strongly growing company can use that dividend money more profitably than you can. A no-dividend policy usually is a plus.

(7) Has it a high degree of profitability? Its per-share earnings should be rising each year by at least 9 per cent. Some professionals put the level for professional selections much higher than that, but for you, the amateur, 9 per cent should be the yardstick.

(8) Is the stock already popular or its product or service already a fad? Then beware: the stock is probably fully priced by now, and you want to beat the mob, not follow it.

(9) Is the company subject to government regulation? If so, avoid it. Regulatory agencies generally limit a company's gains, but they let it chalk up all the losses.

(10) Are you risking too much of your money in this speculation? Don't. The time-honored rule against putting all your eggs in one basket applies particularly to high-risk growth stocks. You could be wrong in your decision. Protect yourself by diversifying.

What About Regional and Second-Tier Stocks?

Most investors are interested in the big national companies with well-known products and names that are household bywords. And in the past the big brokerage firms concentrated their research efforts on analyzing these firms.

But in the late 1970s, attention turned to the so-called regional stocks—issues of companies that basically serve a small geographic area—and "second-tier" stocks—issues of smaller companies listed on exchanges or traded over the counter. Regional stocks, as their name implies, may be well known locally but their products and services aren't known nationally. Second-tier stocks are small but solid companies which may be known nationally, although not as well known as the giants.

What the security analysts discovered—and so did the public—is that many regional and second-tier firms had the makings to become major national companies, yet they were undervalued in price just because not many investors knew about them. In fact, many corporations that have become fairly well known in recent years started out as junior stocks. As a result, Wall Street firms now try to discover the smaller companies that might become the IBMs or Xeroxes of tomorrow.

So, as an investor, do not downgrade a recommendation to buy a stock just because it represents a company you never heard about before. It well may be easier for you to find a real growth stock among the outstanding regional and second-tier firms than on the lists of the national firms which have been carefully and repeatedly studied by countless numbers of analysts.

How to Read an Annual Report

Each year American shareholders receive more than 70 million annual reports from some 11,000 publicly owned U.S. corporations. But a shocking proportion of you will throw away these valuable documents without even opening the envelopes and many others of you simply will skim over the highlights.

If you are among these millions, you are junking the single most important account of the financial health of your company and your single best measure of how well (or how poorly) your savings now are invested. If you are also an employee of the company in which you own stock, your indifference is really inexcusable.

Why do so many stockholders, as many as 40 per cent according to one study, ignore this key document? What are corporations doing to win stockholders' confidence in their annual reports and to make the reports more readable?

Only a couple of decades ago the typical annual report did not contain even a table of contents to guide you through its maze of facts and figures. The typical report told the shareholder how the company did the previous year but gave no figures for other years to help you measure its long-term trends. The untrained shareholder was at the mercy of the professional corporation statisticians and accountants and considerable imagination went into the preparation of the balance sheets.

Now this has changed dramatically. Virtually all major corporations today provide not only detailed indexes in their annual reports but usually also a generous assortment of easy-to-read charts and summaries so you can judge at a glance your company's and its industry's progress. The crucially important ten-year summary of financial highlights, rare ten to fifteen years ago, is now commonplace. A growing number of corporations are printing financial highlights on the covers of their annual reports, to lure more readers to look inside and delve further into their figures.

In Europe, corporation financial reports frequently omit key figures, use outdated information, or fudge statistics beyond semblance of reality. In this country, though, today's shareholder can, with few exceptions, trust every fact, figure, and footnote in every annual report he receives. Helping to assure the accuracy and completeness of financial reports are the rules of the major U.S. stock exchanges, the regulations of the Securities and Exchange Commission, and the accounting principles established by the Financial Accounting Standards Board. Virtually all annual reports now contain a "stamp of approval" of a reputable outside auditing firm or a statement by this firm that it takes issue with some aspect of the report—and why.

Today even the unsophisticated investor can see through most effects a company may still make to obscure bad financial news. In the words of one expert, "When the president's letter to shareholders begins with 'The year was a period of adjustment for your company,' you can assume it was a bad year." Or you can simply turn to the record itself and judge.

Despite the progress, though, it's not easy (and never will be) to understand a corporation annual report. Thus, here is a glossary of key items and the basic rules for interpreting them intelligently.

(1) *The president's letter to stockholders* is the first place to look for a summary of your company's financial highlights for the previous year, plus the reasons why profits were up or down. This letter or the subsequent text also should give you the company's own assessment of its short- and long-term outlook, with supporting facts.

(2) *The "income statement" or "earnings report"* is a summary of the year's sales volume, other income, costs, net profits or losses with comparative figures for the previous year. The crucial figure is the company's net income or net profit and this figure should be compared to profits over the previous five or ten years (usually summarized separately).

(3) *The "price-earnings ratio"* is a measure of how the overall investment community views your company. The ratio won't appear in an annual report, but you can calculate it by dividing the current market price of a share of your stock by the company's per-share earnings noted in the earnings report. A ratio well below the average for the company's industry or for business in general may reflect investor wariness of the future profit potential of the company and/or for the industry.

(4) *The "retained earnings statement"* tells you what share of company profits is being returned to you in the form of dividends and what share is being held back. If the proportion going to you in dividends declines sharply, look for an explanation of how the extra funds are being reinvested.

(5) *Footnotes often reveal important information.* A footnote, for instance, might tell you that an unusually high profit stemmed from a one-shot ("nonrecurring") financial windfall. It may be tedious, but read those footnotes!

If the annual report you receive does not contain at least these basic items of information, or the facts from which to calculate them yourself, ask your stockbroker for further details. Your broker also can provide you with the industrywide record. This is the minimum you should know about the company and the industry in which you are investing your savings.

WHAT IS A "BLUE CHIP"?

Ask a dozen stock market experts to define a "blue chip" and you may get a dozen different answers. I, though, stick to the original rules for spotting a blue chip—for they are basic, time-tested, and always have value.

To begin with, the name "blue chip" is traced easily to the game of poker, in which there are three colors of chips: blue, the highest value; red, next in rank; white, the lowest value.

Now here are four yardsticks for a blue chip:

(1) A long history of good earnings performance in recessions as well as in booms. This does not mean the company's earnings must be skyrocketing. It does mean the company must be turning in a record of solid profits year after year.

(2) A long history of cash dividend payments, and, again, the record must be consistent in bad times as well as good.

(3) Recognition as an established leader in an established industry. There can be several leaders in an established industry. For instance, General Motors and Ford in the auto industry or Eastman Kodak and Polaroid in the camera industry.

(4) A clear prospect for continued earnings growth and dividend payments in the years ahead: a solid—but not flashy—outlook.

Of course, today's red chip can become tomorrow's blue and today's blue can fade into tomorrow's white. The dividend yardstick alone produces some arbitrary divisions. It leaves out many solid and promising corporations operating in the United States today—in terms of recent earnings and dividend payments—simply because they don't have the "ancestry."

These very requirements may make a blue chip stock a dull investment. But, dull or not, the blue chip represents solidity, security, steady growth—precisely what millions of investors cherish most.

WHAT IS A "GROWTH" STOCK?

Several times I have suggested that you buy "growth" stocks for capital gains— but how do you define a "growth" stock? How do you find and invest in this type of stock?

Grasp one point from the start: a growth stock is *not* merely a stock that has gone up in price. A growth stock *is:*

(1) The stock of a company which has shown and is likely to continue to show a record of both consistent and *superior* growth in its earnings per share of stock.

Consistency means year after year, even in the face of business reverses. For instance, many years back the demand for color TV sets was so much larger than the supply that even the marginal producers were prospering. But if that sales pace had continued, there would have been four or five TV sets in every home! When the inevitable slowdown occurred, the stronger companies survived while the sales and earnings of the secondary ones collapsed.

Consistency means a year-in, year-out market for the company's products. Superior growth, in the opinion of many professional investment advisers, means a growth of better than 8 or 9 per cent a year in earnings per share. This on a consistent basis certainly narrows the field from the start.

(2) The stock of a company which dominates its market or is a leading company in a fast-growing field. One expert says he would rather have the stock of the number-one company breeding tropical fish than that of a little firm trying to make a better transistor.

(3) The stock of a company in an emerging field or a company developing new concepts in an established field.

(4) The stock of a company you are convinced is under strong management. You might buy IBM without personally knowing its management, but you should not buy stock in a tiny electronics firm without knowing something about the people running it. The smaller the company, the more crucial is its management's ability.

(5) And it is the stock of a company offering a high return on equity—meaning the company's net profit related to its stockholders' equity is high in comparison to that earned by other firms in the same industry. On an average in the United States today, for every dollar committed in a corporation, the stockholder gets a return on his investment of about 14 cents. The owner of a true growth stock might do better than this.

Admittedly, this merely touches the various aspects of a growth stock and there will be many disagreements with the definitions. But these rules are fundamental, and I trust you notice that each rule assumes that the company has a record to analyze and compare. This last hint alone will help protect you from a lot of "garbage" stocks that will be touted under the banner of "growth" stocks in the years ahead.

WHAT IS A "SPECIAL SITUATION" STOCK?

Attractive as a growth stock is, a "special situation" stock has even more potential for substantial appreciation. But again, how do you define, find, and invest in a "special situation" stock? These questions and answers will guide you:

Q. *What is a special situation stock?*

A. In the modern sense, it is a stock in which you're likely to make a profit as a result of a new or impending specific and unusual development either within the company or in the outside environment affecting the company. What makes this special is that few investors recognize the impending change, and the improvement has not yet been reflected in the price of the stock. In either case, the development is setting the stage for a substantial upsurge in the company's earning— and usually you'll be able to make your profit no matter what the short-term swings in the general stock market.

Q. *How do you identify special situations?*

A. Although they can occur in almost any industry and kind of company, the overriding characteristic of them all is *change*.

The changes within the company itself might include: a new technological breakthrough; a major new process, product, or service; a shift in ownership control; a major acquisition; a fundamental switch in the management philosophy of a previously poorly run company.

Changes in the company's external environment might include: new favorable government action (such as tax breaks); favorable court rulings; new favorable legislation; a significant shift in technological or market trends in the company's industry or related fields; any change which could lead to a dramatic rise in demand for the company's product or service.

Q. *What are the dangers?*

A. You might not be able to analyze the new development or be reasonably sure of its outcome. If you can't do either, it's a sheer speculation, not a special situation.

Also, often, an external environmental change may not produce the expected outcome. If, for instance, you had bought stock of a land development firm which had bought raw land cheap hoping to cash in on the land boom but saw your hopes of a rise in the price of the stock disappear because of accounting practices, your purchase of this special situation stock would have been an expensive mistake.

Or a seemingly great new product may fail in the market place. As one expert points out, "Most potential Xeroxes turn out to be nothing more than an idea for 3-D motion pictures."

Q. *How can you avoid the dangers?*

A. Extreme selectivity and obviously intensive study of the nature of the external or internal changes are vital.

If it's a new management, look for a demonstrated record of superior previous achievement and whether the new managers have competence in the area involved. If it's a new product or service or process, look for some kind of previous track record by the company in introducing such products.

Some of the country's top investment research firms, for instance, rarely even bother to analyze a development until the product's commercial feasibility has been proven.

And whatever the development, it's truly a special situation only when the earnings breakthrough which results is of major proportions and is sustainable for at least several years.

SHOULD YOU BUY ON MARGIN?

Most of the country's millions of investors buy their shares outright and hold them for the long term—that is, they put up 100 per cent cash and hold on no matter what the market does. But there is a sizable minority of active investors and professional traders who use credit from their brokers to help finance their purchases. This, of course, gives the investor a lot more leverage and thus a bigger potential for profits—and losses too.

In the late 1970s individuals held some 950,000 margin accounts with their brokers. The amount of credit customers were receiving from their brokers for this purpose was as high as $12 billion as the decade neared a close.

Just how much credit you can receive from your broker depends on several key elements. First, the Federal Reserve Board sets initial margin requirements. This requirement has ranged from 50 to 100 per cent in the post-World War II period. Say the initial margin rate is 70 per cent. It means if you want to buy $10,000 worth of stock you have to put up $7,000 in cash to buy the stock; you can receive credit for the rest from your broker. Or you have to deposit securities with a loan value of $7,000 in order to purchase $10,000 worth of a listed stock. You must deposit the required cash or securities with your broker within five business days after the purchase to conform to Regulation T of the Federal Reserve Board.

The New York Stock Exchange also has a set of rules covering buying on margin. To open a margin account with an NYSE broker you must deposit at least $2,000 or its equivalent in marginable securities. And on top of this, individual brokerage firms may—and often do—set initial margin requirements higher than those of the Federal Reserve or the Exchange.

Q. *What do you pay for the money you borrow?*
A. The going interest rates vary from time to time but usually were in the 6 to 14½ per cent range in the late 1970s. The amount of interest will show up in the monthly or periodic statement you receive on your margin account.

Q. *How do you open a margin account?*
A. If you have the $2,000 cash deposit or equivalent in securities—or meet the higher standards that your broker sets—there is little problem or paperwork in opening an account. You simply sign a margin agreement and a securities loan consent form. The agreement gives your broker the power to pledge or lend

securities carried for your account. All securities purchased on margin will be held by your broker in "street name." However, you'll be credited with all dividends received on them. Your broker also will send along to you all annual and quarterly reports on the company whose stock you are holding and he will vote your stock in proxy matters the way you direct him.

Once you open a margin account, you must abide by another set of regulations —margin maintenance requirements. The New York Stock Exchange requires that the margin equity of customers be at least 25 per cent of the market value of securities held in the account and some brokerage firms insist on percentages higher than 25 per cent. For example, say you bought that $10,000 worth of stock with an initial margin requirement of 70 per cent. You put up $7,000 and received credit of $3,000 from your broker. Now say the price of the stock drops to the point where it is worth $4,000. Since you owe your broker $3,000, your equity in the securities is only $1,000 and you are right at the 25 per cent limit.

Q. *What happens if the value of your stock approaches the minimum requirement line?*

A. You will get what is termed a margin call. The brokerage firm has a squad of margin clerks whose job is to keep track of the firm's margin accounts and to send out warning phone calls and letters if the value of your account is approaching the minimum requirement line. You'll be asked to put more cash into your account or to put up more marginable securities as collateral. Instead of doing either of these things, you might choose to sell some of the stock in your margin account and pay your broker back part of the money for which he gave you credit.

Q. *What is an undermargined account?*

A. Your account is undermargined when it has definitely fallen below the minimum requirements. If you don't move fast to put it back in order by a transfusion of more cash or securities, your broker has the right to sell the securities in your margin account to replace the credit he advanced to you.

Q. *Should you open a margin account?*

A. Probably not. Margin accounts are generally for individuals who are sophisticated investors, who are active in the market, and who understand the risks as well as the rewards of this type of account.

Also it is difficult to make a profit on small margin purchases. The amount of interest you pay on the borrowed money in your account, plus odd-lot differential charges and commission rates, easily can eat up small trading profits.

And though the leverage in purchasing power you get in a margin account can produce increased profits for you, it also can result in bigger losses if you have guessed wrong on the direction of either the market or an individual stock.

SELLING SHORT

Once you start investing, somewhere along the line the question of whether you should sell short will come up.

What is short selling? It's a technique that reverses most normal attitudes about buying stocks. It starts off on the assumption that you think a certain stock is going to drop in value. So what you do is sell the shares at the current market price, borrow shares of the stock from your broker, and then wait in the hope that the price of the stock will go down. If it does, you buy the same number of shares at a lower price and use these shares to "cover" the stock you borrowed from your broker.

Obviously, the bigger the drop in the price of the stock, the more potential profit you can make. Sounds good? Well, don't jump into short selling, at least until you read on.

Actually, short selling has earned a bad name, mainly because questionable practices of short selling were used by such market manipulators as Dan Drew and Jay Gould in the nineteenth century. They deliberately drove down the prices of stocks in the hopes of buying them back cheap. And short selling still carries a negative, even unpatriotic, connotation. But as a result of some of these shady practices, there are several rules that now govern short selling, the most important of which is the so-called "up-tick" rule.

This means you can sell short only after the previous sale in the stock was one eighth point or more higher than the last sale price. No short sale is permitted except on a rising price. The goal is to make sure that repeated selling waves don't force prices into a down spiral.

At best, though, selling short is a risky business, better left to coldly sophisticated investors. To be specific, the risk is this: You can make money if the stock you are selling short takes a big drop. But what if, instead of dropping, the stock's price takes off in a sharp upturn?

Say you sell short 100 shares at $50 a share, hoping the stock drops, but instead it goes up to $70. You then have a $20-a-share loss which you must take if you then buy shares to cover the stock you've borrowed. And there's no limit at least in theory as to how large your losses can become—whereas in normal trading your loss can never exceed 100 per cent of your investment. Say the stock soars to $100 or $200 a share! Your losses could be catastrophic—200 per cent, 400 per cent . . .

Best bet: don't be tempted to sell short.

WHAT ARE RIGHTS?

A few years ago one of the world's major enterprises, American Telephone & Telegraph Company, raised $1.2 billion in new capital. This was a goodly sum even for AT&T—many governments would have trouble raising as much.

AT&T raised the money through the offering of rights—a common technique employed by a wide range of corporations but, unfortunately, often overlooked by shareowners. A right, in essence, is a privilege given by the issuing corporation to buy its common or preferred stock or bonds or debentures, usually at a favorable price in relation to the price of the outstanding security.

The AT&T offering was a classic illustration of rights. Its several million shareowners were informed that they could buy one additional share for each twenty shares they owned. They would receive one "right" for each share they presently owned. To buy one share, the shareowner would have to have twenty "rights" and pay $100—although at the time of the announcement AT&T was selling at about $146 a share. The rights, of course, immediately acquired a value. (If you have the right to buy a security below its market value, this right has a value.) Theoretically, the rights were worth $46/20 or $2.30 apiece.

AT&T's shareowners had several choices. A shareholder could exercise his rights by paying the company $100 plus giving AT&T twenty rights for each share he wanted and was entitled to. Or he could sell his rights. Or if he owned, say, fifteen shares, and had fifteen rights, he could buy five additional rights, which would allow him to purchase one more share of AT&T at the favorable price.

When it issued the rights, AT&T went on the basis of the privileged subscription or pre-emptive right. Translated, this bafflegab means the company felt its shareowners should have the privilege of buying the additional shares before the stock was offered to the general public. Selling additional shares, of course, dilutes the proportionate equity of the original shareowners—unless the original shareowner has the opportunity to maintain his equity by buying the additional shares.

Rights are often confused with warrants, and admittedly, the difference is a bit hazy. In the broadest terms, a right is a short-term privilege to buy a security at a favorable price; the privilege derives from the security you already own. A warrant is the privilege, usually of a longer term, to buy a security at a specific price. This privilege is usually offered to facilitate the sale of a stock or bond which you do not own. You, the buyer, get the stock or bond plus the warrant.

Caution: check your broker before you ignore your rights or sell them.

ARE YOU BETTER OFF WITH STOCK SPLITS?

If you buy stocks, you probably will find that over a period of time one of the stocks you own will split and soon you will be receiving additional shares from the company. Will these shares make you any richer? In theory, no. In fact, maybe.

To explain just what a stock split means, say you own 100 shares of the 1 million outstanding shares of the XYZ Company. The company votes to split its stock 2 for 1, increasing the number of shares to 2 million. Since you own 100, you get an additional 100 shares—1 for each you own—raising your stake to 200 shares. Before the split you owned 100 shares out of 1 million of the XYZ firm. After the split you own 200 out of 2 million shares of the company. Obviously, in terms of percentage ownership, your position hasn't changed one bit, and generally speaking, since company XYZ hasn't increased its assets in any way, the value of your holding shouldn't be affected.

If the shares sold at $1.00 each before the split the price should drop to 50 cents, making the 200 shares you now have after the split equal to the $100 market value of the 100 shares you owned before the stock split. Theoretically this would be true no matter what the ratio of the split—2 for 1, 3 for 1, 5 for 1, 6 for 1. Yet speculators and investors often respond with enthusiastic buying to news that companies plan to split their stock—and following are the two key reasons why:

(1) It is commonplace for a company to combine a stock split with an increase in its dividend rate. If company A pays 4 cents a year on each of your 100 shares before the split and now pays 3 cents on the split shares you are getting a 50 per cent increase in dividend—6 cents in place of 4 cents.

(2) Usually working to boost the value of split shares to more than the value of the shares before the split is the fact that many investors would rather buy lower-priced stocks than higher-priced stocks. Say, for instance, that you own 10 shares of a stock selling for $150 a share. Many investors will not buy a stock with that high a price simply for psychological reasons. But if your company splits its shares 2 for 1, you now have 20 shares at a market price of $75 per share. Historically, many more investors are interested in buying a stock at $75 than at $150.

And the increased investor demand alone well may help push up the price of the stock beyond its initial $75 level.

WHAT PRICE/EARNINGS RATIOS ARE ALL ABOUT

An old Wall Street adage holds that a stock is worth what somebody is willing to pay for it. In stiffer words, the price at which a stock sells represents the buyer's opinion of its value at a particular time.

Investors use a wide range of yardsticks to try to arrive at this judgment on the worth of a stock. Among them are such factors as book value, net income per share, cash flow, dividend rate, several others. But probably the most widely used measurement is the price/earnings ratio, better known as the P/E ratio.

Q. *What is the price/earnings ratio?*

A. It is the ratio of the current price of the stock to its earnings over the past twelve months. Sometimes experts try to figure price/earnings ratios based on predicted earnings for the next twelve months, but that introduces a speculative element that just complicates matters for the average investor.

Putting an even greater emphasis on price/earnings ratio is the fact that, starting in early 1973, newspapers added price/earnings ratios to the New York and American Stock Exchange tables.

Q. *How do you calculate the price/earnings ratio?*

A. While you can get the ratios in the newspaper stock tables, it also is a simple do-it-yourself task. The current price is in the newspaper tables, and the earnings for the last twelve months are usually available in a Standard & Poor's or other reference work. Divide the current price by the earnings, and you get the P/E ratio. For example, a stock that currently sells for $40 and that earned $2.00 a share over the past twelve months has a P/E ratio of 20.

Another way of saying it is that an investor is paying $20 for each $1.00 of the company's most recent annual earnings.

Q. *How much do price/earnings ratios fluctuate?*

A. Although they don't fluctuate much for stocks in general, they do fluctuate tremendously for individual issues. In the 1960s the average price/earnings ratio for stocks traded on the New York Stock Exchange ran about 18. By the end of the 1970s, this figure had dropped to less than 10. But even as the average P/E ratio fell, ratios on some individual stocks soared and there have been stocks with P/E ratios above 100.

Q. *What can P/E ratios tell you?*

A. As you study price/earnings ratios, several points will soon become clear:

Stocks in a given industry tend to have about the same P/E ratio. For example, most auto companies or international oil companies have the same price/earnings ratios.

In broad market movements, the price/earnings ratios of stocks in an industry group tend to move up and down together. If chemical stocks become depressed, say, the P/E ratio of nearly all chemical stocks will move down.

Companies in growth industries—photographic equipment, computers—tend to have higher price/earnings ratios than firms in such established industries as utilities.

Cyclical stocks in general tend to have lower P/E ratios than companies with more stable earnings.

Obviously, the P/E ratio fluctuates with each change in price and earnings. It also depends on what people active in the market think of the industry's and the company's future earnings prospects.

Q. *Can P/E ratios help you spot bargains in stocks?*

A. Yes. Many analysts and experienced investors use P/E ratios as a tool to find undervalued situations in which they might want to invest.

As an illustration, say that you are interested in a machine tool company. You notice that when the machine tool business is in the doldrums this company's stock (as well as others in its industry) sells for a price/earnings ratio of 9. You also notice that when the industry moves into a favorable business cycle the price/earnings ratio for the company and the group runs around 14. Say the stock is currently selling for $18 and has earned $2.00 a share. You read that prospects for the machine tool industry are bright, and the earnings of the company you are watching are expected to move up to $2.50 next year. So you figure that even with the low P/E average the price of the stock could move up (based on $2.50 earnings) to $22.50. But based on the high P/E ratio of 14, and with $2.50 earnings, it could move as high as $35. Certainly, you now have one very helpful clue to the possible price potential of the stock.

By studying a company's pattern of earnings and P/E ratios you may ultimately see a pattern that will help tell you if you should invest in the stock—and when.

Q. *What about stocks selling at low P/E ratios?*

A. P/E ratios may also give you some idea of the relative profit/loss pattern in an investment. If a stock has historically never had a P/E ratio lower than 5, and its earnings seem headed up, you would seem to be taking little risk in buying the stock when its P/E ratio was 5. The likelihood that the stock will go down further seems fairly slim. On the other hand, the potential upward movement of the stock would seem very promising.

Now take the reverse situation. You are looking at a company which has never had a P/E ratio below 5 or higher than 18. Its earnings outlook appears modestly good, and it presently is selling at a P/E of 18. If you buy that stock when its P/E ratio is at its high point, you obviously are taking a bigger risk, for the likelihood that it will go up depends almost entirely on a sharp increase in its future earnings. On the other hand, the stock would slump before it reaches its historic P/E ratio low.

Huge numbers of investors and speculators have been badly hurt in recent years by buying growth stocks with astronomical P/E ratios. Only a handful of these stocks have been able to maintain their high P/E ratios over the years. The majority with ratios in the 40 to 80 category eventually slide down to realistic levels—but the slide is more akin to a crash for the many who paid fancy prices for the shares.

Q. *What's the safest policy then?*

A. It usually is safest to spot stocks which are selling at low P/E ratios and which are headed for substantial earnings growth. Your downside risk tends to be smaller and your upside opportunities can be very good.

DO OPTIONS MAKE SENSE FOR YOU?

Basically, options are contracts in which a buyer pays a premium (the price of the option) for the right to buy or sell a certain stock at a set price (called the striking price or exercise price) within a set time period. Options to buy shares are termed "call" options; those to sell, "puts."

Option prices fluctuate daily based on the stock market performance of the underlying shares, that is, the shares upon which the options are based. Now that options are traded on exchanges, the expiration date, striking price, and size of each option (100 shares of the underlying stock) have been standardized. This uniformity has helped increase the liquidity of options trading, or the ease with which a buyer or seller of contracts can enter or leave the market.

Q. *Why do people buy options?*

A. There are many reasons, but the main one is that buying an option gives an investor who thinks a stock will move sharply up or down a chance to make a sizable profit while limiting the amount of possible loss.

Say you think that Ajax Mousetrap Company stock, selling for $50, may surge to $100 in three months. It would cost you $5,000 to buy 100 Ajax shares, and you may not want to risk $5,000 or you may not have $5,000 to invest. Still, you would like to take the chance that Ajax will jump in price and as a result will make you a large profit.

In this case, you might go the options route. You ask your broker to buy you one call option with a striking price of $50 and an expiration date three months in the future. Checking the options tables in your newspaper, you find that Ajax call option with a striking price of $50 and an expiration date three months hence, is selling at 3½. That means that the premium, or option purchase price, is $3.50 per share of Ajax stock, or $350 for an option to buy 100 shares. When searching the options tables, however, you notice prices for three calls with the $50 striking price. Of course, you find the option you've purchased—one with an expiration in three months—as well as options with expiration dates six months and nine months away. For example, there might be prices listed for Ajax/Apr/50, Ajax/Jul/50, and Ajax/Oct/50 contracts. All listed options contracts expire on the Saturday following the third Friday of the expiration month.

It is also possible to trade options sharing the same expiration date but having different exercise prices. The prices would reflect the differing expectations of movements in the underlying stock. For example, there could be Ajax 50s, 60s, and 70s all expiring in April. Higher or lower exercise prices are introduced by the exchanges when a significant change occurs in the market price of the underlying security. Normally, new exercise prices are introduced at five-point intervals for stocks trading below $50 a share, at ten-point intervals for stocks trading between $50 and $200, and at twenty-point intervals for stocks trading above $200 a share.

Q. *How can you make money with options?*

A. Go back to the option to buy 100 shares of Ajax stock at $50. Here are some events that could happen:

(1) Ajax stock takes off as anticipated and hits $90 within the option period. Now you exercise your option, buy the 100 shares at $50 per share, turn around and sell the shares you acquired on the market for $90 per share.

You have received $9,000 from the sale of the shares. From this subtract the $5,000 you paid for them, the $350 premium for the option and about $120 in brokerage commissions, and you wind up with a profit of more than $3,500.

(2) Now look at another scenario. You buy the option and three months later Ajax stock nosedives to $40. What do you do? You do nothing, and simply let your option expire. You have lost $370—the price of the option premium and brokerage commission. Compare that to a loss of $1,000—plus commissions— had you bought the Ajax shares at $50 and sold them at $40.

(3) Or suppose that a month after you bought your option, the price of Ajax stock rises to $55. The prices of calls sharing your option's expiration date presumably have become more attractive and the premium is bid, say, to $5.00 a share. You could sell your option, which cost $350, for $500, realizing a $150 profit, less commissions.

The $150 profit on a $350 investment—a 43 per cent return—illustrates the leverage it is possible to achieve through the purchase of calls. Had you instead bought 100 shares of Ajax common at $50 a share and sold it at $55, you would have received a 10 per cent return. For this smaller return, the stock buyer assumed a greater risk since the stock price could have gone down. The option buyer could have lost only the $350 price of the call.

Q. *Are there other ways to make money in options?*

A. Yes. One is through the selling, or writing, of call options. Just as call buyers have a double objective—leverage plus limited risk—sellers, or writers, of calls also seek two basic objectives: additional income from their security investments, coupled with protection against a decline in the market price of those securities.

The call writer is the person from whom the option buyer purchases his option. The writer obligates himself to deliver 100 shares of the underlying stock for each option sold if and when the call is exercised. On delivery of the stock, the writer is paid the exercise price. This is in addition to the premium received.

Let's say an investor owns 100 shares of Ajax, for which he paid $50 a share. He notes that an Ajax call option can be written against the stock at a premium of $5.00 a share. He deposits the stock with his broker and instructs the broker to write an Ajax call option. Within a few business days, his account will be credited in the amount of $500, less commissions. This premium belongs to the writer of the call whether or not the option is ultimately exercised by the buyer. In this example, a $5.00 share premium represents a 10 per cent yield on the $50 investment in stock. In addition, the options writer always retains cash dividends earned on the underlying security during the time prior to exercise.

Writing options on stock you own may be a way to boost your overall return. But if the price of the underlying stock rises close to or above the exercise price, the call owner would exercise his option requiring the option writer to sell the underlying shares. Option writers, therefore, are betting against a rise in the price of their stock. If stock prices do not rise, the option writer increases his total yield; if stock prices exceed the exercise price, the call writer must sell his stock and miss out on the price appreciation. What if the call writer wants to hold on to his stock? He simply can *buy* an identical call at the current premium and close out his position. Even if the call option is exercised, he does not have to deliver the original stock. He can, if he prefers, buy new stock to deliver.

Q. *Are there any other strategies?*

A. Yes, but many are risky, for the same leverage which rewards some options traders wipes out others. One particularly risky maneuver involves writing "naked" options—an option written against stock you don't own. A sharp rise in the market price of the stock will lead to the exercise of the call. To satisfy your delivery obligation, you, the writer of the naked option, would have to acquire the stock in the market at a price substantially above the exercise price. This could result in a large net loss.

Other strategies involve writing and/or buying put options and writing and/or buying a combination of puts and calls. For example, one combination is termed a "straddle" and consists of simultaneously buying (or selling) both a put and a call on the same number of shares of the same stock with the same exercise price and expiration month. By purchasing a straddle, you have an opportunity to profit from either a substantial increase or a substantial decrease in the price of the underlying stock. Obviously, straddles and other complicated options strategies are not for novices. Before trading in options, therefore, arm yourself with as much information as possible!

Q. *Where can I find out more about options?*

A. Introductory material is available free of charge from the options exchanges. The Chicago Board Options Exchange (141 Jackson Boulevard, Chicago, Illinois 60604) offers a variety of pamphlets on options, options writing, options spreading, and tax considerations. The American Stock Exchange (86 Trinity Place, New York, New York 10006) offers similar booklets. Brokerage firms also offer material free of charge.

(Also see pages 1124–26 on commodity options trading.)

FOR YOUR PROTECTION—THE SIPC

The 1967–70 crisis in Wall Street came perilously close—far closer than was ever publicly acknowledged—to wiping out huge numbers of innocent investors who had entrusted their securities to the safekeeping of their brokers. But as a direct result of that nightmare the Securities Investor Protection Act of 1970 went on the statute books. In 1978, the act was amended to provide even greater protection.

The SIPC gives you protection against being hurt by the liquidation of the brokerage firm to which you have entrusted securities and cash almost in the same way that the Federal Deposit Insurance Corporation gives you protection against being hurt by the liquidation of the bank to which you have entrusted your deposits. The difference is that the SIPC is a federally chartered membership organization and the FDIC is an agency of the government.

The SIPC is one of the most important pieces of securities legislation of the past generation and of direct meaning to you. You must know its general outlines, so here goes:

Q. *What is the SIPC?*

A. The Securities Investor Protection Corporation is a non-profit, membership corporation created by Congress to provide financial protection for you—the customers of an over-the-counter broker/dealer or of a member of a national securities exchange. It is not, however, an agency of the U. S. Government.

Q. *What protection does it give you?*

A. Should a SIPC member firm fail, its customers first will receive securities which are registered in their names or which are in the process of being registered. Second, the customers will receive, on a pro rata basis, all remaining cash and securities of customers held by the firm. Third, the SIPC's funds will satisfy the remaining claims of each customer up to a maximum of $100,000. On claims for cash, however, not more than $40,000 may be paid from SIPC's funds.

Q. *Is there any way I can get more than $100,000 protection?*

A. As of the late 1970s, you could have obtained more than $100,000 protection by maintaining accounts with more than one brokerage firm or by holding accounts with the same SIPC member in separate capacities; for example, as an individual and as a trustee for another person.

For more information on the SIPC, write to the Securities Investor Protection Corporation, 900 Seventeenth Street N.W., Suite 800, Washington, D.C. 20006.

Q. *Who are members of the SIPC?*

A. Automatically, members are all registered broker/dealers and members of national securities exchanges, including specialists. Firms excluded from membership are those doing only a mutual fund, insurance, or investment company advisory business—but they can apply for membership in the SIPC if they wish.

Q. *Who puts up the insurance funds for the SIPC?*

A. The securities industry itself. During the first years of the SIPC, assessments on member organizations created a fund of more than $150 million in cash. In 1979, a minimum assessment of $25 a year was imposed on each member. In addition to its $150 million reserve, the SIPC has a $1 billion line of credit with the United States Treasury in case it ever needs it. However, if this credit line is drawn upon, the brokerage firms who are members of the SIPC eventually must repay the Treasury for the loan.

Q. *How does the SIPC work?*

A. When it appears that a large SIPC member firm is in danger of failing to meet its obligations to customers, the SIPC will apply to the appropriate court for appointment of a trustee. Once appointed, the trustee will liquidate the firm, complete open securities transactions, deliver out customers' fully paid securities to the extent that they are on hand and can be identified, and then settle any customer claims up to a limit of $40,000 in cash.

In medium-size cases, the SIPC is permitted to act as a trustee. These are cases in which it appears that the obligations to general creditors and subordinated lenders will be less than $750,000 and there are fewer than five hundred customers.

In cases in which it appears that the claims of all customers will amount to less than $250,000, the SIPC is able to make payments directly to customers if it appears that such direct payments would cost the SIPC less than following the court-appointed trustee methods.

Q. *Who manages the SIPC?*

A. A seven-man board of directors including two representatives of the general public and three of the securities industry appointed by the President of the United States, and one each named by the Secretary of the Treasury and the Federal Reserve Board.

Q. *What does that $1 billion line of Treasury credit mean?*

A. It's an ultimate resource aimed at meeting a crisis far beyond any ever yet experienced. It is to provide for even the most remote danger of financial disaster. The SIPC is indeed for your protection—make sure the firm with which you are dealing is a member.

Q. *In sum, what do these changes mean to you?*

A. They mean that in the process of development is the most comprehensive regulatory program ever devised for the safekeeping of customers' funds and securities by brokerage houses.

Q. *Then can customers be confident of 100 per cent protection against broker-age firm failures?*

A. No, there is no system that is foolproof. For the vast majority of brokerage accounts, though, the $100,000 and $40,000 limits do amount to 100 per cent protection. And this is certainly a spectacular improvement over the defenses of only a few years ago.

Note: several large incorporated brokerage firms also provide insurance of their own that substantially raises the limit on payments to customers—some into the hundreds of thousands of dollars per account.

INVESTMENT BIBLIOGRAPHY

THE STOCK MARKET AND HOW IT WORKS

Dreman, David N. *Psychology and the Stock Market: Investment Strategy Beyond Random Walk.* New York: Amacom, 1977.

Klein, Frederick C., and John A. Prestbo. *News and the Market.* Chicago: Henry Regnery Co., 1974.

Malkiel, Burton G. *A Random Walk down Wall Street.* New York: W. W. Norton & Co., 1973.

Rosen, Lawrence R. *Go Where The Money Is.* Rev. ed. Homewood, Illinois: Dow Jones-Irwin, 1974.

Silk, Leonard. *Economics in Plain English.* New York: Simon & Schuster, 1978.

Sobel, Robert. *Amex: A History of the American Stock Exchange, 1921–1971.* New York: Weybright and Talley, 1975.

———. *Inside Wall Street: Continuity and Change in the Financial District.* New York: W. W. Norton & Co., 1977.

———. *N.Y.S.E. A History of the New York Stock Exchange 1935–1975.* New York: Weybright and Talley, 1975.

Wyckoff, Peter. *Wall Street and the Stock Markets: A Chronology (1644–1971).* Philadelphia, Chilton Book Co., 1972.

LEARNING TO INVEST

Blackman, Richard. *Follow the Leaders; Successful Trading Techniques with Line Drive Stocks.* New York: Simon & Schuster, 1978.

Darst, David M. *The Complete Bond Book; A Guide to All Types of Fixed-Income Securities.* New York: McGraw-Hill, Inc., 1975.

Engel, Louis (in collaboration with Peter Wyckoff). *How to Buy Stocks.* 6th rev. ed. Boston: Little, Brown and Co., 1976.

Gastineau, Gary L. *The Stock Options Manual.* New York: McGraw-Hill, 1975.

Graham, Benjamin. *The Intelligent Investor; A Book of Practical Counsel.* 4th rev. ed. New York: Harper & Row, 1973.

Hardy, C. Colburn. *Dun & Bradstreet's Guide to Your Investments.* New York: Thomas Y. Crowell, 1978.

Holt, Thomas J. *Total Investing.* New York: Arlington House, 1976.

Hoyt, Murray. *The Young Investor's Guide to the Stock Market.* New York: J. B. Lippincott Co., 1972.

Mader, Chris, and Robert Hagin. *The Dow Jones-Irwin Guide to Common Stocks*. Homewood, Illinois: Dow Jones-Irwin, 1976.

Mamis, Justin, and Robert Mamis. *When to Sell: Inside Strategies for Stock Market Profits*. New York: Farrar, Straus and Giroux, 1977.

Metz, Robert. *Jackpot!* New York: Simon & Schuster, 1977.

Newman, Joseph. *Stocks, Bonds and Mutual Funds*. Washington, D.C.: U.S. News & World Report Books, 1977.

Reilly, James F. *Too Good for the Rich Alone*. Englewood Cliffs, New Jersey: Prentice-Hall, 1975.

Rogers, Donald I. *How Not to Buy a Common Stock*. New York: Arlington House, 1972.

Rugg, Donald D. *The Dow Jones-Irwin Guide to Mutual Funds*. Homewood, Illinois: Dow Jones-Irwin, 1976.

Rukeyser, Louis. *How to Make Money in Wall Street*. Rev. ed. New York: Doubleday, 1976.

Sokoloff, Kiril. *The Thinking Investor's Guide to the Stock Market*. New York: McGraw-Hill, 1978.

Tobias, Andrew. *The Only Investment Guide You'll Ever Need*. New York: Harcourt Brace Jovanovich, 1978.

Train, John. *The Dance of the Money Bees: A Professional Speaks Frankly on Investing*. New York: Harper & Row, 1974.

TEXTBOOKS ON THEORY AND PRACTICE

Christy, George A., and John C. Clendenin. *Introduction to Investments*. 7th ed. New York: McGraw-Hill, 1978.

Cohen, Jerome B. *Investment Analysis and Portfolio Management*. 3rd ed. Homewood, Illinois: Dow Jones-Irwin, 1977.

Dougall, Herbert E. *Investments*. 10th ed. Englewood Cliffs, New Jersey: Prentice-Hall, 1978.

Latane, Henry A. *Security Analysis and Portfolio Management*. 2nd ed. New York: Ronald Press, 1975.

FOR THE EXPERIENCED INVESTOR

Blotnick, Srully. *Winning; The Psychology of Successful Investing*. New York: McGraw-Hill, 1978.

Blumenthal, Earl. *Chart for Profit; Point and Figure Trading*. Larchmont, New York: Investors Intelligence, 1975.

Brealey, Richard A. *Security Prices in a Competitive Market; More About Risk and Return from Common Stocks*. Cambridge, Massachusetts: M.I.T. Press, 1972.

Cootner, Paul H., ed. *The Random Character of Stock Market Prices*. Rev. ed. Cambridge, Massachusetts: M.I.T. Press, 1964.

Dines, James. *How the Average Investor Can Use Technical Analysis for Stock Profit*. New York: Dines Chart Corp., 1972.

Edwards, Robert D., and John Magee. *Technical Analysis of Stock Trends*. 5th ed. Springfield, Massachusetts: John Magee, Inc., 1966.

Fosdack, Norman G. *Stock Market Logic; A Sophisticated Approach to Profits on Wall Street.* Fort Lauderdale, Florida: The Institute for Econometric Research, 1976.

Fried, Sidney. *Fortune Building in the 70's with Common Stock Warrants and Low-Price Stocks.* New York: RHM Press, 1974.

Granville, Joseph E. *Granville's New Strategy of Daily Stock Market Timing for Maximum Profit.* Englewood Cliffs, New Jersey: Prentice-Hall, 1976.

Hardy, C. Colburn. *Investor's Guide to Technical Analysis.* New York: McGraw-Hill, 1978.

Noddings, Thomas. *How the Experts Beat the Market.* Homewood, Illinois: Dow Jones-Irwin, 1976.

Thomas, Conrad W. *How to Sell Short and Perform Other Wondrous Feats.* Homewood, Illinois: Dow Jones-Irwin, 1976.

U. S. Industry and Trade Administration. *U.S. Industrial Outlook with 5-Year Projections for 200 Industries* (annual). Available in many libraries. Also, for sale by the Superintendent of Documents, U. S. Government Printing Office, Washington, D.C. 20402.

NEWSPAPERS AND PERIODICALS

Bank and Quotation Record. (monthly magazine) New York

Barron's: National Business and Financial Weekly. (weekly newspaper) New York

Commercial and Financial Chronicle. (weekly newspaper) New York

Dun's Review. (monthly magazine) New York

Finance. (monthly magazine) New York

The Financial Analysts Journal. (bimonthly magazine) New York

Financial Times. (daily newspaper) London

Financial World. (semi-monthly magazine) New York

Forbes. (biweekly magazine) New York

Insiders' Chronicle. (weekly magazine) New York

Investment Dealers' Digest. (weekly magazine) New York

Journal of Commerce. (daily newspaper) New York

M/G Financial Weekly Market Digest. (weekly newspaper) Richmond, Virginia

Money. (monthly magazine) Chicago, Illinois

Money Manager. (weekly newspaper) New York

O-T-C Review. (monthly magazine) Oreland, Pennsylvania

Official Summary of Security Transactions and Holdings. (monthly magazine) Washington, D.C., SEC

Statistical Bulletin. (monthly magazine) Washington, D.C., SEC

Stock Market Magazine. (monthly magazine) Yonkers, New York

Wall Street Journal, The. (daily newspaper) New York

Wall Street Transcript. (weekly newspaper) New York

THE BAFFLEGAB OF STOCKS

The language of Wall Street is colorful and enriched by many idioms. Some of the words and phrases go back more than a century; others are as up-to-date as this year's music. Here is a guide through the bafflegab. I have selected only terms which you will come across fairly frequently and, thus, which you should understand.

ARBITAGE A technique which takes advantage of a temporary price difference between a security or commodity traded on two or more exchanges; or a temporary price difference between new and old securities of the same company; or a temporary price difference between convertible securities and the securities into which they are convertible. The arbitrateur's profit lies in taking almost simultaneous opposite action in two markets to take advantage of the price differentials. You must have detailed technical knowledge of the different prices, excellent communications, be able to take major risks, and be fairly sophisticated in finance to be an arbitrateur. It's not for amateurs. Rather, it is practiced mostly by brokers who are members of exchanges and not subject to their customers' usual commission costs.

AT THE MARKET An order to buy or sell a stated number of shares at the most advantageous price your broker can get when the order is executed. You are ordering immediate execution of your order "at the market," not specifying any price. Also called a "market order."

AVERAGES Yardsticks for measuring broad trends in stock prices. The best-known is the Dow Jones average of the prices of thirty outstanding industrial stocks listed on the New York Stock Exchange. Other widely used market indicators, known as indexes, are issued by Standard & Poor's and the New York Stock Exchange.

The Dow Jones average generally gives you the trends in well-established blue chip stocks but *not* in stocks of service companies, smaller companies, or glamour issues. The New York Stock Exchange index includes *all* common stocks listed on the NYSE and is most representative of the market. The Standard & Poor's indexes of 425 industrial stocks and of 500 stocks (including utilities and rails)—all listed on the NYSE—are also excellent yardsticks.

BEAR An investor who thinks that a stock's price, or the market as a whole, will fall. A bear market is a sharply declining market. See page 1006.

BID AND ASKED The "bid" price for a stock is the highest price that anyone has declared he is willing to pay for a share of the stock at a given time. The "asked" price is the lowest price at which anyone has declared he is willing to sell this same share at a given time. The actual price at which you buy or sell the share usually will be somewhere between the bid and the asked price. "Bid and asked" is usually called a quote.

BIG BOARD Wall Street nickname for the New York Stock Exchange, Inc.

BLOOD BATH In the stock market, this means a horrendous loss suffered by many investors due to a sharp market decline. "Taking a bath" means taking a terrific loss, usually a personal loss but not necessarily a widespread market drop.

BLUE CHIPS Stocks which, like poker chips, have the highest "rank" in terms of: a long history of earnings in both good times and bad times; an unbroken history of paying quarterly cash dividends, for twenty-five years or more, in recessions as well as booms; established leadership in an established industry; a clear, solid prospect for continued earnings, growth, and dividend payments.

BLUE SKY LAWS   A securities industry expression for the laws of various states designed to protect the public against securities frauds. These state regulations prescribe the requirements which must be met for intrastate issue and sale of securities. The term is said to have come into being when a judge ruled that a particular stock had the value of a patch of blue sky.

BOOK VALUE   A company's total assets (exclusive of such intangibles as good will) less its liabilities and the liquidating value of its preferred stock divided by the number of shares of common stock outstanding to put the figure on a per-share basis. Book value is not the same as market value and generally has little or no relation to it.

BROAD TAPE   Wall Street slang for the Dow Jones & Company news ticker displayed in many brokerage houses as a large rectangular screen with lines of copy rolling upward, while the American and Big Board ticker tapes are displayed as narrow rectangles with copy running horizontally from right to left.

BROKER   An agent who executes your orders to buy and sell shares of stock, other securities, or commodity futures contracts for a commission. The word "broker" can refer to the partnership or corporation with whom investors have accounts and, by extension, to its sales employees. A securities salesman is more accurately known as a registered representative, account executive, or customer's man.

BULL   A person who thinks a stock's price, or the market as a whole, will go up. A bull market is a sharply advancing market. See page 1006.

CALL   An option contract that entitles the holder to buy a number of shares of the underlying security at a stated price on or before a fixed expiration date. Calls were the first option contracts to be listed for trading on option exchanges. See PUTS.

CALLABLE   Stock, usually preferred shares, which may be bought back (redeemed) or called by the company, at the option of the company's board of directors, at a certain price within a certain time span and under certain agreed-upon conditions. It is much more usual for bonds and debentures to be callable than stocks. Shares traded on exchanges are usually non-callable.

CAPITAL GAIN (OR LOSS)   Profit (or loss) on the sale of any capital asset, including securities. A long-term capital gain is a gain achieved after the securities have been held for a set period under the law: as of 1978, the period was "more than one year." Long-term gains are taxed at a lower federal rate than short-term gains, which in 1978 were gains achieved in "one year or less." A capital loss occurs when you sell stock (or other capital assets) at a loss. This loss also can be short-term or long-term, and each type is treated differently in income tax reporting.

CATS AND DOGS   Highly speculative and usually very low-priced stocks.

CHURNING   An extraordinary, excessive—and therefore suspicious—amount of trading in a customer's account without adequate or proper justification and probably done only to generate additional commissions for an unscrupulous broker. Such improper conduct is subject to disciplinary action by various regulatory organizations.

CLOSED-END INVESTMENT COMPANY First, let's define an investment company. This is a company which invests in the securities of other companies, holds a diversified list of these securities, and buys and sells them for the purpose of making profits and earning income. It is, in short, a mutual fund.

The closed-end investment company is an investment company with a fixed capitalization and usually a fixed number of shares outstanding which may be traded on a securities exchange. You buy shares of a closed-end investment company in the open market from another owner and sell your shares to another buyer exactly as you would trade in other stocks. In contrast, the familiar open-end investment company (or mutual fund) constantly issues new shares and its capitalization is "open." You buy new shares from the mutual fund itself and redeem them by selling them back to the mutual fund. See Chapter 22 "Mutual Funds" for details on both types.

COMMISSION The broker's basic fee for purchasing or selling securities or property as an agent.

COMMISSION BROKER An agent who executes the public's orders for the purchase or sale of securities or commodities.

CONFIRMATION A form you receive from your brokerage house after you buy or sell securities informing you that your buy or sell order has been executed, the number of shares traded, at what price, in what market, the standing of your account, and the settlement date.

CONGLOMERATE A corporate "supermarket" which has grown externally by rapidly acquiring many unrelated companies primarily through the use of borrowed money and the exchange of securities. In one sense, buying stock in a conglomerate is similar to buying an entire portfolio of different stocks—but at the top a conglomerate, like any other company, is run by a single management team. Basically, therefore, this team's competence and the ability of a conglomerate to grow in size and in earnings per share through both good and bad economic times will determine the prospects for the company as a whole.

CONVERTIBLE A bond or debenture or preferred stock which not only provides a fixed rate of return (in interest or dividends) but which you can also convert into shares of the same company's common stock at a later date if it is to your advantage to do so. Conversion terms often change and are governed by the indenture (contract) covering the original underwriting.

CORNER Buying of a stock or commodity on a scale large enough to give the buyer, or buying group, control over the price. A person who must buy that stock or commodity—for example one who is short—is forced to do business at an arbitrarily high price with those who obtained the corner. Corners are rare these days, since registered exchanges have the power to prevent them.

COVERING A SHORT POSITION What happens when a person who has sold short buys shares of the stock he has "shorted" so he can deliver the shares to the broker from whom he has borrowed the shares. He thereby "covers" his short position. See page 1026.

CURB EXCHANGE   Former name of the American Stock Exchange. Now known as the Amex.

CURRENT YIELD   The dividends or interests paid on a security by a company expressed as a percentage of the current price. A stock with a current market price of $40 a share which has paid $2.00 in dividends in the preceding twelve months is said to return 5 per cent ($2.00÷$40.00). The current yield (also called return) on a bond is figured the same way. A 3 per cent $1,000 bond selling at $600 offers a return of 5 per cent ($30÷$600). Figuring the yield of a bond to maturity calls for a bond yield table.

Yields vary tremendously from stock to stock and often they may be misleading. To illustrate, a very low yield may be a good, not bad, sign, for it may reflect the fact that a company is putting most of its earnings into its own future business and buyers of its stock are banking on that future. A high yield, on the other hand, may be a bad sign, for it may suggest that the company may in time cut the dividend and that investors question its future growth potential.

CUSTOMER'S MAN   Another name for a registered representative, account executive, or securities salesman. See BROKER.

CYCLICAL STOCKS   Stocks which go up and down with the trend of business (the business cycle)—climbing fast in periods of rapidly improving business conditions and sliding fast when business conditions deteriorate. However, cyclical stocks might also follow special cycles related to their own industry which might not parallel the business cycle.

DEALER   An individual in the securities business who acts as a principal, in contrast to a broker, who acts as an agent. A dealer buys securities for his own account and then sells to you, the customer, from his own holdings. His profit or loss is the difference between the price he paid for a security and the price at which he sells the security to you. At different times, an individual or firm may act either as a broker or as a dealer. But he has to alert you to the capacity in which he is acting.

DEBENTURE   A promissory note backed by the general credit of a company and usually not secured by a mortgage or lien on any specific property. See CONVERTIBLE.

DEFENSIVE STOCKS   Stocks which tend to be more stable, in terms of dividends, earnings, and market performance, in periods of recession or economic uncertainty than a general cross section of the market. When the market seems to be entering a major bear phase, portfolio managers and experienced investors attempt to switch from high-growth and speculative stocks to quality stocks, hence the term "defensive."

DISCOUNT   A reduction in market price from the face value or original price of a security. In contrast, a premium means an increase in market price above the face value or original price of a security. Much more commonly used in the bond than the stock markets. For instance, a bond selling at a discount is selling below its face value or original price while a bond selling at a premium is selling above its face value or original price. See Chapter 23, "Your Guide to the Bond Market . . ."

DISCOUNTING THE NEWS   When the price of a stock or the level of a major market indicator rises or falls in anticipation of a specific development—good or bad—and then scarcely moves when the actual development takes place and is announced, this stock, or the market, has "discounted the news." Sometimes the stock or the market moves in a direction opposite to the bullish or bearish news when it is actually published.

DISCRETIONARY ACCOUNT   An account in which you, the investor, give your stockbroker or other agent full or partial authority in writing to buy and sell securities or commodities for you without requiring your specific approval on each transaction. The discretion will include selection, timing, and price to be paid or received for the securities.

DIVIDENDS   A payment distributed to share owners on a proportional basis in amounts and at times voted by a company's board of directors. A dividend may be in cash, additional shares of the company's own stock, or in the securities of another company it owns.

On preferred stock, the dividend amounts are usually fixed. On common stock, dividends may vary throughout a year and from year to year—or may be omitted entirely.

DOLLAR COST AVERAGING   A system in which you invest a fixed amount of money regularly in a given stock or stocks. See pages 1012–13.

DOW THEORY   A theory of market analysis based upon the performance of the Dow Jones industrial and transportation stock price averages. The theory says that the market is in a basic upward trend if one of these averages advances above a previous important high, accompanied or followed by a similar advance in the other. When the averages both dip below previous important lows, this is regarded as confirmation of a basic downward trend. The theory does not attempt to predict how long either trend will continue, although it is widely misinterpreted as a method of forecasting future action. Whatever the merits of the theory, it is sometimes a strong factor in the market because many people believe in the theory—or believe that a great many others do.

EARNINGS (OR INCOME) STATEMENT   A company's statement to shareowners which may appear in an annual, semi-annual, or quarterly report, of its net profits (or "net income") or losses after taxes and expenses, for the period covered by the report.

EQUITY FINANCING   Since stock represents ownership or equity in a company, equity financing is the obtaining of funds by a company through the sale of stock.

EX-DIVIDEND   Means "without dividend" and is usually indicated by the symbol "X" after the company's name in the stock tables. If you buy a stock when it is selling ex-dividend, it means you will not receive a just-declared dividend. Instead, that dividend will go to the previous owner (the seller), who was the stockholder of record.

EX-RIGHTS   Means "without right" that a corporation may have offered stockholders to subscribe to new or additional stock. If you buy a stock selling "ex-rights," you are not entitled to the rights; these remain the property of the seller.

EXTRA The short form of "extra dividend." A dividend in the form of stock or cash in addition to the regular or usual dividend the company has been paying.

FALL OUT OF BED A crash in stock prices. For instance, "the market fell out of bed on the news" means the market declined very sharply.

FISCAL YEAR A company's accounting year, which may coincide with the calendar year or may span some other period—typically July 1 through June 30.

FLOOR The trading area of any of the world's stock exchanges; as of the late 1970s, most particularly the huge trading area where common and preferred stocks were bought and sold on the New York Stock Exchange. Bonds were traded on the New York Stock Exchange in a separate small Bond Room in the building's basement.

FLOOR BROKER A member of an exchange who in the late 1970s executed orders to buy or sell listed securities on that floor.

FOREIGN EXCHANGES Refers to securities exchanges operating in other countries. For instance, the London Stock Exchange is a foreign (securities) exchange.

FORMULA INVESTING An investment technique. One formula calls for the shifting of funds from common shares to preferred shares or bonds as the market, on average, rises above a certain predetermined point—and the return of funds to common share investments as the market average declines.

GOING PUBLIC The underwriting process whereby a privately owned company offers its own stock for sale to the public for the first time and makes it available for trading in the over-the-counter market or an organized exchange.

GROWTH STOCKS Stock in a company with superior prospects in earnings which historically have exceeded the growth rate of the economy or of corporations on the average.

HEDGE In the securities and commodities markets, to hedge means to try to minimize or eliminate a risk by taking certain steps to offset the risk.

HOLDING COMPANY A non-operating company which owns the securities, and usually holds voting control, of another company which does sell products or services. Hence, "holding company."

IN-AND-OUT Buying and selling a stock within a short period of time. In-and-out speculators strive for profits resulting from hour-to-hour and day-to-day stock price changes.

INSIDER Directors, officers, and principal securities holders of a corporation. The latter can be companies or individuals who are beneficial shareholders of 10 per cent or more of a publicly traded company's stock. The Securities and Exchange Commission requires insiders to report their initial position and details of any significant change in their holdings.

INSTITUTIONAL INVESTOR An organization or company with substantial funds invested in securities—i.e., a bank, insurance company, mutual fund, university, labor union, pension plan.

INVESTOR ADVISER OR COUNSEL Individual (or firm) who supervises or manages funds of investors for a fee.

INVESTMENT BANKER (OR UNDERWRITER) Middlemen between companies needing capital and the investing public. To illustrate, when a company wants capital for expansion or modernization, it may sell its securities to an investment banker or underwriter; this firm, in turn, will sell the securities to the public.

INVESTMENT CLUB A group of ten to twenty people who meet regularly and invest together. Most clubs have formal rules and defined investment goals.

INVESTMENT COMPANY Current meaning refers usually to an open-end or a closed-end mutual fund. See Chapter 22, "Mutual Funds."

INVESTOR An individual, owning securities, whose main goals are relatively long-term growth of his principal and/or dividend income. He differs from a speculator in his goals, expectations, risks, and temperament.

LAMB An amateur speculator who blindly follows the flock, buying or selling on tips and rumors, and is easily "fleeced" by the pros or by his own naïveté and greed.

LETTER STOCK A type of unregistered stock—often issued by new small companies to avoid the cost of a formal underwriting—that is sold at a presumed discount to mutual funds and experienced investors specializing in such speculative investments. Letter stock usually carries a proviso that it may not be resold for a considerable period of time.

LIMIT ORDER An order to buy or sell a stated amount of a security at a specified price, or a better price if obtainable, after the order has been placed.

LIQUIDATION Dissolution of a company; process of converting securities and other assets into cash.

LIQUIDITY Capacity of the market in a particular security to absorb a reasonable amount of buying and selling at reasonably limited price changes. An "illiquid" market in a security means you cannot buy or sell with reasonable freedom at reasonable price changes.

LISTED STOCK Stock traded on a national securities exchange. Both the stock and the exchange have been registered with the Securities and Exchange Commission. Detailed information on such stock has been filed with the SEC and the issuing company has met the listing standards of the exchange upon which it is being traded.

LOAD Sales charge which a buyer of mutual funds must pay on top of the actual net asset value of the shares—unless the mutual fund is a no-load fund (meaning the fund is sold without any sales charge to the buyer). See Chapter 22, "Mutual Funds."

LOCKED IN An investor who will not sell stocks in which he has a substantial profit because he would have to pay capital gains tax on the profit. He has a "paper" profit which he is reluctant to take because the tax will consume a good part of it and thus he is "locked in."

LONG Means simply that you have bought a certain number of shares of a stock and hold them in anticipation of higher prices (are "long" of it) or for whatever other goals you have in mind.

MAKING A KILLING Make a spectacular profit.

MANIPULATION Illegal buying and selling of securities in order to create false impression of active trading, or to drive prices up or down as a lure for others to buy or sell while the manipulators are taking profits.

MARGIN Minimum proportion of the purchase price you must pay when you wish to use your broker's credit to buy a security. Initial margins are regulated by the Federal Reserve Board and have ranged in recent years from 50 per cent to 100 per cent of the stock purchase price. A 100 per cent margin means no borrowing is permitted.

You buy on margin when you want to purchase more stock than your cash on hand would permit. You get credit for the balance from your broker at current interest rates because obviously you are hoping to increase your gains. A 50 per cent margin means you put up only 50 per cent of your cash to buy a stock; you get credit for the rest. The New York Stock Exchange also has strict margin maintenance rules that its member organizations are expected to enforce in customer accounts.

MARGIN CALL   A call from your broker asking you to put up additional cash (or collateral) in order to bring your equity in your account at least up to the margin maintenance requirements stipulated by the exchange. You might get this call if your stock declines sharply instead of rising. If you don't meet the call and bring up your equity to the requirement, your stock will be liquidated by your broker.

MARKET ORDER   Order to buy or sell a stated amount of a security at the best price obtainable in the market at the time.

MARKET PRICE   The last reported transaction price of a security.

MEMBER FIRM   A securities brokerage firm organized either as a corporation or a partnership and having at least one executive or general partner who is a member of an exchange.

NASD   The National Association of Securities Dealers, Inc., an association of brokers and dealers in the over-the-counter securities business. The Association has the power to expel members who have been declared guilty of unethical practices. The NASD is dedicated to—among other objectives—"adopt, administer and enforce rules of fair practice and rules to prevent fraudulent and manipulative acts and practices, and in general to promote just and equitable principles of trade for the protection of investors."

NET ASSET VALUE   Most often used by mutual funds which report their net asset value per share every day. The NAV represents the market value of the securities the fund owns on that day plus the cash it holds divided by the total number of the shares the mutual fund has outstanding. "Load" mutual funds charge a sales charge in addition to their net asset value per share. "No load" mutual funds simply sell their shares at the NAV per share.

NEW ISSUE   New stocks or bonds sold for the first time to raise money for just about any purpose. The issuers range from the U. S. Government and foreign governments to the most risky small corporations and cities. If a new issue is in heavy demand and its price rises to a premium over the issue price immediately after the offering, it is called "hot."

NEW YORK STOCK EXCHANGE   The nation's largest securities exchange in the late 1970s was the New York Stock Exchange.

The NYSE is a not-for-profit corporation which does not own the securities traded and does not set prices. Nor does it make or lose money when securities prices rise or fall. It provides a marketplace for the purchase and sale of securities.

ODD LOT   An amount of stock normally less than the 100 shares which make up a "round lot." In seldom-traded "inactive" stocks, 10 shares make up a round lot, and 1 to 9 shares make up an odd lot.

OPTION   A right to buy or sell specific securities, commodities, or properties at a specified price within a specified time.

OVER-THE-COUNTER   By far the biggest securities market in the world, where stocks and bonds which are not listed on securities exchanges are traded. It is the principal area for the trading of U. S. Government securities and municipal bonds. The O-T-C is not a place but mostly a communications network of stock and bond dealers doing business chiefly on a principal basis. This area is supervised by the National Association of Securities Dealers, Inc., which has the power to expel members who have been declared guilty of unethical practices.

PAPER PROFIT   Amount of profit you, the holder of a security, have "on paper" and *would* make *if* you sold this security. Paper loss is the amount of loss you *would* take *if* you sold the security.

PAR VALUE   In a common stock, its nominal value. But many common stocks today are issued without par value, and par value has little meaning to buyers of common stock. Although it has no relation at all to market value or book value, par value for common stock does have legal and corporate significance. In a preferred stock, par value has meaning to the investor because dividends are normally paid on the basis of par value. (A 5 per cent preferred stock might pay that percentage on a par of $100 or a $5.00 dividend.) In a bond, par value is also important to the investor, because par is its face value, the principal on which interest is paid. (A 5 per cent bond might pay that percentage [or $50] every year, usually on a par value of $1,000.) Par value is also the amount usually repaid at the maturity of a bond by the borrower.

PENNY STOCKS   Superspeculative stocks, often of mining companies, which usually sell for $1.00 a share or less.

POINT   In stock prices, one point equals a change of $1.00 and a one-point rise or fall means a $1.00 rise or fall in the stock's price. A half-point rise or fall means a 50 cents change; one quarter means 25 cents, etc.

In bond prices, though, one point equals a change of $10 and a one-point rise or fall in the price per $1,000 face value of bond means a $10 rise or fall in the price of that bond. A two-point change means a $20 change per bond, etc. See Chapter 23, "Your Guide to the Bond Markets . . ."

PORTFOLIO   The collection of securities held by an individual or institutional investor (such as a mutual fund). Term is especially applicable when these securities have been carefully researched and assembled in a deliberate fashion, regarding proportions of: bonds to stocks, growth to income, cyclical to noncyclical, and speculative to conservative issues.

PREFERRED STOCK   A category of stock which is subordinate to the debt a company owes but which has a claim ahead of the company's common stock upon the payment of dividends or the assets of the company in the event the company is liquidated. (Hence the name "preferred stock.") Preferred stock is usually called a "senior" security and its dividend usually is at a set rate—both characteristics similar to those of bonds.

A key difference between preferred stock and bonds is that bonds almost always have a final maturity date (when a bond becomes due and payable), while preferreds do not because these stocks represent ownership. A preferred stock will remain outstanding indefinitely unless called for redemption at a price fixed by the company at the date the stock was issued. Most preferred stocks also are cumulative—meaning that if their dividends are omitted they build up in arrears and then the company must pay these arrears plus current preferred stock dividends before it can pay common stock dividends.

Some preferred stocks are convertible into common stocks just as some bonds are.

PREMIUM   The amount by which a preferred stock or bond may sell above the par value. See DISCOUNT.

PRICE/EARNINGS RATIO   The relationship between the price at which a stock is selling and the company's earnings per share.

PROFIT TAKING   Selling stock which has appreciated in value since purchase in order to realize the profit. The term is often used to explain a downturn in the market following a period of rising prices.

PROSPECTUS   One of the documents filed with the Securities and Exchange Commission by a company when it is planning an issue of securities for public sale totaling $500,000 or more. It is a selling circular containing highlights from the full registration statement, subject to the SEC's disclosure rules, and used by brokers to help investors evaluate the new securities before or at the time of purchase.

PROXY   Authorization you give to a company official or other representative to vote your shares for you at a shareholders' meeting.

PUTS   Options to sell a fixed amount of a specific stock at a specified price within a specified period of time.

QUOTATION   Often shortened to "quote." The highest bid to buy and the lowest offer to sell a security in a given market at a given time. If you ask your broker for a "quote" on a stock, he may come back with something like "45¼ to 45½." This means that $45.25 was the highest price any buyer wanted to pay at the time the quote was given and that $45.50 was the lowest price which any seller would take at the same time.

RALLY   A sharp rapid rise in stock prices or in the price of one particular stock, following a decline.

RED HERRING   A preliminary prospectus. It carries a cautionary statement on the first page, printed in red, which gives rise to the term "red herring."

REGISTERED REPRESENTATIVE   A securities salesman employed by a brokerage firm who has passed certain tests and met certain standards set by the New York Stock Exchange and/or the National Association of Securities Dealers. Also called an account executive, customer's man, a stockbroker, or simply a broker.

REGISTRATION   Before a public offering may be made of new securities offered by a company, or of outstanding securities by controlling stockholders—through the mails or in interstate commerce—the securities must be registered under the Securities Act of 1933 and a registration statement must be filed with the SEC by the issuer. This statement must disclose pertinent information relating to the company's operations, securities, management, and purpose of the public offering. Securities of railroads under jurisdiction of the Interstate Commerce Commission, and certain other types of securities, are exempted. On securities offerings involving less than $500,000, less information is required.

Before a security may be admitted to dealings on a national securities exchange, it must be registered under the Securities Exchange Act of 1934. The application for registration must be filed with the exchange and the SEC by the company issuing the securities. It must disclose pertinent information relating to the company's operations, securities, and management. Registration may become effective thirty days after receipt by the SEC of the certification by the exchange of approval of listing and registration, or sooner by special order of the Commission.

RIGHT   A short-term privilege to buy additional shares at a specified, advantageous price for a short, limited time given to the shareholders on a proportional basis by the issuing company. Rights are often offered by a company seeking to raise additional capital, and may involve bonds, especially debentures. Rights are offered to existing shareholders so that they will continue to hold the same equity position after the change in capitalization has taken place. You, the shareholder receiving rights, have two choices: (1) to buy the security on the terms offered (for example, 1 share for each 20 shares owned); (2) to sell the rights, which, because of the favorable price of the offer, have a value of their own. Failure to exercise or sell your right results in a loss—through dilution of the value of your existing holdings by the issuance of the additional stock. Therefore, you should either exercise your rights or sell them during the allotted time span.

ROUND LOT   A unit of trading in a security. Usually 100 shares for active stocks; 10 shares for inactive stocks.

SEAT   Membership in a stock exchange which entitles the owner to buy and sell securities on that exchange. Big Board seat prices have ranged from $35,000 to $515,000 in recent years.

SEC   The Securities and Exchange Commission, the federal agency established by Congress to help protect investors. The SEC administers the Securities Act of 1933, the Trust Indenture Act, the Investment Company Act, the Investment Advisers Act, and the Public Utility Holding Company Act.

SECONDARY DISTRIBUTION   (Also known as a secondary offering.) The redistribution of a block of stock sometime after it has been sold by the issuing company. The sale is handled off the NYSE by a securities firm or group of firms and the shares are usually offered at a fixed price which is related to the current market price of the stock. Usually the block is a large one, such as might be involved in the settlement of an estate. The security may be listed or unlisted.

SETTLEMENT DAY   The deadline by which a buyer of securities must pay for securities he has purchased and a seller must deliver certificates for securities he has sold. In regular trading, settlement day is the fifth business day after execution of an order.

SHORT POSITION Stocks sold short and not covered as of a particular date. On the NYSE, a tabulation is issued once a month listing all issues on the Exchange in which there was a short position of 5,000 or more shares and issues in which the short position had changed by 2,000 or more shares in the preceding month. Short position or interest also means the total amount of stock an individual has sold short and has not covered as of a particular date. See SHORT SELLING.

SHORT SELLING The reverse of the usual transaction, for instead of buying a stock first and selling it later, the short seller sells it first, then borrows the stock and buys it back later to complete the transaction.

"SMART MONEY" Refers to the so-called professional and sophisticated traders who supposedly exploit alleged "inside" information to make profits at the expense of other investors. In other words, the term implies exceptional contacts, knowledge, timing, and forecasting ability, the special knack of finding the most profitable deals, and use of the newest financing or investing techniques and media.

SPECIALIST A member of an exchange who has two functions. The first is to maintain an orderly market, as far as reasonably practicable, in the stocks in which he is registered as a specialist. In order to maintain an orderly market, the exchange expects the specialist to buy or sell for his own account, to a reasonable degree, when there is a temporary disparity between supply and demand. The second function of the specialist is to act as a broker's broker. When a commission broker on the exchange floor receives a limit order, say, to buy at $50 a stock when selling at $60, he cannot wait at the post where the stock is traded until the price reaches the specified level. So he leaves the order with the specialist, who will try to execute it in the market if and when the stock declines to the specified price. There were some 380 specialists on the NYSE alone in the late 1970s

SPECULATOR A person whose goal in buying and selling securities is to multiply his capital quickly and who is willing to take greater risks than an investor to attain this objective. Differs from an investor in goals, risks, temperament. See IN-AND-OUT.

SPLIT A division of a company's outstanding stock: i.e., if a company has 1 million shares outstanding, currently priced at $50 per share, and splits its stock two for one, it has 2 million shares outstanding which will sell at $25 per share. If you own 100 "old" shares at $50, after the split you own 200 "new" shares at $25. Theoretically, the new shares are worth only half the amount of the old shares, but in actual practice prices tend to rise when a stock is split— at least temporarily. Reason: investors generally are more interested in buying relatively lower-priced stocks than high-priced stocks, hence buying frequently increases after a stock is split.

SPREAD The difference between two prices, between bid and asked or between purchase and sale price.

STOCK DIVIDEND A dividend paid by a company to its stockholders in the form of additional shares of the company's stock instead of in the form of cash (when it is a cash dividend).

STOCK OPTION   A privilege, often conferred as a fringe benefit by a company to its executive and key employees, to buy stock in the company at a specified presumable favorable price, within a specified period of time, and on advantageous terms.

STOP ORDER   Standing instructions to your broker to sell your shares automatically if the price drops to a specified level. The aim is to assure yourself that profits don't disappear or your losses don't exceed a given amount. There is no guarantee that a stop order will be executed exactly as its "trigger" price, because when a stop is activated it becomes a market order and allows the broker to get the best possible price then available in a market. Stops can be used for buy orders too.

STREET   The New York financial community in the Wall Street area.

STREET NAME   Securities left by the owner in his broker's name and custody. Often investors leave all their securities in street name as a matter of choice and convenience, but securities bought on margin must be left in street name.

SYMBOL   The single capital letter or combination of letters given to a company when it is listed on an exchange and by which it is thereafter identified on the tape. For instance, U. S. Steel is "X"; General Motors is "GM"; American Telephone & Telegraph is "T."

TAKEN TO THE CLEANERS   In the stock market, this means the same thing as taking a bath or blood bath. In short, it means being hit by one or many whopping losses.

TENDER   In stock market language, a tender means an offer to acquire a security you own or to exchange stock which you own for stock in another company. Usually a tender is made by a corporation or individual to gain control of a company or to simplify the corporate structure of the company.

THE STREET   Wall Street. But "Wall Street" is not just a street in New York City bounded at one end by a river and at the other by a graveyard. It has been broadened to include all the financial institutions, securities and money markets, and investors on all the Main Streets of the United States from coast to coast.

THIN MARKET   A market in which there are comparatively few bids to buy or offers to sell or both—or an illiquid market. The phrase may apply to a single security or to the entire stock market. In a thin market, price fluctuations between transactions are usually larger than when the market is liquid. A thin market in a particular stock may reflect a lack of interest in that issue or a limited supply of stock in the market.

TICKER   The instrument which prints prices and volume of security transactions in cities and towns throughout the United States and Canada within minutes after each trade on the floor. In recent years it has been complemented by thousands of visual display units on tops of brokers' desks.

TIPS   Recommendations of stocks to buy or sell often given to novices by other novices on the false basis of alleged "inside" information about the stock. Tips may be accurate too, and given in entirely good faith—but these are in a slim minority as far as the general public is concerned. Tipping could be illegal. A tipster, of course, is a person who gives tips.

TRANSFER AGENT   A transfer agent, usually a bank, keeps a record of the name of each registered shareowner, his or her address, the number of shares owned, and sees that certificates presented for transfer are properly canceled and new certificates issued in the name of the transferee.

TURNOVER   The volume of trading on a stock exchange—or in a particular security, or in the entire securities market—on a given day or in a given period.

UNDERWRITER   See INVESTMENT BANKER.

WARRANT   A privilege to buy a security at a specified price—within a specified time limit or perpetually. Usually a long-term offer made by a corporation to pave the way for the eventual sale of stocks or bonds to persons who do not already own its securities. As a rule, it is offered as an inducement to get investors to buy the other securities. A warrant is similar to a right but it normally has a much longer life.

"WHEN ISSUED"   Term used to describe a new issue of securities that has been authorized but not actually issued to purchasers and that is being bought and sold in the market with all transactions settled only when, as, and if the securities are finally issued. "WI" is the label for these issues in the newspaper stock tables.

YIELD   The percentage of return per year on a security. To find the current yield on a stock, you divide the current annual dividend rate by the current price of the stock. (If you bought the stock at $100, and it is paying $3.00 a year in dividends, your current yield is 3 per cent.) Figuring yields on bonds is more complex and determining yields to maturity requires the use of bond tables.

YO-YO STOCKS   Volatile, usually high-priced specialty issues, which fluctuate wildly.

22

MUTUAL FUNDS

WHAT ARE MUTUAL FUNDS?

Probably the best known of the many different types of so-called investment companies, mutual funds are a medium through which you invest your money in a diversified list of stocks and bonds chosen by professional investment managers.

You buy shares in a mutual fund which in turn uses your money to buy the securities of other companies. You can buy and sell mutual fund shares at prices that are calculated once or twice a day on any days that the securities markets are open.

There are "load" and "no-load" funds. There also are the closed-end funds (now known as publicly traded investment funds) and unit trusts, plus many others, most of which are discussed separately later in this chapter. The load funds are sold by salespeople through elaborate marketing systems, and on these shares there is a sales charge (load). The no-load funds have no salespeople, no elaborate distribution systems, and no sales charge. You are not "sold" these shares; you must "buy" them. You usually learn about a no-load fund from another investor, from a banker, a lawyer, an investment adviser, an ad in a financial news section, or from a discussion such as this.

Q. *How many mutual funds are there?*
A. In the closing years of the 1970s, there were more than 700, of which about 255 were no-load funds.

Q. *Who buys mutual funds?*
A. Individuals. Also many institutional investors have in recent years become large holders of fund shares. All together, some 8.5 million individuals and firms had invested in funds as the 1980s neared.

Q. *Where are the prices on mutual funds quoted?*
A. In the financial pages of the major daily newspapers, which usually have a section giving bid and asked prices on mutual funds. On the no-load funds, you will find the same price quoted under "bid" and "asked." On the load funds you will find a higher price under "asked" than under "bid" because the "asked" price

will reflect the sales charge. For example, if the bid on Fund A is $10.50 and the asked is $11.20, the sales charge is 70 cents. Also many major newspapers use the designation "NL" (no-load) next to this type of fund, thereby making it easy to find the no-load funds.

What Fund for You?

Every investor certainly should investigate funds. Many of you will find the funds are suitable for achieving your investment goals.

To help you determine the kind of mutual fund that is best suited for you, here are broad guidelines.

Specifically, if you are:

• *Single,* earning under $15,000, with a savings-oriented (conservative) temperament: you should own an income fund with a dual goal of providing some longer-term capital growth.

• *Single,* earning under $15,000, with a chance-taker's (aggressive) temperament: yours should be a "total return" fund, concentrating on high-growth common stocks or a long-term growth fund.

• *Married,* with two or three dependents, earning $15,000 to $25,000, with a conservative temperament: the best for you would be a blue-chip, common stock fund, for long-term growth of both capital and income.

• *Married,* with two or three dependents, earning $25,000 and up, with a growth-oriented temperament: yours should be either a pure "income" fund, a "money-market" fund, or a bond fund.

• *Working couple,* earning $25,000 and up, with growth-oriented temperament: obviously, a growth fund is for you, so the investments can help you accumulate resources for future tuition needs, travel and other recreation, retirement, etc.

• *Older person,* income coming from Social Security and some savings, with a conservative temperament and a goal of preservation of capital and more current income: ideally, the medium should be an income fund of the more conservative type which pays dividends and has some appreciation possibilities. Or a money-market fund which will preserve capital and offer a satisfactory yield.

Why Should You Buy Mutual Funds?

If I were to tell you that the investment advice given to the small investor in the United States is far inferior to that given to the big guy, and that the men and women who give that advice agree the above is true, wouldn't you be deeply disturbed? Okay, I'm telling you that this is the opinion of an overwhelming percentage of the nation's security analysts. According to a recent survey:

• A shocking seven out of ten security analysts have "reservations about the advice available to the small investor as compared with that given the large one."

• Only one in three believes that "the quality of investment advice now available adequately serves all types of investors."

• Nearly half favor "some form of blanket registration of security analysts" (in short, greater control).

This is a serious indictment of investment advice by the advice industry itself.

By itself, this report would be sobering enough. It becomes even more so in view of the forecasts dramatized in the previous chapter on investing in stocks: first, the fees you pay for Wall Street's service are on the rise while fees the funds pay are declining; second, commissions you pay are more and more determined by the level of the investment advice you request; and third, an investment manager has emerged who supervises the funds of the small investor for a fee on top of the commissions the investor must pay to buy and sell.

What does all this mean to you?

It means you must recognize that you will not get the same high-quality research and advice as an institutional investor and certainly not at the same time the pro gets it—unless you pay extra for it. This in turn means that one possible solution for you lies in joining the pros via buying mutual fund shares.

Here are some of the major advantages of mutual fund ownership versus personal selection by the amateur of a portfolio of stocks and bonds.

Diversification. In general, the greater variety of stocks, bonds, and other types of investments selected by mutual funds lessens the risk of loss due to your making one big mistake in selecting individual stocks.

Mutual funds have to diversify. By federal law, except in instances of special exemption disclosed in the prospectus, they may not invest more than 5 per cent of their assets in the securities of any single issuer. Funds may not own more than 10 per cent of any class of securities issued by a single company.

Professional management. All of the major mutual funds are managed by professionals backed by substantial facilities for research, statistical analysis, and economic research.

Federal regulation. Mutual funds are closely regulated by federal and state laws designed to guard against abuses. By law, mutual funds ordinarily must distribute at least 90 per cent of their net income to shareowners each year. Moreover, there are tight federal restrictions on the amounts of money a mutual fund may borrow.

Convenience. Obviously, it's much simpler for you, the shareowner, to have one single certificate representing your ownership (through a mutual fund) in one hundred or more stocks. Mutual funds have a fine record in handling the paper work of their customers. Many take care of the paper work completely.

Services and easy purchase plans. There are many different, easy, and new ways in which you can buy—and enjoy the ownership of—mutual funds today. This includes automatic reinvestment plans, periodic purchase plans, retirement plans, ordering by telephone, free exchange between funds in "families" of funds, withdrawal plans, and the like.

Liquidity. It's very easy to sell a mutual fund. Nearly all funds will repurchase fund shares at the bid price, and the sell order can be conveniently arranged.

Variety of funds. There are dozens of different types of mutual funds to choose from—including stock, bond, and money-market funds, as well as growth, balanced, income, speculative funds—which means there's probably at least one fund that can meet your specific needs.

WHAT IS THE INVESTMENT RECORD OF MUTUAL FUNDS?

Of course, the performance varies from fund to fund depending on the objective of the fund (growth versus income, for instance) and on the excellence of management. But over the long term, the records of mutual funds compare favorably with the familiar stock averages.

Over the short term, though, the performances of mutual funds can be startlingly good or abysmally poor. For example, in the 1960–74 period, many of the fund shares chalked up dreadful records. Their performance came in for particular criticism in view of the fact that the funds are managed by professionals at a handsome fee and the fact that at a minimum their goal is preservation of capital plus income while, at a maximum, their aim is significant enhancement of capital plus income.

This was the period in which the "go-go" performance funds went into their downward spin. Some of the star fund performers of the 1960s—such as the Manhattan Fund, Mates Investment Fund, Enterprise Fund, and Neuwrith Fund—plummeted from the list of top performers to the also-ran category. It was painful testimony of the extent to which so many of the funds had changed from being a safe, sane haven for the small investor wanting long-term growth into a playground for the fast-moving speculator seeking instant performance.

I repeat, however, that this is short-term, and, in general, mutual funds are much more suited to the long-term investor rather than the trader.

In the latter part of the 1970s, fund managers, stunned by the poor performance earlier in the decade and the investor disenchantment reflected in several consecutive years of net redemptions for the industry, set about developing products, services, and management investment practices designed to win back investor confidence in mutual funds and the basic values mutual funds offer—portfolio diversification, professional management, relatively low entry costs. As a result, fund sales again started to rise, and in the second half of the 1970s mutual funds as a whole were once more outperforming the broad market averages.

On balance, the long-term record of the funds shapes up impressively in the investor's favor.

It would be self-defeating to submit statistics to you at this date to document the excellent long-term performance of mutual funds compared with other forms of investing and saving as well as against other key stock market indexes. You would be only confused as prices of various investment mediums and the returns you can earn fluctuate from month to month. Sources that instead will quickly supply you with up-to-the-minute figures are listed on pages 1069–70 in this chapter.

There may be or may not be a modest charge involved in obtaining the information. Or you may want to subscribe to one or more of the reporting services.

Types of Mutual Funds

As the 1980s begin, you can buy shares in literally dozens of different types of mutual funds—many of them new and little known and many of them highly specialized. These, of course, are in addition to the "old" types of funds, part of the industry since it emerged in the 1920s.

For instance, you can invest your money in shares of a mutual fund specializing in chemical stocks or energy companies. You can choose a fund that gambles in ultra-risky speculative securities, or you can settle for a fund with a conservative investment philosophy. You also can buy shares in funds specializing in tax-exempt short-term securities or bonds, utilities, Canadian securities, options, commodities, the stock market indexes, insurance and bank stocks, or in foreign securities. You even can buy shares in a mutual fund carrying built-in insurance against any loss in your investment—assuming you're willing to pay an insurance premium cost (in addition to the sales charge, if the offering fund is a load fund type).

Mutual funds have now diversified to the point where you can actually lose your way in this financial industry without a guide. Quietly but rapidly, whole new classes of mutual funds have been developed. For example, it was as recently as 1970 that the bond and money-market (liquid asset or cash reserve) funds jumped into the popular class.

To the old-line definitions, it is thus essential to add explanations of some of the new types of funds. In alphabetical order, here is a guide through "old" and "new":

Balanced Funds: among the more conservative funds, with investment portfolios "balanced" at all times among bonds, preferred stocks, and common stocks—as a protection against a roller-coastering stock market. This type of fund is for a person who is seeking safety of principal plus a regular income and who, to get this, is willing to settle for relatively modest growth of his investment.

Bond Funds: funds that invest in portfolios of various types of senior securities to produce relatively high yields. In recent years, the yields on such funds have often substantially outstripped those of savings accounts or even large certificates of deposit. Another attraction of such funds is the possibility of eventual capital gains if some of the bonds in the portfolio were bought at discounts below face value.

Closed-end Funds: see Publicly Traded Investment Funds.

Commodities Funds: funds that seek capital gains through a portfolio consisting of holdings of commodities, as opposed to stocks and bonds.

Common Stock Funds: funds that have limited their portfolios to common stocks. They range from ultra-conservative funds investing primarily in the highest-quality blue chip common stocks to ultra-risky funds investing in speculative stocks.

Convertible Funds: are aimed at producing current income and capital gains by investing in convertible preferred stocks and convertible bonds.

Dual-purpose Funds: type of funds offering two kinds of shares: income shares and capital shares. In most dual-purpose funds, each class of investor at the out-set stands to get double his money's worth. The capital shareholder will reap gains (or losses) on the income shareholder's money as well as his own. The income shareholder collects the capital shareholder's dividends. To obtain this form of leverage, the income shareholder must usually give up all claim to capital appreciation and the capital shareholder must forfeit all income. There are only a handful of such funds and they haven't operated long enough to get a good reading on their performance. They have a long and successful history in England and Holland.

Fund of Funds: these are funds ("multifunds") which invest in shares of other mutual funds, thereby offering shareholders a highly diversified type of investment.

Growth Funds: funds concentrating on purchase of growth stocks. Growth funds involve relatively more risk than income or balanced funds. A growth fund should give you a return ranging from at least 8 per cent to 12 per cent annually over a five-year period or it's not worth the risk.

Hedge Funds: began as private pools of speculative funds formed by groups of wealthy investors, but now there are hedge funds for anyone who wants them. These funds use such unorthodox (for mutual funds) techniques as borrowing against their own stocks in order to buy more shares, speculating in put and call options, and selling shares short in order to profit from stock price declines as well as rises (thus, "hedge" funds). Their major objective is capital gains.

Millions of dollars were put into hedge funds in the 1960s, and until 1969 some turned in dazzling performances. But in the 1969–70 crash, many of the leading hedge funds lost as much as 40 to 50 per cent in value and their reputations were seriously tarnished. Many went out of business. Hedge funds are usually not for the small investor.

Income Funds: the principal goal of these is income to be achieved by investment in high-yielding stocks and bonds. Only an incidental objective is capital gains. These funds tend to be the most conservative—and their popularity swings up and down depending on shifting investor interest in income versus long-term growth.

Index Funds: this type of fund invests in a portfolio that duplicates the Standard & Poor's 500 Stock Index. Through an index fund, the investor is—in effect—buying a prorated interest in all the stocks that make up the S&P Index of Stocks listed on the New York Stock Exchange. By so doing, this type of fund can be expected to about match the performance of the stock market as a whole.

Junk Bond Funds: these funds invest in high-risk corporate bonds and therefore offer investors high yields coupled—inevitably—with high risks. Junk bond funds are not for the conservative!

Letter Stock Funds: highly speculative funds that invest your money in stocks of companies not yet registered with the Securities and Exchange Commission. This stock is called "letter stock" because a buyer (in this case, the mutual fund) must sign an "investment letter" promising not to resell the stock for a specified short-term period and pledging instead to hold it for a longer term. This type of stock is generally sold by small, fledgling companies to finance research, development, expansion.

Look upon any investment in mutual funds specializing in letter stocks as sheer speculation. This is definitely too risky for most mutual fund buyers and the funds virtually disappeared in the market breaks of the early 1970s.

Money-market Funds: funds that invest in short-term money-market instruments. Investors can buy these shares in comparatively small amounts and thus get the same advantages of the relatively high rates on these instruments that big investors get when they buy large blocks in the open market. By the late 1970s, more than $20 billion had been invested in money-market funds by individuals and institutions.

Be sure the money-market funds fit in with your investment objectives. The funds are not meant to be long-term investments nor the keystone of an individual or institutional investment program. But the funds do provide a haven to put your cash to work easily and efficiently at the highest returns consistent with safety.

They invest in short-term money-market paper, are highly conservative, offer returns that usually will rise and fall with the ups and downs of short-term interest rates. Their principal values will show relatively minor changes, reflecting moves in interest rates and credit risks. They usually are used as a safe place to keep money at work that is temporarily out of the stock market or that you must keep in the most liquid form.

Even in this narrow field, investment goals, portfolio policies, and investor services may vary.

Some funds tend to anticipate short-term interest rate fluctuations and change their investments accordingly. Others merely try to maintain their investments at the highest available short-term rates and do not attempt to outguess rate fluctuations.

Some limit themselves to the highest quality U. S. Government securities. Others rely heavily on different types of short-term instruments, such as bank certificates of deposit, commercial paper, other short-term paper of high quality. See "Your Guide to the Bond Markets," Chapter 23. Some impose rigid quality restrictions on their own investments. Others will buy below the highest quality to get a relatively higher yield.

You must check out the funds themselves. Particularly, you must examine the prospectus of each fund for clues to the knowledge, reputation, experience, and resources of the organization and the fund's portfolio managers.

Services the money funds offer include: check writing privileges, immediate phone or wire redemption, exchange privileges, automatic redemption, accounting.

Municipal bond mutual funds: tax-exempt funds popularly called munifunds may be for you *if* income exempt from federal taxes is what you're looking for. That could be if you report at least $16,000 in taxable income on a joint return, or $12,000 on a single return, earn enough to maintain a regular investment program—*and* avoid undue risks by restraining your greed for the highest possible annual returns and vow instead to invest only in quality funds.

• A municipal bond fund follows the basic strategy of buying and selling its investments, just as a stock mutual fund does. The funds are "managed," and your return can vary along with the protection you are given against loss of principal.

Munifunds first appeared in late 1976 and immediately took off, with dozens of investment companies in the field now and others being regularly developed.

If you're a couple filing a joint return on a taxable income in the $20,000–$24,000 bracket, a tax-free 5½ per cent return is the equivalent of a taxable 8.09 per cent; if your bracket is the $28,000–$34,000 range, the 5½ tax free is equal to 9.02 per cent. In the 50 per cent bracket, of course, it's equal to 11 per cent a year. (See chapter 23 on investing in bonds.)

• Never forget that municipal bond funds can decrease as well as increase in value. The cheapest fund may not be the most stable or the best managed; the fund offering the highest return may be investing in very poor bonds. You *can lose* money.

• Profits from increases in asset value are taxable as capital gains.

In munifunds, there are both "load" and no-load funds.

• Before you put up a penny, decide on your goals. And restrain your greed!

Option and Option Income Funds: these funds promise high income and appreciation by investing in options on stocks. This is a relatively new and untested type of fund. Only a few exist. Great caution should be exercised before investing in an option fund.

Publicly Traded Investment Funds: popularly called closed-end funds, these operate like open-end mutual funds except that they issue only a fixed number of shares and will not usually buy back their shares. Shares are bought and sold on the stock market but hardly ever at a price equal to the net asset value per share. As a result, they either sell at a "premium" over their asset price or at a "discount" below it.

Special-purpose Funds: these aren't new, but their number is multiplying. They invest primarily in one specific type of stock or bond or in one particular industry to take advantage of the anticipated faster growth in that area or industry. For example, there are the funds that invest heavily in chemicals, energy, gemstones, minerals, geographic regions or countries—or only in United States Government securities. Within this special-purpose category, too, there are funds adhering to a special stock market forecasting theory or technique.

If you invest in a special-purpose stock fund, a wise precaution would be to seek a fund with an investment portfolio widely diversified among key beneficiaries of any major advance in its chosen area or industry.

Tax-free Exchange Funds: a limited number of funds have been specifically organized to exchange individual securities for a diversified holding of stocks, without incurring immediate taxes. This so-called tax-free exchange through organizations of a mutual fund type of operation was prohibited by the Internal Revenue Service in 1967.

Unit Trusts: UITs were established as far back as 1961. While securities in a mutual fund are actively managed, securities—usually bonds—placed in a unit trust simply remain there for the limited life of the trust or until the bond reaches maturity. Therefore, there is no conventional management role in the performance of a unit trust.

Each UIT is actually a separate trust, with a fixed portfolio of bonds. Though bonds may be sold from the portfolio, if credit-worthiness is adversely affected, no new bonds can be bought to replace them. In short, once the UIT acquires the bonds, it holds them to maturity, thereby assuring you a stable—known in advance—rate of return.

If you have enough of a nest egg to meet the usual minimum investment requirements of $1,000 to $5,000—*and* you also strictly obey the basic rules on greed and quality—UITs may be worth investigating.

UITs charge a one-time sales fee of 3 to 4½ per cent included in the price, but no annual management fee.

Venture Capital Funds: funds that usually invest in securities of smaller companies that are little known and with stock often not yet registered with the Securities and Exchange Commission. These restricted securities cannot be sold publicly until they have been registered. Venture capital funds often provide new and young companies with seed capital. Nowhere is an investor betting more on a manager's ability and judgment than in venture capital funds. Generally, these funds are higher risk investments and should be considered only by more sophisticated investors.

LOAD AND NO-LOAD FUNDS

A load fund will usually be sold to you by a salesperson or selling organization and, for this, you will pay a sales charge, or a "load." A no-load fund you will have to seek out and buy on your own. There are no salespeople, no sales charges—and thus the description "no-load." This is the sole distinction.

Among the no-load funds you will find the same wide selection as among the load funds—in investment goals, in size, in investment record, in quality of management, etc. You can get the same services with no-loads as with loads: systematic purchasing plans, withdrawal plans, dividend reinvestment, retirement plans, payroll deduction, check writing, exchange privileges, and insurance plans. You can sell them easily just by telling the fund's home office you want to redeem your shares. (A few have a redemption charge, usually less than 2 per cent.) The tax status is the same in both cases and so are the SEC's regulations.

Since no-loads have no sales organizations, further information must be obtained by writing directly to the fund, or contacting the No-Load Mutual Fund Association, Valley Forge, Pennsylvania 19481.

When you buy a load fund, you pay the net asset value plus the sales charge. This is generally around 8½ per cent, which translates into something over 9 per cent above the asset value. The charge, however, can range from 1 per cent to more than 9½ per cent. In short, the minute you buy a load fund, the worth of your holdings is less than what you put in. For example, if you buy $1,000 worth of a load fund, you may only get $910 in asset value; $90 went for commission.

With no-loads, all your money goes to work. This gives the no-load investor a head start. Here's why.

Let's assume two $10,000 investments: one in a load fund, the other in a no-load. In the case of the load fund, 8½ per cent, or $850, is deducted, the remaining $9,150 is invested. If both funds grow at the same rate—10 per cent per year, for example—the no-load will be worth $11,000 at the end of the first year, while the load fund will be worth only $10,065. The no-load investor is now $1,000 ahead; the load fund investor is about even. But let's look closer. Originally the no-load investor had $850 more working for him than did the load fund investor. Now the differential is $935 ($11,000 vs. $10,065). What has happened is that the $850 paid out as commission in one case, but invested in the other, is also growing. And over the years this sum will continue to grow and compound, widening the differential. By the end of twenty years, the no-load investment will be worth close to $6,000 more, if both funds continue to grow at the same 10 per cent rate per year.

The long-term records of the no-load funds compare favorably with those of the load funds. The lack of a sales charge has nothing to do with the caliber of the fund's management.

In recent years, no-load funds have become increasingly popular as investors have become aware that they are around and that they provide a savings in commissions. But you well may decide that a specific load fund is right for you and thus you'll ignore the sales charge. The crucial thing is that the specific fund meets your investment goals. Moreover, in time the amount of commissions on "load" funds will go down—in response to the competitive pressure from the "no-loads" plus increasing pressure from the SEC and Congress.

Since this could be your biggest single investment medium for now and the future, the only sensible move is to explore the whole field of loads and no-loads.

WAYS TO BUY AND USE MUTUAL FUNDS

There are not only many different types of mutual funds to choose among, there are also many easy and new ways in which you can buy mutual funds. Just how you buy them depends in part on the way you plan to use them ultimately, for, say, extra regular income, building a retirement fund, or creating a college education fund.

Here's a simple guide through some of the investor programs now available.

Automatic Dividend Reinvestment: under this program all dividends and capital gains distributions are automatically reinvested. In the late seventies, roughly 3 million dividend reinvestment plans were in force.

Withdrawal Plan: an arrangement under which investors in mutual funds can regularly receive monthly or quarterly payments of a specified amount. This may be more or less than the actual investment income.

Letter of Intent: with a pledge to purchase a sufficient amount of mutual fund shares within a limited period of time, you can qualify for the reduced selling charge that would apply to a comparable lump sum purchase.

Periodic Purchase (or Accumulation) Plans: under these, you simply send in checks to invest regularly (usually monthly but sometimes bimonthly or quarterly) in mutual fund shares or you can authorize your bank to invest for you and to deduct the costs from your monthly bank statement. In the late seventies there were about 4 million such plans in force. The minimum investment under these plans is typically between $25 and $50, though some funds have no minimum and some substantially higher; also, in most plans, you can change the dollar amount at any time or stop investing altogether, if you so decide.

A key point here is that, while you're investing identical amounts at regular intervals via these periodic purchase plans, you are also getting the advantage of dollar-cost-averaging—meaning you get more shares when stock prices are depressed and less shares when they are rising. Thus, you average out your costs, which is, as I repeat and stress, an excellent way to invest in stocks over the long term.

403(B) Plans: individuals employed by school districts, hospitals, municipalities, and other non-profit organizations or associations may be eligible to adopt 403(B) plans which will reduce current tax liability and permit earnings in the plan to compound on a tax shelter basis.

Corporate Retirement Plans: many funds make available pension or profit-sharing plans in prototype form for use by corporate employees. Check with your company to find out if it offers this type of plan and the terms for participation.

Keogh Plan: this plan is for the self-employed individual who may contribute 15 per cent of earned income, up to a maximum of $7,500. A retirement plan can be set up by making tax-deductible contributions and at the same time shelter current income dividends and capital gains distributions from current tax liability.

Defined Benefit Keogh: a newer type of Keogh plan that lets you defer income taxes of up to $10,800—a tax deferment on substantially higher income than the $7,500 maximum allowed on regular Keoghs.

Simplified Employee Pension Plan: permitted by the 1978 Tax Reform Act, a SEP eliminates much of the paper work associated with traditional pension plans. Under a SEP an employer contributes to an Individual Retirement Account in the employee's name. The maximum contribution is 15 per cent of earned income, not to exceed $7,500. If your employer's contribution amounts to less than $1,500, you may make up the difference and take that figure as a deduction on your income taxes.

Exchange Privilege: some funds will permit you to shift your investment from one fund to another by telephone. This is permitted only among funds under the same management or with an outside fund under a mutual agreement between the funds. This is a convenience for the shareowner whose investment objective or current needs change.

Individual Retirement Accounts: IRAs were created by passage of the Employee Retirement Security Act of 1974. Individuals not covered by formal corporate, government, or other retirement plans may set up tax-shelter retirement programs of their own with annual funding of 15 per cent of your gross wages, up to a maximum of $1,500 as of the late 1970s, plus an additional $250 is permitted to cover a non-working spouse. And the maximum permissible investment per individual is almost certain to go up.

The Variable Annuity Separate Account: investment vehicles offered by life insurance companies as a means to combine the protection of insurance with the potentials of equity investments.

IRA Roll-over Plan: this permits distributions from a qualified pension or profit-sharing plan to be reinvested within sixty days from the date of the distribution in a qualifying individual retirement account. The amount so invested is not subject to the $1,500 annual IRA limit of the late 1970s. Further, such funds may be later transferred back to a qualified pension or profit-sharing plan, all without incurring a tax liability.

Payroll Deduction Plans: these are among the most rapidly growing fringe benefits offered by U.S. corporations—and, as you might suspect, the payroll plans are being aggressively pushed by the mutual fund industry. Often, by investing this way through your company you will pay a lower load charge—or no sales charge if the plan invests in no-load funds.

Life Insurance-Mutual Fund Plans: you can combine purchase of mutual fund shares and life insurance or invest in a type of plan that will buy X number of shares of a given mutual fund, and then the dividends plus capital gains on your shares will pay your life insurance premiums. If, however, the value of your mutual fund shares drops substantially, you may have to pay your life insurance premium costs out of capital you have invested—or out of your pocket.

Group Life Insurance: some funds offer group life and accident insurance. In this case, you, the shareholders, will be given the opportunity to purchase insurance at special, low group rates, with premium costs being paid optionally from the proceeds of your mutual fund investment or an additional direct payment of the periodic premium cost.

Plan Completion Insurance: also provided optionally by some funds, is a means of ensuring that an intended plan will be completed in the event that the plan holder should die.

Insured Redemption Value Plans: offered by selected funds to protect an investment in a mutual fund against long-term loss. If the total value of your investment at the close of the period, including the value of shares received from reinvested income dividend and capital gains, is less than the insured investment, including the amount of the premium, the insurance company makes up the difference. You, the shareholder, do not have to redeem your shares to collect.

How Mutual Funds Help in Other Ways

You will find a wide variety of uses for mutual funds to help you in planning for your own and your family's financial well-being. To illustrate:

• If your income is at the level suggesting some tax-sheltered income would be valuable, mutual funds that invest in tax-exempt bonds issued by states, cities, and other local governments can be exceedingly attractive. The interest obtained from these bonds is passed through to shareowners free of federal tax.

• If you want to invest in equities but avoid the chance of poor fund management, a fund with a portfolio structured to duplicate the Standard & Poor's 500 Stock Index can be expected to do as least as well—or as poorly—as the stock market as a whole.

• If you want to put your idle cash to work harder for you, you may want to invest some in a money-market fund. Through these so-called liquid asset type funds, you can enjoy competitive interest yields from portfolios that invest primarily in such short-term instruments as those issued or guaranteed by the U. S. Government or its agencies, bank certificates of deposit, commercial paper and short-term corporate obligations. With a money-market fund you can withdraw all or any part of your money at any time for any purpose without penalty, and redemptions often can be accomplished by a simple telephone call. You can use your redemption checks as immediate cash and your investment will still be earning interest, until the checks clear. Money funds are a way to keep your extra savings working for you until the instant they are needed.

• You can buy shares for your children under the "uniform gifts to minors" act and arrange to have dividends and capital gains automatically reinvested to build a college fund. There are significant tax angles, so check them. One major advantage is that you usually have to pay taxes on your fund dividends and capital gains distributions and your youngster doesn't.

• If you are self-employed, you can use mutual funds (among other investments) to create a retirement nest egg for yourself. As of the late seventies, you could contribute up to $7,500 a year under the Keogh law—with the total amount deductible for income tax purposes—and until you retire you need not pay any income tax on any dividends or capital gains distributions paid into your account.

• You can arrange for a second income from your mutual fund shares by setting up a voluntary withdrawal plan. Typically, users of these plans have shares valued at a minimum of $7,500 to $10,000. If you own $10,000 worth of shares and elect to withdraw a typical 6 per cent a year, you'll get about $50 a month. If your shares grow by more than 6 per cent a year, you'll be able to withdraw $50 a month and keep your assets intact.

• You can switch programs. Often so-called families of mutual funds, several of which are run by the same management, permit the owner of one fund to switch to another without paying additional load charges. For example, if a young man buys a growth fund and continues investing in it and then wants to switch to an income fund as he reaches retirement age, he could do this usually without paying additional load charges—if he is investing in load funds—to acquire the income fund. Most no-load fund families offer exchange privileges without any charge for this service. The restriction is that the income fund be in the same "family" as the growth fund. Federal income taxes, though, are applicable on such a switch.

HOW TO BUY MUTUAL FUNDS PROFESSIONALLY

There is far more to the purchase of mutual funds than a simple decision that this is the prudent way for you to invest. There is much more to the wise selection of a fund than a cursory comparison of records and a quick look at a fund's portfolio of investments. Behind a fund's investment record, portfolio makeup, investment philosophy, and investment objectives are many crucial considerations and facts with which you should be thoroughly familiar before you can reach a decision on which fund is the most suitable for you.

Most of the selling of mutual funds focuses on points that *all* funds have in common: management, diversification, services, etc. No one fund has anything unique here. Most mutual fund literature you will see contains similarly persuasive text, photos, and charts. This section is designed to help you become professional in your selection of a fund—so you can, in fact as well as theory, choose the right fund for your needs. You won't get this sort of talk from the average mutual fund salesman; he probably doesn't even know it. Nor will you get it in the average mutual fund literature; it isn't there.

Here are six basic factors in addition to the sales charge to consider before choosing a fund.

(1) *Your own situation.* Don't be deceived by the seeming simplicity of this, for it is the most fundamental consideration of all. Too often, mutual fund salesmen pay only lip service to your circumstances—financial and otherwise. And don't mislead yourself in your eagerness for quick and big profits. Keep in mind that if you pick a fund with the wrong objective and then decide to switch to another fund, it can be costly.

Analyze your own needs and objectives. Do you want a fund for forced savings? College tuition for your child? Long-term financial security? A monthly income supplement? What? Based on these factors, decide on your investment strategy and stick with it in good times and bad.

(2) *Your investment objectives.* This isn't as simple as it sounds either. It's much more complex than finding a fund that has objectives matching yours.

Size of a fund, for instance, can be crucial to whether and how your investment objectives are achieved. A small fund may be less successful in achieving the goals of stability of income than a large fund, for the large fund can buy a more diversified and extensive portfolio and may be able to grow in a more orderly way than the smaller fund. On the other hand, a large fund is likely to be less successful in achieving the goal of big capital gains than a small fund, for it cannot concentrate as a small fund can on a few small companies which have explosive growth potentials. In a small portfolio, say of $10 million to $25 million, two or three hot stocks can do wonders for performance.

Risk. Comparative risk is another factor crucial to weigh in deciding which of the many funds—all with the same investment objectives—is right for you. A fund that diversifies its holdings among many industries and companies is likely to have a less spectacular short-term record than one that concentrates on relatively few industries and companies with spectacular possibilities. The diversified fund's longer-term record, though, can be far superior—particularly if the limited fund's management runs into a period of bad judgment. To illustrate, in 1968 some of the smaller growth funds chalked up superb records—but in the devastating bear markets that followed, these very same funds faded away.

To capsulize, the lesson of the tortoise and the hare should be required reading for mutual fund investors! Size and portfolio makeup are vital in analyzing performance.

(3) *The time factor.* The original idea of the mutual fund was to provide a

means by which the small investor could acquire a diversified investment portfolio under constant management. A fund can produce large gains—or losses—over any short-term period, but it *never* was intended for short-term speculation, and if you try to use it, you are misusing it. Funds are meant for long-term investing objectives.

This leads to the key point that, in buying mutual funds, "timing" of your investments to catch tops or bottoms is much less significant than "consistency" in making your investments. Since the fund's managers are investing to produce continuing results over the long term, whether prices are high or low at a given moment is far less important than your ability to maintain a buying program through good times and bad. (This, again, is the professional approach to dollar-cost-averaging.)

Another point on timing: a fund that raises lots of money from new investors during a bull market will have a hoard of cash which it will feel compelled to invest. This can become a minus factor the instant the markets dip. Thus, "timing" ranks with earlier points as a far more complex and subtle factor than most investors suspect.

(4) *The structure of the management.* Some funds are pretty much one-man operations—and, as with any one-man business, the built-in risks are obvious. Other funds have created strong management teams with diversified brains at the top and with a strong backup in research and other tools essential for successful management of a securities portfolio. You owe it to yourself to find out precisely what sort of management you are buying when you buy mutual fund shares. Since you're buying your shares for the long term, you should make sure your fund has a management structure that can operate successfully over the long term.

In short, an investment program worthy of the name does not consist of just "name" personalities! Many of the famous portfolio managers of the late 1960s have left the business. Also, you may buy into a fund because you understand it has top portfolio managers and find they have left to go to another firm. If you're a truly professional investor in mutual fund shares, you'll do your homework in areas such as this.

(5) *The investment record.* On the face of it, it seems simple enough to say that Fund X has performed better than Fund Y and therefore you should buy X. But as any professional would tell you (and remember, you're trying to become a professional, too), there is far more to an investment record than the simple comparison of percentage gains or losses (which salesmen love to stress when the comparison is in their favor).

To illustrate, for what periods are the investment records being compared? If it is a short-term period, what was the market environment? Was it a market in which speculative issues dominated on the up side? If so, was Fund X, as opposed to Fund Y, in a position to take advantage of this environment?

In recent years, much has been made of the short-term investment record of a limited number of mutual funds. But ask: what actually produced the results? Was it, for instance, the fact that the fund had a very small portfolio with a limited number of holdings and a couple of these happened to be star performers?

Or did the fund come on the scene just when a bull market was starting? Was it because the fund emphasized a given "hot" industry that may soon cool? Was the fund using borrowed capital? Was it invested in highly speculative—and to a great extent unmarketable—securities?

If the answer to any of these questions is in part or in whole yes, proceed with caution. For you must avoid being deluded by short-term percentage figures. Ask and get clear, unqualified answers to such hard questions as I've posed here. The central question is: what has been the fund's long-term record? The importance of this cannot be overemphasized, for you want to see how the fund performs through bad markets as well as good. To the extent that your fund produces relatively favorable results through down markets as well as up markets, you can feel reasonably confident in the management's ability. Figure on a ten-year performance record as a minimum to compare it with another.

And what about the age of the fund? The benefit of a long life is that the fund has had the obvious advantages of navigating through both down and up markets. Its management has become seasoned. A fund that has prospered only in up markets is unseasoned. The acumen of its management must remain open to question. It's generally a good bet to stay clear of mutual funds that have been in business less than five years.

(6) *Makeup of the portfolio.* This point will give you vital clues to the operating philosophy of the fund's management as well as to its investment goals. Among the factors you should analyze in this area are: whether the portfolio includes a great many holdings or just a limited number; the fields of investment in which the fund is primarily involved; the relative emphasis on investments in each of these fields; the size of companies in which the fund invests; the balance between seasoned companies and unseasoned companies; the holdings (or lack) of bonds, preferred stocks, cash.

It is this knowledge and understanding of the portfolio makeup of a fund that will help you assure yourself that this is indeed the fund in which you wish to invest your nest egg and current earnings.

If you'll abide just by the guidance in these pages, you'll be on your way to investing successfully the way the real pros do. You'll also sleep well at night.

OPEN-END FUNDS VERSUS CLOSED-END FUNDS
(Publicly Traded Investment Funds)

Closed-end (publicly traded) funds have been around a long time, but they have never been as popular as the open-end funds—even though these funds operate the same way as open-end mutual funds in terms of diversified portfolio, professional management, and various investment objectives.

The difference is that there are a fixed number of shares in a closed-end fund and their price fluctuates up and down (past its net asset value) just as ordinary common stocks fluctuate up and down on the stock exchanges or in the over-the-counter market. Many closed-ends, in fact, have sold historically at discounts from their net asset value. This has made them at times attractive to some investors who felt they would profit if the discount eventually disappeared.

What are the pros and cons of publicly traded funds or closed-ends as compared to open-end funds?

• If you buy open-end shares, you know precisely on a given day that you can sell your shares back to the mutual fund for the net asset value. If you own publicly traded fund shares, you don't know what price you'll get for your shares on any given day. The price you get can be higher or lower than the net asset value.

• Because closed-end funds do not have to worry about investors redeeming their outstanding shares, they can invest for the long term without some of the concerns that an open-end fund may have.

• On the other hand, the fixed number of shares makes it difficult for publicly traded or closed-end funds to trade their portfolios as aggressively as some open-end mutual funds. Before buying a new stock, a closed-end fund must frequently sell a current holding.

• No one has really solved the mystery of why most closed-end funds sell at a discount. The explanation could be merely that securities salesmen push open-end mutual funds on which they can earn perhaps an 8½ per cent commission rather than closed-end (publicly traded) funds on which there is only a regular (and fluctuating) stockbrokers' commission.

• Open-end funds offer investors a greater flexibility, and range in buying options. There are many more open-end funds from which to choose, and, for instance, they offer more programs as automatic reinvestment and withdrawal plans than do closed-end funds.

• As for whether a closed-end fund selling at a large discount from its asset value is a real bargain, yes, in many cases this is true. However, if you buy a fund for this reason, there is no guarantee that when you sell it other investors will realize it is such a bargain and you might have to sell your shares at the same discount at which you bought them—or worse. Moral of the story: a "bargain" is only a bargain if other investors think it is and ultimately push its price up.

SOURCES OF INFORMATION ON MUTUAL FUNDS

Also to help you with your own homework on mutual funds, as well as to prepare you to discuss your goals intelligently with any adviser or mutual fund salesperson, here are top sources of detailed information on the industry and individual funds. Check what is available in your local library.

(1) *Wiesenberger Financial Services* (210 South Street, Boston, Massachusetts 02111), a division of Warren, Gorham, Lamont, which publishes each year a voluminous book on mutual funds performance—past and present—entitled *Investment Companies*. It also publishes *Wiesenberger Investment Companies Service,* a monthly report on statistics and news, which can be very helpful.

(2) *Moody's Investors Service, Inc.* (99 Church Street, New York, New York 10004), which publishes *Moody's Bank and Finance Manual*—a compendium of details on the hundred largest mutual funds in the United States.

(3) *The Investment Company Institute* (1775 K Street, N.W., Washington, D.C. 20006)—trade organization of the majority of the funds, which publishes

industry statistics, *Mutual Funds Forum,* a bimonthly newsmagazine, and an annual *Fact Book.*

(4) *No-Load Mutual Fund Association, Inc.* (Valley Forge, Pennsylvania 19481)—trade organization of the no-load mutual fund industry, which publishes an annual free directory and investor information book.

(5) *Computer Directions Advisors* (8750 Georgia Ave., Silver Spring, Maryland 20910)—statistical services available in brokerage offices or by $300 annual subscription.

(6) *Forbes Magazine* (60 Fifth Avenue, New York, New York 10011)—annual mutual fund performance issues.

(7) *Lipper Analytical Distributors, Inc.* (74 Trinity Place, New York, New York 10006)—statistical services on the fund industry, available in many brokerage offices.

(8) *Donoghue's Money Fund Report* (Box 540, Hollister, Massachusetts 01746)—publishes a newsletter covering the money-market fund industry.

(9) *Association of Publicly Traded Investment Funds* (666 Fifth Avenue, New York, New York 10019)—trade organization for the closed-end funds, publishes a membership directory and descriptive information which is useful in understanding this type of fund.

(10) *Investment Dealers Digest Mutual Fund Directory* (150 Broadway, New York, New York 10038)—a semiannual directory of investment companies.

(11) *The Hirsch Organization, Inc.* (6 Deer Trail, Old Tappan, New Jersey 07675)—publishes *Mutual Funds Scoreboard,* a quarterly, and the annual *Mutual Funds Almanac.*

In addition, there are other weekly, biweekly, and monthly publications devoted to mutual funds which are written for the public and which often contain valuable data. They are frequently advertised in your daily newspaper's financial pages.

THE BAFFLEGAB OF MUTUAL FUNDS

ACCUMULATION PLAN An increasingly popular arrangement under which you may buy mutual fund shares on a regular basis in small or large amounts—either on your own or through an automatic payroll deduction plan such as a company employee savings plan. Automatic reinvestment of dividends and distributions is commonplace. Many investors are using this type of plan to accumulate funds for retirement, for emergencies, or for the college education of their children.

ASKED OR OFFERING PRICE The price at which a mutual fund's shares can be purchased. The asked or offering price means the net asset value per share plus the sales charge, if any. For no-load funds, the net asset value is the "asked" price.

ASSET VALUE PER SHARE The worth of a share—as you see it quoted in the newspaper financial pages under the heading "bid"—based on the market value of the fund's entire portfolio of stocks and other financial assets, minus the fund's expenses and liabilities, divided by the number of shares that have been issued by the fund. Same as net asset value per share, or NAV.

BID OR REDEMPTION PRICE The price at which a mutual fund's shares are redeemed (bought back) by the fund. The bid or redemption price usually means the net asset value per share.

BLUE SKY LAWS Laws of the various states governing the sale of securities, including mutual fund shares, and the activities of brokers and dealers within the particular states.

BOOK SHARES A modern share recording system which eliminates the need for mutual fund share certificates but gives the fund's shareowner a record of his holdings.

BROKER-DEALER A firm that retails mutual fund shares to the public.

CAPITAL GAINS DISTRIBUTION A distribution to shareholders by the mutual fund from the net long-term capital gains the fund has taken on the sale of securities from its portfolio. Many investors choose to have such distributions automatically reinvested in additional shares of the fund.

CAPITAL GROWTH An increase in market value of a mutual fund's securities which is reflected in the net asset value of fund shares. This is a specific long-term objective of many mutual funds.

CASH EQUIVALENT Includes U. S. Government securities, short-term commercial paper, and short-term municipal and corporate bonds and notes.

CHECK WRITING REDEMPTION PRIVILEGE Some municipal bond and most money-market funds offer redemptions through free check writing privileges.

CLOSED-END INVESTMENT COMPANY See pages 1068–69.

CONTRACTUAL PLAN A type of accumulation plan under which the total amount you intend to invest is stated and you commit yourself to invest regular amounts monthly or quarterly for a specified pay-in period until you reach the total. A substantial amount of the sales charge covering the entire total is sometimes deducted from the first year's payments; this is called a front-end load.

CONVERSION PRIVILEGE See exchange or switch privilege.

DEALER A person or a firm who, as part of a regular business, buys from and sells securities to others. Load mutual fund shares are usually purchased through dealers; no-load shares are usually purchased directly from the fund's distributor.

DISTRIBUTIONS Payments to shareholders from capital gains realized by the fund or dividends paid from the fund's net investment income.

DOLLAR-COST-AVERAGING Investing equal amounts of money in regular intervals regardless of whether the stock market is moving upward or downward. This reduces average share costs because more shares are purchased in periods of lower securities prices and buys fewer shares in periods of higher prices.

DUAL-PURPOSE FUND A type of investment company designed to serve the needs of two distinct types of investors: (1) those interested only in income, and (2) those interested solely in possible capital growth. To accomplish these purposes, this type of fund has two separate classes of shares and an investor can purchase the class of shares in which he or she is interested—the class of shares that seek income or the class of shares that seek possible capital gain.

EXCHANGE PRIVILEGE   The right to exchange the shares of one mutual fund for shares of another fund under the same sponsorship at either little or no cost or a reduced sales charge. However, you are liable to federal taxes on profits realized from first fund.

EXPENSE RATIO   The proportion of annual expenses to average net assets of the fund.

FRONT-END LOADS   Plans under which the investor enters into a contractual investment plan calling for the payment of regular installments for his shares. Sales charges can range up to 50 per cent in the first year.

INVESTMENT ADVISER   The organization that is employed by a mutual fund to give professional advice on its investments.

INVESTMENT COMPANY   A company that invests the funds it obtains from buyers of its shares in a diversified list of securities.

INVESTMENT COMPANY ACT OF 1940   The basic federal law governing the registration and regulation of investment companies.

INVESTMENT MANAGER   The company that provides administrative services for a fund and often also serves as investment adviser to the fund.

INVESTMENT OBJECTIVE   A capsule description of the fund's investment objective, described in greater detail in each fund's prospectus.

INVESTMENT POLICY   A brief description of the policy followed by the investment adviser in aiming at the stated objectives.

INVESTMENT TRUST   Same as Investment Company.

KEOGH PLAN   A retirement program for self-employed persons under which they can save on income taxes while regularly investing funds for their retirement via mutual funds, savings bonds, savings accounts, insurance, etc.

LETTER OF INTENT   A pledge to purchase a sufficient amount of mutual fund shares within a limited period of time in order to qualify for the reduced selling charge that would apply to a comparable lump sum purchase.

LOAD   The sales charge imposed on a mutual fund investor by load funds to cover the costs of the elaborate sales organizations maintained by the majority of the funds. Added to the asset value of the fund's shares (the offering price).

MANAGEMENT FEE   The amount that the managers of mutual fund portfolios charge for their management services—in both load and no-load funds.

MULTIFUNDS   See fund of funds (page 1058).

NO-LOAD FUNDS   See pages 1061–62.

PAYROLL DEDUCTION PLAN   An arrangement whereby an employee may accumulate shares in a mutual fund by authorizing his employer to deduct and transfer to the fund a specified amount from his salary at stated times.

PERIODIC PAYMENT PLAN   Same as Accumulation Plan.

PORTFOLIO   The stocks, bonds, and other assets held by a mutual fund at any given time—and thus, held indirectly by the fund's shareowners.

PORTFOLIO TURNOVER   The dollar value of purchase and sale of portfolio securities, excluding transactions of U. S. Government obligations and commercial paper.

PROSPECTUS   The official document that describes the mutual fund and offers the shares for sale. It contains information as required by the Securities and Exchange Commission on such subjects as the fund's investment objectives, its policies, services, investment restrictions, officers and directors, how shares can be bought and redeemed, its charges and its financial statements.

PROXY STATEMENT   A written power of attorney that stockholders give to another person to vote their stock if they are not present at stockholders' meeting.

PUBLICLY TRADED INVESTMENT FUNDS   See page 1060.

QUALIFIED RETIREMENT PLAN   A private retirement plan that meets the rules and regulations of the Internal Revenue Service. Contributions to a qualified retirement plan are—in almost all cases—tax deductible and earnings on such contributions are always tax sheltered until retirement.

REDEMPTION FEE   About twenty funds charge shareholders a small fee—usually less than 2 per cent—when shares are redeemed.

REDEMPTION IN KIND   Redemption of investment company shares for which payment is made in portfolio securities rather than cash.

REDEMPTION PRICE   The price at which a holder of mutual fund shares may redeem his shares. In most cases of open-end shares, it's the current net asset value per share. Sometimes there is a redemption charge of 2 per cent or less. In the closed-end companies, this would be the highest price offered for the shares in the exchange market, which may be either a premium over or a discount from the net asset value per share.

REINVESTMENT PRIVILEGE   A privilege under which your mutual fund dividends may be automatically invested in additional shares of the fund, without the payment of a sales charge, except for some loads.

SEPARATE ACCOUNT   A portfolio completely separated from the general account of the insurance company, since the assets are generally invested in common stocks.

SPECIALTY FUNDS   A mutual fund specializing in the security of certain industries, special types of securities, or in regional investments.

SPLIT FUNDING   A program that combines the purchase of mutual fund shares with the purchase of life insurance contracts or other products.

STATEMENT OF POLICY   A guide issued by the Securities and Exchange Commission to assist issuers, writers, and dealers in complying with the statutory standards as applied to advertising, sales, literature, reports to sales, and other communication addressed to or intended for distribution to prospective investors.

TELEPHONE REDEMPTION   Some funds allow liquidation by telephone where prearranged and approved agreements have been signed.

TRANSFER AGENT   The organization that is employed by a mutual fund to prepare and maintain records relating to the accounts of its shareholders.

TURNOVER RATIO   The extent to which the portfolio of securities owned by a mutual fund is changed (traded or turned over) within the course of a single year.

UNDERWRITER OR PRINCIPAL UNDERWRITER   The organization that acts as the distributor of mutual fund shares to broker dealers and the public.

VARIABLE ANNUITY   An annuity contract under which the dollar payments received are fixed but fluctuate more or less in line with average common stock prices.

VARIABLE ANNUITY SEPARATE ACCOUNT The funding vehicle for an insurance company's variable annuity contract.

VARIABLE LIFE INSURANCE A contract or plan under which the death benefit and the cash fluctuate in tandem with the investment performance of a separate account generally composed of common stock.

VOLUNTARY PLAN A flexible accumulation plan in which there is no definite time period or total amount to be invested.

WITHDRAWAL PLAN An arrangement under which investors in mutual funds can regularly receive monthly or quarterly payments of a specified amount. This may be more or less than the actual investment income.

YIELD Income received from investments, usually expressed as a percentage of market price, and also referred to as return on the investment.

23

YOUR GUIDE
TO THE BOND MARKETS

Obligations of the U. S. Treasury, Federal Agencies, Guaranteed or Partially Insured Mortgage Pools, States and Cities, U.S. Corporations—Short- and Long-Term

A New Force in the Financial Market

In the early 1970s, a profoundly important new force entered the financial market. It was the historically high interest rates which investors—big and small, institutions and individuals—could earn on bonds, even the highest-quality bonds. This development created competition of the toughest caliber for the stock market. Many investors switched out of common stocks and growth mutual funds and put their money into U. S. Treasury securities, corporate bonds, tax-exempt bonds, new bond and money market funds. Money in savings accounts, too, was shifted into money market instruments and bonds on an impressive scale. And professional investment managers returned to what was a once fashionable investment technique of "balanced" portfolios with both stock and bond holdings.

To understand this fascinating turnabout, you must realize that in the 1940s yields on stocks were about twice those of bonds. By the early 1970s yields on bonds were about twice those of common stocks!

High interest rates have an understandable appeal to investors. If you can invest your money in a bond that pays 9 per cent and if you let the interest accumulate, your nest egg will double in about eight years. If you invest it at 7 per cent, it will double in about ten years. This assumes that you will be reinvesting at the same interest rate and omits tax factors.

These—and higher—fixed annual returns have been available in the bond and money markets of the United States in recent years. Obviously, at these interest rates, high-quality fixed-income investments—in the obligations of the U. S. Treasury, federal agencies, guaranteed or partially insured mortgage pools, our states and cities, U.S. corporations—take on some of the characteristics of "growth" securities. You can also buy low-interest coupon bonds selling at a discount and make long-term capital gains as the bonds rise to their par value.

An investment that can double in ten years is growing by any definition. At the same time this type of investment retains the advantages of fixed annual return and offers greater protection against adverse economic conditions than do stocks. (It is not without hazards, though. And, of course, steep inflation rates which cut deeply into the buying power of fixed dollars can offset and even eliminate the "growth" entirely.)

If buyers can get these high rates, they can count on them every year until their bonds are called or finally mature and that can be five, ten, fifteen, twenty, or even thirty years from purchase date.

Let me be more specific. If a high-grade corporate bond provides an 8 per cent return, it is rivaling the long-term return record for common stocks. Not so many years ago typical interest rates on top-rated corporate bonds were 3½ to 4 per cent.

What will be the level of interest rates on fixed-income securities when *you* are reading this chapter I do not know—and only a fool would pretend to have the capacity to forecast precisely—for the forces which determine interest rate trends are varied and exceedingly complex. However, it is reasonable to assume that in the decade of the 1980s we will maintain a level of interest rates which, regardless of temporary market fluctuations, should be high enough to provide a "living wage" to all investors—meaning the coupons should cover the anticipated annual rise in living costs as well as the income tax bite out of the interest. Under these circumstances, you will need basic information on the fixed-income securities markets so you can carry on to get whatever additional facts you want. And so the following is your *primer on bonds*.

Basic Facts on Bonds and Money Market Instruments

Q. *What's a coupon interest rate on a bond?*

A. This is the specified amount of money the issuer promises to pay you during the life of the bond in return for the use of your money throughout the period. The issuers (borrowers) may be: the federal government, federal agencies, state and local governments, corporations, foreign governments, individuals seeking mortgages.

The interest may be payable to you every six months or every year and in a few cases every month. Or, as in U. S. Government E or EE savings bonds, the interest may accumulate during the life of the bond and be payable to you only when you cash in the bond or when it reaches final maturity date.

Q. *What's the difference between a bond and a stock?*

A. When you buy a bond you are lending your money to its issuer, and thus you become a creditor. When you buy shares of common stock in a corporation you are becoming a part owner of the corporation.

When you buy bonds you expect to earn a fixed rate of return (the interest) as long as you own this type of obligation. When you buy common stocks, you expect to share in the company's profits via the dividends the company pays you— which may vary from year to year. You also own a pro rata share of retained earnings, which can lead to capitalization of earnings in the form of stock dividends or stock splits, hopefully leading to higher values for your stocks—but you can make capital gains on bonds as well as on stocks.

Q. *What's the key to bond prices?*

A. Interest rate levels. When interest rates *rise,* bond prices *fall*—and vice versa. Suppose, for instance, that you held a $1,000 bond paying 6 per cent interest. Because of a variety of factors, interest rates available on new bonds of the same type rise to 7 per cent. Now, your bond will sell for less than $1,000, for if someone can invest $1,000 at 7 per cent by buying a new bond, why should he or she pay you $1,000 for your old bond, which returns only 6 per cent? The lower price and the fixed payment of $60 a year brings the return to about 7 per cent.

Or suppose interest rates fall, so that the rate available on new bonds of this type is now 5 per cent. Your 6 per cent bond will now be worth *more* than $1,000; for if someone can get only 5 per cent interest by investing $1,000 in this type of bond, why should you sell your 6 per cent bond at that $1,000 price?

Interest rates doubled in the last five years of the decade of the 1960s, reached the highest levels in more than a century, then spiraled even higher in the mid— and again in the late—1970s. These upswings have driven down prices of bonds issued at much lower interest rates in earlier years.

Short-term, interest rates tend to fluctuate much more violently than long-term interest rates—reflecting the fact that short-term rates primarily respond to Federal Reserve System maneuvers in fine-tuning monetary policy, while long-term rates primarily respond to investor expectations about inflation well into the future.

But while short-term rates tend to fluctuate more widely, short-term obligations are in a sense much safer than long-term securities. The reason is that an equal change in short-term and long-term rates will have a much larger impact on prices of long-term obligations than on prices of short-term obligations. For instance, a 1 per cent across-the-board rise in interest rates will lower the price of a five-year $1,000 bond about $2.00; on a $1,000 thirty-year bond the cut will be about $12.

Q. *What moves interest rates up or down?*

A. What usually determines the price of any product or service? The demand for and supply of it. When the demand for loans is greater than the available supply of credit, the price for loans (the interest rate) goes up; when the supply of credit is greater than the demand for loans, the price (interest rate) goes down. Expectations of higher or lower interest rates also influence the direction of rates —meaning psychology plays an enormous role too.

But this is by no means the whole story, for a key factor determining the supply of credit in the United States is the monetary policy of the Federal Reserve System (the central bank) of the United States, which regulates the flow of money and credit into our economy.

There is no point in this primer in going into the tortuously complicated, technical details on how the Federal Reserve System attains its credit goals. Suffice it to say that through various devices and operations the Federal Reserve pursues its objective (not always successfully, by any means!) of trying to put just enough credit into the economic stream to promote orderly, sustained growth over the years.

Q. *Why have interest rates risen so much in recent years?*

A. Because, starting in the mid-1960s, the demand for credit exploded—reflecting the prolonged business boom, the Vietnam war, the development of a deep inflation psychology.

At the same time the Federal Reserve tried to curb inflation via the orthodox means of limiting the supply of credit available for expansion. With the demand for loans soaring and the supply of credit restricted, interest rates had to sky-rocket.

Q. *Should we all own bonds?*

A. It would be ridiculous for me to claim that bonds are an appropriate investment for all of you: there are so many different types of fixed-income securities, so many different maturities, so many different grades that even the simple word "bonds" becomes a misleading generality. It also would be utterly out-of-character folly for me to make so superficial a recommendation.

Nevertheless the money and bond markets since the start of the 1970s have appealed to an extraordinarily broad cross section of income and age groups. Many individuals in the $15,000-to-$30,000-a-year income brackets have for the first time ventured into bonds. In fact, in the 1970s many stock brokerage salesmen made a good part of their income selling bonds and money market securities of all types rather than stocks to individuals. That's why this chapter is giving you the fundamentals so you can find out the details on your own.

Q. *What about the income tax factor?*

A. This is vitally important, for you must pay income taxes on interest you earn. Of course, this cuts into your net return and the higher your income bracket the more the cut—except on tax-exempt bonds. For example, if you are in the 40 per cent tax bracket and collect $100 a year in interest on your bonds, you'll pay out $40 of the $100 in taxes, will keep only $60.

Q. *What about inflation?*

A. In judging what your real net rate of return will be on a fixed-income security, you also must consider the erosion in your dollar's buying power caused by the likely annual rate of rise in living costs in coming years.

To illustrate, let's say you buy a $1,000 bond carrying an interest rate of 8 per cent and that the annual rate of inflation in the years ahead turns out to be 6 per cent. Your "real" rate of return—bond interest rate less rate of inflation—would be 2 per cent.

Q. *What about your age?*

A. Of course, this is a vital consideration, for if you are young and can look forward to many years in which you can recoup losses on your investments, you can properly assume more risks in the stock market and speculate for big long-term capital gains. But if you are in the older age brackets, bonds yielding 8 to 10 per cent have indisputable appeal.

Q. *How are bonds quoted?*

A. As a percentage of their par value or face amount—usually in denominations of $1,000. However, many U. S. Government, federal agency, and state and local government issues are now sold with minimum denominations of $5,000 or $10,000. A price of 98 for a $1,000 par value bond means that $980 would be the actual cost (plus any accrued interest).

Since interest is paid on the par value of the bond, your actual percentage return may be more or less than the interest rate specified on the coupon by the issuer of the bond.

To illustrate, say you buy a bond just issued that pays 9 per cent interest or $90 at a price of exactly $1,000. That gives you $90 a year interest on a $1,000 investment or an actual yield of 9 per cent.

But say the bond has already been issued and has been on the market some time and you buy it at 95, or $950. This means your current yield is more than 9 per cent. Current yield is determined by dividing the interest by the price paid for the bond. This means 90/950 or 9.47 per cent.

Or say you bought the same bond for 105, or $1,050. This means your yield is less than 9 per cent. It would be 90/1,050, or 8.57 per cent.

Q. *Is this what is meant by yield?*

A. This is what is meant by current yield. It is interest divided by the price you paid for the bond—that rate of return you receive on the amount of money it cost you to buy the security.

Q. *What's the difference between current yield and yield to maturity?*

A. Yield to maturity takes into consideration the price at which your bond is paid off (redeemed) at maturity as well as the interest coupon it bears and the price at which you bought the obligation.

For example, suppose you bought the 9 per cent bond at a premium, say 105, or $1,050. In figuring yield to maturity it is necessary to amortize the premium until the maturity date. In this case, the yield to maturity will be less than the 9 per cent coupon rate and less than the 8.57 per cent current yield.

In the case of a bond purchased for $950, or at a discount, the yield to maturity will be the coupon rate of 9 per cent, plus the $50 additional money the holder will receive when the bond matures. In this case, the yield to maturity will be greater than 9 per cent and greater than the 9.47 per cent current yield. A reference volume, generally referred to as the *Basis Book,* accurately computes yield to maturity.

Q. *How do you collect interest on your bonds?*

A. There are two major ways you collect your interest. If you own a coupon bond or "bearer" bond you clip a coupon attached to the bond and collect the money by depositing the coupon as if it were a check with the issuer's paying agent or your own bank. If you own a registered bond, your name appears on the bond and also is registered with the issuer. Interest is usually paid by check. Registered bonds offer greater protection from theft than coupon bonds. However, they are tougher to sell because of the bother and delay in arranging transfer of ownership on the registrar's books.

Q. *Do the terms "fixed income" and "bonds" mean the same thing?*

A. Yes, a bond is a fixed-income obligation, but a large percentage of the obligations available to you aren't bonds at all. By definition, they're "notes," "debentures," "certificates," or "bills." And a large percentage aren't traded in the bond markets either. They are bought and sold in the money markets—which are part of the vast over-the-counter markets to start with.

Q. *What are money market securities?*

A. They are the short-term obligations of various borrowers: the U. S. Treasury, federal agencies, state and local governments, banks, corporations of all types.

In general, these are the most marketable, the most liquid, the least risky of fixed-income obligations. Among the obligations in which you might be interested and which you can readily buy and sell in the money markets are:

U. S. Treasury bills, due in up to one year and considered the virtual equivalent of cash.

Short-term federal agency issues, which next to Treasury bills are the most marketable of securities.

Short-term tax-exempt obligations, highly liquid too.

Also traded in the money markets are large ($100,000 and over) commercial bank certificates of deposit; large ($100,000 and more) denominations of commercial paper notes of corporations; bankers' acceptances in denominations of $25,000 and up; Eurodollars; and federal funds (not for individuals, however).

Q. *How can small investors buy in such big amounts?*

A. The smaller investor was effectively barred from the often higher-yielding money market instruments and restricted to the lower-paying "consumer" certificates available from commercial banks and savings institutions for many years, but as interest rates on large certificates of deposit spiraled upward in the 1970s, enterprising firms found ways to get around that patently unfair discrimination against the little fellow.

The concept was simple: the funds of many small investors were "pooled" until the amounts in the pools were large enough to meet the minimums imposed. The "pools" took various forms. Also, as short-term interest rates hit historic peaks in the 1970s new mutual funds came into existence to specialize in these money market instruments and offer small investors a way to share in the juicy returns by purchase of fund shares. The funds were both no-load and load variety—taxable and tax-exempt—and they lured hundreds of millions of dollars out of savings institutions. In 1978, banking regulators allowed banks, savings and loans, and credit unions to issue six-month certificates which can yield up to the same as the latest six-month Treasury bills. (See pages 1076–77.)

Q. *What are bond markets?*

A. In the bond markets, longer-term obligations of various issuers are traded. In turn, the bond markets subdivide into the market for corporate bonds; for U. S. Government bonds and notes and for longer-term federal agency issues; and for tax-exempt municipal bonds. Newer instruments include federally guaranteed Government National Mortgage Association pass-through mortgage pool certificates and private pool certificates.

In only a few places in the 1970s (such as the Bond Trading Room of the New York Stock Exchange) could you visit and watch bond trading in action. Most bonds are handled in the over-the-counter market, where securities are bought and sold by dealers and brokers located all over the nation, communicating with each other via an intricate and immense telephone network and video display terminals.

Q. *What is meant by underwriting syndicates?*

A. These are groups of investment bankers (syndicates) which commit their capital to buy new issues of securities from borrowers at set prices. By doing this, the bankers "underwrite" the issue—provide the total funds at once to the corporation, state, city, or other type of borrower. Then the group reoffers the securities at a higher price to institutional and individual investors. The difference (spread) between what the underwriting syndicate pays for the securities and the higher price at which the group reoffers the securities to you represents the bankers' or syndicate's profit after expenses. Of course, the underwriting syndicate loses money when the bankers misjudge the market and are forced to resell the securities at a lower price than they paid the issuer.

"M1?" "M2?"—"M WHAT?"

Item: Every Thursday shortly after 4:10 P.M. (New York time), financiers in private and government policymaking positions in money centers all over the globe stop whatever they are doing to crowd around their ticker tapes and listen to the tickers clatter out the latest news on M1 and M2 from the Federal Reserve Bank of New York's powerful trading desk.

These weekly reports have assumed enormous significance throughout the world as direct clues to the monetary policy of the Federal Reserve System: whether the U.S. central bank is tightening credit to fight inflation and support the dollar more vigorously; or whether it is easing credit to spur the economy and reduce joblessness more vigorously; or whether it is just standing pat.

"M1?" "M2?" Countless millions of you must have heard of the bafflegab. How many of you honestly can define it?

Item: At a business luncheon of ten men and women from widely varied fields, a Midwestern banker next to me said he thought the growth in M1 in the past few months had been far too rapid and it was contributing to the speedup in inflation in the closing years of the decade. I answered that M1's growth had slowed down substantially, that its weekly gyrations were getting too much attention anyway, and that the concentration on the monetary aggregates from week to week was out of hand.

As we argued, my eyes went around the table. The others listening to us— prominent business leaders, professors in fields outside economics, the like— seemed glassy-eyed.

"How many of you can define M1 or M2?" I asked.

Not one person at the table answered.

"M1?" "M2?" What part do they play in your life?

Item: "When it comes to definitions, money is a little bit like sex appeal," said an analysis in the economic review of the Federal Reserve Bank of Richmond some time ago. "Everyone has a fairly clear intuitive idea of what it is, but defining it in precise language is difficult. Economists have been arguing about the best way to define money for centuries."

Then the Richmond Fed went on to try, for it emphasized that "the concept of money lies at the core of both monetary theory and monetary policy."

Okay, then, I'll rise to the challenge, too. Herewith the accepted definitions of the various "M's" in my simplest language.

• M0. That's just U.S. currency, the dollar bills (of any denomination) and coins in your possession. There's lots of currency circulating in our country today, some for completely legitimate reasons of business and commerce, some for "dirty" deals where tax evasion is a goal.

• M1. That's the total of all U.S. currency in circulation plus the demand deposits all of us—as individuals and organizations—have at commercial banks from coast to coast. This is also known as the "narrowly defined money supply," for it covers a minimum of the money supply affecting our economy and others.

• M1+. Introduced as a "new" measure of the money supply in late 1978 by the Federal Reserve Board in an attempt to offset distortions caused by the development of automatic transfers of funds from savings to checking accounts. Created as only an "interim measure" and immediately dubbed in the sophisticated money markets as "the cold remedy," M1+ consists of M1 (demand deposits and currency) plus savings accounts at commercial banks, NOW (negotiable orders of withdrawal) accounts, checkable deposits at thrift institutions. The purpose of M1+ is to include deposits that are readily usable in transactions for payments to third parties, which is a key aspect of money as distinct from savings.

• M2. That's M1 (defined above) plus all our time deposits at commercial banks, but not including large negotiable certificates of deposit (which usually are bought and sold by very big investors, individuals and institutions). Time deposits include any savings accounts or savings certificates or savings shares you have—but only at commercial banks. The narrowly defined money supply has now been substantially broadened.

• M3. This is M2 (defined directly above) with the additions of all mutual savings bank deposits, savings and loan association shares, and credit union shares. Now the money supply total is truly being broadened.

Now let's say you are thinking for the first time about buying fixed-income securities as an investment . . .

How to Buy Bonds

Q. *How do you buy outstanding fixed-income securities?*

A. Go to your broker, place your order, and pay the principal amount plus the required commission. It usually will run about $10 per $1,000 face value bond, but it can be more, particularly if you buy just one or two bonds. If the investment banker already *owns* the bond, you pay no straight commission, but you do pay the "spread" between the bid and asked prices on the bond. This is often $20 per $1,000 face value if you're buying less than $25,000 worth. If you don't have a broker, establish a relationship with a reputable firm which maintains a retail bond department. Ask questions about commissions and which types of fixed-income securities would be right for you. Or you can buy bonds through your bank but you'll probably pay more in commissions and fees, particularly if you buy a corporate bond that the bank is not permitted to deal in.

Q. *How do you buy new fixed-income securities?*

A. You can subscribe to new issues of corporation or municipal bonds through a firm which is a member of the underwriting group distributing the new issue to the public. If your order is accepted, you'll pay no commission. The issuer of the securities pays the investment banking house through the spread between the selling price and the amount turned over to the issuer.

You can subscribe through your broker or banker to new U. S. Treasury issues and pay a service charge for the convenience. Or you can subscribe to new U. S. Treasury issues through your district Federal Reserve Bank and pay no commission. You'll have to learn the details about forms, minimum deposits required, etc., but they're not difficult.

And you can subscribe to new federal agency issues through the firms which belong to the selling group customarily distributing new agency securities. You'll pay no commission but you'll probably have to pay a service charge if yours is a small subscription.

Check out the details with a broker, bank, or bond dealer who knows you and who will give you a fair deal.

Q. *What firms might you go to?*

A. Some of the great, world-famous investment banking firms won't take your orders. They deal only in large transactions with institutional investors or with wealthy individuals. But many brokerage firms do maintain bond departments and readily accept individual orders. If you're now a customer of one of these firms, ask your own broker about the firm's policy before you go elsewhere. In some areas, however, you might find it more convenient to do business through a bank.

THE CORPORATE BOND MARKET

The corporate bond market is where a lot of the action has been in recent years. Here is where our nation's leading industrial and utility corporations, and finance companies, have borrowed tens of billions of dollars for modernization, expansion, and working capital too. Here is where, during the 1970s, interest rates spiraled up to the highest levels in more than a hundred years. And here is where individual investors began in 1970 to invest aggressively in fixed returns for the first time in decades.

Q. *How many types of corporate bonds are there?*

A. At least a dozen. But the types which will be of most interest to you are:

First mortgage bonds. These are bonds secured by a mortgage on all or a portion of the fixed property of the issuing corporation. These are among the highest-grade corporate bonds because they provide a prime, clear, and indisputable claim on the company's specified assets and earnings. Most utilities issue mortgage bonds.

Debenture bonds. These are bonds backed by the general credit and full faith of the issuing corporation. In short, they represent a pure IOU, a promise to pay. Many of the nation's big, well-established corporations issue debentures. Under the classification of debentures are *subordinated debentures,* which have a claim on a corporation's assets only after senior debt claims have been met, and *income debentures,* on which interest is payable only if it is earned. These are of lower quality than the more senior securities.

Convertible debentures. These are bonds which give the owner the extra privilege of converting the debenture into a certain number of shares of common stock of the same corporation under specified conditions. In other words this is a hybrid, combining some of the features of both a stock and a bond. Convertibles yield less than straight bonds but the conversion sweetener adds speculative appeal because the owner has the chance of making an additional profit if the stock of the issuing company goes up. This makes the conversion privilege more valuable. Of course, the stock can also go down.

Q. *Should I buy only first mortgage bonds, then?*

A. Of course not. The overall strength of a corporation is the key. A debenture of a great, prosperous industrial corporation is far more desirable than a first mortgage bond of a shaky third-rater.

Q. *How can I find out about the quality of bonds?*

A. The quality of bonds ranges from the very highest to the riskiest—with the judgments on the creditworthiness of the various obligations being made by various independent services, such as Moody's and Standard & Poor's. The ratings starting from the top are: Aaa (Moody's) or AAA (Standard & Poor's), Aa or AA, A, Baa or BBB, Ba or BB, B, Caa or CCC, Ca or CC, C. If you're anxious to avoid risks of default, you'll not go below ratings of A. Most dealers will quote the bond ratings along with prices and yields.

Q. *What about call provisions?*

A. This is a key point—for if interest rates decline sharply below the levels at which corporations have sold their bonds they will try to call them in and replace them with new issues bearing lower rates. Thus, you want to make certain that your bond will be protected against redemption by the corporation for a specified period. Usually you can get protection against a call for ten years from issue date on industrial bonds. Treasury bonds and notes are frequently not callable.

Also check with care the price at which the corporation reserves the right to call in its bonds, for this will place an effective ceiling on the price to which your bond can rise in the open market. One way of beating this is to buy bonds that are non-callable.

THE MARKET FOR MORTGAGE-POOL PASS-THROUGH CERTIFICATES
AND MORTGAGE-BACKED BONDS

In the 1970s, a new type of debt obligation involving mortgaged-backed securities rapidly gained investor acceptance. To understand this type of investment, suppose you lend money to a friend to purchase a house—the same as a bank does, with the house mortgaged as security. You know that mortgage loans of this character pay handsome interest, and that your security (residential housing) will tend to retain its value over time. But still, you're nervous; you worry about risking so much of your nest egg on just one person.

Now you have a way to invest money in different mortgages—indirectly. The procedure is this: a bank or institution which lends mortgage money to many home buyers can sell the mortgage IOU's to others. Eventually, the holder of a large total of mortgages can pool these mortgages and sell participations in the pool to you, a public investor. A trustee holds the mortgage pool and passes along interest and principal payments to you.

The mortgage holders which issue mortgage-backed securities can be government agencies or private institutions. The best-known is the Government National Mortgage Association (GNMA, or "Ginnie Mae"). Another is the Federal Home Loan Mortgage Corporation (FHLMC, or "Freddie Mac"). Private institutions include mortgage lenders such as banks and savings and loans.

There are two distinct types of mortgage-backed securities: "pass-through" securities and "mortgage-backed" bonds.

PASS-THROUGH ISSUES

Pass-through issues consist of pools of mortgages which have been sold to a trustee. You, the investor, buy a participation in the pool. The institution continues to collect the monthly interest and principal payments that it receives on its pool of mortgages, and after skimming a small fee passes the money through to you, the security holder—each month. Unlike most fixed-income securities, if you are an investor in pass-through certificates, you are paid interest *and* principal regularly, instead of just interest (with the principal paid at the end).

Most pass-through certificates are backed by pools of mortgages of thirty-year duration, but you should not view them as thirty-year obligations. In fact, pass-throughs usually trade as if they were a unique form of twelve-year obligation. The assumption is that the principal on the certificate is paid down monthly—half before twelve years, the remaining after twelve years—for an average twelve-year life.

Why would this assumption be made?

Because it's the historical experience with mortgages. Often, for instance, houses on which owners still owe money are sold before the mortgages are paid off. So the mortgages end up being prepaid long before the thirty-year expiration date. As far as pass-through certificates are concerned, each pool of mortgages will have a different record of prepayment of principal. The fact that a pass-through *trades* as if it has a twelve-year prepayment doesn't mean that it can't be paid down well before, or after, the twelve-year mark.

MORTGAGE-BACKED BONDS

Mortgage-backed bonds usually are sold in minimum amounts of $10,000 with $1,000 increments. In short, you can buy $11,000 worth—but not $1,000 worth. The maturities of these bonds run five years and more.

Mortgage-backed bonds are much like other bonds—they pay the investor a series of interest payments with a final interest-and-principal payment at the end. They are issued by mortgage-lending institutions, and are obligations of the institution itself. But they are collateralized with large numbers of mortgage IOUs, often a larger dollar amount of mortgages than the total dollar amount of the bonds.

One important fact of which you must be aware if you are considering these bonds: some are government-guaranteed, some not.

The mortgages backing Ginnie Mae pass-through pools are insured by the Federal Housing Administration or the Veterans Administration. In addition, the Ginnie Mae securities themselves are backed by the full faith and credit of the U. S. Government—the same as Treasury obligations. If any mortgages default, the Treasury makes up the payments to the investor.

Freddie Mac mortgages are *not* government-backed, although the FHLMC puts its own guarantee on its securities—which makes them safer than most private mortgage-backed securities. The private pass-through securities, however, often have their mortgage pools insured. These securities are rated by Standard & Poor's and Moody's.

A problem: these securities frequently are marketed in huge dollar chunks. GNMA and private-issue pass-through securities are issued in principal amounts of $25,000; FHLMC pass-throughs are issued in principal amounts of $100,000. But it is possible to buy these pass-throughs for substantially less than the original principal amount, because as the principal amount of the mortgages is paid off, the remaining principal amount shrinks. So you might be able to buy a GNMA pass-through certificate originally issued at $25,000 that now has only $15,000 worth of principal left.

THE TAX-EXEMPT MUNICIPAL MARKET

The great factor favoring purchase of municipal bonds or other tax-exempts is that interest on these obligations is exempt from federal income tax—and if you are a resident of the issuing locality, often from state and local taxes as well. That's the major reason why individuals now own about one third of all the tax-exempt bonds outstanding. A second reason is that tax-exempts of the top-rated issuers have a high degree of safety.

Even if you're only in the 30 per cent tax bracket, a 6½ per cent tax-free return is equal to a taxable rate of 9.29 per cent. And in the 55 per cent bracket, it's the equivalent of a 14.44 per cent return!

There's no doubt that new municipal bonds will be pouring into the market in coming years, for the borrowing needs of states, cities, and towns across the land are and will be enormous. There's no doubt too that this will help place a floor under the rates you can earn and that you'll have a wide variety of types of bonds, of quality of bonds, and of maturity dates from which to choose.

Q. *What are municipal bonds?*

A. These include any obligation issued by a city, town, or village and also by states, territories, U.S. possessions. In addition, they include obligations issued by housing authorities, port authorities, and local government agencies providing and maintaining community services ranging from schools to waterworks. They are all tax-exempt and are all nicknamed "municipals."

Q. *What sets the interest rates on municipals?*

A. First, the general level of interest rates. After that, the credit rating of the issuer—determined by the rating services. Triple A, of course, is the best. I repeat: if you wish to avoid risks of default, don't go below their ratings of A.

Q. *What types of municipals are there?*

A. *General obligation bonds,* secured by the full faith and credit and general unlimited taxing power of the municipal authority. Many bonds of big cities are in this category.

Limited tax or special tax bonds, backed by a limited portion of the issuer's taxing power, or payable only from the proceeds of a single tax.

Revenue bonds, secured by the revenue of a particular municipal department or a special authority created to operate a self-supporting project. Included in this category are toll road and turnpike authority bonds; hospital bonds; many electric and water utility bonds; and housing authority bonds.

Leased revenue bonds, backed by the lease payment made by a governmental unit to a special authority which builds a project (such as a civic center) and issues it back to the municipality.

Industrial revenue bonds, issued by a municipality or authority but secured by the lease payments made by the corporation using the facilities financed by the revenue bond issue. The best quality and most marketable of these are pollution-control issues backed by the creditworthiness of large corporations.

Q. *What are the special characteristics of municipals?*

A. Some are in denominations of $1,000 and up—although the $5,000 minimum denomination is the most common. Most are bearer bonds. The owner's name is not on record with the issuer and if you *hold* the bond the presumption is you *own* it. Usually you'll clip a coupon every six months and collect interest from a paying agency or through your own bank.

You must safeguard bearer bonds as you would cash, for if "your" bonds are in someone else's possession, how can you prove they are yours? If your bearer bonds are stolen, you may be completely out of luck—just as you would be if your cash was stolen. Each bond does have a serial number which may be some help in locating stolen securities.

Most are serial bonds. A certain number will mature each year, will be paid off and retired. The range of maturities may be five, ten, fifteen, twenty years or perhaps thirty or forty years, which means you can decide the date on which you want your capital back and then choose a maturity that fits.

Q. *What about the tax exemption?*

A. You may be able to get eye-popping rates of return—tax-free—on low-quality municipal bonds. But I will not suggest anything second-class—not in this investment area.

The tax advantages are not just for the wealthy! Tax exemption can benefit you to a lesser extent in the lower tax brackets as well. The returns are more attractive than you probably realize, particularly if you're among the millions of us who are subject to state and local as well as federal income taxes.

To the single individual with $15,000 to $18,200 of taxable earnings in a moderate 30 per cent income bracket (including state and local taxes), a tax-free 5

TAX-EXEMPT INCOME VS. TAXABLE INCOME

JOINT RETURN	SINGLE RETURN	TAX BRACKET	TO EQUAL A TAX-FREE YIELD OF:			
			5%	5½%	6%	6½%
$ 20,200- 24,600	$ 15,000- 18,200	28%	6.94%	7.64%	8.33%	9.03%
$ 24,600- 29,900	$ 18,200- 23,500	30%	7.14%	7.86%	8.57%	9.29%
$ 29,900- 35,200	$ 23,500- 28,800	32%	7.35%	8.09%	8.82%	9.56%
	$ 28,800- 34,100	34%	7.58%	8.33%	9.09%	9.85%
	$ 34,100- 41,500	37%	7.94%	8.73%	9.52%	10.32%
$ 35,200- 45,800		39%	8.20%	9.02%	9.84%	10.66%
	$ 41,500- 55,300	43%	8.77%	9.65%	10.53%	11.40%
$ 45,800- 60,000		44%	8.93%	9.82%	10.71%	11.61%
	$ 55,300- 81,800	49%	9.80%	10.78%	11.76%	12.75%
$ 60,000- 85,600		54%	10.87%	11.96%	13.04%	14.13%
	$ 81,800-108,300	55%	11.11%	12.22%	13.33%	14.44%
$ 85,600-109,400		59%	12.20%	13.41%	14.63%	15.85%
	$108,300 & Over	63%	13.51%	14.86%	16.22%	17.57%
$109,400-162,400		64%	13.89%	15.28%	16.67%	18.06%
$162,400-213,400		68%	15.63%	17.19%	18.75%	20.31%
$215,400 & Over		70%	16.67%	18.33%	20.00%	21.67%

per cent bond equals 7.14 per cent on taxable interest; 6 per cent equals 8.57 per cent on taxable interest; 6½ per cent equals 9.29 per cent; and 7 per cent equals 10 per cent.

Q. *What is a moratorium on municipal securities?*

A. Suspension (postponement) by a state or municipality of repayment of principal on a maturing debt. Moratoriums are declared when a debtor hasn't the cash to pay off its obligations when due, even though it continues to pay interest owed on time.

Q. *Is the tax-exempt feature of these bonds safe?*

A. New federal legislation has been proposed from time to time to authorize states and localities to issue taxable bonds—if they so desire—with the federal government providing subsidies to offset the added interest cost to them. The goal: to attract investors who have no incentive now to buy tax-exempts.

Sale of these taxable bond options will not disturb the tax-exempt status of outstanding securities or any new tax-exempts the issuers prefer to sell instead of taxables.

Q. *Aren't some municipals insured to guarantee payment?*

A. Yes, several governmental authorities have taken out insurance to guarantee payment of interest and principal on their obligations in the event of default. The insurance does *not* cover loss due to market fluctuation during the life of the insured bond.

The two major insurers of municipal bonds are the Municipal Bond Insurance Association (MBIA) and the American Municipal Bond Assurance Corporation (AMBAC). An issue that has been insured by the MBIA receives an AAA rating from Standard & Poor's, and an issue insured by the AMBAC receives an "AA" rating. (Moody's does not take account of the insurance coverage in its ratings of municipals.)

The AMBAC also insures mutual bond funds and individual portfolios.

In sum there are three ways to obtain the security of insurance on your tax-exempt bond investments: (1) purchase bonds that the issuing government or underwriter has had insured by the MBIA or AMBAC: (2) purchase shares in a mutual fund that has had its portfolio insured by the AMBAC; (3) insure your own portfolio with the AMBAC.

THE UNITED STATES GOVERNMENT SECURITIES MARKETS

One fixed-income securities market in which the question of quality doesn't even come up is the market for U. S. Government securities. Default on the U. S. Treasury's issues is unthinkable.

Q. *What about U.S. savings bonds?*

A. These are non-marketable bonds and are covered in the following pages.

Q. *What are the marketable types of U.S. securities?*

A. (1) U. S. TREASURY BILLS, the most marketable fixed-income securities in the world, are issued on a discount (sold at less than face value) basis with maturities of three, six, and twelve months and are redeemed at face value at the specified maturity dates. The difference between the lower issue price and the higher maturity price represents your interest. Or if you sell them in the open market before maturity, your income is the difference between the issue price and your sale price.

There are also cash management bills which mature on tax dates and are attractive to investors with large incomes.

(2) U. S. TREASURY NOTES, by definition, securities with maturities of one to ten years. These carry specified coupons.

(3) U. S. TREASURY BONDS, by definition, obligations maturing in more than ten years. Many Treasury bonds outstanding today were sold many years ago at much, much lower than prevailing interest rates. Because of their comparatively low coupons—3 to 4¼ per cent—they sell at deep discounts from par value. Some long-term Treasury bonds issued in recent years, though, carry coupons up to 9⅜ per cent or higher.

Q. *Is buying discount bonds a good idea?*

A. It's a way of helping to guarantee yourself a capital gain if you hold the bond to maturity. You can run a risk of loss if interest rates rise sharply in the meantime and the price of your bonds is down to an even deeper discount if you sell before maturity. Conversely, you can achieve capital gain if interest rates decline and you sell at a profit before maturity. Also, a limited number of U. S. Treasury bonds which can be bought at a discount from par and which are held at death of the owner can be redeemed at par and accrued interest for payment of estate taxes. Of course, you can't have it both ways: these so-called "flower bonds" will be valued in estate at par for inheritance tax purposes too. (See page 1103.)

Q. *How are Treasury securities issued?*

A. Treasury notes and bonds are issued in registered, bearer, and in book entry form. Treasury bills are available only in book entry form.

Q. *How do you buy outstanding U. S. Treasury issues?*

A. You can buy them through your broker or banker and pay the market price plus the current commission or service charge.

A convenient way to obtain the safe returns comparable to those on U. S. Treasury obligations—without actually buying Treasuries—is to substitute an investment in bank "savings certificates," described on page 1081. Savings certificates are covered by U.S. government agency insurance for up to $40,000 per account. But there are substantial penalties for pulling your money out early. Thus you may be better off buying Treasury securities outright, since they are easily marketable at any time.

Q. *How do you buy the new U.S. issues which the Treasury offers to raise cash?*

A. You can submit tenders through your broker or banker and pay whatever service charge is asked. Or you can submit a tender offer through the Bureau of the Public Debt, Securities Transaction Branch, Washington, D.C. 20226 or your district Federal Reserve Bank—and pay no commission.

Q. *What are the minimums you can buy?*

A. At the start of the 1970s, the Treasury raised the minimum purchase on Treasury bills to $10,000 in an obvious move to eliminate the nuisance of the small investor and to protect savings banks from massive deposit withdrawals. The minimum on some Treasury notes and on bonds remained at $1,000 although higher minimums are fixed on most issues.

Q. *If you have the $10,000 minimum, how do you buy U. S. Treasury bills?*

A. You can submit a tender through the Federal Reserve Bank, bank branch in your district, or Bureau of the Public Debt, Securities Transaction Branch, Washington, D.C. 20226. Assuming you're buying less than $500,000 worth, you can buy at the non-competitive tender (bid)—meaning you won't compete with the professionals but will accept the *average* price. The non-competitive bid is the best for you.

Either go in person to your Federal Reserve Bank or branch or write and ask for a "non-competitive tender" covering the bill maturity you want: three, six, or twelve months. Fill out the total you want ($10,000 minimum) and enclose payment in full (face amount). Pay either by certified personal check, bank check, cash, or through Treasury bills you own which mature by the new issue date.

The discount on the bills—the difference between the *average* bid submitted (and the price at which you will therefore buy your bills) and the $10,000 you sent—is your interest. It will be refunded to you on the date the bills are issued. On the maturity date of your bills, when they are worth par or $10,000, you'll either redeem them for cash or exchange them—"roll them over"—for more new bills.

Occasionally the Treasury also offers cash management bills at a discount from face value which you may use at face value to pay income taxes. Once you learn the technique of buying ordinary Treasury bills, you'll find it a cinch to buy these —if you can use them.

Q. *Where do you find a Federal Reserve Bank?*

A. Here are the twelve Federal Reserve Banks, their twenty-nine branches, addresses, and phone numbers. Choose yours.

FEDERAL RESERVE OFFICES

BOARD OF GOVERNORS
Twentieth and Constitution Avenue N.W., Washington, DC 20551
(202) 452-3000

ATLANTA
104 Marietta Street N.W., Atlanta, GA 30303
(404) 586-8500

Birmingham Branch
    1801 Fifth Avenue, North (P.O. Box 10447), Birmingham, AL 35202
    (205) 252-3141

Jacksonville Branch
    515 Julia Street, Jacksonville, FL 32203
    (904) 632-4400

Miami Branch
    3770 S.W. Eighth Street, Coral Gables, FL 33134 (P.O. Box 520847, Miami,
        FL 33152)
    (305) 445-6281

Nashville Branch
    301 Eighth Avenue, North, Nashville, TN 37203
    (615) 259-4006

New Orleans Branch
    525 St. Charles Avenue (P.O. Box 61630), New Orleans, LA 70161
    (504) 586-1505

BOSTON
    600 Atlantic Avenue, Boston, MA 02106
    (617) 973-3000

Lewiston Office
    1775 Lisbon Road, Lewiston, ME 04240
    (207) 784-2381

Windsor Locks Office
    Windsor Locks, CT 06096
    (203) 623-2561

CHICAGO
    230 South LaSalle Street (P.O. Box 834), Chicago, IL 60690
    (312) 322-5322

Detroit Branch
    160 Fort Street, West (P.O. Box 1059), Detroit, MI 48231
    (313) 961-6880

CLEVELAND
    1455 East Sixth Street (P.O. Box 6387), Cleveland, OH 44101
    (216) 241-2800

Cincinnati Branch
    150 East Fourth Street (P.O. Box 999), Cincinnati, OH 45201
    (513) 721-4787

Pittsburgh Branch
    717 Grant Street (P.O. Box 867), Pittsburgh, PA 15230
    (412) 261-7800

DALLAS
    400 South Akard Street (Station K), Dallas, TX 75222
    (214) 651-6111

El Paso Branch
    301 East Main Street (P.O. Box 100), El Paso, TX 79999
    (915) 544-4730

Houston Branch
    1701 San Jacinto Street (P.O. Box 2578), Houston, TX 77001
    (713) 659-4433

San Antonio Branch
    126 East Nueva Street (P.O. Box 1471), San Antonio, TX 78295
    (512) 224-2141

KANSAS CITY
    925 Grand Avenue (Federal Reserve Station), Kansas City, MO 64198
    (816) 881-2000

Denver Branch
    1020 Sixteenth Street (Terminal Annex, P.O. Box 5228), Denver, CO 80217
    (303) 292-4020

Oklahoma City Branch
    226 Northwest Third Street (P.O. Box 25129), Oklahoma City, OK 73125
    (405) 235-1721

Omaha Branch
    1702 Dodge Street, Omaha, NB 68102
    (402) 341-3610

MINNEAPOLIS
    250 Marquette Avenue, Minneapolis, MN 55480
    (612) 340-2345

Helena Branch
    400 North Park Avenue, Helena, MT 59601
    (406) 442-3860

NEW YORK
    33 Liberty Street (Federal Reserve P.O. Station) New York, NY 10045
    (212) 791-5000

Buffalo Branch
> 160 Delaware Avenue (P.O. Box 961), Buffalo, NY 14240
> (716) 849-5000

PHILADELPHIA
> 100 North Sixth Street, Philadelphia, PA 19106 (P.O. Box 66, Philadelphia, PA 19105)
> (215) 574-6000

RICHMOND
> 100 North Ninth Street (P.O. Box 27622), Richmond, VA 23261
> (804) 649-3611

Baltimore Branch
> 114–120 East Lexington Street (P.O. Box 1378), Baltimore, MD 21203
> (301) 539-6552

Charleston Office
> 1200 Airport Road (P.O. Box 2309), Charleston, WV 25311
> (304) 345-8020

Charlotte Branch
> 401 South Tryon Street (P.O. Box 300), Charlotte, NC 28230
> (704) 373-0200

Columbia Office
> 1624 Browning Road (P.O. Box 132), Columbia, SC 29210
> (803) 772-1940

ST. LOUIS
> 411 Locust Street (P.O. Box 442) St. Louis, MO 63166
> (314) 444-8444

Little Rock Branch
> 325 West Capitol Avenue (P.O. Box 1261), Little Rock, AR 72203
> (501) 372-5451

Louisville Branch
> 410 South Fifth Street (P.O. Box 899), Louisville, KY 40232
> (502) 587-7351

Memphis Branch
> 202 North Main Street (P.O. Box 407), Memphis, TN 38101
> (901) 523-7171

SAN FRANCISCO
> 400 Sansome Street (P.O. Box 7702), San Francisco, CA 94120
> (415) 544-2000

Los Angeles Branch
> 409 West Olympic Boulevard (P.O. Box 2077, Terminal Annex), Los Angeles, CA 90051
> (213) 683-8323

Portland Branch
> 915 S.W. Stark Street (P.O. Box 3436), Portland, OR 97208
> (503) 221-5900

Salt Lake City Branch
> 120 South State Street (P.O. Box 30780), Salt Lake City, UT 84125
> (801) 355-3131

Seattle Branch
> 1015 Second Avenue (P.O. Box 3567), Seattle, WA 98124
> (206) 442-1376

THE MARKET FOR FEDERAL AGENCY SECURITIES

Ranking a mere step below the direct obligations of the U. S. Treasury are the obligations of the federal agencies. They are not direct obligations of the U. S. Treasury itself but in one way or another they involve federal government guarantees or sponsorship. They are not outstanding in anywhere near the volume of U. S. Treasury issues but tens of billions of dollars of agency issues already are being traded in the open market and the volume keeps climbing.

What's more, just because they are *not* direct Treasury obligations, the returns available on federal agency issues are usually higher than on Treasuries. As a general rule, at any given time the yield on an agency issue will be above the yield on a Treasury issue of similar maturity.

Q. *Just what are federal agency issues?*

A. They are securities issued by federal agencies created by Congress over the years and operating under federal charter and supervision.

Among the federal agencies concerned with financing the agricultural industry are: the Federal Intermediate Credit Banks (FIC), the District Banks for Cooperatives (Co-ops), and the Federal Land Banks. These are marketed as Consolidated Farm System issues.

Among the agencies concerned with the housing industry are the Federal Home Loan Bank; the Federal Home Loan Mortgage Corporation (Freddie Mac); the Federal National Mortgage Association (FNMA or Fannie Mae); the Government National Mortgage Association (GNMA or Ginnie Mae).

Also, to illustrate the variety and scope among other agencies, there are the Tennessee Valley Authority (TVA) and the Export-Import Bank (ExIm), the Small Business Administration, and more. In addition, new agencies are created from time to time and they too will sell their obligations in the open market—or will have their securities sold for them by the U. S. Treasury.

Q. *What are the minimums on purchases and maturities of the agency issues?*

A. A $10,000 minimum was set in the early 1970s on some federal agency issues also to eliminate the small "nuisance" subscriber. A $5,000 denomination is still fairly typical among the agencies, though, and the minimum on Federal Land Bank issues is $1,000. The maturities of agency issues generally run from a few months to over fifteen years.

Q. *What do federal agency and Treasury issues yield?*

A. Check your daily newspaper for the bid and asked quotes and yields available or call your broker or bank. The quotations and yields change from day to day.

Q. *How do you subscribe to new issues of federal agencies?*

A. Each of the federal agencies has a fiscal agent in New York City which puts together a nationwide selling group when it has a new issue to sell. In the group will be securities dealers, brokerage houses, and dealer banks. The sale will be publicly announced in the newspapers and other media one or two days prior to the offering.

Each of the firms which is a member of the selling group will accept subscriptions from investors on the established terms—and assuming your order is accepted, you will pay no commission on your purchase. You will pay a clearing fee or service charge, however, and this will cut your net return. You must check these details, as stressed over and over in this chapter, with a broker, dealer, or banker who knows *you* and will give you a *fair* deal.

Q. *How do you buy outstanding federal agency issues?*

A. The same way you buy other fixed-income securities trading in the open market: through a broker or banker with whom you have an established relationship. If you buy in the open market, you'll pay the prevailing commission or the offered price.

Q. *In what form are agency securities issued?*

A. Usually in bearer form. You have to assume the responsibility of safeguarding them, collecting interest, and redeeming them at maturity. This can be done through your broker or bank.

LOWER-QUALITY BONDS—OR "JUNK" BONDS

On these, you can really earn some juicy returns. The rate just below A is Baa according to Moody's and BBB according to Standard & Poor's. And these are not low ratings, for those categories go down to Ba or BB, B, Caa or CCC, Ca or CC, or C. In some of these areas, bonds will return a yield ranging up from 10 per cent. But I warn you. Bonds of this caliber *can* turn out to be very risky and you may deeply regret reaching for the rich returns.

"Junk" bonds are risky not only because of the possibility of default by the issue. Their price fluctuations also are sharper and faster than those on higher-quality issues. When interest rates fall—that is, when bond prices rise—most junk bonds appreciate much more than the average fixed-income security. But when interest rates *rise*—and bond prices fall—junk bonds often plummet. The reason is fairly obvious: if you, an investor, can get fairly high yields on good-quality bonds, why should you bother with junk?

At the same time, there has been powerful demand for top-rated obligations, which has widened the spread in interest rates between the quality and the junk.

There has been no mistaking the message: conservative investors clearly prefer the safety of top-caliber obligations at lower rates to the higher income available on lower-quality bonds appealing to speculators. Smaller investors who are willing to take the junk bond risk for the high return can diversify by purchasing high-yield mutual funds, either taxable or tax-exempt.

PITFALLS FOR THE SMALL INVESTOR

Q. *But what if you don't have a big account or a working relationship with a bank?*

A. Unless you have a most extraordinary relationship with your bank, you'll not be able to buy outstanding short-term issues of the U. S. Treasury and federal agencies without meeting some rigid requirements. Specifically:

• You must have a hefty total of cash in your account or be a regular customer. You can't just walk into any bank with a check.

• You must invest at least $100,000 or you'll be considered an odd-lot buyer and have to pay a service charge. You must make sure this service charge doesn't eliminate the interest rate advantage.

• You must meet the minimums—$10,000 on Treasury bills; $5,000 to $10,000 on federal agency issues, depending on the agency. The usual minimum for commercial paper you buy through your bank is $100,000.

• You must keep track of your maturity dates, for if you fail to reinvest your money when your obligations mature, you lose future interest.

Q. *And what about brokers?*

A. You'll have to meet the same rigid requirements. Most brokers also consider you a nuisance to avoid and will slap on a service charge of $20 or more per order. This can more than offset your interest rate advantage.

In short, these are sophisticated markets. You have to seek them out, you have to do your homework, you have to have money, and you have to assume responsibilities.

A BANK OR A BOND? WHICH FOR YOU?

What should you do if you have a fair-size sum to invest and what you primarily want is safety and income?

Should you simply put your money in a corner bank or savings institution, take no risks of the market place at all, and get whatever returns the financial institution offers?

Or should you go into the open market, accept some risks of price fluctuations, and freeze for yourself some of the return available there?

To get your answer, ask yourself:

• How long do you want to freeze your savings in fixed-income mediums? You will certainly not buy long-term bonds if you plan to keep the money invested in the bonds for only a short time—not unless you're trading in and out for quick profits. And that kind of trading is an entirely different matter from what I'm covering in this section.

• What are your investment goals? If all you want is absolute safety and a fair interest rate, you might as well put your money in a nearby savings institution. It's simple and satisfactory.

• What is your age? You can afford to take more risks at a young age.

• What is your judgment on the future pace of inflation? You will want to feel confident that your interest coupon will more than cover the annual loss in the purchasing power of the dollars you have invested.

• Do you have enough money to go into the open market? You must consider the commission charges on buying a few bonds and, of course, there also are the minimums required on many investments.

• How willing are you to accept responsibility for managing your savings in the market? Investing in any of the securities I have discussed in the preceding pages takes more knowledge and responsibility on your part than does a simple deposit in a local bank or savings institution.

These questions will guide you to the proper decision for yourself.

FINANCIAL FUTURES

If you are to invest in bonds or other fixed-income securities, you also must study what might be called the "futures market for interest rates," or "financial futures." Futures are a highly speculative type of investment (more on pages 1124–26), historically associated with such commodities as wheat, corn, copper, etc. In briefest summary, a future is a contract—a contract for a future delivery or purchase at a predetermined price. A typical copper futures contract might require a buyer to purchase 25,000 pounds of copper from the seller next July at X cents a pound. If copper prices have gone up in the meantime, the buyer has a bargain—or if down, vice versa.

There are futures contracts in fixed-income securities, too. The concept behind futures is to hedge against coming price movements—or to place a bet on the way you think the price will go.

A large bond dealer, for instance, may hold a huge supply of U. S. Government bonds paying attractive interest rates; nevertheless, the dealer wants to be protected against a further rise in interest rates—which would cause his supply of bonds to tumble in price. So he sells contracts to deliver U. S. Government bonds in the future. If interest rates do rise, his bonds will be worth less, but he'll make a nice countervailing profit on his futures contracts. Why? Because if bond yields have increased and prices have fallen, he can fulfill the agreement of his futures contract and buy bonds at a lower price for delivery than that at which he originally contracted to sell. Conversely, if interest rates fall, he'll lose money on his futures, but will make a profit on his bonds. (This goal is to guarantee himself the attractive interest payments without fear of capital loss.) The buyer of the contract just may be a speculator betting that interest rates will fall—that is, bond prices will rise or the other participant may be an arbitrageur.

Interest rate futures as the end of the 1970s neared included: Treasury bond and commercial paper futures and two types of GNMA futures, traded on the Chicago Board of Trade; three-month and one-year Treasury bill futures, traded on the International Money Market of the Chicago Mercantile Exchange; and a GNMA certificate delivery contract on the American Commodities Exchange affiliate of the American Stock Exchange. New varieties of similar types of contracts are in the making, and may be actively trading as you read this.

The lure of futures—as opposed merely to buying bonds—is that leverage is tremendous. A tiny change in interest rates will yield a huge profit—or it may wipe out your investment.

For this reason alone, you should trade in *financial futures* only if you are an *experienced investor* able to risk ample sums of money not essential to your well-being!

To suggest how overpowering this leverage is, consider that the typical interest rate futures contract calls for the buyer to buy (and the seller to sell) $100,000* to as much as $1 million† worth of fixed-income instruments at some date in the future. Yet you can buy or sell one of these contracts by *putting up a deposit of only around $1,500,* which is called the "margin." If interest rates move even slightly, the value of the tens of thousands of dollars of bonds involved in the contract can change enough to wipe out your $1,500 deposit—or double your money. (In the case of Treasury bond futures, a fluctuation of only .12 of a point in interest rates would change the value of a single contract by $1,500; in the case of GNMA futures, .12 of a point; in the case of Treasury bill futures .6 of a point.)

By now you may be wondering: Suppose I *do* earn a profit on a $1,500 deposit. Where would I get the money to fulfill a contract calling for me to buy or sell thousands of dollars worth of bonds? Don't worry; very few futures speculators ever have to take over or make "delivery" on their contracts. (To see why, consult pages 1124–26.)

But be warned: even the most sophisticated futures speculators do lose their shirts in this most esoteric of markets.

And the amateurs? I shiver . . .

WHAT SHOULD BE YOUR POLICY ON BONDS?

Let me put it bluntly: unless you know your way around the bond markets, and can afford to take the risks, go and stay first-class.

Don't go into these sophisticated markets blindly.

Don't buy low-grade bonds which might default and wipe you out.

Unless you have at least $5,000 to invest *don't* buy individual bond issues even where there are no minimums. (The alternative here might be to buy into a bond fund, described earlier.)

* For Treasury bond futures and GNMA futures.
† For T-bill futures.

Don't try to diversify too much when you are buying just a few bonds. Commission charges on buying or selling one or two bonds can be steep and in addition the spread on the bid and asked when you are buying just one or two bonds can also be sizable. Some brokers might quote you a spread as much as five points ($50 on a $1,000 par value) if you buy a single bond. If you can, buy several of one issue. You'll probably get a better price and pay less in commissions.

Don't try to make a killing by trading on thin margins.

Do get guidance from a broker or banker you respect and who knows you, your circumstances, and the bond market.

Do make sure you are dealing with a reputable firm. In the 1970s there were far too many scandals in connection with high-pressure bond salesmen in the "Sunbelt" area especially where so many retire with cash to spare and time to fill. Among the shoddy as well as illegal sales tactics were charging excessive prices; quoting deceptive maturities and ratings; providing misleading descriptions of issues.

Do learn the basics of bond yield, maturity, discounts, and ratings before taking the plunge.

Do use your head and curb your greed.

The bond markets are great for wise and cool investors. They can be murder for fools.

THE BAFFLEGAB OF BONDS

ACCRUED INTEREST   Interest which has accumulated on a bond from the last interest payment to the present day. When you buy a bond, you must pay the interest which has accrued from the last interest payment to the seller of the bond. When you in turn sell a bond, the buyer must pay you the interest accrued from the last interest payment. Not all bonds trade with accrued interest. Those in default trade *flat,* and income bonds usually pay interest only when and if it is earned.

AMORTIZE   Fixed periodic charges or credits are scheduled for the specific purpose of adjusting purchaser's cost to redemption.

BASIS   This is another word for yield. The basis of a bond is its yield to maturity. In the financial futures world, though, it is the difference between the price of a nearby contract and the price at which the underlying security can be bought in the cash market.

BASIS POINT $\frac{1}{100}$ of 1 per cent or 0.01. Used in finely describing the yield of a bond.

BEARER BOND   Bond on which the owner's name is not registered with the issuer and thus, in some ways, is equivalent to cash in your possession.

BLUE LIST   Daily trade publication for dealers in municipal bonds listing the names and amounts of municipal bonds that dealers all over the country are offering for sale to other dealers. Printed in blue ink on blue paper, hence *Blue List.* The *Blue List* also includes coupon price, and yield, of offerings.

BOND   Promissory instrument to obtain credit on which principal is to be repaid in usually more than ten years after the loan is made. Interest is to be paid periodically. Bonds are issued by federal, state, and municipal governments as well as corporations and are usually marketable. All non-government bonds are covered by a contract (trust indenture) held by a trustee who—in case of serious violation of the indenture by the bond issuer—can take action to protect the rights of all the bondholders.

BOND MARKETS   Markets in which longer-term debt securities of various borrowers are traded.

CALLABLE BOND   Bonds which include a call provision stating that the issuer may redeem them before their maturity date under specified conditions. Usually the call price is at a premium over par. For example: A corporation has a $10 million bond issue outstanding which carries a 9 per cent coupon maturing in twenty-four years and which is callable at 105. If interest rates drop to, say, 6½ per cent, and the corporation can be assured by its investment bankers that this lower rate is available, it is obvious that the corporation can benefit by paying the slightly additional cost involved in calling the bonds at 105 and floating another loan at a coupon rate so much lower than 9 per cent. Most issues prohibit call to take advantage of lower interest rates in the early years of the issue life.

COMPOUND INTEREST   Interest paid on accumulated interest as well as on the principal and computed on both the accumulated interest and the principal. Over the life of a bond, compounding interest can be equal to more than half the total of realized return.

CONVERTIBLE DEBENTURE   Bond issued on the general credit of the corporation which may be converted into common and sometimes preferred stock of the same corporation at a specified price under stated conditions.

CORPORATES   Corporation bonds.

COUPON   The piece of paper attached to a bearer (or coupon) bond which is evidence that interest is payable on the bond, usually every six months. The coupon rate is the rate of interest which the issuer has pledged to pay you, the bondholder, annually. The coupon amount is the dollar amount you will receive when this paper is submitted to a bank or through your broker for collection.

CURRENT YIELD   The interest paid by a bond expressed as a percentage of the coupon to the current market price. Example: a 3 per cent $1,000 bond selling at $600 offers a current return of 5 per cent ($30/$600).

DEBENTURE   A type of corporate bond which is backed only by the general credit of the issuing corporation and not by any pledge of property.

DISCOUNT   Difference between the lower price at which a bond may be trading and its higher value (par value) at issuance or normally at maturity.

DISCOUNT BOND   Bonds quoted at a price below their face (or par) value. For example: a bond selling at par would be shown in a newspaper bond table at 100, a discount bond would be shown below that (99, 62, 73, etc.).

DISCOUNT RATE   The interest rate the Federal Reserve System charges banks belonging to the Federal Reserve System for loans. It is considered a basic interest rate of the nation because it is the rate banks themselves pay to borrow money. As a result, changes in the discount rate by the Federal Reserve affect all other interest rates in the nation.

EASY MONEY See TIGHT MONEY.

FEDERAL AGENCY ISSUES Securities issued by federal agencies created by Congress over a long span of years and ranking in caliber right below U. S. Government securities themselves. Some are obligations of the government; some are backed by the agency.

FEDERAL RESERVE SYSTEM Established under the Federal Reserve Act of 1913 to regulate the banking system of the United States and to set monetary policy of the country. See MONETARY POLICY.

FINANCIAL FUTURES Contracts traded on major commodities exchanges for the future delivery of large amounts of fixed-income instruments—including Treasury bonds, Treasury bills, GNMA pass-through certificates, and commercial paper.

FIRST MORTGAGE BOND A type of corporate bond which is secured by a mortgage on all or part of the fixed property of the issuing corporation.

FIXED-INCOME SECURITIES Securities which return a fixed income over a specified period. Fixed-income securities may be bonds, notes, bills, preferred stocks, or mortgage-backed securities and pools.

FLOWER BOND Nickname for certain U. S. Treasury bonds which can be turned in at par or face value for payment of federal estate taxes if the bonds are actually owned by the decedent at the time of death. However, because of changes in the tax laws, some of the tax advantages may not be as great as was once the case.

If these bonds can be bought at a deep discount from par, the bonds can be helpful in estate planning. Under a recent law, no more bonds with the special par redemption provision for estate tax purposes will be issued, so the supply of the bonds is limited and growing smaller as the bonds mature or are turned in. Here are flower bonds outstanding and their maturities as the 1980s neared:

COUPON	MATURITY
4	2/80
3½	11/80
3¼	6/83
3¼	5/85
4¼	5/85
3½	2/90
4¼	8/92
4	2/93
4⅛	5/94
3	2/95
3½	11/98

GENERAL-OBLIGATION BOND The major type of municipal bond backed by the full faith and credit of the issuer. These differ from limited-obligation bonds, which rely upon special assessments and specific sources of revenue, and from revenue bonds, which have no call on taxing power.

INTEREST   Money paid for the use of money.

INTEREST RATE   A percentage determined by the amount of money the borrower pledges to pay to the lender of money for the use of the total borrowed. If you pay $80 interest per year on a loan of $1,000, you are paying an 8 per cent interest rate.

INVESTMENT BANKERS   Financial organizations, but usually not commercial banks, raising funds for various types of borrowers often by buying all of the securities and selling them through a selling group of broker-dealers to institutional and individual investors.

LIMITED TAX OR SPECIAL TAX BOND   Also a type of municipal bond.

MATURITY   Specified date on which the stated value of a bond—the principal—becomes payable in full to the bond's owners. Also called due or maturity date.

MONETARY POLICY   Set by the Federal Reserve Board to influence the supply of bank credit and other monetary conditions in the U.S. economy. Monetary policy, therefore, is a key factor in the trend of interest rates and the direction of the entire U.S. economy. Since interest rate changes send the bond and money markets up or down, monetary policy is also obviously a crucial force in these markets. See FEDERAL RESERVE SYSTEM.

MONEY MARKETS   Markets in which the short-term securities of various borrowers are traded.

MORTGAGE-BACKED BONDS   Bonds issued by a bank or institution which lends mortgage money to homeowners. Mortgage-backed bonds have as collateral a sizable amount of mortgages—usually a larger dollar amount than the total dollar amount of the bonds.

MORTGAGE BOND   See FIRST MORTGAGE BOND.

MORTGAGE PASS-THROUGH CERTIFICATE   A certificate of participation in a pool of mortgages that a mortgage-lending institution has sold to a trustee. Investors in pass-through certificates receive monthly payments of interest and principal as the mortgages in the pool are paid off.

MUNICIPAL BONDS   Any obligations issued by a city, town, village, state, territory, U.S. possession, etc. All are exempt from federal income taxation as of the laws in the late 1970s, (and under certain conditions sometimes from state and local taxes too), and all are called municipals.

NATIONAL ASSOCIATION OF SECURITIES DEALERS, INC.   A non-profit membership corporation, established in 1938 by Congress and including thousands of securities dealers and brokers throughout the United States. The NASD is responsible for self-regulation of the over-the-counter securities markets and also, in turn, to the Securities and Exchange Commission.

OBLIGATION   In Wall Street, an IOU, a bond, a note, or a bill.

OFFERING   Principal amount of an obligation or the face value at which an obligation is issued and on which interest is paid. Usually $1,000 or $5,000 per bond.

POINT   In bonds, one point represents a $10 change in the price per $1,000 (face value) bond—in contrast to stocks, where one point is a $1.00 change in price. The reason a point is $10 is that a bond price is quoted as a percentage of $1,000: 1 per cent of $1,000 is $10, 5 per cent is $50, etc., and so one point is $10, five points is $50, etc. To illustrate further, a quotation of 92 is $920 and a five-point rise to 97 would be equal to $50 or a rise to $970.

PREMIUM Difference between higher price above par at which a bond may be selling and the lower price recorded at the time it was issued or to be received at maturity date.

PRINCIPAL Face value of a bond on which interest is paid.

PRUDENT-MAN RULE A standard for investments. Under this standard, states having "prudent-man laws" permit trustees managing other people's money to diversify their investments and include high-quality stocks as well as the highest-quality bonds in the portfolios they manage.

RATINGS The informed judgments of independent rating services (the two major ones are Moody's and Standard & Poor's) on the quality of various obligations. Obligations are ranked from the very highest Aaa (Moody's) and AAA (S&P's) to C and even lower. The ratings of these two services play a key role in evaluating the quality of bonds to investors.

REAL RATE OF RETURN Annual yield derived from fixed-income securities reduced by per cent of yearly rise in cost of living. Sometimes quoted on a pre-tax basis and sometimes on an after-tax basis.

REDEEM Repayment of the par value of a bond at maturity or at the price that has to be paid if the bond is being redeemed earlier at a call date.

REFUNDING The replacement of an outstanding and redeemed obligation with a new obligation. When interest rates decline, an issuer may in advance of maturity date decide to call in securities it sold at higher interest rates and refund them into new lower-interest bonds.

REGISTERED BOND A bond registered in the name of the owner with either the issuer of the bond or the issuer's agent. The owner is mailed a check when interest is due and the bond can be transferred only by endorsement of the certificate. See BEARER BOND.

RETURN Also known as yield. The rate of income derived from an investment—interest in the case of bonds, dividends in the case of stocks.

REVENUE BOND A type of municipal bond relying upon revenues generated by some public facility (bridges, tunnels, roads, transit, etc.) rather than taxes. Industrial revenue bonds are a special sort issued by a government and therefore pay tax-exempt interest to finance a corporate facility. Their main security is the lease rental paid by the industrial corporation.

ROLLOVER Another word for refund, commonly used when the Treasury replaces its short-term bills at their maturity dates with new short-term bills, or a bank replaces maturing certificates of deposit with proceeds of new CDs.

SELLING AT A DISCOUNT A bond selling at a price below its face value. See DISCOUNT.

SELLING AT A PREMIUM A bond selling at a price above its face value. See PREMIUM.

SERIAL BONDS Issues which are redeemed on an installment basis in sequential —usually annual—order. A predetermined amount carry chronological maturity dates so that bonds fall due every period until the full amount is paid up.

SIMPLE INTEREST   Interest that is paid only on the principal and computed only on the principal.

SINKING FUND   A pool of money created through periodic payments by an issuer of bonds that must be used to retire (call in) a certain fixed (or variable) amount of its outstanding bonds at specified intervals. See AMORTIZE.

SPREAD   Difference between two prices. Between bid and asked; or between the price at which an investment banking syndicate buys an issue from the issuer and the price at which the syndicate sells the issue to the public; or between the prices at which top-rated bonds are quoted and the prices at which second-quality bonds are quoted; or just between different types of bonds.

SYNDICATES   Groups of investment bankers formed to underwrite and distribute issues of securities.

TAX-EXEMPTS   Slang name for all types of municipal obligations which are exempt from federal income tax and sometimes from state and local taxation.

TERM   Length of time that a bond is outstanding. A term bond, in comparison with a serial bond, has only a single maturity date.

TIGHT MONEY   Financial conditions that develop when the Federal Reserve adopts a monetary policy under which it restrains the supply of credit and thereby encourages higher interest rates. As the supply of credit becomes more limited while demand remains unaffected, the availability of the credit to would-be borrowers shrinks and there is a feeling of "tightness" in the markets. Easy money describes financial conditions that develop when the Federal Reserve adopts a monetary policy under which it expands the supply of credit and thereby encourages lower interest rates. The policy usually follows a decline in demand for funds, reflecting a slowdown in business activity.

TREASURY   Nickname for the securities of the United States Government: bonds, notes, and bills.

TREASURY BILLS   Short-term marketable U. S. Treasury obligations maturing from ninety days to one year and offered on a discount basis. T-bills are considered in the investment community almost as liquid as cash or as savings in the bank. Minimum denomination is $10,000.

UNDERWRITING SYNDICATES   Groups of investment bankers who buy and market new issues to public.

UNITED STATES GOVERNMENT SECURITIES MARKET   Generally speaking, the vast over-the-counter market in which bills, notes, and bonds of the U. S. Treasury are bought and sold. (Some are listed on the New York Stock and American Exchanges too.)

VARIABLE RATE   The term applied to certain special loans or debt obligations, the interest rates on which vary with overall interest rates or some specific interest rate. Also called Floating Rate notes.

YIELD TO MATURITY   Total, true rate of return you are slated to receive on a debt instrument, taking into consideration the price you paid, the interest to be received, and the price at which your bond will be paid off at its maturity date. This is an exact calculation that must be worked out with aid of specially prepared mathematical tables.

24

YOUR GUIDE
TO UNITED STATES SAVINGS BONDS

INTRODUCTION

"On New Year's morning, my husband and I vowed to save $50 a month, about 10 per cent of his take-home pay. But in the past few weeks an unexpected bunch of expenses has wiped it all out. This has happened over and over again to us, with the result that we haven't accumulated one extra dollar in the past five years. Is there any cure for the habitual non-saver?"

This typed plea for help, sent to me, is far more typical of Americans than any figures on total savings suggest. This is the sort of letter, in fact, which highlights the fact that, despite our ever-rising volume of overall savings, a full one third or more of U.S. families have no savings at all—in the form of bank deposits, stocks, bonds, etc.—and for millions of other families the savings total is less than $500.

If you are among the millions who feel unable to stick to voluntary savings plans, your best answer will be a form of "forced savings." There are literally dozens of different ways to discipline yourself into saving and I've analyzed many of the techniques in these pages. But among the very, very *best* ways to force yourself to save is to buy United States savings bonds under a payroll savings plan at the place where you work—or via a bond-a-month plan at your corner bank. And in fact a fantastic total of approximately 10 million Americans in the late 1970s were buying bonds via these savings plans at their offices or plants or factories.

This advantage is not to be underestimated in any way! By buying savings bonds via these plans, you discipline yourself into saving money you otherwise might easily fritter away. By authorizing regular small deductions from your paycheck, you build over the years a sizable total of savings. By enrolling in a payroll savings or bond-a-month plan you tend to become "frozen" to the savings program and to keep building your nest egg through good times and bad.

This is the "heart" of the United States savings bond program. This is the "magic" by which a few dollars put aside regularly every week becomes hundreds of dollars saved over a year. This is the secret of the program's continuing popularity, for as one of the leading industrialists of the country said to me a while ago:

"Many employees wouldn't save at all unless they were enrolled in a payroll savings plan. It is a lot better to get only a mediocre interest rate on something than a sensational interest rate on nothing!"

To put it another way, there may be better ways to invest—and there are—but there is no better way to save. It's a subtle but significant distinction.

Okay, the above explains why the savings bond program has survived so long. Now what are these bonds?

KEY QUESTIONS ON SAVINGS BONDS

There are two series of U.S. savings bonds currently on sale—Series E and Series H—and in the early 1980s, the EE and HH will replace these. Since savings bonds were originally issued forty years ago, the Treasury raised the interest they paid in successive stages until you could earn up to 6 per cent on the bonds in the late 1970s. As the 1980s neared, it appeared a virtual certainty that the rate again would be increased (for the ninth time since the program was begun in World War II). Congress in 1979 voted to permit a rise up to 7 per cent. Check your local bank for details.

Q. *What are the characteristics of savings bonds?*

A. The familiar E (and EE) bond is an appreciation-type security. This means you buy it at a discount from its face amount, and the gradual increase in the value of the bond, from your purchase price to its face amount (or redemption price), represents your interest.

The less familiar Series H (and HH) bond is a current-income security. This means you buy it at par (face value) and you receive interest in the form of semi-annual checks from the U. S. Treasury.

Both types of bonds are non-marketable bonds—non-negotiable, not acceptable as collateral for loans. Series E and EE bonds may be redeemed by the Treasury or one of its authorized paying agents (most banks and other financial institutions are authorized paying agents and will redeem your bonds). H and HH bonds may be redeemed only by the Treasury or any Federal Reserve Bank branch.

Q. *How do you earn the 6 per cent rate?*

A. Series E and EE bonds increase in redemption value monthly from the third to the thirtieth month after issue, and semi-annually after that. Your interest, represented by these increases, is compounded semi-annually. Your overall rate of return increases on a graduated scale, from 4.54 per cent for bonds redeemed after one year to 6 per cent for bonds held five years after issue. The following table shows you your return on E or EE bonds with issue dates beginning September 1, 1976, if you cash them in before or at original maturity.

E OR EE BONDS
CASHED IN AFTER   YIELD

1 year	4.54 (annual)
1½ years	4.69
2 years	4.76
2½ years	4.86
3 years	4.95
3½ years	5.03
4 years	5.14
4½ years	5.25
5 years	6.00

Series H bonds also return 6 per cent when held to a maturity of ten years. They earn 4.99 per cent the first year; thereafter, their interest increases too, until, at maturity date, they have returned 6 per cent a year over the ten-year span.

The following table shows you your return on H bonds—with issue dates beginning December 1, 1973—if you cash them in before or at original maturity.

(See pages 1115–19 later in this chapter for facts on HH bonds.)

H BONDS CASHED IN AFTER   YIELD

½ year	4.20%
1 year	4.99
1½ years	5.25
2 years	5.38
2½ years	5.46
3 years	5.51
3½ years	5.55
4 years	5.58
4½ years	5.60
5 years	5.62
5½ years	5.69
6 years	5.75
6½ years	5.80
7 years	5.84
7½ years	5.87
8 years	5.91
8½ years	5.93
9 years	5.96
9½ years	5.98
10 years (maturity)	6.00

Q. *Has the rate been increased for older bonds?*

A. Yes. Beginning with 1959, the yields on outstanding savings bonds have been improved several times, bringing them in line with current issues.

The latest increase was effective December 1, 1973, or at the beginning of the first semi-annual interest period thereafter.

Q. *How do the various extensions of maturity apply to E and H bonds?*

A. E bonds, with original maturities ranging from five years to ten years, have been granted one or more ten-year extensions.

DATE OF ISSUE	EXTENDED MATURITY	LIFE OF BOND
May 1941–Apr. 1952	May 1981–Apr. 1992	40 years
May 1952–Jan. 1957	Jan. 1992–Sep. 1996	39 years, 8 months
Feb. 1957–May 1959	Jan. 1996–Apr. 1998	38 years, 11 months
June 1959–Nov. 1965	Mar. 1997–Aug. 2003	37 years, 9 months
Dec. 1965–May 1969	Dec. 1992–May 1996	27 years
June 1969–Nov. 1973	Apr. 1995–Sep. 1999	25 years, 10 months
Dec. 1973–June 1980	Dec. 1998–June 2005	25 years

For H Bonds, the extended maturities are as follows:

DATE OF ISSUE	EXTENDED MATURITY	LIFE OF BOND
June 1952–Jan. 1957	Feb. 1982–Sep. 1986	29 years, 8 months
Feb. 1957–Dec. 1979	Feb. 1987–Dec. 2009	30 years

Q. *Is there any advantage in redeeming older E or H bonds to buy new bonds?*

A. Absolutely none. They all pay the same interest rate schedule and pay off at the same price at maturity. And in fact there is a good reason not to cash in—if the interest for Series E bonds has not been reported each year as it accrued—for then you would be required to report the accumulated interest (the gain in value) for federal income tax purpose during the year you cash in. In addition, the new bonds purchased with the proceeds would initially accrue interest at a lower rate than the bonds that were cashed.

Q. *Are the rates guaranteed?*

A. Yes. The bonds are backed by the full faith and credit of the U. S. Government and the rates are guaranteed to maturity. You can, though, cash in your bonds as you wish after a short time. Interest may be increased but not decreased, once the rate for an extension has been published.

Q. *How do I sell my bonds?*

A. You don't sell savings bonds. You cash them in or redeem them at guaranteed values. E or EE bonds may be redeemed at most banks and other financial institutions at their current redemption value.

At your, the owner's, option, H or HH bonds may be redeemed at any Federal Reserve Bank or Branch, or at the Bureau of the Public Debt, Securities Transactions Branch, Washington, D.C. 20266, at any time after six months from issue date. H bonds received during the month preceding an interest payment date will be held for redemption until that date.

Q. *What about cash-in restrictions?*

A. Savings bonds are, I repeat, liquid assets which may be cashed in after their minimal holding periods—two months for E bonds and six months for all others (EE, H and HH).

Q. *What if a bond is lost or stolen?*

A. Savings bonds are "indestructible." Any bond which is lost, stolen, mutilated, or destroyed will be replaced by the U. S. Treasury upon your application without charge to you. A record of each bond sold is maintained by Social Security account number for those issued on or after October 1, 1973.

The record is kept by the Bureau of Public Debt. More than 3.6 million U.S. savings bonds, valued at more than $294 million—either lost, stolen, damaged, or destroyed—have been replaced by the Treasury, over the past three decades, without charge to their owners.

Q. *You mean all bonds are registered?*

A. Yes. And you have a choice of registration. The bonds may be issued in one name only, in the names of two persons as co-owners, or in the name of one person with a second person as beneficiary (payable on death).

If bonds are registered in co-ownership form, during co-owner's lifetime either of you may cash the bonds, but a co-owner's name cannot be removed without his or her consent. If registered in beneficiary form, during owner's lifetime only he or she may cash an E bond and beneficiary's name cannot be removed without the beneficiary's consent. On an EE bond, this consent clause has been eliminated.

Savings bonds cannot be transferred, sold, or used as collateral.

Q. *How do I make a claim if my bonds are lost?*

A. Write to the Bureau of Public Debt, 200 Third Street, Parkersburg, West Virginia 26101. Provide as much information as you can about the lost, stolen, damaged, or destroyed bonds; serial numbers, issue dates, names and addresses on bonds. The Bureau of Public Debt will send you a special form to execute to receive your "duplicate" bonds. Keep your bonds in a secure place, such as a safe deposit box. *In another location,* maintain a list of your bonds, with their serial numbers, denominations, and dates issued. Get a "Personal Record of Ownership" from any local savings bond division office.

Q. *What about taxation of savings bonds?*

A. Interest on savings bonds is exempt from all state and local income or personal property taxes. Interest on savings bonds is subject to federal income tax, but the tax may be deferred on E and EE bonds until the bonds are cashed, otherwise disposed of, or finally mature. This tax-deferral privilege permits you to create and build up education, retirement, disability funds (or funds for whatever your objective) which—under certain circumstances—may be tax-free. This aspect is also a major "plus" for E and EE bonds.

You cannot similarly postpone paying income tax on interest you earn on marketable Treasury obligations or other taxable obligations. H or HH bond interest, paid semi-annually by Treasury check, must be reported annually for federal income tax purposes.

Q. *Any other important characteristics?*

A. Yes. Unless administration is required for other purposes, probate is not required in order to dispose of a decedent's savings bonds. The Treasury provides special forms, depending on the amount involved, which may be used for the purpose. Bonds registered in co-owner or beneficiary form belong to the survivor and are not a part of the decedent's probate estate; their value may be included in computing the size of the estate for estate and inheritance tax purposes, whether federal or state.

HOW TO USE THE TAX ADVANTAGES OF SAVINGS BONDS TO CREATE A TAX-FREE EDUCATION FUND

The fact that you need not report the interest you receive on E or EE bonds until you cash in the bonds is a vital tax benefit for you. And you can increase these tax savings when you buy the bonds as gifts for your children.

For instance, as a means of saving for your child's education, buy the bonds in your child's name and designate yourself as beneficiary (*not* co-owner). File a federal income tax return in your child's name and state thereon that the child elects to report the interest annually. But it is not necessary that the election to report interest annually be made in the first year the bonds are purchased. You may do that at any time. In the year the election is made, all the interest earned to date on all E or EE bonds held must be declared as interest income for that year. Also the first return should state that it is being filed to establish the taxpayer's intent to be an accrual basis taxpayer for savings bonds under Section 454 of the Internal Revenue Code. A tax return is only required in future years (reporting only that year's bond interest accrual) if your child's total unearned (investment) income exceeds his or her personal exemption *or* his total income exceeds his personal exemption plus his standard deduction.

Thus, when your child cashes his or her bonds to meet the costs of college, all the accrued interest on the bonds will be free from federal income tax. And the interest is also exempt from all state and local income taxes and personal property taxes.

Or you might buy the bonds in your child's name, with yourself as beneficiary, and not file a federal income tax return until your child starts college and begins to cash in the bonds for his or her educational expenses. Your child then would file a tax return each year and report the full amount of interest on the redeemed bonds as income.

As of the tax laws of the late 1970s, if the total amount of your child's investment income was less than $1,000 a year, no income tax would be due. (The tax-free income of the child could increase considerably more if the child had "earned income" in addition to his investment income. In this regard, earned income does not include interest or dividends.)

If you use the first Tax-Free Education Plan, be sure you keep a copy of the tax return you file to prove "intent."

A Financially Intelligent Attitude
Toward Buying and Holding Savings Bonds

If you buy the bonds via payroll savings, they are a superb way to force yourself to save small amounts regularly and, by so doing, to accumulate a basic reserve. But a rate of 6 per cent does not cover the erosion in your return from spiraling living costs and steep income taxes in the late 1970s.

If inflation is to be our way of life in the rest of the twentieth century as it has been in the past, the Treasury will not be fair to buyers of its bonds until it offers a purchasing power guarantee—e.g., a bond with a dollar value that would rise as the cost-of-living index rose.

This is not a new idea—and, in fact, in the United States in recent years we have been moving closer and closer to purchasing power guarantees to give major segments of our population some automatic protections against steadily rising prices. Social Security benefits are now automatically tied to increases in the Consumer Price Index. Cost-of-living escalator clauses have become commonplace in union wage contracts. The record high interest rates of the 1970s reflect, in part at least, efforts to protect investors in marketable fixed-income securities from the erosion of inflation.

The very least the Treasury should do is give the subject the exhaustive study it demands but since even the study is still in the future, once you've accumulated your nest egg, maintain only a modest proportion in savings bonds.

Divide the balance among sound investments which will grow as our economy grows and, thereby, put and keep you well ahead.

In essence, savings bonds will help you create a nest egg. Other investments will help you enhance it.

CHANGES FOR THE 1980s

In 1980, significant changes occur in this great savings program. Briefly, on January 2, 1980, the Treasury is introducing:

• A series EE bond to replace the series E bond that has been on sale since 1941.

• A series HH bond, to replace the current series H bond that has been on sale since 1952.

• An exchange offering, under which owners of E bonds and savings notes (and, later, the EE bonds) can exchange them, with a tax deferral privilege, for series HH bonds.

SERIES EE BONDS

The series EE bond—so named because it will double in value between its purchase and maturity dates—will retain the tax-deferral advantage of the present E bond.

The new features are:

• The purchase price is one half the face value, e.g., $25 will buy a $50 (face value) bond.

• The lowest available denomination is $50, face value. Other denominations are $75, $100, $200, $500, $1,000, $5,000 and $10,000.

• The interest rate of 6 per cent (for five or more years) remains the same as E bonds, while the term to maturity will be eleven years and nine months.

• But assuming a boost in the EE bond rate above 6 per cent, the term to maturity will be shortened.

• The annual limitation on purchases is increased from the present $7,500 (issue amount) to $15,000 (issue amount).

• The new EE bonds can be cashed in six months after purchase.

• The requirement that a bond beneficiary must consent to a change in the bond is eliminated.

Although the familiar $25 savings bond ($18.75 purchase price) no longer will be available after January 2, 1980, the new series EE $50 bond can be purchased for $25, an increase of only $6.25 in the minimum purchase price.

SERIES HH BONDS

The series HH bond has these new features, as compared to the long-outstanding H bond:

• Interest payments are a level 6 per cent from day of purchase, rather than the present graduated scale.

• Bonds purchased for cash (rather than through exchange of other savings bonds) are subject to an interest penalty if redeemed before maturity.

• The annual purchase limitation is increased from $10,000 (face amount) to $20,000 (face amount).

The new series HH bonds can be bought for cash or obtained in exchange for the present series E or EE bonds or savings notes, singly or in combination, in multiples of $500. The new HH bond has the same maturity period as the H bond and the same denominations.

SERIES E AND H BONDS IN THE 1980s

Changes which affect owners of the present E and H bonds are:

• The earliest E bonds—bought between 1941 and April 1952—will not be extended again when they fall due between 1981 and April 1992, after forty years of interest-bearing life.

• Series H bonds bought from June 1952 through May 1959 will receive no further extensions. These bonds reach final maturity between February 1982 and May 1989.

• Owners of E bonds and savings notes can exchange them for the new HH bonds after they go on sale January 2, 1980. This can be done up to a year after final maturity of the old E bonds. This exchange carries the same tax-deferral privilege as the present E to H bond exchange.

The changes should dispel any uncertainty about the Treasury's position on the final maturity of outstanding E and H bonds. Holders of the 1941–52 series E bonds thus will have the opportunity to decide well in advance of their bonds' final maturity whether to redeem them for cash or exchange them for HH bonds.

But the new EE and HH bonds will not be available until January 2, 1980.

The present E and H bonds will continue to be sold at banks and other savings institutions until *December 31, 1979, and up to June 1980* on payroll savings plans, depending on how fast your company converts to the new bonds.

Both the E and EE bonds pay an identical 6 per cent interest rate when held five years or more.

COMPARISON OF TERMS AND CONDITIONS OF SERIES H AND SERIES HH CURRENT INCOME-TYPE SAVINGS BONDS

	SERIES H BONDS	SERIES HH BONDS
Offering date	Terminate December 31, 1979	Begin January 2, 1980
Denominations	$500, $1,000, $5,000, $10,000	Same
Issue price	Face amount	Same
Maturity	10 years with guaranteed 20-year extension	10 years
Interest	Payable semiannually by check	Same
Yield curve	4.2% first 6 months, 5.8% next 4½ years, 6.5% final 5 years to yield 6% if held to maturity. During extension, uniform payments based on rate prevailing when bond enters extended maturity.	Payments based on 6% level rate, however, bonds sold for cash will have an interest penalty applied against redemption value, if redeemed prior to maturity. Bonds issued on exchange will not be penalized for early redemption.
Retention period	Redeemable any time after 6 months from issue date.	Same
Annual limitation	$10,000 face amount	$20,000 face amount
Tax status	Interest is subject to federal income tax reporting in year it is paid. Bonds subject to estate, inheritance and gift taxes — federal and state — but exempt from all other state and local taxes.	Same
Registration	In names of individuals in single, co-ownership or beneficiary form; in names of fiduciaries or organizations in single ownership only.	Same
Transferability	Not eligible for transfer or pledge as collateral.	Same

	SERIES H BONDS	SERIES HH BONDS
Rights of owners	Co-ownership: either owner may redeem; both must join reissue request. Beneficiary: only owner may redeem during lifetime; both must join reissue request.	Co-ownership: same. Beneficiary: same except that consent of beneficiary to reissue not required.
Exchange privilege	Issuable on exchange from Series E bonds and savings notes, in multiples of $500, with continued tax deferral privilege.	Issuable on exchange from Series E, EE, and savings notes, in multiples of $500, with continued tax deferral privilege.

COMPARISON OF TERMS AND CONDITIONS OF
SERIES E AND SERIES EE
ACCRUAL-TYPE SAVINGS BONDS

	SERIES E BONDS	SERIES EE BONDS
Offering date	Close over-the-counter sales December 31, 1979; close payroll sales June 30, 1980	Begin January 2, 1980; phase in payroll sales through June 30, 1980
Denominations	$25, $50, $75, $100, $200, $500, $1,000, $10,000	$50, $75, $100, $200, $500, $1,000, $5,000, $10,000
Issue price	75% of face amount	50% of face amount
Maturity	5 years with guaranteed 20-year extension	11 years and 9 months
Interest	Accrues through periodic increases in redemption value to maturity	Same
Yield curve	4% after 2 months, 4.5% first year, increases gradually thereafter to yield 6% if held 5 years	4% after 2 months, 4.5% first year, increases gradually thereafter to yield 6% if held 5 or more years
Retention period	Redeemable any time after 2 months from issue date	Redeemable any time after 6 months from issue date
Annual limitation	$7,500 issue price	$15,000 issue price
Tax status	Accruals subject to federal income and to estate, inheritance and gift taxes — federal and state — but exempt from all other state and local taxes. Federal income tax may be reported (1) as it accrues, or (2) in year bond matures, is redeemed or otherwise disposed	Same

	SERIES E BONDS	SERIES EE BONDS
Registration	In names of individuals in single, co-ownership or beneficiary form; in names of fiduciaries or organizations in single ownership only	Same
Transferability	Not eligible for transfer or pledge as collateral	Same
Rights of owners	Co-ownership: either owner may redeem, both must join reissue request. Beneficiary: only owner may redeem during lifetime; both must join reissue request	Co-ownership: same Beneficiary: same except that consent of beneficiary to reissue not required
Exchange privilege	Eligible, alone or with savings notes, for exchange for Series H bonds in multiples of $500, with tax deferral privilege	Eligible, alone or with Series E bonds or savings notes, for exchange for Series HH bonds in multiples of $500, with tax deferral privilege

COMPARISON OF THE TERMS AND CONDITIONS OF
CURRENT INCOME BOND EXCHANGE OFFERINGS

	SERIES H EXCHANGE	SERIES HH EXCHANGE
Offering date	Terminate December 31, 1979	Begin January 2, 1980
Eligible securities	Series E Bonds and Savings Notes, singly or in combination	Series E Bonds, Savings Notes, and Series EE Bonds, singly or in combination; E Bonds must be received no later than one year following their final maturity date
Minimum amount	$500 current redemption value of accrual-type securities	Same
Annual purchase limitation	Exempt	Same
Exchange security	Series H Bonds including all terms and conditions thereof	Series HH Bonds, including all terms and conditions thereof except that bonds redeemed prior to maturity will not be subject to the interest penalty

	SERIES H EXCHANGE	SERIES HH EXCHANGE
Eligible owners	Registered owners, co-owners and persons entitled as surviving beneficiaries or next of kin or legatees of deceased owners	Same
Tax treatment	Accrued interest on retired securities may be (1) reported on federal income tax return for year of exchange (or maturity, if earlier), or (2) deferred to the taxable year in which the current income bonds are redeemed, disposed of or mature. Amount of deferred accruals will be shown on face of new bonds	Same
Registration of bonds issued on exchange	Tax deferred: new bonds will be in name of owner and in same forms as securities submitted except that principal coowner, as defined in Circular, may change, add or eliminate co-owner or beneficiary. Non-tax deferred: any authorized form	Same
Cash adjustments	If securities submitted for exchange have current value which is not an even multiple of $500, subscriber may add cash to reach next highest multiple or receive payment of amount in excess of next lower multiple. In the latter case, amount of refund must be reported currently for federal income tax purposes	Same

THE BAFFLEGAB OF SAVINGS BONDS

ACCRUAL-TYPE SECURITY   This is the E or EE bond type—a bond sold at a discount and which gradually increases to above its face amount at maturity. The difference between the purchase price and the amount received for the bond when you redeem it is your interest.

ACCRUED INTEREST   Interest that has been earned on savings bonds but has not been collected, because the bond has not been redeemed by the holder.

APPRECIATION-TYPE SECURITY   Same as Accrual-type Security, above.

CHAIN-LETTER SCHEMES   Illegal get-rich-quick schemes which frequently are built around Series E savings bonds. If you purchase savings bonds as an innocent participant in a fraudulent chain-letter deal, you may request a refund of your money. Get and use Treasury Form PD-2966, available at any local bank.

COLLATERAL Securities or other property pledged by a borrower against the payment of a loan. Savings bonds cannot be used as collateral for loans.

CURRENT-INCOME SECURITY This is the H or HH bond type. A bond sold at face value (par value) on which a specified amount of interest is paid semi-annually.

DENOMINATION Face amount of various savings bonds. Both the E and EE bonds have eight denominations, up to $10,000. The H and HH bonds have four, up to $10,000.

EXTENDED MATURITIES Extension by the U. S. Treasury of original maturity date on savings bonds for an additional ten-year period. Owners need do nothing to take advantage of the extension of maturity. Just hold the bonds.

FREEDOM SHARES U.S. savings notes sold from 1967 through mid-1970. No longer on sale. However, the original savings notes were granted a twenty-year extension beyond their initial four-and-a-half-year maturity date at the 6 per cent current interest rate.

ISSUE PRICE Price actually paid for bond by the buyer. Differs from denominations in E and EE bonds and Freedom Shares, because issue price is at a discount from the denomination, and that difference is the interest which accrues on the bond or share until it finally matures or is redeemed, in advance of final maturity.

NON-MARKETABLE BONDS Non-negotiable securities which cannot be sold or bought in the open market. Savings bonds are non-marketable securities.

PURCHASE LIMIT Maximum of savings bonds which can be bought by one owner in a single year.

REGISTERED BOND Bond with its owner's name recorded on the books of the issuer. With savings bonds, the owner's name is recorded by the United States Treasury.

SAVINGS STAMPS No longer issued by the U. S. Treasury. If you have or find any of these 10-cent to $5.00 stamps, cash them in at your post office or bank (if it will redeem stamps) or add enough cash to acquire a small-denomination E bond.

TAX DEFERMENT Postponement of taxes. Payment of federal income tax on interest accrued on E bonds may be deferred to redemption, other disposition, or final redemption of the bonds.

WAR BONDS Also called Defense Bonds. Series A, B, C, D, F, G, J, K or any other letter of the alphabet, except E and H are no longer being issued and are no longer earning interest. If you hold or find any of these series, redeem them at once. Send them by registered mail to the Federal Reserve Bank or branch in your district or to the Bureau of the Public Debt, Securities Transactions Branch, Washington, D.C. 20226. Many banks are not qualified to handle this redemption for you. (Soon the E and H bonds also no longer will be issued but they will continue to earn interest).

25

YOUR GUIDE TO THE EXPLODING COMMODITY MARKETS —FOR SPECULATORS AND HEDGERS

THE TWO CATEGORIES OF TRADERS

How would you like to buy 5,000 bushels of soybeans, or 38,000 pounds of pork bellies, or 1,000,000 Swiss francs? Does this seem more exotic and "far out" to you than buying, say, American Telephone & Telegraph shares or settling for an account in a nearby savings institution?

If the thought of trading such provocative items does appeal to you, you merely would be joining mounting millions of other Americans in all income and age brackets, at all levels of education, men and women, married and single, living in areas scattered throughout the United States who in the 1970s discovered and became active in the commodity futures markets.

Futures trading boomed during the 1970s and the explosive growth shows no signs of slowing, much less ending.

Commodity traders fall into one of two broad categories—hedgers and speculators—and both groups began their spectacular expansion at the start of the 1970s.

Hedgers are individuals or corporations who use the futures markets in the course of their business operations to protect themselves against adverse price fluctuations. Commodity prices can and do fluctuate dramatically, and these changes can have a significant impact on profit margins. When producers and users of commodities can free themselves from worry in this sphere, they can concentrate on running their businesses more efficiently, and this increased efficiency is of general public benefit. Stripped of all hopped-up hoopla, this probably is the most important reason for the existence of futures exchanges.

The number of hedgers has increased sharply for two important reasons: (1) the heightened volatility of commodity prices during the 1970s made hedge protection especially desirable and, in some industries, virtually indispensable; (2) more and more businessmen have learned both the mechanics and the benefits of hedging. Later in this chapter, you'll find references to several publications that discuss this subject in depth for you.

The speculator category is loaded with individuals (qualified or utterly unqualified) who trade commodities because they hope to make money by so doing. Doctors, lawyers, businessmen, accountants, and just about every other occupational group are among the swelling ranks of futures speculators.

POWERFUL FORCES BEHIND THE BOOM

Why have so many millions turned on to futures trading in recent years? Among the most powerful forces behind the commodity boom:

(a) The combined impact of accelerated inflation and intermittent worldwide shortages of a wide variety of agricultural and industrial items have sparked substantial price moves in many commodities. These increasingly volatile price changes have been widely publicized, alerting more and more people to the profit opportunities open to those who can accurately forecast commodity prices.

(b) Commodity trading is done on relatively small margin requirements. As a general rule, a speculator must post only about 5 to 20 per cent of the value of the commodity traded. This substantial leverage allows huge sums to be made (or lost) very quickly. It is not at all unusual for a commodity speculator to double or lose all his trading capital within a few weeks.

(c) Futures contracts can be sold short in exactly the same manner as they are bought. Thus it makes no difference whether prices are rising or falling—a trader who can predict correctly how prices will change can profit with equal ease in both bull and bear markets.

(d) The number and variety of futures contracts has multiplied dramatically in recent years. In addition to such traditional items as corn, sugar, and soybeans, the futures spectrum now includes such varied "commodities" as gold, silver, live cattle, foreign currencies, and U. S. Treasury Bills (and by the time you read this, there even may be a futures contract based on the Dow Jones Industrial Average!). If you have a firmly held opinion in any economic arena you probably can find a futures contract that will allow you to put your ideas to the toughest test: risking your whole nest egg.

(e) Commodity market information is easy to obtain. Securities traders have trouble finding up-to-the-minute news on any but the most active of the more than three thousand companies listed on the New York and American exchanges alone. Commodity traders have no such trouble. Only about 35 commodities have active futures contracts, and current information on all of them is readily available. Everyone involved with commodities has access to the facts. Whether you succeed or fail depends on whether you know how to understand and use those facts.

(f) Commission costs for futures transactions are very low—usually amounting to much less than 1 per cent of the value of the underlying commodity. What's more, these charges apply only when a position is closed out, not when it is initiated.

Intriguing, isn't it? If you like action and have a few thousand dollars or more with which to *play,* then the commodity futures markets could be for you. But futures trading can be a bewildering and costly experience if you try it without at least a basic concept of what makes it tick. So here goes . . .

How Commodities Are Traded

Commodities are traded on commodity futures exchanges. These exchanges are located in major U.S. cities, plus London, Paris, Hong Kong, and other cities around the world. The biggest of the dozen or so U.S. exchanges is the Chicago Board of Trade (CBOT), which accounts for about half of all the trading done on U.S. futures exchanges. The Board of Trade was founded in 1848, and is the home of trading in the all-important midwestern agricultural commodities, among the most significant of which are wheat, corn, and soybeans. The Chicago Mercantile Exchange (CME) is the second largest commodity exchange, and in recent years has been the fastest growing. It is the hub of the nation's huge livestock activity, and has active futures contracts in live cattle, live hogs, and frozen pork bellies (bacon), among others. The CME also has a subsidiary exchange known as the International Monetary Market (IMM) which trades futures in eight different foreign currencies. The U.S. dollar's well-publicized battering during the late 1970s helped spark interest in these challenging contracts. Both the CBOT and CME also offer interest rate futures contracts, which became increasingly popular among both financial institutions and speculators after their inception in the mid-1970s.

The Commodity Exchange, Inc., of New York offers futures contracts in gold, silver, and copper, and is the third largest U.S. commodity futures exchange. Other important New York exchanges include: the New York Coffee and Sugar Exchange, the New York Cocoa Exchange, the New York Cotton Exchange, and the New York Mercantile Exchange. The Kansas City Board of Trade and the Minneapolis Grain Exchange offer futures contracts in types of wheat different from the CBOT. The Mid-America Commodity Exchange (MACE) in Chicago offers "mini-contracts" in several major commodities. For instance, the MACE soybean contract consists of one thousand bushels compared with the CBOT's five-thousand-bushel contract. Outside the United States, the major futures markets are in London. The most important of these are the London Metal Exchange, the London Cocoa Terminal Market, and the London Sugar Exchange.

Despite the rich variety of commodities and locations, all futures markets operate in much the same fashion. Commodity exchanges, like stock exchanges, are membership organizations. Most members are either engaged in the producing, marketing, or processing of commodities, or are brokers whose principal activity is to execute orders for others. Non-members trade through brokerage firms, which hold memberships through partners or officers. The exchanges are supported by dues and assessments on members.

The basic unit in commodity trading is the futures contract. Futures contracts are standardized in terms of quantity, quality, and location and require delivery of the commodity during a specified month in the future. Thus if you, a trader, buy one contract of December soybean oil, you know that you are taking responsibility for sixty thousand pounds of soybean oil that will be delivered in Decatur, Illinois, or at a specified alternate delivery point, sometime in December. Actually, only 1 or 2 per cent of all futures contracts are settled by physical delivery. The rest are offset by an opposite futures transaction prior to maturity.

Commodity futures trading in the United States is strictly regulated both by the exchanges themselves and by the Commodity Futures Trading Commission (CFTC), which is an agency of the federal government. The long history of active trading and the steady growth of participation in futures are evidence of the diligent supervision by both exchange and government personnel.

Most prospective commodity traders have had experience with securities, and the chances are that their own securities firm also handles futures transactions. In addition to the major, full-service brokerage firms, there are firms which specialize in commodities and handle little or no business in other areas. Some brokerage houses require a minimum initial deposit (usually $3,000 to $5,000) to open a commodity account. Others have no minimums and will accept accounts as small as several hundred dollars.

Once your account is opened, trading commodities becomes a simple matter (at least as far as the mechanics are concerned!). You need only call and tell your broker how many contracts of a particular commodity you wish to buy or sell, and at what price. The broker then will relay your order to the trading floor of the appropriate exchange. After it is executed, the brokerage firm's representatives on the trading floor will report back to your broker, who will relay the information to you. Often, this entire procedure takes no more than several minutes. Within a few days of every transaction, you will receive a written confirmation of your activities.

Every time you initiate a futures position you will be required to post a specific amount of margin money with your brokerage firm. Commodity margins are really performance bonds that guarantee the customer's willingness to accept any profits or losses. In general, you, the customer, are asked to put up an original margin deposit equal to 5 per cent to 20 per cent of the total value of the commodities involved. Minimum margin requirements are set by the commodity exchanges themselves, but brokerage houses are free to require higher margins if they wish. Margin requirements are always specific dollar amounts rather than percentages—e.g., $1,000 per contract of copper or $2,500 per contract of soybeans. Unlike the securities market, there are no interest charges on the difference between margin and full cost.

Another unique feature of futures markets is the existence of daily trading limits. To lessen the likelihood of an overly extreme market response to unusually dramatic news, all U.S. (and most foreign) exchanges have adopted maximum fluctuation limits beyond which prices cannot move in the course of a trading session. For example, the daily limit on silver is 20 cents. Thus if July silver closes at $5.50 one day, its permissible range the following day will be $5.30 to $5.70. If there are no bids at or above the lower end of this range or no offers at or below the upper extreme, no trading will take place.

Minimum price fluctuations also are set by the exchanges, and although these usually appear small, the quantities of the various commodities involved are large enough to make even minor price changes significant.

For instance, the minimum price fluctuation for wheat, corn, and soybeans is

¼ cent per bushel. Doesn't sound like much, does it? But multiply that by 5,000 bushels (the size of a single futures contract) and you'll find that you, as a trader, make or lose $12.50 every time the price changes by the minimum amount—which it often does several times a minute! And if that's not fast enough action, you can always trade five, ten, fifty, or more contracts at a time! To give you a clearer idea of what commodity price changes mean to you in terms of real, out-of-pocket dollars, the following table shows the *effects of a 1-cent price move* (up or down) in a variety of the more actively traded items:

COMMODITY	EXCHANGE	CONTRACT SIZE	EFFECT OF 1¢ PRICE CHANGE
Cattle (Live)	Chicago Mercantile	40,000 lbs.	$ 400
Cocoa	New York Cocoa	30,000 lbs.	300
Copper	COMEX (NY)	25,000 lbs.	250
Corn	Chicago Board of Trade	5,000 bushels	50
Cotton	New York Cotton	50,000 lbs.	500
Hogs	Chicago Mercantile	30,000 lbs.	300
Pork Bellies	Chicago Mercantile	38,000 lbs.	380
Potatoes	New York Mercantile	50,000 lbs.	500
Silver	COMEX (NY)	5,000 troy oz.	500
Soybeans	Chicago Board of Trade	5,000 bushels	50
Sugar	New York Coffee & Sugar	112,000 lbs.	1,120
Swiss francs	IMM of CME	125,000 francs	1,250
Wheat	Chicago Board of Trade	5,000 bushels	50

MARKET ANALYSIS

Commodity traders usually divide market analysis into two general categories —fundamental and technical. Fundamental analysis deals with the basic forces of supply and demand, production and consumption. The fundamentalist wants to know how much is being grown, how much eaten, how much exported, and so forth. He attempts to predict prices by applying basic economic principles to the commodities being traded.

Technicians (or chartists, as they are often called) believe that past market behavior holds the key to successful forecasting. The technician's most important tool is a chart of price action which reflects the interaction of all the various forces of supply and demand. By analyzing various price patterns on their charts, technicians attempt to identify the current trend and project it into the future. Chart analysis has been around since the late nineteenth century, but became especially popular among commodity traders beginning in the mid-1960s.

FUNDAMENTAL ANALYSIS

As a futures trader, you must pay at least some attention to market fundamentals. You may follow only the most general statistics relating to national or international supply and demand considerations. Or you may analyze fundamentals in as much detail as you can, looking at local weather conditions, daily changes in wholesale prices, etc. A general rule is that short-term price movements may depend heavily on minor or localized changes in the supply/demand picture, while long-range trends will be determined by broader forces.

A major attraction of the commodity markets is the fact that so much fundamental information is so readily available. Market news flows from the U. S. Government, the futures exchanges, private research organizations, trade and industry groups, brokerage firms. Through its Departments of Agriculture and Commerce, the U. S. Government is easily the most important source of raw commodity data, releasing huge amounts of data relating to crop production, imports, exports, livestock numbers, etc. Most of the U. S. Government's statistics are carried on the various financial newswires, and the major news releases are printed in the financial section of the big-city newspapers.

Because the output of commodity data is so voluminous, nearly all traders rely to some extent on professional analysts to collect the various pieces of information and put them together in proper perspective. Of the oldest and most respected publications dealing with market fundamentals, two are put out by Commodity Research Bureau, Inc., 1 Liberty Plaza, New York, New York 10006. CRB's Commodity Year Book has been published annually since 1939. The Year Book contains separate statistical sections for each of more than a hundred commodities, more than a hundred charts of long-term price trends, and a wide range of articles each year on subjects of interest to commodity traders.

Commodity Research Bureau also has published a weekly newsletter called Futures Market Service, since 1934, popularly known as the "blue sheet." The blue sheet discusses the current fundamentals affecting each of more than twenty commodities and each week carries an in-depth analysis, complete with charts, of provocative market situations.

Brokerage houses are another worthwhile source of fundamental market information. Most brokerage firms publish weekly or biweekly market letters, and some of the larger firms have internal newswires in each of their branch offices with a portion of the space devoted to commodity news. In addition, nearly every brokerage house branch office that takes its commodity business seriously has at least one of the two major commodity newswires—Reuters and Commodity News Service (CNS). Both of these wire services carry commodity information exclusively and are essential for brokers and traders who want to stay abreast of current market developments. The two services carry virtually the same information, and many brokers choose between them more for reasons of style than substance.

The futures exchanges themselves publish useful information for fundamentally oriented traders as well. The various major exchanges maintain their own statistical departments, which compile and release figures pertinent to their particular futures contracts. Most exchanges publish daily printed market reports disclosing the most important of these statistics along with a summary of the day's trading activity. These letters are available to you, the public, at relatively modest cost.

TECHNICAL ANALYSIS

The central problem which fundamentally oriented traders must face is deciding when a market will respond to the various pieces of its supply/demand puzzle. Few experiences are as frustrating as correctly diagnosing the fundamental outlook and losing money anyway because of poor market timing. After being too early a few times, and too late a few other times, if you are typical of most traders you will turn to technical analysis for assistance.

WHAT IS THE VALUE OF CHARTS?

Here there is a considerable difference of opinion. Some experts hold that price changes in broad, liquid markets are strictly "random" and that price behavior of the past has no relationship whatever to price changes of the future. Others regard charting as some sort of magic key to trading profits, and refuse even to give a passing glance to fundamentals.

The truth must lie somewhere in between. Technical analysis is neither a complete waste of time nor the road to instant wealth. It is an important and valuable forecasting technique used by large and growing numbers of hedgers, speculators, analysts, and others whose businesses require them to anticipate market trends. Technical analysis "took off" in popularity among futures traders starting in the early 1960s, and today even the most diehard fundamentalists pay at least some attention to the charts—even if only to see what the technicians are likely to do next.

The purpose of technical analysis is to measure the relative strengths of buying and selling pressures. The actual forecasting process consists of identifying and interpreting various chart "formations" which, over the years, have correlated with subsequent price moves in a particular direction. Vertical line charts are the most frequently used technical tool. On these charts, each day's price action is represented by a vertical line connecting the high and the low of the session. A short cross line marks the closing price.

Commodity chartists are particularly concerned with identifying *trends,* which play a key role in futures trading. Commodity futures markets have a well-established reputation for extensive moves in one particular direction. Since charts make it possible for you to visualize the presence or absence of a clear trend, no wonder they are popular! The chartist's main objective is to identify the existence of a prevailing trend as quickly as possible after it begins, and to trade with the trend until there is evidence of a reversal.

Do not be dismayed by the following financial bafflegab, but technicians also pay special attention to *support and resistance levels, continuation patterns,* and *reversal formations.*

In simplest explanation, support and resistance areas are price regions in which previous trading activity was especially heavy or meaningful. Because traders have a penchant for "getting even," prices are likely to have difficulty moving above a resistance area or below a support level.

Continuation patterns are pauses of several days to several weeks that usually are followed by a resumption of the previous trend.

Reversal formations, as the name implies, signal major trend changes.

Because constructing charts for the dozens of active futures contracts is such a laborious process, almost all technicians subscribe to a professional chart service. By far the most popular of these services is Commodity Chart Service, published weekly by Commodity Research Bureau, Inc., and containing over two hundred futures charts, analytical comments, and a variety of additional statistical information. As a subscriber you are given (free) booklets explaining the basic principles of chart analysis.

If you want to learn more about chart analysis, you can consult several excellent books on the subject. The so-called bible is *Technical Analysis of Stock Market Trends* by Robert D. Edwards and John Magee (John Magee, Springfield, Massachusetts). While this book deals almost exclusively with securities, most of the technical principles also can be applied to futures. The same is true of William L. Jiler's *How Charts Can Help You in the Stock Market* (Trendline, New York, New York), a more recent work than that of Edwards and Magee. Jiler is president of Commodity Research Bureau and one of the most widely known and respected authorities on the technical analysis of futures markets.

Though there are "pure" fundamentalists and "pure" technicians, if you are to be like nearly all successful traders you will employ a blend of these two techniques.

Thus, if you think the supply/demand picture for wheat points to significantly higher prices, you would be wise to check whether the wheat charts also look bullish before laying any cash on the line.

Even complete agreement between charts and fundamentals cannot ensure profits, but if you avoid market situations where the two approaches disagree markedly, you will have a useful safeguard against catastrophe.

THE GREAT PITFALLS, HOW TO IDENTIFY AND AVOID THEM

Let's say you are intrigued rather than frightened by the pitfalls that confront all futures traders, you are willing to spend the time learning, say, where soybeans are grown, and you've figured out such bafflegab as the difference between an uptrend line and a symmetric triangle. Now you think you are ready to grab the challenges and make your fortune in grains or livestock or precious metals.

But wait! You are *not* ready unless you also have thoroughly grasped the basic rules of successful commodity trading and have taken a solemn, unbreakable vow that you will respect and obey them always. The rules that follow won't *guarantee* you success (no rules can) but they will give you at least a fighting chance to avoid losing your entire capital and even a chance to win.

(1) Before you trade a single commodity futures contract, make a list of several actively traded commodities whose movements you would like to follow.

Learn everything you can about these markets—via United States Department of Agriculture publications, brokerage house letters, and independent advisory services such as Futures Market Service. Keep up-to-date on all basic forces affecting the prices of each item—weather, crop forecasts, consumption trends, etc. You need not know as much as the experts to trade successfully, but even if you rely heavily on the advice of others, you should be able to understand and draw your own conclusions about the advice.

(2) Trade through a reputable brokerage firm that is financially sound and has solid experience in the markets in which you plan to trade too. Most of the major stock brokerage firms have commodity divisions and are well qualified on this score. There also are several well capitalized and highly regarded specialized commodity firms that have national branch office networks.

(3) Do not trade with money that you cannot afford to lose! Commodity trading can be enjoyable, stimulating, and sometimes very profitable. But it is always a *risky* venture. Speculate only with money you can afford to lose without affecting either your financial state or your peace of mind.

(4) Before you begin to speculate, decide on an overall plan and stick to it. Are you a fundamentalist or a technician? Will you be looking for short-term or long-term price moves? How much are you willing to risk before reappraising your trading approach? Answer these and other similar questions as honestly as you can before you risk a single dollar on a futures position.

(5) Be faithful to the old guide: "Cut your losses short and let your profits run." This is the *cardinal* rule of futures trading. The most spectacularly successful commodity speculators have more losing than winning trades, but they come out ahead in the long run because their average profits far exceed their average losses. Many speculators who consistently make money actually profit on only about one third of their trades. Bob Feduniak, now senior vice-president of Commodity Research Bureau, ran the managed commodity account program for one of the largest Wall Street brokerage firms from late 1973 to early 1976. Feduniak told me that during that period he made 215 trades. Of that number, *only 72, or 33 per cent, were profitable,* but his typical account, starting with $15,000–$25,000 showed a net profit of more than $20,000. Taking small losses quickly is the best protection you can have against the one or two ruinous defeats that could remove you from the trading game permanently. Letting profits run is the best way to make the trending tendency of commodity prices work for you rather than against you.

(6) Use stop-loss orders as your most effective safeguard against letting your losses balloon. These orders instruct your broker to offset your position once prices have reached a specified adverse level. Your broker can tell you more about "stops" as they are called, and guide you in placing them. And never—*never*—move your stop order even one penny in the direction of further risk.

(7) Don't try to pick tops and bottoms. While it's only human to try to buy things at their cheapest and sell at their most expensive, in commodity trading that temptation can be suicidal. To repeat it once again, the reason is that futures prices often trend in a particular direction much longer than most people expect. When you spot a trend, ride with it—don't try to guess when it will reverse.

(8) Don't be in the market all the time. Nobody—not even the most astute, full-time professional traders—can understand what is happening in a market day in and day out. At times, fundamentals are confusing, charts look fuzzy, and you can't tell pork bellies from soybean oil. When these times come, as they do for everyone, you belong on the sidelines. Save your money and your energy for the time ahead when you feel confident about where prices are headed.

(9) Don't trade inactive markets. On some futures markets, average daily trading volume totals ten thousand, twenty thousand, or more contracts. On others, only a handful of contracts are traded each week. Learn which markets are which (the newspapers publish volume statistics) and restrict yourself to the most actively traded commodities. You will find thinly traded markets difficult to move into and out of, and the lack of interested traders usually makes it hard to get vital information.

(10) Don't overtrade. No matter how convinced you are that the price of a particular commodity is headed up or down, resist the temptation to risk a large portion of your trading capital on a single position. Any number of unforeseen events, ranging from hurricanes to wars, can violently change a price outlook literally overnight. *There is no sure thing in commodities*, so always try to diversify into at least two or three markets.

(11) Never trade on the basis of tips or rumors. Base your trading on the best factual information you can find, and ignore the advice of anyone doing you a "favor" by offering "inside information."

(12) Approach commodity trading as an avocation and not a one-shot deal. Realize that commodity trading is an exceedingly complex business, and view your first year or two as an educational period. Pace your trading so you'll be able to learn from early errors and still have enough capital left to take advantage of what you will have learned.

MANAGED ACCOUNTS AND COMMODITY FUNDS

If by now you're really impressed by the potential rewards of commodity trading and still undaunted but you lack the time or inclination to follow the markets yourself and you fear making your own decisions, then professional account management may be the answer for you. A sizable and growing number of brokerage firms and private traders will handle futures transactions on a strictly discretionary basis. That is: you put up the money, they do the trading. Not surprisingly, the various programs and managers span the spectrum from excellent to fraudulent, so if you are considering this route, you must investigate each situation with utmost caution before laying any cash on the line.

The two most common ways for you to arrange to have your commodity trading handled by someone else are via (1) managed accounts and (2) commodity funds.

A managed account is simply an ordinary commodity account over which you give the manager limited power of attorney. This allows the manager to transact business in your account without consulting you, while you retain responsibility for all profits and losses.

A commodity fund is similar to a securities mutual fund. Each participant owns shares of the fund (or, more typically, units in a limited partnership) and trading is done in the account of the fund rather than in the accounts of the individual participants.

The principal advantages of a commodity fund are limited liability and increased flexibility. As a limited partner, your losses cannot exceed your original investment, whereas in an ordinary commodity (or security) margin account you are liable for any deficits that might occur. Also, since limited partners' funds are pooled, the trading account has the usual advantages of diversification and handling which very large traders also enjoy.

The main advantage of a managed account over a fund is your retention of some control. In general, limited partners have no say in how their fund is handled and can withdraw only at specified times since the secondary market for these units is virtually non-existent. But as the owner of an individual account, you can close the account or revoke power of attorney at any time—giving you greater continuing voice in the handling of your futures money.

The costs of professional money management in commodities are comparatively reasonable. Several of the large brokerage firms maintain internally run managed programs and impose no charges at all beyond the usual commissions. Private managers generally charge a fee of around 1 to 1½ per cent per quarter of an account's equity, plus 5 to 15 per cent of any profits. Most reputable firms require that managed accounts be of a specified minimum size—usually in the $15,000 to $25,000 range.

Smaller accounts usually don't generate enough commissions or fees to offset handling costs unless they are overtraded, so beware of anyone who says that he will "professionally manage" accounts of only a few thousand dollars. Limited partnership units, however, frequently sell for around $1,000 each, and can provide a way for you to get into futures trading with smaller amounts of risk capital.

Paying a professional to trade commodities for you is an easy and potentially profitable way to participate in these exciting markets, but the admonition *caveat emptor* applies with brutal force.

If you are considering a fund or limited partnership, read the prospectus carefully.

Pay particular attention to the backgrounds and qualifications of the managers, and to their prior trading records.

If you are looking at individual managers, ask each for a written (and preferably audited) record of his actual trading results for other clients.

Beware of "hypothetical" or "simulated" track records, since these have a way of losing their luster under real-life market conditions.

WHERE TO GET INFORMATION ON COMMODITY TRADING

As emphasized earlier, the best sources of commodity information are the United States Department of Agriculture, private research organizations, brokerage houses, and the various futures exchanges.

The Chicago Board of Trade and the Chicago Mercantile Exchange offer the widest selections of basic information of all the exchanges. Write to them at the addresses below for lists of what is available.

Commodity Research Bureau, Inc., with its several publications already discussed, is the leading private publisher of commodity information. CRB offers a wide variety of books, charts, market letters, statistics, and computerized data for all types of traders. You can obtain a complete list of the CRB's products by writing your request to 1 Liberty Plaza, New York, New York 10006.

The USDA publishes vast quantities of commodity material, most available to you free of charge. For catalogs of the most important reports, along with information on ordering them, write to: Crop Reporting Board, U.S.D.A. Room 005, South Building, Washington, D.C. 20250; and to: U.S.D.A. ESCS Information Staff, Publications Unit, Room 0054-South, Washington, D.C. 20250.

Another source of information is the Association of Commodity Exchange Firms, Inc., 1 World Trade Center, New York, New York 10005.

Here are the addresses of the major exchanges to which you might write for additional material:

Chicago Board of Trade
141 West Jackson Boulevard
Chicago, Illinois 60604

Chicago Mercantile Exchange
444 West Jackson Boulevard
Chicago, Illinois 60606

Commodity Exchange, Inc.
4 World Trade Center
New York, New York 10048

New York Coffee and Sugar Exchange, Inc.
4 World Trade Center
New York, New York 10048

Kansas City Board of Trade
4800 Main Street
Kansas City, Missouri 84112

New York Cocoa Exchange, Inc.
127 John Street
New York, New York 10038

New York Cotton Exchange
4 World Trade Center
New York, New York 10048

New York Mercantile Exchange
4 World Trade Center
New York, New York 10048

Mid-America Commodity Exchange
175 West Jackson Boulevard
Chicago, Illinois 60604

Minneapolis Grain Exchange
400 South Fourth Street
Minneapolis, Minnesota 55415

Many books are available that cover the various facets of commodity markets and futures trading in some detail, and are worthwhile reading if you want to pursue the subject more deeply. Among the best and most popular are:

Modern Commodity Futures Trading, by Gerald Gold (Commodity Research Bureau, Inc., New York, New York)

The Commodity Futures Game, by Richard J. Teweles, Charles V. Harlow, and Herbert L. Stone (McGraw-Hill, Inc., New York, New York)

The Economics of Futures Trading, by Thomas Hieronymus (Commodity Research Bureau, Inc., New York, New York)

Most daily newspapers provide no more than sparse coverage of commodity news in their financial sections. Beginning in the mid-1970s, however, the *Wall Street Journal* significantly expanded its coverage of futures markets, and its commodity page is worthwhile daily reading for anyone interested in or involved with futures.

COMMODITIES SWINDLES—BIGGEST INVESTMENT FRAUD OF THE 1970s

The fraudulent sale of London commodity options was one of the giant telephone swindles of the late 1970s. Falsely touted as "investments" these speculations turned into nightmares for countless thousands of the defrauded victims.

The fraud was so widespread that in mid-1978, the industry's regulator, the Commodity Futures Trading Commission, actually banned the sale of London commodity options in the United States! But the profits of fraud were so great that many of the promoters easily modified their boiler-room, hard-sell campaigns and started selling either diamonds or managed commodity accounts. (For the diamond scheme, see pages 1171–73.) As the price of gold soared in this period, the con men moved quickly into fraudulent sales of the leveraged gold contract and the deferred delivery gold contract.

Even though you may be totally disinterested in and ignorant of commodities or metals, options or managed accounts, you still may be the target of some of the cleverest con men who ever have operated in the United States marketplace.

Your ignorance and gullibility can easily betray you. Your greed will steal your savings!

So when your phone rings in early evening and a fast-talking pitchman tells you in glib terms about the fortunes being made in managed commodity accounts, or leveraged gold contracts, be on guard! First some basics.

Some commodities—such as sugar, coffee, copper—are bought and sold in large quantities in auction markets in London and the United States. That is what this whole chapter has been about. And as stressed, it's complicated. Playing with commodities is only for you if (1) you are a sophisticated speculator, (2) you are more than typically familiar with the intricacies of the market, and (3), most important, you can afford to lose all the money you put up.

If this chapter convinces you merely of these three points and compels you to be cautious, I will have achieved my goal.

THE PITCH

In New York, in Florida, in Ohio, all over the Midwest and West Coast, London commodity options were pushed by such sales pitches as the following hypothetical come-on:

"Hello, Mr. Wilson, I'm calling from ZYX Commodities Co. We sell London options. You know what the price of coffee has done lately and we think sugar is about to do the same thing. But I'm not calling to sell you anything. Just to tell you about commodity options. These are an amazing investment opportunity now available to the American public for the first time.

"As an example, several months ago, we were recommending the purchase of $2,000 copper options. Within one month, the option our clients bought was worth $6,000. That's a killing! I will mail you all the facts so you can see in black and white how you can double and triple your money. The sugar move is already on its way . . ."

About eight days and seven calls later, another call:

"Mr. Wilson, you've already made $110. I bought you an option for $2,500, today it went to $2,610. Wire me the money right away to pick up your option in London.

"My commission? Only 10 per cent. Check us out with the Commodities Futures Trading Commission (CFTC). We're registered. And if you want a banking reference, call . . ."

WHAT'S WRONG WITH THIS PITCH?

(1) Again, the often prestigious sounding but meaningless company name; the wild claims of gains across the board—possible, but highly improbable; the con man's comment that he has reserved an option for you in their London office. There probably isn't even a London office.

(2) As for the 10 per cent commission—not likely! Instead, the commission is likely to be at least double. Commission, fees, overhead, and *profits* may take 60 per cent of your outlay. Buying an option from someone else would be a lot, lot cheaper.

(3) Registered with the CFTC? Yes, by law the firm had to be. But some companies operated without registration. The CFTC found enforcement of its regulations to be exceedingly tough and finally just outlawed London commodity options. What's more, registration with the CFTC did not mean you could believe a telephone pitch. And of course, the company will have a pile of money in the bank (perhaps, including yours).

Beware! The biggest commodity sold in these instances is deception.

THE CON MAN

While obviously the convicted felons operating in the London commodity options market are in a minority, the con man element is a large one. Who are some of these con men?

• One high-pressure promoter working for a company denied registration by the Commodities Futures Trading Commission (CFTC) is a felon who was released from jail in mid-1976 after having been convicted of defrauding gullible investors out of hundreds of thousands of dollars in a "business opportunities" scheme in New Jersey. While in options, he advertised for a "partner" to invest $10,000 in a new venture, claiming in his ad that after the partner put up the $10,000, he would earn a salary of $800 a week.

• The principal of another option company, with offices in New York and Florida, was the subject of action by the Florida attorney general while operating a Florida land resale rip-off. This slippery swindler took money from landowners for assistance in helping them to sell their land, then went out of business, leaving the property owners stuck with their land but without their cash. After options he switched into diamonds but that company folded leaving rent unpaid. Present whereabouts? Unknown.

● A Massapequa Park, New York, resident, a former salesperson for a New York options firm, now bankrupt, pleaded guilty in New York State Supreme Court to a felony arising from her securing her salesman's registration without revealing that she had been permanently enjoined previously from offering or selling securities and commodities within and from New York State. In another, an individual who had been convicted for stealing securities first went to work as a salesman for an options house and, when it folded, formed his own options firm, which failed a few months later. He "accomplished" all of this while on parole!

● *The pattern is clear:* the salespeople and boiler-room organizers travel from options house to options house after the firm for which they are working goes out of business leaving large debts to customers. Often their first entrance into commodity options is when the marginal securities house in which they had been employed goes out of business.

● Record-keeping at these firms is, at best, inadequate and, at worst, horrendous and chaotic. Investigators have discovered that even normal books of accounts used by any business aren't established or maintained. Sending confirmations to customers and mailing checks to customers often are delayed for unreasonable periods or, in many instances, never sent.

In one firm, an employee was able to forge his signature to company checks and received more than $80,000 based on the forged checks without being detected. In documented cases, customers who did receive payments due them actually were receiving funds that had been put into the firm by more recent customers—a modern-day version of one of the oldest swindles in finance.

● Salesmen for the firms are practicing "boiler-room" techniques—swindles that most of you almost surely thought were past history by now. Individuals who had been permanently enjoined from dealing in the offer or sale of commodities and securities have been found working for commodity options firms. Some salesmen have had records of felon convictions for interstate transportation of stolen securities, arson, bad checks, assault charges, etc.

There is a thread which ties together many of these gypsters—and they appear to move almost as a group from one area to another, from securities to diamonds to London commodity options, Scotch whisky, or silver.

THE VICTIMS

Who are the victims of commodity options fraud? Who is likely to be ripped off? Is there a chance that you—if you are typically gullible and typically greedy —will get involved?

"I purchased two sugar options at a total price of $7,300 and, as you know, lost the whole thing," wrote a small-town Michigan businessman to the Better Business Bureau in Metropolitan New York. (He expressed no regret.)

"My father-in-law received ten phone calls in ten days from the same saleslady," a bank executive in Ohio reported. The saleslady claimed that the profit on a $6,500 copper option could easily range from $12,000 to $13,000.

A typical victim:

(1) Is not wealthy but has a nest egg in savings;

(2) Is a middle-aged male operating in his own business, quite probably in a rural area;

(3) Has little or no experience making his own investment decisions; and

(4) Before the pitchman phoned, had never heard of London commodity options.

Recognize yourself? Or a close friend or relative?

HOW TO PROTECT YOURSELF

It's your nest egg that's at stake. You must know not only what you are buying, but from whom you are buying as well.

How can you protect yourself from the con men preparing right now to defraud you?

And be warned: London commodity options and phony "managed accounts" in commodities were just the favorites in the late 1970s. In past years, Scotch whisky, diamonds, and silver have been favorites; in the next decade solar energy, insulation, and others will undoubtedly emerge.

Most of you who will get the telephone sales pitch shouldn't be speculating in commodities, and certainly not risking your life's savings.

Because of the volatile nature of the commodity markets, the trading of commodity futures or options was not and is not suitable for most members of the public. You should not, I repeat again, purchase a commodity contract or an option unless you are prepared to sustain a total loss of your commitment.

Here are some simple rules to remember if and when a salesman calls:

(1) Don't discount your own common sense, skepticism, experience. If a stranger promises you over the phone to double your money in several months, ask the obvious question: "If it is so easy to make so much money so fast, why is he letting me in on it?"

(2) Refuse to make an important investment decision over the phone. In the real world, big-time deals transacted over the phone are between people who may never see each other but who know and have respect for each other's credentials. Again, ask the obvious: "If it's so easy to make so much, why does this stranger have to phone me?"

(3) Ask for references for both the salesman and the company. What was the salesman selling last year? For whom did he work in the past? If he was in the business of advising on securities, what was he promoting and how did his recommendations work out? (Don't accept mere verbal assurance; get this in writing.) Compare the answers to your questions with your own knowledge (or the advice of experts) on what actually did happen to the securities he recommended and, again, double-check the answers. If you are an utter innocent in this sphere, move away fast.

(4) Educate yourself in the basics before you risk your savings in any kind of investment—particularly anything as speculative as commodities. Don't be taken in by the alluring promises of a pitchman. Use your head.

(5) Ask any phone salesman at least these questions: How did you get my name? What is the total price I will pay for this option? Commissions, fees, other charges?

(6) Be sure you also are fully aware of how much money you will get back (if any) if the market moves against you or if you will have to put up any more money during the life of the contract. And get it in writing. You can't trust the spoken word!

(7) Ask questions, be tough and persistent in demanding answers in writing on company letterheads signed by a company officer whose credentials you can and you *do* check. That still doesn't protect you completely, but at least it's a starter.

(8) Be on guard from the beginning about prestigious-sounding company names and references. The names may be meaningless; they certainly may be misused. As for excellent banking references, con men usually have solid bank deposits (other people's money).

(9) Freely admit your own gullibility and ignorance. You wouldn't put thousands of dollars in a local bank without asking several key questions. How can you put the money in diamonds and options without seeking at least some fundamental facts?

(10) If you have a question about commodity options, call the CFTC's hotline at (800) 424-9838. You may get a tape message. Leave your name and phone number and your call will be returned.

(11) Never speculate on impulse. Never confuse "speculation" with "investment." An investment carries a modest or minimal risk, offers some return, some degree of security. Inherent in speculation is a "major chance of loss." Never confuse a con game with either.

The Bafflegab of Commodities

ACCUMULATION Building up of either a long or short position in a given commodity by buying or selling contracts over a period of time.

ACTUALS (Spot commodities): Physical commodities. Goods available for immediate delivery, as opposed to futures contracts.

ARBITRAGE Simultaneous buying and selling of the same commodity in two different markets to profit from a temporary price discrepancy.

AT THE MARKET Order to buy or sell a contract at whatever is the best price available at the time the order reaches the pit (or market). Also called "Market Order."

BASIS The price difference over or under a designated futures contract at which a given cash commodity is quoted.

BID Price offer made by a buyer for a specific quantity of a commodity.

BOT Abbreviation for "bought," widely used in the stock and bond as well as commodity markets.

BREAK Sharp price decline for a given commodity.

BULGE Sharp price advance.

BUY ON CLOSE To buy at close of a trading session at a price prevailing at that time. Buying on opening means to buy at a price within the range at the opening of a trading session.

CARRYING CHARGE   Charges incurred in carrying the actual commodity including interest, insurance, and storage.

CASH COMMODITY   Same as actuals.

CCC   Commodity Credit Corporation. Wholly government-owned corporation established in 1933 to assist agriculture through price support programs and other measures.

CFTC   Commodity Futures Trading Commission. The federal agency which regulates trading on the commodity exchanges in this country and also administers the Commodity Exchange Act.

COMMISSION HOUSE   A concern that buys and sells actual commodities or futures contracts for the accounts of customers.

CONTRACT   A unit of the commodity being traded. The amount of the unit is set for each commodity by the exchange where it is traded.

COVER   Shorts are said to "cover" when they buy back the contracts they had previously sold, thereby liquidating their position.

CROP YEAR   Period from harvest of a crop to the same period in the following year. Thus the United States wheat crop year is June 1 to May 31.

DAY ORDERS   Orders that are to be executed the day for which they are effective and are automatically canceled at the close of that day.

DELIVERY MONTH   The calendar month during which a futures contract matures.

DELIVERY NOTICE   A notice of intention to deliver a stated quantity of a commodity in settlement of a futures contract.

DISCRETIONARY ACCOUNT   Account under which you specifically authorize your broker to place buy and sell orders for you—without your having to give the broker your consent prior to each order. Your broker, in short, has "discretion" over your account.

FILL OR KILL ORDER   Order which requires that it be either executed at once or that it be canceled.

FUTURES CONTRACT   Agreement to buy and receive or to sell and deliver a commodity at a future date and in accord with the established rules of a futures exchange.

HARD SPOT   Period of strength in a commodity market usually due to heavy buying.

HEDGE   In its simplest form, a hedge is a sale of a commodity futures contract against a purchase of actuals, or vice versa. It is a medium through which offsetting commitments are employed to eliminate or minimize the impact of an adverse price movement on inventories or other previous commitments.

LIMIT   Maximum fluctuation in the price of a futures contract permitted during one trading session as fixed by the rules of a contract market.

LONG   Person who is on the buying side of the futures contract.

MARGIN   The amount which you deposit with your broker as a guarantee that you will fulfill your financial obligation in cases of losses on contracts being carried or to be carried by the brokers. In the commodity market, margins generally range between 5 and 20 per cent of the actual value of the contract.

MARGIN CALL   Demand by your broker for additional funds to cover losses in the event of a price decline in the commodity for which you own a contract—

in order to restore your deposit to original level required or maintenance requirements. Or a margin call may be the demand to deposit the original margin at the time of the transaction.

MARKET ORDER   Order to your broker to buy or sell a futures contract at the best possible price as soon as received.

OPEN INTEREST   The number of outstanding futures contracts. It refers to the total quantity of unliquidated purchases or sales, and never their combined total.

OPEN ORDER   Buy or sell order which is considered good unless and until you cancel it.

OPEN OUTCRY   Method of registering all bids and offers in the pits.

PAPER PROFIT   Unrealized profit that a holder of a commodity contract has and that can be realized by offsetting his open position.

PITS   Platforms (locations) on the trading floor of a commodity exchange on which traders and brokers stand as they trade in particular commodities.

POSITION   Your stake in the commodity market—via long or short ownership of a futures contract.

PURCHASE AND SALE STATEMENT   A statement sent by a commission house to a customer when his futures position has been wholly or partly offset. It generally shows the quantities and prices involved, the gross profit or loss, commission charges, and the net profit or loss. (Frequently referred to as a P and S.)

PYRAMIDING   Using profits of open or unliquidated positions to add to your original position.

RANGE   The difference between the high and low price of a futures contract during a given period (often a single trading session).

RING   Same as "Pits," above.

ROUND TURN   Completion of your order to buy a futures contract and, later, to sell it as well. Or, vice versa, completion of both a sale and purchase order.

SHORT   Person who is on the selling side of a futures contract.

SPOT COMMODITIES   Same as "Actuals," above.

SPREAD (also STRADDLE)   The simultaneous purchase and sale of two different but related futures contracts. The objective is to profit by forecasting changes in price relationships rather than in absolute price levels.

STOP-LOSS ORDER   Order to buy or to sell a futures contract when the market reaches a given price. Primarily used as a protection to limit your losses or protect profits.

VISIBLE SUPPLY   Amount of a particular commodity in store at trading centers.

VOLUME   The number of futures contracts traded during a particular period (usually a single session).

26

YOUR MOST SIMPLE GUIDE
TO BUYING LAND

What Do You Want?

For profit and as a hedge against inflation over the years, you want desperately to buy land. You are scarcely unusual! *But:*

Know your objectives. Capital appreciation or income? Living space—primary residence, or vacation home?

Know your financial limitations. Investment or speculation? Security or risk?

Do you plan to live on the land? Or do you want to turn a nice profit in seven years without your ever tending it? Or a little of both? Your objective will determine the kind of land you purchase.

If you want to live on the land, it should be habitable and near a job if you need one. If a campsite or a weekend retreat is your objective, *commute* the distance several times in both good weather and bad *before you buy*.

If speculation is your goal, then you must know far more than these few pages will tell you. If the money with which you are speculating is an essential part of your net worth, then stop right here. If you are speculating in land, nothing you read in these pages should be new to you. If you are reading any angles here for the first time, you don't know what you are doing. Put your money elsewhere.

Whatever your objectives in buying land, write all the facts on paper in your own words. Put down the numbers; initial cash outlay; interest charges on the loan; attorney's fees; filing fees; title search. Now add in the costs of using the land: an access road, both building and maintenance costs; site clearing costs; water, sewer, and power installation costs; structural costs; travel expense to and from the location. And the kicker: calculate the interest you would have made had you merely left your initial cash outlay in a savings institution and avoided all the additional expense you have just tallied. Add some reasonable amount for the dollar value of the man-hours you and your family will devote to owning this property.

Put aside all these figures and read them again tomorrow. Make sure you and your family clearly understand your objectives and the costs of achieving them before you buy.

What you are reading is just a brief outline of the kind of careful examination you must make before you proceed with a major purchase in land. And this is designed only for one person or family buying one residential piece of property. Any investment in commercial real estate is far too complex a subject for treatment here. If commercial real estate investment or speculation is what you are seeking, then the basic information in this chapter cannot possibly prepare you to make an intelligent decision. Unless you want to master the material yourself by enrolling in several real estate courses at a university-level business school in your vicinity, or unless you want to try to graduate from the school of hard knocks, you must get professional advice.

WHAT ARE YOU BUYING?

Get a map. A good topographical map will give you a tremendous amount of information about a piece of land before you even see it. It should show natural features such as ground coverage, swamps, lakes, streams, deserts, plus man-made features such as roads, power lines, dams, cultivated land, and towns and building. Check with the United States Geological Survey for the map of the proper section. By studying the map several times prior to visiting the site, you should be prepared to make a thorough and efficient on-site examination.

Plan to spend some time on the site. Perhaps a couple of visits at different times of day would be good over a weekend. Concentrate on critical features: drainage; winds; easements; layout of your planned buildings; septic tanks and water sites on adjacent lots, and the ones you plan for yours.

A pretty view should be a secondary consideration. Other nearby property probably has the same or a similar view.

Make sure *you buy* and are *not sold*. Land developers offer few bargains. Assume a real estate salesman will not tell you the negative characteristics of the property you are looking at. You must know enough to ask the right questions, evaluate the answers, pursue an independent inquiry. But test your real estate salesperson by letting him talk first. Then ask your questions and see how clear and forthcoming his answers are. If his replies concur with the information you get from independent third parties, give him credit. You have an honest real estate salesperson.

HOW CAN YOU FIND IT?

Bargains are rarely advertised. Land is no exception and may be worse than most retail purchases. The bigger the land developers' promotion, the less of a bargain you are getting. You pay for everything: the advertising, the fancy brochures, the dinners, the trips to the development, the free gifts and "vacations," the stock offering and the salesman's hefty commission.

So make sure you understand that a land promotion in which the sellers woo you will rarely turn out a bargain for you.

So, how do you find the bargains? With difficulty. Talk to local people: the mailman, the gas station attendant, the bread man, the milk man, if they still come to the house. They regularly tour the neighborhood. They know the changes, who's moving, who has died, where building is going on. Check the local paper's obituary columns for the last six months. Subscribe to the local paper if you know you want to buy property in a local town or county. Drive out to see a particular site that attracts you and then visit the county courthouse to check the assessor's records for ownership.

WHERE ARE THE BARGAINS?

If you're an amateur, a good place to begin your search for sound investments in land is in your own "back yard." The reasons are obvious. You've been living with local trends in real estate. Here is where you've watched the process of buying and selling among neighbors, friends, and outsiders. You undoubtedly know quite a bit about prices now being paid and about how those prices dwarf those paid five or ten years ago. You have a good idea of what is and what isn't a bargain.

If you live in any major suburb, you almost surely have seen prices climb steeply to levels often double or triple those of the early 1970s (the prices are astronomical in some wealthy suburbs, and thus the dollar totals don't mean much). What's more, there is no sign of anything more than an interruption in these trends in the years directly ahead.

Here, according to the National Association of Real Estate Boards and other key sources, are some of the best places to shop for reasonably priced raw land with a good profit potential:

(1) In the suburbs. Although prices in many areas seem dreadfully inflated, reasonable buys still do exist—and with more than 70 per cent of our expanding population continuing to congregate in the nation's major metropolitan areas, the likelihood is for sustained price advances in the years ahead. Consult local real estate agents on going prices for various types of land in this category; on zoning matters affecting property which appeals to you; on current population growth trends; plans for new or expanded public services, schools, hospitals, bus lines, recreational facilities, etc.

(2) Areas just beyond the suburbs.

(3) Exurbs—areas beyond the suburbs but still accessible to major city facilities—into which increasing numbers of corporations have moved, followed, of course, by the movement of employees and their families, with obvious impact on land values. If you are investing in land with the objective of later resale for industrial use, though, be warned: *musts are adequate transportation facilities,* appropriate utilities, labor sources.

(4) Recreational areas—particularly "water-oriented" land near lakes, rivers, fishing brooks and streams, shorelines within three to five hours' drive of major metropolitan areas.

(5) Commercially zoned real estate near airports and with good accessibility to the airports. Industrial parks are burgeoning in these areas as reliance on air freight increases.

(6) Any land within the boundaries of any U.S. megalopolis with some very

special attribute: a beautiful view, woodlands, a tempting body of water, a very attractive location. You'll have to pay extra for these special aspects. But the future profit potential also is likely to be much greater than the potential for an ordinary parcel of land.

(7) Properties already in the process of change and upgrading by others—through the installation of new public facilities, planned new roads or highway interchanges, parking facilities, an urban renewal or rural beautification project, a new town, a reservoir or park or man-made lake.

BUYING LAND—PROS AND CONS

DISADVANTAGES OF BUYING LAND

(1) In all parts of the country, property taxes have soared—and taxes, of course, are a major part of the cost of land-ownership. Moreover, property taxes tend to leap with each sale.

(2) High interest rates add heavily to the cost of real estate you buy with borrowed money.

(3) To invest in real estate, you generally must be prepared to commit a sizable sum of money—say $10,000 or more—in order to turn any significant profit. You can obtain a stake in securities with much less.

(4) Real estate is one of the least liquid of all investments, and it may take months or years to dispose of a property at a price you approve. Realtors' commissions, when you sell, can cost 10 per cent or more of the selling price.

(5) Some forms of real estate—such as land slated for recreational purposes—are highly vulnerable in any period of business recession. So an investor in this type of land must be prepared to accept such risks and be prepared to sit out a prolonged downturn. In the depression of the 1930s there was simply no market at all and several times in the 1970s the market became exceedingly "sticky." (The "advantage" side of this was that you could pick up tremendous bargains at tax auctions.)

(6) There is no formal market for buying and selling real estate, as there is for trading securities. And there is no really solid way for the small investor to investigate and compare values in various parts of the country.

ADVANTAGES OF BUYING LAND

(1) The key advantage, of course, is the relatively high return you can achieve over the long term on any sound investment in real estate.

(2) By investing in real estate and making your profit on land, you can get favorable tax treatment when you sell because your land profits are treated as capital gains.

(3) You can get the great benefit of "leverage," for you may be able to borrow between 60 and 75 per cent of the cost of the property and thus tie up only a small amount of your own capital. To illustrate how leverage works, let's say you invest in a $10,000 parcel of land with a $3,000 down payment; you get a ten-year mortgage for the remaining $7,000 at 8 per cent interest a year. And let's

say you're able to resell at $15,000 after two years, which isn't an unrealistic achievement. Your monthly mortgage payments on the $7,000 loan are $85 and after two years you've paid off $1,000 in principal and $1,040 in interest (tax-deductible). Your net profit on the deal is $3,960 ($15,000 less $11,040)—but your total outlay has been just $5,040. That's an 80 per cent profit in only two years!

(4) Finally, debt in itself is a hedge against inflation because you borrow "expensive" dollars, repay with increasingly "cheap" dollars over the years.

Let's assume you feel the advantages win. Let's assume, therefore, that even though you're a complete amateur you have decided to try a modest investment in land.

TEN RULES FOR INVESTING IN LAND

What I have given you in this short chapter is only a primer—for if you are going into investing in land in a serious way, what you need most at this beginning stage is an easy-to-read guide outlining the most basic points for you in broad strokes. Then you carry on to find the facts which will tell you whether your specific investment is the right one for you.

What, then, are the fundamental rules for investing in land for you, an amateur?

(1) Before you invest, get answers to this key question: How can the land actually be used when you sell it? For housing? Fishing? Hunting? Swimming? Enjoying a good climate? Skiing? Shopping center? Retirement homes? Summer vacations? Winter vacations? Industrial parks? Your profit when you resell the land will depend largely on the uses to which the buyer can put it.

(2) Also, before you invest, find out from local census statistics, local Realtors, gossipy individual citizens, other sources in the area: Are there local shortages of housing and available land? How fast is the section which interests you growing? (This rate could be obscured by the growth rate for the area as a whole.) Is the land suitable for building? What have similar properties been selling for?

(3) Calculate how much money you would have to invest to turn the property into one which you could resell at a maximum profit. Or will time alone probably bring you adequate profits on a resale? An investment could be brutally costly, entail bringing in telephone lines, building a road, cutting views, clearing, finding and drilling for water, on and on.

(4) Study the possibilities of making the land earn money during the period in which you are waiting to resell. Among the choices: planting trees, raising some other crop, selling timber rights, charging admissions to hunters and campers, renting pasture land. Other ideas will be suggested by what nearby owners do.

(5) If you intend to resell a part of the property right away, sell the less valuable parts first. The more desirable parts of the land tend to grow more rapidly in value.

(6) Be on guard if a property is advertised as a "distress sale." However, notes Don G. Campbell, author of *The Handbook of Real Estate Investment,* "hell

hath no fury like a property owner whose love affair with a piece of real estate has flagged"—so at least investigate the "distress."

(7) Try to gauge what the effect of various national economic developments will be on the value or salability of any land you buy. For instance, if a business recession, fuel shortages, or similar misfortunes dampened sales of vacation properties, could you hold on until the nation was again in a strong upturn?

(8) Shop for the best possible financing deal—a fundamental point which becomes particularly important in any period of high or rising interest rates. If you can arrange a comparatively favorable mortgage rate and if you can pass on this mortgage to a future buyer, this could be a real "plus."

(9) Avoid ultra-cheap, undeveloped land in the middle of nowhere—especially if it's being pushed in high-pressure promotions. There are millions of acres of raw land that are just as unwanted and undeveloped now as they were two hundred years ago.

(10) And study books about land as an investment. Get the most expert advice you can find (and be willing to pay for it). Treat this investment with the respect it demands!

You Must Read the Property Report

Because of the great land frauds in the 1970s, more states require registration of land offerings within the state. In addition, the United States Department of Housing and Urban Development requires that interstate land offerings comply with the Interstate Land Sales Full Disclosure Act. In the past, many victims simply have not bothered to read the information available to them.

The property report is like a prospectus in a stock offering: it should contain all the material facts about the land development and the proposed sale. In the late 1970s, HUD streamlined the property report because the public found it too difficult to understand. But if you're dealing with a land developer, whether selling land intrastate or interstate, you must read the offering statement or property report.

You may find that many of the improvements in the development which the salesman mentioned are in early planning stages and that the developer has no obligation to carry them out. Nor has financing been arranged. The promotional literature might convey a different impression.

You may find that the well-known company whose name is used in the promotion actually has no corporate connection with, nor financial responsibility, for the success of the development.

You surely should be fully aware of the fact that an offering is registered with the state or HUD does *not* mean that the state in any way recommends or endorses the offering.

You also should read that, under certain conditions, you may have forty-eight hours to revoke the contract without penalty.

You may find, too, that there is no regular water service to the land tract; that purchasers must obtain water from private sources at their own expense.

You may learn that the United States Government has a perpetual right to overflow the banks of the river in the development in order to facilitate irrigation operations.

You may discover that temporary structures are prohibited and that no campers will be allowed for permanent residence.

These are just a few of the items that you might find in a property report or offering statement. Never sign a document stating that you have read the property report until you have not only read it but studied it with utmost care as well!

Never sign a document waiving your right to cancel within forty-eight hours.

And never rely on someone else's summary of a property report or offering statement.

If you are unwilling to take the time to read the report yourself, then you are not investing your money to buy land. You are giving your nest egg away.

Are You Being Hustled?

During the 1970s, countless thousands of Americans were swindled out of millions of dollars when con men sold them desert land as an investment. Few of those con men ever went to jail. Few of the companies had to pay back any substantial percentage of the money they made in the form of fines. There was little restitution to any of the victims.

Old people, young people, middle-aged people were sold thousands of acres of desert land as vacation homes, retirement homes, or "great" investments. But their dollars blew away with the sand. The promoters made a killing selling a fraction of an acre for $2,000 to $5,000 after they had bought the land for next to nothing.

Therefore, when you are dealing with a land developer who is pressing you hard to make a cash outlay, be alert to the likelihood that you are being hustled!

• Be suspicious if you get an unsolicited phone call inviting you to a dinner to hear about a great land offering.

• Never sign a contract at a dinner or any other kind of promotional gathering designed to stimulate your emotions and dull your judgment.

• Never buy land without visiting the property.

• Never buy land in another state before thoroughly examining the "property report" which the developer must give you to be in compliance with the Interstate Land Sales Full Disclosure Act.

• Always check on the financial position of the developer by asking for an audited financial statement.

• Determine what improvements, if any, the developer will provide.

• Never make your decision to buy during the first inspection to the site when you're being pitched by a salesman, but don't have adequate time to make a thorough inspection or evaluate the offer.

• Learn the names of the principals and officers of the development and how long they have been associated with this firm or similar firms.

• Before closing any deal, retain an attorney who has had experience in land transactions.

• Never sign an installment contract without fully understanding the interest charges, the monthly payments, the total of the monthly payments, and your ability to maintain them.

• Get a written statement of the consequences if you miss a payment, or several payments. If you miss a payment, do you forfeit your right to own the land or lose any credit for installments already paid?

• Always be suspicious of any high-pressure sales tactics, elaborate promotional dinners, glossy brochures, and starlet-filled movies.

None of these has anything to do with investing in land! Rather, in the past, they have been the hallmarks of the land hustle.

27

YOUR GUIDE TO OFF-BEAT AND ON-TARGET

WHERE THE "SMART MONEY" HAS BEEN GOING

In the late 1960s, stock prices across-the-board stumbled into a plunge so prolonged and at times perpendicular that Wall Street earned the unenviable reputation of being a disaster area. Since then tens of billions of dollars of "smart money" have moved in mounting volume into the off-beat investment spheres.

Among them: coins which are not for spending . . . books which are not for reading . . . paintings which are not for viewing . . . stamps which are not for postage. All are beyond the traditional mediums, involve possibilities for profit and risks for loss that would challenge any imagination. And challenges the mediums have been indeed, and still are in every sense of the word.

In fact, the old gag about the wheeler-dealer who tried to unload a railroad car of rotten sardines on a skeptical buyer was even more appropriate at the end of the 1970s than at the start. For protested the fast-talking salesman:

"These are not *eating* sardines, these are just *buying* and *selling* sardines!"

If off-beat areas intrigue you, the following pages are designed specifically to help you turn your sense of the unusual into maximizing your profits and minimizing your losses . . . as well as having fun . . .

IF YOU WANT TO BUY GOLD, HERE'S HOW

As the worldwide demand for gold as a haven of safety continued powerful and undiminished into the late 1970s, the number of ways you could buy the precious metal multiplied. Some ways make it simpler to buy; others make it less expensive to hold; all are designed as lures to draw you into the gold market.

But do not permit yourself to be lulled into overconfidence by any of the appeals. Gold buying is a speculation; as is true of all speculations, there are traps for the uninformed, pitfalls for the unwary. And while it is indisputable that gold was a great buy in the 1970s—as the new decade neared, its price had more than quintrupled since gold was torn from its long-standing peg of $35 an ounce—it was an utterly sterile and costly holding for a prolonged span of time before the upward move finally began.

FIVE METHODS

Here are five of the ways you can participate in ownership of gold—if you want to despite all the warnings and the determination of many major governments around the world to minimize the role played by gold in the international monetary system:

(1) You can, if you have a hefty bankroll, take part in the periodic auctions of gold held by the United States Government. The smallest amount you can buy is a 400-ounce bar. Merely to submit a bid, you must place a $10-an-ounce deposit. Purchasers at these auctions have been primarily European banks.

(2) You can buy "gold deposit certificates," a new instrument introduced at the end of the 1970s.

You can buy the certificates in minimum units of $2,500, representing an undivided but specific interest in gold bullion with a minimum fineness of 0.995. The metal is registered and stored in bulk at a depositary bank in Zurich. The potential return to you, the buyer of the certificates, lies solely in the market increase in the price of gold. If the price of the metal falls, you, as a gold deposit certificate holder, are the loser.

(3) You can buy "common" gold coins, such as the South African Krugerrand (1.0 ounces), the Mexican 50 peso (1.2057 ounces), and the Austrian 100 crown (0.9802 of an ounce). These coins are attractive solely because of their gold content in contrast to numismatic coins which sell for large premiums over their gold content. American gold coins minted before 1932 sell for a 200 to 300 per cent premium over their gold content. You must have expert guidance and be cautious in buying them.

Common gold coins are rarely counterfeited, are quickly recognizable, and are bought and sold by most dealers at a narrower spread or markup than on small gold bars.

(4) You can buy gold bars, but here you must trade only via a reputable dealer who will guarantee that he will buy back the bars at a fixed markup. It's difficult to sell gold bars to strangers, which accounts for the need to have an advance commitment from the dealer as a protection. Assaying bars before sale can be (and is) cumbersome, time-consuming, and expensive.

(5) You can buy shares of gold mining companies. With the exception of Homestake Mining, located in South Dakota, however, this choice involves buying shares of Canadian or South African mines. And here, there is a clear political risk. But these shares often pay dividends averaging 15 per cent a year—a major advantage over holding gold itself, which can be costly and pays nothing.

I must confess to a long-standing prejudice against gold as an investment (much less, a speculation). But I also agree that gold is sought eagerly when people don't trust paper currency, and the 1970s has been a decade of deep mistrust. Although gold has been officially downgraded in the monetary system, it still constitutes 45 per cent of central bank reserves in the free world. And the supply of gold is not only limited but also it is so widely owned that its price cannot be manipulated by any one country.

So, I bow out of the debate—and leave it up to you—except for the following warning:

BEWARE THE GOLD BUG! IT BITES!

If you are thinking about buying gold as a good investment and as a hedge against inflation, watch out!

Hundreds of telephone con men are luring you to part with your money. The bait includes such exotic speculations as "leveraged gold contracts," "supervised gold accounts," and "deferred delivery gold purchases." Many of these speculations are sold fraudulently by boiler-room, watts-line con men representing firms that were not in business last year and may not be here tomorrow.

Any of these contracts can be legitimately sold as a speculation and most companies selling actual gold or gold stocks are legitimate. But beware of the tipster touting a speculation as a sure thing.

Sound complicated? *It is!* London commodity options were complicated too, yet thousands of you were swindled out of tens of millions of dollars in the late 1970s, despite all warnings.

The same con men with the same boiler rooms then moved into diamonds, art, managed commodity accounts and gold.

Here's how it works:

You get three calls on one day from a pitchman touting gold. He tells you his firm is a gold specialist with dozens of experts watching the minute-by-minute movements in the gold markets and computing and charting future price action. He reminds you that "gold has done well in the recent past and his firm thinks that it will keep reaching new highs year after year."

His firm offers a unique program that, for the first time, makes the profitability of gold available to the small investor with limited risk. The chances are excellent that you can make twice your money in a few months.

You are skeptical but interested. The pitchman sends you the firm's promotional literature, which includes some expensive glossy brochures and numerous reprints from leading business publications. The firm's name sounds prestigious and the address is in New York City's Wall Street area. The company claims to be a leader in the field and lists references, including well-known New York City banks, several commodities exchanges, and even a federal government agency.

Several days later you get another call from the firm. This time the pitchman tells you that "if you had invested last week, you would have made $400 by today. You better get in right away before the price rises. Your investment of $4,000 will control ounces of gold worth over $20,000. We invest the money for you in a supervised account . . . My commission? No commission. We make money when you make money. We take 25 per cent of the profits we make for you . . ."

THE PITFALLS IN THE PITCH

• The glossy promotional literature may look impressive but usually tells you few facts about the firm or the sale.

• The firm is not a "gold specialist" but a telephone sales specialist. Their help-wanted ads reveal their real specialist: "telephone pro . . . heavy closer . . . $2,000 to $4,000 per week."

• Contrary to the pitchman, the chances are not excellent that you will double your money in the following few months. The chances are excellent that you will lose your entire cash outlay.

• The reprints from well-known publications are nearly always used without the publication's authority. References are often misused and are always danger-ous to take at face value.

• As for commissions, a hefty percentage of your cash outlay, sometimes as much as 50 per cent, goes immediately to the firm for fees, commissions, and other charges. The claim that the only cost is 25 per cent of the profits is nearly always a lie. One pitchman allegedly told a Missouri farmer that there was no commission and reiterated it in a second call the same day. The same salesman was telling a Better Business Bureau investigator a few hours later that he had fully disclosed that commissions and fees would take $2,400 of the farmer's $5,000 initial cash outlay.

• What about the "unique program" and the "dozens of experts . . . watching the gold market . . ."? The experts are bucket-shop pros keeping a close eye on their commissions and the "unique program" is being touted by more than a dozen boiler-room operations in New York.

As for the claim that gold will keep hitting new highs, it might happen. But the past is no guide to the future.

Are the con men successful? Yes, they always are. Many of you are sending in thousands of dollars without even knowing what you are buying. Here are the profiles of some pitches and some purchases from people who contacted the New York City Better Business Bureau.

• A California dairy farmer and his wife sent $9,000 to a New York City firm for 200 ounces of gold. They did not know whether they had bought an option, a deferred delivery contract, or the actual gold. They did not consult their broker, banker, or lawyer. A few days later, the salesman called them back with the good news that the price of gold had increased and they had already made money. Didn't they want to invest more? They sent another $13,500. Finally a concerned daughter-in-law called the New York City Better Business Bureau. More than two months after wiring their money bank-to-bank in the overnight federal funds market, the Californians were embroiled in a dispute to get back their $22,500. The company insisted it went for "selling costs."

• A coal mine superintendent in Ferron, Utah, sent $9,500 to a different com-pany. He was unable to get written confirmation of his purchase or even to get anybody at the company, including his salesman, to talk to him When he con-tacted the company he was told the salesman had suffered a nervous breakdown and was in the hospital. The same evening, a company spokesman told the Better Business Bureau investigator that the same salesman was on the telephone. Most of the $9,500 went to fees and commissions but the miner was not told that before he sent in his cash.

Fortunately, few who get calls send money. A construction company owner in Shawnee, Oklahoma, got a pitch to buy $55,000 worth of gold contracts. A messenger would come around in person to pick up the check. A few hours before the messenger's planned arrival, he called the New York City Better Business Bureau. "We told him we had known of the firm three weeks. After a few questions, this man realized he did not know what he had agreed to buy nor how much he was paying for it," said the New York City Better Business Bureau, adding:

"Most people don't know what they are buying, from whom, on what terms, or at what cost. Nearly all are taking savings to buy, at best, a speculation or, at worst, a swindle. To say they are being made fools of may seem unkind. Unfortunately, it's true."

HOW TO PROTECT YOURSELF

When the phone rings and a promoter starts talking about gold contracts, why you should buy one, how much money you can make, and why gold is going to reach new peaks per ounce, let him talk. Follow these suggestions and you will learn a good lesson in how to protect your savings and future earnings from the telephone con men who will swarm all across the nation in the 1980s.

While he is talking, you take notes. Jot down key phrases from his telephone pitch that you can check later. Take notes under these headings: The commodity (gold), the company, the references, the salesman, the cost, the contract, the market. After you are finished, your notes should look something like this:

• The commodity—gold: gold will go to $? by the mid-1980s, Arabs requiring gold clause in oil payment contracts, political unrest in South Africa.

• The company: a subsidiary of a Connecticut firm, long established, one of the biggest in the street, office in Geneva and London for fourteen years, used to be in the jewelry business.

• The references: trade on all commodity exchanges, major New York City banks, licensed by the federal government.

• The cost: no commission to me, take 25 per cent of the profits, no margin calls, risk limited to initial investment.

• The contract: you own the gold but defer delivery, you can get out at any time, store the gold for you and pay 8 per cent interest.

• The market: gold will skyrocket in months ahead.

When the pitchman has finished, casually work into your conversation with him his statements you want to confirm.

Then begin your interrogation. *This* man wants $4,000 of your money. At those rates, you are entitled to ask a lot of questions.

• . . . "gold will skyrocket." Why? You get an answer that is a litany of canned con: "The OPEC nations are requiring payment in gold for oil, the

United States dollar is no longer No. One, inflation continues, South Africa is very unstable, there are new mining difficulties with gold . . ." "But why?" you ask again. And you observe that gold has had its slumps as well as its swings in recent years. "Why won't that repeat?" you ask. Silence from the promoter. You have marshaled a fact. He has no retorts.

• "Mother company in Connecticut has the gold." What is the name, address, and chief executive officer? Is your firm a subsidiary? Affiliate? "Oh, no connection." How long has your firm worked with this firm? (A call to the "mother company" may tell you that there is no connection and the promoter asking for your $4,000 is just a cash-paying customer of the so-called "mother company" or may even be misusing their name.) A check on the "mother company's" reputation may reveal that it was recently accused of fraud by a federal regulator.

• "Firm in business since early 1970s." At what address? Under what name? Same ownership? Who were and are the officers? Same telephone listing? (Check telephone information where the firm is based. You may find the firm has a new listing.)

• "Company has offices in Geneva and London." Where in Geneva and London? Addresses and phone numbers.

• "Trade on all exchanges." What is the exchange name and address? Is the firm a member? How long? If not a member, does the firm trade through a member firm? Who? Name, address, and chief executive officer? (Write to confirm a long-standing satisfactory relationship between the promoter firm and the exchange member.)

• "No commission." How can you live solely on a percentage of unknown profits? (Newspaper ads for "telephone sales pros, heavy closers" often claim annual incomes of $50,000 to $100,000 per year. Something is not right.) How much is the contract price really? But what about the contango fee? The brochure says the $4,000 is the non-refundable contango fee. What about that?

• "Risk is limited to $4,000 investment." If it is an investment, just how risky is it? What is the security? If the risk is limited to $4,000, what is the cost? Is there any additional charge such as a storage fee, an incentive fee based on paper profit, a monthly management fee? Is there any additional cash required from me anytime? (There usually are additional fees over the life of the deferred delivery or leverage gold contract. Get details in writing.)

As you go through the claims of the pitchman, and your notes, you will have basic information that you can check directly with third parties of your choosing, or, as is more likely, you will have a list of vague responses and non-answers. But in either case, you will have spent nothing out of your pocket. You will have developed a technique for foiling the telephone con man who usually triumphs in today's fast-paced market place.

It's your money. You have to protect it. There are a thousand-and-one ways to lose it. Most Americans who are making stupid mistakes think they can beat inflation through gambling.

In fact, they often lose everything. Gold glitters—but don't let it blind you!

OR GOLD JEWELRY

SHOP THE STORES

But you, amateur investor, need not even try to play the awesomely risky, complex world gold markets. You can get a sense of the glitter of gold merely by shopping at your local jewelry store to buy gold jewelry. And that you obviously have been doing.

Sales of gold jewelry have been in a spectacular upsurge.

In the greatest boom ever has been gold jewelry for men—attributed not only to the appeal of gold but also to the return of an era of elegance in men's attire and of romanticism.

KARATS, OTHER TERMS

You, a would-be-buyer, cannot go safely into the gold jewelry market, however, without some basic knowledge of what you're buying in terms of karats, finishings, alloy, etc.

(1) For instance, the karat mark identifies the percentage of gold in an item. (Carat, though, spells out the stone weight in figuring the weight of diamonds.)

If an item is marked 24 K, it means it is made of 100 per cent pure gold, with each karat representing $\frac{1}{24}$ parts gold. Pure, solid gold is 24 karats—too soft to be used by itself in jewelry. It must be alloyed with other metals for strength and hardness.

If a piece of jewelry is marked 14 karat, or "14 K," it has 14 parts of pure gold to 10 parts of alloy. Or as a percentage, it is 58.5 per cent gold. If the jewelry is 18 karat gold, it contains 18 parts of pure gold to 6 parts of alloy. Nothing less than 10 karats can be called "gold," or "karat gold," under U. S. Government regulations. England allows the sale of 9 K "gold" jewelry. Nothing less than 18 karat can be sold in some countries, such as France. Many experts agree that below 10 karats, the metal loses the special characteristics of gold.

There are times when a piece of jewelry will carry the mark "585" or "750." Some Europeans—notably Italians—use this karat marking. It expresses the gold karatage in percentages of 1,000 (750 equals 18K; 585 equals 14K) rather than in the American fractions of 24.

(2) An alloy is a metal composed of two or more metallic elements and it is used to improve its properties. Most alloys are obtained by fusing a mixture of metals.

Gold is an exceedingly versatile metal, and many shades can be made by alloying it with special metals. Karat golds are available in yellow, red, pink, green, and white—with the color variations made by varying the proportions of copper, nickel, zinc, and silver in the alloy. The proportion of pure gold is unchanged.

(3) Fashion jewelry may be gold-plated, gold-electroplated, or gold-washed. These items are defined by law, according to the percentage of real gold in the jewelry—and if you are not familiar with the terms, you could wind up beguiled into paying "karat gold" prices for gold-plated jewelry.

(4) Gold-filled jewelry, also known as "gold overlay," is rated between karat

and costume jewelry and is made by mechanically bonding a gold layer or layers to a base metal such as copper.

It must have a fineness of 10 karats or better; the outer layer must be at least $\frac{1}{20}$ the total weight. Thus, if a 14-karat layer has been used, the jewelry should be marked "14 K gold filled," or "14 K G.F."

(5) Rolled gold plate describes high-quality costume jewelry. Manufactured by the same method as gold-filled jewelry, the gold layer is less than $\frac{1}{20}$ the total weight. Look for the markings that tell you the ratio of gold to the metals used: "$\frac{1}{40}$ 12 K Rolled Gold Plate," or "$\frac{1}{40}$th 12 K R.G.P."

(6) Gold electroplate is jewelry that has been electrolytically coated with at least seven millionths of an inch of karat gold. If the gold coating is thinner, the jewelry should be labeled "gold washed" or "gold flashed." If it is a thicker karat gold label—at least 100 millionths of an inch—the manufacturer can mark the product "heavy gold electroplate."

Preferred in our country in fine jewelry is 18-karat gold, representing 75 per cent pure gold. As for durability, the more karat gold in a piece of jewelry, the longer it will last. King Tutankhamen's gold has survived for thousands of years. Jewelry with a very thin layer isn't meant to endure; it is designed to have a short life-span.

The important point when considering gold jewelry: look for the karat stamp. Only karat gold jewelry is real gold.

How to Buy "Collectables"

BE ON GUARD

The popularity of "collectables"—so-called "limited edition" medallions, coins, records, ingots, plates, spoons, statuary, you-name-it—has rocketed to such peaks in recent years that the mass market has become crowded to the point of saturation. Your chances of finding a "winner," therefore, are steadily diminishing. The signal to you as the 1980s begin is: be on guard!

New editions of artistic pieces that have caught the public's fancy have flooded the market in a flow estimated at more than a thousand a year! Increasing numbers of manufacturers are entering the "limited edition collectables" market. A chilling appraisal by Aetna Life and Casualty, one of the nation's largest insurers of personal property and "objets d'art" is that 80 per cent of all collectables are worth less now than on the day they were purchased.

Reflecting this deterioration in the market's attractiveness was the report in the late 1970s that the Kennedy Memorial medal was still at $40 to $50, higher than the $25 issue price, but no higher than a listing a few years earlier.

A set of fifteen gold medals for the prime ministers of Canada that came out in 1971–72 at $570 was ranging from $1,100 to $1,250 in the late 1970s. That was a gain, obviously, but not so sensational considering what $570 would have earned at 7 per cent simple interest in the same span of time. In fact, not sensational at all.

But of course, some "instant collectables" do and will continue to climb significantly in value over a period. For instance, a limited edition Franklin Mint sterling silver plate, which sold in 1970 for $100, was being offered by one dealer for $550, less than a decade later!

But such increases in value are becoming extremely rare.

(1) There is no established market through which to resell limited edition collectables—which means no established prices and no simple ways to bring potential buyers and sellers together.

(2) With markups at 240–270 per cent on many collectables, you have virtually a built-in loss if an item sells for only the worth of the material from which it is composed.

(3) Manufacturers widely advertise the charms, plates, commemorative coins, statues, etc., in Sunday newspaper supplements but, cautions Aetna, often with incorrect appraisals and sometimes at prices dramatically higher than true market values. Consequently, Aetna, for one, will not insure such items for more than their actual purchase price. In its words, "the price obtainable when the collector decides to sell is often a small fraction of the so-called market price used for appraisals of the collectables."

(4) Despite what you might think, silver—the raw material of many collectables—is not recession-proof. Silver sold at 24 cents an ounce in the mid-1930s, during the Great Depression, its lowest price in a century.

(5) If you are a fledgling collector, you must be wary of outright fraud, when a so-called "floater" will try to sell a replica of famous originals to innocent collectors as the "real thing." "Limited editions" produced after expiration of the production cut-off date also have been foisted upon unsuspecting collectors by unscrupulous manufacturers.

The question you must face is: how much will an assortment of instant collectables, bought today, be worth five years from today? "It is practically certain the collectables advertised will be worth less than they cost, with no market in which to sell," Aetna says bluntly. You, an owner, will be lucky to salvage half your investment if you sell the piece.

In essence, you must heed the time-honored cliché of "let the buyer beware." Aetna suggests you, as a newcomer:

• Buy what pleases your own esthetic taste.

• Buy only from a manufacturer, mint, or dealer whose reputation and integrity you have verified.

• Buy what fits your pocketbook and under no circumstances borrow to purchase the piece.

• Do not view commemorative art as a hedge against inflation or protection against deflation—but rather as a speculation. Some collectors, suddenly pressed for cash and forced to sell, have had to accept as little as 30 cents on the dollar for their collections.

• Insure your collectables against a wide range of losses by an "all risks hobby collection policy," available on listed "collectables" at $15 per $1,000 of insurance coverage for one year. This type of policy provides much broader coverage than you could get under a homeowner's policy.

AND "NOSTALGIA" COLLECTABLES

These are the items that used to be junk—Shirley Temple dolls, windup toys from the 1920s, and, later, old postcards, political campaign buttons, and glass from "nostalgia" collectables.

For instances, those tin boxes in which cigarettes were packed in the early 1930s—the Lucky Strike "flat fifties"—sold to nostalgia buyers for $8.00 and up in the late 1970s. A tin "Li'l Abner" windup toy that retailed at $2.98 in 1946 sold for $40 nearly twenty years ago and is up to more than $250 in the original package. The value of any nostalgia item increases if it is preserved in its original box. A "Mickey Mouse" watch which sold for $2.50 in 1932 was valued at over $300 with the original box as the 1980s neared.

If you are thinking of taking a flier in the nostalgic collectables, be warned: this is a fad business!

It is virtually impossible to guess the next fad that will catch the public eye and by the time a new buying mood becomes general knowledge, it's usually too late to make money.

Some areas that could have promise are:

burlesque-house posters;

early paperback books;

plaster Kewpie dolls—the kind given away at carnival shooting galleries;

glass;

baseball cards, which can range over $1,500 for a Honus Wagner card and have long-lived appeal.

In the "nostalgia" collectables market as differentiated from the new "limited edition" collectables, a big factor in values can be rumor. And that knowledge should be sufficient for you to move with caution.

ANTIQUES AS AN ARENA

AN INSATIABLE TASTE

Of the $2 million raised by a Henry Ford II sale of French furniture and decorations in the late 1970s, half went to individual private Americans bidding against fierce foreign competition.

Dramatizing what is becoming a virtually insatiable thirst for antiques among Americans was the $65,000 paid by a private U.S. collector for a Queen Anne carved walnut highboy, a startling three times the presale estimate. While the antique was of rare, small size, and had belonged to a descendant of General "Mad" Anthony Wayne of Revolutionary War fame, it set a record for a Philadelphia highboy and for miniature American furniture.

Bids for Victorian International have been setting new high marks month after month. Decorative nineteenth-century porcelain, silver, furniture and bronzes, rugs, tapestries, clocks, vertu, etc., again have become fashionable—reflecting the glitter of Victorian International.

A few years ago an eighteenth-century American Paul Revere tea set brought $70,000 at Sotheby's in New York. This was double the amount experts predicted. A five-inch sugar tongs fetched an amazing $5,250. Prices of some antique American silver pieces have doubled in the last ten years and gone on to increase again.

Exceptional pieces of eighteenth-century French furniture were being sold in the late 1970s for more than $100,000. Single eighteenth-century French chairs which brought $5,000 to $10,000 in the early 1970s were going as high as $20,000 with the coming of the 1980s.

Between 1950 and 1980 Chinese porcelain multiplied twenty-three times in value and no end was in sight.

A chief auctioneer at Sotheby Parke Bernet in North America observed:

"We can thank American bidders for putting us into a whole new orbit in attracting fine property for sale."

And should you want a translation of that judgment into dollars, antiques have been rising in value at more than 10 per cent a year—against the "round trip" movements during the 1970s of stocks, bonds, commodities, other more familiar investments.

As still another confirmation, in the face of tough bidding by dealers representing the Mideast and European markets, twelve of the fourteen top prices were paid by Americans at a Sotheby Parke Bernet sale, a while back. Not only was the sale a record for Victorian International, but it was claimed to have been "the most international sale ever to have taken place in America."

What's behind the soaring market for antiques?

KEY FORCES

As always, a key force is the obviously limited supply. In addition, the sophisticated investing public is buying.

It is against this traditionally favorable background of restricted supply and expanding demand that price peaks are tumbling and each record sale brings new buyers stampeding into the market.

Even the summer auction trails have been setting new marks. Prices along the remote country lane locations have been higher than ever. In the straw hat shopping market of rural America, furniture of the 1800s has been appreciated as much as 15 per cent yearly. Tiffany glass has been going up an astounding 25 per cent yearly.

Mechanical toys, vintage photo equipment, and tools dating to the late 1800s have zoomed though the roof (or barn) in price. And more increases are expected in the years ahead. Antique mechanical banks have soared an astronomical 1,000 per cent in the past ten years! And more price increases are predicted.

A longtime collector characterized the market succinctly: "Antiques are better than blue-chip stocks." The observation was made to include lower-price items found on the country circuit.

Thus, every class, period, and price range encompassed the market with the coming of the 1980s.

FUNDAMENTAL RULES

How do *you* get into the antiques arena? What are the fundamental rules you must learn and never disobey?

• As a beginner, advises Sotheby's, concentrate on a specific category—American silver, French tapestries, whatever.

• Read as much available literature in the field of your choice as you can find.

• Attend auctions. Survey dealers for prices. Go to the previews or showings at auctions before the sale.

• If in doubt, hire a dependable dealer or connoisseur to represent you at the auctions—and pay the fee required. (You can save as much as 25 per cent or more by buying at auction vs. retail.)

• Look for quality (is it a good example?); authenticity (can its origin be verified?); condition; rarity; age (is the piece dated and can its date be verified?); area and era (is it from a country and period considered valuable?)

• Buy the best examples. Don't be afraid to go to a major international house because you're a "small" buyer. The average "lot" at one top New York auction house sells for $500.

• In bidding at auctions, first pick a reputable firm. Some sell on consignment —some from their own accounts. Shun the house with a no-touch policy on furniture. The better houses will have experts on the floor for consultation during exhibitions.

• Find out when items you're seeking will go up for bids. You often can leave a bid but this can get sticky. Reputable firms frequently will designate employees to bid for customers. Don't necessarily try to put in a rock-bottom price; most houses have so-called "reserve" prices below which there is no sale.

• Watch—without bidding—the first auction, and look for the dealers who often gather in little knots. In the absence of dealers, be wary.

• Check out trucking arrangements and insurance, storage charges, pickup terms, payment terms, surcharges, and attendance fees. Bring a tape measure when you go to an auction, to make sure the item is in scale with your furnishings and is appealing in your home—in addition to its inherent investment value.

FOUR CATEGORIES FOR BARGAINS IN ANTIQUES

Here are four categories in which experts at New York's Sotheby Parke Bernet Galleries believed bargains still existed in the late 1970s:

(1) Late American Federal (or "Empire") furniture—from the 1830–50 period. In pre-1830 early fine American Federal furniture, too, relatively lower-priced pieces still are available.

(2) Early American textiles, including quilts and flags with some historic association.

(3) Other Americana, such as early hand-carved duck decoys, New England tinware, utensils of the post-Civil War period; late nineteenth-century decorative objects such as candelabra, fixtures, art pottery, and porcelains.

(4) Indian miniatures, often of as fine a quality as Persian works, yet sell for a fraction of the cost. Fine nineteenth-century examples cost a few hundred dollars. Quality eighteenth-century paintings only bring a few thousand at best.

There are disadvantages to antiques as an investment. Among them:

they are perishable;

may be costly to maintain properly;

may have a retail markup of 100 per cent or more;

are subject to price fluctuations based on fashion;

cannot necessarily be sold quickly at top prices.

But the key advantages of investing in antiques are that—aside from the strong chance of substantial increase in values—you also can develop a happy hobby of collecting and you can decorate your home at least temporarily with the antiques you buy.

THE LURE OF ORIENTAL RUGS

UP 10–15 PER CENT ANNUALLY

Whether you are a collector, connoisseur, or window-shopper, mounting numbers of you have been turning to Oriental rugs as investments, with a handsome and perhaps spectacular promise of gain.

Never has the boom in Orientals in the United States been greater. The market for fine Orientals is now appreciating at an annual rate of 10 to 15 per cent and . . . no end appears in sight.

Skilled workers on new Orientals are shifting to other areas of employment throughout the world. Supplies of used Orientals are being snapped up by dealers and at auctions. Sales and auctions—once limited to such major centers as New York and Chicago—are now spreading all over the country. While the big wave of U.S. interest in Orientals dates back only to the past five years or so, experts predict that values of higher-quality rugs easily could double in the next five years.

And on top of the investment appeal, the Western world long has been fascinated by the designs and craftsmanship of Oriental carpets and the visions of the exotic that they inspire.

But while the opportunities for gain in Orientals (particularly used Orientals) seem solid over the next decade, most industry experts agree, there are major pitfalls for the unwary and uninformed. On the resale side, for instance:

PITFALLS FOR SELLERS AND BUYERS

• You should be fully aware that investments in Oriental classics are not for the overnight, get-rich-quick speculator. You must hold for the long-term—up, say, to ten years or more.

• You may have a major liquidity problem since, depending on the market-place, a satisfactory sale could take as much as six months to a full year.

While fine antique and semi-antique rugs are expected to increase in value year after year far into the new decade, many so-called "new" Orientals could have limited upside potential value. These are Middle East rugs that are under twenty years old.

For example, new Kirmans are said to be coming in lacking the quality of ten years ago. Sarouks, too, are inferior to the quality of a few years back. The poorer quality is ascribed to the fact that weavers have been reported not applying the same time as in the past. This, in addition to the fact that the older weavers are dying off.

Even in the face of the fact that values of most better-quality rugs are expected to double in the early-mid 1980s, buying in the market still requires skill. It's really an art.

• Because sales are generally made through dealers or at auction houses which work on a consignment basis with a commission from 25 per cent and up, you must have a satisfactory built-in profit to compensate for your net shrinkage from the market value.

GUIDELINES

On the buying side, there are similar warnings:

• No matter how much knowledge and experience you gain as an amateur in your early stages of studying Orientals, you will have difficulties in judging a rug. You must learn such factors in evaluating an Oriental as the knot count, the quality of the wool used in the pile, the kind of dye employed, the period and place from which the rug came.

• The guidelines will be altered for knot density, design type, and wool quality depending on the region from which the Oriental originated. For instance, a carpet with high knot density could be less valuable than one with low knot density from the same period, depending on the skills of the area where it was produced.

• Learn how to test for the quality of the warp and woof. Fold the carpet face-in; then jerk the fold slightly. If it cracks, hesitate about buying. The warp and woof could be faulty.

• Learn how to value a rug's condition. The better the condition, the more valuable can be the rug. Check for evenly clipped pile, luster of wool along with the quality of the color dye. Examine the rug in full daylight.

• Avoid so-called bargain sales. Pick your dealer with utmost care, for this is the expert in position to consider all factors relative to valuation. Shop several dealers, for prices and advice will vary. As a novice, you must move slowly. Do extensive homework in advance, possibly preparing for a full year before entering the actual market for a purchase.

• Inquire if a dealer has a policy permitting you to buy on approval. Most reputable dealers want you to be satisfied, will allow you to make an exchange if you ask within a reasonable time.

• Study estate sales as a source; these sales ads frequently appear in the Sunday newspapers.

• If you're a beginner, start in a price range of from $500 to $3,000. Stay away from the high end of the price spectrum. If you're attending an auction, get expert opinion and evaluation in advance; the tempo is fast at an auction sale. Never forget you're bidding against professionals in many cases and restrain your eagerness.

Orientals may be grouped as new, used, semi-antique, and antique. Antique rugs are said to be at least a hundred years old; semi-antiques at least a half century; and used rugs can mean just about anything.

Age and name are not necessarily the requisites for guarantee of quality. Regardless of the style or vintage, the condition of the rug can make the big difference. Condition in Orientals can be as vital as condition in a fine painting.

• Learn about maintenance, possible summer storage (if there is any threat of deterioration from bright light), washing, and repairs. The basic of basics is *study*.

• And while you consider your Oriental rug as a valuable investment, treasure its beauty and functionalism as well.

COINS NOT FOR SPENDING

SPECTACULAR UPSURGE

In Chicago a short while ago, a coin collection of 1,530 pieces, one of the most important in the nation, was auctioned off piece by piece for $2.25 million, well above the experts' expectations. A $5 gold piece, 1825-over-1824, went for $140,000 to a coin dealer. Even though only two such coins are known to exist, the price paid was characterized as "way over the estimated value."

This was merely the latest manifestation of the big boom during the 1960s and 1970s in coins not meant for spending, along with the upsurge in books not meant for reading, paintings and sculptures not necessarily for viewing.

Do you own a 1964 50-cent piece, minted in honor of President John F. Kennedy the year after he was assassinated? It was worth $2.00 or four times its face value at the close of the 1970s, a 100 per cent increase just since 1974 when it was worth twice its face value.

Or a 1940 quarter from the Philadelphia mint, all silver and never circulated? It commanded $9.00, or thirty-six times its face value, up from $7.50 just from the mid-1970s.

And how about a 1950 Jefferson nickel, minted in Denver in limited quantities? That nickel would have brought you an astronomical increase of 220 times its face value—or $11. And a 1909 penny V.D.B. (Victor D. Brenner series) uncirculated? This one would have shown a 1,250 times increase over face value, or $12.50. As recently as 1975, it sold at a hefty 500 times its face value.

HOW TO APPRAISE YOUR "COLLECTION"

But how do *you* find out if that box of collected coins in your attic has any real value?

The chances are your "collection" is only an "accumulation," say the experts. But to make sure:

(1) Take the collection to two or three respected dealers, ask each what it would pay for the entire collection, not just best pieces. Dealers will charge for a formal, written appraisal. (A New York-based dealer, for instance, charges a fee of 1 per cent of the total value of your coins, with a minimum fee of $25.) The appraisal is refunded—if you sell the collection through that dealer.

(2) Do not make your own inventory of the coins to present it to a dealer for appraisal. The dealer wants to see the coins.

(3) Under no circumstances, try to clean the coins! A poor cleaning job can drastically slash a coin's value. Using pencil erasers, silver polish, or baking soda won't make the coins more valuable. You can only harm them.

(4) Rare coins, like other antiques, are most desirable in their original condition. What could be a seemingly dirty coin just might appear beautiful to a dealer.

(5) If you are told you have expensive coins, do not keep them at home. Even when insured, put them in a safe deposit box.

IF YOU ARE A BEGINNER

And if you are a beginner in coin collecting?

• Don't try to collect every type of coin. Specialize. Read extensively. Get the advice of acknowledged specialists.

• Buy the best examples of coins you can find. Over the long run, the better coins are likely to climb the most in value.

• Don't succumb to coin "fads." In recent years, as an illustration, foreign governments have been selling virtually worthless proof sets in coins in fancy packaging for as much as $30. The prices then have fallen back to the $5.00 range.

• Don't invest for the short-term. Collections are to be designed for long-term investments.

• Beware of coins which appear grossly underpriced. They almost surely are not "super bargains," but just gyps.

• Don't buy or sell through unknown mail-order coin dealers; obey the prime rule of patronizing only the reputable firms.

• Don't hoard on the basis of rumors. Treasury $1.00 silver certificates were redeemed in 1968 for as much as $1.85. In 1979, they could not be redeemed above the face value.

• Beware of coins that are overgraded. Unless the true condition of the coins is described, you are heading for trouble.

• Finally, note that the value of coins does not depend on the age of the coin, its face value, or the price originally paid. Rather, value is based on rarity, condition, demand, date, mint mark, and authenticity. These are your never-to-be-forgotten yardsticks.

DIAMONDS: A DILEMMA

DIZZYING SPIRAL

Diamonds soared to such dizzying price levels in the late 1970s that some of the world's largest diamond retailers as well as the world's greatest diamond cartel warned publicly that diamond prices had been driven too high.

New York's West Forty-seventh Street—hub of the United States diamond industry—became the center of excitement. A one-carat top stone which had wholesaled, for example, a few years back at roughly $7,500 had doubled or more as the 1980s rolled in. Your cost as a consumer would be double this amount.

What caused the spectacular price run-up? A measure of the impetus came from the action of the world's giant diamond marketing cartel—De Beers Consolidated Mines, Ltd. The company, with next to total control over worldwide "diamond rough," i.e., uncut and unpolished stones, boosted prices 40 per cent. De Beer's action partially came as the result of reduced output which resulted in a cutback on the stones it could market.

Beyond the De Beers action, other factors behind the astronomical increase in the prices of diamonds included:

• Spiraling demand for polished diamonds for investment purposes.

• Diamonds are portable and can be secretly removed if it is necessary to flee a homeland.

• Diamonds are an inflation hedge or a defense against currency devaluation.

So immense and intense has been the interest in diamonds that some stock brokerage firms have been exploring ways to offer customers the opportunity to participate in diamond-investment programs.

CAUTION!

If you, an individual, are intent on buying for investment, proceed with caution.

The big drawback is that those who make profits in diamonds are primarily dealers in the gems who *buy from you at wholesale and sell to you at retail*—a vast disadvantage considering the diamond retailer's markup ranges from 30 to 125 per cent over the wholesale price.

Add to this local sales taxes and annual insurance premiums and it becomes apparent that even with the big increase of the late 1970s, if you bought for a quick profit, you could easily be burned.

There also is the very real possibility that future processes for producing imitation diamonds could undercut demand for and depress the prices of real diamonds.

Then, you must realize that, of the two thousand separate categories of diamonds, an overwhelming 99 per cent have shown gains of less than 15 per cent a year—and only the top 1 per cent of quality grades appreciate at faster rates.

Many firms claiming to sell this high-quality merchandise are in actuality selling the lower-quality gems.

IF YOU BUY

Have the grade of the diamond analyzed by a bonded and insured gem laboratory, with qualified and trained personnel. Be sure the lab guarantees the accuracy by international standards of the grade supplied or guarantees your money back. These are essential protections. In addition:

• Buy only diamonds of the very finest qualities and be aware of the importance of the size you select. Large diamonds appreciate faster than smaller diamonds, but in very top qualities, large diamonds are extremely expensive and often not very liquid. Very fine diamonds of from one-half- to two-carat sizes are the most liquid when you wish to resell all or part of your diamond assets.

• Deal only with companies established in the real diamond industry. If a company says it sells diamonds wholesale, ask if it sells to jewelry stores. Obtain references in the jewelry industry which the company claims to service. Check with the Jewelers Board of Trade, in Providence, Rhode Island, and the Jewelers Vigilance Committee in New York City, to find out if the company is a member of either organization. Ask your local Better Business Bureau if it has any data on the firm.

• Shop and compare prices and grade categories. Do not buy diamonds sealed in plastic or containers which make examination hard.

• Be sure the diamond is sold according to specifications set by the Gemological Institute of America, an international grading standard. If the seller does not have its own gemological lab (bonded and insured), have the diamonds appraised by an outside lab.

• Buy only from companies which guarantee to repurchase the diamonds if you are not totally satisfied—and the guarantee should be unconditional. Many reputable sellers offer this guarantee.

• If you're buying diamonds as a collector, buy merchandise of the highest clarity grade, under GIA grading criteria, in the colorless spectrum of G-H color or better, and of very fine proportion and finish. Only about 1 per cent of all diamonds fall into this high band of excellence. If any one of the scales of quality is lowered even slightly, the merchandise is much less rare, much more abundant, and appreciates at a much, much lower rate. Although many companies advertise that they have ample supplies of this merchandise, few firms in the United States actually do have many gems of this grade.

• Get full disclosure of fees at your initial purchase of the diamond for collection, and in advance of your purchase, full disclosure of fees and charges to resell the diamond at a future date. Avoid any seller unwilling to make, or who is vague about, these disclosures.

HOW TO SPOT A DIAMOND GYP

No agency of the law—federal, state, or local—or any Better Business Bureau or any jewelers' trade association could possibly stringently police the individual sale of diamonds through retail outlets. Even so-called "reputable" jewelers have been known to palm off inferior diamonds to an unknowledgeable consumer, hiding the deception by incorrect and collusive appraisals. Your fundamental guide is obvious: buy only from an established jeweler whose reputation you can trust.

You also may be able to detect an unscrupulous dealer if he tries to sell you:

(1) A perfect blue-white diamond, unless it is truly colorless and flawless. Because the term "blue-white" has been misused so much, most reputable dealers do not use it.

(2) An artificially colored diamond. This is a genuine diamond of poor color. The diamond may be painted or coated to disguise its yellowish color. In either case, a jeweler must state in writing before the diamond is sold what treatment was used, under penalty of fine and jail.

(3) A piggyback diamond. This is a small diamond placed in close proximity to another, with the mounting hiding the separations of the stones and making the two small diamonds look like one large one. Dishonest jewelers will try to sell this as, say, "one carat in diamonds" or some other deceptive advertising.

(4) An imitation or simulated diamond which will look like the real thing. Its chemical term, though, will be "colorless synthetic sapphire," or "synthetic rutile," or "strontium titanite."

When you shop, keep constantly in mind the traditional four "C's" of the trade —color, clarity, carat, and cut—which deeply affect prices.

Carat weight. This is a weight unit for diamonds and other gems. It comes from "carob"—seeds of the Mediterranean trees used in ancient bazaars to balance the scales because they were so uniform in weight. The metric carat of 200 milligrams is standard in most of the world. Some dealers suggest carat weights between one carat and three carats per stone. The majority of carats mined are under one carat. As noted, diamonds over three carats are not as liquid.

Color. A diamond's body ranges from colorless to yellow scale. The absence of color is an important factor in investment of quality diamonds. The most valuable color grades are those diamonds that are colorless.

Clarity. This identifies the relative position of a diamond on the flawless-to-imperfect scale. A number system is used to grade diamonds. Probably the most common begins with flawless or perfect; very, very, slightly imperfect; very slightly imperfect; slightly imperfect; and imperfect.

Cut. These are the facet angles and proportions mathematically calculated to achieve maximum brilliance consistent with a high degree of fire in a round brilliant which is considered the ideal cut.

THE FUTURE

What about the future of diamonds in view of the lofty price peaks already reached?

Dealers are optimistic that prices will rise at a rate matching the pace of inflation in the 1980s. An added hedge is the tremendous role played by De Beers. During the forty-plus years that De Beers has played a dominant role in the industry, it has *never* reduced prices. When demand declined, the company simply withheld stones from the market.

DIAMOND GYPS OVER THE PHONE

The pitch below is a hypothetical sales pitch. Tomorrow you may get one just like it.

It's early in the evening when your home phone rings. "Hello, Mr. Jones, I'm the head buyer with ZYX Gems Exchange in New York City. I would like to talk to you about diamonds. Did you know that investment quality diamonds have increased at a rate of 30 per cent a year for the past ten years? Most people don't. Instead, they buy diamonds at exorbitant retail prices.

"Here at ZYX Gems we are trying to let the average American get in on what professional investors have known all along. That is, you can make your fortune in diamonds. The price always goes up! One company mines 80 per cent of the diamonds in the world and that company controls diamond prices.

"We are calling *you* to offer the highest-quality investment grade diamonds at wholesale prices. We deliver directly to you. The diamonds come with a forty-five-day money-back guarantee. If for any reason you don't like them, just send them back and we will give you your money back . . . And since the diamonds always increase in value, if you want to sell them, we will buy them back. We can resell while you wait on the phone.

"Trust me. You can't go wrong . . ."

How true are these claims?

They are typical of the most deceptive claims used by the few but pervasive high-pressure promoters selling diamonds over the phone. During the 1980s countless thousands of Americans will realize that they have lost millions of dollars to con men touting diamonds as a "sure thing."

WHAT'S WRONG WITH THE PITCH?

The name of the company sounds prestigious enough. But in fact, the company is not an "exchange" in the sense of an auction market; it is not "international" in the sense that it has operations in many countries; and it has been in business for only a short time.

The "head buyer"? He is really a pro, but not at diamonds. He is likely to be what the telephone sales trade calls a "heavy closer," a boiler-room high-pressure professional. To you, he is selling diamonds; last year it was silver; next month it may be sugar options; a few years ago it was Scotch whisky.

Diamonds *in general,* as emphasized earlier, have *not* been increasing in value at the spectacular rate of 30 per cent a year even in this era.

This company is not offering the "highest-quality investment grade" diamonds but frequently is pushing diamonds that are seriously flawed and less than a carat in weight—and that is not investment quality.

The "forty-five-day money-back guarantee" is limited by terms and conditions, such as the fact that the container seals must remain unbroken. How can you examine the stones to see whether or not you want to exercise the money-back guarantee?

The "buy-back agreement" usually is fictitious. The company may try to resell your diamonds—meaning a "best efforts try"—but it doesn't guarantee the resale or the price. And it will charge a commission for the service.

And that giveaway con man's line about "trust me, you can't go wrong"—don't fall for it. A TV repairman in Oklahoma who got that pitch laid out $12,000—and now he has learned his diamonds are worth only a fraction of what he paid for them.

You may call back, find the company's phone is disconnected, and the "trust me" salesman is off on a new venture.

One large New York City diamond promoter may have deceptively sold grossly overpriced diamonds of dubious value to more than five thousand customers, from whom the company grossed in excess of $10 million in ten months. At this writing, the company has been under investigation by federal agents for over a year and a half. Some of the customers may get back a pittance, but they will wait a long time to retrieve even a small percentage of what they so invested because they were so gullible.

Who are these victims? A cross section: the fellow across the back alley, the lady down the block, the person you work with, *and you.*

"I should have my butt kicked!" exclaimed a hospital executive in Ohio when told that he had been swindled out of most of the $2,257 that he had paid for diamonds sold to him over the phone.

"The $8,000 I put up was about 98 per cent of my lifetime savings," moaned a rubber stamp manufacturer in a rural Washington State area when he found out that the company which had sold him the diamonds was no longer in existence to honor its buy-back agreement.

"Most of the people who get pitches to buy diamonds or options have no experience in either," emphasizes the New York Better Business Bureau.

And, says the New York BBB, during the late 1970s, dozens of companies employing hundreds of telephone hucksters operated nationwide. So it was not surprising that diamonds were a top big-ticket phone fraud. Even if you never bought diamonds, and don't trade in stocks, you still may become the victim of a smooth-talking pitchman who will reach you by phone and convince you to take thousands of dollars out of your savings deposits or bonds and buy diamonds.

Gems traditionally glitter in the eyes of the average individual. And all of us have some degree of larceny within ourselves which tends to make us believe we can pile up a fortune by risking a small stake. The con man's success is built on our greed and gullibility.

Of course, there are legitimate companies selling diamonds to the public all over the United States!

But most of you who will get a telephone sales pitch will lack two fundamentals for successful diamond investing: knowledge to measure quality and access to a resale market. If you want to buy diamonds for investment or speculative gain, make sure you can tell the difference between the swindlers and legitimate sellers.

A FEW ADDITIONAL GUIDELINES

• Never buy diamonds over the phone from a company and salesman utterly unfamiliar to you. This is downright stupid.

• Before you buy any diamonds, check and double-check with local, long-established, highly reputable jewelers. You will get sound guidance from these jewelers; they know the market, they know prices, they will be reliable.

• Never clean out your savings account to put the money in diamonds. It has happened. According to one fraud investigator, "People who shop weeks to save $300 on an automobile will send $8,000 for diamonds to a company they never heard of, based on the promises of an unknown salesman they never will even meet."

• Find out about boiler-room markups. All retail markups are hefty. Do a thorough comparative shopping job and give other gem dealers a detailed description of the stone you are considering buying. Describe it in detail by the grading characteristics: clarity, carat, cut, and color. But don't be impressed by a pitchman's expertise when he uses these four C's with seeming authority. These words are in his first lesson. Make sure you are buying quality goods in each grading category. Slightly inferior quality in any one category can have a great adverse impact on the value of the stone.

• Don't kid yourself about any get-rich-quick potential. To make significant profits, you will have to hold your diamonds for at least two or three years of generally rising prices.

• If you get a pitch or think you have been defrauded, write all details to your local U. S. Attorney and to your local BBB. Don't delay. If you have received the diamonds, make sure they are what you actually ordered. Take them to a registered gemologist and have him appraise them. He can give you some kind of an estimate, probably by looking through the container, without breaking the seal.

• If they are not worth what you paid, complain at once. If they are what you ordered, and were sold without misrepresentation, deception, and at a reasonable price, then you might put them away safely and in several years see what you can get for them. You may have made a little money, but make sure you measure what you made in diamonds against what you would have made on your money in a savings account or in a high-yield bond.

• And back to the basics: if you receive a phone call from a stranger who promises get-rich-quick profits in diamonds, shrug him off and hang up the phone!

FEVERISH BOOM IN ART

ALL PRICE RECORDS BROKEN

In all history, there never was a more monumental period for the world of art than the end of the 1970s.

In London, bidders from all over the globe poured out a record $34.1 million at Sotheby Parke Bernet's auction of the Baron Robert von Hirsch collection of splendid art. Walter Feilchenfeldt, a Zurich dealer, paid the highest price ever at auction for a watercolor by any artist—$1,177,600 for an Albrecht Dürer work. "I was amazed at the prices here," said Feilchenfeldt, "but I paid them because we will never have another chance at some of these things."

In New York City, Sotheby Parke Bernet reported that in only one month it chalked up sales of $112 million. Sales skyrocketed 40 per cent on the strength of American bidding in such areas as Impressionist and Modern painting, European Old Masters, French furniture, and jewelry.

In Los Angeles, a new high was set for any American work of art—$980,000 for *The Jolly Flatboatmen,* by George Caleb Dingham, circa 1848. A world peak was reached for an American portrait with the $265,000 sale of a Thomas Eakins.

Sales of paintings of major importance in the $1 million range actually became commonplace! A Van Gogh sold for $1,300,000, a Rembrandt self-portrait, for $1,519,200. These prices were hundreds of thousands of dollars above the levels they would have commanded only a few years back and, if brought again to the feverish auction market, the odds are they would bring substantially more.

Among individual artists, the upsurge also was sensational for Renoirs, Monets, Picassos, and Braques.

You can find art prices published weekly in many newspapers and art departments in big-city department stores.

Franchised art galleries have been set up across the nation. While art investment funds have not multiplied as expected in Paris and in New York, investment counselors are offering advisory services in investment in art works.

Adding to the frenzy is the entrance of the young American into the investment-in-art sphere, investing thousands of dollars a year in paintings and sculptures, for aesthetic as well as moneymaking potentials.

Then there are the corporations—not only the famous giants who display contemporary sculpture and paintings in and around most, if not all, of their buildings, but also small companies following the lead in investing for gain as well as for status.

FORCES AT WORK

What are the key forces behind this raging art boom?

(1) Inflation, obviously. During this whole phase of rapidly climbing living costs, favorite investments have been tangible, rare, valuable assets—ranging from rare books to old wines.

(2) The growing American sophistication along with the funds to satisfy the yearning for culture. As museums and universities buy art works, they, too, help drive up prices.

(3) And there are the basics behind every price upspiral: a growing demand coming head-up against a steadily shrinking supply of the acknowledged, familiar masters.

TEN RULES TO GUIDE YOU IN ART INVESTING

Say "art" is your choice of the wide variety of areas covered in this chapter. Here are ten rules to guide you.

(1) Before you put down a penny, invest as much time as you can reading art catalogs in the field which interests you, visiting galleries to see what works are available and how much they cost, inspecting art works before auctions, attend-

ing auctions to get the feel of them. You even might subscribe to art auction catalogs published by major galleries in the field of your interest.

Many of these catalogs will give you, after each auction, prices paid for each item which appeared in the pre-auction catalog. Keep these catalogs for later comparisons of prices for various items.

Try to read all the scholarly books you can find on your specialty to help give you a feel for "good," "better," and "best" in quality and value.

(2) When you decide to buy, be cautious at least to start. Don't spend all you have on one item you think is a good buy.

(3) Make sure you have, also before you buy, a really special feeling about a painting or sculpture—a sense which tells you it has quality. Or have somebody who has this type of instinctive feeling represent you as a buyer or bidder at an art auction.

(4) Deal with a top gallery or art dealer. Don't be afraid to frequent the very best. Also, a top dealer is interested in earning and holding your patronage. If you are not satisfied, he will make every effort to resell anything you bought for at least what you paid. Some dealers and major galleries will guarantee the authenticity of the art works they sell, in fact, so check this point as well. Don't patronize galleries or dealers whose large ads proclaim their merchandise to be "art investments" (they often are not).

(5) Have an understanding with your dealer or gallery about trading up—so he'll repurchase or resell your works as you have more money to invest in high-quality art. Also find out whether he'll let you and your prospective purchase have a "trial marriage"—by taking a picture home for a week or so before you make a final decision.

(6) Be wary of works by modern artists in current fashion. Inflated prices easily can result from an exhibit by a single major museum. But after the excitement of the show has subsided, prices tend to drop as well. Buying art works because they are a current rage is akin to buying stocks on tips at a cocktail party.

(7) If there is a museum director or curator in your community, ask for his advice on buying. Or use the services of specially assigned personnel at large art galleries whose job is to guide you.

(8) Decide, before you buy, how much money you can afford to invest and stick to that ceiling. If you find a more expensive work irresistible, arrange to pay for it over a period of time.

(9) Unless you are an expert, spread your financial risks by investing in the works of a variety of different artists. But try at the same time to maintain a theme or unifying force in your collection.

(10) Buy the best examples you can afford in any category. For buyers with limited funds, a good drawing by a given artist may be a better buy than a poor painting. You well may find artists who were overshadowed by the greats in the era in which they lived a better buy than new artists who have not been tested by time.

FIVE TYPES OF ART FOR RAPID "GROWTH"

As a newcomer, what types of art should you seek? What is expected to grow at a relatively rapid rate in the years coming up? These, according to spokesmen for Sotheby's, New York, are among your best bets:

(1) Old master paintings or drawings. Their value is virtually guaranteed to continue rising, despite today's high prices. However, they'll probably increase in value at a slower rate than other art categories. While there are still some excellent old master drawings ranging up to $50,000 and more, a substantial number are available at a fraction of this amount. Always turn to a reputable dealer for counsel on what good drawings by superb artists can be bought at reasonable prices.

(2) Almost any good American painting of unusual historical, social, or geographic interest. Bargains may still be had, dealers say, in late nineteenth- and early twentieth-century paintings by respected American artists of the Hudson River School (Thomas Cole, Thomas Doughty, Asher Durand, and their associates) and in good marine paintings by many American artists. Prices range from $1,000 to $10,000 and up.

(3) German artists of the nineteenth century. Good examples of their works are said to be worthwhile buys at prices ranging from $600 to $6,000.

(4) Primitive art works. Authentic African wood carvings, pre-Columbian works, such as sculptured figures, vessels, and ceramics, are regarded as good investments. Go only to top-name galleries for these items. Prices will vary from a few hundred dollars to a few thousand. Primitive oceanic carvings from the Southwest Pacific islands range from $50 to $100 and into the thousands for the more elaborate, large carvings. Beware of modern reproductions and fakes, which have flooded the market.

(5) Classical antiquities. These include small bronzes, pottery, and sculptures from the Mediterranean which should appreciate. You can create a fairly large collection of significance for about $50,000 today. Only five years ago, a collection could have been established for around $30,000. You can still buy most individual art objects in this area for an investment of a few hundred dollars or so.

A crucial guideline: specialize in a specific field and become acquainted with other art lovers in it.

PRINTS ROAR ON TOO

BIG WINNER

"Art used to be a place to spend extra money," said the president of Associated American Artists, in New York, as the 1980s neared. "Now taxi magnates are investing their profits in art."

And high on the list of winners in the art market are prints—which have moved way out of what was once second-class status into an artistic niche of their own. To illustrate:

• A Picasso linoleum cut, entitled "After Cranach," went for $600 in 1960, commanded $60,000 in the late 1970s.

• A Toulouse-Lautrec print, entitled "La Grande Loge," soared to world record of $175,000, while Rembrandt etchings startled the art world with price runups as high as $80,000 to an almost incredible seven figures.

• In the early 1960s, an original, signed Matisse lithograph entitled "Seated Odalisque" from an edition of 50, was priced at $350, rocketed to the $50,000 range.

FACTORS BEHIND BUYING EXPLOSION

Why the churning of prices in the print explosion?

(1) Print dealers have been multiplying. In turn, they have bought up prints to build their inventories. The impact on prices has been obvious. For example, in the early 1960s, there were no more than twenty top print dealers in the United States. Today, they number in the hundreds. This includes not only galleries and print shops but also department store boutiques, bookstores, picture frame and gift shops.

(2) The ranks of collectors have been greatly expanded by young Americans who find the tag for paintings and sculptures by major artists prohibitive. They have added immensely to the demand and, in doing so, have lifted prints out of a second-class status into an artistic niche of their own. Status has become identifiable by a collection of fine prints.

(3) Art investors and art funds have been flocking to the print market. This has opened competition with the collectors of art.

(4) Availability of material from the old masters has been diminishing. Prints done from the fifteenth to the eighteenth century have grown in value due to their antiquity and rarity. There has been a tremendous drain on the old masters by institutions augmenting or beginning new study collections.

(5) Middle East oil wealth has upped prices. For example, Iran, in opening a museum, has bought paintings, sculpture—anything in the market place of artistic value. This material will never return to the market place. In the United States, universities continue to develop important museums.

(6) The absence of a property tax has been an important consideration in contributing to demand for art, also. Another appeal to many people is the fact that, in contrast, say, to real estate, prints are portable and virtually maintenance free.

BASIC RULES FOR BUYING PRINTS

The print market—like other similar markets—is plagued by its share of fly-by-nights, forgers, and unscrupulous dealers. Hundreds of Chagall "original" lithographs have been clipped out of books and French publications, dressed up with fake signatures and "limited edition" numbers, and sold for ridiculously inflated prices.

High-pressure auctioneers have been known to offer examples from large editions (300 to 400 impressions) by artists who are described as fabulous and famous by the auctioneers—but who are, in fact, unknown to the rest of the art world.

How then can you avoid paying big sums for forged prints and other non-originals? How can you find etchings, engravings, lithographs, or other types of prints to adorn your living-room walls and at the same time see your purchases grow in value in coming years?

A fundamental point is that prints can be either originals or reproductions. An original print, as defined by the prestigious Print Council of America, comes from a plate, block, stone, or other medium on which an image has been created by the artist himself. A reproduction, however, is a copy of a print or other art work made by photographic techniques, seldom under supervision by the artist.

Here are the basic rules for buying prints, both for their artistic rewards and for their profit potential:

(1) Before buying, consult established sources of information, including auction catalogs, art books, and "catalogues raisonnés," which are comprehensive, well-annotated compilations of all the prints of various artists. Also, to get a basic education, visit museum print cabinets. Often you must make an appointment to do so but don't fail to do this, for many of the finest examples of prints are to be found today in museums.

(2) Browse in galleries and shops, both in the United States and abroad, to get an idea of the range of prints available and prices being charged by various outlets for similar works. Try to find an era or an artist or a school of artists really attractive to you and then focus your interests and attention on your choices.

(3) When you are ready to buy, stick to established print dealers—preferably those who have been in business at least five years. Seek their guidance on the quality and authenticity of the prints you are considering purchasing.

(4) Avoid one-shot print exhibitions in hotel suites and sales by unknown auctioneers. Frequently, experts say, fly-by-night auctioneers will hold up a page which has been torn out of an art book, announce flatly, "This is worth $250 but let's start the bidding at $25"—and succeed in selling it for a distinctly non-bargain price of $50.

"Small-time auctions," dealers warn, "can be a great place to buy prints, but only if you know exactly what you are doing." A cardinal rule on this type of auction is to attend the exhibition beforehand and examine the prints, since they are generally sold "as is."

(5) Also avoid the "bargains" advertised in your neighborhood picture frame shop unless the dealer has an established reputation in the field of prints and you know what you want.

(6) Be on the lookout for "restrikes"—which are reruns of the original plates. These plates may have been rediscovered long after an artist's death, sometimes with cancellation lines drawn through them by the artist so that further prints supposedly could not be made.

(7) Finally, examine catalogs at auctions and art print exhibitions. Descriptions of individual prints should include whether or not they are signed by the artist, the condition and quality of each print, the number of impressions in the entire edition (for modern prints), the print's size and date, the process or processes used. Reputable dealers also should be happy to put whatever descriptive data you wish on the invoice or give a certificate of authenticity.

SEVEN CATEGORIES FOR INVESTING

With these basic rules for shopping for profit firmly in mind, what might you find the most provocative areas for investing in the print market? Seven specific categories underlined by leading dealers are:

(1) French nineteenth-century artists such as Jean Baptiste Camille Corot, Jean François Millet, Adolphe Appian, Albert Besnard, Félix Buhot, and Charles François Daubigny. In the late 1970s, you could buy good Corots and Millets for $300 to $600 and good examples of others for $20 to $200—a fraction of the prices which were paid for other major artists of this era such as Toulouse-Lautrec, Manet, Cézanne, Renoir.

(2) American early twentieth-century artists and especially those who worked in the 1930s. Good prints by Thomas Hart Benton, John Steuart Curry, Grant Wood, George Bellows, John Sloan, and Reginald Marsh could be bought for $300 to $1,500.

(3) The celebrated British "triumvirate" of the 1920s—D. Y. Cameron, Muirhead Bone, and James McBey. Works by these once fantastically popular artists were available in the closing days of the 1970s for only 10 per cent of the prices they commanded a half century ago ($200 to $3,000 in the expensive dollars of the 1920s). "Whether the prices for works by these artists will ever come back to the levels of the 1920s is anybody's guess," says one print dealer. "But they might possibly be an interesting school to explore." Similarly, works by Seymour Haden, Whistler's brother-in-law, well may start to rise on Whistler's coattails. Prices of major Whistler prints have passed the $3,000 mark.

(4) High-quality works by lesser-known printmakers of the fifteenth, sixteenth, and seventeenth centuries—e.g., Lievens, Hollar, Waterloo, to name just a few. Outstanding examples of prints by these artists could be bought in the late 1970s for $50 to $500. But choosing among these lesser-knowns takes expert knowledge and if you don't possess it consult someone who does have the required know-how.

(5) Other lesser masters with appeal—Van Leyden, Callot, Adriaen Van Ostade, and Raimondi. Outstanding examples of these artists are now $2,000 to $3,000. However, you can buy fine examples of these lesser-known artists in the $100 to $500 range as opposed to the outstanding examples.

(6) Ultramodern art. This can be riskier, for time has not tested the durability of many of today's avant-garde. Among the most important contemporary artists are Robert Motherwell, Jasper Johns, Helen Frankenthaler (one of her prints fetched over $3,000 at auction as the 1980s neared), David Hockney, Richard Estes, Andy Warhol, and Jim Dine (his etchings have passed the $2,000 mark).

(7) Old masters. Price increases notwithstanding, there are still some attractive investment areas. Prints from the old masters such as Rembrandt and Dürer are in big demand, bringing $10,000 and up. Old masters require a vast amount of expertise. Beware of buying an old master that was printed in the nineteenth century—even though it was from an original plate. It could be of minor monetary value and hardly worth the investment.

WHAT DETERMINES VALUES OF PRINTS?

Print values in all categories are based on these four factors: the artist, the image or subject of the print, the rarity of the print, and the print's condition.

But an artist's standing as an oil painter or a sculptor has little to do with his stature as a printmaker. Aristide Maillol, for instance—whose sculptures are valued in the tens of thousands of dollars—is considered a minor printmaker.

Rarity is the key to the upswing in prices for fine examples of prints by such artists as Rembrandt, Dürer, Cranach, Callot. And a print from an edition of only fifty may cost four times the price of an example from an edition of two hundred, everything else being equal.

As an illustration of the importance of a print's condition, a Toulouse-Lautrec poster which normally would sell for $7,000 might fetch less than $2,000 if it is torn or wrinkled or otherwise in poor condition.

If you are considering buying an old master, shop and consult with an expert. One fine print by Dürer may be worth upward of $25,000. Late impressions of the same print in poor condition may be worth less than $1,000. This rule applies particularly to Rembrandt. Late impressions can be worth only a fraction of the value of early impressions.

If you invest in lesser prints, don't underestimate the problem of liquidity. You may have to wait for years to get the price that you believe is fair for such prints. Auctions are getting choosy and are turning down the hard-to-sell items.

Before you buy, study sources of information on the category of prints which interests you, e.g., museum print cabinets, print galleries, auction catalogs, art books, and "catalogues raisonnés"—the latter are complete compilations of all the prints of a single given artist.

Be on guard against today's ever-broadening array of questionable print offers such as one-shot print exhibitions in hotel suites, small-time auctions conducted by unknown auctioneers, and books of prints by well-known artists offered at grossly inflated prices.

Buy only from established dealers who will be your best guides to quality, authenticity, and fair prices.

Beware of vendors who indicate "regular price $1,000, special price $500" on a print. In all probability, the $1,000 is exaggerated and the $500 is overpriced. Beware of such terms as "Fine Arts Print," "Museum Quality Print." These have little to do with the print's intrinsic value.

A final guide: If you do decide to choose prints as an investment medium as well as a source of great personal pleasure, avoid the hottest print fads and concentrate on the temporarily less fashionable but still high-quality artists and epochs. In fact, here—among the less fashionable eras and less fashionable artists —is where you'll find real price bargains.

STAMPS AS INVESTMENTS

UPSWING YEAR AFTER YEAR

While the stock market was mostly a disaster area during the 1970s and stock values lagged far behind inflation's erosion of your dollar's buying power, stamps continued to climb as much as 20 per cent year after year. In many instances, the upsurge in values was even more spectacular—and no reversal in the escalation is foreseen.

Item: A top-quality inverted U.S. airmail 24-cent stamp, familiar to generations of collectors and considered among the world's fifty most valuable, was auctioned in the late 1970s for $100,000 and another similar stamp went for $72,500. As recently as the mid-1970s, the upside-down airplane was quoted at $35,000 to $40,000—and even conservative experts predict this stamp's price could rang up to $120,000 in the 1980s.

Item: A New Orleans stamp dealer paid $380,000 for a couple of 1847 one-penny stamps from the Indian Ocean island of Mauritius a few years back. The Mauritius stamps epitomized all the elements that go into the value of stamps: rarity, demand, and good condition.

Item: Since World War II, classic U.S. stamps have risen in value an average of 20 per cent a year. Other increases have been even more spectacular. A British Guiana 1-cent stamp, for example, was sold in 1940 for $45,000. Thirty years later it went at auction for $280,000. In the late 1970s it had soared to an astronomical $1 million in value!

Item: A new force behind the spiraling of stamp prices has been the emergence of the big-money syndicate. Added to the approximately one million serious individual stamp collectors in this country, the big-money syndicates put high leverage on prices as well as provide a price floor. The stamp market has moved way beyond the hobby of grade school and high school youngsters and into the area of major investments.

THREE LEVELS OF INVESTMENT

There are three levels of investment in stamps.

(1) $500 to $1,000. While they have no great lure as big money-makers, if you invest wisely by investing in ten or so items costing around $50 each, you can have a nice appreciation potential. You should avoid stamps in the $2 to $10 area and new issues that are mass produced.

(2) $1,000 to $10,000. Here is where more expensive stamps show their greater rapid appreciation. Concentrate on issues costing from $100 to as high as $5,000. Intensive research and a bit of luck could get you a real money-maker. Develop a specialty in buying at these prices. You can get burned with random buys.

(3) $10,000 to $50,000. Here you enter the real investment arena with stamps involving outlays of $100 to $500 or more. In assembling a collection in this area, concentrate on a philatelic theme. Your rewards could be healthy. Or, limit

yourself to a limited number of rare items that could range from $5,000 and up. In this price range the emphasis is on scarcity for ultimate significant appreciation.

Postage stamps have long been considered a traditional hedge against inflation and economic-political catastrophe.

Their small size makes them easy to hide.

Stamps are readily convertible into cash.

Many wealthy foreign investors—frightened that they will be subjected to government seizure of their assets—have been turning to stamp acquisitions as a way to handle their resources. Wealthy South Africans, for instance, are extensively "plowing money into stamps," reported the chief executive officer of the American Stamp Dealers Association in New York City. "It's a seller's market," he adds.

DO'S AND DON'TS FOR INVESTING IN STAMPS

How then can you, the amateur, intelligently invest a portion of your capital in stamps to protect your savings against inflation and probably to make substantial profits too?

(1) Do start as a general collector, investing only small sums. Then develop a specialty—such as stamps of one type—airmail stamps or classic stamps, stamps from a particular country or region, stamps from a particular era. Study as much reliable literature as possible and attend as many auctions in your area as you can. Join a local stamp club and learn from experienced collectors.

(2) Don't waste your money on cheap packets of stamps. The odds that you'll find a valuable one are virtually nil because these packets are put together by experts who almost surely have snagged any valuable stamps before they get into the packet. The wholesale price of a typical collection of five thousand stamps may be only $12.50.

(3) Don't buy up whole sheets of ordinary new stamps from this or that country—where a currency devaluation could slash their value. This goes for the United States too: the value of post-1943 U.S. stamps as collector's items has remained at or below their face value and their sole use as postage.

(4) Do stick to the higher-price specimens and avoid the typical 50 per cent retail markup on inexpensive examples. The big increases in values are taking place today in this high-priced category—particularly, nineteenth-century quality stamps and early airmail stamps.

(5) Do, if you find an old stamp collection in the attic and want to sell it, take it to one or two reputable stamp dealers and/or auctioneers. Ask each how much he considers the whole collection to be worth. If the stamps are attached to the original letters, don't remove them, or you may slash their value to next to nothing. A stamp professional may legitimately charge you for an assessment of your collection, if you do not end up selling it to him. Typically an auctioneer will charge you a commission of 20 per cent of the sale price of the collection for auctioning it, less if the collection is very valuable.

To make sure a stamp dealer is reputable, check names with the American

Stamp Dealers Association in New York City or one of its chapters in other big cities.

(6) Do, if you know nothing about stamps but still want to invest for profit, employ a knowledgeable dealer or other expert to advise you, to buy stamps for you at auction, or simply to sell you stamps he deems investment-worthy. Such agents today are representing increasing numbers of investors; their fees generally run about 5 to 10 per cent of the cost price of stamps bought. Serious collectors and top stamp auctioneers can steer you to good advisers or, in the case of some auctioneers, advise you.

(7) Do beware of improbable "bargains" of any sort. Errors and varieties can be manufactured and apparent quality improved by a "stamp doctor" for the sole purpose of fleecing the unwary. On such "bargains," get advice from a reputable dealer, a trusted expert friend, or a reputable committee of stamp experts (usually part of the large philatelic societies) which issues certificates of stamp authenticity.

Stamps are not for the short-term investor. Experts agree that the key to success for the amateur collector is to follow up on top-grade stamps and establish a specialty. In this environment, you should achieve impressive appreciation in three to five years.

BOOKS NOT FOR READING

ONE OF THE RICHEST ERAS EVER

For the first time in more than a half century, individual collectors had a chance to bid at auction in the late 1970s for a Gutenberg Bible, the book of books that rare book collectors covet beyond all others as the greatest masterpiece of printing in world history. It fetched $2.2 million.

It was the second example of the work of Johannes Gutenberg (the fifteenth-century inventor of moveable type) to have changed hands in the late 1970s. A New York-based rare book dealer had earlier sold his copy to the Gutenberg Museum in Mainz, West Germany, for $1.8 million.

This was one of the richest eras ever for rare book collectors and dealers, with the marketing of such coveted rarities as a fifteenth-century Flemish Book of Hours; a first edition of Mark Catesby's *The Natural History of Carolina, Florida, and the Bahama Islands,* the earliest known book on American birds with colored illustrations; Ezra Pound's first book, *A Lume Spento,* plus a large collection of Ernest Hemingway correspondence.

Never had interest in this type of investing been so acute, reported the president of Swann Galleries, New York, largest specialty rare book auctioneers in the United States. The signs: increased membership in the industry trade association, the Antiquarian Booksellers Association of America (ABAA); mushrooming of new dealers; multiplication of book fairs; accelerating auction activity.

Long neglected by the public, rare book collecting has been viewed in the past as a classical form of investing, a rich man's hobby. While old coins, stamps, and art have boomed, rare books have climbed in value at a steady but unspectacular price.

But now . . . a copy of James Joyce's first edition of *Ulysses,* in good condition, one of a hundred, and signed by Joyce, was auctioned at $10,000 in the closing years of the 1970s against $2,100 in 1968. William Faulkner's first book, *The Marble Faun,* published in 1924, inscribed, sold for $6,250. An art book by Chagall, published as recently as the 1950s for $35, sold for $1,000.

While the soaring value of rare books and manuscripts rarely make the front page or the business news, book collecting for profit has become so attractive that it now ranks third in popularity behind stamps and coins. It is a solid, relatively low-risk investment that requires less cash outlay than, say, art and antiques, and there is every likelihood that values will continue to climb in the next five to ten years.

The biggest profits are made in anticipating what collectors will want at some future date. For example, Ian Fleming, the late British author of the popular James Bond books and one of England's leading book collectors at his death, collected manuscripts by Karl Marx. These items ultimately proved to be the most valuable in his impressive collection.

Similarly, some prices shift. The reason in not quite clear. An illustration is Edward S. Curtis' *The North American Indian,* a 20-volume set, with twenty portfolios of illustrations, published in 1935. The set sold for $20,000 in 1972, was auctioned for $60,000 five years later, was down to $50,000 as the 1980s opened. The reason? Either the unusually sharp rise of the Curtis set pushed the volumes out of reach of collectors, or it motivated other owners to offer their copies. Hence, the element of supply and demand possibly entered to lower the set's value.

BASIC RULES FOR NEOPHYTES

If you are a neophyte, don't enter this area to make a quick killing. Buy rare books and manuscripts first for the love of the items, the pleasure of ownership—and view moneymaking as a corollary, after you've educated yourself on how to collect.

You can collect in many fields: paperbacks (the first Penguin Paperback is now worth over $100); mysteries, science, telephone books, directories (the first New York City Directory sold a short while ago for more than $1,000).

The most active areas of book collecting are first editions, books of Chinese and Japanese art, medical books, maps and atlases, children's books, travel, cooking and wine books. Also, books on geology, crime, whaling, the American Indian, and early works on scientific subjects.

You can create your own field. "Why not collect every book published in Cleveland in 1931, for instance?" asks one expert.

Another area might be imprints. "I've known people who collected Swedish cookbooks published in France or books on a variety of subjects published in the year of their birth," the expert adds. "There are no limits to individual taste or interest."

Or:

(1) You may specialize in scientific and medical papers describing vital discoveries and inventions. *De Revolutionibus,* Copernicus (1543), went from $11,000 in 1963 to $40,000 in 1974, is now over $100,000. H. D. W. Smyth's report, heralding the Atomic Age, published in 1945, is now at the $1,000 mark.

(2) Modern first editions. In addition to Faulkner, other hot authors are F. Scott Fitzgerald, John Steinbeck, and Ernest Hemingway. (Hemingway's high school yearbook of February 1916, containing his first published story, "Judgment of Manitou," recently sold for $1,000.)

(3) Press Books, with examples of fine printing. Important names are Doves Press, Kelmscott Press, The Limited Editions Club.

(4) Children's books with "a certain eternity." A first edition of *Pinocchio* by Carlo Lorenzini, published in Italian in 1883, and in English in 1892, sells for $500 to $800. Lewis Carroll's *Alice's Adventures in Wonderland* sells for $10–20,000. These high values can be ascribed to the fact that perfect copies of children's books are rare.

(5) Books on photography, maps, atlases, and nineteenth-century literature in fine condition command good prices.

(6) Limited and signed art books. In addition to Chagall, Picasso, Calder, and Dali books draw premiums.

(7) Comic books. If you want to save these, make sure your copies are in perfect condition.

In general, for the uninitiated, the watchwords are condition and collection. Therefore, as a newcomer, buy the best you can afford. Bargain hunting is false economizing when condition is so important a factor. One prime book is better than a room full of instant libraries which will have little appeal to knowledgable dealers later.

Value lies in the collection. The more complete it is, so much the better. Single copies seldom bring much money on resale, since the market wants collections.

If you try collecting first editions, handle with care! If the pages are uncut, don't cut them. Don't remove the dust jacket. Wrap them in plastic and carefully put them away. Don't touch (much less read).

Form a good relationship with a dealer and book collector, particularly one who specializes in the subject you've chosen. The guidance you receive can pay huge dividends in the long run.

Finally, educate yourself. You can't go it alone. Read dealer and auction catalogs. Attend courses on rare books being offered across the country.

VINTAGE CARS—FOR FUN AND PROFIT

ANOTHER LOVE AFFAIR WITH CARS

How would you treasure an investment of $30,000 that doubled itself in the next five years? And, then increased again by more than your original outlay in the second five years?

What would you think of doubling your money on a $6,000 investment by the mid-1980s?

Would you be happy if your investment of $12,000 today is worth $20,000 in the next five years?

Hard to believe? Got to be a catch? Not at all.

These are the past and projected growths in the value of restored collector cars —vintage automobiles for which the boom also appears relentless. Spurred by America's thirst for the nostalgic and coupled with a love affair with the automobile, thousands of car buffs are finding fortunes in vintage autos.

Residents on Main Street and in mansions, alike, have taken to this profitable and fascinating hobby in unprecedented numbers. Collecting vintage cars looms as the great social "leveling" influence of a generation of Americans in the 1980s.

As with all booms, speculators have entered the field in numbers that virtually guarantee price spiraling and warn you to be on guard. Add to that a new breed of car counterfeiters whose clandestine operations span the Atlantic, and who copy original parts, assemble them to a bogus body, fake in manufacturer's serial number identity—then sell the finished item for $25,000 to $30,000 and up.

Conversion of expensive sedans into rare, limited editions of exotic models through counterfeiting of parts is not unknown, either.

An estimated 800,000 vintage-car buffs swelled demand for these cars in the 1970s. Now, it is predicted that the ranks will be enlarged by another 200,000 in the 1980s.

Lovers of nostalgic cars fan out to club rallies and car shows—all turned on by a hobby that has become rich bounty for old-car hunters. Their vocabulary is spiced with references to "antique cars," "classic cars," and "milestone models."

An important factor in the expansion of the vintage-car market was the national obsession that swept the country in the late 1970s for anything that reflected nostalgia. From collecting of antiques to the exchange of old bubble-gum baseball cards, millions of Americans have found new pleasure in turning back to yesteryears.

Whole new industries have sprung up in recent years to mirror the American obsession. In automobiles, of course, it could only be the real thing. And that meant turning back to the "Rembrandts" of the car world, the vintage car.

A second spur to the soaring market for cars of a bygone era has been the attraction of this hobby for the very wealthy. The polo set of the 1920s found a new hobby in the 1970s in the assemblage of a stable of cars from the turn of the century, or later. The result: dwindling supplies of the "good oldies" established a hydraulic lift of base market prices.

Latter-day self-made millionaires also have embraced vintage car-collecting. A Nevada casino operator was noted for his outstanding assemblage of these automobiles as museum pieces.

But the contagion of vintage-car collecting has not been limited to the wealthy. For the millions of American men who envision themselves as "tire kickers," the appeal of owning (and driving) a refurbished old car with a patent-leather shine and dazzling polished hardware has proved a strong lure too.

In fact, the boom in vintage-car collecting reflects not only a yearning for the past, but also the American identity with the automobile and the highway which began with the burgeoning of the Ford assembly line and the guaranteed $5.00 per day minimum salary.

All of this has been stimulated even more by the gathering of the car buffs; the explosion of antique-car societies; the regional and national meets; and the mushrooming of periodicals reporting enthusiastically about the field.

Collecting the cars is only a part of the busy world of the vintage-car owner and prospect. Restoration has become an important business.

PITFALLS!

The financial and aesthetic appeal of the vintage-car market can become magic. But, to the unwary, its pitfalls are risky. For the impatient it can be downright dangerous, since this is a hobby that requires expert knowledge, careful appraisal, and controlled bidding.

While big profits are being made by the informed, racing into this fascinating field for pure "moneymaking" can be very treacherous. You can get stung—perhaps badly—because, as a neophyte, you fail to take time to study the field.

A fun-filled avocation with the potential of profits can turn into a financial mudhole. The uninitiated can be caught in an escalating price market against a background of misleading advertising, revved-up salesmanship, and overpriced restoration jobs.

Restoration poses particular problems for the uninitiated, according to those experienced in the vintage-car market. Old-car buffs admonish beginners to watch with care the balancing of costs against maintenance of authenticity in the car's restoration.

THREE CLASSIFICATIONS

The vintage-car market actually covers three classifications of nostalgic cars:

Antiques. Can be traced to the beginning years of this century through World War I. The market turned lackluster on this category in the late 1970s.

Classics. Cars that span the era of the 1920s and 1930s. These have attracted substantial totals of sophisticated money in the past few years. Prices have been climbing, and experts agree that they could advance smartly into the mid-1980s.

Milestones. Post-World War II models with their preponderance of heavy metal trims. Interest has been great in cars from a quarter of a century ago—these gas-guzzling models of the 1950s. For the buyer with $10–$15,000 to invest, milestones have been particularly attractive, with appreciation possibilities still good.

GUIDELINES

Getting into the collectable car hobby requires homework. If you are tempted by this field of investing for fun and profit, here are a few guidelines to set you on the right road:

(1) Absorb as much education as possible. Read magazines in the field. Read the catalogs, anything to learn the market. Do research. *Hemmings Motor News* often is cited as a major source. *The Old Car Value Guide* is another important source.

(2) Develop a "feel" for ads. Knowing the values inherent in the market will be especially helpful in helping you to negotiate a price.

(3) Join local vintage-car clubs, a popular meeting place for old-car buffs. You can get a wealth of information from your associates in the field.

(4) Train yourself to be thoroughly familiar with the basic values in vintage cars. Become a student of rarity, condition of the car, engineering and aesthetic excellence as you also gain knowledge on makes and models. You should, for example, know that any classic car which was regarded as a masterpiece when it was built is still highly thought of by the old-car buffs. Convertibles could rise steadily in price if they fail to appear again in significant numbers from the Detroit assembly lines. Open cars such as roadsters are considerably more valuable than sedans.

(5) Approach auction markets with caution. Certainly until you learn your way around this field, take along an experienced friend. Watch out for the high-pressure auctioneer. Vintage-car auctions can turn out to be sheer folly for the untried and uninitiated shopper. Inspect cars ahead of sale and put a limit on your bidding budget. Don't allow yourself to be swept away. Consider bringing along a professional car restorer who can be retained for a fee in the $100 range to make an inspection of the car you have under consideration.

(6) Ask the advice of established dealers on types and prices of cars before you invest. Again, if you have a particular car in mind, get a professional appraisal.

(7) Undertake vintage restoration only if you are prepared to devote an inordinate amount of time to the job. It can be a big task and consume five hundred to two thousand hours of your so-called "free" time depending on the size of the car and how mechanically expert you are. Be warned: not only will your ability be involved, but you also may need costly special tools.

(8) If you restore—don't overdo. Being sensible is as important as being authentic.

(9) Consider a professional restorer. Depending on your car and its condition, restoration costs could run well into five figures. You could sink more into the restoration than you will ever recoup on a resale—even in a rising market. Restorers frequently will take monthly payments of a quarter to a third of the price of the job.

(10) Make sure that you are adequately covered by liability and collision insurance. Some policies will cover you for parading your vintage cars at a show or similar festive event—but you could be banned from driving on major highways. Understand the limitations and restrictions of your policy.

Finding vintage cars outside the established market place can be fun and potentially profitable for the neophyte shopper. Consider making a few car-searching trips into the countryside, for the cars still could be sitting in some barns. Try touring the back roads. Keep looking for a potential bonanza that might be rusting away in some yard. Ask local residents about old cars: some could be abandoned; some could be on blocks.

Search for semi-restored cars which their owners halfheartedly gave up midway through the spruce-up job.

Pass the word among your friends to be on the lookout for you. This way you'll have several emissaries working in your behalf.

And above all, go slow! Don't be overeager. Learn the rules. Abide by them. Vintage cars can be a great hobby. But you must study the cars and the market—as you would any investment.

How to Choose an Appraiser

WHO ARE THE APPRAISERS

An accurate appraisal of any asset you own (all those mentioned in this chapter, for example) often is imperative—if only for your own protection. And certainly this will be the case if you're selling or buying, if taxes are at stake, if estate values are involved. How much do you know about this vast area?

Who are the appraisers? How are they organized, educated, monitored? When you need their services, how do you find and select the right one?

• There are five leading, nationwide testing/certifying appraisal societies in the United States, with an estimated 30,000 members of whom perhaps 15,000 have been tested and certified as being professionally expert and experienced. In addition, about 25 national, regional, local groups represent appraisal practitioners; and there are about 100,000 non-organized, or non-affiliated practitioners.

• Since the early 1900s, United States appraisers have been trained and monitored mainly by these five major societies, together with "in-house" training by some government agencies. Seminars, guidelines, tests, similar learning tools have been prepared by their educational leaders. A code of ethics has been published and is enforced by each of the five societies.

• But few states bother with monitoring appraisers. And there are *no* states which license, certify, or register appraisers in personal property appraising (or machinery/equipment, utilities, etc.). Only a couple specifically license even real estate appraisers.

• Your growing awareness, however, is stimulating appraisers to look seriously at themselves and some are taking steps to improve their educational, monitoring, and public service programs. As one example, the Washington-headquartered American Society of Appraisers is involved in a nationwide effort to create for the first time in the United States a valuation sciences degree program under which the education of appraisers will be placed with colleges and universities. As of the late 1970s, five colleges were offering the program.

This action will facilitate access to the most current data on statistics, economics, data processing, ethical criteria, and reporting techniques, says the ASA's executive officer, and it "will emphasize the great need for participation in appraising by minority members, whose participation we need to strengthen our professional ability to serve the public.

"Some form of licensing/certification/registration should be legislated," the ASA stresses, "for the benefit of the public, and all appraisers should be included in all fields."

The ASA also has adopted a "recertification concept," which would require continuing education criteria for every designated appraiser.

Thus, appraisers are moving to improve their profession, upgrade educational methods, encourage minority participation, require continuing education.

QUESTIONS TO ASK

But—how do you learn to select the best service you can? By asking these questions of the appraiser before you hire him or her:

What are your special qualifications to appraise this particular property? Are you a member of an appraisal society? Have you been tested by written exams? How long is it since you have been examined? May I see a list of clients for whom you have worked?

Ask for the name of the appraisal society. Call the organization for a double-check.

The names and addresses of the five major societies, each with chapters and members in major cities from coast to coast, are:

American Society of Appraisers, Dulles International Airport, P.O. Box 17256, Washington, D.C. 20041; American Society of Farm Managers and Rural Appraisers, P.O. Box 6857, Denver, Colorado 80206; American Institute of Real Estate Appraisers, 430 North Michigan, Chicago, Illinois 60611; National Association of Independent Fee Appraisers, 7501 Murdoch Street, St. Louis, Missouri 63119; Society of Real Estate Appraisers, 7 South Dearborn Street, Chicago, Illinois 60606.

28

KNOW YOUR RIGHTS!—AND HOW TO USE THEM!

THE CONSUMER MOVEMENT AT THE START OF THE 1980s

As the 1980s begin, the consumer movement is being viewed by millions of Americans with a new mix of disappointment and suspicion. Ironically, the aggressive consumer advocacy of the past decade has itself contributed to the disillusionment.

For "consumerism" has moved beyond the easy black-and-white issues of banning flammable children's sleepware and into the gray areas that do not inspire your instant support or lead to quick solutions.

It is hard, for example, for average citizens to get excited about legislation that would enable public interest groups to take part in government proceedings. And there is no clear or easy answer as to where the line should be drawn between the constitutionally protected right of commercial free speech and invasions of an individual's privacy. This is the sticky issue which the Federal Communications Commission and other state government bodies are up against as they weigh whether and how to control unsolicited "junk" phone calls.

In many respects, the consumer movement has evolved from a crusade against blatant outrages into an attempt to change the way institutions work, to open them up, to make them more responsive to a variety of viewpoints and interests.

But in this maturing process, the consumer movement has made serious mistakes.

It has failed to celebrate its successes with the same relish that it has cataloged its failures and unfinished business.

It also has failed to make clear that its major goal is not "more government" or a form of "big brother" protectionism but to establish rules of conduct in the market place which enable you to help yourself, to make your own choices and decisions based on information that is accurate and easy to understand.

In 1962, President John F. Kennedy outlined in a consumer message to Congress four basic consumer rights that underlie today's consumer advocacy and which warrant repetition:

• The right to safety—to be protected against the marketing of goods and services which are dangerous to your health, life, or limb.

• The right to be informed—to know enough to guard yourself against fraudulent advertising, inaccurate labeling, unfair and deceptive practices, and to have facts which enable you to get full value for your dollar.

• The right to choose—to have, as far as possible, access to a variety of products at reasonable prices.

• The right to be heard—to obtain legal redress of complaints and grievances when the market place fails.

One of the basic challenges facing the consumer movement in the 1980s is to re-emphasize these original goals and to make clear that its aim is to disperse power and information to you, the individual, not consolidate it within a bureaucracy.

HELPING YOU TO HELP YOURSELF

Do you know what your rights are when you have a dispute with the automobile repair shop?

Are you aware that you can take legal action against a dealer in any type of merchandise who unjustifiably threatens your credit rating?

Do you know what protection the law gives you if you receive unsolicited goods in the mail?

Test your ability to take care of yourself in today's market place, your awareness of important consumer rights, by answering this consumer rights quiz. True or False:

CONSUMER RIGHTS QUIZ

(1) Mail order firms generally must fill orders within thirty days or offer your money back. (True)

(2) Parents and students over eighteen have the right to see most school records and get inaccurate information corrected. (True)

(3) A consumer in Small Claims Court in all states must be represented by a lawyer. (False)

(4) Food labels must list their contents in order of quantity. (True)

(5) If your credit card is lost or stolen, you are liable for any amount until you notify the issuer. (False. You're liable until you notify the issuer or up to a maximum of $50, whichever is less.)

(6) There is a thirty-day cooling-off period on door-to-door sales contracts. (False. There's a three-day cooling-off period during which you can cancel door-to-door sales.)

(7) All wearing apparel selling for more than $3.00 is required to carry care labels. (True)

(8) Anyone seeking classified data from the government must receive a reply to his or her inquiry within ten working days. (True)

(9) If a moving company fails to pick up and deliver your household goods

when it agreed to and as a result your family incurs motel and dining expenses, the moving company must pick up the bills. (True)

(10) If you complain about an error in your bill to a creditor and don't hear from him for two months, you are entitled to keep the disputed amount up to $50, whether or not an error has been made. (True)

(11) If you have overpaid or returned an item and forgot you have credit outstanding, the store can pocket the money after thirty days. (False. You must be sent a refund or a notice of your credit during each billing period.)

(12) A creditor can ask if you are divorced or widowed if you're seeking individual credit. (False. A creditor may only ask if you are married, unmarried, or separated.)

(13) The Consumer Leasing Act requires leasing companies to tell you the facts about the cost and terms of their contracts, when you lease cars, furniture, appliances, and other personal property (not apartments or houses) for more than four months. (True)

(14) If you are covered by a private pension plan and have worked long enough to get a pension, it will automatically go to your spouse if you should die before retirement. (False. It will be so directed only if your plan has early retirement provisions, you opt for a surviving spouse reduction, and you have reached a certain age.)

(15) The Federal Wage Garnishment law limits the amount of your wages that your employer may withhold to repay a creditor to whom you owe money. (True)

(16) The Fair Debt Collection Practices Act prohibits anyone from harassing or abusing you, calling you repeatedly at odd hours, or telling anybody other than you that you owe money. (False. It applies only to debt collectors who regularly collect money for others, not the creditor himself or his lawyer.)

(17) If you are turned down for credit, insurance, or a job, you have the right to be told the name and address of the consumer reporting agency that prepared the report which resulted in the turndown. (True)

(18) If you are "bumped" involuntarily from an overbooked airline flight and the airline puts you on another flight to your destination within minutes you are still entitled to receive a refund. (True)

(19) With a few exceptions, no law prevents a private organization from demanding your Social Security number, but no law says you have to provide it either. (True)

(20) Federal law sets the minimum interest rates which banks, credit unions, and savings and loans must pay on deposits. (False. The maximum is set by law.)

How did you score?

If you found that you did poorly, review the quiz and the basic protections which federal law provides you, and which are discussed in virtually all the chapters of this book.

Also check what types of consumer protection rules your state and city now have on the books.

State and Local Government Protections for You

Various states and localities, for instance, prohibit:

• Selling used goods (such as demonstrator cars and worn furniture floor models) as new.

• Presenting you with a non-itemized repair bill.

• Stating that an item has been "marked down" when it normally has been priced at its current level.

• Changing the term of an advertised guarantee when you come to the store to look over the item.

Some areas also require that:

• All grocery items be marked with their individual prices, regardless of whether the store has an automated computer checkout system.

• All trade schools and auto repair shops be licensed or registered.

• Landlords place rent deposits into escrow accounts that cannot be used as income until disposition of the deposit is determined.

• Mobile home park tenants must be given a sixty-day written notice if the management wants to evict you, the tenant, and you must be told why.

A survey comparing laws and regulations in all fifty states and the District of Columbia on fifteen consumer issues disclosed that California and Massachusetts rated the highest, Wyoming and North Carolina the lowest.

How to Complain—and Get Action!

The fact that we in the United States are the owners of more than one billion home appliances, small and large, is convenience carried to a new dimension. But the miseries of repairing and servicing all these appliances also can be agony in a new dimension.

When was the last time you brought home some brand-new gadget, found it to be a lemon, then struggled through the utterly frustrating experience of having the dealer who sold it to you pass the buck to some huge and distant manufacturer, who maintained a stony silence for weeks before even acknowledging your complaint, much less fixing the appliance?

When was the last time you registered a complaint during the warranty period, then watched the dealer welch out of the warranty because he failed to cope with the problem before the warranty ran out?

But do you know what to do about these infuriating situations? Do you know how to complain—and get action?

BASIC RULES ON COMPLAINING

Here's what—and how:

(1) Go back to the dealer who sold you the product, or to the service agency to which he directs you, and complain—loudly. Take the ailing product with you (unless it's a refrigerator or a stove or some other monolith) and the original sales slip. Give the dealer all such pertinent details as the date of the purchase, the date on which the problem arose, a description of the problem and, if you

could not take the appliance for any reason, the identification number of the machine. Don't threaten; this will only turn people off. Let the facts speak for themselves. And don't accost an innocent salesgirl who has neither the know-how nor the authority to handle your problem. If you document your case well, the normal channels of complaint usually will work.

(2) If the dealer or service agency refuses to help, then write or telephone the manufacturer's customer relations department. Again, state the key facts clearly —including dates, serial numbers, place of purchase, amount paid, what went wrong. Send photocopies of canceled checks and previous correspondence if you can. *Never, never send your only and original documents.*

(3) If this doesn't produce results, write to the company's president, again coldly stating the facts. Indicate at the bottom of your letter that copies are being sent to a variety of consumer organizations. If you do not know the name of the company president or the address of the company, ask your state or local consumer protection agency how and where you can find this information. Or go to your local library and look them up in Poor's Register of Corporations, Directors, and Executives or Moody's Industrial Manual. If these directories are not available in your local library, ask for the "directory" issues of such business publications as *Fortune, Business Week,* or *Forbes.*

(4) Send copies of your letter to your local consumer protection organization and also to such organizations as the Office of Consumer Affairs in Washington, Consumers Union, and your local Better Business Bureau. (See pages 1243–64, for addresses of agencies and organizations which are eager to hear about your problems and in *some* cases prepared to assist you.)

When the Better Business Bureau receives a complaint, it contacts the company involved and tries to arrange a settlement. In some cases, arbitration is used. Because the Better Business Bureau makes contact with a company's top managers, reasonable complaints are fairly often settled satisfactorily.

However, there are limits to what the BBBs can or will do.

A BBB can only be a negotiator, not a judge.

It cannot force a firm to make an equitable settlement.

It can rarely even negotiate a settlement of a complaint with an unscrupulous enterprise, and it cannot force it out of business.

It will not handle complaints involving legal matters, credit matters, collection of accounts, or wages owed.

It will not pass judgment on prices or quality of goods or services.

To make the best use of a Better Business Bureau, request a Bureau report on a company—summarizing its past methods of operation—before committing yourself to any expensive proposition.

(5) Be constructive all along the line. If you have a suggestion on how the company or the dealer or the manufacturer could avoid the problems you are complaining about, include this suggestion in your correspondence. Propose a specific remedy. Do you want a refund? Repairs? Replacement? An apology? Be fair and realistic about what you propose.

(6) Don't try to be an amateur lawyer or insist on your "rights." The company

or person to whom you are complaining probably knows a lot more about your rights than you do.

(7) If you are complaining in writing for the umpteenth time, give the dates of previous complaints.

(8) If you have bought the unsatisfactory or undelivered merchandise on a charge account, tell the store you don't intend to pay for it until a fair adjustment has been made.

(9) If it's an appliance, and if the manufacturer is unresponsive, send all pertinent information to the Major Appliance Consumer Action Panel or "complaint exchange" operated by the Association of Home Appliance Manufacturers in Chicago. MACAP has a staff of consumer specialists equipped to get action on your complaints on both small and large appliances. Also appeal directly to a local consumer organization, and if no such organization exists, ask the Consumer Federation of America in Washington for help in locating one.

(10) Tell your problem to your local newspaper in the form of a letter to the city editor, a tip to the consumer "action line" desk, a telephone request for help. Don't exaggerate, don't dramatize: just tell it the way it is. If your problem is real and other consumers also are victims, most newspapers or TV or radio stations will rise to your defense. There is no more powerful weapon than publicity.

Above all: Don't fail to complain if you feel you have a valid gripe—not only about a money loss but also about rude salespeople, deceptive advertising, late deliveries, confusing warranties, or outright gyps. It may be embarrassing to admit you've been had, but your complaints—if you make them fairly and coolly —will win better products and better service over the long range not only for yourself but also for other shoppers.

WHY YOU NEVER GET YOUR MONEY BACK

The 1980s will have the unenviable reputation as a bonanza decade for the nation's schemers and probably will be the worse decade ever for the millions of you who will become victims of your own ignorance and greed.

Equally dismaying, you'll not even have the excuse that you have been the target of a "new" gyp. The most successful of the rackets are and will be perennials that you should have learned to recognize and avoid in elementary school, and that I have tried to warn you about repeatedly throughout this book.

And worst of all, despite the growing numbers and power of consumer protection bureaus, law enforcement agencies, regulatory bodies at all levels of government, if you become a victim, the odds are overwhelming you won't get one cent —not one—of your money back.

But, "I want my money back!" is understandably the anguished cry that almost always comes after a victim of a consumer fraud discovers he/she has been ripped off and his/her precious "investment" has simply vanished.

Q. *Why do you rarely get it back?*

A. Because your money is, in fact, gone. Many schemes have profit margins no higher than their legitimate business counterparts. (Racketeers are not usually good money managers). If a promoter does make a bundle, he/she siphons it off, so it's hard to find or recover.

Q. *"Where did the company go?"*

A. Bankrupt or closed. Or unknown to you, the gypsters start up again in a new city/town under a new name while you try (without a chance of success) to recover from the defunct firm.

Q. *"I'll get the law involved!"*

A. "Money back" still requires a voluntary agreement, usually under pressure, or a suit and a court order. Either requires a thorough investigation. A court order requires prosecution. Since few law enforcement agencies have adequate resources, they pick among frauds to investigate and prosecute. Your individual complaint may be neither carefully investigated nor prosecuted.

Q. *"But can't the court order restitution?"*

A. Yes, but far, far too often it is not paid. Con men frequently are "judgment proof." Unlike most of us who own property, a car, a house, etc., they have no assets that can be seized.

Q. *"But fraud is a crime!"*

A. Yes, even though these schemes seem outright frauds to you and me, it's tough to prove to a jury "beyond a reasonable doubt" that the intent of the defendant was to defraud. While it may be easy to show that you, a victim, have lost, this is not proof of fraud. The defense attorney simply may argue the business failed.

Q. *"He's convicted. At least send him to jail!"*

A. He may or may not go to jail. But no one gets any money back unless the judge orders restitution as part of the sentence. And often the judge does not so order.

Q. *"Any other reasons why I don't get my money back?"*

A. Yes. You won't get your money back from the 1980s' record total of consumer frauds unless you, the victim, complain loudly enough. A veteran postal inspector says that even in fraud cases fewer than 5 per cent of the victims complain. And often if you do complain, you are up against a professional con man.

On a scale beyond anything ever known in the United States, the "con man" will be spreading out across the nation in the 1980s—snaring countless numbers of you as victims in the market place. The circumstances of the 1980s will be made to order for these shrewd, slippery swindlers: tens of millions itching to use their nest eggs to get-rich-quicker side-by-side with steep unemployment and other millions desperately seeking ways to earn a living wage.

If you are caught in a con man's web, the odds are he (or she) will escape unpunished and free to go on to other schemes. The odds also are you'll rarely, if ever, recover a single penny.

Your only real protection is being sufficiently informed to be on guard. Below, therefore, is a profile of a real-life con man, L.D., who has been operating throughout the 1970s without ever being put away by law enforcement agencies.

(1) In 1972, working out of New Jersey, L.D. touted a nationwide consumer discount buying service to alert members to ecological hazards, unsafe products,

misleading ads, and even frauds. In reality, L.D.'s scheme was a straight distributorship and he, with his accomplices, conned more than $500,000 from hundreds of victims. The promoters misrepresented earnings, told distributors to claim they were making a survey in order to pitch other distributors, failed to disclose that so-called "account manager" jobs had to be purchased, and pressured the gullible into falsifying loan applications at banks. In 1974 a New Jersey court ordered L.D. to pay restitution of $503,000 plus fines and costs of $10,000. For itself, the state collected less than $1,000. Not one of the 312 victims got a cent.

(2) In 1975, L.D. crossed the Hudson to a swanky Central Park South cooperative apartment/office in New York City. His business-opportunity ads claimed: "Tired of working for someone else? Tired of giving all of yourself and not receiving? Call us . . . We Can Help! . . . A product every motorist needs. No competition. Guaranteed location and buy back." The product was a tire sealant to be vended from ten gas stations. But there was no merchandise. There were no locations. A promotional quote from a Chicago banker who headed "the nation's 2nd largest bank" was a complete fabrication. Neither the bank nor banker existed. In November 1976 a New York state court ordered the return of $36,000 to victims of the scheme plus payment of $4,000 in state courts. L.D. has paid zero.

(3) The U. S. Government was next in the web, through the Commodity Futures Trading Commission (CFTC), a federal agency which was then fighting the nation's biggest investment swindle—the fraudulent sale of London commodity options. L.D. registered with the CFTC as a salesman (omitting mention of his phony schemes in his application). The CFTC has since revoked his license and fined him $10,000. But as of this writing, the CFTC is waiting for its $10,000. (And it always will be waiting.)

(4) In late 1977, L.D. advertised for an "associate or partner, $40,000 1st year guaranteed with better potential the second year. My marketing firm is growing . . . I am seeking a working partner with $10,000 to invest. Serious inquiries only." Among his victims was a Long Island business products salesman who grabbed a distributorship selling artificial flowers made of silk to be sold from display racks. The victim's loss: $4,500.

The law affords little protection and less recourse. So:

• Avoid any promise of quick money which involves your putting up cash first. That combination is almost always lethal.

• Don't be fooled by plush offices, handsome clothes, an expensive car. Victims' money bankrolls the con man, and his bank accounts are usually newly opened. Check the longevity of the account; it's more important than the balance.

• Never take references, even the most impressive, at face value. Ask the promoter what they mean, then check the references. You may get two entirely different stories.

• Don't be impressed either by such words as "national," "international," "consumers," etc. How many cities does "national" mean? Which ones? Be skeptical about any claims of affiliates, subsidiaries, suppliers, customer relationships. They may not exist. Get letters, names, addresses, question every claim.

• Insist on any promise in writing. Even then, be wary. Once a con man parts you from your money, you're out. But L.D.? He's still around, with several schemes going at once.

HOW TO FILE A FORMAL COMPLAINT

If you are filing a formal complaint with a government agency—say the Food and Drug Administration—be reasonably sure there is a violation of a law for which that agency has responsibility to avoid wasting your and the agency's time. (See pages 1243–64 on where to get help, for the addresses of all key federal agencies you might want to write or call.)

To be effective, your complaint should be prompt and should contain the following information:

• Your name, address, phone number, and directions to your home or where you work.

• A clear description of the problem.

• A description of the label on the product and any code marks on it (such as the numbers stamped on a tin can).

• The name and address of the store which sold you the product, and the date you bought it.

Save whatever is left of the offending product, and save any unopened containers, for your doctor's use or for possible inspection by the agency.

Also report the suspect product to its manufacturer, the packer or distributor shown on the product label, and to the store where you bought it.

HOW TO WRITE YOUR REPRESENTATIVES

Finally, you may strongly support current consumer legislation to protect you and others in the future. If so, the first thing to do is to write your representatives —both in your state legislature and in Washington. Good, thoughtful, constructive letters may have a great impact on your senator's or congressman's thinking, and ultimately on legislation.

Here are five key rules for writing your representative:

(1) Identify the issue or bill that concerns you—by either its official or its popular title.

(2) Write as soon as possible after a bill has been introduced—but in any event before it comes out of the committee that is holding hearings on it and is responsible for shaping it into the form in which it will be put before the entire Senate or House.

(3) Make your comments constructive: if you oppose a bill, offer sound alternatives; if you approve, say why.

(4) If you are especially knowledgeable in the area about which you are writing, or if you have significant personal experience related to the legislation to report, share your knowledge and your experience.

(5) Keep your letter short—and clearly written.

The address at which you write (or telegraph) all senators and representatives are:

The Honorable ————— —————   The Honorable ————— —————
Senate Office Building   House Office Building
Washington, D.C. 20510   Washington, D.C. 20515

How to Avoid Mail Order Agonies

One of the convenient but also potentially the most agony-laden ways to shop is by mail either from mail order catalogs or in response to advertisements. Among the worst agonies are late deliveries, non-deliveries, broken merchandise, and refusal to honor warranties on products which do not perform as they are supposed to.

RULES FOR SHOPPING BY MAIL

You can avoid this type of bitter disappointment, though, by following these basic rules:

• Order at least three to four weeks before the date on which you want delivery —particularly during the Christmas season. Look in the catalog for a notation on the deadline for guaranteed delivery for Christmas.

• Be explicit in your instructions. Be sure to include your name and address (surprisingly, many don't), and any other information required. Also tell the store how to include your name if the gift is being sent by you to a friend.

• Don't rely solely on the picture of the merchandise you want to order. Read the description of its size, dimensions, weight, contents. And if key dimensions are missing, skip it.

• Look into the conditions of sale and/or guarantees. Are all sales final? Are products guaranteed to satisfy? To grow? To work? What will the company do if you are not satisfied—especially with expensive items? Give your money back? Replace the item? Or, least desirable, give you credit toward another purchase? Do you have anything specific to get the guarantee fulfilled—such as keeping the shipping label?

• Pay by check or money order, not cash. If you are ordering from a department store, charge the order if you can, then pay promptly after you have received your order intact and on time. If you must return an item, do so promptly, stating your reasons in a letter attached to the package. Give your name, address, account number, date of your order, description and cost of the item. If you complain "properly," most reliable companies will replace unsatisfactory merchandise or refund your money. And if your order does not arrive until after the time when you need it, the company will almost always accept return of the merchandise.

• Inspect mail order packages as soon as you receive them to be sure no parts are missing and to confirm the contents.

• If your complaints don't get a response within a reasonable period of time, write the Postal Inspection Service of the U. S. Postal Service in Washington to start an investigation into possible fraud, the Bureau of Consumer Protection, Federal Trade Commission, Washington, D.C. 20580, and the Direct Mail Marketing Association Consumer Service Director, 6 East 43rd Street, New York,

New York 10017. This trade association will bring pressure on any member violating its standards of ethics.

In sum, be at least as wise a shopper by mail as you are in a store.

WHAT TO DO WITH UNORDERED MERCHANDISE

What should you do if you receive, say, a clutch of ugly neckties either through the mail or delivered to your door, which you have not ordered, do not want, and certainly do not wish to pay for? You also do not want to go to the trouble of rewrapping them, trundling them to the post office, and paying return postage to return them to their sender.

You have no obligation to accept the merchandise, return it, pay for it, or give it any special care. So feel free to ignore any dunning letters for payment for any unordered merchandise you may receive. If you receive any such merchandise C.O.D. through the mail this is a postal violation and should be reported immediately to your post office.

Of course, first be sure that the merchandise was not sent to you by a merchandiser—such as a book or record club—which has signed you up for "negative option" selling. Under this arrangement you, the member of the "club," must return a reply card to the company if you do not want the merchandise, and are obligated to pay for the items if you fail to return the card within the allotted time. Under a Federal Trade Commission "Trade Regulation Rule," dating back to the mid-1970s, you have at least ten days in which to return the form rejecting an offer of merchandise. The FTC also requires the merchandiser to tell you "clearly and conspicuously" on all promotion materials:

how to reject the offer of a selection;

whether you are required by your agreement to buy a certain number of items in a certain time;

that you have the right to cancel your membership in the plan at any time.

If you would like to reduce the volume of unsolicited mail you receive, write to the Direct Mail Marketing Association and request a form to remove your name from the mailing lists of their 1,600 member firms.

WHAT IS A WARRANTY WORTH?

WHAT IS A WARRANTY?

You buy a new TV set from a neighborhood store, the set is "guaranteed," and it breaks down within the guarantee's time limit. Who is responsible for repairs—the store or the manufacturer?

Will you have to pay labor costs and other charges which would amount to the bulk of the repair bill?

Does the guarantee cover all the parts, or will you find out that the part which broke down wasn't warranteed?

Do you have to send the product a long distance to be repaired and at whose cost?

If you are promised "satisfaction or your money back," do they really mean they'll give you a refund if the product is defective?

And how much red tape do you have to endure before you get your money?

If an appliance is guaranteed for a "lifetime," what does "lifetime" mean?

Does the guarantee cover problems rising from faulty installation or only the manufacturer's defects?

What if the installer and manufacturer disagree on the cause of the problem?

These are merely a few of the annoying, often frustrating questions facing you when one of those sixteen appliances in your "average" household quits, collapses, or goes up in flames. It's no more than common sense to inform yourself about the basic provisions of warranties and on the fundamental rule for protecting yourself against worthless "guarantees."

Consumer product warranty law now gives you a basic floor of warranty coverage and requires that all warranties on virtually all types of products "mean what they say and say what they mean."

There is no difference between a warranty and a guarantee. They are the same: a maker or seller backs the product you buy. But there are two main types of warranties: an "express" warranty and an "implied" warranty. The usual express warranty is the one you see in writing—the type you find on most automobiles, small and large appliances, other household and around-the-house equipment. The implied warranty, which goes automatically with all purchases (except "as is") that you make, is the *unwritten* protection *implied* by the seller when he offers to sell to you. It is created by law. It simply says that when you buy something, it should perform the job it is supposed to perform, whether there is a written warranty or not. If it doesn't work, it's up to the seller to repair it or replace it or give you a refund.

TRAPS IN A WRITTEN WARRANTY

With any express or written warranty, what is *not* covered often tends to be more important that what *is* covered. In one study by a Presidential Task Force, no fewer than thirty-four different types of disclaimers were found on appliance warranties! A toaster you buy, for instance, may have a single defective part which is costly to replace or have repaired. That part may be excluded from coverage.

Be skeptical about products advertised as covered by an "unconditional guarantee" or a "lifetime guarantee." "Lifetime" guarantees almost never refer to the life of you the buyer. A product with a "lifetime" warranty is usually warranted for *its* own life (whatever that means!) or for the life of the product with which it is used (such as a muffler on a car), or for as long as the first purchasers continue to own the product. You also often may be led to believe a "lifetime" guarantee means the product is especially durable. This isn't necessarily so. Manufacturers are well aware how soon you're likely to sell, say, a car or lose a bicycle.

KEY QUESTIONS TO ASK ABOUT WARRANTIES

Here are the key questions you should ask about *any* warranty or guarantee:

Who will be responsible for repairing the product? The dealer? A service agency? The manufacturer? A repairman designated by the manufacturer? Does whatever source responsible have a good reputation for living up to warranties?

Does the warranty cover the entire product—or only certain parts? Are any kinds of failures excluded? Once you know the scope of the warranty learn its terms.

Is it a full warranty or a limited one? What do you get if the warranteed product is defective?

Is labor included or only replacement parts?

Is there a provision for prorating the guarantee—e.g., paying only an allowance toward replacement of an item such as the motor of a year-old food blender which has somewhat depreciated?

If the product you have bought is defective and must be removed from your home for repair, will the dealer or manufacturer substitute an equivalent appliance in the interim?

Do you have to pay to return it to the shop or pay shipping charges to the factory?

How and by whom would the warranty be honored if you should move? Is there an authorized service agency at your destination which could perform the needed repairs?

Note: In warranties offered on many cars, tires, bikes, furnitures, and appliances, there may be two different sets of rules—one set covering the first year and the other set covering the remaining one, two, four, or nine years.

WHAT YOU MUST DO TO MAKE YOUR WARRANTY WORK

You, the buyer, must protect your warranty coverage by informing yourself thoroughly and *before you buy* about what a product's warranty does and does not cover. Consider the warranty coverage offered on products made by different manufacturers as you comparison shop. And do *your* part to keep the warranty valid.

Most important, keep your sales slip. You almost always have to prove the date of purchase. If you must mail a special warranty card before the warranty is valid, do so, although very few companies insist on this; they use these cards mostly for marketing information. Keep any guarantee you may have seen in an advertisement. Don't lose the guarantee card which may have come with the product. It tells you what you get and how to get it. If you must submit the product for special inspections or servicing to make the guarantee good, do so.

Also, be sure to keep a written record of the dates you request service and your service receipts so that if your warranty period runs out before repairs are performed, you'll be able to establish the fact that the problem started while the warranty was still in effect. If it did, it is covered under the warranty.

And be on guard:

"Do-it-yourself" repairs on an appliance within the warranty period will probably make the warranty invalid. So leave such work strictly to the seller or his authorized service company.

Put in a file the exact name and address of the company or individual making the guarantee or keep the warranty.

How to Get the Most Out of Your Car Warranty

There are probably few problems quite as frustrating as those you encounter if and when you find yourself stuck with a car that's a "lemon." One Chicago woman, for instance, was forced to take her new expensive model car back to the dealer eight times to be repaired. The car was two months old. Despite her efforts, the car's transmission did not move in gear, it leaked oil, died frequently, and was infested with so many ants her seven-year-old son was afraid to ride in it!

If you are typical of many new-car buyers, you believe you are stuck with a "lemon" so long as the dealer continues to try to repair the defects.

This isn't so.

By law, all products, including cars, have an "implied warranty" that there are no defects interfering with the use and value of the product.

An "implied warranty of merchantability" is yours automatically by law when you buy any product, except one at an "as is" sale. As applied to cars, it basically guarantees that your automobile will be fit for safe, efficient, and trouble-free transportation. It covers defects that exist in the car at the time of sale and show up then or any time thereafter.

There is a catch to this "protection," though. Most states (with a few notable exceptions) allow dealers and manufacturers to limit the "implied warranty" to the duration of the written warranty. Say, for instance, one month after your 12,000-mile or 12-month written warranty runs out, your car's engine explodes. Under the manufacturer's written warranty you are out of luck. But under the "implied warranty of merchantability" if you bought your car in a state which does not limit it, you still have the right to file suit to have your engine replaced. In other states you may be stuck, although people in other states have sued—and won—in such cases.

If you or your lawyer are considering legal action, send for a free fact sheet on private consumer remedies, prepared by the staff of the Federal Trade Commission and available from Room 130, FTC, Washington D.C. 20580. Another helpful booklet is "The Down Easter's Lemon Guide," from the Bureau of Consumer Protection, State House, Box 692, Augusta, Maine, 04330. It is free to Maine residents, but if you live out of state, it cost $1.00 in the late 1970s.

GUIDES BEFORE GOING TO COURT

But before you consider going to court be sure that:

• Once you have bought a car, you do your part by maintaining it according to the schedule in the owner's manual. Have the shop doing the work note it in the schedule.

● You keep copies of all work orders to show when you first had problems and whether or not they were fixed properly.

● If you believe that you have a problem covered under the warranty, you take the car to the dealer from whom you bought it. Get a written estimate on what must be done and on whether or not the work will be covered by the warranty— *before* you authorize the dealer to proceed with it. Give him adequate time to do the necessary repairs.

● If you do not get satisfaction, you write or call the manufacturer's zone manager or factory zone manager. You can get his name and address from the dealer (simply asking him for this may make him more cooperative). A courteous and objective letter—giving full, appropriate details—will have the best chance of success. Be clear about what you want—a repair, replacement, refund, loaner car, etc.

● If your car is out of warranty but the problem arose during the warranty period, you mention this and that you are well aware the company is obligated to fix it. The firm cannot get out of its responsibility by saying "sorry your car is out of warranty." The same applies if your problem was "fixed" once and reoccurred. The company has to keep trying to repair the defect.

● You keep in mind, too, that many problems are the result of faulty design and may result in recalls. If the problem affects the safety of the car, you might want to call the Department of Transportation's toll-free hotline (800-424-9393) for recall information and to report safety problems.

● You realize that in many places you can take your problem to a small claims court, magistrate's court, county court, etc., where you do not need to be represented by a lawyer. You should use these courts for disputes involving cars if:

(1) the problem is repairable but the shop hasn't made the repairs.

(2) the shop or dealer charged you for the repair but shouldn't have.

(3) you went to another repair shop to have work done that should have been done under warranty but wasn't.

● You take advantage of the fact that you can work through a local consumer group to spur a dealer to act by, say, running an ad in your local newspaper detailing how the dealer shortchanged you. But *don't* attempt this on your own without legal advice. You can get into major legal trouble.

● You consider writing to the Federal Trade Commission, Warranties Division, Washington, D C. 20580, telling the agency of your problem. Do not expect the staff, however, to help you directly or to get involved in your case. They cannot do so

● You inform the dealer that you are doing all this.

● You are fully aware that court action is your last resort. It's here that "lemons" get replaced or money refunded. It does happen, and federal warranty law allows the court to require that your lawyer's fees be paid by the warrantor. One more guide: often manufacturers settle after a lawsuit is filed. Fear of a court battle frequently is enough to make them act.

USED CAR WARRANTIES

In some states, used car dealers must offer a guarantee that their cars will pass state inspection. In others used cars must pass inspection before they leave the lot. But most states leave the condition of a used car offered for sale pretty much up to the dealer. Any used car warranty has the same remedies as one supplied on a new car, but implied warranties on used cars are all but worthless.

If you financed your car *through the dealer,* however, you can stop payment until he honors the warranty. Before you do this, contact the bank or finance company where you make payments and the dealer to inform them you'll not be making any additional payments until the problem is resolved.

This step, as well as those outlined above, should improve your chances of fair treatment.

SHOPPING FOR LEGAL SERVICES

LAWYERS ALLOWED TO ADVERTISE

Each American adult will have at least three serious legal problems in a lifetime. Yet 30 per cent of adult Americans have *never* consulted a lawyer and an additional 30 per cent have talked with a lawyer only once, according to an American Bar Association report in the late 1970s.

Why, when law schools are graduating thirty thousand lawyers a year?

Because millions of you simply do not know how to find the right lawyer for you. You are utterly befuddled about which lawyers specialize in handling what types of problems and at what prices.

This was the prime reason for a 1977 Supreme Court decision striking down state and local bans against lawyers' advertising. As one result, you now can get more facts than ever before about lawyers—their availability, specialties, and fees—through TV, radio, newspaper, and magazine advertisements.

Another significant result has been the development of legal clinics—supermarket-like law firms that specialize in offering routine legal services at cut-rate prices. As the 1980s neared, there were a thousand of these clinics in operation throughout the country and more are springing up all the time. They often are located in shopping centers and offer their services during evenings and on Saturdays. Because they handle so many clients, use paralegals to do much of the work, and concentrate on such relatively simple matters as uncontested divorces, personal bankruptcy cases, and uncomplicated wills, their fees almost always are lower than those of individual lawyers associated with big law firms or practicing alone.

Many lawyers still are reluctant to advertise but this resistance undoubtedly will be whittled down as more prominent firms take the plunge. Some state bar associations already have begun to set aside advertising budgets to stimulate business for the whole profession and to encourage widespread use of lawyers' services.

BASIC RULES FOR FINDING AND CHOOSING A LAWYER

The wisest time to decide who will be your family lawyer is *before* you need one. If you are new in town or have never before used the services of a lawyer, there are a variety of ways you can find a lawyer to meet your needs.

Check the Yellow Pages for the number of your local bar association. Many bars have prepared lawyer directories—books which list lawyers by their specialties: criminal law, general practice, consumer law, etc. The directories also contain information about the lawyer's education, whether he speaks any foreign languages, and his fees. Many lawyers give details on how much they will charge for an initial consultation.

• Instead of or in addition to these directories, even more local bar associations maintain lawyer referral services. The best of these advise you whether your particular problem actually requires legal help. This alone can solve your case immediately. If your problem does require a lawyer, the service then refers you to one, or perhaps several lawyers, who have indicated experience in your problem area. The referral service also may help you arrange an appointment, and often can tell you about other legal services and social service organizations in your area which might be able to assist you. The fees for such referral services usually range between $5 and $25.

• Ask your friends, doctor, minister, bank officers, or your company lawyer for suggestions. Any of these may have had some experience with your kind of problem and can refer you to an appropriate lawyer.

• Investigate local public interest groups which may provide legal services in certain specialized areas of law. If they cannot help you directly, often they will know of lawyers who are the most experienced in the field of your problem.

• When asking for referrals, be as specific as you can about the nature of your problem and be honest about the limits of your ability to pay.

IF YOU CANNOT AFFORD THE FEE

But what if you cannot afford to pay the fee a lawyer asks to help you solve a serious legal problem? Then . . .

• Go to one of the nation's five-hundred-plus Legal Aid Society offices. Look in the Yellow Pages under "Legal Aid" or "Lawyers" or call the local bar association for the address and phone. These societies are backed by community funds and offer legal aid at low or no cost. (In criminal cases, the best source of free help is the Public Defender.)

• Ask for help at one of the many federally funded Legal Service Corporation offices around the country. The LSC is the largest provider of legal aid to the poor and indigent. To locate an office near you, also look in the Yellow Pages under "lawyers," call your local bar or write directly to the Legal Service Corporation, 733 Fifteenth Street, N.W., Washington, D.C. 20005.

• Find out if any local law schools have set up legal service facilities for ordinary consumers or low-income groups.

• Check whether your company or labor union offers free legal advice or group "lawyer insurance." As the 1980s approach, few do. Premiums for these services are deducted from your paycheck. You may be able to buy a prepaid legal plan on the open market, too. These are similar to health insurance plans. If you would like to join a prepaid plan or have questions about a specific one, write to the National Resource Center for Consumers of Legal Services, 1302 Eighteenth Street, N.W., Washington, D.C. 20036.

HOW TO SLASH LEGAL COSTS

To keep your legal costs to a minimum, first find the best lawyer you can afford to handle your problem, and check with all potential lawyers to whom you are referred through any of the sources previously mentioned. Call and talk to several of them before you make your first appointment.

When you phone, find out if the lawyer has experience with your kind of case. Learn what he charges for an initial interview, if anything. If you believe your matter is routine, ask if he has a standard fee and what it covers. If your problem is more complicated, ask what the lawyer's hourly fee is. Inquire if the lawyer provides written agreements describing the fees and the services he will give in return.

Consider these answers from each of the lawyers, then make an appointment with those whose replies suit you the best.

During your first interview, keep in mind that the attorney works for you. He or she should be anxious to help you solve your problem in the best way possible —which well might mean avoiding court action. Your lawyer also should be able to explain simply what he can do for you and how he will accomplish it. You should feel that you can tell the lawyer everything about your problem, including information that might be unfavorable. He can only assess your problem and his ability to solve it accurately if you are completely honest and straightforward.

When talking about your case, it will save you time (and therefore money) if you are as organized as possible. Prepare in advance a clear summary of your needs. Bring with you the names and addresses of all parties involved, their attorneys and insurance companies, if you know them. Have all pertinent documents —medical bills, receipts, contracts, etc.—in order too. Some lawyers may ask you for these before your interview so they can review them in advance of your actual meeting.

If you have decided to seek an interview with a law firm, ask who will actually be working on your case. If the firm uses paraprofessional help (law students, paralegals, etc.) to prepare certain routine legal documents or background information, decide if you should talk directly with those people. Increasingly, such individuals are doing more routine legal work. Their hourly rate is considerably less than an attorney's, so if they handle much of the work on your problem you should know it and the cost should be less.

If you want to be actively involved in your own case, you should be allowed to be. Make this clear to the lawyer at the first interview and tell him you want to:

• Receive copies of all documents involved in the case or have them available to you at his office.

• Be told of all developments in the case.

• Be consulted before decisions in the case are made and the major instances in which you can make these decisions yourself.

• Ask the lawyer for a list of events that are likely to occur in your case and a timetable for them. You should have some idea of how long he will need to resolve the matter.

UNDERSTAND THE FEES!

Perhaps the most common cause of dissatisfaction between lawyers and their clients revolves around fees.

It is essential—even if the lawyer is your friend or is taking the matter on a reduced-fee basis—to understand fully his fees and how you will pay them.

Most lawyers charge on an hourly basis, with fees ranging from about $20 per hour to more than $100, as the 1980s approached. You can see about a reduced rate if the lawyer you want to hire normally charges more than you can afford. You also can ask that a lawyer not exceed a certain amount of time or amount of money on your case without first getting your permission.

More and more, both clients and lawyers are spelling out fee agreements in writing to avoid possible misunderstandings. Make sure that your agreement not only explains the fees your lawyer charges but also expenses that he's likely to incur and for which you will pay and the services he will provide in exchange.

Some lawyers require an advance fee called a retainer. It usually represents a number of hours of the attorney's time at his usual hourly rate. If the time your lawyer spends on the case exceeds the amount paid for by the retainer, he will bill you for the additional charges. You both should agree beforehand on how billing and payment for such excess will be made. If the attorney spends less time than is covered by the retainer, you both should agree that a refund will be made.

If the retainer is for a flat fee, covering the entire cost of the case no matter how much or how little time it takes, you may be unable to get a refund.

In accident or personal injury and some other types of cases, some lawyers agree to accept as their fee a percentage of the money you may get if you win. If you lose, you pay the lawyer only for the expenses associated with the case—telephone calls, court costs, postage, copying costs, etc. Cases handled on such a basis are called contingency fee cases.

If you agree to such an arrangement, be certain you understand what portion of the recovery you and your lawyer will each receive and how expenses will be covered.

The Citizens Advisory Committee to the Washington, D.C., Bar has prepared an excellent guide, "Finding and Hiring a Lawyer" (available by writing D. C. Bar, 1426 H Street, N.W., Suite 840, Washington, D.C. 20005). The guide recommends you ask your lawyer the following questions regarding any type of legal fee arrangement:

• Can you prepare for me an estimate of how much this legal problem will cost?

• Can you give me a written fee agreement which sets forth not only my obligation to pay but also exactly what you will do for me?

• How often will I be billed? Will you agree to let me know when a specific dollar amount of your time has been spent on my case so that I can authorize further payments?

• Can you estimate how much court costs, witness and deposition fees and other costs will run, aside from your fees? How will I be required to pay these costs?

• When will I have to pay? (Explain to your lawyer the payment schedule which is best suited to you.)

In your final analysis of any lawyer you should trust your own common sense and feelings as you judge a lawyer's personality, experience, how you communicate with one another.

These aspects are well outside of the money area, but fundamentally may be just as important as, or even more important than, the fees you will have to pay.

WHICH LEGAL SERVICES DO YOU NEED?

Inquire about what services and specialties are and are not provided by the law firm as a whole. If services important to you are not provided, ask whether the lawyer or firm has access to top-notch outside legal specialists.

Here's a list of five legal services a family lawyer should be able to provide.

(1) Deed preparation, title searches, and other details in real estate transactions. (See chapter on housing for description of legal mechanics of home buying.)

(2) Drawing up a will and perhaps later serving as executor or legal adviser for your estate. (See "What You Should Know About Wills, Estates, and Trusts.")

(3) Representing you in and out of court if you should be arrested or sued or if you should decide to sue someone else.

(4) Preparing a separation agreement and other documents associated with a divorce and, if necessary, representing you in a divorce court. (See chapter on "Sex and Money" for discussion of can you afford a divorce?)

(5) Steering you to a competent insurance agent, tax adviser, accountant, and other experts whose fees are favorable to you or who will make special arrangements with you.

YOUR RIGHTS AS A BORROWER

SHOPPING FOR CREDIT

The 1968 Truth in Lending Act is one of the most important consumer protection measures ever signed into law. It requires creditors to provide you with information that tells you exactly what credit will cost. With these facts you can compare the *real* cost of credit from Lender A with that available from Lender B. Furthermore, the act also covers professional services, such as those provided by your physician, dentist, or lawyer, if you pay for them in more than four installments.

In order to help you comparison shop, the law requires that the same terms be disclosed by all creditors. The two most important disclosures required are the *finance charge* and the *annual percentage rate*.

The finance charge is the amount of money you pay to get credit. It includes interest as well as such other charges as loan or finder's fees, points, service charges, or premiums for required credit life, accident/health, or property insurance.

The annual percentage rate (APR) is the charge for credit expressed as a percentage. The lowest APR is always the best credit buy, *regardless* of the amount of the debt or the length of the time over which payments are to be made. Comparing the APR on credit deals and choosing the lowest one gives you the most for the least amount of money.

The APR is not always the same as the interest rate. Like the finance charge, it also includes other charges which may increase the cost to you and expresses them in a manner which allows you to compare one deal with another.

Basically, you, a consumer, can obtain two major types of credit.

One type is called "closed end" credit. It is frequently used to finance the purchase of such relatively expensive items as cars, furniture, TV sets, or for personal loans. You usually ask for this type of credit for a specified period of time and agree in advance on the amount, number, and due dates of payments, as well as the dollar amount of the finance charge.

The second major type of credit is called "open end" credit. You generally use this sort with revolving charge accounts or credit cards to pay for such less costly items as clothes, meals, and hotel rooms. Another example of "open end" credit is the overdraft checking account. With this type of credit, you pay finance charges periodically on your unpaid balance, and you may obtain new extensions of credit at any time.

Depending on the type of credit you get—open or closed end—the Truth in Lending Act requires you be provided with certain facts. Here is a sampling of the information you must be given for each type of credit:

CLOSED END CREDIT DISCLOSURES

All closed end credit disclosures must be given to you *before* any credit agreement is made. You must be given a copy of the document on which the disclosures appear. Below is what you *must* be told:

• The total finance charge—the amount of money the credit will cost you.

• The annual percentage rate.

• The number, amount, and due dates of payments, plus the sum total of all the payments.

• The amount or method of figuring out what penalty fee you may be charged if your payments are late.

• A description of any security interest and clear identification of the property to which it applies.

• A description of any penalty charge that you might have to pay if you pay off your account before the agreed-upon time limit.

• A statement of whether you will get any rebate of unearned finance charges for early payment and, if so, the method used to compute the amount of such a rebate.

OPEN END CREDIT DISCLOSURES

Before any transaction is made on an open end credit account, creditors must disclose a number of important facts to you. Among these are:

• A description of when a finance charge may be imposed and the time within which you can pay without having to pay any finance charge.

• The method the creditor will use to determine the balance on which a finance charge may be imposed, as well as how he'll determine the amount of the finance charge.

• The periodic rate or rates which he will use to compute finance charges and the range of balances to which each rate applies, and the corresponding annual percentage rate.

• The minimum periodic payment required.

• A notice describing your rights under the Fair Credit Billing Act (see pages 1225–26).

When you open a new open end account, you must be given this information. In addition, you also must be sent a periodic statement (usually monthly) that tells you: your previous balance, the date and amount of each of your purchases, a recognizable description of each item you charged, credits for returns, the amount of the finance charge for the period, the address to which billing inquiries should be mailed, and other items.

If, under the open end credit plan, you can avoid a finance or other charge by repaying any portion of your new balance before a certain time has elapsed, your periodic statement must be sent to you at least fourteen days before the cutoff date.

CREDIT ADVERTISING

The Truth in Lending Act regulates credit advertising, too, including deals with no finance charges but payable in more than four installments. If a creditor or seller advertises any specific credit term in newspapers, magazines, radio, television, promotional material, or on the price tags attached to merchandise, he must include other pertinent credit information. For example, he may not simply say that "you'll pay only $30 a month" without telling you such facts as the "cash price," the "cash down payment required" (even if zero), the annual percentage rate, and other pertinent information.

OTHER PROTECTIONS UNDER TRUTH IN LENDING

In any credit transaction in which your home is to be used as security, a creditor must give you three business days during which you can back out of the deal and cancel the contract you have signed.

You must be given a written notice explaining you have the right to this "cooling off" period.

If you decide not to go through with the transaction, you must tell the creditor in writing. This three-day cooling off or "rescission" period applies to such credit arrangements as second mortgages and home repair or home improvements loans (some of these involve mechanics' and similar liens; see pages 250–51 for a description of such liens).

The right to cancel does *not* apply to a first mortgage loan used to purchase your home.

YOUR REMEDIES

If a creditor fails to give you any of the information outlined above (except the disclosures required in credit advertisements), you have the right to sue.

You can sue for damages plus twice the amount of the finance charge (not less than $100 or more than $1,000). You can also be reimbursed for court costs and attorney's fees if you win the lawsuit.

However, even if you should win, you still must pay off the debt, including the finance charges. Creditors who deliberately violate the law may be hit with criminal charges, including fines of up to $5,000 or a maximum of one year in prison, or both.

LEASING VS. BUYING ON CREDIT

When shopping for your next car or furniture for an apartment that you plan to use for only a short time, you well may wonder if you should buy on credit or lease. The Consumer Leasing Act, which became law in 1977, will help you decide. It will also help you compare the terms of one leasing arrangement with another.

As with credit transactions, there are two main types of leases: "open end" and "closed end."

In an open end lease you run the risk of owing extra money depending on the value of the property when you return it. This payment is called a "balloon payment."

In a closed end lease you are not responsible for the value of the property when you return it and will not have to make a balloon payment. Consequently, closed end leases usually have higher monthly payments than open end leases.

The Consumer Leasing Act applies to both open and closed end leases. It requires that certain facts be disclosed to you, the individual, when you lease property for more than four months for your personal, family, or household use.

Before you sign a lease you must, for instance, be told:

• The amount of any advance payment or security deposit.

• The amount and dates of regular payments and the total amount of those payments.

• The kind of insurance you'll need, who is responsible for maintaining and servicing the property, and whether or not you can buy the goods, when and at what price.

• The amount you must pay for taxes, license, registration.

• How you or the leasing company may cancel the lease and what the charge is for doing so.

If you choose an open end lease, the leasing company also must tell you that you may face a balloon payment and how it is determined. You have the right when such a lease is over to get an independent appraiser's estimate of what the property is worth. Both you and the leasing company must abide by the estimate.

Say, for instance, you sign an open end lease for a car. At the end of the lease, the leasing company figures the car will be worth $2,000. If, when you return the car, the leasing company claims it is worth only $1,500, you can ask an outside appraiser to determine the car's value. If he agrees with the leasing company, you probably will have to pay a balloon payment of $500.

There are limits on the size of balloon payments, however. The law says that in an open end lease they may not exceed three times the average monthly payment, unless you agree to make a higher payment or have, in the case of a car, driven more than average mileage. The leasing company may seek a bigger payment by going to court. If it does go to court, it must pay your attorney's fees, whether it wins or loses.

To compare the cost of buying on credit with the cost of open end leasing, you will need to know:

The annual percentage rate you must pay on your loan and the finance charge;

The total amount for which you are responsible under the lease—that is, total periodic payments, the estimated value of the property at the beginning and end of the lease, and the difference between the two.

All of this information must, by law, be given to you.

To illustrate, here is a rundown on a three-year open end car lease. The lease might show:

36 monthly payments of $125	$4,500
+Estimated value of car at lease end	2,000
Amount for which you are responsible	$6,500
—Value of car at beginning of lease	5,800
Difference	$ 700

If you bought this same $5,800 car and financed it over a period of thirty-six months by obtaining a loan with an annual percentage rate of 12¼ per cent, you would pay a finance charge of about $1,160. Compare this finance charge figure with the difference shown in the example above. This permits you to compare the two costs.

Of course, the costs of buying the car on credit depend on the annual percentage rate of your loan. The higher your credit costs, the more appealing leasing may seem. But before making up your mind, take into account the cost of insurance, maintenance, and other special fees associated with both leases and loans.

APPLYING FOR CREDIT

Credit—the right to incur debt and to defer paying for goods and services—is an important privilege, not a right. Banks, department stores, gasoline companies, credit unions, and other creditors set their own standards for judging your creditworthiness or ability and willingness to repay.

Under the Equal Credit Opportunity Act, however, they cannot deny you credit on the basis of your sex, marital status, religion, natural origin, or (with limited exceptions) your age.

In general, creditors assess your ability to repay your debts by asking how much money you earn; if you have other outside income, say from such investments as stocks and bonds; and if your earnings are steady. Often creditors inquire how long you have held your present job. Usually you have to be employed for at least six months before a creditor will consider you sufficiently reliable to receive credit.

The best indication of your willingness to repay your debts is your credit history—whether you've paid your credit card bills and loans on time, any outstanding debts you may have, if you've ever gone bankrupt or had actions taken against you by a collection agency, etc.

Creditors also will ask about your assets: whether you have a savings and/or checking account, a home, a car. They use other criteria to judge your stability: your occupation, whether you own or rent your home, how long you have lived at your present and previous address, whether you have a telephone.

Many firms, particularly large ones, have replaced the above more traditional, rule-of-thumb measures of an applicant's creditworthiness with a mathematically developed credit scoring system.

These systems are based on the information in a particular creditor's own accounts, and certain characteristics which have been selected to predict your financial trustworthiness. Whether you are considered a good risk or bad depends on your total score.

While these systems have been praised for their statistical accuracy, they also have been criticized by some legislators and consumer groups for being incomprehensible.

For example, when an applicant has been turned down by some creditors using such systems, he has been told that the "reason" for denial was geographical area, occupation, type of residence, or other explanations which give him no chance to take corrective action in order to qualify for credit. These incomplete and ambiguous statements have led some critics to charge that creditors are still practicing discrimination.

WOMEN AND CREDIT

Until relatively recently, many creditors discriminated against women, not because they lacked steady jobs or were burdened with debts, but simply because they were women. The Equal Credit Opportunity Act, which became law in 1975, makes discrimination on the basis of sex or marital status illegal. The act gives women these important protections:

• A creditor may not refuse you credit because you use your maiden name, a combined or hyphenated last name, or your first name with your husband's last name that you have assumed—"Anne Smith," for example, rather than "Mrs. John Smith."

• If you are married, divorced, widowed, or separated or change your name, a creditor may not require you to reapply for credit because of this change. He may not require you to change the terms of your account or stop reporting your credit history.

• Creditors cannot ask any questions regarding your childbearing or birth control practices. They may not assume that because you are of childbearing age and statistically apt to stop working that your income will fall, and for that reason deny you credit.

• A creditor may not refuse to consider alimony, child support, or separate maintenance payments as income for you as long as the payments are regular or reliable. Each creditor has a different idea of what constitutes reliability for this sort of income, so you should ask what evidence or proof he might want (copy of a court order or checks sent to you) before you apply. However, you do not have to reveal that some of your income comes from these sources unless you think you won't obtain credit without them.

• A creditor may not refuse to consider your income because it comes from regular part-time work.

• A creditor cannot require your husband to co-sign or guarantee credit or a loan, unless you are depending on his income to support your application or jointly held property is being put up as collateral for a secured loan.

• Creditors cannot ask you what your marital status is if you are applying for a separate, unsecured account unless you live in a community property state (Arizona, California, Idaho, Louisiana, Nevada, New Mexico, Texas, and Washington). In fact, if you don't live in one of these states, are not relying on your spouse's income, alimony, or support payments and your spouse will not be using the account, creditors cannot ask for any information about your spouse.

Many private groups and public agencies have written excellent, easy-to-understand booklets about women's credit rights. Among these are:

"Equal Credit Opportunity" and "Women and Credit Histories," available free from the Federal Trade Commission, Legal and Public Records, Room 130, Washington, D.C. 20580.

"A Woman's Guide to Personal and Business Credit" by Susan Ingram ($2.95) from Pilot Books, 347 Fifth Avenue, New York, New York 10016.

"New Credit Rights for Women" ($2.00) from The Consumer Credit Project, Inc., 267 Kimberly, Barrington, Illinois 60010.

"Borrowing Basics for Women," free from the Public Affairs Department of Citibank, Box 939, Church Street Station, New York, New York 10008.

"How Women Can Get Credit" (20 cents) from National Organization for Women, 2000 P Street N.W., Washington, D.C. 20036.

"Women to Your Credit," free from your nearest Commercial Credit office or Commercial Credit Corp., 300 St. Paul Place, Baltimore, Maryland 21202.

"The Credit Handbook for Women," free from the American Express Co., American Express Plaza, New York, New York 10004.

CREDIT AND THE ELDERLY

You have just turned sixty-five and receive a notice to reapply for credit at a local department store. You are seventy-eight years old, still have a steady job, a savings and checking account, home and car, yet your application for a major credit card is turned down.

Experiences such as these led to the 1977 amendments to the Equal Credit Opportunity (ECOA) Act. These amendments extend the ban on credit discrimination to include race, national origin, religion, receipt of public assistance, as well as age.

The ECOA permits creditors to consider age only if:

You are too young (usually under eighteen) to sign contracts;

You are sixty-two years or older and the creditor provides special credit help or consideration because of your age;

The creditor uses a statistically sound credit scoring system which *favors* applicants sixty-two years old and over. (See "Applying for Credit" for an explanation of credit scoring systems.)

Because age has its economic consequences, creditors can use it to consider factors that clearly bear on your ability and willingness to repay a debt. They may, for instance, determine if your income is about to drop because you are close to retirement.

However, creditors may *not:*

• Refuse to consider your retirement income (money from a pension or annuity plan) in rating your credit application.

• Require you to reapply, change the terms, or close your account just because you reach a certain age or retire.

• Deny you credit or close an account because credit life insurance or other credit-related insurance is not available to someone your age.

CREDIT AND MINORITIES

The ECOA prohibits you from being denied credit because of your race, color, religion, and national origin, because you receive income from any public assistance program or because you have exercised your rights under consumer credit laws.

Under the law, too, lenders may not consider the race or national origin of the people who live in the neighborhood where you want to buy or fix up a home with the help of a loan.

You also might want to know where most lending institutions in your city make mortgage and home improvement loans. The Home Mortgage Disclosure Act requires most major lenders in metropolitan areas to make this information available annually. You can ask to see the disclosure statement at your bank, credit union, or savings and loan association.

REMEDIES

If you believe you have been the target of discrimination, you can sue for actual damages and up to $10,000 in punitive damages. Before taking legal action, complain to the creditor. Let him know you are aware of your rights. Request the reason for your denial in writing. If still unsatisfied, speak with the credit manager or loan officer.

If the problem cannot be solved, you can file a complaint with one of a number of federal agencies which have enforcement responsibility.

If the creditor is a retail store, small loan and finance company, gasoline or travel card firm or state-chartered credit union, contact the Federal Trade Commission, Equal Opportunity Division, Washington, D.C. 20580.

If the creditor is a bank, write to one of the bank regulatory agencies. (See pages 1248–49 for a discussion of which agencies are responsible for which types of banks.)

If the creditor is a federally chartered credit union, alert the regional office of the National Credit Union Administration.

Your Right to an Honest Credit Rating

Because of the Fair Credit Reporting Act, which became effective in 1971, you can take action if you believe you have been denied credit, insurance, or a job or had difficulties obtaining any of these due to a consumer report on you.

There are two basic kinds of consumer reports. The most common is a credit report or credit history assembled by a credit bureau. It contains information about your credit accounts and bill-paying habits, which comes from creditors who use the services of the credit bureau. This type of consumer report costs little, and merchants, banks, credit card companies, and other creditors request thousands of them on applicants every day.

The other type of consumer report is an investigative report. It usually is requested by insurance companies or employers. This type of report involves personal interviews with third parties who may know something about the consumer's character, general reputation, or style of living. As a rule, the consumer is entitled to be told when he is the subject of such a report. These investigative reports are costly and relatively rare.

The Fair Credit Reporting Act is designed to protect consumer privacy and safeguard the accuracy of credit bureau reports. Under the Act you have the right:

• To learn the name and address of the consumer reporting agency responsible for the report which caused you to be denied credit or a job.

• To discover upon request and proper identification of yourself the nature and substance of the information (except medical) that a credit bureau or other consumer reporting agency has on file about you.

• To know the sources of such information, except for investigative-type sources.

• To get the names of all who have received reports on you within the last six months or within the past two years if the report was furnished for employment reasons.

• To have incomplete or incorrect information reinvestigated and, if it's found to be inaccurate or cannot be checked, to have it removed from your file.

• To make certain that if an item is deleted or added to your file, the credit bureau (at no cost to you) notifies those firms which you name of the inaccuracies.

• To have your side of a disputed fact or story included in your file and future reports, if a disagreement between you and the agency cannot be resolved.

The law forbids reporting agencies from sending out adverse information about you that is more than seven years old, although bankruptcies may be reported for fourteen years. There are no time limits for sending information on you if you apply for a loan or insurance policy of $40,000 or more or apply for a job with a salary of $20,000 or more.

HOW TO REVIEW YOUR OWN FILE

It is simple to learn what is in your credit file. You may visit in person or possibly receive the information by mail or over the phone.

Check the Yellow Pages under such headings as "credit" or "reporting agencies" to get the name and address of the major credit bureau in your area. Or call your bank or department store and ask which credit bureau it uses.

Call to arrange a personal or telephone interview. Some, but not all, bureaus will send you a report by mail once you send them a release form and probably a small fee ($2.00 to $5.00). Technically, you have the right to be told what is in your file, not to receive a copy of it.

If you visit the credit bureau, have some personal identification with you. You also may bring one person with you when looking over or discussing your file. That person must furnish identification, too, and you may have to give the bureau written permission for his or her presence. If you have any questions, the law requires that the credit bureau provide you with a trained counselor who can help you read and understand your file.

CREDIT HISTORIES FOR WOMEN

Frequently when women are rejected for credit, the reason is "lack of sufficient credit history." In the past, credit accounts often were recorded only under the husband's name, even though the wife used the accounts and took charge of paying the monthly bills.

If you are a woman—single, married, divorced, separated, or widowed—you owe it to yourself and your family to establish a credit history in your own name!

Why? Because the chances are very high that at some point in your life you will want and need to get a mortgage loan, department store charge account, or credit card. The day almost surely will come when you will be on your own with an income of some sort and obtaining credit will be important to you. To obtain it, you will need to establish your creditworthiness.

To develop your own credit record, take these steps:

• Open a checking and/or savings account in your own name (e.g., "Mrs. Susan Smith," not "Mrs. John Smith," which is a social title and could possibly refer to more than one woman. You may use your maiden name, a hyphenated last name or whatever name you wish and use legally). Establishing a separate checking and/or savings account doesn't mean you have to close out a joint account that you share with your husband. Just open a new one for your own use. Don't overdraw on it.

• Apply for a retail, bank, or credit card in your own name. This is one of the least expensive ways to start a credit history, since you can use the cards without paying any interest if you pay your bills within a certain period of time. You may have to accept a limited credit line until you prove your willingness to repay. You don't have to borrow on these lines of credit. They will appear on your credit history and establish you as soon as they are approved.

Don't apply for too many accounts at one time. Some creditors may deny your application if they think you are opening too many new accounts in a short space of time. If you are turned down, though, the Equal Credit Opportunity Act gives you the right to request the specific reasons why.

Make certain that your local credit bureau has complete and accurate information about *you* in a file in *your* name, if you have had credit before, alone or with your husband. (Look in the Yellow Pages under "credit" or "credit rating" or "reporting agencies" for the name and address of major credit bureaus in your area. Contact them and arrange to find out what is in your file. The bureau may charge you a small fee, but it's worth it.)

• Be sure that the creditor is reporting information on any shared accounts in both spouses' names, if you opened an account with your husband after June 1977. This is the law under an ECOA amendment.

• Ask to have any accounts opened before June 1977 added to your file—if these accounts were reported only in your husband's or former husband's name, whether the accounts are active or closed.

• Notify the creditor that you want the account history reported to the credit bureau in your name, if the accounts are still open.

• Ask the bureau to add them to your file, too, if the accounts are presently closed.

• Give a creditor any information which shows that a derogatory credit history from your marriage should not be used against you.

DEBT COLLECTION PROTECTIONS FOR BORROWERS

The Fair Debt Collection Practices Act prohibits debt collectors from harassing, oppressing, or abusing you, from using any false statements, such as implying that they are attorneys or work for a credit bureau, and from engaging in such unfair practices as making you accept collect calls or threatening to take your property without the right to do so.

The law applies to any personal, family, or household debts—money owed for a car, for charge accounts or medical care. It covers debt collectors who regularly collect debts for others, not the creditor himself or his lawyer.

The law forbids debt collectors from contacting you at inconvenient times or places—before 8 A.M. or after 9 P.M., unless you agree. A collector may not contact you at work if your employer disapproves, and he must not tell anybody other than you that you are behind on your bills. He may contact other persons about your debt only in order to find your whereabouts, and he generally must not talk to a second party more than once.

Once you tell a debt collector in writing to stop trying to reach you, he must stop except to let you know he will not be in touch again or that he or the creditor will take some specific action on which he usually carries through.

You have the right to sue a debt collector within one year from the date the law was broken. You may recover up to $1,000 for any violation, as well as money for actual damages, court costs, and attorney's fees.

If you wish to learn more about this act or wish to complain about collectors other than banks and other financial institutions, write to the Federal Trade Commission, Debt Collection Practices, Washington, D.C. 20580 or to one of its regional offices.

WAGE GARNISHMENT PROTECTIONS

The Federal Wage Garnishment law, in effect since July 1970, limits the amount of your earnings that your employer may withhold to repay a creditor to whom you are in debt.

The amount is limited either to 25 per cent of your after-tax (disposable) weekly earnings; or the amount by which your disposable earnings exceed thirty times the federal minimum hourly wage, whichever is less.

For example, if the minimum wage is $2.90 an hour, an employee's earnings may not be garnisheed at all if his disposable earnings in a given week are $87.00 or less. (If you are paid on a monthly basis, the figure is $374.10; on a semi-monthly basis, it is $188.49.) If your weekly disposable earnings amount to more than $87.00 but less than $116, only the sum above $87.00 may be garnisheed. (As the federal minimum wage rises, naturally so will these numbers.)

An employer may not fire you because your earnings have been subjected to garnishment for a single debt, regardless of the number of garnishment proceedings brought to collect the debt. Anyone willfully violating this law may be fined up to $1,000 or imprisoned for as long as one year, or both. State laws with more restrictive provisions take precedence over the federal law.

If you believe any portions of this law have been broken, contact the Labor Department's Wage and Hour Division. The nearest office should be listed in your telephone directory under the Labor Department in the U. S. Government listing section.

IF YOUR CREDIT CARD IS LOST OR STOLEN

Under the Truth in Lending Act, it is illegal to mail or otherwise issue unsolicited credit cards. This protects you against credit card thieves who steal and use credit cards that you didn't even know had been issued in your name. If this happens, you are not responsible for any charges made with the card.

You also are protected from *unauthorized* use of credit cards that you have accepted. If you lose your card or it is stolen, you are liable only for the lesser of $50 or the amount charged before you report the loss to the card issuer. The $50 maximum applies even if you fail to discover and report the loss or theft for months. However, if the credit card company failed to provide you with a notice of the potential $50 liability or neglected to give you a self-addressed postage-paid notification form, you have no liability at all. You also are not liable if the card issuer provided no method to identify you as the person authorized to use your card, such as by signature or photograph on the card. (For discussion of your liability for lost or stolen debit cards used to make electronic fund tranfers see Chapter 15 on "Your Personal Banking Business.")

BILLING ERRORS

The computer at the local department store bills you for goods you have returned to the store or fails to credit your account for payments made. How do you get that computer to listen to reason?

Your credit card company's computer makes a mistake in figuring your finance charge. How should you approach this problem?

Or you are billed $90 for two tires you never bought. Or the bank's electronic billing brain raises the price of a $25 loan on your overdraft checking account to $250.

Billing errors are a common and major nuisance. But as a result of the Fair Credit Billing Act (FCBA), much of the onus for clearing up disputes is now on the creditor—provided you, the customer, take certain steps. Furthermore, you can fight over a bill that you believe is unfair with reasonable protection of your credit rating.

HOW TO ARGUE WITH A COMPUTER

Under the Fair Credit Billing Act, which went into effect in the fall of 1975, you have sixty days from when the first bill containing the error is mailed to *write* the store, credit card company, or bank about a billing error. This notice need not be long. Just identify yourself and your account number; indicate that your bill contains an error. State the amount involved and briefly explain why you think a mistake has been made.

Do not send in your copy of a sales slip or other document unless you have a duplicate copy for your records.

Send this letter to the address given on your bill for billing error notices. It's wise to send the letter by certified mail with a return receipt requested, so you have proof of the date it was mailed and received.

The notification letter is essential. It triggers protections provided by the Fair Credit Billing Act, and shifts the burden of resolving the dispute from you to the creditor.

The creditor has thirty days to let you know that he has received your letter, and two billing cycles (not more than ninety days) to resolve the dispute by correcting your account or explaining why he felt it was accurate.

Once your letter is received, the creditor cannot:

close your account;

send you collection letters;

threaten to damage your credit rating or sue you;

report the disputed amount as delinquent to a credit bureau (although it *can* be reported as in dispute);

turn the matter over to a collection agency or attorney.

Furthermore, once you have sent this letter, you do not have to pay the amount in dispute or make any minimum payments or finance charges connected with it until the matter is resolved. (You are still obligated, however, to pay all parts of the bill that are not questioned.)

If it turns out that the creditor or his computer is in the wrong, you won't have to pay any finance charges on the disputed amount. If the reverse is true—you have made an error—then you may have to pay for any finance charges which accumulated on the amount in question and you will have to make up any minimum payments on the disputed amount that you missed.

If the creditor fails to follow these rules, he may not collect the amount indicated by the customer to be a billing error, up to $50, and finance charges, even if the bill turns out to be correct. You also have the right to sue for actual damages, and twice the amount of any finance charges, not less than $100 or more than $1,000, plus reasonable attorney fees.

FASTER ERROR RESOLUTION

While it is important to write a letter about a suspected error in your bill in order to preserve your rights under the FCBA, you may want to use the telephone as well. Most questions and disputes involving major credit cards are handled over the phone. (Usually there is a toll-free customer service number given on your monthly statement.)

These credit card company telephone lines tend to be busiest Monday mornings. So call in the afternoons and at the end of the week, if you can. Get the name of the person to whom you are talking.

But caution! Using the telephone does not preserve your legal rights—only a letter does that.

Two other tips: keep your own receipts when you make charges, and check them against your monthly statements. And be sure to check large bills, especially ones for hotel rooms, before charging them. Hotel and airline bills are sources of many arguments.

PROTECTION AGAINST DEFECTIVE OR SHODDY GOODS OR SERVICES

Before the FCBA took effect, if you used a credit card to buy an item that you later discovered was a piece of junk, you might have been required to continue making payments to the bank or credit card issuer, while trying to seek satisfaction from the seller—sometimes a fly-by-night operator who had since skipped town or gone out of business or who simply was unwilling to make good on defective merchandise.

While the FCBA does not treat such cases as "billing errors" subject to its resolution requirements, it may allow you to withhold payment from the credit card issuer, *if* you first try in good faith to return the goods or to convince the merchant to correct the problem.

There are two limitations on this right: first, the purchase price must be more than $50; second, you must have made the purchase within your home state or within a hundred miles of your current address. These limitations do not apply if the retailer is owned or operated by the creditor—a department store on whose charge you made a purchase, for instance, or if the creditor sent or participated in an advertisement for the goods or services that you bought.

This protection against poor goods and services is important and useful, especially in certain instances. An example: because automobile repair work is the source of many consumer complaints, some consumers try to insure themselves satisfaction by paying for such repair work with a credit card. If they discover, as many car owners do, that no repairs have been made or that they have been done improperly or inadequately, they withhold payment. Of course, you first must earnestly request the car repair shop to meet its obligations. You also should notify the credit card company of the dispute, so it won't report the disputed amount as delinquent until the matter is settled.

DISCOUNTS ALLOWED FOR CASH-PAYING CUSTOMERS

The law also allows stores, hotels, restaurants, and other retailers who honor credit cards to give discounts of up to 5 per cent to customers who choose to pay by cash or check. Previously, many credit card issuers had prevented member merchants from giving these discounts. Such agreements are now prohibited.

Nothing requires merchants to give discounts to customers paying cash, but if they do, they must post signs telling you about it. Presently, few stores offer their customers cash discounts. But it's probable the granting of discounts will spread during the 1980s, as prices continue to rise and more cash-paying people question why they have to finance the cost of a credit system that they do not use.

YOUR RIGHTS AS A VETERAN

In the late 1970s, about 100 million Americans, including veterans, their families, and survivors of deceased veterans, were eligible for benefits distributed by the Veterans Administration—ranging from low-cost life insurance to VA hospital and medical care, VA-guaranteed home loans, GI Bill benefits for education and training, disability and death compensation, pension payment.

Details on most of these are in other sections of this book—covering life insurance, college scholarships, loan programs, funerals, pensions—and you'll find a full range of veterans' benefits spelled out in a VA booklet entitled "Federal Benefits for Veterans and Dependents." Listed too are the locations of VA offices, hospitals, drug treatment centers, national cemeteries, and veterans' programs administered by other government agencies, such as the Civil Service Commission's federal job preference (to veterans) rules, and loan programs run by the Small Business Administration. Copies of the booklet are available for a small sum from the Superintendent of Documents, Washington, D.C. 20420.

Every eligible veteran (man or woman) has a right to these benefits. But among the most important rights a veteran has are those connected with the job he or she left to enter military service.

If you are a veteran now re-entering the job market, it will be crucially important for you to be thoroughly aware of these rights to your former job, as well as to promotions, fringe benefits, seniority, etc.

Under the law, if you apply within ninety days after discharge you are entitled to get back the job you left to go into service—with the same pay, seniority, and status. This rule also applies if you can't do your old job because of physical disability or because the job has been changed. It doesn't matter if the company has been sold, as long as the business still goes on.

If your employer has a seniority system—in a contract or in practice—you must be credited with seniority for your time in service. If there has been a general pay raise or increase in benefits, you are entitled to these too. If promotions are automatic, based on length of employment, you are entitled to any promotion you would have received if you hadn't been in service. If fringe benefits depend on length of service, you must be credited for the time you were away. If your right to a pension or a longer vacation depends on the period of your employment, your military service must be counted. For other benefits, you're like any other employee who has been on leave. You also share in pay losses or changes in working conditions which occurred while you were away.

You can't be fired or demoted for one year (six months in the case of National Guardsmen) except for misconduct or other good reason. Your seniority and other rights last as long as you stay on the job.

If your employer refuses to rehire you, you can bring a lawsuit in a federal district court and ask the United States Attorney to represent you. You can get help or further information at the Office of Veterans' Reemployment Rights, which is part of the United States Labor Department and has offices in cities all over the United States. Also, you can go to the local VA, state employment service, or any veterans' organization for guidance. To make sure you know and get all your job rights, register with one of the state employment service offices throughout the country. By law, you will get preference and priority in both job counseling and placement.

Check with your nearest Veterans Administration regional office on your rights and eligibility for a wide range of education, employment, and training programs. These change frequently; keep up to date.

And most important: do not ignore or downgrade the full range of benefits available. Make sure you explore all the possibilities.

VETERANS' BENEFITS

The Veterans Administration pays a dependency and indemnity compensation to widows of veterans who died while in service or from a service-connected disability, based on the husband's pay grade while he was in service. In the late 1970s this ranged from $297 to $760 a month for a widow, with an additional $35 a month for each child under age eighteen.

If your husband died while on active duty (including training) or within 120 days after discharge and from a service-connected cause, there also is an award of a six months' death gratuity. This is a lump-sum payment of six times the veteran's monthly pay, but not more than $3,000 or less than $800, payable by his military service.

Under the law after the amendments of 1978, the surviving spouse of a veteran could qualify for a Veterans Administration "death pension" in an amount sufficient to bring her (or his) income up to $2,379 per year, to $3,116 for a surviving spouse and one child, and with $600 added for each additional child. If the surviving spouse is so disabled that he or she is confined to the home, there is an extra allowance of $1,427 per year to cover needed aid and attendance.

These survivors benefits, like veterans' pension benefits (see pages 952–53), are to be increased to keep up with the cost of living.

There also is a burial expense grant of $300 for veterans whose death was not service-connected, and up to $1,100 if the death was service-connected. (See pages 991–92 for more details on veterans' death benefits.)

If the funeral director does not alert the VA insurance division of your husband's death, contact the nearest VA center.

Unremarried widows of men who served in World War II, the Korean war, or the Vietnam war and who died in service or from service-connected disabilities also may qualify for GI home loans and educational benefits. (See page 189 for more on the GI home loan program, and also pages 537–38 on financing an education.)

In addition, widows are entitled, until they remarry, to special preference when applying for Civil Service positions. If the widow is the mother of a veteran who lost his life or became totally disabled, she also is entitled to special preference.

For answers to other questions you may have, or assistance you may need, write, phone, or visit your nearest VA regional office.

YOUR RIGHTS AS A HOSPITAL PATIENT

The American Hospital Association a few years ago adopted the first nation-wide "Patient's Bill of Rights"—a milestone for you in view of the probability that sooner or later you'll be hospitalized for one reason or another and, if you're unlucky, you'll be confronted with a long series of unnecessary indignities, confusion, secrecy, arrogance, and frustrating lack of responsiveness to your needs.

Yet you, the patient, are the one paying the nation's multibillion-a-year health care bill—with a huge share of this for hospital services. Your life and limb and comfort are at stake—not anybody else's. You, therefore, have every right to insist on certain basic rights while you're hospitalized—even if they are not specifically spelled out in any lawbook.

According to the American Hospital Association's Bill of Rights you, the patient, should have the right:

(1) To considerate and respectful care.

(2) To get complete information from your physician concerning your diagnosis, treatment, and prognosis, in terms you understand.

(3) To receive whatever information is necessary for you to give your informed advance consent for any procedure and/or treatment.

(4) To every consideration for your privacy concerning your medical care program.

(5) To refuse treatment to the extent permitted by law, and to be informed of the medical consequences of your action. (This would mean that, as an adult, you have the right to die if your condition is hopeless.)

(6) To expect that all communications and records pertaining to your care will be treated as confidential.

(7) To expect a hospital to respond, within reason, to your request for services.

(8) To get information about any relationship between your hospital and other health care and educational institutions in so far as your care is concerned and to get information (including names) on the existence of any professional relationship between individuals who are treating you. (This means that you, the patient, have the right to know whether you are being treated by a member of a university hospital or by your physician's student.)

(9) To be advised if the hospital proposes to engage in or perform human experimentation on you in the course of your care or treatment.

(10) To expect reasonable continuity of care.

(11) To examine and receive an explanation of your bill, regardless of the source of payment.

(12) To know what hospital rules and regulations apply to your conduct as patient.

WHAT IS HAPPENING

What has happened in the years since the Hospital Association made its formal move?

Only a fraction of the nation's hospitals have offered all the rights to their patients, although "a few have made it a policy to distribute copies of the AHA's Bill of Rights" to patients—and some others have developed their own statements of rights.

The State of New York Hospital Code mandates the posting of a Patient's Bill of Rights and states that it also must be made available to individual patients upon request.

Meanwhile, other major moves on behalf of us as patients are being made. For instance, state legislatures are now considering a variety of bills giving terminally ill or injured people the right to order doctors to permit them to die.

The United States Department of Health, Education and Welfare in the mid 1970s issued a major set of regulations to protect subjects of medical research experimentation financed by the federal government in or out of hospitals. Under the regulations, would-be subjects must be fully informed of the risks, discomforts, and benefits of the experimentation. Special review committees in research institutes must consist not only of reviewers from within the institution but also of outsiders who might well be more objective.

Ralph Nader's Health Research Group has issued a guide to choosing a dentist and is promoting the preparation of local directories of physicians.

In the late 1970s, the Health Research Group published *Getting Yours: A Consumer's Guide to Obtaining Your Medical Records.*

The book notes that patient access to health records enables you to protect your privacy by knowing what is there. In addition, access improves patient education and understanding of medical conditions.

It improves the patient-doctor relationship and also continuity of care.

There are step-by-step, state-by-state instructions for getting patient records. All patients in federal facilities such as VA or Public Health Service hospitals, it points out, are entitled to see their records under the federal Privacy and Freedom of Information Acts. In only fourteen states, however, did patients have the right of direct access to medical records held by physicians or hospitals or both, in the late 1970s.

Getting Yours, available from the Health Research Group, Dept MR, 2000 P Street N.W., Washington, D.C. 20036, for a moderate price, tells how consumers might work to change state laws to provide for freer patient access.

The surgery releases which hospitals require patients to sign waiving any liability on the part of hospitals for surgical bungling—and more—are being challenged by consumer protection lawyers. Says one of these lawyers: "A court would never enforce this type of contract."

THE "PATIENT ADVOCATE"

Another aspect of consumer choice is going through dramatic change.

Prior to the 1970s, the physician's legal obligation to disclose information to his patient was measured by a professional community standard. The doctor could be held liable for non-disclosure only if he revealed significantly less than other doctors would have disclosed under similar circumstances. A court case in the early 1970s changed that. In the case of Canterbury vs. Sponce, the United States Court of Appeals for the District Court Circuit set the stage for a shift to a patient-based standard. Under the Canterbury decision and the large number of state court opinions which it influenced, the doctor must reveal all that a "reasonable patient" in the position of the person he is treating would consider "material" to his decision as to whether to accept the doctor's proposed treatment.

If you or a loved one have been hospitalized recently, you may have encountered a new type of consumer representative known as the "patient advocate." About 20 per cent of all hospitals now employ such ombudsmen to try to help humanize the hospital, to enable patients to get action on their complaints, and to recommend changes in policy or procedure which will benefit patients.

Some of these patient advocates simply try to enforce the Patient's Bill of Rights; others have considerable authority, including the power to adjust bills. Some have been criticized as merely cosmetic attempts to smooth over problems. They are gaining a stronger foothold, though, and their organization, the Society of Patient Representatives, is the most rapidly growing professional society affiliated with the American Hospital Association. Their supporters point out that they can help to head off malpractice suits, have improved hospital billing and collection procedures—and even meal menus.

YOUR RIGHTS AS A DISABLED PERSON

Taking a leaf out of the book of the civil rights activists of the 1970s, the nation's 30 million disabled—the blind, the deaf, the crippled, and all those with other physical or mental handicaps—are now demanding a place in society. Backed by federal law, they are demanding improved access to education and jobs and easier physical access to public buildings and transportation.

Under Section 504 of the Rehabilitation Act of 1973, all institutions and agencies that accept federal aid in the form of funds, services, or property must make their programs accessible to the handicapped—or risk having the federal aid withheld.

Another law, the Education for All Handicapped Children Act, assures a disabled child's right to a free appropriate education and gives the parent of the child a right to participate with the public school in planning and evaluating the education programs.

The Rehabilitation Act identifies a handicapped person as anyone with a physical or mental disability that substantially impairs or restricts the person in one or more of such major life activities as walking, seeing, hearing, speaking, working, or learning. Epilepsy is considered to be such a condition; so are perceptual handicaps such as dyslexia, minimal brain dysfunction, and developmental apasia. The U. S. Attorney General has ruled that alcoholism and drug addiction are physical or mental impairments that are handicapping conditions if they limit one or more of life's major activities.

YOUR RIGHT TO EMPLOYMENT

An employer who is receiving federal funds or other federal assistance may not discriminate against you, the disabled person, in hiring, promotion, demotion, transfer, layoff, or rehiring. You must be given an even break with the non-disabled in job assignments and on career ladders—as well the same treatment on leaves of absence, sick leave, training programs, etc.

Once you have been hired, your employer must take reasonable steps to take account of your disability, supplying a reader if you are blind, for example, and reading is essential to the job, or giving you adequate workspace and a way of getting to it if you use a wheelchair.

YOUR RIGHT TO EDUCATION

Your disability cannot be a factor when you apply to enroll in any private or public educational institution that receives assistance from the Department of Health, Education and Welfare.

Your application must be considered on the basis of your academic or other school records.

Once you are enrolled, the college is not required to lower its standards or degree requirements, but it may have to give you more time to earn a degree. It also must provide braille books or other aids you may need if they are not obtainable from another source.

YOUR DISABLED CHILD'S RIGHT TO EDUCATION

Under Section 504 of the Rehabilitation Act, your state and local school districts are responsible for providing an appropriate elementary and secondary education for your physically or mentally disabled child.

The type of disability and the severity of the disability do not alter this responsibility. Further, the education must be provided at a cost to you that is not more than the cost to parents of children who are not handicapped.

You and your public school district decide whether it shall be:

- A regular public school classroom
- A special education program of the public school
- A boarding school if the public school has no appropriate program
- Appropriate education in a hospital if the child is a long-term patient

The Education for All Handicapped Children Act is even more specific. The public school is required by that legislation to develop with your advice and consent a tailor-made education program for your child and to give you in writing a list of the special aids that will be provided, such as braille books or a desk that can be used with a wheelchair.

You also must be given a schedule for the periodic review of your child's progress and an explanation of your rights, including your right to a written notice of major changes proposed in your child's program or the location of that program.

IF YOUR RIGHTS ARE NOT RESPECTED

If you believe that your rights as a disabled person (or the rights of your disabled child) have been violated by any business, hospital, physician, school, college, or any other institution which receives federal funds from the Department of Health, Education and Welfare, write to the Office of Civil Rights in the HEW Regional Office in your part of the country. Submit full details.

Your local post office or your nearest Social Security Office can give you the address.

YOUR RIGHTS AS A TAXPAYER

You have just come home from an infuriating afternoon at the local office of the Internal Revenue Service—during which you tried with increasing desperation to convince an IRS agent that you *do not* owe an extra $300 on your latest income tax return. But the IRS agent won't concede a dollar, even though you are convinced of your right to deduct $1,000 of disputed contributions to your church. Further appeals within the IRS have been abysmal failures.

You are incensed. You want to fight the IRS, not to give in with a whimper. What do you do? Your basic right, as a taxpayer, is to pay *only* the federal income tax which you actually owe—and to pay not one cent more. To protect this basic right, you, as a taxpayer, have a distinct and formal set of legal procedures you can use.

HOW TO FIGHT THE IRS

You may fight the IRS—via the Small Tax Case procedure of the U. S. Tax Court, the court which Congress created specifically to help you, the taxpayer, and which came into existence in 1971 under a minor provision of the Tax Reform Act of 1969.

The provision authorized the Tax Court to hear and decide small claims—now defined as any dispute about income, gift, or estate taxes involving not more than $1,500. You argue your own case without a lawyer and without filing any technical and time-consuming forms. Under the Small Tax Case procedure, the technical rules of evidence are off and the dominant rule instead is informality. However, if you wish, you may hire a lawyer or file a brief or do both.

You have no worries about strangulating red tape or masses of paper work. Both are at a minimum. You will not be placed at an immediate disadvantage by being forced to travel far from your home for your informal hearing and the decision. A hearing on your case will be held as near your home as the court finds possible, and you'll get advance notice of when your case is coming up. The Tax Court judges hold hearings in more than a hundred cities across the nation each year. You won't have to wait long for a decision either. The judge hearing your case probably will decide whether you win or lose against the IRS within thirty days.

Of course, since this is a Tax Court procedure, you can fight your own case there without first paying the tax deficiency claimed by the IRS. Only if and when you lose or settle will you have to pay up. If you were to use the other courts—a district court or the Court of Claims—you would have to pay the deficiency claimed by the IRS first and then bring suit for a refund to get that money back.

You can be relaxed when telling your side of the dispute, trusting the judge hearing you to give you any benefit of the doubt. In fact the judge probably will help you to bring out points in your own favor which, in your innocence, you might overlook or shrug off on your own.

Moreover, the decisions of the judge are not subject to review by any other court. This means that neither party—neither the taxpayer nor the IRS—can appeal the decision to any higher court. This encourages the judges to rule more speedily and freely, for they do not face the possibility of being overruled by another court.

And the fact that the decisions set no precedents means that a judge's ruling in one case will have no effect on future cases in any court. This encourages judges to be more lenient with taxpayers, for they need not fear that their rulings will open the way for cases which would cost the Treasury countless tens of millions of dollars.

So, what if you are the reasonable taxpayer described above and you want to fight the IRS's claim that you owe $300 more on your last year's taxes?

WHAT TO DO

Here's what you do:

(1) Get a ninety-day letter (its official name is a "notice of deficiency") from the IRS office that is handling your case. You must start your case in the Tax Court within ninety days after the date on which that ninety-day letter is mailed to you. If you do not, you lose your right to litigate in the Tax Court.

(2) Write to the Clerk of the Court, U. S. Tax Court, 400 Second Street N.W., Washington, D.C. 20217, and ask for a Small Tax Case kit. The clerk will send you this kit, which includes an instruction pamphlet, a return envelope, and four copies each of these two forms:

Form 2, Petition (Small Tax Case);

Form 4, Request for Place of Trial.

(3) Fill out the forms. They are very simple.

In paragraph one of Form 2 Petition fill in the taxable year or years for which the deficiency is claimed and the city and state of the IRS office that sent you the ninety-day letter.

To illustrate, in your case it would read: "John and Mary Doe, Petitioners v. Commissioner of Internal Revenue, Respondent. Petitioners request the court to redetermine the tax deficiency for the year 19 . . . , as set forth in the notice of deficiency, dated (blank), a copy of which is attached. The notice was issued by the Office of the Internal Revenue Service at 120 Church Street, New York, New York 10007."

In paragraph two, fill in your Social Security number and your spouse's if a joint return is involved. In your case, it would read: "Petitioners' taxpayer identification (e.g., Social Security) numbers are 012-34-5678 and 876-54-3210."

In paragraph three, tell how you disagree with the IRS deficiency notice. In your case, it would read: "Year, 19 . . . Amount of deficiency disputed, $300."

In paragraph four, state briefly where you think the IRS agent went wrong in claiming you owe more taxes. In your case you might write: "The Commissioner of Internal Revenue made the following error in determining this tax deficiency: he mistakenly disallowed the entire $1,000 amount that I deducted as a charitable contribution."

Also, give facts to support your claim that the Commissioner was wrong. In your case, you might write: "We have witnesses who saw me give $1,000 in cash to my church as part of a special fund-raising drive on May 6, 19 . . ."

Now you sign the petition, with your spouse if it is a joint return, and give your present address. For example:

"John Doe, 105 Main Street, New York, N.Y. 10010

"Mary Doe, 105 Main Street, New York, N.Y. 10010."

The official form has this paragraph above your signatures: "Petitioners request that the proceedings in this case be conducted as a 'small tax case' under section 7463 of the Internal Revenue Code of 1954, as amended, and Rule 172 of the Rules of Practice of the United States Tax Court."

There also is room for the signature and address of your lawyer if you retain one—but I'm assuming you're battling the IRS in this instance all on your own with a minimum of expense and red tape. For that's the central idea of this Small Tax Case Division. And don't mark an "X" in the box at the bottom of the petition, because that would make your case a regular Tax Court Case instead of a Small Tax Case.

Now make three identical copies of the Petition and set them aside. Attach a copy of your deficiency notice to the original of the Petition.

(4) Turn to Form 4 Request for Place of Trial, of which you also have four copies. Fill out one form by listing the city and state in which you would like to have your trial and by signing it where required.

To illustrate in your case, the form would read: "John and Mary Doe, Petitioners v. Commissioner of Internal Revenue, Respondent. Petitioners hereby request that trial of this case be held at New York City, New York State. (Signed) John Doe, husband, Mary Doe, wife." And that's all there is to it!

Make three identical copies of this form too.

(5) Make out a check or money order for $10 payable to "Clerk, U. S. Tax Court."

(6) Mail this check together with the original and two copies of your Petition and the original and two copies of your Request for Place of Trial to: United States Tax Court, 400 Second Street N.W., Washington, D.C. 20217.

Keep one copy of each form for yourself.

(7) The Commissioner will answer your petition and, almost surely, will make some concession or compromise suggestion—assuming you have a fairly reasonable case.

If there is still a disagreement between the IRS and you after the commissioner's answer, your case will be set for trial at a time and place of which you will be notified by the court.

(8) The size and location of the city you have selected for trial will determine whether the Tax Court will be able to comply with your request in your Form 4. (New York City is a cinch). But, if the court cannot comply, it will pick a place that is as close and convenient to your choice as possible and it will then notify you.

A crucial point is that the judge will try to persuade you to settle the case without going to trial if your case has any validity. If you are satisfied with any settlement offer, that will end the case. A fat majority of taxpayers, incidentally, do settle before trial.

A caution, however: even though the Small Tax Case procedure is informal, easygoing, relaxed, and designed to help *you,* the taxpayer, you still must have a reasonable case to win.

YOUR RIGHTS AS A WORKER

Today there are federal and state laws covering just about every aspect of work —minimum wage laws, equal-pay-for-equal-work rules, overtime pay requirements, on-the-job safety and health standards, wage garnishment protections, and many others. Because there are so many such laws and enforcement of them is spread over dozens of separate state and federal agencies, departments, and divisions, many are neglected or violated. Thus, you, the employee, must be the watchdog of your own workplace. To help you, here is a brief rundown on major employee protection laws:

YOUR RIGHT TO A JOB

The Employment Act of 1946 and its successor, The Humphrey-Hawkins Full-Employment Act of 1978, make the federal government responsible for fostering general economic and financial conditions that will promote high employment. These laws are not really enforceable but resemble proclamations of good intentions. The Humphrey-Hawkins Bill, for instance, sets the government goals of bringing the unemployment rate down to 4 per cent by 1983, and the overall inflation rate to 3 per cent by the same date.

YOUR RIGHT TO A MINIMUM WAGE

A federal law signed in November 1977 set a uniform minimum wage for virtually all workers. As of January 1, 1979, this wage was at $2.90 an hour and it will jump to $3.10 in 1980 and to $3.35 in 1981, unless amended by Congress.

The law also requires that workers receive one and a half times their regular pay if they work overtime—more than forty hours a week. Some states have higher minimum wage laws, and these supersede the federal law. Any questions or complaints regarding wages should be directed to the U. S. Department of Labor, Wage and Hour Division, Washington, D.C. 20210, or your state employment office.

YOUR RIGHT TO JOIN A UNION

The 1934 National Labor Relations Act and amendments guarantee employees in private industry the right to organize, to bargain collectively, and to strike.

YOUR RIGHTS AS AN OLDER WORKER

Employers of twenty or more workers cannot fire or refuse to hire individuals age forty to sixty-five simply because of their age, unless the job—say, modeling dresses—requires someone within a certain age range. Firms cannot favor younger workers in pay, promotion, and fringe benefits, and unions cannot deny membership to older persons or refuse to refer them to jobs.

Furthermore, employment agencies cannot refuse to refer a job applicant to an opening because of his or her age. "Help-wanted" ads, too, cannot contain such statements of age preference as "Boy Wanted," "Girl Wanted," or "Only under thirties Need Apply."

The 1978 Age Discrimination Act also protects most workers from mandatory retirement before age seventy. (See pages 895–96.) These protections are enforced by the Labor Department's Wage and Hour Division, Washington, D.C. 20210.

EQUAL EMPLOYMENT OPPORTUNITY

Women and minorities receive most of their equal employment protection under Title VII of the Civil Rights Act. It specifically bans job discrimination in private employment on account of race, sex, religion, or national origin. It also prohibits discrimination against anyone who wants to join a union or who seeks the services of an employment agency. It bars discrimination in help wanted ads, pay scales, fringe benefits, promotions, and other aspects of employment.

A 1978 amendment to the Civil Rights Act, the Pregnancy Discrimination Act, provided specific protections for pregnant workers. It said that pregnant women who are able to work must be permitted to do so on the same conditions as other employees. When they are unable to work for medical reasons, they must be given the same rights, leave privileges, and other benefits as disabled workers. The condition of pregnancy may not be singled out for reduced coverage in medical, sick leave, or disability benefit plans.

However, the law permits abortions to be excluded from employee health insurance plans, unless the abortion was necessary to save the life of the mother. This exception applies to health insurance only. Employers are required to provide for women who have abortions sick leave and disability benefits as they would for workers with any other disability. Furthermore, they must cover health costs involved in treating medical complications that result from non-therapeutic abortions.

Complaints of discrimination by private employers, unions, or employment agencies should be directed to the Equal Employment Opportunity Commission, Washington, D.C. 20606.

Discrimination complaints involving the federal government should first be taken to the individual agency's equal employment office. If it cannot be resolved within the agency, contact the Board of Appeals and Review, U. S. Civil Service Commission, Washington, D.C. 20415.

Firms which have contracts with the federal government are subject to special non-discrimination and affirmative action requirements. Complaints involving the employment practices of companies with federal contracts should go to the Office of Federal Contract Compliance, U. S. Department of Labor, Washington, D.C. 20210.

WOMEN'S RIGHT TO EQUAL PAY

Your key defense against salary discrimination on the basis of sex is the Equal Pay Act of 1963 and its amendments. This law requires that men and women performing under similar working conditions receive the same wages, overtime pay, and benefits when their jobs demand "substantially" equal (not "identical") skill, effort, and responsibility. It is enforced by the Equal Employment Opportunity Commission, Washington, D.C. 20506.

Despite this law and despite the increasing number of women doctors, lawyers, construction workers, and astronauts, women still earn only around 60 per cent of the money that men do. This proportion has been relatively constant for the last twenty to thirty years. Today, the median (half above, half below) salary of full-time working women is $166 a week. The median salary for full time working men is $272 a week.

The major reason for this pay gap is that the majority of women still hold lower-paying and traditionally "female" jobs as secretaries, service workers, salespeople, and household helpers.

Some women's groups feel that many jobs routinely filled by women are "comparable" to higher paying ones usually held by men. They argue that a nurse, for instance, exercises as much skill and responsibility as a factory manager and should earn as much. Their arguments have not as yet been upheld by the courts. But "comparable pay for comparable work" may become the rallying cry for working women in the 1980s just as "equal pay for equal work" was in the 1960s and '70s.

YOUR UNEMPLOYMENT INSURANCE PROTECTION

And if you lose your job?

An important source of between-job financial assistance for workers in all pay brackets is unemployment insurance benefits. To qualify for this aid you usually must have left your job involuntarily and be able, willing, and looking for work. With some exceptions, most states do not provide unemployment insurance benefits to workers on strike.

Basically, unemployment benefits are paid for twenty-six weeks, but in some states under certain conditions they are stretched out an additional thirteen weeks. The size of your benefits depends on the amount of your earnings, your marital status, and the number of dependents you have.

In the late 1970s, covered out-of-work Americans were getting benefits ranging from a low of $10 a week in Mississippi to a high of $183 a week in Connecticut. The national average payment in fiscal year 1978 was in the $80 to $90 per week range. And the unemployed averaged twelve to thirteen weeks on the federal insurance program.

Unemployment insurance benefits were tax-free until 1979. They are now subject to federal taxes and to taxation in some states. Each state operates its own unemployment compensation system. To find out if you qualify for benefits and if so, how to apply, contact your local unemployment insurance office. It is listed in your telephone directory under the heading for state government agencies.

If you are an executive and lose your job, your former employer almost surely provides for some amount of severance pay. In addition, the company planning to lay you off may permit you to continue working until you have located a suitable new job, and thus keep you covered by its group insurance plans.

YOUR RIGHT TO WORKER'S COMPENSATION

Since the first workman's compensation law was passed in 1911, an increasing number of workers (and their survivors) have become entitled to receive benefits in the event of a job-related injury, disability, or illness.

With the exception of three groups of workers—federal employees, coal miners, and harbor workmen and longshoremen—each state administers its own workman's compensation program. These programs vary enormously.

Several states provide coverage for all job related injuries or diseases, while a few recognize only certain occupational illnesses. Some states exempt employers with a small number of workers. Some fail to cover such categories of workers as farm laborers or domestics. The amount of compensation that you, an injured worker, may receive also varies widely as does the time it takes to process an injury or disability claim.

Basically, compensation claims fall into three major categories: temporary, permanent, and death.

If you are injured and are out of work temporarily as a result, most states provide you with benefits equal to a maximum of 66⅔ of the average weekly wage in your state. In the late 1970s, this maximum ranged from about $60 a week in Oklahoma to about $600 a week in Alaska. Some state laws provide no benefit payments for the first three to seven days you are off the job, unless your time off exceeds a certain period, ranging again from four to forty-one days.

If you are disabled permanently—say, you've lost an arm or have contracted a lung disease from inhaling factory dust—both the size of the benefits you receive and the period for which you'll receive them depend on the laws in your state. If your injuries are permanent and you lived in Alabama in the 1970s, you could get a maximum benefit of $120 per week. In Maine you could get a maximum of $220 a week. The loss of an arm might be worth two hundred weeks' worth of compensation. Partial loss of your arm might entitle you to fifty weeks' worth of benefits. Again, the "schedules" vary, as do the size of death benefits, maximum burial allowances, and the ways in which the programs are administered.

If you are injured or contract a disease through a job-related activity or exposure, you should take the precaution of reporting your claim to your state worker's compensation commission. You may be required to support your claim with medical data. Also report your injury or illness to your employer. In most instances, he in turn will file a report with the appropriate state agency and/or his private insurer.

The amount of time you must wait until your claim is processed depends on where you live, your claim, your doctor's medical reports, whether your employer disputes the claim, and other factors.

Although each state has jurisdiction over its own worker's compensation program, the U. S. Department of Labor's Office of Workers Compensation (within the Employment Standards Administration) has a state standards division. This division is trying to coordinate state programs and has offices within each of the Labor Department's ten regional bureaus.

IF YOU LOSE YOUR JOB THROUGH COMPETITION FROM IMPORTS

If you lose your job because of increased competition from abroad—in short, from imports—you may be entitled to adjustment assistance from the Department of Labor.

Under the 1975 Trade Act, groups of three or more workers or their union representative may petition the Secretary of Labor for various types of aid. By writing the Office of Trade Adjustment Assistance, Bureau of International Labor Affairs, U. S. Department of Labor, Washington, D.C. 20210, you may receive:
- employment training assistance
- relocation allowances
- employment counseling, testing, and job placement help
- cash trade adjustment allowances amounting to 70 per cent of your average weekly wage, up to a maximum of about $230 a week. You can obtain such funds for as long as fifty-two weeks and up to seventy-eight weeks if you are sixty years of age or older or enrolled in a qualified training program.

At the end of 1978, about 400,000 American workers—many of them from the steel, automobile, electronics, and shoe industries—had received a total of $560 million under the Trade Adjustment program. Like unemployment insurance benefits, these trade adjustment payments are newly subject to federal income taxes. They, too, are administered by your state employment security office.

YOUR RIGHT TO SAFE AND HEALTHFUL WORKING CONDITIONS

When the Occupational Safety and Health Act was passed in 1970, and the Occupational Safety and Health Administration (OSHA) established to run and enforce it, they were hailed as the most important sources of protection for U.S. workers in this half of the twentieth century.

Nearly ten years later, OSHA is the prime contender for the title of most disliked government agency. From one side, business groups complain its standards are costly and even ridiculous (one spelled out how "exit" signs were to be designed). From the other, public interest and union groups charged the agency had done little to implement the 1970 law, which promised "as far as possible every working man and woman in the nation safe and healthful working conditions." By May 1977, OSHA had issued only seventeen health standards.

Despite its poor record to date, OSHA has stepped up its action on major health hazards. It has grouped suspected cancer-causing agents according to importance, required warning notices in the workplace and on products, and proposed that much tougher penalties be levied on firms that violate safety rules. In addition, the National Institute for Occupational Safety and Health (NIOSH) that acts as a research agency has been authorized to inform workers who have been exposed to certain dangers on the job. NIOSH can obtain the names and addresses of affected workers from the Internal Revenue Service.

Among the obvious potential hazards for which you should be on guard in your workplace are: dust, fumes, gases, vapors, and mists that you breathe; asbestos; microwaves; lasers; drugs and hormones; molds; parasites, or bacteria from animals or animal products; materials that irritate your skin; and excessive noise.

OSHA has several hundred inspectors in the field, and if you report a complaint it is up to the agency's representatives to visit your plant or office, explore the details, and set in works the machinery to right the situation. Inspectors are supposed to arrive unannounced, and you can ask to have your complaint kept confidential. OSHA's main address is Department of Labor, Washington, D.C. 20210; phone: 202-523-8151.

YOUR RIGHTS AS A VOCATIONAL SCHOOL STUDENT

If you, a vocational school student, decide for any reason to quit your pilot training, secretarial, beautician, or any other trade course, the school must give you your money back. It is permitted to keep only a $75 enrollment fee and a portion of your tuition covering the lessons you have completed.

If, however, you drop out of the school within *fourteen days* of signing your enrollment agreement, the school must refund *all* your money. Furthermore, at the time you sign up you must be told that you have fourteen days during which to cancel and receive your money back.

These important protections are part of a Federal Trade Commission rule in effect in January 1980. The rule covers all seven thousand of this country's vocation schools, including those which provide correspondence courses.

The only sort of instruction excluded from the rule's requirements are self-improvement courses and ones leading to either high school equivalency certificates or standard college-level degrees.

Also under the rule, you must receive the following information from the vocational school:

• the number of students who have dropped out, as well as the number or percentage who have graduated.

• the rate at which the school has actually found jobs for its graduates and their earnings. This information must be given you, if the school makes any claims about the availability of jobs or earning potential of its graduates. (It might, for instance, advertise "Our grads earn $20,000 a year or more.")

If you pull out of a vocational school, be certain to return any equipment that the school may have supplied you as part of the course. If you don't return it, the school may charge you for it. If the course has started when you cancel, the school may keep a portion of the equipment charge based on how long you have used it, even if you return it.

Schools which fail to comply with this rule can be required to pay $10,000 per violation and damages to injured students.

YOUR RIGHTS AS A FRANCHISEE

If you ever thought about owning your own business, you probably have toyed with the idea of buying a franchise.

Franchises often provide your business with instant name-recognition, and good operations supply quite a lot of advertising and technical support. It is possible to buy a small franchise operation for as little as $1,500. Or you can spend as much as $500,000 for a popular restaurant franchise.

The biggest mistake that people make in buying a franchise is failing to investigate the business thoroughly. They also neglect to spend time with people already in business to find out where potential pitfalls and problems lie.

A new Federal Trade Commission rule, effective in mid-1979, goes a long way toward helping you, potential franchisees, by requiring franchise operators to give potential investors the following facts:

• A list of key executives in the operation and their employment background.

• A rundown on all lawsuits and bankruptcies involving the company.

• A full description of any financial help that the franchiser has given to the franchisee.

• A complete disclosure of all money that the franchisee has to pay both at the start and during the life of the business.

• A list of all suppliers with whom the franchisee must do business and the amount of money these suppliers pay to the franchise operator.

• A clear explanation of why your franchise might be revoked. Generally, you risk losing your business if you don't make the kind of profit the franchiser expects.

If you are misled by a franchiser, complain to the FTC. It won't be able to help you get your money back. You have to go to court for that. But your complaints will help the agency build a case against the franchiser.

For background information on nearly eight hundred franchise operations, write to the U. S. Department of Commerce, Industry and Trade Administration, Room 1104, Washington, D.C. 20230. Their franchise booklet is free. For more information on this topic, see chapter on your job, career, or business of your own.

29

HOW AND WHERE TO GET HELP

A Record Number of Allies for You

Never before have you had so many allies to assist you in finding your way through our increasingly gargantuan, endlessly complex market place and in dealing with your complaints. Numerous public interest organizations, specializing in areas ranging from the overall environment to the individual problems of the disabled, have been started in recent years. These groups initiate and pursue research projects, testify before Congressional committees, participate in federal agency proceedings, bring lawsuits, publicize issues, pinpoint problems, distribute newsletters and other information. Not all handle your complaints as an individual, but some do, and many can give you valuable advice.

Directly below are the names of the broadly based, nationwide private groups and government agencies which are concerned with many types of problems.

This is followed by a list of agencies and organizations which concentrate on one or a few categories of issues, broken down so you easily can find the subject of importance to you. Neither list is by any means exhaustive.

But by contacting one or more of the organizations mentioned, you have a head start toward solving your problem or at least learning how to begin.

Nationwide Organizations

Bureau of Consumer Protection, Federal Trade Commission, Washington, D.C. 20580. Rides herd over deceptive advertising, illegal sales tactics, violations of the Truth in Lending law, and a host of other consumer frauds, deceptions, unfair sales, and trade practices. Telephone: (202) 523-3727.

Center for Science in the Public Interest, 1755 S Street N.W., Washington, D.C. 20009. Specializes in promoting food and health safety, energy conservation, and good nutrition through publications and participation in government proceedings. Telephone: (202) 332-9110.

Center for the Study of Responsive Law, P. O. Box 19367, Washington, D.C. 20036. Subjects of study range from mental health to aviation to coal mining. This is Ralph Nader's working address. Telephone: (202) 833-3400.

Citizen Action Group, 1346 Connecticut Avenue N.W., Washington, D.C. 20036. Helps students and citizens organize state and local consumer action groups and public interest research groups. Telephone: (202) 833-3935.

Common Cause, 2030 M Street N.W., Washington, D.C. 20036. Largest citizen's lobby in the country. Concentrates on "structure and process" issues to improve function and accountability of government. Also, in the late 1970s, key issues were tax reform, energy policy, consumer and environmental protection. Telephone: (202) 833-1200.

Congress Watch, 133 C Street S.E., Washington, D.C. 20003. Lobby groups which keeps tabs on voting records, committee performance, and responsiveness by senators and representatives to their constituents and to the public generally. Telephone: (202) 546-4936 or (202) 546-4996.

Consumer Opposed to Inflation in the Necessities (COIN), Suite 413, 2000 P Street N.W., Washington, D.C. 20036. A coalition of consumer, labor, senior citizen and other public interest groups dedicated to fighting inflation in food, energy, health and housing. Telephone: (202) 659-0800.

Consumer Federation of America, Suite 406, 1012 14th Street N.W., Washington, D.C. 20005. Private, non-profit national federation of hundreds of state and local consumer groups which helps groups organize and act, testifies and lobbies on any proposed consumer legislation, and publicizes important issues. Telephone: (202) 737-3732.

Consumers Union, 256 Washington Street, Mount Vernon, New York 10550. Publishes *Consumer Reports* magazine, the classic shopper's guide, which includes results of Consumers Union tests of products ranging from cars to contraceptives—for safety, convenience, effectiveness. Also participates in lawsuits on behalf of consumers. Telephone: (914) MO4-6400.

Corporate Accountability Research Group, 1346 Connecticut Avenue N.W., Washington, D.C. 20036. Contests corporate power, violation of anti-trust laws, seeks to make corporations accountable to shareowners and the public. Telephone: (202) 833-3931.

Council of Better Business Bureaus, 1150 17th Street N.W., Washington, D.C. 20036. Headquarters of the well-known Better Business Bureaus. Can put you in touch with the right local Bureau for you. Telephone: (202) 862-1200.

Disability Rights Center, 1346 Connecticut Avenue N.W., Washington, D.C. 20036. Works to strengthen rights of the disabled through legal action and monitoring of federal actions. Telephone: (202) 223-3304.

Energy Action, 1523 L Street N.W., Washington, D.C. 20005. Consumer oriented group that watches federal energy legislation and publishes a newsletter. Telephone: (202) 737-6220.

Office of Consumer Affairs, 626 Reporters Building, Washington, D.C. 20201. The consumer's "man in Washington"; government agency concerned with all kinds of consumer problems, consumer education and legislation. Telephones: consumer complaints (202) 755-8820; state and local programs (202) 755-8892.

Public Citizen Litigation Group, 7th Floor, 2000 P Street N.W., Washington, D.C. 20036. Initiates lawsuits against corporations, government agencies on behalf of the public. Telephone: (202) 785-3704.

STATE AND LOCAL CONSUMER PROTECTIVE ORGANIZATIONS

All states—and many cities and counties as well—now have a central department or agency to deal with consumer fraud and also with less dramatic problems and gripes. Frequently this office is a part of the state attorney general's office. Or it may be listed under: Department (or Division) of Consumer Protection; Consumer Affairs Bureau; Consumer Protection Agency; Department of Weights and Measures; or perhaps some other name.

Each state also has at least one privately sponsored consumer organization. It may be called Consumers Council or Consumer Association or Consumer Information Center. Most states have a Ralph Nader-affiliated Public Interest Research Group, which may be called CALPIRG (in California) or VPIRG (in Vermont)—depending on the state.

Look for the agencies and organizations in your city or state—both government and non-government—under "Consumer . . ." in the government agencies section of your telephone book, as well as in the regular telephone listings.

In addition to seeking help from these organizations, you may find it helpful to get in touch with:

> your city department of consumer affairs (see the telephone directory, or call City Hall to find out whether there is such an agency);
>
> your local chamber of commerce;
>
> your local Better Business Bureau;
>
> the "Action Line" of your local newspaper, radio, or TV station;
>
> the Consumer Education Department of a local college or university;
>
> the Extension Service of the U. S. Department of Agriculture.

WHERE TO TAKE YOUR PROBLEM: BY CATEGORY OR SUBJECT

Aging. See Retirement.

Air Travel. If you have a complaint which you have been unable to resolve with an airline—about mishandled baggage, or failure to deliver you to your destination, or being illegally "bumped" off a flight, or being overcharged on a fare—write: Bureau of Consumer Protection, Civil Aeronautics Board, 1825 Connecticut Avenue N.W., Washington, D.C. 20428. Telephone: (202) 673-5482.

Or you may use the CAB hot line, (202) 673-5158, at any hour of the day or night. You will be billed for a three-minute call, but after that the CAB will call back to finish discussing your problem.

Aviation Consumer Action Project (ACAP), 1346 Connecticut Avenue N.W., Washington, D C 20036, works on problems in air carrier safety and regulation as well as passenger treatment.

Appliances. First try to settle your complaint with the dealer or manufacturer. Among the toll-free lines that you may be able to use are Whirlpool: (800) 253-1301; Westinghouse: (800) 523-5222.

If the appliance dealer, manufacturer, or serviceman fails to act on any legitimate complaint you have, write: Major Appliance Consumer Action Panel (MACAP), Complaint Exchange, Room 1500, 20 North Wacker Drive, Chicago, Illinois 60606.

Or telephone MACAP at: (312) 984-5858.

Auto Insurance. See Insurance.

Automobiles. Owners can write:

American Motors Corporation, 14250 Plymouth Road, Detroit, Michigan 48232; telephone: (313) 493-2344; or, in Canada, 350 Kennedy Road South, Brampton, Ontario.

Chrysler Corporation, P.O. Box 857, Detroit, Michigan 48231; telephone: (313) 956-5970; in Canada, the Chrysler Center, Windsor, Ontario.

Ford Motor Company, Owner Relations Department, Park Lane Tower West, Dearborn, Michigan 48126, about warranty problems; telephone: (313) 322-8055.

General Motors car owners should contact the appropriate division's Consumer-Relations Manager. Division addresses are:

Buick Motor Division, 902 East Hamilton Avenue, Flint, Michigan 48550. Telephone: (313) 766-1240.

Cadillac Motor Car Division, 2860 Clark Avenue, Detroit, Michigan 48232. Telephone: (313) 554-5536.

Chevrolet Motor Division, 3044 West Grand Boulevard, Detroit, Michigan 48202. Telephone: (313) 556-5219.

Oldsmobile Division, 920 Townsend Street, Lansing, Michigan 48921. Telephone (517) 373-5546.

Pontiac Motor Division, 1 Pontiac Plaza, Pontiac, Michigan 48505. Telephone: (313) 857-1321.

AUTOCAP is an automobile owner complaint service of the National Automobile Dealers Association. Programs are located throughout the country. To find out if an AUTOCAP is in your area, contact National Automobile Dealers Association, 8400 West Park Drive, McLean, Virginia 22101. Telephone: (703) 821-7070.

Auto Safety. If your complaint has to do with automobile safety (or lack of safety)—which may affect other car owners as well—address your question, gripe, or suggestion to:

National Transportation Safety Board, U. S. Department of Transportation, 400 7th Street S.W., Washington, D.C. 20591.

Director, Office of Public and Consumer Affairs, Department of Transportation, Washington, D.C. 20590. Telephone: (202) 426-4570.

National Highway Safety Administration; toll-free hotline (800) 424-9393; in Washington, D.C., call (202) 416-0123.

National Highway Traffic Safety Administration, Public Affairs, Room 5232, 400 7th Street S.W., Washington, D.C. 20590. Telephone: (202) 426-9550.

Center for Auto Safety, 1346 Connecticut Avenue N.W., Washington, D.C. 20036. Telephone: (202) 659-1126.

If you are a truck or bus driver and would like to contribute information and ideas for improved truck or bus safety, contact: Professional Drivers Council (PROD), 7th Floor, 2000 P Street N.W., Washington, D.C. 20036. Telephone: (202) 785-3707.

Borrowing. If you suspect a store, a dealer, a finance company, or a small loan company of violating the federal Truth in Lending law—for example, by not clearly stating the true simple annual interest rate on an installment loan or a purchase agreement on time—call or write the nearest regional office of the Federal Trade Commission. National headquarters of the FTC is Washington, D.C. 20580 (address complaints and inquiries to the Bureau of Consumer Protection).

The FTC's regional offices are at these addresses:

John F. Kennedy Federal Building
Government Center
Boston, MA 02203

Federal Building
26 Federal Plaza
New York, NY 10007

6 Pennsylvania Avenue
Washington, DC 20580

Suite 500
The Mall Building
118 St. Clair Avenue
Cleveland, OH 44114

1718 Peachtree Street N.W.
Atlanta, GA 30308

55 East Monroe Street
Chicago, IL 60603

2001 Bryan Street
Dallas, TX 75201

450 Golden Gate Avenue
Box 36005
San Francisco, CA 94102

Federal Building
11000 Wilshire Boulevard
Los Angeles, CA 90024

915 Second Avenue
Seattle, WA 98101

1405 Curtis Street
Denver, CO 80202

If you have any reason to believe that your *bank* is not clearly spelling out full details of the loan you are negotiating, and if it's a national bank, check with Consumer Affairs, Office of the Comptroller of the Currency, Washington, D.C. 20219. Telephone: (202) 566-2000.

Or if it's a state-chartered bank which is a member of the Federal Reserve System get in touch with the Truth-in-Lending Officer of the Federal Reserve Bank in the city closest to you. Federal Reserve Banks are located at these addresses:

600 Atlantic Avenue
Boston, MA 02106

230 South LaSalle Street
Chicago, IL 60690

33 Liberty Street	411 Locust Street
New York, NY 10045	St. Louis, MO 63166
100 North Sixth Street	250 Marquette Avenue
Philadelphia, PA 19105	Minneapolis, MN 55480
1455 East Sixth Street	925 Grand Avenue
Cleveland, OH 44101	Kansas City, MO 64198
100 North Ninth Street	400 South Akard Street
Richmond, VA 23261	Dallas, TX 75222
104 Marietta Street N.W.	400 Sansome Street
Atlanta, GA 30303	San Francisco, CA 94120

NON-MEMBER INSURED BANKS. If it's a bank which is not a member of the Federal Reserve System but is federally insured contact the Office of Bank Customer Affairs, Federal Deposit Insurance Corporation, Washington, D.C. 20429. Telephone: (202) 389-4427.

Or call the FDIC Supervising Examiner for the district in which bank is located.

If it is a federally insured savings and loan association get in touch with the Federal Home Loan Bank Board's Supervisory Agent in the district in which the association is located. Or write Office of the General Counsel, Federal Home Loan Bank Board, N.W., Washington, D.C. 20552. Telephone: (202) 377-6000.

Addresses of the FHLBB's twelve districts are:

(Connecticut, Maine, Massachusetts, New Hampshire, Rhode Island, and Vermont): P.O. Box 2196, Boston, Massachusetts 02106.

(New Jersey, New York, Puerto Rico, and Virgin Islands): 1 World Trade Center, Floor 103, New York, New York 10048.

(Delaware, Pennsylvania, and West Virginia): 4th Floor, 11 Stanwix Street, Gateway Center, Pittsburgh, Pennsylvania 15222.

(Alabama, District of Columbia, Florida, Georgia, Maryland, North Carolina, South Carolina, and Virginia): P.O. Box 56527, Atlanta, Georgia 30343.

(Kentucky, Ohio, Tennessee): P.O. Box 598, Cincinnati, Ohio 45201.

(Indiana and Michigan): 2900 Indiana Tower, 1 Indiana Square, Indianapolis, Indiana 46204.

(Illinois and Wisconsin): 111 East Wacker Drive, Chicago, Illinois 60601.

(Iowa, Minnesota, Missouri, North Dakota, and South Dakota): Second Avenue at Center Street, Des Moines, Iowa 50309.

(Arkansas, Louisiana, Mississippi, New Mexico, and Texas): 1400 Tower Building, Little Rock, Arkansas 72201.

(Colorado, Kansas, Nebraska, and Oklahoma): P.O. Box 176, Topeka, Kansas 66601.

(Arizona, Nevada, and California): P.O. Box 7948, San Francisco, California 94120.

(Alaska, Hawaii and Guam, Idaho, Montana, Oregon, Utah, Washington, and Wyoming): 600 Stewart Street, Seattle, Washington 98101.

FEDERAL CREDIT UNIONS. If it is a federally chartered credit union, write National Credit Union Administration, 2025 M Street N.W., Washington, D.C. 20456. Telephone: (202) 254-9800.

Or contact the NCUA's regional office serving the area in which the federal credit union is located. Regional offices are located in Boston, Atlanta, Toledo, San Francisco, Harrisburg, and Austin.

If it is a state-chartered credit union, get in touch with the appropriate state supervising agency—either the Department of Banking or the Finance Department or the state agency covering credit unions.

Another federal agency enforcing various aspects of the Truth in Lending law is the Civil Aeronautics Board, Bureau of Enforcement, 1825 Connecticut Avenue N.W., Washington, D.C. 20428.

And if the problem involves interstate transportation (trucking companies and railroads that cross state lines), write the Office of Proceedings, Interstate Commerce Commission, Constitution Avenue and 12th Street N.W., Washington, D.C. 20423.

Finally, if you believe you have been illegally fired or otherwise harmed because your wages have been garnisheed—a possible violation of the Truth in Lending law—contact the Labor Department's Wage and Hour Division, which is in charge of enforcing this part of the law.

Broadcasting. Send your complaints about radio or television broadcasting or business practices to: Federal Communications Commission, 1919 M Street N.W., Washington, D.C. 20554.

The National Citizens Committee for Broadcasting, 1028 Connecticut Avenue N.W., Washington, D.C. 20036, tries to encourage citizens and groups to take a more active role in the media and regulation of these forms of communication.

Action for Children's Television (ACT), 46 Austin Street, Newton Center, Massachusetts 02159, tries to reduce offensive TV ads aimed at child viewers. Telephone: (617) 527-7870.

The Consumer Assistance Office, Federal Communications Commission, also may deal directly with your complaints as a consumer. (Address above.) Telephone: (202) 632-7000.

Civil Liberties. If you believe there has been a serious infringement of your civil liberties, contact: American Civil Liberties Union, 22 East 40th Street, New York, New York 10016. (see also Discrimination.)

Counseling. If you need counseling on subjects ranging from wage garnishment to problems in your child's school to psychiatric needs, call a local voluntary Family Service agency. For names and other specifics on such agencies in the area where you live, write: Family Service Association of America, 44 East 23rd Street, New York, New York 10010.

Or contact: Office of Human Development, Department of Health, Education, and Welfare, 300 Independence Avenue S.W., Washington, D.C. 20201. Telephone (202) 472-7257.

Or get in touch with your local YMCA or YWCA. For the address of the branch nearest you, write: Young Men's Christian Association, 291 Broadway, New York, New York 10007, or the Young Women's Christian Association of the U.S.A., 600 Lexington Avenue, New York, New York 10022.

For counseling on runaway children, call the National Runaway Hotline: toll-free (800) 621-4000. In Illinois, call (800) 972-6004.

Credit Rating. If you are unfairly rated a bad credit risk, write for help directly to: Associated Credit Bureaus, Inc., 6767 Southwest Freeway, Houston, Texas 77036. Telephone (713) 774-8701. Or appeal to the nearest office of the Federal Trade Commission, which enforces the Fair Credit Reporting Act.

If you need help setting up a program to repay your debts and manage your finances properly in the future, visit a credit counseling service in your area. (See Yellow Pages for addresses of a local service.) Or write the National Foundation for Consumer Credit, Inc., 1819 H Street N.W., Washington, D.C. 20006, for names and addresses of credit counseling services convenient to where you live.

Discrimination. If you believe you are the victim of illegal discrimination—on the basis of race, age, sex, or national origin—at your job, in your pay, in your search for housing, in trying to borrow money, in the courts, or in any aspect of your constitutional rights, there are a number of organizations ready to help you.

If your problem is racial discrimination:

National Association for the Advancement of Colored People, 1790 Broadway, New York, New York 10019.

NAACP Legal Defense and Education Fund, 10 Columbus Circle, New York, New York 10019.

American Civil Liberties Union, 22 East 40th Street, New York, New York 10016 (or your state's branch of the ACLU).

If the problem is sex discrimination, in jobs, credit, pay:

Women's Bureau, United States Department of Labor, 200 Constitution Avenue N.W., Washington, D.C. 20210.

Center for Women's Policy Studies, 2000 P Street N.W., Washington, D.C. 20036. Telephone (202) 872-1770.

National Organization for Women, 705 G Street S.E., Washington, D.C. 20003. Telephone (202) 347-2279.

If your problem is discrimination in housing, call the housing discrimination hotline: (808) 424-8590. In Washington D.C. call (202) 755-5490.

If your problem is employment discrimination:

Equal Employment Opportunity Commission, Washington, D.C. 20506 (or any of the EEOC field offices).

Wage and Hour Division, Employment Standards Administration, U. S. Department of Labor, 200 Constitution Avenue N.W., Washington, D.C 20210 (or any of the 350-plus field or regional offices listed under "United States Government—Department of Labor, Wage and Hour Division" in the telephone book).

If you are an applicant, trainee, or apprentice in a program covered by federal regulations, and you believe you have been discriminated against: Bureau of Apprenticeship and Training, United States Department of Labor, Washington, D.C. 20210.

If your employer is a federal government contractor or subcontractor: Office of Federal Contract Compliance, Employment Standards Administration, United States Department of Labor, Washington, D.C. 20210, or: Assistant Attorney General, Civil Rights Division, United States Department of Justice, Washington, D.C. 20415.

You can also address a complaint to your state Fair Employment Commission or Human Rights Agency or your city's Commission on Civil Rights.

If you feel immediate action is in order, report the matter to the nearest office of the Federal Bureau of Investigation or to your nearest United States Attorney.

If your complaint goes unanswered or if you don't get satisfactory action, write or call: United States Commission on Civil Rights, 1121 Vermont Avenue N.W., Washington, D.C. 20425. Telephone: (202) 655-4000.

Door-to-Door Sales. If your problem or dispute involves a door-to-door salesperson, or the goods or services he is selling: Direct Selling Association, 1730 M Street N.W., Washington, D.C. 20036.

Drugs. See Food and Drugs.

Electronic Equipment. If you haven't been able to resolve a problem involving a TV, stereo, or calculator, the Electronic Industries Association, 2001 I Street N.W., Washington, D.C. 20006, will forward the complaint to the company involved and follow up for you until you receive a response.

Environment. If you believe court action is warranted against a person or corporation destroying some aspect of your environment, go first to your local environmental board or write Office of Public Affairs, Environmental Protection Agency, 401 M Street S.W., Washington, D.C. 20460. Telephone: (202) 755-0707. If you fail to get satisfaction, get in touch with one of these groups of lawyers and scientists dedicated to preserving a healthful environment through court action: Environmental Defense Fund, 1525 18th Street N.W., Washington, D.C. 20036; or: Natural Resources Defense Council, Inc., 122 East 42nd Street, New York, New York 10036.

For advice on how to change your buying habits to minimize their adverse environmental effects: Concern, Inc., 2233 Wisconsin Avenue N.W., Washington, D.C. 20007.

If you want to share in efforts to prevent further pollution or depletion of the earth's natural resources, among the leading environmental and conservation organizations you can join:

Environmental Action, Inc., 1346 Connecticut Avenue N.W., Washington, D.C. 20036. Publishes biweekly *Environmental Action.* Lobbies and educates for stronger laws and enforcement.

A good source of environmental news is the weekly *Environmental Action Bulletin* (Rodale Press, Emmaus, Pennsylvania 18049).

Friends of the Earth, 620 C Street S.E., Washington, D.C. 20003. Publishes monthly *Not Man Part*, publicizes issues, lobbies, brings suits.

National Audubon Society, 950 Third Avenue, New York, New York 10022. Publishes monthly *Audubon* magazine, educates, researches environmental problems.

National Wildlife Federation, 1412 16th Street N.W., Washington, D.C. 20036. Publishes bimonthly *National Wildlife* and *International Wildlife*. Concerned with all environmental problems affecting wildlife.

Sierra Club, 530 Bush Street, San Francisco, California 94108. Publishes monthly *Sierra Club Bulletin*. Local chapters sponsor outdoor activities, lobbying, legal action.

Wilderness Society, 1901 Pennsylvania Avenue N.W., Washington, D.C. 20006. Publishes quarterly *Living Wilderness*, lobbies, educates, sues, conducts outings.

If your environmental problem involves solar heating, one advice source is the National Solar Heating and Cooling Information Center, Box 1607, Rockville, Maryland 20850. Toll-free hotline: (800) 523-2929. In Pennsylvania: (800) 462-4983.

Flammable Fabrics. Use the Consumer Product Safety Commission's hotline, (800) 638-2666, to report cases of dangerously flammable fabrics on the market or to get safety-related information on fabrics you suspect of being dangerously flammable—including names of offending brands and retailers.

Food and Drugs. If you find you have bought any contaminated or otherwise harmful food, drugs, or cosmetics, report it to your nearest FDA regional or district office or resident post.

The FDA's national headquarters is: Consumer Inquiry Section, Food and Drug Administration, 5600 Fishers Lane, Rockville, Maryland 20852. Telephone: (301) 443-3170.

The FDA's district offices are:

DISTRICT OFFICE	ADDRESS	AREA CODE AND NUMBER
Atlanta, GA 30309	880 West Peachtree Street N.W.	(404) 881-3576
Baltimore, MD 21201	900 Madison Avenue	(301) 962-3731
Boston, MA 02109	585 Commercial Street	(617) 223-5857
Brooklyn, NY 11232	Room 700 850 Third Avenue	(212) 965-5529
Buffalo, NY 14202	599 Delaware Avenue	(716) 846-4483
Chicago, IL 60607	Room 1222, Main Post Office 433 West Van Buren Street	(312) 353-7126
Cincinnati, OH 45202	1141 Central Parkway	(513) 684-3501
Dallas, TX 75204	3032 Bryan Street	(214) 749-2735

DISTRICT OFFICE	ADDRESS	AREA CODE AND NUMBER
Denver, CO 80202	721 19th Street U. S. Customhouse Room 500	(303) 837-4915
Detroit, MI 48207	1560 East Jefferson Avenue	(313) 226-6260
East Orange, NJ 07018	20 Evergreen Place	(201) 645-3023
Kansas City, MO 64106	1009 Cherry Street	(816) 374-3817
Los Angeles, CA 90015	1521 West Pico Boulevard	(213) 688-3771
Minneapolis, MN 55401	240 Hennipin Avenue	(612) 725-2121
New Orleans, LA 70122	4298 Elysian Fields Avenue	(504) 589-2401
Philadelphia, PA 19106	Room 900 2nd and Chestnut	(215) 597-4390
San Francisco, CA 94102	Room 568 United Nations Plaza Federal Office Building	(415) 556-2062
San Juan, PR 00905	P.O. Box S 4427 Old San Juan Station	(809) 967-1221
Seattle, WA 98104	Room 5003 Federal Office Building 909 First Avenue	(206) 442-5304

The Health Research Group, 2000 P Street N.W., Washington, D.C. 20036, is a consumer advocate group concerned with occupational safety, food and drugs, and health care delivery.

The Community Nutritional Institute, 1146 19th Street N.W., Washington, D.C. 20036, provides information and technical aid on a wide range of food programs and policy issues.

The Children's Foundation, 1028 Connecticut Avenue N.W., Washington, D.C. 20036, monitors federal food assistance programs and helps eligible women and children to participate.

(Also see Health Care.)

If you have reason to believe that your butcher's or supermarket's or grocer's scales are rigged to show a heavier weight for meats, fruits, vegetables, or other products—or that the weight of a product you have bought is misstated on the label—alert your state Bureau of Weights and Measures or: Office of Weights and Measures, National Bureau of Standards, Washington, D.C. 20234, or Assistant Secretary for Food and Consumer Services, U. S. Department of Agriculture, Administrative Building, Room 2018, Washington, D.C. 20250; telephone: (202) 447-4623.

Furniture. If you cannot clear up a dispute with a furniture dealer within a reasonable time:

Furniture Industry Consumer Advisory Panel (FICAP), P.O. Box 951, High Point, North Carolina 27261. Telephone: (919) 885-5065.

The National Association of Furniture Manufacturers, 8401 Connecticut Avenue N.W., Washington, D.C. 20015, represents more manufacturers than the Consumer Advisory Panel. Telephone: (202) 657-4442.

Health Care. If you have a problem or question or serious complaint about medical service, tell it to:
- your state's office of Consumer Health Affairs (if there is one);
- your local and/or state Health Department;
- your state or county Medical Society;
- the local private Health and Welfare Council (in major cities);
- the local chapter of the Medical Committee for Human Rights based at P.O. Box 7155, Pittsburgh, Pennsylvania 15213 (but with chapters in other major cities);
- the nearest Comprehensive Health Planning agency;
- your state insurance commissioner;
- state or local consumer protection agencies;
- your state's Public Interest Research Group;
- the local offices of the Blue Cross and Blue Shield organizations, Social Security Administration, the Welfare Department;
- or to one of these key national organizations:

American Medical Association
535 North Dearborn Street
Chicago, IL 60610

National Medical Association
1720 Massachusetts Avenue N.W.
Washington, DC 20036

American Dental Association
211 East Chicago Avenue
Chicago, IL 60611

United States Public Health Service
5600 Fishers Lane
Rockville, MD 20852

American Psychiatric Association
1700 18th Street N.W.
Washington, DC 20009

American Hospital Association
840 North Lake Shore Drive
Chicago, IL 60611

American Public Health Association
1015 18th Street N.W.
Washington, DC 20036

Find out whether the hospital has a patient advocacy system or any other type of grievance mechanism.

Get a copy of the American Hospital Association's Patient's Bill of Rights (see pages 1229–30) and show it to hospital authorities.

A few states have special "grievance panels" which function as alternatives to malpractice suits. Inquire about whether your problem could be handled by such a panel.

For quick referral to a nearby specialist who can give you a second medical opinion about your problem, call HEW-funded (800) 325-6400.

If venereal disease is your worry, call VD, toll-free hotline (800) 523-1885. In Pennsylvania, call (800) 462-4966.

Finally, you can get a variety of excellent "Shopper's Guides"—to surgery, dentistry, and health insurance—published by the Pennsylvania Insurance Department. If you are a Pennsylvania resident, send a self-addressed 9×12-inch envelope with 20 cents postage per guide to the Pennsylvania Insurance Department, Harrisburg, Pennsylvania 17120. Non-residents can get copies of these and other guides for $1.00 each from Consumer News, Inc., 813 National Press Building, Washington, D.C. 20045.

Immigration and Naturalization. If your problem is in this area, your source for help is: Information Services, Immigration and Naturalization Service, 425 I Street N.W., Washington, D.C. 20536. Telephone: (202) 376-8449.

Information. For help in prying loose government information under the Freedom of Information Act: Freedom of Information Clearinghouse, 2000 P Street N.W., Washington, D.C. 20036.

If you need advice or information on such close-to-home matters as child care, gardens, nutrition, health, clothes care, food storage, "do it yourself" projects, farm subsidies, financial problems, or dozens of other subjects, three superb sources of pamphlets, instructions, and guidance are: Extension Service, U. S. Department of Agriculture, 14th Street and Independence Avenue S.W., Washington, D.C. 20250; Superintendent of Documents, U. S. Government Printing Office, Washington, D.C. 20402; and Consumer Information Center, Pueblo, Colorado 81009.

Of the three, the Center is your best one-step source for getting low-cost or free publications on subjects ranging from warranties to myths about vitamins. You can get a free Consumer Information Index, listing the more than 250 publications available, by writing the Consumer Information Center, Pueblo, Colorado 81009. The Index is also available in Spanish. It is published four times a year.

To get information quickly about which federal, state, or local agency can help you with a problem or to obtain help directly, the General Services Administration in co-operation with the Civil Service Commission operates Federal Information Centers in cities across the country. They also have toll-free numbers linking nearby cities to the centers. Here are the toll-free numbers:

ALABAMA			San Diego	(714) 293-6030
Birmingham	(205) 322-8591		San Francisco	(415) 556-6600
Mobile	(205) 438-1421		San Jose	(408) 275-7422
ARIZONA			COLORADO	
Phoenix	(602) 261-3313		Colorado	
Tucson	(602) 622-1511		Springs	(303) 471-9491
			Denver	(303) 837-3602
ARKANSAS			Pueblo	(303) 544-9523
Little Rock	(501) 378-6177			
CALIFORNIA			CONNECTICUT	
Los Angeles	(213) 688-3800		Hartford	(203) 527-2617
Sacramento	(916) 440-3344		New Haven	(203) 624-4720

DISTRICT OF COLUMBIA
Washington   (202) 755-8660

FLORIDA
Fort Lauder-
    dale   (305) 522-8531
Jacksonville   (904) 354-4756
Miami   (305) 350-4155
Orlando   (305) 422-1800
St. Petersburg   (813) 893-3495
Tampa   (813) 229-7911
West Palm
    Beach   (305) 833-7566

GEORGIA
Atlanta   (404) 221-6891

HAWAII
Honolulu   (808) 546-8620

ILLINOIS
Chicago   (312) 353-4242

INDIANA
Indianapolis   (317) 269-7373

IOWA
Des Moines   (515) 284-4448

KANSAS
Topeka   (913) 295-2866
Wichita   (316) 263-6931

KENTUCKY
Louisville   (502) 582-6261

LOUISIANA
New Orleans   (504) 589-6696

MARYLAND
Baltimore   (301) 962-4980

MASSACHUSETTS
Boston   (617) 223-7121

MICHIGAN
Detroit   (313) 226-7016

MINNESOTA
Minneapolis   (612) 725-2073

MISSOURI
Kansas City   (816) 374-2466

St. Joseph   (816) 233-8206
St. Louis   (314) 425-4106

NEBRASKA
Omaha   (402) 221-3353

NEW JERSEY
Newark   (201) 645-3600
Trenton   (609) 396-4400

NEW MEXICO
Albuquerque   (505) 766-3091
Santa Fe   (505) 983-7743

NEW YORK
Albany   (518) 463-4421
Buffalo   (716) 842-5770
New York   (212) 264-4464
Rochester   (716) 546-5075
Syracuse   (315) 476-8545

NORTH CAROLINA
Charlotte   (704) 376-3600

OHIO
Akron   (216) 375-5638
Cincinnati   (513) 684-2801
Cleveland   (216) 522-4040
Columbus   (614) 221-1014
Dayton   (513) 223-7377
Toledo   (419) 241-3223

OKLAHOMA
Oklahoma
    City   (405) 231-4868
Tulsa   (918) 584-4193

OREGON
Portland   (503) 221-2222

PENNSYLVANIA
Allentown/
    Bethlehem   (215) 821-7785
Philadelphia   (215) 597-7042
Pittsburgh   (412) 644-3456
Scranton   (717) 346-7081

RHODE ISLAND
Providence   (401) 331-5565

TENNESSEE

Chattanooga	(615) 265-8231
Memphis	(901) 521-3285
Nashville	(615) 242-5056

TEXAS

Austin	(512) 472-5494
Dallas	(214) 749-2131
Fort Worth	(817) 334-3624
Houston	(713) 226-5711
San Antonio	(512) 224-4471

UTAH

Ogden	(801) 399-1347

Salt Lake
City   (801) 524-5353

VIRGINIA
Newport
News   (804) 244-0480
Norfolk   (804) 441-6723

WASHINGTON
Seattle   (206) 442-0570
Tacoma   (206) 383-5230

WISCONSIN
Milwaukee   (414) 271-2273

One good source of more addresses of organizations which stand ready to help you and accept your help is:

Help: The Useful Almanac (available for $4.95 from Consumer News, Inc., 813 National Press Building, Washington, D.C. 20045, or at a reference library), which lists and describes hundreds of private and government agencies across the country. A detailed guide to what you can *do* to secure your rights is *A Public Citizen's Action Manual,* by Donald Ross ($1.95 from Grossman Publishers, 625 Madison Avenue, New York, New York 10022).

Insurance. If your question is about insurance, an insurance agency, or insurance salesman, write direct to the State Insurance Department in your state capital, or to one of these private trade associations:

FOR LIFE INSURANCE
American Council of Life Insurance
1850 K Street N.W.
Washington, DC 20006

FOR CRIME INSURANCE
Federal Crime Insurance
P.O. Box 41033
Washington, DC 20014
Free hotline: (800) 638-8780

FOR AUTOMOBILE AND LIABILITY INSURANCE
Insurance Information Institute
110 William Street
New York, NY 10038

1266 National Press Building
529 14th Street N.W.
Washington, DC 20004

400 Montgomery Street
San Francisco, CA 94104

You can get excellent, no-nonsense advice on how to buy insurance by sending small sums for *Shopper's Guide to Term Insurance; Shopper's Guide to Cash Value Life Insurance; Shopper's Guide to Health Insurance;* and *Shopper's Guide to Mobile Home Insurance* (Consumer News, Inc., 813 National Press Building, Washington, D.C. 20045). *The Shopper's Guidebook* by Herbert Denenberg also is available from this source ($3.50).

FOR FLOOD INSURANCE
National Flood Insurance,
Department of Housing and Urban Development
Washington, DC 20410
Toll-free hotline: (800) 424-8872

Job Safety. If you think you are being exposed to a hazardous substance or other dangerous condition in your workplace, contact the nearest field office of the Occupational Safety and Health Administration, listed in the phone book under "United States Government, Department of Labor." The main office address is: OSHA, Department of Labor, Washington, D.C. 20101. Employees covered by the law can request inspection of their workplace, and the OSHA must agree not to reveal the names of any complaints to employers. Also, contact the Health Research Group, 2000 P Street N.W., Washington, D.C. 20036, which has written about how workers can become involved in OSHA proceedings.

Job Training and Employment. Check your phone book under "State Government" for your State Employment Service. Or write Employment and Training Adminstration, Department of Labor, Washington, D.C. 20201.

Legal Services. The National Consumers Center for Legal Services, 1302 18th Street N.W., Washington, D.C. 20036, gives information about legal service plans. The National Legal Aid and Defender Association, 2100 M Street N.W., Washington, D.C. 20037, helps provide the poor with quality legal services. The Legal Services Corporation, 733 15th Street N.W., Washington, D.C. 20005, is federally funded and is the largest provider of legal aid to the poor and indigent. Also call your local bar association, Legal Aid Society office, law school, or legal clinics for referrals.

Life Insurance. See Insurance.

Magazine Action Line. This organization resolves complaints about any magazine. It is a service of Publishers Clearing House, a large direct-mail, discount seller of subscriptions. Address: 382 Channel Drive, Port Washington, New York 11050.

Mail Order. If you suspect mail fraud of any description or if you receive unordered merchandise through the mails, or even if you simply receive a piece of highly deceptive advertising, ask your local post office whether a formal complaint is in order, or write: Office of the Chief Postal Inspector, U. S. Postal Service, Washington, D.C. 20260. Telephone: (202) 245-5445.

If you have complaints about postal service (e.g., packages lost or damaged, surly clerks, long lines), take them first to your local postmaster. If he can't help you, write: Consumer Advocate, at the United States Postal Service, Washington, D.C. 20260. Telephone: (202) 245-4514.

If you have an unresolved disagreement with a mail-order house, or would like to reduce the amount of junk mail you get, write: Consumer Service Director, Direct Mail Marketing Association, 6 East 43rd Street, New York, New York 10017. Telephone: (212) 689-4977.

Mortgages. If you have problems about a home mortgage insured by the Veterans Administration or the Federal Housing Administration, or a home improvement contractor who is working on a project involving a federally guaranteed loan, ask your bank for the address of the nearest office of the VA or FHA. The FHA's national headquarters are: Federal Housing Administration, Department of Housing and Urban Development, 451 7th Street S.W., Washington, D.C. 20410.

The VA's headquarters are: Veterans Administration, 810 Vermont Avenue, Washington, D.C. 20420.

All HUD field offices give free counseling to people who have housing problems.

Moving. Send your complaints about movers to: Bureau of Operations, Interstate Commerce Commission, Constitution Avenue and 12th Street N.W., Washington, D.C. 20423, or call the ICC on its hot line: (800) 424-9312. In Washington, D.C., call (202) 275-7301. In Florida, call (800) 432-4537.

Occupational Health. See Health Care and Job Safety.

Pensions. The Department of Labor keeps tabs on pension plans and has legal responsibility, under the 1974 pension reform law to initiate action to correct abuses. If you have a complaint about your pension plan, send it to the Office of Communications and Public Services, Pension, Welfare and Benefit Programs, 200 Constitution Avenue N.W., Room S4522, Washington, D.C. 20216. It also has a representative at your nearest area office of the Labor-Management Services Administration. Or send your complaint to: Administrator of Pension, Welfare, and Benefit Programs, 200 Constitution Avenue, N.W., Room S4522, Washington, D.C. 20216.

The Internal Revenue Service also regulates pension plans and can terminate a plan and split its assets among the participants if it is being improperly administered. So send a copy of your complaint to: Office of Employee Plans and Exempt Organizations, Internal Revenue Service, 1111 Constitution Avenue N.W., Washington, D.C. 20224.

If you're thinking of taking a pension case to court, you or your lawyer may want to contact: National Senior Citizens Law Center, Suite 201, 1636 West

Eighth Street, Los Angeles, California 90017, or: National Senior Citizens Law Center, 1200 Fifteenth Street N.W., Washington, D.C. 20005, or Pension Rights Center, 1346 Connecticut Avenue N.W., Washington, D.C. 20036. The latter publishes excellent "Pension Fact Sheets" that you can receive for 25 cents upon request.

Another group concerned with your pension rights is:

American Pension Conference, 358 Fifth Avenue, New York, New York 10001.

See also Social Security and Veterans' Benefits.

Pollution. If you believe that a local industry or individual is illegally polluting the air or water in your community, check with one or all of these agencies:

The state or local Environmental Control Board or pollution control board;

The state or local Health Department;

The U. S. Environmental Protection Agency, 401 M Street S.W., Washington, D.C. 20460.

Consumer Protection and Environmental Health Service, Public Health Service, Department of Health, Education and Welfare, 5600 Fishers Lane, Rockville, Maryland 20852.

Product Labeling. See Food and Drugs.

Product Safety. If you have found an unsafe product of almost any kind, get in touch with the Consumer Product Safety Commission Team, 1750 K Street, N.W., Washington, D.C. 20207. Toll-free hotline: (800) 638-8326. In Maryland, call: (800) 492-8363.

Addresses and phone numbers of the commission's regional offices are:

1330 West Peachtree Street, N.W.
Atlanta, GA 30309
  (404) 881-2259

100 Summer Street
Boston, MA 02210
  (617) 223-5576

230 South Dearborn Street
Room 2945
Chicago, IL 60614
  (312) 353-8260

Room 410-C
500 South Ervay
P.O. Box 15035
Dallas, TX 75201
  (214) 749-3871

Suite 938
Guaranty Bank Building
817 17th Street
Denver, CO 80202
c/o Food and Drug Administration
  (303) 837-2904

Room 1500
1125 Grand Avenue
Kansas City, MO 64106
  (816) 374-2034

Suite 1100
3660 Wilshire Boulevard
Los Angeles, CA 90010
  (213) 688-7272

SYLVIA PORTER'S NEW MONEY BOOK FOR THE 80's

Room 1905
911 Walnut Street
Kansas City, MO 64106
  (816) 374-2034

Suite 1100
3660 Wilshire Boulevard
Los Angeles, CA 90010
  (213) 688-7272

Room 650
Federal Building, Fort Snelling
Twin Cities, MN 55111
  (612) 725-3424

International Trade Mart, Suite 414
2 Canal Street
New Orleans, LA 70013
  (504) 527-2102

Building 1, 8th Floor, Bay 7
830 Third Avenue

Brooklyn, NY 11232
  (212) 788-5000, Ext. 1166

Continental Building, 10th Floor
400 Market Street
Philadelphia, PA 19106
  (215) 597-9105

Room 558
50 Fulton Street
San Francisco, CA 94102
  (415) 556-1816

1131 Federal Building
909 First Avenue
Seattle, WA 98104
  (206) 442-5276

DEB Annex 21046
Brookpark Road
Cleveland, OH 44135
  (216) 522-3886

For Alaska, Hawaii, Virgin Islands, and Puerto Rico, phone (800) 638-8333.

Retirement. Here are key organizations and agencies concerned with the special needs of elderly citizens (see pensions too):

Your state's Commission on Aging

United States Administration on
  Aging

National Council of Senior Citizens
1511 K Street, N.W.
Washington, DC 20005

Social and Rehabilitation Service
Department of Health, Education
  and Welfare
Washington, DC 20201

National Council on the Aging, Inc.
60 East 42 Street
New York, NY 10010

Senate Special Committee on Aging
Senate Office Building
Washington, DC 20510

American Association of Retired
  Persons
1909 K Street, N.W.
Washington, DC 20006

Social Security. If you have any questions about Social Security, contact your local Social Security office first (look for it in the phone book under "United States Government"). If the local office cannot or will not resolve your problem, contact: Social Security Administration, 6401 Security Boulevard, Baltimore, Maryland 21235.

If you disagree with a decision on a claim for Social Security benefits or for Supplemental Security Income (SSI), you have sixty days from the date you are notified of the decision in which to request a reconsideration.

You can file your request at any Social Security office, but it must be in writing, either in a letter, or on a form your Social Security office can supply.

If, after you have received the results of that reconsideration, you still are not satisfied, you may ask for a hearing before an officer of Bureau of Hearings and Appeals. This request, too, must be made within sixty days of the time you receive notice of the reconsideration decision.

If, when you have been notified of the hearings officer's decision, you still disagree, you may ask for a review by the Appeals Council. The hearing decision notice will show how much time you have to file for that review.

Claimants who disagree with an Appeals Council decision may take the final step and bring suit in Federal Court.

Stocks and Securities. If you are the victim (or even suspect you may be the victim) of a shady deal involving a transaction in securities, get in touch with the nearest regional office of the Securities and Exchange Commission, or write: Securities and Exchange Commission, 500 North Capital Street N.W., Washington, D.C. 20549.

Taxes. If you have a question or complaint about your federal income tax, call your local Internal Revenue Service office. To learn where this office is, check your Form 1040 Instructions, or contact: Internal Revenue Service, 1111 Constitution Avenue N.W., Washington, D.C. 20224.

Or use one of the IRS's toll-free information numbers. These are listed on the Form 1040 Instructions, and in many telephone books under "United States Government." You also can get the number for your area by calling "Information."

For information on tax court procedures, contact: Clerk of the Court, United States Tax Court, Washington, D.C. 20217.

If you feel you have been the victim of inequities or abuse in any aspect of the tax system—sales, property, income, etc., contact: Tax Reform Research Group, 133 C Street, S.E., Washington, D.C. 20003.

Tenants' Rights. If you are, for any reason, served with an eviction notice, consult your lawyer. Or, if you don't have a lawyer and can't afford to hire one, go to the local tenants' association for advice on what to do about it. Or get in touch with: National Tenants Organization, 1025 Fifteenth Street N.W., Fifth Floor, Washington, D.C. 20005; telephone: (202) 783-0711.

Toy Safety. See Health Care and Product Safety.

Unemployment Insurance. To sign up for benefits or to resolve a problem concerning benefits, go to the nearest state employment service office (look for the address in the telephone book under the listing for your state government).

Utilities. If you are dissatisfied with the service or business policies of your phone, gas, water, or electricity company and cannot resolve the matter with the company itself, complain to your state utility regulating body. This may be called the public utility commission, the public service board, or some similar name; its address will be under the state government listing in the capital phone book.

Warranties. If your warranty is not honored, contact your regional office of the Federal Trade Commission or its main office, Division of Special Statutes, FTC, Washington, D.C. 20580; telephone: (202) 523-3598.

EPILOGUE

How Much Do *YOU* Know About Your Economic System?

The subject really isn't nearly as confusing as it might seem, once you understand the fundamentals. Test your knowledge of our system with the following quiz. There is just one right answer to each question. Answers appear at the end of the quiz, along with a brief explanation of some points.

Give yourself one point for every correct answer. If you score between 13 and 16, you are indeed well informed on economic matters. If you score between 9 and 12, you are above average and you can probably debate the issues with just about anyone. If you score between 5 and 9, you're average. But if you score 6 or less, you might want to make an effort to learn more about the United States economic system and the forces that often play tug-of-war with your family income.

MONEY

1. The value of the U.S. dollar is determined by
(a) the amount of government-held gold reserves
(b) the amount of goods and services the dollar will buy
(c) the Federal Reserve

2. Of the total American money supply, checking account money represents about
(a) 75 per cent
(b) 45 per cent
(c) 30 per cent

3. The "prime rate" refers to
(a) the interest that banks charge on business loans to their best corporate customers at a given time
(b) the going rate most banks and savings and loans charge on residential mortgages
(c) the highest interest rate banks are permitted to pay on savings deposits

4. A Federal Reserve Bank is any bank that offers checking and savings accounts. True or false?

ECONOMIC TERMS

5. Our gross national product refers to
(a) the total market value of goods and services produced by the United States in a given period of time
(b) the total amount of goods and services sold by the United States in a given period of time
(c) the total market value of goods and services exported by the United States in a given period of time

6. The consumer price index measures changes in prices paid for goods and services by urban consumers. True or false?

7. When the dollar is "down" against the Japanese yen, it takes fewer yen to equal one dollar. True or false?

8. Baseball great Babe Ruth was able to earn $80,000 at the depth of the Depression when millions of other Americans were unemployed. This illustrates the economic principle of
(a) supply and demand
(b) scarcity and choice
(c) income distribution

CONSUMERS

9. The buying public largely determines the type and amount of goods and services produced in the U.S. economy. True or false?

10. The availability and widespread use of consumer credit helps makes possible a higher standard of living for all Americans. True or false?

11. A shortage of business capital has little effect on the average consumer. True or false?

12. When you invest money in something, your "return on investment" is the total profit you make on the transaction, or your gain. True or false?

WORK AND WAGES

13. The U.S. standard of living is closely tied to worker productivity. True or false?

14. If a company goes bankrupt, stockholders are among the first in line to divide up available assets. True or false?

15. Of all American workers, those who belong to a union represent
(a) 1 out of 4
(b) 1 out of 2
(c) 1 out of 3

16. Your "disposable income" is
(a) your annual salary
(b) your take-home pay after income taxes
(c) money you spend on entertainment and recreation.

THE ANSWERS

1. (b)

2. (a)

3. (a) The prime rate tends to rise and fall with the cost of money banks must borrow from the Federal Reserve and other sources to meet the corporate credit demand.

4. (False) All national banks and many state-chartered banks are members of the Federal Reserve System. However, Federal Reserve Banks are "central banks" that conduct business mainly with the federal government and with their member banks, rather than with the general public.

5. (a)

6. (True)

7. (True)

8. (a)

9. (True)

10. (True) With credit, consumers are able to purchase many more goods than they could pay for with cash. Therefore, more goods are produced, more factories are built, and more jobs are created.

11. (False) A scarcity of business capital affects your life as a worker and consumer in important ways. When business has difficulty building new plants, it may be forced to manufacture products at greater per unit cost with outdated equipment. This means productivity is restricted even though consumer demand for some goods may be on the increase. As always, when demand is high and supply is low, prices go up and *you* feel the pinch in your pocketbook.

12. (False) Don't forget taxes. Your actual "return on investment" is your profit *after* you've paid Uncle Sam and any other state or local taxes that might be applicable.

13. (True) As productivity increases, more goods and services flow into the market place, and availability of these products helps reduce cost. The amount of goods and services produced by the average American worker continues to increase at a rate of almost 3 per cent a year, and innovations in production methods, along with the discovery and use of cheaper resources, allow families to buy more goods and services and enjoy a higher standard of living.

14. (False) Stockholders go to the rear when a company goes under. Bondholders have the better chance of recovering all or part of their investment by claiming a share of any available assets.

15. (a) At present, union memberships account for nearly 23 million workers, or about 25 per cent of the entire American work force.

16. (b)

SOURCE: Continental Illinois National Bank and Trust Company of Chicago

The Hidden Threat to America's Economic System

THE THREE FUNDAMENTAL POINTS

Out of a lifetime specializing in my chosen field of economics-financial reporting, I have learned these three fundamental points:

The first fundamental point is that the American market place is an economic jungle. As is true of all jungles, this market place easily can destroy all who are ignorant of the basic guides for survival. Millions of you easily can fall into dangerous traps from which you cannot escape unharmed if you are not on the alert and aware of the maneuvers to avoid them. But you also can come through safely, in fine shape, and can even conquer the jungle—if you learn the rules, heed them, and refine them for your own use.

My second fundamental point is that we are a nation of economic illiterates and our illiteracy is a threat to the survival of the system we profess to love so much.

My third fundamental point follows the second and leads to the fear I've always had that if our system ever dies, it will be because in our ignorance we didn't know it was dying—or that we were killing it.

OUR ECONOMIC ILLITERACY

In our Congress, policies vitally affecting the survival of our form of economic system have for decades been made by economic illiterates, and probably still are being made.

In the executive suites of great financial and business concerns and in union headquarters across the nation, decisions directly involving our paychecks, profits, and prosperity have been made and probably still are being made by men and women who have only the vaguest idea of what creates paychecks, profits, and furthers prosperity.

In most of our high schools and colleges, the future leaders of America are either being taught nothing about our economic system or given courses woefully superficial, appallingly inadequate.

We are a nation of economic illiterates.

Few students in our high schools learn anything at all about our economic system in their classrooms.

The vast majority of American adults are not only ill informed on economic issues: worse, just because they are ignorant, they don't care about being better informed.

Most of our lawmakers are loaded with misconceptions about the economic issues on which they are passing laws.

And this indictment goes to the very top of our nation at this start of the 1980s, a time when more than ever before, understanding of our own economy and what's right with it, what's wrong with it, what might be done to make it stronger, more virile, more productive of basic values and of everyday things that make life more comfortable—such understanding has been and is absolutely imperative.

Harsh words? They certainly are. And I could make them even harsher.

THE HARSH DOCUMENTATION

Heed these simple dreadful statistics:

• Less than four out of ten U.S. high schools offer separate courses in economics—and only about two out of ten of those require students to take the course.

• The total time spent in high schools is about 3,557 hours. Thus, those students who *do* take the economics course will devote only a little over 1 per cent of their total hours in high schools to studying economics.

Only about 65 per cent of the colleges with teacher trainees require economics of social studies majors—the teachers usually assigned to teach economics. Where economics is not required, rarely does more than one out of ten take it voluntarily.

As an illustration of how this frightening lack of teaching and training works out, consider this test statement about a hypothetical country:

"GRASSLAND"

"Grassland is a country in which there is very little government ownership of farms and businesses. People may train for jobs and start businesses as best they can. The government does not usually control prices and wages."

What type of economic system does Grassland have?

The shocker here is that only a minority of students in 13,000 junior high school systems confronted with this statement by testers for the Joint Council on Economics Education recognized Grassland's as a "capitalistic" system. The majority opted for "communistic," "socialistic," "co-operative"—or "don't know."

As other illustrations of economic ignorance:

• A test was administered to over 21,000 high school students by a professor at Georgia State University. Over half did not know that the U.S. economy is based upon private enterprise.

• The New York University Center for Economic Education administered a test (twelfth-grade level) to several hundred students in community colleges in the New York area. The majority missed questions on: (a) government and freedom of choice in a free enterprise economy; (b) the characteristics of communism and free enterprise; (c) the relationship between productivity and wages.

• The same test used with the New York Community College students was given to 540 college students in Rhode Island with these partial results: 85 per cent did not understand the impact of inflation on creditors; 82 per cent did not understand the relationship between changes in business spending and recessions; 81 per cent did not understand the simple opportunity cost concept.

• The same test was administered to a group of young adults employed by a major U.S. bank. All were college graduates but had not taken economics. Their overall knowledge of economics was no better than that of high school students who had not taken a course in economics. Indeed, most of them missed questions of the functions of the Federal Reserve and on the differences between capitalism and communism.

Enough. Research studies underline the almost incredible ignorance of the so-called man in the street—but what about *educated* adults whose formal education did *not* include economics? The best example is the large group of bank employees tested. All were college graduates (with top scholastic records); all were in positions of responsibility (relations with important bank clients); all were picked by their supervisors as being "the best" in their departments. All claimed to be interested in economic matters and all read such papers as the New York *Times*. Results:

The average score on the test of economic understanding was little better than that of the average high school student who had taken no economics.

The majority missed questions on money and banking (origin of commercial bank deposits)!

The majority missed questions of functions of the Federal Reserve!

The majority did not understand the balance of payments problem.

THE HEART OF THE MATTER

And that brings me to the heart of my message about the "real" world in which you live.

Both "pure" and consumer economics are horribly neglected fields—and the neglect you pay it and others pay it is dangerous, terribly dangerous.

Behind every war, there is an economic cause. Never have wars been fought strictly for ideological reasons or for political reasons or for religious reasons.

Behind every social change, there is an economic cause. It's simply impossible to understand the modern world and its trends without understanding the key part economic changes are playing in our lives and our futures.

Now: Whose fault is it that of all the spheres in our lives, the sphere of economics is the least understood, the least covered, and certainly the least attractively presented?

First, I admit it is the fault of the individual reporter and commentator, people in positions like mine—and, I repeat and re-emphasize, of the education system that produced us.

Since our teachers cannot and do not begin to give us the fundamental information to help us understand our economy, and do not even teach the fundamentals of family finance, when you, the student, graduate, you haven't even the elementary facts to guide you to understanding. As a result, few of you think of economics as the very core of your lives.

Or those who do try to teach you often are economists who turn to writing as an afterthought. They cannot write; they do not even begin to recognize the extent to which simplicity is an art. They write down to you; they hide their own confusions behind fancy words, incomprehensible jargon, what I call bafflegab.

Second, it is the fault of the educators who belittle this type of news or who are bored to death with it or who don't understand.

In too many instances, editors cater to tastes you've already developed or which are obviously there—juicy scandals, personal or political.

It's not so obvious that what is happening to your dollar and jobs and savings is mighty important and interesting—to you—too.

The need is there, the taste is there—but it cannot be met and will not be until and unless the need and taste are fully appreciated (as my entire life and this book symbolize my appreciation).

Let me give you a personal anecdote that illustrates the general lack of appreciation in a painful way.

In the late 1970s, the head of a nationwide organization phoned to tell me that a blue-ribbon volunteer committee had been formed to help combat public ignorance of how our system works. It had plans to distribute millions of pamphlets, each dealing with a frequently misunderstood aspect of our economy. The gentleman offered me the story on an exclusive basis because he knew of my dedication to fighting economic illiteracy.

"Will the pamphlets be free?" I asked.

When he said that there would be a small charge, I responded that if he could work out a way to distribute them free, I would enthusiastically help publicize the effort. He got the permission for free distribution, so I asked him to send me copies of the pamphlets at once.

When I saw the pocket-size booklets, I was appalled. The looking-down-the-nose approach was so apparent that my first reaction was embarrassment plus resentment. The effort to achieve simplicity had led only to a "cutesie-tootsie" result.

End of my effort to help as originally planned. As for the pamphlets, I don't know where they are.

"Cute" writing must never be confused with simplicity. Simplicity of writing or talking about economic matters, I often have thought, can be compared to an iceberg. Two-thirds is beneath the surface, only one-third is visible.

And incidentally, how much do *you* really know?

The average U.S. citizen thinks corporation profits amount to 28 cents out of every sales dollar and even stockholders think after-tax corporation profits average 23 cents on the sales dollar, according to an opinion research corporation poll.

The average actually ranges between 3 cents and 5 cents out of a full dollar.

I guess I could boil all this down to two four-word sentences.

You have to understand. You have to care.

And that's what this whole book has been designed to help you do—understand, protect yourself. And care enough to fight the hidden enemy of our system —before it does indeed destroy us.

INDEX